Dutton's Navigation and Piloting

Dutton's Navigation and Piloting

TWELFTH EDITION BY

G. D. Dunlap

AND

H. H. Shufeldt

Captain, USNR (Retired)

NAVAL INSTITUTE PRESS

ANNAPOLIS, MARYLAND

Foreword

To men who go to sea, either off shore or on soundings, there is no skill more basic or more important than finding the position of the vessel. The ancient art of navigation has not been superseded in the Atomic Age.

In today's Navy, there is the natural danger that new, exciting areas of knowledge, such as missilery and nuclear propulsion, will claim an undue share of attention—significant as they are—to the detriment of the older sciences. Even a casual reading of this book, however, should convince the seaman that navigation has its own share of the new and the exciting. Yet the book also underlines the fact that neither the sextant nor common sense has been replaced by any black box.

In every man-of-war, in every commercial or pleasure vessel, there must still be a man—the Navigator—who takes exceptional pains with his work, who seeks and uses every possible scrap of information to check his work, and who scrupulously avoids making an assumption unsupported by facts. Anything less than the utmost devotion to duty by the Navigator means his vessel will be unsafe and her mission may be left undone.

THOMAS H. MOORER
Admiral, U. S. Navy
Chief of Naval Operations

Washington, D. C.
May 1969

Publisher's Preface

The original *Navigation and Nautical Astronomy* was prepared in 1926 by Commander Benjamin Dutton, U. S. Navy, for the instruction of midshipmen at the United States Naval Academy. Dutton himself wrote five editions under that title before he died in 1937. The eleventh edition was titled *Dutton's Navigation and Piloting,* both to perpetuate the work of the original author and to more accurately describe the contents. This name is retained for the present edition, which includes data on navigational methods and instrumentation that have been developed since the publication of the previous edition. Widely recognized as the standard authority in its field, *Dutton's* is familiar to hundreds of thousands of students of the art and science of navigation.

This new edition has been almost completely rewritten, and chapters have been added giving brief descriptions of navigational systems that have been developed recently; among these systems are navigational satellites, inertial navigation, Doppler, Omega, Loran-C, and bathymetric navigation. Great emphasis is placed on the practice of celestial navigation, since for many naval operations it is the only available method of determining position. In addition, celestial navigation remains the basic back-up system for the sophisticated electronic methods.

Like its predecessors, the current edition is intended as a basic text for the instruction of midshipmen at the U. S. Naval Academy, for those enrolled in the NROTC program, and for students at other schools and academies teaching marine navigation. It is used as the navigation textbook for the United States Power Squadrons, and is suitable for home study and for use as a reference in training at sea. It is not intended to be an all-inclusive reference book in its field, but rather a text for instruction in the basic elements of marine navigation as practiced in the Navy today. Sections of tables from the almanacs used throughout the text are illustrative only and are not to be used for actual navigation.

This text was prepared by Mr. G. D. Dunlap, president of Weems and Plath, Inc., and Captain H. H. Shufeldt, U. S. Naval Reserve (Retired). Grateful acknowledgment is made to the many individuals who contributed technical data, suggestions, and illustrations for the revision. The list of corporate representatives is too long for complete individual listing here. The U. S. Naval Observatory, the U. S. Naval Oceanographic Office, U. S. Naval Academy, U. S. Coast Guard, U. S. Coast and Geodetic Survey, U. S. Naval Ships Systems Command, NASA, Applied Physics Laboratory of Johns Hopkins University, and Her Majesty's Nautical Almanac Office also contributed data or illustrations for the text. Special thanks are extended to Mr. T. C. Lyon for his contribution on cartographic information; Lieutenant Commander Lawrence White, U. S. Coast

Guard, for polar navigation; Mr. John Larsen for background material on electronic navigation systems; Mr. Earl McCartney, Mr. Edward Gold, Mr. T. S. Stansell, Dr. Raynor Duncombe, Dr. Gene Marner, and Mr. William Rowan for their special contributions in various technical areas; and to Mr. H. C. Ketts, III, for his assistance in many areas of the text and for preparing the index.

UNITED STATES NAVAL INSTITUTE

Annapolis, Maryland
April 1969

Contents

Dutton's Navigation and Piloting

CHAPTER 1

Introduction to Navigation

101. *Navigation* (from the Latin *navis*, a ship, and *agere*, to direct) is the process of directing the movement of a ship or aircraft from one point to another. Both art and science are involved in conducting a ship safely to its destination. Art is involved in the proficient use of all available aids and methods and the interpretation of data with judgment to determine position and the ship's course. The science of navigation includes the computation of solutions for various navigational problems, and the design and development of instruments, methods, tables and almanacs intended to facilitate the work of the navigator, and to increase the accuracy of the results he may obtain. Great progress has been made during the twentieth century in advancing the science of navigation, but such progress is in vain if the navigator is not skilled in the art of his trade.

Definition.

102. Navigation may be divided into four principal classifications: piloting, dead reckoning, electronic navigation, and celestial navigation.

Principal classifications of navigation.

Piloting is defined as navigation involving frequent or continuous determination of position or line of position relative to geographical points, to a high order of accuracy. It is used to direct a vessel from place to place by observations of visual landmarks on the earth's surface, such as lighthouses, beacons, buoys, prominent rocks and cliffs, etc., and by determinations of depth of water, called soundings. Piloting once depended upon individual use of the senses of sight and hearing. Modern radio, radar, and other electronic systems have vastly extended the range of human visual and aural perception, far beyond the horizon, into the depth of the sea, and into space.

Piloting.

Dead Reckoning (DR) is the determination of present position by advancing a previous position for known courses and distances. The term is derived from "deduced reckoning" of sailing days, which was abbreviated to ded. reckoning. In dead reckoning, course and speed are generally computed without allowance for wind or current. Courses were once determined from the magnetic compass, and later from the gyro compass, and speed from a log, or a count of engine revolutions, and these values were plotted by hand on a chart. On modern vessels a dead reckoning analyser is often used to compute the ship's movement through the water and a dead reckoning tracer (DRT) will compute and automatically plot the position. The modern inertial navigation and doppler navigation systems are, in effect, dead reckoning systems which are gradually coming into use as technology advances in these fields.

Dead reckoning.

Electronic Navigation—navigation by means of electronic equipment—is essentially a form of piloting. It has now assumed such importance that it

3

Electronic navigation.

should be considered as a separate division of navigation. Many earlier text-books contained sections on radio navigation—the use of radio direction finders to obtain bearings on radio broadcast stations—as the earliest form of electronic navigation. Modern usage of the term includes navigation involving any electronic device or instrument. Radar and Loran A still constitute the most widely used methods of electronic navigation. This text will discuss these basic systems, as well as new developments ranging from worldwide systems to high accuracy short range methods.

Celestial navigation.

Celestial Navigation involves the determining of position through observations of the celestial bodies—the sun, moon, planets and stars. It is the most widely used method of determining position at sea, and the great majority of celestial observations are still obtained by means of the marine sextant as described in Chapter 22. Somewhat more sophisticated observing instruments now being introduced will also be discussed.

Early history of navigation.

103. Before discussing the modern practice of navigation, it might be well to consider briefly navigation as practiced by early mariners. Although their tools were few and very crude, they dared to venture out into unknown oceans, generally to return safely. The science of navigation was primitive, but the art was already developed, and had many outstandingly able practitioners. Among them, Columbus, Magellan and Drake will always remain an inspiration, and their names should serve to remind future navigators of the importance of mastering the art.

Archeologists believe that the art of navigation originated some 8,000 years ago in the eastern Mediterranean. The first American Indians probably reached the continent by a water crossing from Siberia as early as 4000 B.C. A written "sailing direction" existed in the Mediterranean Sea several hundred years before Christ and may well have been accompanied by a crude form of chart. This was the "Periplus" of Scylax, written between the sixth and fourth centuries B.C. Its contents were similar to the modern sailing directions; it furnished the navigator information on distances between ports and navigational aids, and it cautioned him against dangers. Data on port facilities were also included, as well as other useful information; for example, it advised the mariner that there were good natural harbors on the island of Pharos, but that no drinking water could be found there.

There still exists the record of a voyage made about 325 B.C. by Pytheas of Massilia, a Greek astronomer and navigator. He sailed from the Mediterranean to England; from there he went on to explore the coast of Scotland and then sailed to Thule, the legendary land of the midnight sun, the Norwegian fjords, and the coast of Germany along the North Sea. While this is one of the earliest known accounts of such a voyage, the route from the Mediterranean to England was well travelled even then, and a lively trade existed between the two areas.

Pytheas' voyage, and others like it, are astounding now in that they were made without benefit of what would be considered the bare essentials of navigational equipment—compass, accurate charts, and sextant for determining latitude. But such early mariners did have a good idea of the apparent motion of the sun and stars and were able to steer by them, and they developed their powers of perception until their navigation became a well advanced art.

Pytheas wrote a book, *Ports Around the World*, on observations made during the voyage. By modern standards, his descriptions of coast lines and estimates of distances would be considered crude, but the book served as an invaluable aid to subsequent voyagers in those previously unknown waters.

As far as is known, no works of comparable value appeared for about 1500 years, until the "portolanos" came into use in the Mediterranean. They were, in effect, sailing directions: surprisingly accurate charts were usually included. The portolanos were followed by the French "routiers," which the English called "rutters," and an excellent Dutch text, *Spieghel der Zeevaert* (The Mariner's Mirror) by Waghenaer, which the English called a "Waggoner."

In 1557, the *Brieve Compendio del Arte del Navigar* was published in Italy. This was designed to be a general text on navigation, rather than a sailing direction, and was intended to serve the navigator both on and off soundings.

Little is known of the navigational methods used by the ancients; it seems probable that they relied almost entirely on the seaman's eye. The first effective instrument was the magnetic compass which in its earliest form consisted of a needle, magnetized by being rubbed against a lodestone, and floated on water by means of a straw. Where and when the magnetic compass was first used is not known, but probably the Vikings were familiar with it in the eleventh century. Examples of early compasses are shown in Figure 103a.

Early navigational instruments.

Magnetic compass.

Figure 103a: Early magnetic compasses.

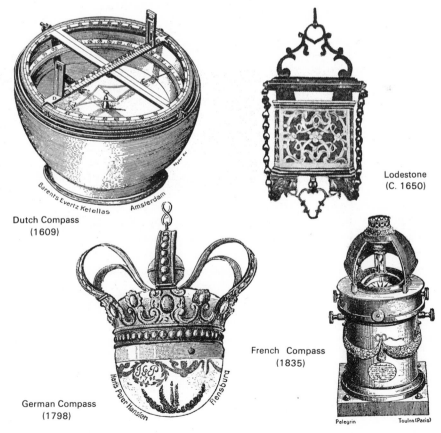

Dutch Compass
(1609)

Lodestone
(C. 1650)

German Compass
(1798)

French Compass
(1835)

5

Cross-staff.

The next advancement was the invention of the cross-staff, the first successful instrument developed for measuring the altitude of celestial bodies at sea. It was unique in that it measured altitude from the sea horizon; its drawback was that it required the observer to look at the horizon and the body at the same time. This must have been quite a feat, particularly when the body was well above the horizon; however, a practiced navigator could for the first time determine the altitude of a body at sea with an accuracy of about a degree.

Backstaff.

In 1590 the backstaff or Davis's quadrant, shown in Figure 103b, was invented by John Davis. This was a great advance over the cross-staff. To use the instrument, the observer turned his back to the sun, and aligned a shadow cast by the sun with the horizon. Later models of the instrument were fitted with a mirror, to permit observations of bodies other than the sun.

Figure 103b: Davis quadrant, 1775.

The sun was the body the navigator observed most frequently. Early Greek astronomers had been able to determine the sun's declination with considerable accuracy for every day of the year. Knowing the sun's declination for the date, the navigator could deduce his latitude by observing the sun's altitude when it transited his meridian. In the northern hemisphere he could also obtain his latitude by measuring the altitude of Polaris. However, the determination of longitude at sea had to await the invention of the chronometer.

The usual practice was to sail to the latitude of the ship's destination, and then head due east or west to make a landfall. This was called running down one's easting or westing.

The *leadline*, used since time immemorial to determine the depth of water, was of great assistance in coming up on the land. Frequently it was armed; that is, a depression in the lower end was filled with tallow. Small particles of the bottom sediment adhered to the tallow; on a known coast, identification of this material was often of further assistance in determining position.

The *chip log*, or *ship log*, to determine a ship's speed, was invented about the same time as the backstaff. It consisted of a piece of wood, in the shape of a quadrant, weighted with lead at the center of the circular side. This log chip, as it was called, was secured to a bridle at each corner; the bridle, in turn, was secured to the log line. At one corner of the log chip, the bridle was held by a wooden peg so arranged that a sharp tug on the log line would pull out the peg, allowing the chip to be hauled back on board readily.

Chip log.

The log line was stored on a free turning reel. To determine speed, the log chip was put overboard where it floated vertically due to its ballasting. A considerable length of log line was allowed to get the log chip into undisturbed water astern. When the first knotted marker worked into the log line passed off the reel, timing was started; at the end of a definite period, the line was seized and the number of knots in the line that had paid out were counted to determine the vessel's speed. From this arose the present use of the term *knot* to designate one nautical mile per hour.

The timing was originally done by reciting certain religious sentences, which, in theory, required an exact amount of time. Later, a sand glass was employed. This was usually a 30-second timer, and gave far more accurate results.

The keeping of accurate time aboard ship was impossible until the invention of the chronometer by John Harrison in the early eighteenth century. Hour or sand glasses were satisfactory for establishing the length of the watch aboard ship, but were useless for sustained time keeping. Probably the best shipboard timekeeper before the eighteenth century was the compass. Many compasses were designed especially for this purpose, with a vertical pin at the center of the card. The compass card was in effect a sundial, and the pin was the gnomon.

The *sextant* and the *chronometer*, the two instruments which made accurate navigation possible, were invented within a few years of one another. Interestingly enough, the design of the sextant was arrived at in the year 1730 by John Hadley in England and Thomas Godfrey in Philadelphia, working independently.

Sextant.

The chronometer was important because it was sufficiently accurate to permit determining longitude afloat. The sextant offered both convenience and accuracy in measuring altitudes, not only of the sun, but also of the moon, planets and stars. Until about 1880, it was the general practice to compute position by the time sight method. A latitude was obtained from an observation of Polaris or of the sun's transit. This latitude was carried forward by dead reckoning and used in determining longitude by a subsequent observation; latitude and longitude were both calculated, rather than being determined from plotting lines of position (LOP) on a chart, as is done today.

Chronometer.

An American, Captain Thomas H. Sumner, discovered the line of position in 1837. Due to thick weather, when approaching the English coast, he had been unable to obtain any observations. About 10 AM the sun broke through, and he procured an altitude which he reduced to obtain the longitude. However, the latitude he used for the reduction was in doubt; he solved for longitude twice more, each time using a different latitude. After plotting the three positions on a chart he was surprised to find that a straight line could be drawn through them. He correctly deduced that his position must lie somewhere along this

Line of position.

line, which happened to pass through a light off the English coast. He turned the ship and sailed along that line until the light appeared, thus establishing his position exactly.

Sumner's discovery of the line of position was a great step forward in celestial navigation. Its greatest weakness lies in the fact that to obtain a line of position, a sight must be worked twice, using different latitudes. In 1875, Commander Marcq de St. Hilaire, of the French Navy, introduced the altitude difference, or intercept method, which has become the basis of virtually all celestial navigation. In this method, the altitude and azimuth, or direction of a body, are calculated for a given instant of time and for a location where the vessel is supposed to be. The difference between the altitude as observed by sextant, and the calculated altitude is then determined: this difference, which is called the intercept, will be in minutes of arc.

A line is then drawn through the position, corresponding in direction to the calculated azimuth. The intercept is next laid off along the azimuth line, one nautical mile being equal to one minute of arc. It is measured towards the body if the observed altitude is greater than the calculated, and away if it is less. All that remains is to draw the line of position at right angles to the azimuth line.

Electronics.   The twentieth century may well be called the century of electronics, and nowhere has electronics had a greater impact than in navigation. The modern navigator has many electronic aids. The depth finder gives him a continuous record of the depth of water, and radar facilitates piloting in thick weather. Loran permits him to fix his position in any weather over a small portion of the globe. New electronic systems now under development are expected to provide accurate positioning anywhere on the earth's surface.

Despite their sophistication, these electronic aids may become ineffective due to loss of ship's power, propagation irregularities and equipment malfunction. It is essential that the navigator be skilled in piloting, dead reckoning and celestial navigation. He cannot place his reliance solely on electronic navigational systems; he must be able to navigate successfully with the basic tools of the trade—the compass and the sextant. In the words of the Bible, he must know "the way of a ship in the midst of the sea."

CHAPTER 2

The Earth and its Coordinates

201. It is well known that the earth is round—but it is not perfectly so. The earth is described more exactly as a "spheroid," which simply means a less-than-perfect sphere. The equatorial diameter of the earth is not quite 6,888 nautical miles; the polar diameter is nearly 6,865 nautical miles, or about 23 miles less.

Size and shape of the earth.

If the earth is represented by a terrestial globe with an equatorial diameter of 12 inches, the polar diameter, to be exact, should be 11.96 inches, or 0.04 inches less.

As a further comparison, Mt. Everest reaches a little less than 30,000 feet above mean sea level; the greatest ocean depths yet known extend a little more than 35,000 feet below mean sea level. On the same 12-inch globe those depths would be only about 0.01 inch below the surface.

Since these variations from a truly spherical shape are so slight, for most navigational purposes the earth is considered as a sphere, and solutions of navigational problems on this basis are of practical accuracy.

202. On a sphere at rest, any point is similar to every other point; all points on the surface are defined simply as being equidistant from the center. Since all points are alike, there can be no reference point or line as a starting point for measurements.

Reference lines on the earth.

As soon as rotation is introduced, the sphere acquires one line that is different from every other line: the *axis* on which it rotates. The axis of the earth meets its surface at the *north pole* and the *south pole*.

Axis.

Halfway between the two poles, a plane perpendicular to the axis intersects the surface of the earth in a line known as the *equator*. All points on the equator are equidistant between the two poles, and the plane of the equator divides the earth into two equal hemispheres.

Equator.

Other planes can be passed through the earth, all perpendicular to the axis and parallel to the plane of the equator. Such planes intersect the surface of the earth in lines known as *parallels of latitude* (or *parallels*). Figure 202a shows the earth's axis, the north pole, the equator, and parallels of latitude at intervals of 15°. The *latitude* of a point on the surface of the earth is its angular distance north or south of the equator, an arc of the earth's surface, as measured at the center of the earth, from the equator toward either pole. In the figure, measurement of the angles for 15° and 45° *north* latitude and for 30° *south* latitude are shown.

Parallels.

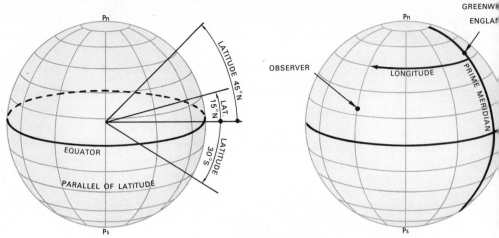

Figure 202a: Equa-
tor, parallels of lati-
tude and latitude.

Figure 202b: Merid-
ians, prime merid-
ian and longitude.

Any number of planes can be passed through the earth with the axis and both poles lying in the plane. Such a plane intersects the earth's surface in a complete circle which is a *meridian*. That half of a meridian extending from the north to the south pole on the same side of the earth as an observer is considered by him as the *upper branch* of the meridian. The other half of the meridian, which is on the other side of the earth and seems to the observer to be beneath him, is referred to as the *lower branch*.

Meridian.

It will be important to remember that, since each parallel of latitude is parallel to the equator, the planes of *all* parallels are parallel to each other. Also, all parallels intersect each meridian on the earth's surface at 90° angles.

Meridians are used for the measurement of *longitude*, but first some particular meridian must be selected as the starting point. In the early days of map making a number of meridians were chosen for this purpose, but for many years the British have considered the "prime meridian" to be the meridian passing through the original position of the Royal Greenwich Observatory. On almost all modern nautical charts that meridian is used as the starting point for the measurement of longitude.

Figure 202b illustrates the measurement of longitude. The longitude of a point may be defined as the angular distance between the meridian of Greenwich and the meridian passing through the point. It is measured in degrees of arc, from 0° to 180° east (*east longitude*) or west (*west longitude*) from the prime meridian (Greenwich). It may be thought of:

(1) as measured along a parallel of latitude, as in the figure;
(2) as measured along the equator; or
(3) as the angle between the two meridians as they converge and meet at the pole.

Having established a set of reference lines for the sphere (meridians and parallels) any position on earth may be precisely pin-pointed as "so many degrees north (or south) latitude, and so many degrees east (or west) longitude."

One difference between the measurement of latitude and of longitude is important:

The length of a degree of latitude (measured *along* a meridian) is every- where the same on a sphere, from the equator to the poles. On the earth, for navigational purposes, it is equal to 60 nautical miles, and 1 minute of latitude is equal to 1 nautical mile.

Degree length.

The length of a degree of longitude (measured along a parallel), decreases from 60 nautical miles at the equator, to 30 nautical miles at latitude 60°, and to zero at the poles. See Figure 202c. This linear distance is referred to as *departure* (p).

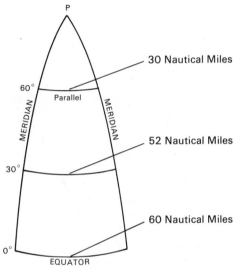

Figure 202c: Length of a degree of longitude at various latitudes.

203. In some problems of navigation it is necessary to know the *difference of latitude (l)*, or the *difference of longitude* (DLo) between two points.

Difference of lati- tude and longitude.

In determining the difference of latitude, the two points may both be on the same side of the equator, in which case they are said to be of the "same name" (that is, both are *north* latitude, or both are *south* latitude), or they may be on opposite sides of the equator, and of "contrary name" (one *north* latitude, one *south*). The difference of latitude (*l*) is always measured as though the two points were both on the same meridian, with one point due north or south of the other, regardless of the direction between them. Thus, in Figure 203a, *A* is 45° north, *B* at 30° south (*contrary name*); obviously, the total difference of latitude between them is obtained by *adding* the two distances from the equator: 45° + 30° = 75° = *l*. This gives rise to the formal rule:

for latitudes of contrary name, Add.

Again, in Figure 203a, *A* is 45° north, *C* at 15° north (*same name*) and the difference of latitude, 30° is obtained by subtracting the smaller from the larger. The rule in this case becomes:

for latitudes of same name, Subtract

In the same way, the *difference of longitude (DLo)* is always measured as though both points were on the same parallel, or were both on the equator.

11

Both points may be on the same side of the prime meridian (Greenwich), and therefore of the "same name:" both *east* longitude, or both *west* longitude. They may also be on opposite sides of the prime meridian, and therefore of "contrary name:"—one in *east* longitude, the other in *west* longitude.

In Figure 203a, *B* is at longitude 30° west, *C* at 30° east (*contrary name*); the total *DLo* is obtained by adding the two distances from the prime meridian: 30° + 30° = 60° = *DLo*, and the rule is still:

for contrary name, Add

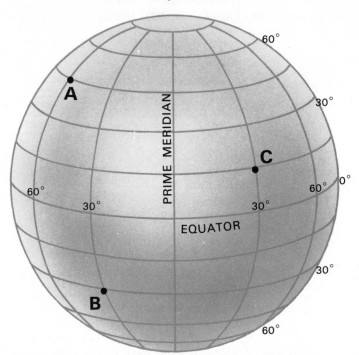

Figure 203a: Difference of latitude (l) and Difference of longitude (DLo).

A slight complication may appear if the sum of the two longitudes is greater than 180°, but in this case the *DLo* is *360° minus the sum*. This may be seen from Figure 203b, in which the circumference *GWE* is the equator, and *P* is the north pole. *PG* is the meridian of Greenwich. *PW* is the meridian through the point *W*, at 120° west longitude, *PE* the meridian through *E*, at 90° east longitude (*contrary name*): sum, 120° + 90° = 210°. Obviously, the *DLo* sought is the *shorter* arc between them (*WXE*), or 360° − 210° = 150°, not the longer arc of 210°.

Again, in Figure 203a, *A* is at 60° west longitude, *B* at 30° west longitude (*same name*). *DLo*, 30° is obtained by subtracting the smaller from the larger, and the rule again is the same.

for same name, Subtract

Some navigation problems are solved by means of "latitude and departure." "Latitude," here, is the difference of latitude already discussed. "Departure" is the *DLo*, but for this special problem *DLo* is in nautical miles, not in degrees and minutes of arc. As described in Chapter 5, *DLo* in miles can be found graphically; it can be computed; or it can be found in Table 3 of Bowditch.

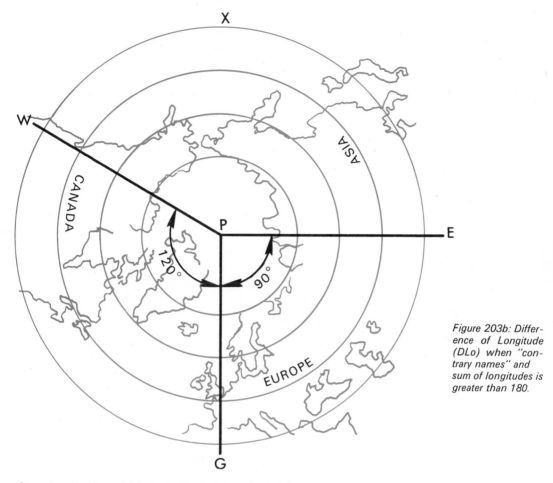

Figure 203b: Difference of Longitude (DLo) when "contrary names" and sum of longitudes is greater than 180.

Occasionally the *mid-latitude* (*Lm*) is required. When both points are on the same side of the equator this is obviously the arithmetical mean of the two latitudes. For example, in Figure 203a, *Lm* for points *A* and *C* is 45° + 15° ÷ 2 = 60° ÷ 2 = 30°.

If *Lm* is ever required for points on opposite sides of the equator, the procedure is readily apparent in Figure 203a. Thus, *Lm* for *A* and *B* (contrary names), is: 45° + 30° ÷ 2 = 75° ÷ 2 = 37°30′. In this case, however, 37°30′ is not the *Lm* sought. It is the difference of latitude between *either* of the two points and the desired *Lm*; that is, it is either

45° − 37°30′ = 7°30′ north latitude; or
30° − 37°30′ = −7°30′ (that is, 7°30′ on the other side of the equator
from *B*, which is, as before, at 7°30′ north latitude).

204. On a *plane* surface, a straight line is defined as "the shortest distance between two points." With the help of a protractor or straightedge such a line may be drawn on an engineering plan and the *distance* measured at the scale of the drawing. Similarly, the *direction* between the two points may be measured with an ordinary protractor as the angle which the line makes with the rectangular reference lines of the drawing.

Great circles and small circles.

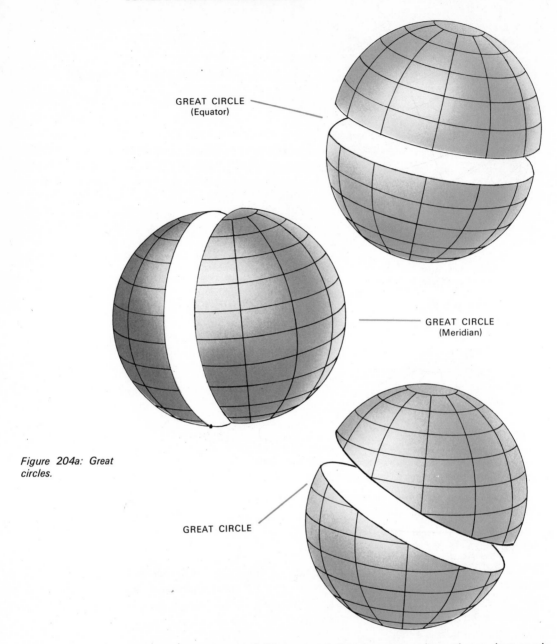

GREAT CIRCLE
(Equator)

GREAT CIRCLE
(Meridian)

GREAT CIRCLE

Figure 204a: Great circles.

For the measurement of distance and direction on a sphere, the student needs to become familiar with *great circles, small circles* and *rhumb lines,* also known as loxodromes, or loxodromic spirals; (article 205).

Great circle.

A *great circle* is that line on the surface of a sphere which divides the sphere into two equal parts; it is formed by the intersection of its surface with any plane passing through its center. Great circles are illustrated in Figure 204a.

Small circle.

A *small circle*, regardless of how large it may be, is a line on the surface of a sphere formed by the intersection of its surface with any plane which does *not* pass through the center of the sphere and does not divide the sphere into two equal parts. See Figure 204b.

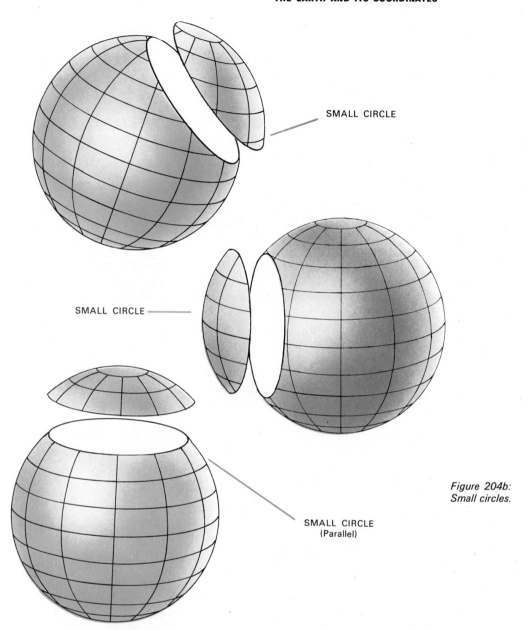

SMALL CIRCLE

SMALL CIRCLE

Figure 204b:
Small circles.

SMALL CIRCLE
(Parallel)

The shortest distance between any two points on the surface of a sphere is always along the great circle between them. The more closely the plane of a small circle approaches the center of the earth, the more closely will distance measured along it approach the shortest distance. The converse is also true, of course.

From Figures 204a and 204b it is seen that the equator and all meridians are great circles; all parallels (excluding the equator) are small circles. It is also apparent that either a great circle or a small circle need not trend with meridians or parallels, but may be diagonal (transverse), crossing the meridians and parallels at any required angle.

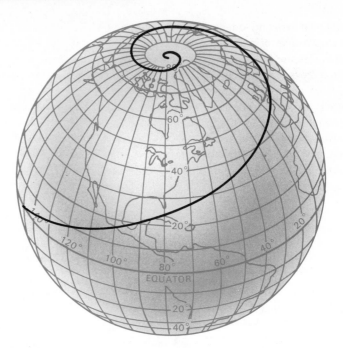

*Figure 205a:
A rhumb line or
loxodrome.*

Rhumb line.

205. Since a great circle is the shortest distance between two points on the surface of a sphere, it might be supposed that it would always be the route selected unless there were intervening dangers, such as reefs or shoals. The practical objection to following a great circle route is that the direction of a great circle is constantly changing ; it makes a different angle with each meridian it crosses from starting point to destination. This means that the ship's heading on a great circle route would be subject to continual alterations.

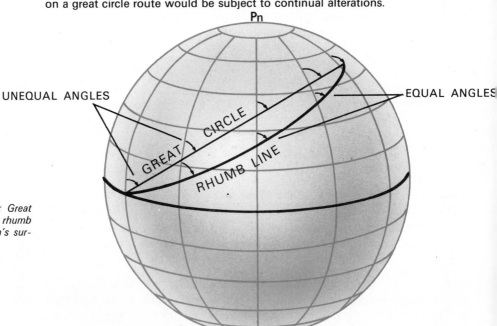

*Figure 205b: Great
circle and rhumb
line on earth's sur-
face.*

Since continual heading changes are scarcely practical, it is customary to follow a *rhumb line*, or a series of rhumb lines, rather than a great circle, as described in Chapter 3. For practical purposes, a rhumb line may be defined as a line which crosses every meridian of the sphere at the same constant angle. In other words, one true heading of the ship may be maintained without change from starting point to destination (if, for the moment, one disregards factors such as currents, wind, and changing magnetic variation). A rhumb line is also known as a loxodrome, or as a "loxodromic spiral." Figure 205a shows a rhumb line extending in a continuous spiral from the equator to the north pole, crossing each meridian throughout its length at a constant angle near 70°.

Figure 205b shows the sphere with its meridians and parallels. A great circle and the corresponding rhumb line are also shown, both lines from a point on the equator to a point about 135° of longitude toward the east and at a latitude near 52° north. In this rendition of the sphere it is not possible to show angular relationships correctly, but reference to a globe will show that the great circle leaves the equator at an angle of a little less than 30° with the meridian there; near the middle of the route, the angle with the meridian has increased to about 50° and, near the end of the route, to more than 100°. The rhumb line crosses each successive meridian at a constant angle of about 65°.

206. From the preceding it is apparent that there are two kinds of direction, both of which are of interest to the navigator:

Directions in navigation.

Rhumb line directions are most commonly used in determining the course to be followed, or the track made good.

Great circle directions are used chiefly in connection with radio direction finding or star sights, and are generally referred to as *bearings* or *azimuths*.

In navigation, direction is measured as the angle between the plotted route and

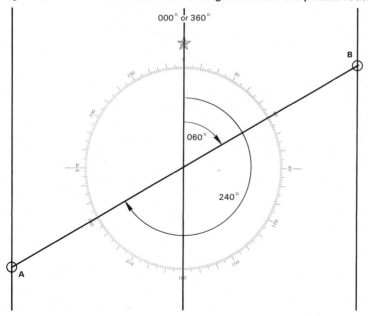

Figure 206: Measurement of direction (course or track) in navigation.

a selected meridian, from 000° at true north, clockwise to 360°: Direction is always expressed in three figures. True north may be considered either as 000° or as 360°, according to the problem.

In Figure 206, the true direction from *A* to *B* is 060°; the true direction from *B* to *A* is 240° (the *reciprocal* of 060°). It is axiomatic that every line has two directions, hence the direction intended should be clearly indicated by arrow heads or some system of labeling. Direction can be shown as clearly by the *order of letters* used: thus *AB* is the direction from *A* to *B*; the reciprocal direction from *B* to *A* is *BA*.

All directions, whether great circle, rhumb line, or other, are *true* directions when measured from the true geographic meridian printed on the chart; *magnetic* directions when measured from magnetic north; and *relative* directions when measured from the ship's head (the direction in which the ship is pointed).

Distances in navigation.

207. As with direction, the navigator is also concerned with *great circle* distances and *rhumb line* distances. Except for a few special cases, great circle distances are shorter than rhumb line distances, the difference depending on various combinations of *latitude* and *direction*.

In article 204 it was seen that the equator is a great circle. But the equator is also a rhumb line, with constant direction of 090° or 270°. Along the equator, then, great circle distance and rhumb line distance are identical, and there is no difference at all.

As a ship moves farther from the equator toward either pole, the saving in distance by way of the great circle becomes greater, and is always greatest for east-west courses (090° or 270°).

All meridians, too, are great circles by definition; they are also rhumb lines of constant direction 000° or 180°. It should be obvious that along a meridian (as along the equator) great circle distance and rhumb line distance are identical, and there is no difference. The difference begins to increase as the great circle direction moves away from the north-south direction, reaching a maximum in an east-west direction.

Near the equator, then, the saving in distance by way of a great circle is negligible. For an east-west distance of 1,000 nautical miles, the saving is only about 1.5 miles at latitude 40°, and 10.5 miles at latitude 60°. For the diagonal route from New York to London (mid-latitude about 46°), the great circle distance is 3,016 nautical miles and rhumb line distance is 3,139 nautical miles —a difference of 123 nautical miles.

Great circle distances are sometimes computed, rather than measured on the chart. In this case, they are obtained in degrees and minutes of arc. As is true of any great circle (such as a meridian), one degree of arc is equal to 60 nautical miles, and 1 minute equals 1 nautical mile. The total number of minutes, then, is also the distance in nautical miles.

Definitions and symbols.

208. For convenient reference in problems in navigation, certain definitions and symbols are commonly used. A few that have already been treated in some detail, together with several related ones, are given here with their commonly accepted symbols:

Azimuth (Zn): the great circle direction of any place or object from a given point; chiefly used to designate the direction of a heavenly body in celestial navigation. When referred to true north, azimuth is written as Zn. Azimuth angle (Az) is measured either east or west using either north or south as the reference direction.

Basic definitions used in navigation.

Bearing (B): same as azimuth, but commonly used in radio direction finding, or in visual sights. As mentioned in article 206, azimuths and bearings (or any other directional term) may be true, magnetic, or relative, according to the reference line or point used.

Course (C): A rhumb line direction. The horizontal direction of travel through still water, expressed in angular units from a reference direction, from 000° at the reference direction clockwise through 360°. The course is often designated as *true, magnetic, compass,* or *grid* as the reference direction is true, magnetic, compass, or grid north, respectively. Course can be either an anticipated or an accomplished direction of travel with respect to the water.

Heading (Hdg. or SH): The horizontal direction in which a ship points or heads at any instant, expressed in angular units, 000° clockwise through 360°, from a reference direction. The heading of a ship is also called ship's head. Heading is a constantly changing value as a ship oscillates or yaws across the course due to effects of the sea and of steering error.

Knot (Kn): the unit of speed, one knot being equal to a speed of one nautical mile an hour. It is *never* permissible to refer to a speed of "30 knots *an hour*".

Mile: the *statute mile* (St.M), commonly used on land, is 5,280 feet; the *nautical mile* (Nt.M), always used in navigation, is 6,076.1 feet. It is always considered as equal to 1 minute of latitude, or to 1 minute of arc of any great circle.

Track (TR): as used in navigation, is the rhumb line or lines describing the path of a vessel actually made good relative to the earth. (In some texts referred to as *Course Made Good*).

Latitude (L: also designated by ϕ, the Greek letter *phi)*, the arc distance of a point measured from the equator toward either pole. In problems involving latitude at two or more points, latitude of the first point is usually written as L_1; second point L_2, etc. *Difference* of latitude between two places is indicated by *l; mid-latitude* (the mean latitude) by *Lm.*

Longitude (Long. sometimes indicated by λ, *lambda)* the angular distance along the equator or a parallel, between the meridian of Greenwich and the meridian passing through the particular point. *Difference* of longitude *(DLo)*. *Departure (p)* is the difference of longitude in nautical miles.

209. This chapter has described the basic reference lines of the sphere, which are essential to determining geographical position in terms of latitude and longitude. It has also outlined the general problems of distance and direction, and their solutions by way of great circles, small circles, and rhumb lines. This information is basic and fundamental. Without it, solution of the problems of navigation is impossible.

Summary.

CHAPTER 3

Chart Projections and Chart Interpretation

301. The nautical chart is one of the mariner's oldest and most widely used navigational aids. The Greeks used sailing directions several hundred years before the birth of Christ. They may also have had charts, as it is easier to draw a diagram to show how to get to a place than it is to explain the process in writing; however, there is no proof that such charts actually existed.

In the third century B.C., the Greek scientific writer, Eratosthenes of Alexandria, reasoned that the earth must be a sphere, as at high noon on the day of the summer solstice objects of the same height at two locations on the same meridian did not cause shadows of the same length. He proceeded to determine the zenith distances at Alexandria and Syene (now Aswan), which he estimated to be 500 miles apart, and found them to differ by about 7.5°. Since 7.5° is 1/48 of the circumference of a circle, he calculated that the earth's circumference must be 48 × 500 or 24,000 statute miles. This was a surprisingly accurate determination, as the actual circumference is about 24,900 statute miles. This seems to be the first measurement of latitude using the degree as a standard of measurement.

In the second century A.D., the great astronomer and mathematician, Ptolemy, constructed many maps, among them a famous world map which listed several thousand places by latitude and longitude. Unfortunately, he did not use Eratosthenes' calculations but those of a Greek philosopher, who had estimated the earth's circumference to be only 18,000 miles. Ptolemy's work remained a standard through the middle ages, and led Columbus to believe that he had reached the East Indies in 1492.

The earliest charts of the middle ages still in existence are the Portolan charts prepared in Spain in the fourteenth century. They are remarkably accurate in their portrayal of the Mediterranean. In 1515, Leonardo da Vinci drew his famous map of the world, which shows America extending further east and west than north and south.

Gerardus Mercator, the Flemish cartographer who produced a world chart constructed on the basis of the projection which bears his name, is the father of modern cartography. The accuracy of charts continued to improve, but as they had to be printed by hand, they were extremely expensive. The mariner considered them much too valuable to be used for plotting; this led to wide use of the sailings and calculated dead reckoning. These mathematical methods of determining DR position remained in wide use aboard ship through much of the nineteenth century.

The *U. S. Coast and Geodetic Survey* was established by Congress in 1807 and charged with making a survey of the coast, harbors, and off-lying islands of the United States. The Navy, in 1830, established the *Depot of Charts and Instruments* which later became the *Hydrographic Office*, and currently the *U. S. Naval Oceanographic Office*. The mission of the National Ocean Survey, the new designation for the Coast and Geodetic Survey, remains much the same ; but now includes the waters off U. S. territories. The Oceanographic Office is charged with the preparation of charts of the remaining waters of the world. Both agencies conduct continuing surveys, and their highly accurate charts are available to the mariners of all nations. Specialized charts for aviators and for other purposes are prepared by various Government agencies.

A *map* is a representation of some part of the earth's surface, showing political boundaries, physical features, cities and towns, and other geographic information. *Maps and charts.*

A *chart* is also a representation of a portion of the earth's surface, but has been specially designed for convenient use in navigation. It is intended to be worked upon, not merely to be looked at, and must readily permit the graphic solution of navigation problems such as distance and direction, or position determination in terms of latitude and longitude.

A *nautical chart* is primarily concerned with navigable water areas. It includes information such as coastlines and harbors, channels and obstructions, currents, depths of water, and aids to navigation.

Aeronautical charts show elevations, obstructions, prominent landmarks, airports, and aids to navigation. Although frequently depicting only land areas, they may differ from ordinary maps of the same areas by emphasizing or exaggerating landmarks or other features of special importance to air navigators.

For use at sea there are also a number of "special purpose" charts, such as pilot charts to provide weather and other information, tidal current charts, star charts, etc. In the remainder of this chapter, primary consideration will be given to nautical charts, to the projections upon which they are constructed, and to the navigator's use of them.

302. Experiment will prove that no considerable portion of a rubber ball can be spread out flat without some stretching or tearing. Conversely, a sheet of tissue paper cannot be wrapped smoothly around a sphere ; there will be numerous wrinkles and overlaps of excess paper. *The round earth on flat paper.*

The earth also being round (a "spheroid"), it cannot be represented on a flat piece of paper without some distortion. The smaller the portion of the globe to be mapped, the less the distortion that will be present—conversely, the greater the area, the greater the distortion.

Because the surface of a sphere cannot be represented accurately upon a plane surface, it is called "non-developable." There are other surfaces, however, which *are* developable, and can be spread out flat without change in any design or pattern drawn upon them. Two such surfaces are those of a cone and of a cylinder. A paper cone or cylinder can be cut from top to bottom and rolled out flat without distortion of any kind, as indicated in Figure 302. It is also true that a *limited portion* of the earth's surface can be shown ("projected")

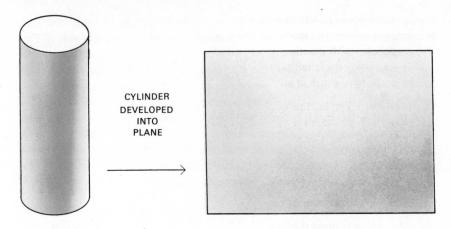

CYLINDER
DEVELOPED
INTO
PLANE

Figure 302: The
cylinder and cone.

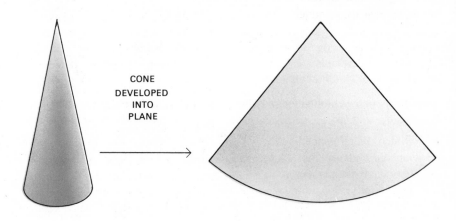

CONE
DEVELOPED
INTO
PLANE

Reference lines.

directly upon a plane surface while keeping distortion within acceptable limits. It is customary, therefore, to think of the reference lines of the nondevelopable sphere as first projected upon some developable surface (a plane, cone, or cylinder) and then developed or spread out flat. A chart projection may be loosely defined as any orderly arrangement of the meridians and parallels of the sphere.

There are several hundred projections, each with some particular property that may make it desirable for some specific purpose. Of these, not more than about half a dozen have ever been of much use for navigation.

*Properties and
projections.*

303. For navigation, certain properties are desirable in a projection. Among them are: *true shape* of physical features; *correct angular relationships* (a projection with these two features is said to be *conformal*); *true scale,* for measuring distances; *great circles* as straight lines; *rhumb lines* as straight lines.

One or more of these properties may be obtained in any one chart, according to the projection chosen. *All* can be obtained only upon a spherical surface.

Conformal charts.

Except for the *gnomonic,* all the projections commonly used in navigation are *conformal*. This is generally said to mean both *true shape* and *correct angular relationships,* but this is true only in a very limited sense.

22

Conformality does provide true shape for small areas. For example, the Mercator projection is conformal; along the rugged coast of Alaska it preserves the shape of a single inlet with practical accuracy, but for Alaska as a whole the northerly portion has been stretched out much more than the southerly portion, and the overall shape is not true at all.

Conformality is also said to afford correct angular relationships. It might therefore be expected that on a Lambert conformal map of the United States, one might draw a straight line from Miami to Seattle, and that the line so drawn would make the correct angle with each of the meridians between, but this is not the case (see article 312). With only minor exceptions, no straight line "from *A* to *B*" can be said to represent *exactly* correct angular relationships, even on a conformal map or chart.

304. Perhaps it is most practical to classify projections in accordance with the developable surface from which they are thought of as derived: that is, as plane, conical, or cylindrical.

Classification of projections.

The *plane* projections best known to navigators are the gnomonic and the stereographic.

Conic projections include the Lambert and Albers.

The best known *cylindrical* projection is the Mercator.

This general classification can be further broken down according to the point from which the reference lines (meridians and parallels) are projected upon the developable surface. Thus, Figure 304a shows the method of projection for the *gnomonic* and *stereographic* projections.

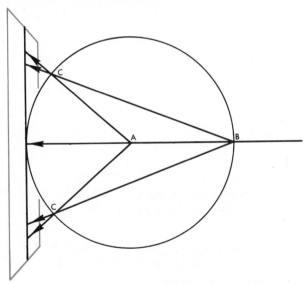

Figure 304a: Gnomonic projection projected from center of sphere, A; stereographic, projected from B.

For the *gnomonic* projection the points *C, C* on the sphere in Figure 304a are projected from *A*, the center of the sphere, upon a plane tangent at the equator. Because of the point of projection this is classed as a *central perspective* (or geometrical) projection. Since the plane is tangent at the equator, it is also known as the *equatorial* gnomonic. For a chart of the north polar regions the plane could have been made tangent at the pole, and the resulting projection

23

from *A* would have been a *polar* gnomonic. The plane could also have been made tangent at any point between the equator and either pole, in which case the projection obtained from the same central point *A* would have been an *oblique* gnomonic.

Figure 304a also shows the method of projection for the *stereographic*. Instead of being projected from the center of the sphere, points are projected upon the tangent plane from the opposite end of the diameter from the point of tangency (from *B* in the figure). As described in the preceding paragraph, the case shown in the figure affords an equatorial stereographic. A *polar* stereographic or an *oblique* stereographic is as readily obtained. In each case, the point of projection is always the opposite end of the diameter from the point of tangency.

A central perspective projection can readily be obtained by projecting the reference lines of the sphere upon a cylinder tangent to the sphere along the equator. The resulting projection is shown in Figure 304b (at left), with the meridians represented by a series of equally spaced vertical lines, the parallels by a series of lines at right angles to the meridians; spacing between the parallels expands rapidly with increasing distance from the equator. This expansion is, in fact, so great that the *central perspective cylindrical* projection is never used.

The Mercator projection (Figure 304b, right), because of the general similarity in appearance, is considered as a cylindrical projection, but it is related to the central perspective cylindrical in no other way. The Mercator is conformal, and its distortion in high latitudes is less than the distortion that occurs in the central perspective projection. The Mercator is derived from rigid mathematical formulae such that a straight line between any two points represents the rhumb line between them, a property which the central perspective does not possess.

Accepting the general classification of the Mercator as a cylindrical projection, the "cylinder" may be thought of as tangent along the equator (its most common form), and become the *equatorial* case. The "cylinder" may also be turned through 90° and become tangent along a selected meridian, and thus tangent also at both poles. According to previous terminology, this should be known as the polar case, but is actually called the *transverse Mercator*—and, sometimes, the *inverse Mercator.*

The "cylinder" may also be made tangent to some selected great circle, in any direction, anywhere on the surface of the sphere, as along a great circle route between San Francisco and Honolulu. This is generally known as the *oblique Mercator*, since the "cylinder" in this case is neither vertical nor horizontal with reference to the earth's axis, and only the area containing the line of tangency is used.

For conic projections, the axis of the cone usually coincides with the axis of the sphere, but it also may be turned to any other position, resulting in a transverse or oblique conic.

Azimuthal projections.

Other classifications are common. For example, most polar projections are *azimuthal* (or zenithal). By this it is meant that all directions (azimuths) from the center of the projection are true. The polar stereographic projection is azimuthal as well as conformal. All gnomonic projections are azimuthal, affording true directions from the point of tangency, regardless of its position on the surface of the sphere.

In any family of projections it is possible to obtain different properties simply by varying the spacing of the parallels. The *polar stereographic* projection is conformal, and scale along the meridians varies. The *polar equidistant* affords true scale along each meridian. A *polar equal area* projection is also obtainable by another variation in the spacing of the parallels. All three are azimuthal.

In the same way, a cylindrical projection may be conformal (the ordinary Mercator) or equal area, by varying the spacing of the parallels. Conic projections, too, may be either conformal (as the Lambert conformal) or equal area (as the Albers).

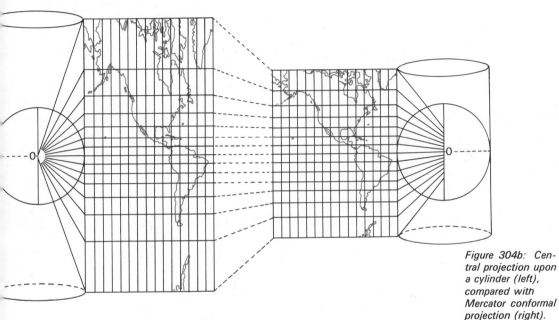

Figure 304b: Central projection upon a cylinder (left), compared with Mercator conformal projection (right).

305. Most of the charts used for marine navigation, and a good many of those used for air navigation, are based on the Mercator projection. In many cases this is completely justifiable; in others, its use appears to be based in part on its past success, and on a reluctance to adopt more suitable projections because of slightly different procedures from those which have become habitual. It is thought by some that modern methods of electronic navigation might be better adapted to a projection on which a straight line represents a great circle rather than a rhumb line. It has also been pointed out that, even for ordinary nautical charts, other projections could replace the Mercator with appreciable advantage, especially in higher latitudes.

Mercator projection.

For conventional methods of navigation—largely based on dead reckoning, or the determination of position by course and distance from some charted point— the Mercator projection has its advantages. On its rectangular graticule latitude and longitude are conveniently plotted; the *rhumb line* (see article 205) between any two points is the straight line between them; and the direction of a rhumb line may be measured at any convenient meridian.

Rhumb lines.

Distances along a course line can be determined without great difficulty although not with the same ease of measurement as on a Lambert. Great circle distances and directions are not readily determinable without first plotting the great circle on a gnomonic chart (article 309) and transferring points along the line to the Mercator.

When compared with a globe, a Mercator projection shows great exaggeration of shape and area in high latitudes. The example most often cited is that Greenland, when shown complete on the Mercator, appears to be larger than South America, although the latter has an area nine times as great.

Figure 305 may help in understanding this weakness of the projection. In the figure, at *A*, one gore or section of an ordinary school room globe has been peeled off and stands vertically. Two true circles have been drawn on the gore, to serve as "test patterns."

Figure 305:
Relation between
a globe and the
Mercator
projection.

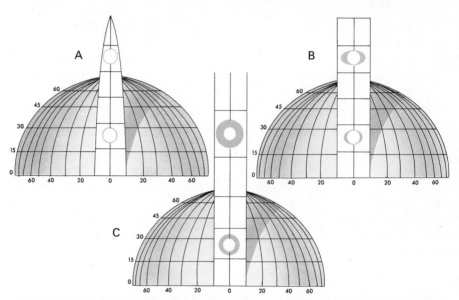

At *B* the sides of the gore have been stretched horizontally so that the two outer meridians are parallel to the central meridian of the gore. In the stretching the two circles have become ellipses (represented by the shaded areas), the northerly one having been stretched much more than the southern one.

Since the Mercator projection is conformal, true shapes of small areas must be preserved, so the horizontally stretched gore must now be stretched vertically until the ellipses again become (approximately) circles, the diameter in each case approximating the major axis of the ellipse. The result is shown at *C* in Figure 305.

Distortion.

Note that, since the upper part of the gore has been stretched more than the lower part, the upper circle has become appreciably greater in diameter than the lower one. Also, the upper edge of the gore at *C* is shown ragged and broken. It can no longer be extended all the way to the pole, for the pole has been stretched northward all the way to infinity. Consequently, most Mercator projections extend no farther from the equator than about 70°; rarely beyond 80°.

Part of the definition of *conformality* is that the scale at any point must be the same in all directions. This means that when a given parallel of latitude has been expanded from its length as shown at *A* to the length indicated in *B*, the scale of the meridian at that latitude must be expanded proportionately. It can be shown mathematically that the expansion at any place on the Mercator approximates the secant of the latitude of the place. Figure 304b shows the graticule of a Mercator projection for the western hemisphere.

Navigation charts generally cover a much smaller area, on which the distance scale is almost constant and there is little variation between the rhumb line and great circle. It is on the small scale charts of large areas (see article 321) that these distinctive features become evident.

306. A position of known latitude and longitude can be quickly plotted on a Mercator projection, using a plotter or straightedge and a pair of dividers. For example, a navigator's 2000 fix (L 41°09'.0 N, λ70°44'.0 W) may be plotted as follows: Note the given latitude, 41°09'.0 N, on the latitude scale. Place a straightedge through this point parallel to any convenient parallel of latitude, aligning it in an east-west direction. Then set one point of the dividers at 71°00'.0 W on the longitude scale and the other at 70°44'.0 W, a spread of 16.0 minutes of longitude. Without changing the setting of the dividers, lay off this distance along the straightedge from the 71st meridian eastward, in the direction of the fix. Circle this point (Figure 306) and label as appropriate (2000 fix).

Position on a Mercator chart.

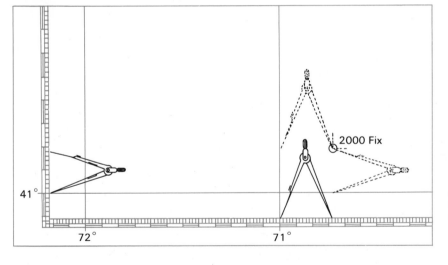

Figure 306: Locating position on a Mercator chart.

The reverse problem—determining the latitude and longitude of a fix that has been plotted at the intersection of two or more lines of position—is also easily accomplished. Place one point of the dividers on the 2000 fix and swing the other point in an arc, while adjusting its radius, until it becomes tangent to a parallel of latitude. The spread of the dividers then equals the difference of latitude from this reference parallel. Transfer the dividers to the latitude scale and, placing one point at the reference parallel, read the latitude of the fix at the other point. A similar procedure, measuring from the fix to a meridian of longitude, will provide the longitude of the point. Be careful in each case to lay off the difference of latitude and longitude in the proper direction from the reference parallel or meridian. With practice, this may easily be done with one hand while aligning the straightedge or recording with the other.

27

Direction on a Mercator chart.

307. As pointed out in article 205, two kinds of direction are important to a navigator: *great circle* directions and *rhumb line* directions.

On a sphere the great circle is the direct (shortest) route, and may be thought of as a straight line, while the rhumb line is a longer curved line, always between the great circle and the equator. The one purpose of the Mercator is to introduce exactly the right amount of distortion to show every rhumb line as a straight line. When this has been done, in order to keep all parts of the chart in their correct *relative* positions, the great circle has been distorted into a curved line, always farther from the equator than the rhumb line, and always concave toward the equator. If a mental picture of this relationship is kept in mind, it will help in the solution of navigation problems which will be met later.

The practical advantage of "sailing the rhumb" has already been mentioned. For routes where the saving in distance is sufficient to justify it, the advantages of great circle sailing *and* rhumb line navigation can be combined. This is done by first plotting the great circle route on a *gnomonic* chart, on which every straight line is a great circle (article 309). The great circle route is then transferred to the Mercator chart by plotting the latitude and longitude of a number of points lying on the great circle. Finally, the great circle as plotted on the Mercator is divided into sections of convenient length; and the rhumb line direction of each section is measured, and *followed* in turn. In this way the great circle route is approximated by a number of rhumb line "chords". On these long routes the advantages of using a Lambert projection for the chart work becomes apparent.

Figure 307: Measuring direction on a Mercator chart.

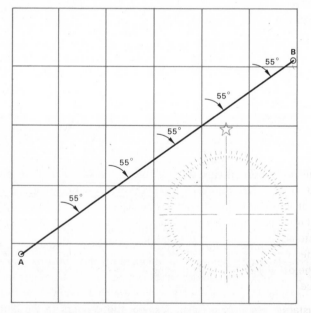

Measurement of the rhumb line direction (Figure 307) can be made at any convenient meridian, with any available protractor; or the direction of the rhumb line can be transferred to a nearby compass rose by means of parallel rulers, or a drafting machine, and read from the compass rose. In any case, care must be taken to read the direction at the circumference of the compass rose *toward* the destination, not at the opposite direction which is 180° different.

308. For practical purposes, 1° of latitude everywhere on the earth's surface may be considered to be 60 nautical miles in length; the length of 1° of longitude varies with the latitude, from 60 miles at the equator to zero at the poles (Figure 202c). Since 1 *minute* of latitude, then, is everywhere equal to 1 *mile*, it is the *latitude scale* that must be used for measuring distance—*never the longitude scale*.

Distance on a Mercator chart.

Because the latitude scale of a Mercator chart expands increasingly with distance from the equator, the scale of miles is increasing accordingly. That is, in the northerly part of a Mercator chart the length of each mile has been stretched, and there are fewer miles in an inch than in the southerly part. That part of the latitude scale should be used which is at the mean latitude of the distance to be measured (Figure 308a). Except for small scale charts, this may usually be done with sufficient accuracy by placing one point of a pair of dividers at *A*, the other point at *B*; then placing the dividers on the latitude scale with the middle of the dividers at about the mid-latitude. The difference of latitude in minutes on the latitude scale, is the distance in nautical miles, of course.

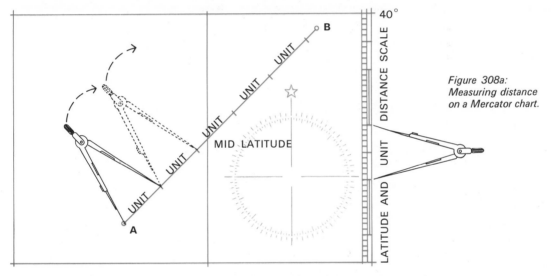

Figure 308a: Measuring distance on a Mercator chart.

When the distance is great enough that the dividers cannot reach all the way from *A* to *B* in one step, one point of the dividers might be placed at *A*, the other point at a position about halfway between *A* and *B*. The length of this portion of the route could then be measured from the latitude scale with the dividers centered at about the mid-latitude of that part. Similarly, the length of the remainder could be read with the dividers centered at about the mid-latitude of the other part. The two distances then would be added to obtain the total distance.

Distance measured at mid-latitude of route.

When the distance is too great for one or two settings of the dividers then some convenient unit (10 miles, in Figure 308a) can be taken from the latitude scale at the mid-latitude and stepped off along the route, as shown. In the figure it was stepped off five times: 5 × 10 = 50 miles, with a little left over. The small amount left over is then set on the dividers and referred to the latitude scale, where it is found to measure 2 miles: 50 + 2 = 52 miles, the total distance from *A* to *B*.

29

Large scale charts, which cover a limited area, so that there is little change of scale, often carry a simple "bar scale" for measuring distance. This may be simply a line, or a double line, divided into miles, or some other appropriate unit, to the right of zero, and into fractions of a mile to the left of zero.

When using the bar scale, a distance to be measured between two points on the chart is set on the dividers and referred to the bar scale. Assume that the distance is between 2 and 3 miles; one point of the dividers is set on the graduation for 2 miles, and the other point falls at 0.5 miles to the left of zero. The total distance is determined as 2.5 miles.

For smaller scale charts covering a wide band of latitude a "scale diagram" (Figure 308b) is sometimes used. This is, in effect, simply a series of bar scales, in parallel lines, with zero of each scale in the same vertical line. Smooth curves are then drawn through the corresponding graduations of each scale.

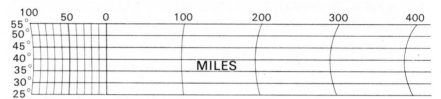

Figure 308b: Scale diagram for Lambert chart of the United States; scale 1:5,000,000.

Each scale in the diagram is correct for the latitude indicated, and distances should be measured with the scale for the average latitude of the distance required. Obviously, the correct scale for any latitude intermediate between two adjacent lines is also available. For example, if the average latitude between *A* and *B* is determined as about 27°30′ the dividers can be set on the diagram about halfway between the scales for 25° and 30°.

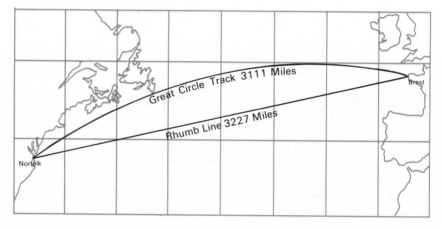

Figure 308c: Great circle and rhumb line on a Mercator chart.

Figure 308c is a portion of a Mercator chart showing both the great circle route and the rhumb line between Norfolk, Virginia, and Brest, France. As always on a Mercator chart, the great circle route *appears* to be appreciably longer but, when measured as shown in Figure 308a, the longer line is found to cover fewer miles.

Transverse and *oblique* Mercator projections are described in article 314.

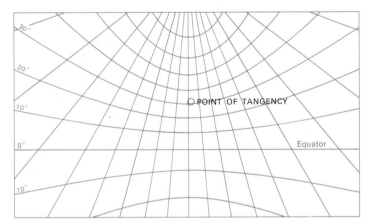

Figure 309a:
Gnomonic great
circle chart.

309. The gnomonic projection (Figure 304a) is a perspective (geometrical) projection in which the reference lines of the sphere are projected from the center of the earth upon a tangent plane. The point of tangency may be on the equator (*equatorial*); at either pole (*polar*); or at any other latitude (*oblique* gnomonic). For the oblique gnomonic, shown in Figure 309a, convergency of the meridians increases with the latitude of the point of tangency, from 0° in the equatorial case to 1° for each degree of longitude in the polar case.

Gnomonic projection.

The Mercator projection was invented for the sole purpose of showing every rhumb line as a straight line. The gnomonic projection has been adapted to a number of special uses, but in navigation it is chiefly used because it shows every *great circle* as a straight line. Figure 309b shows the great circle and rhumb line of Figure 308c. For the latter figure, the great circle was first drawn as a straight line on the gnomonic, then transferred to the Mercator by plotting a number of geographic positions along it. For the navigator, this is the principal use of the gnomonic or great circle charts. If a rhumb line is desired on the gnomonic, this process must be reversed: a straight line is first drawn on the Mercator, then transferred to its geographic position on the gnomonic.

Great circle as a straight line.

In all three cases of the gnomonic, distortion of shape and scale increases as distance from the center of the projection (the point of tangency) increases. Within about 1,000 miles of the point of tangency, this is not greatly objectionable; beyond that, it increases rapidly. Distance and direction cannot be measured directly, but instructions are usually printed on the chart for determining great circle distances and the initial direction of a great circle. It is useless as a working chart for normal plotting of navigational data.

It is impossible to include as much as a hemisphere in a single gnomonic chart. At 90 degrees from the center of the projection (the point of tangency) the projecting line is parallel to the plane of the projection, and will meet it only at infinity.

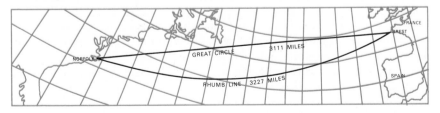

Figure 309b: Great
circle and rhumb
line on a gnomonic
chart.

31

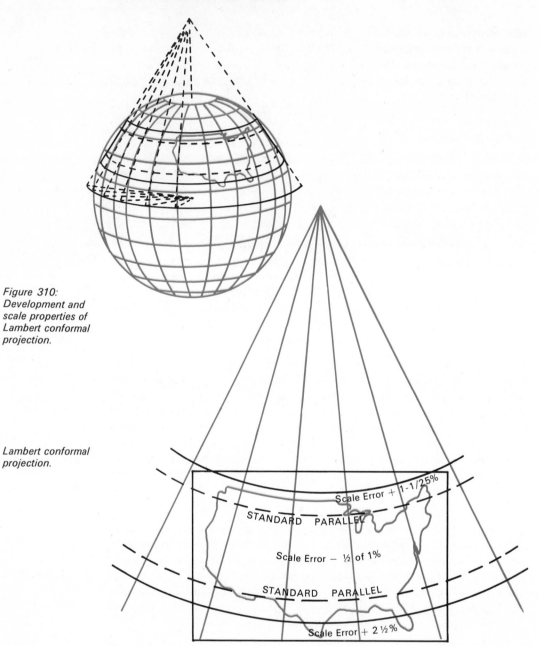

Figure 310: Development and scale properties of Lambert conformal projection.

Lambert conformal projection.

Parallels and meridians.

310. Like the Mercator, the Lambert is derived from rigid mathematical formulae. To aid in visualizing the general form of the projection, it is convenient to think of it as in Figure 310, illustrating a Lambert chart of the United States.

The cone is represented, not as tangent to the earth, but as *intersecting* the earth along two *standard parallels* of true scale. Between the standard parallels the scale is somewhat compressed, the maximum error being about 1/2 of 1 per cent (minus); outside them, the scale is slightly expanded, reaching a maximum of nearly $2\frac{1}{2}$ per cent at the tip of Florida. Stated another way, the *total* change in scale within the United States is about 3 per cent. That is, from a point in the central United States to the tip of Florida, each 100-mile section would measure about 103 miles (Figure 310). By way of comparison, the total change of scale for a Mercator chart of the United States would be approximately 40 per cent.

As illustrated in Figure 310, all parallels are concentric circles, all meridians are straight line radii of the parallels, meeting when extended at a common point, the apex of the developed cone.

This projection first came into use during World War I, for military maps. Since then, it has been widely used for aeronautical charts; very seldom for nautical charts. In article 305 it was suggested that projections other than the Mercator might well be considered for modern electronic navigation. With this in mind, special attention should be given to the desirable properties afforded by the Lambert.

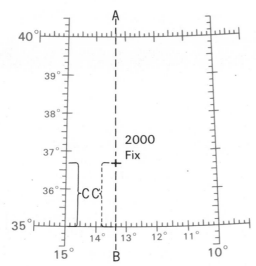

Figure 311: Position on a Lambert chart.

311. Many meridians and parallels of a Lambert chart are subdivided for easy plotting of latitude and longitude. The subdivision interval varies with the scale of the particular chart, or chart series. Figure 311 represents a portion of the projection of the Coast and Geodetic Survey's "Aircraft Position Chart No. 3071," at scale 1 : 6,250,000 (85.72 Nt. M to 1inch); meridians and parallels are both clearly subdivided into 10' intervals.

Position on a Lambert chart.

Assume that a fix has been obtained at 2000, as L 36°40' N, λ13°20' W, and is to be plotted on the chart. First, the longitude is plotted by laying a straight-edge through the appropriate subdivisions for 13°20' W, on the parallel for 35° N and on the parallel for 40° N, and drawing at least a part of the line *AB* (Figure 311). Plot the latitude by setting the dividers for the distance from the parallel for 35° to the subdivision for 36°40', along any meridian, as at *C*; then lay off the same distance from the 35th parallel along the line *AB* (as at *C'*) to obtain the position of the fix.

The problem of determining the geographic position of a fix obtained on the chart by graphic methods is arrived at quite easily by reversing the procedure just outlined.

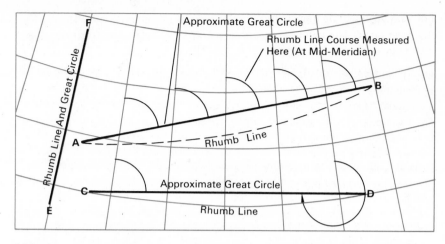

Figure 312a: Directions on a Lambert chart.

Direction on a Lambert chart.

312. On a Lambert chart, for most practical purposes, a straight line may be considered as a great circle; a rhumb line is a curved line, as on the sphere itself. In Figure 312a the straight lines *AB* and *CD* are approximate great circles; the line *EF*, which coincides with a meridian, *is* a great circle, and also a rhumb line.

Radio bearings travel great circle routes. Assume *C* is a radio station; the angle indicated at the meridian nearest *C* is the direction of a ship *D*, as measured at *C*. The angle with the meridian nearest *D*, is the direction of *C* as measured by radio direction finder aboard ship. This procedure is further illustrated in Figure 312b, showing measurement of the bearing of point *B from* point *A*. The protractor scale on a standard plotter is used to measure the bearing at the meridian nearest to point *A* on the Lambert chart.

As with great circles on the sphere, straight lines such as *AB* intersect each successive meridian at a different angle, but the direction of the rhumb line course may be measured at the intersection of the straight line with the meridian nearest halfway between *A* and *B*, as in Figure 312b.

Figure 312b: Measuring a bearing on a Lambert conformal chart, by AN plotter. Note that measurement is made at the meridian nearest the ship.

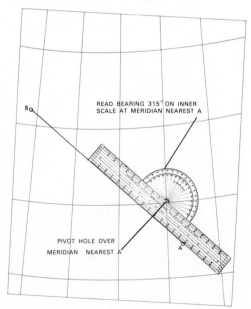

For long voyages the track will appear as a series of rhumb lines approximating the great circle. The course is changed every few degrees of longitude and the new course is measured at the center of each segment.

Series of rhumb lines.

Using the Lambert this is accomplished by drawing a single line on the chart representing the great circle and measuring the rhumb line courses at various meridians. This is a far simpler process than using a great circle gnomonic chart to determine the great circle, then determining the latitude and longitude of a number of points and transferring these to a Mercator where they are re-plotted and the rhumb line courses measured. When the course is measured as illustrated, a ship sailing that course does not exactly track the straight line, but follows a curved rhumb line, which is always between the straight line and the equator.

The higher the latitude the greater is the departure of the rhumb line from a great circle. This is due to the increasing curvature of the parallels with increasing distance from the equator. As the equator is approached, the curvature of the parallels becomes less; the distance between great circle and rhumb line also decreases until, at the equator, as along the meridians, they become identical.

In the central part of the projection, about halfway between the standard parallels, there is less distortion than in any other area. This also has a bearing on the relation between a straight line on the Lambert, which *approximates* a great circle, and a *true* great circle.

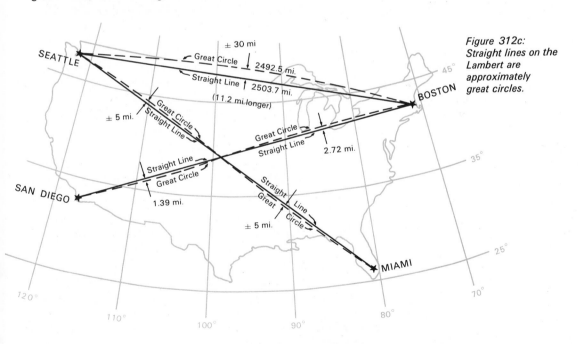

Figure 312c: Straight lines on the Lambert are approximately great circles.

Figure 312c shows the results of careful tests on a Lambert chart of the United States with standard parallels at latitudes 33° and 45°, the center of the projection being about latitude 39°. This illustrates maximum error of a great circle on the Lambert. Most navigational charts will cover a smaller area and have less distortion.

35

Distance on a Lambert chart.

313. On a Lambert chart selected meridians are subdivided into degrees and minutes of latitude (Figure 311), the subdivision interval varying according to the scale of the particular chart. As with the Mercator projection, the subdivided meridians provide convenient scales of nautical miles. In general, distances are measured as though on a chart with constant scale. As shown in Figure 310, however, there *is* some variation in scale. If a distance to be measured is long and is appreciably far from the center of the projection, more accurate results may be obtained by using that part of the meridional scale at about the same latitude as the line between the two points in question, although this is by no means as necessary as in the case of the Mercator (article 308).

Bar scales and scale diagrams similar to Figure 308b are printed on many Lambert charts. Special plotters are available which combine the functions of protractor, parallel rule, and a straightedge graduated to show mileage scales for some of the most commonly used charts. In aircraft navigation, dividers and parallel rules have been almost completely replaced by these special plotters for measuring course and distance. Even on a small scale chart of the entire North Atlantic practical accuracy can be attained.

Aircraft position charts.

Articles 310 and 311 referred to the series of Aircraft Position Charts. Three of these are on the Lambert projection : No. 3071, for the North Atlantic, and Nos. 3087 and 3094 for the North Pacific. Other charts of the series, on generally similar projections, are available for other areas.

The Aircraft Position Charts, among other data, show Loran lines of position, Consolan, and other radio aids. While designed primarily for air navigation, they are also suitable for surface navigation, in long range planning and cruising.

Because of the smaller scale and consequent greater extent of latitude, as compared with the chart of the United States, the total variation of scale in any one of these charts is slightly greater than that indicated in Figure 310. By any of the procedures just described, however, distances may be measured directly from the chart with practical accuracy. Even the slightly greater distance by way of the Lambert straight line, as compared with the true great circle distance, is seldom great enough to be important. Figure 312b shows that for a route completely across the northern United States, in the poorest area of the projection, the straight line distance is only about 11 miles greater than the great circle distance.

Aeronautical charts on the Lambert projection are available for almost the entire earth, in a number of series and in several projection bands. In all cases, the standard parallels of the band of which the chart is a part are noted in the margin. For most of the smaller scale charts of the band, the standard parallels actually appear on the chart. Larger scale charts of the same area are constructed as though they were pieces cut out of the small scale charts. In this case, the marginal notes indicate the standard parallels of the projection band, but the graphic scales printed on the chart are based on the true scale for the mid-latitude of the chart on which they appear. Consequently, they may generally be used anywhere on the chart with negligible error.

Transverse and oblique Mercator projections.

314. Mercator also devised projections other than the Mercator conformal described in articles 305–308. In speaking or writing of some other projection bearing his name, one must take care to give the complete designation, as

Mercator equal area. Whenever reference is made to the Mercator, it is always understood as applying to the Mercator conformal, by all means his best known projection and the one most commonly used in navigation.

It might seem that the transverse or oblique forms of the Mercator should have directly followed the description of the latter. While they are derived from the Mercator, they are in fact generally similar to the Lambert (articles 310 to 313) in appearance and use, and are therefore treated at this point.

The Mercator is commonly pictured as being developed from a cylinder tangent to the earth's equator. For the transverse Mercator, the cylinder has been turned through 90° and is tangent along a selected meridian.

Figure 314a shows a transverse Mercator chart. For the polar regions it possesses the excellent properties that the original Mercator possesses near the equator. The distortion of areas of the original Mercator in latitudes distant from the equator are still the regions of distortion in the new transverse projection, but it is apparent that they are now in regions *distant from the pole.*

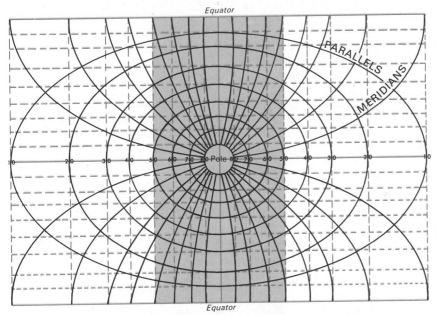

Figure 314a: Transverse Mercator projection, derived from Mercator conformal.

The transverse Mercator has been used for some charts of the polar regions, where its properties and methods of use are practically identical with those of the Lambert. Its chief disadvantage is the curvature of the meridians, making them less suitable for measurements with a protractor. Within the limits of a single chart, however, this is usually negligible. The transverse Mercator is also known, confusingly enough, as the *inverse* Mercator. If its use is confined to regions not too far removed from the central (vertical) meridian of Figure 314a, it represents meridians and parallels with little distortion, and it is sometimes used by cartographers for general maps.

Oblique Mercator.

The cylinder of the Mercator *could* have been turned through some angle other than 90°—any angle, and at any latitude between the equator and either pole. In this case it is often known as the *oblique Mercator*, though—and probably just as often—it is also referred to as the transverse Mercator.

37

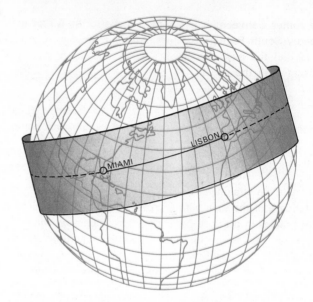

Figure 314b:
Oblique Mercator
projection in which
a selected great
circle (Miami to Lis-
bon) serves as the
"equator" of the
projection.

Figure 314b shows a portion of a cylinder tangent to the great circle from Miami to Lisbon. On the resulting oblique Mercator projection, whether it is visible or not, the great circle is in effect the *equator* of the projection. Meridians will be "S" curves, the direction of curvature reversing as a meridian crosses the *equator*, but the curvature is scarcely apparent for areas within 700 or 800 miles of the *equator*. Parallels are also curved lines.

In appearance, in the properties it affords, and in methods of use, the oblique is also generally similar to the Lambert. It has been used for several of the Aircraft Position Charts: No. 3097, for great circle routes between the west coast of the United States and the west coast of Europe; and No. 3096 for

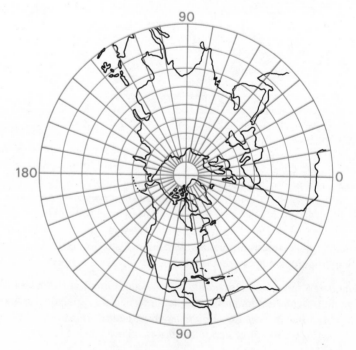

Figure 315: The
polar stereographic
projection.

great circle routes between the west coast of the United States and Tahiti, and the nearby South Pacific. For each chart, within about 15 degrees (900 nautical miles) of the new equator (or selected great circle), the new projection possesses all the excellent properties afforded by the Mercator conformal within about 15 degrees of the earth's equator—that is, all *except* the straight line meridians of the latter.

315. The polar stereographic is used for aeronautical charts of the polar regions, from about latitude 75° to the pole. It is also used for a few charts of interest in marine navigation. Figure 315 shows a polar stereographic map of the Northern hemisphere. Note that in this case the parallels are concentric circles, and all meridians are straight line radii. The polar form of the projection is, in fact, a special case of the Lambert projection. It possesses all the properties of the latter and is used in the same way.

Stereographic projection.

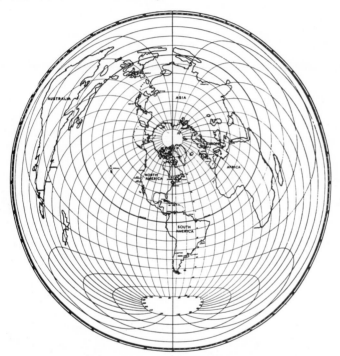

Figure 316: The azimuthal equidistant projection.

316. This is a mathematically derived projection. It is always centered on some place of strategic importance, such as Washington, D. C., or a selected naval base. On this projection it is possible to show the entire surface of the earth in one flat chart, though with great distortion. For example, the *point* at the opposite end of the earth's diameter from the central point of the projection is stretched into a *line* throughout the entire 360° of the limiting circle, as in Figure 316.

Azimuthal equidistant projection.

From the chosen central point of the projection all distances are true (equidistant), and the distance to any place on earth may be measured as accurately as the scale of the chart permits.

From the same central point all directions are true, and the direction (azimuth) of any place on earth may also be measured directly. A 360° scale is usually printed around the edge of the chart for this purpose.

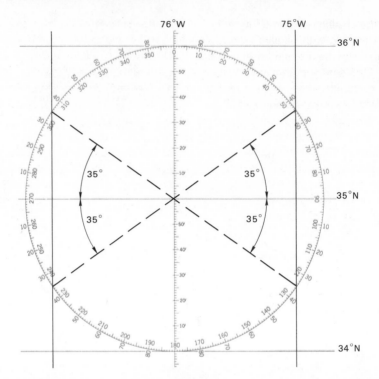

*Figure 317:
Universal plotting
sheet.*

Plotting sheets.

317. Plotting sheets are designed for use by the navigator at sea where no large scale charts are available. They are basically Mercator charts showing only the graticule of meridians and parallels with a compass rose, without any other chart data. Plotting sheets are particularly useful in plotting celestial fixes on a large scale. The position of the fix is then transferred to the working chart. There are two types available; those printed for a given band of latitude, and Universal Plotting Sheets (UPS) which can be used at any latitude.

The Hydrographic Office publishes several series of plotting sheets at different scales; the value of the latitude is printed on the parallels of latitude. The meridians are left blank and the navigator inserts the longitude of his area of operations. When labeling the meridian it must be remembered that in west longitude the longitude becomes numerically greater towards the west, to the left on the sheet. In east longitude it increases numerically to the east, to the right on the sheet. The same plotting sheets can be used for either north or south latitudes by inverting the sheet. As on any sheet north is always at the top. When plotting sheets are used in north latitude the value of the latitude becomes numerically larger towards the north or top of the sheet. In south latitude the reverse is true. The Oceanographic Office's 3000 series of plotting sheets covers 8° of latitude per sheet at a scale of 1° longitude = 4 inches. The 3000Z series covers 5° of latitude at the same scale. A special plotting sheet has been prepared to be used at the Naval Academy for classroom work, covering 2° of latitude.

Universal plotting sheets contain a compass rose, unnumbered parallels of latitude, and a single meridian in the center of the sheet. They are unusual in that they can be used for any latitude and longitude, exclusive of the polar areas where a Mercator chart is not practical. From Figure 317 it is obvious that in the absence of printed sheets they can be hand constructed simply by drawing a circle with parallel horizontal lines through the center of the circle, and tangent to the top and bottom of the circle, to serve as parallels of latitude. On the UPS the navigator draws in meridians properly spaced for the mid-latitude of the area to be covered. To draw meridians on the UPS the mid-latitude of the area desired is determined and the parallels labeled accordingly. Points on the compass rose, representing angles from the horizontal numerically equal to the mid-latitude, are determined and a meridian drawn through these points, as in Figure 317. The universal plotting sheets issued by the Oceanographic Office are at a scale of 20 miles per inch. The AN plotter shown in Figure 312b has distance scales to fit the UPS which greatly facilitates plotting direction and distance. The Weems Universal Plotting Charts are similar but constructed so as to be used with the Department of Commerce type plotter Mark II at a scale of 1 : 1,000,000.

318. In this chapter the basic principles of chart projection have been presented, with a treatment of the methods of use.

Comparison of chart projections.

By way of summary, the items of practical importance for selected projections have been combined into the following table, for further study and convenient reference.

Property	MERCATOR	LAMBERT*	OBLIQUE GNOMONIC
Parallels	Horizontal straight lines	Arcs of concentric circles	Curved (conic sections), except equator
Meridians	Vertical straight lines perpendicular to parallels	Straight-line radii of parallels, converging at the pole	Straight lines
Appearance	See Figure 304b	See Figure 310	See Figure 309a
Conformal	Yes	Yes	No
Great circle	Curved lines (except meridians and equator)	Approximates straight line	Straight line
Rhumb line	Straight line; course angle measured with *any* meridian	Curved line; course angle measured at intersection of straight line and mid-meridian	Curved line
Distance scale	Varies; scale at mid-latitude of a particular course to be used	Nearly constant	No constant scale; can be measured by rules printed on most charts
Increase of scale	Increases with distance from equator	Increases with distance from central parallel of projection	Increases with distance from center of projection (point of tangency)
Derivation	Mathematical; tables available (only one table required)	Mathematical; tables available for various standard parallels	Graphic or mathematical
Navigational uses	Dead reckoning; may be adapted to almost any type	Dead reckoning and electronic; may be used for almost any type	Great circle route determination

* Includes Lambert conformal, transverse and oblique Mercator, and polar stereographic. Statements in this column are true for the Lambert conformal; approximately correct for others.

Sources of charts. **319.** The principal sources from which nautical charts may be obtained are:

> The National Ocean Survey, Washington, D. C., which is responsible for charts of the ocean areas and waterways adjacent to and within the United States.

> Defense Mapping Agency, Hydrographic Center (formerly the U. S. Naval Oceanographic Office), Washington, D. C., which is responsible for charts and related publications for all other areas of the world.

Further details are given in Chapter 4.

CHART INTERPRETATION

Accuracy of charts. **320.** A chart is no more accurate than the survey on which it is based. In order to judge the accuracy and completeness of a survey, note its source and date, which are generally given in the title. Besides the changes that may have taken place since the date of the survey, the earlier surveys often were made under circumstances that precluded great accuracy of detail. Until a chart based on such a survey is tested, it should be regarded with caution. Except in well frequented waters, few surveys have been so thorough as to make certain that all dangers have been found. The fullness or scantiness of the soundings is another method of estimating the completeness of the survey, but it must be remembered that the chart seldom shows all soundings that were obtained. If the soundings are sparse or unevenly distributed, it should be taken for granted, as a precautionary measure, that the survey was not in great detail.

Large or irregular blank spaces among soundings mean that no soundings were obtained in these spots. When the nearby soundings are deep, it may logically be assumed that in the blanks the water is also deep, but when the surrounding water is shallow, or if it can be seen from the rest of the chart that reefs or banks are present in the vicinity, such blanks should be regarded with suspicion. This is particularly true in coral regions and off rocky coasts. These areas should be given a wide berth.

Large and small scale charts. **321.** The terms "large scale" and "small scale" cause much confusion to many who are not accustomed to using charts.

For example, if a chart is printed at scale 1:5,000,000 the very bigness of the number makes it seem of larger scale than one at 1:150,000. Remember that these scales can also be written as fractions,—1/5,000,000 or 1/150,000— and the larger the denominator of a fraction the smaller the part.

At a scale of 1:5,000,000, one mile is only 0.01 inch in length; at 1:150,000 it is 0.49 inches—nearly 50 times as long.

The 1:5,000,000 means that 1 inch on the chart represents 5,000,000 inches on the earth's surface; or 1 centimeter represents 5,000,000 cm.; or 1 of any other unit represents 5,000,000 of the same units.

There is no firm definition for the terms large scale charts and small scale charts; the two terms are only relative. Thus, as compared with a chart at 1:150,000, the chart at 1:5,000,000 is a *small* scale chart; it becomes a *large* scale chart, when compared with one at 1 :10,000,000. The chart that shows any particular feature, such as an island, or bay, at a larger size and in more detail is considered—comparatively, at least—as the *large scale* chart.

A chart may also carry a statement of scale such as "1 inch equals 16 miles"— that is, 1 inch on the chart represents 16 miles on the surface of the earth. On a Mercator chart it may be stated that "1° of longitude equals 1.25 inches." Scale is stated in this form because the spacing between meridians is the one constant on a Mercator projection.

322. The scales of nautical charts range from 1 :2,500 to about 1 :5,000,000. Graphic scales are generally shown on charts of scale 1 :80,000 and larger, and numerical scales are given in the upper right border for smaller scale charts. For convenient reference, charts may be classified according to scale as follows: *Scales of principal chart series.*

> *Sailing charts.* Scales 1 :600,000 and smaller. These are planned for use in fixing the mariner's position as he approaches the coast from the open ocean, or for sailing between distant coastwise ports. On such charts the shoreline and topography are generalized and only offshore soundings, the principal lights, outer buoys, and landmarks visible at considerable distances are shown.

> *General charts.* Scale 1 :100,000 to 1 :600,000. These are planned for coastwise navigation outside of outlying reefs and shoals.

> *Coast charts.* Scale 1 :50,000 to 1 :100,000. These are planned for inshore navigation, for entering bays and harbors of considerable width, and for navigating large inland waterways.

> *Harbor charts.* Scales larger than 1 :50,000. These are planned for harbors, anchorage areas, and the smaller waterways.

> *Intracoastal Waterway (inside route) charts.* Scale 1 :40,000. This is a special series of charts embracing the inside route in New Jersey, the route from Norfolk, Virginia, to Key West, Florida, on the Atlantic Coast and from Key West, Florida, to the Mexican Boundary on the Gulf Coast.

Mariners are urged to obtain and study thoroughly the largest scale charts available for a particular route, even if a smaller scale is used for keeping track of position in passage.

Read carefully all notes appearing on the chart. Do not merely look at it as though it were a picture. Check the scale, determine the date of the survey on which it is based, and see whether or not it is corrected up to date. Check to see whether soundings are in feet, fathoms, or meters. Check that the sounding coverage is complete and, if not, note the areas where lack of information may indicate danger. Note the system of projection used, so that you can be sure of how to measure direction and distance when using it. Check the tidal reference plane. Remember that a chart is a basic tool in the art of navigation. Learn to use it skillfully.

323. Many symbols and abbreviations are used on charts. These constitute a kind of shorthand which tells the navigator the physical characteristics of the charted area, and details of the available aids to navigation. The symbols used are quite standardized, but are subject to some variation, depending on the *Chart symbols and abbreviations.*

scale of the particular chart or chart series. It simply is not possible on a small scale chart to show all the details that can be shown on a large scale chart.

Many pages of text would be needed to describe all the symbols and abbreviations employed to present the detailed information available on a modern chart. Instead of a written description, these symbols and abbreviations are shown in "Chart No. 1" of the U. S. Naval Oceanographic Office, which is appended to this text. It should be studied until complete familiarity is attained.

Even the style of lettering on a chart affords information. For example, features that are dry at high water are identified in roman lettering such as this; submerged and floating hydrographic features (except the sounding figures, showing depths) are identified in *italic* lettering. Often, on small scale charts, it may be difficult to distinguish a small reef from a small islet, but the style of lettering will indicate the difference.

Metric system.   **324.** The U. S. Naval Oceanographic Office, in 1970, started a program of using the metric system of measurements on nautical charts to conform to bilateral chart reproduction agreements with other nations. On all new charts produced, water depths and the height of lights will be in meters. Land contours will be shown in meters if the source information is in meters; when source information is in feet this measurement will be retained. As the program progresses this change to the metric system will have widespread effects and will necessitate changes in echo sounder equipment to provide dual scales for use with either the English or the metric system.

To distinguish nautical charts being produced with depths in meters, the new color *green* on land areas will be used for all nautical charts produced in meters after October 1971. In addition, nautical charts produced in meters will carry in *bold purple* type the legends "Soundings in Meters" on the upper and lower chart margins and the word "Meters" superimposed over the metric depths when space allows on the face of the charts. *Gray* tint will continue to be used for land areas on those charts which express depths in fathoms and feet.

Summary.   **325.** This chapter has described the basic frameworks, or chart projections, on which almost all the nautical charts of the world are, or are likely to be, constructed. Only by becoming familiar with the way in which one type of chart may be used to complement another, and by learning the weaknesses, advantages and methods of use of the different projections, may the various available charts be used to the best advantage.

Chart symbols have been referred to as a kind of shorthand. For these who can read this shorthand, it provides all the information that mariners long familiar with the area could offer. Until the navigator can relate the appearance of objects he observes around him to their corresponding symbols on the chart, the chart will remain merely a piece of paper.

Any tool, regardless of form, requires intelligent and practised use in order that the most efficient service may be gained from it. In no other area of navigation is this more true than in regard to the mariner's chart—a basic tool in the art of navigation.

CHAPTER 4

Navigational Publications

401. The U. S. Naval Oceanographic Office exists for the improvement of the *Introduction.* means for navigating safely the vessels of the United States Navy and of the merchant marine by providing accurate and inexpensive nautical charts, Sailing Directions, and manuals of instructions for the use of all vessels of the United States and for the benefit and use of navigators generally. The office maintains several specially equipped vessels that conduct hydrographic surveys in areas where accurate charts are most needed, and keeps in touch with hydrographic developments in all parts of the world in order that its published charts and descriptive nautical documents may contain the most recent and accurate information available.

Hydrographic services of varying degrees of completeness are maintained by practically all maritime countries. The smaller countries restrict such service to their own coastal waters, but the larger countries, whose maritime interests embrace large parts of the globe, issue charts and other publications that cover the entire world. Most of these institutions are associated in the International Hydrographic Bureau, Monaco, and hold periodic conferences for the purpose of promoting international agreement in the form of nautical publications and effecting collaboration in the common task of collecting and disseminating hydrographic information. The result of this effort is an improvement in the quality and coverage of hydrographic surveys in many parts of the world and increasing uniformity in charts and nautical books which facilitates their use by mariners of all nations. There is a free exchange of hydrographic publications among the various maritime countries. As a result of this arrangement, the U. S. Naval Oceanographic Office, in preparing nautical documents for any particular area, makes full use of the hydrographic information that has been compiled and published by the country having jurisdiction.

The Oceanographic Office does not depend solely upon official sources of information. It serves as a clearing house for nautical information from any and all sources and in this way gives navigators in general the benefit of observations noted by ships' officers in the routine performance of their duties. Many observers contribute from time to time valuable data concerning currents, aids, and dangers to navigation, port facilities, and related subjects, which help materially in keeping the charts, Sailing Directions, and Light Lists in agreement with prevailing conditions. The office solicits such cooperation and greatly appreciates the receipt of any data that may increase the accuracy and completeness of its publications. Direct contact with ships' officers is facilitated by branch offices maintained at a number of ports in the United States and possessions, where the most recent hydrographic information is placed at the disposal of commanding officers and masters.

The Oceanographic Office is the principal source of navigational publications. Others in the United States are the Coast Guard, National Ocean Survey, Naval Observatory, National Weather Service, Federal Aviation Administration, miscellaneous government agencies, and private sources.

Navigational publications are supplied to naval vessels in accordance with *allowance lists*, which are established by the various type commanders. In addition, the navigator of a naval vessel should consult the Fleet Commander's applicable allowance list, and the 5600 series of the Navy Department's *Instructions and Notices* for specific information of immediate concern to the administrative management procedures pertaining to the navigation department of a public vessel.

Nautical charts.   **402.** The principal sources from which nautical charts may be obtained are:

The National Ocean Survey, Washington, D. C., and

The U. S. Naval Oceanographic Office, Washington, D. C.

Both agencies have branch offices in many other places, and both have many authorized agents from whom charts and publications can be obtained. Two other minor sources of charts and maps for the U. S. Navy are:

The Lake Survey Center, National Ocean Survey, Detroit, Michigan, and

Department of the Army, Corps of Engineers, Army Map Service, Washington, D. C., (for topographical maps).

Nautical charts may be categorized as follows:

Charts by geographic area.   Charts of the coasts of the United States, its territories and possessions; published by the National Ocean Survey and distributed through its sales agents. These charts are listed in the NOS *Nautical Chart Catalog of the Atlantic and Gulf Coasts, including Puerto Rico and the Virgin Islands* (Vol. 1), *Nautical Chart Catalog of the Pacific Coast, including Hawaii, Guam and Samoa Islands* (Vol. 2), and *Nautical Chart Catalog of Alaska, including the Aleutian Islands* (Vol. 3).

Charts of the Great Lakes, Lake Champlain, and the St. Lawrence River above St. Regis and Cornwall, Canada; published by, and obtained from the Lake Survey Center, National Ocean Survey, Detroit, Michigan. These charts are listed in the *Lake Survey Center Catalogue of the Great Lakes and Connecting Waterways*.

Charts covering the coasts of foreign countries; distributed through the U. S. Naval Oceanographic Office sales agents. These charts, together with world coverage of charts and publications of other agencies, are listed in the *Catalog of Nautical Charts*, N. O. Pub. No. 1-N-A.

Portfolios.   Because of the thousands of charts published by various agencies (such as Oceanographic Office, National Ocean Survey, and British Admiralty), there must be a system of filing and identification. The *Portfolio Chart List*, N. O. Pub 1-PCL, is prepared by the Naval Oceanographic Office for use by the U. S. Navy, U. S. Coast Guard, and Merchant Marine in maintaining nautical navigational charts in a current status, and in logical geographical sequence to facilitate filing and access aboard ship, thereby assisting the navigators in the performance of their functions.

The publication is produced in two parts consisting of individual Atlantic and Pacific area coverages. Within the Atlantic area, coverage includes the North and South Atlantic Ocean, Arctic Ocean, Barents and Mediterranean Seas. Coverage of the Pacific area includes the North and South Pacific Ocean, and Bering Sea. (Coverage of the Antarctic and Indian Oceans is included in both parts of the publication.) The publication provides guidelines and procedures for the correction of nautical charts and publications, instructions for establishing a chart correction card system, general information of interest to navigational personnel, and a comprehensive listing of portfolios covering selected geographic areas of the world. In addition, with the advent of the new chart numbering system, all charts are arranged in sequence within a regional subarea designated as a numbered portfolio listing the title, edition number, and date of each chart. Within each regional subarea a further grouping is made to show all available charts within that precise area. Symbols are used to show if a chart is or is not a part of a portfolio and charts which are not for sale.

The nautical chart portfolio system groups nautical navigational charts covering a specific geographical area of the world. Portfolio areas are identical to the breakdown of the subregions established within a regional chart catalog. This system divides the world into 52 geographical areas and assigns a two-digit designator representing a portfolio number to each area. This portfolio number is synonymous with the five-digit chart number, in that the first number also represents a catalog index region, and the second digit represents the subregion within that region. An A and/or B prefix is also used. The "A" series of portfolios contain all the general charts, and principal harbor and approach charts for each of the numbered areas, and the "B" series supplement the "A" coverage of nautical charts within the area. Accordingly, a portfolio identified as "A&B 14" will contain all standard navigational charts applicable to Portfolio 14. If only "A" or "B" types of portfolios are desired, identification would be Portfolio "A14" or Portfolio "B14". Charts within a subregion (Portfolio) are also categorized by a "C" prefix which includes all remaining (special type) charts of the area that do not comprise part of a portfolio.

Numbering of portfolios.

The numbering of nautical charts is predicated on a system which generally identifies a chart through a scale range and geographical location. Charts are numbered from 1 to a maximum of 5 digits as follows: 1 digit—flag chart and symbol sheets; 2 digits—charts with a scale of 1:9,000,000 and smaller; 3 digits—all charts of scale 1:2,000,000 to 1:9,000,000; 4 digits—miscellaneous charts; 5 digits—all charts with scales larger than 1:2,000,000.

Numbering system for oceanographic charts.

403. Perhaps the best known of all manuals is H. O. Pub. No. 9, *The American Practical Navigator*, originally written by Nathaniel Bowditch. It first appeared in 1802 and has since been revised many times. The book was originally published because of the need for a simply written, complete text on navigation, with the necessary tables and explanations to permit the relatively uneducated mariner of a century and a half ago to navigate. The book immediately became popular because it was so much better and more reliable than any other book of its time. It has now become primarily a reference book, and will be found in any collection of books on navigation.

Manuals.

The British Admiralty *Manual of Navigation*, in 3 volumes, is also an excellent reference work on navigation.

Varous manuals on specific phases of navigation are available to the mariner. Among these are the following : N. O. Pub. No. 1310, *Radar Navigation Manual,* H. O. Pub. No. 217, *Maneuvering Board Manual;* H. O. Pub. 226, *Handbook of Magnetic Compass Adjustment;* H. O. Pub. 150, *World Port Index; Naval Arctic Operations Hand Book, Vols. 1 and 2; Electronic Aids to Navigation;* and manuals of instruction for equipment, published principally by the Naval Ship Systems Command and the Air Systems Command.

Navigational tables. **404.** Most navigational tables used by American navigators today are published by the Oceanographic Office, but a few are published by private sources. Perhaps the most widely used of all such tables are known simply as "H. O. 214," though the title is *Tables of Computed Altitude and Azimuth.* There are 9 volumes, one for each 10° of latitude. In these books the solutions of the navigational triangle for celestial altitudes of 5° or greater are tabulated. Answers are given to a precision of 0'.1 of altitude and 0°.1 of azimuth. A complete description of these tables is given in Chapter 25.

A new set of somewhat similar tables, H. O. 229, *Sight Reduction Tables for Marine Navigation,* is now available and scheduled as an eventual replacement in the Navy for H. O. 214. These tables are also described in Chapter 25.

Other volumes of tables for reduction of the navigational triangle which are still in use, but which will not be republished when present supplies are exhausted are H.O. 208, *Dreisenstok,* and H.O. 211, *Ageton.* While H.O. 249, *Sight Reduction Tables for Air Navigation,* is widely used by air navigators, the range of declination covered, and the fact that it does not permit sufficiently precise reduction makes it less desirable for general marine navigation.

Two volumes of azimuths are available : H. O. Pub. No. 260, *Azimuths of the Sun,* for declinations from 0° to 23° ; and H. O. Pub. No. 261, *Azimuths of Celestial Bodies,* for declinations from 24° to 70°.

Other books of navigational tables available are the tables of *Bowditch,* and H.O. Pub. No. 151, *Table of Distances Between Ports.*

Almanacs. **405.** Books giving the positions of the various celestial bodies used by navigators, times of sunrise, sunset, moonrise, and moonset, and other astronomical information of interest to navigators are prepared by the Naval Observatory and published by the Government Printing Office. The *Nautical Almanac,* published annually, and the *Air Almanac,* published three times each year, gives ephemeristic data for air and marine navigation respectively. These almanacs are discussed in Chapter 24. The *American Ephemeris and Nautical Almanac* contains the information given in the *Nautical Almanac* and a great deal of additional information of interest primarily to astronomers and is published annually.

Sailing Directions and Coast Pilots. **406.** The *Sailing Directions,* also called "Pilots," consist of 69 separate volumes, each of which describes a foreign geographic area and is identified by a publication number and an appropriate title. These volumes contain descriptions of coast lines, harbors, dangers, navigational aids, winds, currents, tides, directions for navigating, approaching, and entering restricted waters and harbors, port facilities, signal systems, pilotage service, and other data that cannot be conveniently shown on the charts of the area. *Sailing Directions* are issued as looseleaf publications. A new series of 43 *Sailing Directions*, compiled under an entirely new concept which is intended to assist mariners in planning a voyage of any extent, was started in 1971 and is scheduled to be completed by 1 January 1977, replacing the older *Sailing Directions*. The new *Sailing Directions* are divided into two groups:

Planning Guides. Each covers an arbitrary division of the world's seaways, often called "ocean basins," containing chapters of useful information about countries adjacent to that particular ocean basin; information relative to the physical environment and local coastal phenomena; references to publications and periodicals listing danger areas; recommended ship routes; detailed electronic navigation systems pertaining to that ocean basin.

En route. Each includes detailed coastal and port approach information, supplementing the largest scale chart for sale by the Naval Oceanographic Office. It should be used along with the Planning Guide of that particular ocean basin.

The port facilities data, now scattered throughout the old *Sailing Directions*, has been computerized and tabulated in a new expanded edition of N. O. Pub. 150, *World Port Index*, designed as a companion volume to be used in conjunction with the new *Sailing Directions*.

The coasts of the United States and its possessions are described in a similar set of 8 publications called *Coast Pilots* published by the National Ocean Survey. They are reprinted annually, and supplement the navigational information shown on the marine charts of the area. They should be updated by information published in the *Notice to Mariners*. The appendix includes additional useful information such as climatological tables of the area, various conversion tables, and distances between ports in the area covered by the particular volume.

407. The Naval Oceanographic Office publishes, for U. S. Navy use only, a series of 23 publications entitled *Fleet Guides*, designed to acquaint naval vessels with important command, navigational, repair, and logistic information relating to each major United States base as well as those overseas ports frequently visited by ships of the United States Navy, such as Pearl Harbor, Tokyo Bay, Sangley Point, and Roosevelt Roads. As originally published, information contained in Fleet Guides is based on the best source material available in the Oceanographic Office on the date of printing. Corrections are published at frequent intervals in the form of consecutively numbered changes, with interim corrective information published in the Navy *Notice to Mariners*. The prudent naval navigator will pay the same careful attention to the *Fleet Guide* as he does to *Sailing Directions* and *Coast Pilots*, prior to entry into port. *Fleet Guides.*

408. Seven publications, each called *List of Lights*, are published by the Oceanographic Office. These give detailed information on the positions and characteristics of foreign navigational lights, with a brief description of the light structures and of any accompanying fog signals. These volumes list the lights in geographical order along the various coasts of the world, except those of the United States and its possessions. These coasts are covered by five volumes of *Light Lights* prepared by the Coast Guard and published by the Govern- *Light Lists.*

ment Printing Office; the *Light Lists* also list unlighted buoys; both *Light Lists* and *Lists of Lights* are kept corrected to date by means of the *Notice to Mariners*.

Periodicals. **409.** Various publications are made available regularly to keep the mariner informed of the latest changes in navigational aids, dangers to navigation, etc.

Notice to Mariners is issued weekly in one pamphlet covering the world. Specific sections list changes in aids to navigation (lights, buoyage, harbor constructions), dangers to navigation (rocks, shoals, banks, bars), important new soundings, corrections to radio aids, broadcast warnings, route information, and, in general, all such information as affects the mariner's charts, manuals, and *Sailing Directions* (Pilots). The Notices are mailed to all United States vessels in commission, cooperating observers, Branch Oceanographic Offices and agencies, and United States consulates.

U. S. Navy Notice to Mariners, a separate publication, is published weekly for the correction of certain charts and publications issued by the Oceanographic Office to official users. Its distribution is limited to those naval activities and commands who hold such navigation material. This publication is designated "for official use only" and, as with the regular Notices, contains specific corrections to be made to special charts and publications affecting safety of navigation.

Hydrolants and *Hydropacs* are navigational warnings broadcast by the Naval Oceanographic Office. Hydrolants cover the Atlantic Ocean, Gulf of Mexico, Caribbean Sea, and contiguous areas. Hydropacs cover the Pacific Ocean, Indian Ocean, and contiguous areas. Each contains navigational information of such importance and urgency to the mariner that radio transmission is essential to its prompt dissemination. The locations affected by the information contained in Hydrolants and Hydropacs messages are indicated by the N. O. chart numbering system, region or subregion numerical designators as part of the Hydrolants/Hydropacs numbers. *Naveams* are urgent messages pertaining to the eastern Atlantic and the Mediterranean and broadcast by the British Admiralty. All information contained in Naveam messages affecting the safety of navigation is repromulgated as consecutively numbered Hydrolants.

Special Warnings supplement Oceanographic Office radio broadcasts of Hydrolants and Hydropacs as necessity arises. These warnings are numbered consecutively and given further publicity by the *Daily Memorandum and Notice to Mariners*. They are used primarily for the dissemination of official governmental proclamations affecting commercial shipping restrictions.

Local Notices to Mariners are promulgated by each of the twelve U. S. Coast Guard District Offices within its area of responsibility, using Fleet broadcast transmission facilities listed in H.O. 117-A and B when appropriate. They are issued in addition to the warnings broadcast by the Oceanographic Office. Copies of these warnings are made available to vessels arriving in an area upon application at the District Office. A complete file of local notices should also always be maintained by the navigator.

Daily Memorandum contains reprints of *Hydrolants* or *Hydropacs* messages which were previously broadcast, with the exception of messages containing satellite ephemeral data. An East Coast edition is prepared by the main office; the West Coast by the branch Oceanographic Office, San Pedro; the Pacific edition by the branch Oceanographic Office, Honolulu; and the Canal Zone edition by the branch Oceanographic Office, Cristobal, C. Z.

410. The following various miscellaneous publications of interest to navigators are issued by the Oceanographic Office, Coast Guard, or National Weather Service as indicated.

Miscellaneous publications.

H. O. Pub. No. 117-A, Atlantic Coast and Mediterranean area, *H. O. Pub. No. 117-B*, Pacific Coast and Indian Ocean, *Radio Navigational Aids* contains information on marine direction-finder stations, radio beacons, Consol and Consolan stations, Loran, Decca, Racon, Radar, time signals, times and transmission frequencies of navigational warnings, the delineation of Hydrolant and Hydropac areas, medical advice and quarantine stations, long range navigational aids, and radio regulations for territorial waters.

H. O. Pub. No. 118, Radio Weather Aids contains general weather information and broadcast schedules, weather codes, code forms, and international index numbers with location of stations, key groups, and call signs. World coverage of this data is now in a single volume.

H. O. Pub. No. 150, World Port Index provides a convenient means of locating maritime ports and shipping places in all parts of the world and of presenting information as to their type, general facilities, available services, and other information of an operational nature. Reference is also made to the appropriate volume of *Sailing Directions* or *Coast Pilot*, and to the best-scale chart of the particular port as a source for more detailed information concerning the port.

Pilot charts of the North Atlantic Ocean N. O. 16 (formerly H. O. 1400) and North Pacific Ocean N. O. 55 (formerly H. O. 1401) are issued by the Oceanographic Office each month. These charts present available data in graphic form which will assist the mariner in choosing the safest and quickest routes. Besides timely information of a varied nature, they show average winds, currents, the percentage of gales, calms, storm tracks, sea surface temperature, visibility, and average conditions of wind and weather for each month, the presence of ice and derelicts, isobaric and isothermic lines, lines of equal variation of the compass for each degree and their annual change, and recommended routes for steamers and sailing vessels. They are furnished free to cooperating observers, and automatically to naval vessels after the initial request. Pilot charts are published in atlas form for the Northern North Atlantic Ocean, H. O. 108; the South Atlantic Ocean and Central American Waters, H. O. 106; and the South Pacific and Indian Ocean, H. O. 107.

N. O. Pub. *No. 1-N, Catalog of Nautical Charts.*

H. O. Pub. *No. 102, International Code of Signals, Visual and Radio Signals.*

H. O. Pub. *No. 220, Navigation Dictionary.*

N. O. Pub. *No. 1-P, Catalogue of Publications.*

N. O. Pub. *No. 1-PCL, Portfolio Chart List.*

51

Atlases and charts depicting graphically such hydrographic and oceanographic information as sea surface temperatures, surface and ocean currents, ice limits, and sea and swell conditions are also available from the Oceanographic Office.

C.G. 169, *Rules of the Road, International and Inland.* U. S. Coast Guard pamphlet.

Buoys in Waters of the United States. U. S. Coast Guard pamphlet.

The Significance of Aids to Marine Navigation. U. S. Coast Guard pamphlet.

Tide Tables, Tidal Current Tables, Tidal Current Charts, and *Tables of Distances Between United States Ports* are all issued by the National Ocean Survey.

Mariners Weather Log, a pamphlet, and other publications of primary interest in weather observing, instruments, forecasting, cloud forms, etc., are issued by the National Weather Service, National Oceanic and Atmospheric Administration (NOAA), Department of Commerce.

Defense Mapping Agency Effective July 1, 1972, the Department of Defense established a new Defense Mapping Agency. The Hydrographic functions of the U. S. Naval Oceanographic Office, the USAF Aeronautical Chart and Information Center, and the U. S. Army Topographic Command were incorporated into the new agency and redesignated as follows: Defense Mapping Agency, Hydrographic Center; Defense Mapping Agency, Aerospace Center; and Defense Mapping Agency, Topographic Center.

Although the names have been changed, no changes are being made at the present time that would affect the distribution and requisitioning of nautical charts, publications, and periodicals.

CHAPTER 5

The Sailings

501. The term *the sailings* refers collectively to the various mathematical methods of solving problems involving course, distance, difference of latitude, difference of longitude, and departure. These mathematical solutions were in general use until comparatively recent years due to a lack of adequate chart coverage of much of the world. The modern navigator usually solves these problems by measurement on a chart, as this graphic method provides a rapid solution of practical accuracy. Occasionally, however, it becomes necessary to obtain the solution by computation or by table.

Introduction.

Great-circle, mid-latitude, and Mercator are the only sailings to be discussed in this chapter. *American Practical Navigator* (Bowditch), H. O. Pub. No. 9, contains a more complete discussion of the various sailings.

502. It must be kept constantly in mind that all solutions are made with true directions. Throughout this text *all directions given are true unless otherwise stated.*

Preliminary considerations.

Before proceeding with a discussion of the sailings, it will be advisable to become familiar with the terms to be employed. In Chapter 2 the following terms were introduced: latitude (L), difference of latitude (*l*), longitude (λ), difference of longitude (DLo), distance (*d* or dist.), departure (*p*), course (C or Cn), rhumb lines, and great circles. Latitude and longitude of the point of departure will be designated L_1 and λ_1 respectively, and the coordinates of the destination, L_2 and λ_2.

Course angle (symbol C) is the inclination of the course line to the meridian, measured from 0° at the reference direction (*north* or *south*) *clockwise* or *counterclockwise* through 90° or 180°. It is labeled with the reference direction (N or S) as a prefix, and the direction of measurement from the reference direction (E or W) as a suffix, and is converted to *course* by following the instructions of the labels. The rules for determining the labels and the numerical limits vary with the method of solution.

Departure (symbol *p*) is the linear measure, in nautical miles, of an arc of a parallel included between two meridians. The term distinguishes it from difference of longitude (DLo) which is the *angular* measure of the same arc. Regardless of the latitude, the difference of longitude between two meridians remains the same, but the departure between those meridians varies with the parallel on which it is measured. Thus, in Figure 502 the difference of longitude between the meridians is constant, whereas the departure becomes less as the

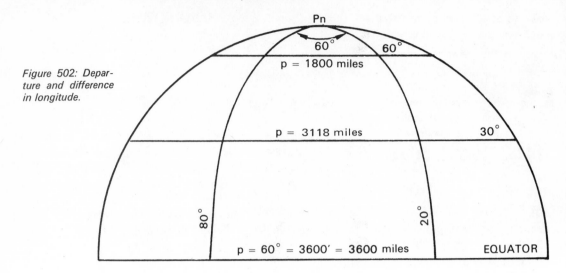

Figure 502: Departure and difference in longitude.

poles are approached. Departure may be marked east (E) or west (W) according as it is made to the east or to the west.

Figure 502 illustrates the relationship of DLo and departure at various latitudes. At the equator DLo and departure are identical and equal to the difference in longitude in minutes. The distance between the meridians becomes less with increased latitude and varies as the *cosine* of the latitude—at 60° then, the departure is one half of that at the equator (cos 60° = $\frac{1}{2}$), and the distance around the earth at the sixtieth parallel is one half the distance around the earth at the equator. The relationship of DLo and p is expressed by the formula, $p = DLo \cos L$, $DLo = p \sec L$.

Comparison of rhumb lines and great circles.

503. A course line plotted on a Mercator chart is a rhumb line; it makes the same angle with all the meridians it crosses. The chief advantage the rhumb line offers is that a ship following it does not change course between departure and destination. It is adequate for most purposes of navigation, except in high latitudes, and except for long bearing lines, such as those obtained by a radio direction finder.

A *great circle* is formed by the intersection of the surface of a sphere and a plane passing through the center of the sphere. The shortest distance between two places is measured along the great circle arc passing through them. However, this arc will cross each meridian at a slightly different angle; it cannot be drawn on a Mercator chart as a straight line, but would be represented by a curve. The *vertex* is the point of greatest latitude through which the great circle arc passes.

The equator and meridians are great circles, but they may also be considered as special cases of the rhumb line. Arcs of both meridians and of the equator appear as straight lines on a Mercator chart.

The difference between the great circle distance and the rhumb line distance between two places may amount to several hundred miles. For example, the great circle distance from Sydney, Australia, to Valparaiso, Chile, is 748 miles shorter than the rhumb line distance. It is obvious that while the rhumb line is most convenient, it should not be used for all long voyages.

Decision as to whether or not to use great circle sailing depends on whether the distance to be saved is sufficient to justify the trouble involved, as well as on other considerations, such as the latitude of the vertex, and anticipated weather, currents, etc., along the alternate routes.

504. This sailing is based on approximations which simplify solution, but which yield somewhat less accurate answers than are obtainable by more rigorous and time-consuming reductions. For ordinary purposes, however, it yields results more accurate than are obtainable in ordinary navigation. *Mid-latitude sailing.*

In mid-latitude sailing, the difference of latitude and departure are found when course and distance are known; alternately, the rhumb line course and distance may be found if the difference of latitude and departure are known. Departure and difference of longitude may be interconverted, using the mean or *mid-Latitude* (Lm).

The basic formulae for mid-Latitude sailing are:

$$p = \text{DLo (in minutes of arc)} \times \cos \text{Lm} \qquad (1)$$

$$\tan C = p/l, \text{ where } l = \text{the difference of} \qquad (2)$$
$$\text{latitude in minutes of arc}$$

$$d \text{ (distance)} = l \times \sec C \qquad (3)$$

The use of these formulae is shown in the following example:

Example: A vessel at lat. 8°48'.9 S, long. 89°53'.3 W is to proceed to lat. 17°06'.9 S, long. 104°51'.6 W.

Required: (1) Course, (2) distance.

Solution:

L_1	8°48'.9 S	λ_1	89°53'.3 W
L_2	17°06'.9 S	λ_2	104°51'.6 W
l	8°18'.0 S	DLo	14°58'.3 W
$\frac{1}{2}l$	4°09'.0 S	DLo	898'.3 W
Lm	12°57'.9 S		

DLo 898'.3 W	log	2.95342	
Lm 12°57'.9 S	l cos	9.98878	
p 875.4 mi. W	log	2.94220	
l 498'.0 S	log (−)	2.69723	log 2.69723
C S 60°21'.9 W	l tan	0.24497	l sec 0.30586
(2) d 1007.1 mi.			log 3.00309
(1) Cn 240°.4			

A mid-Latitude sailing problem can be computed rapidly and with sufficient accuracy for most purposes with a slide rule. Formulae (1) and (2) are used as stated above, but $d = l/\cos C$ is substituted for formula (3).

When the latitude and longitude of the point of departure, and the course and distance steamed are given, the latitude and longitude of the point of arrival may be found by using the following formulae:

$$l = d \times \cos C \qquad (4)$$

$$p = d \times \sin C \qquad (5)$$

$$\text{DLo} = p \times \sec \text{Lm} \qquad (6)$$

With l having been found, $\frac{1}{2}l$ is applied to the latitude of the point of departure to find Lm. The latitude and longitude of the point of arrival are found by applying l and DLo in accordance with their names to the latitude and longitude respectively of the point of departure.

Note that in the computation of mid-Latitude sailings, if a course line crosses the equator the triangles on the North and South sides should be solved separately.

Mercator sailing.

505. The determination of course and distance on a Mercator chart constitutes a graphic solution of a *Mercator sailing* problem. This sailing may also be solved mathematically; however, two terms not defined in article 502 are involved. These are:

Meridional parts (M). The length of a meridian on a Mercator chart, as expanded between the equator and any given latitude, expressed in units of 1' of arc of the equator, constitutes the number of meridional parts of that latitude. The meridional parts used in the construction of Mercator charts and in Mercator sailing are tabulated in Table 5 in Bowditch. In Mercator sailing, M_1 represents the meridional parts of the latitude of the point of departure, and M_2 the parts of the latitude of the destination.

The *meridional difference* (m), which represents the absolute difference $M_1 \sim M_2$.

The formulae of Mercator sailing are:

$$\tan C = \frac{DLo}{m} \qquad (1)$$

$$d = l \sec C \qquad (2)$$

These formulae can be conveniently arranged for solution as shown in the following example:

Example: Find the course and distance by Mercator sailing from Cape Flattery Light, Washington, to Diamond Head, Oahu, Hawaiian Islands.

Cape Flattery Light	L_1	48°23'.5 N	Diamond Head	L_2	21°15'.1 N
	λ_1	124°44'.1 W		λ_2	157°48'.7 W

Solution:

L_1	48°23'.5 N	M_1	3309.2	λ_2	157°48'.7 W
L_2	21°15'.1 N	M_2	1296.9	λ_1	124°44'.1 W
l	27°08'.4 S	m	2012.3	DLo	33°04'.6 W
l	1628'.4 S			DLo	1984'.6 W
DLo	1984'.6 W	log	3.29767		
m	2012.3	log (−)	3.30369		
C	S 44°36'.2 W	l tan	9.99398	sec	10.14752
l	1628'.4			log (+)	3.21176
d	2287.0 mi.			log	3.35928
Cn	224°.6				

In Mercator sailing the limits of C are 0° to 90°. It is labeled N or S to agree with l, and E or W to agree with DLo. To convert C to Cn, follow the instructions of the labels. In this example, start at S (180°). The course is 44°36'.2 to the west, or 180° + 44°36′.2 = 224°36′.2 or 224°.6. It is customary to solve for C and *d* to an accuracy of 0′.1, but to record Cn to an accuracy of 0°.1, as shown.

These formulae can also be used for determining the latitude and longitude of the destination if the course and distance are known, but if the course is near 090° or 270°, an appreciable error in DLo may result.

Mercator sailing problems can be solved by means of Table 3, Bowditch, in accordance with instructions contained therein.

506. Every great circle of a sphere bisects every other great circle. Therefore, every great circle, if extended around the earth, will lie half in the northern hemisphere and half in the southern hemisphere, and the midpoint of either half will be farthest from the equator. This point, where a great circle reaches its highest latitude, is called the *vertex*. *Characteristics of great circles.*

A great circle between two places on the same side of the equator is everywhere nearer the pole than the rhumb line. If the two places are on different sides of the equator, the great circle between them changes its direction of curvature, relative to the rhumb line, at the equator. If the two places are equal distances on opposite sides of the equator, the great circle will bisect the rhumb line between them at the equator.

Since the direction of a great circle is constantly changing, the course of a ship attempting to follow such a curved path would have to be continually changed. As this is obviously impractical, the course is changed at intervals, so that a ship follows a series of rhumb lines. Since for a short distance a rhumb line and a great circle are nearly coincident, the result is a close approximation of the great circle. This is generally accomplished by determining points at regular intervals along the great circle, plotting them on a Mercator chart or plotting sheet, and steaming the rhumb lines between the points (see Figure 506).

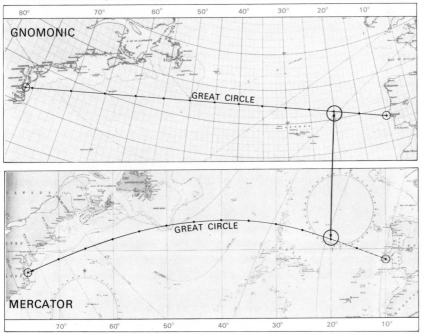

Figure 506: Transferring a great circle from a gnomonic chart to a Mercator chart.

It should be apparent that the equator and the meridians are special cases, and that many of the statements regarding great circles do not apply to them. If the course lies along one of these great circles, the solution may be made mentally, since the course is constant (these special great circles being also rhumb lines), and the distance is the number of minutes of DLo in the case of the equator and *l* in the case of a meridian.

Great circle sailing by chart: gnomonic projection.

507. The Oceanographic Office publishes several charts on the gnomonic projection, covering the usually navigated portions of the earth. The point of tangency is chosen for each chart to give the least distortion for the area to be covered. Any great circle appears on this type chart as a straight line. Because of this property, the chart is useful in great circle sailing.

However, since the meridians are not shown as parallel lines, no ordinary compass rose can be provided for use in measuring direction over the entire chart, and since angles are distorted, they cannot be measured by protractor. Latitude and longitude at a particular point on the chart must be determined by reference to the meridians and parallels in the immediate vicinity of the point. Hence, a gnomonic chart is not convenient for ordinary navigational purposes. Its practical use is limited to solution of great circle sailing problems.

In use, a straight line connecting the point of departure and the destination is drawn on the chart (upper half of Figure 506). The great circle is then inspected to see that it passes clear of all dangers to navigation. If this requirement is met, the courses are then transferred to a Mercator chart by selecting a number of points along the great circle, determining their latitude and longitude, and plotting these points on the Mercator chart. These points are then connected by straight lines to represent the rhumb line courses to be steered. The two arrows of Figure 506 indicate a corresponding position on the two charts. It can be seen in Figure 506 that points have been chosen at intervals of 5° of longitude to facilitate the picking off of points and plotting them on the Mercator chart. At this interval the error in using rhumb lines to approximate the great circle is small.

It will be noted that the rhumb line segments determined in the manner just described are chords of the great circle, as plotted on the Mercator chart. The course and distance for steaming each segment can be determined by measurement on the Mercator chart. Courses and distances of tangents to the great circle can be determined directly from the great circle charts, but the method is somewhat involved and can best be understood by studying the explanation given on each gnomonic chart. The chord method is easier and is commonly used in practice. The great circle distance of the entire trip is sometimes determined from the gnomonic chart for comparison with the rhumb line distance in making a decision as to which method to use.

Great circle sailing by chart: Lambert conformal projection.

508. Although most marine navigators use the combination of gnomonic and Mercator charts for great circle sailing, the use of the Lambert conformal projection is beginning to receive attention. The advantage of the Lambert conformal chart for this purpose is that both great circle distance and courses for segments of the great circle may be obtained by direct measurement, saving a transfer of points from the gnomonic to the Mercator projection. As stated earlier, any straight line on a Lambert conformal chart is a close approximation

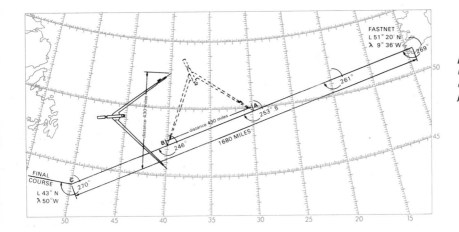

Figure 508:
Great circle sailing
on the Lambert pro-
jection.

to a great circle, and angles are truly represented on this projection. Although direction can therefore be measured directly on the chart, protractors or plotters must be used, as the meridians are not shown as parallel lines. The course, a rhumb line, of each segment of a great circle is measured at its midpoint.

Since the distance scale of a Lambert conformal chart is so nearly constant that a fixed scale can be used without appreciable error, distance may be measured either by means of the latitude scale (as on a Mercator chart), by distance scales which are sometimes printed on the chart, or by use of a special protractor plotter made to the scale of the chart. This latter method permits rapid measurement of both course and distance.

The illustration in Figure 508 is on the base plate of Coast and Geodetic Survey chart 3071. This chart, which contains Loran lines and other information, was designed originally for air navigation, but is extremely useful for marine navigation. The Coast and Geodetic Survey prints a series of these charts covering areas of the world with high density air traffic. Note that distance from *A* to *B* (430 miles) is measured with dividers directly on the latitude scale, while the course at any point is determined by use of a protractor to measure the angle with the meridian at that point. Weems & Plath of Annapolis, Maryland, has developed an APC protractor-plotter specifically designed for use with the chart, which facilitates rapid and accurate measurement of both direction and distance.

Because of the advantages noted, and since this projection is suitable for general navigational purposes, charts based on this projection are replacing both gnomonic and Mercator charts to some extent, especially for air navigation. Plotting charts are commercially available on the Lambert conformal projection, made for specific latitudes, which may be used for any longitude.

509. If the difference in the direction of the great circle and rhumb line is known, this difference, called the conversion angle, can be applied to either one to obtain the other. In any great circle sailing the angle which the great circle makes with the meridian at the starting point is referred to as the initial great circle direction. In many texts it is referred to as the initial great circle course even though the course by definition must be a rhumb line.

Great circle sailing
by conversion angle.

59

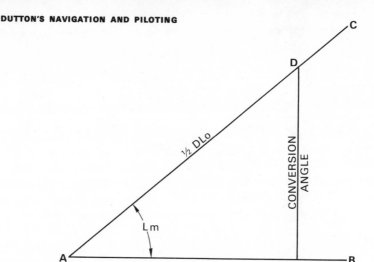

Figure 509: Conversion angle determined graphically.

Conversion angles are tabulated in Table 1, Bowditch. If the distance does not exceed 2000 miles and both points lie on the same side of the equator, the conversion angle can be found to practical accuracy by this formula:

$$\text{tan conversion angle} = \text{sin Lm tan } \tfrac{1}{2}\text{DLo}$$

This formula can be solved graphically by a simple construction as shown in Figure 509. Draw any line, *AB*. Draw a second line, *AC*, making an angle with *AB* equal to the mid latitude between the point of departure and the destination. From the intersection measure, to any convenient scale, a number of linear units equal to one half the number of degrees of DLo, thus locating *D*. From *D* drop a perpendicular to the line *AB*. The number of linear units in this perpendicular, to the same scale used for $\tfrac{1}{2}$DLo, is the number of degrees of the conversion angle.

The sign of the conversion angle in any given case will be apparent if it is remembered that the great circle is nearer the pole than the rhumb line. For instance, in north latitude if the destination is east of the point of departure, the conversion angle is minus (−); if to the west, it is plus (+).

In practice the conversion angle is usually modified to provide chord courses. This is done by dividing the conversion angle by the number of legs to be used and *subtracting* this from the conversion angle before it is applied to the Mercator (rhumb line) course. At the end of the first leg a new solution must be made for the next leg. This is somewhat more trouble than using a great circle chart, but eliminates the necessity of a lengthy computation if no great circle chart is available.

Distance is determined by measuring the length of each rhumb line leg.

Great circle sailing by computation: the problem.

510. In Figure 510, *C* represents the point of departure, *B* the destination, *P* the pole nearest *C*, and *EQ* the equator. The great circles through *PC* and *PB* are meridians. Since latitude is the angular distance of a place north or south of the equator, measured along a meridian, *PC*, the angular distance from the pole to *C*, the point of departure, is 90° −L_1, or the co-latitude. Similarly, *PB* is the co-latitude of the destination. However, the term *co-latitude*, as used with respect to the destination, is 90°± L_2, since *P* is chosen as the pole nearest the point of departure. That is, if *B* and *C* are on the same side of the equator, or of the same *name*, the latitude of *B* may be considered (+) and the co-

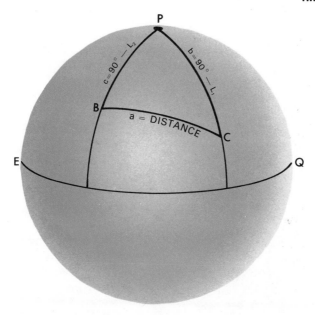

Figure 510: The navigational triangle, as used in great circle sailing.

latitude $= 90° - L_2$. However, if B is of opposite name, or on the opposite side of the equator from C, it may be considered $(-)$ in which case the co-latitude is $90° - (-L_2)$, or $90° + L_2$.

If C and B are connected by a great circle, a spherical triangle is formed. The length of the arc of the great circle between C and B is the great circle distance between these two points. The initial direction from C to B is the angle PCB. The angle BPC is the DLo, designated t when used in the special case as part of the navigational triangle illustrated in Figure 510. This is the same triangle used in the solution of celestial observations, C then being the assumed position of the observer and B the point on the earth directly under the celestial body observed. Hence, any method of solution devised for one of these problems can be used for the other. However, some methods devised for solution of celestial observations are better adapted to the solution of great circle sailing problems than others.

The solution of a great circle sailing problem involves computation for the distance and initial direction, the position of the vertex, and the coordinates of points along the track. Computation is somewhat tedious, but the results are accurate and this method sometimes constitutes the only method available.

511. Refer to Figure 511. A perpendicular dropped from the destination, B, to the meridian, PC, through the point of departure, C, will divide the oblique navigational triangle PBC into two right spherical triangles. The length of the perpendicular is designated R, and the foot of the perpendicular y. The latitude of point y is designated K, which is always on the same side of the equator as B. The arc Cy represents the *difference* of latitude of points C and y, regardless of which is greater or whether or not both are on the same side of the equator. This is designated K $\sim$ L_1. The symbol $\sim$ is used to mean the *algebraic difference*. Thus, if both K and L_1 have the same name, the smaller is subtracted from the larger, but if they are of opposite name, their numerical values are added. The value K $\sim L_1$ has no sign or name, being merely a difference. The side Py is co $-$ K.

Great circle sailing by computation; distance and initial direction.

61

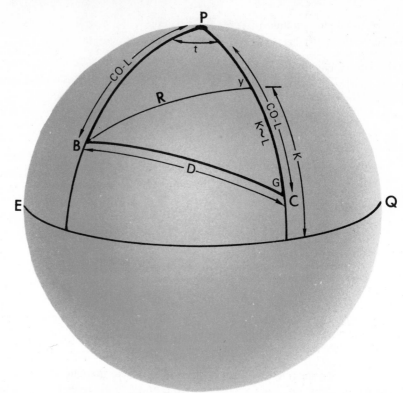

Figure 511: The navigational triangle divided into two right spherical triangles by a perpendicular from the point of destination to the meridian of the point of departure.

If the point of departure and the destination are known, L_1, L_2, and t are the values available for solution. The problem is to find d (the side D of Figure 511) and the angle at C.

These can be found by the following formulae:

$$\csc R = \csc t \sec L_2 \tag{1}$$

$$\csc K = \frac{\csc L_2}{\sec R} \tag{2}$$

$$\sec d = \sec R \sec (K \sim L_1) \tag{3}$$

$$\csc C = \frac{\csc R}{\csc d} \tag{4}$$

The derivation of these formulae is explained in Bowditch. Any table of log secants and log cosecants can be used for the solution by these formulae, but they are most conveniently arranged in H. O. Pub No. 211, in which column "A" contains log cosecants multiplied by 10^5 and column "B" contains log secants multiplied by 10^5. H. O. 211 is intended to be used without interpolation, the accuracy obtained in this way being sufficient for practical problems. However, the results are least accurate if t is near 90°. It is advisable to interpolate if t is between 87°30' and 92°30'.

Numerous rules for naming the triangle parts north or south, and for entering the tables at the top or bottom of the page must be carefully followed. These rules and the formulae and method of solution for determining the great circle distance, the initial direction, the vertex, and additional points along the track are given in the introductory pages of H. O. 211 and will not be repeated here.

A single complete solution is given for illustrative purposes in the following article.

512. The complete solution for all aspects of the great circle sailing problem, using H. O. 211 *Dead Reckoning Altitude and Azimuth Tables*, by Ageton, is given in the following example. The formulae used and the terminology are given in the instructions printed in each volume of H. O. 211.

Great circle sailing by computation: complete solution.

Example:

(1) Find the initial great circle direction and distance from Land's End, England, L 50°04'.0 N, λ 5°45'.0 W, to St. John's Newfoundland, L 47°34'.0 N, λ 52°40'.0 W, using H. O. 211.

(2) Find the latitude and longitude of the vertex.

(3) Find the latitude and longitude of points along the great circle at distance intervals of 5° (300 nm along the great circle), measured in both directions from the vertex.

Solution:

(1)			ADD	SUBTRACT	ADD	SUBTRACT
λ_2	52°40'.0 W					
λ_1	5°45'.0 W					
t	46°55'.0 W	A 13646			
L_2	47°34'.0 N	B 17087	A 13191		
		A 30733	B 6041	B 6041	A 30733
K	58°01'.0 N		A 7150		
L_1	50°04'.0 N				
$K \sim L_1$	7°57'.0			B 419	
d	30°29'.0			B 6460	A 29475
Cn	283.7		C N76°16'.5 W		A 1258
d	1829.0 mi.				

(2)		ADD	SUBTRACT
L_1	50°04'.0	B 19253	
C	N 76°16'.5 W	A 1258	B 62477
L_v	51°25'.5 N	B 20511	A 10691
t_v	17°40'.0 W		A 51786
λ_1	5°45'.0 W		
λ_v	23°25'.0 W		

(3) d_{v-x}	5°	10°	15°	20°	
L_v	A 10691	10691	10691	10691	
$d_{v-x}(+)$ B	165.6	665	1506	2701	
L_x	A 10856.6	11356	12197	13392	
L_x	51°09'.0 N	50°21'.0 N	49°02.5 N	47°16'.5 N	
d_{v-x}	A 105970	76033	58700	46595	
$L_x(-)$ B	20254	19511	18342	16846	
t_{v-x}	A 85716	56522	40358	29749	
t_{v-x}	7°59'.0	15°47'.5	23°15'.5	30°16'.5	
λ_v	23°25'.0 W	23°25'.0 W	23°25'.0 W	23°25'.0 W	
λ_x	15°26'.0 W	7°37'.5 W	—	—	$(\lambda_v - t_{v-x})$
λ_x	31°24'.0 W	39°12'.5 W	46°40'.5 W	53°41'.5 W	$(\lambda_v + t_{v-x})$

In a solution of this type it is well to write down the entire form for all parts before doing any of the computation. The mind is thus freed of thinking of what to do next and can focus on the mechanics of the computation. Also, it will be noted that the same quantity sometimes appears in several places. In part (1), for instance, C is found from its A function. In part (2) both A and B functions are needed. If the B function is picked out at the same time C is being found, it will save a table entry in the solution of (2). The same A value found in part (1) is used in part (2) regardless of whether it is a tabulated number.

It will be noted that but one point is found at distances of 15° and 20° from the vertex, since the points to the east are beyond the point of departure. The number of points needed can be determined by dividing the distance interval (in this example 5° or 300 miles) into the total distance. In determining the number of computations the position of the vertex must be considered. In some problems the vertex will be located beyond the destination but its position must be determined in order to calculate the points along the great circle.

Checking great circle computations.

513. Mathematical errors frequently occur when a great circle problem is computed in the foregoing manner. It is advisable to check the answers for gross errors with a slide rule, using the following formulae. Distances over 1,800 miles and course angles between 0° and 70° and 110° and 180° can be solved with considerable accuracy.

$$\text{Cos } d = \sin L_1 \times \sin L_2 \pm \cos L_1 \times \cos L_2 \times \cos \text{DLo} \tag{1}$$

$$\text{Sin } C = \frac{\cos L_2 \times \sin \text{DLo}}{\sin d} \tag{2}$$

$$\text{Cos } L_v = \cos L_1 \times \sin C \tag{3}$$

$$\text{Sin } t_v = \frac{\cos C}{\sin L_v} \tag{4}$$

$$\text{Sin } d_v = \cos L_1 \times \sin t_v \tag{5}$$

$$\text{Sin } L_x = \sin L_v \times \cos d_{v-x} \tag{6}$$

$$\text{Sin } t_{v-x} = \frac{\sin d_{v-x}}{\cos L_x} \tag{7}$$

Great circle sailing; computation by H.O. 229.

514. These tables are highly adaptable to great circle solution, as the point of departure and the destination can always be found on the same page.

H. O. Pub. No. 229, and the use of its interpolation tables, is described at some length in article 2505; it will be dealt with only briefly here, in describing its use for finding the great circle distance and initial direction.

Example: A navigator in Lat. 75°31'.0 N, Long. 139°52'.0 W desires to determine the great circle distance and initial direction to a point located in Lat. 1°28'.0 N, Long. 110°44'.0 W by means of H. O. 229.

Solution: The DLo is first determined

$$\lambda_1 \quad 139°52'.0 \text{ W}$$
$$\lambda_2 \quad 110°44'.0 \text{ W}$$
$$\text{DLo} \quad 29°08'.0 \text{ E (called LHA in H. O. 229)}$$

The appropriate volume of H. O. 229 is now selected for L_1; this will be volume 6, which covers the range of latitude from 75° to 90°. Entry in this volume is made for LHA 29°; a portion of the appropriate page is reproduced in part in Figure 514a. The integral degree of L_2 is found in the vertical column labeled

"Dec."; as L_1 and L_2 are of the same name (north), the page titled "Latitude Same Name as Declination" will be used. On this page, for L 75° and Dec. 1°,

29°, 331° L.H.A.   LATITUDE SAME NAME AS DECLINATION

	75°			76°			77°			78°			79°			80°		
Dec.	Hc	d	Z	Hc	d	Z	Hc	d	Z	Hc	d	Z	Hc	d	Z	Hc	d	Z
°	° ′	′	°	° ′	′	°	° ′	′	°	° ′	′	°	° ′	′	°	° ′	′	°
0	13 05.0	+59 5	150.2	12 12.9	+59 6	150.3	11 20.8	+59 6	150.4	10 28.6	+59 7	150.5	9 36.4	+59 7	150.5	8 44.1	+59 8	150.6
1	14 04.5	59 5	150.0	13 12.5	59 6	150.1	12 20.4	59 7	150.3	11 28.3	59 7	150.4	10 36.1	59 8	150.5	9 43.9	59 8	150.5

Figure 514a: Portion of a "same name" page H.O. 229.

three values are tabulated under the headings Hc, d, and Z; these are 14°04′.5, (+) 59′.5, and 150°.0 respectively. The first of these, 14°04′.5 represents the codistance, (90°-distance or, in the celestial problem, altitude) expressed in degrees and minutes from a point in Lat. 75° to a second point in Lat. 1° (both latitudes being of the same name, north), and 29° away in longitude.

The second tabulated figure, 59′.5, in this problem represents the change in the codistance for an increase of 1° in the latitude of the destination.

The third figure, 150°.0, is the course angle for the initial direction. This must be labeled, the prefix being the name of the elevated pole and the suffix the direction of the change of longitude. In this example, as the navigator is in north latitude, and his destination is to the east, it would be N 150°.0 E, and course angle and initial direction are the same.

Dec. Inc.	Altitude difference (d)														Double Second Diff. and Corr.	
	Tens				Decimals	Units									
	10′	20′	30′	40′	50′		0′	1′	2′	3′	4′	5′	6′	7′	8′	9′	
28.0	4.6	9.3	14.0	18.6	23.3	.0	0.0 0.5	0.9 1.4	1.9 2.4	2.8 3.3	3.8 4.3	0.8	
28.1	4.7	9.3	14.0	18.7	23.4	.1	0.0 0.5	1.0 1.5	1.9 2.4	2.9 3.4	3.8 4.3	2.4	01
28.2	4.7	9.4	14.1	18.8	23.5	.2	0.1 0.6	1.0 1.5	2.0 2.5	2.9 3.4	3.9 4.4	4.0	02
28.3	4.7	9.4	1.1	18.9	23.6	.3	0.1 0.6	1.1 1.6	2.0 2.5	3.0 3.5	3.9 4.4	5.6	03
28.4	4.7	9.5	14.2	18.9	23.7	.4	0.2 0.7	1.1 1.6	2.1 2.6	3.0 3.5	4.0 4.5	7.2	04
													8.8	05
28.5	4.8	9.5	14.3	19.0	23.8	.5	0.2 0.7	1.2 1.7	2.1 2.6	3.1 3.6	4.0 4.5	10.4	06
28.6	4.8	9.5	14.3	19.1	23.8	.6	0.3 0.8	1.2 1.7	2.2 2.7	3.1 3.6	4.1 4.6	12.0	07
28.7	4.8	9.6	14.4	19.2	23.9	.7	0.3 0.8	1.3 1.8	2.2 2.7	3.2 3.7	4.1 4.6	13.6	08
28.8	4.8	9.6	14.4	19.2	24.0	.8	0.4 0.9	1.3 1.8	2.3 2.8	3.2 3.7	4.2 4.7	15.2	09
28.9	4.9	9.7	14.5	19.3	24.1	.9	0.4 0.9	1.4 1.9	2.3 2.8	3.3 3.8	4.2 4.7	16.8	10

Figure 514b: Interpolation Table.

The next step is to correct the angular *codistance* for the difference of 28.′0 between the actual latitude of the destination, and the latitude, 1°, used in entering the tables. This correction is obtained by using the *d* factor (+) 59′.5, in two increments from the Interpolation Table, a portion of which is reproduced in Figure 514b; the first increment 23′.3, and the second is 4′.5. As the sign in the *d* column was (+), both are additive.

Next, correct the angular *codistance* for the 31′.0 increment of latitude of the initial position beyond the 75° with which the tables were entered, and also for the 8′.0 increment of a DLo beyond the 29° used in entering the tables.

These corrections are obtained from a nomogram appearing in each volume of H. O. 229; it is not reproduced here. These two corrections are subtractive, and total − 27′.8. It may be noted that it is purely coincidental that this correction should have the same numerical value as the first; in most cases the corrections would not cancel out.

65

	Hc	d	Z
Lat. 75° N			
LHA 29°	14°04'.5	+59'.5	150°.0
Dec. 1° N			

Corr. for 28'   +   23.3
Increment of L_2 +   4.5
using d factor
+59.5
                                    _____
                                    14°32'.3
Corr. for 31'.0
of L_1 + 8'.0 of   −27'.8
DLo obtained
from nomogram   _____
            Codistance 14°04'.5

The fully corrected codistance is next subtracted from 90° to obtain the angular distance, 75°55'.5. This converted into nautical miles equals 4555.5, and the initial direction is 150°.0.

In this instance, an inspection of the tables indicates no appreciable change in the value of Z in adjoining entries. The tabulated value of Z may therefore be taken as the value of the initial direction without correction. However, in some instances, where the adjoining values of Z differ considerably from the selected value, correction will be necessary. Corrections to the initial direction (Z) for increments of latitude of the point of departure (L_1) and destination (L_2—Dec. in the tables) as well as for the increments of the difference of longitude (LHA) may be made by interpolation between the various tabulated values of Z.

Answer: Great circle distance is 4555.5 miles, and the initial direction is 150°.0.

The accuracy of H. O. 229 in computing great circle distance and direction is indicated by the fact that the actual distance, rigorously computed, is 4555.6 miles, and the initial direction is 149°53', giving an error of only 0.1 miles, and 0.1 degrees.

CHAPTER 6

Aids to Navigation

601. As used in this chapter, the term "aids to navigation" includes lighthouses, *Introduction.* lightships, buoys, day beacons, and fog signals. Electronic aids to navigation, such as Omega, Loran, and Consolan are discussed in later chapters.

The U. S. Coast Guard, with which the Lighthouse Service was amalgamated in 1939, is now charged with the operation and maintenance of all lighthouses and other aids to navigation along 40,000 miles of coastline in the United States and its possessions. This includes more than 13,000 lighthouses and minor lights, and over 22,000 lighted and unlighted buoys.

These aids are of tremendous assistance to the navigator in making a landfall when approaching from seaward, and in all coastal navigation. Their importance was first recognized by the ancient Mediterranean mariners; a lighthouse was built at Sigeum, near Troy, before 600 B.C., and the famous Pharos of Alexandria was built in the third century B.C. Wood fires furnished their illumination, and wood and sometimes coal remained in general use for this purpose until the eighteenth century. The first lighthouse in the United States was built at Boston in 1716, and logs and kegs were used as buoys in the Delaware in 1767.

602. Light Lists for the United States and its possessions, including the Intra- *Light lists.* coastal Waterway, the Mississippi and its navigable tributaries, and the Great Lakes including both the U. S. and Canadian shores, are published annually by the U. S. Coast Guard. A portion of a sample page is reproduced in Figure 602.

Similar publications, called *Lists of Lights,* covering foreign coasts are published in looseleaf form by the U. S. Naval Oceanographic Office as H. O. Pub. Nos. 111A, 111B, and 112–116; page changes are published periodically. Corrections to both sets of light lists are published weekly in the *Notice to Mariners.*

These light lists give detailed information regarding navigational lights, light structures, radio beacons, and fog signals. In addition, the Light Lists for the United States, published by the Coast Guard, give data on lighted and unlighted buoys.

It is of the utmost importance that corrections be entered promptly in the appropriate light lists, as well as on any applicable charts.

603. The primary function of buoys is to warn the mariner of some danger, some *Significance of* obstruction, or change in the contours of the sea bottom, and to delineate the *buoys.* channels leading to various points, so that he may avoid the dangers and continue his voyage safely. The utmost advantage is obtained from buoys when they are considered as marking definitely identified spots, for if a mariner

(1) No.	(2) Name / Characteristic	(3) Location / Lat. N. Long. W.	(4) Nominal Range	(5) Ht. above water	(6) Structure / Ht. above ground Daymark	(7) Remarks Year
		MAINE				FIRST DISTRICT
	SEACOAST (Chart 1106) (For Gulf of Maine, see No.199)					
1 227 J 48	MOUNT DESERT LIGHT .... Gp. Fl. W., 15ˢ 0.2ˢfl., 3.0ˢec. 0.2ˢfl., 11.6ˢec. 2 flashes.	On Mount Desert Rock, 20 miles south of Mount Desert Island. 43 58.1 68 07.7	25	75	Conical gray granite tower..... 58	RADIOBEACON: Antenna at light tower. Distance finding station. (See p. XVIII for explanation.) HORN, 2 blasts ev 30ˢ (2ˢbl-2ˢsi-2ˢbl-24ˢsi). 1830
2 239 J 116	MATINICUS ROCK LIGHT .... Gp. Fl. W. (1 + 2), 15ˢ 0.2ˢfl., 5.8ˢec. 0.2ˢfl., 2.8ˢec. 0.2ˢfl., 5.8ˢec. 3 flashes.	On south part of rock. 43 47.0 68 51.3	23	90	Cylindrical gray granite tower and dwelling. 48	RADIOBEACON: Antenna 105 feet 053° from light tower. Distance finding station. (See p. XVIII for explanation). HORN, 1 blast ev 15ˢ (2ˢbl). Bell, hand, 1 stroke ev 20ˢ if horn is inoperative. 1827–1857
3 282 J 128	MONHEGAN ISLAND LIGHT....... Fl. W., 30ˢ(2.8ˢfl)	Near center of island. 43 45.9 69 19.0	21	178	Gray conical tower covered way to dwelling. 47	Within 3 miles of island the light is obscured between west and southwest. 1824–1850
4 283 J 130	Manana Island Fog Signal Station ..	On west side of island, close to Monhegan Island. 43 45.8 69 19.7	....	....	Brown brick house....	RADIOBEACON: Antenna 2,880 feet 259° from Monhegan Island Light tower. Distance finding station (See p. XVIII for explanation.) HORN, 2 blasts ev 60ˢ (3ˢbl-3ˢsi-3ˢbl-51ˢsi). 1855–1870
5 297 J 146	SEGUIN LIGHT .... F. W.	On island, 2 miles south of mouth of Kennebec River. 43 42.5 69 45.5	19	180	White cylindrical granite tower connected to dwelling. 53	HORN, 2 blasts ev 20ˢ (2ˢbl-2ˢsi-2ˢbl-14ˢsi). 1795–1857
6 320 J 176	HALFWAY ROCK LIGHT .... Alt. F. W., R., and Fl. R. 90ˢ(F. W., 59ˢ,F .R ., 14ˢ,R.fl., 3ˢ (high intensity), F. R., 14ˢ).	On rock, midway between Cape Small Point and Cape Elizabeth. 43 39.4 70 02.2	21W 16R 25 Fl. R.	76	White granite tower attached to dwelling. 77	RADIOBEACON: Antenna 30 feet 160° from light tower. Distance finding station (See p. XVIII for explanation.) HORN, 2 blasts ev 60ˢ (3ˢbl-3ˢsi-3ˢbl-51ˢsi). 1871

Figure 602: Excerpt from Light List.

knows his precise location at the moment and is properly equipped with charts, he can plot a safe course on which to proceed. Such features as size, shape, coloring, numbering, and signaling equipment of buoys are but means to these ends of warning, guiding, and orienting the navigator.

The waters of the United States are marked for safe navigation by the *lateral system* of buoyage. This system employs a simple arrangement of colors, shapes, numbers, and light characteristics to show the side on which a buoy should be passed when proceeding in a given direction. The characteristics are determined by the position of the buoy with respect to the navigable channels as the channels are entered *from seaward*. As all channels do not lead from seaward, arbitrary assumptions must at times be made in order that the system may be consistently applied.

The characteristics of buoys maintained by the United states are based on the assumption that a ship is returning "from seaward" when proceeding in a westerly and southerly direction along the Maine coast, and in a southerly direction along the remainder of the Atlantic coast, in a northerly and westerly direction along the Gulf coast, in a northerly direction on the Pacific coast, and in a northerly and westerly direction on the Great Lakes.

Canada maintains a buoyage system which is in general accord with that of the United States.

604. The buoyage system adopted for the waters of the United States provides several different types of buoys, each kind designed to serve under definite conditions. All buoys serve as daymarks; those having lights are also available for navigation at night; those having sound signals are more readily located in time of fog, as well as by night.

Types of buoys.

All new buoys are fitted with radar reflectors which return a clear, sharp echo on the radar screen. All unlighted buoys are fitted with reflection tape, in order that they may be more readily located at night by means of a searchlight. The colors of such reflectors have the same significance as the colors of lights.

The principal general types of buoys are:

Can Buoys. Buoys built up of steel plates having the shape of a tin can.

Nun Buoys. Buoys built up of steel plates, the portion above water having the shape of a truncated cone.

Bell Buoys. Steel floats surmounted by short skeleton towers in which the bells are fixed. Most bell buoys are sounded by the motion of the buoy in the sea. In newer types, the bells are struck by compressed gas or electrically operated hammers.

Gong Buoys. Similar in construction to bell buoys, but sounding a distinctive note caused by sets of gongs, of which each gong has a different tone.

Whistle Buoys. These buoys provide a sound signal which is useful at night and also during fog and low visibility. As the whistle mechanism is operated by the motion of the buoy in the sea, these buoys are used principally in exposed locations. A type of sound buoy is also in use in which a horn is sounded at regular intervals by mechanical means.

Lighted Buoys. A metal float on which is mounted a short skeleton tower at the top of which the light is placed. Electric batteries, by which the light is operated, are placed in the body of the buoy.

Combination Buoys. These are buoys in which a light and a sound signal are combined, such as a lighted bell buoy, lighted gong buoy, or a lighted whistle buoy.

Special purpose buoys. In addition to the lateral system of buoyage, several special purpose buoyage characteristics, which have no lateral significance, are utilized to mark dredging areas, quarantine areas, fish net areas, anchorages, race courses, experiments or tests, etc.

Identification of
buoys.

605. In the United States, the following system of daytime buoy identification is used :

Coloring of buoys. All buoys in the lateral system are painted distinctive colors to indicate their purpose or the side on which they should be passed. The meaning of these buoys, *when returning* from *seaward*, is indicated by their colors as follows :

Buoy colors.

Black Buoys mark the port (left) sides of channels, or the location of wrecks or obstructions which must be passed by keeping the buoy on the port (left) hand.

Red Buoys mark the starboard (right) sides of channels, or the location of wrecks or obstructions which must be passed by keeping the buoy on the starboard (right) hand.

Red and Black Horizontally Banded Buoys mark junctions in the channel, or wrecks or obstructions which may be passed on either side. If the topmost band is black, the preferred channel will be followed by keeping the buoy on the port (left) hand. If the topmost band is red, the preferred channel will be followed by keeping the buoy on the starboard (right) hand.

However, in some instances it may not be feasible for larger vessels to pass on either side of such a buoy, and the chart should always be consulted.

Black and White Vertically Striped Buoys mark the fairway or mid-channel.

Special-purpose buoys.—These buoys are not part of the lateral system. Their meaning is indicated by their colors as follows :

White buoys mark anchorage areas.

Yellow buoys mark quarantine anchorage areas.

White buoys with green tops are used in connection with dredging and survey operations.

White and black horizontally banded buoys mark fish net areas.

White and international orange buoys alternately banded, either horizontally or vertically, are for special purposes to which neither the lateral-system colors nor the other special-purpose colors apply.

Yellow and black vertically striped buoys are used for seadrome markings and have no marine significance.

Buoy numbers.

Most buoys are given numbers, letters, or combinations of numbers and letters which are painted conspicuously upon them. These markings facilitate identification and location of the buoys on the charts.

All solid-colored red or black buoys are given numbers, or combinations of numbers and letters. Other colored buoys may be given letters. Numbers increase from seaward and are kept in approximate sequence on both sides of a channel by omitting numbers where required. Odd numbers are used *only* on solid black

LATERAL SYSTEM AS SEEN ENTERING FROM SEAWARD

PORT SIDE
Odd numbered buoys or structures with white or green lights.

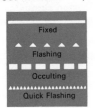

Fixed
Flashing
Occulting
Quick Flashing

LIGHTED BUOY   CAN

MID CHANNEL
No numbers, may be lettered, white light only.

Morse Code A

CAN   LIGHTED   NUN

STARBOARD SIDE
Even numbered buoys or structures with white or red lights.

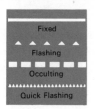

Fixed
Flashing
Occulting
Quick Flashing

LIGHTED BUOY   NUN

JUNCTION
Marks junction or obstructions. No numbers, pass on either side. May be lettered.
Interrupted quick flashing. White or Green—White or Red.

Interrupted
Quick Flashing

LIGHTED   CAN   LIGHTED   NUN

Figure 605: Buoy identification. A complete illustration is provided in Chart 1 in the back of the book.

BUOYS HAVING NO LATERAL SIGNIFICANCE—ALL WATERS
No special shapes, no numbers, white lights only. (May be lettered.)

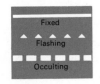

Fixed
Flashing
Occulting

Special Purpose   Quarantine Anchorage   Anchorage   Fish Net   Dredging

WOr: White and Orange
Y: Yellow
W: White
BW: Black and White
GW: Green and White

71

buoys. Even numbers are used *only* on solid red buoys. Numbers followed by letters are used on solid-colored red or black buoys when a letter is required so as not to disturb the sequence of numbering; or on important buoys, particularly those marking isolated offshore dangers. An example of the latter case would be a buoy marked "1DR." In this instance the number has the usual significance, while the letters "DR" indicate the place as Duxbury Reef. Letters without numbers are applied in some cases to black and white vertically striped buoys, red and black horizontally banded buoys, solid yellow buoys, and other buoys not solid-colored red or black.

In order to provide ready identification, certain *unlighted* buoys are differentiated by shape.

Buoy shapes. *Conical* shaped buoys are called *nun buoys;* they may be Red Buoys, or Red and Black Horizontally Banded Buoys with the topmost band red.

Cylindrical shaped buoys are called *can buoys;* they may be Black Buoys, or Red and Black Horizontally Banded Buoys with the topmost band black.

Black and White Vertically Striped Buoys may be either *nun* or *can* buoys. The shape has no significance in this case.

Lighted buoys, sound buoys and spar buoys painted with the same characteristics may take the place of any of the buoys described.

Full reliance should not be placed on the shape of an unlighted buoy alone. Charts and light lists should be consulted to ascertain the significance of unlighted buoys as determined by their colors.

Lighted buoys, sound buoys, and spar buoys are not differentiated by shape to indicate the side on which they should be passed. Since no special significance is attached to the shapes of these buoys, *their purpose is indicated by the coloring, numbering,* or *light characteristics.*

Daybeacons. Many aids to navigation are not lighted. Structures (not buoys) of this type are called *daybeacons.* They vary greatly in design and construction, depending upon their location, and the distance from which they may be seen. A daybeacon may consist of a single pile with a *daymark* at the top, a spar with a *cask* at the top, a slatted tower, or a structure of masonry. Daybeacons are colored, as are lighthouses, to distinguish them from their surroundings and to provide a means of identification. Daybeacons marking the sides of channels are colored and numbered in the same manner as buoys and minor light structures; red indicating the right side entering, and black the left side entering. All daybeacons are fitted with reflecting tape and identified by numbers or letters to facilitate locating them at night by means of a searchlight.

Buoy light colors. **606.** In the United States, the following system of nighttime buoy identification is used:

Color of lights. The three standard light colors used for lighted aids to navigation are white, red, and green. *Red lights* on buoys are used only on red buoys, or red and black horizontally banded buoys with the topmost band red. *Green lights* on buoys are used only on black buoys, or red and black horizontally banded buoys with the topmost band black. *White lights* are used on any color

Illustration and phase description	Symbols and meaning	
	Lights which do not change color	Lights which show color variations
A continuous steady light.	F. = Fixed . . .	Alt. = Alternating.
A fixed light varied at regular intervals by a flash of greater brilliance.	F.Fl. = Fixed and flashing.	Alt.F.Fl. = Alternating fixed and flashing.
A fixed light varied at regular intervals by groups of 2 or more flashes of greater brilliance.	F.Gp.Fl. = Fixed and group flashing.	Alt.F.Gp.Fl. = Alternating fixed and group flashing.
Showing a single flash at regular intervals, the duration of light always being less than the duration of darkness.	Fl. = Flashing	Alt.Fl. = Alternating flashing.
Showing at regular intervals groups of 2 or more flashes.	Gp.Fl. = Group flashing.	Alt.Gp.Fl. = Alternating group flashing.
Light flashes are combined in alternate groups of different numbers.	Gp.Fl. (1 + 2) = Composite group flashing.	. . . .
Light in which flashes of different duration are grouped in such a manner as to produce a Morse character or characters.	Mo.(A) = Morse Code.	. . . .
Shows not less than 60 flashes per minute.	Qk.Fl. = Quick flashing.	. . . .
Shows quick flashes for about 4 seconds, followed by a dark period of about 4 seconds.	I.Qk.Fl. = Interrupted quick flashing.	. . . .
Light with all durations of light and darkness equal.	E.Int. = Equal interval. (Isophase)	. . . .
A light totally eclipsed at regular intervals, the duration of light always greater than the duration of darkness.	Occ. = Occulting.	Alt.Occ. = Alternating occulting.
A light with a group of 2 or more eclipses at regular intervals.	Gp.Occ. = Group occulting.	. . . .
A light in which the occultations are combined in alternate groups of different numbers.	Gp.Occ. (2 + 3) = Composite group occulting.	. . . .
Light colors used and abbreviations: W = white, R = red, G = green.		

Figure 606:
Light phase characteristics.

buoy. No special significance is attached to a white light on a buoy; the purpose of the buoy is indicated by its color, number, or its light phase characteristic.

Light phase characteristics. Lights displayed from navigational aids are given distinct characteristics to aid in identification. These are indicated by standardized abbreviations as shown in Figure 606. The *period* of a flashing or an occulting light is the time required for it to go through a full set (cycle) of changes. Lights are referred to as *flashing* when the light period is shorter than the dark period, as *occulting* when the light period is longer than the dark period, and as *Isophase* when the intervals are equal. By varying the length of the periods of light and darkness of any of the flashing or occulting characteristics and by varying the colors of lights, a great variety of characteristics may be obtained. Advantage is taken of this to secure the necessary distinction between aids in a given area.

Buoy light phase characteristics.

The following general rules pertain to light phase characteristics exhibited from lighted buoys in United States waters:

Fixed Lights may be shown on any buoy except a fairway buoy, a junction buoy, or an obstruction buoy.

Flashing Lights (flashing at regular intervals and at the rate of not more than 30 flashes per minute) are placed only on black buoys, red buoys, or special purpose buoys.

Quick Flashing Lights (not less than 60 flashes per minute) are placed only on black buoys and on red buoys, at points where it is desired to indicate that special caution is required, as at sharp turns or sudden constrictions, or where used to mark wrecks or dangerous obstructions which must be passed *only on one side.*

Interrupted Quick Flashing Lights (the groups consisting of a series of quick flashes, with dark intervals of about 5 seconds between groups) are placed only on buoys painted with red and black horizontal bands, at points where it is desired to indicate junctions in channels, or wrecks or obstructions which may be passed on *either* side.

Morse (A) Lights (groups consisting of a short flash and a long flash, the flashes recurring at the rate of about eight per minute) are placed only on buoys painted in black and white vertical stripes, at points where it is desired to indicate fairways or midchannels and should be passed close to, on either side. The lights are always white.

Reflectors.

All unlighted buoys are fitted with reflective tape. This greatly facilitates locating the buoys at night by means of a searchlight. Reflectors may be white, red, or green, and have the same significance as lights of these colors.

Miscellaneous buoyage information.

607. The lights on buoys are operated by means of electricity supplied by batteries stored in the body of the buoy and wired to a flashing mechanism in the base of the lantern.

In order that lighted buoys may function for a reasonably long period of time without requiring a replacement of the batteries, the length of the light flashes as compared with the intervening periods of darkness is made quite short. Buoys at isolated points frequently function for 6 months or more without attention and the batteries frequently can flash the light for 3 years or more without replacement.

Whenever practicable, the towers, beacons, buoys, spindles, and all other aids to navigation are arranged in the buoy list of the U. S. Coast Guard in regular order as they are passed by vessels entering from sea.

The navigator should keep in mind that the buoys in thoroughfares and passages between the islands along the coast of Maine are numbered and colored for entering *from eastward*.

The buoyage systems of the other principal maritime nations are quite similar to that of the United States *but there are differences of importance*. Information as to the buoyage systems of any country may be found in the publication of the Oceanographic Office *Sailing Directions* referring to that country. For the buoyage systems of the British Islands, for instance, see the British Islands sailing directions.

Buoys do not always maintain exact positions; therefore, they should always be regarded as warnings and not as fixed navigational marks, especially during the winter months or when moored in exposed waters. A smaller nun or can buoy called a *station buoy*, is sometimes placed in close proximity to a major aid, such as a sea buoy, to mark the station in case the regular aid is accidentally shifted from station. Station buoys are colored and numbered the same as the regular aid to navigation. Lightship station buoys bear the letters *"LS"* above the initials of the station.

A ship's position, when possible, should not be plotted using buoys exclusively, but by bearings or by horizontal angles of fixed objects on shore. Lighted buoys cannot always be relied on, because the light may become extinguished or, if periodic, the apparatus may fail to operate. Many whistle and bell buoys are sounded by the action of the sea; therefore in calm weather they are less effective and at times may not sound.

Buoys on the chart. Harbor buoys are normally shown only on the harbor chart. An approach chart will display sea buoys, approach buoys, and the beginning of buoyed channels. Smaller scale charts will show sea buoys only. The position of a buoy is indicated on the chart by a diamond symbol with a dot marking its location. A larger overprinted magneta dot indicates a lighted buoy and the legend will include information as to the color of the light and its characteristics. Additional printed information is used to advise of warning features such as a sound signal (WHIS, BELL, GONG, etc.), or a radar reflector (Ra Ref). The number or letter designation is given in quotation marks near the symbol for the buoy. For unlighted buoys, the letter C, N, or S by the buoy indicates a can, nun, or spar respectively. As a general rule, the amount of printed information applicable to a charted buoy will depend upon the space available on the chart to print it. For details see Figure 604 and the nautical chart symbols in the appendix.

Sea buoys. Typical of a new type of buoy placed in operation by the U. S. Coast Guard in 1967 is the large navigational sea buoy shown in Figure 607. This buoy is 40 feet in diameter, 42 feet high, exclusive of its antennae, and draws 4 feet. It has a 5,000 candlepower light with a visibility range of 10 miles in clear weather, a fog horn signal with an audible range of 3 miles and oceanographic and meteor-

Figure 607: Large navigational sea buoy.

ological telemetry systems, and will operate unattended for one year. The first of these sea buoys replaced Scotland Lightship guarding the approach to Lower New York Bay.

Fog signals.

608. Any sound-producing instrument operated in time of reduced visibility (caused by fog, snow, haze, smoke, etc) from a definite point shown on the charts, such as a lighthouse, lightship, or buoy, serves as a useful fog signal. To be effective as an aid to navigation, a mariner must be able to identify it and to know from what point it originates. The simpler fog signals are bells or gongs and whistles on buoys, and bells at lighthouses. As signals on buoys which are operated by the action of the sea do not produce sounds on a regular time schedule, positive identification is not always possible.

At most lighthouses and lightships, fog signals are operated by mechanical means and are sounded on definite time schedules, providing the desirable feature of positive identification.

The various types of apparatus employed for sounding fog signals are of interest to the mariner principally because each type produces distinctive sounds, familiarity with which assists in identification.

Types of fog signals.

The various types of fog signals differ in tone, and this facilitates the recognition of the respective stations. The type of fog signal apparatus for each station is stated in the light lists.

> *Diaphones* produce sound by means of a slotted reciprocating piston actuated by compressed air. Blasts may consist of two tones of different pitch, in which case the first part of the blast is high and the last part is low. These alternate-pitch signals are called "two-tone."

Diaphragm horns produce sound by means of a disc diaphragm vibrated by compressed air, steam, or electricity. Duplex or triplex horn units of differing pitch produce a chime signal.

Reed horns produce sound by means of a steel reed vibrated by compressed air.

Sirens produce sound by means of either a disc or a cup-shaped rotor actuated by compressed air, steam, or electricity.

Whistles produce sound by compressed air or steam directed through a circumferential slot into a cylindrical bell chamber.

Bells are sounded by means of a hammer actuated by hand, by a descending weight, compressed gas, or electricity.

The navigator must always bear in mind that sound signals, in fog, can be very deceptive. At times, they may be completely inaudible even when near at hand. Again, they may be somewhat refracted; that is, they may appear to be coming from a direction other than the actual bearing of the signal source. Constant soundings should be obtained when operating in fog in coastal areas. *Warning.*

609. Lighthouses called "lights" in the Light Lists are found along most of the world's navigable coastlines and many of the interior waterways of the various countries. Such structures are so well known as to require little description. Lighthouses are placed where they will be of most use, on prominent headlands, at entrances, on isolated dangers, or at other points where it is necessary that mariners be warned or guided. Their principal purpose is to support a light at a considerable height above the water. The same structure may also house a fog signal and radiobeacon equipment, and contain quarters for the keepers. However, in the majority of instances, the fog signal, the radiobeacon equipment, and the operating personnel are housed in separate buildings grouped around the tower. Such a group of buildings constitutes a *light station*. *Lighthouses.*

The location of a lighthouse, whether in the water or on shore, the importance of the light, the kind of soil upon which it is to be built, and the prevalence of violent storms, have a direct bearing upon the type of structure erected and on the materials of which it will be built. Engineering problems will not be entered into here, but it is important to note that the materials used and types of construction differentiate one lighthouse from another and hence aid in identification.

Lighthouses vary markedly in their outward appearance because of the points already mentioned and also because of the great difference in the distances to which their lights should be seen. Where the need for a powerful light is great and the importance and density of traffic warrants, a tall tower with a light of great candlepower is erected. Conversely, at points intermediate to the major lights, where the traffic is light, and where long range is not so necessary, a less expensive structure of more modest dimensions suffices.

The terms *secondary* lights, *minor* lights, and *automatic* lights indicate in a general way a wide variety of lights, each class shading imperceptibly into the next. These lights may be displayed from towers resembling the important seacoast lighthouses, or may be shown from almost any type of inexpensive structure. The essentials of a light structure where keepers are not in residence, as for *Classes of lights.*

all lights, are: best possible location dependent on physical conditions of the site, sufficient height for the location, a rugged support for the lantern, and a housing for the tanks of compressed gas or electric batteries by which the light is operated. Meeting these essentials are many types of structures—small tank houses surmounted by a short skeleton tower, a cluster of piles supporting a battery box and the light, and countless other forms.

Lighthouses and automatic light structures are painted to make them readily distinguishable from the background against which they are seen, and to distinguish one structure from others in the same vicinity. Solid colors, bands of color, and various other patterns are applied for these purposes.

Minor light structures are sometimes painted black or red, to indicate the sides of the channel which they mark, following the same lateral system used in the coloring of buoys. When so painted, red structures mark the right side of the channel, and black structures the left side of the channel, entering from seaward.

Lightships.

Lightships serve the same purpose as lighthouses, being equipped with lights, fog signals, and radio beacons. Ships are used only when it is impracticable or impossible to construct a lighthouse at the desired location. Lightships mark the entrances to important harbors or estuaries, dangerous shoals lying in much frequented waters, and also serve as leading marks for both transoceanic and coastwise traffic.

All lightships in United States waters are painted red with the name of the station in white on both sides, except for Lake Huron Lightship which is painted black with the name of the station in white on both sides. Superstructures are white; masts, lantern galleries, ventilators, and stacks are painted buff. Relief lightships are painted the same color as the regular station ships, with the word "RELIEF" in white letters on the sides.

Relief vessels may be placed at any of the lightship stations, and when practicable, will exhibit lights and sound signals having the characteristics of the station. Relief ships may differ in outward appearance from the regular station ships in certain minor details.

The masthead lights, fog signals, and radio beacon signals of lightships all have definite characteristics, so that each lightship may be distinguished from others and also from nearby lighthouses. As with lighthouses, details regarding these signals are shown briefly on charts and more completely in the light lists.

A lightship under way or off station will fly the International Code signal flags "*LO*," signifying that the light ship is not at anchor on her station. It will not show or sound any of the signals of a lightship, but will display the lights prescribed by the International or Inland Rules for a vessel of its class. While on station a lightship shows only the masthead light and a less brilliant light on the forestay; as lightships ride to a single anchor, the light on the forestay indicates the direction from which the combined wind and current effect is acting and the direction in which the ship is heading. By day, whenever it appears that an approaching vessel does not recognize the lightship or requests the information, the lightship will display the International Code call letters of the station.

Light towers.

As of 1967, some lightships are being replaced by offshore light towers, The Ambrose Offshore Light Tower, shown in Figure 609, is painted red with the

Figure 609: Ambrose offshore light tower and the former Ambrose Lightship.

exception of the radiobeacon antenna, which is painted in accordance with the Federal Aviation Administration requirements. The quarters in the upper deck, just below the helicopter platform, are painted white. The Ambrose tower is located at the entrance to New York Harbor approximately seven miles east of Sandy Hook, New Jersey, in 74 feet of water. The main light beacon operates at a high intensity of six million candlepower and at a low intensity of 600,000 candlepower, with a visibility of 18 miles. An electronic fog signal with an audible range of 4 miles and a radiobeacon with a range of 100 miles are mounted on the tower. An oceanographic laboratory is also located on the tower.

610. In order to obtain full benefit from lights the navigator must not only understand their use and be able to interpret all data concerning them given in lights lists and on charts, but be able definitely to identify each light.

Identification lights.

One of the most frequent sources of groundings is the failure to identify lights correctly. When making a landfall, the charts and the Light Lists should be consulted to learn the exact characteristics of the light or lights which it is expected will be first seen. When a light is observed, its color is noted and, by means of a watch or clock with a second hand, a note is made of the time required for the light to perform its full cycle of changes. If color, cycle, and number of flashes per cycle agree with the information in the Light List, correct identification has been made. The Light List should be examined to ascertain if any other light in the general locality might be seen and mistaken for the desired light. If there is doubt, a careful timing of the length of all flashes and dark intervals, for comparison with the Light List, is usually conclusive.

In approaching a light of varying intensity, such as fixed varied by flashes, or alternating white and red, due allowance must be made for the inferior brightness of the less powerful color of the light. The first-named light may, on account of distance or haze, show flashes only, and the true characteristic will not develop until the observer comes within range of the fixed light; similarly, the second-named may show as occulting white until the observer comes within range of the red light. At short distances and in clear weather flashing lights may show a faint continuous light.

It is well worth noting that in Light Lists all bearings are stated in degrees true, reading clockwise from 000° at north; bearings relating to visibility of lights are given as observed *from a vessel;* distances are in nautical miles unless otherwise stated; heights are referred to mean high water; depths are referred to the plane of reference on charts. The great majority of lights have no resident crew tending them; such lights are called "unwatched." Unwatched lights have a high degree of reliability; however, they may become irregular or extinguished. Where a light is tended, the Light List states: "Resident Personnel." Latitudes and longitudes in the Light Lists are approximate, and are intended only to facilitate reference to a chart.

Light sectors.   **611.** Sectors of colored glass are placed in the lanterns of certain lighted aids to navigation to mark shoals or to warn mariners off the nearby land. Lights so equipped show one color from most directions and a different color or colors over definite arcs of the horizon indicated in the light lists and upon the charts. A sector changes the color of a light, when viewed from certain directions, but *not* the characteristic. For example, a flashing white light having a red sector, when viewed from within the sector, will appear flashing red.

Sectors may be but a few degrees in width, marking an isolated rock or shoal, or of such width as to extend from the direction of the deep water toward shore. Bearings referring to sectors are expressed in degrees as observed from a vessel *toward* the light.

For example, the *List of Lights* describes a certain light as displaying a red sector from 045° clockwise to 120°. Both are true bearings as observed from seaward. Figure 611 is a sketch of this light indicating the limits through which the light would appear red as observed from aboard ship.

In the majority of cases, water areas covered by red sectors should be avoided, the exact extent of the danger being determined from an examination of the charts. In some cases instead of indicating danger a narrow sector may mark the best water across a shoal.

In some conditions of the atmosphere white lights may have a reddish hue; the mariner therefore should not trust solely to color where there are sectors, but should verify the position by taking a bearing of the light. On either side of the line of demarcation between white and a colored sector there is always a small sector of uncertain color, as the edges of a sector cannot be cut off sharply. Note here also that the bearings given on the lines of demarcation on the chart are true bearings of the light as seen from the ship.

When a light is cut off by adjoining land, and the arc of visibility is given, the bearing on which the light disappears may vary with the distance of the vessel from which the light is observed, and the height of eye.

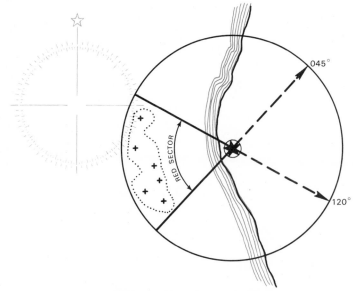

Figure 611: Red sector marking a reef.

612. Two lights, located some distance apart, visible usually in one direction only, are known as *range lights*. They are so located that the mariner, by bringing his ship into line with them, when they will appear one over the other, places his ship on the axis of the channel. If he steers his ship so that the lights remain continuously in line, he will remain within the confines of the channel. Entrance channels are frequently marked by range lights. The Delaware River and the St. Johns River on the Atlantic coast, and the Columbia River on the Pacific coast are examples of successive straight reaches marked in this manner.

Range lights.

The lights of ranges may be any of the three standard colors, and may also be fixed, flashing, or occulting, the principal requirement being that they stand out distinctly from their surroundings. Range light structures are always fitted with conspicuously colored daymarks for daytime use. Most range lights lose brilliance rapidly as a ship diverges from the range line. On some ranges, the sector of visibility of the lights is very narrow; for example, the Cape May harbor range lights are visible only for 2° on each side of the center-line of the channel. Ranges should be used only after a careful examination of the charts, and it is particularly important to determine for what distance the range line can be followed safely; this information is not always obtainable from the Light Lists themselves.

613. For a lighted navigational aid, such as a lighthouse, to be seen at a distance, it must have sufficient elevation above sea level, and sufficient intensity or power. The navigator frequently desires to know at what specific distance he can expect to sight a given light. The first step is always to refer to the appropriate *Light List* for the necessary data.

Visibility of lights.

Height Feet	Nautical Miles	Height Feet	Nautical Miles	Height Feet	Nautical Miles
1	1.1	33	6.6	125	12.8
2	1.6	34	6.7	130	13.0
3	2.0	35	6.8	135	13.3
4	2.3	36	6.9	140	13.5
5	2.6	37	7.0	145	13.8
6	2.8	38	7.1	150	14.0
7	3.0	39	7.1	160	14.5
8	3.2	40	7.2	170	14.9
9	3.4	41	7.3	180	15.3
10	3.6	42	7.4	190	15.8
11	3.8	43	7.5	200	16.2
12	4.0	44	7.6	210	16.6
13	4.1	45	7.7	220	17.0
14	4.3	46	7.8	230	17.3
15	4.4	47	7.8	240	17.7
16	4.6	48	7.9	250	18.1
17	4.7	49	8.0	260	18.4
18	4.9	50	8.1	270	18.8
19	5.0	55	8.5	280	19.1
20	5.1	60	8.9	290	19.5
21	5.2	65	9.2	300	19.8
22	5.4	70	9.6	310	20.1
23	5.5	75	9.9	320	20.5
24	5.6	80	10.2	330	20.8
25	5.7	85	10.5	340	21.1
26	5.8	90	10.9	350	21.4
27	5.9	95	11.2	360	21.7
28	6.1	100	11.4	370	22.0
29	6.2	105	11.7	380	22.3
30	6.3	110	12.0	390	22.6
31	6.4	115	12.3	400	22.9
32	6.5	120	12.5	410	23.2

Figure 613: Table of Horizon Distances.

The following terms and their definitions as used in current editions of the *Light List* are employed in connection with the range of visibility of a light.

Horizon distance is the distance, expressed in nautical miles, from a position above the surface of the earth, measured along the line of sight to the horizon. Horizon distances for various heights of eye are given in Table 8 in Bowditch; an extract from this table appears in Figure 613. A similar table is located in the introductory pages of each *Light List*. These tables, as well as the following formula, allow for refraction as calculated for standard weather conditions.

Horizon distance may be calculated by the formula $D = 1.144\sqrt{h}$, where h is the height of the eye in feet.

Nominal range is the maximum distance at which a light may be seen in clear weather (meteorological visibility of 10 nautical miles—see International Visibility Code, Figure 616a) expressed in nautical miles. Nominal range is listed for all Coast Guard lighted aids except range and directional lights.

Luminous range is the maximum distance at which a light may be seen under the existing visibility conditions. By use of the diagram in Figure 616b, luminous range may be determined from the known nominal range and the existing visibility conditions. Nominal and luminous ranges take no account of elevation, observer's height of eye, or the curvature of the earth.

Geographic range is the maximum distance at which a light may be seen under conditions of perfect visibility, limited only by the curvature of the earth. It is expressed in nautical miles for a height of observer's eye at sea level. It is necessary, therefore, to add to these a distance of visibility corresponding to the height of the observer's eye above sea level.

Computed visibility is the visibility determined for a particular light, taking into consideration its height and nominal range, and the height of eye of the observer. In computing the visibility of a light, it is assumed that the computed visibility will never exceed the light's nominal range: however, under certain atmospheric conditions a light may occasionally be visible far beyond its nominal range.

614. The following examples illustrate the recommended form for determining the visibility of a light. *Bear in mind that computed visibility cannot be greater than the nominal range.*

Determining visibility.

Example 1: Determine the visibility of Mount Desert Light (L. L. No. 1) for an observer with a height of eye of 70 feet.

Solution: From the *Light List,* determine the nominal range (column 4), 25 miles, and the height above water (column 5), 75 feet, of the light. Determine horizon distance from Figure 613, and place in form shown below.

Geographic Range for 75 feet	9.9 miles
Horizon Distance for 70 feet	9.6 miles
	———
Computed visibility	19.5 miles
Nominal range	25　miles

Answer: 19.5 miles

Example 2: Determine the visibility of Cape Nedick Light (L. L. No. 14) for an observer with a height of eye of 33 feet.

Solution: From Light List, determine the nominal range, 13 miles, and the height above water of the light, 88 feet. Determine horizon distances from Figure 613, interpolating for 88 feet.

Geographic Range for 88 feet	10.7 miles
Horizon Distance for 33 feet	6.6 miles
	———
Computed visibility	17.3 miles
Nominal range	13　miles

Answer: 13 miles.

As stated earlier the distance at which a light may be sighted may, due to abnormal atmospheric refraction, be far greater than its nominal range. Conversely, the nominal range may be greatly lessened by fog, haze, rain, snow, or smoke. In clear weather, the loom of a powerful light may appear before the light itself comes into sight.

The *Light Lists* include graphs for determining the visibility of lights under various standard conditions of visibility, as defined in the International Visibility Code (Figure 616a). The entering arguments are the visibility code number and the nominal range, or the intensity, as given in the *Light List.* By means of these arguments, the existing luminous range may be determined.

Intensity (candlepowers) given for lights are approximate and are the equivalent fixed intensity values (calculated from the Blondel-Rey formulas) based on the International Standard Candela. When the intensity of a light varies, as in the case of a white light with a red sector, or a fixed light varied by flashes, the candlepower of both white and red, or fixed light and flash, is given. From the stated candlepowers the mariner may judge the relative brilliancy and power of the various lights.

Predicting time and bearing for sighting a light.

615. When the visibility of a light for the appropriate height of eye has been determined, an arc is drawn on the chart; this arc is centered at the charted position of the light, and its radius is the range of visibility. It is labeled with the name of the light above the arc, and the visibility below it. The point at which this circle intersects the dead reckoning plot indicates the position at which the light should become visible. The time of arrival at this point is determined by dead reckoning; the bearing on which the light should be sighted is its direction from this point. Such a plot is illustrated in Figure 615. The true bearing obtained from the chart is frequently converted to a relative bearing to assist lookouts in locating the light. If the dead reckoning plot crosses the visibility arc at an acute angle, the predicted time and bearing may be considerably in error, as a small set to the right or left will make a considerable difference in the location of the point of intersection.

Figure 615: Predicting the time and bearing for sighting a light.

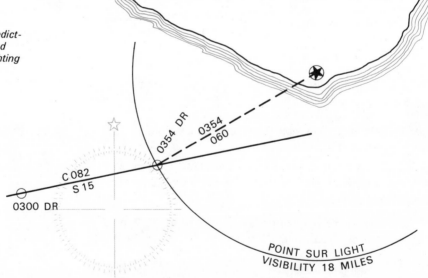

Bobbing a light.

When a light is first seen on the horizon, it will disappear if the observer tries to sight it from a point several feet, or one deck, lower, and reappear when he returns to his original position. This is called *bobbing a light*, and can be helpful in estimating its distance. When a light can be bobbed it is at the limit of its visibility for the observer's height of eye. By determining horizon distance for

METEOROLOGICAL OPTICAL RANGE					
Code	Weather	Yards	Code	Weather	Nautical Miles
0	Dense fog	Less than 50	4	Thin fog	$\frac{1}{2}$ to 1
1	Thick fog	50 to 200	5	Haze	1 to 2
2	Moderate fog	200 to 500	6	Light haze	2 to $5\frac{1}{2}$
3	Light fog	500 to 1000	7	Clear	$5\frac{1}{2}$ to 11
			8	Very clear	11.0 to 27.0
			9	Exceptionally clear	Over 27.0

Figure 616a: International Visibility Code.

the height of the light, and for the observer's height of eye, and combining these two values, an approximation of the distance may be obtained. This distance, combined with a bearing will give an *estimated position;* distances obtained in this way are not sufficiently accurate to yield a fix.

616. The nominal ranges, tabulated in column 4 of the *Light Lists* for major lights, are predicted on the existence of "clear" weather, with a meteorological visibility of 10 nautical miles; this falls in code No. 7 of the International Visibility Code, reproduced in Figure 616a. It may be noted that under "Very clear" and "Exceptionally clear" conditions, visibility is greatly increased, and the luminous range of a given light may be increased by several miles. Conversely, in the lower range of code, visibility tends to fall off very rapidly. By means of the diagram in Figure 616b, the luminous range of a given light may be approximated for existing conditions of visibility. The diagram is entered vertically from the top, using the nominal range listed in column 4. The selected vertical line is followed until the appropriate curve for the existing visibility is reached. Opposite this point, on the vertical scale at the left of the diagram, the luminous range for the existing meterorological conditions may be read off.

Visibility of lights.

When a light is sighted, it should be identified immediately (see article 610). Its characteristics as tabulated in the *Light List* are compared with the observed characteristics and timed with a stop watch. In identifying lights, it must be borne

Figure 616b: Luminous visibility diagram.

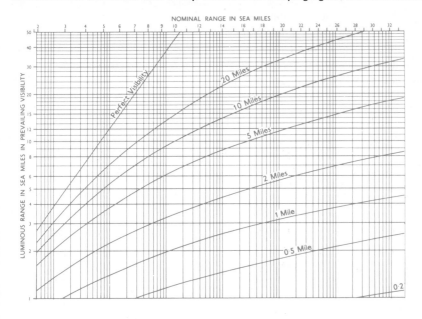

in mind that in the case of a fixed and flashing light, the flashes may, depending on atmospheric conditions, be seen well before the fixed light, and that the white flashes of an alternating white and colored light may become visible before the colored flashes.

Aids to navigation on ICW.

617. The Intracoastal Waterway (ICW) is a free, largely sheltered waterway, suitable for year-round use, extending some 2,400 miles along the Atlantic and Gulf coasts of the United States. In general it follows natural waterways.

The ICW aids to navigation may readily be identified by their yellow borders. The various types of aids that are in use are shown on page 23 of the Nautical Chart Symbols and Abbreviations included in Oceanographic Chart No. 1 appended to this text.

Colors.

The colors used for ICW aids are governed by the following rules:

> The *left side* of the channel, entering from the north and east, and traversing towards the south and west, is marked with *black aids*, bearing *odd numbers*.

> The *right side* of the channel, entering from the north and east, is marked with *red aids*, bearing *even numbers*

> All *black* markers on piles, etc. are *square*, while the *red* markers are *triangular* in shape.

In certain areas, the ICW coincides with other waterways, which are buoyed in accordance with the standard practice, that is black buoys on the left hand when proceeding from seaward, and red buoys on the right, as described in article 605. In such joint waterways the standard system of coloring prevails for buoys, and the ICW numbers and yellow borders are omitted, but the yellow triangle or squares are used on the regular aids to designate the ICW. The system of marking where the ICW and another waterway coincide is shown on page 23 of Chart 1. An inspection of the sketch on that page shows that the color of aids may be reversed under such conditions. A vessel proceeding south down the ICW has red aids on her right hand until the nun "6" is reached where the channel becomes a joint waterway; at this point the red aids will be on her left hand. However, along this reach of the channel the yellow shapes painted on the buoys can be of assistance, as the squares will be on the red buoys as a reminder that in this joint waterway a red buoy may be on the left-hand for vessels proceeding south.

CHAPTER 7

Dead Reckoning and Current Sailing

701. *Dead reckoning* (DR), as previously stated, is one of the four main divisions of navigation. The term is derived from *deduced* or *ded*. reckoning, the process by which a ship's position was *deduced* or computed trigonometrically, with relation to a known point of departure. Although highly accurate modern charts permit solution by graphic methods, rather than by laborious mathematics, the term, in its present form, continues in use. While treated as a separate division of navigation in this text, dead reckoning is basic to all phases of navigation.

Introduction to DR.

702. Dead reckoning is the process of determining a ship's approximate position by applying to its last well-determined position a vector or a series of consecutive vectors representing the run that has since been made, using only the true courses steered, and the distance steamed, as determined by the ordered engine speed, *without considering current.* By projecting these course and speed vectors ahead of the present position, the ship's predicted DR position for any desired time can be determined.

DR defined.

The key elements of dead reckoning may be summarized as follows:

Only the true courses steered are used to determine a DR position.

The distance run used in obtaining a DR position is obtained by multiplying the ordered engine speed by the time it has acted or will act.

An intended DR plot is always plotted from a known position, that is, a fix or running fix.

The effects of current are not considered in determining a DR position.

703. The importance of maintaining an accurate dead reckoning plot cannot be overemphasized. The means of fixing the ship's position is not always available, due to weather, equipment failure, etc. Under such conditions the navigator must rely on his dead reckoning for an indication of his position. It is obvious that a DR position must be used with extreme caution in the vicinity of shoal water, or other dangers to navigation.

The importance of DR.

If the ship made good exactly the ordered course and speed, and there was no wind or current, dead reckoning would at all times provide an accurate indication of position. However, since such conditions rarely exist, a DR must be considered as only an approximation of the true position. This serves to show the need for maintaining a constant and accurate dead reckoning plot. It is most important that the best approximation of position be constantly available; this information is required for determing when to make turns, predicting the time of sighting lights or other aids to navigation, and identifying landmarks.

Dead reckoning is customarily done graphically on a chart or plotting sheet appropriate to the area in which the ship is steaming. Graphic solution enables the navigator to visualize his ship's position in relation to dangers to navigation, or to landmarks.

DR terms defined.

704. Definitions of terms used in dead reckoning vary greatly in different texts and have thus far not been standardized. Various adjectives can be used to clarify specific uses of basic terms, but confusion in terminology can be avoided by remembering that in marine navigation *course* is always used as a direction with reference to the water, while *track* is used with reference to the earth. This usage is standard in this text, is used at the U. S. Naval Academy in teaching navigation and concurred with by the U. S. Naval Oceanographic Office.

Heading (Hdg. or SH). The horizontal direction in which a ship points or heads at any instant, expressed in angular units, clockwise from 000° through 360°, from a reference direction (Figure 704). The heading of a ship is also called ship's head. Heading is a constantly changing value as a ship oscillates or yaws across the course due to effects of the sea and of steering error.

Figure 704: Course, heading, and track.

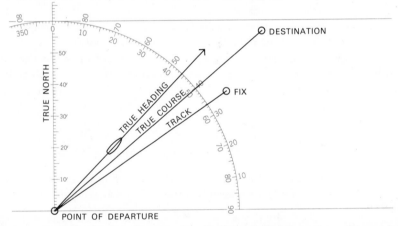

Course (C). A rhumb line direction. The horizontal direction of travel through still water, expressed in angular units from a reference direction, from 000° at the reference direction clockwise through 360°. The course is often designated as true, magnetic, compass, or grid as the reference direction is true, magnetic, compass, or grid North, respectively. Course can be either an anticipated or an accomplished direction of travel with respect to the water.

Course Line. In marine navigation, the graphic representation of a ship's course, normally used in the construction of a dead reckoning plot.

Track (TR). As used in navigation, track is the rhumb line or lines describing the path of a vessel actually made good relative to the earth. (In some texts referred to as Course Made Good, CMG, or Course Over Ground, COG.)

Intended Track (ITR). The anticipated path of a vessel relative to the earth. When used in constructing vector diagrams the direction of the resultant side after drawing the vectors for course and speed, and estimated current set and drift, is termed the intended track.

Speed (S). The rate of travel of a ship through the water, in knots. It is used in conjunction with time to establish a distance run on each of the consecutive segments or vectors of the DR plot.

Speed Made Good (SMG). The speed along the track, representing the *speed made good* over the surface of the earth. It differs from the ship's speed (S) through the water by a vector of the current velocity. Sometimes called *Speed Over The Ground* (SOG).

Speed of Advance (SOA). The average speed in knots which must be maintained on a voyage to arrive at a destination at an appointed time.

DR Position. A position determined by plotting a vector or series of consecutive vectors using only the true course, and distance determined by speed through the water, without consideration of current.

Estimated Position (EP). The most probable position of a ship, determined from incomplete data or data of questionable accuracy. In practical usage it is often the DR position as modified by the best information available.

Dead Reckoning Plot. Commonly called DR plot. In marine navigation it is the graphical representation on the nautical chart of the line or series of lines representing the vectors of the ordered true courses, and distance run on these courses at the ordered speeds, while proceeding from a fixed point. The DR plot originates at a fix or running fix; it is suitably labeled as to courses, speeds and times of various dead reckoning positions, usually at hourly time intervals or at times of change of course or speed. The DR plot may represent courses and speeds to be used or those that have been used.

Estimated Time of Departure (ETD). The estimate of the time of departure from a specified location in accordance with a scheduled movement.

Estimated Time of Arrival (ETA). The best estimate of the time of arrival at a specified location in accordance with a scheduled movement.

705. It is of the utmost importance that all points and lines plotted on the chart be properly labeled. Employing a standard method of labeling enables the commanding officer and the officer of the deck readily to understand the navigator's chart work. The principal rules for labeling DR plots are:

Labeling a DR plot.

Immediately after drawing any line or plotting any point, label it.

The label for any point on a line should not be along the line, but should make a sufficient angle with the line to be well clear of it.

The labels indicating direction and rate of movement along a course line should lie *along* that line.

The label indicating the direction of a course line *C*, should appear along the *top* of the line, followed by three numerals indicating the true course in degrees.

The label indicating the rate of travel along the line, *S*, should appear along the *bottom* of the line *underneath the direction label*, followed by numerals indicating the speed in knots.

Habitually print all labels clearly and neatly.

The label for a point on a DR plot is a semicircle which locates the point, and is labeled with the time. A fix or running fix requires a circled dot around the point and the time. A running fix is differentiated from a fix by adding RFIX to the label, as shown in Figure 705a.

Figure 705a: Labels of points used in dead reckoning.

A WELL-DETERMINED POSITION (FIX):

A WELL-DETERMINED POSITION (RUNNING FIX):

A DEAD RECKONING (DR) POSITION:

As summarized, the method of labeling a course line consists of noting the *true course* with the prefix *C above* the line and noting the *speed* with the prefix *S below* the line, in addition to the labeled points along the line. Course lines, properly labeled, are shown in Figure 705b, as a part of the complete DR plot.

Figure 705b: Labeling a DR course line.

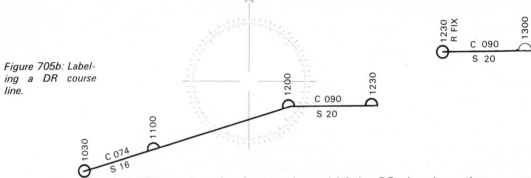

In addition to knowing *how* to plot and label a DR plot, the navigator must know *when* it should be plotted. The following rules have been developed which, when combined with the standard labeling, will result in a plot that can be understood by any conning officer:

A DR position shall be plotted every hour on the hour.

A DR position shall be plotted at the time of every course change.

A DR position shall be plotted at the time of every speed change.

A DR position shall be plotted at the time of obtaining a fix or a running fix.

A DR position shall be plotted at the time of obtaining a single line of position.

A new course line shall be plotted from each fix or running fix as soon as the fix or running fix has been determined and plotted on the chart.

Figure 706: The navigator's DR plot.

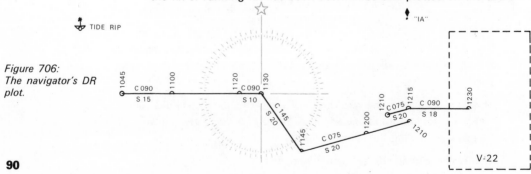

These rules of dead reckoning are considered adequate to meet the needs and requirements of navigation in the open waters of the sea. There are occasions, however, when a more frequent plot of the ship's dead reckoning position is essential to safe navigation, as when in the confined waters of channels, bays, straits and harbors. Knowledge of when to plot frequent fixes and even more frequent dead reckoning positions when in such waters will come with experience and judgment. This subject will be discussed more fully in Chapter 14.

706. The following example outlines a typical dead reckoning problem; its complete solution is illustrated in Figure 706. *Example of a DR plot.*

A partial extract from a deck log reads as follows:

> "1045. With Tide Rip Lightship bearing 315°, distant 6 miles, took departure for operating area V-22 on course 090°, speed 15 knots. 1120-Changed speed to 10 knots to blow tubes. 1130-Changed course to 145° and increased speed to 20 knots. 1145-Changed course to 075°. 1210-Made radar contact on Buoy 1A bearing 010°, distant 8 miles. 1215-Changed course to 090° and changed speed to 18 knots to arrive at the rendezvous point at 1230 . . . "

It is well to review at this point the applicability of the rules for dead reckoning as they pertain to this example. Commencing at the initial known position, the 1045 fix, the navigator plotted the course line in a direction of 090° corresponding to the ordered course. The rate of travel, speed 15 knots, for an elapsed time of 15 minutes and then 20 minutes enabled the navigator to make a scaled plot of the 1100 DR and 1120 DR positions respectively on his chart. Labeling the fix, the 1100 DR, the 1120 DR, and the course line itself completes the graphic description of the ship's travel to 1120. At 1120, only the speed was changed. At 1130, both the course and speed were changed, while at 1145, only the course was changed. Each of these occurrences requires a separate DR position on the plot, while segments of the course lines are labeled to indicate what specific change of the course and speed occurred at that time. The 1200 DR was plotted on the whole hour as prescribed. At 1210, since the navigator fixed his position by radar, he must then plot both the 1210 DR on the former course line and the 1210 radar fix from which he commences a new course line. The navigator plots the ship from the fix on a course of 075° at a speed of 20 knots to 1215, at which time the course is changed to 090° and the speed is reduced to 18 knots in order to arrive at the operating area at 1230 as scheduled. The DR plot reflects the course and speed change and includes the 1230 DR as shown.

707. In actual practice, a preliminary DR course line was plotted on a tentative basis before the ship ever got underway for the operating area. Called navigational planning, it introduced a fundamental principle of safe navigation. Every cruise, every departure from and entry into port must be planned in advance, based on all information available to the navigator. The material studied in the course of this planning includes the charts of the areas to be traversed, the navigational aids expected to be sighted, the availability of electronic coverage, estimates of currents and weather to be encountered, the contour of the bottom, and other factors which will be discussed later in this text. The following description of a short voyage will serve to illustrate many of the principles and concepts enumerated so far in this chapter. *DR plot in practice.*

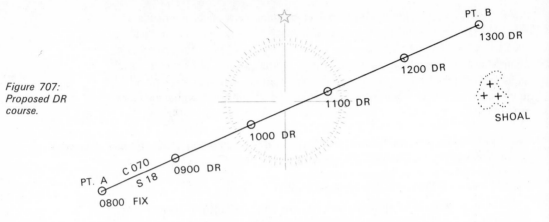

*Figure 707:
Proposed DR
course.*

Referring to Figure 707, assume that a ship is located at point A, and receives orders to depart at 0800 for point B, 90 miles distant, arriving at 1300. Immediately upon receipt of this information, the navigator located points *A* and *B* on the appropriate small-scale chart of the area. By measuring the direction of *B* from *A*, the course of 070° is determined and noted on the DR plot as "C 070." Dividing the rhumb line distance between *A* and *B* by five hours, SOA is computed to be 18 knots and labeled accordingly. Next, starting at the known position, or fix, at 0800, the navigator stepped off and marked the successive hourly positions which the ship is expected to occupy. The plot is now a complete and graphical picture. The plan is complete and, barring any unforeseen circumstances, represents the movement which the ship will follow from the point of departure to its destination. The technique of handling departures from plan comprise the subject of the next article.

*Departures from
plan.*

708. The ship gets underway as scheduled and sets course 070° true and speed 18 knots to arrive at *B* at 1300. If the calculations are correct and there is no current or change of course to avoid shipping, the ship should arrive at *B* as planned. The navigator's work now consists of trying to establish his actual position from time to time, in order to be sure that the ship is following the intended track, or, if it is not following it, to recommend changes in course or speed, or both, which will bring the ship safely back to the intended track or to any selected point on it.

The navigator had poor weather and was unable to establish his position until about noon at which time he obtained a 1200 fix. When the fix was plotted, he found the ship was at point *X* in Figure 708. He further noted that if the ship maintained the same course from point *X* as it had between *A* and *X*, the ship would be standing into danger of grounding at the indicated shoal. This illustrates the fundamental danger and the inherent weakness of relying solely on DR positions.

Since the ship will not reach its destination on a course of 070° and a speed of 18 knots, the navigator must determine a new course and speed to arrive at point *B* by 1300, based upon the relationship between point *B* and the latest fix, point *X*.

In this example, it took the navigator until 1215 to make and record his observations, plot the fix, and inform the captain of the new course and speed recommendations to arrive at point *B* at the specified ETA. Therefore he plotted the 1215 DR position from the fix, point *X*, using the ordered course of 070° and speed 18 to locate the position from which the recommendation will take effect. This is a concept which should be remembered : *The course line will continue in the direction and at the speed originally ordered during the time required to obtain and plot the fix and decide upon a new course of action.* Upon the advice of the navigator in this instance, the captain ordered a course of 028° and a speed of 24 knots at 1215 to direct the ship to point *B* to arrive at 1300. Although it is apparent that a current existed, it is not considered in this example. The technique and procedures of computing and allowing for current are explained later in this chapter and would be used by the navigator.

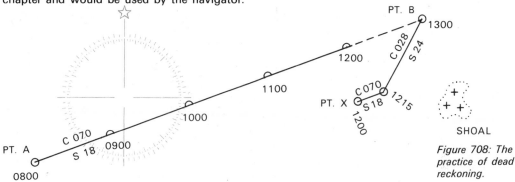

Figure 708: The practice of dead reckoning.

The navigator believed that the ship was following the intended track until he obtained and plotted his 1200 fix. This illustrates the fundamental weakness of relying solely on dead reckoning, for dead reckoning is dependent on the assumption that the ship makes good over the ground the same direction that it is traveling through the water, and that the ship makes good over the ground the same speed that it is traveling through the water. Therefore the dead reckoning position should not be relied upon if it is possible to obtain information to determine the position by other means. There are on file in the Navy Department numerous reports of instances of naval vessels having been put aground and lost because of a navigator's adherence to a course which was laid in safe waters, while the actual track was an unknown path leading to danger.

709. Experience has shown that the mechanics of plotting presents many difficulties for the beginner. These helpful hints will increase both accuracy and speed in plotting :

Plotting techniques.

A drafting machine should be used whenever available to determine the direction of a line, as it is both more rapid and accurate than other methods. When a drafting machine is not available, a protractor is used. Various types are shown in Chapter 10.

Tape the chart to the desk before plotting. This will maintain proper orientation of the chart. Tape is preferable to thumbtacks for this purpose.

If the chart is too large to fit on the desk used, determine the extent of the chart which must be used, then fold under the portions of the chart which will not be required to be exposed. Be sure to leave one latitude scale and one longitude scale available for measurement.

Use a *sharp* No. 2 pencil. A harder pencil will not erase well, and a softer pencil will smear.

Draw lines heavy enough to be seen readily, but light enough so that they do not indent the chart paper.

Avoid drawing unnecessary lines, and erase any lines used only for the purpose of measurement. Do not extend lines excessively beyond the point at which their direction is to be changed.

Hold the pencil against the straight edge in a vertical position throughout the entire length of a line when drawing it.

Measure all directions and distances carefully. Accuracy is the mark of good navigation. On Mercator charts, measure distance on the latitude scale using the portion of the scale which is opposite the line which is being measured. Be neat and exact in plotting work. Use standard symbols, and print all labels neatly.

Learn to use dividers with one hand and with either hand if possible.

Lay down a new DR track from each new fix or running fix. Plot a DR position at every change of course, at every change of speed, at the time of obtaining a fix, a running fix, or a single line of position, and on the whole hour.

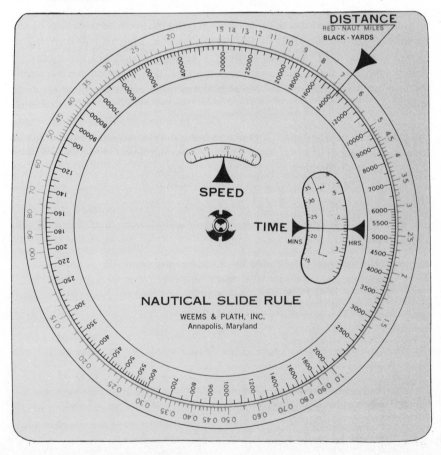

*Figure 710a:
Nautical Slide Rule.*

710. The navigator may find it convenient to use a nautical slide rule, Figure 710a, or computer for the solution of time speed, and distance problems. Alternately, he may use tables such as those in Bowditch, or in H. O. 214, for this purpose. However, he should be able to solve these problems without the use of such devices.

Time, speed, and distance solutions.

Time, distance, or speed can be rapidly determined by means of the logarithmic scale printed on Oceanographic Office plotting sheets, and on the top line of the nomogram at the bottom of the maneuvering board, illustrated in Figure 710b. The scale, together with a pair of dividers, is used as a slide rule. Let the right leg of a pair of dividers represent time in minutes and the left leg, distance. Consider speed as distance in 60 minutes.

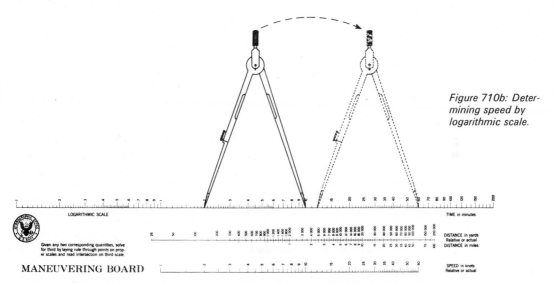

Figure 710b: Determining speed by logarithmic scale.

Thus, to obtain time, place the left leg of the dividers on the speed and the right leg on 60. Without changing the spread of the dividers, place the left leg on the required distance and read off the time at the right leg. If distance in a given time is desired, place the right leg on the given time and read off the distance at the left leg. If speed is required, set the left leg of the dividers at distance and the right leg at time and then, without changing the spread, place the right leg on 60 and read the speed at the left leg.

If the problem runs off the scale, solution can be made by using a fraction of the speed, or distance (only one) and multiplying the answer by the inverse of the same fraction.

If in doubt as to the accuracy of a solution, check it mentally or by simple arithmetic using the formula $D = S \times T$, where D is distance in miles, S is speed in knots, and T, is time in hours.

A useful rule to use in plotting in confined waters where frequent fixes and DR positions are required is the so-called "*three minute rule*," applied as follows: The travel of a ship *in yards* in three minutes is equal to the speed of the ship in knots multiplied by 100. Where a six-minute DR would be more appropriate than a three minute plot, the travel of a ship *in miles* in six minutes is equal to the speed of the ship in knots multiplied by 1/10.

95

Example 1: A navigator desires to plot a three-minute DR from his last fix in Brewerton Channel. The ship is making a speed of 12 knots. To compute the travel of the ship in yards in three minutes, he multiplies the speed in knots, 12, by the factor 100 and determines the DR advance to be 1200 yards.

Answer: Distance 1200 yards.

Example 2: A navigator desires to plot a six-minute DR from his last fix in Chesapeake Bay. The ship is making a speed of 15 knots. To compute the travel of the ship in miles in six minutes, he multiplies the speed in knots, 15, by the factor 1/10 and determines the DR advance to be 1.5 miles.

Answer: Distance 1.5 mile.

DR summary.

711. This chapter has thus far presented the data required to understand the elements of the dead reckoning process. The mechanics of dead reckoning, the standard method of labeling, and when to plot DR positions have been discussed. Facility in the graphic portrayal of the ship's travel will come with practice.

The need for maintaining an accurate and readily understandable dead reckoning plot cannot be overemphasized. It is axiomatic that the navigator who demonstrates neatness and accuracy in plotting can be expected to demonstrate the same qualities in the other phases of navigation. It is the converse of these qualities which is frequently found to be the basic cause of groundings.

Introduction to current sailing.

712. So far in this chapter, the effect of current has not been discussed. This omission was intentional, as current complicates the navigational problem; it was deemed desirable first to cover some of the fundamentals of DR navigation. This section deals with *current sailing*. How the current is determined, and what use of this knowledge is made by the navigator will be discussed.

In discussing dead reckoning, it was stated that a DR position only represents the actual position of the ship if the steering is accurate, the engine calibration or speed log is correct, and if no external forces have acted on the ship. In navigation, the total of all the factors which may cause a ship to depart from its intended course and DR are termed *current*. Among the factors included in the term are:

Ocean current
Tidal current
Wind current
Windage on the ship
Heavy seas
Inaccurate steering
Undetermined compass error
Error in engine calibration
Errors in log calibration
Excessively fouled bottom
Unusual conditions of trim

From the foregoing, it can be seen that *current*, unfortunately, has two meanings as commonly used in marine navigation. First. it refers to the horizontal movement of water due to ocean currents, tidal currents, or wind currents. Second, in common usage it refers to the combined effect of all the factors listed above. Thus the term current, as used in navigation, may or may not include the motion of the water through which the ship is passing; in most cases, however, this factor, if it exists, will have the greatest effect on the travel of the ship.

713. *Current sailing* is the art of determining course and speed through the water, making due allowance for the effect of a predicted or estimated current, so that upon completion of travel, the intended track and the actual track will coincide.

Current sailing defined.

Current sailing may also be interpreted to include the determination of an existing current. Primarily, however, current sailing is the application of the best available current information to the intended track to determine what course and speed to order. Conversely, similar techniques are used to determine the actual current which has acted upon the ship.

714. Three primary types of currents are of interest to the navigator:

Types of currents.

Ocean current is a well defined current, extending over a considerable oceanic area.

Tidal current is one due to tidal action. Its effect is often marked in harbors, estuaries, etc., but tidal currents are also encountered along coasts.

Wind current is one affecting a limited area created by the action of a strong wind blowing for twelve hours or more; it usually does not flow in the direction of the wind, as it tends to be deflected by Coriolis force. The nature of this deflection is discussed in Chapter 8, which also includes much useful information on currents.

Estimated current is determined by evaluating all the known forces which will contribute to make up the sum total of current effects in a given area.

Current terms defined.

Actual current is determined by the displacement of the ship from the DR position to a fix. It is determined when an accurate position can be obtained, the difference in direction and distance between the fix and the DR position for the time of the fix establishes the actual current.

Set of a current is the direction *towards* which it flows. It is expressed in degrees true.

Set and drift.

Drift of a current is its velocity, usually stated in knots. However, some publications, notably pilot charts and current atlases, express drift in terms of nautical miles per day.

Estimated position (EP) is the most probable position of a vessel, determined from all available data, when a fix or running fix are unobtainable, and includes the effect of the estimated current.

Current triangle is a graphic *vector diagram*, in which one side represents the set and drift of the current, one side represents the ship's course and speed, and the third side represents the track. If any two sides are known, the third can be determined by measurement.

97

715. Point *D* (Figure 715) bears 090° distant 20 miles from Point *A*. A current with an estimated set of 180°, and drift of 4 knots flows between the two points. If a ship were ordered to steam from *A* to *D* in a total elapsed time of two hours, the navigator would be faced with a typical problem in current sailing. It is obvious that the direction of the *ITR* is 090°, and the *SOA* is 10.0 knots. It is equally obvious that if course 090°, and speed 10.0 knots were ordered, the ship two hours later would be some eight miles south of *D*. To allow for the estimated current on this two hour trip, the ship should be steered on a course somewhat into the current in the direction of Point *C* some eight miles to the north of *D* (Point *C*), and at a speed slightly greater than 10 knots. *Provided the estimate of the current was correct*, the ship would arrive at *D* in two hours, the current effects having exactly countered the course and speed offset from the intended track.

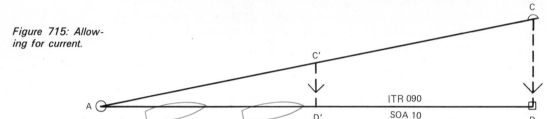

Figure 715 illustrates what has occurred. The ship headed for Point *C*, on course 070°, but making good 090°, and constantly "crabbing" into the current, as shown. At the end of the first hour she reached *D'*, rather than *C'*, and at the end of the second hour she reached Point *D* rather than *C*. The track, *AD*, is the resultant of the vector sum of the velocity of the ship with respect to the water (*AC*) and the velocity of the current with respect to the earth, (*CD*), both of which were in action for the same length of time.

Point *C* represents the ship's DR position at the end of two hours, and Point *D* represents the *estimated position*, EP, which is the most probable position, short of a fix or running fix. Note that *actual current* has not entered into this problem; this will be discussed in article 718.

716. It has been pointed out that in the absence of a fix or running fix, the navigator, on the basis of available information, may often estimate the ship's position to greater accuracy than that indicated by the DR. For instance, if a navigator has good reason to believe that a current of well determined set and drift exists, he can find the EP for a given time by plotting the predicted movement of the ship away from the DR position for a given time, due to the effect of the current. To do this, he plots the set and measures off along this line the *drift* multiplied by the number of hours it has been or will be acting. An alternate method, used chiefy when the ship steams on a single course at a constant speed, is to solve graphically a current triangle.

Example: (Figure 716) The 0500 fix of a ship is as shown. The ship is on course 300°, speed 6 knots. A current has been estimated with a set of 250°, drift 1.0 knot.

Required: Plot and label the hourly DR positions and hourly EP's from 0500 to 0800.

Solution: Plot the course and the hourly DR positions up to 0800. From each DR position plot a line in the direction 250° and measure off 1 mile from the 0600 DR, 2 miles from the 0700 DR, and 3 miles from the 0800 DR. Enclose the points so obtained in small squares and label as shown in Figure 716.

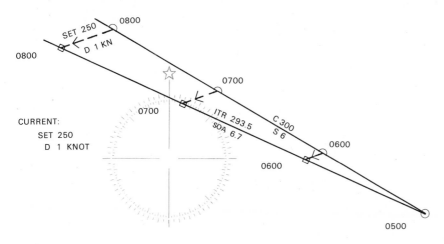

Figure 716: The EP plot.

The accuracy of an estimated position depends on the accuracy with which the current is estimated. It is not safe to assume that a current determined by the last fix will continue, unless there is evidence to indicate that this is so. Unless there is information available to permit a reasonably accurate estimate of the current, it is best to assume zero current. It is especially unwise to expect a current to be regular and uniform near a coast, for local conditions are likely to cause irregularity, and tidal currents have greater effects here than on the open sea. When approaching pilot waters, it is often desirable to maintain two plots, allowing for anticipated current in one (the EP plot) and not in the other (the DR plot), and to consider both plots when laying a course to avoid danger.

717. Three problems frequently arise in connection with currents of estimated set and drift: *Allowing for current.*

To find what course a ship steaming at a given speed through such a current should take to make good an intended track.

To find what course and speed must be ordered to steam through an estimated current to arrive at the destination on time.

To find the intended track and speed over the ground by a ship when steaming a given course and a given speed through a current.

If a current is setting the same direction as the course, or its reciprocal, the track is the same as the course through the water. The effect on speed can be found by addition or subtraction; if in the same direction the speeds are added, and if in opposite directions, the smaller is subtracted from the larger. This situation happens frequently when a ship encounters tidal currents upon entering or leaving port. If a ship is *crossing* a current, the solution can be made graphically by a vector diagram since the velocity over the ground is the vector sum of the ship's velocity through the water and the current effects over the ground.

Such vector solution can be made to any convenient scale and at any convenient place, such as the center of a compass rose, on a separate sheet, or directly on the plot. The following examples will show the method of graphic solution:

Example 1: (Figure 717a) Given the estimated set and drift of the current and ordered speed of the ship, find what course must be steered to make good a given intended track.

Figure 717a: Finding course to steer to make good an intended track.

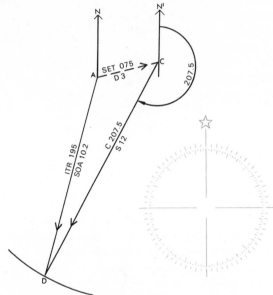

Let the estimated set of the current be 075°, drift 3 knots. The ship has boiler power available for a speed of 12 knots. The direction of the intended track is 195°.

Solution: In Figure 717a *N* and *N'* indicate the direction of true north. From *A*, the position of the ship, lay off the line *AD* of indefinite length in the direction 195°. Plot the current vector, *AC*, in the direction of the set, 075°, for a distance equal to the velocity of the drift, 3 knots. With *C* as a center, swing an arc of radius equal to the ship's speed through the water, 12 knots, intersecting *AD* at *D*. The direction, *CD*, 207°.5, is the course to order and the length *AD*, 10.2 knots, is the estimated SOA. Notice that vectors *AD* and *AC*, representing intended track and current respectively, have been plotted with respect to the earth (Point *A*), while vector *CD* has been plotted with respect to the water.

Example 2: (Figure 717b) Given the estimated set and drift of the current, the direction of the intended track, and the intended *speed of advance* (SOA), find the course and speed to order.

Figure 717b: Finding course and speed to use to make good an intended track.

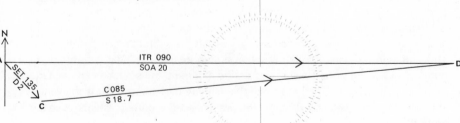

A ship at 1300 is 100 miles due west of her desired destination. If the ship is to arrive at her destination at 1800, find the course and speed to order if a 2 knot current setting southeast (135°) is predicted.

Solution: In Figure 717b, let N be the meridian of the ship located at Point A. The distance to the destination is 100 miles due east. With five hours to reach this destination, the ship obviously must maintain a speed of advance of 20 knots. Lay off AD in the direction 090° to represent the intended track and of a length equal to the intended SOA, 20 knots. Lay off the current vector, AC, in the direction of its set, 135°, from Point A and of a length equal to the drift, 2 knots. Complete the current sailing vector diagram by drawing CD. The direction of CD, 085°, is the course to order while its length, 18.7 knots, is the speed to order to make the passage. Again notice that vectors AD and AC, representing *intended track* and current respectively, have been plotted with respect to the earth while vector CD has been plotted with respect to the water.

Example 3: (Figure 717c) Given course and speed of the ship, and the estimated set and drift of the current, find the intended track and the estimated speed of advance. This example illustrates the procedure whereby a navigator is solving only incidentally for intended track and SOA. His primary concern is to establish an estimated position defined by track and SOA. It is included here to illustrate the third case of current sailing stated initially in this article.

A ship steams at 12 knots on course 211° true, through a current estimated to be setting 075° at a drift of three knots. Find the intended track and the SOA.

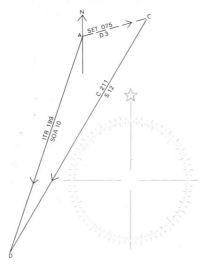

Figure 717c: Finding intended track and speed of advance to determine an estimated position.

Solution: In Figure 717c, let N be the meridian through the ship located at Point A. Lay off AC, the vector representing the direction of the set of the current, 075°, and a length equal to the drift of 3 knots. From C, lay off the vector CD in the direction of the course, 211°, at a length equal to the speed, 12 knots. Complete the current sailing vector diagram by drawing AD. The direction of AD, 199°, is the direction of the intended track while its length, 10 knots, represents the estimated SOA.

The navigator is now able to apply this solution to his last fix to obtain an estimated position.

Determining actual current.

718. If a course line is laid down from a fix (not a running fix) and at a later time a new fix is obtained which does not agree with the DR position for the same time, the difference between the DR position and the fix must represent the actual current encountered during passage. It is immediately apparent that current so determined will include all of the factors mentioned in article 712 and, in addition, any errors in the fixes. It should also be apparent that if the estimated position on the intended track coincides with the fix on the actual track, the estimated current computed prior to departure was exactly equal to the actual current encountered during passage. If the two positions are *not* identical, then the estimated current was in error by an amount directly proportional to the rate and direction of separation of the two positions.

Three problems most frequently arise in determining the set and drift of an actual current:

> To find set and drift of an actual current, given the DR position based on on an earlier fix, and a fix for the same time.

> To find set and drift of an actual current, given the DR position based on an earlier *running* fix, and a fix at the same time.

> To find set and drift of an actual current, given the DR position and an estimated position based on an earlier fix, and a fix at the same time.

Example 1: (Figure 718a) Given the DR position based on an earlier fix and a fix for the same time, find the set and drift of the actual current.

The 1815 DR position has been run forward from a fix obtained at 0545 the same day. At 1815 a fix is obtained and when plotted, is located 7.5 miles from the 1815 DR.

Required: The set and drift of the actual current.

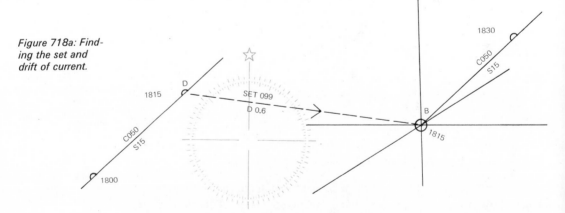

Figure 718a: Finding the set and drift of current.

Solution: The set is the direction *from the DR position to the fix* for the same time. Drift is determined by measuring the distance between the DR position and the fix for the same time, and dividing it by the number of hours *since the last fix.* This is true regardless of the number of changes of course and speed since the last fix. Since the 1815 DR position represents the position the ship would have occupied had there been no current, and the 1815 fix represents the actual position of the ship, the line *DB* joining them is the direction and distance the ship has been moved by current. The direction of this line from the DR to the fix, 099°, is the *set* of the current. The *drift* is its distance, 7.5 miles, divided by the time between the fixes, 12.5 hours, or 7.5/12.5 = 0.6 knots

Answer: Set 099°, drift 0.6 knots.

Example 2: (Figure 718b) Given the DR position based on an earlier running fix, and a fix for the same time, find the set and drift of the actual current.

Two methods may be used to determine the actual current when the DR position has been run forward from a running fix. Each method is explained below. At 0700 the navigator obtained a fix as shown. At 1152 a running fix is obtained from two LOP's, one at 0919, and the other at 1152, and a new DR plot is begun. At 1710 another fix is obtained as shown.

Required: The set and drift of the current.

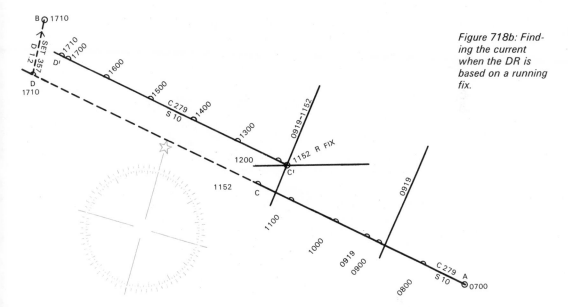

Figure 718b: Finding the current when the DR is based on a running fix.

Solution: (Method 1). The plotted DR position at 1710 (point *D'*) has been run forward from a running fix, and therefore cannot be used to obtain the set and drift of the current. Ignore the 1152 running fix, and continue the original DR course from point *C* until the DR position for time 1710 (point *D*) is determined. The set of the current is the direction from point *D*, to the 1710 fix (point *B*), 357°, and the drift is this distance, 12.7 miles, divided by the time since the last fix, 10.2 hours, or 1.2 knots. (In this example the extension of the original course from *C* to *D* is shown as a broken line for clarity.)

Solution: (Method 2). Measure the direction and distance *CC'* from the original 1152 DR to the 1152 running fix. By applying the reciprocal of this direction and the same distance to the 1710 DR position, point *D* is established. It is noted that this is the same position as determined in method 1. The set of 357° and drift of 1.2 knots are obtained as before.

Answer: Set 357°, drift 1.2 knots.

Example 3: (Figure 718c) Given a DR position and an estimated position based on an earlier fix, and a fix for the same time, find the set and drift of the actual current.

At 0900, a navigator fixed his position at *A* as shown. While proceeding to Point *D* bearing 090°, 20 miles from *A*, the navigator estimated that the current would be 135°, 6 knots, and therefore he set course 075° speed 16.3 knots to make good the intended track to Point *D*. At 1000, the navigator fixed his position at Point *B*.

Required: The set and drift of the actual current.

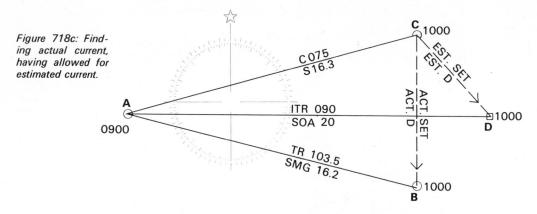

Figure 718c: Finding actual current, having allowed for estimated current.

Solution: Since the 1000 DR represents the position the ship would have occupied had there been no current, and the 1000 Fix represents the actual position of the ship, the line *CB* joining them is the direction and distance the ship has been moved by the actual current. The direction of this line from the DR to the fix, 180°, is the set of the current. The drift is its distance 8.0 miles, divided by the time between fixes, 1 hour, or drift = 8.0 knots.

As is evident from an inspection of the figure, the navigator's estimate of current was in error by the vector difference of *CD* and *CB*.

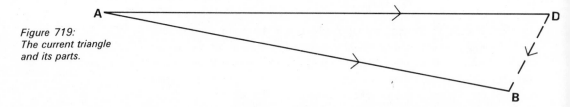

*Figure 719:
The current triangle and its parts.*

Part	Using Estimated Current	Using Actual Current
Point A	Present position (fix) of ship	Previous position (fix) of ship
Point D	DR position of ship at future time	DR position of ship at present time
Point B	Estimated position at future time	Present position (fix) at present time
Side AD	Course and speed vector	Course and speed vector
Side AB	Intended track and SOA	Actual track and SMG
Side DB	Anticipated or expected current	Actual current encountered

Note: Points B and D are always for the *same* time.

719. Many times it is desirable to construct a current sailing vector triangle to assist in the graphic solution of the problem. However, as has been demonstrated, the solution of the unknown parts of the triangle must be in terms of the given information of the known parts.

Labeling the current triangle.

A complete current triangle equally applicable to the solutions of the current problem prior to departure, as well as to its solution after arrival, is illustrated in Figure 719. A tabulation of the respective parts of each triangle is given in the accompanying table.

720. Article 718 discussed the fact that a running fix could not be used in the determination of current, as the earlier LOP used to obtain the running fix had in fact been acted upon by current during the time intervening between it and the second LOP. It follows, therefore, that if the navigator believes he knows the set and drift of the current within reasonable limits, he can increase the accuracy of the running fix by allowing for it when he advances the earlier LOP.

The running fix with known current.

The following example illustrates the technique of plotting a running fix with a known current

Example 1: (Figure 720) The navigator of a ship on course 012°, speed 12 knots observes Light *E* bearing 311° at 1500. He has reason to believe that a current exists with set 030°, drift 3.0 knots. Light *E* is subsequently observed bearing 245° at 1520.

Required: Plot the 1520 running fix, allowing for current.

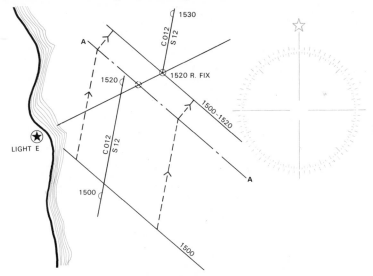

Figure 720: Plotting a running fix with known current.

Solution: In the twenty minutes between LOP's, the ship advanced 4.0 miles in the direction 012°, so the navigator advances the 1500 LOP as shown by line *AA'*. During this time the current has also moved the ship 1.0 mile in the direction 030°. The navigator must further advance the 1500 LOP to represent the additional travel of the ship caused by the current, or to the 1500–1520 LOP shown in the figure. The intersection of the 1500 LOP so advanced and the 1520 LOP marks the 1520 running fix. Had current not been taken into consideration, the running fix (see article 1111) would have been located at the dotted circle, over one mile from the established running fix.

105

Errors inherent in running fixes.

721. In working with current, the inexperienced navigator is likely to make one of two errors, about equally dangerous. He either allows for too little or no current, or expects a current to continue when he is not justified in so doing. Judgment born of experience is the best guide. However, there are some considerations that even the beginner can learn to apply. The estimates of current given in current tables, pilot charts, etc., are usually quite accurate and should not be ignored. When there is a strong steady wind, its effect both in forming a temporary wind-driven current and in blowing the ship to leeward should be considered. The effect of wind on ships differs with the type of ship, her draft, and the relative direction of the wind. The current acting on a ship is generally changing because of the tidal cycle, changes in wind, changes of geographical position, etc. The error in steering usually changes with a change of helmsman. Hence, it is generally unwise to assume that the current that has acted since the last fix will continue. All the factors mentioned above should go into the estimate of the current. In estimating current the most unfavorable conditions possible should be assumed. It must be remembered that a running fix obtained by two bearings not taken simultaneously will be in error unless the course and distance are correctly estimated, the track and the distance over the ground being required. Difficulty will occur in estimating the exact course when there is bad steering, a cross current, or when the ship is making leeway; errors in the estimated run will arise when the vessel is being set ahead or back by a current or when the logging is inaccurate. Since the current is rarely known, the run between two bearings will often be in error, and therefore the running fix will give a false position, the amount and direction of the error depending upon the current that has *not* been taken into consideration during the run. Some indication of the current may be obtained by taking more than two successive bearings of the same object and plotting three-line running fixes. If the current is parallel to the course its presence will not be revealed by this method since the fix will be a point either too far in toward the light or too far out, depending on whether the current is with or against the ship, respectively, and successive fixes will show a course parallel to that steered (Figure 721a). If there is a cross current, however, the fix

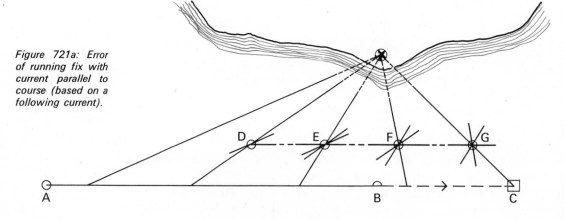

Figure 721a: Error of running fix with current parallel to course (based on a following current).

A-B   RUN BY DR
B-C   CURRENT
A-C   TRACK
D, E, F, G   POSITION SHOWN BY RUNNING FIXES

will result in a triangle, the size of which depends upon the cross component of the current, and the line through the mean points of the successive fixes will show a track oblique to the course steered, to the right or left depending upon whether the current is setting to the right or left, and it will plot between the course steered and the actual track (Figure 721b).

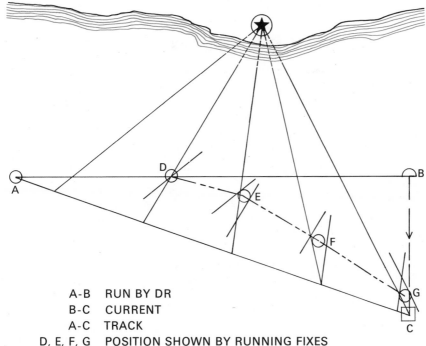

Figure 721b: Error of a running fix with cross current.

A-B   RUN BY DR
B-C   CURRENT
A-C   TRACK
D, E, F, G   POSITION SHOWN BY RUNNING FIXES

Obviously, the presence of a current acting against the ship presents a hazard, since in this case the ship's positions as plotted by running fixes indicate a greater margin of safety to shoals, rocks, etc. extending out from the shore than actually exists. Hence, when there is a possibility that a head current exists, all dangers to navigation should be given a wider berth than indicated by running fixes. A better plan, when possible, is to obtain frequent fixes by simultaneous bearings of two or more fixed objects.

722. This discussion on current sailing has involved aspects of DR and of piloting which are inseparable. The perfect example is seldom encountered in actual navigation aboard ship. The illustrated classroom problems were given to show the vector analysis involved. A DR plot must always be maintained. If data on *current* is unavailable or considered to be in error the course and intended track are considered one and the same. All possible data should be evaluated to give an estimated position, as it is a rare occasion when a fix is obtained that coincides precisely with the DR position, indicating no current effect whatsoever.

Summary.

CHAPTER 8

Currents and Tides

Introduction.

801. Previous chapters have used the term "estimated current" frequently; the first part of this chapter will deal with the known ocean current systems, their location, and where data concerning them may be found, as well as with tides and tidal currents. In considering these current systems it must be borne in mind that strong winds, blowing contrary to the prevailing wind pattern for prolonged periods, can have a marked effect on the drift of an ocean current and to a lesser degree on the set, in the affected area. When the weather returns to normal, the current system will also return to its normal flow, which often can be predicted with considerable accuracy.

Figure 802:
The principal ocean
currents.

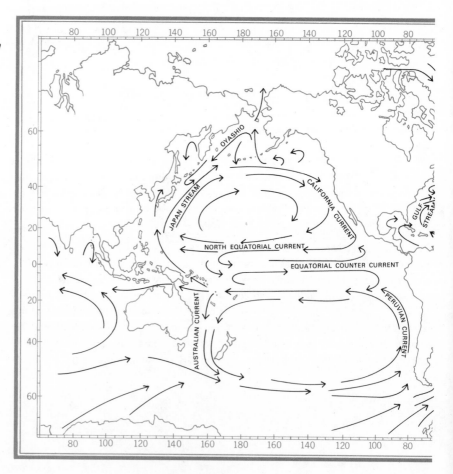

802. A number of well defined permanent current systems exist in the open oceans, as charted in Figure 802. The chief cause of these currents is wind. Winds, such as the various *trade winds*, blow almost continuously with considerable force, and in the same general direction over large areas of the globe. The direction, steadiness, and force of a prevailing wind determine to a large extent the set, drift, depth, and permanence of the current it generates. However, currents with a generally northerly or southerly drift are considerably affected by the Coriolis force. This is an apparent force, acting on a body in motion, caused by the rotation of the earth. In the northern hemisphere deflection is to the right, in a clockwise direction; in the southern hemisphere the deflection is counterclockwise. The *Coriolis force* is largely responsible for the circular pattern of the slow flow of currents in the North and South Atlantic, the North and South Pacific, and in the Indian Ocean. Because of seasonal variations in the wind systems, and due to other seasonal changes, the characteristics of most ocean currents change considerably, but quite predictably, at certain times of the year.

Ocean current systems.

Currents are often described as warm or cold. These terms are relative, and are based on the latitudes in which they originate, and on the effect they have on climate. For example, the northeast drift current off the northern coast of Norway is a "warm" current, although it may be lower in temperature than the southern extremity of the cold Labrador current off the New England coast.

Warm and cold currents.

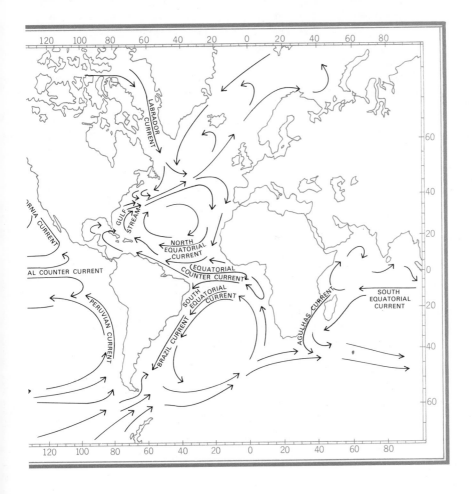

Currents as well as winds were of great importance in the days of sail. Clipper ships in the nineteenth century wool trade, bound from England for Australia, would go out via the Cape of Good Hope, but return via Cape Horn, thus taking advantage of both the strong prevailing westerlies in the "Roaring Forties" and the resultant westerly wind drift. Similarly, the sixteenth century Spanish "treasure galleons" sailed from Acapulco, Mexico, for Manila, via the north equatorial current, but returned via the Japan Stream and the California current.

Much useful information on these currents may be obtained from the Pilot Charts, and surface current atlases, published by the U. S. Naval Oceanographic Office. The atlases, covering the principal ocean areas of the world, are usually arranged to show for each month the mean direction and force of the surface currents in each one degree quadrangle of latitude and longitude, as well as the frequency of direction, and average drifts. Brief summaries of the chief ocean currents of the Atlantic, Pacific, and Indian Oceans follow.

Atlantic Ocean currents.

803. The effect of the trade winds is to form two *equatorial currents* flowing westward across the Atlantic at the rate of about two thirds of a knot. Between the *north* and *south* equatorial currents the somewhat weaker *equatorial counter current* flows to the eastward under the influence of the southwest monsoon.

At the western edge of the Atlantic the south equatorial current divides, part of it flowing southward and part continuing on into the Caribbean or northwestward along the West Indies. Under the influence of the land, the Caribbean and northwesterly currents curve to the northward and then to the northeastward and combine in the Florida Straits, being joined there by the curving north equatorial current to form the well known *Gulf Stream*, which flows along the eastern coast of the United States.

The indigo-blue water of this sharply defined current of warm water roughly follows the coast line as far as Cape Hatteras, where it curves to the eastward, widens, and gradually loses some of its velocity.

Off the Grand Banks the Gulf Stream loses its identity as such, but continues on to the eastward as a general circulatory flow or drift. It meets the cold water of the *Labrador current* in this area, part of which accompanies it towards the east. However, the water mass remains comparatively warm, and has a very marked effect on the climate of northwestern Europe. On the eastern side of the Atlantic it divides to form the *northeast, easterly,* and *southeast drift currents*.

The circulation of the south Atlantic is somewhat similar. That part of the south equatorial current curving southward forms the *Brazil current*, which roughly follows the coast of South America. Off the coast of Uruguay the current divides further, part of it continuing on to the south and part curving to the eastward across the south Atlantic. The part, known as the *southern current,* is joined in the eastern Atlantic by water flowing northward from the Antarctic and flows along the western coast of Africa to connect with the south equatorial current and complete the circulation, much as does the southeast drift current in the North Atlantic. The principal Atlantic Ocean currents are:

north equatorial (warm)	Gulf Stream (warm)
south equatorial (warm)	Labrador (cold)
equatorial counter (warm)	Brazil (warm)

804. The circulation in the Pacific is similar to that in the Atlantic. Here, as in the Atlantic, the *north* and *south equatorial currents* set to the westward, with the *equatorial counter current* between them setting to the east.

Pacific Ocean currents.

In the western Pacific the north equatorial current curves northward forming the *Japan Stream,* similar to the Gulf Stream, which roughly follows the coastline of the Japanese islands. The Japanese name for this current is *Kuroshio,* or "black stream," named for the dark color of the water. Part of this stream flows to the westward of Japan into the Sea of Japan, but the main stream passes east of Japan and flows northward and eastward, widening as it does so, with a loss of velocity.

Part of the stream continues northerly as well as easterly to the region of the Aleutian Islands, and part continues on to the eastward where it joins the weak north and northeast drift currents in this area.

Similar to the Labrador current, the cold *Oyashio* flows out of the Bering Sea to the southward and westward close to the shores of the Kuril Islands and Japan. Like the Labrador current, the Oyashio often brings ice from the Arctic Ocean.

Along the Pacific coast of the United States the cold *California current* flows southward, generally following the coast line. This current, being 200 to 300 miles wide, is not as strong as narrower currents, but flows with an average velocity of about 0.8 knot.

In the western Pacific the south equatorial current divides, part of it continuing on to the west and part of it, the *Australia current*, curving southward past the east coast of Australia, where it bends toward the east and spreads out and is lost as a well defined stream.

A current of cold water sets out of the Antarctic southwest of South America. The current divides at the southern tip of Patagonia, part of it, the *Cape Horn current,* crossing into the southern Atlantic and part of it continuing up the west coast of South America, as the *Peruvian current.* Near Cape Blanco the stream curves to the westward, past the Galapagos Islands and finally joins the south equatorial current. The principal Pacific Ocean currents are:

north equatorial (warm)	Oyashio (cold)
south equatorial (warm)	California (cold)
equatorial counter (warm)	Australia (warm)
Japan stream (warm)	Peruvian or Humboldt (cold)

805. The Indian Ocean circulation bears a strong resemblance to that of the southern Atlantic and Pacific. North of the equator the currents are weak and variable with the seasons. To the southward the *south equatorial current* flows westward as in the other oceans.

Indian Ocean currents.

Near the African coast this current divides, part of it curving northward and eastward, but the main part curving to the southward, where part of it flows on each side of Madagascar, at the southern end of which they combine and narrow to form the warm *Agulhas* current, which bears strong resemblance to the Gulf and Japan streams. Near the southern end of Africa this current curves more to the southward and then eastward, when it widens and is generally lost as a well defined current.

111

Across the southern Indian Ocean the drift is generally eastward, the flow being fed by the Agulhas current and a weak flow from the Atlantic past the Cape of Good Hope. Near Australia this flow divides, part of it continuing on along the southern coast into the Pacific and part curving northward along the west coast.

As in the Atlantic and Pacific, there is a general weak flow from the Antarctic into the Indian Ocean. The Indian Ocean compares with the southern Atlantic or Pacific in size and general circulation, but lacks the cold currents of the others. The principal Indian Ocean currents are:

<blockquote>
south equatorial (warm)   Agulhas (warm)
</blockquote>

Temporary wind-driven currents. **806.** Local and temporary wind-driven currents at times develop outside the well defined ocean current systems. The drift of such a current depends largely on the force of the wind and its duration. However, if a wind has been blowing fairly steadily for some time at sea, a reasonable assumption would be that the drift of the current roughly equalled 2 per cent of the wind speed.

In the open ocean the set of a temporary wind current is not in the direction the wind is blowing. It is deflected by the *Coriolis force* (article 802); in the northern hemisphere, this deflection is to the right; in the southern hemisphere it is to the left. In the open sea, the deflection is about 40°; near a coast line it is considerably less, probably near 20°. However, deflection of the current is affected by the land structure. The Current Tables give information on the local conditions to be expected.

Tidal currents. **807.** The rise and fall of the water level due to the tidal effect of the sun and moon sets up currents along the coast and in its bays and estuaries. These are called *tidal currents* to distinguish them from ocean currents. The horizontal movement of the water toward the land is called *flood current*, and the horizontal movement away from the land is called *ebb current*. Between these two, when the current changes direction, there is a brief period when no horizontal motion can be detected. This is called *slack water*.

Along a relatively straight coast with shallow indentations there is usually little difference between the time of slack water and high or low tide, but where a large bay connects with the ocean through a narrow channel, the tide and current may be out of phase by as much as seven hours.

The effect of the tide in causing currents may be illustrated by two cases:

Where there is a small tidal basin connected with the sea by a large opening.
Where there is a large tidal basin connected with the sea by a small opening.

In the first case, the velocity of the current in the opening has its maximum value when the height of the tide within is changing most rapidly, i.e., at a time about midway between high and low water. The water in the basin keeps at approximately the same level as the water outside. The flood current corresponds with the rising and the ebb current with the falling of the tide.

In the second case, the velocity of the current in the opening has its maximum value when it is high water or low water without, for then there is the greatest head of water for producing motion. The flood current in such cases generally begins about three hours after low water and the ebb current about three hours after high water, slack water thus occurring about midway between the tides.

Along most shores not much affected by bays, tidal rivers, etc., the current usually turns soon after high water and low water.

The swiftest current in straight portions of tidal rivers is usually in the middle of the river, but in curved portions the most rapid current is toward the outer edge of the curve, and here the deepest water will generally be found.

Counter currents and eddies may occur near the shores of straits, especially in bights and near points. A knowledge of them is useful, that they may be used or avoided.

A swift current often occurs in a narrow passage connecting two large bodies of water, owing to their considerable difference of level at the same instant. The several passages between Vineyard Sound and Buzzards Bay are cases in point.

Tide rips are generally made by a rapid current setting over an irregular bottom, as at the edges of banks where the change of depth is considerable, but they sometimes occur on the high seas.

808. The National Ocean Survey publishes *Tidal Current Charts* (article 817) each containing 12 charts printed in color which depict, by arrows and numbers, the direction and velocity of the tidal currents for each hour of the tidal cycle. The charts, which are good for any year, present a comprehensive view of the tidal current movement in the respective waterways as a whole, and also supply a means for readily determining for any time the direction and velocity of the current at various localities throughout the area covered. Current Tables (article 816), giving tabular data on tidal currents, are published annually. *Tidal current charts.*

809. A proper consideration of current will result in improved estimated positions. However, any allowance for current must be tempered with judgment. Charted and tabulated data on currents give an average condition, and the prudent navigator must always be alert to variations from such an average. *Summary.*

For example, *meanders,* or eddies, originate along the eastern border of the Gulf Stream; these are off-shoots of warm Gulf Stream water curving away from the main axis of the stream. They may take a direction almost contrary to the axis, and have a speed only slightly slower than the body of the stream.

Tidal currents, particularly, can be markedly affected by strong winds; their direction may, for a time, actually be reversed from that given in the Current Tables. The navigator must take all factors into consideration in predicting the effect of a current. He must also consider the lateral drift of his ship through the water, due to wind pressure. The direction of leeway depends on the relative direction of the wind; the amount depends on the relationship between freeboard and draft. It varies with the type of ship, and with the loading.

810. The vertical rise and fall of the ocean level due to the gravitational force between the earth and moon, and to a lesser extent the sun, is called *tide.* In general, this rise and fall takes place twice during a lunar day. *High tide* or *high water* is the highest level reached by an ascending tide. From high tide the level of the water decreases until it reaches a minimum level called *low tide* or *low* *Tides.*

113

water. At *high water* and *low water* there is a brief period when no change in the water level can be detected. This period is called *stand*. The total rise or fall from low water to high water, or vice versa, is called the *range* of the tide. *Mean sea level* is the average level of the ocean, differing slightly from *half-tide level*, which is the plane midway between mean high water and mean low water.

A knowledge of the times of high and low water and of the amount of vertical rise and fall of the tide is of great importance in the case of vessels entering or leaving port, especially when the low water is less than or near their draft. Such knowledge is also useful at times to vessels running close along a coast, in enabling them to anticipate the effect of the tidal currents in setting them on or off shore. This is especially important in fog or thick weather.

Types of tide.   **811.** A body of water has a natural period of oscillation that is dependent upon its dimensions. No ocean appears to be a single oscillating body, but rather each one is made up of a number of oscillating basins. As such basins are acted upon by the tide producing forces, some respond more readily to daily or diurnal forces, others to semidiurnal forces, and still others respond almost equally to both. Hence, tides at a given place are classified as *semidiurnal, diurnal,* or *mixed*—according to the characteristics of the tidal pattern occurring at that place.

Semidiurnal. In this type of tide, there are two high and two low waters each tidal day with relatively small inequality in the consecutive high and low water heights. Tides on the Atlantic coast of the United States are representative of the semidiurnal type, which is illustrated in Figure 811a.

Diurnal. In this type of tide, only a single high and a single low water occur each tidal day. Tides of the diurnal type occur along the northern shore of the Gulf of Mexico, in the Java Sea, in the Gulf of Tonkin (off the North Vietnamese-Chinese coast), and in a few other localities. The tide curve for Pakhoi, China, illustrated in Figure 811b is an example of the diurnal type.

Mixed. In this type of tide the diurnal and semidiurnal oscillations are both important factors, and the tide is characterized by a large inequality in the high water heights, low water heights, or in both. There are usually two high and two low waters each day, but occasionally the tide may become diurnal. Such tides are prevalent along the Pacific Coast of the United States, and in many other parts of the world. Examples of mixed types of tides are shown in Figure 811c. At Los Angeles, it is typical that the inequalities in the high and low waters are about the same. At Seattle the greater inequalities are typically in the low waters, while at Honolulu the high waters have the greater inequalities.

Reference planes for tidal data.   **812.** The expression *height of tide* is not to be confused with *depth of water*. The latter refers to the vertical distance from the surface of the water to the bottom; the former refers to the vertical distance from the surface of the water to an arbitrarily chosen *reference plane* or *datum plane*, such plane being based on a selected *low water* average. The *charted depth* is the vertical distance from this reference plane to the ocean bottom. A second reference plane based on a selected *high water* average is used as a basis for the measurement of *charted heights* and *vertical clearances* of objects above the water. If the selected low water average is mean low water, and the selected high water

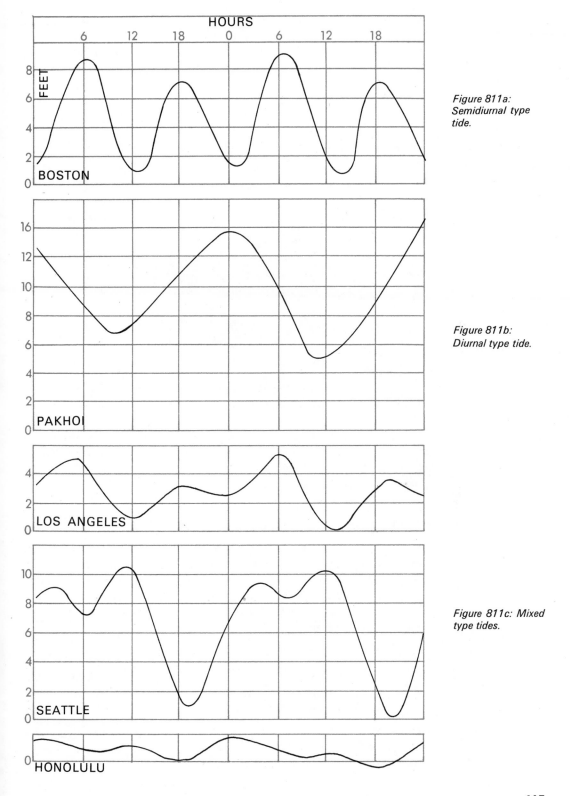

Figure 811a:
Semidiurnal type
tide.

Figure 811b:
Diurnal type tide.

Figure 811c: Mixed
type tides.

average is mean high water, then the difference between these two planes is called the *mean range of the tide*. The relationship of these terms is shown in Figure 812.

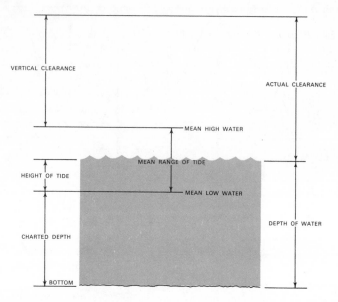

Figure 812: Relationship of terms, measuring depths, and heights.

Reference planes.

It is important to remember that the water level is occasionally *below the reference plane*. That is, *the depth of water can be less than the charted depth*. This is indicated by a minus sign (−) placed before the height of tide as shown in the tide tables. The depth of water is equal to the algebraic sum of the charted depth and the height of tide, so that when there is a negative tide, the numerical value of the height of tide is subtracted from the charted depth to find the depth of water. Because of wind, primarily, the water level sometimes differs from the predicted height.

The arbitrarily chosen reference plane differs with the locality and the country making the survey on which the chart is based.

Spring tides occur near the time of full moon and new moon when the tidal effects of sun and moon are in phase. When the sun and moon are thus acting together, high tides are higher than average and low tides are lower. When the moon is at quadrature, at first and last quarter, the tidal effects of the two bodies are opposing each other and the range of the tide is less than average. These are called *neap* tides.

The principal planes of reference used are derived from the approximation of:

Mean low water, the average of all low tides. This plane is used on charts of the Atlantic and Gulf coasts of the United States, and on nearly all Oceanographic Office charts based on its own surveys.

Mean lower low water, the average of the lower of the two daily tides. This plane is used on charts of the Pacific coast of the United States, the Hawaiian Islands, the Philippines, and Alaska.

Mean low water springs, the average of the low waters at spring tides. Most British Admiralty charts are based on this reference plane.

It is not necessary to know the reference planes of various localities, for the tide tables are always based on the same plane used for the largest scale charts of the locality, as stated in the tables. The reference plane for a given locality, when not one of the three listed above, is stated in reference to one of them.

Each chart generally carries a statement of the reference plane used for soundings. However, the plane of reference may be in doubt on charts compiled from old or various sources. When there is any doubt, assume that it is mean low water, for this assumption allows for the greatest margin of safety in that it is the *highest* of the low water datum planes in use on nautical charts. A cautious navigator knows that the depth of the water at a low tide (mean low water springs, for example) can be *less* than the depth charted with reference to mean low water. He also is aware that the depth of the water will seldom be lower than the charted depth, *regardless of the state of the tide* if, for example, mean lower low water springs had been assumed as a tidal reference plane. Proceeding on this latter assumption, the decision to take a ship drawing 24 feet over a shoal charted at a depth of 26 feet would prove disastrous if the height of the tide had been (−) 3 feet from mean low water, the actual reference plane used, but not noted, in the chart survey and printing.

813. Tide tables are published annually by the National Ocean Survey of the Department of Commerce in four volumes as follows: *Europe* and *West Coast of Africa (including the Mediterranean Sea); East Coast, North and South America (including Greenland); West Coast, North and South America (including the Hawaiian Islands); Central* and *Western Pacific Ocean* and *Indian Ocean.* Together they contain daily predictions for 188 reference ports and difference data for about 5000 stations.

Tide tables.

The make-up of the tables is illustrated in Figure 813a. Table 1 lists the time and height of the tide at each high water and low water in chronological order for each day of the year at a number of places which are designated as *reference stations.* Because the lunar or tidal day is a little more than 24 hours in length (an average of about 24^h50^m), the time between successive high or low tides is a little more than 12 hours. When a high (or low) tide occurs just before midnight, the next high (or low) tide occurs about noon of the following day, and the next one occurs just after midnight. Under these conditions, three consecutive high (or low) tides may occur on three different dates, although the total interval may be no more than the average period of a lunar day, 24^h50^m. This means that on the middle of the three days, there is but one high (or low) water. An example of this occurrence can be seen in Figure 813a; only one high tide occurs at the Battery on 1 January. During portions of each month the tide becomes diurnal at some stations; that is, there is only one high tide and one low tide each lunar or tidal day. This fact is indicated by blank entries in the tabulated data.

Secondary or *subordinate stations* are listed in geographical order in Table 2. Given for each station are the latitude and longitude to the nearest minute, and certain information to be applied to the predictions at a stated reference station to obtain the tidal information for the subordinate station.

A separate time difference is tabulated for high and low water as shown in Figure 813b. Each time difference is added to or subtracted from the time of

117

NEW YORK (THE BATTERY), N.Y.   TIMES AND HEIGHTS OF HIGH AND LOW WATERS

JANUARY

DAY	TIME H.M.	HT. FT.	DAY	TIME H.M.	HT. FT.
1 SU	0524	-0.2	16 M	0012	3.6
	1154	4.6		0548	0.5
	1812	-0.5		1212	3.7
				1818	0.1
2 M	0036	4.1	17 TU	0054	3.6
	0630	-0.1		0642	0.7
	1248	4.4		1248	3.5
	1906	-0.4		1906	0.3
5 TH	0324	4.5	20 F	0306	3.7
	1000	-0.1		0954	0.6
	1548	3.7		1512	3.0
	2212	-0.4		2154	0.4
6 F	0424	4.6	21 SA	0400	3.9
	1100	-0.3		1048	0.4
	1654	3.7		1624	3.0
	2306	-0.4		2242	0.3
7 SA	0524	4.8	22 SU	0500	4.1
	1154	-0.4		1142	0.1
	1754	3.7		1730	3.2
				2336	0.1
8 SU	0000	-0.4	23 M	0554	4.4
	0624	4.9		1230	-0.2
	1248	-0.5		1824	3.4
	1848	3.7			
9 M	0048	-0.5	24 TU	0024	-0.1
	0712	5.0		0642	4.7
	1336	-0.6		1318	-0.5
	1936	3.8		1912	3.7
10 TU	0136	-0.5	25 W	0118	-0.3
	0754	5.0		0730	5.0
	1424	-0.7		1406	-0.7
	2024	3.8		2000	3.9
11 W	0224	-0.4	26 TH	0206	-0.6
	0842	4.9		0812	5.1
	1506	-0.7		1448	-1.0
	2112	3.8		2042	4.1
12 TH	0312	-0.3	27 F	0254	-0.8
	0924	4.7		0900	5.2
	1548	-0.6		1530	-1.1
	2200	3.7		2130	4.3
13 F	0348	-0.2	28 SA	0336	-0.9
	1006	4.5		0954	5.1
	1624	-0.5		1612	-1.1
	2242	3.7		2224	4.5
14 SA	0430	0.0	29 SU	0424	-0.8
	1048	4.2		1042	4.9
	1706	-0.3		1654	-1.0
	2330	3.7		2318	4.5
15 SU	0506	0.3	30 M	0512	-0.7
	1130	4.0		1136	4.7
	1742	-0.1		1742	-0.8
			31 TU	0012	4.6
				0612	-0.4
				1230	4.4
				1836	-0.5

FEBRUARY

DAY	TIME H.M.	HT. FT.	DAY	TIME H.M.	HT. FT.
1 W	0106	4.6	16 TH	0030	3.8
	0718	-0.1		0624	0.7
	1324	4.0		1230	3.3
	1942	-0.2		1812	0.5
2 TH	0200	4.5	17 F	0106	3.8
	0836	0.0		0748	0.8
	1424	3.7		1318	3.1
	2048	-0.1		1900	0.7
5 SU	0512	4.5	20 M	0418	4.0
	1136	-0.2		1112	0.3
	1742	3.5		1700	3.2
	2342	-0.1		2306	0.3
6 M	0606	4.6	21 TU	0524	4.4
	1230	-0.3		1200	-0.1
	1836	3.6		1800	3.5
7 TU	0036	-0.2	22 W	0006	-0.1
	0700	4.7		0618	4.7
	1318	-0.5		1254	-0.4
	1924	3.8		1848	4.0
8 W	0124	-0.3	23 TH	0054	-0.4
	0742	4.7		0706	5.0
	1406	-0.6		1336	-0.8
	2012	3.9		1936	4.4
9 TH	0212	-0.3	24 F	0148	-0.8
	0824	4.7		0754	5.2
	1442	-0.6		1424	-1.0
	2054	4.0		2024	4.7
10 F	0254	-0.3	25 SA	0236	-1.1
	0900	4.6		0842	5.3
	1524	-0.6		1506	-1.2
	2130	4.0		2106	5.0
11 SA	0330	-0.3	26 SU	0324	-1.2
	0942	4.4		0930	5.2
	1554	-0.5		1548	-1.2
	2212	4.0		2200	5.1
12 SU	0406	-0.1	27 M	0412	-1.1
	1018	4.2		1024	5.0
	1630	-0.4		1630	-1.1
	2248	4.0		2254	5.1
13 M	0442	0.0	28 TU	0500	-0.9
	1054	4.0		1118	4.7
	1654	-0.2		1718	-0.8
	2324	3.9		2348	5.0
14 TU	0512	0.2			
	1124	3.8			
	1718	0.1			
15 W	0000	3.8			
	0542	0.5			
	1200	3.5			
	1742	0.3			

MARCH

DAY	TIME H.M.	HT. FT.	DAY	TIME H.M.	HT. FT.
1 W	0554	-0.5	16 TH	0512	0.3
	1212	4.3		1118	3.5
	1806	-0.4		1654	0.4
				2330	4.1
2 TH	0042	4.8	17 F	0542	0.5
	0700	-0.2		1154	3.3
	1306	3.9		1730	0.6
	1912	0.0			
5 SU	0342	4.2	20 M	0218	4.0
	1024	0.1		0942	0.6
	1624	3.4		1500	3.2
	2236	0.3		2142	0.8
6 M	0454	4.3	21 TU	0336	4.1
	1118	0.0		1036	0.3
	1730	3.5		1630	3.5
	2330	0.2		2248	0.4
7 TU	0548	4.4	22 W	0454	4.4
	1206	-0.1		1130	0.0
	1824	3.8		1730	3.9
				2342	0.0
8 W	0024	0.0	23 TH	0554	4.7
	0636	4.5		1218	-0.4
	1254	-0.3		1824	4.5
	1906	4.0			
9 TH	0106	-0.1	24 F	0036	-0.5
	0724	4.6		0642	5.0
	1336	-0.4		1306	-0.7
	1948	4.2		1912	5.0
10 F	0154	-0.2	25 SA	0130	-0.9
	0800	4.6		0736	5.2
	1418	-0.5		1354	-1.0
	2024	4.4		1954	5.3
11 SA	0230	-0.3	26 SU	0218	-1.2
	0836	4.5		0818	5.3
	1454	-0.5		1436	-1.1
	2100	4.4		2042	5.5
12 SU	0306	-0.3	27 M	0306	-1.3
	0912	4.4		0912	5.2
	1524	-0.4		1524	-1.1
	2130	4.4		2130	5.6
13 M	0342	-0.2	28 TU	0354	-1.2
	0942	4.2		1000	4.9
	1554	-0.2		1606	-0.9
	2206	4.3		2224	5.4
14 TU	0412	-0.1	29 W	0442	-0.9
	1018	4.0		1054	4.6
	1618	0.0		1648	-0.5
	2236	4.2		2318	5.2
15 W	0442	0.1	30 TH	0536	-0.5
	1042	3.7		1154	4.2
	1636	0.2		1742	-0.1
	2300	4.2			
			31 F	0018	4.9
				0636	-0.1
				1254	3.9
				1842	0.4

Figure 813a:
Tide Table 1, N.Y.

TIME MERIDIAN 75° W. 0000 IS MIDNIGHT. 1200 IS NOON.
HEIGHTS ARE RECKONED FROM THE DATUM OF SOUNDINGS ON CHARTS OF THE LOCALITY WHICH IS MEAN LOW WATER.

the respective high or low water at the reference station in accordance with its sign. Be alert to changes of date when the time difference is applied. For example, if a high water occurs at a reference station at 2200 on 23 March and the tide at the subordinate station occurs 3 hours later, then high water will occur at 0100 on 24 March at the subordinate station. Conversely, if a high water at a reference station occurs at 0200 on 29 March, and the tide at the subordinate station occurs 5 hours earlier, the high water at the subordinate station will occur at 2100 on 28 March.

The height of the tide is found in several ways, depending on local conditions. If the difference for height of high water is given, with 0.0 feet tabulated as the low water difference, apply the high water difference in accordance with its sign to the height of high water at the reference station. The height of low water will be, of course, the same as at the reference station. If a difference for

TABLE 2.—TIDAL DIFFERENCES AND OTHER CONSTANTS

No.	PLACE	POSITION		DIFFERENCES				RANGES		Mean Tide Level
		Lat.	Long.	Time		Height		Mean	Spring	
				High water	Low water	High water	Low water			
		° ′	° ′	h. m.	h. m.	feet	feet	feet	feet	feet
1451	Deep Creek Meadow	40 36	73 32	+1 02	+1 09	*0.52	*0.52	2.4	2.9	1.2
1453	Green Island	40 37	73 30	+1 22	+1 29	*0.41	*0.41	1.9	2.3	0.9
1455	Cuba Island	40 37	73 31	+1 08	+1 20	*0.50	*0.50	2.3	2.8	1.1
1457	Bellmore, Bellmore Creek	40 40	73 31	+1 29	+1 56	*0.43	*0.43	2.0	2.4	1.0
1459	Neds Creek	40 37	73 33	+0 50	+0 52	-1.9	0.0	2.7	3.3	1.3
1461	Freeport Creek	40 38	73 34	+0 34	+0 27	-1.5	0.0	3.1	3.8	1.5
1463	Freeport, Baldwin Bay	40 38	73 35	+0 38	+0 53	-1.6	0.0	3.0	3.6	1.5
1465	Long Beach	40 36	73 39	+0 19	0 00	-0.7	0.0	3.9	4.7	1.9
1467	Long Beach, outer coast	40 35	73 39	-0 29	-0 35	-0.1	0.0	4.5	5.4	2.2
	Hempstead Bay—Continued									
1469	East Rockaway	40 38	73 40	+0 42	+0 45	-0.7	0.0	3.9	4.7	1.9
1471	Woodmere, Brosewere Bay	40 37	73 42	+0 35	+0 48	-0.7	0.0	3.9	4.7	1.9
1473	East Rockaway Inlet	40 36	73 44	-0 06	-0 16	-0.5	0.0	4.1	5.0	2.0
	Jamaica Bay									
1475	Plumb Beach Channel	40 35	73 55	+0 03	-0 05	+0.3	0.0	4.9	5.9	2.4
1477	Barren Island, Rockaway Inlet	40 35	73 53	0 00	-0 06	+0.4	0.0	5.0	6.0	2.5
1479	Beach Channel (bridge)	40 35	73 49	+0 38	+0 22	+0.5	0.0	5.1	6.2	2.5
1481	Motts Basin	40 37	73 46	+0 40	+0 46	+0.8	0.0	5.4	6.5	2.7
1483	Norton Point, Head of Bay	40 38	73 45	+0 39	+0 43	+0.8	0.0	5.4	6.5	2.7
1485	New York International Airport	40 37	73 47	+0 26	+0 43	+0.7	0.0	5.3	6.4	2.6
1487	Grassy Bay (bridge)	40 39	73 50	+0 44	+0 45	+0.6	0.0	5.2	6.3	2.6
1489	Canarsie	40 38	73 53	+0 28	+0 06	+0.6	0.0	5.2	6.3	2.6
1491	Mill Basin	40 37	73 55	+0 29	+0 02	+0.6	0.0	5.2	6.3	2.6
	NEW YORK and NEW JERSEY **New York Harbor**									
1493	Coney Island	40 34	73 59	-0 03	-0 19	+0.1	0.0	4.7	5.7	2.3
1495	Norton Point, Gravesend Bay	40 35	74 00	-0 03	+0 01	+0.1	0.0	4.7	5.7	2.3
1497	Fort Wadsworth, The Narrows	40 36	74 03	+0 02	+0 12	-0.3	0.0	4.3	5.2	2.1
1499	Fort Hamilton, The Narrows	40 37	74 02	+0 03	+0 05	+0.1	0.0	4.7	5.7	2.3
				on NEW YORK, p.62						
1501	Bay Ridge	40 38	74 02	-0 24	-0 24	+0.1	0.0	4.6	5.5	2.3
1503	St. George, Staten Island	40 39	74 04	-0 21	-0 18	0.0	0.0	4.5	5.4	2.2
1505	Bayonne, New Jersey	40 41	74 06	-0 19	-0 08	0.0	0.0	4.5	5.4	2.2
1507	Gowanus Bay	40 40	74 01	-0 19	-0 15	-0.1	0.0	4.4	5.3	2.2
1509	Governors Island	40 42	74 01	-0 11	-0 06	-0.1	·0.0	4.4	5.3	2.2
1511	NEW YORK (The Battery)	40 42	74 01	Daily predictions				4.5	5.4	2.2
	Hudson River‡									
1513	Jersey City, Pa. RR. Ferry, N. J	40 43	74 02	+0 07	+0 07	-0.1	0.0	4.4	5.3	2.2
1515	New York, Desbrosses Street	40 43	74 01	+0 10	+0 10	-0.1	0.0	4.4	5.3	2.2
1517	New York, Chelsea Docks	40 45	74 01	+0 17	+0 16	-0.2	0.0	4.3	5.2	2.1
1519	Hoboken, Castle Point, N. J	40 45	74 01	+0 17	+0 16	-0.2	0.0	4.3	5.2	2.1
1521	Weehawken, Days Point, N. J	40 46	74 01	+0 24	+0 23	-0.3	0.0	4.2	5.0	2.1
1523	New York, Union Stock Yards	40 47	74 00	+0 27	+0 26	-0.3	0.0	4.2	5.0	2.1
1525	New York, 130th Street	40 49	73 58	+0 37	+0 35	-0.5	0.0	4.0	4.8	2.0
1527	George Washington Bridge	40 51	73 57	+0 46	+0 43	-0.6	0.0	3.9	4.6	1.9
1529	Spuyten Duyvil, West of RR. bridge	40 53	73 56	+0 58	+0 53	-0.7	0.0	3.8	4.5	1.9
1531	Yonkers	40 56	73 54	+1 09	+1 10	-0.8	0.0	3.7	4.4	1.8
1533	Dobbs Ferry	41 01	73 53	+1 29	+1 40	-1.1	0.0	3.4	4.0	1.7
1535	Tarrytown	41 05	73 52	+1 45	+1 54	-1.3	0.0	3.2	3.7	1.6

Figure 813b: Tide Table 2, Differences and constants.

height of low as well as high water is given, each must be applied in accordance with its sign to the height of the corresponding tide at the reference station, adding the difference if its sign is plus (+) and subtracting if its sign is minus (−). If a ratio of ranges is given, the height of the tides at the subordinate station can be obtained by multiplying the heights of both high and low tides at the reference station by the respective ratios. If a ratio of ranges and an arithmetical difference are given in a form such as "*0.7–5.4 feet," multiply the heights of high and lower water at the reference station by the ratio, 0.7, and then apply the correction, 5.4 feet, in accordance with its sign, (−).

Any unusual conditions pertaining to the subordinate stations are listed in keyed footnotes.

The mean tide level and the ranges of tide given in the last three columns are not generally used. An explanation of them is given in the tide tables.

TABLE 3.—HEIGHT OF TIDE AT ANY TIME

		Time from the nearest high water or low water															
Duration of rise or fall, see footnote	h. m.	h. m.	h. m.	h. m.	h. m.	h. m.	h. m.	h. m.	h. m.	h. m.	h. m.	h. m.	h. m.	h. m.	h. m.	h. m.	h. m.
	4 00	0 08	0 16	0 24	0 32	0 40	0 48	0 56	1 04	1 12	1 20	1 28	1 36	1 44	1 52	2 00
	4 20	0 09	0 17	0 26	0 35	0 43	0 52	1 01	1 09	1 18	1 27	1 35	1 44	1 53	2 01	2 10
	4 40	0 09	0 19	0 28	0 37	0 47	0 56	1 05	1 15	1 24	1 33	1 43	1 52	2 01	2 11	2 20
	5 00	0 10	0 20	0 30	0 40	0 50	1 00	1 10	1 20	1 30	1 40	1 50	2 00	2 10	2 20	2 30
	5 20	0 11	0 21	0 32	0 43	0 53	1 04	1 15	1 25	1 36	1 47	1 57	2 08	2 19	2 29	2 40
	5 40	0 11	0 23	0 34	0 45	0 57	1 08	1 19	1 31	1 42	1 53	2 05	2 16	2 27	2 39	2 50
	6 00	0 12	0 24	0 36	0 48	1 00	1 12	1 24	1 36	1 48	2 00	2 12	2 24	2 36	2 48	3 00
	6 20	0 13	0 25	0 38	0 51	1 03	1 16	1 29	1 41	1 54	2 07	2 19	2 32	2 45	2 57	3 10
	6 40	0 13	0 27	0 40	0 53	1 07	1 20	1 33	1 47	2 00	2 13	2 27	2 40	2 53	3 07	3 20
	7 00	0 14	0 28	0 42	0 56	1 10	1 24	1 38	1 52	2 06	2 20	2 34	2 48	3 02	3 16	3 30
	10 40	0 21	0 43	1 04	1 25	1 47	2 08	2 29	2 51	3 12	3 33	3 55	4 16	4 37	4 59	5 20

		Correction to height															
Range of tide, see footnote	Ft.	Ft.	Ft.	Ft.	Ft.	Ft.	Ft.	Ft.	Ft.	Ft.	Ft.	Ft.	Ft.	Ft.	Ft.	Ft.
	0.5	0.0	0.0	0.0	0.0	0.0	0.0	0.1	0.1	0.1	0.1	0.1	0.2	0.2	0.2	0.2
	1.0	0.0	0.0	0.0	0.0	0.1	0.1	0.1	0.2	0.2	0.2	0.3	0.3	0.4	0.4	0.5
	1.5	0.0	0.0	0.0	0.1	0.1	0.1	0.2	0.2	0.3	0.4	0.4	0.5	0.6	0.7	0.8
	2.0	0.0	0.0	0.0	0.1	0.1	0.2	0.3	0.3	0.4	0.5	0.6	0.7	0.8	0.9	1.0
	2.5	0.0	0.0	0.1	0.1	0.2	0.2	0.3	0.4	0.5	0.6	0.7	0.9	1.0	1.1	1.2
	3.0	0.0	0.0	0.1	0.1	0.2	0.3	0.4	0.5	0.6	0.8	0.9	1.0	1.2	1.3	1.5
	3.5	0.0	0.0	0.1	0.2	0.2	0.3	0.4	0.6	0.7	0.9	1.0	1.2	1.4	1.6	1.8
	4.0	0.0	0.0	0.1	0.2	0 3	0.4	0.5	0.7	0.8	1.0	1.2	1.4	1.6	1.8	2.0
	4.5	0.0	0.0	0.1	0.2	0.3	0.4	0.6	0.7	0.9	1.1	1.3	1.6	1.8	2.0	2.2
	5.0	0.0	0.1	0.1	0.2	0.3	0.5	0.6	0.8	1.0	1.2	1.5	1.7	2.0	2.2	2.5
	5.5	0.0	0.1	0.1	0.2	0.4	0.5	0.7	0.9	1.1	1.4	1.6	1.9	2.2	2.5	2.8
	6.0	0.0	0.1	0.1	0.3	0.4	0.6	0.8	1.0	1.2	1.5	1.8	2.1	2.4	2.7	3.0
	6.5	0.0	0.1	0.2	0.3	0.4	0.6	0.8	1.1	1.3	1.6	1.9	2.2	2.6	2.9	3.2
	7.0	0.0	0.1	0.2	0.3	0.5	0.7	0.9	1.2	1.4	1.8	2.1	2.4	2.8	3.1	3.5
	7.5	0.0	0.1	0.2	0.3	0.5	0.7	1.0	1.2	1.5	1.9	2.2	2.6	3.0	3.4	3.8
	8.0	0.0	0.1	0.2	0.3	0.5	0.8	1.0	1.3	1.6	2.0	2.4	2.8	3.2	3.6	4.0
	8.5	0.0	0.1	0.2	0.4	0.6	0.8	1.1	1.4	1.8	2.1	2.5	2.9	3.4	3.8	4.2
	20.0	0.1	0.2	0.5	0.9	1.3	1.9	2.6	3.3	4.1	5.0	5.9	6.9	7.9	9.0	10.0

Figure 813c: Tide Table 3, corrections.

Obtain from the predictions the high water and low water, one of which is before and the other after the time for which the height is required. The difference between the times of occurrence of these tides is the duration of rise or fall, and the difference between their heights is the range of tide for the above table. Find the difference between the nearest high or low water and the time for which the height is required.

Enter the table with the duration of rise or fall, printed in heavy-faced type, which most nearly agrees with the actual value, and on that horizontal line find the time from the nearest high or low water which agrees most nearly with the corresponding actual difference. The correction sought is in the column directly below, on the line with the range of tide.

When the nearest tide is high water, subtract the correction.
When the nearest tide is low water, add the correction.

The height of the tide at a specific time other than those tabulated in Table 1 or computed using Table 2 can be found by means of Table 3, illustrated in Figure 813c, which is normally used without interpolation. This table is easy to use and the instructions given below the table are explicit.

The local mean time of sunrise and sunset is given in Table 4. While this information is usually obtained from an *almanac*, it is well to note that the values given in Table 4 extend to L 76° N, 4° beyond the latitude range of American almanacs.

The following example illustrates the use of tide tables. While the form may seem to be somewhat lengthy, its use is recommended to avoid errors.

Example 1: Use the illustrations (Figure 813a, b, c) to determine the following:

Required: (1) Tabulate the times and heights of all tides at Bayonne, N. J. on 26 Jan.

(2) Find the height of the tide at Bayonne at 0600 and 1300 on 26 Jan.

(3) If the charted depth of water at a certain point in the harbor off Bayonne is 26 feet, find the depth of water at that point at 0600 and 1300 on 26 Jan.

(4) If the draft of a ship is 18.5 feet, find the depth of water under the keel at 0600, 1300, and 1440.

COMPLETE TIDE TABLE

Substation_ BAYONNE, N.J. Date_ 26 JAN.

Reference Station_ NEW YORK

HW time difference_ — 0 h 19 m

LW time difference_ — 0 h 08 m

Difference in height of HW_ 0

Difference in height of LW_ 0

Reference Station		Substation	
LW	0206	-0.6	0158	-0.6
HW	0812	5.1	0753	5.1
LW	1448	-1.0	1440	-1.0
HW	2042	4.1	2023	4.1

HEIGHT OF TIDE at_ BAYONNE N.J. Date_ 26 JAN.

Time	0600	1300
Duration rise/fall	5h 55m	6h 47m
Time from nearest tide	1h 53m	1h 40m
Range of tide	5.7 ft.	6.1 ft.
Height of nearest tide	5.1 ft.	-1.0 ft.
Correction from table 3	-1.1 ft.	+0.9 ft.
Height of tide	4.0 ft.	-0.1 ft.

DEPTH OF WATER at_ BAYONNE N.J. Date_ 26 JAN.

Time	0600	1300
Height of tide	4.0 ft.	-0.1 ft.
Charted depth	26.0 ft.	26.0 ft.
Depth of water	30.0 ft	25.9 ft.

WATER UNDER KEEL at_ BAYONNE N.J. Date_ 26 JAN.

Time	0600	1300	1440
Depth of water	30.0 ft.	25.9 ft.	25.0 ft.
Draft of vessel	18.5 ft.	18.5 ft.	18.5 ft.
Depth under keel	11.5 ft.	7.4 ft.	6.5 ft.

121

Notes on the solution: The key to accuracy in working either a tide or a current problem can be found in the consistent use of a logically arranged, well-organized form. Once the form has been made, the tide problem and current problem are easily completed using simple arithmetic.

In cases of doubt, particularly in working with Table 3 in the Tide Tables, and Tables 3 and 4 in the Current Tables, reference to the explanatory notes accompanying the tables will clarify the method of solution.

The most common errors in the completion of a tide table for a subordinate station are: applying the high water difference to the height of low water at the reference station as well as to the height of high water; not being alert to a change in date at the subordinate station after applying the high water or low water time difference to the reference station; and failure to apply the difference factor from Table 3 with proper sign to a rising or a falling tide at the station in question. When the nearest tide is high water, subtract the correction factor of Table 3 from nearest high tide; when the nearest tide is low water, add the correction to nearest low tide.

Tidal current.

814. The periodic horizontal flow of water accompanying the rise and fall of the tide, and resulting from the same cause, is called *tidal current*. However, the times of the phenomena of tidal currents do not always coincide with the tidal height of water. Non-tidal currents are currents not caused by the tidal movement; they include the permanent currents in the general circulatory system of the oceans, as well as temporary currents rising from local meteorological conditions. In general, the current experienced at any time is a combination of tidal and non-tidal currents.

In navigation, the effect of the tidal current is often of more importance than the changing depth due to the tide. Many mariners speak of "the tide," when they refer to the flow of the tidal current.

General features.

Rotary current.

815. Offshore, where the direction of flow is not restricted by any barriers, the tidal current is *rotary;* that is, it flows continuously, with the direction changing through all points of the compass during the tidal period. Due to the effect of the earth's rotation, the change is clockwise in the northern hemisphere, and counterclockwise in the southern hemisphere except where modified by local conditions. The speed usually varies throughout the tidal cycle, passing through two maximums in approximately opposite directions, and two minimums about halfway between the maximums in time and direction. Rotary currents can be depicted as in Figure 815a by a series of arrows representing the direction and speed of the current at each hour. This is sometimes called a *current rose*.

Reversing current.

In rivers or straits, where the direction of flow is more or less restricted to certain channels, the tidal current is called a *reversing current;* that is, it flows alternately in approximately opposite directions, with a short period of little or no current, called *slack water*, at each reversal of the current. During the flow in each direction, the speed varies from zero at the time of slack water to the *maximum flood* or *ebb* about midway between the slacks. The symmetry of reversing currents is affected in certain areas by the configuration of the land. Reversing currents can be represented graphically by arrows or curves that indicate the speed of the current at each hour, as in Figure 815b.

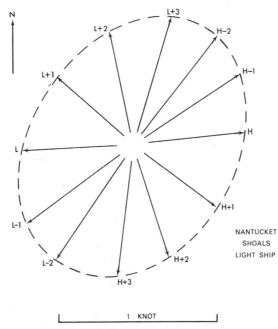

Figure 815a: Rotary tidal currents. Times are hours before and after high and low tide at Nantucket Shoals Lightship. The bearing and length of each arrow represents the hourly direction and speed of the current.

The movement toward shore or upstream is the *flood*, the movement away from shore or downstream is the *ebb*. The *direction toward* which the current flows is termed the *set*. While the speed of ocean currents is called the *drift* and is stated in either knots or miles per day, the speed of tidal currents for any given time is usually stated as speed in knots.

Flood, ebb, set and drift.

At many places where current and tide are both semidiurnal, there is a definite relation between times of current and times of high and low water in the locality. Elsewhere the relationship is not constant, and it may be hazardous to predict the times of current from the times of tide.

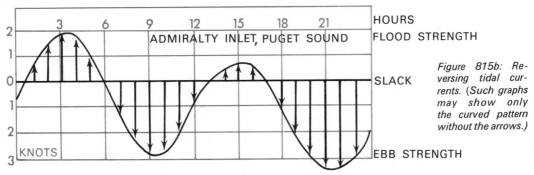

Figure 815b: Reversing tidal currents. (Such graphs may show only the curved pattern without the arrows.)

816. Current Tables are published annually by the Department of Commerce (Coast and Geodetic Survey) in two volumes; one for the Atlantic Coast of North America and the other for the Pacific Coast of North America and Asia.

Current Tables.

For a number of principal ports, called *reference stations*, Table 1 of these tables (Figure 816a) lists the predicted times of slack water in chronological order in the left-hand column, and the predicted times and velocities of maximum flood (*f*) and ebb (*e*) currents, also in chronological order, in the center and right-hand columns respectively for each day of the year. Flood and ebb current directions appear at the top of each page.

123

THE NARROWS, NEW YORK HARBOR, N.Y.   F-FLOOD, DIR. 340° TRUE   E-EBB, DIR. 160° TRUE

Figure 816a: Current Table 1, reference station.

JANUARY

DAY	SLACK WATER TIME H.M.	MAXIMUM CURRENT TIME H.M.	VEL. KNOTS	DAY	SLACK WATER TIME H.M.	MAXIMUM CURRENT TIME H.M.	VEL. KNOTS
1 SU	0100	0406	2.0E	16 M	0130	0436	1.6E
	0736	1018	1.9F		0818	1042	1.4F
	1324	1636	2.2E		1342	1700	1.8E
	2024	2254	1.7F		2048	2312	1.4F
2 M	0154	0506	1.9E	17 TU	0218	0524	1.5E
	0842	1112	1.8F		0912	1130	1.3F
	1412	1736	2.1E		1424	1748	1.7E
	2118	2348	1.8F		2136		
3 TU	0248	0606	1.9E	18 W		0000	1.4F
	0948	1212	1.6F		0306	0624	1.5E
	1506	1830	2.0E		1012	1218	1.1F
	2206				1512	1842	1.6E
					2224		
10 TU		0000	1.9E	25 W	0306	0554	2.1F
	0330	0624	2.1F		0906	1224	2.2E
	0924	1248	2.2E		1606	1824	1.5F
	1624	1854	1.5F		2112		
	2130						
11 W		0054	1.9E	26 TH		0030	2.0E
	0412	0700	2.0F		0354	0636	2.2F
	1012	1330	2.2E		0954	1312	2.3E
	1712	1936	1.4F		1648	1906	1.7F
	2218				2200		
12 TH		0142	1.9E	27 F		0124	2.2E
	0500	0742	1.9F		0442	0724	2.2F
	1054	1412	2.2E		1036	1400	2.4E
	1754	2018	1.4F		1730	1954	1.8F
	2306				2254		
13 F		0224	1.8E	28 SA		0212	2.3E
	0548	0824	1.8F		0530	0812	2.2F
	1136	1454	2.1E		1124	1442	2.5E
	1836	2100	1.4F		1812	2042	1.9F
	2354				2348		
14 SA		0306	1.8E	29 SU		0300	2.3E
	0630	0906	1.6F		0624	0906	2.1F
	1218	1536	2.0E		1212	1524	2.4E
	1918	2148	1.4F		1900	2136	1.9F
15 SU	0042	0348	1.7E	30 M	0036	0348	2.3E
	0724	0954	1.5F		0718	0954	1.9F
	1300	1612	1.9E		1300	1612	2.3E
	2006	2230	1.4F		1948	2230	2.0F
				31 TU	0130	0442	2.2E
					0824	1054	1.8F
					1348	1706	2.1E
					2042	2318	2.0F

FEBRUARY

DAY	SLACK WATER TIME H.M.	MAXIMUM CURRENT TIME H.M.	VEL. KNOTS	DAY	SLACK WATER TIME H.M.	MAXIMUM CURRENT TIME H.M.	VEL. KNOTS
1 W	0230	0542	2.0E	16 TH	0224	0536	1.5E
	0924	1148	1.6F		0936	1142	1.1F
	1442	1806	2.0F		1430	1748	1.5E
	2142				2136		
2 TH		0018	1.9F	17 F		0006	1.5F
	0330	0648	1.9E		0318	0642	1.5E
	1030	1242	1.4F		1036	1230	1.0F
	1542	1906	1.9E		1518	1848	1.4E
	2236				2224		
3 F		0118	1.9F	25 SA		0100	2.4E
	0436	0754	1.9E		0424	0706	2.3F
	1136	1354	1.2F		1012	1330	2.5E
	1642	2006	1.8E		1700	1930	2.1F
	2336				2236		
10 F		0118	1.9E	26 SU		0154	2.5E
	0442	0724	1.8F		0512	0748	2.2F
	1024	1348	2.1E		1100	1418	2.5E
	1724	1948	1.5F		1742	2018	2.2F
	2242				2324		
11 SA		0200	1.9E	27 M		0242	2.5E
	0524	0800	1.7F		0606	0842	2.1F
	1106	1424	2.1E		1148	1500	2.5E
	1800	2024	1.5F		1824	2106	2.2F
	2330						
12 SU		0242	1.9E	28 TU	0018	0330	2.5E
	0606	0836	1.6F		0700	0936	1.9F
	1142	1500	2.0E		1236	1548	2.3E
	1836	2106	1.5F		1918	2200	2.1F
13 M	0012	0318	1.8E				
	0654	0918	1.5F				
	1224	1536	1.9E				
	1918	2148	1.5F				
14 TU	0054	0400	1.7E				
	0742	1006	1.3F				
	1300	1618	1.8E				
	2000	2230	1.5F				
15 W	0136	0448	1.6E				
	0836	1054	1.2F				
	1342	1700	1.6E				
	2048	2318	1.5F				

TIME MERIDIAN 75° W.   0000 IS MIDNIGHT.   1200 IS NOON.

Figure 816b: Current Table 2, differences of constants.

TABLE 2.—CURRENT DIFFERENCES AND OTHER CONSTANTS

No.	PLACE	POSITION		TIME DIFFERENCES		VELOCITY RATIOS		MAXIMUM CURRENTS			
								Flood		Ebb	
		Lat.	Long.	Slack water	Maximum current	Maximum flood	Maximum ebb	Direction (true)	Average velocity	Direction (true)	Average velocity
		° '	° '	h. m.	h. m.			deg.	knots	deg.	knots
	JAMAICA BAY	N.	W.	on THE NARROWS, p.52 Time meridian, 75°W.							
797	Rockaway Inlet --	40 34	73 56	-1 45	-2 15	1.1	1.3	85	1.8	245	2.7
799	Barren Island, east of --	40 35	73 53	-2 00	-2 25	0.7	0.9	5	1.2	190	1.7
801	Canarsie (midchannel, off Pier) --	40 38	73 53	-1 35	-1 50	0.3	0.3	45	0.5	220	0.7
803	Beach Channel (bridge) --	40 35	73 49	-1 20	-1 20	1.1	1.0	60	1.9	225	2.0
805	Grass Hassock Channel --	40 37	73 47	-1 10	-1 00	0.6	0.5	50	1.0	230	1.0
	NEW YORK HARBOR ENTRANCE										
807	Ambrose Channel entrance --	40 30	73 58	-1 10	-1 05	1.0	1.2	310	1.7	110	2.3
809	Ambrose Channel, SE. of West Bank Lt --	40 32	74 01	[1]	-0 25	0.8	0.9	5	1.3	170	1.8
810	Coney Island Lt., 1.6 miles SSW. of --	40 33	74 01	-0 10	[2]	0.5	0.8	330	0.8	145	1.5
811	Ambrose Channel, north end --	40 34	74 02	+0 05	+0 15	0.8	0.9	330	1.3	175	1.9
813	Coney Island, 0.2 mile west of --	40 35	74 01	-0 55	-0 55	0.9	1.0	330	1.5	170	2.0
815	Ft. Lafayette, channel east of --	40 36	74 02	[3]	[3]	0.6	0.5	345	1.1	195	2.0
817	THE NARROWS, midchannel --	40 37	74 03	Daily predictions				340	1.7	160	2.0

TABLE 3.—VELOCITY OF CURRENT AT ANY TIME

		TABLE A													
		Interval between slack and maximum current													
		h. m. 1 20	h. m. 1 40	h. m. 2 00	h. m. 2 20	h. m. 2 40	h. m. 3 00	h. m. 3 20	h. m. 3 40	h. m. 4 00	h. m. 4 20	h. m. 4 40	h. m. 5 00	h. m. 5 20	h. m. 5 40
	h. m.	f.	f.	f.	f.	f.	f.	f.	f.	f.	f.	f.	f.	f.	f.
	0 20	0.4	0.3	0.3	0.2	0.2	0.2	0.2	0.1	0.1	0.1	0.1	0.1	0.1	0.1
	0 40	0.7	0.6	0.5	0.4	0.4	0.3	0.3	0.3	0.3	0.2	0.2	0.2	0.2	0.2
	1 00	0.9	0.8	0.7	0.6	0.6	0.5	0.5	0.4	0.4	0.4	0.3	0.3	0.3	0.3
	1 20	1.0	1.0	0.9	0.8	0.7	0.6	0.6	0.5	0.5	0.5	0.4	0.4	0.4	0.4
	1 40	---	1.0	1.0	0.9	0.8	0.8	0.7	0.7	0.6	0.6	0.5	0.5	0.5	0.4
	2 00	---	---	1.0	1.0	0.9	0.9	0.8	0.8	0.7	0.7	0.6	0.6	0.6	0.5
	2 20	---	---	---	1.0	1.0	0.9	0.9	0.8	0.8	0.7	0.7	0.7	0.6	0.6
	2 40	---	---	---	---	1.0	1.0	1.0	0.9	0.9	0.8	0.8	0.7	0.7	0.7
	3 00	---	---	---	---	---	1.0	1.0	1.0	0.9	0.9	0.8	0.8	0.8	0.7
	3 20	---	---	---	---	---	---	1.0	1.0	1.0	0.9	0.9	0.9	0.8	0.8
	3 40	---	---	---	---	---	---	---	1.0	1.0	1.0	0.9	0.9	0.9	0.9
	4 00	---	---	---	---	---	---	---	_._	1.0	1.0	1.0	1.0	0.9	0.9
	4 20	---	---	---	---	---	---	---	---	---	1.0	1.0	1.0	1.0	0.9
	4 40	---	---	---	---	---	---	---	---	---	---	1.0	1.0	1.0	1.0
	5 00	---	---	---	---	---	---	---	---	---	---	---	1.0	1.0	1.0
	5 20	---	---	---	---	---	---	---	---	---	---	---	---	1.0	1.0
	5 40	---	---	---	---	---	---	---	---	---	---	---	---	---	1.0

Interval between slack and desired time (left axis label)

1. From predictions find the time of slack water and the time and velocity of maximum current (flood or ebb), one of which is immediately before and the other after the time for which the velocity is desired.

2. Find the interval of time between the above slack and maximum current, and enter the top of Table A or B with the interval which most nearly agrees with this value.

3. Find the interval of time between the above slack and the time desired, and enter the side of Table A or B with the interval which most nearly agrees with this value.

4. Find, in the table, the factor corresponding to the above two intervals, and multiply the maximum velocity by this factor. The result will be the approximate velocity at the time desired.

Figure 816c: Current Table 3, velocity of current.

Table 2 (Figure 816b) contains a list of secondary or *subordinate stations*, arranged in geographic order. Given for each station is its position in terms of latitude and longitude to the nearest minute, its reference station, the difference in time of slack water and time of maximum current in hours and minutes with respect to its reference station, the maximum flood and maximum ebb velocity ratios with respect to similar current at the reference station, and the direction and average velocities of the maximum flood and ebb currents. Keyed footnotes, applicable to specific subordinate stations, appear at the bottom of the page. The arrangement of Table 2 is illustrated in Figure 816b. Note particularly the bold-face printing of the name of the reference station above the group of subordinate stations to which it applies.

The respective time differences are added to or subtracted from, according to their signs, the time of slack water and strength of current (maximum flood or ebb) at the reference station to obtain the times of occurrence of the respective events in the current cycle at the subordinate station. The velocity of the maximum currents at the subordinate station is found by multiplying the velocity of either the flood or ebb current at the reference station by the respective velocity ratio listed for the subordinate station.

The set of maximum ebb tabulated in Table 2 generally differs from the flood direction by about 180°, as an examination will indicate. Where direction of ebb is not listed in Table 2, it is assumed to be 180° from the tabulated flood direction. The average flood velocity is the mean of all the maximum flood currents, while the average ebb velocity is the mean of all the maximum ebb currents.

Table 3 (Figure 816c) is used to find the velocity of the current at a specific time. Full instructions for its use are given below the table.

Figure 816d:
Current Table 4,
duration of weak
current.

Maximum current	Period with a velocity not more than—				
	0.1 knot	0.2 knot	0.3 knot	0.4 knot	0.5 knot
Knots	*Minutes*	*Minutes*	*Minutes*	*Minutes*	*Minutes*
1.0	23	46	70	94	120
1.5	15	31	46	62	78
2.0	11	23	35	46	58
3.0	8	15	23	31	38
4.0	6	11	17	23	29
5.0	5	9	14	18	23
6.0	4	8	11	15	19
7.0	3	7	10	13	16
8.0	3	6	9	11	14
9.0	3	5	8	10	13
10.0	2	5	7	9	11

Table 4 (Figure 816d) is used to find the duration of slack. Although slack water, or the time of zero velocity, lasts but an instant, there is a period each side of slack during which the current is so weak that for practical purposes it can be considered as negligible. From Table 4, the period (half on each side of slack) during which the current does not exceed a given velocity (0.1 to 0.5 knot) is tabulated for various maximum currents.

Table 5 (Atlantic tables only—no figure shown) gives information regarding *rotary tidal currents*, or currents which change their direction continually, and never come to a slack, so that in a tidal cycle of about $12\frac{1}{2}$ hours they set in all directions successively. Such currents occur offshore and in some wide indentations of the coast. The values given are average velocities due to tidal action only. When a steady wind is blowing, the effect of the current due to wind should be added vectorially to the current due to tidal action. This table is seldom used. Instructions for the use of this table as well as for Tables 1 through 4 are given in the publications themselves.

The following example illustrates the use of the current tables. While the form may appear to be somewhat lengthy, its use is recommended to avoid errors.

Example 1: A ship expects to arrive at Rockaway Inlet at 1400, 28 January. Use the figures of this article to solve for the following:

Required: (1) A complete current table for the Narrows, New York Harbor, and for Rockaway Inlet for 28 January.

(2) The velocity and the direction of the current at Rockaway Inlet at 1400.

(3) The length of the period during the 1627 slack water at Rockaway Inlet when the velocity will be 0.5 knot or less.

Note that in *Solution* (3) the total period of 46 minutes during which the current is 0.5 knot or less, 23 minutes of an ebb current occur before 1627, and 23 minutes of a flood current occur after 1627. The current has zero velocity at 1627.

Because of the difference of time between the reference and subordinate stations, it is sometimes necessary to pick one or more values from the day

COMPLETE CURRENT TABLE

Locality ROCKAWAY INLET Date 28 JAN.

Reference Station THE NARROWS (N·Y·)

Time Difference   Slack water   — 1h 45m

Max. current   — 2h 15m

Velocity ratio   Max. flood   1·1

Max. ebb   1·3

Flood direction 085°T   Ebb direction 245°T

Reference station		Locality	
0212	2·3 E	(27) 2357	3·0 E
0530	0	0345	0
0812	2·2 F	0557	2·4 F
1124	0	0939	0
1442	2.5 E	1227	3.25 E
1812	0	1627	0
2042	1·9 F	1827	2·1 F
2348	0	2203	0

VELOCITY OF CURRENT at ROCKAWAY Date 28 JAN

Time 1400

Interval between slack and desired time   2 h 27 m

Interval between slack and max. current   4 h 0 m

Max. current   Ebb/Flood   3·3

Factor from table 3   0·8

Velocity 2·6 E   Direction 245° T

DURATION OF SLACK WATER at ROCKAWAY Date 28 JAN

Nearest time 1627

Times of max. current	1227	1827
Max. current	3·25 °E	2·1° F
Desired Max.	0·5 K	0·5 K
Period from table 4	36 m	56 m
Sum of periods		92 m
Average period		46 m
Duration of period		1604 – 1650

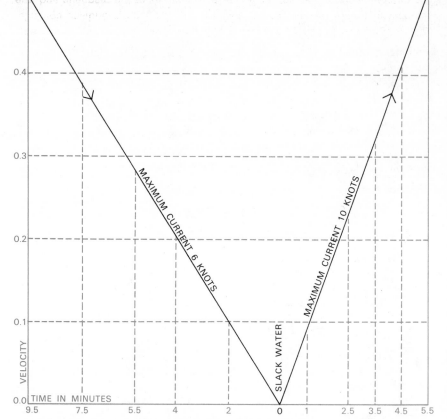

Figure 816e: Graph of duration of weak current.

preceding or the day following at the reference station to obtain the values for the desired day at the subordinate station.

Tidal cycle. Since the tidal cycle is about $12\frac{1}{2}$ hours, there are not quite two complete cycles per day; hence, on some days one entry is left blank. For instance note in Figure 816a that only one entry is given for maximum flood for 3 January; the next maximum flood occurring shortly after midnight (0042) on 4 January.

It must be remembered that values taken from the current tables are *predictions* only. The actual current encountered at any place seldom is exactly as predicted, because of wind. Since the predicted current is thus an approximation of actual conditions, it is standard practice to use Table 3 without interpolation.

Unless precise results are desired, use Table 4 without interpolation. (Interpolation was used in the preceding problem.) Figure 816e illustrates graphically the period during which a current slows down from a maximum of 6 knots, reaches the slack period, and then commences its run in the opposite direction with increasing velocity to a new maximum, 10 knots.

For practical purposes, this graph has expressed the relationship between current velocity and time as a straight line function.

When there is a difference between the velocities of the maximum flood and ebb preceding and following the slack for which the duration is desired, it will be sufficiently accurate for practical purposes to find a separate duration for each maximum velocity and take the average of the two as the duration of the weak current as illustrated in the preceding example.

128

817. Current diagrams for the principal tidal waterways of the coasts of the United States are also printed in the current tables. A "current diagram," as used in these publications, is "a graphic table which shows the velocities of the flood and ebb currents and the times of slack and strength over a considerable stretch of the channel of a tidal waterway." At definite points along the channel the velocities of the current are shown with reference to the times of turning of the current at a *reference station*. This makes it a simple matter to determine the velocity of the current at any point in the channel or the average current along the channel for any desired time, as well as the desired time for leaving a place to take maximum advantage of a favorable current.

Current diagrams.

The Current Tables contain diagrams for these areas on the Atlantic Coast with instructions for their use: Boston Harbor; Vineyard and Nantucket Sounds; East River, New York; New York Harbor (via Ambrose Channel); Delaware Bay; and Chesapeake Bay. Examine the diagrams closely and be sure you understand them before attempting to use them. They can be helpful and simple to use, but only if thoroughly understood.

The Current Tables also give data on rotary tidal currents at various stations off the Atlantic coast of the United States, as well as in the Gulf Stream, wind driven currents, and the preparation of vectors to show the effect of two currents, together with explanatory text. Separate tidal current charts published by the National Ocean Survey are also available for the following principal areas: Boston Harbor, Long Island Sound and Block Island Sound, Narragansett Bay to Nantucket Sound, New York Harbor, Delaware Bay and River, San Francisco Bay, and Puget Sound.

Tidal current charts.

CHAPTER 9

Compasses

THE MAGNETIC COMPASS

Introduction.

901. The magnetic compass is one of the oldest of the navigator's instruments. Its origin is unknown, but apparently the Vikings were familiar with it in the eleventh century. The earliest compass probably consisted of a needle thrust through a straw and floated in a container of water. A lodestone, or piece of iron ore having magnetic properties, was used to magnetize the needle. By the thirteenth century there were two new types of compasses, one with the needle supported by two floats, the other fitted with a *lubber's line*, or reference, to indicate the ship's head. The compass card is believed to have come into use in the fourteenth century.

The magnetic compass still retains its importance, despite the invention of the gyrocompass. While the latter is an extremely accurate instrument, it is highly complex, dependent on an electrical power supply, and subject to mechanical damage. The magnetic compass, on the other hand, is entirely self contained, simple, comparatively rugged, and not easily damaged.

Standard and steering compasses.

Most vessels of any size carry at least two magnetic compasses; these are the *standard compass* and the *steering compass*. The standard compass, where possible, is located on the ship's centerline, and on a weather deck near the bridge, at a point where it will be least affected by unfavorable magnetic influences. Headings read from this compass are termed *per standard compass* (*psc*). The steering compass in most ships is also located on the centerline, just forward of the steering wheel, where it can be seen conveniently by the helmsman. Its headings are termed *per steering compass (p stg c)*.

This section is intended primarily to stress the continuing importance of the magnetic compass, despite the great advances made in the field of the gyro compass. It will deal only briefly with the theory of magnetism, and is not intended as a treatise for the professional compass adjustor. The theory of compass adjustment is covered in detail in the *Handbook of Magnetic Compass Adjustment*, H. O. 226.

The following terms used in connection with the magnetic compass should be thoroughly understood:

Definitions.

Variation. The angle between the magnetic and geographic meridian at any place, expressed in degrees east or west to indicate the direction of magnetic north from true north.

Dip. The angle between the horizontal and the lines of force of the earth's magnetic field at any given point. The maximum dip, 90°, occurs at the magnetic poles.

Magnetic equator. The line on the surface of the earth connecting all points at which the magnetic dip is zero.

Magnetic meridians. Horizontal lines of the earth's magnetic force. The direction of the horizontal component at any place defines the magnetic meridian at that place.

Isogonic lines. Lines connecting points of equal magnetic variation. They must not be confused with magnetic meridians.

Deviation. The angle between the magnetic meridian and the compass card, expressed in degrees east or west to indicate the direction in which the north mark of the compass card is offset from magnetic north.

Compass error. The angle by which a compass direction differs from the true direction; it is the algebraic sum of the variation and the deviation.

Compass adjustment. The principal purpose of compass adjustment is to eliminate the deviation as far as possible. Other purposes are to make the residual deviation as nearly constant as possible under all conditions of dip, and to improve the directive force of the compass.

Residual deviation. The deviation of a magnetic compass, remaining after the compass is adjusted.

902. The basic principle of operation of the magnetic compass is that magnetic materials of the same polarity repel each other, and those of the opposite polarity attract. In its simplest form, the magnetic compass consists of a magnetized needle freely suspended so that it can turn horizontally in any direction. Such a needle tends to align itself with the magnetic field of the earth, which lies in a roughly north-south direction; it so serves to indicate direction. Allowance must, however, be made for the variation of these magnetic lines of force from the geographic or true meridians, and for the magnetic influences within the ship which cause the needle to deviate away from magnetic north. These factors will be discussed in subsequent articles.

The earth as a magnet.

Figure 902a illustrates the concept of the earth as a magnet. The magnetic north pole is in the vicinity of latitude 74° N, longitude 101° W, and the magnetic south pole is situated near latitude 68° S, longitude 144° E; the exact locations have not been established. Recent observations seem to indicate that the magnetic north pole is not stationary, but is in constant daily motion within an ellipse having a major axis of about 50 miles, being at the southernmost point about noon, and at the northernmost about midnight local time.

As stated in the previous article, the earth's magnetic field in general lies in a roughly north-south direction; it is *focused* at the north and south magnetic poles. It may be considered to be composed of *lines of force* with which a compass needle free to rotate in a horizontal plane aligns itself. These lines of force are called *magnetic meridians;* they must not be confused with *isogonic* lines, which connect points of equal magnetic variation, and are shown on some navigational charts. The magnetic meridians are irregular lines which can-

Magnetic meridians.

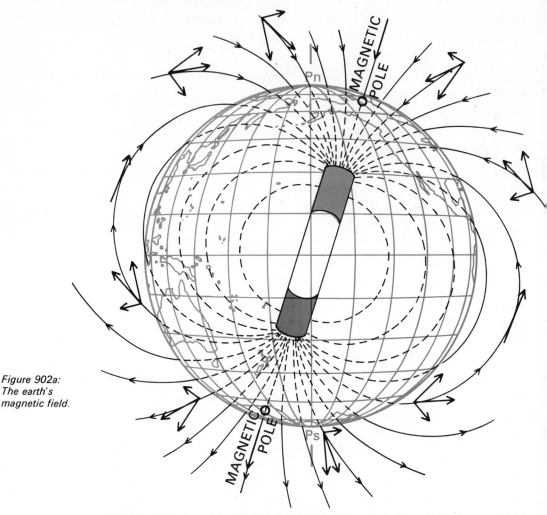

Figure 902a:
The earth's
magnetic field.

not be printed on charts covering large areas; their irregularity is caused by the non-uniform distribution of magnetic material in the earth.

The magnetic lines of force can be divided into components. For the navigator, the horizontal and vertical components are important, and are discussed as *variation* and *dip* in subsequent articles.

Secular change. The earth's magnetic field is not constant in either intensity or direction. The changes are *diurnal* (daily), *yearly*, and *secular* (pertaining to a long period of time). The changes in intensity are too small to have any effect in navigation. The same is true of diurnal changes in direction, except in polar regions, where diurnal changes of 7° have been observed.

The secular change, however, is a real factor in navigation. Although it has been under observation for more than 300 years, the length of its period has not been fully established. The change generally consists of a reasonably steady increase or decrease in the *variation*, which is the inclination of the magnetic meridian to the true meridian at a given place. This change may continue for many years, sometimes reaching large values, remain nearly stationary for a few years, and then reverse its trend.

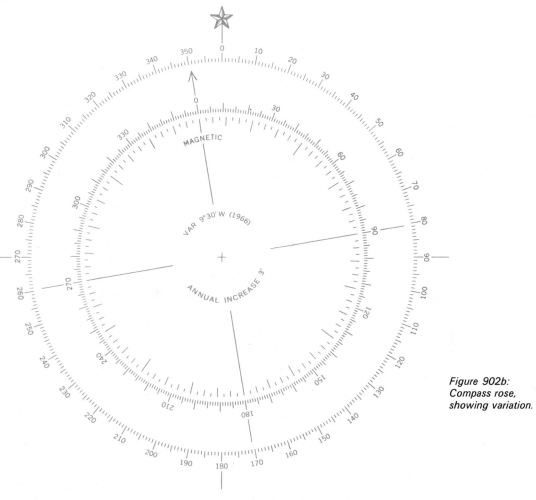

Figure 902b:
Compass rose,
showing variation.

The secular change is extremely complex. However, if the change of inclination
of the magnetic meridian to the true meridian is measured over a period of several
years at a given location, its future values for the next few years can be predicted with considerable accuracy. Charts generally indicate the values of the
variation for a stated year, and note the annual amount and direction of the
secular change, so that the value for any subsequent year, within a reasonable
period, may be calculated. This annual change is printed within the compass
rose on the chart as shown in Figure 902b. Predictions of the change of variation
are intended for short term use—a period of a few years. Values derived from
the predictions on an old chart may be considerably in error; the latest charts
available should always be used.

Change in magnetic field.

903. Magnetic meridians indicate the direction of the earth's magnetic field;
but only in a very few places do the magnetic and true meridians coincide.
The difference at any location between the directions of the magnetic and true
meridians is the *variation*, sometimes called *magnetic declination*, at that
location. It is called easterly (E) if the compass needle, aligned with the magnetic meridian, points eastward or to the right of true north, and westerly (W),
if it points to the left. Variation is the horizontal component of a magnetic
line of force.

Variation.

Variation is of importance to the navigator, as the magnetic compass, responding to the earth's magnetic field, is in error in measuring true direction by the amount of the variation. The magnetic variation and its annual change are shown on charts, so that directions indicated by the magnetic compass can be corrected to true directions. Since variation is caused by the earth's magnetic field, its value changes with the geographic location of the ship, but is the same for all headings of the ship.

Dip.

904. The earth and its surrounding magnetic field are illustrated in Figure 902a. Note that the lines of force are horizontal, or parallel to the earth's surface only at the *magnetic equator*, which is defined as the line connecting points of zero dip. At all other points they are inclined to the horizontal, the degree of inclination increasing as the magnetic poles are approached, where the inclination reaches 90°. The amount of this inclination is called the *dip, magnetic inclination*, or *magnetic latitude*, and the instrument which measures it is called a *dip circle*.

As the compass magnets are constrained to remain essentially horizontal, they are acted on only by the horizontal component of the earth's total magnetic force. This is greatest at the magnetic equator, where the dip is 0°, and disappears altogether at the magnetic poles, where the dip is 90°.

Magnetic charts.

905. A series of magnetic charts of the world are published by the Oceanographic Office. Chart 1700 shows the dip, 1701 the intensity of the horizontal component of the earth's magnetic force, 1702 the intensity of the vertical component, 1703 the total force, and 1706 the variation. On each of these, the world is shown on the Mercator projection. Two separate charts (bearing the same number followed by N or S) on the polar azimuthal equidistant projection are published for the polar regions. Of these the chart of chief interest to the navigator is No. 1706, a simplified adaptation of which is shown in Figure 905.

Figure 905: Simplified chart of magnetic variation of the world, from H.O. Chart 1706. The lines shown are isogonic lines.

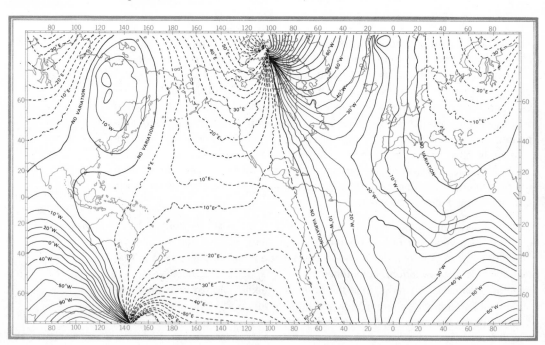

While these charts are useful for planning purposes, the large scale chart of the area involved should always be consulted in setting a course by magnetic compass or converting a magnetic compass bearing to a true bearing for plotting, since there are many small irregularities in variation that cannot be shown on the small scale world charts. In addition, there are regions of local magnetic disturbance over a very small area that may or may not be indicated on the chart. At one place off the coast of Australia, near Cossack, the variation changes from 56° E to 26° W in a distance of about 180 yards, less than the length of a cruiser. This area of local disturbance extends over nearly 3 miles of navigable water.

906. As stated in article 902, a compass needle free to turn horizontally tends to align itself with the earth's magnetic lines of force. Unfortunately, it is not free to do so in a steel ship; such ships have marked magnetic properties of their own, and these tend to deflect the compass from the magnetic meridian. The divergence thus caused between the north-south axis of the compass card and the magnetic meridian is called *deviation*.

Deviation.

Although deviation differs from variation in that the latter is caused by the *earth's* magnetism, the two are named and labeled in the same manner. Thus, if no deviation is present, the compass card lies with its axis in the magnetic meridian and its north point indicates the direction of *magnetic* north. If deviation is present and the north point of the compass points eastward of magnetic north, the deviation is named *easterly* and marked E. If it points westward of magnetic north, the deviation is named *westerly* and marked W.

The navigator can easily find the correct variation by referring to the chart of his locality. Deviation, however, is not so simple to ascertain. It varies not only on different ships, but on any particular ship it varies with changes in the ship's heading. Also, it often changes with large changes in latitude.

From the foregoing it should be apparent that there are three ways in which a direction can be expressed:

As *true*, when referred to the *true* (geographic) meridian as the reference of measurement.

As *magnetic*, when referred to the *magnetic* meridian as the reference of measurement.

As *compass*, when referred to the axis of the *compass* card as the reference of measurement.

907. Much research has gone into the development of the magnetic compass to bring it to its present high state of accuracy and reliability. Metallic alloys have been intensively studied in order that magnets of increased strength and retentivity might be produced. Alloys of nickel, cobalt, and other metals have proven far superior in both these respects to the iron formerly used. In addition, great advances have been made in protecting the needle from mechanical disturbances, in order to reduce its oscillations, or *hunting*, and in the presentation of the directional readout.

Requirements for a marine compass.

On some modern compasses a circular or ring magnet is used, replacing the bar magnets attached to the compass card. The ring magnet, due to its circular

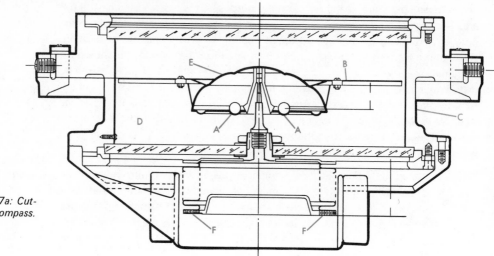

Figure 907a: Cut-away of compass.

shape, causes less friction with the fluid in the compass bowl as the ship turns; this produces an exceptionally steady card.

Compass components.

The modern marine magnetic compass is contained in a glass-topped bowl made of non-magnetic material. Figure 907a presents a sectional view, and Figure 907b a photograph, of a Navy standard No. 1 seven and one-half inch compass. The letter *C* indicates the bowl; the letters in the following description refer to the corresponding components in this illustration. At the forward side of the bowl is the *lubber's line*, which indicates the direction of the ship's head (355° in the photograph). At the center of the bottom of the bowl is a vertical pin, the pivot, upon which the compass card (B) rests. To the bottom of this card are attached two or more magnets (A) aligned with the north-south axis of the compass card.

In order to reduce friction on the pivot and to dampen vibration, the compass bowl is filled with a clear fluid (D), which is not subject to freezing at normal temperatures. The card has a *float* or air chamber (E), designed so that it will support all but a minute percentage of the weight of the card with the attached magnets. Lastly, the bowl is fitted with an *expansion bellows* (F), which permits the bowl to remain completely filled as the liquid expands and contracts with temperature changes.

The bowl is supported in *gimbals*, or double rings, hinged on both the fore and aft and athwartships axes. These gimbals permit the compass bowl to remain horizontal or nearly so, regardless of the ship's rolling or pitching. A gimbal is illustrated in Figure 907b.

The gimbaled compass is mounted in a *binnacle*, or stand, made of non-magnetic metal. A typical Navy binnacle is shown in Figure 907c. The balls on either side are called quadrantal spheres.

When the compass is mounted in its binnacle, the magnets, being free to respond to the influence of the earth's magnetic field, align themselves approximately with the horizontal component of this field. *They maintain this alignment irrespective of the ship's heading.*

Figure 907b: U. S. Navy standard No. 1 7½-inch varsol-filled compass.

As the compass card is attached to the magnets, the 000° mark on the card always points in the direction of the magnetic north, and the magnetic direction of the ship's head is indicated by the lubber's line, if there is no deviation. When the compass is installed, great care is taken to align the lubber's line exactly parallel to the center line of the ship. The compass bowl and lubber's line are constrained to turn with the ship, thus the direction of the lubber's line from the center of the compass always represents the direction of the ship's head. Since the 000° mark on the card is always toward the magnetic north, the direction indicated on the compass card opposite the lubber's line is the ship's heading. As the ship turns, the lubber's line turns with it, while the compass card remains aligned with the magnetic meridian, so that the heading at any moment is indicated at the lubber's line. *Remember that it is the lubber's line, and not the compass card, which turns.*

Figure 907c: Binnacle for standard Navy compass.

137

Figure 908a: U. S. Navy standard No. 3 5-inch alcohol-filled compass and binnacle.

Typical marine compasses.

908. The *No. 1 seven and one-half inch compass* described in article 907 is the magnetic compass used most widely in the Navy. It has proven itself to be an excellent instrument. Two other compasses used by the Navy are the *No. 3 five-inch compass*, shown in Figure 908a, and the *No. 5 three-inch compass*, shown in Figure 908b.

Periscopic compass.

The periscopic reflection compass and binnacle is coming into increasing use as a combined steering and bearing compass on most maritime vessels. It permits installing the compass on the level above the wheel house; the image of the compass card is reflected down periscopically and presented in the field of view of the helmsman. This type of installation has several advantages. The

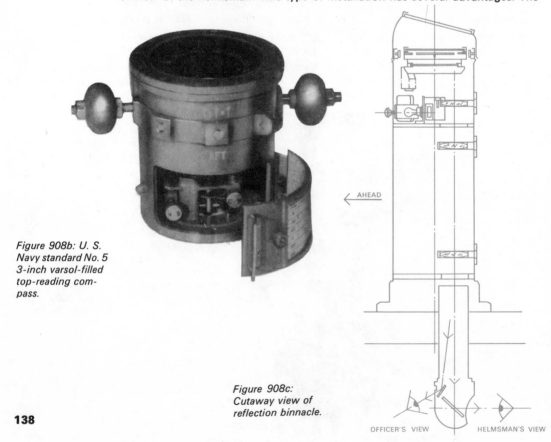

Figure 908b: U. S. Navy standard No. 5 3-inch varsol-filled top-reading compass.

AHEAD

Figure 908c: Cutaway view of reflection binnacle.

OFFICER'S VIEW   HELMSMAN'S VIEW

compass itself is removed from the enclosed wheelhouse, where it would be surrounded by metal, and much electric and electronic equipment. Also, on the open deck above, bearings and azimuths may be obtained directly on the compass itself, either for navigation, or for checking the compass. A schematic representation of a typical perioscopic reflection compass is shown in Figure 908c.

Figure 908d: A spherical compass.

A *spherical compass* is illustrated in Figure 908d. This type of compass is becoming increasingly popular among yachtsmen, as well as with commercial operators, as it offers several advantages compared to the conventional flat-topped compass. These compasses are internally gimbaled, and the compass card is pivoted at the center of the sphere, assuring maximum stability for the card in all conditions of pitch, roll, and heave. In addition, the transparent spherical dome of the compass acts as a powerful magnifying glass, and greatly increases the apparent size of the compass card in the area of the lubber's line. When fitted with shock mounting supports, the spherical compass gives excellent results in high speed boats, despite continuous vibration and shock in heavy seas.

909. The algebraic sum of variation (article 903) and deviation (article 906) is *compass error*. The navigator must understand thoroughly how to apply variation, deviation, and compass error, as he is frequently required to use them in converting one kind of direction to another.   *Compass error.*

At this point, review the three ways of expressing direction outlined in article 906. Direction may be expressed as:

> *True,* when the earth's true meridian is used as a reference.

> *Magnetic,* when the magnetic meridian is used as a reference.

> *Compass,* when the axis of the compass card is the reference.

Any given direction may be expressed in all three of these ways, if it is understood that:

> *True* differs from *magnetic* by *variation*.

> *Magnetic* differs from *compass* by *deviation*.

> *Compass* differs from *true* by *compass error*.

139

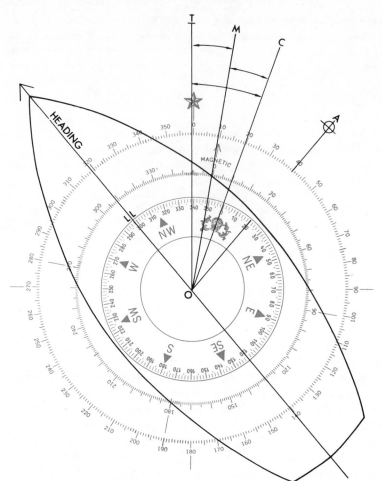

Figure 909:
Compass errors.

Figure 909 outlines a ship in which is shown the card of the standard compass. *OC* is the direction of the compass needle. *OM* is the magnetic meridian, and *OT* the true meridian. The two outer circles, concentric with the standard compass card, represent magnetic and true compass roses, thus indicating magnetic and true directions. The observer is at *O*. The magnetic meridian is 10° eastward (right) of the true meridian; therefore, the variation of the locality is 10° E. It is additive to the magnetic direction of *M* (0° on magnetic rose) to obtain the true direction of *M* (10° on true rose). The compass needle is 10° eastward (right) of the magnetic meridian; therefore, the deviation is 10° E on the ship's heading shown. It is additive to the compass direction of *C* (0° on compass card) to obtain the magnetic direction of *C* (10° on magnetic rose). The compass error is the algebraic sum of the variation and deviation or CE = 20° E. It is additive to the compass direction of *C* (0° on compass card) to obtain the true direction of *C* (20° on true rose). The bearing of object *A* from the ship is shown as 20° psc, 30° magnetic, and 40° true. In practice, bearings are expressed in three-numeral groups—e.g., 020°, 030° and 040°. The ship's heading is 300° psc (note lubber's line *LL*), 310° magnetic, and 320° true.

As already noted, easterly deviation is additive (+) to compass in converting to magnetic, easterly variation is additive (+) to magnetic in converting to true, and easterly compass error is additive (+) to compass in converting to true. Conversely, they are subtractive (−) when converting in the reverse order.

A similar figure may be drawn to show westerly variation and deviation, which would show that the above rules of application should be reversed for westerly errors.

It is convenient to have a thumb rule to serve as an aid to the memory in applying the above principles. The following will serve: *When correcting, easterly errors are additive,* or simply, *correcting add east.* When applying this rule, it is necessary to consider a *compass* direction as the least correct expression, since it contains two errors, variation and deviation. *Magnetic* direction is considered more correct than compass, since the error deviation has been removed, leaving only the one error, variation. This is true even when the axis of the compass card is closer to the true meridian than is the magnetic meridian. When this one remaining error is removed, the correct *true* direction remains. Hence, the process of converting a compass direction to a magnetic or true direction or of converting a magnetic direction to a true direction is one of "correcting," or removing errors. If easterly errors are additive, it is obvious that westerly errors are subtractive, and no separate rule is needed.

The opposite of *correcting* is called *uncorrecting*. The process of uncorrecting is one of converting a true direction to a magnetic or compass direction or a magnetic direction to a compass direction by applying errors. If easterly errors are additive when correcting, they must be subtractive and westerly errors must be additive when uncorrecting. Hence, the one rule, *correcting add east* is sufficient to cover all four possible situations:

When correcting,   Easterly errors are additive.
                    Westerly errors are subtractive.
When uncorrecting, Easterly errors are subtractive.
                    Westerly errors are additive.

Rules for applying compass errors.

The process of correcting is one of starting with compass direction, applying deviation to obtain magnetic direction, and then applying variation to obtain true direction. Take the first letter of each key word in this process, Compass, Deviation, Magnetic, Variation, and True and let it be the initial letter of another word such that a sentence is formed. A convenient one to use is *Can Dead Men Vote Twice?* Using this sentence to remember the order, write just the initial letters vertically down the page:

```
W    C  _____
↑    D  _____
+    M  _____
↓    V  _____
E    T  _____
```

To the left of the column, draw a double-ended arrow, placing a "W" at the top, and "E" at the bottom and a *plus* sign in the center as illustrated. The arrow heads have nothing to do with actual direction but apply only to the direction of proceeding through the initial letters of the memory phrase, whether correcting from compass to true or uncorrecting from true to compass.

Now by placing the given information in the corresponding blanks, the unknown values can easily be computed following the rule of the form.

Examples of
correcting and
uncorrecting.

Example 1: A ship is heading 127° per standard compass. For this heading the deviation is 16° E and the variation is 4° W in the area.

Required: (1) The magnetic heading. (2) The true heading.

Solution: The problem is one of correcting. Since the deviation is easterly, it must be added. Hence, the magnetic heading is 127° + 16° = 143°. To find the true direction we are again correcting, and since the variation is westerly, it is subtractive. Hence, the true heading is 143° − 4° = 139°. In this case the compass error is 16° E − 4° W = 12° E. Applying this directly to the compass heading, we find the true heading is 127° + 12° = 139° as previously determined.

Answers: (1) MH 143°, (2) TH 139°.

Example 2: A ship's course is 347° psc. The deviation is 4° W and the variation is 12° E.

Required: (1) The magnetic course. (2) The true course.

Solution: Again the problem is one of correcting. The deviation is subtractive and the magnetic course is 347° − 4° = 343°. The variation is additive and the true course is 343° + 12° = 355°.

Answers: (1) MC 343°, (2) TC 355°.

Example 3: A ship's course is 009° psc. The deviation is 2° W and the variation is 19° W.

Required: (1) The magnetic course. (2) The true course.

Solution: The problem is one of correcting and since both errors are westerly, they are subtractive. The magnetic course is 009° − 2° = 007°. The true course is 007° − 19° = 348°. Since 0° is also 360°, this is the same as 367° − 19° = 348°.

Answers: (1) MC 007°, (2) TC 348°.

Example 4: From a chart the true course between two places is found to be 221°. The variation is 9° E and the deviation is 2° W.

Required: (1) The magnetic course. (2) The compass course.

Solution: For both requirements uncorrect so that the easterly variation is subtractive and the westerly deviation is additive. The magnetic course is 221° − 9° = 212°. The compass course is 212° + 2° = 214°.

Answers: (1) MC 212°, (2) CC 214°.

Example 5: A navigator sets up a compass at a spot on shore near the ship's anchorage. This compass, not being affected by the iron and steel of the ship, is free from deviation and indicates magnetic direction. From the chart the navigator determines the true bearing of a distant mountain peak to be 320°. By compass it bears 337°. The ship bears 076° by compass from the observation spot ashore.

Required: (1) The variation. (2) The true bearing of the ship.

Solution: The numerical difference between the true and magnetic bearings is 17°. Since the magnetic bearing is the greater, the difference is subtractive when applied to the magnetic bearing to obtain the true bearing, or when correcting. Hence, the variation is 17° W. To find the true bearing of the ship, correct. The true direction is 076° − 17° = 059°.

Answers: (1) V 17° W, (2) TB 059°.

Example 6: Two beacons are so placed ashore that when seen in line from seaward they mark the direction of a channel, 161° T. Seen in line from a ship heading up the channel, they bear 157°.5 by compass. The chart shows the variation for the locality to be 2°.5 E.

Required: (1) The compass error. (2) The deviation.

Solution: The compass error is 161° − 157°.5 = 3°.5 E. Since the true direction is greater than the compass direction, the error is easterly. The compass error is the algebraic sum of the variation and deviation. Hence, the deviation is the algebraic *difference* or 3°.5 − 2°.5 = 1°.0 E.

Answers: (1) CE 3°.5 E, (2) D 1°.0 E.

Example 7: Make a table of the first six examples, filling in the given values and solving for the missing ones where sufficient information is available. At the bottom of the form add a space for compass error (abbreviated CE), and fill in this column for each problem where sufficient information is given.

		1	2	3	4	5	6
W	C	127°	347°	009°	214°	337°	157°.5
↑	D	16° E	4° W	2° W	2° W	0°	1° E
+	M	143°	343°	007°	212°	337°	158°.5
↓	V	4° W	12° E	19° W	9° E	17° W	2°.5 E
E	T	139°	355°	348°	221°	320°	161°
	CE	12° E	8° E	21° W	7° E	17° W	3°.5 E

910. As stated in article 906, the deviation changes with a change in the ship's heading. The deviation is determined by comparing a direction determined by compass with the known magnetic direction. Several methods of accomplishing this will be explained later. The deviation on various headings is tabulated on a form called a *deviation table*, or *magnetic compass table*, and posted near the compass. A copy of the table should also be kept posted in the chart house.

Deviation table.

Figures 910a and 910b illustrate the standard Navy form, used for tabulating deviation, compass history, and performance data.

It provides blanks for filling in certain information regarding the compass and correctors used to reduce the deviation. Two different columns of deviation are shown, one marked "DG OFF" and the other "DG ON." "DG" refers to the ship's degaussing coils. Since the deviation may be somewhat different when the degaussing coils are energized, it is necessary to determine the deviation under both conditions. The deviations shown in the tables are somewhat larger than might normally be expected for a well-adjusted compass. Large deviations are shown to provide practice in interpolating.

A deviation table can be made for ship's heading by compass as in Figure 910c or, more commonly, by ship's heading magnetic as shown in Figure 910a. *When*

MAGNETIC COMPASS TABLE
NAVSHIPS 3120/4 (REV. 6-67) (FRONT) *(Formerly NAVSHIPS 1104)*
S/N 0105-601-9520

NAVSHIPS RPT. 3530-2

U.S.S. Compass Island ___ NO. EAG 153
(BB, CL, DD, etc.)

[X] PILOT HOUSE [ ] SECONDARY CONNING STATION [ ] OTHER

BINNACLE TYPE: [ ] NAVY ST'D [ ] OTHER

COMPASS 7½" MAKE Lionel ___ SERIAL NO. 12792

TYPE CC COILS K ___ DATE 15 Sept 1968

READ INSTRUCTIONS ON BACK BEFORE STARTING ADJUSTMENT

SHIPS HEAD MAGNETIC	DEVIATIONS DG OFF	DG ON	SHIPS HEAD MAGNETIC	DEVIATIONS DG OFF	DG ON
0	4.0 W	4.5 W	180	4.0 E	3.5 E
15	4.0 W	4.0 W	195	5.5 E	5.0 E
30	3.5 W	4.0 W	210	6.5 E	6.0 E
45	3.0 W	3.5 W	225	6.5 E	6.0 E
60	2.5 W	3.0 W	240	6.0 E	5.5 E
75	2.5 W	2.5 W	255	4.5 E	4.0 E
90	2.0 W	2.5 W	270	3.0 E	2.5 E
105	2.0 W	2.0 W	285	0.5 E	0.5 E
120	2.0 W	2.0 W	300	1.0 W	1.0 W
135	1.5 W	1.5 W	315	2.5 W	3.0 W
150	0.5 W	0.5 W	330	3.5 W	3.5 W
165	1.5 E	1.5 E	345	4.0 W	4.0 W

DEVIATIONS DETERMINED BY: [ ] SUN'S AZIMUTH [X] GYRO [ ] SHORE BEARINGS

B 4 MAGNETS RED [ ] FORE [ ] AFT AT 13" FROM COMPASS CARD

C 6 MAGNETS RED [ ] PORT [ ] STBD AT 15" FROM COMPASS CARD

D 2-7" [X] SPHERES [ ] CYLS AT 12" [X] ATHWART-SHIP [ ] SLEWED [ ] CLOCKWISE [ ] CTR. CLOCKWISE

HEELING MAGNET: [X] RED UP [ ] BLUE UP 18" FROM COMPASS CARD FLINDERS BAR: [X] FORE [ ] AFT 15"

[ ] LAT 0.190 [ ] LONG +0.530
[X] H [ ] Z

SIGNED *(Adjuster or Navigator)* APPROVED *(Commanding)*

VERTICAL INDUCTION DATA
(Fill out completely before adjusting)

RECORD DEVIATION ON AT LEAST TWO ADJACENT CARDINAL HEADINGS

BEFORE STATING ADJUSTMENT: N 5.5W ; E 4.0W ; S 5.5E ; W 6.0E .

RECORD BELOW INFORMATION FROM LAST NAVSHIPS 3120/4 DEVIATION TABLE:

DATE 1 Mar 1968 [ ] LAT 41° 22' N [ ] LONG 71° 18'W
[ ] H [ ] Z

15" FLINDERS BAR [X] FORWARD [ ] AFT
DEVIATIONS N 4.5W ; E 2.0W ; S 4.5E ; W 3.0E

RECORD HERE DATA ON RECENT OVERHAULS, GUNFIRE, STRUCTURAL CHANGES, FLASHING, DEPERMING, WITH DATES AND EFFECT ON MAGNETIC COMPASSES:

Annual shipyard overhaul:
3 June – 7 Sept 1968
Depermed Boston NSY: 12 Sept 1968

Abnormal deviation observed

PERFORMANCE DATA

COMPASS AT SEA:	[ ] UNSTEADY	[ ] STEADY
COMPASS ACTION:	[ ] SLOW	[X] SATISFACTORY
NORMAL DEVIATIONS:	[X] CHANGE	[ ] REMAIN RELIABLE
DEGAUSSED DEVIATIONS:	[X] VARY	[ ] DO NOT VARY

REMARKS

None

INSTRUCTIONS

1. This form shall be filled out by the Navigator for each magnetic compass as set forth in Chapter 9240 of NAVAL SHIPS TECHNICAL MANUAL.

2. When a swing for deviations is made, the deviations should be recorded both with degaussing coils off and with degaussing coils energized at the proper currents for heading and magnetic zone.

3. Each time this form is filled out after a swing for deviations, a copy shall be submitted to the Naval Ship Engineering Center. A letter of transmittal is not required.

4. When choice of box is given, check applicable box.

5. Before adjusting, fill out section on "Vertical Induction Data" above.

NAVSHIPS 3120/4 (REV. 6-67) (REVERSE)   C-3054

Figure 910a: Deviation Table (front) Navships 3120/4.

Figure 910b: Deviation Table (reverse) Navships 3120/4.

the deviations are small (5° or less), *compass and magnetic courses being close together, little significant error is introduced in entering the deviation table with either compass or magnetic heading.* When the deviations are large and change rapidly, great care must be exercised in using the table of deviation to insure that the proper deviation is obtained for the heading desired.

If it is desired to find compass course when a magnetic heading deviation table is available, proceed in the manner discussed in the following examples.

Example 1: A ship is to steer course 201° true. The variation is 10°.5 W. DG is off.

Required: The compass course using deviation table of Figure 910a.

Solution: Applying the variation, the magnetic course is 201° + 10°.5 = 211°.5.

SHIPS HEAD COMPASS	DEVIATIONS		SHIPS HEAD COMPASS	DEVIATIONS	
	DG OFF	DG ON		DG OFF	DG ON
0	4.0 W	4.5 W	180	4.5 E	4.0 E
15	4.0 W	4.0 W	195	6.0 E	5.5 E
30	3.5 W	4.0 W	210	7.0 E	6.0 E
45	3.0 W	3.5 W	225	6.5 E	6.0 E
60	2.5 W	3.0 W	240	5.5 E	5.5 E
75	2.5 W	2.5 W	255	4.0 E	3.5 E
90	2.0 W	2.5 W	270	2.5 E	2.5 E
105	2.0 W	2.0 W	285	0.5 E	0.5 E
120	2.0 W	2.0 W	300	1.0 W	1.0 W
135	1.5 W	1.5 W	315	2.5 W	3.0 W
150	0.5 W	0.5 W	330	3.5 W	3.5 W
165	2.0 E	1.5 E	345	4.0 W	4.0 W

Figure 910c: Deviations tabulated by compass headings.

Enter the table with 211°.5. The deviation is 6°.5 E. The compass course is 211°.5 − 6°.5 = 205°.0.

Answer: CC 205°.0.

Example 2: The ship's head is 210° magnetic. A lighthouse bears 136° by compass. The variation is 3° E. DG is off.

Required: The true bearing using deviation table of Figure 910a.

Solution: The deviation depends on the ship's head, *not* the bearing. Hence, we enter the table with 210°. The deviation is 6°.5 E + 3°.0 E = 9°.5 E. The true bearing is then 136° + 9°.5 = 145°.5.

Answer: TB 145°.5.

Example 3: Using the deviation table of Figure 910a, determine the compass courses corresponding to the following true courses in an area where the variation is 12° W and with DG off: 093°, 168°, 238°.

Answers: CC 107°, CC 176°, CC 245°.

When it is desired to find a compass course if deviations for compass headings only (Figure 910c) are available, proceed as shown in Example 4.

Example 4: A ship is to steer course 187° true. The variation is 6° E. DG off.

Required: The compass course (CC) using the deviation table of Figure 910c.

Solution: Find the magnetic course first: 187° − 6° = 181°. Enter the deviation table with the compass courses, which when converted to magnetic courses, will bracket the desired magnetic course of 181° as follows:

Ships Hd. Compass	Deviation	Ships Hd. Magnetic
165°	2°.0 E	167°.0
		181°.0
180°	4°.5 E	184°.5

145

Interpolate between 167°.0 and 184°.5 to find the deviation corresponding to MH 181° as follows: for a change in magnetic heading of 17°.5 (184°.5 − 167°.0), the corresponding change of deviation is + 2°.5 E. For a change of magnetic heading of 14° (181°.0 − 167°.0), the change of deviation is found by the ratio 2.5/17.5 = Δd/14, and Δd = 2°.0 E. The deviation for MH 181° is then the deviation for MH 167° plus Δd determined above, or 2°.0 E + (+2°.0 E) = 4°.0 E. Combining this deviation with the magnetic course of 181° corresponding to the true course given of 187°, the compass course is found to be 177°.

Answer: CC 177°.

The required standard at the U. S. Naval Academy is to interpolate for values of compass deviation to the nearest 0°.5 and to use the value of magnetic variation to the same standard of accuracy. The answers to magnetic compass problems involving the computation of compass course, magnetic heading, true course, and compass error are also recorded to the nearest 0°.5 as it is assumed that the ability of a helmsman to steer a given course within closer tolerances is not customarily required nor usually possible.

It should be noted that the deviation tables illustrated tabulate deviations for either compass or magnetic headings. Usually only one or the other is prepared by the navigator and is available.

If the deviations are large, interpolating for headings between those tabulated can be difficult. A convenient way of interpolating for large deviations is to use a *Napier diagram,* as discussed in the following article.

Napier diagram or Curve of Deviations.

911. When the maximum deviation is considerable, say near 10° or more, the *Napier diagram* or *Curve of Deviations* is a convenience to the navigator, as it permits accurate interpolation between the tabulated values of deviation in a deviation table. The user can find the deviation for any heading, compass or magnetic, and obtain the magnetic course corresponding to a compass course, or vice versa, simply by drawing two short lines.

Figure 911 shows a Napier diagram. The heavy curves are drawn through the points established by plotting the deviations given in the following table:

Compass		Magnetic	Deviation
N	000°	012°	12° E
NE	045°	049°	4° E
E	090°	087°	3° W
SE	135°	128°	7° W
S	180°	174°	6° W
SW	225°	224°	1° W
W	270°	278°	8° E
NW	315°	328°	13° E

For simplicity, only whole degrees are used. The table of deviations indicates that the compass is in need of adjustment: however, it serves to illustrate the use of the Napier diagram.

The central dotted line of the diagram with the numerals of every fifth degree represents the rim of a compass card cut at the north point and straightened into a vertical column. For convenience, it is usually arranged into two halves, as shown in the illustration. The method of construction and use of the curve can best be explained by describing the preparation of the *curve of deviations* shown in the figure, and by examples.

Just above the left half of the curve is the precept, "compass courses on dotted lines." This means that to plot the deviation of 12° E on north (000) by compass, dotted line is followed toward "deviation east" from the "0" to the twelfth dot. This dot is enclosed in a small circle. Because the table is in two halves, the full circle back to zero ends with the "360" at bottom of the right half of the diagram; here again the twelfth dot toward "deviation east" is circled for the deviation of

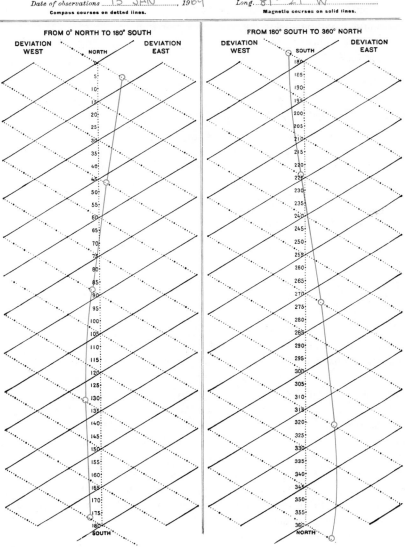

CURVE OF DEVIATIONS
(Constructed upon the Napier Diagram.)

Of the .... STANDARD .... *Compass No.* 12826 , *on board the*

.... S. S. GOODCHILD ....
(Name and Number)

Date of observations .... 15 JAN ...., 1969

Lat. 30° 24' N
Long. 81° 21 W

Compass courses on dotted lines.

Magnetic courses on solid lines.

FROM 0° NORTH TO 180° SOUTH	FROM 180° SOUTH TO 360° NORTH
DEVIATION WEST — NORTH — DEVIATION EAST	DEVIATION WEST — SOUTH — DEVIATION EAST

Figure 911: Napier diagram with curves drawn.

12° E. In similar fashion the deviation of 4° E on compass heading of 045 is represented by a circle around the fourth dot from the "45" toward "deviation east," and the 3° W on 090 by compass is shown by the circle around the third dot from the "90" toward "deviation west," etc. A faired curve is drawn through all the circled points. When a deviation to a fraction of a degree is to be plotted, the correct position between the dots for the whole degrees on each side is estimated by eye and marked by a circled dot.

Wherever the curve crosses a dotted line, the deviation for that 15° rhumb of the compass headings may be read directly, as 15° E for 330° and 345° and 5° W for 105°. For a compass heading which does not have a diagonal dotted line through it, a broken line drawn parallel to those dotted lines, from the dot of the desired heading to the curve, will give the deviation. For example, for compass heading 009° the broken line, from the ninth dot on the central line to the curve, will be found to be about 11 dots long toward "deviation east," showing the deviation to be 11° E.

The second precept "magnetic courses on solid lines" is applied this way: A *solid* line drawn parallel to the *solid* lines, say, from the 323rd dot to the curve will be found to be 13 dots long toward "deviation east." This shows that the deviation for 323° *magnetic* is 13° E.

When using the "curve of deviations" to determine directly the magnetic courses corresponding to compass courses, or vice versa, the following old jingle may help in applying the two precepts:

> "From compass course, magnetic course to gain,
> Depart by dotted and return by plain.
> From magnetic course to steer the course allotted,
> Depart by plain and then return by dotted."

Example 1: What compass course is indicated in Figure 911 for a magnetic course of 020°? *Answer:* 009°.

Example 2: The compass heading is 310°. What is the correct magnetic heading? *Answer:* 323°.

PRACTICAL COMPASS ADJUSTMENT

Introduction.

912. Article 906 stated that the deviation of the magnetic compass is caused by the magnetic properties of a steel ship. A complete analysis of the many separate magnetic components which combine to cause deviation is beyond the scope of this text; however, an understanding of the basic concepts and terminology is desirable. The various magnetic components or parameters of the total magnetic field of a vessel are referred to as coefficients, and different correcting magnets are used to compensate for their effects on the compass. Figure 902 illustrates the concept of the earth as a magnet, with the north magnetic pole colored blue, in accordance with the usual practice. Article 902 states that materials of opposite polarity attract each other; the polarity of the magnetic hemisphere and the north-seeking end of a compass magnet are therefore opposite. To identify their polarity, the ends of compensating bar magnets used in binnacles are color-coded, the *north* end being painted *red*, and the *south, blue*.

Coefficient A is constant on all headings and may be a combination of other parameters or may be mechanical, as from an incorrectly placed lubber's line.

Coefficient B is maximum on compass headings east or west and zero on compass headings north or south.

Coefficient C is maximum on compass headings north or south and zero on east or west. *Coefficients B and C* are caused by permanent magnetism and to some extent by induced magnetism in vertical soft iron. On small craft and yachts constructed mainly of wood or fiberglass only the B and C correctors are used. These are the so called built-in correcting magnets used in many small binnacles for spherical domed compasses.

Coefficient D is quadrantal deviation. It is maximum on intercardinal headings: 045°—135°—225°—315°, and zero on cardinal compass headings: north—south—east—west.

Coefficient E is quadrantal deviation which is maximum on the cardinal compass headings and zero on the intercardinal headings.

Coefficients D and E are caused by induced magnetism in horizontal soft iron and are compensated for by the use of the soft iron *quadrantal spheres* normally mounted on brackets athwartship on the binnacle. On all vessels constructed of steel these spheres should be used.

Coefficient J is defined as the change of deviation for a heel of 1° while the vessel is on compass heading 000°. It is, in effect, the error caused by the compass with its gimballing arrangement, remaining in a horizontal plane while the ship, with its magnetic field, rolls and pitches with relation to the compass. A slight change in their relative positions is therefore introduced. This change in deviation caused by the motion of the ship can cause the compass card to oscillate. Coefficient J is compensated for by a heeling magnet placed in a vertical tube directly below the center of the compass.

On the magnetic equator (article 904) there is no vertical component of the earth's magnetic field and consequently no induced magnetism in vertical soft iron. At other locations, notably in higher latitudes, the vertical component can cause the compass to become unreliable in a much larger area than if the force is neutralized. This statement represents an oversimplification of the problem as the various coefficients are of course interrelated. To compensate for or neutralize the induced magnetism in vertical soft iron, a *Flinders bar* is installed outside the compass binnacle, generally on the forward side for convenience. The Flinders bar consists of sections of soft iron having no permanent magnetism.

The theory of compass adjustment hinges on a more complete analysis. The following articles will dispense with theory, and follow empirically the procedure which experience indicates is satisfactory for adjusting the great majority of compasses. It is assumed that the compass is aboard a vessel which has been in commission for some time, that the compass is approximately correct, and that only comparatively minor adjustment is required.

If the procedure outlined hereafter does not give acceptable results, the services of a professional compass adjustor should be sought. For a detailed discussion of compass adjustment, see *Handbook of Magnetic Compass Adjustment and Compensation*, H. O. 226.

*Compass binnacle
and correctors.*

913. The *compass binnacle* is the case in which the magnetic compass is mounted. The type used by the Navy for mounting the standard $7\frac{1}{2}$ inch compasses was illustrated in Figures 907a, 907b, and 907c. It consists of a casting of nonmagnetic material about $3\frac{1}{2}$ feet high with an opening in the top to receive the compass, and provision for holding the correctors used for adjusting the compass. Inside the binnacle, which has access doors, are trays or holders for fore-and-aft magnets and for athwartship magnets. The trays are supported on screws so they can be raised or lowered with about 12 inches of motion available, and provision is made for as many as eight 4-inch magnets in each set of trays. These are the B and C correcting magnets. Most modern binnacles now have provision for under-lighting the compass. In the center of the interior of the binnacle a tube is located to hold the heeling magnets, which can be moved up and down in the tube and secured as desired. The soft iron spheres are readily identified, and are mounted on either side of the binnacle in grooved brackets which permit the spheres to be moved in a horizontal plane, toward or away from the binnacle. The binnacle in Figure 907c is also equipped with degaussing compensating coils mounted around the binnacle at the level of the compass with the junction boxes for the coils shown near the base of the binnacle.

*Preparations
adjustment.*

914. The preparatory steps for adjusting the compass can be made before getting under way. The vessel should be on an even keel. All moveable magnetic gear in the vicinity of the compass should be secured in the position it will occupy at sea. Two types of personal articles occasionally left on the bridge— small transistor radios and photoelectric light meters—are highly magnetic, and should never be permitted in the vicinity of the compass.

Be sure degaussing coils are secured and compass coils have been given a "dockside" compensation.

The binnacle should be exactly on the midship line and should be so solidly secured as to avoid any chance of movement.

The compass bowl should be in the center of the binnacle. To center a compass bowl in its binnacle, with the ship heading north or south or nearly so, put the compass bowl in place and adjust its position by the screws at the ends of the outer gimbal ring knife-edges, until no change of heading by compass is observed as the heeling magnet is raised and lowered, the vessel being on an even keel. Secure the compass bowl in this position by setting in on the screws to prevent any sliding back and forth athwartships. In case there is lost motion in the gimbal rings, they should be repaired or new ones obtained. The compass bowl should not move either fore-and-aft or athwartships in the gimbal rings.
The lubber's line of the compass should be exactly in the fore-and-aft plane of the ship. This should be carefully verified. It is best done by sighting with the azimuth circle on straightedges erected on the midship line at some distance forward and abaft the compass. It may also be done in dry dock, using the battens rigged for checking directors and other instruments.

The lubber's line of each pelorus should also be checked. This can be done by taking simultaneous bearings of a distant object from the magnetic compass and the pelorus.

150

Be prepared to record details of the adjustment.

915. If the *Flinders bar* is in place, it should be left there. If not, do not use it until expert advice has been obtained. *Flinders bar.*

The *quadrantal spheres* should be left in the same position in which they were placed when the compass was last adjusted. If there is uncertainty as to where they should be located, place them in the amidships position on each athwartships arm. *Quadrantal spheres.*

If the *heeling magnet* is in place, with the correct end up—*red* end *up, north* of the magnetic equator, and *blue* end *up, south* of the magnetic equator—leave it in place. If not, place it in the bottom of the tube with the appropriate end up. The proper height for the heeling magnet can be determined after the other steps of the adjustment are completed, by heading north or south when the ship has a steady roll. Observe the oscillations of the compass, and raise the magnet until the compass steadies. This can readily be accomplished on smaller vessels; it is more difficult on larger ones. The position of the heeling magnet may have to be readjusted to keep the compass steady, if the ship changes magnetic latitude materially. *Heeling magnet.*

Remove all others correctors, except the degaussing coils.

916. Having arrived in a clear area, with plenty of room to maneuver, the ship must be steadied *accurately* on selected *magnetic* headings in a definite sequence. Then when the proper corrector described below is so placed as to cause the compass to read the known *magnetic* heading, the deviation becomes zero. For example, if the ship is on magnetic north but the compass shows the heading as 358°, when it should read 000°, the deviation is 2° E, and the corrector should be so placed as to cause the compass to read 000°. Various methods of putting the ship on the desired magnetic headings are given later in this chapter. *Underway procedure.*

The sequence of magnetic headings is as follows:

1. A cardinal point—N, S, E, or W.
2. The cardinal point 180° from the first point.
3. A cardinal point 90° from the first.
4. The cardinal point 180° from the third.
5. An intercardinal point—NE, SE, SW or NW.
6. An intercardinal point 90° from the point used in step 5.
7. Swing ship, steadying for at least one minute on headings 15° apart —000°, 015°, 030° etc. through 360°—to find the residual deviations.

Assume the first heading is north. After the ship has been steadied on 000° magnetic, note the deviation. The required correcting magnets will go in the *athwartships* holders below the compass, which should be cranked down, near the bottom range of their travel. *Several magnets near the bottom of the travel are preferable to one or two close to the compass card*. The correct direction in which to place the red ends of the magnets may be determined by holding one magnet above the compass card parallel to the position it will have in the holder. If the card swings in the proper direction, magnets should be inserted symmetrically in the holders with all red ends facing the same way; if the swing is in the wrong direction, the red ends should be reversed. The number of magnets to use is determined by trial and error. When enough magnets have been inserted to remove nearly all the deviation, the holders are cranked up or down until the compass indicates the correct magnetic heading.

151

The ship is now brought to the second heading—south. After she steadies down, the deviation, which should be small, is again noted. *Half* the deviation is removed, by cranking the holders containing the athwartship magnets up or down, as necessary.

Proceed next to the third heading, which in this case will be east or west. All deviation on this heading is removed, using magnets in the fore-and-aft holders. The correct direction of the red ends is determined as on the first heading. The holders should again be cranked down towards the lower end of their travel; magnets will be inserted as required. The holders are cranked up or down to remove all deviation.

The ship now comes to the fourth heading, 180° from that of the third. *Half* the deviation is removed, by cranking the fore-and-aft magnets up or down as required.

She is next brought to the fifth heading, an intercardinal point, and all deviation found on this heading is removed by moving the two iron spheres. *Both the spheres are moved in or both out,* as required, until the magnetic heading and heading by compass are identical.

Come next to the sixth heading, an intercardinal point 90° from the one used for the fifth heading, and remove *half* the deviation found by moving the iron spheres. Both spheres must be moved in, or out, and by the same amount.

At this point the number and positions of all correctors should be carefully logged.

Finally, the ship is swung through 360°, steadying on each 15° heading *for not less than a minute;* If the compass appears sluggish, steady up for at least two minutes on each heading. The *residual deviation*, that is the deviation remaining after adjustment, is recorded for each 15° change of heading. If time is very short, or the residuals are small, say 2° or less, they may be taken on only 8 headings, or every 45°.

If the ship is fitted with degaussing gear, all circuits for normal operation are now energized, the ship is swung again and the residuals for degaussing on (DG ON) are noted on each 15° heading.

The degaussing equipment is intended to give the ship some measure of protection against magnetic mines and torpedoes, by reducing the ship's magnetic field. Degaussing is normally accomplished by permanently installed cables in the form of coils through which an electric current is passed, thus setting up a magnetic field which tends to neutralize the ship's field. The degaussing currents do, however, have a strong effect on the magnetic compass, and the deviation caused by these currents is usually larger than that caused by the ship's magnetism. Some of the deviation caused by the degaussing circuits is offset by degaussing compensating coils mounted on the binnacle as described in article 913. They are not completely efficient, hence the deviation must also be determined with the degaussing gear activated.

A deviation table, as described in article 910, and if desired, a Napier diagram, are now completed. Copies of the deviation table should be posted at the compass, in the compass record book, and in the ship's log.

917. Five methods of coming to a magnetic heading and for finding the devia- *Coming to a mag-*
tion are in use, with the first listed being probably the most accurate, as well as *netic heading and*
the one most commonly employed. *finding deviation.*

> Azimuths of a celestial body.
> Comparison with a gyro compass.
> Comparison with a magnetic compass having known deviations.
> Bearings of a distant object.
> Ranges.

918. The body most frequently used for this purpose is the sun. A time of day *Azimuths of a*
should be selected when the sun's altitude is below about 30°, as it is difficult *celestial body.*
to measure its azimuth, or horizontal direction, accurately at high altitudes.
The azimuths must be computed in advance, usually for every 8 minutes of the
period required for adjustment. By using H. O. 214 or H. O. 229, the computation
is rendered quite simple. Having computed the true azimuth at 8 minute intervals, the variation for the locality is applied to obtain magnetic azimuths. These
are plotted on graph paper, and a smooth curve is drawn through the various
points; the coordinates are true and magnetic azimuths. The method of computing the azimuths and plotting the curve is discussed in Chapter 29.

To put the ship on a desired magnetic heading, pick the magnetic azimuth off
the curve for the appropriate time, then find the angle between the desired magnetic heading, and the magnetic azimuth. Rotate the azimuth circle on the
compass so that the line of sight through the vanes forms this same angle with
the lubber's line. Adjust course right or left until the sun appears in the vanes.
Recheck the time and the corresponding magnetic azimuth, and adjust the setting
of the azimuth circle, if necessary.

Example: How would you place a ship on magnetic heading 225° when the
magnetic azimuth of the sun is 101°?

Solution: When the ship is on the required heading, the sun will be 225° − 101°
= 124° to the *left* of the ship's head. See Figure 918.

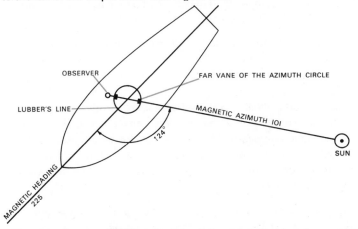

*Figure 918: Placing
a ship on heading
225° magnetic by
azimuth of the sun.*

Answer: Place the far vane 124° to the left of the ship's head and maneuver the
ship until the sun is in line with the vanes.

If a pelorus is used, it can be set with the required magnetic heading, 225°, at the
lubber's line and the far vane at the magnetic azimuth, 101°.

The deviation is determined by comparing the observed azimuth with its computed value at that moment. The difference is the deviation, which is easterly if the computed azimuth is the greater, and westerly if the observed azimuth is the greater.

Example: At a given time the azimuth of the sun is observed by the standard compass, and is found to be 105°.5. The magnetic azimuth taken from the curve for the same moment is 103°.5.

Redquired: The deviation of the standard compass on the present heading.

Answer: Dev. 2°.0 W.

By comparison with a gyrocompass.

919. When a gyrocompass is available, the comparison of the course as shown by gyro and the course as shown by magnetic compass will give the compass error, provided the gyro is running true. If the gyro has an error it must be allowed for. The deviation can then be found by combining the compass error thus determined and the charted variation. This is the method most frequently used by ships with a reliable gyrocompass.

To bring the ship to a desired magnetic heading, apply the variation to the desired magnetic heading to obtain the corresponding true heading, and bring the ship to this heading by gyro.

Example 1: A ship is heading 214° by gyro compass and 201° by magnetic compass. The gyro error is 1° W and the variation is 5° E.

Required: The deviation of the standard compass on the present heading.

Solution: If the ship is heading 214° by gyrocompass and the gyro error is 1° W, the heading is 213° true. Applying the variation, the magnetic heading is found to be 213° − 5° = 208°. The deviation is 208° − 201° = 7° E.

Answer: Dev. 7° E.

Example 2: Find the gyro heading to place a ship on magnetic heading 000°, if the variation is 23° E and the gyro error is 1° W.

Solution: The true heading is 000° + 23° = 023°. The gyro heading is 023° + 1° = 0.24°.

Answer: GH 024°.

By comparison with a magnetic compass of known deviation.

920. This method is similar to that of comparison with a gyrocompass, except that it is not necessary to know the variation. The method is often used when two or more magnetic compasses are adjusted at the same time. For example, the deviation of the standard compass may be found by a curve of magnetic azimuths or some other method and the steering compass then compared with it. This is a method frequently used when there is no gyrocompass installed in the ship.

To bring the ship to a desired magnetic heading apply the deviation to the desired magnetic heading to obtain the compass heading.

Example 1: A ship is heading 173° by standard compass and 175° by steering compass. The deviation of the standard compass on this heading is 4° E.

Required: The deviation of the steering compass.

Solution: The magnetic heading is 173° + 4° = 177°. The deviation of the steering compass is 177° − 175° = 2° E.

Answer: Dev. 2° E.

Example 2: Find the compass heading to place a ship on magnetic heading 180°, using the deviation table of Figure 920 (DG OFF).

SHIPS HEAD COMPASS	DEVIATIONS		SHIPS HEAD COMPASS	DEVIATIONS	
	DG OFF	DG ON		DG OFF	DG ON
0	4.0 W	4.5 W	180	4.5 E	4.0 E
15	4.0 W	4.0 W	195	6.0 E	5.5 E
30	3.5 W	4.0 W	210	7.0 E	6.0 E
45	3.0 W	3.5 W	225	6.5 E	6.0 E
60	2.5 W	3.0 W	240	5.5 E	5.5 E
75	2.5 W	2.5 W	255	4.0 E	3.5 E
90	2.0 W	2.5 W	270	2.5 E	2.5 E
105	2.0 W	2.0 W	285	0.5 E	0.5 E
120	2.0 W	2.0 W	300	1.0 W	1.0 W
135	1.5 W	1.5 W	315	2.5 W	3.0 W
150	0.5 W	0.5 W	330	3.5 W	3.5 W
165	2.0 E	1.5 E	345	4.0 W	4.0 W

Figure 920: Deviation table.

Solution: The deviation table is made out for compass headings. Interpolating, the deviation is found to be 4°.0 E on magnetic heading 180°. Applying this to the magnetic heading, the required compass heading is 180° − 4° = 176°.

Answer: CH 176°.

921. If a ship swings about an anchor, the bearings of a fixed object at least six miles distant will not change materially during the swing. By observing the bearing of the object by a magnetic compass as the ship heads in various directions, the deviation can be obtained for each heading for which an observation is taken, by comparison with the magnetic bearing. *By bearings of a distant object.*

If the distant object is shown on the chart, its magnetic bearing is obtained simply by applying the charted variation to the true bearing by compass rose. If not charted, its magnetic bearing may be taken as the average of a round of compass bearings of the object, observed on equidistant headings of the ship. The explanation of the last statement is that, theoretically, if a ship is swung through a circle and deviations are determined on equidistant compass headings, the sum of the easterly deviations found will equal numerically the sum of the westerly deviations, the resulting net deviation for all headings being zero. The error introduced by this assumption is generally very small unless there is a constant error.

A ship may be under way when obtaining a table of deviations by this method. In this case an object at a great distance must be chosen, and the ship should remain in as small an area as possible while making the observations. A buoy may be anchored and the ship maneuvered to keep as close as possible to this buoy while taking the observations.

Example 1: A ship plants a buoy, and, remaining close to this buoy, takes bearings of an unidentified prominent peak on a distant mountain.

Required: The deviations of the standard and steering compasses, the observations being as shown in the columns below.

Solution:

A	B	C	D	E	F	G
Ship's head psc	Bearing of peak psc	Magnetic bearing of peak	Deviation standard compass	Ship's head magnetic	Ship's head per steering compass	Deviation of steering compass
°	°	°	°	°	°	°
000	340.7	330.5	10.2 W	349.8	342.4	7.4 E
045	338.0	330.5	7.5 W	037.5	038.0	0.5 W
090	332.5	330.5	2.0 W	088.0	097.0	9.0 W
135	328.0	330.5	2.5 E	137.5	154.0	16.5 W
180	325.0	330.5	5.5 E	185.5	193.7	8.2 W
225	321.5	330.5	9.0 E	234.0	232.6	1.4 E
270	326.0	330.5	4.5 E	274.5	263.5	11.0 E
315	332.3	330.5	1.8 W	313.2	294.0	19.2 E
Sum	2644.0					
Mean	330.5					

Columns *A*, *B*, and *F* are observed during the swing. Column *C* is the average of column *B*. Column *D* is the difference between columns *B* and *C*. Column *E* is found by applying column *D* to column *A*. Column *G* is the difference between columns *E* and *F*.

It is good practice to determine deviation to the nearest tenth of a degree and round off to the nearest half degree when making out the deviation table. When the deviation has been determined for headings at irregular intervals, as for the steering compass, it is good practice to plot the deviations on cross section paper and fair a curve through the points. The deviation at the various headings can then be read from the curve to the nearest half degree.

With deviations as large as those shown, the ship should be swung on headings differing by 15°, rather than 45° as shown, if it is not possible to adjust the compasses and reduce the deviations. The example uses headings differing by 45° for brevity.

Note that this example includes the method of comparing a compass with one of known deviation.

To bring the ship to a desired magnetic heading, determine the magnetic bearing of the object, and find the difference between this and the desired magnetic heading. Set the far vane to the right or to the left as with an azimuth of a celestial body, and maneuver the ship until the distant object is in line with the vanes.

Example 2: How would you place a ship on magnetic heading 180° if the true bearing of a distant mountain peak is 227°. and the variation is 12° W?

Solution: The magnetic bearing is 227° + 12° = 239°. Set the far vane 239° − 180° = 59° to the *right* of the ship's head. See Figure 921.

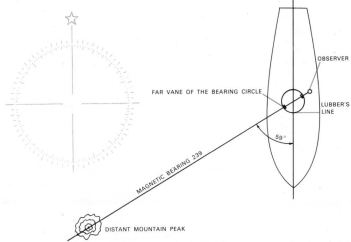

Figure 921: Placing a ship on heading 180° magnetic by bearings of a distant object.

Answer: Set the far vane 59° to the right of the ship's head and maneuver until the mountain is in line with the vanes.

922. Two fixed objects appearing in line constitute a range. Prepared ranges are placed in position to mark mid-channels, turning points, measured mile limits, etc. Natural ranges will often be found. A position that will not interfere with normal ship traffic should be selected. The true direction of the range selected is determined by measurement on the chart. The magnetic direction is then determined by applying the variation of the locality. The deviation is found by crossing the range on the desired heading and observing the compass bearing at the instant the objects are in line.

Refer to Figure 922. Beacons *A* and *B* form a range, the direction of which is 030°.5 true. The local variation is 20° W. Hence, the magnetic direction of the range is 050°.5. If the observed bearing of the range is 045°, the deviation is 050°.5 − 045°.0 = 5°.5 E.

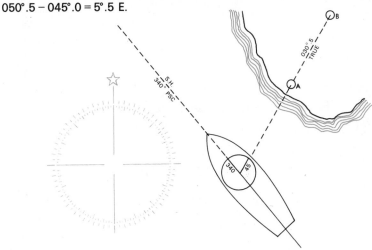

Figure 922: Finding the deviation by ranges.

To bring the ship to a desired magnetic heading, proceed as outlined in article 921.

Example: For determining the deviations of the standard compass, a ship uses the two ranges marking the measured mile off Kent Island, Chesapeake Bay. The true direction of the ranges is 091°.5 and the variation for the locality is 7°.8 W. As the ship crosses a range on the headings shown in the first column of the following table, the navigator observes corresponding directions of the range as noted in the fifth column.

Required: The deviations of the standard compass.

Ship's head psc	True direction of range	Variation	Magnetic direction of range	Direction of range psc	Deviation
°	°	°	°	°	°
000	091.5	7.8 W	099.3	103.2	3.9 W
015				103.1	3.8 W
030				102.6	3.3 W
045				102.1	2.8 W
060				101.8	2.5 W
075				101.7	2.4 W
090				101.5	2.2 W
105				101.4	2.1 W
120				101.3	2.0 W
135				100.8	1.5 W
150				099.9	0.6 W
165				097.2	2.1 E
180				094.8	4.5 E
195				093.3	6.0 E
210				092.5	6.8 E
225				092.9	6.4 E
240				093.8	5.5 E
255				095.3	4.0 E
270				096.8	2.5 E
285				098.8	0.5 E
330				100.3	1.0 W
315				101.8	2.5 W
330				102.7	3.4 W
345				103.3	4.0 W

The solution for the magnetic direction can be made first and columns 2 and 3 omitted from the form.

The deviation table (Figure 910c—DG OFF) is made up from this solution, by rounding off the deviations to the nearest half degree.

THE GYROCOMPASS

923. The first section of this chapter was devoted to the magnetic compass which was for many centuries the only instrument available at sea for the determination of direction. In the search for an instrument which would indicate true north rather than magnetic north, the gyrocompass was developed early in this century. Parallel advances have been made in America and Europe; the American Sperry Gyro-Compass was developed on the basis of the use of a single rotor or spinning wheel as compared with the multiple rotors of the early Anschutz compasses built in Germany.

Introduction to the gyrocompass.

As will be explained in article 929, the gyrocompass inherently is capable of oscillating about its vertical, or azimuth-indicating, axis. Damping is employed to suppress this tendency. Professor Max Schuler showed that the effects of accelerations, due to speed and course changes, are minimized when the period of this oscillation is made equal to approximately 84 minutes. This is the period a simple pendulum would have if its length were equal to the radius of the earth. This has come to be known as the Schuler pendulum, and the principle has basic application in all inertial navigation systems.

Schuler pendulum.

The gyro is used increasingly in navigation aboard ships today, not only as a steering or heading reference, but also for indicating the vertical in terms of ship's roll and pitch data for celestial observing instruments (Chapter 38) and as a basic component of inertial navigation systems (Chapter 36).

Of the four natural laws or facts upon which gyrocompass operation depends, the first two are inherent properties of the gyroscope, namely, gyroscopic inertia (rigidity in space) and precession. The third and fourth relate to the earth and are, namely, the earth's rotation and gravitation. The interrelation of these natural phenomena is explained briefly in this chapter to enable the navigator to understand the basic concept of a gyrocompass and, more important, to enable him to realize the limitations of practical accuracy, and the source of inherent error of the gyroscope when used as a compass in the shipboard environment.

Gyroscopic laws.

924. A rapidly spinning body having three axes of angular freedom constitutes a gyroscope (from the Greek *gyro*, meaning turn or revolution, and *skopein*, meaning to view). This is illustrated by a heavy wheel rotating at high speed in supporting rings or gimbals, as shown in Figure 924. One degree of freedom for the mass of the wheel or rotor is provided by the spin axis (1) itself. The remaining two degrees of freedom, which allow the spin axis to be pointed in any direction, are provided by the axes of the supporting gimbals. Corresponding to the arrangement used in a simple gyrocompass, these are designated as the horizontal (2) or inner axis, and the vertical (3) or outer axis.

Basic gyroscope.

925. Newton's first law of motion states that a body in motion will continue to move at constant speed in the same direction unless it is acted upon by an outside force. If the gyroscope could be constructed entirely free of mechanical error, with no bearing friction on the axis of the rotating wheel or its gimbals, and operated in a vacuum with no air friction on the rotating wheel, the result would be a perpetual motion machine. The direction of the spin axis would be fixed in inertial space parallel to its original position when placed in motion, and

Gyroscopic inertia.

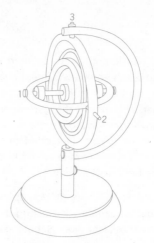

Figure 924:
The gyroscope has
three axes of
angular freedom.

the gyroscope would rotate forever. Obviously this perfection has not been accomplished, although electrostatically supported gyros have been constructed which will spin, or coast, for many months. Gyroscopic inertia thus tends to keep the rotating wheel in the same plane and resists any force which tries to change its plane of rotation. The strength of this force depends on the moment of inertia and velocity of the spinning rotor.

A basic model of the gyroscope as shown in Figure 924 can be used to illustrate the principle if the rotor is kept spinning with sufficient velocity. If the base of the gyroscope is slowly tipped the rotor or wheel will maintain its original plane of rotation as the base is moved about it in any direction with the relative position of the gimbals changing. A simple model of this type is useful in demonstrating gyroscopic inertia and precession.

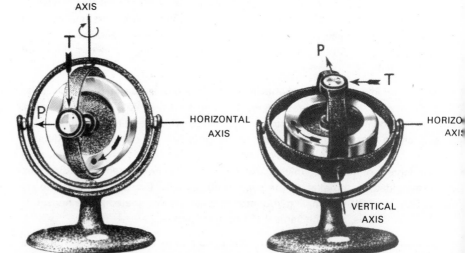

Figure 926a:
Precession about
the vertical axis.

Figure 926b:
Precession about
the horizontal axis.

Precession.

926. If force is applied to the axis of the spinning gyroscope, the axis rotates not in the direction in which the force is applied, but 90° from this. This reaction is known as precession, which is defined as that property of a gyroscope which causes the spin axis to change direction when a torque or force is applied to the gyro. The phenomenon was observed by Foucault, the French physicist who first observed the laws of the gyroscope and gave it its name. Figure 926a illustrates precession when a force is applied to the horizontal axis. The applied torque meets with resistance and the gyro instead of responding to the applied torque by turning about the horizontal axis turns or precesses about its vertical axis in the direction indicated by the arrow P in the figure. The arrow labeled T indicates the direction in which the torque was applied. Similarly in Figure 926b, if a torque is applied around the vertical axis in the direction of the arrow T, the gyro turns or precesses around its horizontal axis as shown by P. A convenient way to remember the direction in which precession takes place is to regard the pressure or torque as though it acted at a single point on the rim of the wheel, as indicated by the black dot in Figures 926a and 926b. This point will not move in response to the pressure, but a point 90° beyond (in the direction of the wheel's rotation) will move away instead.

927. As stated in article 925, the direction of the spin axis tends to be fixed in inertial space due to gyroscopic inertia. Inertial space may be conceived as a region in which the sum of all acceleration and gravity forces is zero. For purposes of illustration, if the spin axis were directed toward a star the axis would continue to point toward the star during its apparent motion across the sky.

Effect of earth's rotation.

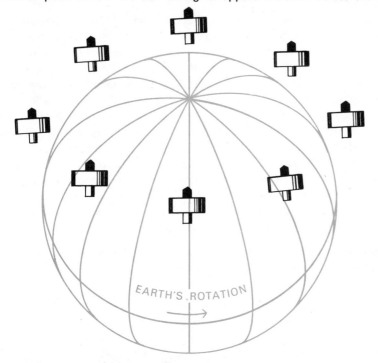

EARTH'S ROTATION

Figure 927a: A gyroscope with its spin axis set horizontal at any point away from the equator; observed from a point in space above the gyroscope.

To an observer on earth the spin axis would appear to change direction as the earth rotated eastward. This is illustrated in Figure 927a, in which it can be seen that with one rotation of the earth the direction of the spin axis relative to the earth would have moved through a complete 360°; it therefore becomes apparent that, if the gyroscope is to be used as a compass to indicate true north relative to the earth, a torque must be applied which causes it to precess an amount exactly opposite to the apparent movement caused by the rotation of the earth. In Figure 927b, the gyroscope is considered to be mounted at the equator with its spin axis pointing east and west. From a point in space beyond

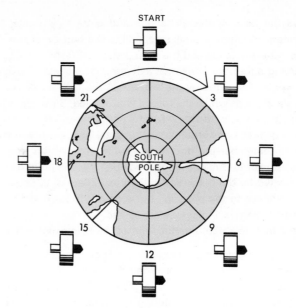

Figure 927b: A gyroscope with its spin axis set in the east-west position at the equator observed from a point in space beyond the south pole.

the south pole the relative position of the gyro and of the earth is illustrated for a 24-hour period. If observed while standing on the earth the gyro appears to rotate about its horizontal axis with a velocity equal to but in the opposite direction of the rotation of the earth. This effect is commonly referred to as *horizontal earth rate*. Similarly, if the gyro is assumed to be mounted at the north or south pole with its axis horizontal as shown in Figure 927c, the gyro will appear to rotate about its vertical axis. This effect is commonly referred to as *vertical earth rate*. At points between the poles and the equator the gyro appears to turn partly about the horizontal axis and partly about the vertical axis. This can be visualized in Figure 927a. The relative magnitudes of the vertical and horizontal rates are a function of latitude. The effect of horizontal earth rate is maximum at the equator and zero at the poles, and varies as the cosine of the latitude. The effect of the vertical earth rate will vary as the sine of the latitude being maximum at the poles and zero at the equator.

Earth rate.

In general the horizontal earth rate causes the gyro to tilt and the vertical earth rate causes it to move in azimuth with respect to the earth.

Figure 927c: A gyroscope with its spin axis set horizontal at the north pole; observed from a point in space beyond the equator.

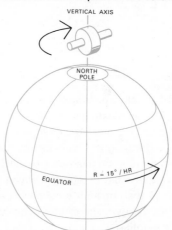

928. As previously stated, the horizontal earth rate causes the gyro spin axis *Gravity effect.* to tilt in relation to the surface of the earth. The precession effect on a gyroscope when a force or torque is applied has been discussed briefly. The effect of this application of force is precisely the same whether it be a force applied mechanically or whether it be the force of gravity, or of acceleration. The use of gravity to cause the spin axis to precess into a north-south plane, in a pendulous type gyro, can be visualized in an overly simplified manner as follows: picture the spinning gyroscope mounted in a hollow sphere with the spin axis horizontal and aligned in an east-west direction and with a weight mounted in the bottom of the sphere. The unit is located on the equator (Figure 928 at A). As the earth rotates, the spin axis, which is fixed in space, tends to become inclined to the horizontal, with the east end rising. The weight applied to the bottom of the sphere is therefore raised against the pull of gravity and consequently causes a torque about the horizontal axis of the gyro, as at position B.

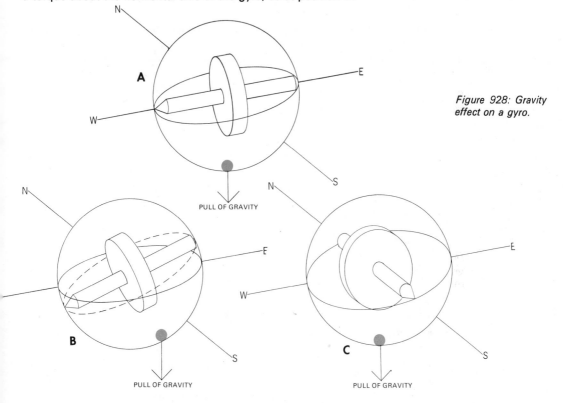

Figure 928: Gravity effect on a gyro.

This torque causes a precession about the vertical axis causing the spin axis of the gyroscope to align itself with the axis of rotation of the earth, the north-south direction, position C. When this alignment has taken place there will no longer be a tendency for the heavy bottom of the sphere to rise and produce further precession. The gyroscope now performs as a crude north-seeking instrument or gyrocompass. Gravity reference systems vary with different compass designs as will be discussed in the following articles. They were formerly classified as pendulous and non-pendulous according to the type of mechanical device used. The latest designs use an electrical gravity reference system. There are, however, other essential features of a practical compass, such as damping, and latitude and speed compensation.

Basic gyrocompass.

929. A gyrocompass is essentially one or more north-seeking gyroscopes with a suitable compass rose, housing, etc.

Various mechanical and electrical arrangements have been devised to take advantage of the natural laws described in the four previous articles. The mercury ballistic described here constitutes a basic method which produces the non-pendulous system used in older Sperry compasses. A pendulous system is used in Arma compasses and by some European manufacturers to achieve the same results.

One method of utilizing precession to cause a gyroscope to seek north is illustrated in Figure 929a. Two reservoirs connected by a tube are attached to the bottom of the case enclosing the gyro rotor, with one reservoir north of the rotor and the other south of it. The reservoirs are filled with mercury to such a level that the weight below the spin axis is equal to the weight above it, so that the gyroscope is nonpendulus. The system of reservoirs and connecting tubes is called a mercury ballistic. In practice, there are usually four symmetrically placed reservoirs.

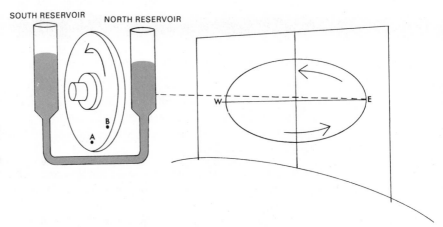

SOUTH RESERVOIR   NORTH RESERVOIR

Figure 929a: The mercury ballistic (left) and the elliptical path (right) of the axis of spin without damping.

Suppose that the spin axis is horizontal but is directed to the eastward of north. As the earth rotates eastward on its axis, the spin axis tends to maintain its direction in space; that is, it appears to follow a point, such as a star rising in the northeastern sky. With respect to the earth, the north reservoir rises and some of the mercury flows under the force of gravity into the south reservoir. The south side becomes heavier than the north side, and a force is applied to the bottom of the rotor case at point *A*. If the gyro rotor is spinning in the direction shown, the north end of the spin axis precesses slowly to the westward, following an elliptical path. When it reaches the meridian, upward tilt reaches a maximum. Precession continues, so that the axis is carried past the meridian and commences to sink as the earth continues to rotate. When the sinking has continued to the point where the axis is horizontal again, the excess mercury has returned to the north reservoir and precession stops. As sinking continues, due to continued rotation of the earth, an excess of mercury accumulates in the north reservoir, thus reversing the direction of precession and causing the spin axis to return slowly to its original position with respect to the earth, following the path shown at the right of the illustration. One circuit of the ellipse requires about 84 minutes. This is the Schuler period mentioned previously.

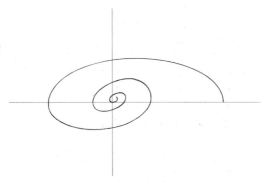

The elliptical path is symmetrical with respect to the meridian, and, neglecting friction, would be retraced indefinitely, unless some method of damping the oscillation were found. One method is by offsetting the point of application of the force from the mercury ballistic. Thus, if the force is applied not in the vertical plane, but at a point to the eastward of it, as at B in Figure 929a, the resulting precession causes the spin axis to trace a spiral path as shown in Figure 929b, and eventually to settle near the meridian. The gyroscope is now north-seeking and can be used as a compass. Some compasses are provided with automatic means for moving the point of application to the center line during a large change of course or speed, to avoid introduction of a temporary error.

Another method of damping the oscillations caused by the rotation of the earth is to reduce the precessing force of a pendulous gyro as the spin axis approaches

the meridian. One way of accomplishing this is to cause oil to flow from one damping tank to another in such a manner as to counteract some of the tendency of an offset pendulous weight to cause precession. Oscillations are completely damped out in approximately one and one-half swings.

Details of construction differ considerably in the various models. Each instrument is provided with a manual giving such information and operating instructions. In the latest gyrocompasses, methods have been devised to measure the tilt of the gyro axle, due to earth rate, and to use control devices to produce torques proportional to the tilt, about the vertical and horizontal axes. This eliminates the necessity for using weights or a mercury ballistic to produce torques and damping.

On the Mark 19 gyrocompass, now in wide use in naval vessels, this is accomplished by the use of a special electrolytic level which transmits an electrical signal with magnitude and sense according to tilt. The gravity reference and the gyro axle are parallel and rigidly fixed with respect to one another. The signal emitted by the gravity reference is amplified and applied to the control fields of electrical torquers which are used to precess the gyro.

Detailed descriptions of various systems using sensing devices in the form of electrolytic levels, special pendulums and electromagnetic pick-off units for sensing orientation are included in the operating manuals provided with the compass. A comparative analysis of mechanical and electrical features of different compass designs is beyond the scope of this text.

Fundamentally, a gyrocompass is a gyroscope to which has been added control elements to apply *torques* of the correct magnitude and sense to the gyroscope in order that: the gyroscope will precess in such manner that the spinning axis is brought parallel to the meridian within a reasonable time after the wheel is set spinning, and quickly returned to the meridian if it becomes displaced. The gyroscope will precess about the vertical axis at the proper rate and direction so as to cancel the effect of the earth's rotation; the *spinning axis* will remain nearly level when parallel to the meridian and prevent the instrument from oscillating across the meridian.

Gyrocompass components.

930. A modern gyrocompass system consists of a *master unit,* a *control cabinet,* a *power supply unit,* a *speed unit,* and *auxiliary electrical transmission* and *alarm units.*

The master unit is the heart of the compass system and contains the gyroscopic north-seeking, and in the more complex newer compasses, the vertical-seeking sensitive elements, necessary gimballing, and related electrical components and wiring.

The control cabinet is the "nerve center" of the system. It contains all the computing and amplifying circuitry and components, and in addition provides on its front panel all the controls, meters, and dials necessary for proper control of the operation of the compass.

On the major ships, present standards provide for two master compasses with the necessary control units and auxiliary apparatus. On smaller naval vessels frequently only one gyrocompass is provided. Repeater compasses are supplied as necessary for navigational and fire control uses. At steering stations two repeaters are provided in order that indications of both master compasses may be constantly available at those stations for purposes of comparison and checking.

Most naval ships are also supplied with dead reckoning equipment to plot automatically, to the scale of various charts, the track of the vessel during action or maneuvers. Latitude and longitude indicators and course recorders are also included in the tracer equipment. Self-synchronous alidades, which remain in the direction pointed until again moved by the observer, are also installed, (article 1005).

By being employed to actuate a contact maker, which causes the rudder to respond instantly to slight variations of the vessel's head from the prescribed course, the gyrocompass has become the control element of the gyro pilot for mechanical steering, and for the mechanical recording of the courses pursued.

Gyro repeater compasses mounted as peloruses on the wings of the bridge give true bearings. Self-synchronous alidades also include gyro repeaters. In the event of gyrocompass failure, gyro or self-synchronous alidade repeaters, set to the true course, may be used as ordinary peloruses.

Gyrocompass transmission system.

931. One of the features of the gyrocompass system is the ability of the master compass to transmit to remotely located indicators electrical data representing the ship's heading, and on the more complex newer compasses, electrical data representing ship's roll and pitch. These data are utilized in navigating the ship and are supplied as a necessary input to sonar, radar, fire-control, and other vital ship's equipment.

Gyrocompass repeaters (ship's course indicators).

932. Modern ship's course gyro repeaters are accurate electronic servo mechanisms which reproduce the master gyrocompass readings at remote locations.

Older types of repeater compasses consist essentially of a compass card fixed to the end of the shaft of a step or synchro motor, the rotor of which turns in synchronism with the transmitter indications of the master gyrocompass. In appearance it looks much the same as any compass, but it may be mounted rigidly in any position; it may be attached to a bulkhead as well as placed horizontally in a pelorus stand or binnacle. There are several models, each best adapted to the use intended.

Most repeaters are entirely self-synchronous, so that if they become out of step with the master gyro, as through temporary power failure, they will automatically line up with the transmitter when power is restored. Repeaters are generally provided with a damping device to prevent undesirable oscillation when the heading is changed rapidly.

A gyro repeater is used as a compass. As far as the user is concerned, the repeater *is* a compass. Lighting is provided by making the dial of translucent material with dark or colored markings or of opaque material with translucent markings, and placing a light behind the dial.

There is no practical limit to the number of repeators that can operate from a single master gyrocompass.

933. The gyrocompass is normally kept in continuous operation at sea. Most compasses are equipped with a stand-by power supply and a compass failure annunciator to indicate any malfunction of the compass, or failure of the ship's electrical power supply. The stand-by power supply will automatically operate the compass for a short period of time until ship's power can be restored. When in port for a considerable period of time the gyro can be switched off. The navigator must be aware of the fact that when the gyro is restarted several hours may be required for the rotor to attain operating speed and for the compass to settle on the meridian. The instruction manual contains methods to precess the compass to speed up this settling period. If the ship may be required to get under way on short notice the gyrocompass should be kept running.

Preparation for use.

934. When a vessel is under way, the movement over the earth resulting from course and speed, as well as the latitude in which the vessel is operating, is detected by the gyroscope as a change in horizontal and vertical earth rate (article 927). The gyro cannot distinguish between a force caused by movement of the vessel and that caused by rotation of the earth. On an east or west course there is no effect on the gyrocompass as the vessel's movement merely adds to or subtracts from the rate of rotation of the earth. This motion is in the plane of the rotor when the spin axis is settled on a meridian and therefore causes no precession. A vessel steaming north or south produces a maximum effect upon the compass indication. On older model compasses speed and latitude were compensated for by applying a torque which could be set by hand, and, generally by moving pointers along speed and latitude scales. Course was compensated for by the use of a built in cosine cam automatically driven by the compass itself. On the Mark 19, and other new models no insertion of latitude and speed correction by the navigator is necessary. The control cabinet contains a computer (Figure 934), which generates en electrical signal to torque the gyro. The computer has an input for speed directly from the pit log or EM log, and heading generated by the compass itself. The computer, properly set for latitude when started, pro-

Latitude, speed, and course correction.

Applying corrections.

Figure 934:
Computer
indicators.

duces a constant readout of latitude and an electrical compensating torque to the gyroscope.

Sperry Mark 11 Mod 6 gyrocompass.

935. This gyrocompass is used aboard many destroyers. The complete system consists of the master compass, the control system, alarm system, follow-up system, the transmission system, and repeaters. The master compass includes five major components: sensitive element, mercury ballistic, phantom element, spider, and binnacle and gimbal rings. The mounting arrangement within the binnacle is illustrated in Figure 935. The sensitive element is the north-seeking element. The mercury ballistic is the group of parts which applies the gravity controlling force, and makes the compass north-seeking. The phantom element is a group of parts that acts to support the sensitive element. The spider is a circular table of cast aluminum alloy that supports the entire inner, or moving member by means of the hub on which the phantom element rests. The binnacle is the case for the master compass; in it are pivoted the gimbals which support the spider.

Figure 935: Sperry
Mark 11 Mod 6
gyrocompass show-
ing binnacle and
gimbal rings.

Figure 936a: Mark 19 Mod 3 gyrocompass equipment.

936. This is the gyrocompass in general use aboard larger modern naval vessels. It constitutes a system which includes two gyroscopes, the meridian and slave gyros, to which certain control devices have been added. The system's four components are the master compass, the control cabinet, shown in Figure 936a, the compass failure annunciator, and the standby power supply.

Sperry Mark XIX Mod 3 gyrocompass.

The Mark 19 has, within a sensitive element, two gyroscopes. The spin axis of the meridian gyro is aligned with the earth meridian as in any gyro compass. The slave gyro mounted on the same phantom or support has its spin axis oriented in an east-west direction. In addition to indicating the meridian, this arrangement defines the true vertical, useful for fire control and other purposes. This two-gyro arrangement should not be confused with the multiple gyro arrangement originated by Anschutz in Germany, wherein a two- or three-gyro configuration is used to produce heading information.

The force of gravity, instead of acting directly to control the compass, merely acts on a special type of electrolytic bubble level, called the gravity reference, which generates a signal proportional to the tilt of the gyro axle. This signal is used to apply torque electromagnetically about the vertical or horizontal axes to give the compass the desired period and damping. The gyro unit is enclosed in a gyrosphere.

The gyrosphere is the heart of the meridian gyro assembly, as it is the north-seeking component of the compass. It derives its name from the fact that the gyro wheel is mounted within a spherical enclosure. The gyrosphere is immersed in oil, and is of the same specific gravity as the oil. It is therefore in neutral buoyancy, and exerts no load on the vertical bearings, which serve only as guides. This flotation not only reduces pivot friction, but also serves to protect the gyrosphere from destructive shock.

169

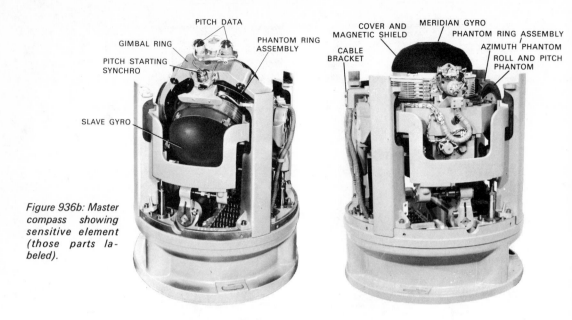

PITCH DATA

GIMBAL RING

PHANTOM RING
ASSEMBLY

PITCH STARTING
SYNCHRO

SLAVE GYRO

COVER AND
MAGNETIC SHIELD

MERIDIAN GYRO

PHANTOM RING ASSEMBLY

AZIMUTH PHANTOM

CABLE
BRACKET

ROLL AND PITCH
PHANTOM

Figure 936b: Master compass showing sensitive element (those parts labeled).

Figure 936b shows the sensitive element in the master compass; the gyrosphere for the meridian gyro in the upper part of the sensitive element, and that for the slave gyro in the lower portion.

Sperry Mark XXIII Mod O gyrocompass.

937. This instrument was designed as a small compass capable of withstanding the severe operating conditions encountered by amphibious craft, such as LSTs, without sacrificing the primary function of furnishing accurate heading data. It is also used as an auxiliary compass aboard larger ships. It combines electronic compass control and oil flotation, and uses an electronic control to make it north-seeking.

The electrolytic bubble level is used to sense the force of gravity in the same manner as on the Mark 19 compass.

Figure 937: Sperry Mark 23 Mod O gyrocompass.

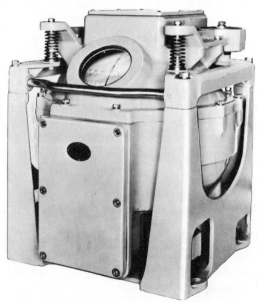

938. The gyrocompass has the following advantages over the magnetic com- *Advantages.*
pass:

It seeks the true meridian instead of the magnetic meridian.

It can be used near the earth's magnetic poles, when the magnetic compass is useless.

It is not affected by surrounding magnetic material which might seriously reduce the directive force of the magnetic compass.

It is preferable to the magnetic compass for use in connection with fire control equipment, dead reckoning equipment, course recording and automatic steering devices.

939. In spite of the many advantages and undoubted capabilities of a modern *Limitations.*
gyrocompass, there are certain disadvantages inherent in its design:

It requires a constant source of electrical power.

It requires intelligent care and attention if it is to give the kind of service of which it is inherently capable.

The accuracy decreases with increased latitude above 75 degrees.

Despite these limitations, the modern gyrocompass, if given proper attention, will render reliable and satisfactory service. This should not cause the navigating officer to neglect his magnetic compass. When the gyrocompass does fail, as any intricate instrument may, the prudent navigator who has a properly adjusted magnetic compass, with an accurate deviation table, will be well repaid for his efforts.

940. When a gyrocompass is mounted on land, it is affected only by gravity *Errors.*
and the earth's motion. When it is mounted in a ship at sea, consideration must be given to additional factors due to motions of the ship such as roll, pitch, turning, speed over the ground, course being steered, and the latitude. The effect of these factors differs in compasses of different basic design. Reference should be made to the appropriate instruction books for a detailed exposition of the theory of a particular compass design, including a description of the automatic and manual error-corrective features incorporated in the design.

941. Even after all the corrections have been made, a gyrocompass is not *Accuracy.*
perfect. However, the error of a modern, properly adjusted gyrocompass seldom exceeds 1°, and is usually such a small fraction of this that for practical purposes it can be considered zero. This does not mean that it must not be checked frequently. A small error carried for a long time will take a ship far to one side of the desired objective. Large errors introduced by temporary mechanical failure, when undetected, have meant disaster.

942. Whenever a new course is set, and at regular intervals thereafter, the mag- *Comparing gyro*
netic compass, master gyrocompass, and gyro repeaters should be compared. *and magnetic*
A record of these comparisons should be kept in a compass comparison book. *compasses.*
Any erratic operation of either gyrocompass, or the getting out of step of either steering repeater, will be apparent at once by such comparisons.

943. The compass card (Figure 943) is attached to or actuated by the sensitive *Determing gyro*
element and is graduated in degrees from 0° to 360°. The direction of the ship's *error.*

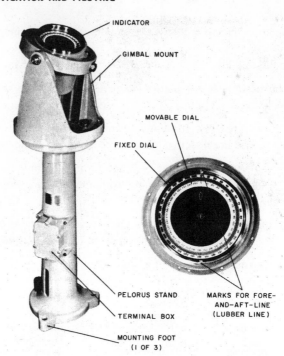

INDICATOR

GIMBAL MOUNT

MOVABLE DIAL

FIXED DIAL

PELORUS STAND

TERMINAL BOX

MARKS FOR FORE-
AND-AFT-LINE
(LUBBER LINE)

MOUNTING FOOT
(1 OF 3)

Figure 943:
Gyro repeater.

head is indicated by the *lubber's line*, a vertical line on the compass housing exactly aligned in the fore and aft axis of the ship. As the ship turns, the lubber's line turns with it so that the changing heading is properly indicated on the card. *It is the lubber's line and not the compass card* which actually turns. The 0° point on the card always points toward true north if there is no compass error. If there is compass error, the 0° point on the compass will not indicate true north but a direction either to the left or to the right of the meridian. If the 0° point is to the left or west of the meridian, gyro error (GE) is the numerical difference between the two directions and is labeled west (W). If the 0° point is to the right or east of the meridian, gyro error is again the numerical difference between the two directions and is labeled east (E).

Navy Regulations require that, when the ship is under way, the navigator determine the error of the gyrocompass at least once each day. Over and above this bare minimum, the prudent navigator will take advantage of every opportunity to check the accuracy of his gyro. The importance of so doing is emphasized by a grounding case on record where the failure of a ship's gyro went undetected for a period of over twelve hours, with the result that, at the time of grounding, the vessel was more than 110° off course and more than 200 miles from the DR position.

There are several methods of checking the accuracy of a gyrocompass, the most important of which are summarized and briefly discussed as follows:

By comparing the observed gyro bearing of an artificial or natural range with the charted true bearing of the range. When entering or leaving a port, the method of checking the gyrocompass by ranges should be used regularly, as the varying speed of the ship, even though compensated for by the proper setting of the speed corrector, causes the compass to oscillate to a certain extent across the meridian. This makes it necessary for the navigator to be constantly on the alert to note in which direction and by what amount his compass is swinging off, and to correct his bearings accordingly.

By comparing the gyro bearing of an object ashore with the charted true bearing of the same object from a fixed position. The fixed position is obtained by means of the three-point problem using a sextant and a 3-arm protractor. The right and left angles for any three well-defined objects are taken with the sextant at the gyro repeater which is to be used in the checking. At the same time, the bearings of the three objects are taken with the repeater. By means of the sextant angles set on the 3-arm protractor, the position of the ship at the time of observation can be accurately plotted on the chart. From this position, the bearings of the three objects can be found by plotting. A comparison of the bearings so found, with the bearing taken by the repeater, shows the error of the compass. Be sure to check the repeater with the master gyro each time a set of checking observations is made.

By comparing the gyro bearing of a celestial body, usually the sun, with the computed true bearing (azimuth) of the same body. At sea, the azimuth method is the only one available and any time a sight of a celestial body is taken for a line of position, the bearing of the body observed may be taken at the same instant. Azimuths of the sun, when the altitude is low in the early morning and late evening, are particularly useful for this purpose. The azimuth obtained by computation, when compared with the gyro azimuth, gives a check on the accuracy of the compass. Polaris is very useful for checking the azimuth at night in low northern latitudes.

By "trial and error" adjustment of the observed bearings of three or more lines of position obtained on charted objects equally spaced around the ship until a point fix results. Take three bearings with the repeater and plot them on the chart. If they meet in a point, the repeater is "on" and there is no gyro error. If the three lines form a triangle, the lines can be adjusted to meet in a point by trial and error; that is, 1° is added to or subtracted from each bearing, and they are again plotted. If the size of the triangle is reduced, the proper estimate of the direction of the error has been made, and after a sufficient correction is applied, the lines should meet in a point. When they do meet, the total amount of correction applied to any one bearing is the error of the compass.

By comparison with a compass of known error, as for example, a standby gyro compared with a master gyro. If a compass of known error be compared with one whose error is to be determined, the comparison of the unknown to the standard will indicate the error of the former. This comparison is generally only possible in ships having two gyrocompasses installed aboard.

As previously mentioned, error as determined using one of these methods is known as *westerly* or *easterly* gyro error, depending upon its direction. If the 0° point on the compass card is to the *west* of true north, the card has been rotated counter-clockwise and all readings of course and bearing made with this error will be too high. If the 0° point on the compass card is to the *east* of true north, the card has been rotated clockwise and all readings will be too low. The principles of applying compass error to obtain true course and bearing hold true both for the application of magnetic compass error discussed in article 917, and for the application of gyro error discussed in the next article.

Applying gyro error.   **944.** By one of the several methods available to the navigator, it is a relatively simple process to determine the numerical value of gyro error using simple arithmetic. The difficulty arises in determining the sign or *label* of the error, and in its subsequent application. The two basic rules to follow in this process can be stated as follows:

> When converting from gyro to true, *add* easterly gyro error and, conversely,

> When converting from gyro to true, *subtract* westerly gyro error. Reference to the following examples will explain the principles involved.

Example 1: Two beacons in line are sighted with a gyrocompass repeater, and found to be bearing 136°.5 per gyro compass. According to the chart, the bearing of these beacons when in line is 138° true.

Required: The gyro error (GE).

Solution: Numerically, the gyro error is the difference between gyro and true bearings of the objects in range, or 138° − 136°.5 = 1°.5. Since this 1°.5 would have to be added to the gyro bearing to obtain true bearing, the direction of the error is easterly.

Answer: GE 1°.5 E.

Example 2: A light ashore is sighted, and by gyrocompass repeater is observed to bear 310°.0 per gyrocompass. From the ship's fixed position, the charted true bearing of the light is measured as 308°.5 true.

Required: The gyro error (GE).

Solution: As before, the gyro error is the difference between the gyro and the true bearing, or 310° − 308°.5 = 1°.5. Since this 1°.5 would have to be subtracted from the gyro bearing to obtain true bearing, and since westerly errors are subtractive, the direction of the error is westerly.

Answer: GE 1°.5 W.

Example 3: A round of gyro bearings was taken on three terrestrial objects with results as follows:

Tower:	058°.0
Light:	183'.0
Beacon:	310°.0

The three lines of position, when plotted, formed a small triangle. By trial and error, it was found that when 2°.0 was *added* to each bearing, a point fix resulted.

Required: The gyro error (GE).

Solution: Since 2°.0 had to be added to each bearing to obtain a perfect fix, and since easterly errors are additive, the gyro error is 2°.0 E.

Answer: GE 2°.0 E.

Example 4: A ship is heading 130° per gyrocompass (GH). The gyro error (GE) is 1° E.

174   *Required:* The true heading (TH).

Solution: Since error is easterly, it must be added. Hence the true heading is $130° + 1° = 131°$.

Answer: TH 131°.

Example 5: A ship is heading 020° per gyrocompass. The gyro error is 1° W.

Required: the true heading.

Solution: Since the error is west it must be subtracted. Hence, the true heading is $020° - 1° = 019°$.

Answer: TH 019°.

Example 6: From a chart the true course between two places is found to be 151°; the GE is 1° E.

Required: The heading per gyro compass to steer 151° true.

Solution: Since easterly errors are added to gyro to obtain true, they must be subtracted when converting from true to gyro, or $151° - 1° = 150°$.

Answer: GH 150°.

A rule-of-thumb sometimes used as a memory aid in applying compass error is:

> **"Error east, compass least:**
> **error west, compass best."**

Another such aid combines the first letters of the words Gyro Error True to form the one word **GET.** In applying the gyro error to gyro heading to obtain true heading, add easterly error and subtract westerly error, or in abbreviated form: $G + E = T$, where G represents gyro heading or gyro bearing, E represents *easterly* gyro error and T represents true heading or true bearing respectively. Westerly error, of course, reverses the sign in the expression.

945. Primary emphasis in this section has been placed on the basic concept of *Summary.* the gyro and the determination of errors affecting the accuracy of the gyrocompass, and their application once the errors are known. When properly operated, serviced, and maintained, the gyrocompass is an extremely accurate instrument, but as is the case with all such instruments it is subject to failure and error. Total failure of the gyrocompass is immediately evident and corrective measures can be taken quickly to eliminate the trouble, or to shift to the stand-by compass. Even with known error, the gyrocompass is eminently serviceable, since account can be taken of this error, and correction to course and bearing can be applied accordingly. It is the unknown error which contributes to marine disasters, particularly so in those instances in which the dead reckoning plot was laid in navigable water whereas the actual track finally terminated at the point of grounding. For example, were a ship to have an undetected error in its gyrocompass of 2° during a 24-hour run at 18 knots, the 24-hour DR position would be in error by more than 15 miles, a margin which, if planned to clear a charted reef, might not be sufficient.

The gyrocompass is a tool of the navigator and, as with any other tool, it demands intelligent operation to obtain the accurate directional reference which it is designed to supply.

CHAPTER 10

The Navigator's Instruments

Introduction. **1001.** Navigation is both a science and an art, and the navigator must be both a scientist and practitioner in the performance of his duties. This chapter will describe some of the instruments and devices available to the navigator in his practice of the science and art of navigation. These are the tools of his profession, which he uses in determining the position of his ship and in guiding it safely on its way.

Navigational instruments may be classified in various ways, any of which will result in some overlap. They will be considered here in groups according to their primary purpose—for measuring *direction, distance* and *speed; depth; weather conditions;* for *plotting;* and for *miscellaneous* use. Other chapters discuss aids to navigation, such as buoys and lights, the publications, and the sextant and chronometer used in celestial navigation.

DIRECTION

Compasses. **1002.** The two general types of compasses are: *magnetic compass,* which depends on the earth's magnetic field for its directive force; and *gyrocompass,* which depends on the mechanical or electrical torquing of a gyroscope to align its axis with that of the earth. Marine compasses were discussed in Chapter 9.

Gyrocompass repeaters. **1003.** A gyrocompass transmits constant indications of true headings electrically to *gyrocompass repeaters* located at various positions throughout the ship. It resembles a magnetic compass in appearance, but unlike a magnetic compass it may be mounted in any position.

Azimuth circle. **1004.** The term *azimuth,* as generally used, means the *bearing* of a celestial body. The terms *azimuth* and *bearing* are often used interchangeably to mean the *direction* of an object from the observer. It is expressed in degrees, using three digits, from 000° at north clockwise through 360°. True azimuth or bearing refers to the direction with respect to true north, magnetic azimuth with respect to magnetic north, and compass azimuth as measured by a magnetic compass. A *relative* bearing or azimuth is reckoned from the ship's head, measuring clockwise with 000° being dead ahead.

An *azimuth circle* is an instrument for determining both *bearings* of terrestrial objects and *azimuths* of celestial objects. It consists of a non-magnetic ring, formed to fit snugly over the compass bowl, about which it can be turned to any desired direction. Its inner lip is graduated from 0° to 360°, *counterclockwise,* for measuring relative bearings. On one diameter of this ring is mounted a pair of sighting vanes, consisting of a peep vane at one end of the diameter and a vertical wire mounted in a suitable frame at the other end. To observe the bearing of a terrestrial object the observer looks through the peep vane in the direction of the object and by means of the finger lugs provided on the circle, he turns the latter until the observed object appears on the vertical wire of the opposite vane. At the base of the opposite vane is a mirror marked with a center line agreeing with the vertical wire of the vane. This mirror reflects the compass card into the field of view of the observer so that he can see the observed object and the compass card at the same time. The compass bearing of the observed object is then read by the position of the vertical wire on the compass card.

The pair of sighting vanes carries a reflector of dark glass attached to the far vane (called *far* vane because it is *farther* from the eye, in observing, than the peep vane). The reflector is movable about a horizontal axis, enabling the observer to adjust it so that the reflected image of a celestial body can be brought to his eye, and a compass azimuth obtained as has been described for a terrestrial object.

At right angles to the line of sight of the vanes there is placed a second set of observing devices, designed especially for obtaining the compass azimuth of the sun. At one extremity of the diameter on which these appliances are mounted is a 45° reflecting prism encased in a metal housing. This housing is provided with a narrow slit in which light may be received from a concave mirror diametrically opposite, the slit being in the focus of the concave mirror. Light so received is reflected downward by the prism and appears on the graduations of the compass card as a bright narrow band. To observe the compass bearing of the sun with this arrangement the observer turns the azimuth circle until the sun's rays are reflected by the mirror across the card to the prism, when the bearing can be read on the compass card by means of the narrow band of light.

Figure 1004:
Azimuth circle to fit
Navy 7 1/2-inch
standard compass.

Two leveling bubbles are provided, for the azimuth circle should be truly horizontal at the moment of observation if accurate azimuths or bearings are to be obtained.

Relative bearings or azimuths can be obtained by reading the graduations of the azimuth circle against a mark on the bezel ring, colinear with the lubber's line of the compass. An azimuth circle is shown in Figure 1004.

An azimuth circle without the prism-mirror appliance for sun observation is called a *bearing circle.* It serves the same purpose as an azimuth circle except that azimuths of the sun are not as conveniently measured.

Telescopic alidade.

1005. A *telescopic alidade* is similar to a bearing circle except that the azimuth circle mounts a telescope instead of the sighting vanes. The telescope contains a reticle for greater precision in taking bearings. The image is magnified, making distant objects appear larger to the observer. A prism arrangement which reflects the bearing of the object from the compass card enables the observer to sight the object and its bearing simultaneously.

Self-synchronous alidade.

Because of the constant motion of the ship, it is sometimes difficult to keep an object in the telescopic field of vision. This problem has been overcome by development of the self-synchronous alidade illustrated in Figure 1005. The self-synchronous alidade is mounted on a gyro repeater card and is stabilized by a synchro-motor driven by the master gyrocompass. Once it is set to a true bearing it remains fixed in this direction until reset. Accurate bearings can be obtained far more easily than with previous equipment especially when a ship is yawing badly, or on a dark night when there is no horizon for a visual reference.

Figure 1005: Self-synchronous alidade.

Figure 1006: A pelorus.

Pelorus.

1006. Since a clear view in all directions may be unobtainable from the compass, *peloruses* (Figure 1006) or dumb compasses may be mounted at convenient points, such as the wings of the bridge. In most modern installations, a gyro repeater is mounted in the pelorus stand in place of the pelorus card so that gyro bearings can be obtained directly; this unit is also called a *pelorus.*

A pelorus consists essentially of a flat, non-magnetic, metallic ring mounted in gimbals on a vertical stand. The inner edge of the ring is graduated in degrees from 0° at the ship's head clockwise through 360°. This ring snugly encloses a compass card called a *pelorus card.* The card, flush with the ring and the top of the bowl, is rotatable, so that any chosen degree of its graduation may be set to the lubber's line. A small set screw is provided for temporarily securing the card to the ring. Upon the card is mounted a pair of sighting vanes similar to those of a bearing circle. They may be revolved about the center of the card, *independently of the card itself,* and held in any desired position by a central clamp screw. On some models an electric light inside the stand illuminates the card from underneath for night work.

True bearings are obtained as follows: set the pelorus to the ship's *true* course, by turning the card until its true-course graduation coincides with the lubber's line. Secure the card. Line up the sighting vanes approximately on the object to be observed. Direct the steersman to sing out "Mark! Mark! Mark!" when he is steady on his steering compass course, and when he does so, take the bearing exactly, and read the degree on the card as indicated by the sighting vanes.

As an alternative method of obtaining a true bearing, the navigator gives the steersman a warning "Stand by!" followed by a "Mark!" at the instant of the observation. If the steersman was on his course, the bearing was *true.* If not, it may be corrected by applying the number of degrees the steersman was off, being careful to apply the correction in the right direction.

Magnetic or compass bearings are taken in exactly the same manner as true bearings, the pelorus card being set beforehand to the magnetic or compass course, respectively. By applying to such bearings the variation or the compass error, as appropriate, they can be converted to true bearings (article 909) for plotting on a chart.

Magnetic bearing.

The pelorus is used for taking relative bearings by setting the 0° graduation of the card to the lubber's line and observing the object. Relative bearings are converted to true bearings for plotting by adding to the bearings observed the true heading of the ship.

SPEED AND DISTANCE

1007. The instrument used to measure the speed of a ship and the distance traveled through the water is called a *log.* Three types are in general use: the pitot-static log, the impeller type, and the electro magnetic (EM) log. These logs all require the use of a *rodmeter* projecting through the bottom of the ship into the water. The rodmeter contains the sensing device used to determine speed. As the rodmeter can be damaged by striking submerged objects, it may be necessary to retract the unit in shallow water. A sea valve forms a support for the rodmeter and provides a means for closing the hull opening when the rodmeter is withdrawn or housed. The various logs have a remotely located *indicator-transmitter* housing the electrical or electro-mechanical parts. The signal received from the sensing device is converted into a readout of speed and distance traveled which can be transmitted by synchronous motors to display units throughout the ship.

Types of logs.

The dead reckoning analyzer (article 1023), the modern gyrocompass, and various navigational computers require an automatic input of speed which is also transmitted from the indicator-transmitter unit.

1008. The rodmeter assembly of the pitot-static log detects both dynamic and static pressure. As a ship moves through the water, the forward side of the rod-

Pitot-static log.

meter is exposed to *dynamic* pressure which is proportional to the speed of the ship. Dynamic pressure is defined as the pressure on a surface at which a flowing fluid is brought to rest in excess of the pressure on it when the fluid is not flowing. The pressure of still water is called *static* pressure. A *pitot tube* is a device by which the difference in dynamic and static pressures may be detected. Obviously, the difference of the two pressures will vary with the speed of the ship. The device consists of two tubes, one inside the other. One tube opens forward and is subjected to dynamic pressure, when the ship is in motion; the other opens athwartship and is exposed only to static pressure.

The control unit for converting the pressure indications into speed units consists of a sensitive bellows arrangement connected to the dynamic and static orifices of the rodmeter. Suitable mechanical and electrical linkage converts the movement of the bellows into rotary motion for transmission to the speed and distance indicators by self-synchronous motors.

Two types differing slightly in construction but using the pitot-static principle are in general use. They are commonly known as the Pitometer Log and the Bendix Underwater Log.

Impeller-type logs. **1009.** The *Impeller Type* Underwater Log System uses a propeller to produce an electrical impulse by which the speed and distance traveled are indicated. The rodmeter head is projected about 2 feet from the vessel through the sea valve. The head assembly contains an 8-pole, two-phase, propeller driven, frequency generator. The impeller is driven by the water as the impeller moves through it. The frequency generated is directly proportional to ship's speed.

The output of the generator is amplified and passed to a master transmitter indicator where the number of alternations, reduced by gears, shows the mileage on a dial. The frequency of the alternating current, being proportional

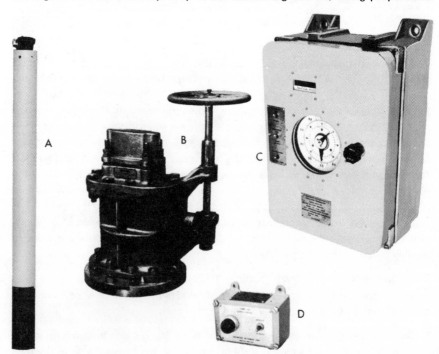

*Figure 1010a:
Underwater log
equipment, electro-
magnetic type,
0–40 knots.*

to the speed of the ship, is transmitted to the tachometer mechanism which indicates the speed of the ship.

The speed and distance readings at the master transmitter indicator are repeated at remote indicators by means of electrical synchro transmission.

1010. The *electro magnetic* (EM) log is generally calibrated for speeds from 0 to 40 knots. Components are shown in Figure 1010a. The rodmeter (A), which can be mounted fixed to the hull, is generally retractable through a sea valve (B), as described in article 1007. It is an induction device which produces a signal voltage that varies with the speed of the ship through the water. Any conductor will produce an electro magnetic field or voltage when it is moved across a magnetic field, or when a magnetic field is moved with respect to the conductor. It is this relative movement of the conductor and the magnetic field producing a measurable induced signal voltage which is used in the EM log. Figure 1010b shows a cutaway view of the sensing unit in the rodmeter. The magnetic field, produced by a coil in the sensing unit, is set up in the water in which the ship is floating. Two Monel buttons, one on each side of the rodmeter, pick up the induced voltage as the ship moves through the water. A complete discussion of the principle involved and instructions for adjustment and repair is included in the manual supplied with each instrument.

Electro magnetic log.

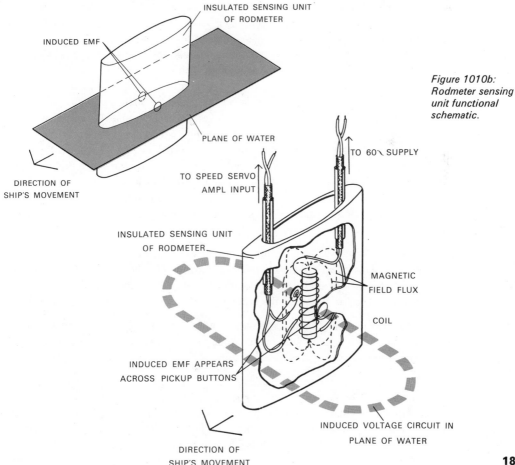

Figure 1010b: Rodmeter sensing unit functional schematic.

The *indicator-transmitter*—labeled (C) in Figure 1010a—contains all the electrical and electromechanical parts of the log except the components in the rodmeter and remote control unit. It indicates the ship's speed on a dial, and operates synchro transmitters to generate corresponding synchro signals for transmission to receivers located elsewhere in the ship. It also registers the number of miles the ship has steamed. Provision is made in the indicator-transmitter for calibrating the log.

The *remote control unit*—labeled (D) in Figure 1010a—is used to set speed into the indicator-transmitter when the equipment is being operated as a dummy log.

In addition to the ship's forward motion, pitching and rolling will produce output signals from the rodmeter, which could lead to a too high indicated speed. Provision is made in the indicator-transmitter so that these undesirable signals can be rejected.

RPM counters.

1011. The *engine revolution counters* provide a convenient means of determining speed and distance. One of these instruments is provided for each propeller shaft in the engine rooms. They automatically count the revolutions of the propellers, and show continuously on their dials the total count. By means of a master counter, connected to the individual counters, the average revolutions made by all propellers can be obtained. The number of revolutions made during any interval of time can be determined by taking the difference in the readings at the beginning and the end of the interval, and if such difference is divided by the number of revolutions required to drive the ship one mile, then the distance traveled in miles is obtained. The records of the acceptance speed trials of a ship furnish data as to the revolutions required for a mile, as well as revolutions per minute (RPM) for various speeds. Such data can also be derived from trial runs made by the ship over a measured mile, a number of which are available for the purpose. This information is used to construct a curve with RPM as ordinates and corresponding speed in knots as abscissas. From the curve, a *revolution table* is made out for use on the bridge while under way. It gives the RPM required for each knot of speed. In making use of engine revolutions as speed indicators, the draft of the ship, the condition of its bottom as to cleanliness, and the state of the sea must be considered and corrections applied, if necessary.

The *dummy log* is used underway when the ship's regular log is inoperative, to supply speed information to the Dead Reckoning Tracer (DRT) (article 1023), the gyrocompass and various computers throughout the ship. An estimate of the ship's speed, based on the propeller RPM, is set by hand on the dummy log.

Yacht logs and speedometers.

1012. In yachting circles, the term "log" usually is applied to a device which *indicates distance sailed;* instruments to indicate speed are usually termed *speedometers*.

The log most commonly used aboard small vessels to determine distance traveled is the *taffrail log*. This consists essentially of a rotor, streamed at the end of a braided log line sufficiently far astern to be clear of the wake effect. The log line is connected to an indicating device, usually reading nautical miles and tenths on two separate dials. In sailing ships, this indicator was frequently attached to the taffrail, the hand rail at the after end of the ship, hence the name.

Figure 1012: Yacht speedometer.

Good taffrail logs are quite reliable; although all logs tend to over-read slightly when moving through a head sea, and to under-read with a following sea.

Speedometers aboard small craft are in general actuated by one of three basic types of underwater sensing units: these are the pitot tube, a propeller or rotating device, and a strut or finger, which is deflected as the boat moves through the water.

The pitot tube type has generally been limited to use in fast outboard runabouts, as it lacks sensitivity at the lower speed ranges.

The propeller type, when well designed, has proven very satisfactory; but is subject to fouling by sea weed.

The strut type is the most widely used. The strut at the zero speed position is raked aft at an angle of about 45°, which tends to prevent its being fouled by weed. As the boat moves forward, water pressure tends to deflect the strut; this deflection is sensed and converted to a speed reading. Hydraulic sensing was employed originally, and is still in use. However, the best speedometers today use electric sensing, which is ultra-sensitive. A speedometer of the latter type is illustrated in Figure 1012, which shows the strut and sensing element, the speed readout, and the control box. This latter unit permits calibration adjustment, a switch for expanding the readout, so that the most minute changes of speed may be read, and a damping control for use in rough seas.

The speedometer illustrated is the KMX, manufactured by Kenyon Marine, Guilford, Connecticut.

Most manufacturers of high quality yacht speedometers also produce distance measuring logs for use with their speedometers. These integrate speed readings, and convert them to distance traveled.

Stadimeters.

1013. The *stadimeter* is an instrument for measuring the distance of objects of known heights, between 50 and 200 feet, covering ranges from 200 to 10,000 yards. Other ranges can be measured by using a scale factor for the graduations. The two general types in use, the Fisk and the Brandon sextant type, are illustrated in Figure 1013.

Figure 1013: Sta-dimeters. Brandon sextant type (on right); Fisk type (on left).

The Fisk type stadimeter consists of a rectangular metal frame upon which is pivoted an index arm graduated in feet. The arm bears an index mirror directly above the pivot. By moving the arm this mirror is rotated through a small arc, providing the necessary adjustment between the direct and reflected images as viewed through the sighting telescope. The stadimeter measures the angle sub-tended by the object of known height, and converts it into range, which is read directly from a micrometer drum attached to a pointer which moves the index arm. The instrument is initially set for the known height of the object by moving the carriage holding the drum and pointer along the index arm. The drum is then turned until the top of the reflected image is brought into co-incidence with the bottom of the direct image, and the range read.

The Brandon sextant type stadimeter uses the same principle as the Fisk type, but the construction is different. The frame, similar in appearance to a sextant frame, has mounted upon it two pivoted arms, the index arm and radius arm. The index arm bears the index mirror directly above the pivot. Rotation of the micrometer drum moves the index arm, accomplishing the rotation of the index mirror necessary for the desired coincidence of images.

The adjustment of the stadimeter is similar to that of a sextant as described in Chapter 22.

Distances of objects can also be ascertained by determining the angle subtended by an object of known height, as measured by a sextant. The angle so measured can be converted to distance by means of trigonometry or Table 9, Bowditch.

DEPTH

1014. The *lead*, for ascertaining the depth of water, consists essentially of a lead weight attached to one end of a suitably marked line. It is an invaluable aid to the navigator in shallow water, particularly in thick or foggy weather, and may be of service when the vessel is out of sight of land.

Hand lead and deep sea lead.

Two leads are used for soundings: the hand lead, weighing from 7 to 14 pounds, with a line marked to about 25 fathoms; and the deep-sea lead, weighing from 30 to 100 pounds, the line being 100 fathoms or upward in length.

Lines are generally marked as follows:	*Metric Equivalent*
2 fathoms from the lead, with 2 strips of leather	3.66
3 fathoms from the lead, with 3 strips of leather	5.49
5 fathoms from the lead, with a white rag	9.14
7 fathoms from the lead, with a red rag	12.80
10 fathoms from the lead, with leather having a hole in it	18.29
13 fathoms from the lead, same as at 3 fathoms	23.77
15 fathoms from the lead, same as at 5 fathoms	27.43
17 fathoms from the lead, same as at 7 fathoms	31.09
20 fathoms from the lead, a line with 2 knots	36.58
25 fathoms from the lead, a line with 1 knot	45.72
30 fathoms from the lead, a line with 3 knots	54.86
35 fathoms from the lead, a line with 1 knot	64.01
40 fathoms from the lead, a line with 4 knots	73.15

Fathoms which correspond with the depths marked are called *marks* and intermediate fathoms are called *deeps*. The only fractions of a fathom used are a half and a quarter.

A practice sometimes followed is to mark the hand lead line in feet at the critical depths of the vessel using it.

Lead lines should be measured frequently while wet and the correctness of the marking verified. The distance from the leadsman's hand to the water's edge should be ascertained in order that proper allowance may be made in taking soundings at night.

The deep-sea lead may be *armed* by filling its hollow lower end with tallow or salt water soap, by which means a sample of the bottom sediment is brought up.

1015. A sound generated in the water will echo from the bottom and can be received by a microphone. Since the approximate speed of sound in water is known, the depth can be determined by measuring the time interval between the generation of the sound and the return of the echo, according to the formula, depth = speed $\times \frac{1}{2}$ time interval between sound and echo.

Echo sounder.

Figure 1015a: AN/ UQN-1 Echo Sounder.

The speed of sound waves in water varies with temperature, salinity, and pressure; but an average value of 4,800 feet per second is sufficiently accurate for navigational depth finding. This being equivalent to 800 fathoms per second, an elapsed time of one second would indicate a depth of 400 fathoms.

The essential parts of an echo sounder are a transmitter, a receiver, and a depth indicator. Echo sounders fall into two general classes, (1) sonic, those using sound waves in the audible range and (2) ultrasonic, those using sound waves in the high pitch range above audibility. In the first category, the sound is produced mechanically or by an oscillator, which is a diaphragm built into the

Figure 1015b: Depth recording on three scales, showing a steady decrease in depth.

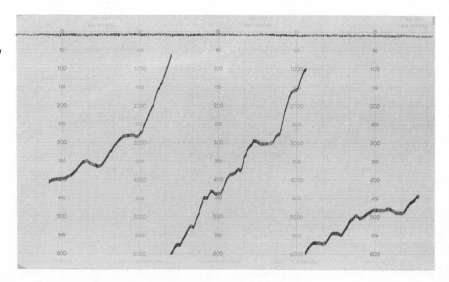

ship's bottom. The echo is received by a microphone, amplified, and the energy thus obtained is used to flash a lamp in the depth indicator. In the second type, a diaphragm in contact with the water is vibrated by the contraction of quartz crystals in an electric circuit. The same diaphragm is used to receive the echo, which is amplified and fed into the depth indicator.

Echo sounders vary greatly in detail, but all operate on the same principle and measure the elapsed time for a signal to go to the bottom and echo back. A shaft driven by a constant speed motor carries a contact maker and a device on an arm to illuminate the depth scale. The illuminating device, thus traveling in a circle, is just under a transparent scale graduated in fathoms or feet. When the arm passes under the zero of the scale, the contact maker closes and the signal is transmitted. When the echo is received a flash of light is thrown on the scale, indicating the depth.

Many echo sounding instruments are also equipped to record the depth graphically, usually by means of a hot stylus and sensitized paper. The AN/UQN-1 installed aboard many vessels is such an instrument. With this instrument, the operator has a choice of two indicators or direct depth readouts, one to a maximum depth of 100 feet, and the other to 100 fathoms. Alternately, he has the choice of three graphic or recorder readouts, these depth ranges being to 600 feet, 600 fathoms, or 6,000 fathoms. Figure 1015b illustrates depths recorded on these three scales. The trace of the outgoing pulse, generated by the instrument, is the horizontal trace at the top of the paper.

A new precision echo sounder, the AN/UQN-4, is described in article 4103.

PLOTTING EQUIPMENT

1016. Most lines on a chart are ruled by means of a straightedge. Because *Plotting tools.* of the width of the pencil lead and the conical shape of the sharpened end, the line ruled on the chart is some distance from the straightedge. Allowance for this distance must be made when placing the straightedge in position. The actual amount is easily determined by trial and error under any given circumstances. The important point to remember is that the pencil must make the same angle with respect to the straightedge throughout the length of the line.

Use No. 2 pencils for plotting and keep a number of them handy, well sharpened. Draw only light lines on the chart, so that they can be easily erased. Avoid drawing lines longer than necessary and erase extra lengths. Label all lines and points as soon as drawn. An unlabeled line on a chart is a possible source of error. Avoid drawing lines through chart symbols for navigational aids, so that the symbols will not be rendered indistinct when the line is erased.

An art gum eraser is best for cleaning the chart. An additional soft eraser should be used for making small erasures.

1017. Dividers are frequently used by the navigator. He keeps them handy for *Dividers.* immediate use, primarily for measuring distance on the chart, but they have many other uses, also.

Learn to use the dividers with one hand, keeping the other hand free for other purposes. With a little practice this can be done easily and it will speed up plotting considerably. The dividers should be tight enough to remain as set, but not so tight that setting is difficult. If there is any choice of dividers, pick

187

a pair with long legs, so that considerable distances can be measured with one setting.

Compasses.

1018. Compasses are convenient for drawing distance circles. They are used most frequently for drawing in computed visibility circles of lights, but they are also useful in drawing circles of position when the range of an object is known, for drawing circles of position for high altitude celestial observations, and other purposes.

The statement regarding the use, adjustment, and selection of dividers applies also to compasses. The navigators of naval vessels are provided with a "navigator's case" containing a pair of dividers and compasses.

Parallel rulers.

1019. Although various types of plotters have appeared, and some of these are widely used, parallel rulers are still a widely used instrument for measuring direction on a chart. Several types of parallel rulers are available. The best known consists of two bars of the same length connected in such a manner that when one is held in place on the chart and the other moved, it will move parallel to itself, or to its original direction.

Parallel rulers are used for drawing straight lines, moving lines parallel to themselves, as in advancing lines of position, and for measuring direction. When the direction of a line is to be measured, the line is moved parallel to itself to the center of a *compass rose* and its direction is read from the graduations of the compass rose. To measure a given direction from a point, the direction is transferred from the compass rose to the point.

Plotters.

1020. Parallel rulers are somewhat slow and it is sometimes difficult to keep them from slipping when a direction is to be moved a considerable distance across the chart. Moreover, they are of little value for measuring direction when

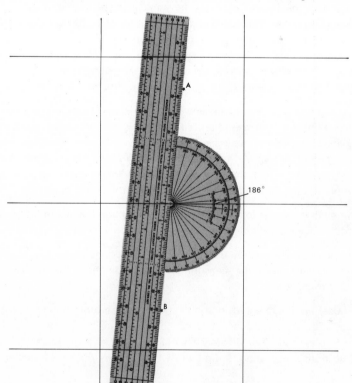

Figure 1020a:
Mk II Plotter.

186°

no compass rose is shown on the chart, as on those of the Lambert conformal projection.

For these reasons and as a matter of personal preference, many navigators use one of the many plotters that are available. Most of these consist of some form of protractor and a straightedge.

One of the most commonly used plotters is the *Weems Mark II* (Federal Stock Catalog No. FSN 6605-693-8388). It is a plotter-protractor of 180°, mounted on a scaled straight edge, intended primarily for measuring courses or bearings relative to a meridian. An auxiliary scale is included, which permits measuring from a parallel.

In Figure 1020a this auxiliary scale is being used on a parallel of latitude to measure a true course from *A* to *B* of 186°. The Mark II Plotter was designed primarily for aircraft use; it can be used on any chart or on the Universal Plotting Chart which contains distance scales to match. A similar plotter, the No. 641, contains distance scales at 20 miles per inch matching the Oceanographic Office Universal Plotting Charts.

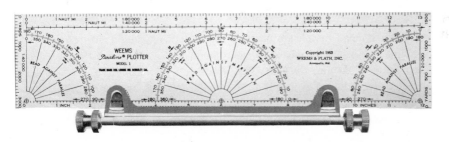

Figure 1020b: Weems Paraline Plotter.

The *Paraline Plotter*, Figure 1020b, is a comparatively new plotter-protractor, which may be used either as a plotter, or roller-type parallel ruler. It is gaining favor rapidly for use aboard small craft, and has been adopted by the U. S. Coast Guard. Its Federal Stock Catalog No. is CG-6605-600-2320.

A pair of ordinary draftsman's triangles are also often useful in plotting.

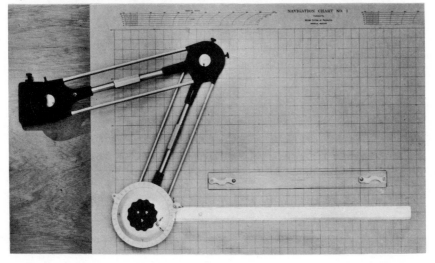

Figure 1021: Universal drafting machine.

189

Universal drafting machine.

1021. Chart plotting is done on most large naval ships by means of a drafting machine, one type of which is illustrated in Figure 1021.

The instrument consists of a protractor carried by a parallel-motion system fastened to the upper left-hand corner of the chart table. The linkage permits the movement of the protractor to any part of the chart without change of orientation. Several graduated rulers of different length are provided. On some models any two of these can be mounted, one as shown and the other at right angles to the first, to facilitate plotting of lines of position from celestial observations. However, most navigators prefer to use a right triangle to obtain the perpendicular. The graduated protractor rim, or compass rose, can be rotated and clamped in any position desired. Hence, it can be oriented to directions on the chart.

Protractors.

1022. While not essential, a common protractor is sometimes useful for measuring angles. Any type will do, but a fairly large one made of transparent plastic is most desirable. A special type of protractor with three arms is useful for plotting the position of a ship. The middle arm is fixed and the others movable so that they can be set at essentially any angle to the fixed arm. A complete description of this instrument and the method of using it is given in article 1110; the instrument is illustrated in Figure 1110a.

Dead reckoning equipment

1023. Most naval vessels are supplied with a dead reckoning electromechanical computer. The basic part of this equipment is the *analyzer* (DRA); heading information is fed into the DRA from the ship's gyro compass, and speed information is supplied by the log. The speed input is integrated with time to read distance. The DRA has three readouts: miles steamed north or south, miles steamed east or west, and total number of miles steamed.

Some DRAs also give latitude and longitude readouts, in which case they are

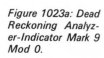

Figure 1023a: Dead Reckoning Analyzer-Indicator Mark 9 Mod 0.

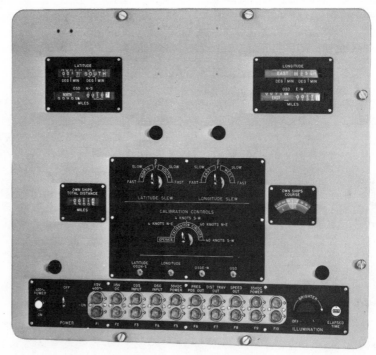

usually called Dead Reckoning Analyzer-Indicator (DRAI). A Mark 9 Mod 0 DRAI is shown in Figure 1023a.

The *Dead Reckoning Tracer* (DRT) receives its heading and speed inputs from the DRA, and provides a graphic trace of the ship's travel through the water. Some new models also trace the paths of two or more targets, permitting a constant readout of target range and bearing; target data are supplied from radar or sonar inputs. The DRT permits the choice of one of a number of scales, depending on the tactical situation, and the trace may be on a Mercator chart or a polar coordinate chart. The "own ship" trace may be made by a pencil moved across the chart; alternately the ship's position as well as that of the targets may be indicated by spots of light focused on the chart from under-neath. Such a DRT is shown in Figure 1023b; it is the Mark NC-2, Mod 2 plotting table, designed primarily for use aboard ASW vessels. This plotting table permits a choice of 8 scales, ranging from 200 yards per inch to 5 miles per inch, and gives a plotting area of 30 by 30 inches.

This DRT, like many others, may be used either in the geographical or relative plot mode. In the former, own ship's projected image moves across the chart; in the latter, usually used in tactical problems, own ship remains at the center of the plotting surface, and the tactical situation appears as on a radar PPI display.

In many ships, the DRA is in the chart house, while the DRT is in Combat Information Center. The DRT can be a convenience to the navigator when the ship is manuevering; however, he must bear in mind that it makes no allowance

Figure 1023b: Mark NC-2, Mod 2 Plotting Table.

for current, and in no way relieves him of his responsibility for keeping an accurate check on his position by other means.

Nautical slide rule.

1024. This is a circular plastic slide rule, illustrated in Figure 710a, which is widely employed throughout the Navy for solution of time, distance, and speed problems. Given any two of these factors, the third may be obtained. The time scale gives hours in red figures, and minutes and seconds in black figures. Seconds are shown separately to 120; this scale must be used only for times of 120 seconds or less. Hours and minutes are both stated in units and decimals. If the hour scale is set to 2.5, the minute scale will read 150. Similarly, if the minute scale is set to 1.5, 90 seconds may also be read.

The distance scale gives nautical miles in red figures, and yards in black figures. The latter are stated on the assumption that one nautical mile equals 2,000 yards; this is an assumption frequently used in tactical problems. Therefore, if the distance scale is set at 3 miles, it will also read 6,000 yards. The figures on the distance scale may also be used in solving problems involving statute miles; however, in this case, the yard scale must *not* be used.

In using the slide rule, when the distance is one of the known factors, the distance setting should be made *first*. When speed is a known factor, it should always be set last, as the speed scale is read through both dials.

Conventional slide rule.

1025. A conventional slide rule, particularly one having sine and tangent scales, can be of great assistance to the navigator in solving incidental problems, such as transfer for a given change of course, interpolation, etc.

WEATHER

Barometer.

1026. A *barometer* is an instrument for determining the atmospheric pressure, a meteorological element of considerable interest to a mariner, as its fluctuations provide an index useful in predicting weather, an important factor in navigation and ship handling. Because bad weather is usually associated with regions of low atmospheric pressure and good weather with areas of high pressure, a rapidly falling barometer usually indicates the approach of a storm.

Two general types of barometer are used. The *mercurial* barometer consists essentially of a column of mercury in a tube, the upper end of which is closed and the lower end open to the atmosphere. The height of the column of mercury supported by the atmosphere is read by a suitable scale. Readings are in inches of mercury. The *standard* atmospheric pressure is 29.92 inches.

The *aneroid* barometer consists essentially of a short metal cylinder from which the air has been partly exhausted. The ends of the cylinder, being of thin metal, expand or contract as the external pressure changes. This motion is transferred by a suitable linkage to a registering device which may be graduated in either inches of mercury or *millibars*, a metric unit of measurement. The reading of one scale can be converted to those of the other by table or arithmetically, since 29.92 inches of mercury is equivalent to 1013.2 millibars.

A *barograph* is a self-recording instrument that provides a permanent record of atmospheric pressure over a period of time.

Thermometer.

1027. Temperature is determined by means of a *thermometer*. Shipboard thermometers are generally graduated to the Fahrenheit scale (water freezes at 32° and boils at 212° at standard atmospheric pressure), but aviators sometimes use the Centigrade scale (0° is freezing and 100° boiling). The reading of one can be easily converted to that of the other by means of Table 15, Bowditch, or mathematically, since

$$F° = \tfrac{9}{5} C° + 32°$$

$$C° = \tfrac{5}{9}(F° - 32°)$$

in which F° = degrees Fahrenheit and C° = degrees Centigrade.

Two thermometers are often mounted together in an *instrument shelter*, a wooden box with louvered sides to protect the instruments from direct rays of the sun and other conditions that would render their readings inaccurate. The instrument shelter is installed at some exposed position aboard ship. One of the thermometers has its bulb covered with a wet fabric and the other is exposed to the air. The rate of evaporation of the water is dependent on the *relative humidity* of the air, or the relative amount of water vapor in the air. The evaporating water cools the bulb of the thermometer, resulting in a lower temperature. Knowing the air temperature (reading of the *dry bulb thermometer*) and the difference between this and the reading of the *wet bulb thermometer*, the relative humidity and *dew point* (the temperature to which the air must be cooled for condensation to take place) can be easily determined. Tables for this purpose are given in Bowditch. The wet and dry bulb combination is known as a *pyschrometer*.

1028. An *anemometer* is an instrument for measuring wind force or speed, *Anemometer.* usually in miles per hour. It must be remembered that wind speed measured on a moving ship is *apparent* wind, or wind relative to the moving ship. Apparent wind can be converted to true wind, or vice versa, by means of a simple graphic solution or by tables provided for the purpose.

MISCELLANEOUS EQUIPMENT

1029. A pair of good binoculars is useful in picking up aids to navigation, *Binoculars.* especially small ones such as buoys, and in reading their identifying markings. The navigator should have a pair of binoculars for his own exclusive use, and they should be in a handy location, but sufficiently protected to prevent damage from dropping, being knocked off a table by motion of the ship, or by weather. When they are being used, the strap should be placed around the user's neck. Like the other instruments used by the navigator, binoculars must receive proper care if they are to give reliable service.

The Navy has standardized on 7 × 50 binoculars—glasses with a magnification of 7 powers, and an objective lens 50 mm in diameter. This ratio of magnification to objective diameter permits excellent light gathering characteristics particularly suitable for night use. The less bulky and less costly 6 × 30 binoculars, if manufactured to high standards, are very well adapted to use aboard small craft.

1030. At least one good flashlight should be kept handy for accurate reading *Flashlight.* of the watch and sextant, during twilight observations, if the latter is not equipped with its own readout light, and for timing light characteristics, etc., during the hours of darkness. To protect dark-adapted vision, this flashlight should be equipped with a red bulb, or a red lens. Lacking these, a red plastic or cellophane filter should be fitted.

If accurate twilight or night observations are to be made, the navigator must protect his eyes from any direct light. If no red flashlight is available, the quartermaster who is acting as recorder should stand with his back to the observer, with his light on the watch. If the sextant has no readout light, after the altitude is obtained, it should be handed to the recorder for reading.

Timing devices.

1031. A stopwatch or a navigational timer, which can be started and stopped at will, is of particular value in timing the period of a navigational light to determine its characteristic for purposes of identification. When equipped with a luminous dial and sweep-second hand, the watch may be read without the use of artificial light thereby maintaining night-adapted vision.

Figure 1031: A stop watch and a chronograph containing the split second feature.

Split second timers, sometimes referred to as split action stopwatches, are now available. With this feature the watch continues to run and measure elapsed time; there are, in effect, two second hands that run together. When the side push button on the stop watch is depressed one of these second hands is stopped so that the exact interval can be read from the face of the watch. A second depression of the side push button causes the second hands to run together. This feature is also available on chronographs which can be kept running on GMT with the split second feature being used to determine the exact time of an event, such as celestial sight, without disturbing the time keeping function of the watch.

Summary.

1032. This chapter has classified many of the usual navigation instruments used by the navigator in making his observations. This chapter has not described all of the instruments and equipment with which the navigator must be familiar but only those which *are considered essential to basic instruction* in elementary navigation and those not covered in detail elsewhere in the text. For this reason, instruments of direct concern to celestial navigation are discussed in the celestial navigation section, while various electronic instruments are described in separate chapters. The construction and operation of the gyro and magnetic compasses is described in Chapter 9.

CHAPTER 11

Elements of Piloting

1101. The direction of the movements of a vessel by reference to land and seamarks, by soundings, or by radar, is called piloting. All electronic methods of navigation may, in a broad sense, be considered to be forms of piloting. The electronic methods, including radar, are discussed elsewhere in this text; this chapter deals with visual piloting. *Piloting defined.*

Piloting requires the greatest experience and nicest judgment of any form of navigation. Constant vigilance, unfailing mental alertness, and a thorough knowledge of the principles involved are essential. Mistakes in navigation on the open sea can generally be discovered and corrected before the next landfall. In piloting there is little or no opportunity to correct errors. Even a slight blunder may result in serious disaster involving perhaps the loss of life. The problems of piloting are fundamentally very simple, both in principle and in application. It is the proximity of danger which makes piloting so important. The question of avoiding collision in the heavy traffic of harbors and along coast lines is essentially a problem of *seamanship*. The navigator is concerned with the problem of keeping his ship in navigable waters. Throughout this chapter a deep-draft vessel is visualized. The principles and procedures which will keep sufficient water under the keel of a large vessel will unquestionably bring safety to a smaller one.

In all phases of piloting, the navigator must constantly realize that he is dealing with both the present and the future. He must continually analyze the situation which exists at present to plan for the future. He should constantly use every logical means at his disposal to:

> *obtain warnings* of approaching danger
> *fix the position* of the ship accurately and frequently
> *determine the proper course* of immediate action.

1102. In piloting, as in almost all phases of navigation, the navigator must deal with lines of position. A single observation does not provide a position; it does provide the observer with a line on some point of which he is located. This line is a segment of a great circle but in visual pilotage the segment is relatively so short that it may be plotted as a straight, or rhumb, line on a Mercator chart. In this chapter, only visual lines of position established by various methods will be discussed. *Lines of position (LOP).*

It must be borne in mind that there is no connection between the DR course line and lines of position. The DR course line and DR positions may be considered as statements of *intention*, or a graphic representation of ordered courses and speeds. The lines of position are statements of *fact*, as the ship is actually somewhere on the line of position, regardless of courses steered, and speeds used.

Labeling lines of position.

1103. A single line of position, whether a bearing (article 1105), a range (article 1104) or a distance (article 1106), is labeled on the upper side of the line with the time of observation expressed in four digits. A single line of position advanced to form a running fix (article 1111) is labeled with the original time of observation and the time to which it has been advanced. Simultaneous lines of position forming a fix are not labeled, the time of the fix being sufficient. Similarly the second line of position in a running fix is not labeled, taking its time as that of the running fix.

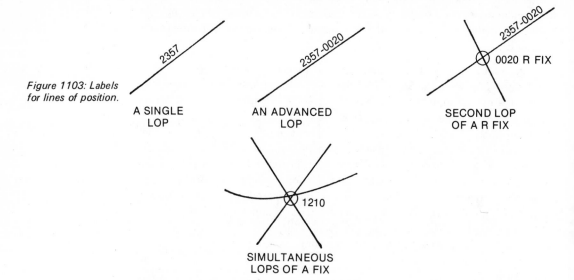

Figure 1103: Labels for lines of position.

A SINGLE
LOP

AN ADVANCED
LOP

SECOND LOP
OF A R FIX

SIMULTANEOUS
LOPS OF A FIX

Every line should be labeled when it is plotted; an unlabeled line can be a source of error. There is enough uncertainty in piloting without adding to it by leaving doubt as to the meaning of a line. Care must be taken not to confuse a course line with a line of position (article 1409).

Observing a range.

1104. The simplest way of establishing a line of position is by observing a range. If two fixed objects of known position appear to the observer to be in line, he must at that instant be somewhere on the line passing through the objects.

Example: (Figure 1104). At 1205 a beacon and stack appear in line. The ship must then be somewhere along the straight line drawn through the symbols for the two objects on the chart.

Draw light lines on the chart and make them no longer than necessary. Particularly avoid drawing them through the chart symbols for aids to navigation, which may be rendered indistinct by erasures. In illustrations for this chapter, broken lines will be extended from the symbols on the chart to illustrate principles. *The solid segment of the line of position is all that is normally plotted on the chart.*

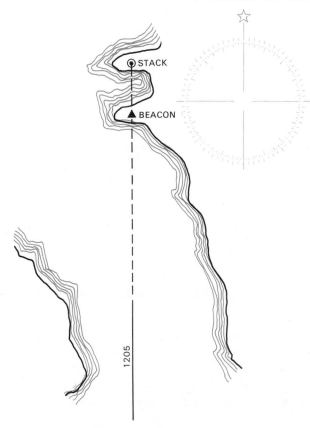

Figure 1104: Plotting the range.

1105. It is not always possible to find two fixed known objects in line at the time the navigator wishes to make an observation. Consequently, the line of position is usually obtained by plotting a *bearing* on the chart. The observer sights across his pelorus, hand bearing compass, bearing circle, or gyro repeater toward a fixed known object and thus determines the direction of the line of sight to the object; this is the *bearing* of the object. He then plots this bearing to the fixed known object on his chart.

Plotting bearings.

Example: (Figure 1105). At 1200 a spire bears 050°. The navigator plots this line as shown; at 1200 the ship must be somewhere on this line.

Figure 1105: A bearing line of position.

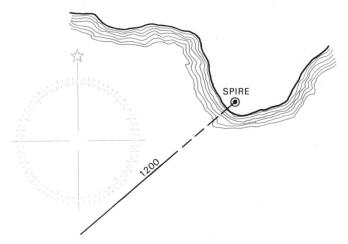

197

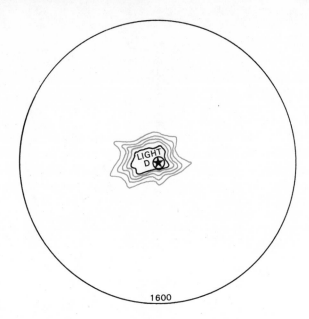

Figure 1106:
A distance circle
of position.

Distance.

1106. If the distance to an object is known, the ship must lie somewhere on a circle centered on the object, and with the known distance as the radius. This circle is termed a *distance circle of position.* Figure 1106 illustrates a distance circle; at 1600, the navigator found the distance of the lighthouse, *D*, to be six miles. Obviously, the ship must be somewhere on a circle of six mile radius, centered on the light. In most cases only a segment of the circle will be drawn on the chart. Distance may be obtained by radar, by range finder, by synchronized radio and air or submarine sound signals, and if the height of the object is known, by stadimeter or sextant; the latter two instruments are used for measuring angles by which distance may be determined. Table 9 in Bowditch permits a rapid solution for sextant angles. If the object observed is a lighthouse, the known height may be stated either as "height above water" or "height of structure"; the angle must be measured accordingly.

A distance circle is frequently combined with a bearing, as described in article 1107 (example 6).

Figure 1107a:
Plotting a fix
by cross bearings.

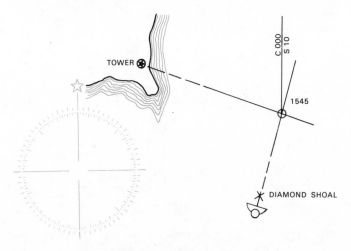

1107. There are an infinite number of possible positions on any single line of *Plotting a fix.*
position; to fix the ship's position the navigator must therefore plot at least
two lines of position which intersect, preferably at angles as nearly 90° as possible. Three or more LOP's should be used whenever possible.

Lines of position can be combined to obtain fixes as follows:

Example 1: Two cross bearings (Figure 1107a). At 1545 a ship steaming on
course 000°, speed 10, observes a tower bearing 288°, and Diamond Shoal
Lightship bearing 194°.

The 1545 fix must lie at the intersection of the two lines of position; it is obtained by plotting the reciprocals of the observed bearings from the symbols
of the tower and lightship on the chart of the area.

The intersection of the two lines of position at the 1545 fix is labeled as shown
in Figure 1107a. A new DR course is then started from this position.

Example 2: Three cross bearings (Figure 1107b). At 1351, with the ship on
course 285°, speed 15 knots, the navigator observes the following bearings by
gyrocompass (gyro error is zero): Left tangent of Smith Point, 005°; left
tangent of Jones Bluff, 130°; Hall Reef Lightship, 265°.

Required: Plot and label the 1351 fix.

Solution: See Figure 1107b.

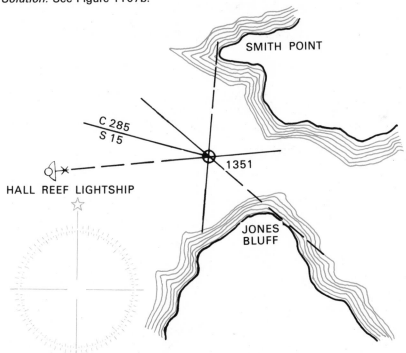

Figure 1107b:
A fix by three
cross bearings.

Note that in Examples (1) and (2) the bearings were taken simultaneously to
obtain the fix, which is often the case in observing terrestrial objects. However,
as will be explained more fully in article 1111, if the bearings are taken at *different* times, they may be adjusted to a common time to determine what is
known as a *running fix.*

199

Example 3: Two ranges. A ship entering a harbor at ten knots steams so as to keep range lights *W* and *X* (Figure 1107c) in line. At 2153, with *W* and *X* exactly in line, light *Y* and Airport Beacon *Z* are observed to be in line and the ship changes course to 057°.

Required: Plot and label the 2153 fix.

Solution: See Figure 1107c. The 2153 fix is at the intersection of the two range lines of position.

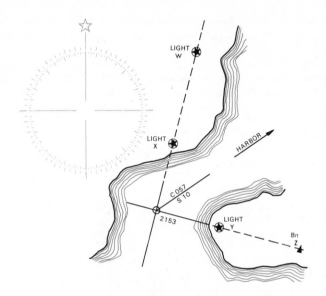

Figure 1107c: A fix by two ranges.

Example 4: One range and a bearing (Figure 1107d). A ship is on course 090°, speed 10 knots. At 1227 Radio Tower *A* and a cupola are in range. At the same time the right tangent of Burke Point bears 057°.

Required: Plot and label the 1227 fix.

Solution: The 1227 fix is at the intersection of the two lines of position.

Figure 1107d: A fix by one range and a bearing.

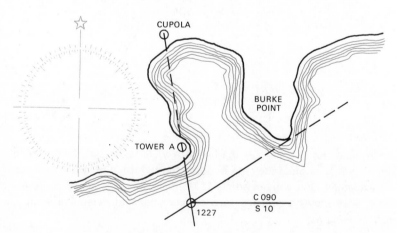

Example 5: Bearing and distance on different objects (Figure 1107e). At 1425 radio tower *A* bears 350 degrees. At the same time, the radar range to Sandy Point Lightship is four miles. The ship is on course 050°, speed 18 knots.

Required: Plot and label the 1425 fix.

Solution: The 1425 fix is at the intersection of the line of position and the distance circle of position.

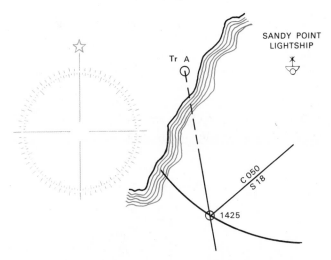

Figure 1107e: A fix by bearing and distance on different objects.

Example 6: Bearing and distance of the same object (Figure 1107f). At 1314, Double Point Lighthouse bears 347°. From a 1314 sextant observation its distance is computed to be 3 miles. Ship is on course 225°, speed 10 knots.

Required: Plot and label the 1314 fix.

Solution: Plot the observed bearing, 347°. With the lighthouse as the center, plot the distance circle of position. The point where the line of position is intersected by the circle of position is the 1314 fix.

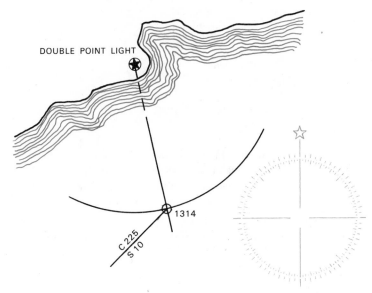

Figure 1107f: A fix by bearing and distance of the same objects.

201

Example 7: Passing close aboard an aid to navigation: The ship's position can also be fixed approximately by passing close aboard a navigational aid, such as a buoy or lightship, the position of which is indicated on the chart. This is a type of fix frequently employed by the navigator when plotting on a small scale chart. The accuracy of a position obtained in this manner depends upon two factors: the accuracy of the measurement of the relationship between the ship and the observed aid, and the amount of displacement between the actual and plotted positions of the aid. This procedure is recommended only when other navigational aids are not available to establish a more accurate position.

Relative bearings.

1108. The *relative bearing* of an object is its direction from the ship, relative to the ship's head. It is the angle between the fore-and-aft line of the ship and the bearing line of the object, measured clockwise from 000° at the ship's head through 360°. In Figure 1108 the relative bearings of objects *A, B, C,* and *D* are 135°, 180°, 270°, and 340°, respectively. The pelorus can be used for taking relative bearings by setting the 000° graduation of the pelorus card to the lubber's line, then observing the object and reading the card. The azimuth circle or the bearing circle are more frequently used, however.

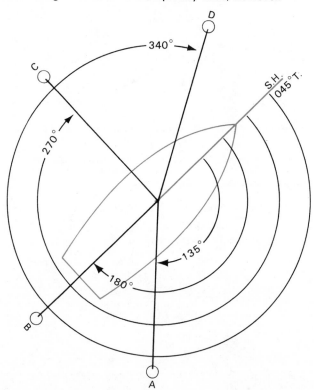

Figure 1108:
Relative bearings.

Frequently in practice, and always before plotting, relative bearings are converted to true bearings. This is done simply by adding to them the ship's true heading when the relative bearings were taken, subtracting 360° if the sum equals or exceeds that amount. Thus, assuming the ship is steady on 045° true during observations, the corresponding true bearings of *A, B, C,* and *D* are 180°, 225°, 315°, and 025°. Conversely, true bearings can be converted to relative bearings by subtracting from them the ship's true heading, first adding 360° if necessary.

1109. When selecting objects from which to obtain a fix, the primary consideration is the angle between the bearings. If only two visual bearings are available, the best fix results from two bearings crossing at 90°, in which case an error in either bearing results in minimal error in the plotted fix. As the angle between the objects decreases, a small error in either bearing throws the fix out by an increasing amount. Bearings of objects intersecting at less than 30° should be used only when no other objects are available, and the resulting fix should be regarded with caution. Figure 1109 illustrates the deterioration in accuracy of a fix caused by a given error in one bearing. *Selecting objects for obtaining a fix.*

To check two bearings and to obviate fix error, three or more bearings should always be taken if possible. If three are taken, the optimum angle is 60° between bearings.

Figure 1109 compares the errors to a fix arising from a 5° error in one bearing, when the observed objects differ 90° in bearing and when they differ 20°. *A*, *B*, and *C* each represent known objects. *O* is the observer's true position. *AOC* = 20°, and *AOB* = 90°. If a 5° error is made in plotting the bearing of *B*, *OX* shows the resulting error; however if a 5° error is made in plotting the bearing of *C*, *OY* is the error.

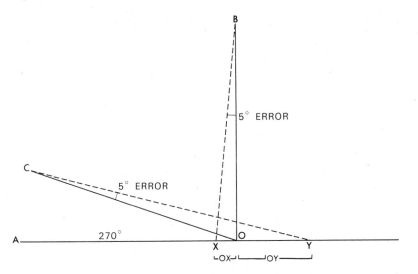

Figure 1109: Fix errors.

5° ERROR IN ANGLE AOB = DISTANCE ERROR OX
5° ERROR IN ANGLE AOC = DISTANCE ERROR OY

1110. This instrument is used in conjunction with the sextant, usually when the ship has no way on, to fix position accurately when three or more fixed and known objects are in view. *The three-arm protractor.*

The protractor, of brass or plastic, consists of a circular scale which can be read to minutes of arc, and to which the three arms are attached (Figure 1110a). The center or index arm is fixed, and the zero graduation of the protractor coincides with the straight edge of this arm. The other arms are rotatable, and can be set and locked at any angle relative to the fixed arm.

To obtain a fix, three fixed objects, which can be identified on the chart, must be visible. The angles between the right and central objects, and the left and central objects, are measured with the sextant. The two movable arms are set to these angles, and locked, and the protractor is placed on the chart, with the index arm passing through the center object. The instrument is now moved slowly across the chart until all three arms are aligned with the three objects. The ship's position may now be marked on the chart with the point of a pencil through the hole at the center of the protractor. Care must be used in selecting the three objects to be observed; if they and the ship all lie on the circumference of a circle, no fix can be obtained. To avoid this possibility, the objects should be so selected, if a choice is available, that the center one is closer to the estimated position than the right and left objects.

Figure 1110a: The 3-arm protractor.

The three-arm protractor gives chart positions of great accuracy; these positions are not affected by any error of the compass. If a three-arm protractor is not available, the method can be used by drawing a straight line on clear plastic or tracing paper, and laying off the two required angles from one end of this line.

On vessels not carrying a sextant the position finder can be substituted, as the accuracy required, for purposes other than surveying, is considerably less than the inherent accuracy of the sextant. The position finder is, in effect, a three-arm protractor with mirrors attached which permit using one instrument for observing and plotting. It is unnecessary to read the value of the angles measured as the plotting arms are properly positioned for plotting when making the observations. Figure 1110b illustrates the optics of the position finder and Figure 1110c shows it positioned on the chart for plotting.

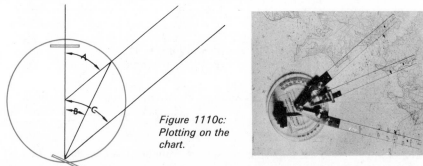

Figure 1110b: Optical principle of position finder.
$B = \frac{1}{2}A$.
$C = A$.

Figure 1110c: Plotting on the chart.

The running fix.

1111. It is not always possible to obtain two simultaneous observations. At such times the navigator must resort to a *running fix*, using two lines of position which are obtained by observations at *different times*. In order to plot a running fix, he must make allowance for the time elapsed between the first observation and the second. This is done by *advancing* the earlier line of position to the time of the second observation.

The navigator assumes that, for the limited period of time between the two observations, the ship makes good over the ground a definite distance in a definite direction. He moves the earlier line of position, parallel to itself, to this advanced position. The new, advanced, line now represents the possible positions of the ship at the time of the second observation.

When an accurate position has been determined by fix or good running fix, a new DR plot is started and the old one discontinued.

There is no rule as to how far a line of position can be advanced and still give a well determined position. This is a matter of judgment and depends upon individual circumstances. But until judgment is developed, a good general rule is to avoid advancing a terrestrial line of position more than 30 minutes. The length of time should be kept as short as consistent with other considerations.

In the examples below current effects are not considered.

Example 1: Advancing a line of position (Figure 1111a). A ship on course 012°, speed 12 knots, observes Light *E*, at 1500, bearing 245°. A subsequent observation on another object is made at 1520, at which time light *E* is no longer visible.

Required: Advance the 1500 line of position until it becomes a 1520 line of position.

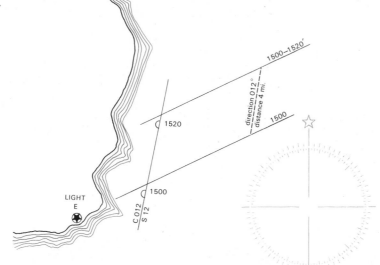

Figure 1111a: Advancing a line of position without current.

Solution: In this case the navigator assumes that for the limited period of time (20 minutes) involved, the ship makes good both course 012° and speed 12 knots, or 4 miles in the direction of 012°. Plot and label the 1500 DR and the 1500 line of position. This line represents all possible positions of the ship at 1500. Note that the 1500 DR is not on the 1500 line of position, indicating that the DR position does not coincide with the true position of the ship, the location of which is not as yet known. From *any* point on the 1500 line of position (including but not limited to the point where the course line intersects this line of position), measure off 4 miles in the direction of 012° and draw a line through this point parallel to the original 1500 line. Label the new line with both the original time of observation, 1500, and the time to which the line has been advanced, 1520, as shown. Note that *any point* on the 1500 line advanced 4 miles in direction 012° arrives at the advanced line.

205

The label "1500–1520" really means "a 1500 line which has become a 1520 line by allowing all points of the 1500 line to steam in a given direction at a given speed for the time interval indicated (1500–1520)." The given direction and given speed are the ordered course and the ordered speed respectively.

Consider now the full problem of determining a ship's position by running fix.

Example 2: A running fix with bearings on different objects (Figure 1111b). The 1440 DR position of a ship is as shown. The ship is on course 012°, speed 12 knots. The weather is foggy. At 1500 light *E* is sighted through a rift in the fog bearing 245°. No other landmark is visible at this time. At 1520 stack *F* is sighted bearing 340°. Light *E* is no longer visible.

Required: Plot and label the running fix (1520 R Fix).

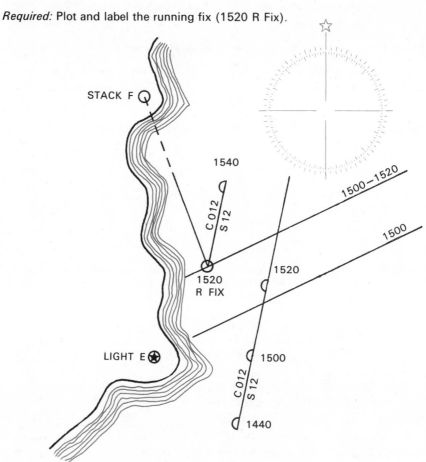

Figure 1111b:
A running fix.

Solution: Plot and label both the 1500 and 1520 DR positions. (A DR position should actually be determined and plotted every time an LOP or fix is obtained.) Plot the bearing of Light *E* as a line of position and label with time. Advance this line parallel to itself in the direction (012°) of the ship's course being steered and a distance (4 miles) determined by the speed of the ship divided by elapsed time. This distance will be the same as that between the 1500 and 1520 DR positions. Label this advanced line of position as shown in 1111b. Plot the second line of position through stack *F* bearing 340°. It is only necessary to draw a segment of this line, long enough to intersect the advanced LOP. The intersection of the two

LOPs is the 1520 running fix. Since the position of the ship has been definitely established a new DR plot can be started from this position.

Care must always be exercised when plotting a running fix to insure that the earlier line is advanced in the proper direction. This may be ascertained by inspection of the labels of both the DR plot and the lines of position.

Example 3: A running fix with bearings on the same object (Figure 1111c). A running fix can also be obtained by plotting two bearings of the same object as illustrated in this example.

A ship is on course 018°, speed 12 knots. At 1430, Light *G* bears 042° and at 1452, it is observed to bear 083°.

Required: Plot and label the 1452 running fix.

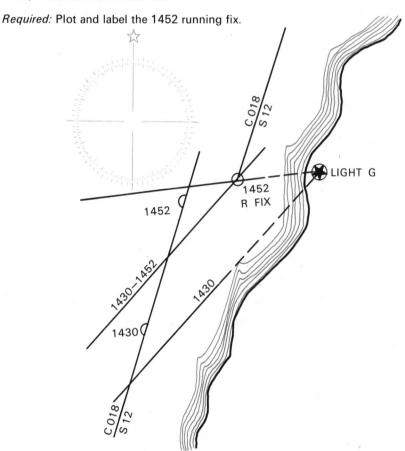

Figure 1111c:
A running fix by two
bearings on the
same object.

Solution: Plot the 1430 DR position on the course line which corresponds with the time of the first observation and plot the 1430 line of position on a bearing of 042° to the light, labeling the plot as indicated. In a like manner, plot the 1452 DR and its corresponding line of position on a bearing of 083°. Then advance any point on the earlier line of position in the direction of the course, 018°, for a distance of 4.4 miles ($\frac{22}{60} \times 12$ kts = 4.4 miles). Through this point advanced, construct a line parallel to the original 1430 line of position. The intersection of the 1430 LOP advanced to 1452 with the 1452 LOP determines the 1452 running fix. A new course line is started from the 1452 running fix as indicated.

207

Example 4: A running fix advancing a distance circle of position (Figure 1111d). A distance circle of position is advanced by moving the center of the circle as illustrated in this example.

A ship is on course 076°, speed 15 knots. The 1440 DR position has been plotted as shown. At 1440, the distance to Lightship *J*, obscured by fog, is found by radar to be 4.7 miles. At 1508, Light *H* is sighted bearing 040°, and the radar has become inoperable.

Required: Plot and label the 1508 running fix.

Figure 1111d:
Advancing a
distance circle
of position.

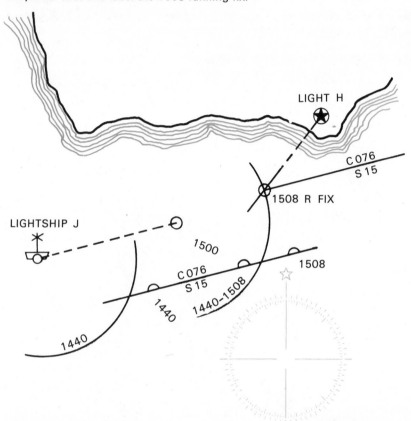

Solution: Note that the center of the circle (the lightship) is advanced in the direction 076° for a distance of seven miles ($\frac{28}{60} \times 15$ knots = 7 miles). From this point, the distance circle of position is constructed again with a radius of 4.7 miles and labeled as indicated. The 1508 line of position to Light *H* is plotted on a bearing of 040°. The intersection of this line of position with the advanced distance circle of position determines the 1508 running fix, from which a new course line is started.

Note that there are two possible intersections of a bearing line of position with a distance circle of position, only one of which is shown. In ordinary circumstances, that intersection nearer the DR position is termed the running fix. In cases of doubt and in the absence of additional information which will confirm either one as the true running fix, commence a DR plot from both positions, assume the ship to be on that course which is potentially more dangerous, and govern future actions accordingly.

1112. A line can be advanced to determine a running fix even though the ship's course or speed is changed in the period between the two observations, as illustrated in the following examples.

The running fix with changes of course and speed.

Example 1: A running fix with a single course change (Figure 1112a). A ship is on course 063°, speed 18 knots. The 2100 DR position is plotted as shown. At 2105 Light *P* bears 340° and disappears shortly thereafter. The 2105 DR position is plotted. At 2120 the course is changed to 138° and the 2120 DR position plotted. At 2132 Light *Q* is sighted bearing 047°.

Required: Plot and label the 2132 running fix.

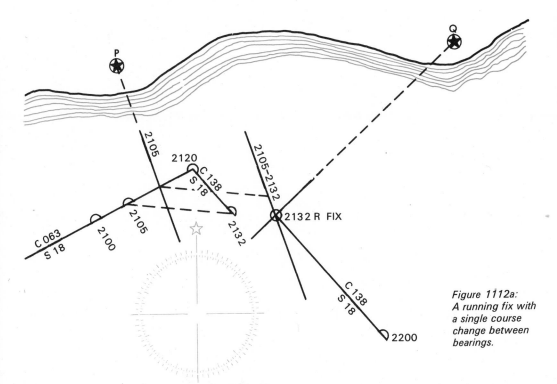

Figure 1112a: A running fix with a single course change between bearings.

Solution: Plot the 2105 DR and 2132 DR positions. The 2105 line of position is advanced by using the course and distance made good through the water between the DR positions corresponding to the time of each visual observation. This is shown by a dashed line, usually not drawn in practice but used here for clarity, connecting the 2105 DR and the 2132 DR. By advancing the 2105 line of position parallel to itself in the direction of the *course made good* a distance equal to the *distance made good* between the 2105 and the 2132 DR, the 2105 line of position advanced becomes the 2105–2132 line of position. In this example, the point of origin for the measurement of this advance was at the intersection of the 2105 LOP with the DR course line as shown. Similar advance of any other point on the 2105 LOP would have produced the identical result.

Plot the 2132 line of position to Light *Q* on a bearing of 047°. The intersection of this line of position with the 2105–2132 LOP determines the 2132 running fix, from which a new DR is started. The plot is labeled as indicated.

Example 2: A running fix with multiple course and speed changes (Figure 1112b). At 0300, a ship is on course 125°, speed 20 knots. At 0302, Light *A* is observed on a bearing of 040° and is soon lost sight of in the haze. At 0310 course is changed to 195° and speed is reduced to 18 knots. At 0315, course is changed to 220°. At 0319, course is changed to 090° and speed is increased to 24 knots. At 0332, Light *B* is sighted on a bearing of 006°.

Required: Plot and label the 0332 running fix.

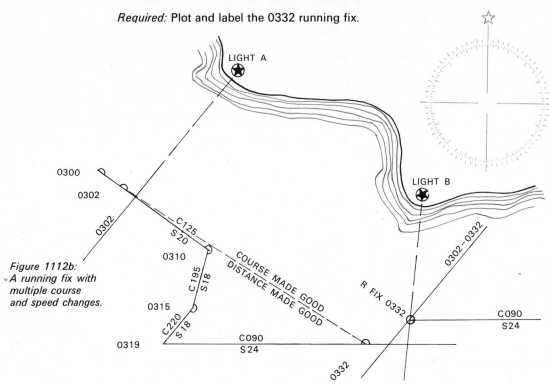

Figure 1112b: *A running fix with multiple course and speed changes.*

Solution: Use the "course and distance made good" technique described in the foregoing example to construct the 0332 running fix. The accuracy of measurement of "course made good—distance made good" displacement will depend, of course, upon the accuracy with which the DR plot was maintained between 0302 and 0332. *This principle is true for any running fix obtained by construction.*

The 0302 line of position is advanced parallel to itself in the direction of the course made good a distance equal to the distance made good between the 0302 and 0332 DR positions. This advanced line now defines the 0302–0332 LOP. The intersection of this line of position with the 0332 line of position on a bearing of 006° to Light *B* establishes the 0332 running fix, from which a new DR plot is started. The plot is labeled as indicated.

Example 3: A running fix using the DRT (Figure 1112c). A ship is maneuvering with frequent changes of course and speed. The 0900 DR position is as shown. At 0900, Light *D* bears 220° by visual observation and at 0925 it bears 150°, at which time the ship is on course 270°, speed 10 knots. The DRT (article 1023) indicates that between 0900 and 0925 the ship makes good 2.5 miles north and 4.0 miles west.

Required: Plot and label the 0925 running fix.

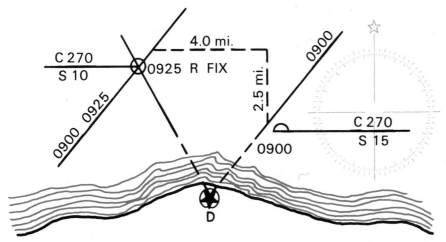

Figure 1112c: A running fix using the DRT.

Solution: Any point on the 0900 bearing line is advanced 2.5 miles north and 4.0 miles west, as indicated by the dashed line, and the advanced line of position is drawn through the point thus determined. A new DR track is started from the 0925 running fix.

1113. It is possible to solve the running fix by trigonometry; two angles are determined by measurement, and the length of the side between them is determined by the ship's run between the bearings. The distance off at the time of the second bearing can readily be found as can the predicted distance off when the object is abeam. A slide rule lends itself well to this solution.

Solution by Table 7, Bowditch.

It is not necessary to resort to trigonometry to obtain the solution. Table 7, Bowditch (Figure 1113), tabulates both distance off at the second bearing and predicted distance off when abeam, for a run of one mile between relative

Figure 1113: Extract from Table 7, Bowditch.

TABLE 7
Distance of an Object by Two Bearings.

Difference between the course and second bearing.	Difference between the course and first bearing.													
	20°		22°		24°		26°		28°		30°		32°	
30°	1.97	0.98												
32	1.64	0.87	2.16	1.14										
34	1.41	0.79	1.80	1.01	2.34	1.31								
36	1.24	0.73	1.55	0.91	1.96	1.15	2.52	1.48						
38	1.11	0.68	1.36	0.84	1.68	1.04	2.11	1.30	2.70	1.66				
40	1.00	0.64	1.21	0.78	1.48	0.95	1.81	1.16	2.26	1.45	2.88	1.85		
42	0.91	0.61	1.10	0.73	1.32	0.88	1.59	1.06	1.94	1.30	2.40	1.61	3.05	2.04
44	0.84	0.58	1.00	0.69	1.19	0.83	1.42	0.98	1.70	1.18	2.07	1.44	2.55	1.77
46	0.78	0.56	0.92	0.66	1.09	0.78	1.28	0.92	1.52	1.09	1.81	1.30	2.19	1.58
48	0.73	0.54	0.85	0.64	1.00	0.74	1.17	0.87	1.37	1.02	1.62	1.20	1.92	1.43
50	0.68	0.52	0.80	0.61	0.93	0.71	1.08	0.83	1.25	0.96	1.46	1.12	1.71	1.31
52	0.65	0.51	0.75	0.59	0.87	0.68	1.00	0.79	1.15	0.91	1.33	1.05	1.55	1.22
54	0.61	0.49	0.71	0.57	0.81	0.66	0.93	0.76	1.07	0.87	1.23	0.99	1.41	1.14
56	0.58	0.48	0.67	0.56	0.77	0.64	0.88	0.73	1.00	0.83	1.14	0.95	1.30	1.08
58	0.56	0.47	0.64	0.54	0.73	0.62	0.83	0.70	0.94	0.80	1.07	0.90	1.21	1.03
60	0.53	0.46	0.61	0.53	0.69	0.60	0.78	0.68	0.89	0.77	1.00	0.87	1.13	0.98
62	0.51	0.45	0.58	0.51	0.66	0.58	0.75	0.66	0.84	0.74	0.94	0.83	1.06	0.94

bearings from 20° on the bow to 30° on the quarter. Since the distance rarely equals exactly one mile, the tabulations are in reality multipliers or factors, which, when multiplied by the actual run give the distance from the object at the time of the second bearing and the predicted distance at which the object should be passed abeam.

Arguments for entering Table 7 are arranged across the top and down the left side of each page. The multipliers or factors are arranged in *double columns*. The left-hand column lists the factors for finding the distance at the time of the second bearing. The right-hand column contains the factors for finding the predicted distance abeam.

Whenever the second bearing is 90° (relative), the two factors are the same. In this case the second bearing *is* the beam bearing and the element of *prediction* no longer exists.

In case the second bearing is greater than 90° (relative), the right-hand factor obviously no longer gives a *predicted* distance abeam, but the estimated distance at which the object *was* passed abeam.

There is usually no need to interpolate when using Table 7, even though only the even-numbered relative bearings are given. As a rule it is easy to obtain even-numbered relative bearings if the bearing-taker or navigator exercises a little patience.

Example 1: A ship is on course 187°, speed 12 knots. At 1319 Lighthouse *A* bears 161° and 1334 it bears 129° true.

Required: (1) Distance from Lighthouse *A* at 1334.

(2) Predicted distance at which Lighthouse *A* should be passed abeam.

Solution: (Figure 1113) Difference between course and *first* bearing (first relative bearing or first angle on the bow) = 26°. Difference between course and *second* bearing (second relative bearing or second angle on the bow) = 58°.

Factors (multipliers) = 0.83 and 0.70.

Run (1319 to 1334) = 15 minutes = 3 miles ($12 \times \frac{15}{60}$). (1) $3 \times 0.83 = 2.49$ = 2.5 miles (distance at 1334). (2) $3 \times 0.70 = 2.10 = 2.1$ miles (predicted distance abeam).

Example 2: A ship is on course 235° psc, speed 14 knots. At 2054 Light *X* bears 267° psc, at which time the patent log reads 26.7. At 2129 Light *X* bears 289° psc, at which time the patent log reads 34.9.

Required: (1) Distance from Light *X* at 2129.

(2) Predicted distance at which Light *X* should be passed abeam.

Solution: (Figure 1113) Difference between course and *first* bearing (first relative bearing or first angle on the bow) = 32°. Difference between course and *second* bearing (second relative bearing or second angle on the bow) = 54°.

Factors = 1.41 and 1.14.

Distance run = 8.2 miles. (1) Distance at 2129 (time of second bearing) = 11.6 miles. (2) Predicted distance abeam = 9.3 miles.

1114. Certain cases of this problem (two bearings of an object and the inter- *Special cases.* vening run) do not require the use of tables. Some of these *special cases* are as follows:

The *bow and beam* bearing (Figure 1114a and 1114b) in which the known run between the bow (45°) and beam (90°) bearings equals the object's distance abeam.

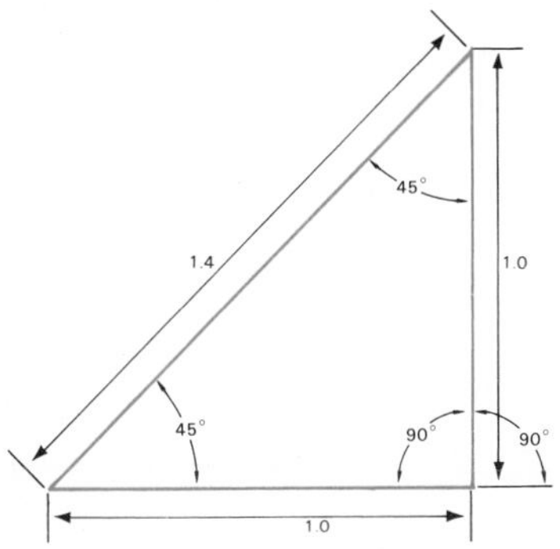

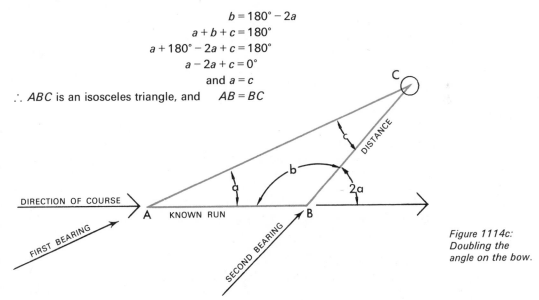

Figure 1114a: Proportion of a right isosceles triangle.

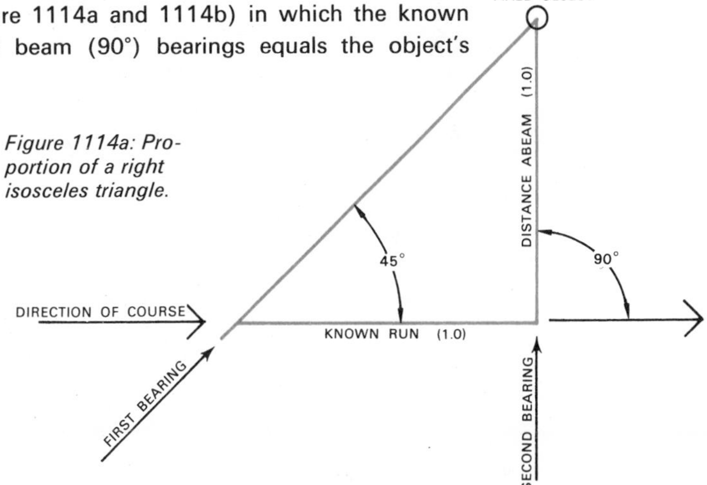

Figure 1114b: The bow and beam bearing.

Doubling the angle on the bow (Figure 1114c). This is developed as follows:

$$b = 180° - 2a$$
$$a + b + c = 180°$$
$$a + 180° - 2a + c = 180°$$
$$a - 2a + c = 0°$$
$$\text{and } a = c$$

∴ *ABC* is an isosceles triangle, and $AB = BC$

Figure 1114c: Doubling the angle on the bow.

Hence, when the angular distance of the object on the bow is doubled, the run between bearings equals the object's distance at the second bearing.

The *$22\frac{1}{2}°-45°$ case,* or $\frac{7}{10}$ *rule.* This is a case of doubling the angle on the bow, explained in the preceding case, the distance run being equal to the object's distance at second bearing. Also, in this particular case, $\frac{7}{10}$ of the distance run equals the distance the object will be passed abeam.

213

The *30°–60° case*, or $\frac{7}{8}$ *rule*, in which the relative bearings are 30° and 60° on the bow. This being another case of doubling the angle on the bow, the distance run between bearings equals the object's distance at second bearing. Also, $\frac{7}{8}$ of the distance run equals the distance the object will be passed abeam.

The *26½°–45° case*. If the first bearing is 26½° on the bow and the second is 45°, the object's distance when abeam equals the run between bearings. This is true in other combinations of angles whose natural cotangents differ by unity. Some of these combinations are listed below in tabular form. The asterisked pairs are the most convenient to use, since they involve whole degrees only. In each case, the distance run between bearings equals the distance of passing the object abeam.

1st Bearing	2d Bearing	1st Bearing	2d Bearing	1st Bearing	2d Bearing
°	°	°	°	°	°
20	29$\frac{3}{4}$	28	48$\frac{1}{2}$	37	71$\frac{1}{4}$
21	31$\frac{3}{4}$	*29	51	38	74$\frac{1}{4}$
*22	34	30	53$\frac{3}{4}$	39	76$\frac{3}{4}$
23	36$\frac{1}{4}$	31	56$\frac{1}{4}$	*40	79
24	38$\frac{3}{4}$	*32	59	41	81$\frac{1}{4}$
*25	41	33	61$\frac{1}{2}$	42	83$\frac{1}{2}$
26	43$\frac{1}{2}$	34	64$\frac{1}{4}$	43	85$\frac{3}{4}$
26$\frac{1}{2}$	45	35	66$\frac{3}{4}$	*44	88
*27	46	36	69$\frac{1}{4}$	*45	90

Figure 1115: Relative bearings.

Keeping in safe water without a fix.

1115. It is sometimes possible to insure the safety of a ship without obtaining a fix, and under some conditions such a method might be even more certain and yet easier to use than those discussed previously.

Along a straight coast where the various depth curves roughly parallel the shore, the echo sounder or lead can be kept going and any tendency of the ship to be set in toward the beach will soon be apparent. Such a method, of course, must be used intelligently. If a given fathom curve is blindly followed, it may lead into trouble. It is necessary to look ahead and anticipate the results. If the given fathom curve makes a sharp turn, for instance, a ship following a steady course might find itself in rapidly shoaling water before it could make the turn. The given fathom line, while affording plenty of water under the keel, might pass close to isolated dangers, such as wrecks, shoals, or rocks.

In following a narrow channel, particularly one that is not well marked, a constant bearing on a distant object ahead or a range can be of inestimable value. A very slight deviation from the desired track is immediately apparent when navigating by means of a range dead ahead. Beacons are often installed in such a position as to form ranges to guide ships along channels, but when such an aid has not been made available, natural ranges can sometimes be found. The navigator should be alert to recognize such a situation, for the value of ranges, either artificial or natural, as guides in navigation cannot be overemphasized. In using a range, it is important to know how far the range can be followed; that is, when to turn. Turns in a channel are usually marked by turn buoys. Excellent fixes to check the progress of a ship can be obtained by following a range and noting the instant other objects near the beam are in range. A study of the chart in advance will often reveal several good natural ranges to use as check points along a channel. One near a turn is especially valuable.

Danger bearings and danger angles are also very useful under certain conditions. These will be discussed separately in the next two articles.

1116. A *danger bearing* is used by the navigator to keep his ship clear of an outlying area of danger close to which the ship must pass. The area has been previously surveyed and is plotted on his chart but, in the vast majority of cases, it will give no warning of its presence to the eye. Examples of such dangers are submerged rocks, reefs, wrecks, and shoals. A danger bearing must be established between two fixed objects, one of which is the danger area. The other object must be selected to satisfy these conditions: *Danger bearings.*

    visible to the eye,
    indicated on the chart,
    true bearing from the danger area should be in the same general direction as the course of the ship as it proceeds past the area.

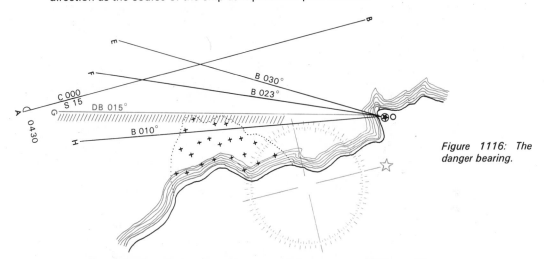

Figure 1116: The danger bearing.

As shown in Figure 1116, a ship is standing up a coast on course 000°, speed 15 knots. The 0430 DR is at Point *A*. A charted danger area of shoal water and sunken rocks off the coast must be avoided. On the chart draw line *GO* from Light *O* (the visible object), tangent to the danger area (the invisible object). The measured direction of this line from *G* to *O*, 015°, is the danger bearing. It is habitually drawn in red pencil, hachured on the dangerous side, and labeled also in red pencil with the abbreviation "*DB*" followed by the numerical value of the danger bearing—"*DB* 015°" in this example.

As the ship proceeds up the coast, frequent visual bearings of Light *O* are taken. If each such bearing is numerically *greater* than the charted bearings *GO*, such as *EO* or *FO*, the ship must be in safe water. If, however, a bearing is observed to be *less* than *GO*, such as *HO*, the ship may be standing into danger as illustrated. In this case, if the position of the ship cannot be determined by a fix, the ship should change course radically to the left until the danger bearing is reached, when it is safe to resume the original course.

215

The value of this method decreases as the angle between the course and the danger bearing increases. Unless the object is nearly *dead ahead*, the danger bearing is of little value in keeping the ship in safe water as the danger is approached. If there is a large angle between the course and the danger bearing, the object might better be used to obtain running fixes as the ship proceeds. However, if there is but one object in sight and that nearly ahead, it would be very difficult to get an exact position, but a danger bearing will show whether or not the ship is on a good course, and will, in consequence, be of the greatest value. Even if there were other objects visible by which to plot accurate fixes, it is a simple matter to note, by an occasional glance over the sight vane of the pelorus or compass, between fixes, that the ship is making good a safe course It occasionally will occur that two natural objects will so lie that, when in range, they mark a danger bearing. Advantage should be· taken of all such ranges.

When stated or recorded for use, a "danger bearing" should include not only the numerical value of the bearing, but also an amplifying statement of whether the bearing tendency should be greater or less for safety. In this example, the Captain and the Officer of the Deck should be informed that *"bearings to Light O greater than 015° are safe"* or *"bearings to Light O less than 015° are dangerous,"* in order that the danger bearing be meaningful.

Danger angle.

1117. To avoid sunken rocks or shoals, or other dangerous obstructions which are marked on the chart, the navigator may use what is known as a *danger angle.* There are two kinds, the horizontal and the vertical danger angle. The former requires two well-marked objects indicated on the chart, lying in the direction of the coast, and sufficiently distant from each other to give a fair-sized horizontal angle; the latter requires a well-charted object of known height. In Figure 1117a, let *AMB* be a portion of the coast along which a vessel is steaming on the course *CD*. *A* and *B* are two prominent objects shown on the chart; *S* and *S'* are two outlying shoals, reefs, or other dangers. In order to pass outside danger *S'*, take the middle point of the danger as a center and the given distance from the center it is desired to pass as a radius, and describe a circle. Pass a circle through *A* and *B* tangent to the seaward side of the first circle. To do this it is only necessary to join *A* and *B* and draw a line perpendic-

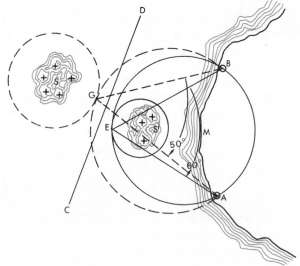

ular to the middle of *AB*, and then ascertain by trial the location of the center of the circle *AEB*. Measure the angle *AEB*, set the sextant to this angle, and remembering that *AB* subtends the same angle at all points of the arc *AEB*, the ship will be outside the arc *AEB*, and clear the danger *S'*, as long as *AB* does not subtend an angle greater than *AEB*, to which the sextant is set. At the same time in order to avoid the danger *S*, take the middle point of the danger *S* and with the desired distance as a radius describe a circle. Pass a second circle through *A* and *B* tangent to this circle at *G* and measure the angle *AGB* with a protractor. Then, as long as the chord *AB* subtends an angle greater than *AGB*, the ship will be inside the circle *AGB*. Therefore, the ship will pass between the dangers *S* and *S'* if the angle subtended by *AB* is less than *AEB* and greater than *AGB*. To simplify reference to these angles and to make the plot more meaningful, make a notation in red pencil on the chart of the numerical values of angles *AEB* and *AGB* at the point of measurement. In addition, trace over in red pencil the arc of the inscribed circle about shoal *S* and the arc of the circle *AEB* adjacent to which the ship will pass in the safe passage corridor between the danger areas. Unless the danger covers a large area, it is generally not necessary to draw the circles as described above. In many cases points *E* and *G* can be selected by eye a safe distance from the dangers.

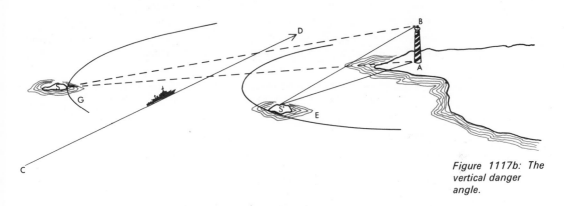

Figure 1117b: The vertical danger angle.

The vertical danger angle involves the same general principle, as can be seen by reference to Figure 1117b, in which *AB* represents a vertical object of known height. In this case the tangent circles are drawn with the charted position of the object as a center. The limiting angles are determined by computation or by means of Table 9, Bowditch. The addition of the measured values of the respective vertical danger angles and the marking of the limits of the safe passage corridor between the shoals in red pencil will measureably improve the graphic value of the plot.

1118. The information available is sometimes inadequate to fix the position of the ship accurately. However, under these conditions it is often possible to improve on the DR by using the data at hand. A position determined under these conditions is called an *estimated position* (EP). An EP is indicated on the chart by a small square and the corresponding time.

The estimated position.

Estimated positions are determined in a variety of ways. In a heavy sea, it is sometimes impossible to obtain accurate bearings. Bearing lines determined

217

electronically may vary considerably in accuracy; they are almost never as reliable as good visual bearings. It is often difficult to determine distance by distance finding stations with accuracy. Bearings obtained by magnetic compass are no more accurate than the deviation table. Estimates of current and leeway due to wind are rarely accurate enough to use in obtaining a fix. However, any of these factors may supply information, which, while not exactly correct, will tend to indicate a more probable position for the ship than that indicated by the DR.

An estimated position is the best position obtainable short of a fix or good running fix. A doubtful fix or running fix might appropriately be considered an EP. An estimated position is determined by considering all information available, giving due consideration to each factor. Each additional item of information results in a reconsideration of the estimated position, and the possible revision of the estimate.

One important method of estimating position by means of soundings has yet to be explained. With modern developments in surveying and navigation instruments, there has been introduced a nautical chart which the navigator can use to great advantage. On these charts depth contours (curves of equal depth) are shown by blue lines at selected intervals to delineate important submarine features, in the same manner that a topographic map shows the land relief by means of contours. Navigation on ships equipped with echo sounding devices can utilize submarine features to obtain position, frequently without recourse to other conventional methods. However, the value of a position determined in this way depends largely on the contour and nature of the bottom and the ability of the navigator to interpret the available information. Soundings of a flat bottom are worthless in determining position, unless samples of the bottom are taken, but when the bottom is very uneven, an accurate position can sometimes be determined by means of soundings alone.

One of the best ways to establish an estimated position by depth curve navigation using soundings is as follows:

Draw a straight line on a piece of transparent paper or plastic. Along this line mark off distances between soundings according to the speed of the ship and the scale of the chart. For this purpose it is usually best to record soundings at regular intervals: every 6 or 10 minutes, or every mile, or oftener if desired. Record the times and corresponding soundings consecutively at the marks along the line. Then adjust the line of soundings on the paper to match the depth contours or individual soundings on the chart, using the DR plot and line of EP's, if there is one, as a guide and moving the paper so that it remains approximately parallel to the true course. Do not forget the possibility of a current setting the ship to one side of its course or affecting the speed made good. Soundings corresponding to depth curves shown on the chart are particularly valuable. These should be recorded even when they do not fall at the appointed time. Where tides are appreciable they must naturally be taken into account.

It is suggested that navigators use depth contours for position determination and for planning courses in advance, particularly where characteristic bottom features are available. They may be combined with other information such as radio bearings, visual bearings, or lines of position from celestial bodies.

In thick weather or at time of poor radio reception, depth curve navigation provides a highly practical means of obtaining a good estimated position.

Another important method of graphically obtaining an estimated position depends upon the relationship existing between a single line of position and the ship's DR position. The DR position at the time of observation represents the best position available before a line of position is plotted. Once plotted, a line of position represents the loci of all the possible points the ship could have occupied at the time of the observation. The most probable position or estimated position (EP) of the ship is defined as that point on the line of position which is closest to the DR position.

Example 1: (Figure 1118) The 0600 DR of a ship is as indicated. Course is 025°, speed 10 knots. At 0627, Lighthouse *A* was observed through a rift in the fog, bearing 260°.

Required: Plot and label the 0627 EP.

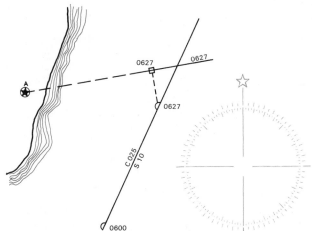

Figure 1118: The estimated position (EP).

Solution: Plot the 0627 LOP and the corresponding 0627 DR. From the 0627 DR, drop a perpendicular to the LOP. The intersection of the LOP and the perpendicular locates the 0627 EP, labeled as shown. This is the most probable position of the ship on the 0627 LOP, as it is not only on the observed line of position but it also represents the nearest point thereon to the 0627 DR.

Combining this method with an estimation of current and a series of soundings will often result in a very accurate position.

Since an EP is not a well determined position, it is not customary to run a new DR plot from such a position. However, a line representing the estimated course and speed being made good should be run from an EP to indicate the possibility of the ship standing into danger, allowing the navigator to take appropriate avoiding action before a dangerous situation develops.

It is emphasized that the navigator *must* gather all the information possible to determine the best estimate of his position. This is particularly true when adverse conditions exist. Single LOP's, soundings, danger bearings, and estimated set and drift, can all be used to good advantage by the navigator. Each situation is different and a careful analysis of the existing information will aid in keeping the ship out of danger.

CHAPTER 12

Tactical Characteristics
in Piloting

Introduction. **1201.** The phrase "tactical characteristics of a ship" refers to the manner in which a given ship responds to engine and rudder orders. So far, in this text, it was assumed that at the instant of an ordered course change the ship came immediately to the new course, and that when a new speed was ordered, the ship attained that speed instantly. Such, of course, is not the case. To increase or decrease speed by 10 knots may require from one to twenty minutes, depending on the initial speed, the power available, and the flexibility of the engineering plant. A course change of 90° may require as much as a half mile of sea room to complete, depending on the type of ship, the rudder angle used, the wind and sea, and on other factors. Each ship reacts in a different way to a given rudder or speed order, and reacts differently under different conditions of wind and sea.

When his ship is steaming singly at sea, the navigator may ignore the time and travel required to effect course and speed changes, for the scale of his plot is too small to be affected by the resulting errors.

Speed and course changes in restricted waters. In restricted waters the situation is entirely different. Here, the navigator frequently needs to know his position within 10 yards, and the effect of the ship's travel in the time required to complete a change of course or speed is so comparatively large that it must be taken into account. The navigator must know his ship's tactical characteristics; that is, how she will respond to a given order under existing conditions.

This chapter is concerned with the quantitive effects of course and speed changes on the travel of the ship, and the techniques and methods which a navigator uses to allow for these effects when piloting a ship in restricted waters. Bringing a ship to anchor in an assigned berth, which requires the use of these same techniques, will also be discussed in some detail.

Turning characteristics. **1202.** When approaching an anchorage, turning onto a range, piloting in a restricted channel, maintaining an intended track, or at any time when precise piloting is necessary, the navigator must allow for the *turning characteristics* of the ship. The standard method of finding a ship's turning characteristics is to turn her in a number of complete circles under varying conditions and to record the results for each. The variables used are: right and left rudder of specified angles, steady speeds of different value, and differences in draft and trim. When taking turning data, effects of wind and sea are allowed for. Most course changes are not as much as 360°, but by studying the complete turning circle, the ship's behavior for turns of any extent can be determined.

In considering the track actually followed by a ship during a turn, an understanding of the following definitions is essential. These terms may be understood more easily by reference to Figure 1202.

Turning circle is the path followed by the pivoting point of a ship in making a turn of 360° or more at constant rudder angle. For the typical ship, the stem will be inside and the stern outside this circle.

Advance is the distance gained in the direction of the original course, measured from the point at which the rudder is put over. The advance will be a maximum when the ship has turned through 90°.

Transfer is the distance gained at right angles to the original course, measured from the line representing the original direction of travel to the point of completion of the turn.

Tactical diameter is the distance gained to the right or left of the original course when a turn of 180° has been completed.

Final diameter is the distance perpendicular to the original course between tangents drawn at the points where 180° and 360° of the turn have been completed. Should the ship continue turning indefinitely with the same speed and rudder angle, she will keep on turning in a circle of this diameter. It will always be less than the tactical diameter.

Standard tactical diameter is a specific distance which varies according to ship type. It is laid down in tactical publications and is used when ships are maneuvering in company.

Standard rudder is the amount of rudder angle necessary to cause the ship to turn in the standard tactical diameter at standard speed.

Angle of turn (Figure 1204) is the arc, measured in degrees, through which the ship turns from the original course to the final course.

Definitions.

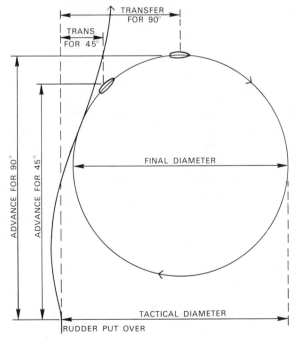

TRANSFER FOR 90°

TRANS. FOR 45°

ADVANCE FOR 90°

ADVANCE FOR 45°

FINAL DIAMETER

TACTICAL DIAMETER

RUDDER PUT OVER

Figure 1202: Advance, transfer, and tactical diameter.

221

The speed at which a ship makes a turn may affect the turning diameter markedly if the "speed-length ratio" (ratio of speed to the square root of the length) is high enough. Thus a 300-foot ship at 30 knots has a considerably larger turning circle than at 15 knots. Tactical diameters are not inversely proportional to the rudder angle. While turning diameters decrease with increase in rudder angle (up to a certain point), the relationship is not an inverse proportion. Furthermore, the rudder angle for minimum turning diameter varies from one design to another. The rudder angle for minimum diameter depends upon many factors of ship and appendage form as well as speed. The majority of ships have a limiting rudder angle of 35°; some have larger ones. A short vessel will have a smaller turning circle than a longer one with the same general characteristics.

Sample tactical data for turning.

1203. The following is a sample of the type table prepared after taking tactical data for the turning characteristics of a ship. The data included herein is representative, and is to be used solely for solving problems used in this course. It must be understood that the proper tactical data for the specific ship in which embarked must be used when actually working under service conditions.

Standard Tactical Diameter, 1500 Yards—Standard Rudder 15°

Angle of Turn	Advance	Transfer	Angle of Turn	Advance	Transfer
15°	500	38	105°	993	853
30°	680	100	120°	933	1013
45°	827	207	135°	827	1140
60°	940	347	150°	687	1247
75°	1007	513	165°	533	1413
90°	1020	687	180°	367	1500

It will be noted that the above table is prepared for every 15° of turn. Data required for increments between these fifteen-degree points may be obtained by interpolation. Instructions for obtaining tactical data for U. S. Navy ships are contained in NWP 50-A, *Shipboard Procedures*, and in the *Technical Manual*, Navships 0901-000-0020.

Computing the turning bearing.

1204. From the preceding discussion it can be seen that during conditions when precise piloting is required the navigator must know at what point the rudder must be put over, so that when allowance has been made for the advance and transfer of the ship, the ship will steady on the desired heading at the time the desired track or point is reached. To accomplish this, the navigator must predetermine the bearing to a known object from a point on the original track line

Determining turning bearing.

at which the rudder must be put over. When this *turning bearing* is reached, the appropriate rudder angle for the turn is given.

In allowing for the advance and transfer, the navigator should use standard tactical diameter and commence the turn using standard rudder. By so doing a margin for error remains and the rudder angle can be increased if the turn is commenced too late.

Example: (Figure 1204) A ship is standing up a channel on course 000° T and must round a point of land by changing course to 075° T.

Required: The turning bearing on Light *M* so as to be on course 075° upon arriving at Point *B*.

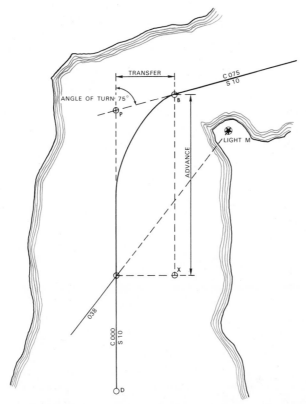

Figure 1204:
Turning bearing.

Solution: Draw a line parallel to the ship's present course being made good (000° T), at a perpendicular distance equal to the transfer for a 75° turn (513 yards). The intersection of this line with the final course, 075° T, will be the point *B* at which the turn must be completed. From this point, measure back along the line a distance equal to the advance, 1007 yards, locating point *X*. From point *X*, drop a perpendicular to the original course line. This will locate the point at which the rudder must be put over to complete the turn at the required point. The bearing, 038°, from that point to Light *M* is the *turning bearing.*

The problem is now complete and the data obtained are: The ship continuing on course 000° T arrives at a point when Light *M* bears 038° T, distant 650 yards, where the command *"Right standard rudder"* is given. The turn is completed and the ship is heading on the final course at point *B*. The solid line *DB* represents the actual track of the ship.

1205. Speed changes are usually of less concern to the navigator than are course changes. There are many times, however, when one may desire to allow for the acceleration or deceleration as in the cases described here.

Acceleration and deceleration.

Example 1: A ship is standing up a channel at speed 15 knots, and the captain desires to slow to 10 knots at the latest possible time so as to pass a construction barge at that speed.

Determining time to change speed.

Required: How far before reaching the barge should speed 10 knots be rung up so as to slow the ship to actual speed of 10 knots at the time the barge is abeam?

223

Knots		Minutes		Rate
Change of Speed		Time Required	Total Elapsed	Knots Change
From	To	for Change	Time	per Minute
Acceleration				
0	10	3	3	$3\frac{1}{3}$
10	15	1	4	5
15	20	2	6	$2\frac{1}{2}$
20	24	4	10	1
24	28	6	16	$\frac{2}{3}$
28	31	9	25	$\frac{1}{3}$
Deceleration				
31	28	3	3	1
28	24	4	7	1
24	20	2	9	2
20	15	1	10	5
15	10	1	11	5
10	0	2	13	5

*Figure 1205:
Acceleration and
deceleration table.*

Typical acceleration and deceleration table; values differ for every ship.

Solution: The table in Figure 1205 shows that to decelerate from 15 to 10 knots requires 1 minute. Since the rate of deceleration between these speeds is assumed to be constant, the average of the initial speed and the final speed will be the average speed for that minute, or $12\frac{1}{2}$ knots. In 1 minute at $12\frac{1}{2}$ knots a ship will travel 417 yards. Measure back 417 yards along the DR track from a point abeam of the construction barge to locate the point at which speed 10 knots should be rung up on the engines.

Example 2: A ship is standing down the channel at speed 10 knots. The captain has stated that he desires to order speed 24 knots as soon as the ship is clear of the channel, in order to make a rendezvous on time.

Required: How far along the DR track line should the navigator consider the ship to have traveled between the time speed 24 is rung up on the engines, and the time the ship actually gets up to speed 24 knots through the water and how much time is required?

Solution: (Figure 1205) Note that three different rates of acceleration will be used for this speed change. For this reason it will be necessary to calculate the distance traveled during the period of acceleration in three separate parts, one part for each rate of acceleration. From speed 10 to speed 15 knots requires 1 minute, at an average speed of $12\frac{1}{2}$ knots. During this time the ship will travel 417 yards. From speed 15 to speed 20 requires 2 minutes at an average speed of $17\frac{1}{2}$ knots. During this time the ship will travel 1167 yards. From speed 20 to speed 24 requires 4 minutes at an average speed of 22 knots. During this time the ship will travel 2933 yards. Add the three distances computed to find the total distance traveled from the time the new speed is rung up until the ship is actually making it; the answer is 4517 yards, or about $2\frac{1}{4}$ miles. Elapsed time, the total of that noted in the table and used above, is 7 minutes.

As can be seen from these examples, the determination of distance traveled between the time a speed is ordered and the time a ship actually is making it good through the water, is easily accomplished, and can be quite accurate. The time involved can be determined by direct reading from the table. Many navigators use the average of the initial and final speeds as the effective average speed during the time of acceleration or deceleration. Although this is not as accurate as the method used in the examples above, it is usually sufficiently accurate for most navigational work.

1206. The Oceanographic Office issues anchorage charts for the principal ports of the United States and its possessions. They are simply harbor charts with anchorage berths over-printed in colored circles of various diameters corresponding to the swinging area required by naval ships of various types and sizes. On these charts, series of berths of like size are laid out in straight lines, referred to as *lines of anchorages*. Usually, adjacent circles are tangent to each other. The center of the circle marks the center of the berth, and each berth is designated by a number or letter printed inside the circle.

Anchoring in an assigned berth.

This orderly arrangement greatly simplifies the assignment of anchorages, especially when a large task group, or other tactical unit, is to occupy a harbor in company. In harbors for which no standard anchorage chart is available, berths are assigned by giving the bearing and distance from a known object to the center of the berth, together with the diameter of the berth. It is the duty of the navigator to cause the ship to be maneuvered in such a manner that the anchor may be let go in the center of the ship's assigned berth. This should be accomplished with a maximum permissible error of ten yards.

For this discussion the following terms are defined:

Definitions of anchoring terms.

Letting go circle is a circle drawn around the center of the berth with a radius equal to the horizontal distance between the alidade and the hawse pipe.

Approach track is the track a ship must make good in order to arrive at the center of the berth.

The *letting go bearing* is the bearing from the point of intersection of the letting go circle and the final approach track to any convenient landmark, generally selected near the beam.

Range circles are distance circles of varying radii from the center of the berth, with distance measured from the letting go circle.

When the ship has been ordered to anchor in a specific berth (Figure 1206) the navigator consults the chart and prepares for the approach to the anchorage by laying off from the center of the berth the following:

The letting go circle, with a radius equal to the horizontal distance between the alidade in use and the hawse pipe.

The intended track, selecting appropriate approach courses and navigational aids for fixing the ship's position en route, and locating turning bearing marks at predetermined points where turns are necessary. The final approach should, if possible, be made with the ship heading into the current, or if the wind has the greater effect, then into the wind. In either case the ship should, if possible, be steadied on the final approach track 500 yards before the letting go point is reached. It is also of great value if an approach track can be selected which runs through the center of the berth to a navigational aid or to a range. As the approach is made the constant bearing of the aid or range from the center of the berth can then be maintained. If no such aid is available, or if the aid previously selected becomes obscured, the positions of consecutive fixes with respect to the approach track (to the right of it or to the left of it) will permit the navigator to recommend a change of course to conn the ship back on the approach course.

Range circles of varying radii, including the radius of the letting go circle. In most cases it is necessary to draw in only the arcs of the range circle adjacent to the approach track. In practice it is usual to draw arcs every 100 yards out to 1000 yards; then at 1200 yards, 1500 yards and 2000 yards. The *letting go circle* is labeled 0 yards; the range circles are measured from the letting go circle, and labeled 100 yards, 200 yards, etc. as the case may be.

When bringing a ship to anchor, the navigator should advise the commanding officer, the officer of the deck, and the first lieutenant of the depth of water and the character of the bottom in the assigned or selected anchorage. In addition, they should be notified of the distance and location of the nearest (and other) shoal water in the vicinity of the anchorage.

Example: (Figure 1206) A ship has been assigned Berth 21 for anchoring. The initial approach into the harbor is on a course of 350°. The approach track to the berth is to be such that Light *M* is dead ahead. Distance from the hawse pipe to the alidade is 75 yards.

Required: (1) Approach track to the berth.
        (2) Letting go bearing on Light *H*.
        (3) Turning point.
        (4) Turning bearing on Light *H*.

Solution: Plot the approach track from Light *M* back through the center of the berth. Measure the direction (295°). Plot the initial approach track into the harbor. Plot the letting go circle (75 yards), using the center of the berth for the center of this circle. This circle is labeled 0 yards. The intersection of the letting go circle and the approach track is the "letting go" point, and is the point from which to determine the letting go bearing on Light *H* (170°).

Range circles are plotted from the center of the berth but the ranges are measured from the letting go point. Thus the distance from the letting go circle to the first range circle is 100 yards, but the radius used in plotting this circle is 175 yards; the radius of the letting go circle plus the 100 yard range circle.

By use of his ship's table of tactical data the navigator can determine the advance and transfer and plot this information, locating the point at which the rudder must be put over, and the point at which the turn will be completed. The turning bearing (291°) on light *H* is thus determined.

As the ship enters the harbor and proceeds along the track, the navigator takes frequent fixes to insure that the desired track is maintained. As the range circles are crossed the navigator advises the captain of the distance to the letting go point so that the speed may be adjusted to bring the ship nearly dead in the water when the letting go point is reached.

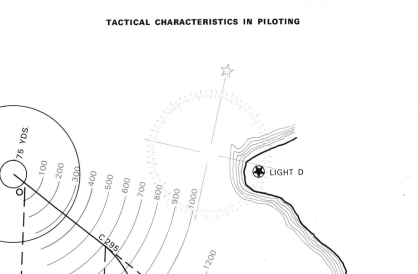

*Figure 1206:
anchoring in an
assigned berth.*

When Light *H* bears 291° the rudder is put over and the turn commenced. The rate of turn is adjusted so that upon completion Light *M* bears 295°, dead ahead. The heading of the ship is adjusted so that a constant bearing of 295° is maintained on Light *M*. Bearings on Lights *H* and *M* are plotted continuously, and the captain advised of the distance to go. When Light *H* bears 170° and Light *M* 295°, the anchor is let go, and at that instant bearings are taken on all navigational aids visible, in order that the exact location of the anchor can be accurately determined. The ship's exact heading at the time of the final fix is also observed. A distance of 75 yards is then plotted from the fix, in the direction of the observed heading. The exact position of the anchor is then known. The anchor should be within ten yards of the center of the berth.

Answers: (1) Approach track 295°;

(2) Letting go bearing 170°;

(3) See Figure 1206;

(4) Turning bearing 291°.

Effect of wind and current.

1207. In discussing the computation of the turning bearing, the effects of acceleration and deceleration, and anchoring in an assigned berth, the assumption was made that these maneuvers were being carried out under conditions when there was no wind or current. In actual practice there almost always is some wind or current, and frequently both. Before entering or leaving harbor, and particularly if the channel is restricted in any way, the navigator must determine what currents may be encountered, and what effect they may have on the ship as she negotiates the channel. The effect of wind must also be taken into consideration; at times a strong wind may have a greater effect than the existing current. The navigator must always be prepared to modify his original plans to meet existing conditions.

When possible, constricted channels should be negotiated at slack water, or if this is impractical, when the ship can head into the current.

Summary.

1208. This chapter has outlined the methods by which the navigator can use the known tactical data pertaining to his ship to keep it on the intended track in pilot waters and to bring it to anchor safely and accurately in its assigned berth. Every naval vessel has its own tactical characteristics; the data for each will be slightly different. The tactical data for the ship must be available on the bridge at all times when under way, and in the most convenient form for use by the captain, the officer of the deck, and the navigator.

CHAPTER 13

Graphic Solution for Relative Motion Problems

1301. Most of the text is concerned with the art of directing a ship safely to its destination by avoiding fixed hazards such as shoals. These are stationary hazards; to avoid them, the navigator must know the actual or geographic movement of his ship. But moving hazards, such as other ships under way, are also encountered in the course of a voyage, and introduce a second kind of movement with which the navigator must become familiar. This is *relative movement* which deals with the apparent motion of moving objects. Sometimes, as when meeting another ship under way in constricted waters, both types of motion must be considered simultaneously. *Introduction.*

The purpose of this chapter is to define the movement of a ship under way with respect to another moving vessel, and to the earth, and to show how the relationship between these two motions can be solved accurately and quickly, primarily to avoid the hazard of collision. For this purpose, it is assumed that all bearings and ranges on other vessels are obtained by radar. The use of radar is described in Chapter 16.

The maneuvering board here described can be used for many additional types of problems involving relative motion. In naval formations the conning officer is required to maintain a position relative to the guide, and to determine course and speed to move to a new station. These ship handling problems and many other uses are discussed in H. O. 217, *Maneuvering Board Manual*, published by the U. S. Naval Oceanographic Office.

1302. Motion is the movement of an object from one point to another; it can be measured in terms of the direction and distance from the first point to the second. Alternately, it can be measured in terms of the direction and speed of the object, as it moves from the first point to the second. All motion is relative to some reference, and it is necessary when discussing motion to define the reference. For purposes of this discussion, all fixed objects on the earth will be considered as being without motion. *Motion.*

To the navigator, the motion of his ship over the earth's surface is of primary importance. Assuming that there is no current the course and speed of the ship through the water represents its movement *over the ground.* This is called *actual movement;* it is defined as *motion measured with respect to the earth.*

Relative movement is motion measured *with respect to a specified object,* which may or may not have actual movement.

To illustrate the difference between relative and actual motion, suppose two ships are proceeding on the same course and at the same speed. Relative to each other, there is no motion, and the ships are at rest; however, both have the same actual movement relative to the earth.

Problems in relative movement are solved subconsciously in everyday life. A pedestrian wishing to cross the street sees a car coming. Without conscious thought he determines the car's approximate speed and converts it to speed relative to himself when walking; based on this determination he either crosses ahead of the car or waits for it to pass. The same type of reasoning, but at a conscious level, applies to the solution of problems of relative motion at sea.

In general, aboard ship, the problem is to determine the course and speed required to bring about the desired change in relative position. The navigator must learn to plot the position of any ship relative to any other ship. How this is done is discussed in the following articles.

General considerations regarding the use of radar and relative plotting in navigation.

1303. The student may question what sort of accuracy can be achieved at sea, using radar bearings and ranges, and relative plots similar to those described in this chapter. The answer depends on three factors—the characteristics of the radar set, the navigator's ability to read bearings and ranges accurately, and his care in plotting. Time, incidentally, should be stated to the nearest whole minute.

Assuming that the radar, when set on the 20-mile scale, gives bearings accurate to 0°.5, and ranges accurate to ± 0.2 miles, and that the navigator uses reasonable care in plotting, he should be able to determine the closest point of approach (CPA), within 0.5 miles, the target's course within 2°, and her speed within 0.2 knots.

It is most important that bearings and ranges be obtained on a continuing basis; the more there are, the more accurate the plot will be. Also, the target ship has been known to change course or speed or both, just after a navigator had decided that no more bearings were required, as the range at the CPA was sufficient to be safe.

It is vital that the *Rules of the Road* be observed in making any decisions on course or speed changes based on radar or any other information. Article 1312 describes a situation in which two vessels are on a collision course, and one correctly changes course to the right. while the other changes to the left, contrary to the rules and common sense. But such things do happen. A few years ago the *Andrea Doria* and the *Stockholm*, both large passenger liners, and both equipped with radar, collided under rather similar conditions, resulting in the loss of the *Andrea Doria*. The admonition to motorists: "drive defensively" applies equally well on the high seas.

These suggestions are offered to simplify the task of relative plotting: A stop watch is a great convenience in timing. It, as well as a pad of Maneuvering Board sheets or plastic Maneuvering Board, pencils, dividers, and plotting instruments should be ready to use at a moment's notice.

Aboard most ships moving targets are picked up at 20 miles or less and since most speeds at sea are less than 20 knots, a scale of 2:1 is generally convenient for plotting both ranges and speeds.

A series of readings should be made at convenient, but constant, time intervals. Readings should be made as long as there is any possibility that a change of course and speed on the part of the target ship might result in collision.

If the risk of collision exists, and action on your part is called for, make *big* changes in course and or speed, rather than small ones.

Tips on plotting.

If the radar has concentric range rings, but no other range indicator, take bearings of the echo as it crosses these rings, and record the times.

Plot all bearings as true. If the radar does not have a gyro repeater, set the movable azimuth circle so that the bearings are true.

Plot all targets.

1304. The plotting connected with problems in relative motion in order to obtain a solution can be done on plain paper. The solution is greatly facilitated if the work is done on a polar coordinate form or "board."

Aids for the graphic solution of relative movement problems.

Three such forms or boards designed especially for solving relative movement problems are available. They are the *Maneuvering Board,* the *Navy Mark I Mod 0 Plastic Maneuvering Board,* and the *Radar Plotting Sheet.* All are available commercially. The first two are intended to assist in the solution of all types of relative movement problems; the third is intended primarily for plotting radar contacts. Where a good deal of relative plotting is to be done, the Mark I Mod 0 Plastic Maneuvering Board is recommended, as its design permits an extremely rapid problem solution.

The Maneuvering Board comes in pads of 50 sheets; each sheet can be used on both sides. It is published by the U. S. Naval Oceanographic Office as the H. O. 2665 series. H. O. 2665-10, used to illustrate problems in this chapter, has equally spaced concentric circles numbered from 1 to 10 which may be used to represent any desired increment either of speed or distance. Arranged vertically on either side of the paper are scales designed for rapid conversion when a ratio of other than 1:1 in circle spacing is desired, for measuring distance or the length of vectors.

A nomogram is provided at the bottom of the maneuvering board, consisting of three logarithmic scales: one each for time, distance, and speed. If any two are known, the third may be determined by connecting the two known points with a straight line and extending it as necessary to intersect the third scale. The point so determined is the unknown quantity.

Time, speed, distance problems may also be solved by using only the top logarithmic scale of the nomogram as a slide rule. This method is more accurate than using all three scales, and should be understood; see article 710.

The *Mark I Mod 0 Plastic Maneuvering Board* illustrated in Figure 1314 offers the most rapid method of solving problems in relative motion. Solutions may be obtained without dividers or parallel rulers; only a pencil is required. This board consists of a transparent plastic plotting board upon which is engraved a compass rose. Beneath the board, and centered with the compass rose is a rotatable circular grid upon which are printed concentric circles, and a cross-section grid, as well as a compass rose. A transparent cursor, rotatable about the center, and mounted above the plotting board, is provided to facilitate the measure-

231

ment of courses and bearings. A Speed-Time-Distance conversion computer is secured to the lower right-hand corner of the board. This computer or the nautical slide rule (article 1024) represents the most convenient method of solving the STD problem. The navigator should not depend on mental conversion of the problem when a simple mechanical solution is readily at hand. A speed conversion scale from knots to yards per minute, appears at the upper right-hand corner. A detachable ruler clipped to the upper section carries a distance scale.

The Radar Plotting Sheet (Figure 1310) is, in size and general format, similar to the Maneuvering Board. It is published by the U. S. Naval Oceanographic Office, as the H. O. 4665 series. It differs from the Maneuvering Board primarily in the selection and arrangement of the speed and distance scales, and in that only four concentric circles, rather than ten, are shown. Also, the radii shown at 10° intervals on the Maneuvering Board are omitted in the Radar Plotting Sheet, which lends itself extremely well to the solution of radar plotting problems; solution is obtained in the same manner as by the Maneuvering Board. For relative movement problems other than those involving radar plots, the Maneuvering Board is generally more convenient. H. O. No. 257, *Radar Plotting Manual,* covers the use of these sheets in detail.

The geographical plot.

1305. A plot showing the successive positions of one or more ships, moving over the earth's surface, is called a geographical or navigational plot; this represents motion with reference to the earth. Such a plot is presented in Figure 1305; it can best be illustrated by an example. Your ship is on course 000°, speed 10.0 knots. At 2200, your ship is at point A, and a radar contact on another ship is obtained, bearing 067°, distance 10.8 miles.

Required: The other ship's course and speed, and the *closest point of approach* (CPA).

Solution: Draw your ship's course line from A, marking off the distance run for convenient periods of time; for this example, use 8 minutes. Then plot the target ship's 2200 position, bearing 067° distant 10.8 miles from A. Radar ranges and bearings on the target are obtained every eight minutes, as shown in the table, and plotted from the position of your ship at that time.

Time	Bearing	Range (Miles)
2200	067°	10.8
2208	063°	9.4
2216	058°	8.2
2224	052°	7.2
2232	043°	6.2
2240	032°	5.4
2248	017°	4.9
2256	001°	4.8
2300	352°	4.9

Inspection will show that the bearing changed to the left, and that the range closed steadily until the target crossed ahead at about 2256, the CPA being about 4.8 miles (the actual CPA was about 4.75 miles, on bearing 004°). The

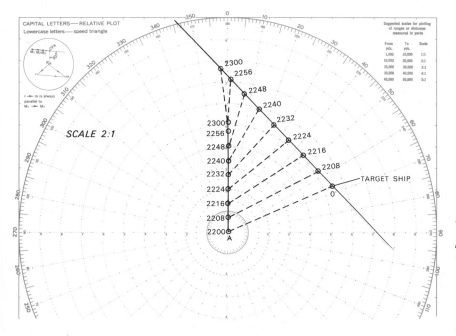

Figure 1305: Geographical plot shown on Maneuvering Board.

plot will show that the target was on course 315°, speed 15.2 knots. Actually, all this information could have been predicted, after the first few points were plotted.

This geographical plot provides the required information; the difficulty is that its construction is extremely time consuming, some 30-odd steps being required. Fortunately, there is a simpler method of obtaining the desired information by means of the relative plot.

1306. In the geographical plot, the positions of both ships were plotted, using the earth as a reference; that is, course lines had to be drawn for both ships. But the requirement in that problem was the movement of the target ship, *relative* to your own. Now consider that your ship remains fixed at the center of the maneuvering board, which, of course, is the way it appears on most radar screens, and plot only the position of the target relative to your ship, using the bearings and ranges given in article 1305.

The relative plot.

This plot is shown in Figure 1306. The line M_1 and M_2, M_3, etc., represents the movement of the target in one hour, relative to your ship; it is the *relative movement line,* and the direction of relative movement (DRM) is 274°. Measurement shows it is 10.6 miles long; as the target moved this distance in 60 minutes, target speed along this line must be 10.6 knots. This is the target speed with respect to your ship, or *speed of relative movement* (SRM).

Relative motion.

This plot has provided data necessary to determine the CPA (about 4.8 miles on bearing 004° at 2256) and with a minimum amount of work, as well as the SRM, and the DRM. It is frequently desirable to determine the distance at which another ship will pass ahead or astern of your ship. This is done by drawing a line from your ship's position (R, at center of the maneuvering board) in the direction of the course; where this line crosses the direction of relative movement line locates the point where the other vessel will be directly ahead or astern.

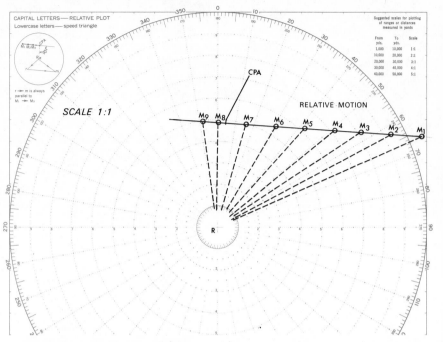

Figure 1306:
Relative plot.

Problems in relative motion require the use of two diagrams; the relative plot just discussed, and the speed triangle which will be discussed in the following article. These diagrams are entirely separate, although the solution of the problem consists of developing one diagram with the information gained from the other until the desired result is reached. Inasmuch as this development of the two diagrams consists largely in transferring similar directions from one to the other it simplifies matters to use a common origin of direction (north) for the two so that these similar directions become parallel lines, readily transferred with parallel rules, protractors, or a drafting machine. It may also prove more convenient and will also save space if both diagrams are constructed from a common point of origin, but the diagrams as such remain separate and distinct nevertheless, and must not be confused. To help prevent confusion it is wise to use different types of lettering in the two diagrams. The common practice is to use small letters in the speed diagram and capital letters in the relative plot, but the same letter of the alphabet should be used to represent the same unit in both diagrams. In this text *e* is used for earth, *r* for own ship, and *m* for the target vessel.

The relative plot is a diagram comprising a fixed point of origin and one or more straight lines called relative movement lines. In the problems concerning collision avoidance, illustrated in this chapter, own ship is used as the point of origin as movement and position of other ships *relative to own ship* is the basis of the problem. In tactical naval maneuvers a guide ship is generally used as the origin, as the position and movement of your ship and others in the formation *relative to the guide* is the primary concern. The fixed point of origin is always plotted at the center of the maneuvering board.

The speed triangle. **1307.** So far, use of the relative plot has determined the relative speed and the direction of relative movement of the target, as well as the CPA. Still to be obtained are the target's course and actual speed; these may be determined by means of the *speed triangle,* sometimes called the vector triangle.

234

The speed triangle or vector diagram consists of a system of properly related straight lines called vectors. Each vector has a pointed end called the "head," and a plain end called the "foot," both appropriately lettered to indicate the units represented. These vectors indicate direction and rate of travel in accordance with the following vector definition applying to relative movement: "A vector is a straight line indicating by its inclination the direction, and by its length, the ratio of travel of a moving element, represented by the head of the vector, with respect to another element which is represented by the foot of the vector." It is essential that the distinction between the head and the foot of a vector be kept clearly in mind—the element or unit represented by the head moves relative to the element or unit represented by the foot of the vector. In order to form a vector diagram, the component vectors must represent movement taking place concurrently, they must be referred to a common origin of direction, and they must all be to the same scale. Since the vector diagram is composed entirely of vectors, and since vectors indicate only direction and velocity, it follows that the diagram deals exclusively with direction and velocity and will therefore yield only what is called course and speed.

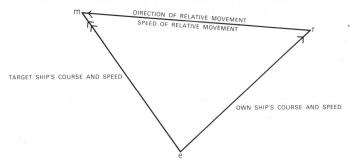

Figure 1307: The speed or vector triangle.

The center of the plot is labeled with the small letter, *e*, for the "earth," since that is the reference for actual movement. The course and actual speed of own ship is represented by the vector *er*, while the course and actual speed of the target ship is represented by the vector *em*. The vector *rm* can be remembered as standing for relative movement; it represents both the direction of relative movement (DRM), and the speed of relative movement (SRM). *All actual course and speed vectors are drawn from e.* The direction of the vectors are also shown by arrows; the vector *rm* is always drawn in the direction from *r* towards *m*.

It is important not to confuse the speed triangle with the relative plot. The *relative plot* represents direction and *distance;* the *speed triangle* represents direction and *speed*.

Having plotted any two sides or vectors of the speed triangle, it is obvious that the third side can be determined, thus obtaining the direction and speed that is required.

1308. Procedure for obtaining required data from the relative plot and speed triangle is illustrated in the following example.

The speed triangle and relative plot in use.

Example: (Figure 1308) Own ship is on course 020°, speed 10.0 knots, at 2312, radar picks up a contact bearing 337°, distant 16.0 miles.

Required: The time and distance of the CPA, and course and speed of the target ship.

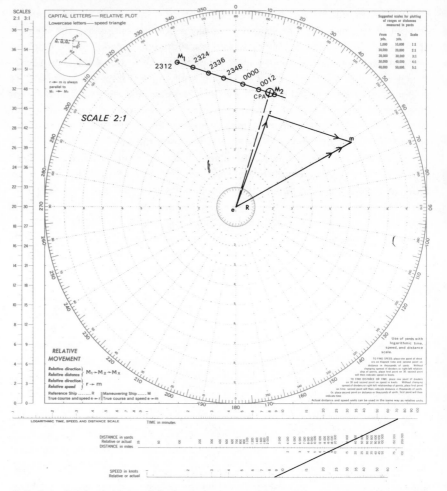

Figure 1308:
Speed triangle
and relative plot.

Solution: As the initial range to the target is 16.0 miles, 2:1 appears to be a convenient scale for distance. Accordingly, plot M_1 bearing 337° in the 8 circle; this is the first step in preparing the relative plot. As own ship speed is 10.0 knots, 2:1 also is a convenient scale for the speed triangle; draw *er*, course and speed vector.

Bearings and ranges are obtained on the target as tabulated below: the successive positions of the target are plotted as soon as noted.

Time	Bearing	Range (Miles)
2312	337°	16.0
2324	342°	15.0
2336	348°	14.0
2348	354°	13.3
0000	002°.5	12.6
0012	011°	12.3
0024	019°	12.2

When the third bearing is obtained, it is evident that the bearing is changing quite rapidly, and that *no danger* of collision exists, *as long as both ships maintain their present course and speed.* When the 019° bearing and range are plotted at 0024, sufficient data are on hand to furnish answers of acceptable accuracy. A line is drawn in through all the bearings and range points that have been plotted and labeled M_1–M_2. Measure it, remembering to use a 2:1 scale to find the relative distance of 10.8 miles. The target ship, therefore, has traveled a *relative distance* of 10.8 miles in 72 minutes; by simple arithmetic, determine the *relative speed,* which is 9.0 knots $(\frac{10.8}{72} \times 60)$, and check this answer by putting a straight edge across the nomogram, at the bottom of the board, as indicated.

Now draw the second vector or side in the speed triangle. From *r*, the head of own ship's course and speed vector, draw a line parallel to M_1–M_2, and to the *right,* as this is the direction of relative movement. This line is $4\frac{1}{2}$ units in length, to correspond to the relative speed of 9.0 K. The head of this line is labeled *m* and a line is drawn joining *em* to complete the triangle. This line, or vector, represents the target ship's course and speed; inspection shows target course 060°.5, speed 13.8 knots.

Data on the CPA is obtained by dropping a perpendicular from *e* to the line of relative movement, M_1–M_2. Measurement of this perpendicular shows that at the CPA, the target will be distant 12.2 miles, and the bearing will be 017°.5. To determine the time of the CPA, first determine its relative distance from M_1 which is 5.2 units or 10.4 miles. As the relative speed is 9.0 knots, it will take 68 minutes to move 10.4 miles. The time of CPA is 0020 (2312 + 68 min.). The nomograph or log scale may also be used to advantage in determining the time of CPA.

1309. The preceding article used an example in which the target was crossing the bow of your own ship, but the CPA was 12.2 miles. This is a comfortable distance at which to pass another ship and obviously no change of course or speed was indicated in the interests of safety.

Relative movement problem involving a change of course.

Now consider the relative movement problem, when it appears that at the CPA, the target ship will be uncomfortably close to your ship, and you desire to take corrective action.

Example: (Figure 1309) Your ship is on course 200°, speed 14.0 K. A pip appears on the radar screen, bearing 212°, range 20.0 miles. Plot the contact on the maneuvering board, using a scale of 2:1 and label it M_1, as shown. Observation of the pip shows that it is drawing left slowly, and that the range is closing. Ten minutes after the first contact, the bearing is 211°.5, range 18.2 miles. At time 20 minutes, the bearing is 211°, range 16.3 miles.

Enough data is now available to determine the CPA if both ships maintain present course and speed. Draw the relative movement line through the three points marking the target's bearings and ranges, and extend it past *e*, at the center of the maneuvering board. Note that this relative movement line shows that the range at the CPA will be slightly less than 2 miles.

The decision is made to pass the target at a range of 4.0 miles, by altering course immediately to starboard. To obtain the new course, first determine the target's course and speed. To do this, plot *er* own ship's present course and speed vector. Measure the relative distance traveled by the target between the first and third bearings (20 min); it is 3.6 miles. This gives a relative speed of 10.8 knots.

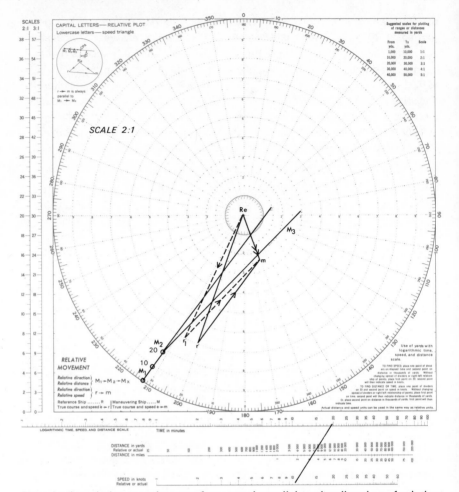

Figure 1309:
Own ship
changes course.

Draw in the relative speed vector from *r* and parallel to the direction of relative movement (M_1–M_2). Now draw the target's course and speed vector from *e* to the end of the relative speed vector *m*. By inspection, the target is on course 160°, speed 5 knots.

To determine the new course, draw a line from M_2 tangent to the circle centered on *e*, and representing a distance of 4 miles. This line, M_2–M_3 will be the new direction of relative movement. From *m* the end of the target's course and speed vector, draw the new relative speed vector parallel to the new line of relative movement, M_2–M_3. The point where this relative speed vector crosses the speed circle (14.0 K) defines the new course, 206°.

Note that the target's range can be determined for the moment it crosses your ship's bow. The range is 12.3 miles.

Collision situation.
Own ship stops.

1310. The following example requires both a relative and geographical plot.

Example: (Figure 1310) Your ship is on course 145°, speed 10.0 knots. A radar contact is picked up, bearing 220°, range 18.0 miles and a relative plot of the target is commenced, with its present position labeled M_1. The range is closing, and there is no apparent change in the bearing. After 17 minutes, the range has closed to 14.0 miles but the bearing remains unchanged. At 34 minutes after the first contact the range is 10.0 miles; this position is M_3. Immediate corrective

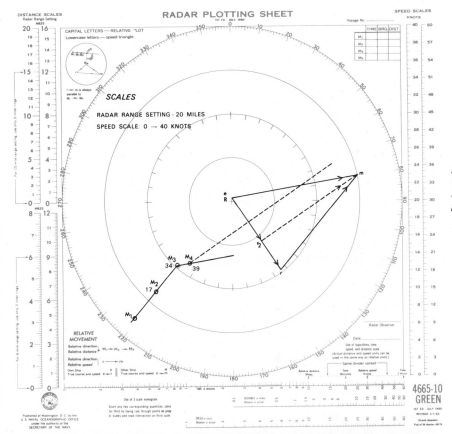

Figure 1310:
Collision situation
shown on radar
plotting sheet.

action is obviously required—it is not possible for your ship to change course to starboard—so stop all engines, then back them until the ship has lost all way. First, determine the target's course and speed. The direction of the relative movement is indicated by the successive plots of the target's position, along the line M_1–M_3, 040° as shown, and the relative distance traveled by the target is indicated by the length of the line M_1–M_3, which is 8.0 miles. The relative speed is 14.0 knots. With this data and own ships course and speed vector, er, construct the speed triangle, erm. From the target's vector, em, determine the target to be on course 080°, speed 15.0 knots.

Next determine what the bearing and range of the target will be at 39 minutes, 5 minutes after your ship stopped. (For purposes of this problem, assume that your ship stopped short, with no advance while losing way.) Remember that your ship is now dead in the water and the situation has become a geographical plot rather than a relative movement plot. Draw a line in the direction 080°, the target's course, from M_3, its position at 34 minutes. Target speed is 15.0 knots, therefore in 5 minutes it will have moved 1.25 miles along this course line, and its position will be at M_4, bearing 215°, distant 9.2 miles.

At 39 minutes, you decide to go ahead on the original course, but at speed 6.0 knots. You wish to determine how far ahead of you the target will pass. You return to the speed triangle; the target's vector, em, remains the same, as it has

239

not changed course or speed. Your own ship's vector, *er*, remains unchanged in direction, but is shortened to represent the new speed of 6.0 knots; call this vector er_2. By drawing in r_2m, obtain the new direction of relative motion, as well as the relative speed. Draw a line through M_4, the thirty-nine minute position, parallel to r_2m; this crosses your own ship's course line at a distance of 3.2 miles, which will be the range when the target crosses ahead of you.

Collision situation.
Target alters course.

1311. This problem requires only a relative plot; by now you should begin to grasp the principles involved in solving relative movement problems. With this problem, a geographical plot is included, below the relative, which may be helpful if any confusion still exists.

Example: (Figure 1311) Your ship is on course 350°, speed 12.0 knots. At 00 minutes a pip is seen on the radar screen, bearing 308°, range 20.0 miles. At 10 minutes, the range has closed to 16.5 miles; the bearing remains the same, and a plot is commenced. Subsequent plots show the bearing falling off to the left, and at 20 minutes, the target bears 303°, range 14.0 miles, indicating a new relative movement line. A partial list of bearings and ranges appears below. (In actual practice, many additional bearings would have been obtained. Only the more important ones are included here.)

Time	Bearing	Range (Miles)
00 (M_1)	308°	20.0
10 (M_2)	308°	16.5
20 (M_3)	303°	14.0
35 (M_4)	300°	8.8
50 (M_5)	290°	3.7
63.5 (M_6)	170°	1.7

Required: (1) Target's course and speed from time 00 to 10.
(2) What maneuver the target made at time 10.
(3) What the target did at time 20.
(4) The CPA.
(5) The time of the CPA.

Solution: (Figure 1311) (1) Construct the speed triangle, *erm*. From your vector, *er* lay off *rm* parallel to M_1–M_2, and for a relative speed of 21.0 knots (M_1–M_2 equals 3.5 miles; this distance was covered in 10 minutes). The vector *em* gives the target's course, 094°, and speed, 14.5 knots.

(2) Draw a new relative speed vector from *r*. This vector, rm_2, is parallel to M_2–M_3, and for a relative speed of 16.8 knots. The vector em_2 shows that the target came right to course 120°, and slowed to 6.4 knots.

(3) Use the relative movement line M_3–M_5, to obtain a new vector *rm*. This falls on the first vector *rm*, and is of the same length; the target therefore returned to her original course, 094°, and speed, 14.5 knots, at times 20 minutes.

(4) Drop a perpendicular from *e* to the line M_3–M_5 extended, and find that the range at the CPA will be 1.2 miles, on bearing 217°.5.

(5) Measure the relative distance from M_3 to the CPA. It is 14.0 miles; 14.0 miles at the relative speed of 21.0 knots will require 40 minutes, so the CPA will be reached at 60 minutes (40 + 20).

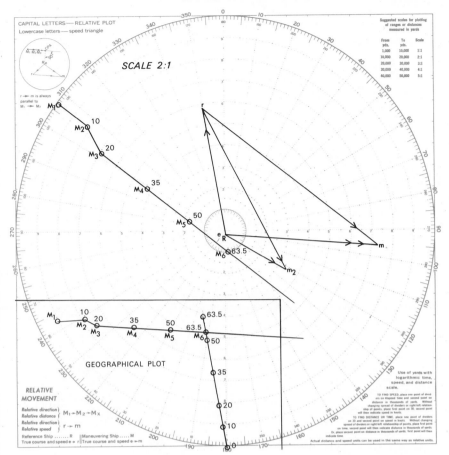

Figure 1311:
Target ship
changes course.

It should be pointed out again that considerably more bearings and ranges must be obtained than those tabulated in this example. There would have been considerable doubt as to the direction of the short leg, M_2-M_3, if only these two bearings had been obtained.

1312. This problem highlights the need to keep a constant check on a radar contact when danger of collision exists, and for plotting at frequent intervals.

Relative movement problem, with both ships changing course.

Example: (Figure 1312) Your ship is steaming on course 000°, speed 10.0 knots. You obtain a radar contact bearing 029°, range 20.0 miles, start your stop watch, and plot the target's relative position, M_1, as shown. At time 10 minutes the bearing has not changed, but the range has closed to 16.7 miles (M_2). You must obtain the target's course and speed. The relative speed is 19.8 knots (3.3 miles in 10 minutes) and the direction of relative movement is 209°. From the speed triangle, you determine that the target is on course 233°, speed 12.0 knots. The plot of the target's relative position is continued. At time 20 minutes, the bearing remains unchanged at 029°, but the range has closed at 13.4 miles (M_3). An immediate 20° course change to the right is ordered, and your ship steadies on course 020°.

This change of course should, of course, change the direction of the line of relative movement, as the latter is generated by the movement of one ship with relation to another, and any change in course or speed by either ship will change

241

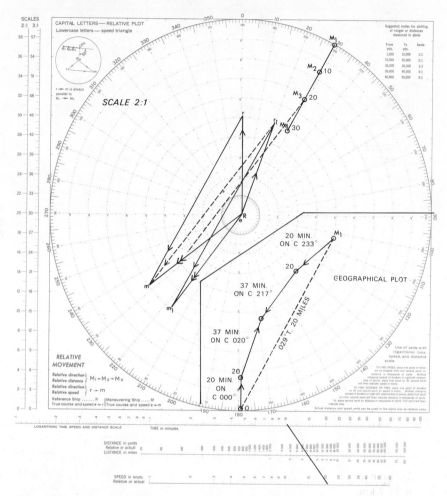

*Figure 1312:
Own ship and
target ship
change course.*

the relative movement line. You plot a er_1m vector.

Obviously, your ship's change of course to the right should cause the bearing to change to the left. This can be checked from the plot r_1m, which will now be the direction of relative movement; this direction, laid down from M_3, passes to the left of e. The CPA, incidentally, should be slightly more than 2 miles.

With your ship on her new course, 020°, you continue to watch the radar contact. Surprisingly, the range steadily decreases but the bearing remains unchanged. This can be due only to the fact that the target has also changed course or speed. You believe that it is probably maintaining speed of 12.0 knots, and that a course change is causing the bearing to remain constant. The target's new course must be determined.

Construct a new speed triangle, starting with the vector of your ship's new course, and speed of 10.0 knots; this is er_1. The relative speed line (r_1m_1) is then drawn in parallel to the direction of the relative movement, which has not changed. The terminus of the line, m_1, is determined by where the line cuts the 12 knot speed circle, at 217°. This shows the target's new course to be 217°, *and both ships are again on a collision course.*

242 Figure 1312 shows a geographical plot of the developing situation.

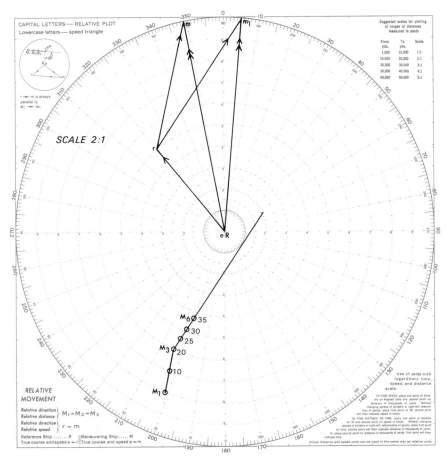

Figure 1313:
Own ship is
being overtaken.

At this time you must take drastic evasive action, as the range is closing at about 21.7 knots. At time 30 minutes, the bearing is still 029°, but the range has decreased to 9.8 miles. If your ship maintains speed of 10.0 knots, but comes right to 080°, can you determine the range and bearing at the CPA, assuming that the target makes no further changes in course or speed? The plotting necessary for this solution is not included in Figure 1312, which is already sufficiently complete. The answer is: Range 4.4 miles; bearing 327°.

1313. This is a problem that is frequently encountered aboard ship.

Relative movement problem. Own ship is being overtaken.

Example: (Fig. 1313) You are at sea, on course 320°, speed 10.0 knots. At 00 minutes a radar contact is made, bearing 201°, range 16.0 miles. You continue to track and plot the target. A partial list of bearings and ranges is tabulated as follows:

Time (Min.)	Bearing	Range (Miles)
00	201°	16.0
10	202°	14.0
20 M_3	204°	12.0
25	203°	10.9
30	202°	9.7
35	200°	8.5

243

At time 20 minutes you decide to determine the target's course and speed based on the data so far obtained. The relative distance, M_1-M_3, is 4.1 miles, and this distance was traversed in 20 minutes: the relative speed is 12.3 knots, and the direction of relative movement is 012°. With these data draw the *rm* vector of the triangle: the target's vector, *em*, shows that it is on course 349°, speed 20.0 knots.

However, the bearings obtained after that are now changing in the opposite direction. As your ship has maintained course and speed, the target must have changed course and speed or both. With the data obtained after time 20 minutes, you must determine the target's new course and speed. The relative speed is 14.8 knots. By means of parallel rulers, the direction of relative movement is determined to be 033°. With these data, plot a new relative speed vector, rm_1, and determine that the target is now on course 005°, speed remaining at 20 knots.

All that remains is to determine the range, the bearing, and the time of the CPA. Extend the M_3-M_6 line; it is tangent to the 2.0 mile circle, on bearing 123°. The target will reach the CPA at time 68 minutes (M_3–CPA = 11.8 miles). The relative speed is 14.6 knots; 11.8 miles at 14.6 knots requires 48 minutes; 48 + 20 minutes (M_3) = 68 minutes.

Plotting multiple targets.

1314. Particularly in coastal waters, several targets may be on the radar screen at one time. The following example illustrates the plot for two targets which are on the screen at the same time.

Example: (Figure 1314) Your ship is on course 000°, speed 8.0 knots. At time 00 there is a radar contact bearing 280°.5, range 10.0 miles. At time 43 there is another contact, bearing 070°, range 11 miles. Bearings and ranges are tabulated as follows:

TARGET M			TARGET M'		
Time (Min.)	Brg.	Range (Miles)	Time (Min.)	Brg.	Range (Miles)
00	280°.5	10.0	43	070°	11.0
30	286°	7.7	62	072°	8.1
45	291°	6.5	76	074°	6.3
61	300°	5.0	94	080°	3.8
87	313°	4.0	103	090°	2.5
105	336°	3.2			

As the plot develops, it becomes obvious from the two lines of relative movement M_1-M_6, $M'_1-M'_5$, that both ships are going to pass clear of you. The speed triangles are interesting, as they are both based on your ship's vector.

The course and speed of target M, from its triangle, are 030° and 10.0 knots. (The relative distance M_1-M_6 is 8.6 miles, the time is 105 minutes; the relative speed is 5 knots.)

Target M' is on course 298°, speed 9 knots. (The relative distance $M'_1-M'_5$ is 8.5 miles, the time is 60 minutes; the relative speed is 8.5 knots.)

You must determine the time each vessel will be at CPA, and the range at that time.

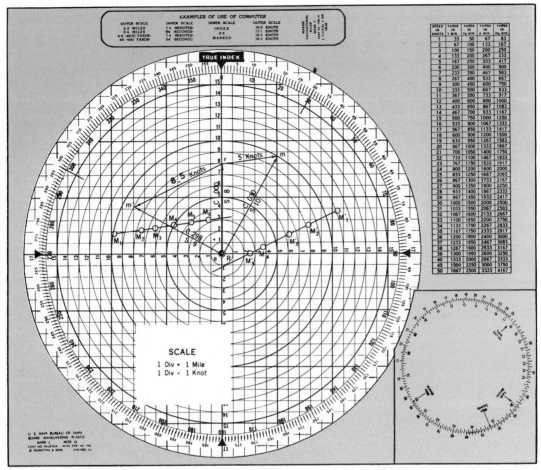

Figure 1314:
Multiple targets
as shown on
plastic
Maneuvering
Board.

Target *M* will be at CPA at time 114 minutes, range 3.1 miles.

Target *M'* will be at CPA at time 117 minutes, range 1.2 miles.

Again it should be pointed out that considerably more bearings and ranges must be obtained than those tabulated here, and that the information would have been computed several times in the period that actually elapsed.

1315. This is a common problem for Naval and Coast Guard vessels; it arises at times for other ships, as when called on to lend assistance. It is not based on radar data.

Relative movement problem. To intercept a moving ship on known course and speed.

Example: Your ship at sea receives a message from ship A that she requires assistance. She gives her position, and states that she will remain on course 090°, speed 6.0 knots. The plot shows her to bear 030° from your position, distant 200 miles. Your ship can maintain 20 knots.

Required: (Figure 1315) (1) The course to reach A in minimum time,

(2) How long will it take to rendezvous?

This is merely a new application of the other problems in this chapter. The relative plot differs in that A is at the center, and that this will also be your final position,

245

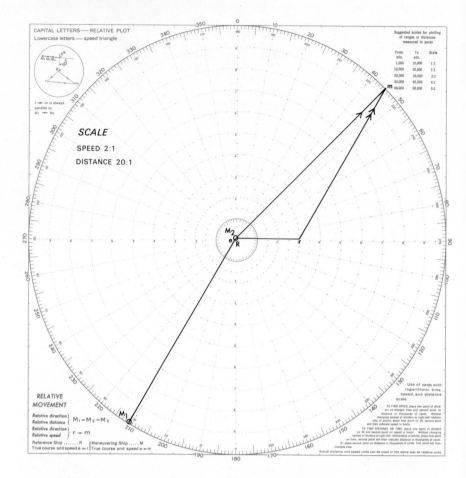

Figure 1315:
Rendezvous
problem.

M_2. In the speed triangle, A's course and speed vector will establish the base with which to determine your ship's course, at 20.0 knots.

Solution: Plot initial position, M_1 bearing 210°, and distant 200 miles from e using a scale 20:1. Plot A's course and speed vector, 090°, 6.0 knots, using a scale 2:1. The direction of relative motion is from M_1 towards M_2(e), this is 030°. Plot the relative speed vector parallel to M_1–M_2 from r to where it intersects the relative speed circle at 20.0 knots; this intersection establishes the point m.

Answer: (1) The vector em establishes the course, 045°, to steer at 20.0 knots.

Your course is now established: all that remains is to determine how long it will take to come alongside A. The relative distance is 200 miles, the relative speed, rm, is found to be 16.3 knots.

(2) The time required will therefore be 12.3 hours, to the nearest tenth.

Other information can be obtained for this plot. For example, how many miles must your ship steam to reach A? The answer is 246—12.3 hours at 20.0 knots. Again, when should you pick up A on radar, at a range of 20.0 miles? A's echo should appear in slightly over 11 hours (180 miles at 16.3 knots).

Changing station
when in formation.

1316. A common problem on board naval vessels is that of changing station within a formation.

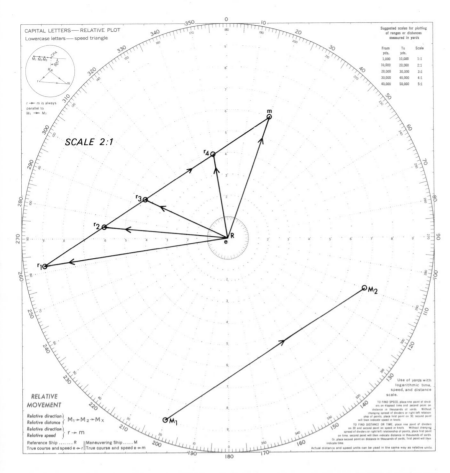

Figure 1316:
Changing station
maneuver.

Example: (Figure 1316) Your ship is in formation on course 020°, speed 12 knots, 9 miles ahead of the guide. The formation commander orders her to take station on the port beam of the guide, at a distance of 7 miles. The following information will be necessary before you can decide the most expedient way to make the maneuver.

      (1) Direction or relative movement of the guide with respect to your ship;
      (2) Own ship course at 18 knots;
      (3) Own ship course at 12 knots;
      (4) Own ship speed if you steer 295°;
      (5) Own ship speed if you steer 350°.

Solution: (a) Draw vector *em* to represent the true course, 020°, and speed 12 knots of the guide. Locate M_1 and M_2 as follows. Convert your relative bearing from the guide to true bearing as described above; which is 020°. Since own ship is the reference, M_1 bears the reciprocal of 020°, or 200° from the center. Hence, M_1 is located on the 9 circle in the direction 200° from the center. Similarly, M_2 is located on the 7 circle in the direction 110° from the center. The DRM can now be determined.

(b) Draw vector r_1m parallel to M_1M_2. Since the direction of relative movement is from *r* to *m*, and *r* is to be found, the reciprocal of *rm* is drawn from *m* until it intersects the 18 knot circle. Thus, *rm* is in the required direction M_1M_2.

247

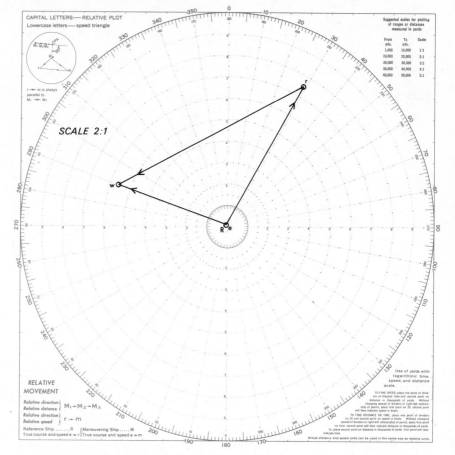

Figure 1317:
Wind triangle.

SCALE 2:1

(c) Complete the speed triangle by drawing vector er_1 from the center of the diagram to r_1.

(d) Draw vector er_2 from the center to the intersection of the r_1m vector with the 12 knot circle.

(e) Draw vector er_3 in the direction 295°.

(f) Draw vector er_4 in the direction 350°.

Answer: It can be seen that the DRM is 058°, the course at 18 knots is 262°, the course at 12 knots is 276°, the speed when steering 295° would be 8.8 knots and the speed for course 350° would be 7.9 knots. From this information you would be able to pick the course and speed to put your ship on the new station in the smartest manner.

Determining the true wind.

1317. The Maneuvering Board lends itself well to determining both the speed (force) and the direction of the true wind aboard ship by means of the speed triangle.

In this triangle, the vector *er* represents the course and speed of the ship, the vector *rw* the direction and speed of the relative or apparent wind, and the vector *ew* is the direction and speed of the true wind. The vector *er* is plotted first, the vector *rw* is then plotted from *r* in the direction the apparent wind is blowing, the length of *rw* representing the speed of the apparent wind. The

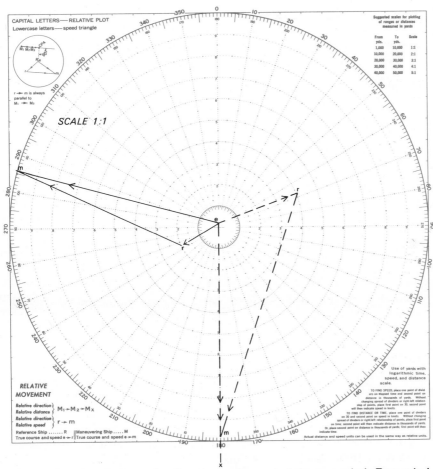

Figure 1318:
Current vector
problem.

third vector *ew* represents the direction and speed of the true wind. *True wind* is the force and the true direction from which the wind blows, as measured at a fixed point on the earth.

Apparent wind is the force and the relative direction from which the wind blows, as measured from a moving vessel. It can also be expressed as a true direction.

Example: (Figure 1317) Assume the ship is underway, on course 030°, speed 15 knots, and that true direction of the apparent wind is from 062° at 20 knots.

Required: Direction and speed of the true wind.

Solution: Draw the speed triangle as shown, using a scale of 2:1. The vector *er* represents your course and speed. From *r*, plot the relative speed vector *rw* in the direction of 242° (the apparent wind direction, 062° plus 180°), and to a length representing 20 knots; the terminus of this vector is labeled *w;* join *e* and *w;* this vector, *ew*, represents the true wind direction, from 109°.5, and its speed, 10.8 knots.

1318. It is easy to determine the course to steer at a given speed, and the speed over the bottom, when the set and drift of a current are known. Solution is by the speed triangle method.

Allowing for known current.

In this example, *er* is the vector representing the set and drift of the current; it is

249

the vector on which the speed triangle is constructed. The vector *em* represents the intended track (ITR) and speed over ground (SOG) to make good, and *rm* represents the course to steer and the speed through the water, to reach a given point at a desired time.

Example 1: (Figure 1318) You have an intended track of 285° at a speed of 10.0 knots. The current is setting 240°, drift 2.0 knots.

Required: Course and speed to make to stay on the track line.

Solution: First draw the current vector *er* as shown in Figure 1318 (solid lines). Next, draw in the vector *em* for the intended track line in the direction 285°

Answer: The vector *rm* represents the course to steer, 294°.5, and the speed to make, 8.6 knots, to travel along a track in the direction 285°, making 10.0 knots over the ground.

A similar problem arises when you want to travel along a given track line, and at a given speed, through a known current, and must determine the course to steer, and what will be the speed made good over the ground.

Example 2: (Figure 1318) A current sets 070°, drift 4.0 knots. You have an intended track of 180°, using a speed of 12.0 knots.

Required: Course to steer to stay on the track line, and speed made good over the ground.

Solution: Plot the current vector, *er*, in the direction 070°, and for a speed of 4 knots. Next, from *e*, plot a vector *ex* in the direction 180°, but of indefinite length Now from *r* swing an arc of a radius equal to 12.0 knots; the point at which this arc cuts *ex* is labeled *m*, and draw in *rm*, the vector representing the course you must steer. It is in the direction 198°, and its length indicates that you will make good 10.0 knots over the ground.

CHAPTER 14

The Piloting Team

1401. Thus far, this text has described most of the primary techniques and skills *Introduction.* which enable a navigator to conduct his ship safely in pilot waters. The student has learned piloting techniques used in restricted waters provided the bearings, ranges, and echo sounder readings were given. To obtain these data in a systematic manner requires several men, each trained to do a small part of the overall job, and organized as a group to provide the navigator with the proper information at the proper time. This group, known as the *piloting team,* is stationed whenever the ship gets under way in or enters into pilot waters, usually shortly before the *special sea detail* is set.

Aboard most naval vessels, the Combat Information Center (CIC) will also supply bearings and ranges, obtained by radar, to conn. The DRT in CIC will also be in operation, and will be updated frequently. However, the navigator must always bear in mind that he is charged with the safe navigation of the ship; and the information passed on from CIC is for "back-up" purposes.

This chapter is concerned with how the navigator obtains the necessary information in a timely and orderly manner from the various people on this team, how the team is organized to furnish this information, and some elements of doctrine and methods which have proven to be of assistance in the fleet in solving this problem. Not all of the combinations of information available to the navigator are used in the illustration herein; only a representative sampling of the everyday uses to show a typical method is given. It should be emphasized at the outset that the methods outlined here are only *one* way of accomplishing the results desired—namely, a smooth and timely flow of essential information to the navigator. Any method of organization will do, provided it achieves this desired result.

1402. The navigator is charged with using all available sources of information *Sources of* to fix the ship's position. The kinds of information needed, and the various places *information.* in a typical ship where it may be obtained, are listed in subsequent paragraphs.

Bearings of objects can be obtained by any of the following means in most ships of the Navy:

> *Visually,* by means of a gyro compass repeater, magnetic compass, pelorus, a self-synchronous alidade, or a gun director (5" or larger).

> *By radar,* using the surface search radar equipment (either in CIC or the bridge PPI), or using a fire control radar in a gun director.

By sonar, using the echo ranging equipment.

Ranges (distances) of objects can be obtained in most ships of the Navy by the following means:

Optically, using an optical rangefinder in a gun director (5" battery or larger).

Visually, by use of the stadimeter.

By radar, using the surface search radar equipment (either in CIC or the bridge PPI), or using fire control radar in a gun director.

By sonar, using the echo ranging equipment.

By sound, by computing ranges using the time difference of receipt at the ship between simultaneous audio and submarine sound signals, or simultaneous audio and radio signals transmitted from *a distance finding station*.

Depths of water can usually be obtained for most ships of the Navy, by:

Echo sounder readings.
Lead line soundings.

1403. Navy Regulations require that a permanent record must be maintained

Required records.

of all observations and computations made for the purpose of navigating the ship. This means that any organization established by the navigator to obtain navigational information must be so organized that the necessary information is recorded without hampering its flow to the navigator. Since, in piloting, the navigator normally relies on visual bearings of landmarks and other aids to navigation to fix the position of the ship, the primary record that must be

---

Figure 1403:
Bearing Book.

RECORD GYRO BEARINGS

Date: *23 June 1969*   Gyro Error *1°W*
Place: *Entering Norfolk, Va.*

Time	Cape Henry Light	Cape Charles Light	Thimble Shoals Light	Lynn-Haven Bridge Tower	Checkered Tank	Echo Sounder Reading
0946	205.5	010.0	287.0			4
0949	201.0	012.5	287.0			
0952	197.0	016.0	287.0			3
			10870			
0955	192.5		287.0			3
0958	186.0		287.0			
1001	178.0		287.0	222.5		
1004	171.0		286.5	217.0		3
1007	164.0		287.0	211.0		
1010	155.0		287.0	206.5		3
1013	147.3		287.0	201.0		
1016	*stack*		287.0	195.0	263.0	3
1019	236.7		287.0	188.0		

maintained is of the bearings used to navigate the ship. To be complete, the time of the bearings and identification of the objects used must also be included. To accomplish this, a *Bearing Book* is maintained in each ship of the Navy. Each ship may have its own form for this record, but all are essentially the same, since the same information is recorded by all. A sample page of a Bearing Book is shown in Figure 1403. Note that there is a place for the date, the port which the ship is leaving or entering, and the gyro error. If ranges are taken, they are recorded under the bearing (or in place of it) in the column for the object on which they were taken. An entry of this nature is seen for 0952 under Thimble Shoals.

When bearings on one object are discontinued, the column previously used is relabeled when it is desired to use it for an object which is not already provided for, as was done in the *Cape Henry* column at 1016. Any bearing recorded in the Cape Henry column after the time when that column was re-labeled *Stack* are bearings on the stack, and not on Cape Henry. Using this manner of re-labeling, any number and sequence of landmarks employed for piloting can be recorded. The right hand column should also be carefully noted, for it provides a record of depth readings sent to the navigator at the times indicated.

Bearing Book.

Any book of convenient size may be used as a bearing book by simply ruling off the columns desired, and printing the appropriate information at the top of the page. There is normally one column for *time*, one for *depth* readings, and at least four columns for *bearings*. On most ships it is customary for the man keeping the bearing book to sign his name when the piloting is completed, to indicate that the record made is a true one. In addition, most navigators have standing instructions posted in the front of the book prohibiting erasures, and directing the bearing recorder to draw a line through any mistake and to rewrite the correct bearing so that both are still legible. This is done to preserve the legality of the record, and to prevent any confusion as to the correct bearing.

Sounding Book.

All depth readings may not be sent to the navigator, for reasons which will be discussed later. However, all readings taken must be recorded, and a special *Sounding Book* is established for this purpose. Note that the right hand column of the Bearing Book (Figure 1403) indicates the observed depth sounding reading. This reading may or may not be the depth of water under the keel depending upon the location of the sounding head of the sonic depth finder. Since it is the comparison of the observed depth with the charted depth in which the navigator is primarily interested, a correction factor must be applied in any event to each reading to account for the distance from the sounding head to the water line. A record of this correction should be made on the inside front cover of the Sounding Book for ready reference. A recommended procedure least subject to error is to require the echo sounder operator to record and report depth measurements as read, to which the navigator shall apply the correction factor previously determined. The result will be the measured depth from the water line which can be compared directly with the charted depth corresponding to the estimate of the ship's position.

Selection of information.

1404. Article 1402 lists the considerable number of sources of information available to the navigator in piloting. It is essential that he organize his piloting team so that the navigational aids are known in advance, and that he receives

253

only the information which he requires at any particular time.

For normal piloting in good visibility, the navigator can accurately fix the position of the ship using two or three bearings or LOP's. As visual bearings are most accurate and normally the most easily obtained, they are the first choice. Should visibility become poor, the use of *radar ranges* (article 1608) is the next most accurate method of positioning the ship.

When the ship is in pilot waters, continuous use of the echo sounder should be required. Depths obtained by the hand lead are useful in doubtful situations when the ship is proceeding slowly enough to permit accurate casts and readings. Both may then be used in comparison with charted depths to insure safety. In practice, the depth finder is manned in addition to the chains.

From this brief summary of the effectiveness and accuracy of different types of fixes, it has been determined that provision should be made for obtaining the following sources of piloting information in the basic organization of a piloting team:

> *Visual bearings.*

> *Radar information* (ranges and bearings) from CIC and the bridge PPI.

> *Soundings* by the lead line and echo sounder.

Stationing of personnel.

1405. Since the chains are required to be manned in pilot waters, and the echo sounder is also manned at the same time, two members of the team are stationed. As the typical ship has at least two peloruses or alidades, a man is assigned to each to obtain visual bearings. The careful navigator will request the operations officer to station his radar navigation team in CIC, which will include two additional surface plotters and an additional officer to supervise radar navigation, augmenting the normal watch personnel. Means must also be provided to transmit piloting information to the bridge on designated circuits. The echo sounder operator can maintain the Sounding Book as well as operate the equipment, but an additional man is required to maintain the Bearing Book. Using these personnel, the basic team consists of the following:

> One leadsman in the chains.

> One echo sounder operator.

> Two or more bearing takers, each assigned to a pelorus.

> One bearing recorder to maintain the bearing book.

> One or more men to maintain communication with and receive radar information from CIC.

Should information be required from gun directors, special provision for this information must be made with the weapons officer. Sonar information is usually available through CIC, or by a direct broadcast system to the bridge.

Communications.

1406. Communications must be established between the various members of the team and the navigator. This is done in such a manner that the navigator has positive control of the communications used to reach any member of the team at any time. It is therefore customary for the piloting team to be connected by means of sound-powered telephones, with the bearing recorder acting as the navigator's talker on the circuit. In this way, the bearing recorder can obtain all information sent to the navigator and enter it in the bearing book as it is received. He can also act as a communication link with CIC, requesting and recording all radar data considered pertinent by the navigator. In practice, the leadsman is not normally on this telephone circuit with the other members of the team but sends his soundings over the anchoring and maneuvering circuit to the bridge. This information is usually desired by the captain and the officer of the deck as well as by the navigator. The lead line soundings are repeated by the telephone talker on the bridge so that all can hear them, and the navigator notes the information as it is heard.

Thus a piloting telephone circuit has been established with the following stations:

The *bearing recorder* (who is the navigator's talker and controls the circuit).

A *bearing taker* at each pelorus.

The *echo sounder operator.*

A *talker* in CIC.

The specific circuit used for this purpose will vary from ship to ship, but most ships have provision for such communications. In addition to sound-powered communications, many ships have and use voice tubes connecting these stations. Many navigators have found it helpful to use a call-bell system to indicate to the bearing takers the times to take a round of bearings. This system limits talking on the circuit, thereby reducing the noise level on the bridge which is always desirable.

In addition, a separate circuit from CIC to bridge is usually established to provide a clear channel for the transmission of evaluated radar information during reduced visibility piloting.

1407. For these stations it is desirable to establish specific reporting doctrine to assist the navigator in the advance selection of information that he will receive while piloting. *Duties and doctrine.*

The *bearing recorder* is charged with four main duties: *Bearing recorder.*

Controlling the communication circuit and acting as the navigator's talker on that circuit.

Relaying all information received to the navigator.

Recording all bearings, ranges, and depths as he receives them.

At the direction of the navigator, giving *marks* to the bearing takers and CIC to indicate when to take bearings or ranges. In ships so equipped, the *"mark"* can be indicated by sounding a bell or buzzer installed on the bridge for that purpose. If this latter system is used, the officer doing the plotting frequently gives his own marks.

Bearing takers. The primary duty of these men is to take bearings on objects at times specified by the navigator, and to report them over the phone. In addition, a good bearing taker will be familiar with the landmarks and aids to *Bearing taker.*

navigation expected to be used, and will assist the navigator by reporting when they are in sight. He will also assist the navigator in identifying each landmark or aid as it is sighted. In addition, the bearing taker can assist the navigator by reporting other information, such as the set of current past buoys, shipping which may lie along the intended track, when buoys and landmarks pass abeam, etc.

In most ships only two gyro repeaters are available, and since the navigator usually desires three LOP's to plot his fix, one bearing taker must take bearings on two objects. If it can be determined beforehand that a majority of the aids to navigation to be used will lie either to port or to starboard for the major part of the travel of the ship in pilot waters, the most experienced bearing taker should be assigned to the repeater on that side. In taking bearings of two objects from the same repeater, it is desirable that the two bearings be taken simultaneously insofar as possible. The bearing taker is trained to take the fastest moving bearing first. By this is meant taking the bearing of an object closest to the beam first, as it will be changing bearing most rapidly, and then taking the bearing of the object more nearly ahead or astern. In this manner the effects of the advance of the ship in the time between the two bearings will be minimized.

Sound operator.

Echo sounder operator. The echo sounder is sometimes not on the bridge where the navigator can personally oversee the work of the operator. For this reason, the man assigned as operator should be thoroughly trained, and should realize the importance of his duties. As depths are normally used by the navigator only as a safety factor, readings are not actually required to be sent continuously to the bridge. Most ships establish a doctrine directing the operator to take soundings continuously, to record the soundings every minute, to send soundings to the bridge at regular specified intervals and whenever called for, or when a limiting depth is encountered. This depth is a safety factor determined by each navigator for his ship, and will depend upon the draft of the ship and the distance of the sonic transmitter below the water line. For instance, in a destroyer with a draft of 18 feet and with the sounding head located 12 feet below the water line, the navigator may direct the echo sounder operator to report to the bridge immediately any reading less than 4 fathoms, while the doctrine on a carrier may prescribe a report at 8 fathoms. In addition, most navigators have a standing order to the operator to report immediately any rapid shoaling of the water. These limiting factors must occasionally be changed depending on the depth of water in which the ship expects to steam, for a minimum reading doctrine of 4 fathoms would have little practical significance if the destroyer were steaming inside the 5 fathom curve.

CIC talker.

Talker in CIC. The navigator does not provide the talker in CIC in most ships, as he is assigned from the CIC personnel. The talker usually sends up to the bridge only the information requested, in accordance with doctrine established by the navigator and approved by the commanding officer.

Frequency of fixes.

1408. No fixed policy on the frequency of taking bearings and obtaining fixes by a navigator can be established. In practice, the frequency will vary with the situation, the navigator, and the wishes of the captain. If the ship is steaming comparatively slowly in coastal waters with no immediate dangers to navigation in the vicinity, a fix every 15 minutes could be sufficient; but if the ship is coming to anchor and exact accuracy is required, fixes should probably be taken every 30 seconds. However, a good rule for normal piloting in restricted waters, and at normal speeds, is to obtain a fix every three minutes. This will allow a navigator sufficient time to extend the DR track ahead for at least 6 minutes, to compute the current effects and to keep the captain advised accordingly.

While so occupied, it is a practice in many ships to require the assistant naviga- *Assistant navigator.*
tor to assist in plotting under the supervision of the navigator. This procedure frees the navigator for overall piloting supervision, giving him the opportunity personally to check the identification of new landmarks and aids to navigation as they are sighted, and to instruct the team regarding shifting from one object to another. The task of a navigator in pilot waters is an exacting one, and is a full time duty, even with the assistance of a well-trained piloting team. The frequency of fixes to keep the ship in safe waters will depend upon the navi-navigator's judgment. An international conference on this subject several years ago resulted in compilation of the table reproduced here for information.

Area	Distance From Nearest Danger	General Order of Depth of Water	Order of Accuracy	Fix Frequency
Pilot waters	Less than 3 miles	Up to 20 fathoms	$\pm$ 50 yds.	Every minute
Coastal waters	3–50 miles	20–100 fathoms	$\pm \frac{1}{4}$ mi.	Every 3–10 minutes
Ocean passage	Over 50 miles	Over 100 fathoms	$\pm$ 2–3 mi.	As conditions warrant, and at least 3 times daily

1409. A sketch of the bridge and related navigational positions on a typical *The team in*
destroyer-type ship is shown in Figure 1409. Personnel who wear sound- *operation.*
powered telephone headsets are shown, as are the telephone circuits. It should be noted in this diagram that the bearing recorder is located next to the navigator at the chart table. Frequently no provision has been made for the navigator to be on the open bridge, and consequently he must operate from inside the pilot house. This is acceptable if there is sufficient visibility, but it is preferable to have his chart desk on the open bridge. The chart table should have a clock mounted over it, or readily visible from it, as a record of time is important in piloting.

The chart selected for plotting will be a large scale chart; ordinarily, it is ad- *Charts.*
visable to use a single chart for the entire approach, as changing charts can be dangerously time consuming. It is very helpful if the water area on the chart, too shallow to permit safe navigation, has been shaded in advance. This will permit the navigator to determine at a glance if the ship is standing into danger.

Suppose that a destroyer is entering Chesapeake Bay en route Norfolk, and is

Figure 1409: Navi-
gational positions
on destroyer-type
ship.

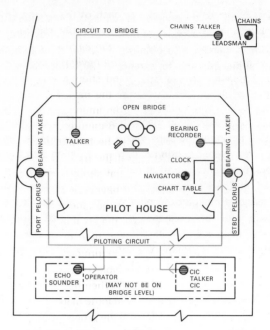

*Piloting team
routine.*

about to pass into *Inland Waters*. The piloting team has been stationed. The navigator has a man stationed on both the port and the starboard gyro repeaters, the echo sounder is manned, a talker is in CIC, and the bearing recorder is at his station. Communications as shown in Figure 1409 have been established. It is a clear day, and Cape Charles, Cape Henry, and Thimble Shoals Lights are in sight. The bearing book has been set up as shown in Figure 1403 with columns headed by the names of the navigational aids expected to be used. The navigator directs the bearing recorder to sound the buzzer or to give a "mark" over the circuit every third minute, being careful to mark exactly when the second hand of the clock reaches the whole minute. The navigator also directs the bearing recorder to tell the port bearing taker to report Cape Henry and Thimble Shoals Lights, and the starboard bearing taker to report Cape Charles Light.

Plotting procedure.

When he is ready to plot, he directs the bearing recorder to obtain a round of bearings. At about ten seconds before the minute, the bearing recorder informs the personnel on the circuit to *"standby."* When the second hand reaches 60, he sounds the buzzer or sings out *"mark"* over the circuit. The man on the port repeater who has two bearings to take, will report first. The first bearing, which he took on the *mark*, will be the object nearest the beam, Cape Henry Light. He reports, "Cape Henry bearing 205°.5." The starboard bearing taker has taken a bearing of Cape Charles Light when the *mark* was heard but does not report until the port bearing taker has reported his first reading. The quarter-master on the starboard side now reports "Cape Charles bearing 010°.0." While this report was being made, the port bearing taker has taken a bearing of Thimble Shoals Light, which he now reports: "Thimble Shoals bearing 287°.0." Since Thimble Shoals is nearly dead ahead, its bearing will *not* have changed appreciably during the time delay between the *mark* and the actual taking of the bearing.

258   When the bearing recorder gave the "mark," the time was noted and recorded in the time column of the bearing book. As each of the bearings was reported by the bearing takers, the recorder wrote it down in the appropriate column of the bearing book, *and repeated it back over the circuit for confirmation*. This procedure enabled the navigator to hear it. The navigator commenced plotting as soon as the first bearing was reported, and should have all three bearings plotted in less than 30 seconds. As soon as the navigator has the fix plotted and labeled, he inspects it to see if it is on the intended track. If it is, he plots DR positions ahead from the fix for the next 6 minutes, which will enable him to be reasonably sure of his position should he be unable to obtain a fix for any reason at the next three-minute mark. If the fix is not along the intended track, the navigator determines the course that should be steered, and recommends the new course to the captain. The navigator plots the DR, using the old course, up to the time of the course change, and then lays down the DR plot for the new course for the remainder of the six minutes from this position. In addition, an extended DR to compute the time of arrival at an expected turning point along the track, the identity of the turning point in terms of relative or true bearing, and range from an identifiable object, and the new course recommendation can be given to the captain. When the recorder, who has been watching the clock, sees that the next three-minute mark is about due, he gives "standby" and "mark" at the proper time, and the procedure continues as before.

Students have learned to label each LOP in a specified manner, by placing the time and the true bearing along the line. The purpose of this is to insure identification and provide a record of data used to plot the LOP. On board ship, the time and true bearing of each LOP are recorded in the Bearing Book, as described above, and by using the information recorded therein, all plotting can be reconstructed should it become necessary. To facilitate speed in plotting, then, the labels may be left off LOP's in fleet practice, and symbolism used. In general usage a fix is marked with a circle, a DR position with a half circle, an EP with a square. If the fix is by electronic methods a triangle is often substituted for the circle.

Plotting the LOP.

Suppose that at about this time the echo sounder operator reports "depth 4 fathoms." He has made this report in compliance with standard doctrine established in this particular ship for reporting a limiting reading of 4 fathoms, and a 6 fathom spot has just been crossed. Since 4 fathoms is the depth of water from the sounding head, the navigator must add to it the distance from the water line to the sounding head before he can compare it with the charted depth. If this distance is 12 feet, then the total depth of water according to the depth finder is 36 feet. The chart at the DR position for the time of the reading showed 34 feet; therefore, the two depths are basically in agreement, for the chart is probably constructed using a low water datum as a sounding reference and two feet of difference can be expected. Height of tide must also be checked, as this can cause a considerable difference from the charted depth.

Soundings.

In addition to the echo sounder, the leadsman in the chains has also been getting soundings, if the speed of the ship permitted it. The navigator must remember that it is extremely difficult for a man to heave a lead and get a sounding in 30 feet of water at speeds much above 3 or 4 knots. In shallower water, the speed can be increased slightly, but usually never above 5 knots and still get accurate soundings by lead line. This is mentioned here, as a navigator should bear this restriction in mind and recommend slowing or stopping at any time

259

when the position of the ship is in real doubt and soundings by the hand lead are essential for the safe navigation of the ship. In this example, assume that the ship was making a speed of 5 knots and the leadsman had obtained a sounding of 6 fathoms. This information was sent to the bridge over the circuit, and the talker on the bridge repeated it to the navigator. The navigator noted this depth, and checked it against the other two to see that they all agreed. If there had been major disagreement between any two of them, he should recommend slowing and checking, until he is absolutely sure of his position obtained by other means. The navigator is responsible for the safe navigation of the ship, and if he is in doubt, *for any reason*, as to the ship's position, the only safe thing to do is so advise the captain and recommend slowing or stopping.

The navigator in piloting.

1410. The foregoing example does not show all of the preparation which the navigator and his assistants made to achieve smooth results.

Prior to entering Chesapeake Bay, the navigator had studied the charts of the area, read and digested the material in the Coast Pilot, Light List, Tide and Current Tables, and had marked on the chart those landmarks and aids to navigation which he expected to use. He had noted on the chart the physical appearance of each of these aids to navigation in order that he might have the information readily available and would be able to utilize it in recognizing the landmarks as they were sighted. With this information firmly in mind, and with necessary notes on the charts, he assembled the bearing takers and the bearing recorder for a briefing. During this briefing he pointed out to each the location of every landmark expected to be used, its name, its appearance, and the order of expected sighting. In so doing he enabled each member of his team to become familiar, in some degree, with the objects which they would be using. The bearing takers knew in advance where to look and what to look for, and the bearing recorder knew the names of the landmarks which he would have to record and transmit over the phones. In cases of entry into unfamiliar pilot waters, there is particular benefit to be gained from preparing and issuing a written brief to each man on the team in order that he can later refer to the printed information rather than trust it to memory. The brief should contain a written description of each expected navigational aid as recorded in the Light List, and appropriate extracts from the Coast Pilot or Sailing Directions. Such a brief materially helps in the smooth operation of a piloting team, and is of particular importance when entering a strange port. If the port is a familiar one, this briefing is usually not necessary.

When on the bridge, the navigator utilizes the knowledge he has gained in preparation. As each landmark and aid to navigation is sighted, he personally checks its appearance to be sure it is correctly identified and compares it with the description in the Light List, not trusting to memory alone. The bearing takers, having been briefed in advance, can be of considerable help in preliminary identification, but the burden of final identification rests on the navigator. As the navigator plots his fixes, and as the ship proceeds up the channel, the prudent navigator visually checks all landmarks and aids to make sure that his ship is where it appears to be on the chart. The quick appraisal and good judgment of an experienced navigator have kept many ships out of danger even though objects—particularly buoys—may previously have been incorrectly identified.

CHAPTER 15

The Practice of Piloting

1501. The preceding chapters have discussed in detail the various charts, publications, instruments, procedures, and techniques customarily required for the safe piloting of a ship. The purpose of this chapter is to relate each of these individual treatments to the actual practice of piloting in order that the inter-relationship of each may be understood, and the importance of each to intelligent voyage planning and execution may be appreciated. To accomplish this purpose, the initial articles discuss the steps which must be taken by a navigator in planning and executing any voyage in pilot waters, while the latter articles illustrate how these general requirements are applied to a specific piloting situation.

Introduction.

1502. As soon as it is known that the ship will get under way for a specified destination, the navigator assembles various data, charts and publications for study so that he can *plan* the voyage in detail before submitting his plan to the commanding officer for approval. Once under way, the navigator and his assistants will find that their time is well occupied with the routine mechanics and techniques of piloting, and that little or no time is available for completing the planning phase. For this reason, it is essential that all planning be done well in advance of the sailing date. In the following paragraphs, all essentials to the completion of adequate and safe planning are discussed. The order of accomplishing these steps is optional, although an attempt has been made to place the various items in the sequence most frequently encountered in practice.

Preliminary preparations.

Authority for a ship to get under way and proceed to a specified destination will usually be in the form of a message, fleet or type employment schedule, or operation order. This authority should be carefully studied, with dates and times of departure and arrival noted, as well as the route which may also be designated. It is customary for the authority directing the movement to specify only *dates* of departure and arrival, leaving the *times* of departure or arrival to the discretion of the commanding officer. This permits him to take advantage of the most favorable conditions of tide, current, and weather. Movement orders may specify other limiting factors such as time, date and SOA; or perhaps only the time and date of arrival will be prescribed. Where exact ETA and ETD are not given, the navigator must complete his study of the various charts and publications as outlined below before these times may be accurately determined.

Determining ETD and ETA.

Once the destination and other information prescribed in the movement order are known, the navigator must determine the charts available for use during the voyage. These are located by reference to the appropriate *Catalog of Charts.*

Determining chart requirements.

Most charts for United States waters are listed in the National Ocean Survey catalog, while the Oceanographic Office Catalog 1N lists all charts issued for for foreign waters and Loran charts.

Using the appropriate catalog, the navigator examines the *index diagrams* covering the area to be traveled. Each index diagram shows by colored outlines the area covered by each chart, with its corresponding number. On the reverse side of these index diagrams is tabulated information giving the edition, date of printing, scale, and purchase price of the several charts.

From this information, the navigator compiles a list of the numbers of all available charts which cover any part of the proposed route. Using these chart numbers, N. O. Pub. No. 1-PCL, the *Portfolio Chart List* is then consulted, and the consecutive numbers of each of the charts previously noted is obtained. With these consecutive numbers, the navigator is able to obtain the charts desired from the portfolio chart stowage, since charts are stowed by consecutive numbers within each portfolio.

Publications required.

The navigator should have available all pertinent Light Lists, Lists of Lights, Coast Pilots, Sailing Directions, and other navigational publications for the area to be traversed. On board naval ships, the current allowances established for the type ship and the fleet to which assigned will normally be adequate. The various publications are described in detail in Chapter 4. After all necessary charts and publications have been assembled, they must be checked to ensure that each is the latest edition, and that the latest pertinent corrections have been entered.

Checking editions of charts. The edition number and date of each chart is checked against that given in the portfolio listings in N. O. 1-PCL to insure that the latest edition is actually on board. Since most naval vessels are on the automatic mailing list maintained by the Oceanographic Distribution Offices, it is usual for the portfolios on board to contain the latest editions. If the latest edition is not on board, it should be obtained from the nearest Oceanographic Distribution Office through normal channels, or from a Branch Oceanographic Office using emergency procedures if time does not permit routine methods.

Chart corrections. The Fleet Chart Correction Record H. O. 5610/2 for each chart to be used is consulted to determine corrections which have been charged on the card, but which have not been entered on the chart. Each of these charged but unmade corrections must be completed before the chart can be used with safety.

Corrections to publications. Each publication to be used must be checked to ensure that the latest corrections are available or have been made. Sailing Directions are corrected by page changes issued periodically, plus corrections published in Notices to Mariners since the effective date of the last page changes. Coast Pilots are corrected by yearly supplements, amended by information in Notices to Mariners. Notes are made on individual pages affected by these corrections, and care must be taken to insure that both the current supplements and appropriate Notices to Mariners are available. Light Lists are also corrected by supplements and Notices to Mariners, and have a special page for recording the numbers of Notices which pertain.

It is usually desirable to get under way or enter port at high water stand, and as near as possible to the time of slack water, although they seldom coincide. A large ship entering a harbor with comparatively shallow water will be primarily concerned with the time of high water, while a smaller ship entering a harbor with deep water but variable current, will be more interested in times when the current is slack.

Tides and limiting conditions.

Occasionally the draft of the ship will be greater than the charted depth (low water) of the harbor. This requires use of Table 3 in the Tide Tables to determine how long before and after high water the depth of the water will be sufficient to permit safe passage of the ship. Extreme care must be used in such cases, as the tide tables are only predictions, and there can be considerable difference between the predicted and the actual conditions.

Draft.

Many ports with large naval concentrations place sortie plans in effect on certain days of the week, specifying times and order for ships to get under way. This plan is normally arranged so that ships nearer the harbor entrance get under way first. The SOPA (Senior Officer Present Afloat) instructions should be consulted for such standing procedures.

Sortie plans.

Since the navigator normally recommends the times of departure and arrival and the SOA to the commanding officer, it is first essential that he determine the total distance to be steamed. This distance may be obtained by measurement from the charts to be used, or, in many cases, by reference to available publications. H. O. Pub. No. 151, *Table of Distance Between Ports* covering foreign ports throughout the world, or *Distance Between U. S. Ports*, a pamphlet published by the National Ocean Survey, should be consulted. Distances between many other combinations of ports will also be found in the pertinent Coast Pilots and Sailing Directions. If it is intended to travel the regular route between ports, the distance given in these publications should be used, as it is more accurate than can normally be determined by chart measurement. The Coast Pilots also include some data on distance between ports.

Determining distance and SOA.

Once favorable hours of departure and arrival have been decided upon, the required SOA can be determined. Care must be taken not to exceed the maximum steaming speeds prescribed by fleet or type commanders in current directives. After the SOA has been computed, the speed to order can be determined, taking into account the ship's displacement, condition of bottom and trim, currents expected to be encountered, and so forth.

1503. After completing the preliminary preparations described above, the navigator is now ready to plan the voyage. Only by commencing the planning phase as far in advance as possible will the navigator have sufficient time to study the various publications and charts, and to give the proposed track careful consideration.

Voyage planning.

Most commanding officers and navigators prefer an overall plot of the entire voyage on one chart. This permits rapid determination of distance made good and distance to go at any desired time during the voyage, and presents clearly the relationship between the route selected and the coastline or adjacent land masses. Unless the voyage is very short, it is not possible to plot the entire track on one chart which is also suitable for piloting. For this reason, a small scale (large area) chart is initially used.

Small scale (large area) charts.

*Large scale
(small area) charts.*

When the route has been established, the navigator must select those charts he will use for piloting. Many areas, such as the east coast of the United States, have charts available to three different scales. The largest scale chart is suitable for harbor piloting, but not for offshore piloting. The most commonly used scale for coastal piloting is 1:80,000, which is the scale of the 1200 chart series issued by the National Ocean Survey. In selecting the scale of the chart to use for a voyage in pilot waters, consideration should be given to the scale used, ascertaining that it includes all of the landmarks and aids to navigation desired or required in any one area. If the scale is too small, the chart coverage may exclude features best suited for visual observation and fixes.

Once the charts to be used are selected, the navigator should insure that he is familiar with the details shown on each. The following should particularly be noted:

Whether depths are indicated in feet or fathoms.

Whether heights are indicated in feet or meters.

The distance indicated by the smallest division of the latitude scale.

The distance indicated by the alternately shaded divisions of the latitude scale.

The significance of the length of the ship and its turning characteristics in relation to the scale of the chart.

The geographical limits covered by each chart.

Variation of the magnetic compass, correction thereto since printing of the chart due to annual change, and the differences in variation at different points along the track.

The patterns of shoal and deep water, and depths, as indicated by the fathom lines.

Abnormal patterns of bottom contour lines which may be useful for determining positions by echo sounder.

Land contours, marshes, bluffs, prominent mountain peaks, and landmarks which may be useful for radar piloting or identification, or which may affect radar PPI interpretation.

Intended track.

Having selected his charts, the navigator now plots the route to be followed on both the large and the small scale charts. The route is normally plotted first on the small scale (large area) chart or charts, and labeled as to track, speed, and distance between points. This permits the navigator to check visually the safety of the track initially laid down, and to make any adjustments which become apparent at this time.

DR positions for selected times are then plotted along the track, using the speed previously determined. The frequency with which these DR positions are plotted on the large area chart will depend upon the judgment of the navigator, the proximity of land masses, and the course desired to be made good. When making an ocean passage, DR positions every twelve hours are normally sufficient; in coastal piloting, a DR position every hour is common practice.

At this time, any special information of interest in the broad planning of the voyage should be noted on the chart. These items may include limits of operational control areas, changes in communications responsibility, limits of special strategic or restricted areas, etc. This information should be noted on the chart in the vicinity of the position at which the event is expected to occur.

The navigator should next translate the general voyage information portrayed on the small scale chart into detailed graphic representations on the large scale charts covering the same areas. At this time, careful reference should be made to the instructions and information given in the Coast Pilots and Sailing Directions for the areas of each chart. If specific routes are recommended or overprinted on the charts, these should be used insofar as possible, for they represent known safe tracks which have been tested over many years. In deciding on details of the final track, the careful navigator will not only avoid all obvious dangers, but will allow himself as much sea room as possible in the areas of these dangers.

Turning points, or points at which the course will be changed, are of particular interest to navigators and should always be marked on the chart. In operational movements of ships in company, it is frequently desirable to assign a name or number designation to these points for ease of reference. The ETA at each turning point should be plainly marked on the charts.

Frequently the intended track may of necessity place the ship in close proximity to dangers to navigation during the voyage. In addition to such natural dangers as rocks, shoals, and bars, various governmental agencies have declared certain designated areas reserved for hazardous operations. Gunnery practice and testing ranges, ammunition disposal areas, special anchorages, and spoil grounds are a few examples. Where particularly confined waters or heavy shipping concentrations prevail, special rules may be in effect to limit maximum speed and to prevent collisions. Each of these areas, whether natural or man-made, constitutes an additional hazard for the mariner. Each chart should be carefully inspected to determine these dangers, the Coast Pilot, Sailing Directions, and Notices to Mariners consulted for detailed information concerning them, and appropriate amplifying notations made on each chart in question. In addition, it is a good practice to outline these danger areas and the limits of water considered safe for the draft of the ship, using a colored pencil. Do not use a red pencil if the chart will be used under a red light on the bridge at night, as the red marking will not be visible. For this reason, magenta is frequently used instead.

Danger areas, danger bearings, and limits of safe water.

Where appropriate, danger bearings should be located, plotted, and the information noted on the chart.

Special attention should be given to the aids to navigation expected to be sighted during the voyage. A list in which has been recorded a complete description of the structure and its light characteristics, the expected time of sighting, and the approximate bearing at sighting will be of particular use to the navigator.

Aids to navigation.

Daytime identification. Under normal conditions of visibility, a lighthouse may be seen in daytime at its geographic range and may be identified by its color and structural appearance. A complete description of the distinctive features of

Lighthouses.

265

each is given in the appropriate Light List and, since this information seldom appears on the chart, notation should be made thereon. Photographs or drawings of many lights appear in the Sailing Directions, while many foreign charts include a sketch of the light near its symbol.

Buoys.

While the color and shape of buoys that are a part of the lateral system used in United States waters are evident from the printed chart symbol, it is not always possible to predict the characteristics of a special purpose buoy by chart inspection alone. In like manner it is not possible to apply the rules pertaining to United States buoyage to interpret the various buoyage systems in use in foreign countries, for each system is dissimilar except by coincidence. In such cases careful reference to List of Lights and Sailing Directions is necessary to avoid misinterpretation.

Lights.

Nighttime identification. The majority of harbors, bays, coastal and danger areas are well-marked with lighted aids which the navigator should personally and positively identify on each occasion of sighting. Accurate identification of buoys is particularly important and should not be a matter of delegation, chance, or guesswork. The characteristic period of lighted buoys is not printed on recent charts and, even when using large-scale charts, information such as the length of each flash and eclipse of major aids does not always appear. Only by use of the Light List, comparing the recorded information with those characteristics actually observed, can the navigator be absolutely certain of the identification of a lighted navigational aid. Supplementary information appearing *only* in the Light List should be the subject of a special entry in a box adjacent to the charted symbol.

Visibility of lights. While preparing for the voyage, computed visibility for all lights expected to be sighted en route are plotted and labeled on the charts. In United States waters, the *nominal range* is the extreme distance in nautical miles at which a light may be seen in clear weather with an unlimited height of eye, as set forth in article 613. In computing the range at which the light should be sighted in clear weather, the navigator must allow for his, or the lookout's, height of eye, as described in article 614.

Tide and current data.

Times and heights of the tides, and times and strengths of the currents for the points of departure and arrival are computed for the respective dates. This information should be carefully studied before reaching a decision as to the time of departure and arrival. Some ports may have shoals or bars that can be crossed only near the time of high water, while others may have bridges of such vertical clearance that high-masted ships may be required to transit the channel at low water. Ships arriving at or leaving their berths will be assisted by a favorable current, while an unfavorable current may make the evolution very difficult, especially for a single screw ship.

When the decision as to the times of arrival and departure has been made, the navigator should consult the applicable National Ocean Survey tidal current chart, if available, for the ports or channels in question, and the velocity and direction of the current at selected reference points along the track noted on the chart. Similarly, the current diagrams contained in the Current Tables should be consulted to determine the average current expected en route. This information, combined with the selected speed of advance, can be used to determine ordered speed at selected stages of the voyage. Occasionally these diagrams may be used to plan the time of departure in order that advantage may be taken of a favorable channel current.

For ocean passages, the estimates of predicted currents contained in the monthly Pilot Chart and in the various current atlases should also be taken into consideration. These estimates have evolved after years of current observations, and warrant careful attention by the navigator.

Information concerning the anchorage or berthing space assigned to the ship may not be received until the ship has reported its ETA to the port authority. If the destination is a port frequently used by naval vessels, an anchorage chart is usually available showing the exact location of all berths, the radius of each, and the range and bearing of its center from a prominent point or light. Additional information concerning the port such as pier space, tugs, pilots, communications, harbor facilities and other pertinent items of interest are contained in the Coast Pilot, Sailing Directions, and Fleet Guides which should be carefully examined prior to arrival. In addition, the Hydrolant or Hydropac file and the local Coast Guard Notices to Mariners should be checked to ascertain if any recent changes to navigational aids have been made, or special warnings concerning dangers to navigation have been issued for the area. *Port information.*

Upon arrival, the latest copies of the daily memorandum and any other pertinent information available in the Branch Oceanographic Office should be obtained. Every week, the office of the Port Director distributes a list of the exercises to be conducted in the designated operating and training area. This list should be carefully checked to make sure that the ship, upon departure, does not interfere with scheduled exercises in the area.

The requirements for pilot and tug assistance vary from port to port, and the Coast Pilot, Sailing Directions, or Fleet Guide must be consulted to determine the procedures in effect at each. Some ports with an elaborate pilot association require separate pilots for the approach to the harbor, the harbor itself, and the final berthing, whereas other ports may have no regular pilots engaged. In such cases, local fishermen, familiar with local conditions, can be of invaluable assistance to a ship making its first passage in strange waters. *Berthing assistance.*

Depending upon weather and other considerations, a large ship may require the assistance of two or more tugs, and smaller ships one, when berthing or undocking, and forehanded arrangements must be made in such cases.

1504. The preceding articles have dealt with the preparations made in the planning stages by the navigator in advance of the day prescribed for getting under way. It is assumed that the navigator has conferred with the commanding officer and that the latter has approved of the details of the plan proposed by the navigator, or that any changes directed by him have been incorporated into the final plan. There remain, however, certain other preparatory steps to be taken which are properly postponed until the overall plan has been decided upon, the systematic accomplishment of which are no less important to the execution of a safe passage than was careful voyage planning. *Preparing to get under way.*

A typical ship's organization book prescribes that the gyrocompass be started at least four hours before getting under way in order that the gyro may settle *Gyrocompass.*

on the meridian. Many experienced navigators prefer to start the gyrocompass well in advance of this minimum. This provides sufficient time to detect and correct any minor mechanical or electrical malfunctioning before getting under way.

Degaussing equipment.

Prior to getting under way, the proper settings for the ship's degaussing equipment should be determined by reference to the special charts prepared for that purpose, and the engineering department informed of the coil readings to be pre-set before departure. This equipment is always used in wartime and at any other time when it is known that influence mines may be encountered in a specified area. At the direction of the navigator, the degaussing equipment is energized before leaving protected waters and periodic adjustments made thereafter to the coil settings to maintain protection at a maximum.

Piloting team.

Prior to entering or leaving port, the navigator should assemble his piloting team for a briefing. While the bearing takers and the bearing recorder will be most vitally concerned with the briefing, all other members of the piloting team and all members of the navigation department should also attend. During the briefing the navigator should point out all aids to navigation expected to be used, their name, appearance, and about where and when they will be sighted. All natural and man-made ranges are located in order that a check on the gyro-compass may be made whenever one is crossed. Any special information concerning soundings should be given to the echo sounder operator at this time. This is also an excellent opportunity to brief the CIC officer on the plans for entering or leaving port.

It is advantageous that key members of the team be given the material covered in the briefing in written form in order that the detailed plan, characteristics, name, and appearance of lights and other important features to be encountered not be trusted entirely to memory.

Equipment checking.

The organization book of a ship as well as the navigator's sea detail bill will prescribe certain readiness tests of various items of ship's equipment in accordance with a pre-under way time schedule. Again, forehanded testing will permit time to repair casualties uncovered during this phase. The master gyro is first checked for error, after which the gyro repeaters on the bridge are checked against the master gyro. The steering engine and related electric and hydraulic transmission systems are tested as is the engine order telegraph, the depth finder, the bridge radio, the navigation and signal searchlights, and the navigational lighting circuits, and appropriate check-off notations made in the list maintained to record the test results. After the special sea detail has been set and all stations are manned, this equipment should be re-checked and all remaining items on the check-off list attended to, such as external and internal communication circuits, the bridge PPI, and the whistle and siren. In addition, the navigator should personally ascertain that all necessary charts, publications, and plotting instruments are available at his chart desk and are ready for use.

Gyro error.

With the piloting team on station, a round of bearings is taken and plotted on the chart or a gyro observation of a range is obtained and the amount and direction of gyro error, if any is present, is determined. When known, CIC should be notified of the results and an appropriate entry made in the bearing book. When the gyro error steadies down and remains constant, the navigator may offset the parallel motion protractor by the amount of the error. This procedure permits plotting the reported bearings as they are received from the bearing takers without the necessity of applying gyro error before plotting each line of position.

The navigator should personally check to see that his piloting team is on station and in all respects, both personnel and material, ready to function. A well organized and efficient team requires a minimum of supervision, but the navigator should insure that the more experienced bearing taker is on that side of the ship by which will pass the majority of navigational aids. Any final instructions pertaining to frequency of fixes, depth readings, draft, minor changes in plan, or bearing order should be announced at this time. The draft report should be made to the conning officer and the officer of the deck, and entered in the ship's log. To conclude all of the multitudinous preparations made by the navigator since the receipt of the original movement order, the navigator reports his department "ready for sea" to the executive officer, signifying that every phase of navigational planning and final checking under his cognizance has been accomplished to the best of his knowledge and ability. *Final preparation.*

So far the navigator has been primarily concerned with the science of navigation in extracting information from a number of publications which will be of great value to him once the ship is under way. The manner in which the navigator employs the art of navigation—the practical use of the information made available to him from whatever source—will be the subject of the remainder of the chapter.

1505. The destroyer *Glennon*, moored starboard side to Pier 4, U. S. Naval Shipyard, Philadelphia, Pennsylvania, had completed its overhaul and was awaiting orders to proceed to Norfolk, Virginia. On the afternoon of 7 August, the following message was received: *Voyage planning.*

```
TO:   USS GLENNON   DD-840

FROM:   COMDESRON

        R-071900Z-GR   18-BT

WHEN RFS DEPART PHILANSY FOR NOB NORVA
DIRECT X SOA15 X MOOR PIER 4 PRIOR 090800Q
```

The navigator noted that both the time of arrival and speed of advance had been specified. Estimating that the trip will take about 16 hours, the ship should depart Philadelphia during the afternoon of 8 August in order to arrive on schedule. This is the navigator's initial estimate of the time of departure which will be corrected after the exact length of the trip and current data has been determined.

Since both Philadelphia and Norfolk are deep water ports, there are no restrictions placed on the times of departure or arrival by the state of the tide. As the time of arrival at Norfolk is specified, only the time of departure can be varied to allow for conditions en route. On consulting the commanding officer, the navigator learns that he desires to take departure from the Delaware Light

Ship, and make a landfall on Chesapeake Light, off the entrance to Chesapeake Bay, rather than to follow the coast line. The voyage is planned accordingly.

SOA.

By reference to Table 1, "Atlantic Ocean Distances for Deep-Draft Vessels, Quebec, Canada to Panama Canal Zone," in Volume 3 of the Coast Pilot, the distance from Philadelphia to Norfolk was found to be 269 miles. As the speed of advance was specified as 15 knots, the navigator decided to allow about 19 hours for the trip. This is more than the time computed using distance and SOA, but makes allowance for time expected to be lost in the Delaware River transit due to speed regulations and heavy traffic.

ETD.

The time of departure from Philadelphia is now determined by subtracting 19 hours from the ETA, 0800, on 9 August.

Time of arrival Norfolk	9 August	0800 (Plus 4)
Length of trip		19 hours
Time of departure Phila.	8 August	1300 (Plus 4)

Both Philadelphia and Norfolk are keeping Daylight Saving Time. If Norfolk were keeping Standard Time (+5), departure from Philadelphia could have been delayed by one hour. In such planning the navigator must always allow for a possible difference in the time kept at the port of departure, and that at the port of arrival.

Tides and currents.

The appropriate *Current Tables* and *Current Diagram*, as well as the *Tidal Current Charts* are next inspected. The Current Table gives the time of Slack, Ebb Begins, as 1112 (+5), and that of Maximum Ebb as 1412 (+5), the velocity of the maximum ebb being 1.8 knots. Slack water at Delaware Bay Entrance will therefore occur about an hour before the ship gets under way at 1300 (+4), and the maximum ebb at the entrance will occur about two hours after getting under way. The Current diagram indicates that the ship will encounter a flood tide for approximately the first two and a half hours after departing Philadelphia, until in the vicinity of Newcastle. The Current Charts show that this current will average about one knot, using the factor of 0.8 for a maximum current of 1.8 knots at the entrance.

Chart preparation.

1506. Next, the navigator located the number of every chart on the direct route from Philadelphia to Norfolk by reference to Volume 1, U. S. Department of Commerce Nautical Chart Catalog of the Atlantic and Gulf Coasts (Figure 1506a) and, using H. O. Pub 1-PCL, listed the consecutive number of each:

Numerical Index of Coast Survey Charts					
CHART	CONSEC	CHART	CONSEC	CHART	CONSEC
280	A 1343	1219	A 1338		
295	A 1342	1220	B 1345A	562	A 1348
294	A 1340	1221	B 1346	481	A 1350
1218	A 1330	1222	A 1347	400	A 1352

Since the list indicated that every chart was located in Portfolio 13, it was a simple matter to obtain the charts from the portfolio chart stowage. Comparing each chart with the edition data contained in the portfolio summary section of H. O. 1-PCL, Figure 1506b, the navigator determined that the charts he intends to use are in fact the latest Oceanographic Office issue.

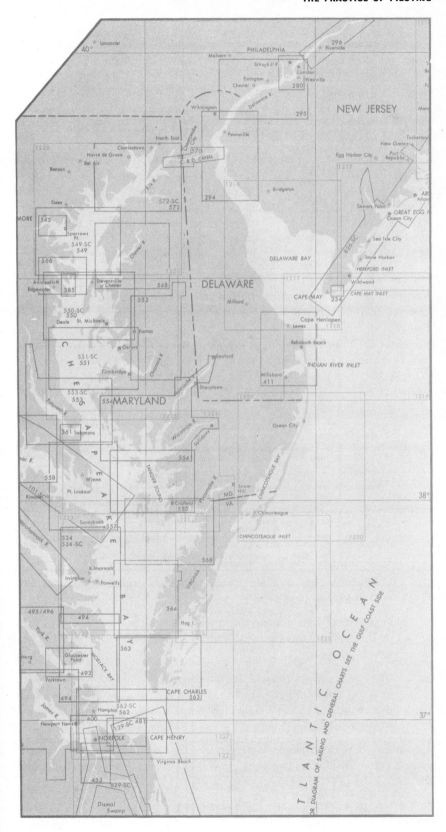

Figure 1506a: Portion of National Ocean Survey Nautical Chart Catalog of the Atlantic and Gulf Coasts, Volume 1

271

NEW YORK TO CAPE HENRY INCL. DELAWARE BAY AND RIVER

CONSEC	CHART	ED. NO.	ED. DATE	ABBREVIATED DATE
B1336	CS 1216	011	09 65	Sea Girt Light to Little Egg Inlet
B1337	CS 1217	018	05 66	Little Egg Inlet to Hereford Inlet
A1338	CS 1219	018	06 64	Cape May to Fenwick I. light
A1339	CS 1218*	013	09 66	Delaware Bay
A1340	CS 0294*	015	11 66	Delaware R. Smyrna R. to Wilmington
B1341	CS 0570	003	03 60	Chesapeake and Delaware Canal
A1342	CS 0295	022	06 65	Delaware R. Wilmington to Phila.
A1343	CS 0280	018	04 65	Phila. and Camden Waterfronts
A1344	CS 0296*	016	09 66	Delaware R. Phila. to Trenton
A1345	HO 5672 OA	009	04 66	Opera. Areas Vic. of Virginia Capes
B1345A	CS 1220*	013	10 66	Fenwick I. light to Chincoteague Inlet

Figure 1506b: Extract from N. O. pub. No. I-PCL.

Next the Fleet Chart Correction Record for each chart on the list is removed from file and checked to determine the status of chart corrections. With all chart corrections made, the navigator is ready to plot his intended track, using as a guide the information contained in the Coast Pilot, Volume 3. This publication, as well as all others to be used, has first been examined to insure that the latest changes have been entered therein and that the latest supplements are available.

The section of the Coast Pilot dealing with Delaware Bay and the Delaware River passage is carefully studied to obtain all pertinent information relating to these waterways. The navigator made particular note of the following:

Channels. Federal project depth is 40 feet from the sea through the main channel in Delaware Bay and River to the Philadelphia Naval Shipyard.

Speed. The Corps of Engineers has requested masters to limit speed to 6 knots when passing piers and wharves along the Delaware River in order to avoid damage caused by excessive wave action.

Obstructions. Delaware Memorial Bridge has a suspension main channel span clearance of 188 feet.

Fogs. Most frequent along this part of the Atlantic coast during months of December, January, and February, but may be encountered at any time of the year.

Rules of the Road. Inland Pilot Rules shall be followed from Cape May Inlet East Jetty Light to Cape May Harbor Inlet Lighted Bell Buoy 2 CM; thence to South Shoal Lighted Bell Buoy 4; thence to the northernmost extremity of Cape Henlopen.

Ranges.

A wealth of other information is available in the Coast Pilot, but only that of direct concern in plotting the track down the bay has been included in this chapter.

As the navigator plotted the recommended track on the chart, he observed that the Delaware River Main Channel was exceptionally well marked with buoys

Figure 1506c: Example of intended track chart notations on Chart No. 280.

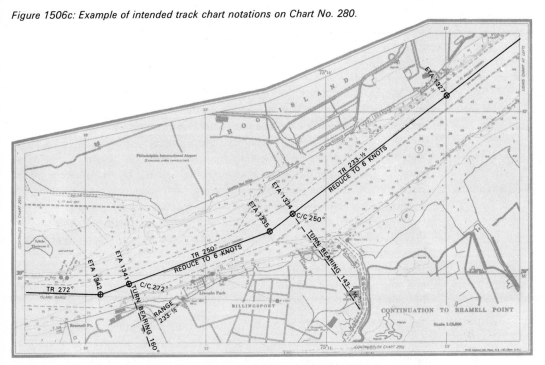

and that every leg of the channel was marked by both day and night ranges. A notation was made on the chart of the bearing of each of the fifteen ranges, observation of which would permit a continuous check of the gyro while in the confined waters of the river.

It was also noted that it would be necessary to reduce speed to six knots when passing Hog Island, Billingsport, Paulsboro, Chester, Marcus Hook, Edgemoor and New Castle. Due to this speed restriction, and considering it advisable not to exceed 15 knots while in confined waters, the navigator estimated that the speed would be 10 knots until abreast of New Castle. Using a time of departure of 1300 and a speed of 10 knots, the ETA at every turn point was computed and noted on the chart. After passing New Castle a speed of 15 knots was assumed for determining the ETA at the remainder of the turning points.

After plotting the track on all charts, the navigator computed the amount of advance and transfer for every turn, plotted the point at which the turn should commence, and located a landmark as near the beam as possible for use as a turning bearing. The turning point, turning bearing and ETA were all noted on the chart. Two of these notations are illustrated in Figure 1506c.

Continuing this procedure, all notations concerning tracks, ranges, turning points, turning bearings, areas requiring a speed reduction, and the ETA at the various points were made on the remaining charts to be used.

After passing Chohansey River, N. O. S. Chart 1218 must then be used to plot the track until abeam of Cape Henlopen. Subsequently, the track is plotted successively on N. O. S. Charts 1219, 1220, 1221, and 1222 as far as Cape Henry. N. O. S. Chart 1109 is used for planning the section of the voyage from the mouth of Delaware Bay to the Virginia Capes. Departure is to be taken from the

273

Delaware Light Ship for Lighted Whistle Buoy "2JS" and hence direct to the Chesapeake Light.

N. O. S. Chart 400 is prepared for entry into Hampton Roads, in the same manner that Chart 280 was prepared for departure from Philadelphia.

Danger bearings.

While proceeding down the river for the first forty miles, every channel axis is marked by ranges providing a ready means of observing the ship's position in relation to the center of the channel. After leaving the Liston Range, no more ranges are available and the navigator must employ other means to keep the ship in safe water. Besides taking frequent fixes, the navigator previously decided that danger bearings would be very useful. An examination of the chart showed that the red sectors of the principal lights coincided with danger bearings. The limits of these sectors were outlined in magenta and the exact bearing obtained from the light list. The information concerning the sectors, danger bearings, and the description of each light structure, were placed in a box adjacent to the light symbol on the chart. A list of all lights that would be seen from sunset until sunrise was then prepared giving information as to name and number of the light, light characteristics, length of flash and eclipse, and its sound signal.

Lights.

Figure 1506d: Arcs of visibility.

The computed visibility of all lights that would be sighted after sunset was determined for this ship, using a height of eye of 36 feet, and the arcs of visibility plotted on the chart as in Figure 1506d. From the intersection of the track

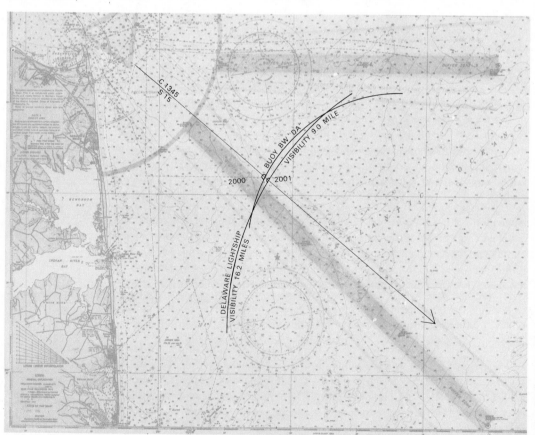

with the arc of visibility, the predicted bearing and time of sighting was computed and added to the summary, an extract of which follows:

Expected Time of Sighting	Bearing	Name of Aid	Characteristics	Fog Signal
2000	125°	BW "DA" Buoy	MO' (A) vis. 9.0	Whistle Radar Reflector
2001	137°	Delaware Lightship	Gp Fl (4) ev. 30 sec vis. 16.2	Diaphone
2243	270°	Red "2JS" Buoy	Fl ev. 4 sec vis. 9.0	Whistle
0343	315°	Chesapeake Light	Gp Fl (2) ev. 5 sec. vis. 19.3	Horn

Arcs of visibility of the first two of these lights are shown in Figure 1506d. Since sunset occurs at 2005 both of these lights will become visible almost immediately after sunset. In this figure note the safety lanes laid down for entering and departing Delaware Bay. The appropriate lanes must be used by all major vessels.

Tide tables for Philadelphia and Norfolk were prepared as follows: *Other data.*

	8 August			9 August	
Philadelphia			**Norfolk (Sewell's Point)**		
Low water	1118 (+4)	0.1 ft.	Low water	0612 (+4)	(−)0.2 ft.
High water	1624 (+4)	6.2 ft.	High water	1230 (+4)	3.0 ft.

Current tables for Delaware Bay Entrance and Chesapeake Bay Entrance were prepared in the following form:

	8 August			9 August	
Delaware Bay Entrance			**Chesapeake Bay Entrance**		
Max. Flood	0912 (+4) 1.8 K				
Slack, Ebb Begins	1212 (+4)		Slack, Ebb Begins	0248 (+4)	
Max. Ebb	1512 (+4) 1.8 K		Max. Ebb	0612 (+4) 1.6 K	
Slack, Flood Begins	1818 (+4)		Slack, Flood Begins	0930 (+4)	
Max. Flood	2118 (+4) 1.9 K		Max. Flood	1200 (+4) 1.1 K	

Using the publication *Tidal Currents Charts—Delaware Bay and River*, the navigator determined the velocity and direction of the current at various points along the river for the estimated time of passage. Figure 1506e is the tidal current chart used during the first hour of the trip. These charts are related to the time of maximum current at the entrance, and the appropriate one must be used for each hour in the current cycle.

From the Current Tables the navigator determined that the maximum flood will occur at the Schuylkill River entrance, near the Navy Yard, at 1257 (+4) with a velocity of 0.5 knots, setting in the direction 355°.

He further computed from the Current Tables that the current at Sewell's Point at Norfolk will be slack at 0800 (+4) on 9 August.

With the time of departure fixed, and the speed in Delaware River and Bay estimated, the navigator may use the current diagram in the current tables to determine the direction and velocity of the current which will be encountered at various stages during the river and bay passage. The under way time is 1300 (+4) 48 minutes before the time of slack water preceding the ebb current at the entrance to the Bay. Using the current diagram in the current tables, the navigator drew a line with a slope equal to that given for a speed of ten knots, the estimated SOA for the first part of the river passage. (An example of the slopes of speed lines furnished for use with this type of diagram is shown in Figure 1506f.) This line originates at the intersection of the PHILA (Chestnut St.) station with the vertical grid of "1 hour after ebb begins." This speed line terminates at the NEW CASTLE station, where it is estimated that a speed of 15 knots can be ordered. A new speed line for speed 15 knots is originated and extended to the entrance of the Bay, called "Overfalls" in the current diagram. By inspection, the navigator finds that the ship will encounter a flood current until almost abeam of New Castle, and that the average velocity of this current will be about 1.2 knots. Below New Castle, the current will be ebbing, with an average velocity of about 1.4 knots until the ship reaches Brandywine Shoal Light, at which point a flood current with an average velocity of about 0.6 knots will be encountered until the ship clears the Bay.

The navigator now prepared his notebook, listing in chronological order every event of interest for the passage. Examples of typical entries is as follows :

Estimated Time	Event
1300	Under way.
1315	Set course 274°, speed 10.
1318	C/C to 233°.5 on the Miflin Range.
1328	Reduce speed to 6 knots off Hog Island Billingsport.
1334	C/C to 250° on the Billingsport Range.
1341	C/C to 272° on the Tinicum Range.
	(Intervening entries omitted)
1723	R "32" Qk Fl Bell abeam. C/C to 156° (Cross Ledge Range)
1736	Cross Ledge Lt abeam. C/C to 145° (Miah Maull Range)
	(Intervening entries omitted)
1919	"4" Fl Bell abeam. Special sea and anchor detail secured.
2005	Sunset.

Based on the navigational planning as completed, a listing of all navigational events for the entire voyage is prepared, similar to that shown above. Such a listing is invaluable, especially when it is expected that the ship will be in pilot waters for an extended period of time, for it permits the assistant navigator or the officer of the deck to anticipate each item as the passage progresses, and permits the navigator greater freedom for supervision and observation.

Under way from Philadelphia to Norfolk.

Prior to getting under way, all equipment checks mentioned in article 1504 were completed, and all personnel concerned in the piloting team and the CIC piloting team were briefed and given last minute instructions. Gyro error was determined to be zero.

The ship got under way on time, and as the trip down the bay progressed, the assistant navigator plotted fixes on the chart every three minutes, while the navigator exercised supervision over the entire team, evaluated the information, and made recommendations to the commanding officer regarding changes

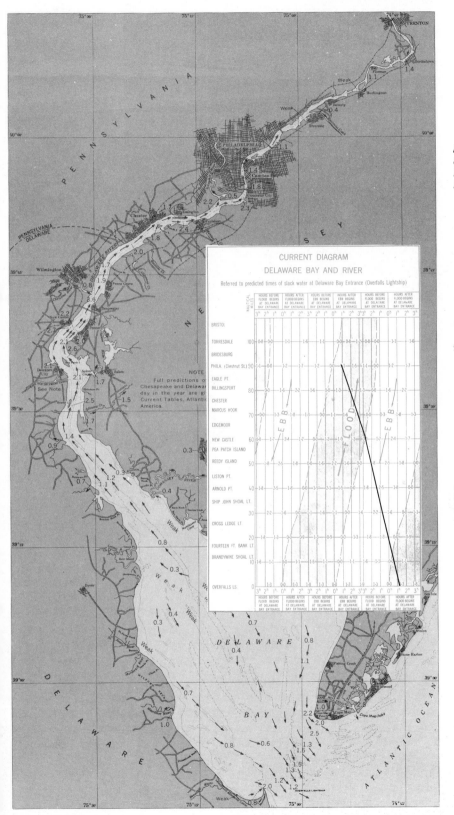

Figure 1506e: Tidal current chart for Delaware Bay and River. (Background)

Figure 1506f: Current diagram for Delaware Bay and River. (Insert)

of course and speed to carry out the voyage safely. Heavy river traffic slowed the ship so that by the time New Castle was reached, an SOA of eight rather than ten knots had been maintained. Since sufficient leeway had been allowed in the navigational planning, this occasioned no difficulty, and the schedule of events was adjusted accordingly. At 2105 departure was taken on Overfalls Lightship, and the SOA to Chesapeake Light was adjusted to arrive abeam at 0500 (+4).

Once the adjusted SOA for the next phase of the trip was known, the expected time of sighting each light was inserted in the summary prepared earlier, and one copy provided for the commanding officer, one for the officer of the deck, and one retained for the navigator's use. Using this same information, the data for the Captain's Night Orders were prepared and sent to the commanding officer. See Figure 1506g. This data included the time and bearing of sighting each navigational aid, the expected times of arrival at each turning point, with the new course and the bearing of aids used as markers for the course change, and any other pertinent data of interest to the safe navigation of the ship.

Figure 1506g: Extracts from navigation data for preparation of night orders.

ETA	C/C to:	Name	Distance	Bearing
2105	200°	Delaware Lt. V.	2.0 miles	044°
2232	213°	Buoy R "2JS" Fl. Whis.	0.5 miles	270°
		No other lights are expected to be sighted before Chesapeake Lt.		
0500		Chesapeake Lt.	0.7 miles	315°

Entering port at Norfolk.

At 0603 Cape Henry Light was passed abeam to port and the special sea detail was set. Since Norfolk was the home port of the ship, no further briefing of the piloting team was necessary. Again the assistant navigator did the actual plotting on the chart, while the navigator kept a continuous check on all the various phases of navigating the ship into port.

The piloting team was functioning smoothly and the ship proceeded up the channel without incident. At 0705, speed was reduced after passing Fort Wool.

The tug and pilot met the ship as scheduled, and the first line was secured to the pier at 0749. The piloting team and all equipment except the gyro were secured after all lines were doubled-up. The navigator, knowing that the stay in Norfolk would be short, decided not to secure the gyro.

Summary.

1507. The first part of this chapter was devoted to summarizing in general terms the preparation and planning necessary for the safe travel of a ship from one port to another. The latter part of the chapter demonstrated the application of these procedures to a typical voyage from Philadelphia to Norfolk, primarily emphasizing the navigational planning aspects of the passage. Although much of this chapter is typical, the procedures used are not exclusive, and no attempt has been made to describe all of the work done by the navigator and the piloting team. Navigation, like any other professional skill, requires thorough preparation and careful execution to be successful. Careless or incomplete work can endanger not only ships, but the lives of many people and is a blemish on the pride and record of a professional mariner. If you understand all of the procedures and techniques necessary to completion of a voyage such as is described here, you have mastered the mechanics of the navigational profession in pilot waters; the polish and precision of the professional navigator will come only with experience.

CHAPTER 16

Radar Navigation

Introduction.

1601. Radar (*RA*dio *D*etecting *A*nd *R*anging) as used for navigation is a system of determining distances by measuring the time between the transmission and return of an electromagnetic signal which has been reflected back to the receiver by a "target." The returned signal may be reflected as an "echo"; alternately, it may be retransmitted by a *transponder* triggered by the original signal. A transponder generates a signal automatically, when interrogated by a signal of the appropriate frequency. Bearings may also be obtained by radar.

Radar equipment consists essentially of these five parts:

Equipment.

Transmitter. An oscillator which produces electromagnetic waves of energy. Extremely high frequencies, generally 3,000 to 10,000 though sometimes as high as 30,000 MHz, are used.

Modulation generator (*keyer*). It turns the transmitter on and off so that the energy is sent out in pulses of about one *microsecond* (one millionth of a second) or less. Approximately 500 to 3,000 pulses per second are transmitted by most surface radars, depending on the range scale in use.

Antenna. Used both for transmitting the signal and receiving the reflected signal, or *echo.* A suitable antenna must be directional and so mounted that it can be rotated.

Preamplifier. Amplifies the echo and sends it on to the *receiver,* where it is further amplified for display. An electronic switch, *transmitter/receiver cell* (T/R cell) is provided between the receiver and antenna to disconnect the receiver and thereby prevent damage during the interval of transmission of the energy pulse.

Indicator. Presents the information in a form for interpretation. It consists essentially of a cathode ray tube (CRT), the face or screen of which is commonly referred to as the *scope* (Figure 1601a), and various timing circuits and controls. In the scope a stream of electrons is directed toward a fluorescent screen, appearing there as a dot of light.

A typical system arrangement for the five parts of a radar system is shown in Figure 1601b, with the range unit, or travel time to distance converter, shown.

Various types of presentation are used on CRTs, but for radar navigation only one type is generally employed; this presentation is called the *PPI* for *Plan Position Indicator.*

Figure 1601a: Dia-grammatic sketch of a cathode ray tube (CRT) and electro-static deflector. Many radars use magnetic deflection which is accom-plished by exciting a coil located at the neck of the CRT.

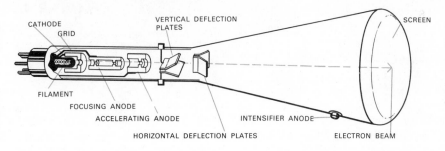

Figure 1601b: Typical radar system arrangement.

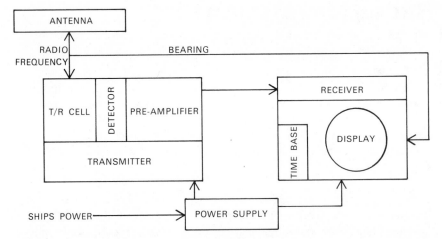

On the PPI, the transmitted beam of energy is presented as a radial line, originat-ing at the "own ship" position at the center of the screen, and rotating in bearing in synchronism with the antenna's rotation. When the radiated energy from the antenna strikes a target, the returning energy is amplified and causes a small area of the screen to glow. As the radial line is synchronized to the bearing of the antenna to which own ships course has been added from the gyrocompass, the true bearing of the target is indicated. Navy surface search radars present the PPI picture with north at the top of the screen when in *true bearing* position. When in *relative bearing* position ship's head is presented at the top. The bearing graduation is placed around the PPI, permitting direct reading of bearings. The time base sweeps the beam across the CRT at a rate synchronized to the propagation rate of radar energy to the range scale selected therefore

Figure 1601c: PPI presentation of radar.

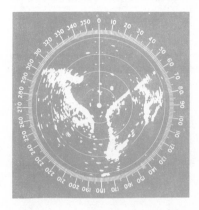

providing for determining range or dis-tance of the target from own ship. The screen phosphor is selected to have the required *persistence;* that is, echoes con-tinue to glow, after the radial line has passed them. By selecting the proper phosphor decay a continuous chart-like picture of the surrounding area is thus presented without the smearing of the old traces into the new. The lighted area surrounding own ship at the center of the screen is *clutter* caused by *sea return,* which is described in article 1604.

1602. Radar has several advantages over other navigational aids for piloting: *Advantages of radar.*

It can be used at night and during periods of low visibility, when most other methods are not available.

A fix can be obtained from a single object, since both range and bearing are provided.

Fixes can be obtained rapidly. With the PPI, a continuous position is available.

Navigation by radar is often more accurate than other methods of piloting during periods of reduced visibility.

Fixes may be available at greater distances from land than in most methods of piloting.

It may be used with great effect to assist in the prevention of collision during periods of low visibility.

It can be used to locate and track violent tropical storms.

1603. As a navigational aid, radar is subject to certain limitations and dis- *Limitations of radar.* advantages:

It is subject to mechanical and electrical failure.

There are both minimum and maximum range limitations.

Interpretation of the information presented on the scope is not always easy, even after considerable training.

It is less accurate than visual piloting, i.e., a visual bearing is more accurate than a radar bearing.

It requires transmission from the ship.

Charts do not always give information necessary for identification of radar echoes.

Small boats, buoys, etc., may not be detected, especially if a high sea is running, or if they are near the shore.

1604. Many factors affect the operational characteristics of radar. The accuracy *Accuracy.* of positions obtained by radar varies considerably with different types of radar and with the skill of the operator. In general, the accuracy of radar fixes compares favorably with those obtained by other methods. The limitations of each radar set should be thoroughly understood by those who are depending on its information. Some of the factors affecting the accuracy are beam width, pulse length, mechanical adjustment, and interpretation of return. Radar signals, while *Beam width.* directional, are transmitted as narrow, fan-shaped beams. Echoes are received continuously as the beam sweeps across a *target*, or reflecting surface. The center of the arc thus indicated is the desired bearing. On the PPI scope the effect is to cause a target to appear wider than it actually is. On each side its width is increased by about half the beam width, or slightly less. If two or more *Resolution in bearing.* targets are relatively close together at about the same range, their widened pips may merge, appearing as a single pip of a larger target. The minimum difference in bearing between two objects at the same range that can be separated by a radar is called its *resolution in bearing.* The ability to make this separation is directly dependent on beam width. A number of piles, rocks, or small boats near a shore may appear as a solid line, giving a false impression of the position of the actual shore line.

Pulse length.

This factor affects the depth of the reflected signal in a manner similar to the widening by the beam width. Thus, a signal of one microsecond duration reflected from a flat, perpendicular surface, continues to be received for one microsecond. The depth of such a pip is equal to half the distance traveled by the signal in one microsecond, or 492 feet. The shorter the signal, the more accurate is the depth of the pip. This is the minimum difference in range between two objects on the same bearing that can be separated by a radar. The ability to make this separation is dependent primarily on pulse length, but to some extent also on the pulse shape and the fidelity of the receiver. False interpretation may occur when two or more targets appear as a single long one, or when a ship, buoy, or rock is near shore and is not separated from it on the PPI.

Resolution in range.

Frequency.

It may be stated as a generality that radars operating near the top of the normal radar frequency range of 9500 MHz may easily be designed to have shorter pulse length and narrower beam width and therefore to give rather better resolution in both bearing and range than do those operating at lower frequency. On the other hand, for an equal output of power, sets operating at lower frequencies can acquire targets at somewhat longer ranges. The useful operational range of a given set depends not only on the frequency employed, but also on the height of the antenna above water, the power output, and its power of resolution. Low frequency radar, as a rule, permits better target acquisition in areas of heavy rain, and also tends to have a smaller area masked by *sea return* or *clutter.* Sea return is caused by a portion of the transmitted signal being reflected by waves. It occurs principally in the area immediately surrounding the ship, and can mask targets within its area. On the other hand 3 cm radars operating at peak pulse powers far below the allowable maximum can detect targets at the horizon range of most radar antenna installations. A 3 cm radar at 25 kw peak pulse power can detect large ships at ranges above 60 miles under certain atmospheric conditions.

Sea return.

Sensitivity time control.

On modern radar sets special circuits are included with appropriate manual settings to permit improved resolution in both range and bearing. A *sensitivity time control* (STC) circuit (for clutter control) changes the gain characteristics of the receiver at close-in ranges. This circuit is valuable in reducing sea return saturation at close ranges so that nearby targets can be seen; it does not affect targets beyond the limit of its time base. A *fast time constant* (FTC) circuit (for differentiation) provides differentiation of the received signals and also helps to reduce *rain clutter,* the pale echoes on the PPI scope caused by rainfall.

Fast time constant circuit.

The pulse length and repetitive rate can also be adjusted for best resolution at given ranges. For example, a pulse repetition rate of 1500 pulses per second and a pulse length of 0.1 microseconds is used on some sets for ranges under approximately 4 miles; this is changed to 750 pulses per second and 0.5 microseconds for longer ranges.

Frequency and wavelength.

1605. The great majority of marine surface search radars, as well as the radar beacons designed for use in conjunction with them, operate in the frequency band of 3,000 to 10,000 MHz. Radars are frequently described by the approximate wavelength they employ. Thus, a *10 cm* radar is one operating in the frequency range of *3,000 to 3,246 MHz,* a *5 cm* radar uses the *5,450 to 5,825 MHz* band, and a *3 cm* radar is in the *9,320 to 9,500 MHz* band. Most of the surface search radar employed by the U. S. armed forces operates in the 5 cm band.

Most small craft, such as yachts and the smaller commercial fishermen, use 3 cm radar so as to obtain maximum resolution in bearing and range; in most instances, they have neither the antenna height nor the power available to work at long ranges. Liners, large tankers and freighters frequently are equipped with both 10 cm radar for target acquisition at maximum ranges, and 3 cm radar for use in piloting during periods of poor visibility.

In radar design, selecting the frequency band to use for a given service is a complex problem. Some of the important factors involved are:

Propagation conditions for the different wave lengths.

Size of antenna systems for the desired resolution and necessary gain (concentration of energy).

Comparative cost of components and complexity of design.

The first factor, propagation, is the one factor affecting radar performance over which man has no control. Reliability of coverage regardless of meteorological conditions is an important consideration for navigational radars. Fog has negligible effect on the strength of either 3, 5 or 10 centimeter signals. Rainfall is more serious, as the signal strength weakens more-or-less linearly with the density of the precipitation. The amount the signal is weakened is called the *attenuation constant* and varies approximately as the square of the frequency. This means that the effective range of the higher frequency 3 centimeter sets may be considerably less than the 10 centimeter sets during periods of rainfall. When the precipitation is heavy and the distance to the target is great, the effect becomes more serious. During cloudbursts a complete radar blackout may temporarily occur on the 3 centimeter scope.

Another early disadvantage of the 3 centimeter sets was the great sea return, or clutter, that is inherent at this shorter wavelength. The main beam, or *major lobe,* at 3 centimeters "grazes" the surface of the sea at a very low angle. Rough seas near the ship reflect more of the incident energy which tend to clutter up the scope, masking the weaker targets images. However, the higher "grazing" angle of a 10 centimeter beam is more likely to miss buoys and other small targets. In favor of the 3 centimeter sets, it should be added that the effect of sea return and heavy rain which were so detrimental in early sets, have largely been overcome by the development of the special operating circuits and controls described, and by the use of circular polarized antennas and high power. It is also generally held that the total percentage of time during which heavy rainfall occurs is so small that reduced performance during these limited periods is acceptable as a trade-off in return for better definition and resolution of targets for navigational purposes.

1606. Radar sets are sensitive instruments requiring accurate adjustment. Any error in the adjustment causes an error in echo interpretation. It is of the utmost

Mechanical adjustment.

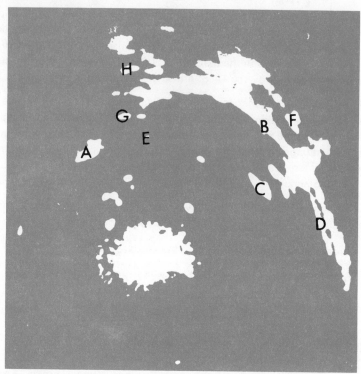

Figure 1607a: A PPI pattern, ship off Pt. Loma, California.

importance that every user be completely familiar with the operator's manual for that set. Repairs should only be attempted by thoroughly experienced and licensed personnel.

Interpretation. **1607.** Even with considerable training an operator may not always find it easy to interpret an echo properly. Here are some of the factors which make the problem more difficult:

As stated earlier, beam width limits *resolution in bearing* and will cause a target to appear wider than it actually is. False interpretation may occur when two or more targets appear as a single long one, or when a ship, buoy, or rock is near shore and is not separated from it due to the resolution in range of the radar set.

False shore lines may appear on a PPI for any of several reasons. In Figure 1607a false shore lines appear at *B* because of a pier, at *C* because of several small boats, and at *D* because of heavy surf over a shoal. Figure 1607b is a chart of the area shown in Figure 1607a. The shore line may appear some distance inland at bluffs or cliffs back of a low, flat, or sloping beach.

Shadows (Figure 1607c) occur behind prominent objects. That is, no echo is returned from a surface that is completely shielded from radar pulses by higher targets nearer the antenna. Hence, mountains, towers, etc., inshore can be seen only if they extend above nearer objects by essentially direct line of sight. Thus, a valley parallel to a high shore line will not return an echo, although the higher land on either side may be seen. Similarly, a rock or small boat too far beyond the horizon to be seen will not return an echo, although a high mountain beyond it can be picked up. Until the operator is thoroughly familiar with the interpretation of all echoes on the radar screen, he should take every opportunity to compare the picture shown on the PPI with the actual land area it portrays. Particular

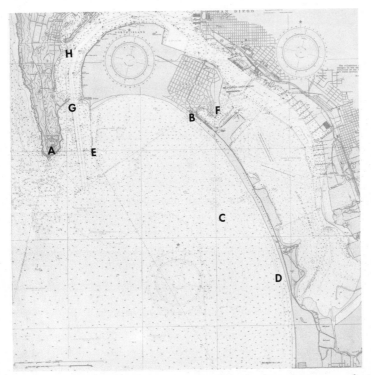

Figure 1607b: Chart of area shown in Figure 1607a.

attention should be given to noting the difference in the appearance of echoes caused by buoys and by ships.

By comparing the screen with a chart of the area it will be noted that shore lines and prominent points will appear as bright areas against a dark background. The reflected echo will be very much like the actual view of the area. Small objects such as buoys will appear as small illuminated areas when picked up at a distance. The image will increase in size as range decreases in much the same way that it would appear visually larger at close range. At close range a buoy might give a stronger return than a small vessel situated at a greater distance; this is particularly true if the buoy is fitted with a *radar reflector*. Such a reflector, despite its comparatively small size, returns a very strong echo. With practice, the size of different vessels can be estimated by the relative size of their images on the screen; allowance must be made for range. Low flying aircraft can be identified by their speed of travel. High coastlines and mountain areas near the sea can be picked up at the extreme range of the equipment. Storm areas and rain squalls are easily recognized by their mass and hazy definition.

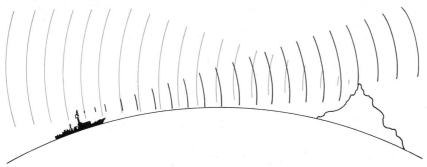

Figure 1607c: Radar shadows.

Radar interference. Interference from another radar-equipped vessel may occasionally appear on the screen as a patterned series of small dots. This effect is especially pronounced at the longer range scales. These dots appear to move to and from the center of the screen, often in long sweeping curves, sometimes in a straight line.

Ghost images of several types appear occasionally. They are easy to identify as they maintain a fixed relationship with respect to the true image, they have more of an arc-like appearance than the true image, and they have a tendency to "smear." They are not generally troublesome, as they are easily recognized. They should be noted, with their probable cause, to assist in future recognition.

Range limitations. **1608.** Both minimum and maximum range is limited. The minimum range is dependent on several factors. Excessive *sea return*, or echo from nearby water, and other obstructions nearby also affect the minimum effective range. Sea return can be reduced by judicious tuning, reducing the signal strength of close-in echoes which, however, reduces maximum range. Sea return becomes less with increased range because of the change in the angle of incidence, more of the signal being reflected away from the ship and less returned in the form of an echo. The minimum range is to a considerable extent a function of the frequency; a 3 cm radar may have a minimum range as low as 15 yards.

Sea-return saturation at close range. The STC (sensitivity time control) provides the operator with a means of controlling the receiver sensitivity near minimum operating range. The best results in reducing sea return and other clutter such as that caused by rain, snow, or sleet can generally be achieved by careful adjustment of both the STC and the fast time constant control (FTC).

Maximum range is usually limited by the curvature of the earth to the line of sight or slightly more, because high frequency radio waves travel in a straight line and do not follow the earth's curvature, except under abnormal atmospheric conditions. The approximate maximum range at which any given target will return an echo can be determined by means of Table 8, Bowditch, in the same manner used for determining the distance at which lights can be expected to be seen at sea (article 613).

The navigator should be alert to unusual ranges which may be obtained when temperature inversion exists in the atmosphere.

Radar fixes. **1609.** Radar can be used in several ways to obtain position. Well determined positions are labeled as *fixes* and less reliable ones as *EPs*, depending on the judgment of the navigator after experience with his equipment.

The accuracy of radar or radar-assisted position fixes follows in descending order:

Radar ranges and visual bearings of prominent isolated objects;

Radar ranges of several radar-conspicuous objects plotted as position circles;

Radar range and radar bearing of a single charted feature;

Radar bearings of two or more charted features.

Radar positions, no matter how they are determined, are plotted in the same manner as visual fixes (Chapter 11). The only difference occurs in plotting radar bearings of tangents when the radar beam width must be taken into consideration. For this specific case a correction of one-half the beam width may be applied in the direction of the land. An example of this would be a radar with a beam width of 4° giving a bearing of 045° on the left tangent of a point of land. The actual bearing to be plotted on the chart would be 047°.

1610. Radar, while consisting of the major components listed in article 1601, varies according to the specific use for which it is designed. In the U. S. Navy the modifications run from extremely high frequency, high power, line-of-sight radar for control of the ship's armament, to a much lower frequency, long range radar for tracking aircraft. Somewhere in between lies navigational radar. Radar aboard naval vessels usually employs a *north up* presentation, that is, true north appears at the center of the top of the scope. Many commercial radar sets are relative only (own ships head up) or have a switch to change from north up to a *ship's head up* presentation. Most military radars show own ship at the center of the scope with both fixed and moving targets having relative motion on the scope when own ship is in motion. Several commercial models now present *true motion* with both own ship and other moving target images moving across the scope while land areas, fixed buoys, etc., remain motionless. Still another innovation permits an off-center relative motion display with own ship position remaining motionless but offset from the center of the scope to permit a maximum view of the area lying in a desired relative direction, usually ahead.

Military and commercial radar innovations.

1611. The 3 cm band radar (9500 MHz range) is coming into general use both in the navies of the world, and with the merchant services as an adjunct to longer wave radar. The high quality of the resolution it gives makes it particularly useful in pilotage.

Use of short wave, high-definition radar.

The Royal Navy has adopted it for use aboard all ships of destroyer type and larger. All vessels of the Royal Navy, equipped with this radar, are prepared to enter or leave any port under conditions of zero visibility.

Many merchantmen are now equipped with dual radar installations consisting of either a 10 cm and a 3 cm radar or two 3 cm sets. This practice is even gaining favor with many operators of seagoing tugs and larger fishing vessels in the United States.

Fishing fleets operating from U. S. ports are now widely equipped with the 3 cm band radar in order to allow greater mobility when fog, haze or darkness might otherwise hinder operation. Smaller transistorized versions of the 3 cm band radar are available for use by yachtsmen in boats as small as 30 feet.

1612. The Navy's search radar, like that used by the Coast Guard, Army, and Air Force, differs from commercial radar, in that it is almost invariably equipped for Identification, Friend or Foe (IFF) operation, which is described in article 1613. In addition, the surface search radar sets such as the SPS-10 and SPS-53 found aboard most combat vessels, have a *range cursor* for the accurate determination of range. The cursor is moved in or out by means of a handle, until it touches the near side of an echo: the range is then read from a dial, and transmitted directly to the navigational and command plotting stations.

Navy surface radar.

The radars for navigation and tracking most commonly found in U. S. Naval and military vessels are the SPS-5 and SPS-10 series. The new SPS-53 series, a

3 cm radar, is appearing in the fleet in increasing numbers, particularly aboard new construction. A brief discussion of these three radars follows.

SPS-10 series radar.

1613. The SPS-10D operates in the 5450 to 5825 MHz band; the beacon receiver uses 5450 MHz. It is a 5 cm radar, and currently the most widely used surface search set in the U. S. Navy. Range and bearing information is displayed on a 10-inch PPI scope, and provision is made for transponder beacon and IFF operation. IFF returns a predetermined coded identification signal automatically. Similarly, if own ship's IFF is properly challenged, it will also return such a signal automatically. A pulse type of emission is used, the pulse length varying from 0.25 to 1.3 microseconds; the beacon pulse length is 2.5 microseconds. Depending upon the pulse length employed, pulse rate varies between 625 and 650 cycles per second, while the beacon uses 312 to 325 cycles per second. Bearing resolution is less than one degree with a range resolution on the short pulse of 50 yards and on the long pulse of 275 yards. This radar is generally supplied without the transponder beacon interrogator, but when used for beacon operation it constitutes a complete electronic navigation system. In beacon operation the radar set generates and transmits electromagnetic microwave pulses which activate the strategically located navigational aid beacons. These beacons, when activated, transmit a microwave signal, coded for identification which is received by the radar thus permitting the ship to be precisely located relative to an exactly known position. The SPS-10 presents either north or ship's heading at the top of the scope. Heading from the ship's gyrocompass can be used to show a ship's heading marker (SHM) on the PPI. This circuit provides a momentary marker flash on the PPI the instant the reflector faces the direction of the ship's heading. On relative bearing the ship's heading marker appears at 000° on the PPI; on true bearing it indicates own ship's course relative to true north. Either true or relative bearing can therefore be read from the screen. Normally, the set will acquire surface targets at ranges slightly greater than the visual line of sight from the antenna. Except under unusual conditions, it permits target identification within a rain area. The SPS-10 may be described as a medium range, high-definition surface-search radar.

IFF.

SPS-5.

1614. The SPS-5, generally similar to the SPS-10, but lighter in weight, is also a 5 cm radar, operating in the 5450 to 5825 MHz band. The PPI scope has a diameter of 10 inches. The SPS-5D, as currently in use, provides simultaneous surface search and limited air search. Figure 1614a and Figure 1614b show the antenna, and the control indicator containing the scope.

Figure 1614c: Vertical radiation pattern

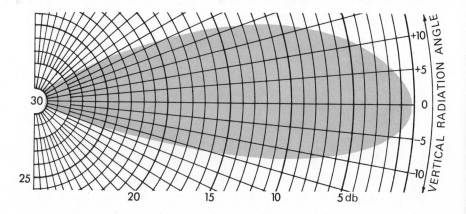

*Figure 1614a:
SPS-5 antenna.*

*Figure 1614b:
Control
indicator.*

The horizontal beam width is 1°.7 and the vertical beam width is 15°. Normally, the beam is centered horizontally, so that it scans from 7°.5 below to 7°.5 above the horizontal. In order to obtain some air search capability, it can be adjusted to scan from 7°.5 to 22°.5 above the horizontal. The antenna rotates at 17 RPM. Figures 1614c and 1614d illustrate the vertical and horizontal radiation patterns of the antenna beam. These are generally similar to those of most surface radars.

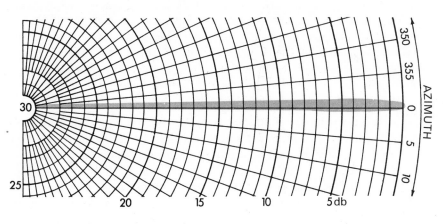

*Figure 1614d:
Horizontal
radiation
pattern.*

SPS-53.

1615. The SPS-53 is a surface search radar in the 9345–9405 MHz band; its maximum range is 32 miles. Since it is typical of late model radars now being introduced in the U. S. Navy and U. S. Coast Guard, the function of the various components will be discussed in greater detail than for other models. The pedestal mounted antenna contains a horizontally polarized, slotted waveguide radiating element. The "control-indicator" unit contains a 10-inch PPI tube. A signal data converter provides true and relative bearing inputs to the control-indicator for display.

The RF energy output of the transmitter is conducted by a waveguide to the antenna where, after making a transition in the antenna pedestal, the energy is applied to the slotted array and then radiated in a fan beam pattern. The antenna rotates at 15 RPM and provides search capability for both surface and low flying targets.

The transmitted energy which strikes a target is reflected back to the antenna. The antenna returns a portion of this reflected energy to the receiver via the waveguide. The detected echo pulse is amplified in the receiver and delivered to the control-indicator unit as a video signal whose amplitude is controlled at a desired level. The amplified video signal is coupled to the grid of the cathode ray tube, causing the echo signal to be converted into visual intelligence on the PPI screen where the signal appears as a bright spot.

Antenna.

The feedhorn, containing the slotted array radiating element, produces a vertical beam width of 20° and a horizontal beam width of 1°.6 at the half power points. The 20° height of the beam is sufficient to allow for the ship's pitch and roll which might otherwise cause the radar beam to miss a target. The above parameters are based on a 5 ft. antenna. Larger antennas which produce a smaller horizontal beam width are supplied on some models of the SPS-53A.

Receiver transmitter.

The RF pulse width of 0.1 microsecond with a pulse repetition rate of 1500 pulses per second used at short range, may be switched to 0.5 microseconds and 750 pulses per second for improved long range performance.

Control indicator.

The main display unit, shown in Fig 1615, contains all the system controls. The set is turned on at this unit, the receiver is controlled, and true or relative bearing operation may be selected. The unit can be pedestal mounted. Provision is also made for table-top, overhead, or bulkhead mounting.

A 10-inch magnetic-deflection, electrostatic-focus cathode-ray tube provides a PPI presentation. A hood is provided for daytime viewing. Range scales available are: 0.5, 1, 2, 4, 8, 16, and 32 nautical miles, providing a wide choice of areas to be scanned. Scales are multiples of 2, so that perspective is not lost when switching scales. Calibrated range markers are provided; the distance represented by the range markers varies with the setting of the range switch. For example, the four markers will be at 1,000 yard intervals with a range setting of 2 miles, and at 16,000 yards with a range setting of 32 miles.

Surrounding the radar screen is an azimuthal or bearing ring calibrated in degrees. A bearing cursor which intersects the azimuth ring can be rotated in either direction and aligned with an object on the screen to determine the object's bearing relative to the ship's heading. A ship's heading flasher momentarily brightens the screen each time the PPI sweep goes through zero degrees relative, creating a definite line on the screen to indicate the ship's heading. Figure

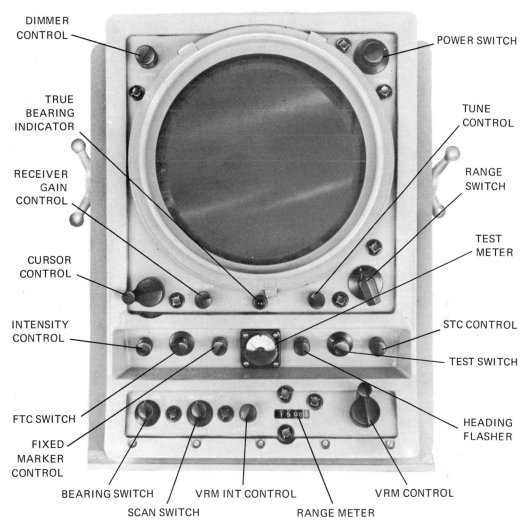

DIMMER CONTROL

POWER SWITCH

TRUE BEARING INDICATOR

TUNE CONTROL

RECEIVER GAIN CONTROL

RANGE SWITCH

CURSOR CONTROL

TEST METER

INTENSITY CONTROL

STC CONTROL

TEST SWITCH

FTC SWITCH

HEADING FLASHER

FIXED MARKER CONTROL

BEARING SWITCH   VRM INT CONTROL   VRM CONTROL

SCAN SWITCH   RANGE METER

Figure 1615: SPS-53 control locations.

1615 shows the location of controls on the SPS 53-A. The operator must be completely familiar with the use of these controls, if he is to obtain optimum information from the scope picture.

1616. Typical of modern merchant marine radar is the Kelvin Hughes Type 14 3 cm radar illustrated in Figure 1616. This equipment can be operated in either the true bearing (north up) mode or the relative bearing (own ship head up) mode. Plotting can be accomplished directly over the tube by using a reflection plotter. Range is determined by matching a range cursor to the target and reading the range on a dial presentation. A clutter control (sensitivity time control) and differentiation control (fast time constant) are incorporated as standard equipment as well as transmit and receive monitors. Pulse length is switched automatically with range to provide equivalent range discrimination with antenna beam width and to provide greater pulse power for the longer ranges.

Commercial radar.

The same basic equipment is also available as a true motion radar in which own ship moves across the display tube at scale course and speed. Both range and bearing of targets are then measured by electronic cursors and fixed targets remain stationary while moving targets are presented as true target course and speed tracks. This function is most useful where own ship is maneuvering in channels or other restricted waters. Own ship's position may be reset either automatically when it reaches a pre-set limit of travel or manually at any time the operator selects. This manual reset is accomplished by using N-S and E-W controls provided on the display.

One of the most interesting features of this radar is that it may be fitted with a "Photoplot," a second display accomplished by photographing a small 3-inch, high resolution, flat-faced, radar cathode ray tube sequentially on 16 mm strip film. The resultant photographs, processed in $3\frac{3}{4}$ seconds and rear projected onto a 25 inch diameter flat, bright display screen, allow plotting directly over the displayed targets.

Several alternative film exposure times are available. As an example, when own ship is not operating in congested waters, the display cathode ray tube may be photographed for up to 6 minutes before processing the exposure in $3\frac{3}{4}$ seconds and displaying it. In this case, the last target positions displayed are only one antenna rotation old while the integration and correlation of the target track makes them both easy to detect and simple to evaluate.

Figure 1616: Kelvin Hughes Type 14 3 cm radar.

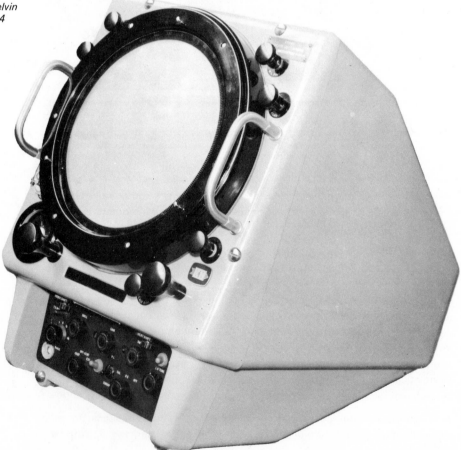

This presentation can be relative bearing, true bearing, or true motion at the operator's selection. The processed film is then a stored record of continuous radar observation for whatever period the display is used. This film may be projected for display at a later time for training or analysis.

1617. Radar adapts itself quite readily to uses other than for navigation. As was previously pointed out, the military uses vary from fire control to tracking aircraft at long distances. Other uses include tracking weather disturbances, surveying, etc. However, in all probability, the most important use of radar is to avoid the danger of collision.

By means of radar supplied data, proper plotting procedures, and common sense, information on the movements of other vessels can be properly evaluated. The conning officer can thus make decisions regarding course and speed changes in sufficient time to avoid the risk of collision.

Collision avoidance.

The mariner must always bear in mind that even though other vessels may be detected by radar, there are no absolutely positive means of relating fog signals to objects detected by radar. The International Rules state in part "the possession of information obtained from radar does not relieve any vessel of the obligation of conforming strictly with the rules. . . ." The use of radar does not legally justify greater speeds under conditions of restricted visibility.

One of the most essential factors in the use of radar for collision avoidance is the use of proper procedures for all available plotting information, as described in Chapter 13. As one knowledgeable mariner so aptly stated : "Many collisions have occurred because ships officers were too busy to plot; but none, of which I have knowledge, has occurred because the officers were too busy plotting."

Warning on use of radar.

1618. The future outlook for radar and for radar-associated navigation is extremely bright. Research and development in the field of high resolution radar, combined with VHF (Very High Frequency) voice radio communications appears to offer a partial answer to the problem of collision avoidance during reduced visibility, as well as for in-port pilotage. Utilization of enlarged and brightened pictures on the PPI scope for examination of the presentation by several persons at the same time, day or night, without the restriction of the viewing hood and visor, is coming into increasingly wide use in commercial radar and may see eventual application to military radar. Surveillance radar for harbors and canals is being used in several locations throughout the world and is being investigated by the U. S. Army Corps of Engineers for use in the United States; such a surveillance system may be combined with closed-circuit television. Charts especially prepared for radar navigation in restricted waters are coming into use. These charts show buoys and other aids to navigation, as well as the shore line and radar-visible landmarks as they would appear on the radar screen of a vessel in the channel, with the range scale set to a stated distance. Such charts permit the navigator to locate himself both accurately and rapidly, and also permit ready differentiation between buoys and small craft. More and more use is being made of radar beacons on prominent navigational landmarks. When this equipment must be designed to respond to all radar frequencies which may be employed, even in the 3 cm band, the problem becomes quite complicated; but many believe well worth the effort. Typically, a beacon located in a coastal lighthouse which would otherwise be difficult to detect in the surrounding land return, would be clearly marked by a coded return

Future outlook.

Radar beacon.

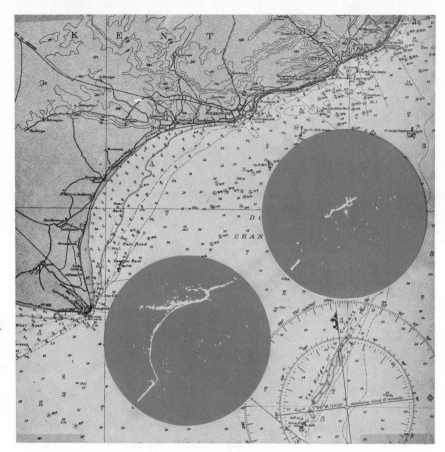

Figure 1618: Dungeness, England, radar beacon presentation.

pulse drawing a short, bright line radially outward on the PPI with the near end of the line pointing to the navigational landmark. One such 3 cm installation is shown as Dungeness, England, (Figure 1618) with the radar presentation which would be observed at the two locations marked by the inserts.

With these developments radar will come into ever increasing use both for navigation and collision avoidance aboard the great majority of vessels plying the rivers, bays, and oceans of the world. Transistors and microminiaturization will help to bring down both size and cost to the point where radar can be used aboard almost all powered vessels, regardless of size.

CHAPTER 17

Electronics

1701. *Electronics* may be defined as the science and technology relating to the emission, flow, and effects of electrons in a vacuum, through a semiconductor, and through appropriate circuitry. *Electronic navigation*, as discussed in the main in this chapter, is considered to mean navigation by means of electronic equipment, and radio wave emissions received from an outside source. *Introduction.*

The *radio time signal* was the first such aid to come into use. It made precise time available to the navigator for use in connection with celestial navigation. Subsequently, he was able, on request, to obtain radio bearings from a limited number of shore stations; usually only one such bearing was available to him at a time. This system was replaced by the shipborne *radio direction finder* (RDF), which permitted the navigator to obtain a bearing on any radio station which was transmitting signals. In many coastal areas, he was able to obtain several such bearings, which enabled him to determine his position with considerable accuracy. The wide employment of radio direction finders led to the introduction of the term *radio navigation.*

With the design of subsequent highly sophisticated electronic systems in navigation, the term *electronic navigation* replaced the previously used term radio navigation.

Extensive research has been carried out in this field over the past several decades. The development of long range airplanes established a need for suitable electronic navigational systems. Subsequently, the need arose for systems suitable for the Fleet Ballistic Missile submarines, and recently systems have been required for the navigation and guidance of space vehicles.

These needs were, in each instance, twofold: systems for maintaining dead reckoning position (inertial systems, Chapter 36), and systems for position fixing (electronic navigational systems). Under the first heading, extremely sensitive and accurate, but expensive, gyros and accelerometers were designed. For position fixing, highly accurate instruments for determining the time of travel of radio signals have been produced, as well as for the measurement of altitude angles of celestial bodies by automatic electro-optical and radiometric tracking. In addition, equipment for measuring the *Doppler shift* of very precisely timed radio signals transmitted by artificial satellites has yielded excellent results. *Dead reckoning and positioning systems.*

The Doppler shift (named for the Austrian scientist who reported the effect in 1842) is the apparent change in frequency of radiated energy when the distance between the source and the receiver is changing. *Doppler shift.*

In piloting, excellent position fixing is being achieved by both radar and sonar, as currently instrumented. Bathymetric navigation, or navigation by means of continuous soundings of the ocean bottom analyzed by a computer, holds great promise. However, it requires data in the form of very precise bathymetric charting of the operating area.

The ideal navigation system has yet to be developed. Such a system should be world-wide, self-contained, passive, completely reliable, and highly accurate. Currently, the most promising systems, although they do not meet all the above requirements are Omega, discussed in Chapter 31, and Satellite Navigation, discussed in Chapter 37. Omega uses radio signals from land based transmitting systems, while the Satellite Navigation system depends on signals from a satellite travelling in a precisely determined orbit.

Basic phenomena.

1702. The following brief discussion of electronic terminology assumes that the student has some knowledge of basic physics, or has access to appropriate textbooks, as it is not possible to cover the field of electromagnetism in detail in this volume.

Hertz (Hz) and cycle(s) per second.

For many decades, alternating current frequency was expressed in "cycles per second." This seemed the natural term to indicate the complete reversal of the polarity of the voltage, and the direction of flow of the current in alternating current circuits. Use of this term has decreased in recent years and it is being replaced by *Hertz*, which is synonymous with "cycles per second," in many countries, including the United States. It honors the German scientist Heinrich Hertz, a pioneer in the field of electromagnetic radiation. The official definition is: "A unit of frequency equivalent to one cycle per second. The term Hertz (Hz) and cycle(s) per second are synonymous and may be used interchangeably."

Basic alternating current theory provides that a varying magnetic field, resulting from the flow of alternating current in a circuit, induces a voltage in a conductor placed within the field. In fact, voltage is induced even when there is no conductor in the field. Such a voltage, induced into space is, in effect, an electric field. Thus, a varying electric field is created in space by a varying magnetic field. The varying electric field in turn sets up a displacement current, which gives rise to a magnetic field. The varying magnetic field creates an electric field and so on. The process whereby they mutually induce one another is called *electromagnetic induction.* The combination is called the *electromagnetic field;* this effect occurs at all alternating frequencies.

Electromagnetic induction.

Once the initial field is created, it becomes independent of further electrical input. When the current stops, the field can continue to survive and to propagate itself on out into space, because of the self-sustaining exchange process.

In an electromagnetic radiation field, the electric field lines close on themselves. They are not attached to charges, and the magnetic field lines are not related to current in conductors. The fields are truly independent, as if cut adrift in space.

There is also a connotation of motion in the process. The complete theory was developed about a hundred years ago by James Clerk Maxwell. He correlated a set of four simultaneous partial differential equations, which describe the interrelation of the electric and magnetic components of electromagnetic fields, and their relation to electric currents and voltages. These equations stand today as the theoretical basis of electromagnetism, and by their use all problems of electromagnetic fields and radiation can be solved. They are: Ampere's circuital law; Gauss's theorem for the electric field; Gauss's theorem for the magnetic field; and Faraday's law on electromotive force.

These laws, formulated by others, but combined by Maxwell within the concept of the displacement current, facilitate the computation of electromagnetic propagation. To compute the velocity of waves of electromagnetic energy traveling outward into space from the point at which they are created, the characteristics of the medium through which they travel must be considered. The Maxwell equations predict that electromagnetic field velocity should be equal to the reciprocal of the square root of the product of the permeability and the permittivity of the medium in rationalized meter-kilogram-second (RMKS) units.

Permeability may be defined as the ratio of magnetic induction to magnetizing force. It is a measure of the magnetic induction produced by a unit value of magnetizing force. Permeability is expressed in *henrys* per meter (a term named after Joseph Henry, an American physicist), and may be considered an inductance value.

Permittivity is the ratio of electric flux density to electric field intensity. Relative permittivity of a medium is the ratio of its value of permittivity to that of empty space. It is sometimes referred to as dielectric constant, and may be considered a capacitance value. The permittivity of a substance is expressed in *farads* per meter.

Permeability.

Permittivity.

Permeability of empty space is considered to be equal to 1.26×10^{-6} *henrys* per meter; permittivity of empty space is equal to 8.85×10^{-12} *farads* per meter. Then, in accordance with Maxwell's laws, in empty space:

$$\text{electromagnetic wave velocity} = \frac{1}{\sqrt{1.26 \times 8.85 \times 10^{-18}}}$$

or 3×10^8 meters per second.

Maxwell noted that this velocity very closely approximated the measured velocity of light, suggesting that light is a form of electromagnetic radiation. To illustrate the relationship of velocity, wave length and frequency, consider the measurement of time in the transit of one complete cycle of an electromagnetic field at a specific point on the earth's surface. In the period of time of this measurement, a minute fraction of a second, a complete wavelength of the electromagnetic field would have moved across the point at which the measurement was made. The measured time is the elapsed time required for the electromagnetic field to be moved a distance equal to the wavelength of the field.

The time of completion of one full cycle is therefore equal to the velocity divided by the wavelength. The frequency, the number of times *per second* the signal completes one full cycle, is given in Hertz units. The relationship can be visualized as the greater the wavelength the lower the frequency. The transmission characteristic of a given electronic system is stated either as wavelength or frequency. The relationship as discussed briefly above can be stated as a simple formula:

Wavelength vs. frequency.

$$\lambda = \frac{300}{F}$$

in which λ is the wavelength in meters, F is the frequency in megahertz, and the constant 300 is the velocity of light in meters per microsecond.

Absorption.

Absorption accounts for the loss of some of the energy of electromagnetic waves propagated through space which contains material which is not a perfect insulator. In both radio and light waves, the losses caused by absorption are the result of the conversion of some of the field energy into heat, through the collisions of electrons, excited by the electric field, with other particles in the material. The computation of this loss is similar to the computation of power loss in an electrical circuit due to resistance. If the electromagnetic field were radiated into a pure vacuum, no work would be performed by the energy of the field, and its intensity would be maintained. The alternating electric and magnetic fields would continue to be propagated by each other with the same magnitude of energy as that of the initial radiation.

For example, if an electromagnetic field is radiated from an antenna near the surface of the earth, the electrons in the gas atoms of the atmosphere begin to move under the force of the electric field. The greater the length of time that the force continues in one direction, i.e., the lower the frequency of the radiated field, the greater will be the velocity attained by the electrons during each half cycle of the radiated energy. If the movement of the freed electrons were unobstructed, the power expended in their acceleration would be returned to the electromagnetic wave by the magnetic field which their own motion would produce. However, the electrons, moving at high velocity, collide with atoms of gas and other particles in the atmosphere, thus dissipating significant power in the heat generated by the collisions.

Permittivity and permeability values vary slightly with atmospheric density. Therefore, in accordance with Maxwell's rules, electromagnetic radiation velocity is slightly reduced by increased atmospheric density, or by other material in the propagation medium.

Ground waves and sky waves.

1703. The preceding article has discussed briefly the radiation of an electromagnetic field from an antenna into the atmosphere. It seems desirable at this point to consider how this field travels outward.

Electromagnetic energy, as transmitted from the antenna, radiates outward in all directions. A portion of this energy proceeds out parallel to the earth's surface, while the remainder travels upwards as well as outwards, until it strikes the *ionosphere*, and is reflected back to earth; this latter process may be repeated as illustrated in Figure 1703a. (Sky wave "1" in this figure is called a "one hop" wave; sky wave "2" is a "two hop" wave.) That portion of the energy which follows the surface of the earth is called the *ground waves;* the portions that are reflected back are termed *sky waves.*

In the employment of low frequencies, ground waves become very important, and the conductivity of the earth's crust becomes a major factor in signal attenuation (the decrease in amplitude of a wave or current with increasing distance from the source of transmission) by absorption, and its effects on propagation velocity. Because of this conductivity, the electromagnetic field to some extent penetrates the earth's surface. The lower limit of the wave is slightly impeded by its penetration into this medium of increased conductivity, while the upper portion of the wave is not so affected. This results in the lines of force leaning away

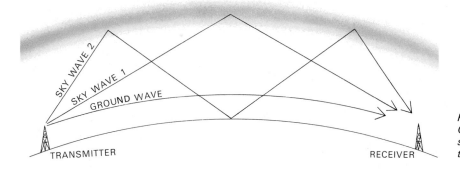

*Figure 1703a:
Ground wave and
sky wave propaga-
tion paths.*

*(The vertical distances in this figure have been exaggerated for clarity as the distance be-
tween the transmitter and receiver is normally hundreds of miles while the ionosphere is only
85 to 100 miles above the earth.)*

from the signal source, causing the movement of the electromagnetic wave to
curve with the curvature of the earth's surface. It must be remembered that the
lines of force of the electric field are perpendicular to the lines of force of the
magnetic field, and the direction of motion of the electromagnetic wave is
perpendicular to both. (Figure 1703b).

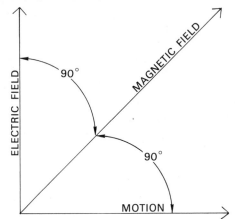

*Figure 1703b: Vec-
tor relationship of
the electric and
magnetic fields and
of the motion of
the electromagnetic
wave.*

It is this tendency to follow the earth's curvature that makes possible the transmission of ground waves over great distances. Combined with this curvature of
the motion of the electromagnetic wave is the energy dissipation through absorption in the penetration of the earth's surface. This latter effect necessitates
the use of high power to achieve long distance transmission of the ground wave.

The variation in the characteristics of the surface of land areas complicates the
prediction of its effects on ground wave transmission. The conductivity of the
ocean surface is quite constant and propagation velocity over ocean areas can
be predicted with considerable accuracy.

Only the low frequency radio transmissions curve sufficiently to follow the
earth's surface over great distances. Electromagnetic fields at higher frequencies
do not penetrate as deeply into the surface, and so encounter less impedance of
velocity from the ground. They are slightly curved, but not enough to provide
ground wave signals at great distances from the transmitting antenna.

299

1704. Long distance communications by means of high frequency radio waves are achieved by reflection and refraction of the electromagnetic waves from ionized layers in the upper atmosphere.

Radio waves and light waves are both forms of electromagnetic waves, differing only in frequency. Some of the laws learned in the science of optics are also applicable to radio waves.

Any surface can reflect light waves. If the surface is smooth and polished, the light is reflected in a *specular* fashion, as by a mirror. Reflection from a rough surface is *diffuse*. Dull, dark colored surfaces reflect poorly. When a surface reflects only a portion of the light, the rest is absorbed, and the energy of the absorbed light wave is converted into heat in the material.

Radio waves are also reflected, specularly from smooth surfaces and diffusely from rough surfaces. Surfaces of good conductors reflect, and poor conductors absorb. The waves pass through some materials which are electrical insulators, such as glass. Most materials do not completely reflect or completely absorb radio waves, but are imperfect reflectors, or, as poor conductors, still reflect a small portion of the wave.

In both light and radio waves, the reflection capability depends upon the magnitude of the surface irregularities, as compared to the wavelength of the electromagnetic wave. A sea of ten-foot waves would reflect specularly a radio wave of several hundred meters in length, but a radio wave of a few centimeters would be reflected diffusely.

When a radio wave is reflected specularly, the character of the wave front is unchanged. As in the behavior of light rays reflected from a sextant mirror, the angle of reflection is equal to the angle of incidence. When reflected from a rough surface, the incident wave front breaks up and is randomly reflected in different directions.

In free space, an electromagnetic wave travels in a straight line; however, when traveling through an area containing matter or material particles, the wave may be bent or *refracted*. The light from a celestial body, entering the atmosphere at an oblique angle, bends increasingly downward as it continues into an atmosphere of increasing density. Similarly, bending in the direction of travel of a radio wave occurs when the wave passes from one medium to another of different permittivity of permeability. Thus, when a wave front enters a medium of different characteristic at an oblique angle, the change in velocity affects the first portion of the wave front entering the new medium before the remainder of the wave is affected, and the alignment of the wave front is changed. The direction of travel, as previously stated, is perpendicular to the wave front, therefore the direction of travel changes toward the direction of reduced velocity.

1705. When an electromagnetic wave, either radio or light, is partially obstructed by an object of opaque material, the area behind the object is shadowed as the unobstructed portion of the wave front continues in its original direction. In the case of light waves, a shadow is cast by the object; waves which would otherwise reach this area are blocked.

According to Maxwell's equations, the wave front portion at the edge of the obstructing object does not completely hold to its original direction. A small

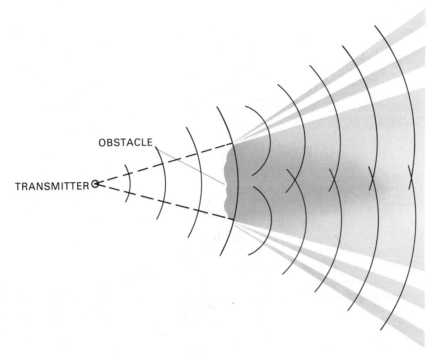

OBSTACLE

TRANSMITTER

Figure 1705:
Diffraction.

portion of the energy is propagated into the shadow area. This phenomenon is called *diffraction* (Figure 1705). Maxwell's equations predict the intensity of the field to be found in the shadow area.

1706. If two or more radio waves arrive simultaneously at the same point in space, *interference* results. The combination of such waves is in accordance with the principle of superposition of fields. Each field may be represented by a vector, indicating spatial direction and intensity.

Interference.

The resultant field direction and intensity of either the electric fields or of the magnetic fields may then be determined by following the rules for vector addition.

1707. The daylight portion of the earth's atmosphere is subjected to bombardment by intense ultra-violet rays of the sun. At extremely high altitudes in the atmosphere, the gas atoms are comparatively sparse. Electrons are excited by the powerful ultra-violet electromagnetic forces which reverse polarity approximately 10^{17} times per second. This violent oscillation causes the electrons to separate from the positive ions with which they were combined. These freed electrons would eventually find their way to other electron-deficient atoms, but this is prevented by the continuing forces of the ultra-violet rays while in direct sunlight. Thus, the freed electrons form ionized layers, reach their maximum intensity when the sun is at its highest.

Ionization.

Ionization has a tendency to form layers in the atmosphere and these layers change, disappear, combine, and separate, as they are affected by the local time of day, the time of the year, and the phase of the eleven year sun-spot cycle; the layers are also affected by apparent random changes from moment to moment. Four such ionized layers (Figure 1707) are important to the study of radio wave propagation.

Layers of ionization.

301

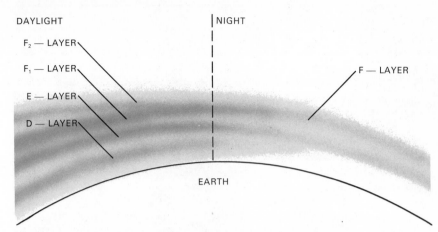

Figure 1707: Layers of ionization.

D-Layer.

This is the ionized layer nearest the earth's surface. Its density is considerably less than that of either of the other three layers. This D-layer, which is found 60 to 90 kilometers (1 KM = .54 nautical miles) above the earth's surface apparently exists only during daylight hours, and disappears completely at night.

E-Layer.

Located at a height of about 110 kilometers, this layer remains during the night but with somewhat decreased intensity. Its density is greatest in the region beneath the sun. Irregular areas of very high ionization occur during a large percentage of the time. These areas are referred to as *Sporadic E;* they occur at night as well as in daylight.

F_1-Layer.

This layer occurs only in daylight, the freed electrons and ions apparently re-joining to form the normal atoms of the rarefied air as the stress of the sun's ultra-violet rays diminishes. This layer is usually between 175 and 250 kilometers above the earth's surface.

F_2-Layer.

This layer varies in height and in density; the variation is diurnal, seasonal, and by sunspot cycle. It is found at altitudes of 250 to 400 kilometers, where the atmospheric density is extremely low and results in a more complicated diurnal pattern. Due to the molecular collision rates in the very low density of the air at these altitudes, solar energy may be stored for many hours. The gas atoms are relatively few and far between. The release of electrons during the periods of high ultra-violet intensity leaves them moving freely for hours after the sun has disappeared below the horizon. In this condition collisions between free electrons and gas atoms cause other electrons to be dislodged, even during the hours of darkness. Solar energy may be stored in this manner for many hours at these levels.

Some diurnal pattern is discernible at the high levels of the atmosphere. There is a tendency for the F_1 and the F_2 layers to merge during darkness, at a height of about 300 kilometers. After sunrise, the upper portion of the layer is again intensified by the sun's rays, and the F_1 layer increases in density as it lowers.

Radio wave propagation is affected by the various ionized layers in accordance with the wave length or frequency of the radio transmission, and the height and density of the layers of ionization. The ionized layers may either be conducive to the sky wave transmission of the electromagnetic energy to the area of desired reception, or may hinder or even prevent such transmission, as will be discussed in the following paragraphs.

1708. Radiation in electronics is in the form of electromagnetic waves called *radio waves.* Electromagnetic fields occur at all alternating frequencies. The electromagnetic frequency spectrum extends from a single reversal of polarity per second, through the radio frequency spectrum, infra-red frequencies, visible light frequencies ultra-violet ray, X-ray, and Gamma-ray spectrums to approximately 10^{15} mHz. The electromagnetic frequency spectrum is shown in Figure 1708a.

Electromagnetic frequency spectrum.

The radio frequency spectrum extends from about 5 kHz to 300 gigahertz (3×10^5 MHz). This spectrum is divided into eight frequency bands.

Radio frequency spectrum.

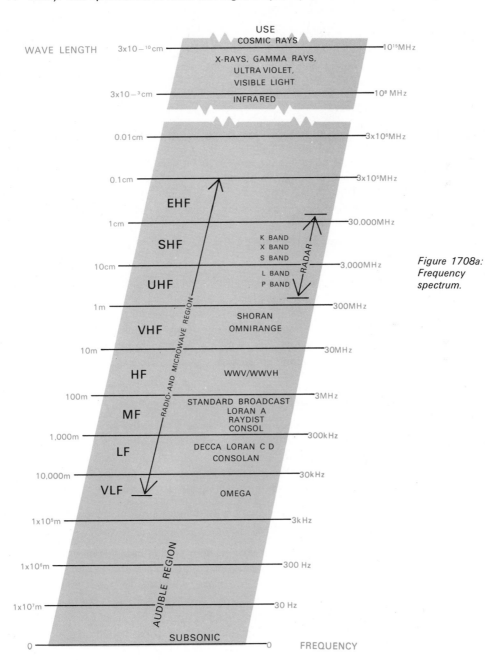

Figure 1708a:
Frequency
spectrum.

Very Low Frequency (VLF).

The *VLF band* includes those frequencies below 30 kHz. The primary advantage in employing frequencies in this band is the reliability of propagation over great distances by the use of high power. VLF ground waves may be propagated for distances of 4,000 to 8,000 miles facilitating accurate determination of distance by measuring the time of travel of the wave.

VLF sky waves are reflected from the ionosphere with comparatively little loss of energy due to the short distance traveled within the ionized layer. However, the ensuing reflection from the earth's surface undergoes significant loss by absorption, especially over land areas. Diffraction is also greater in the VLF frequencies than in the higher frequencies.

It is much more difficult and expensive to obtain antenna efficiency at these frequencies than at higher ones. Radiation of high power, which is required if good reliability over long distances is to be realized, becomes very costly.

The primary navigational use of the VLF band is for the Omega system discussed in Chapter 31.

Low frequency (LF).

The *LF band* (30 to 300 kHz) is not reflected as efficiently by the ionosphere. Ground losses increase as the frequency is increased and diffraction decreases. However, the antennas for use in the LF band are usually more efficient than those in the VLF band. Good ground wave propagation is still possible over moderate distances. Both VLF and LF radio waves penetrate ocean water to some extent, making possible the transmission of signals to submerged submarines. In the 10 kHz region, signals may be received with good reliability at depths of 40 to 50 feet; at 100 kHz, the signals are available a few feet below the surface.

Navigational time measurement systems employing the LF band are able to use first hop sky waves, by applying a correction to compensate for the additional distance of travel of the sky wave. The accuracy obtainable by use of first hop sky waves is not as good as that obtained with ground waves, although satisfactory for most navigational purposes. For positioning accuracy of less than a mile, ground wave reception is necessary.

The primary navigational use of the LF band is for Decca (Chapter 33), Loran-C and D (Chapter 32), and Consol (Chapter 18).

Medium frequency (MF).

The *MF band* extends from 300 kHz to 3 megahertz (MHz). Frequencies in this band provide reliable ground wave propagation over distances of up to approximately 700 miles. Daytime ionosphere absorption is high, and limits sky wave propagation. Long distance skywave transmission is possible at night. Antenna requirements are not as stringent as for use in the VLF and LF bands.

The primary navigational use of the MF band is for Consol, Raydist (Chapter 33), and Loran-A (Chapter 18).

High frequency (HF).

The *HF band* (3 MHz to 30 MHz) is employed in long distance communication, which is made possible by the ionized layers in the ionosphere. At these frequencies, antenna efficiency is much more easily obtained than at the lower frequencies. Communications over long distances are possible with moderate transmitter power. However, frequencies must be selected with respect to the conditions prevailing at the moment. Under some conditions, the higher fre-

quencies travel great distances in the ionosphere before being refracted sufficiently to reflect the wave back to earth. Signals entering the ionosphere at an
angle of incidence which prevents their being refracted back towards the earth
penetrate the ionized layers and are lost in space. In daylight, energy propagated
at the lower frequencies of this band has high absorption losses and fades out
a short distance from the source. Higher frequencies, during hours of darkness,
if reflected at all, return to earth at great distances from the transmitting antenna,
so that they skip over distances of perhaps several hundred miles. No sky wave
signal will be received in this "skip" distance (Figure 1708b).

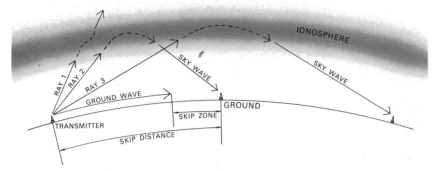

*Figure 1708b: The
effect of the iono-
sphere on radio
waves.*

An example of this phenomenon is found when using the U. S. Naval Observatory time signal on Station WWV. This signal is readily obtainable on a standard
radio set on the 19 meter band during the daytime hours, but the 59 meter band
must be used at night, for good reception in some areas.

This frequency band does not lend itself well to distance or azimuth navigational systems; it is chiefly used for communications.

Frequencies in the *VHF band* (30 to 300 MHz) and the *UHF band* (300 to 3,000
MHz) are widely used for communications. They are basically *line-of-sight* frequencies as their range is ordinarily limited by the curvature of the earth to
distances approximately equal to those at which the top of one antenna could
be seen from the top of the other under ideal weather conditions. VHF and
UHF frequencies are also used to some extent for communications over several
hundred miles in what is termed a *scatter mode* of operation. A small portion of
very high power electromagnetic waves in the 30 to 60 MHz frequency range
are scattered by particles in the ionosphere and returned to earth, permitting
signal reception at ranges of 600 to 1,200 miles.

*Very High
Frequency (VHF)
and Ultra High
Frequency (UHF).*

A similar scatter effect can be obtained in the *troposphere* by emissions in the
400 to 4,000 MHz range. The troposphere is much nearer the earth than the
ionosphere, being situated below the stratosphere. By means of tropospheric
scatter, ranges of about 600 miles have been obtained.

Scatter effect.

For navigational purposes, these frequencies provide good line-of-sight propagation at moderate transmitter power. Shoran (Chapter 33) employs frequencies
in the VHF band with accuracies possible to a few feet. The UHF band is
primarily used for radar.

The *SHF band* (3,000 to 30,000 MHz) and the *EHF band* (30,000 to 300,000
MHz) are used for precise distance measurements and for radar, within line-of-
sight range. The employment of SHF frequencies for radar has resulted in sig-

*Super High
Frequency (SHF)
and Extremely High
Frequency (EHF).*

nificantly improved definition over the UHF systems. Power requirements are moderate, and very efficient antennas are employed.

Ducting and irregularities. **1709.** Many irregularities occur, especially at the higher frequencies, in the propagation of electro-magnetic waves. A phenomenon called *radio refractive ducting* occurs over much of the radio frequency spectrum, but particularly on frequencies of the VHF and UHF bands. This phenomenon seems to occur more over oceans than over land, and is generally associated with a temperature inversion at a very low altitude, perhaps 200 or 300 feet, and a sharp decrease in moisture content of the warm air. Very long ranges have been reported when low power UHF transmitters were employed in experiments with this phenomenon. Ducting can be responsible for limiting as well as extending the range of radio transmissions.

Hyperbolic navigation systems. **1710.** *Hyperbolic navigation systems* are based on the theory that the known velocity of travel of electromagnetic waves through space is constant, within acceptable limits. The capability of measuring the difference in time of the arrival of signals from two separate sources makes possible the determination of position.

A major advantage of the hyperbolic navigation systems is that position line data may be computed in advance of its use, and plotted or printed on charts, at convenient units of time difference value, eliminating the necessity for the navigator to make such computations. A disadvantage lies in the deterioration of accuracy inherent in spherical hyperbolic system geometry.

The hyperbola is the locus of the points at which synchronized signals from the two transmitters comprising a system will arrive at a constant time difference. This time difference is expressed in *microseconds*, or millionths of a second. The receivers employed in these systems therefore provide a readout in microseconds of time difference.

In Figure 1710 signals from stations *S* and *M* transmitted simultaneously would have no time difference but would arrive simultaneously at any point along the center line, as all points along this line are equidistant from points *S* and *M*. All other lines, represented by hyperbolas, would represent points of equal time difference. In actual hyperbolic navigation systems the transmission for the slave station *S* is delayed rather than being simultaneous with the master *M*. The figure represents hyperbolic lines on a plane surface. The appearance of the lines on a navigation chart, which represents a portion of the spherical surface of the earth, will vary somewhat with the chart projection used.

The computation of hyperbolas for a given pair of stations are tabulated for the navigator, giving the coordinates at which each hyperbola intersects a whole meridian or parallel, whichever is applicable. Charts, on which the hyperbolas are printed, are commonly employed. At least one receiver is now available, which includes a digital computer and coordinate converter, thus providing a readout in geographical coordinates.

Two types of time-difference measurement are employed in hyperbolic systems. In one, the matching of electromagnetic wave envelopes of pulses transmitted from the two stations is measured in time difference, resulting in a coarse measurement which locates the receiver on a hyperbolic line with known geographical coordinates. In the other system, matching the electromagnetic wave *phase*

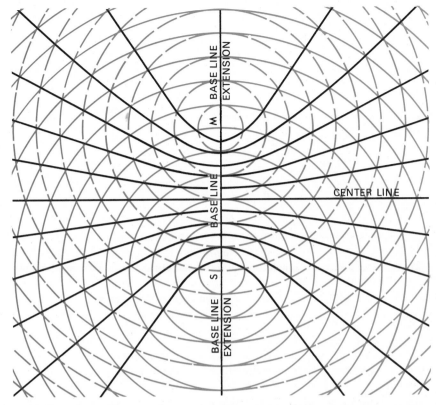

Figure 1710: A family of hyperbolic lines of position.

provides a fine measurement within an area or lane defined by two time-difference hyperbolas, in addition to the coarse measurement obtained by time difference. In phase matching systems, extreme accuracy is possible under favorable conditions. A precision of about 0.05 microseconds can be obtained, which is equivalent to about 50 feet. This precision is, of course, degraded by system geometry as distance from the base line increases.

To establish position, a ship or aircraft employs two or more pairs of stations to acquire two or more intersecting position lines. As with other methods of determining position by means of intersecting lines of position, precision in positioning varies with the angle of intersection of the lines. Where lines cross at right angles, the area of most probable position is circular, with its center at the intersection of the lines. Where the lines intersect at an acute angle, the area of most probable position is elliptical; the minor axis of this ellipse will be equal to the diameter of the circle formed when the intersection is at 90°. The major axis will be greater, the ratio of its length to the diameter of the circle varies with the cosine of the angle of the intersection.

The development of the first electronic hyperbolic navigational systems began about 1940. Due to the urgent requirements brought about by World War II, Loran-A came into general military use only a few years later. Hyperbolic navigation systems in use today include Loran-A, Loran-C, Loran-D, Decca, and, to a more limited extent, Omega.

Short range hyperbolic systems designed for survey and oceanographic use are Decca Survey and Raydist, among other specialized equipment.

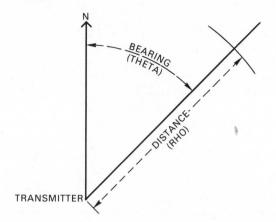

**Rho-Theta
navigation.**

1711. *Rho-Theta navigation*, or, more specifically, range-direction navigation utilizes a combination of circular, or ranging systems for distance measurements, with azimuthal, or directional measuring systems (Figure 1711). The *Omnirange* (VOR) system in general use for aviation throughout the U. S. provides bearing information. A large number of the stations are equipped with distance measuring equipment (DME) to provide a complete rho-theta system. The military version is known as TACAN. These systems are sufficiently accurate for general navigation purposes, but are limited to a line of sight range.

The principle of Omnirange navigation is based on the phase comparison between two radiated radio frequency signals, with the phase varying with a change in azimuth. One of these two signals is nondirectional, with a constant phase throughout 360° of azimuth. This signal is utilized as the reference phase. The other signal rotates and varies in phase with change in azimuth; it is the variable phase signal.

Special receiver and display equipment, on the aircraft, translates the received signal into usable information for the pilot including "TO" or "FROM" the ground station.

**Repeatability
and predictability.**

1712. In the design of all electronic position systems two major factors are carefully taken into consideration for precision work: *repeatability* and *predictability*. The first problem, repeatability, is the ability of a system to repeat a position. In other words, if the position of a point on the surface of the earth is given in coordinates of the system at one time, "how closely may we return to that exact position at some later time?"

The second problem, that of predictability, is one of knowing, given the atmospheric conditions, the propagation characteristics of the signal. Predictability is influenced primarily by refraction in the atmospheric medium, and by the conductivity of the surface. One of the basic limitations on predictability versus repeatability is the integrity of the geodetic positioning of the transmitter stations. A minor displacement of an antenna position can cause a major error in prediction of a service area point. Of interest is the geodetic datum, method of measuring geodetics, the spheroid used, etc. Also a problem in predictability is the translation of coordinates, i.e., hyperbolic to orthogonal and the rigor of the mathematics used.

CHAPTER 18

Basic Electronic Navigation Systems

1801. Some background information on electronic navigation and the principles involved are discussed in Chapter 17. It is recommended the student study that chapter as a basis for a more complete understanding of the electronic systems described in this and subsequent chapters.

Introduction.

Even the most enthusiastic supporters of electronic navigation recognize it has limitations and that it will probably never supersede other methods any more than the gyrocompass, valuable as it is, has replaced the magnetic compass. Keep constantly in mind that the methods discussed in this chapter are navigational *aids* and that it is still important to know how to use other methods.

1802. Besides being a method of general communication, radio provides means of obtaining certain specific information of interest to the navigator. From a navigational standpoint perhaps the most important are radio time signals. Collection and dissemination of weather information, particularly regarding tropical hurricanes, is made possible by radio. Urgent navigational warnings are broadcast daily by the Oceanographic Office. Even medical information is obtainable by radio. Full information, instructions, and regulations regarding the use of radio navigational aids are given in H. O. Pub. No. 117, *Radio Navigational Aids* and H. O. Pub. No. 118 *Radio Weather Aids,* which should be familiar to every navigator. Radio beacon locations are also listed in the several H. O. Pubs. No. 111 to 116, *Lists of Lights.*

Information by radio.

1803. Loran (LOng RAnge Navigation) encompasses pulsed hyperbolic radio aids to navigation. Loran-A is often referred to as Standard Loran.

Loran-A.

Expansion of the original Loran concept to meet operational requirements for greater accuracy and greater service range has resulted in the development of three related systems designated as Loran-A, Loran-C, and Loran-D. (See Chapter 32 for explanations of Loran-C and -D). All Loran systems provide navigational-fix data in the form of hyperbolic lines of position (Article 1710) determined by the time difference between the reception of pulse signals from widely separated shore transmitting stations. In 1974, the Department of Transportation, in its implementation of the National Plan for Navigation, announced a scheduled phase-out of the operation of Loran-A chains. The replacement system, Loran-C, has been chosen as the government-provided radio navigation system of the U.S. coastal /confluence zone.

1804. The technical principle that distinguishes the various versions of Loran from most other hyperbolic navigation systems is the use of pulse emissions. This permits the non-ambiguous measurement of time-differences of signals from different stations and further provides the means for discrimination at the

Theory of operation.

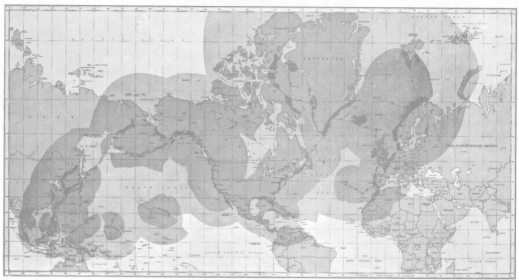

Figure 1803:
Loran-A coverage
diagram.

receiving location between ground waves and skywaves. The ability to select and utilize a particular transmission provides maximum accuracy consistent with the inherent system geometric accuracy.

Loran requires transmitting stations at fixed points, which send carefully synchronized signals. These travel at the speed of light (about 186,218 miles per second) and cover one nautical mile in 6.18 microseconds (μs) or 6.18 millionths of a second.

The time interval between transmission of signals from a pair of Loran stations is controlled to an accuracy of about 2 μs. To understand the principle of operation, assume this difference is zero and that two stations, M and S (Figure 1804) broadcast signals simultaneously. A ship at A, equidistant from the two stations, receives both signals at the same time. A ship at A' also receives the signals

Figure 1804: The
principle of Loran.

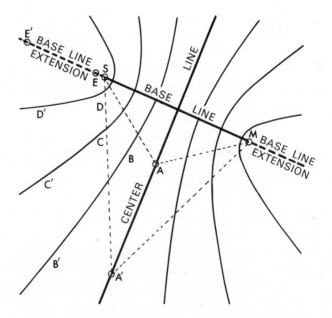

simultaneously, since it is also equidistant from the stations. The locus of all points equidistant from the two stations is called the *center line.* It is the perpendicular bisector of the *base line*, the great circle joining the two stations.

Consider, now, a ship at *B*, closer to *S* than *M*. The signal from *S* is received first. At some other point *B'*, where the difference in distance from *M* and *S* is the same as at *B*, the time difference is the same. The locus of all points with this time difference is a hyperbola, since this curve defines all points with a constant difference in distance from two fixed points. These lines do not appear as true hyperbolas on most charts because of chart distortion and the Earth's spheroidal shape.

If the time difference is greater, the ship is on another hyperbola, at *C* or *C'*, still closer to *S*. A still greater difference puts the ship at *D* or *D'*. If the difference is equal to exactly the time needed for a signal to travel from *M* to *S*, the ship is somewhere on the *base line extension* at *E* or *E'*.

Any number of hyperbolas could thus be drawn indicating various time differences.

If the signal from *M* is received first, the ship is nearer *M*. For every curve to the left of the center line there is a similar but reversed curve to the right. Since the time differences thus define definite fixed curves, they can be either plotted on a chart or their coordinates tabulated. In practice, both methods are used. In actual practice there is a precise time delay between the transmission of the signal from the master and the slave.

At any given point, then, one line of position can be obtained from one pair of stations. To obtain a fix at least one additional line is needed from another pair of stations or from other means, such as celestial observations.

1805. Since a Loran receiver may pick up signals from a number of station pairs at the same time, some method of identification becomes necessary. Station pairs are identified by their broadcast frequency and the rate at which signals are transmitted. The signal rate is broken down into two parts, a *basic pulse recurrence rate* (repetition rate) and a *specific pulse recurrence rate*, both of which are variables that can be used for identification. In effect there are three such variables: *Identification of station pairs.*

> Frequency
> Basic pulse (signal) recurrence rate.
> Specific pulse recurrent rate.

Three frequency channels are available: *Frequency.*

> Channel 1: 1950 kHz
> Channel 2: 1850 kHz
> Channel 3: 1900 kHz

Three basic rates are used: *Basic pulse recurrence rate.*

> S=special=20 pulses per second, 50,000 μs intervals
> L=low=25 pulses per second, 40,000 μs intervals.
> H=high=$33\frac{1}{3}$ pulses per second, 30,000 μs intervals.

Eight stations may use the same frequency and same basic rate, each specific rate varying slightly from the basic rate: the specific pulse rates differ by 100 *ms*.

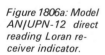

Station No.	L basic rate	H basic rate	S basic rate
0	40,000 μs interval	30,000 μs interval	50,000 μs interval
1	39,900 μs interval	29,900 μs interval	49,900 μs interval
2	39,800 μs interval	29,800 μs interval	49,800 μs interval
3	39,700 μs interval	29,700 μs interval	49,700 μs interval
4	39,600 μs interval	29,600 μs interval	49,600 μs interval
5	39,500 μs interval	29,500 μs interval	49,500 μs interval
6	39,400 μs interval	29,400 μs interval	49,400 μs interval
7	39,300 μs interval	29,300 μs interval	49,300 μs interval

A pair of stations or its signals are identified by giving all three variables. Thus, stations on *rate* 1L0 operate on a frequency of 1950 kHz at a pulse recurrence rate of 25 per second. Rate 2H5 operates on a frequency of 1850 kHz at a pulse recurrence rate of about $33\frac{8}{9}$ per second. It is not essential to remember the figures. To receive signals, the operator need only know that rate 1L0 means channel 1, low basic pulse recurrence rate, station pair 0; while rate 2H5 means channel 2, high basic pulse recurrence rate, station pair 5. Receivers are marked for identification in this way.

Receivers and indicators.

1806. The Loran receiver currently in wide use in the Navy is designated the AN/UPN 12, (Figure 1806a), and employs a cathode ray tube (CRT) presentation. This instrument gives a direct reading in microseconds (at the Loran receiver) of the time difference in arrival of signal pulses from master and slave transmitters of a Loran transmitting group.

Figure 1806a: Model AN/UPN-12 direct reading Loran receiver indicator.

In the Loran system it is not necessary to know the exact location of the transmitting station, or to measure the direction of arrival of the radio signals. The short synchronized radio signal pulses are received through the wire or whip type antenna installed on the receiving vessel, where they are amplified, matched and read from the time-difference dial on the face of the receiving set.

In nearly all military and commercial Loran receiver sets the method of obtaining the time-difference reading is the same. The power is turned on, the sweep or function selector is set in the number *1* position and the proper frequency and pulse recurrence rates are set. Some receivers require that the power switch be placed in the standby position for at least 15 minutes, before the power is turned on, to allow for proper warm-up of the instrument. This procedure is not necessary in the newer transistorized instruments.

Operation of Loran-A receiver.

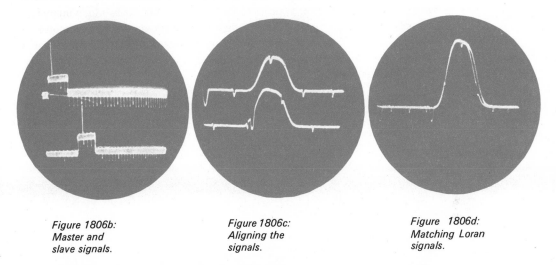

Figure 1806b:
Master and
slave signals.

Figure 1806c:
Aligning the
signals.

Figure 1806d:
Matching Loran
signals.

In the sweep or first function position the master signal will appear on the upper line (A) and the slave signal on the lower line (B) as shown in Figure 1806b. With the delay knob the master and slave signals are moved to the left edge of the pedestals. The drift knob is adjusted to stop the movement or drift of these signals. The sweep or function switch is then turned to the number *2* position, which will enlarge the left part of the pedestal, and with the delay knob the signals are aligned one under the other as illustrated in Figure 1806c. By adjusting the drift knob both signals are moved to the left hand side of the scope. The drift control is often referred to as the left–right control, with the drift knob being used for fine adjustment.

The final step is to set the function switch to the number *3* position, bringing the image of the two signals together on the same line. With the fine delay knob, the left hand edges are aligned, as in Figure 1806d, and the time-difference is read off the dial. During each of the steps some increase or decrease may be necessary in the gain or balance control settings in order to obtain proper amplitude on one or the other of the signals. The maximum amplitude that will not cause distortion should be used for the third function.

Extreme caution must be employed by the operator to insure that ground waves are matched with ground waves and sky waves matched with sky waves. Sky waves can usually be identified by watching the signals, or pips. Since the reflecting surface is irregular, the signals are irregular. Two principal effects are noted:

Sky waves.

Fading. Since the ionosphere is composed of shifting patches of ionized air (Article 1707), rather than a homogeneous layer, the reflecting power varies, causing the strength of the incoming signal to vary in intensity; that is, to change

313

in height as seen on the scope. It may even disappear altogether for a short time. Hence, do not be in too much of a hurry in identifying signals, and use plenty of gain to find weak signals. If the ship is rolling considerably, a ground wave may appear to fade, but this will be regular and in time with the period of roll.

Splitting. Since the patches of ionized air shift about, somewhat like clouds, only part of a signal may be reflected by the first surface it strikes. The other part may penetrate and be reflected by a higher patch of the same layer. When this happens, the signal splits, or appears to have two or more peaks. Such splitting is usually temporary. Figure 1806e shows the appearance of a typical ground wave signal (at greatest magnification) and two forms of split sky wave signals. The relative size of the pips and of the peaks of the split sky wave signals have no significance, for they vary greatly.

If readings are taken at regular intervals, such as hourly, identification is made easier by noting the changing pattern.

Figure 1806e: Scope appearance of ground wave and two forms of sky waves.

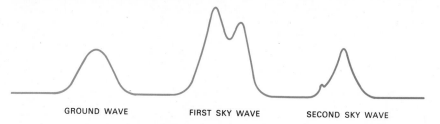

GROUND WAVE   FIRST SKY WAVE   SECOND SKY WAVE

Transmission delays.

1807. To facilitate measurement, it is desired that one signal appear on each trace. This means that instead of signals from both stations being sent at the same time, one signal must be delayed for a period equal to half the pulse recurrence rate, or 20,000 μs for rate 1LO. If both stations were the same distance away, one signal would then appear directly above the other. In this case the reading would be 0, since this delay is not included in the reading.

If the stations were not the same distance away, one signal would appear to the right of the other, but since there would be no way of being sure which signal came from station *M* and which from *S*, there might be some question as to which of two possible curves represented the true line of position of the ship (Figure 1804), especially if the ship were near the center line, where the DR position would not resolve the ambiguity. Hence, a second delay is introduced.

Station *M* is designated the *master* station and station *S* the *slave* station. The signal is sent first from *M*. The half pulse recurrence rate delay begins, not at the instant *M* transmits its signal, but when the signal from *M* is received at *S*, or 6.18 $\mu s \times$ the length of the base line after transmission of the *M* signal. Hence, the signal from *S* always appears to the right of the signal from *M* (since time is measured from left to right) when the *M* signal appears on the *A* trace and the *S* Signal on the *B* trace.

A third delay, usually of 950 or 1000 μs, called the *coding delay*, is also introduced to prevent any reading from being 0 (as it would on or near the base line extension from *S* (Figure 1804), so there will be no question of which signal is right, and which is left. This delay may be changed at will and provides a means of security in wartime.

The delays may be summarized as follows:

Half pulse recurrence rate delay—to put one signal on each trace.

Base line delay (6.18 × length of base line in miles)—to insure *M* signal being received first.

Coding delay (usually 950 or 1000 *μs*)—to help operator distinguish between *M* and *S* signals at small readings, and for purposes of security.

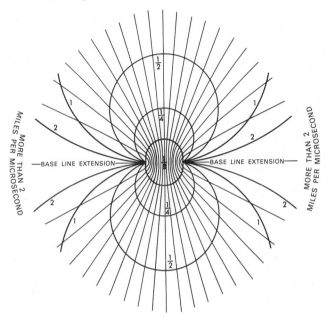

Figure 1808: Accuracy of Loran-A lines of position. The numbers refer to the number of miles per microsecond time difference.

1808. The accuracy of a Loran line of position varies considerably over the area covered by a single rate. It will be seen from Figure 1808 that the lines of position are closest together along the base line and draw farther apart as the lines extend outward from the line.

Accuracy.

Greatest accuracy may be expected near the base line, where one *μs* reading in time difference represents less than 0.1 mile. This increases as shown in Figure 1808 to the base line extension, where one *μs* represents more than 2 miles. At a considerable distance, one *μs* could represent 10 miles or more.

In general, ground waves produce a line of position accurate to 1.5 miles or better over 80 per cent of the area covered by the stations. Sky waves produce a maximum error of 5 to 7 miles for 80 per cent of the coverage area; sky and ground waves are described in article 1703. The accuracy of a position is increased, of course, if three or more lines of position are used and the various lines weighted by their position relative to the stations, type of wave, angle of cutting other lines, etc.

The actual reading of the signals should be accurate to ±2 *μs* for 90 per cent of the time if ground waves are used. If sky waves are used, the accuracy of reading 90 per cent of the time should be ±5 *μs*, when located more than 800 miles from the stations. The accuracy of sky waves decreases as the stations are approached. At 250 miles, an error of ±20 *μs* may be expected. Sky waves should not be used closer than 250 miles.

The greatest source of error in Loran fixes is the small crossing angles of lines of position in many areas.

Advantage of Loran. **1809.** Loran, like many of the hyperbolic navigational systems, has several advantages over some other methods.

Rapid readings. A single reading for one line of position can generally be obtained in about a minute; at critical ranges, using sky waves, several minutes may be required. Plotting Loran lines of position is extremely rapid. When the Loran tables are used, and the resulting line of position is plotted on a conventional chart or plotting sheet, the time required is somewhat longer. However, the tables should always be used when the available Loran charts are of small scale. Loran lines of position are advanced and retired to a common time, in the same way as any lines of position.

Operator training. Quartermasters may be trained in a few days to become proficient Loran operators. At Loran schools, they learn how to check the receiver for alignment, and are instructed in the identification of ground and sky waves, etc.

Reliability. Like the other hyperbolic systems, readings can be obtained in almost any weather; severe thunderstorms occasionally make it impossible to obtain readings. Loran signals are broadcast 24 hours a day, making a reading available at any time, except in the event of a mechanical or electrical failure.

Wide coverage. Most of the commonly used ocean routes lie within an area of Loran coverage.

Accuracy. The accuracy of a signal is not reduced when it crosses land; however, the distances at which Loran signals may be received are somewhat reduced, when traveling across land.

Independent of time. Hyperbolic navigational systems are independent of real time. Time is used only with respect to the movement of the vessel.

Homing. Hyperbolic lines of position may be used for homing, when a line passes through the destination. It is only necessary to reach the required line, and then steam along it, keeping the count reading constant.

Jamming not practical. Loran signals are very difficult to jam. While jamming causes interference it is usually possible to receive and identify the signals.

Security. By changing the coding delay, it is possible to restrict the use of Loran to friendly nations.

Disadvantages of Loran. **1810.** As with all navigation systems, certain disadvantages are inherent in Loran.

Equipment failure. Failure is possible in both the transmitting and receiving equipment.

Range is critical. Loran is far from being a world-wide system, and many areas of operational interest to the U. S. Navy have either poor coverage, or are out of range of any Loran stations. At critical ranges there is the possibility of incorrect station identification.

Equipment damage. The transmitting stations are subject to damage by weather or enemy action.

Interference. **1811.** Like other forms of radio, Loran is subject to interference. However, in most forms of radio, interference is *heard;* in Loran it is *seen*.

Ordinary static appears as *grass* on the traces. If signals are strong enough to appear above the grass, a reading can be made. Flashes of lightning and CW transmission by radio produce interference which momentarily obscures the Loran signals, but with patience the process can be carried on between the disturbances.

Radar produces a series of signals somewhat resembling Loran signals, but they can easily be distinguished by their regular spacing across the traces and need not interfere with obtaining a reading.

Two other forms of interference come from Loran itself. These are known as *spillover* and *ghost pulses*.

Spillover. When a ship is near one Loran station and is tuned to a station of a different channel (wave length), weak signals from the nearby station may appear, just as the program of a strong commercial station nearby can sometimes be heard in the background when a home radio is tuned to a distant station of a wave length differing slightly from the closer station. If the commercial radio dial was extended a little, Loran signals of channel 1 (1950 kHz) would be picked up as a low hum at 195 on the dial. Channel 2 signals would come in at 185, channel 3 at 190 and channel 4 at 175. From this it can be seen that the frequency separation is not great. A mistake can easily be made by matching such signals and the Loran operator must be on the alert for such interference if he is in an area where it may reasonably be expected. If spillover is suspected, shift to the frequency of the nearby station; the spillover signal becomes stronger, while the one of the correct frequency disappears.

Ghost pulses appear when the Loran set is tuned to the wrong basic pulse recurrence rate. They appear as ordinary Loran signals, but flicker and may be further identified by the fact that the trace itself appears unbroken at the pip. With the true pulse the trace appears interrupted across the base of the pip. Ghost pulses may be matched, but the reading is meaningless.

1812. Loran synchronization is constantly monitored and if the timing of the signals becomes inaccurate by as much as two microseconds, the receiver operator is warned by *blinking* of one or both signals of the rate. Two forms of blinking are used. The signal may be turned on and off at short intervals or moved right and left, both forms being regularly timed. No reading should be taken at such a time. The synchronization of signals is usually corrected within a few minutes and readings may then be resumed. *Blinking.*

1813. Special charts are published for plotting Loran lines of position. On these charts Loran lines of position from stations within probable range are drawn in at intervals, usually 20 to 200 μs. The lines of each rate have a distinctive color. To further facilitate identification each line is labeled with the rate as well as the reading. Charts are made to several different scales. Part of one of the smallest scale charts, approximately 70 miles to an inch, is illustrated in Figure 1813. This small scale, which has been further reduced in reproduction, was chosen for illustration because of its relatively simple pattern, good crossing angles over most of its area, and the fact that it illustrates the characteristic pattern of the hyperbolic lines of position. *Plotting Loran lines of position by chart.*

To plot a line of position, it is necessary only to draw in a portion of the line

317

near the DR, interpolating between lines as necessary. If it need be advanced, do this in the usual way, the time label indicating both times, as with any line of position.

Lines shown on the charts are for ground waves. If sky waves are matched, a different reading is obtained, since the waves travel longer paths, the extent of the lengthening being inversely proportional to the distance from the station. Hence, if sky waves are used, a correction must be applied before a line is plotted. The correction appears at intersections of latitude and longitude on the chart. Eye interpolation is used for the area at which the line of position is to be drawn.

Example (Figure 1813). The 1130 DR position of a plane is L 23°26′ N, λ 159°46′ W. At this time Loran readings are taken in quick succession, as follows: 2L5 T$_G$ 1184, 2L6 T$_G$ 1775. (2L5 T$_G$ 1184 means "a reading of 1184 μs on ground waves of rate 2L5.")

Required: Using the chart shown, plot, label and record the 1130 Loran fix.

Solution: Plot the DR position. Interpolating between the 1100 and 1200 lines, draw a small part of the line of position of rate 2L5 (1184 μs). Label this line with the time, 1130, above the line and 2L5 below the line. Similarly plot and label the other line in such a position that it will cross the first line. Label the intersection of these lines "1130 Loran Fix." (Plot carefully, but do not expect extreme accuracy on such a small scale.)

Answer: 1130 Loran Fix; L 23°22′ N, λ 159°45′ W.

Plotting Loran lines of position by table. Tables issued by the Oceanographic Office (H. O. Pub. No. 221) provide the necessary data for plotting Loran lines of position on navigational charts or plotting sheets.

The arguments for entering these tables are the Loran reading (corrected for sky wave, if necessary) to the nearest 20 ot 50 μs and the latitude *or* longitude, depending on the direction of the line. Entries are given for every 15′, 30′, or 1° of latitude or longitude, depending on the amount of curvature of the line which is illustrated in Figure 1813.

The sky wave corrections for each rate are given at the front of the pages of tables of that rate.

Enter the tables in the column of the nearest Loran reading with the latitude or longitude on each side of or bracketing the DR value, and pick out the corresponding values of longitude or latitude for these two points. Interpolation for the exact Loran reading is provided by means of a Δ value which represents the change (to the nearest 0′.01) of longitude or latitude for a change of 1 μs of Loran reading. The total correction is equal to this Δ value times the number of microseconds by which the Loran reading differs from the tabular value. Although a multiplication table is available for performing this step, it can usually be done mentally. The correction, to the nearest 0′.1, is applied to the tabulated longitude or latitude in accordance with the sign of the Δ value if the Loran reading is greater than the tabular value; otherwise the sign is reversed.

Plot two points thus found and connect them with a straight line. Label the lines as above.

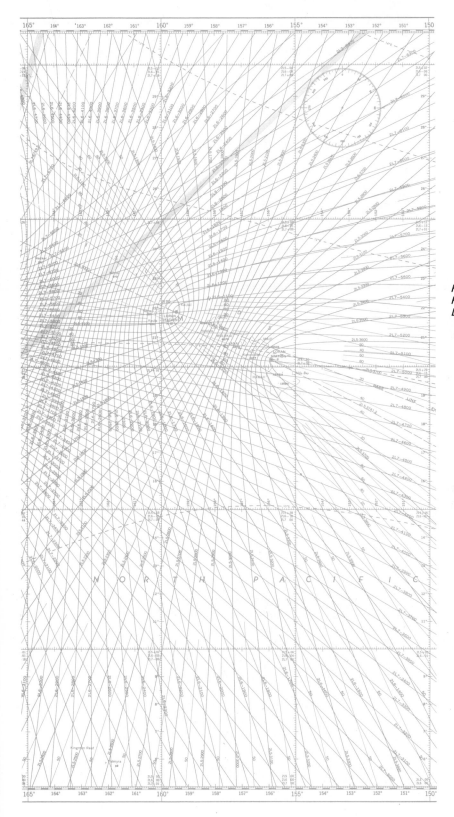

Figure 1813:
Portion of a
Loran chart.

To obtain a fix it is necessary to have at least two lines of position, and it is desirable to have three or more. Loran lines can be crossed with other Loran lines or lines of position determined in any other manner, as by celestial observation, RDF, etc. The accuracy of the fix thus obtained depends on the accuracy of the individual lines and their angle of crossing.

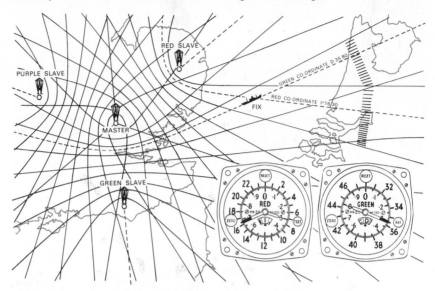

Figure 1814a:
Decca lattice of
English Channel.

Decca.

1814. This is a British hyperbolic navigation system (Figure 1814a), using phase comparison for determining the distance from the transmitters. Each chain consists of one master and three slaves. Ideally, the slaves are equally spaced around the circumference of a circle having a radius of 70 to 80 miles, and centered on the master.

For purposes of identification, the slaves are designated *purple*, *red*, and *green*. Each of the four stations transmits a continuous wave at a different frequency; these frequencies are in the ratio 5, 6, 8 and 9. The signals are in the 70–130 kHz band. With the continuous harmonically related carrier frequencies the phase relationship of the signals conveys the information necessary to determine hyperbolic position.

The receiving unit consists of four receivers (Figure 1814b), one for each frequency. Circuits are installed for comparing the phase of each slave with that of the master.

Decca charts are published, showing hyperbolas printed in colors to agree with the colors of the slaves. Two slaves provide a fix; the third provides a check on the others, and permits positioning in areas unfavorable to one of the other slaves. To determine a position, it is only necessary to read three dials called *Decometers*, and locate the intersection of the two or three lines indicated. No matching of signals, or manipulation of dials is required. As with any phase relationship system the phases of the signals transmitted by master and slave are compared, rather than the travel times. The phase comparison gives a precise measure of the fractional part of a wave-length, or lane, but no indication of the total number of whole lanes existing. An auxiliary means of keeping track of the number of whole lanes is essential. This is accomplished

Figure 1814b: Mark XII marine Decometers and pictorial display unit.

by a counter on the receiver equipment or by accurate dead reckoning on the chart.

The average reliable operational day and night range of Decca is about 250 miles. At this distance the average error in a line of position is approximately 150 yards in daytime, and about 800 yards at night.

Decca coverage extends over much of Western Europe, the Persian Gulf, the Bay of Bengal, and parts of Eastern Canada and Northeastern United States. Ships of the U. S. Navy operating in these areas at times employ Decca receivers.

For air navigation a Decca roller map display (Figure 1814c) is available when an automatic system is installed in the aircraft. This roller map display is an X-Y plotter using true coordinates and a strip map showing the exact location of the aircraft at all times.

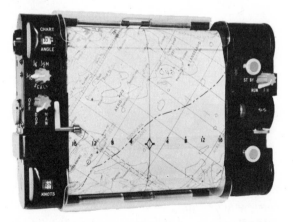

Figure 1814c: Decca roller map Mark IV (Type 9275).

1815. Radio Direction Finding (RDF) systems, in spite of advances in radio navigation systems that have occurred in recent years, have remained in common use. Most RDF systems utilize a non-directional transmitter and a direction-sensitive antenna system for the receiver. RDF sets aboard ship enable *bearings* to be taken from other ships, aircraft, and shore stations, marine radio beacons, and the coastal stations of the radio communication network, as well as from commercial broadcasting stations. A bearing thus obtained can be used in the same manner as any other line of position when the location of the transmitting antenna is known.

Radio Direction Finders.

321

A radio direction finder makes use of the directional properties of a loop antenna. If such an antenna is parallel to the direction of travel of the radio waves, the signal received is of maximum strength. If the loop is perpendicular to the direction of travel, the signal is of minimum strength or entirely missing. When a dial is attached to such a loop antenna, the direction of the antenna and hence the direction of the transmitter can be determined. The pointer indicates the direction of the transmitter from the receiver when the loop is perpendicular to this direction, when the minimum signal is heard. The minimum, generally called the "null," rather than the maximum, is used because a sharper reading is thus obtained. Since radio waves travel a great circle, a correction must be applied for plotting on a Mercator chart. A Lambert chart permits direct plotting of all radio bearings.

The correction to be applied to convert a great circle direction to the rhumb line direction for plotting on a Mercator chart can be obtained from the correction table given in H. O. 117 or Table 1 in Bowditch.

Arbitrary rules are sometimes given to determine whether or not a radio bearing should be corrected before plotting, but these are always based on certain assumptions. The amount of the correction depends on the latitude and the difference of longitude. A bearing from a transmitter 200 miles away near the equator or in a nearly north-south direction from the receiver may require a smaller correction than if the distance is 25 miles in an east-west direction in high latitudes. The only way to be sure is to enter a correction table and determine the magnitude of the correction.

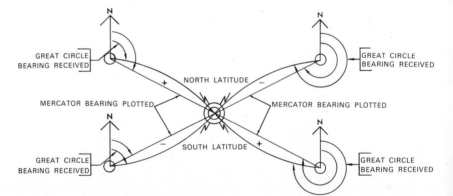

Figure 1815: Diagram for determining the sign of a conversion angle.

Having found the correction, it is necessary to determine its sign before applying it to the observed bearing. This is easy to determine if it is remembered that the *great circle direction is always nearer the pole than the mercator direction.* Do not try to remember any other rule. Draw a small diagram, mentally or otherwise, for each problem and determine the sign from it. Figure 1815 illustrates the four possible situations. The important thing to remember is that the sign depends on the relative position of the *receiver* and the *transmitter*, regardless of which is the ship.

Marine radiobeacons.

1816. These electronic aids to navigation are provided in many parts of the world. Full information as to their locations, frequency, identifying signals, hours of operation, and type of service is given in H. O. 117, *Radio Navigational Aids.* Their locations are marked on nautical charts by the letters RBn near a general chart symbol which is *not* indicative of the expected range of radio reception.

Reference to H. O. 117 or the Light List for the specific characteristics and range of each station is recommended. Although any transmitting station can be used, the station must first be properly identified and its antenna accurately located. Particular care must be used if commercial broadcasting stations are used, not only to be sure the position indicated is the transmitter rather than the studio, but also to be sure that the signal being received is not being re-broadcast from another station.

Since radio signals may normally be received in darkness and during periods of poor visibility, radiobeacons primarily serve when visual aids cannot be used. They operate "continuously" during fog and reduced visibility and also at specified times during clear weather to provide an opportunity for the calibration of direction finders within visual range of the beacon. Radiobeacons transmit in the medium frequency range. For purpose of station identification, simple characteristics consisting of dots and dashes—not to be construed as code letters—are used.

Radio beacons have been divided into three specific classifications.

> *Directional radiobeacons* which transmit radio waves in beams along fixed bearings.

> *Rotating radiobeacons* by which a beam of radio waves is revolved in azimuth in a manner similar to the beam of light sent out by certain lighthouses.

> *Circular radiobeacons* which send out waves of approximately uniform strength in all directions so that ships may take radio bearings of them by means of the ship's radio direction-finder sets. This is the most common type of radiobeacon.

To extend the usefulness of marine radiobeacons to ships and aircraft employing automatic radio direction finders, U. S. marine radiobeacons on the Great Lakes, Atlantic, and Pacific coasts have been modified to transmit a continuous carrier signal during the entire radiobeacon operating period with keyed modulation providing the characteristic signal. Unless a beat frequency oscillator is installed, the continuous carrier signals are not audible to the operator of an aural null direction finder. A 10-second dash has been included in the characteristic of these radio-beacons, to enable the navigator using a conventional aural null direction finder to refine his bearing. Vessels with direction finders will be able to use the United States radiobeacons located on the Great Lakes, and the Atlantic and Pacific coasts at any time in their assigned sequence.

For convenience in studying the time of operation by radiobeacons, they may be divided into three categories:

> *Stations*, such as the United States Government stations mentioned, which maintain a continuous carrier wave on which is superimposed the characteristic code signal;
> *Unattended marker beacons*, of low power and short range, which

operate 24 hours a day;

Group sequence stations, identified on a radiobeacon map with the Roman numerals I, II, III, etc.

These stations are said to operate "continuously" during reduced visibility, but actually they are *on* one minute, during which they transmit the individual code signal, and *off* for the period of time necessary for the other stations in the sequence to transmit. Many stations in a given area operate in groups such as this each using the same frequency, but with only one station on the air at a time, each for one minute.

A typical group, near the approaches to New York Harbor, consists of the following:

Position within the transmission sequence of the group	Name	Frequency	Approximate range in miles	Characteristic code
I	Ambrose Light Station	286 kHz	100	— etc.
II	Fire Island Light	286 kHz	100	·—·—
III	Barnegat Light Station	286 kHz	75	———
V	Block Island Southeast Light	286 kHz	70	··—·

Two other stations, Stratford Shoal Light, and Execution Rocks Light, both located in Long Island Sound, occupy positions IV and VI in this group. Both are of comparatively low power, with a service range of 20 miles, and would be of doubtful value to a mariner approaching New York from the Atlantic.

Radio direction finder stations.

1817. In certain foreign countries radio direction finder equipment is installed at points ashore and these radio direction finder stations obtain and furnish bearings of ships upon request. Such stations are also called radio compass stations, and can be located by reference to H. O. 117 or by the letters RDF placed near the radio station symbol on the chart. The former Radio Direction Finder Service, which was under the control of the U. S. Coast Guard, has been discontinued.

Bearings taken by radio direction finder stations, and reported to the ships, are corrected for all determinable errors except the difference between a great circle and a rhumb, and are normally accurate within 2° for distances under 50 nautical miles.

Accuracy of RDF bearing depends on the following factors:

Strength of signals. The best bearings can be taken on vessels whose signals are steady, clear and strong. Weak signals give inaccurate bearings at best.

Personal error. The skill of the operator is perhaps the most important factor in obtaining accurate readings. Frequent practice is essential if this source of error is to be reduced to a minimum.

Calibration error. Direction finders are subject to errors of calibration, particularly on metal ships. Calibration can be accomplished near a radio station by observing simultaneous radio and visual bearings on various headings. Errors should be checked at intervals, particularly after the ship's structure has been altered or magnetic material has been taken aboard. Bearings should be taken when other antennas and movable equipment such as davits, cranes, etc. are in the same condition as during calibration.

Reciprocal bearings. With some equipment it is not apparent from which side the bearing is coming. The best known grounding case in U. S. history, the Point Honda disaster, took place in 1923 when seven destroyers were lost because they used a reciprocal bearing taken by the radio compass station then located at Point Conception, California. It is usually possible to tell which bearing to use by the dead reckoning position of the ship, but if there is any doubt, take several bearings and note the direction of change. The station should draw aft. *If a reciprocal bearing is obtained, do not attempt to obtain the correct bearing by adding or subtracting 180°.* The calibration correction will probably not be the same.

Night effect. Within half an hour of sunrise and sunset, and to a lesser extent throughout the night, radio bearings may be less accurate than at other times, due largely to polarization effect. This is manifest by a broadening and shifting of the minimum signal.

Land effect. When a radio signal crosses a shore line at an oblique angle, or if it passes over an island or peninsula of high land, the direction of travel may be bent a slight amount in a manner similar to the refraction of light. When a bearing is taken under these conditions, it should be considered of doubtful accuracy.

Quadrantal error. Radio bearings are subject to certain errors due to a disturbing or refracting influence caused by the metal in a ship's structure, electric currents, other antennas, wire rigging, etc. This is called *quadrantal error,* being maximum on relative bearing 45° and 135° on each side.

Plotting errors. In addition to the usual errors of plotting, two sources of error must be guarded against. First, be careful to plot from the correct position. If the bearing is observed aboard ship, it must be plotted from the position of the transmitting antenna ; if observed at a radio compass station, it must be plotted from the position of the *receiving* antenna. *These locations are not always the same,* nor do they always coincide with a light having the same name. Second, radio waves travel great circles and if they are to be plotted on a Mercator chart, a correction may have to be applied to convert the great circle to the corresponding rhumb line between the broadcasting and receiving antennas. A correction is usually not necessary providing the range is under 50 miles. If necessary, the correction may be found in Table 1 in Bowditch, or in H. O. 117.

1818. Radio bearings are plotted and labeled in the same manner as visual bearings. However, radio bearings are usually much less accurate and a position determined with the aid of one or more of them is generally called an *estimated position* and labeled EP. A new DR is not customarily plotted from an EP, but a course line may be plotted from such a position to determine whether or not there is a possibility of the ship standing into danger. A series of estimated positions obtained by radio and supplemented by a line of soundings can often fix the ship's position with considerable accuracy.

Plotting radio bearings.

1819. Omnirange, frequently called "Omni," is of comparatively recent develop-

Omnirange.

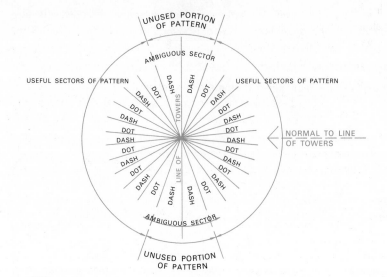

Figure 1820a: Polar diagram of Consolan pattern.

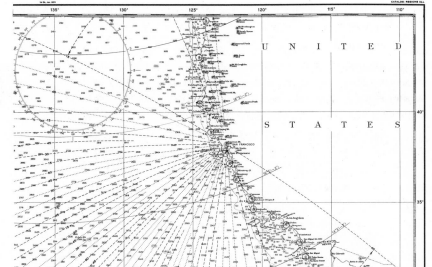

Figure 1820b: Portion of N. O. chart 520 showing Consolan station at San Francisco.

7600.3. San Francisco Consolan Station–Dash Sectors

Count of Dashes	True bearing from station													
0	344.9	14.7	35.6	54.7	74.4	97.9			182.1	205.6	225.3	244.4	265.3	295.1
1	344.5	14.5	35.4	54.6	74.2	97.6			182.4	205.7	225.5	244.6	265.5	295.5
2	344.1	14.3	35.2	54.5	74.1	97.4			182.6	205.9	225.7	244.8	265.7	295.9
3	343.7	14.1	35.0	54.3	73.9	97.2			182.8	206.1	225.8	245.0	265.9	296.3
4	343.3	13.9	34.9	54.1	73.7	97.0			183.1	206.3	226.0	245.1	266.1	296.7
5	342.9	13.7	34.7	54.0	73.5	96.8			183.3	206.4	226.2	245.3	266.3	297.1
6	342.5	13.5	34.5	53.8	73.4	96.6			183.5	206.6	226.4	245.5	266.5	297.5
51		4.1	26.9	46.7	65.9	87.1	118.7	161.2	192.9	214.1	233.3	253.1	276.0	
52		3.9	26.8	46.5	65.7	86.9	118.3	161.6	193.1	214.2	233.5	253.2	276.2	
53		3.7	26.6	46.3	65.5	86.7	117.9	162.0	193.3	214.4	233.7	253.4	276.3	
54		3.4	26.4	46.2	65.3	86.5	117.5	162.4	193.5	214.5	233.8	253.6	276.5	
55		3.2	26.3	46.0	65.2	86.3	117.1	162.8	193.7	214.7	234.0	253.7	276.7	
56		3.0	26.1	45.9	65.0	86.1	116.7	163.2	193.9	214.8	234.1	253.9	277.0	
57		2.8	25.9	45.7	64.9	85.9	116.3	163.6	194.1	215.0	234.3	254.1	277.2	
58		2.5	25.8	45.5	64.7	85.7	115.9	164.0	194.3	215.2	234.5	254.2	277.4	
59		2.3	25.7	45.4	64.6	85.5	115.5	164.4	194.5	215.4	234.6	254.3	277.6	
60		2.1	25.6	45.3	64.4	85.3	115.1	164.9	194.7	215.6	234.7	254.4	277.9	

Figure 1820c: Dash to bearing conversion table.

ment, intended for the use of aircraft. However, Omniranges have been installed along considerable stretches of the U. S. coast, and an increasing number of small vessels, particularly pleasure craft, are installing Omni receivers.

The older aircraft beacons were limited in their utility, in that each could only indicate four "beams" or flight paths. The Omniranges are not so limited. They broadcast a rotating or omni-directional pattern (article 1711) and the magnetic direction of the station can be read directly from a dial.

The Omni signals are broadcast on very high frequencies, and their range is thus limited to approximately the line of sight. Small vessels, as a rule, can obtain signals up to a distance of about 25 miles from the transmitting station.

1820. Consolan is essentially a long range navigational aid requiring no special receiving equipment. Currently, only one Consolan station is operative; it is located at San Francisco, operating on a frequency of 192 kHz. Signals may be received on any low frequency radio receiver including most radio direction finders. The receiver must have a beat frequency oscillator. If a loop antenna is used best results will be obtained by adjusting the antenna near the maximum signal position. If a communications receiver is used the continuous wave (CW) beat frequency oscillator should be cut in and the automatic volume control should not be used.

Consolan.

Consolan employs a pattern of alternating dot sectors and dash sectors separated by an equisignal. The width of the sector averages about 12° differing slightly with the position relative to the line of the towers. It is most accurate at a position 90° from the line of the towers and has an unusable ambiguous sector off both ends of the line of the towers (Figure 1820a). Charts giving the various dot-dash sectors are available (Figure 1820b). H. O. 117 contains tables giving true bearings from the station for various counts (Figure 1820c).

If these bearings are plotted on a Mercator chart, an additional correction must be made since a radio wave follows the great circle, a curved line on the Mercator projection. A portion of this conversion table is shown in Figure 1820d. On a Lambert chart the bearings are plotted direct.

7600. San Francisco (SFI).
FREQ.: 192 kHz.
CHARACTERISTIC SIGNAL: 7.5 seconds call signal, 2.5 seconds silent, 30 seconds keying cycle (See Fig. 1).
HOURS OF TRANSMISSION: Continuous.

38°12'13"N., 122°34'08"W.

Figure 1820d: Excerpt from a radio bearing conversion table.

7600.1.   San Francisco Consolan Station—Conversion Table

Difference of longitude	Latitude of Observer																		
	0°	5°	10°	15°	20°	25°	30°	35°	40°	45°	50°	55°	60°	65°	70°	75°	80°	85°	90°
0°	0°.0	0°.0	0°.0	0°.0	0°.0	0°.0	0°.0	0°.0	0°.0	0°.0	0°.0	0°.0	0°.0	0°.0	0°.0	0°.0	0°.0	0°.0	0°.0
5°	1°.1	1°.2	1°.2	1°.3	1°.3	1°.4	1°.4	1°.4	1°.7	1°.7	1°.7	1°.7	1°.7	1°.7	1°.7	1°.7	1°.6	1°.5	0°.0
10°	2°.3	2°.4	2°.5	2°.6	2°.7	2°.7	2°.8	3°.0	3°.2	3°.3	3°.4	3°.4	3°.4	3°.4	3°.4	3°.4	3°.2	3°.0	0°.0
75°	19°.3	20°.4	21°.3	22°.2	23°.0	23°.7	24°.4	25°.0	25°.6	26°.0	26°.4	26°.7	26°.8	26°.8	26°.5	25°.9	24°.7	22°.3	0°.0
80°	21°.0	22°.1	23°.1	24°.0	24°.9	25°.7	26°.4	27°.1	27°.6	28°.1	28°.5	28°.7	28°.8	28°.8	28°.5	27°.8	26°.5	23°.8	0°.0
85°	22°.7	23°.9	25°.0	26°.0	26°.9	27°.7	28°.5	29°.2	29°.7	30°.2	30°.6	30°.8	30°.8	30°.8	30°.4	29°.6	28°.2	25°.3	0°.0
90°	24°.6	25°.8	27°.0	28°.1	29°.0	29°.9	30°.7	31°.3	31°.9	32°.4	32°.8	33°.0	33°.0	32°.8	32°.4	31°.5	29°.9	26°.8	0°.0

Corrections to be *added* to the true bearing to obtain the Mercator bearing when the observer is to the East of the station and *subtracted* when the observer is to the West of the station.

Range and
accuracy.

1821. Consolan is basically a CW system in respect to both identification and navigation system transmissions and may be useable to long ranges. As with all aural systems, operator experience is the limiting factor. An experienced operator can pick up the Consolan signal, with good accuracy, under adverse conditions of signal and noise when voice communications may be unintelligible. Therefore range depends on such variables as noise, ground conductivity, ionospheric conditions, frequency and power of ground stations, and the ability of the operator. Since the greatest range would be over sea-water paths, due to the high conductivity, the Consolan stations, operating in the neighborhood of 190 kHz, can be expected to provide coverage at ranges up to 1400 nautical miles, or more. The system is not usable within 50 nautical miles of the station.

The greatest accuracy is obtained in a direction normal to the line of towers, as illustrated in Figure 1820a, with the general accuracy averaging 0.3° during the daylight hours, and 0.7° during the night.

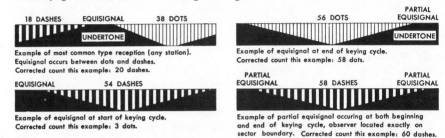

*Figure 1822:
Examples of keying
cycles received.*

Consolan bearings.

1822. It is not difficult to obtain a Consolan bearing. The following procedure is taken from H. O. 117 A.

To obtain a Consolan Bearing the desired Consolan Station is tuned using the DF receiver or a communications receiver with the (BFO) beat frequency oscillator turned ON and the (AVC) automatic volume control turned OFF. The station is identified by the Morse Code identification signal. Immediately following one of the 2.5 seconds silent periods the operator must count the dots and dashes heard until the equisignal is heard, then continue counting until the next silent period is reached. Add the two counts together which will produce a figure less than 60. The unheard dots and dashes were lost in the equisignal zone and may be determined by subtracting the total heard from 60. *One half* of the remainder is then added to the dots or dashes which were heard first immediately following the silent period.

Example:

Dots (heard first) counted	15	Equisignal (60–54)	6
Dashes counted	39	Total dots (15 plus 3)	18
Total	54	Total dashes (39 plus 3)	42

The observer is, therefore, located on the line represented by 18 dots after the end of the silent period. This total count has been identified as a "dot" count. If the transmission should begin with the equisignal or partial equisignal, care should be exercised in interpretation of the signal count. For instance, the 3 dot example (Figure 1822) shows a condition where the beginning 3 dots were masked by the equisignal yet the count is a "dot" count. Should an instance of this kind result in interpretation as a "dash" count, reference to the conversion table would yield a bearing of such great discrepancy that it would be readily recognized as an error. The 60 dot count and the 60 dash count (shown in Figure 1822) are repetitive exceptions to the rule. Fortunately this condition holds the probability of infrequent occurrence and even so, if it should result in misinterpretation of 59 instead of a 60 dash count, the error in the resulting bearing derived from the tables would be less than $\frac{1}{2}°$.

Ambiguous signal counts occur in alternate dot-dash sectors. It is necessary, therefore, to determine the sector by known approximate position, maps, charts, dead reckoning, or direction finding. Practical experience indicates that the possibility of using the wrong sector is rather small but care should be taken. A direction finder check will usually suffice to identify the proper sector.

Referring to the Consolan Table for the particular station being received, the dot-dash signal count converts to the true bearing of the observer's position from the station. Consolan charts give the location of the station, the "zero" line (through the towers) and the normals (90° to the zero line). A line of position, therefore, may be readily plotted. The intersection of two bearings or LOPs will give an accurate indication of position. The Mercator bearing from the station is obtained by entering the conversion table with the difference of longitude and latitude of the observer, interpolating if necessary, and applying the resulting correction to the true bearing according to the rules given. See tables for individual stations.

Caution: At night, always take a series of readings, particularly when 300 to 700 miles from the station. Wide variation in successive counts is an indication of sky wave or ground wave interference. These bearings should be handled with great caution or disregarded altogether.

1823. Consol is generally similar to Consolan, in that it is a long-range, short base line, hyperbolic system. It operates in the 250–350 kHz frequency range. In actual use, it is considered a directional system, and the hyperbolic portions of the lines are not used. It differs from Consolan in that cycles of varying lengths, rather than CW, are employed, and the keying cycle may be up to 30 seconds in duration.

Consol.

Five Consol stations are established along or near the western coast of Europe at Seville in southern Spain, Lugo in northern Spain, Ploneis on the west coast of France, Bushmills in North Ireland, and Verhang in southern Norway. Two stations are also in operation along the Arctic coast of Russia.

Under favorable conditions the area of coverage of a Consol station over water extends outward for about 1000 to 1200 miles in the daytime, and 1200 to 1500 miles at night. In general, when ground waves are received, the error over water does not exceed about one-third degree along the perpendicular, and about two-thirds of a degree at an angle of 60° to the perpendicular. Stated in miles, this is an error of about one mile for each 180 miles from the station along the perpendicular, and for each 90 miles along the bearing line 60° from the perpendicular. This error can usually be considerably reduced by taking a number of bearings, and averaging the results.

While Consol cannot be considered a precision system, its bearings can be highly useful at times, particularly for ships approaching the Straits of Gibraltar from the westward in overcast weather, and when operating in the western Mediterranean.

CHAPTER 19

Navigational Astronomy

Introduction.

1901. Astronomy is perhaps the oldest science to which man has devoted his attention. Probably primitive men gazed at the night sky in awe and wonderment, and folklore and legend reflect their interest in the heavenly bodies. The progress of the science of astronomy is closely associated with the history of the human race. Each of the great civilizations of the ancient world has recorded its findings in this field. The Egyptians, Babylonians, Chinese, Hindus, Mayas and Aztecs all pursued the science of astronomy, which they associated with their religious beliefs. This history is documented and classified and the science of astronomy has been greatly advanced by modern scientists.

The universe.

1902. The universe is generally considered to be infinite in size. Modern technology has made possible giant telescopes which have greatly increased man's ability to see farther into the vast reaches of space. As a result, an immense number of galaxies have been discovered. Galaxies of stars are now observed at distances of approximately ten billion trillion (10^{22}) miles.

Units of distance.

Special units of measurement have been created for expressing such vast distances. In the measurement of distances within the solar system, the *astronomical unit* (AU) is used. To express distances to bodies outside the solar system, two terms are used, the *light-year,* and the *parsec.*

Figure 1902: Photograph of a typical spiral galaxy.

The value of the astronomical unit is approximately 93 million statute miles, the mean distance between the earth and the sun. The light-year is about 5.87 trillion (5.87×10^{12}) statute miles. This is the distance light travels in one year. The speed of light is 186,281 miles per second, and one year is equivalent to approximately 31.6 million seconds. Parsec (from the words *parallax* and *second*) is the distance at which a body, viewed from the earth and from the sun will differ in apparent position by one second of arc. This amounts to about 19.1 trillion (19.1×10^{12}) statute miles or 3.26 light years. Since this value is less than the distance from earth to Rigil Kentaurus, the navigational star nearest to our solar system at a distance of about 4.3 light years, any star viewed from the sun and from the earth will differ in direction by less than one second of arc. This small angle is known as the star's *heliocentric parallax* (not to be confused with *geocentric parallax)*.

Parsec.

Each galaxy is an assemblage of perhaps 100 billion stars, dust clouds, and masses of thin gas in rotation, held together by gravitational force in a lens-shaped formation. A typical galaxy may be some 100,000 light years in diameter, tapering in thickness from 15,000 light years at the center to about 5,000 light years near the rim. Most galaxies are spiral in shape (see Figure 1902).

The brightness of a celestial body is expressed in terms of magnitude. The magnitude ratio is derived from Ptolemy's division of the visible stars into six groups according to brightness. The first group is considered to be 100 times brighter than the sixth group. Thus, the magnitude ratio is computed as the fifth root of 100 or 2.512, and a zero magnitude body is 2.512 times brighter than a first magnitude body, which is 2.512 times brighter than a second magnitude body, etc. With this scale, the two brightest stars, Sirius and Canopus, have negative magnitudes of −1.6 and −0.9 respectively.

Magnitude.

1903. Our own galaxy, the Milky Way, derives its name from the milky appearance of the night sky to the unaided eye as the observer looks along its major axis. This milky appearance is caused by the myriad of stars in this area.

The Milky Way.

The Milky Way is considered to be about average among galaxies in star population. The stars are not evenly distributed; they tend to be concentrated in two spiral arms extending outward from the center, with the whole galaxy in rotation. Our solar system is located roughly two-thirds of the way from the center to the rim, and rotates about the galaxy center in about 200 million years.

The stars comprising this galaxy vary greatly in size. The largest known star is Antares (Alpha Scorpii) with a diameter about 428 times that of the sun, while the smallest has a diameter of only about 1730 miles, or roughly one-quarter that of the earth. This small star, 48 light years distant, was only recently discovered, and to date has not received a name. Our sun, an average sized star, is approximately 864,400 miles in diameter.

Apart from our own star, the sun, the navigator is concerned only with stars within our galaxy and, astronomically speaking, in our immediate neighborhood. The Nautical Almanac tabulates data on a total of 173 stars suitable for use in celestial navigation. Only 58 of this total are normally used; these are the 57 so-called "selected stars," plus Polaris, which is conveniently located for the determination of latitude in the northern hemisphere.

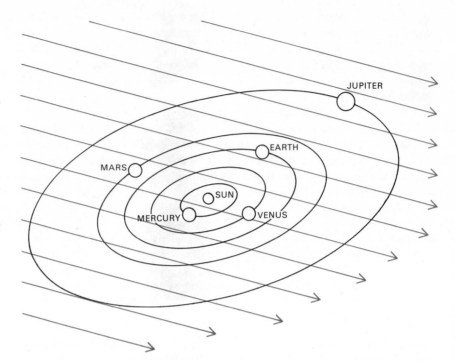

Figure 1903: Light rays from star parallel across entire solar system.

The stars are not the only celestial bodies employed in navigation. The planets of the solar system and the moon are also valuable to the navigator. These bodies, with the sun, are frequently suitable for daylight observations. However, the navigator's use of the bodies within the solar system differs from his use of the stars in two respects, both due to the vast difference in distance.

First, for navigation purposes, rays of light from any star may be considered to be parallel throughout the solar system. For example, Rigil Kentaurus, the nearest navigational star, is more than four light-years distant; the second nearest navigational star and the brightest in the sky, Sirius, is twice that distance. Rigil Kentaurus observed from opposite points on the earth's orbit around the sun (Figure 1903) would differ in angle by approximately 1.5 seconds of arc. The navigator is not equipped to measure angles to this precision. Thus, in the observation of a star, *geocentric parallax,* also called horizontal parallax, that difference in the apparent direction or position of a celestial body as observed from the center of the earth and a point on its surface, may be disregarded. For navigational purposes the stars can be considered as being at an infinite distance, while the sun, moon and planets are at finite distances. The moon is only about $1\frac{1}{4}$ light seconds distant from the earth, and the sun is less than $8\frac{1}{2}$ light minutes away, necessitating a correction for parallax.

Second, for navigational purposes, stars may be considered as point sources of light with no measurable diameter when viewed through a sextant telescope. The sun, at an average distance from the earth of 93,000,000 miles, is considered to be equivalent in mass to the average star. Thus, semi-diameter, not visually observable in bodies outside our solar system, is applied in the use of the sun and the moon. The semi-diameter of planets, limited to about 32 *seconds* of arc, is seldom considered in marine navigation.

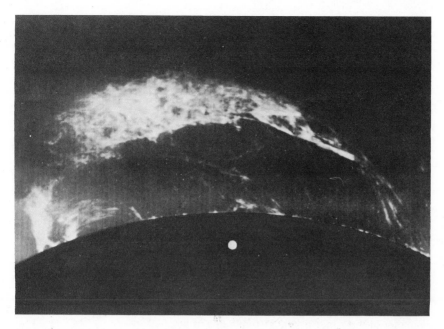

Figure 1904: The surface of the sun. Dot represents comparative size of earth.

1904. The center of our solar system, a rotating mass of burning gases radiating energy at a fantastic rate, is called the sun. Every second it converts millions of tons of matter into energy, and it has been doing this for some five billion years. Its surface temperature is about 10,000 degrees Fahrenheit, and it is in a constant state of agitation, emitting eruptions of burning gas to distances sometimes as much as hundreds of thousands of miles, before they fall back to the surface.   *The sun.*

Another solar phenomenon is the *sun spot*, which appears dark on the surface of the sun. Sun spots are masses of comparatively cooler gas, sometimes 50,000 miles in diameter.

Magnetic storms on the earth, which interfere with the propagation and reception of radio signals, are related to sun spots, which occur in an eleven-year cycle.

The sun rotates about its axis, but due to its gaseous composition, the rotation is faster near the equator (25 days) than near the poles (34 days).

1905. The solar system consists of nine major planets and thousands of planetoids or asteroids, traveling in elliptical orbits about the sun. Of these major planets, only Venus, Mars, Jupiter, and Saturn are normally used in navigation. Mean distances from the sun, for the navigational planets, in millions of miles, range from 67 million miles for Venus, to 886 million miles for Saturn, and the periods required by each to complete a revolution around the sun vary from about 225 days for Venus, to $29\frac{1}{2}$ years for Saturn.   *The solar system.*

Pluto, the most remote of the planets, is about $5\frac{1}{4}$ light hours, or about 3,670 million miles, from the sun and requires 248 years to complete a revolution.

The ellipticity of the earth's orbit about the sun results in a substantial change in the latter's apparent diameter. At perihelion, the point of nearest approach (Figure 1905a) which follows the winter solstice by ten to twelve days, the apparent diameter of the sun is approximately 32.6 minutes of arc; at aphelion,

333

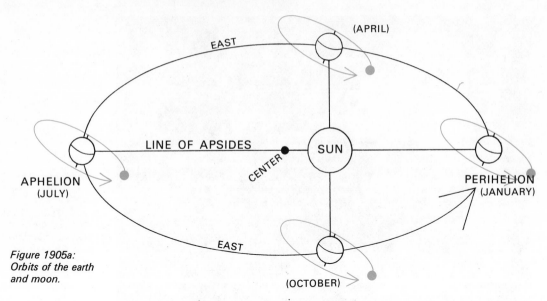

Figure 1905a:
Orbits of the earth
and moon.

following summer solstice by about the same period of time, the apparent diameter of the sun is about 31.5 minutes of arc.

The moon.

The earth's only satellite, the moon, is at an average distance of about 239,000 miles from the earth. Its orbit is elliptical; at perigee it is approximately 221,000 miles from the earth's center, at apogee about 253,000. As with the sun, this change in distance causes a change in the apparent diameter of the moon as observed from the earth, varying between about 29.4 and 33.4 minutes of arc. The actual diameter of the moon is about 2,160 miles. Its period of rotation about the earth and its axial rotation are the same, $27\frac{1}{3}$ days, thus it always presents essentially the same face to the earth.

The moon illustrates why the navigator, in measuring altitudes, cannot use the nearer bodies in the solar system exactly as he does the stars. The altitude of the upper or lower limb of the body, as measured with the sextant, must be corrected to read as though made to the center of the body. The moon's visible diameter changes in value as it moves in orbit from perigee to apogee. The semidiameter, illustrated in Figure 1905b, must be applied as a correction to the sextant altitude.

Figure 1905b: Semidiameter, scale greatly exaggerated.

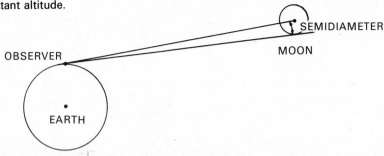

The altitude observed by the navigator is measured up from the sea horizon, but it must be corrected to read as though it had been made at the center of the earth. This correction for horizontal parallax (Figure 1905c) has a maximum value for bodies near the horizon, decreasing to zero for a body directly overhead.

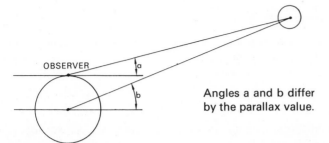

OBSERVER

Angles a and b differ
by the parallax value.

Figure 1905c:
Parallax due to
observer's not being
at earth's center.

The nearer planets, Venus and Mars, are at times observed at distances less than
that of the sun. The distance of Venus varies from 0.28 astronomical units to
1.72 astronomical units; Mars, from 0.38 to 2.66 astronomical units. Venus,
almost equal in diameter to the earth, provides an observable disc when nearest
the earth. The sidereal period of revolution for Venus is only 224.7 days; for the
earth it is 365.2 days. The maximum brilliance, as observed from the earth,
occurs about 36 days prior to and after the inferior conjunction of the two
planets, at which time it approaches a magnitude of −4.4. The minimum magnitude is about −3.3. For a considerable portion of the time, Venus is favorably
situated for daytime celestial fixes in combination with lines of position acquired
by sun or moon observations. Geocentric parallax is a small factor in planet
observations.

Other planets may be observed during daylight hours, subject to the telescope
used and atmospheric conditions. Jupiter varies in magnitude from −1.4 to
−2.5, Mars from 1.6 to −2.8, Mercury from 1.1 to −1.2. These bodies compare
very favorably in brilliance with the 57 selected stars which range from comparatively faint Zubenelgenubi, with a magnitude of 2.9 to the brightest star, Sirius,
with a magnitude of −1.6. The full moon has a magnitude varying somewhat
around − 12.6; the magnitude of the sun is about − 26.7.

Like the moon, the sun varies in apparent size, depending on the earth's position
in its elliptical orbit. Geocentric parallax, a value much smaller than that involved
in moon observations, due to the much greater distance of the sun, amounts to
approximately 0'.1 between altitudes 0° and 65°.

Data on the nine principal planets are given in Figure 1905d. It is interesting to
note that the majority of the principal planets have satellites, or "moons" rotating
about them. These satellites, like the planets themselves, are relatively cold
bodies, and shine only due to the light reflected from them.

Planet	Mean Distance from Sun		Mean Diameter (in miles)	Sidereal Period	Axial Rotation	Known Satellites
	Millions of Miles	Astro-nomical Units				
Mercury	36	0.4	3,008	88 days	60^d	none
Venus	67	0.7	7,700	224.7 days	$247^d \pm 5$	none
Earth	93	1.0	7,918	365.24 days	23^h56^m	1
Mars	142	1.5	4,215	687 days	24^h37^m	2
Jupiter	484	5.2	86,800	11.86 years	9^h50^m	12
Saturn	887	9.5	71,500	29.46 years	10^h14^m	10
Uranus	1783	19.2	31,700	84.02 years	10^h49^m	5
Neptune	2794	30.1	31,000	164.8 years	15^h40^m	2
Pluto	3666	39.4	3,500±	248.4 years	6.4^d?	none

Figure 1905d:
Planet data.

Minor planets and asteroids.

1906. Minor planets and asteroids differ from the principal planets chiefly in size and number. While Mercury, the smallest principal planet, is only about 3,100 miles in diameter, the largest minor planet has a diameter of only about 480 miles. Over 3,000 minor planets have been discovered, but many thousands more are believed to be circling the sun.

Most of the minor planets are in orbits lying between those of Mars and Jupiter. It is speculated that they may be the remains of a former principal planet, as there is mathematical support for the theory that such a planet once orbited there.

Meteors and meteorites.

1907. The so-called "shooting stars" are small, solid bodies of the solar system, usually no larger than a grain of sand, which enter the earth's atmosphere, and are heated to incandescence by friction. They are observed only when they enter the atmosphere. Most *meteors* are completely vaporized as they travel through the atmosphere. The small percentage which are not completely destroyed and strike the surface as solid particles are called *meteorites.* Most are composed largely of nickel and iron; the remainder are stone.

Some meteors are apparently small asteroids, which were drawn out of their elliptical orbits about the sun by the earth's gravity. Others, possibly remnants of comets, seem to travel in quasi-parabolic orbits; these latter are believed to cause the "showers of shooting stars" which occur periodically. Most meteors are believed to weigh only a small fraction of an ounce, but some can be of great size, and it seems probable that the large crater near Winslow, Arizona, was caused by a meteorite which weighed some 50,000 tons.

Meteors enter the atmosphere at an estimated rate of 100 million a day. The dates of prominent annual meteor showers are listed in most astronomical texts. At such times, the observer may see ten or more, and on rare occasions sometimes hundreds, in an hour; the hours between midnight and dawn are the most favorable for observation.

Comets.

1908. Comets are composed chiefly of frozen methane, ammonia, and water, with clusters of meteoric material in the nucleus. They travel in orbits which are elliptical (if periodic), parabolic, or hyperbolic. When a comet first becomes visible, it shines only by light reflected from the sun but, as it approaches the sun, solar radiation excites the gases within the comet and it becomes partly self-luminous.

Figure 1908: Path of Cunningham's Comet. The tail of a comet always points away from the sun.

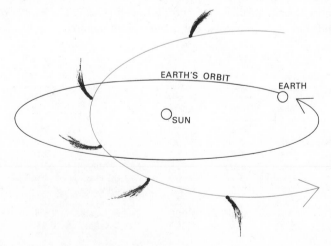

EARTH'S ORBIT

EARTH

SUN

As the comet approaches within 100 to 200 million miles of the sun a tail generally begins to form, the result of the impact of the nucleus of the comet with charged particles of the solar wind. The tail may grow in length to 100 million miles at perihelion and gradually recedes as the comet moves away from the sun. This tail is always directed away from the sun (Figure 1908) so that it precedes the comet as the latter gets farther away from the sun. Occasionally a comet is sufficiently brilliant to be seen in broad daylight, although this is a rare occurrence.

Comets are fairly plentiful in the solar system, and on most nights during the year at least one can be seen with a telescope. In general, they take many years to complete their orbits about the sun. Halley's comet, which is the best known, has a period of 76 years, and will next be visible in 1986.

1909. The earth revolves about the sun in a slightly elliptical orbit; it is about 91,400,000 miles from the sun in January, and 94,500,000 miles in July. It rotates 360° about its axis once in 23 hours 56 minutes; this is termed the *sidereal day,* and differs from the solar day, which averages 24 full hours, because of the earth's motion in its orbit. This difference between the sidereal and solar days is illustrated in Figure 1909.

Revolution and rotation of the earth.

At position (1) the sun is over the meridian M; rotation is counterclockwise in this diagram. When the earth has arrived at position (2) in its orbit, it has rotated 360° on its axis, but the sun is still east of the meridian M, and will not be on the meridian until the earth has rotated for an additional period averaging four minutes. This period varies slightly during the year, and depends on the earth's position in its orbit.

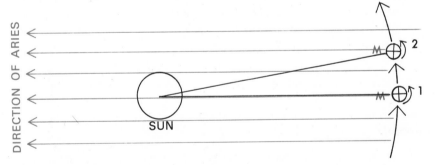

DIRECTION OF ARIES

SUN

Figure 1909: Sidereal and solar days.

The earth's equator is inclined about 23°.5 to its orbit (Figure 1913a), the north pole being inclined towards the sun from the latter part of March to the latter part of September. During the balance of the year, the south pole is inclined towards the sun. The resultant apparent annual path of the sun among the stars is called the *ecliptic.* This inclination of the equator causes the change of seasons. The earth's axis remains rigidly inclined in space due to rotation of the mass, just as a spinning gyroscope's axis is rigid.

Inclination of the earth.

In the ordinary practice of navigation, the earth is considered to be a sphere. In fact, however, it approaches an *oblate spheroid,* in that it is somewhat flattened at the poles, and bulges slightly at the equator; its exact shape is still under study. The polar diameter is approximately 26 statute miles less than the equatorial diameter.

Shape of the earth.

337

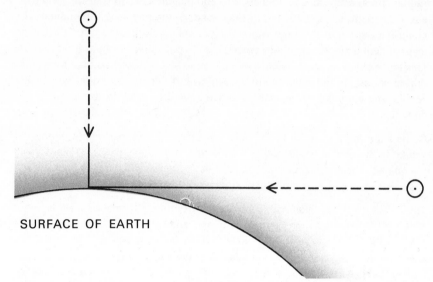

SURFACE OF EARTH

The earth's atmosphere.

1910. The atmosphere is a great blanket of air, consisting principally of 78 per cent of nitrogen and 21 per cent of oxygen. Half the atmosphere is concentrated within a very few miles of the surface; the remainder thins out to an altitude of perhaps 1,000 miles.

Atmospheric diffusion.

Without the diffusing effect of the atmosphere, the stars and the sun would be visible at the same time. However, the molecules which make up the atmosphere, aided by suspended dust, scatter the sun's light in all directions, and make it difficult to see the stars. Astronauts report that at altitudes over 100 miles they are still unable to see the stars in daytime. The short wave-length blue light from the sun is particularly affected by this scattering, thus giving the sky its characteristic blue color.

When a celestial body is near the horizon, its light must pass through a greater volume of air than when it is overhead, as is shown in Figure 1910. This causes additional scattering, and permits very little blue light to reach the observer, leaving only the long wave-length red light. This causes the reddish-orange appearance of the sun and moon near the horizon.

Refraction of light.

The atmosphere also causes light rays to be *refracted*, or bent, as they enter it from space; this refraction of the sun's rays prolongs the twilight. In addition, except when a celestial body is directly overhead, refraction affects its apparent altitude, causing it to appear higher than it actually is. Refraction increases as altitude decreases; under "standard" atmospheric conditions it amounts to 34'.5 at zero altitude. The entire disc of the sun can be visible after the upper limb has, in fact, passed below the horizon. The atmosphere also reduces the apparent brightness of celestial bodies, again having its greatest effect when the body is on the horizon, and its light rays are passing through the maximum distance and density of air. As its altitude decreases from 90° to 5°, a star's brightness may be reduced by a full magnitude. Atmospheric turbulence often causes the light from a star to twinkle; the light from planets usually does not appear to do so, as they are comparatively near the earth, and have appreciable size, rather than being mere point sources of light.

1911. The earth in company with the entire solar system revolves around the axis of our galaxy. This motion has very little effect upon the apparent motion of the celestial bodies across the heavens. But there are three major and two minor types of earth motion or changes which affect the apparent paths of these bodies. The three major motions of the earth are *rotation* about its axis, *revolution* around the sun, and *precession*. The two minor motions are *wandering* of the terrestial poles, and *variations* in the speed of rotation (article 1916).

Motions of the earth.

1912. This daily rotation on its axis causes the principal apparent motion of the heavenly bodies across the sky from east to west. This motion is: parallel to the plane of the earth's equator; occurs in circles whose centers are on the earth's axis or its extension; and is at an almost constant rate. These circles are called diurnal or daily circles. To be visible to an observer a body must, of course, be above his *celestial horizon*, which may be considered as a plane passing through the center of the earth, and perpendicular to a line connecting the observer's position and the earth's center (see Figure 1912b). The plane of his horizon therefore changes as he changes latitude. If he is located at one of the poles his horizon is parallel to the equator. If the body's brightness and atmospheric conditions are ignored its visibility depends both upon the position of the body's diurnal circle, relative to the observer's latitude, and its location on that circle. The *declination* of a body on the celestial sphere is identical to the latitude of the point on earth directly under the celestial body. This is referred to as the *geographical position* (GP) of the body. Declination and GP will be discussed in greater detail in Chapter 20. The apparent motion of the celestial bodies caused by the rotation of the earth on its axis results in the GP of the body moving westward along a parallel of latitude equivalent in angular value to the declination of the body.

Effects of the earth's rotation.

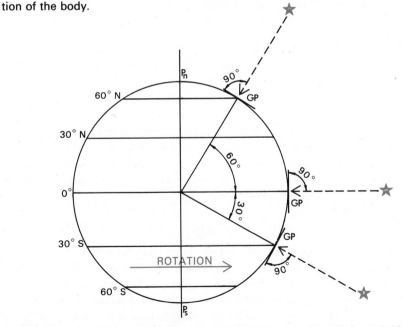

Figure 1912a:
Declination of star
equals latitude of
its GP.

Figure 1912a illustrates three stars with declinations of 0°, 30° S, and 60° N. As the earth rotates the GPs of the bodies will trace lines across the earth following the equator, the 30° south parallel of latitude, and the 60° north parallel of latitude respectively.

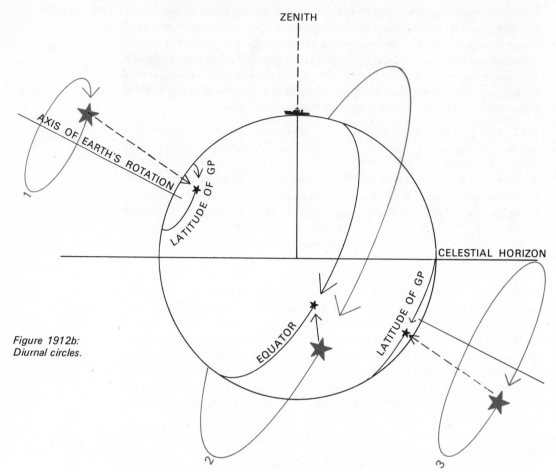

Figure 1912b:
Diurnal circles.

As illustrated in Figure 1912b, an observer is in 30° north latitude; the plane of his horizon is shown as passing through the earth's center; circle 1 represents the apparent daily path or diurnal circle of a body having a declination of approximately 80° north. In moving along its diurnal circle it is therefore constantly above some point on the 80th parallel of north latitude. Note that for the observer in latitude 30° north this body never sets below the horizon. This of course will be equally true of all bodies having a declination of 60° north or more. All such bodies will bear due north of the observer at the highest and lowest points on their diurnal circles and since they do not set below the horizon they are referred to as *circumpolar* stars. Figure 1912c depicts the trace of circumpolar stars, showing their path around the earth's axis extended.

The star with a declination of 30° north will be above the horizon for about 14 hours and 40 minutes of the day. It rises over the horizon well north of east and will pass directly overhead and set north of west. Circle 2 represents the diurnal circle of a star having a declination of 0°; it circles the equator. It rises due east of the observer, is due south of him when it reaches its maximum altitude of 60° and sets due west. It is above the horizon for 12 hours. Circle 3 represents the diurnal circle of a body with 60° south declination. Such a body or any with a declination greater than 60° south would never appear above the horizon for an observer in latitude 30° north.

Figure 1912c:
Observatory
photograph of
circumpolar stars.

The declination of the stars changes so slowly that over many years an observer in a given latitude has essentially the same view of the diurnal circle of each star. On the contrary, the declinations of the bodies of the solar system change with comparative rapidity and apparent motions of the body change accordingly. The declination of the sun, moon, and navigational planets vary between approximately 25° north and 25° south, and at any time their diurnal circles will lie between these values.

One of the principal effects of the earth's rotation on its axis is the alternating phenomena known as day and night. Since the earth is approximately a sphere, half of it will be in sunlight and half in darkness at any given time. The length of the period of day or night varies with location on the surface of the earth due to the inclination of the poles, as discussed in article 1909 and below.

Day and night.

1913. The annual revolution of the earth about the sun is illustrated in Figure 1913a which also shows the 23°.5 inclination of the equator to the earth's orbit. About 21 June each year the north pole is at its maximum inclination towards the sun, and the declination of the latter is 23°.5 *north.* As the earth moves on in its orbit about the sun, the northerly declination of the sun decreases slowly, and reaches 0° about 23 September; it continues to decrease algebraically until about 22 December, when it reaches 23°.5 *south,* its maximum southerly declination. Moving on from this point, the declination increases algebraically, reaching 0° again about 21 March, and 23°.5 north on 21 June.

Effects of the earth's revolution.

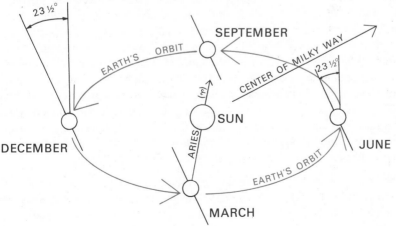

Figure 1913a: The annual revolution of the earth around the sun.

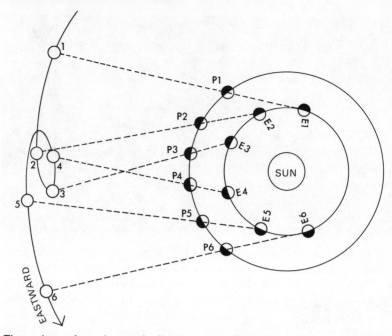

Figure 1913b: Retrograde motion of a superior planet.

First point of Aries ♈.

The points of maximum declination are called the *solstices;* the points of 0° declination are called the *equinoxes.* These words are derived from the Latin, solstice meaning "sun standing still," and equinox meaning "equal night." The point in space at which the March equinox occurs is also called the *first point of Aries* (♈), or simply *Aries;* it is an important point in the measurement of celestial coordinates. It derives its name from the fact that, when this system of measurement was first established, the sun entered the constellation Aries, as it passed from south to north declination. It has kept the name although this point has moved due to the earth's precession (article 1915).

The annual change in the sun's declination explains the changing seasons experienced on earth; they are caused by the angle at which the sun's rays strike the earth, and the comparative length of daylight and darkness. In this connection the times of 0° declination are generally termed the vernal (spring) and autumnal equinoxes; the time of maximum north declination is the summer solstice, and the time of maximum south declination is the winter solstice.

The revolution of the earth about the sun also affects the apparent positions of the stars, which surround the system on all sides. The ones which can be seen from the earth on a given night are those in a direction generally opposite to that of the sun. Because of this the stars appear to make one complete revolution around the earth each year independently of their nighly revolution due to the earth's rotation on its axis; each succeeding night at the same time at a given place, each star will be almost one degree farther west; it requires an average of $365\frac{1}{4}$ days to complete the revolution of 360°. The early astronomers grouped the stars into arbitrary *constellations;* the 12 constellations along the plane of the ecliptic through which the sun passes during the year are called the *zodiac.* The zodiac as such has no navigational significance.

The combination of the revolutions of the earth and of the planets about the sun results in the comparatively rapid change of position of the planets. Mars, Jupiter and Saturn, whose orbits lie outside that of the earth, are termed *superior planets.* The superior planets appear to move steadily westward with respect to *Superior planets.* the sun, meaning that they rise earlier and cross the observer's meridian earlier on each succeeding day. They emerge from behind the sun as morning twilight bodies and continue to rise earlier each day until they again disappear behind *Motion of planets.* the sun, last being seen as evening twilight bodies. With respect to the stars, the superior planets appear to move constantly eastward from night to night, except when they are nearest the earth. At this time their motion is *retrograde,* appearing to move westward among the stars. Figure 1913b illustrates the retrograde motion of a superior planet. When the earth is at E_1, E_2, E_3, etc., the superior planet is at P_1, P_2, P_3 etc., and appears at positions 1, 2, 3, etc., at the left.

Mercury and Venus are termed *inferior planets,* as their orbits lie inside that of *Inferior planets.* the earth. They appear to oscillate with respect to the sun. Venus always appears comparatively near the sun, it alternates as a morning and evening planet, (Figure 1913c) and rises and sets within about three hours of sunrise and sunset. Mercury is a bright celestial body, but because of its closeness to the sun it can be seen only rarely, and its coordinates are therefore not listed in the Nautical Almanac.

The planets shine by the reflected light of the sun; the inferior planets go through all the same phases as the moon (article 1914), being "full" when on the opposite side of the sun from the earth, and "new" when on the same side. The superior planets never pass between the earth and sun, and are never seen in the "new" phase.

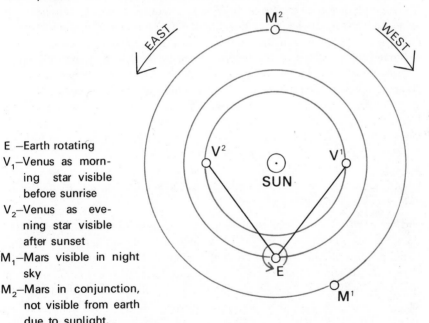

Figure 1913c: Venus as morning and evening star.

E —Earth rotating
V_1—Venus as morning star visible before sunrise
V_2—Venus as evening star visible after sunset
M_1—Mars visible in night sky
M_2—Mars in conjunction, not visible from earth due to sunlight.

1914. The most obvious effect of the moon's revolution about the earth is the *Effects of the* cycle of *phases* through which it passes. Like the planets, the moon shines by *moon's revolution.* the sun's reflected light. Excluding possible eclipses, the side facing the sun is lit, and the opposite side is dark; the moon's appearance from the earth depends on its orientation relative to the earth and sun.

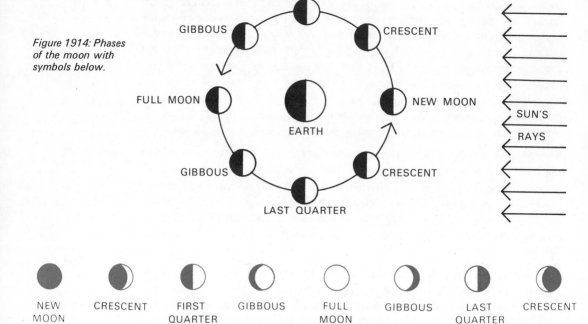

Figure 1914: Phases of the moon with symbols below.

FIRST QUARTER		
GIBBOUS		CRESCENT
FULL MOON	EARTH	NEW MOON
GIBBOUS		CRESCENT
LAST QUARTER		

SUN'S RAYS

| NEW MOON | CRESCENT | FIRST QUARTER | GIBBOUS | FULL MOON | GIBBOUS | LAST QUARTER | CRESCENT |

Phases of the moon.

The moon passes through its cycle of phases during a 29.5 day *synodic period*. The synodic period of a celestial body is its average period of revolution with respect to the sun, as seen from the earth. It differs from the 360° sidereal period because of the motions of the earth and the body in their orbits. Figure 1914 illustrates the positions of the moon relative to the sun and earth during its synodic period, and the resulting phases. When the moon is between the sun and the earth, its sunlit half faces away from the earth, and the body cannot be seen; this is the *new moon*. As it revolves in its orbit, (counterclockwise in Figure 1914) an observer on earth first sees a part of the sunlit half as a thin crescent, which will then *wax* or grow slowly through first quarter, when it appears as a semicircle. After passing through the first quarter, it enters the *gibbous* phase until it becomes full, and the entire sunlit half can be seen. From full it is said to *wane*, becoming gibbous to the last quarter, and then crescent until the cycle is completed.

Age of the moon.

The *age of the moon* at a given time is the number of days which have passed since the preceding new moon, and is an indication of the phase, and therefore of the amount of light it sheds. The full moon rises in most latitudes about the same time the sun sets, and sets when the sun rises; the new moon rises and sets with the sun. On the average, the moon rises about 50 minutes later each day, although the interval varies considerably. The full moon which occurs near the time of the autumnal equinox actually has a small retardation, rising earlier each day. The illuminated limb of the moon is always towards the sun with the *cusps* or points directed away from the sun.

Solar and lunar eclipses.

Other effects of the moon's revolution about the earth are *solar* and *lunar eclipses*, which occur when the sun, the earth, and the moon are in line. The earth and the moon both cast shadows into space, in a direction away from the sun. A solar eclipse occurs whenever the shadow of the moon falls on a part of the surface

344

of the earth. Depending on the alignment of the three bodies an observer on earth may witness a total eclipse, or only a partial eclipse if part of the disc of the sun is visible. A solar eclipse is defined as *annular* when the moon's distance from the earth is sufficiently great to permit a narrow ring of sunlight to appear around the moon. A lunar eclipse occurs when the moon passes through the shadow of the earth.

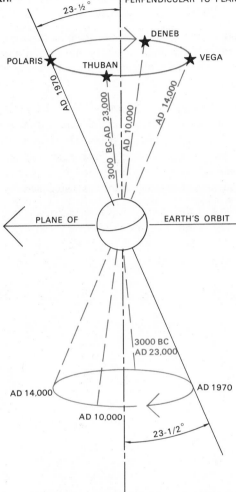

Figure 1915: Precession of the earth.

1915. The earth is, in effect, a gigantic gyroscope, and is subject to the laws of gyroscopic motion. However, it is not a perfect sphere and has a bulge about its equator which is inclined at 23°.5 to the plane of its orbit. The moon and sun exert gravitational forces on the earth, and these forces would tend to make the polar axis perpendicular to the plane of its orbit. Due to its rotation the earth resists these strong forces but reacts like a gyroscope when external force is applied. It precesses in a direction which is at right angles to the direction of the external force.

Effects of precession.

This precession causes a slow rotation of the earth's axis about an axis projected outward at right angles to the plane of its orbit, therefore slowly tracing a circle on the celestial sphere. The period of precession is about 25,800 years. Figure 1915 shows this path in space, and indicates various stars with the dates at which they will replace Polaris as the Pole Star.

345

Nutation.

This precession is usually called the *precession of the equinoxes,* the latter being the points among the stars occupied by the sun when its declination is 0° in the spring and fall. The annual precession is about 50 seconds of arc per year and is in a westerly direction—that is, clockwise from the north pole. This is the opposite direction to both the earth's rotation and revolution. The period of earth precession is not uniform due principally to the variant positions of the moon relative to its orbit. This slight variation is termed *nutation.*

Minor earth motions.

1916. In addition to the major motions described above, there are several motions of the earth of minor importance. Two of the more significant in navigation are the *wandering of the terrestrial poles* and the *variations in speed of rotation* of the earth.

The north and south terrestrial poles, or the points where the earth's axis of rotation theoretically pierces the earth's surface, are not stationary. Instead, they wander slightly in somewhat circular paths. The movement is believed to be caused partly by meteorological effects. Each pole wanders in an area smaller than a baseball diamond, and neither has been known to move more than 40 feet from its average position. The phenomenon is also called "variation in latitude."

The rotational speed of the earth on its axis is steadily decreasing by a small amount, causing the length of the day to increase at the rate of about 0.001 second a century. There are also small irregular changes in the rotational period, the causes of which are unknown.

CHAPTER 20

Introduction to Celestial Navigation

2001. Celestial navigation may be defined as the art of navigation with the aid of the sun, moon, planets, and the major stars. In order to practice this art, the navigator, until comparatively recent times, had to be well versed in spherical trigonometry. Now, due to the advent of the modern inspection tables, which offer precomputed solutions of the spherical triangle, he needs little mathematical skill beyond the ability to add or subtract two or three digits. He must, however, be familiar with the various concepts and assumptions upon which celestial navigation is based; these will be discussed in this and subsequent chapters.

Definition.

2002. In celestial navigation, the earth is assumed to be a perfect sphere, located at the center of the universe. The universe is assumed to be a second sphere of infinite radius concentric with the earth. It is called the *celestial sphere,* and all heavenly bodies are held to be located on it. The nearest of the "fixed stars" is at a distance of over six billion times the radius of the earth, resulting in this radius being negligible when using the "fixed stars" in celestial navigation.

Earth and the celestial sphere.

The earth's rotation from west to east causes the celestial sphere to appear to rotate slowly in the opposite direction, causing the bodies to rise in the east, cross the meridian, and then set in the west.

Rotation of the earth.

These assumptions ignore the vast variation in the distances of these bodies, and the fact that the earth is an oblate spheroid rather than a true sphere. Because of the latter, a number of the relationships stated herein are close approximations, rather than exact statements of fact. However, no significant error is introduced in celestial navigation, as it is usually practiced, by considering the earth as a sphere.

The earth's center is thus considered to be at the center of the celestial sphere, and the axis of its poles, extended outward, form the north and south celestial poles. Similarly, the plane of the equator is extended outward to form the celestial equator on the sphere, and any of the earth's meridians can also be projected out to form celestial meridians.

2003. In Chapter 2, the earth system of coordinates—latitude and longitude— was discussed; by means of these coordinates the location of any spot on earth can be precisely stated. A similar system of coordinates exists for the celestial sphere, by means of which a heavenly body can be located exactly on that sphere. The plane of reference is the *celestial equator* (the equinoctial) which is perpendicular to the axis formed by a line extending from the north celestial pole through the center of the earth and its poles to the south celestial

Celestial equator system of coordinates.

Celestial equator.

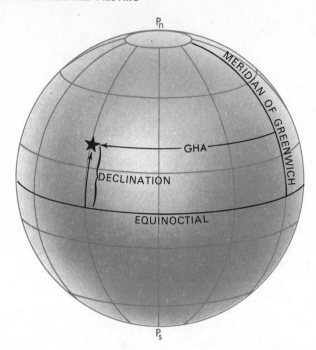

*Figure 2003a: Equi-
noctial coordinates.*

Declination.

pole. The celestial equivalent of latitude is *declination* (Dec.). It may be defined as angular distance north or south of the celestial equator (Figure 2003a). It is expressed in degrees and minutes of arc, generally to the nearest tenth of a minute, and is labeled N or S to indicate the direction of measurement. Declination is one of the coordinates for stating the location of any heavenly body.

Hour angle.

The other celestial coordinate, equivalent to longitude on earth, is *hour angle*. *Greenwich hour angle* (GHA) is the angular distance of a celestial body west of the celestial meridian of Greenwich. GHA is measured in arc from 0° to 360° and is stated in degrees and minutes to the nearest tenth; in this it differs from longitude which is measured east or west to 180°. This *celestial meridian* is

Celestial meridian.

formed by projecting the plane of the meridian of Greenwich outward to the celestial sphere. Like all meridians, it is a great circle, in that it is formed on the sphere by a plane passing through the center of the sphere, as discussed in Chapter 2.

The observer's meridian is also projected out to the celestial sphere (Fig. 2003b) and, like the meridian of Greenwich, it forms an important reference in celestial navigation. Just as the special name of celestial meridian is given to the arc of a great circle on the celestial sphere which passes through the poles and remains

Hour circle.

fixed with respect to the earth, so the special name of *hour circle* is given to the arc of a great circle on the celestial sphere which passes through the celestial poles and a celestial body, and moves with the body.

Local hour angle (LHA) is measured from 0° to 360° in arc *westward* from the observer's meridian to the hour circle of the celestial body. However, in most

Meridian angle (t).

celestial computations *meridian angle* (t) is used. It is equivalent to LHA except that it is measured from 0° to 180° east or west from the observer's meridian to the hour circle of the body. Meridian angle, like longitude, is labeled with the suffix E or W, depending on whether the direction of measurement is east or

348

west.

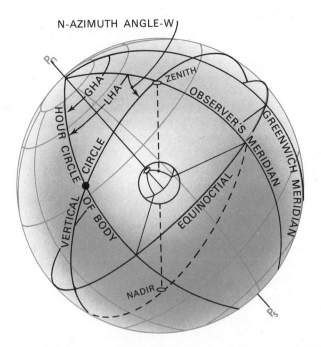

Figure 2003b:
Celestial meridians,
hour circles, and
hour angle.

To determine LHA of a body apply longitude to the value of GHA by *adding* east longitude or *subtracting* west longitude.

The use of GHA relates the celestial sphere to the revolving earth by referring all values of hour angle to the earth's Greenwich meridian. The GHA of every celestial body is therefore constantly changing with time, as the earth containing the Greenwich meridian rotates around its axis. If the solar system, with the earth and navigational planets revolving around the sun, is ignored, there is a reference coordinate for locating the star positions in their east-west relationship

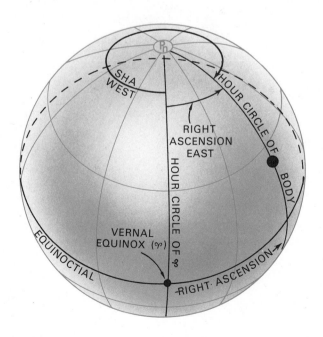

Figure 2003c:
Sidereal hour
angle (SHA).

to each other. Just as the meridian of Greenwich serves as the fixed reference on earth for terrestrial coordinates, so, on the celestial sphere, the hour circle through the *first point of Aries* (♈) is the fixed reference. In Chapter 19 on Navigational Astronomy, Aries was described as the point in space represented by the vernal equinox.

Sidereal hour angle (SHA) is measured westward from the hour circle of Aries from 0° through 360°. All of the fixed stars can be positioned in space by their SHA and declination (see Figure 2003c). Astronomers use *right ascension* (RA) which is equivalent to SHA but measured eastward from the hour circle of Aries and expressed in units of time rather than arc, but the navigator need not be concerned with the use of right ascension. To tabulate the GHA of all the navigational stars in the Almanac would require publishing extremely large volumes. The GHA of the first point of Aries is therefore tabulated for each instant of time and the slowly changing SHA and Dec. of the navigational stars are listed separately. GHA of a star equals the GHA of Aries plus the SHA of the star. GHA of the sun, moon, and navigational planets are tabulated separately as they move through the fixed pattern of the stars on the celestial sphere.

Horizon system of coordinates.

2004. A second system of coordinates is required in the practice of celestial navigation; this is termed the *horizon system of coordinates.* It differs from the celestial system in that it is based on the position of the observer, rather than on the celestial equator. The reference plane of the horizon system is the observer's *celestial horizon* (Figure 2004a); this plane passes through the center of the earth, and is perpendicular to a line drawn from the position of the observer to the earth's center. This line, when extended outward from the earth's center through the observer's position, defines his *zenith* on the celestial sphere (Figure 2004a). The zenith will be exactly 90° above the celestial horizon; it could also be defined as the point on the celestial sphere directly above the observer. Extended in the opposite direction through the earth's center, this line

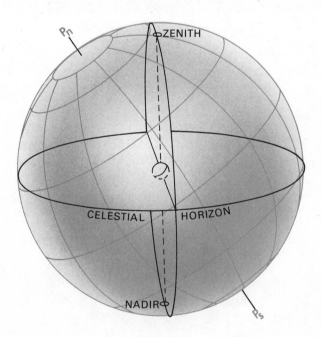

Figure 2004a: Zenith, nadir, and celestial horizon.

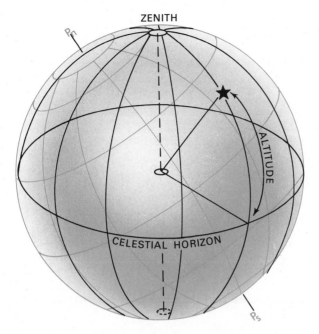

ZENITH

ALTITUDE

CELESTIAL HORIZON

Figure 2004b:
Altitude measured
above the celestial
horizon.

marks the observer's *nadir* on the celestial sphere. The imaginary line from zenith to nadir forms the axis of the observer's celestial horizon system. The celestial horizon is parallel to the plane of the observer's visible horizon at sea. The visible horizon, also called the sea horizon, and sometimes the natural horizon, is the line at which, to an observer, sea and sky appear to meet.

This concept is important, as the celestial horizon is the reference plane to which the navigator's observations are referred. It is illustrated in Figure 2004b.

Altitudes of *all* celestial bodies above the celestial horizon differ from those measured with the marine sextant aboard ship because of the height of the observer's eye above the visible horizon. The higher above the ocean surface the observer is situated, the more the visible horizon will be depressed below the true horizontal plane at his eye level. This causes the measured altitude of the body observed to read higher than its true altitude. A correction for the *dip of the horizon*, as it is termed, must be made to the measured altitude, as will be described in Chapter 22.

A second correction is required for observations of the bodies within the solar system—the sun, moon, and planets. These bodies are much nearer the earth than are the fixed stars, which are considered to be at infinity; the light from such a body does not reach the earth in parallel rays, but diverges from a point at a finite distance. The altitude of the body above the celestial horizon will be greater than its altitude above the horizontal at the observer's eye, except when the body is on his zenith. This difference in altitude is called *parallax*. The required correction to the altitude as measured above the visible horizon is described in Chapter 22.

Altitudes of celestial bodies, as measured with the sextant, are angles above the plane of the celestial horizon, measured along a great circle, called the *vertical circle*, passing through the body as well as the observer's zenith and nadir. In the celestial equator system of coordinates there can be an infinite number of

351

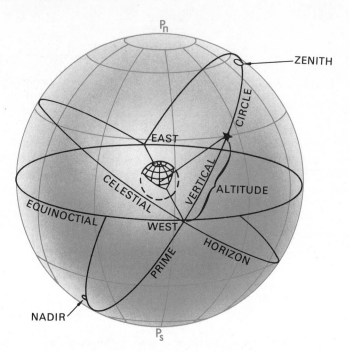

hour circles, so, in the horizon system of coordinates, there can be an infinite number of vertical circles passing through various bodies on the celestial sphere. In addition to the vertical circle passing through the celestial body being observed, there is one other important vertical circle. This is termed the *prime vertical* and is that vertical circle which passes through the east and west points of the observer's celestial horizon. Figure 2004c shows the two systems of coordinates superimposed, with the altitude of a star shown on the prime vertical.

The astronomical
triangle on the
celestial sphere.

2005. The *astronomical* or *celestial triangle* is an area on the celestial sphere defined by the observer's celestial meridian, the hour circle passing through the observed celestial body, and the vertical circle passing through that body. The celestial triangle is illustrated in Figure 2005. The vertices of the triangle are the celestial pole, the observer's zenith, and the position of the celestial body.

In Figure 2005 both the observer's zenith and the star being observed are shown in the northern hemisphere. The relationship of other possible positions will be discussed later in detail. It will be noted from this illustration that the angular distances representing two sides of the triangle are determined from the celestial equator system of coordinates, namely, the side defined as 90° minus Dec. and the one defined as 90° minus Lat. The third side, 90° minus altitude, has its angular distance determined by the altitude of the body above the celestial horizon and therefore it utilizes the horizon system of coordinates. The relationship of the two systems, as projected on the celestial sphere, should now be obvious. Only two of the angles within the celestial triangle are used in celestial navigation. Meridian angle (t), previously defined, is shown in Figure 2005 as the angle at the pole between the observer's meridian and the hour circle of the body. *Azimuth Angle* is the angle at the zenith between the celestial meridian of the observer and the vertical circle passing through the celestial body. Altitude and azimuth form the two horizon coordinates by means of which a celestial body is located with reference to the observer.

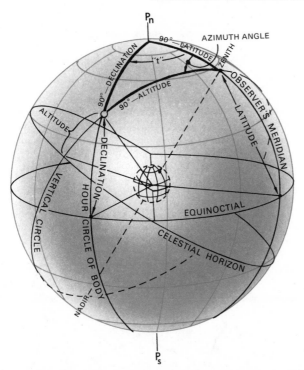

Figure 2005:
Astronomical or
celestial triangle.

2006. This chapter has considered the heavenly bodies only in relation to their positions on the celestial sphere, in order to show the fundamentals of the celestial triangle concept, and to define the terms used in celestial navigation. The understanding of celestial navigation is greatly simplified if the apparent position of each heavenly body is considered to lie on the surface of the earth, rather than on another sphere. Imagine the earth to be a glass globe, with the observer located at its center. As the observer looks at a star or other celestial body its light rays pass through a single point on the earth's surface. This point is called the *geographic position* (GP) of the body (Figure 2006); it is moving constantly westward, but its precise position on the earth's surface can be determined for any instant of time from the Nautical Almanac. Knowing the exact location of the GP of a body, the navigator can develop a line of position, by

*Geographic
position (GP).*

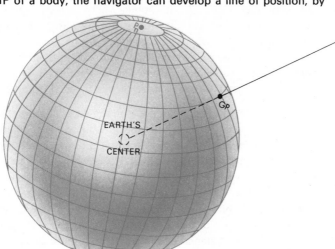

Figure 2006: Geographical position (GP) of a celestial body.

353

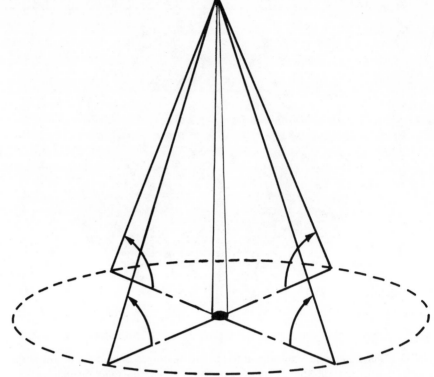

*Figure 2007a: Circle
of equal altitude
around a pole.*

means of a sextant observation, very much as an LOP is obtained from observation of any landmark of known position on the earth's surface. To develop a
celestial line of position, the navigator must obtain an accurate measurement of
the altitude of a celestial body above the horizon. The following sections of this
chapter will explain the principles of developing such an LOP.

*Circles of equal
altitude.*

2007. To illustrate the basic concept involved in measuring an altitude, consider a pole of known height erected vertically on level ground, and stayed with
a number of guy wires of equal length attached to the top of the pole and
stretched taut to points on the ground equidistant from the base. The base of the
pole establishes its GP. At the points where the guy wires meet the ground,
angles are formed between the ground and the wires; these angles will be equal
in value at each guy wire, and the points on the ground will describe a circle
with the base of the pole at its center. It is evident then that anywhere on this
circle the angle subtended by the height of the pole will be the same. This
circle of equal altitude around the pole is illustrated in Figure 2007a.

In the case of the pole of known height, the distance from the base of the pole
can be determined by plane trigonometry, if the angle it subtends is known. This
is *partially analogous* to determining a ship's distance from the GP of a star by
observing the star's altitude. However, the analogy is not completely valid, as
the ship is on the curved surface of the earth, rather than on a flat plane, and
instead of dealing with a pole of known height, the navigator is concerned with
a celestial body considered to be situated at an infinite distance above its GP.
It is, in fact, because of the curvature of the earth's surface that the navigator
can determine his distance from the GP of a celestial body by measuring its
altitude above the visible horizon.

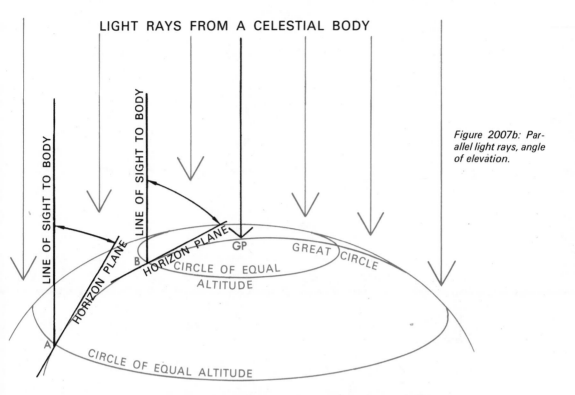

LIGHT RAYS FROM A CELESTIAL BODY

LINE OF SIGHT TO BODY

LINE OF SIGHT TO BODY

HORIZON PLANE

HORIZON PLANE

HORIZON PLANE

GP

GREAT CIRCLE

B

CIRCLE OF EQUAL ALTITUDE

A

CIRCLE OF EQUAL ALTITUDE

Figure 2007b: Parallel light rays, angle of elevation.

The problem now involves spherical trigonometry and angular measurements from a horizontal plane (the horizon) tangent to the earth's surface at the point of observation. As previously stated, most of the celestial bodies used in navigation are at such great distances that their rays of light are parallel when they reach the earth. If the earth were flat, the angular altitude of each of these bodies would be the same at any point on the plane, regardless of distance from the GP, and the concept of circles of equal altitude would not be valid. However, the angular altitude the navigator actually uses is the angle between the line of sight to the body and that to the sea horizon. Because the earth's surface is curved, the observer's horizontal plane is tangent to the earth's surface at his position, and only at that one position on the surface of the earth. Hence, the angle between his horizon and the line of sight to a celestial body will vary if he moves his position toward or away from the GP of the body. This is illustrated in Figure 2007b, which shows the light rays from a celestial body intersecting two different horizon planes on the surface of the earth at the same instant of time. At point A the altitude of the body above the horizon plane is considerably less than at point B and the circle of equal altitude on which point A is located is further away from the GP of the body than the circle of equal altitude passing through point B.

As the altitude varies in proportion to the observer's distance from the GP, he can convert coaltitude (an angular distance on a great circle) into linear distance from the GP, and this distance will in turn be the radius of the circle of equal altitude as 1' of arc on a great circle equals 1 nautical mile. The entire circle is seldom drawn on the plotting chart as only a very short segment of its arc, in the area of the DR position, is needed. Due to the usually large radius of the

355

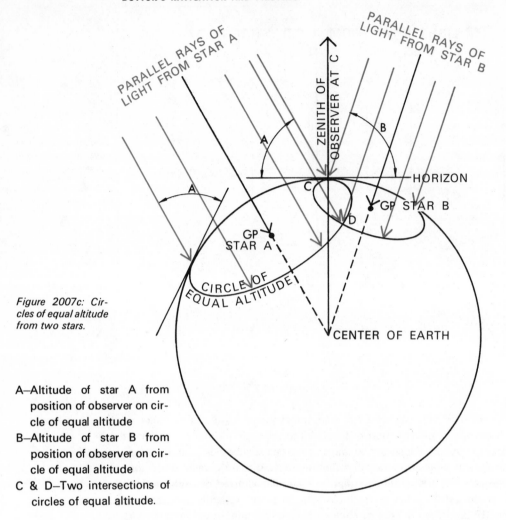

Figure 2007c: Circles of equal altitude from two stars.

A—Altitude of star A from position of observer on circle of equal altitude

B—Altitude of star B from position of observer on circle of equal altitude

C & D—Two intersections of circles of equal altitude.

circle, this short segment can, for practical purposes, be represented as a straight line, without causing material distortion. This small segment of a circle of equal altitude is a *celestial line of position*. Figure 2007c illustrates circles of equal altitude, or of position, derived from observations of two stars. One of the intersections of these two circles on the surface of the earth represents the navigator's position or "Fix." The other intersection of the two circles is located so far away from the DR position that in practical navigation there is no chance of error due to choosing the wrong intersection.

The navigational triangle represented on the earth's surface.

2008. The *navigational triangle*, described briefly as the astronomical triangle in article 2005, is the basis of celestial navigation, and understanding of it is essential to the student. It is defined by three points on the earth's surface, and formed by the arcs of the great circles connecting these points (Figure 2009). These points are the position of the observer (*M*), the geographical position of the celestial body (GP), and the elevated pole. The elevated pole is the pole nearer the observer; it is in the north pole for an observer in north latitude, and the south pole if he is in the southern hemisphere. It is called the elevated pole because it is the celestial pole above the observer's horizon. The GP may be in either the same or the opposite hemisphere to that of the observer.

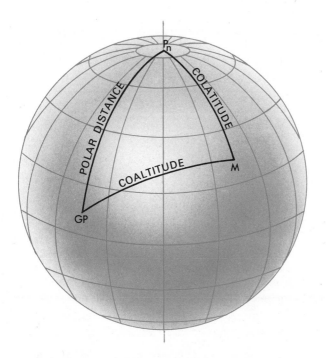

Figure 2009: Navigational triangle with sides labeled.

Since the possible positions of M and GP are almost unlimited, the triangle may take a great variety of shapes. For any particular moment of time, a navigational triangle can be constructed connecting an observer at any location on the earth, the elevated pole, and the GP of any celestial body within the observer's field of view. Having a complete understanding of the triangle, the navigator is able to solve any problem of celestial navigation. He can fix his position at sea, check the accuracy of his compasses, predict the time of rising or setting of any body in the heavens, determine the times of the beginning and ending of twilight, and locate and identify celestial bodies. The solution of the navigational triangle *is* celestial navigation.

2009. The side of the triangle joining the observer and the elevated or nearer pole is called the *colatitude;* it is equal to 90° minus his latitude. The side joining the GP and the pole is called the *polar distance;* it is equal to 90° minus the body's declination, or 90° minus the latitude of the body's GP when referred to the surface of the earth. The side joining the GP and M, the position of the observer, is the *coaltitude*, sometimes called zenith distance, and it is equal to 90° minus the altitude of the body. Each of these sides is an arc of a great circle through the two points it connects, and its angular distance in minutes of arc is the distance in nautical miles between the two points on the surface of the earth. The triangle shown in Figure 2009 is for an observer in north latitude, with a celestial body setting to his west. Remember that two sides of the triangle, polar distance and colatitude, are defined by using the celestial equator system of coordinates, and the third side, coaltitude, is an arc of the vertical circle of the horizon system of coordinates. The three sides of the navigational triangle are illustrated and discussed in more detail in the following paragraphs.

The sides of the navigational triangle.

2010. Latitude, described in Chapter 2, is the angular distance north or south of the equator. It may also be defined as an angle at the center of the earth, measured along the observer's meridian from the equator to his position. Figure

Colatitude.

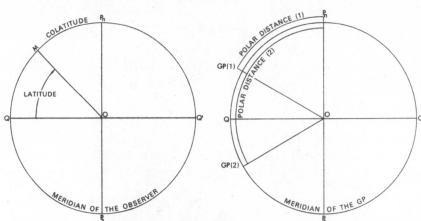

Figure 2010:
Colatitude shown
as angle at center
of earth.

Figure 2011:
Polar distance of
GP_1 90° − Lat.,
of GP_2 90° + Lat.
of GP.

2010 illustrates latitude and colatitude shown on the plane of the meridian of the observer. The line QQ' represents the equator and 0 the center of the earth. Since the maximum angle in the measurement of latitude is 90° (the latitude of the pole) it can be seen from the illustrations that colatitude will always be 90° minus the latitude.

Polar distance.

2011. The GP of a celestial body is expressed in terms of latitude and longitude. Thus, the side of the navigational triangle joining the GP and the pole is similar to the side connecting the observer's position, M, and the pole. Although the observer is always on the same side of the equator as the elevated pole, at times he may observe a celestial body having a GP with a latitude of contrary name; that is, a navigator in north latitude may observe a celestial body whose GP is in south latitude or vice versa.

Polar distance, for a body having a GP in the same hemisphere as the observer's position, is shown in Figure 2011 to be 90° *minus* the latitude of the GP. For any body observed with a GP in the latitude of opposite name, the polar distance will be 90° *plus* the latitude of the GP, as illustrated in Figure 2011. In this illustration the line QQ' again represents the equator and point 0 the center of the earth.

Figure 2012a:
Coaltitude=
90°−Altitude.

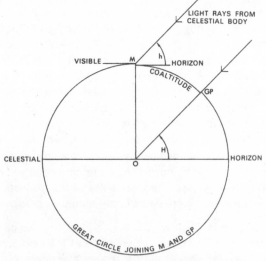

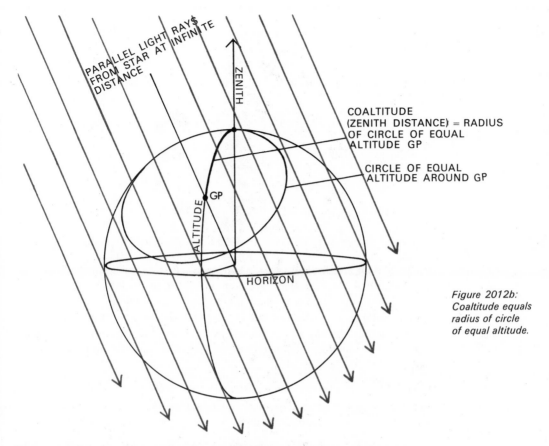

COALTITUDE
(ZENITH DISTANCE) = RADIUS
OF CIRCLE OF EQUAL
ALTITUDE GP

CIRCLE OF EQUAL
ALTITUDE AROUND GP

PARALLEL LIGHT RAYS
FROM STAR AT INFINITE
DISTANCE

ZENITH

GP

ALTITUDE

HORIZON

*Figure 2012b:
Coaltitude equals
radius of circle
of equal altitude.*

2012. When a navigator observes a celestial body, he measures its angular altitude above the horizon. In Figure 2012a the observer, M, is shown at the top of a great circle representing the earth's circumference. This great circle joins the position of the observer and the GP of the celestial body; it is not a meridian (except in the rare case in which the GP falls on the observer's meridian) but a vertical circle on which the body's altitude is measured from the celestial horizon toward the zenith.

Coaltitude.

In Figure 2012a it can be seen that the light rays of a celestial body are assumed to be parallel, and that the angle (h) at the observer's visible horizon is the same as angle (H) at the center of the earth, measured from the celestial horizon. If altitude is illustrated as angle (H) in this figure, then it follows that coaltitude must be 90° minus the altitude. Although this presents no problem in the mathematical solution of the triangle, it is often difficult for the student to relate the circle of equal altitude to this third side of the navigational triangle. Figure 2012b presents a graphic illustration in which the arc segment labeled coaltitude is shown as both 90° minus altitude and as the radius of the circle of equal altitude. This is true in all cases when using the basic relationship of one minute of arc on a great circle on the surface of the earth equals one nautical mile.

2013. In the navigational triangle the angle at the pole between the meridian of the observer and the meridian of the GP is called the *meridian angle*, and labeled "t." Refer back to Figure 2003b, where this angle was labeled LHA.

The angles in the navigational triangles.

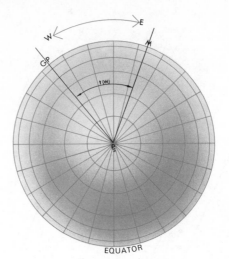

Figure 2013a:
Meridian angle (t)
measured.

The local hour angle, LHA, is always measured in a westerly direction from the meridian of the observer to the meridian of the GP, extending through an angle of 0° to 360°. In the computations involved in sight reduction it is more convenient to be able to measure this angle either east or west from the meridian of the observer, therefore the designation meridian angle. Meridian angle is the "difference of longitude" between the position of the observer and the GP of the body.

Meridian angle.

The use of the *time diagram* is explained in chapter 23. The meridian angle (t) is a vital part of the diagram. Figure 2013a illustrates the meridians of the observer and of the GP, with the resultant angle (t) as they will appear on a time diagram.

The outer circle in this illustration represents the earth's equator as viewed from a point in a space on an extension of the earth's axis beyond the south pole. The center of this circle is labeled Ps to indicate the south pole. The lines in the illustration which connect both M and GP with the pole represent projections of meridians. M represents the intersection of the observer's meridian with the equator and GP represents the intersection of the meridian of the GP with the equator. In this diagram and in actual practice the meridian angle (t) is always measured from the observer's meridian toward the meridian of the GP and is labeled with the suffix "E" east or "W" west to indicate the direction of measurement. In a diagram of this type the use of the south pole does not imply that it is the elevated pole. The angle of intersection of the two meridians is idential at both poles.

Azimuth angle.

The other important angle within the navigational triangle is the *azimuth angle* (Az), measured at the observer's position, between the observer's meridian and the vertical circle running through the position of the GP and that of the observer (Figures 2003b and 2005). Azimuth angle is always measured from the observer's meridian toward the vertical circle joining the observer and the GP. It is labeled with the prefix "N" north or "S" south, to agree with the name of the observer's elevated pole, and with the suffix "E" east or "W" west to indicate the direction of measurement. Labeling the azimuth angle in this manner is necessary as it may be measured from either the north or south poles, and either in an easterly or westerly direction. In the final plotting of position this angle is converted to *true azimuth* (Zn), which is measured clockwise from the north through 360°, as illustrated in Figure 2013b.

True azimuth.

The third angle in the navigational triangle is called the *parallactic angle*. It is not used directly in the ordinary practice of celestial navigation, and need not be considered here.

Parallactic angle.

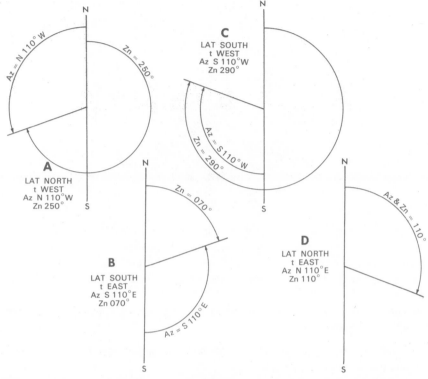

C
LAT SOUTH
t WEST
Az S 110°W
Zn 290°

A
LAT NORTH
t WEST
Az N 110°W
Zn 250°

Az = N 110° W
Zn = 250°
Az = S 110° W
Zn = 290°

B
LAT SOUTH
t EAST
Az S 110°E
Zn 070°

Zn = 070°
Az = S 110° E

D
LAT NORTH
t EAST
Az N 110°E
Zn 110°

Az & Zn = 110°

Figure 2013b: Azimuth angle (Az) and true Azimuth (Zn).

2014. To obtain a position at sea the navigator observes the altitude of a celestial body and notes the instant of time of the observation. The time enables him to determine the exact position of the GP of the body from data in the Nautical Almanac. Since the coaltitude has been previously described as equal to the radius of the circle of equal altitude, the position of the observer lies somewhere on the circumference of the circle of equal altitude. The observer's exact position cannot be determined by a single observation. If the bearing of the GP at the instant of observation could be obtained with the same accuracy as the altitude measurement, the position of the observer could be fixed mathematically. Unfortunately, at present it is not possible to measure azimuth with this degree of accuracy. A single observation only establishes that the observer is on the circle of equal altitude, a small segment of which can be assumed to be a straight line forming a line of position in the close vicinity of his most probable position at the time of the sight. To use the navigational triangle to determine position, the navigator begins by assuming that he is located at some selected point. This *assumed position* (AP) will be near the best *estimated position* (EP) that the navigator can determine. For convenience in using the tables and in plotting, both of which will be discussed in later chapters, the assumed position is rarely the same as either the estimated or DR position, but is chosen so that the latitude and meridian angle are both whole degrees.

Use of the navigational triangle.

Assumed position.

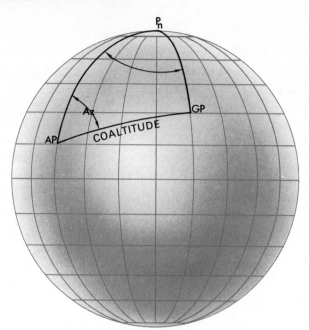

Figure 2014: Two
sides and included
angle known, solve
for Az and coalti-
tude.

Having selected an assumed position and knowing the GP of the celestial body at the instant of observation, the colatitude, polar distance, and meridian angle can easily be computed. Knowing these two sides and the included angle of the navigational triangle, the "sight reduction" is to determine coaltitude and azimuth angle as illustrated in Figure 2014. Modern inspection tables for sight reduction are conveniently arranged in that the value for altitude rather than coaltitude is stated.

Although the navigator will seldom use spherical trigonometry to solve the triangle, the classic formulae are:

Altitude $\qquad \sin h = \sin L \sin d \pm \cos L \cos d \cos t$

Azimuth $\qquad \sin Z = \dfrac{\cos d \sin t}{\cos h}$

Computed altitude (Hc).

Observed altitude (Ho).

Altitude intercept (a).

2015. As outlined in the foregoing article, by using an assumed position for the observer and the actual position of the GP of the celestial body, the spherical triangle can be solved to produce a *computed altitude;* this is labeled Hc. The *observed altitude* obtained from the sextant observation with all corrections applied is labeled *Ho.* Hc and Ho are each proportional to the value of the radius of a circle of equal altitude, centered at the GP of the body, the first circle passing through the assumed position, the second through the observer's actual position. The difference betwen Hc and Ho is known as *altitude intercept (a);* this intercept represents the difference in length of the radii of the computed and observed circles of equal altitude. In article 2007 it was shown that a small altitude angle places the circle of equal altitude, and therefore the LOP, farther away from the GP of the body than does a larger altitude. Accordingly if Hc— the computed altitude—for the assumed position is greater than Ho—the observed altitude—the actual position from which the observation was made would be farther from the GP of the body than the assumed position. Similarly, if Ho is the greater, the actual position would be nearer the GP. The intercept

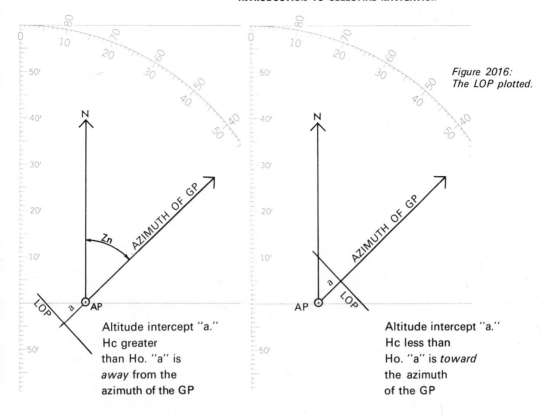

Altitude intercept "a."
Hc greater
than Ho. "a" is
away from the
azimuth of the GP

Altitude intercept "a."
Hc less than
Ho. "a" is *toward*
the azimuth
of the GP

*Figure 2016:
The LOP plotted.*

must always be labeled either with the suffix T (towards) or A (away) as plotted
from the AP (Figure 2016).

2016. In addition to obtaining the value and direction of the intercept (*a*) in
miles by solving the navigational triangle containing the AP, the navigator obtains the computed value of the azimuth angle (Az). By converting Az to direction measured from north (Zn), the navigator can conveniently plot on his chart
the bearing of the GP from the AP. This azimuth line drawn through the assumed
position would indicate the direction of the GP even though the latter is, in most
cases, off the area of the chart being used. Since *a* is the difference in miles
between the lines of position passing through the actual and assumed positions,
the navigator can plot either toward or away for the value of *a* along this azimuth
line. It is necessary to remember the direction of the intercept. From the description given in the preceding paragraph the phrase "computed greater away" can
be derived and remembered. The point on the azimuth line represented by
marking off the intercept *a* is a point on the observer's circle of equal altitude.
The celestial line of position is then drawn through this point and perpendicular
to the azimuth line as shown in Figure 2016. Since a celestial LOP does not
produce an absolute position or fix but merely a line on which the observer is
located, a minimum of two LOPs are required to obtain a fix. Four or five LOPs
derived from different celestial bodies are highly desirable. The position of the
ship is determined by the point at which the LOPs intersect, assuming there is
no error. In actual practice they will seldom intersect at a point but will produce
a small polygon, often referred to as a "cocked hat," which usually contains the
position of the ship. For exterior fixes see Figure 3009.

*Determining the
vessel's position.*

363

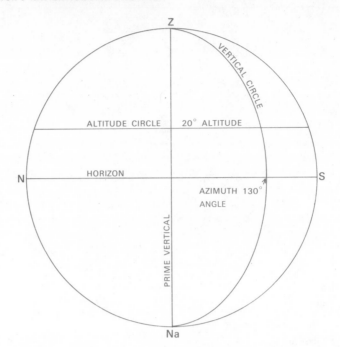

Figure 2017a:
Horizon
coordinates
on plane of
meridian.

Coordinates on the plane of the observer's meridian.

2017. The two systems of coordinates have been illustrated in this text to show their appearance both on the celestial sphere, and on earth. Both the horizon system and the celestial equator system of coordinates contain the celestial meridian of the observer, and celestial problems can be illustrated conveniently on the plane of the observer's meridian. Students usually find it convenient to make sketches similar to these illustrations to clarify specific problems.

Horizon system of coordinates.

In Figure 2017a the horizon system of coordinates is used. The circle represents the plane of the observer's meridian, the line NS is the celestial horizon with

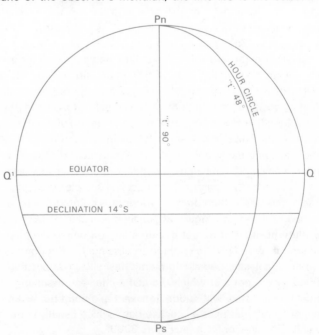

Figure 2017b:
Celestial equator
coordinates on
plane of meridian.

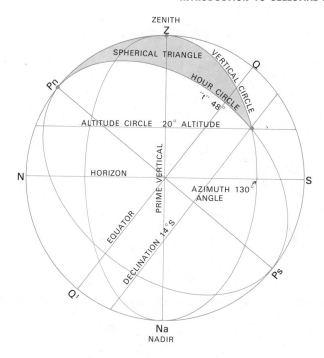

Figure 2017c:
Combined
systems.

north at the left and south at the right. It is obvious that the center of the circle can be either the east or west point on the horizon, and the N-S line contains a locus of points representing all azimuths. Z represents the zenith of the observer, and *Na* the nadir. The line Z-Na passing through the zenith-nadir and the east-west point of the horizon is then, by definition, the prime vertical. Other vertical circles through celestial bodies will be shown on the diagram as ellipses passing through the observer's zenith, his nadir, and the celestial position of each body. The point where this line intersects the celestial horizon determines the azimuth angle of the body. Lines parallel to the horizon will represent lines of equal altitude. The position of any body can be plotted on the diagram in terms of altitude and azimuth.

Figure 2017b illustrates the celestial equator system of coordinates on the plane of the celestial meridian. In this case the line Q-Q' is the celestial equator containing a locus of points representing a position on all hour circles. Pn and Ps are the north and south poles respectively. The hour circle 90° from the meridian of the observer appears as the straight line Pn-Ps (its LHA is 90° or 270° and *t* is 90° E or W); all other hour circles appear as curved lines. Lines parallel to the celestial equator are lines of equal declination. The position of any body can then be located on this diagram in terms of declination and hour angle.

Celestial equator system of coordinates.

Combining the two systems of coordinates, if the observer were located at the north pole where his zenith and the north pole were identical, the diagrams could be superimposed on each other as drawn. For all other positions of the observer the elevated pole must be placed on the plane of the observer's celestial meridian at a point above the horizon equal to the latitude of the observer. Figure 2017c illustrates the diagrams of Figures 2017a and 2017b superimposed for a latitude of 40° N ; with the area covered by the celestial triangle shaded.

Combining the coordinate systems.

Summary.

2018. The basic theory of celestial navigation as it is usually practiced aboard ship has been presented in this chapter. The manner in which celestial navigation is practiced afloat is explained in detail in subsequent chapters. Celestial navigation continues to be the only basic self-contained passive method for obtaining a position at sea. The art of celestial navigation is well documented and will be presented in a step by step operation involving the four basic tools: sextant, time piece, almanac, and sight reduction tables. To master the art of navigation requires a thorough understanding of the basic concepts presented herein, as well as much practice in the use of the sextant.

CHAPTER 21

Identification of Celestial Bodies

2101. In order to solve the navigational triangle, the navigator must know the name of the celestial body he has observed, so that he can obtain its GHA and declination from the almanac. No difficulty is experienced in identifying the sun or moon, but the stars and planets can present a problem. Both appear to be point sources of light, and the only apparent differences between any two are in position, brightness, and, much less obviously, color.

Introduction.

The usual procedure in identifying stars and planets is to select, in advance of twilight, a number of these bodies, so located that lines of position obtained from them will result in a good fix. Occasionally an unknown body is observed and identified afterward.

Most experienced navigators pride themselves on their ability to locate and identify the navigational stars; a portion of this chapter is intended to assist the student in learning the elements of star identification. However, he must also learn to predetermine the approximate altitude and azimuth of the navigational bodies, so that they may be located without reference to other bodies. The modern sextant telescope enables the observer to sight a star in a comparatively bright sky when it is not visible to the unaided eye. Under such conditions he usually has the benefit of sharp horizon contrast, which permits accurate observations.

2102. 2102-D is usually referred to simply as the "Star Finder." It is designed to permit the user to determine the approximate altitude and azimuth of those of the 57 "selected stars" listed on the daily pages of the *Nautical Almanac* which are above the horizon at any given place and time. It is the most widely used device of its kind.

The "Star Finder and Identifier" 2102-D.

The Star Finder consists of a base, and ten circular templates. The base is a white opaque plastic disc, with a small pin at its center. On one side, the north celestial pole is shown at the center; on the opposite side the south celestial pole is at the center. On both sides the circumference is graduated in half degrees of LHA♈; and labeled towards the east, at 5° intervals. All the stars are shown on each side of the base on a polar azimuthal equidistant projection extending towards the opposite pole. Each star is named, and the approximate magnitude—first, second, or third—is indicated by symbol. Because of the distortion caused by the projection, the relative positions of the stars shown on the base do not correspond to their apparent positions in the sky, and the device cannot be compared directly with the heavens.

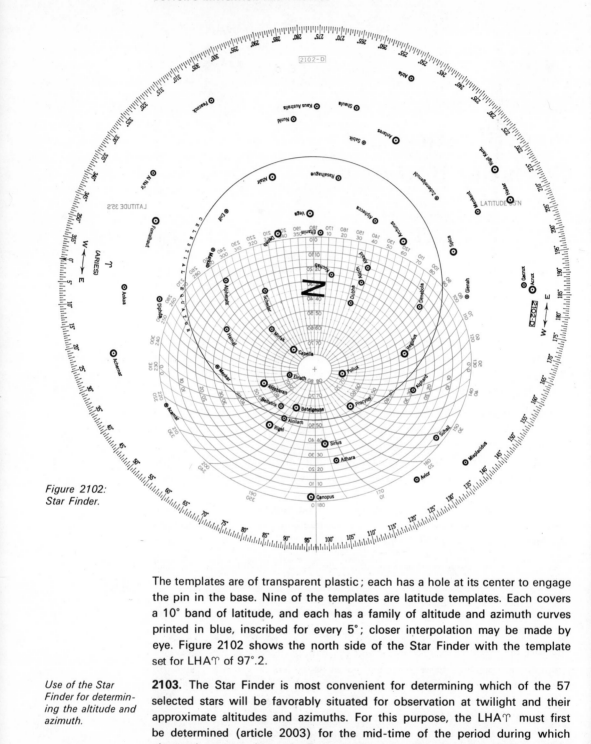

Figure 2102:
Star Finder.

The templates are of transparent plastic; each has a hole at its center to engage the pin in the base. Nine of the templates are latitude templates. Each covers a 10° band of latitude, and each has a family of altitude and azimuth curves printed in blue, inscribed for every 5°; closer interpolation may be made by eye. Figure 2102 shows the north side of the Star Finder with the template set for LHA♈ of 97°.2.

Use of the Star Finder for determining the altitude and azimuth.

2103. The Star Finder is most convenient for determining which of the 57 selected stars will be favorably situated for observation at twilight and their approximate altitudes and azimuths. For this purpose, the LHA♈ must first be determined (article 2003) for the mid-time of the period during which observations are to be made. For morning sights, the beginning of civil twilight or a time shortly thereafter is often used. For the evening, the time would be based on the ending of civil twilight. The most suitable time to select depends largely on the ability of the observer and the quality of his sextant, and can best be determined by experience.

The Star Finder is used as follows:

Example: A navigator whose DR position at the time of the ending of civil twilight will be Lat. 37°14'.8 N, Long. 144°25'.6 E, determines the GHA of Aries to be 312°46'.8 at that time.

Required: The approximate altitudes and azimuths of all first magnitude stars which will be above the horizon at that time, using 2102-D.

Solution: (Figure 2102). First, determine LHA♈ in the usual manner. In this case it is 97°12'.4. Select the blue latitude template closest to the DR latitude, and place it over the star base so that the labels on each correspond to the name of the DR latitude. In this case the template for LATITUDE 35° N is selected and placed over the side of the star base which has the letter "N" at the center, as shown. Orient the template so that the arrow extending from the 0°–180° azimuth line points to the value on the base plate of LHA♈ for the time desired. In this case the arrow is aligned, approximately, with 97°.2. Finally, note the approximate altitudes and azimuths of the desired celestial bodies. The approximate altitudes and azimuths of the first magnitude stars are tabulated below, in order of increasing azimuth.

Body	ha	Zn
Regulus	36°	101°
Pollux	73°	106°
Procyon	57°	148°
Sirius	39°	176°
Canopus	2°	181°
Betelgeuse	62°	200°
Rigel	43°	207°
Aldebaran	58°	243°
Capella	72°	315°

GHA ♈ 312°46'.8
λ   144°25'.6 E
LHA ♈   97°12'.4

In this instance, there are a considerable number of first magnitude stars above the horizon; but they are not evenly distributed in azimuth. In practice, the navigator would include some tabulated stars of lesser magnitude to his north, such as Dubhe, Kochab, etc. He would probably not observe Canopus, except from necessity, due to its low altitude. Pollux and Capella might be difficult to observe, both being above 70° in altitude; Regulus and Mirfak would be easier to observe and give equivalent coverage in azimuth.

It is always wise to list more stars than the navigator actually expects to observe, as some may be obscured by clouds. The stars listed for observation should not be limited to those of the first magnitude; all the stars shown on the Star Finder are readily visible in clear weather. The stars should be selected so that good distribution in azimuth is obtained, and on the basis of altitude. The most convenient altitude band for observation lies roughly between 15° and 60°, but it is preferable to obtain observations considerably lower or higher than these approximate limits, rather than to have poor distribution in azimuth.

2104. The Star Finder may be used in the same manner to predetermine the position in the heavens of the planets—or of additional fixed stars, should this be required—if their positions are plotted on the star base. While the planets move in position relative to the stars, their positions so plotted will be satis-

Using the Star Finder for determining the approximate altitude and azimuth of planets.

factory over a period of several days. Thus, for a vessel departing on a two week cruise, the positions of the planets could be plotted on the star base for a date approximately one week after departure.

To plot the position of a planet on the star base, the navigator first determines its declination for the desired time, as well as 360° minus its sidereal hour angle (SHA) as the relative position of the stars are determined by their SHAs. This latter quantity is obtained by subtracting the GHA♈ for the desired time from the GHA of the planet at that time, adding 360° to the GHA when necessary. For example, suppose a navigator in south latitude wishes to plot Venus on the star base. From the Nautical Almanac he obtains the data shown below, and then determines 360° − SHA.

GHA Venus	222°40'.2	Dec. S 4°39'.6
GHA ♈	− 213°29'.3	
SHA Venus	9°10'.9	
360° − SHA	350°49'.1	

This angle, with the declination, would be required to locate Venus on the star base: for plotting purposes, he would call them 350°.8 and 4°.5 south, respectively.

He places the colored template south side up on the south side of the star base, and sets the index arrow of the template at 350°.8. He then plots Venus on the star base, using the cut out slot, with the declination scale printed beside it. Figure 2104 shows the star base with the template set at 350°.8 and Venus plotted at Dec. 4°.5 south.

Identifying unknown celestial bodies.

2105. At times, the navigator will obtain an observation of an unknown body which is not marked on the star base. In such a case, if *both its altitude and azimuth* are noted as well as the time of the observation, it may be identified by means of the Star Finder.

If the star is one of those listed on the base plate of the star finder the identification is quite simple. The index arrow of the blue template is aligned to the appropriate LHA of Aries for the time of the observation. The point of intersection of the altitude and azimuth curve of the body is then located on the blue template and the body listed on the star base at or quite near this position can usually be assumed to be the one observed.

The visible planets should have been plotted on the star base as outlined above, as the observed body may have been a planet rather than a star.

If no star or planet appears at or near that point, the red template can be used to determine the approximate Dec. and Sidereal Hour Angle (SHA) of the star. These two arguments can be located in the list of stars in the Almanac for proper identification.

To determine the SHA and Dec., the blue template is left in place properly aligned with LHA of Aries; the red template is then placed over the blue template and rotated until the slotted meridian is over the intersection of the altitude and azimuth curve obtained from the observation of the star. The Dec. is read off the scale along the slotted meridian; or its imaginary extension for large values of Dec. 360° minus SHA is read from the base plate underneath the

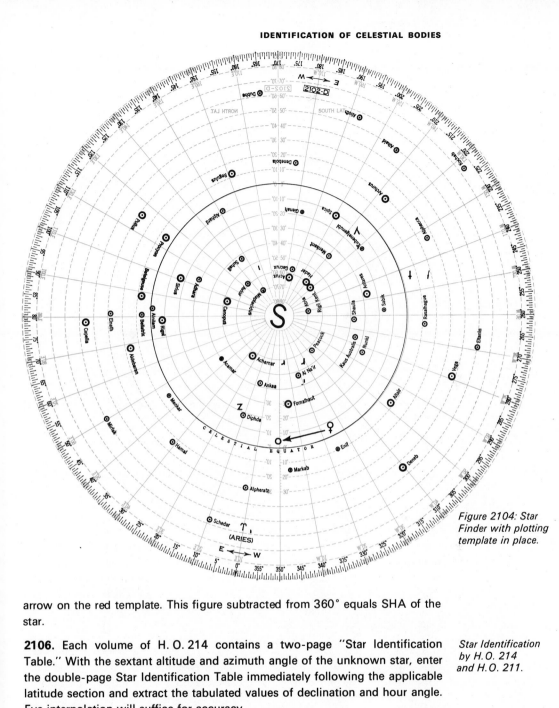

Figure 2104: Star Finder with plotting template in place.

arrow on the red template. This figure subtracted from 360° equals SHA of the star.

2106. Each volume of H. O. 214 contains a two-page "Star Identification Table." With the sextant altitude and azimuth angle of the unknown star, enter the double-page Star Identification Table immediately following the applicable latitude section and extract the tabulated values of declination and hour angle. Eye interpolation will suffice for accuracy.

Star Identification by H.O. 214 and H.O. 211.

Combine the LHA with the longitude to determine the GHA of the star, and from this subtract the GHA♈ to obtain the SHA. Enter the *Nautical Almanac* with the declination and SHA, and identify the star.

H. O. 211 may also be used for star identification by computation. Directions will be found on page 10 of the tables. Note that in the example given Greenwich Sidereal Time (GST) and Right Ascension (RA) are stated. GHA♈ and SHA should be substituted for GST and RA; GST is GHA♈ expressed as time, and SHA = 360° − RA (expressed in arc).

371

Identification by star chart.

2107. Star charts are representations of the celestial sphere, or of parts of it, on a flat surface. On most charts, north is at the top and south at the bottom, but east is at the *left*, and west at the *right;* this is the reverse of the terrestrial chart presentation. If the chart is held overhead, and the N-S axis is properly oriented, this presentation approximates the appearance of the heavens. Some star charts are polar projections; these show the star groups around the pole and are especially helpful in visualizing the movement and relations of circumpolar stars. Primarily, star charts are of value to the student only in learning to identify stars by sight.

Nautical Almanac *Star Charts.*

The *Nautical Almanac* star charts consist of four charts; one polar projection for each hemisphere, covering declinations 10° through 90°, of the same name, and two rectangular projections covering Dec. 30° N to 30° S, around the celestial sphere.

A planetary diagram giving LMT of meridional passage of the planets is also given in the *Nautical Almanac*. By means of this diagram the approximate positions of the planets relative to the sun, and to each other, may be determined.

Air Almanac *Star Charts*

A fold-in, white-on-black star chart is located in the back of the *Air Almanac*. It presents the entire celestial sphere on a rectangular projection, the top and bottom edges representing the north and south celestial poles, respectively. This causes great distortion in the relative positions of stars near the poles, but provides an excellent reference of the order of appearance of the stars and constellations as they move across the heavens.

Star Charts.

2108. Six numbered star charts are included in this chapter as Figures 2109 to 2114. They show all the brighter stars, necessarily with some repetition. The two charts of the polar regions are on the azimuthal equidistant polar projections; the others are on the transverse Mercator projection.

To use a polar chart, face the elevated pole and hold the correct chart with the name of the month on top. It will then be correctly oriented for LMT 2200 for that month. For each hour the LMT differs from 2200, rotate the chart one hour, as shown by the radial lines. These are labeled for LHA in *time units*, in which case it is called *local sidereal time* (LST), and for sidereal hour angle (SHA). The sidereal time indicates the direction of rotation, as earlier sidereal times occur at earlier solar times. The region about the *elevated* pole will be the only polar region visible.

To use a transverse Mercator star chart, hold it overhead with the top of the page toward north. The left edge will then be east, the right edge west, and the bottom south. The numbers along the central hour circle indicate declination and can be used to orient for latitude. The charts are made for LMT 2200 on the dates specified. For each half month later, subtract one hour to determine the time at which the heavens appear as depicted in the chart; for each half month earlier, add one hour to LMT 2200. The numbers below the celestial equator indicate local sidereal time; those above indicate sidereal hour angle. If the LMT of observation is not 2200, these can be used to determine which hour circle coincides with the celestial meridian. The dotted lines connect stars of some of the more easily distinguished constellations. The dashed lines are shown to aid in the identification of stars of different constellations.

It must be kept in mind that the apparent positions of the stars are constantly changing because of the motions of the earth. If the observer changes his position on the earth, a further change in the apparent positions of the stars will result. Remember too, that the limits of the transverse Mercator charts represent the approximate limits of observation only at the equator. Observers elsewhere will see below their elevated pole, and an equal amount of the opposite polar region will be hidden from view.

The approximate appearance of the heavens at any given time can be determined by obtaining LHA♈ (from GHA♈, tabulated in the almanacs, and λ) and converting it to time units. The resulting LST is then found on the star charts. The celestial meridian on the transverse Mercator chart which is labeled with that time is the one which is approximately overhead. The same celestial meridian on the polar charts, labeled in the same way, is the one which is *up*. Thus if LHA♈ is 225°, LST is 15^h. This appears on the transverse Mercator charts of both Figures 2110 and 2111. The stars to the east of the celestial meridian at this time appear in Figure 2111 (in the direction of increasing LST and decreasing SHA), and the stars to the west of the celestial meridian at this time appear in Figure 2110 (in the direction of decreasing LST and increasing SHA). By orienting each polar chart so that the celestial meridian labeled 15^h is up, the stars toward and beyond each celestial pole can be seen. An observer can view only half of the celestial sphere at a given time, of course, and the stars actually visible depend upon his latitude.

2109. The north polar region (Star Chart 1, Figure 2109). Nearly everyone is familiar with the *big dipper*, part of the constellation of *Ursa Major* (the big bear). This is composed of seven stars in the shape of a dipper, with the open part toward the north celestial pole. For observers in the United States, most of the dipper is circumpolar and is therefore visible the year around. Dubhe, Alioth, and Alkaid are the stars of this constellation most used by navigators. Dubhe and Merak, forming part of the bowl of the dipper, are called the pointers, for if the line connecting them is extended northward, it passes very near Polaris, less than one degree from the north celestial pole. If the line is extended across the pole it leads very near to Caph in *Cassiopeia*. These stars point straight *down* to Polaris in the evening sky of mid-April. By the middle of July they are to the left of Polaris. In mid-October they are directly below the pole, and three months later, in the middle of January, they are to the right. For other stars identified by means of the big dipper, see article 2110. *Ursa Major.*

Little dipper. Polaris is part of the little dipper, *Ursa Minor* (the little bear), which is not conspicuous until the sky has become quite dark. Only Polaris at one end and Kochab at the other, both second magnitude stars, are used by the navigator. The little dipper is roughly parallel to the big dipper, but upside down with respect to it. In the autumn the big dipper is under the little dipper and there is a folk saying that liquid spilling out of the little one will be caught by the big one. The handles of the two dippers curve in opposite directions, relative to their bowls. *Ursa Minor.*

Cassiopeia (the queen). Across the pole from the handle of the big dipper, and approximately the same distance from Polaris, will be found Cassiopeia's chair. The principal stars of this constellation form a well-defined W or M, depending on their position with respect to the pole. Schedar, the second star from the right when the figure appears as a W, is a second magnitude star *Cassiopeia.*

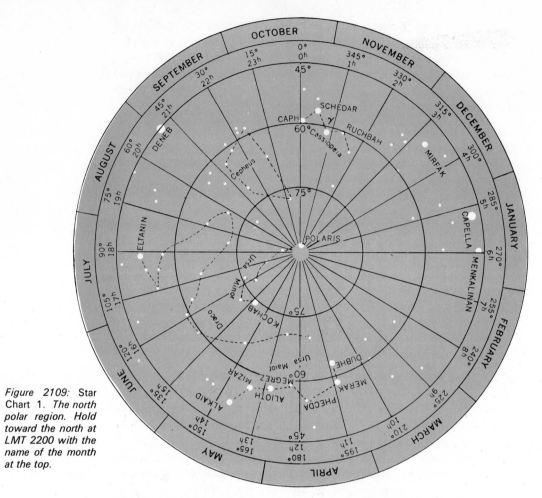

Figure 2109: Star Chart 1. *The north polar region. Hold toward the north at LMT 2200 with the name of the month at the top.*

sometimes used by navigators. Second magnitude Caph, the right-hand star when the figure appears as a W, is of interest because it lies close to the hour circle of the vernal equinox.

Draco.

Draco is about halfway from Cassiopeia to the big dipper in a westerly direction, but its navigational star Eltanin probably is most easy to identify by following the western arm of the Northern Cross as described in the Scorpio group (article 2111).

2110. The spring sky (Star Chart 2, Fig. 2110). In the spring, the big dipper is above the pole, high in the sky, and serves to point out several excellent navigational stars. Starting at the bowl, follow the curvature of the handle. If this curved arc is continued, it leads first to Arcturus, the only navigational star in *Boötes* (the herdsman) and then to Spica in *Virgo* (the virgin), both first magnitude stars much used by the navigator. A line northward through the pointers of the big dipper leads to Polaris. If this line is followed in the opposite direction, it leads in the general direction of Regulus, the end of the handle of the sickle in the constellation *Leo* (the lion). This much used navigational star is of the first magnitude and the brightest star in its part of the sky. A line connecting Regulus and Arcturus passes close to second magnitude Denebola (tail of the lion) sometimes used by navigators, which marks the tail of *Leo.*

Boötes.   *Virgo.*

Leo.

374

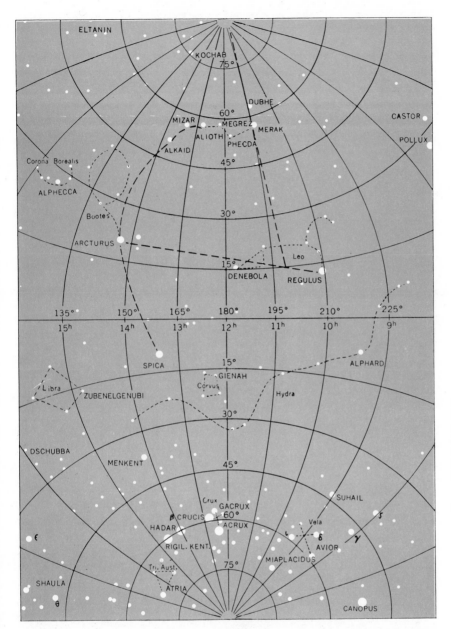

Figure 2110: Star Chart 2. *The spring sky as seen at LMT 2200 on 22 April. Hold overhead with the top of the page toward the north.*

Corvus (the crow) resembles more nearly a quadrilateral sail. It is not difficult to find and contains the third magnitude navigational star Gienah. Due south of *Corvus* is the southern cross (article 2114).

Corvus.

The only navigational star in *Hydra* (the serpent), a long, inconspicuous constellation near Corvus, is the second magnitude Alphard. This star is more easily identified by its being close to the extension of a line from the pointer of the big dipper through Regulus and extending southward.

Hydra.

Alphecca and *Corona Borealis* (the northern crown), located to the east of Arcturus, form a distinctive pattern and connect the dipper group to the northern cross to the east.

Corona Borealis.

375

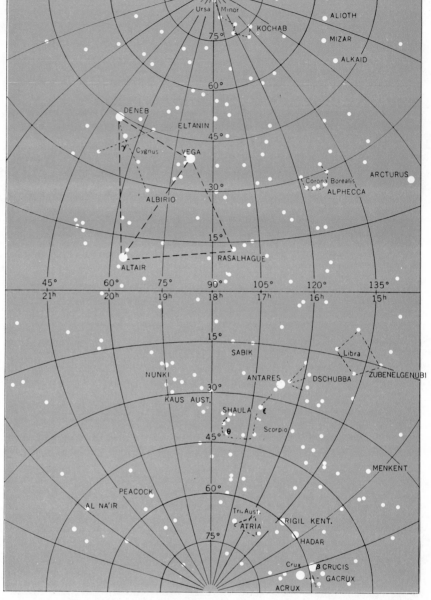

Figure 2111: Star Chart 3. *The summer sky as seen at LMT 2200 on 22 July. Hold overhead with the top of the page toward the north.*

Scorpio.

2111. The summer sky (Star Chart 3, Figure 2111). *Scorpio* (the scorpion) is one constellation which resembles the animal for which it is named without too much stretch of the imagination. The curve from Antares, the main navigational star, to Shaula is particularly suggestive of a scorpion's tail. Immediately to the east is a group forming the shape of a teapot with the star Nunki in the handle.

To the north of these are the first magnitude stars, Vega, Deneb, and Altair. They form a distinct right triangle (right angle at Vega) which many people use as an identification feature. However, each one is in a different constellation which should enable one to identify it without reference to any other stars. Deneb is in the northern cross (*Cygnus*); the eastern arm of the cross points to Enif, the western arm to Eltanin, and the bisectors of the lower right

Cygnus.

376

angles point to Altair and Vega. Altair is readily identified by the small stars on either side of it, sometimes called the guardians. It should be kept in mind, however, that the southern guardian is only a fourth magnitude star and may not show too plainly on very hazy or bright moonlight nights. This configuration is unique and should identify Altair through a break in the overcast with no other stars showing. Vega may be identified under these conditions by an almost perfect parallelogram slightly to the south and east of it. Again, however, these are fourth magnitude stars and are not too distinct if conditions are unfavorable.

The northern crown (*Corona Borealis*) is a group of stars shaped like a bowl about two thirds of the distance from Vega toward Arcturus. Second magnitude Alphecca in this group is sometimes used by navigators.

Corona Borealis.

Rasalhague forms nearly an equilateral triangle with Vega and Altair. This second magnitude star and third magnitude Sabik, to the south, are occasionally used by navigators.

2112. The autumn sky (Star Chart 4, Figure 2112) is marked by an absence of first magnitude stars. The northern cross has moved to a position low in the western sky, and *Cassiopeia* is nearly on the meridian to the north. A little south of the zenith for most observers in the United States the great square of *Pegasus* (the winged horse) appears nearly on the meridian. The eastern side of this square, and Caph in *Cassiopeia*, nearly mark the hour circle of the vernal equinox. Alpheratz and Markab, second magnitude stars at opposite corners of the square, are the principal navigational stars of this constellation. Second magnitude Enif is occasionally used.

The Pegasus Group.

The square of *Pegasus* is useful in locating several navigational stars. The line joining the stars of the eastern side of the square, if continued southward, leads close to second magnitude Diphda in *Cetus* (the sea monster). Similarly, a line joining the stars of the western side of the square, if continued southward, leads close to first magnitude Fomalhaut. A line through the center of the square, if continued eastward, leads close to second magnitude Hamal, in *Aries* (the ram). This was the location of the vernal equinox some 2000 years ago, when it was designated the "first point of Aries."

Aries.

A curved line from Alpheratz through *Andromeda* leads to *Perseus*. The only navigational star in Perseus frequently used is the second magnitude Mirfak. The curved line from Mirfak to Alpheratz forms a handle to a huge dipper of which the square of *Pegasus* is the bowl.

A line from Fomalhaut through Diphda extended about forty degrees leads to Menkar, an inconspicuous third magnitude star in *Cetus;* and Ankaa, a second magnitude star in *Phoenix*, is found about twenty degrees southeasterly from Fomalhaut. Both stars are listed among the navigational stars.

The navigational stars associated with *Pegasus* are Alpheratz, Markab, Diphda, Fomalhaut, and Hamal.

Capella, rising in the east as *Pegasus* is overhead, connects this group to the *Orion* group while Enif acts as a link to the west.

2113. The winter sky (Star Chart 5, Figure 2113). No other part of the sky contains so many bright stars. The principal constellation of this region is

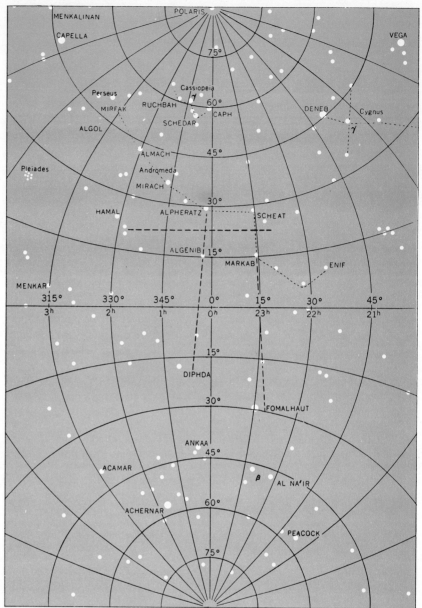

Figure 2112: Star Chart 4. *The autumn sky as seen at LMT 2200 on 21 October. Hold overhead with the top of the page toward the north.*

Orion.

Orion (the hunter), probably the best known constellation in the entire sky, with the exception of the big dipper. This figure is well known to observers in both northern and southern hemispheres, as the belt of *Orion* lies almost exactly on the celestial equator. Brilliant Rigel and first magnitude Betelgeuse lie approximately equal distances below and above the belt, respectively.

Pleiades.

Taurus.

Canis Major.

Several good navigational stars may be found by the use of *Orion*. If the line of the belt is continued to the westward, it leads near first magnitude reddish Aldebaran (the "follower", so named because it follows the "seven sisters" of *Pleiades*), in the V-shaped head of *Taurus* (the bull). If the line of the belt is followed in the opposite direction, it leads almost to Sirius, the brightest of all the stars. This is the principal star in the constellation of *Canis Major*, the hunter's large dog. Starting with Sirius, a rough circle can be drawn through

378

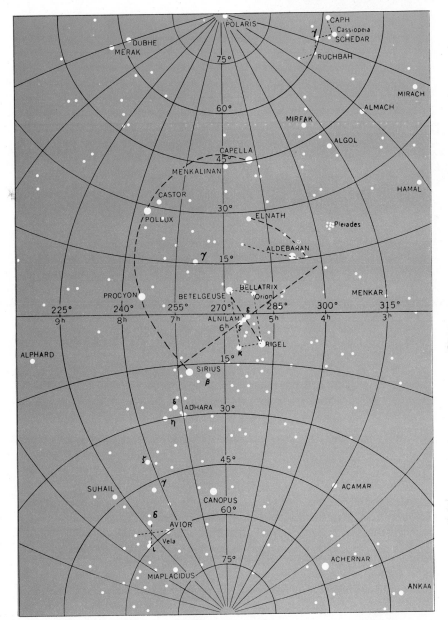

Figure 2113: Star Chart 5. *The winter sky as seen at LMT 2200 on 21 January. Hold overhead with the top of the page toward the north.*

Procyon in *Canis Minor* (the little dog), Pollux and Castor in *Gemini* (the twins), Capella in *Auriga* (the charioteer), Aldebaran, Rigel, and back to Sirius. All of these except Castor are first magnitude stars.

Several second magnitude stars in the general area of *Orion* are bright enough for navigational purposes, but are seldom used because there are so many first magnitude stars nearby. Four of these second magnitude stars are listed among the principal navigational stars of the almanac. These are Bellatrix, just west of Betelgeuse; Alnilam, the middle star (actually, a spiral nebulae) in the belt; Elnath, in *Taurus;* and Adhara, part of a triangle in *Canis Major,* and just south of Sirius.

Nearly on the meridian far to the south the brilliant Canopus, second brightest

Canis Minor.

379

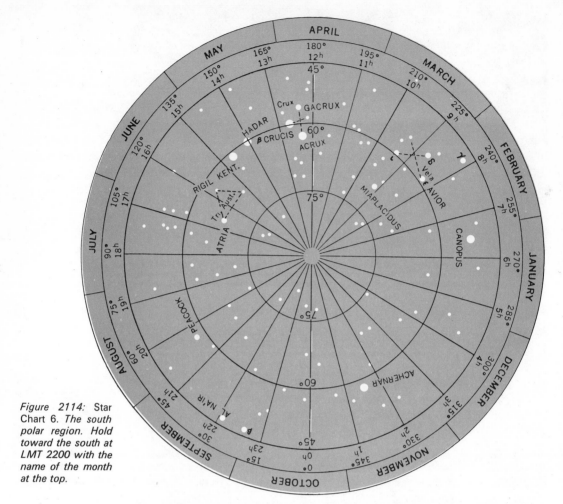

Figure 2114: Star Chart 6. *The south polar region. Hold toward the south at LMT 2200 with the name of the month at the top.*

star, is visible only to observers in the United States south of latitude $37\frac{1}{2}$ degrees. This star is part of the constellation *Carina* (the keel).

2114. The south polar region (Star Chart 6, Figure 2114). While the south polar region contains a number of bright stars, the person who travels to the southern hemisphere for the first time is likely to be disappointed by the absence of any striking configuration of stars similar to those with which he is familiar. The famed southern cross (*Crux*) is far from an impressive constellation and such a poor cross it might easily be overlooked if two of its stars were not of the first magnitude. A somewhat similar "false cross" in the constellation *Vela* may be easily mistaken for the southern cross.

Crux.

Canopus is almost due south of Sirius. The constellation *Carina*, of which Canopus is a part, was originally part of a larger constellation *Argo* (the ship), which is now generally divided into *Carina* (the keel), *Puppis* (the stern), *Pyxis* (the mariner's compass), and *Vela* (the sails). Navigational stars included in *Argo* are, besides first magnitude Canopus, Avior (part of the "false cross"), Suhail (Figure 2110 and 2113) and Miaplacidus, all second magnitude stars.

Counterclockwise from *Argo* is *Crux*, the true southern cross. Acrux and Gacrux are listed among the principal navigational stars of the almanac. This constellation also contains the first magnitude star β Crucis.

Two more good first magnitude stars lie in nearby *Centaurus* (the centaur). These are Rigil Kentaurus and Hadar. The second magnitude Menkent at the other end of the constellation (Figures 2110 and 2111) is listed among the principal navigational stars and is used occasionally by navigators.

Centaurus.

Near *Centaurus* and still in a counterclockwise direction around the pole is Atria, a commonly used navigational star in *Triangulum Australe*.

The half of the south polar region thus far described has a relatively large number of first and second magnitude stars. This area is actually a continuation of the bright area around *Orion*, as can be seen by referring to Figure 2113.

In the remaining section of the south polar region there are relatively few navigational stars. These are second magnitude Peacock in *Pavo* (the peacock), second magnitude Al Na'ir in *Grus* (the crane), and first magnitude Achernar and third magnitude Acamar (Figures 2112 and 2113) in *Eridanus* (the river). All of these constellations are faint and poorly defined. Of these stars Achernar and Peacock are good navigational stars. The other two are seldom used.

CHAPTER 22

The Marine Sextant: Its Use, Adjustment, and Corrections

Introduction.

2201. The sextant is an instrument designed to permit measurement of the angle between two objects with great precision. It derives its name from the fact that its arc is approximately one-sixth of a circle; because of its optical principle, it can measure angles up to about 120°, or twice the value of the arc itself. Quintants and octants are similar instruments, named for the lengths of their arcs, but today it is the general practice to refer to all such instruments as sextants, regardless of the precise lengths of their arcs.

The optical principle of the sextant was first described by Sir Isaac Newton. However, its importance was not realized, and the information was long forgotten until it was applied to celestial navigation.

The double reflecting principle of the sextant, described hereafter, was independently rediscovered in 1731 by Hadley in England, and Godfrey in Philadelphia; it made possible a high standard of accuracy in celestial navigation. The sextant and the compass remain the navigator's most important tools.

The marine sextant's components.

2202. A marine sextant is illustrated in Figure 2202 with the principal parts labeled as follows:

A. The *frame*, on which the other parts are mounted.

B. The *arc* or *limb* is a part of the frame, and is graduated in degrees.

C. The *index arm* is mounted at the center of the arc, and is free to move along it. Its lower end carries an index mark to indicate the reading in degrees on the arc. A spring release, shown at the bottom of the index arm, permits it to be moved to any portion of the arc.

D. The *micrometer drum* is used to make fine adjustments of the index arm. It is mounted on a shaft, having a pinion gear at the other end called the *tangent screw*. This tangent screw engages the worm teeth cut in the arc, and one full turn moves the index arm by one-half degree on the arc, thus adjusting the observed altitude by exactly one degree. The micrometer drum is generally graduated in minutes of arc, and on some sextants a vernier scale permits it to be read to 0'.1. On other models a single index mark is used and tenths are estimated between the even minute graduations.

E. The *index mirror* is mounted at the upper end of the index arm. It is perpendicular to the plane of the arc.

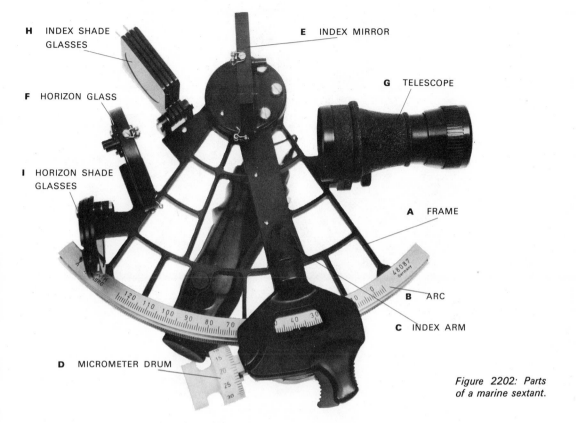

H INDEX SHADE GLASSES

E INDEX MIRROR

G TELESCOPE

F HORIZON GLASS

I HORIZON SHADE GLASSES

A FRAME

B ARC

C INDEX ARM

D MICROMETER DRUM

Figure 2202: Parts of a marine sextant.

F. The *horizon glass* is mounted on the frame. Like the index mirror, it is perpendicular to the arc. When the index arm is set exactly at 0°, the horizon glass is parallel to the index mirror. The horizon glass is divided vertically into two halves. The part lying nearest the frame is silvered as a mirror, the other half is clear optical glass.

G. The *telescope* is mounted with its axis parallel to the plane of the arc. The magnification of the telescope permits the observer to judge contact between the celestial body and the sea horizon much more exactly than is possible with the unaided eye, and often makes it possible to pick up the image of a star when it cannot be seen by the unaided eye. On some sextants the telescope can be moved towards or away from the frame as conditions warrant.

H. The *index shade glasses* are of optically ground glass mounted perpendicular to the arc, and are pivoted, so that they can be swung out of the line of sight between the index and horizon mirrors. Two types of index shade glasses are employed on sextants. The first is a variable density polarizing filter; the second consists of four or more shade glasses of neutral tint, and increasing density. The shade glasses are employed when making observations of the sun, and sometimes when observing a bright planet or star above a dimly lighted horizon.

I. The *horizon shades* are similar to the index shades, and serve to reduce the glare of reflected sunlight on the horizon.

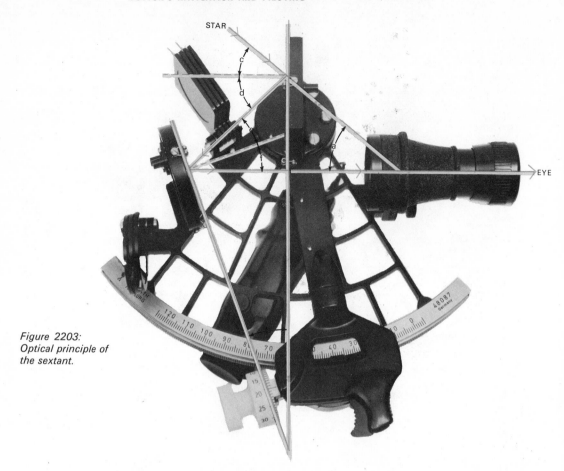

Figure 2203:
Optical principle of
the sextant.

Optical principle of
the sextant.

2203. The optics of the sextant are based on a system of double reflection, in that the image of the body observed is reflected from the upper, or index mirror, to the lower, or horizon mirror, and thence into the field of view of the sextant telescope, where it is brought into coincidence with the sea horizon, which is seen through the clear portion of the horizon mirror. The principle of optics involved is stated: *The angle between the first and last directions of a ray of light that has undergone two reflections in the same plane is twice the angle that the two reflecting surfaces make with each other.* This principle can be proven by geometry, and is illustrated in Figure 2203. The sextant arc, however, is engraved to show the actual altitude of the body, rather than the number of degrees the index arm has been moved from the 0° setting. in Figure 2203, angle *a,* the difference between first and last reflection, equals twice angle *b,* the angle between the reflecting surfaces. Angle *c* equals angle *d* and angle *e* equals angle *f,* the angles of incidence and reflection respectively, of the index and horizon mirrors.

Reading the sextant
altitude.

2204. In using the sextant to obtain a celestial altitude, the spring release at the bottom of the index arm is disengaged, and the arm is moved until the body and the horizon are both seen in the field of view. The release is then freed so that the tangent screw re-engages the worm teeth on the arc, and the micrometer drum is turned until the body is brought into coincidence with the horizon.

*Figure 2204:
Micrometer drum
and index.*

To read the altitude, the position of the arm's index mark against the scale of degrees on the arc is first read. In Figure 2204, the index mark is located between 77° and 78°, indicating that the altitude will be 77°, plus the reading of minutes and tenths obtained from the micrometer drum.

The index mark for the micrometer drum is the zero mark on the vernier; in Figure 2204, this falls between 0' and 1', indicating that 0' plus the number of tenths obtained from the vernier must be added to 77°. To read the vernier, the graduation most nearly in line with a graduation on the drum is noted. In Figure 2204, the first mark on the vernier is aligned with a graduation on the drum; the number of tenths to be added is therefore one. The altitude is 77°00'.1.

2205. The sextant is an instrument of great precision; it is also fragile. To be kept in alignment, *it must at all times be handled most carefully*. When not in use, it should be kept in its box, and the box must be stowed so that it cannot come adrift at sea.

Sextant care.

Moisture and salt must be wiped off the mirrors and the telescope objective lens; fogged optics make it extremely difficult to pick up stars. Salt spray, particularly, can damage the sextant if it is not removed, and should be rinsed off with a little fresh water. The sextant should then be gently wiped with a soft cotton cloth. The mirrors and objective lens should next be gently polished with lens paper. Silk should never be used, as it is liable to scratch the mirrors.

Sextant adjustments detailed in article 2213 should be undertaken only by an experienced person, and must be made with great care.

2206. The "bubble sextant" has long been used by aviators for celestial observations. The vertical is established in these instruments by bringing the center of the observed body into coincidence with the center of a free floating bubble. Most aviation artificial horizon sextants are fitted with an averaging device. This provides the determination of a mean of observations made over a considerable period of time, usually two minutes. On the latest models the observation may be discontinued at any time after the first thirty seconds and the average altitude determined. However, it is generally assumed that a full two-minute observation will at least cover the complete natural oscillation of the aircraft in pitch and roll.

*Artificial horizon
sextants.*

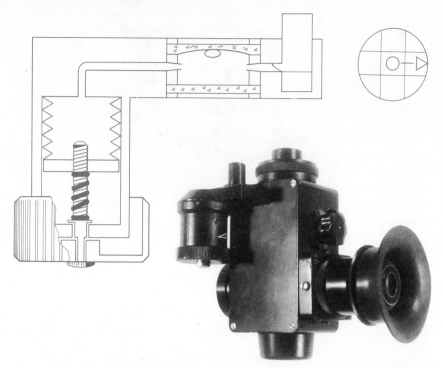

Figure 2206:
Plath Marine sextant
bubble attachment.

The aircraft bubble sextant is difficult to use aboard most surface vessels, particularly in a seaway, due to the constant and often violent accelerations that occur and the relatively short period of roll of a ship as compared to an aircraft. However, useful results have been obtained with them aboard large carriers, and partially surfaced submarines. The fleet ballistic missile submarines are now issued a marine sextant with special bubble attachment (Figure 2206).

In the past thirty years considerable experimentation has been conducted with sextants fitted with gyroscopic artificial horizon systems. Such a system holds great promise but has not come into current usage.

The great advantage of an artificial horizon sextant is that it permits observations of celestial bodies when the sea horizon is obscured by darkness, fog, or haze. The accuracy obtainable with the bubble sextant lies in the range of minutes of arc, rather than in tenths, as is the case with the marine sextant using the natural horizon.

SEXTANT OBSERVATIONS

Horizon system coordinates.

2207. As stated in article 2004, celestial observations are made with reference to the horizon system of coordinates. The axis of this system is dependent on the position of the observer, and its reference plane is the celestial horizon. The celestial horizon passes through the center of the earth, and is perpendicular to the vertical circle passing from the observer's zenith on the celestial sphere, through his position and through the earth's center on to the observer's nadir.

Observing altitudes.

2208. Altitude observations of celestial bodies are made in the plane perpendicular to the celestial horizon, along the vertical circle passing through the body. They are measured upward from the visible, or sea horizon, and a correction is applied which adjusts the sextant altitude to read as though the observed

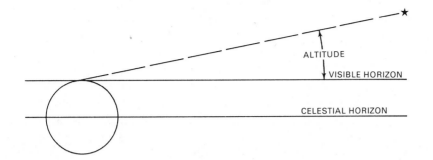

Figure 2208a:
An altitude
measurement.

angle had been measured from the earth's center, above the celestial horizon. The plane of the visible horizon may, for all practical purposes, be considered to be parallel to the celestial horizon. Figure 2208a illustrates the principle of a celestial altitude measurement.

The altitude of a body above the visible horizon as read from the sextant, is termed the sextant altitude; its symbol is hs.

To make an observation, the observer stands facing the body, holding the sextant vertically in his right hand, and centers the horizon in his field of view. He then frees the spring release, and moves the index arm until the body also appears in the field of view. The tangent screw is next allowed to engage the worm teeth on the arc, and the micrometer drum is turned until the horizon and the body are in coincidence.

The sextant is next rotated slightly about the axis of the line of sight to the horizon, causing the body to swing like a pendulum along the horizon, as illustrated in Figure 2208b. The lowest point traced by the body on this arc marks its intersection with the body's vertical circle, and the micrometer drum is again rotated until the body makes contact with the horizon at the bottom of its swing. At this instant the time is noted and the sextant altitude is read off.

Figure 2208b:
Swinging the arc.

The rotation of the sextant described in the last paragraph is called *swinging the arc.* With practice, it is easy to determine when the body is on the vertical. The eye tends to extend the line of the sea horizon into the mirrored portions of the horizon glass, and the arc of the reflected image appears not only in the mirrored half of the horizon glass, but in the clear half as well.

Graphing sights.   Skill in obtaining accurate altitudes comes only with practice. Some individuals are markedly more accurate observers than others, but experiments conducted for the Office of Naval Research clearly indicate that the accuracy of the best observers tends to increase with practice. Each of five observers made over 3,000 sextant observations, and for each observer the mean of his second thousand observations was better than his first thousand, and the third thousand showed still further improvement. The novice observer may find that his sights do not yield satisfactory lines of position. Working with an experienced navigator may improve his technique, and it may be helpful for him to make simultaneous observations with an able observer. It is also helpful to make a string of 10 or more observations of the same body in a period of less than three minutes. These sights should then be plotted on a large sheet of plotting paper, using a horizontal scale of one inch to ten seconds of time, and a vertical scale of one inch to one minute of arc, if possible. A "line of best fit" is then drawn through the string. The divergence of the individual sights from this line will tend to indicate the magnitude of the observer's random errors. The random error of a single sight is the greatest hazard to the accuracy of celestial naviga-

Multiple observations.   tion. Where accuracy is required, a single observation should not be relied on to obtain a line of position. It is far better practice to take at least three sights of each body, and for maximum accuracy an even greater number of observations should be made and graphed as described above. A convenient altitude and time can then be selected for the sight from the graph.

Observing LAN.   The student, when practicing with the sextant, will be wise to observe the sun at local apparent noon (LAN). In most latitudes, the sun changes altitude but little for a period of several minutes before and after LAN. A string of 12 or more observations should be made, and the altitudes noted. After each sight, the micrometer drum should be moved, so that the sun's image appears alternately above and below the horizon. It should then be brought to the horizon, and the arc should be swung until the sun's image is brought into coincidence with the horizon on the vertical. When the student is able to obtain a consistent string of altitudes at LAN, he may obtain a string of sun sights in the afternoon—or morning—when the sun is moving rapidly in altitude. The procedure for making sun sights is outlined in article 2209.

These should, if possible, be graphed as outlined above; otherwise it should be determined that the change in altitude is consistent with the time interval between.

Suggestions that may be helpful in obtaining good sights are included in the following articles.

Sun observations.   **2209.** As described in article 2202, the sextant is fitted with index shade glasses, either of the variable density polarizing type, or neutrally tinted filters of varying degree of density. To determine the degree of density best suited to the observer's eye under existing conditions, it is usually best first to look at the sun through the darkest index shade; if this dims the image too much, the next lightest shade should be tried. It should be noted that sometimes the best results are achieved by using two of the light filters, rather than a single dark one. When a polarizing filter is used, it should be set to full dark before looking at the sun; the rotatable portion can then be turned to lighten the image until the eye sees the image comfortably and clearly.

On a calm day, when the sun is low in altitude, the sea short of the horizon may reflect the sunlight so glaringly that it is desirable to employ a horizon shade. The most desirable shade must again be selected by trial and error.

After the proper shade or shades are selected, the observer sets the index arm to 0°, faces the sun, and proceeds as described in article 2208 until the sun's *lower limb* is on the horizon; during this process the arc must be swung to establish the vertical. (The term "limb" is used to denote a portion of the circumference of the sun or moon.) At most altitudes, the best results are obtained by observing the sun's lower limb; however, at altitudes below about 5°, it is more desirable to observe the upper limb. In this case, the correction for *irradiation effect* should be applied to the sextant altitude, in addition to the other corrections. The procedure for observing the sun's upper limb is the same as for the lower limb. Figure 2209 shows the sun's lower limb on the horizon, as seen through the sextant telescope.

The sun's limb.

Figure 2209: Observing the sun.

2210. Observations of the moon are made in the same manner as those of the sun, except that shades are not required during the daylight hours.

Moon observations.

Because of the phases of the moon, upper limb observations are made about as frequently as those of the lower limb. Accurate observations of the moon can only be obtained if the upper or lower limb is brought to the horizon. This is not always possible, due to the moon's phase, and its position in the sky.

Carefully made moon observations, obtained during daylight hours, under good observational conditions, yield excellent LOPs. If the moon is observed at night, it may be desirable to shade its image somewhat, in order that the horizon not be obscured by the moon's brilliance.

Star and planet observations.

2211. Observations of stars and planets are made at twilight. More experience in the use of the sextant is required to obtain good twilight sights than is needed in daylight. This is chiefly due to the fact that a star appears only as a point of light in the sextant telescope, rather than appearing as a body of considerable size, as does the sun or moon. In addition, the stars fade out in the morning, as the horizon brightens; in the evening this condition is reversed, and it is sometimes difficult to obtain a good star image and a well defined horizon at the same time. However, the problem is considerably simplified when a well designed sextant, fitted with a good telescope, is employed.

Three methods of bringing the star and the horizon together are possible. The first is to bring the star's image down to the horizon, the second is to bring the horizon up to the star, and the third is to predetermine the approximate altitude and azimuth of the selected star. Of the three methods, the third is usually the most satisfactory, as it often permits locating the star before it can be seen by the unaided eye.

Bringing a star down.

To employ the first method, the sextant is set within about 2' of 0°, and the line of sight is directed at the star, which will then appear as a double image. The index arm is then slowly pushed forward, while the sextant is moved downward, in order to keep the image of the body in the field of the telescope. When the index arm has reached the star's approximate altitude on the arc, the horizon will appear in the field. The micrometer drum is then allowed to engage the teeth on the arc, and the final contact is made by means of turning the drum, while rocking the arc to establish the vertical.

Some observers, when using a sextant with a small optical field of view, prefer to remove the telescope from the sextant while bringing the star down. The telescope should always be reinstalled before the altitude is read in order to obtain maximum accuracy.

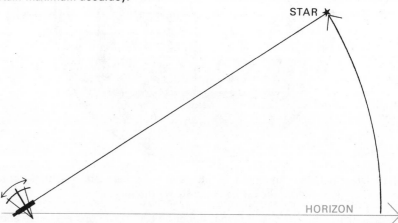

Figure 2211: Using the sextant inverted.

The second method is sometimes employed when the horizon is bright, and the star is dim. To bring the horizon up to the star, the sextant is set at approximately 0°, and then held inverted in the left hand. The line of sight is then directed at the body, which will be seen through the clear portion of the horizon glass as shown in Figure 2211. The index arm is next adjusted until the horizon appears in the field of view and then allowed to lock to the arc, the sextant is righted, and the altitude is determined in the usual way.

The best practice for star observations, in most cases, is to determine in advance the approximate altitude and azimuth of the stars to be observed, by means of a star finder, such as the "Star Finder and Identifier" H. O. 2102-D, which is described in article 2102. This predetermination of the approximate altitude permits full use to be made of the sextant telescope, which will usually make it possible to sight a star when it cannot be seen with the naked eye. Stars can thus be located at evening twilight, while the horizon is still clearly defined, and can be observed in the morning after they have faded from view of the unaided eye. *Precomputed altitudes for sextant observations.*

When using this method, the altitude of the body to be observed is taken from the star finder, and set on the sextant. The observer then faces in the direction of the body's azimuth, usually determined by sighting over a gyro repeater or magnetic compass, and directs his line of sight at the horizon. After locating the star, its altitude is determined in the regular manner.

2212. At times it is necessary to seize every opportunity to obtain one or more celestial observations, even under adverse conditions. Hints which may be helpful to the student navigator in observing various bodies follows: *Notes regarding celestial observations.*

Sun. During extended periods of overcast, the sun may occasionally break through, appearing for only a minute or so. Under such conditions it is advisable to have a sextant set to the approximate altitude, and with the telescope mounted, located in a convenient spot where it can be picked up instantly if the sun appears. If necessary, the observer should be prepared to note his own time of observation rather than using a quartermaster for this. At times the sun shows through thin overcast, but its image is not sharply defined. It can nevertheless supply a helpful line of position.

When the sun is high in altitude, as it transits the observer's meridian at LAN, its change in azimuth during the hour or so preceding and following LAN is very rapid. This permits obtaining excellent running fixes over a comparative short period of time. The first observation should be made when the sun bears about 45° east of the meridian. This should be followed by the conventional noon sight and another set of observations can be made when the sun is about 45° west of the meridian.

Low altitude sights of the sun (i.e., altitudes of 5° more or less) can be extremely helpful at times, and under most observational conditions will yield lines of position accurate to two miles or less, when carefully corrected. When making low altitude sun sights, the upper limb will usually yield better observations than the lower. The correction for refraction listed for stars in the *Nautical Almanac* should be used, as well as a correction for semidiameter, as found in the daily pages of the *Nautical Almanac*. The correction for index error, dip of the horizon, and an additional refraction correction for non-standard conditions, all given in the *Nautical Almanac*, should be used. When the sun's upper limb is observed and the Star Refraction correction table in the *Nautical Almanac* is used, an additional correction for irradiation should be employed (article 2225). *Low altitude sun observations.*

H. O. Publication No. 214 does not list altitudes below 5°, and such observations must be reduced by some other method.

Moon. The moon can often be used for valuable daylight fixes when combined with observation of the sun. When moon observations are to be made at night, it is advisable to make them from a point as low in the ship as possible. This will minimize errors caused by cloud shadows, which can shade the true horizon, and make the moon appear below its true position, causing the sextant altitude to read higher than it should.

Planets. Venus can frequently be observed with a sextant during daylight, particularly when its altitude is greater than that of the sun, and it is not too close to the latter in hour angle.

Daylight planet observations.

To locate Venus during daylight, its position (declination and angle relative to Aries) should be carefully plotted on the "Star Finder and Identifier" H. O. 2102-D, as discussed in article 2102. The latter is then set in the regular manner for the time of the desired observation and the corresponding DR position, and the approximate altitude and azimuth are read off.

Fixes based on sights of the sun, moon, and Venus made during daylight hours should be employed whenever possible.

The other planets, which are not as brilliant as Venus, are ordinarily observed only at twilight. Their positions may also be plotted on the Star Finder and Identifier, to aid in locating them in the sky. Twilight observation techniques, applicable to planets, are described in the following paragraph.

Stars. When the Star Finder and Identifier is employed, altitudes and azimuths of twelve or more stars, preferably with altitudes of 20° or more, should be listed in advance for the time of twilight. It is desirable to list considerably more stars than will actually be observed, as not all the stars may be visible at twilight, due to clouds.

The visibility of a star at twilight depends primarily on its magnitude, or brilliance, and on its altitude; to a considerably lesser extent it depends on its azimuth relative to that of the sun. Remember that the lower the tabulated magnitude of a star, the greater the brilliance. All other factors being equal, a low magnitude star will be visible against a brighter sky than one of higher magnitude, and hence of less brilliance. If two stars are of equal magnitude, and have the same azimuth, the star with the higher altitude will appear to be the brighter. Due to the polarization of the sun's light rays, stars situated at 90° to the sun's azimuth will appear to be slightly brighter than stars of the same magnitude and altitude having nearly the same azimuth as the sun or lying about 180° from it. This is equally true, whether the sun be below or above the horizon.

The visibility of stars also depends on the sextant's mirrors, and on the quality and magnification of the telescope. The mirrors must be a size that permits using the full angular field of view of the telescope, as the larger the mirror, the larger is the bundle of light rays transmitted to the observer's eye; this is another way of saying the brighter will be the star's reflected image. In addition, the greater the magnification of the telescope, the more easily can the star be located against a bright sky; full daylight observations have been made of Sirius (Mag. −1.6) and Arcturus (Mag. 0.2) with a sextant fitted with a 20-power telescope.

The position of the telescope relative to the sextant frame may be adjusted to suit varying conditions of illumination at twilight. Article 2202G stated that some sextant telescopes are not permanently fixed relative to the frame, but that their axis may be moved in or out. This is generally true of sextants with small mirrors which have less light gathering power. When the telescope is moved as close as possible to the frame, the maximum amount of light is reflected from the sky into the field of view. Conversely, when it is moved out from the frame, more light is transmitted from the horizon, and less from the sky. With a dim horizon, the telescope is moved out to the end of its travel. When the horizon is very dim, it may even be desirable to use a pale index screen, when observing a brilliant star or planet; this will facilitate obtaining an accurate contact between the body and the horizon. The student should experiment in positioning the telescope, in order to obtain the optimum balance of lighting between the body and the horizon. It should be noted that a telescope with good light gathering powers will permit the observer to see a sharply defined horizon, when it appears "fuzzy" to the naked eye.

It is, of course, desirable to observe stars against a sharply defined horizon, which implies a fairly bright sky. At evening twilight, the eastern horizon will fade first; as a general rule, it is therefore best to observe stars situated to the eastward first. At morning twilight, the eastern horizon will brighten first. With practice, the student will be able to determine the order of observation of stars, balancing off the various factors involved—star magnitude and altitude, and horizon lighting.

With a sextant telescope of good magnification and optical characteristics, it is possible to observe stars at any time on a clear night. However, the observer's vision must be completely dark adapted. Submariners during World War II regularly obtained very good star fixes in the middle of the night, using a sextant fitted with a 6-power prismatic telescope, having an objective lens 30 mm in diameter. Night vision telescopes are now available which use an electronic unit to amplify the small amount of ambient light available at night. These light amplification scopes can be adapted to sextants for night observations.

Observations at night.

2213. The sextant, being an optical-mechanical instrument, cannot be manufactured error-free. When a sextant is assembled by the manufacturer it is tested for *fixed instrument errors* and the combined values are recorded on a certificate attached to the inside of the sextant case. The error is usually listed for each 10° of the arc. Some manufacturers merely certify the instrument to be free of errors for practical use. This implies that the error nowhere exceeds approximately 10 seconds of arc. In modern precision sextants these non-adjustable errors are small, and may usually be ignored. Specifications for the Navy Mark II sextant require that no errors be greater than 35 seconds of arc. Since this exceeds a half minute of arc, or half mile on the earth's surface, correction should be applied to the hs for any errors approaching this magnitude.

Sextant adjustment.

Instrument errors.

The mirrors are mounted in a manner permitting adjustment to maintain their perpendicularity to the sextant frame, and parallelism to each other. The line of sight of the telescope must be parallel to the plane of the sextant frame, but any necessary adjustment should, whenever possible, be accomplished in an optical repair shop.

2214. *Index error* should be determined each time the sextant is used. In the daytime, this is usually done by an observation of the horizon. The index arm is first set at 0° and with the sextant held in a vertical position, the micrometer

Index error.

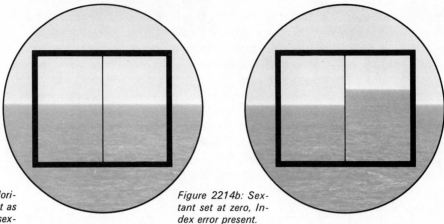

Figure 2214a: Horizon in alignment as seen through sextant telescope.

Figure 2214b: Sextant set at zero, Index error present.

drum is adjusted until the reflected and direct images of the horizon are brought into coincidence, forming a straight unbroken line, as is shown in Figure 2214a. This operation should be repeated several times, the reflected image of the horizon being alternately brought down and up to the direct image. The value of the index error is read in minutes and tenths after each alignment, and the

Sign of IC. average of the readings is taken and used as the *index correction* (IC), with the appropriate sign. If the error is positive—the micrometer drum reads more than 0'.0—the sign is negative; conversely, if the error is negative, the sign is positive. If the average reading of the micrometer drum is 58'.5, the error is (−)1'.5 and the IC is (+)1'.5. If the index error is small, say less than 4'.0, it is best not to try to remove it. Where the error is negative, it is sometimes said to be "off the arc," conversely, when positive it is "on the arc."

At night the index error may be determined by observing a star. The direct and reflected images are brought into coincidence, or directly adjoining each other horizontally in the manner described above for the horizon. Quite frequently two observers will not obtain the same value for the index error; their findings will represent a combination of the actual index error and of each personal error.

The index error is caused by a lack of perfect parallelism between the index mirror and horizon glass, when the sextant is set at 0°. This lack of parallelism causes a greater error in observations than would a slight error in the perpendicularity of the mirrors.

Adjusting the mirrors. To eliminate or reduce excessive index error, the *horizon* glass must be adjusted. On the Mark II Navy sextant the mirror is fixed within the mirror frame; adjustment is accomplished by moving the frame by means of two adjusting screws as shown in Figure 2214c. This adjustment is a trial and error process; one screw is first loosened by a small fraction of a revolution, and the other is tightened by an equal amount, and the process is repeated until the error is removed, or brought within an acceptable limit.

With the Plath and several other fine commercial sextants, the horizon glass is adjusted within the mirror frame. When holding the sextant vertical only the upper screw is used, as illustrated in Figure 2214d. The procedure just described is followed except that only the one adjusting screw is turned slightly; this moves the mirror against the mounting springs. When the sextant is properly adjusted the horizon will appear as in Figure 2214a with the sextant reading zero.

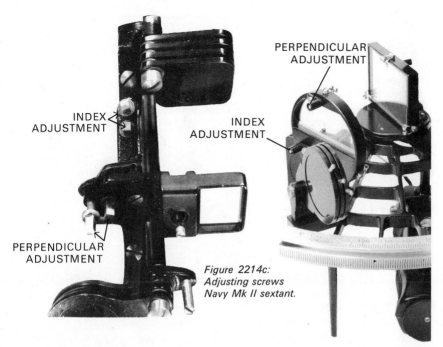

PERPENDICULAR
ADJUSTMENT

INDEX
ADJUSTMENT

INDEX
ADJUSTMENT

PERPENDICULAR
ADJUSTMENT

Figure 2214c:
Adjusting screws
Navy Mk II sextant.

Figure 2214d:
Adjusting screws
Plath sextant.

2215. The sextant should occasionally be checked to see that the mirrors are perpendicular to the sextant frame, and adjusted if a misalignment is found to exist. Index mirror alignment is checked by holding the sextant in the left hand with the index mirror towards the observer; he then looks into the index mirror and shifts the position of the sextant until the reflected image of the limb in the index mirror appears as a continuation of the limb as seen directly, looking past the index mirror. This is illustrated in Figure 2215a. If the reflected image is inclined to the limb as seen directly or is not in alignment with it the index mirror is not perpendicular to the plane of the limb, and the alignment should be corrected by use of the adjusting screws on the back of the index mirror frame. Again, some sextants have two adjusting screws, one of which must first be loosened and the other tightened. On other sextants one adjusting screw is used which moves the mirror against retaining springs.

Perpendicularity of mirrors.

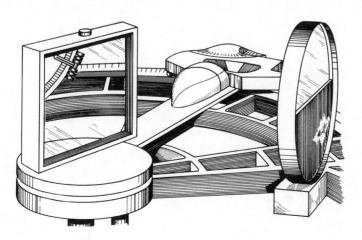

Figure 2215a:
Checking perpendicularity of index mirror.

Here the mirror is not perpendicular.

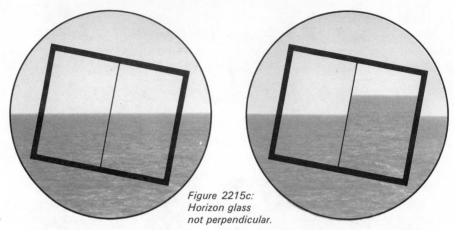

Figure 2215b:
Horizon glass
perpendicular to
sextant frame.

Figure 2215c:
Horizon glass
not perpendicular.

To check the perpendicularity of the horizon glass, the horizon should be sighted in the same manner as discussed in article 2214, for determining the index error. The tangent screw is adjusted until the reflected and direct images of the horizon appear as a straight line with the sextant in a vertical position. The sextant is then turned or rocked around the line of sight; the reflected horizon and the direct horizon should remain in exact alignment as in Figure 2215b. If they do not, as in Figure 2215c, the horizon glass needs adjustment to make it perpendicular to the plane of the limb. On the Navy Mark II sextant the two adjusting screws (Figure 2214c), are used to move the mirror frame assembly. Again, care must be used to loosen one before tightening the other. On sextants where the mirror is adjusted within the frame the adjusting screw furthest away from the sextant frame is used (Figure 2214d). When the mirror is properly adjusted the horizon will appear as a straight line while the sextant is rotated around the line of sight. To accomplish the adjustment at night the sextant is sighted directly at a star with the index set at 0°. When the tangent screw is turned, the reflected image of the star should move in a vertical line exactly through the direct image. If the line of movement is to one side or other of the direct image the horizon mirror is not perpendicular to the frame and should be adjusted (Figures 2215d and 2215e).

Since two different adjustments are made on the horizon glass, it is obvious that these adjustments are interrelated, and in making adjustment for the per-

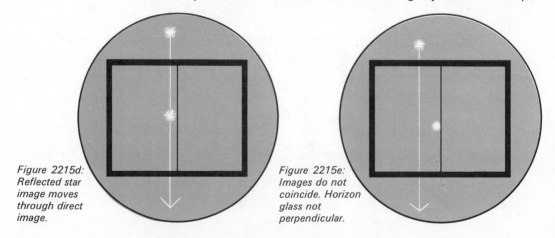

Figure 2215d:
Reflected star
image moves
through direct
image.

Figure 2215e:
Images do not
coincide. Horizon
glass not
perpendicular.

pendicularity of the mirror, the index error will be affected. As a general rule it is best to remove the index error first, adjust for perpendicularity, and then check again for index error. Several consecutive adjustments may be necessary if the mirror is badly mis-aligned.

2216. If extreme difficulty is encountered in bringing a star down to the horizon as discussed in article 2211, it is possible the line of sight of the telescope is not parallel to the plane of the sextant frame. This is usually difficult to adjust aboard ship, but there is a quick practical check to determine if the telescope is out of alignment. The sextant is held in a horizontal position in the left hand with the horizon glass toward the observer, and the index arm set near 0°. The observer looks into the index mirror, holding the sextant in a position so that the reflected image of the center line of the horizon mirror is directly in line with the actual center line. In this position it should be possible to see straight through the telescope, the line of sight being the same as the path of light rays of a star when an observation is being made. If the telescope is out of alignment the observer will be unable to look straight through it (Figure 2216). Some sextants have adjusting screws on the telescope for adjusting the line of sight. In general this should be accomplished in an optical shop.

Telescope alignment

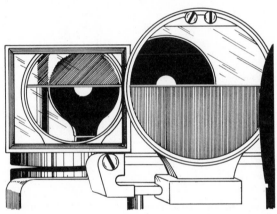

Figure 2216: Checking telescope alignment.

2217. The altitude of a celestial body, as measured with a marine sextant, is termed the *sextant altitude* (hs). It is the angle at the eye of the observer as measured on a vertical plane between the line of sight to the visible horizon, and the line of sight to the body. The *observed altitude* (Ho) of a celestial body is the hs corrected to read as though the altitude had been measured above the celestial horizon, at the earth's center, on a perpendicular plane passing through the observer's zenith and the body. The Ho is the altitude used in all celestial navigation. The significant corrections, and the order of their application to obtain Ho from hs are described in the following articles. In order that these corrections may be applied in the correct order, an intermediate between hs and Ho is sometimes used. This intermediate is the *apparent altitude* (ha); its use is discussed in article 2220.

Sextant altitude corrections.

Sextant altitude.

Observed altitude.

In addition to those listed in the following articles, other corrections are theoretically necessary in order to obtain Ho; however, they are so small (and in some cases so difficult to determine), that no appreciable error arises from omitting their use. These additional corrections are described in Bowditch, H. O. Pub. 9.

Non-adjustable
instrument error.

Instrument
correction

Index error.

Index correction.

Dip of the
horizon (D).

2218. Non-adjustable instrument error is the sum of the non-adjustable errors—prismatic, graduation, and centering—of a sextant (article 2213). The correction for these errors is called the *instrument* correction (I); it is determined by the manufacturer, and recorded on a certificate framed in the sextant box. It varies with the angle, may be either positive or negative, and is applied to all angles measured by that particular sextant.

2219. Index error is the residual error in a particular sextant, after the four adjustable errors have been corrected in so far as possible, as described in article 2214. It is primarily caused by a slight lack of parallelism between the index mirror and horizon glass, when the instrument is set at zero. It is compensated for by applying the *index correction* (IC).

The IC may be *positive* or *negative*, and is applied to *all* observations, whether celestial or geographic. When the IC is applied to the hs, the altitude is corrected to the value it would have, if the instrument had no index error. The IC is not fixed, and its value should be determined each time the sextant is used.

2220. Dip of the horizon is customarily referred to merely as "the dip." The D correction is required because of the height of the observer's eye above the level of the sea.

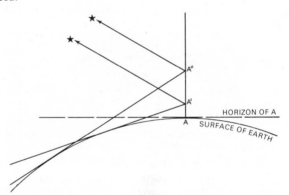

Figure 2220: Dip increases with height of observer above water.

Celestial altitudes obtained with the marine sextant are measured relative to the visible, or sea horizon. As the earth is a spheroid, the higher the observer is situated above the surface, the more depressed the visible horizon will be below the celestial horizon or true horizontal at his eye. Figure 2220 shows two observers, sharing a common zenith, but the observer at A" is situated considerably higher than the observer at A'; both are observing the same star, X. The observer's height of eye is greatly exaggerated in this figure, for illustrative purposes. It is obvious that the star's hs will be considerably larger for the observer at A", than for the one at A', and that the latter will have a larger hs than he would at the point A, on the water surface directly beneath him. The value of the dip may be defined as the excess over 90° of the angular distance from the observer's zenith to his visible horizon, as the reference plane for determining altitudes of celestial bodies is the observer's celestial horizon, which is perpendicular to his zenith. The D correction must be made for this excess. As the magnitude of the correction depends upon the observer's height above the water, it is sometimes called the "height of eye correction."

The value of the dip correction is somewhat decreased by atmospheric refraction between the observer and the horizon. Refraction causes the visible horizon to appear slightly higher than it would if the earth had no atmosphere. This refractive effect is not constant, but depends on atmospheric and sea conditions, chiefly on the difference between the temperature of the air at the observer's eye level, and that directly adjacent to the surface of the water. If the air is colder at the observer's level, the horizon tends to be depressed slightly; conversely, if it is warmer it tends to be slightly elevated (article 2227).

The *D* correction is always *negative*, and is applied to all celestial altitude observations. Its application to the hs corrects the latter to the value it would have if the visible horizon were a plane passing through the eye of the observer, and perpendicular to the line of his zenith.

For routine navigation purposes corrections to the sextant altitude can be applied in any order using the hs as entering argument in the various correction tables. Where great accuracy is desired however, or at low altitudes where small changes in altitude can result in significant changes in the correction, the order of applying the corrections is important. To obtain greater accuracy the three corrections so far discussed, for non-adjustable instrument error (I), index error (IC), and dip (D), are first applied to the hs. The hs so corrected is termed the *apparent altitude* (ha), and the value of ha is used in entering the tables to obtain corrections discussed in the following articles. For illustrative purposes in this chapter most of the corrections are shown as applied directly to hs. In Chapter 27 the forms for sight reduction currently used at the U. S. Naval Academy are illustrated, and the student will note that on these forms the apparent altitude, ha, is utilized.

Apparent altitude (ha).

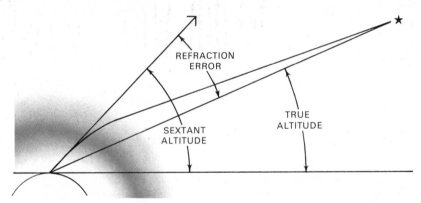

REFRACTION ERROR

TRUE ALTITUDE

SEXTANT ALTITUDE

Figure 2221: Atmospheric refraction causes bending of light rays.

2221. Refraction is caused by the bending of a light ray as it passes from a medium of one density into one of a different density. The increasingly dense layers of the earth's atmosphere cause the rays to be bent more and more downward in the vertical plane, as they approach the surface. Refraction, therefore, causes a heavenly body to appear higher than its actual position, as shown in Figure 2221, except when the body is at the observer's zenith. In such a case, the light rays are traveling vertically, and there is no refraction.

Refraction (R).

The lower a body is located in altitude, the more atmosphere its light rays will penetrate in reaching the observer, and the greater therefore will be the refraction. This effect reaches its maximum at the horizon; in fact, when the sun's lower limb appears to touch the visible horizon at sunset, its upper limb is actually below the horizon.

The refractive effect is not absolutely constant but varies slightly with the density of the atmosphere. This is discussed further in article 2222.

The *R* correction is always *negative*, and it is applied to all celestial altitude observations. Its application to the hs corrects the hs to the value it would have if the light rays from the body were not refracted by the earth's atmosphere.

Air temperature (T) and atmospheric pressure (B) corrections.

2222. The R correction varies slightly with the density of the atmosphere; this, in turn, depends upon the air temperature and atmospheric pressure. The refraction correction table given in the *Nautical Almanac* is based on a standard, or average atmospheric density, with a temperature of 50° Fahrenheit (10°C) and atmospheric pressure of 29.83 inches (1010 mb). An additional table of corrections is given in the *Almanac* to permit further correction for variations of temperature and pressure from the selected norms. The T and B corrections are ordinarily not required, except for low altitude observations, unless temperature and pressure vary materially from the standard values. All observations at altitudes of 10° or less should be corrected for temperature and barometric pressure.

The *combined T and B* correction may be *positive* or *negative*, and is applied to all celestial altitudes when conditions require it, in addition to the R correction. When applied to the hs, the sextant altitude is corrected to the value it would have under conditions of a standard atmospheric density.

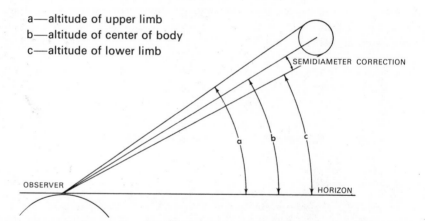

a—altitude of upper limb
b—altitude of center of body
c—altitude of lower limb

Figure 2223: Semidiameter correction for sun or moon.

Semidiameter (SD).

2223. The values of Greenwich Hour Angle and Declination tabulated in all almanacs are for the centers of the various celestial bodies. As an observer, using a marine sextant, cannot readily determine the center of the sun or moon, he measures the altitude of one of the limbs of these two bodies. The *semidiameter* (SD) is the angular distance between the limb of the sun or moon and the center as illustrated in Figure 2223. If a lower limb observation is made, the SD must be added to the hs to obtain the altitude of the center of the body; conversely, it is subtracted if the upper limb is observed.

The semidiameter varies with the distance of the body from the earth. The moon is comparatively near the earth and the changes in its distance as it revolves about the earth have a comparatively large effect on its SD. At certain times, the moon's SD may change significantly from day to day. The sun is much more distant and the eccentricity of the earth's orbit has a less pronounced effect on the sun's SD, which varies between about 15'.8 and 16'.3.

The *SD* correction is *positive* for a *lower limb* observation and *negative* for the upper limb. It is applied only to observations of the sun and moon when their altitudes are measured above the visible horizon. It is not applied to observations of stars or planets, as they have no significant apparent diameter when viewed through the telescopes normally used with sextants. When the SD is applied to the hs, the sextant altitude is corrected to the value it would have if the center of the body had been observed.

2224. The semidiameter of a body varies with its distance from the observer. When a body is on the observer's horizon, its distance from him is greater than when it is at the zenith, the difference in distance being equal to the earth's radius. As the earth's radius is so small, compared to the distance to the sun and planets, augmentation has no significant effect on sextant altitudes of these bodies. However, due to the comparative nearness of the moon, its augmentation from the observer's horizon to his zenith is about 0'.3 at mean lunar distance. Allowance for the moon's augmentation is made in the moon altitude correction tables given in the *Nautical Almanac.*

2225. *Irradiation* is the name applied to the optical illusion that causes the apparent size of a bright or light-colored object in juxtaposition with a darker one to appear larger than it actually is; conversely, the darker one appears smaller.

Some twenty years ago, the U. S. Naval Observatory decided to obtain an empirical check on the values of the refraction corrections for low altitude observations presently listed in the *Nautical Almanac.* Accordingly several hundred observations of the sun's lower and upper limbs at altitudes between 0° and 5° were made by a considerable number of observers. In analyzing these observations, it was found that the upper limb sights were consistently too high while no such error was evident in the lower limb observations. This was caused by the irradiation effect, which tended to increase the sun's apparent diameter, as seen against the sky. At the same time, irradiation tended to depress the horizon slightly, as the sky is usually brighter than the water. For upper limb sun sights, the two effects were therefore additive, whereas for the lower limb they tended to cancel one another.

The size of the error caused by irradiation varies with the magnification of the sextant telescope; the greater the magnification, the smaller the error. For telescopes having a magnification of three powers, the combined irradiation effect for upper limb observations was found to average (+) 1'.2, while for a six power telescope it averaged about half this amount.

It was assumed that the error caused by irradiation would remain constant for upper limb sun observations at all altitudes, and the "Altitude Correction Tables for the Sun" were accordingly prepared for use in the *Nautical Almanac,* incorporating corrections for mean refraction, average semidiameter for a six month period, parallax, and in the case of upper limb sights, for irradiation. The quantity 1'.2 was used for the latter correction, as the sextants in general use at that time were fitted with 3 × telescopes.

Within the past few years the British undertook a study of the irradiation effect on upper limb observations of the sun at normal working altitudes. An analysis of several thousand such observations showed the irradiation effect to average 0'.1. Concurrently, the effect of irradiation at altitudes below 10° was studied, and for these observations, the effect was found to average (+) 0'.8.

It was therefore decided to drop the sun altitude correction tables in their present form from the *Nautical Almanac*, after the 1969 edition.

The correction for irradiation to observations of the sun's upper limb is subtractive. Quantitatively, it decreases with increased telescope magnification, and with increased altitude.

Until the average value for irradiation corrections at various altitudes can be determined with some precision, its omission is recommended in correcting upper limb sun sights, except at altitudes below 10°, for which the values given in this article may be helpful.

Phase (F). **2226.** The planets go through phases which are quite similar to those of the moon. A planet's phase is not obvious to the naked eye, but a telescope does increase the phase effect, and affects the positioning of a planet on the horizon by the observer using a sextant. The phase correction is similar to the semidiameter correction for the sun and moon.

The phase correction (F) tabulated in the *Almanac* may be positive or negative. It is applied only to observations of Venus and Mars, as it is not significant for the other planets. When applied to hs, the sextant altitude is corrected to the value it would have if the center of the planet had been observed. A method of computing the phase and parallax correction for daylight observations of Venus is given in the *Nautical Almanac*.

Sea-air temperature difference correction (S). **2227.** In discussing the dip of the horizon, it was pointed out that refraction affected the value of the dip. The various dip correction tables allow for this refraction, the allowance being based on a standard rate of decrease of pressure and temperature in the atmosphere with increased height above the surface. However, when there is a difference between the sea water and the air temperature *at the water surface,* the air in contact with the sea is warmed or cooled by the water, and the normal rate of decrease is upset.

This may alter the value of the dip. If the water is warmer than the air, the horizon is depressed and the dip is increased, resulting in sextant altitudes that are too great. As a correction to the hs, the sea-air temperature difference correction is negative when the water is warmer than the air. Conversely, when the air is warmer, the reverse is true, and the correction is positive. It is seldom used in routine navigation.

In practice, the air temperature is measured at the observer's height of eye, and the water temperature is determined preferably from a sample picked up by dip bucket, or from the intake water temperature. This is usually the most convenient method of approximating the temperatures. Various values have been placed on the effect resulting from this difference of temperatures. The Japanese Hydrographic Office, by considerable empiric testing, found the value to be 0'.11 per degree Fahrenheit; other values, ranging up to 0'.21 per degree Fahrenheit have been suggested.

To date the U. S. Navy has not taken an official stand on the use of sea-air temperature difference corrections. When the Japanese value of 0'.11 was applied to several hundred observations made along the Atlantic coast between the Virgin Islands and New England throughout a year, it proved to be generally satisfactory and improved some 98 per cent of the observations.

2228. *Parallax* is the difference in the direction of an object at a finite distance when viewed simultaneously from two different positions. It enters into the sextant altitude corrections because hs is measured from the earth's surface, but Ho is calculated from the earth's center. Since the moon is the celestial body nearest the earth parallax has its greatest effect on lunar observations.   *Parallax (P).*

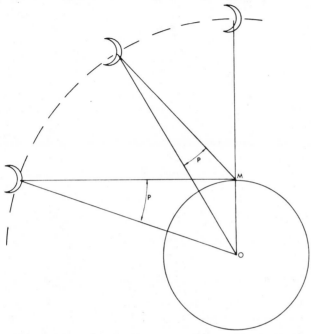

Figure 2228: Parallax correction varies with altitude of observed body.

The effect of parallax is illustrated in Figure 2228. If the moon is directly over-head, that is, with an altitude of 90°, there is no parallax, as its direction is the same at the center of the earth as for the observer. As the moon decreases in altitude its direction from the observer begins to differ with its direction from the earth's center, and the difference in direction increases continuously until the moon sets. The same effect, of course, occurs in reverse when a body is rising. Parallax ranges from zero for a body with an altitude of 90° to a maximum when the body is on the horizon, with 0° altitude. At altitude 0°, it is called horizontal parallax (HP).

In addition to increasing as altitude decreases, parallax increases as distance to a celestial body decreases. Venus and Mars, when close to the earth, are also appreciably affected by parallax. The sun is slightly affected, the parallax correction for the sun being (+)0'.1 from zero altitude to 65°. All other celestial bodies are too far from the earth to require correction for parallax when observed with the sextant.

The correction for parallax is always positive, and is applied only to observations of the moon, sun, Venus, and Mars. When it is applied to hs, the sextant altitude is corrected to the value it would have if the observer were at the center of the earth.

403

Summary of corrections.

2229. The foregoing sextant altitude corrections are summarized in Figure 2229. In the following section a description of the tables used to determine the corrections is given.

Figure 2229: Sextant corrections.

Correction	Symbol	Sign	Increases with	Bodies*	Sextants*	Source
Instrument	I	±	changing altitude	S, M, P, ☆	M, A	sextant box
Index	IC	±	constant	S, M, P, ☆	M, A	measurement
Personal	PC	±	constant	S, M, P, ☆	M, A	measurement
Dip	D	−	higher height of eye	S, M, P, ☆	M	almanacs
Sea-air temp. diff.	S	±	greater temp. diff.	S, M, P, ☆	M	computation
Refraction	R	−	lower altitude	S, M, P, ☆	M, A	almanacs
Air temp.	T	±	greater diff. from 50° F	S, M, P, ☆	M, A	almanacs, table 23 H.O. 9
Atmospheric pressure	B	±	greater diff. from 29.83 in. mercury	S, M, P, ☆	M, A	Nautical Almanac table 24 H.O. 9
Irradiation	J	−	constant	S	M, A	Nautical Almanac
Semidiameter	SD	±	lesser dist. from earth	S, M	M, A	almanacs
Phase	F	±	phase	P	M, A	Nautical Almanac
Augmentation	A	±	higher altitude	M	M, A	Nautical Almanac
Parallax	P	+	lower altitude	S, M, P	M, A	almanacs

*Bodies: S refers to sun, M to moon, P to planets, ☆ to stars.
*Sextants: M refers to Marine, A to artificial horizon.

Applying corrections from the Nautical Almanac.

2230. All observations made with the marine sextant must first be corrected for fixed or instrumental error (I), index error (IC) and Dip (D). The sextant altitude thus corrected is termed the *apparent or rectified altitude*, (ha). This apparent altitude is used as the argument for entering the appropriate correction tables described in the following articles.

Determining apparent altitude.

The I correction is obtained from the maker's certificate, furnished with the sextant. The IC should be determined each time the sextant is used, as described in article 2214. The correction for dip is found in a table on the inside front cover of the *Nautical Almanac*, as well as on the book mark. This table, shown in Figure 2230, is entered with the observer's height of eye above the water in feet; it is a *critical table* in that the tabulated value of dip is correct for any height of eye between those printed half a line above and half a line below. If the entering height of eye is an exact tabulated value, the correction half a line *above* it should be used.

Correcting observations of the sun.

2231. The *Nautical Almanac* gives critical tables for the correction of observations of the sun, as illustrated in Figure 2230. The corrections are tabulated separately for the lower (☉) and upper limb sun (☉̄) sights, and are in two columns, titled Oct.–Mar., and Apr.–Sept., to approximate the change in the sun's semidiameter throughout the year. These tables incorporate corrections for *refraction, semidiameter,* and *parallax;* in the case of the upper limb tables, an additional correction of (−)1'.2 for irradiation effect was included in the *Nautical Almanac* through 1969, but has been omitted from subsequent editions.

A2 ALTITUDE CORRECTION TABLES 10°–90°—SUN, STARS, PLANETS

OCT.–MAR.	SUN	APR.–SEPT.		STARS AND PLANETS			DIP					
App. Alt.	Lower Limb	Upper Limb	App. Alt.	Lower Limb	Upper Limb	App. Alt.	Corrⁿ	App. Alt.	Additional Corrⁿ	Ht. of Eye	Corrⁿ	Ht. of Eye	Corrⁿ	Ht. of Eye	Corrⁿ

OCT.–MAR. SUN App. Alt.	Lower Limb	Upper Limb	APR.–SEPT. App. Alt.	Lower Limb	Upper Limb	App. Alt.	Corrⁿ	App. Alt. Additional Corrⁿ	Ht. of Eye	Corrⁿ	Ht. of Eye	Corrⁿ	Ht. of Eye	Corrⁿ
9 34	+10·8	−22·7	9 39	+10·6	−22·4	9 56	−5·3	**1969**	m		ft.		m	
9 45	+10·9	−22·6	9 51	+10·7	−22·3	10 08	−5·2	**VENUS**	2·4	−2·8	8·0		1·0	−1·8
9 56	+11·0	−22·5	10 03	+10·8	−22·2	10 20	−5·1	Jan. 1–Feb. 1	2·6		8·6		1·5	−2·2
10 08	+11·1	−22·4	10 15	+10·9	−22·1	10 33	−5·0	0° +0′2	2·8	−2·9	9·2		2·0	−2·5
10 21	+11·2	−22·3	10 27	+11·0	−22·0	10 46	−4·9	47	3·0	−3·0	9·8		2·5	−2·8
10 34	+11·3	−22·2	10 40	+11·1	−21·9	11 00	−4·8	Feb. 2–Feb. 28	3·2	−3·1	10·5		3·0	−3·0
10 47	+11·4	−22·1	10 54	+11·2	−21·8	11 14	−4·7	0° +0′3	3·4	−3·2	11·2		See table	
11 01	+11·5	−22·0	11 08	+11·3	−21·7	11 29	−4·6	46	3·6	−3·3	11·9		←	
11 15	+11·6	−21·9	11 23	+11·4	−21·6	11 45	−4·5	Mar. 1–Mar. 17	3·8	−3·4	12·6			
11 30	+11·7	−21·8	11 38	+11·5	−21·5	12 01	−4·4	0° +0′4	4·0	−3·5	13·3		m	
11 46	+11·8	−21·7	11 54	+11·6	−21·4	12 18	−4·3	11 +0·5	4·3	−3·6	14·1		20	−7·9
12 02	+11·9	−21·6	12 10	+11·7	−21·3	12 35	−4·2	41	4·5	−3·7	14·9		22	−8·3
12 19	+12·0	−21·5	12 28	+11·8	−21·2	12 54	−4·1	Mar. 18–Mar. 25	4·7	−3·8	15·7		24	−8·6
12 37	+12·1	−21·4	12 46	+11·9	−21·1	13 13	−4·0	0° +0′5	5·0	−3·9	16·5		26	−9·0
12 55	+12·2	−21·3	13 05	+12·0	−21·0	13 33	−3·9	6 +0·6	5·2	−4·0	17·4		28	−9·3
13 14	+12·3	−21·2	13 24	+12·1	−20·9	13 54	−3·8	20 +0·7	5·5	−4·1	18·3			
13 35	+12·4	−21·1	13 45	+12·2	−20·8	14 16	−3·7	31	5·8	−4·2	19·1		30	−9·6
13 56	+12·5	−21·0	14 07	+12·3	−20·7	14 40	−3·6	Mar. 26–Apr. 22	6·1	−4·3	20·1		32	−10·0
14 18	+12·6	−20·9	14 30	+12·4	−20·6	15 04	−3·5	0° +0′6	6·3	−4·4	21·0		34	−10·3
14 42	+12·7	−20·8	14 54	+12·5	−20·5	15 30	−3·4	4 +0·7	6·6	−4·5	22·0		36	−10·6
15 06	+12·8	−20·7	15 19	+12·6	−20·4	15 57	−3·3	12 +0·8	6·9	−4·6	22·9		38	−10·8
15 32	+12·9	−20·6	15 46	+12·7	−20·3	16 26	−3·2	22	7·2	−4·7	23·9			
15 59	+13·0	−20·5	16 14	+12·8	−20·2	16 56	−3·1	Apr. 23–Apr. 30	7·5	−4·8	24·9		40	−11·1
16 28	+13·1	−20·4	16 44	+12·9	−20·1	17 28	−3·0	0° +0′5	7·9	−4·9	26·0		42	−11·4
16 59	+13·2	−20·3	17 15	+13·0	−20·0	18 02	−2·9	6 +0·6	8·2	−5·0	27·1		44	−11·7
17 32	+13·3	−20·2	17 48	+13·1	−19·9	18 38	−2·8	20 +0·7	8·5	−5·1	28·1		46	−11·9
18 06	+13·4	−20·1	18 24	+13·2	−19·8	19 17	−2·7	31	8·8	−5·2	29·2		48	−12·2
18 42	+13·5	−20·0	19 01	+13·3	−19·7	19 58	−2·6	May 1–May 16	9·2	−5·3	30·4			
19 21	+13·6	−19·9	19 42	+13·4	−19·6	20 42	−2·5	0° +0′4	9·5	−5·4	31·5		ft.	
20 03	+13·7	−19·8	20 25	+13·5	−19·5	21 28	−2·4	11 +0·5	9·9	−5·5	32·7		2	−1·4
20 48	+13·8	−19·7	21 11	+13·6	−19·4	22 19	−2·3	41	10·3	−5·6	33·9		4	−1·9
21 35	+13·9	−19·6	22 00	+13·7	−19·3	23 13	−2·2	May 17–June 29	10·6	−5·7	35·1		6	−2·4
22 26	+14·0	−19·5	22 54	+13·8	−19·2	24 11	−2·1	0° +0′3	11·0	−5·8	36·3		8	−2·7
23 22	+14·1	−19·4	23 51	+13·9	−19·1	25 14	−2·0	46	11·4	−5·9	37·6		10	−3·1
24 21	+14·2	−19·3	24 53	+14·0	−19·0	26 22	−1·9	June 30–Dec. 31	11·8	−6·0	38·9			
25 26	+14·3	−19·2	26 00	+14·1	−18·9	27 36	−1·8	0° +0′1	12·2	−6·1	40·1		See table	
26 36	+14·4	−19·1	27 13	+14·2	−18·8	28 56	−1·7	42	12·6	−6·2	41·5		←	
27 52	+14·5	−19·0	28 33	+14·3	−18·7	30 24	−1·6		13·0	−6·3	42·8		ft.	
29 15	+14·6	−18·9	30 00	+14·4	−18·6	32 00	−1·5	**MARS**	13·4	−6·4	44·2		70	−8·1
30 46	+14·7	−18·8	31 35	+14·5	−18·5	33 45	−1·4	Jan. 1–Mar. 14	13·8	−6·5	45·5		75	−8·4
32 26	+14·8	−18·7	33 20	+14·6	−18·4	35 40	−1·3	0° +0′1	14·2	−6·6	46·9		80	−8·7
34 17	+14·9	−18·6	35 17	+14·7	−18·3	37 48	−1·2	60	14·7	−6·7	48·4		85	−8·9
36 20	+15·0	−18·5	37 26	+14·8	−18·2	40 08	−1·1	Mar. 15–May 4	15·1	−6·8	49·8		90	−9·2
38 36	+15·1	−18·4	39 50	+14·9	−18·1	42 44	−1·0	0° +0′2	15·5	−6·9	51·3		95	−9·5
41 08	+15·2	−18·3	42 31	+15·0	−18·0	45 36	−0·9	41 +0·1	16·0	−7·0	52·8		100	−9·7
43 59	+15·3	−18·2	45 31	+15·1	−17·9	48 47	−0·8	75	16·5	−7·1	54·3		105	−9·9
47 10	+15·4	−18·1	48 55	+15·2	−17·8	52 18	−0·7	May 5–July 19	16·9	−7·2	55·8		110	−10·2
50 46	+15·5	−18·0	52 44	+15·3	−17·7	56 11	−0·6	0° +0′3	17·4	−7·3	57·4		115	−10·4
54 49	+15·6	−17·9	57 02	+15·4	−17·6	60 28	−0·5	34 +0·2	17·9	−7·4	58·9		120	−10·6
59 23	+15·7	−17·8	61 51	+15·5	−17·5	65 08	−0·4	60 +0·1	18·4	−7·5	60·5		125	−10·8
64 30	+15·8	−17·7	67 17	+15·6	−17·4	70 11	−0·3	80	18·8	−7·6	62·1			
70 12	+15·9	−17·6	73 16	+15·7	−17·3	75 34	−0·2	July 20–Oct. 3	19·3	−7·7	63·8		130	−11·1
76 26	+16·0	−17·5	79 43	+15·8	−17·2	81 13	−0·1	0° +0′2	19·8	−7·8	65·4		135	−11·3
83 05	+16·1	−17·4	86 32	+15·9	−17·1	87 03	0·0	41 +0·1	20·4	−7·9	67·1		140	−11·5
90 00			90 00			90 00		75	20·9	−8·0	68·8		145	−11·7
								Oct. 4–Dec. 31	21·4	−8·1	70·5		150	−11·9
								0° +0′1					155	−12·1
								60						

App. Alt. = Apparent altitude = Sextant altitude corrected for index error and dip.
For daylight observations of Venus, see page 260.

Figure 2230: Nautical Almanac *altitude correction tables for the sun, stars, and planets when at altitudes between approximately 10° and 90°.*

If the navigator wants maximum accuracy he may apply the corrections individually, using the actual value of the semi-diameter for the date, obtained from the bottom of the sun column in the daily pages of the Almanac. The small error that may arise due to using a mean value for the semi-diameter is thus avoided.

The steps to follow are:

Apply I, IC, and D corrections to obtain ha.

With the apparent altitude thus found, extract the R correction from the "Stars and Planets" correction table (Figure 2230).

Apply the SD correction obtained from the daily pages; this correction is positive for lower limb sights and negative for upper limb sights.

For altitudes below 65°, apply a positive correction of 0'.1 for parallax (P).

Example: A navigator observes the upper limb of the sun with a marine sextant on 26 April, from a height of eye of 48 feet. The sextant altitude is 51°58'.4 and 1 correction is (−)0'.2 and the instrument has an index error of 2'2 "off the arc." (Use standard corrections from page 698.)

Required: Ho at the time of the observation.

Solution: (1) Record I and IC. In this case they are (−)0'.2 and (+)2.2. (2) Enter the Nautical Almanac "Dip" table with height of eye and extract and record the D correction. In this case, it is (−)6.7. (3) Determine the net correction and apply to hs to obtain ha. (4) Using ha, in this instance 51°53'.7, enter table A-2 in the inside front cover of the Nautical Almanac—SUN, Apr–Sept, Upper limb. Extract the combined correction for refraction, parallax, and semidiameter. In this instance (−)16'.6. (5) Algebraically add this correction to hs to obtain Ho 51°37'.1.

	+	☉	−
I			0'.2
IC	2'.2		
D			6'.7
Sum	2'.2		6'.9
Corr.		−4.7	
hs		51°58'.4	
ha		51°53'.7	
A2			16'.6
Corr.		−16'.6	
Ho		51°37'.1	

Answer: Ho 51°37'.1.

Correcting star observations.

2232. In addition to the I, IC, and D corrections, star observations require only a correction for refraction, R. This is found in the appropriate table of the *Nautical Almanac,* headed "Stars and Planets."

Example: (Figure 2230) A navigator observes the star Zubenelgenubi with a marine sextant from a height of eye of 40 feet. The sextant altitude is 64°52'.7, and the instrument has an index error of 1'.7 "off the arc."

Required: Ho at the time of observation.

Solution: (1) Record the IC. In this case it is (+)1'.7. (2) Enter the *Nautical Almanac* "Dip" table with height of eye, and extract and record the D correction. In this case it is (−)6'.1. (3) Determine the net correction and apply to hs to obtain ha. (4) Using ha, in this instance 64°48′.3, enter table A2 in the *Nautical Almanac—Stars and Planets*. Extract the refraction correction, in this case (−)0′.5 and apply it algebraically to ha. Ho is found to be 64°47′.8.

Answer: Ho 64°47′.8.

	+	☆	−
IC	1′.7		
D			6′.1
Sum	1′.7		6′.1
Corr.		−4′.4	
hs		64°52′.7	
ha		64°48′.3	
A2 -P			0′.5
Corr.		−0′.5	
Ho		64°47′.8	

2233. The planets Jupiter and Saturn, due to their comparatively great distance from the earth, may be treated as stars in the ordinary practice of navigation.

Correcting observations of Jupiter and Saturn.

Example: A navigator observes the planet Jupiter with a marine sextant from a height of eye of 29 feet. The sextant altitude is 18°20′.2, and the instrument has an IC of (+)2′.2.

Required: Ho at the time of the observation.

Solution: (1) Record the IC. In this case, it is (+)2′.2. (2) Enter the "Dip" table with height of eye and extract and record the D correction. In this case, it is (−)5′.2. (3) Determine the net correction and apply it to hs to determine ha. (4) Using ha, in this case 18°17′.2, enter the Nautical Almanac —Table A2, Stars and Planets—extract the correction for refraction, in this instance (−) 2′.9. (5) Algebraically add this correction to ha to obtain Ho which is 18°14′.3.

	+ JUPITER	−
IC	2′.2	
D		5′.2
Sum	2′.2	5′.2
Corr.	−3′.0	
hs	18°20′.2	
ha	18°17′.2	
A2 -P		2′.9
Corr.	−2′.9	
Ho	18°14′.3	

Answer: Ho 18°14′.3.

2234. Observations of Venus and Mars, in addition to being corrected for I, IC, D, and R, should be corrected for phase and parallax for observations made during the period of twilight. These latter two corrections are combined, under the names of the planets, in the "Stars and Planets" correction table shown in Figure 2230.

Correcting observations of Venus and Mars.

Example: During morning twilight on 22 January 1969 a navigator observes the planet Venus with a marine sextant from a height of eye of 53 feet. The sextant altitude is 41°17′.6, and the instrument has an IC of (−)0′.5.

Required: Ho at the time of the observation.

Solution: (1) Record the IC. In this case, it is (−)0'.5. (2) Enter the "Dip" table with height of eye and extract and record the D correction. In this case, it is (−)7.1. (3) Determine the net correction and apply it to hs to obtain ha, in this case 41°10'.0. (4) Enter the Nautical Almanac Table A2—Stars and Planets—left-hand column and extract the refraction correction which is (+) 1'.1. (5) Enter the right-hand column of Stars and Planets and extract the additional correction. In this case (+)0'.2. (6) Determine the net correction to ha and apply it algebraically to determine Ho.

	+	VENUS	−
IC			0'.5
D			7'.1
Sum			7'.6
Corr.		−7'.0	
hs		41°17'.6	
ha		41°10'.0	
A2 -P			1'.1
P add'l	0'.2		
Sum	0'.2		1'.1
Corr.		−0'.9	
Ho		41°09'.1	

Answer: Ho 41°09'.1.

Venus is frequently observed in the daytime; for such observations the tabulated additional correction found in this table should *not* be used, as the magnitude and sign of the phase correction may differ from the tabulated value. If desired, for daylight observations of Venus, an additional correction may be derived from the formula given in the explanation section of the *Nautical Almanac*.

Correcting observations of the moon.

2235. The tables for correcting observations of the moon are found on the inside back cover and the facing page of the *Nautical Almanac*, as shown in Figure 2235. These tables combine the corrections for refraction, semidiameter, augmentation, and parallax.

To correct observations of the moon, the I, IC and D corrections are applied to the sextant altitude. The upper portion of the moon correction tables are then entered with the apparent altitude thus obtained, and the first correction is found under the appropriate altitude heading. The moon's H.P. (Horizontal Parallax) is next obtained from the daily pages of the Almanac for the time of the observation. H.P. is the entering argument to obtain the second correction from the lower portion of the tables. These tables are entered in the same vertical column as was used to obtain the first correction. Two values are listed in each column under the headings L. and U. for each tabulated value of H.P.; the L value is for observations of the moon's lower limb (☾), and the U for those of the upper limb (☾). The second correction is extracted under the appropriate heading. It should be noted that as H.P. is tabulated in increments of 0'.3, it is desirable to interpolate for non-tabulated values of H.P. in obtaining the second correction.

Both the first and second corrections are *added* to the apparent altitude of all moon observations, but for *observations of the upper limb, 30'.0 is to be subtracted from the sum of the corrections.*

Example: A navigator observes the lower limb of the moon with a marine sextant

ALTITUDE CORRECTION TABLES 35°–90°—MOON

App. Alt.	35°–39° Corrⁿ	40°–44° Corrⁿ	45°–49° Corrⁿ	50°–54° Corrⁿ	55°–59° Corrⁿ	60°–64° Corrⁿ	65°–69° Corrⁿ	70°–74° Corrⁿ	75°–79° Corrⁿ	80°–84° Corrⁿ	85°–89° Corrⁿ	App. Alt.
00	35 56·5	40 53·7	45 50·5	50 46·9	55 43·1	60 38·9	65 34·6	70 30·1	75 25·3	80 20·5	85 15·6	00
10	56·4	53·6	50·4	46·8	42·9	38·8	34·4	29·9	25·2	20·4	15·5	10
20	56·3	53·5	50·2	46·7	42·8	38·7	34·3	29·7	25·0	20·2	15·3	20
30	56·2	53·4	50·1	46·5	42·7	38·5	34·1	29·6	24·9	20·0	15·1	30
40	56·2	53·3	50·0	46·4	42·5	38·4	34·0	29·4	24·7	19·9	15·0	40
50	56·1	53·2	49·9	46·3	42·4	38·2	33·8	29·3	24·5	19·7	14·8	50
00	36 56·0	41 53·1	46 49·8	51 46·2	56 42·3	61 38·1	66 33·7	71 29·1	76 24·4	81 19·6	86 14·6	00
10	55·9	53·0	49·7	46·0	42·1	37·9	33·5	29·0	24·2	19·4	14·5	10
20	55·8	52·8	49·5	45·9	42·0	37·8	33·4	28·8	24·1	19·2	14·3	20
30	55·7	52·7	49·4	45·8	41·8	37·7	33·2	28·7	23·9	19·1	14·1	30
40	55·6	52·6	49·3	45·7	41·7	37·5	33·1	28·5	23·8	18·9	14·0	40
50	55·5	52·5	49·2	45·5	41·6	37·4	32·9	28·3	23·6	18·7	13·8	50

H.P.	L U	L U	L U	L U	L U	L U	L U	L U	L U	L U	L U	H.P.
57·0	4·3 3·2	4·3 3·3	4·3 3·3	4·4 3·4	4·4 3·4	4·5 3·5	4·5 3·5	4·6 3·6	4·7 3·6	4·7 3·7	4·8 3·8	57·0
57·3	4·6 3·4	4·6 3·4	4·6 3·5	4·7 3·5	4·7 3·5	4·7 3·6	4·8 3·6	4·8 3·6	4·8 3·7	4·9 3·7		57·3
57·6	4·9 3·6	4·9 3·6	4·9 3·6	4·9 3·6	4·9 3·6	4·9 3·6	4·9 3·6	5·0 3·6	5·0 3·6	5·0 3·6		57·6
57·9	5·2 3·7	5·2 3·7	5·2 3·7	5·2 3·7	5·2 3·7	5·1 3·6	5·1 3·6	5·1 3·6	5·1 3·6	5·1 3·6	5·1 3·6	57·9
58·2	5·5 3·9	5·5 3·8	5·5 3·8	5·4 3·8	5·4 3·7	5·4 3·7	5·3 3·7	5·3 3·6	5·2 3·6	5·2 3·5	5·2 3·5	58·2

Figure 2235: Moon correction tables.

from a height of eye of 25 feet. The sextant altitude is 56°39′.7, and the instrument has no index error. The H.P. is 57′.6.

Required: Ho at the time of the observation.

Solution: (1) Record the IC. In this case there is no IC. (2) Enter the *Nautical Almanac* "Dip" table with height of eye, and extract and record the D correction. In this case it is (−)4′.9. (3) Apply the D correction to hs to obtain ha of 56°34′.8. (4) Enter the upper portion of the *Nautical Almanac* "moon" tables with ha and extract and record the first correction. In this case it is (+)41′.8. (5) Follow down the altitude column used in (4) above, and extract and record from the lower portion of the "moon" table the L correction for the HP found on the daily page. In this case HP is 57′.6 and L is (+)4′.9. (6) Determine the sums of the positive and negative corrections separately, and apply the algebraic sum as a correction to ha to obtain Ho.

	+ MOON −	
H.P.☾	57′.6	
IC	0	
Dip (Ht 25′)		4′.9
hs	56°39′.7	
ha	56°34′.8	
First Corr.	41′.8	
L/U☾	4′.9	
add'l ♀ ♂		
TB (ha<10°)		
sum	+46′.7	0−
corr.	+	46.7
ha	56°34.8	
Ho	57°21.5	

Answer: Ho 57°21′.5.

2236. The refraction corrections included in the various altitude corrections tables in the *Nautical Almanac* are based on an air temperature of 50°F (10°C), and an atmospheric pressure of 29.83 inches (1010 millibars) of mercury. When atmospheric conditions vary from these standard values, the light from celestial bodies is refracted to a greater or lesser value than is stated in the tables.

Correcting for non-standard refraction.

A table of additional corrections for non-standard conditions of refraction is given in the *Nautical Almanac,* and is reproduced in Figure 2236. It is entered at the top with the temperature and a line is projected down vertically until it intersects with a horizontal line drawn in from the appropriate point on the

409

Figure 2236:

ALTITUDE CORRECTION TABLES—ADDITIONAL CORRECTIONS

ADDITIONAL REFRACTION CORRECTIONS FOR NON-STANDARD CONDITIONS

The graph is entered with arguments temperature and pressure to find a zone letter; using as arguments this zone letter and apparent altitude (sextant altitude corrected for dip), a correction is taken from the table. This correction is to be applied to the sextant altitude in addition to the corrections for standard conditions (for the sun, planets and stars from the inside front cover and for the moon from the inside back cover).

Temperature

−20°F. −10° 0° +10° 20° 30° 40° 50° 60° 70° 80° 90° 100°F.
−30°C. −20° −10° 0° +10° 20° 30° 40°C.

Pressure in millibars: 1050, 1030, 1010, 990, 970
Pressure in inches: 31.0, 30.5, 30.0, 29.5, 29.0

Zones: A B C D E F G H J K L M N

App. Alt.	A	B	C	D	E	F	G	H	J	K	L	M	N	App. Alt.
0 00	−6·9	−5·7	−4·6	−3·4	−2·3	−1·1	0·0	+1·1	+2·3	+3·4	+4·6	+5·7	+6·9	0 00
0 30	5·2	4·4	3·5	2·6	1·7	0·9	0·0	0·9	1·7	2·6	3·5	4·4	5·2	0 30
1 00	4·3	3·5	2·8	2·1	1·4	0·7	0·0	0·7	1·4	2·1	2·8	3·5	4·3	1 00
1 30	3·5	2·9	2·4	1·8	1·2	0·6	0·0	0·6	1·2	1·8	2·4	2·9	3·5	1 30
2 00	3·0	2·5	2·0	1·5	1·0	0·5	0·0	0·5	1·0	1·5	2·0	2·5	3·0	2 00
2 30	−2·5	−2·1	−1·6	−1·2	−0·8	−0·4	0·0	+0·4	+0·8	+1·2	+1·6	+2·1	+2·5	2 30
3 00	2·2	1·8	1·5	1·1	0·7	0·4	0·0	0·4	0·7	1·1	1·5	1·8	2·2	3 00
3 30	2·0	1·6	1·3	1·0	0·7	0·3	0·0	0·3	0·7	1·0	1·3	1·6	2·0	3 30
4 00	1·8	1·5	1·2	0·9	0·6	0·3	0·0	0·3	0·6	0·9	1·2	1·5	1·8	4 00
4 30	1·6	1·4	1·1	0·8	0·5	0·3	0·0	0·3	0·5	0·8	1·1	1·4	1·6	4 30
5 00	−1·5	−1·3	−1·0	−0·8	−0·5	−0·2	0·0	+0·2	+0·5	+0·8	+1·0	+1·3	+1·5	5 00
6	1·3	1·1	0·9	0·6	0·4	0·2	0·0	0·2	0·4	0·6	0·9	1·1	1·3	6
7	1·1	0·9	0·7	0·6	0·4	0·2	0·0	0·2	0·4	0·6	0·7	0·9	1·1	7
8	1·0	0·8	0·7	0·5	0·3	0·2	0·0	0·2	0·3	0·5	0·7	0·8	1·0	8
9	0·9	0·7	0·6	0·4	0·3	0·1	0·0	0·1	0·3	0·4	0·6	0·7	0·9	9
10 00	−0·8	−0·7	−0·5	−0·4	−0·3	−0·1	0·0	+0·1	+0·3	+0·4	+0·5	+0·7	+0·8	10 00
12	0·7	0·6	0·5	0·3	0·2	0·1	0·0	0·1	0·2	0·3	0·5	0·6	0·7	12
14	0·6	0·5	0·4	0·3	0·2	0·1	0·0	0·1	0·2	0·3	0·4	0·5	0·6	14
16	0·5	0·4	0·3	0·3	0·2	0·1	0·0	0·1	0·2	0·3	0·3	0·4	0·5	16
18	0·4	0·4	0·3	0·2	0·2	0·1	0·0	0·1	0·2	0·2	0·3	0·4	0·4	18
20 00	−0·4	−0·3	−0·3	−0·2	−0·1	−0·1	0·0	+0·1	+0·1	+0·2	+0·3	+0·3	+0·4	20 00
25	0·3	0·3	0·2	0·2	0·1	−0·1	0·0	+0·1	0·1	0·2	0·2	0·3	0·3	25
30	0·3	0·2	0·2	0·1	0·1	0·0	0·0	0·0	0·1	0·1	0·2	0·2	0·3	30
35	0·2	0·2	0·1	0·1	0·1	−0·1	0·0	0·0	0·1	0·1	0·1	0·2	0·2	35
40	0·2	0·1	0·1	0·1	−0·1	0·0	0·0	0·0	+0·1	0·1	0·1	0·1	0·2	40
50 00	−0·1	−0·1	−0·1	−0·1	0·0	0·0	0·0	0·0	0·0	+0·1	+0·1	+0·1	+0·1	50 00

pressure scale. The intersection of these two lines will fall within one of the diagonal lettered zones; the name of this letter establishes the vertical correction column to be used. Using the apparent altitude as the entering argument, the additional refraction correction is then found.

Ordinarily, except under extreme conditions, it is not necessary to use this table for altitudes above about 10°. However, due to the extremely rapid change in the value of the refraction at very low altitudes, it is desirable that this table be used for correcting such observations. Interpolation may be desirable at extremely low altitudes.

CHAPTER 23

Time

2301. This chapter will discuss the concept of time, and the manner in which the navigator uses time as a factor in his daily work, particularly in determining the coordinates of celestial bodies. It might well be said that all navigation is based on time.

2302. Most forms of time are based on the rotation of the earth, as referred to various celestial bodies. Due to the different rates of motion (article 1909) these various forms of time may differ in the lengths of their standard unit, the *day*, which represents one rotation of the earth relative to the reference body.

The sun is the reference body most commonly used by man, and which continues as the one chiefly used by the navigator; the period of the earth's rotation relative to the sun is called the *solar day*. The solar year is based on the period of the earth's revolution about the sun, which requires approximately 365¼ days. The *common year* is 365 days in length. In years exactly divisible by four, such as 1968 and 1972, and known as *leap years*, an additional day—February 29—is usually inserted to adjust the calendar to the actual period of revolution. As the fraction in this period is not exactly ¼ of a day—it is some 11 minutes 14 seconds less—years ending in two zeros (1900, 2100) are not leap years, unless they are exactly divisible by 400 as in the years 2000 and 2400.

The *month* is an irregular unit of time derived from the moon's period of revolution about the earth.

2303. As stated in article 2302, the sun has been the chief body by which man has controlled his life, since prehistoric times. He used *apparent solar time*, which he read from his sundial, as his criterion. Unfortunately, the apparent rotation of the sun around the earth, actually caused by the rotation of the earth on its axis, is not a constant speed (article 1913); as a result, the length of the apparent day varies throughout the year. This variation is caused primarily by the fact that the axis of the earth's rotation is tilted in respect to its plane of rotation around the sun (Figure 2303), causing the apparent path of the sun to be along the ecliptic.

This irregularity introduced numerous difficulties in an advancing civilization, and led to the introduction of "mean solar time."

2304. To overcome the difficulties introduced by the non-uniform rate of apparent solar time, *mean solar time* was invented. This is based on an imaginary sun, termed the *mean sun*, which has an hour circle moving westward along the celestial equator at a constant rate. Mean solar time is nearly equal to the average apparent solar time; it is the time kept by ship's chronometers and the

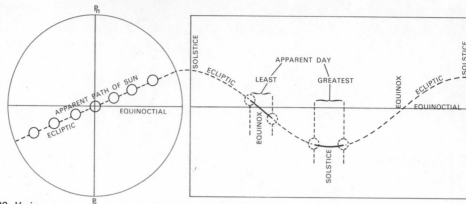

Figure 2303: Variation in length of apparent day due to obliquity of ecliptic.

Figure 2304: Relationship of mean time to solar time.

great majority of timepieces, and is also the argument used in almanacs in tabulating the coordinates of celestial bodies (Figure 2304).

The difference in length between the apparent and the mean day is never as great as a minute, but it is cumulative, and amounts to approximately a quarter hour at certain times of the year.

Equation of Time.

The difference between mean and apparent time at any instant is called the *equation of time*. Although it is tabulated in the *Nautical Almanac*, it is of little direct use in modern navigation, except in the determining of the time of local apparent noon.

Notation of time in navigation.

2305. The navigator states time on the basis of a 24-hour rather than on a 12-hour timepiece; this removes the danger of confusing "AM" and "PM" time. Also, he customarily works to the nearest second of time. To simplify handling and writing, hours, minutes, and seconds are expressed in that order, and are separated by dashes. Thus, a clock time of 10 hours, 57 minutes and 17 seconds P.M. is written 22-57-17. If the number of hours, minutes, or seconds is less than 10, a "0" is placed in front of each so that the hour, minutes, and seconds are each expressed by two digits; a time of 4 hours, 9 minutes, and 7 seconds A.M. is written as 04-09-07. Since the connotation of hours, minutes, and seconds is understood, no further labeling is required.

Upper and lower transit.

2306. Transit signifies the instant a celestial body crosses or transits a given meridian. A meridian on the earth is a great circle, passing through the earth's geographical poles, and any given position.

The passage of a celestial body across the upper branch of the observer's meridian is called *upper transit;* in Figure 2306, the sun at M is shown at upper transit. Depending on the observer's latitude and the body's declination, at this instant the body is either due north, due south, or directly overhead of the observer. The passage of a celestial body across the lower branch of an observer's meridian is called *lower transit;* in Figure 2306, the sun is also shown at lower transit, at m. At this instant, the body will be either directly to his north, or south, or directly below him, again depending on his latitude and the body's declination. Bodies visible at the observer's position will be above the horizon at upper transit; the majority will be below the horizon at lower transit. Circumpolar stars may be above the horizon for both upper and lower transit for an observer who is not at the equator (article 1912).

At all times, that hemisphere of the earth facing the sun is in sunlight, and the other is in darkness. The sun will be in upper transit on the central meridian of the half that is in sunlight, and it will be *midday* at that meridian; on the lower branch of the same meridian the sun will be in lower transit; at that instant it will be *midnight*. Lower transit of the mean sun simultaneously marks the end of one day (24-00-00), and the beginning of the next (00-00-00). For the observer at M in Figure 2306, this occurs when the mean sun is at *m*.

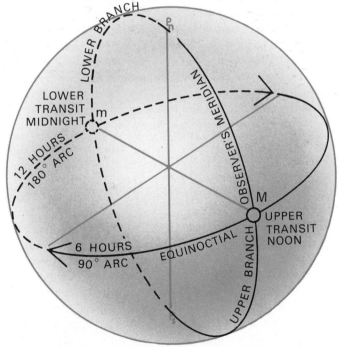

Figure 2306: Upper and lower transit.

As the mean sun is considered to complete a revolution of 360° of arc about the earth in exactly 24 hours, it is evident that in one hour it will have traveled through 15°. In 6 hours it will have traveled through 90°, etc. Thus, there is a definite relationship between time and longitude; this will be discussed in article 2308. The transits of celestial bodies and the resultant time-arc relationships are, for navigational purposes, generally sketched on a time diagram rather than schematically as in Figure 2306. The use of a time diagram will be taken up in the following article.

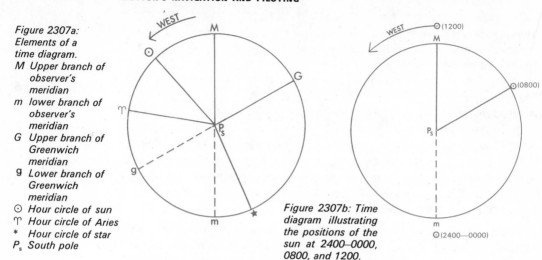

Figure 2307a:
Elements of a
time diagram.
M Upper branch of
    observer's
    meridian
m lower branch of
    observer's
    meridian
G Upper branch of
    Greenwich
    meridian
g Lower branch of
    Greenwich
    meridian
⊙ Hour circle of sun
♈ Hour circle of Aries
* Hour circle of star
P_s South pole

Figure 2307b: Time
diagram illustrating
the positions of the
sun at 2400–0000,
0800, and 1200.

Time diagrams.

2307. The *time diagram* is a most useful aid in visualizing any time and date problem, and the student should be thoroughly familiar with the preparation of such a diagram.

Essentially, it is a simple sketch showing the relative positions of the meridians and hour circles involved in a particular problem. It consists of a circle representing the equator, straight lines from the center to the circumference, representing the meridians and hour circles of the problem, and appropriate labels. In drawing a time diagram, the earth is always considered to be viewed from a point in space beyond the south pole. *East* is in a *clockwise*, and *west* in a *counterclockwise* direction; all celestial bodies are therefore considered to revolve in a counterclockwise direction about the circle. All time problems in this text are illustrated with the use of a time diagram prepared in this manner. The basic elements of the time diagram are shown in Figure 2307a.

By convention, the observer's meridian is always drawn vertically, with the upper branch, *M*, shown as a solid line extending upward from the center. The lower branch, *m*, is shown as a broken line, extended downwards. In problems in which it is necessary to distinguish between local mean time and zone time (article 2318), the *M-m* line represents the observer's meridian, and a *Z-z* line represents the central meridian of his time zone, and these meridians will be quite close together. However, local mean time is involved in only a comparatively small percentage of problems. In the majority of cases the central meridian of the zone is omitted. The approximate zone time (ZT) at *M* is shown by drawing in the hour circle of the sun (⊙) for the time in question. As shown in Figure 2307b, for an observer on the meridian *M-m*, the sun's 2400-0000 hour circle coincides with *m*, at 0800 it is 120° west or counterclockwise from *m*, and at 1200 it coincides with *M*, as it has moved through 180°.

The time diagram may be thought of as the face of a 24-hour clock, with *m* representing ZT 2400-0000, while *M* represents 1200, and the hour circles of the sun and other celestial bodies moving in a counterclockwise direction.

Time and longitude.

2308. The mean sun circles the earth's 360° of longitude in 24 hours, moving from east to west. In *one hour*, it passes over $\frac{1}{24}$ of the earth's meridians, or 15°. In *one minute* it covers $\frac{1}{60}$ of 15°, or 15 minutes of arc; in *four seconds* of time it covers one minute of arc, and in *one second*, it covers 0'.25 of arc.

The time-arc relationship may be summarized in tabular form.

Time	Arc
24 hours	360°
1 hour	15°
1 minute	15'
4 seconds	1'
1 second	0'.25

Due to the mean sun's motion from east to west, it is always *later* by local mean time at places to the observer's *east*, and *earlier* at those to his *west*.

The relationship between time and longitude can be used to determine the difference in local mean time between places in different longitudes. Consider a ship in the Mediterranean at longitude 19°58'.0 E, the U. S. Naval Observatory, Washington, D. C., at longitude 77°04'.0 W, and a lighthouse at Pt. Loma, California, at longitude 117°15'.0 W. These meridians are shown in Figure 2308a, which again depicts the earth on a time diagram. West, the direction of the sun's motion, is in a counterclockwise direction. Ps-G represents the meridian of Greenwich, Ps-S that of the ship, Ps-N that of the Naval Observatory, and Ps-L that of the lighthouse. The difference in longitude between the ship and the observatory is 97°02'.0, since 19°58'.0 E + 77°04'.0 W = 97°02'.0, and the difference between the observatory and the lighthouse is 40°11'.0, since 117°15'.0 W − 77°04'.0 W = 40°11'.0. Converting these differences in longitude to time, we find that the difference in local time between the ship and the observatory is 6 hours, 28 minutes, and 08 seconds, and the difference between the observatory and the lighthouse is 2 hours, 40 minutes, and 44 seconds. Due to the sun's westerly motion, it is always later at the ship than at the other two positions. For example, when the local mean time at the observatory is 12-00-00, as shown by the sun over the meridian Ps-N in Figure 2308a, the local mean time at S is 18-28-08, and that at L is 09-19-16. If subtracting a time difference results in a change of date, it is convenient to add 24 hours to the numerically smaller time in making the computation. For example, if the local mean time at the observatory were 01-00-00, that at the lighthouse would be 22-19-16 the *preceding* day, since 01-00-00 minus 02-40-44 = 25-00-00 minus 02-40-44, or 22-19-16.

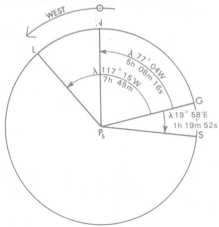

Figure 2308a: The difference in time between places is equal to their differences of longitude, converted to time units.

415

0°–59°		60°–119°		120°–179°		180°–239°		240°–299°		300°–359°			0'·00	0'·25	0'·50	0'·75
°	h m	°	h m	°	h m	°	h m	°	h m	°	h m	'	m s	m s	m s	m s
0	0 00	60	4 00	120	8 00	180	12 00	240	16 00	300	20 00	0	0 00	0 01	0 02	0 03
1	0 04	61	4 04	121	8 04	181	12 04	241	16 04	301	20 04	1	0 04	0 05	0 06	0 07
2	0 08	62	4 08	122	8 08	182	12 08	242	16 08	302	20 08	2	0 08	0 09	0 10	0 11
3	0 12	63	4 12	123	8 12	183	12 12	243	16 12	303	20 12	3	0 12	0 13	0 14	0 15
4	0 16	64	4 16	124	8 16	184	12 16	244	16 16	304	20 16	4	0 16	0 17	0 18	0 19
5	0 20	65	4 20	125	8 20	185	12 20	245	16 20	305	20 20	5	0 20	0 21	0 22	0 23
6	0 24	66	4 24	126	8 24	186	12 24	246	16 24	306	20 24	6	0 24	0 25	0 26	0 27
7	0 28	67	4 28	127	8 28	187	12 28	247	16 28	307	20 28	7	0 28	0 29	0 30	0 31
8	0 32	68	4 32	128	8 32	188	12 32	248	16 32	308	20 32	8	0 32	0 33	0 34	0 35
9	0 36	69	4 36	129	8 36	189	12 36	249	16 36	309	20 36	9	0 36	0 37	0 38	0 39
10	0 40	70	4 40	130	8 40	190	12 40	250	16 40	310	20 40	10	0 40	0 41	0 42	0 43
11	0 44	71	4 44	131	8 44	191	12 44	251	16 44	311	20 44	11	0 44	0 45	0 46	0 47
12	0 48	72	4 48	132	8 48	192	12 48	252	16 48	312	20 48	12	0 48	0 49	0 50	0 51
13	0 52	73	4 52	133	8 52	193	12 52	253	16 52	313	20 52	13	0 52	0 53	0 54	0 55
14	0 56	74	4 56	134	8 56	194	12 56	254	16 56	314	20 56	14	0 56	0 57	0 58	0 59

Figure 2308b: Extract from the "Conversion of Arc to Time" table in the Nautical Almanac.

In the interconversion of time and arc, the navigator is aided by a conversion table published in the *Nautical Almanac*, an extract of which is shown in Figure 2308b.

Greenwich Mean Time (GMT).

2309. *Greenwich Mean Time* (GMT) is mean solar time measured with reference to the meridian of Greenwich. The mean sun transits the lower branch of the meridian of Greenwich at GMT 24-00-00—00-00-00 each day, and the upper branch at GMT 12-00-00. GMT, which is sometimes called *Universal Time* (UT), is of the utmost importance to the navigator, as it is the time used in almanacs as the argument for tabulating the coordinates of all celestial bodies. The choice of the meridian of Greenwich as the reference meridian for time is logical, as it is also the reference meridian used in reckoning longitude.

Local mean time (LMT).

2310. Just as Greenwich Mean Time is mean solar time measured with reference to the meridian of Greenwich, so *local mean time* (LMT) is mean solar time measured with reference to a given local meridian; this is the kind of time discussed in article 2308.

Local mean time was the standard generally used after the introduction of time based on a mean sun, and every city kept time based on the mean sun's transit of its meridian. As a result, a number of different time standards were used in a comparatively small geographic area. The rapid improvement in transportation and communications rendered local mean time completely unsatisfactory, and led to the introduction of zone time.

Zone time (ZT).

2311. The introduction of *zone time* served to straighten out the confusion caused by the multiplicity of different local mean times in a given area. In zone time, all the places in a given zone, or band of longitude, keep the same time, based on the local mean time of a single specified meridian, frequently the central meridian of the zone. Timepieces are reset only when moving into an adjoining time zone; they are advanced an hour if travel is to the east, and retarded an hour if to the west.

As a general rule, these zones are laid out so that they are not excessively wide; therefore at no given place in the zone will the ZT vary greatly from the LMT, and the time will be in reasonably good agreement with the motions of the sun. At sea, the zones are usually bands of longitude 15° in width.

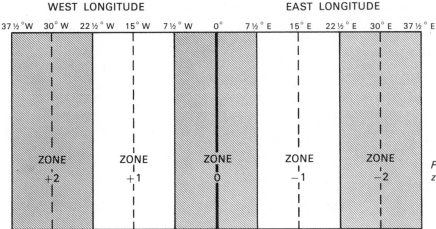

WEST LONGITUDE   EAST LONGITUDE

| 37½°W | 30° W | 22½°W | 15° W | 7½°W | 0° | 7½°E | 15° E | 22½°E | 30° E | 37½°E |

ZONE +2   ZONE +1   ZONE 0   ZONE −1   ZONE −2

Figure 2312a: Time zone boundaries.

2312. In general at sea the central meridians selected for time zones are longitudes which are exact multiples of 15°. There are 24 of these central or "standard" meridians, each one hour apart, and the longitude boundaries of each zone are 7½° on each side of the zone's standard meridian, as shown in Figure 2312a.

Zone description (ZD).

The *zone description* (ZD) of a zone is the correction to be applied to the time of that zone to obtain GMT. For example, between longitudes 7½° east and 7½° west, the ZD is zero, and GMT will be used throughout the zone. In the zone bordered by longitudes 7°30′ E and 22°30′ E, the standard meridian is λ 15° E. ZT in this zone will differ from GMT by one hour, and the zone being *east* of the meridian of Greenwich, it will be one hour *later*. One hour is *subtracted* from ZT to obtain GMT, and the ZD is (−1). Similarly, in the zone bordered by longitudes 7°30′ W and 22°30′ W, the ZT differs from GMT by one hour. But as this zone is *west* of Greenwich, it is one hour earlier, and the ZD is (+1), as one hour must be added to obtain GMT.

This procedure for determining the sign of time corrections for various zones is valid for any longitude; the sign of the ZD of any zone in *east* longitude is *minus*, and that of the ZD of any zone in *west* longitude is *plus*. The numerical value of the correction for a zone can be determined by dividing the longitude of its standard meridian by 15°. Thus, the zone having λ 135° W as its standard meridian will have a ZD of (+9), the zone having λ 75° E as its standard meridian will have a ZD description of (−5).

The ZD at a given position can be similarly determined. The longitude of the place is divided by 15°, and the whole number of the quotient is determined. If the remainder is less than 7°30′, the whole number quotient establishes the numerical value of the ZD; if it is greater than 7°30′, the numerical value of the ZD is one more than the whole number of the quotient. Thus, in λ 37°25′.4 W, the ZD will be (+2), while in λ 37°43.6′ W, the ZD will be (+3).

Time zone plotter.

In Figure 2312b the time zones are illustrated on the Time Zone Plotter (FSN 6605-967-8973). On this plotter, which could more appropriately be described as a computer, the time zones, and their variations, which will be described in article 2314 are shown for both hemispheres. U. S. Naval Oceanographic Office Chart #5192 also portrays this information on a Mercator chart of the world.

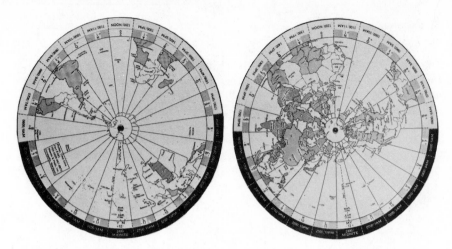

Figure 2312b:
Time zone plotter.

It will be noted that the 15° wide zone centered on the 180th meridian is divided into two parts. The half in east longitude has a ZD of (−12), and that in west longitude has a ZD of (+12). This division of the zone having the 180th meridian as its standard is necessitated by the convention of the international date line, discussed in article 2315.

The letter designations shown in each time zone in Figure 2312b are those used by the Navy in communications and operational planning for identification of the ZT maintained in the various zones. GMT, which is zone time at Greenwich, is designated *Z* time. Zones to the east of Greenwich are designated alphabetically in order of increasing east longitude, commencing with *A*, and ending with *M*; the letter *J* is not used. Zones to the west of Greenwich are similarly designated, commencing with *N*, and ending with *Y* for the zone with ZD (+12). The use of these designations is discussed more fully in article 2313.

Recording time and date in the Navy.

2313. In article 2305, the notation of time on a 24-hour basis in *navigation* was described, and it was stated that the navigator customarily worked and noted time to the nearest second; 23 hours, 14 minutes, and 21 seconds being written as 23-14-21.

A similar system of time notation is used throughout the Navy, except that for *general use* it is sufficient to state time to the nearest minute. Time is expressed by means of a four-digit system, the first two representing hours, from 00 to 24, and the last two minutes, from 00 to 59.

Hours and minutes less than ten are preceded by a zero, to maintain the four-digit system. Thus, 9:30 AM is written 0930, and 4:37 PM becomes 1637. When spoken, the former would be "oh-nine-thirty," and the latter "sixteen-thirty-seven." It is incorrect to add "hours" to the expression, as in "sixteen hundred hours." Even hours are "oh-five-hundred," "oh-nine-hundred," etc.

Because routine activities aboard naval vessels and at shore establishments are usually based on the zone time being used, it is necessary to specify the basis of the time used in naval communications. As discussed briefly in article 2312, and illustrated in Figure 2312b, the various time zones have each been given a letter designator, corresponding to the ZD. In naval communications this letter designator is added at the end of the four-digit time group, to designate the proper time-reference. Thus, a ship operating on the east coast of the United

States, and keeping ZD (+5) time, might report the occurrence of some incident at 1715 R, R being the designator for ZD (+5).

The most commonly used time zone indicator in naval communication is "Z," the designator for the Greenwich time zone. In designating or reporting events which require coordination in more than one time zone, it is general practice to reduce all times to GMT, and so indicate by suffixing the time zone indicator for "Z."

With the use of the Time Zone Plotter one can easily determine the time at any other location in the world. The time zone diagram is pivoted to rotate over the base of the instrument which contains a 24-hour time scale. Example: With the instrument set as in Fig. 2312b, it is 0700 in Washington, D. C., Zone (+5). In Kodiak, Alaska, it is 0200, Zone (+10). In Tokyo it is 2100 the following day (article 2315). If a message were received from a vessel near Kodiak with the designation 0200 W it is therefore easy to convert this to time at any other location, by reading time on the base plate opposite time zone description on the movable dial.

It is also frequently desirable in communications to indicate the date as well as time. This is accomplished by prefixing the time group, with its letter designator, by two digits which indicate the date of the current month. Thus, "121725 Z" would indicate a date/time of GMT 1725 on the 12th of the current month. If a month other than the current one is to be described, the date/time group with the appropriate designator is used, and the name of the desired month is added as a suffix. If a year other than the current one is to be indicated, it is indicated after the month.

2314. Zone time, based upon 15° bands of longitude, is a convenience at sea, but it could lead to complications ashore. For example, a city might lie astride the dividing line between zones.

Variations in zone description, standard and daylight saving time.

To avoid such inconvenience, territorial groups often keep zone times which do not agree with the standard system discussed above, and the boundaries between zones are quite irregular. The form of zone time which does not conform to the usual 15° rule is called *standard time.* Across the United States it is further designated as Eastern, Central, Mountain, and Pacific standard time, the standard meridians of these regions being the 75th, 90th, 105th, and 120th of west longitude, respectively. Similarly, a country which overlaps into two or three time zones may choose to keep one single ZT throughout its territory, thus eliminating any time difference problem within the country (Figure 2312b).

Some places, for convenience, maintain a standard time which results in a ZD which is not a whole hour. The *Nautical Almanac*, under the heading "Standard Times," tabulates the ZD in use in many areas of the world. However, the use of daylight saving time may at times affect the given ZD values.

Daylight saving time (DST), also called *summer* time, is another variation of zone time. Due to the early rising of the sun in summer, a certain amount of daylight would be lost to most people if the ZD were not adjusted. To avoid this loss, in many areas it is customary to adopt the time of the next adjacent zone to the *east*, during the period DST is in effect. This results in sunrise and sunset occurring one hour later. Along the east coast of the United States, where

419

the ZD is usually (+5), based on the 75th meridian, during daylight saving the ZD becomes (+4). Similarly, a place ordinarily using a ZD of (−9) might in summer advance its time so that the ZD is (−10).

Changing time and date aboard ship.

2315. When a ship passes from one time zone into the next, it enters an area where it is desirable to keep a ZT differing by one hour from the previous one; if travel is towards the west, the ZT of the new zone will be one hour earlier than that of the old, and the ship's clocks would be set back one hour. If the ship were traveling toward the east, the reverse would be true, and the clocks would be advanced one hour.

It is the navigator's duty to advise the captain when a new time zone is about to be entered; the latter will determine the time at which the ship's clocks will be reset. Zone time is used as a matter of convenience, and the time change is usually made with this in mind, to cause minimal dislocation of the ship's routine. The ZD does not change until the ZT is changed.

A ship steaming to the west sets its clocks back one hour in each new time zone; in a circumnavigation of the earth, it would therefore "lose" 24 hours. Conversely, if it were steaming around the world in an easterly direction it would "gain" 24 hours in circling the globe. A method of adjusting for the day lost or gained is necessary.

International Date Line.

The *International Date Line* follows the 180th meridian, with some offsets or variations so that it does not bisect an inhabited territory. The adjustment to the date is made at some convenient time before or after the vessel crosses the date line. If a vessel has been steaming *east*, its clocks have been steadily advanced, and this is compensated for by *reducing* the date one day. Conversely, a vessel steaming *west* has been setting back its clocks, so that the date is *advanced* one day. This date change is made by every vessel crossing the date line, regardless of the length of the voyage.

The change of date accounts for the two zone descriptions associated with the 15° band of longitude centered on the 180th meridian. That part of the zone in west longitude has a ZD of (+12), and that part in east longitude has a ZD of (−12). The ZT is the same throughout the zone, but the date is *one day later* in the half which is in east longitude than it is in the half which is in west longitude. For example, aboard a ship in λ 175° W at 0900 ZT on 3 February, GMT is determined to be 2100, 3 February, by applying the ZD of (+12). At the same instant, aboard a ship in λ 175° E and ZT is 0900 on 4 February; by applying the ZD (−12), GMT is also found to be 2100, 3 February.

The date line is used as a convenience, just as zone time is used as a convenience, and the change of date is made in the area of the date line at a time when the ship's routine will be disturbed as little as possible. Frequently, it is convenient to change the date at the midnight falling closest to the time the ship crosses the date line. However, it would generally be considered undesirable either to repeat a Sunday, or a holiday, or to drop it. Under such conditions, ships have found it convenient to operate for a period using a ZD of either (+13), or (−13). Regardless of when the line is crossed, the sign of the ZD remains unchanged until the date is changed.

To sum up: all changes in time and date are made solely for the purpose of convenience. The value of the zone time and the date used aboard ship are of comparatively little importance in themselves; what is important is that the navigator be able to determine the time and date at Greenwich, so that he can obtain the coordinates of celestial bodies from the almanac. Also, the student should remember that the day which is added or subtracted when crossing the date line has no effect on the Greenwich date.

2316. In practical navigation problems the navigator is concerned with using the preceding information on time to determine the GMT and date. The Time Diagram, introduced in article 2307, is generally drawn roughly by the navigator for each celestial problem to assist in visualizing the problem. Since GMT is used, the Greenwich meridian is used on the diagram at an angular distance appropriate for the observer's longitude, east or clockwise from *M* if he is in west longitude, and west of *M*, if his longitude is east. The upper branch of the Greenwich meridian is drawn as a solid line, and is labeled *G*, and the lower branch as a broken line and labeled *g*.

Using the Time Diagram.

Figure 2316a shows on the left a time diagram for an observer in λ 60° W, with a ZT of about 1800. On the right, it shows a ZT of about 1800 for an observer in λ 15° E.

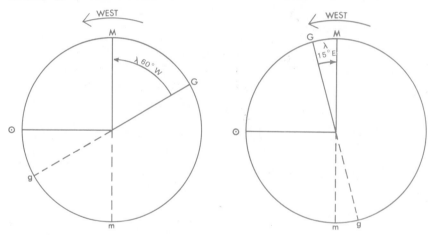

Figure 2316a: East and West longitude on the Time Diagram.

Since the sun is the basis of GMT as well as ZT, the approximate GMT can also be determined from a time diagram. In the time diagram in Figure 2316a, with the observer at λ 60° W, the sun ($\odot$) is approximately 90° west of the upper branch of the observer's meridian, *M*, and 150° or 10 hours west of the upper branch of the Greenwich meridian *G*; the GMT is therefore approximately 2200. Similarly, in the diagram at the right in this figure with the observer at λ 15° E, the sun is about 90° or six hours west of the local meridian *M*, but it is only about 75° or five hours west of the upper branch of the Greenwich meridian, *G*; the GMT is therefore about 1700. In this case, the sun will be at *g* in seven hours, which will signal the start of the next day for Greenwich.

The time diagram is particularly helpful when the date at the observer's meridian differs from that at another meridian, such as Greenwich. The time diagram in Figure 2316b shows an observer in λ 115° E, at approximately 0500 ZT. Here the sun has already passed the lower branch of the observer's meridian *m*, and a new day has begun for him. At this moment the sun must travel approximately 40°, or some 2 hours and 40 minutes, before it transits the lower branch of the meridian of Greenwich to start the new day there; the date at Greenwich is there-

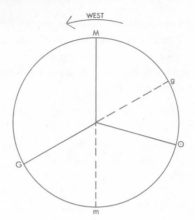

fore *the day preceding* the date for the observer at *M*. Thus, if it is ZT 0500, 10 January for the observer at *M*, the GMT is 2200, January 9.

A difference in date is readily apparent when a time diagram is used, as *the dates at two meridians are always different if the sun's hour circle* falls between their lower branches, and the meridian whose lower branch is to the west of the sun's hour circle will always have the earlier date.

Zone Time (ZT) and Greenwich Mean Time (GMT).

2317. Zone time differs from Greenwich mean time by the zone description. To convert ZT to GMT, the ZD is applied to ZT with the sign as shown. To convert GMT to ZT, the ZD is applied to GMT with the *sign reversed.*

These conversions are illustrated in the following examples.

Example 1: A navigator aboard a ship at longitude 156°19'.5 E observes the sun at 16-36-14 ZT on 26 April.

Required: GMT and date at the time of the observation.

Body	Sun
Date (Z)	26 April
ZT	16-36-14
ZD	(−)10
GMT	06-36-14
Date (G)	26 April

Solution: First record the name of the body, the date based on ZT, and the ZT of the observation. Then sketch on a time diagram the relative positions of the observer, Greenwich, and the sun, to assist in visualizing the problem. Next, determine the ZD by dividing the longitude by 15°, to the nearest whole number. (In practice, the navigator would know the ZD of the ZT his ship was keeping, but the student is asked to determine it here for drill purposes.) The ZD is (−)10 ("minus" because the observer is in east longitude; "10" because 156°19'.5 ÷ 15° = 10, remainder less than 7°30'). Then apply the ZD to ZT in accordance with its sign to determine GMT. Finally, record the date at Greenwich, which in this case is the same as the local date.

Answer: GMT 06-36-14 on 26 April.

Example 2: A navigator aboard a ship at longitude 83°17'.9 W observes the star Arcturus at 19-15-29 ZT on 14 June.

Required: GMT and date at the time of the observation.

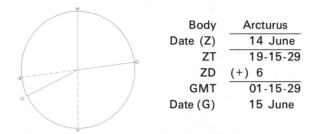

Body	Arcturus
Date (Z)	14 June
ZT	19-15-29
ZD	(+) 6
GMT	01-15-29
Date (G)	15 June

Solution: First record the name of the body, the date based upon ZT, and the ZT. Then sketch on a time diagram the relative positions of the observer, Greenwich, and the sun, to assist in visualizing the problem. Next, determine the ZD by dividing the longitude by 15°, to the nearest whole number. The ZD is (+)6 ("plus" because the observer is in west longitude; "6" because 83°17'.9 ÷ 15° = 5, remainder more than 7°30'). Then apply the ZD to ZT in accordance with its sign to determine GMT. Finally, record the date at Greenwich, which in this case is one day later than the local date.

Answer: GMT 01-15-29 on 15 June.

2318. *Local mean time* (LMT) differs from zone time by the difference of longitude $(d\lambda)$, expressed as time, between the meridian of the observer and the standard meridian of the zone. Local mean time is primarily of interest to the navigator in determining the zone time of phenomena such as sunrise and set, and moonrise and set.

Zone Time (ZT) and Local Mean Time (LMT).

If the observer is *east* of the central meridian of his zone, the phenomenon will occur earlier for him than it will at the zone's central meridian, and LMT at his position will be *later* than ZT, which is LMT at the central meridian. Conversely, if he is *west* of the standard meridian the phenomenon will occur *later*, and LMT at his position will be earlier than ZT.

The following examples will serve to clarify the use of LMT, and its relationship to ZT.

Example 1: The navigator of a ship at longitude 117°19'.4 W determines from the almanac that sunrise is at LMT 0658 on 26 October. (The times of phenomena such as sunrise are given in the almanacs only to the nearest minute.)

Required: ZT of sunrise and local date.

Solution: First, record the phenomenon, the date based upon LMT, and the LMT of a phenomenon. Then sketch on a time diagram the relative positions of the observer, the central meridian of the zone *(Z-z)*, and the sun, to assist in visualizing the problem. Next determine the difference of longitude $(d\lambda)$ between the meridian of the observer and that of the central meridian of the zone and convert to time units, to the nearest minute. In this case, the central meridian of the zone is λ 120° W (the nearest whole multiple of 15°) and $d\lambda$ equals 2°40'.6. Converting this value to time units by the rules of article 2308, $d\lambda$ equals

423

	Sunrise
Date (M)	26 October
LMT	0658
$d\lambda$	(−)11
ZT	0647
Date (Z)	26 October

11^m, to the nearest minute. Since the observer is east of the central meridian, ZT is earlier than LMT, and the $d\lambda$ value must be subtracted from LMT to obtain ZT.

Answer: ZT 0647 on 26 October.

Example 2: The navigator of a ship at longitude 38°58'.5 E determines from the almanac that moonset is at LMT 2347 on 26 January.

	Moonset
Date (M)	26 January
LMT	2347
$d\lambda$	(+)24
ZT	0011
Date (Z)	27 January

Solution: First record the phenomenon, the date based upon LMT, and the LMT of the phenomenon. Then sketch on a time diagram the relative positions of the observer, the central meridian of the zone, and the sun, to assist in visualizing the problem. Next, determine the difference of longitude between the meridian of the observer and that of the central meridian of the zone and convert to time units, to the nearest minute. In this case, the central meridian of the zone is λ 45° E, and $d\lambda$ equals 6°01'.5. Converting this to time units, $d\lambda$ equals 24^m, to the nearest minute. Since the observer is west of the central meridian, ZT is later than LMT, and the $d\lambda$ value must be added to LMT to obtain ZT. Finally, record the date in the zone, which in this case is one day later than the date based upon LMT.

Answer: ZT 0011 on 27 January.

In the practice of modern navigation, the navigator ordinarily has little occasion to convert ZT to LMT.

Timing celestial observations.

2319. The coordinates of celestial bodies are tabulated with respect to GMT and date; it is therefore necessary that the navigator know the GMT and Greenwich date of each celestial observation. This is accomplished most simply by using a timepiece set precisely to GMT, and noting the time at the instant of each observation. This is far superior to using a watch set either to zone or chronometer time, as it both speeds the operation, and reduces the hazard of error.

A split second timer, or lacking such, a stop watch, should be used for celestial observations. The watch should, if possible, be started against a radio signal, using the tick denoting the start of a five-minute increment, and the GMT and Greenwich date at which the watch was started should be noted. If a radio time signal is unavailable, the watch should be started against the best chronometer. To do this, the local time zone description is applied to the ship's time to determine the Greenwich date, and whether the time there is AM or PM. The current chronometer error is then determined. With this, the chronometer time which will give a five-minute increment of GMT is determined, and the watch is started when the chronometer shows this instant of time. This procedure is illustrated in the following example.

Morning star observations are to be obtained, and the recorder's watch is to be started on a 5-minute increment of GMT. The ship's clocks are set to Zone (−10) time (Figure 2319).

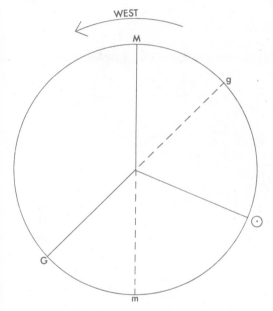

WEST

Ship's time and date   *Figure 2319.*

        0543(−10) 7 April

GMT and date

        1943   6 April

Chronometer error + (fast)

        2 min 41.5 sec

At GMT 19-45-00, a chronometer with a 12-hour dial will read 7 hours, 47 minutes, 41.5 seconds, and the watch is started at this chronometer reading.

2320. The chronometer is a very accurate spring driven timepiece, usually   *Chronometer.* about 4 or 5 inches in diameter, mounted in a heavy brass case, which is supported in gimbals in a wooden case. The gimbals take up much of the ship's motion, so that the chronometer remains in a nearly horizontal position. The wooden case is usually mounted in a very heavily padded second case, designed to give maximum protection against shock, and sudden fluctuations of temperature. Chronometers are usually fitted with a detent escapement, and beat, or tick, half-seconds, as compared to the five beats per second of most watches. This slow beat is of great convenience when comparing the instrument with other chronometers, or with radio time signals.

The great majority of chronometers carry a 12-hour dial, although instruments with 24-hour dials have been produced. A "wind indicator," showing how many hours have elapsed since the instrument was wound, is universally employed. Most chronometers will run for 56 hours before running down, although 8-day models have been produced. However, *it is essential that the instrument be wound at the same time every day.*

*Figure 2320: Hamil-
ton chronometer.*

Naval vessels of destroyer type and larger customarily carry three chronometers, as illustrated in Figure 2320.

Marine chronometers are almost invariably set to GMT; they may, however, be adjusted to keep sidereal time. They are never reset aboard ship; once the chronometer is started, the setting of the hands is not changed until it is scheduled for cleaning and overhaul. Due to the design of the escapement, a fully-wound chronometer will not start of its own accord. When a chronometer is to be started, the hands are set to the appropriate hour and minute of GMT. When the elapsed seconds of GMT agree with the second hand on the chronometer, the chronometer case is given a brisk horizontal turn through about 45°, and immediately turned back to its original position; this will start the movement.

The time indicated by the chronometer is chronometer time (C).

*Quartz crystal
oscillator clock.*

2321. The *quartz crystal oscillator clock* is becoming popular as a substitute for the marine chronometer. It is electrically powered, usually by a self-contained small battery pack, as the current drain is very low.

The quartz oscillator clock is highly resistant to shock and vibration, and does not need to be gimbaled. Among its other virtues is that it can be set while running. Most models have a sweep second hand, which can be advanced or retarded electronically in increments of one-tenth or one one-hundredth of a second while the clock is running.

Kept at a reasonably steady temperature, these clocks are capable of maintaining an excellent rate. The better models, under stable temperature conditions, can be expected to deviate less than 0.01 seconds from their average daily rate.

2322. The *comparing watch* is a watch employed to time celestial observations, and to assist in checking a chronometer against a radio time signal. It is also sometimes called a *hack watch*. A good quality *split-second timer* makes the best comparing watch. It has two sweep second hands, one directly below the other, which can be started and stopped together, by means of a push button, usually mounted in the center of the winding stem. A second push button stops the lower of the two sweephands, permitting an accurate readout. When this button is pushed again, the stopped hand catches up with the running hand. These watches are also fitted with a small dial to indicate the elapsed time since the continuously running sweep hand was started.

Comparing watch.

Lacking a split-second timer, any fine watch with a sweep second hand makes a good comparing watch, as it facilitates reading time to the nearest second. A standard *stop watch* may be used to advantage for this purpose.

A *second-setting watch* also makes a satisfactory comparing watch. In these watches, the hour, minute, and second hand are all mounted concentrically; the hour hand usually reads out to 24 hours. On this type of watch, the second hand is stopped when the winding stem is pulled out, and the hour and minute hands can then be set to any desired time by turning the stem. When the stem is pushed back in, the watch is restarted. This type of watch may be set very accurately by means of a radio time tick. Other models combine the features of keeping GMT with a stop watch mechanism and are referred to as navigational time and stop watches. Due to the ready availability of the radio time tick for checking purposes, many smaller vessels and seagoing pleasure craft do not carry a marine chronometer but depend on a high quality watch or a mounted chronometer watch.

Second setting watch.

To time celestial observations by means of a split-second timer or stop watch, the best practice is to start the watch on a whole 5-minute increment of GMT, either by marking a radio time signal, or against a chronometer. In the latter event, the chronometer error should be applied to the chronometer time, *with sign reversed,* in order to obtain GMT.

Timing celestial observations.

Every watch used as a comparing watch should be checked regularly to determine that it will run free of appreciable error for the period of its normal maximum use; ordinarily this would be about 60 minutes.

2323. All timepieces are subject to certain errors, and at any given time every timepiece probably will indicate a time which is somewhat fast or slow with respect to the correct time.

Errors in timepieces.

If the *error* (E) of a timepiece is *fast* (F), meaning that the time indicated is later than the correct time, the amount of error must be *subtracted* to obtain the correct time. If the error is *slow* (S), meaning that the time indicated is earlier than the correct time, the amount of error must be *added* to obtain the correct time.

Watch error (WE) is the difference between the indication of a watch and the correct time at any instant. *Watch rate* is the amount by which a watch gains or loses in a specified time, usually 24 hours.

427

The watch error can be determined directly by means of a radio time signal, making due allowance for any difference of ZD of watch and radio transmitter, or by means of a chronometer. When the second method is used, the watch and chronometer readings are obtained simultaneously. The chronometer error (article 2324) is then applied to the chronometer time to obtain GMT and the ZD (reversed) is applied to find the correct ZT. The watch time is then compared with the ZT.

Example: During the morning of 3 October, when the DR longitude of a ship is 55°18'.6 E, the navigator compares his watch with the chronometer to determine the watch error on ZT. When the chronometer reads 5-31-00, the watch reads 9-43-28. The chronometer is 12^m56^s slow on GMT.

Required: WE on ZT.

Solution:

C	5-31-00	3 Oct.
CE	(S) 12-56	
GMT	5-43-56	3 Oct.
ZD	(−)4	(rev.)
ZT	9-43-56	
W	9-43-28	
WE	(S) 28	

Answer: WE 28^s slow on ZT.

Chronometer error. **2324.** The difference between chronometer time and GMT at any instant is called *chronometer error,* labeled (F) or (S) as the chronometer is fast or slow on the correct (Greenwich) time. Since chronometers are not reset aboard ship, the accumulated error may become quite large. This is not important if the error is accurately known.

Chronometer error is usually determined by means of a radio time signal. The chronometer may be compared directly, or a watch may be used to avoid moving the chronometer.

Example 1: On 31 October, the navigator of a ship at λ 138°36'.6 W desires to determine the chronometer error by means of a radio time signal, by direct comparison. The time signal is transmitted from Mare Island, λ 122°16'.4 W, at ZT 1200. At the moment of the signal the chronometer reads 7-46-27.

Required: The chronometer error on GMT.

Solution:

ZT	12-00-00	31 Oct.
ZD	(+) 8	
GMT	20-00-00	31 Oct.
C	7-46-27	
CE	(S) 13-33	

Answer: The chronometer is 13^m33^s slow on GMT.

Note that the GMT is 20^h, while the chronometer reads 7-46-27. The CE shown is correct, since the chronometer face is graduated to only 12^h. Hence, at GMT 20^h, the time in Greenwich is 8 PM, as indicated approximately by the chronometer.

Example 2: On 10 July, the navigator of a ship at λ 46°30′.4 W desires to obtain the chronometer error by means of a radio signal. A comparing watch, set approximately to ZT (+3) zone, is used in the radio room to note the watch time of the signal, which is transmitted from Washington, D. C., λ 77°03′.9 W, at ZT 1200. At the moment of the signal the comparing watch reads 2-01-30 PM. A little later the comparing watch reads 2-04-20 PM at the instant the chronometer reads 4-38-00.

Required: The chronometer error on GMT.

Solution:

ZT_w	12-00-00	10 July
ZD_w	(+) 5	
GMT	17-00-00	10 July
ZD_s	(+) 3	(rev.)
ZT_s	14-00-00	
W	2-01-30	PM
WE	(F) 1-30	
W	2-04-20	PM 10 July
WE	(F) 1-30	
ZT_s	14-02-50	
ZD_s	(+) 3	
GMT	17-02-50	10 July
C	4-38-00	
CE	(S) 24-50	

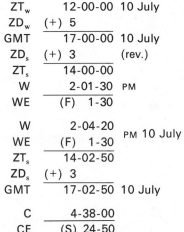

Answer: The chronometer is 24^m50^s slow on GMT.

2325. The *rate* of a timepiece is the amount it gains or loses in a specified time. It is usually expressed as seconds and tenths of seconds per day, and is labeled "gaining" or "losing." Temperature is the main factor affecting fine timepieces; in general, their rates will increase with rising temperatures.   *Chronometer rate.*

The nearly constant rate of a fine chronometer is its most important feature, as it makes safe navigation possible on a long voyage without dependence on time signals.

The chronometer rate is determined by comparison with radio time signals obtained several days apart.

Example 1: A navigator, desiring to determine the chronometer rate, compares the chronometer directly with the Washington, D. C. 1200 radio time signal on different days. On 6 April the chronometer reads 5-25-05 and on 16 April it reads 5-25-51.

Required: The chronometer error on each date and chronometer rate.

Solution:

ZT	12-00-00	6 April		GMT	17-00-00	16 April
ZD	(+) 5			C	5-25-51	
GMT	17-00-00	6 April		CE	(F) 25-51	16 April
C	5-25-05			CE	(F) 25-05	6 April
CE	(F) 25-05	6 April		diff.	46	
				rate	4.6 gaining	

Answers: CE on 6 April is 25^m05^s fast on GMT. CE on 16 April is 25^m51^s fast on GMT. Chronometer rate on 16 April is $4^s.6$ per day, gaining.

429

The chronometer rate provides a means of determining the chronometer error at any instant between time signals.

Example 2: At 1620 on 2 December the DR λ of a ship is 147°40'.6 W when the navigator prepares to observe the sun. He compares his watch with a chronometer which was 17^m27^s fast on GMT at ZT 1200 (when the ship was keeping (+5) zone time on 20 November. The chronometer rate is $0^s.7$ gaining.

Required: The chronometer error.

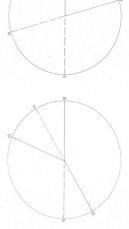

Solution:

ZT		12-00-00	20 Nov.
ZD	(+)	5	
GMT		17-00-00	20 Nov.
ZT		16-20-00	2 Dec.
ZD	(+)	10	
GMT		2-20-00	3 Dec.
GMT		17-00-00	20 Nov.
Elapsed time		9-20-00	+12 days
		= 12.4 days	
CE	(F)	17-27	20 Nov.
corr.		(+) 9	(12.4×0.7)
CE	(F)	17-36	2 Dec.

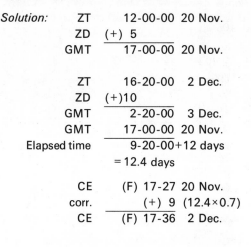

Answer: CE on 2 Dec. is 17^m36^s fast on GMT.

TIME SIGNALS

Radio time signals.

2326. *Radio time signals,* often called time ticks, are broadcast from many stations throughout the world. Complete information on the time signals of all countries is given in *Radio Navigational Aids,* H. O. 117-A and 117-B.

The signals most commonly used by United States vessels are broadcast from the Bureau of Standards, radio stations WWV at Fort Collins, Colorado, from WWVH on the island of Kauai, Hawaii, and from the Navy's stations, NAM at Norfolk, Virginia, NPG at San Francisco, California, NPM at Honolulu, Hawaii, and NPM at Guam. These signals have an accuracy far greater than is required in ordinary navigation.

Stations WWV and WWVH.

WWV and WWVH broadcast time signals continuously during each day. Frequencies and radiated power in kilowatts are as follows:

Frequency mHz	Radiated power, Kw.	
	WWV	WWVH
2.5	2.5	5
5	10	10
10	10	10
15	10	10
20	2.5	2.5
25	2.5	—

Each second is marked by a tick; however, the 29th and 59th second ticks are omitted. Once every minute, time is announced by voice during the last 15 seconds of the minute. The two stations are distinguished by a female voice from WWVH at 15 seconds before the minute, and a male voice from WWV at $7\frac{1}{2}$ seconds before the minute. The time is stated as "Coordinated Universal Time," which for ordinary navigation is the same as GMT. Just before 2235 GMT, for instance, the announcement would be: "At the tone, 22 hours 35 minutes Coordinated Universal Time."

The selection of frequency for best reception will depend on the time of day, and on atmospheric conditions. As a general rule, the 15 mHz band is satisfactory during the daylight hours, while the 5 mHz band is usually better at night.

The signals broadcast from WWV and WWVH are in extremely useful form for the navigator. The tick transmitted every second is most useful for starting a stop watch accurately. By beating every second with the incoming signal for about the final 15 seconds of the minute, with a little practice it is possible to start a stop watch without a readable error; that is, with an error of less than one-fifth of a second.

In addition to the time signals, the storm warnings provided by WWV and WWVH by voice can be very helpful to the navigator. Starting at the 8th minute past the hour, and for the following 3 minutes, WWV gives information on any storms in the North Atlantic west of λ 30°W, for the Gulf of Mexico, the Caribbean Sea, and the western North Pacific Ocean. Starting at the 48th minute, and for the following 3 minutes, WWVH advises of any storms in the Pacific Ocean, south to L 25°S, and west to λ 160°E.

Time signals are broadcast by stations NAM, NPG, NPM and NPN on several frequencies beginning 5 minutes before the hour, four times a day, using the United States system of time signal transmission; no voice announcement is made. Data on this system will be found in *Radio Navigational Aids*, 117A and 117B; these volumes also list the times and frequencies of the transmissions.

Stations NAM, NPG, NPM, NPN.

Continuous time signals are broadcast by the Canadian station CHU, on 3330, 7335 and 14.670KHZ. Voice announcements of the upcoming minute and hour of Eastern Standard Time (ZD+5) are made both in English and French. The 29th second tick is omitted, as are the 51st to 59th; during this latter period the voice announcement is made. These transmissions can be very useful to vessels off the Atlantic coast of North America.

Station CHU.

The U. S. Naval Observatory is officially designated by the Department of Defense as the organization responsible for support and management services for precise time and time interval standards, and the following definitions have been established, under the DOD instruction.

Responsibility for time standards.

Time signifies epoch, that is the designation of an instant on a selected time scale, astronomical or atomic. The word is used in the sense of time of day.

Definitions.

Time interval indicates the duration of a segment of time without reference to when the time interval begins and ends. Time interval may be given in seconds of time.

Precise time signifies a time requirement within ten milliseconds.

431

Precise frequency signifies a frequency requirement within one part in 10^9 of an established time scale.

Standards refers to the reference values of time and time interval determined by astronomical observation and the operation of atomic clocks, and disseminated by a transport of clocks, radio transmissions and other means.

In certain ports a telegraphic time signal is repeated by a visual signal, which usually consists of dropping a large ball or shape, which has previously been hoisted in a conspicuous place ashore, and is released upon receipt of the telegraphic time signal. A gun is discharged as a signal in some ports, the flash of the gun being the signal. The sound of the report should not be used, for it may not reach the observer until several seconds after the flash and smoke are visible. Such signals are usually made at 1200 zone time.

Chronometer record.

2327. The *Navigation Timepiece Rate Book* is issued to every naval vessel; it permits maintenance of complete records on three chronometers or other timepieces. These data include the daily error and the daily rate; each page has space for 31 daily entries. A portion of a sample page is reproduced in Figure 2327.

Figure 2327: Page extract filled in, from the Navigation Time-Piece Book *(NavShips 4270).*

DATE	A				B				C				OBSERVATION	
YEAR 19 58	MAKE HAMILTON / TYPE SC / SERIAL NO. 4327				MAKE HAMILTON / TYPE SC / SERIAL NO. 1278				MAKE HAMILTON / TYPE GCW / SERIAL NO. 843					
MONTH July	ERROR RELATIVE TO G.C.T. +=FAST −=SLOW		SUCCESSIVE DAILY RATES		ERROR RELATIVE TO G.C.T. +=FAST −=SLOW		SUCCESSIVE DAILY RATES		ERROR RELATIVE TO G.C.T. +=FAST −=SLOW		SUCCESSIVE DAILY RATES		LOCAL TIME TO NEAREST MINUTE	
DAY	± MIN.	SECONDS	±	SECONDS	± MIN.	SECONDS	±	SECONDS	± MIN.	SECONDS	±	SECONDS	TIME	INITIALS
1	+ 1	4.5		.	− 2	4.6		.	+ 12	42.4		.	1155	
2	+ 1	6.0	+	1.5	− 2	3.8	+	0.8	+ 12	40.0	−	2.4	1205	
3	+ 1	7.5	+	1.5	− 2	3.0	+	0.8	+ 12	37.5	−	2.5	1140	
4	+ 1	9.0	+	1.5	− 2	2.2	+	0.8	+ 12	35.1	−	2.4	1135	
5	+ 1	10.6	+	1.6	− 2	1.4	+	0.8	+ 12	32.7	−	2.4	1120	
6	+ 1	12.1	+	1.5	− 2	0.5	+	0.9	+ 12	30.2	−	2.5	1200	

Complete instructions for the care, winding, and transportation of chronometers are given in the Navigation Timepiece Rate Book. An officer assuming navigational duty should familiarize himself with these instructions, as well as pertinent information contained in *U. S. Navy Regulations.*

The standard chronometer in the Navy is returned to a chronometer pool every three years for cleaning, lubrication, and any other work that may be necessary.

It is the custom in the U. S. Navy for the senior quartermaster to wind the chronometers and check the rates every day at about 1130. This is reported to the officer of the deck, who, in turn advises the captain that "the chronometers have been wound and compared" as part of the routine 1200 report.

Summary.

2328. The navigator makes direct use of three different kinds of time. These are Greenwich mean time, GMT; local mean time, LMT; and zone time, ZT. All three are based upon the motions of the fictitious "mean sun." The mean sun is considered to revolve about the earth at the average rate of the apparent sun, making one complete revolution in 24 hours.

The reckoning of time is based upon the motion of the sun relative to a given meridian, the time being 2400–0000 at lower transit and 1200 at upper transit. In Greenwich mean time, the reference meridian is that of Greenwich; in local mean time, the reference meridian is that of a given place; in zone time, the reference meridian is the standard meridian of a given zone.

Solar time.

Article 1909 explained why the *sidereal day*, which is the time required for the earth to complete one rotation on its axis relative to the vernal equinox, is about 3 minutes and 56.6 seconds shorter than the mean solar day. As sidereal time indicates the position of the stars, their daily shift westward is therefore almost one degree every night. Because of *nutation,* (see article 1915) sidereal time is not perfectly constant in rate. Time based on the average rate is called *mean sidereal time*. There is no sidereal date.

Sidereal time.

Greenwich sidereal time (GST) uses the meridian of Greenwich as its terrestrial reference, while the observer's meridian is the reference for *local sidereal time* (LST).

Some timepieces, often reading in arc rather than in time, are adjusted to keep sidereal time. If set to GST they permit the navigator to read the GHA ♈, which is GST expressed in units of arc, directly from the timepiece at the instant of making a star observation, thus obviating the need to extract GHA ♈ and a correction thereto from the *Almanac*.

The difference between two times is equal to the difference of longitude of their reference meridians, expressed in units of time. GMT differs from LMT by the longitude of the place; GMT differs from ZT by the longitude of the standard meridian of the zone; LMT differs from ZT by the difference of longitude between the standard meridian of the zone and the meridian of the place. In applying a time difference, a place which is east of another place has a later time than that place, and a place which is west of another place has an earlier time than that place. In interconverting ZT and GMT, the navigator makes use of zone description in applying these rules. The ZD of a zone is the time difference between its standard meridian and GMT, and is given a sign to indicate the correction to ZT to obtain GMT. The sign is plus (+) for places in west longitude and minus (−) for places in east longitude.

Time and longitude.

In this chapter we have discussed time as measured by the rotation of the earth. Unfortunately, this rotation is not at an absolutely uniform rate, but varies slightly due to tidal friction, internal causes, and seasonal variations in the atmosphere. The need has developed for a uniform time standard for some new and highly sophisticated navigation systems, and this need has been met by atomic physicists. The new standard second is based on 9,192,631,770 periods of the microwave transition between the hyperfine levels of the ground state of the cesium atom 133. Time signals as broadcast by WWV, WWVH, etc., are periodically adjusted to be in accord with the new standard. In the ordinary practice of celestial navigation aboard ship the navigator need not concern himself with the effect of this change in the time standard.

Atomic time standard

CHAPTER 24

Almanacs

Introduction. **2401.** The purpose of this chapter is to explain how the navigator, having observed a celestial body at a given time, obtains the Greenwich Hour Angle (GHA) and declination (Dec.) of the body at that time.

While the *Air Almanac* is also discussed, the *Nautical Almanac* should be the primary choice of the surface navigator.

Almanac history. **2402.** The Danish astronomer, Tycho Brahe, during the last half of the sixteenth century, spent over 20 years making accurate observations of the heavenly bodies. On the data thus amassed, Kepler based his laws of motion, which were the foundation both of modern astronomy and celestial navigation. An almanac intended primarily for the use of mariners did not appear until 1767, when the *British Nautical Almanac* was first published. In 1852, the United States Navy's Depot of Charts and Instruments published the first *American Ephemeris and Nautical Almanac* for the year 1855. This volume has appeared annually since then. In 1858, the *American Nautical Almanac* was published; the ephemeris section, of primary interest to astronomers, being omitted.

In 1933, the *Air Almanac* was first published in the United States. It was revolutionary, as Greenwich Hour Angle was substituted for Right Ascension; the hour angle, incidentally, was stated to 0.̇1. This *Almanac* was discontinued in 1934, but produced again in 1937 by the Royal Greenwich Observatory in somewhat modified form, and published in the United States by the Weems System of Navigation. In 1941, the U. S. Naval Observatory resumed the publication of the *Air Almanac* in the United States.

The British and American editions of the *Nautical Almanac*, which are now identical in content, are produced jointly by Her Majesty's Nautical Almanac Office, Royal Greenwich Observatory, and by the Nautical Almanac Office, U. S. Naval Observatory, but are printed separately in the United States and Britain. The *Nautical Almanac* is prepared to the general requirements of the British Admiralty and the United States Navy; its purpose is to provide, in convenient form, the data required for the practice of celestial navigation at sea.

Contents of the Nautical Almanac. **2403.** To find an observer's position on earth by observations of celestial bodies it is necessary to determine the position of the observer relative to the geographical positions of these bodies. The *Nautical Almanac* consists principally of data from which the Greenwich Hour Angle (GHA) and declination (Dec.) of all the celestial bodies used in navigation can be obtained for any instant of Greenwich Mean Time (GMT). In general these data are presented to the nearest one-tenth minute of arc, and one second of time. The Local Hour Angle (LHA) can then be obtained by means of the formulae:

LHA.

$$LHA = GHA - \text{west longitude}$$

and

$$LHA = GHA + \text{east longitude,}$$

bearing in mind that 360° may be added or subtracted as required. LHA, like GHA, is always calculated in a westerly direction. For many methods of sight reduction *meridian angle* (t) is required; this is measured east or west from the observer's meridian to 180°, as discussed in Chapter 20. Meridian angle may readily be determined from the LHA. Determination of the LHA is illustrated in Figure 2403a.

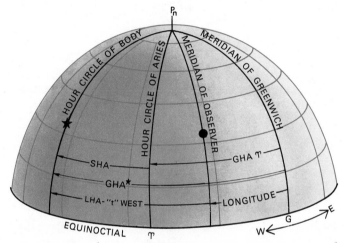

Figure 2403a: Hour angles illustrated on a sphere.

For the sun, moon and planets the GHA and declination are tabulated directly for each hour of Greenwich Mean Time (GMT) throughout the year. GHA of Aries (♈), the vernal equinox, is also tabulated for each hour. For the stars the sidereal hour angle (SHA) is listed and the GHA is obtained from:

Tabulated GHA.

$$GHA \text{ star} = GHA \text{ Aries} + SHA \text{ star}$$

if this value exceeds 360°, 360° is subtracted from the answer. The SHA and declination of the stars change slowly and may be regarded as constant over a period of several days. Interpolation tables give the appropriate increments and corrections to the tabulated hourly value of GHA and declination for the minute and seconds of GMT.

The basic ephemeristic data for all navigational bodies covering a 3-day period are presented on facing pages of the almanac. The left hand pages are devoted principally to the tabulation of data for the stars and navigational planets. These bodies are of navigational interest primarily during morning and evening twilight. The right hand page presents the ephemeristic data for the sun and moon, together with the times of twilight, sunrise, sunset, moonrise and moonset. In Figures 2403b and 2403c sample almanac pages are shown. The extreme left hand column of each page tabulates the dates, the days of the week, as well as the hours of GMT for the three days. Since the date at Greenwich is stated it will, in some instances, be one day different from the local date, as was explained in article 2316.

1969 APRIL 25, 26, 27 (FRI., SAT., SUN.)

G.M.T.	ARIES G.H.A.	VENUS −4·0 G.H.A.	Dec.	MARS −1·0 G.H.A.	Dec.	JUPITER −1·9 G.H.A.	Dec.	SATURN +0·6 G.H.A.	Dec.	STARS Name	S.H.A.	Dec.
d h	° ′	° ′	° ′	° ′	° ′	° ′	° ′	° ′	° ′		° ′	° ′
25 00	212 49·9	204 20·3 N 8 00·4		317 16·1 S 22 54·1		34 42·0 N 2 28·8		184 43·1 N 9 09·7		Acamar	315 43·9	S 40 25·6
01	227 52·4	219 22·9	7 59·7	332 18·5	54·3	49 44·7	28·9	199 45·3	09·8	Achernar	335 51·8	S 57 23·5
02	242 54·8	234 25·6	58·9	347 20·9	54·4	64 47·3	29·0	214 47·4	09·9	Acrux	173 46·5	S 62 56·0
03	257 57·3	249 28·3 ··	58·2	2 23·3 ··	54·5	79 50·0 ··	29·1	229 49·6 ··	10·0	Adhara	255 38·9	S 28 55·9
04	272 59·8	264 30·9	57·5	17 25·7	54·6	94 52·6	29·1	244 51·7	10·2	Aldebaran	291 28·0	N 16 27·0
05	288 02·2	279 33·6	56·7	32 28·1	54·7	109 55·3	29·2	259 53·9	10·3			
06	303 04·7	294 36·2 N 7 56·0		47 30·5 S 22 54·8		124 58·0 N 2 29·3		274 56·1 N 9 10·4		Alioth	166 49·0	N 56 07·6
07	318 07·2	309 38·9	55·3	62 32·9	54·9	140 00·6	29·3	289 58·2	10·5	Alkaid	153 24·4	N 49 27·9
08	333 09·6	324 41·5	54·6	77 35·3	55·0	155 03·3	29·4	305 00·4	10·6	Al Na'ir	28 25·5	S 47 06·5
F 09	348 12·1	339 44·2 ··	53·9	92 37·8 ··	55·1	170 05·9 ··	29·5	320 02·6 ··	10·7	Alnilam	276 20·4	S 1 13·2
R 10	3 14·6	354 46·8	53·2	107 40·2	55·2	185 08·6	29·6	335 04·7	10·8	Alphard	218 28·8	S 8 31·5
I 11	18 17·0	9 49·5	52·4	122 42·6	55·3	200 11·2	29·6	350 06·9	10·9			
D 12	33 19·5	24 52·1 N 7 51·7		137 45·0 S 22 55·4		215 13·9 N 2 29·7		5 09·1 N 9 11·0		Alphecca	126 38·8	N 26 48·8
A 13	48 21·9	39 54·7	51·0	152 47·4	55·5	230 16·5	29·8	20 11·2	11·1	Alpheratz	358 18·4	N 28 55·1
Y 14	63 24·4	54 57·3	50·3	167 49·8	55·6	245 19·2	29·9	35 13·4	11·3	Altair	62 40·7	N 8 46·9
15	78 26·9	70 00·0 ··	49·6	182 52·2 ··	55·8	260 21·8 ··	29·9	50 15·5 ··	11·4	Ankaa	353 48·7	S 42 28·3
16	93 29·3	85 02·6	48·9	197 54·6	55·9	275 24·5	30·0	65 17·7	11·5	Antares	113 06·9	S 26 22·1
17	108 31·8	100 05·2	48·2	212 57·1	56·0	290 27·1	30·1	80 19·9	11·6			
18	123 34·3	115 07·8 N 7 47·5		227 59·5 S 22 56·1		305 29·8 N 2 30·2		95 22·0 N 9 11·7		Arcturus	146 25·7	N 19 20·3
19	138 36·7	130 10·4	46·8	243 01·9	56·2	320 32·4	30·2	110 24·2	11·8	Atria	108 38·4	S 68 58·4
20	153 39·2	145 13·0	46·1	258 04·3	56·3	335 35·1	30·3	125 26·4	11·9	Avior	234 31·9	S 59 24·8
21	168 41·7	160 15·6 ··	45·4	273 06·7 ··	56·4	350 37·7 ··	30·4	140 28·5 ··	12·0	Bellatrix	279 08·0	N 6 19·5
22	183 44·1	175 18·2	44·7	288 09·2	56·5	5 40·4	30·4	155 30·7	12·1	Betelgeuse	271 37·6	N 7 24·2
23	198 46·6	190 20·8	44·0	303 11·6	56·6	20 43·0	30·5	170 32·9	12·3			
26 00	213 49·1	205 23·4 N 7 43·3		318 14·0 S 22 56·7		35 45·7 N 2 30·6		185 35·0 N 9 12·4		Canopus	264 11·2	S 52 40·8
01	228 51·5	220 26·0	42·6	333 16·4	56·8	50 48·3	30·7	200 37·2	12·5	Capella	281 24·1	N 45 58·3
02	243 54·0	235 28·5	41·9	348 18·9	56·9	65 51·0	30·7	215 39·3	12·6	Deneb	49 54·3	N 45 09·8
03	258 56·4	250 31·1 ··	41·2	3 21·3 ··	57·0	80 53·6 ··	30·8	230 41·5 ··	12·7	Denebola	183 07·3	N 14 44·6
04	273 58·9	265 33·7	40·6	18 23·7	57·1	95 56·3	30·9	245 43·7	12·8	Diphda	349 29·5	S 18 09·3
05	289 01·4	280 36·2	39·9	33 26·2	57·3	110 58·9	31·0	260 45·8	12·9			
06	304 03·8	295 38·8 N 7 39·2		48 28·6 S 22 57·4		126 01·6 N 2 31·0		275 48·0 N 9 13·0		Dubhe	194 31·6	N 61 55·2
07	319 06·3	310 41·4	38·5	63 31·0	57·5	141 04·2	31·1	290 50·2	13·1	Elnath	278 55·0	N 28 35·1
S 08	334 08·8	325 43·9	37·8	78 33·5	57·6	156 06·9	31·2	305 52·3	13·2	Eltanin	91 01·3	N 51 29·1
A 09	349 11·2	340 46·5 ··	37·2	93 35·9 ··	57·7	171 09·5 ··	31·2	320 54·5 ··	13·4	Enif	34 20·0	N 9 43·8
T 10	4 13·7	355 49·0	36·5	108 38·3	57·8	186 12·2	31·3	335 56·6	13·5	Fomalhaut	16 00·8	S 29 47·1
U 11	19 16·2	10 51·6	35·8	123 40·8	57·9	201 14·8	31·4	350 58·8	13·6			
R 12	34 18·6	25 54·1 N 7 35·2		138 43·2 S 22 58·0		216 17·5 N 2 31·5		6 01·0 N 9 13·7		Gacrux	172 38·0	S 56 56·7
D 13	49 21·1	40 56·6	34·5	153 45·7	58·1	231 20·1	31·5	21 03·1	13·8	Gienah	176 26·4	S 17 22·5
A 14	64 23·5	55 59·2	33·8	168 48·1	58·2	246 22·7	31·6	36 05·3	13·9	Hadar	149 35·0	S 60 13·7
Y 15	79 26·0	71 01·7 ··	33·2	183 50·6 ··	58·3	261 25·4 ··	31·7	51 07·5 ··	14·0	Hamal	328 38·8	N 23 19·0
16	94 28·5	86 04·2	32·5	198 53·0	58·4	276 28·0	31·7	66 09·6	14·1	Kaus Aust.	84 27·8	S 34 24·1
17	109 30·9	101 06·7	31·8	213 55·5	58·5	291 30·7	31·8	81 11·8	14·2			
18	124 33·4	116 09·3 N 7 31·2		228 57·9 S 22 58·6		306 33·3 N 2 31·9		96 14·0 N 9 14·4		Kochab	137 16·8	N 74 16·7
19	139 35·9	131 11·8	30·5	244 00·4	58·7	321 36·0	31·9	111 16·1	14·5	Markab	14 11·8	N 15 02·2
20	154 38·3	146 14·3	29·9	259 02·8	58·8	336 38·6	32·0	126 18·3	14·6	Menkar	314 50·2	N 3 58·2
21	169 40·8	161 16·8 ··	29·2	274 05·3 ··	59·0	351 41·3 ··	32·1	141 20·4 ··	14·7	Menkent	148 46·7	S 36 13·4
22	184 43·3	176 19·3	28·6	289 07·7	59·1	6 43·9	32·2	156 22·6	14·8	Miaplacidus	221 47·1	S 69 35·6
23	199 45·7	191 21·8	27·9	304 10·2	59·2	21 46·6	32·2	171 24·8	14·9			
27 00	214 48·2	206 24·3 N 7 27·3		319 12·6 S 22 59·3		36 49·2 N 2 32·3		186 26·9 N 9 15·0		Mirfak	309 28·8	N 49 45·3
01	229 50·7	221 26·8	26·6	334 15·1	59·4	51 51·8	32·4	201 29·1	15·1	Nunki	76 39·4	S 26 20·3
02	244 53·1	236 29·3	26·0	349 17·6	59·5	66 54·5	32·4	216 31·3	15·2	Peacock	54 11·4	S 56 50·0
03	259 55·6	251 31·7 ··	25·3	4 20·0 ··	59·6	81 57·1 ··	32·5	231 33·4 ··	15·3	Pollux	244 08·5	N 28 06·3
04	274 58·0	266 34·2	24·7	19 22·5	59·7	96 59·8	32·6	246 35·6	15·5	Procyon	245 34·6	N 5 18·3
05	290 00·5	281 36·7	24·1	34 25·0	59·8	112 02·4	32·6	261 37·8	15·6			
06	305 03·0	296 39·2 N 7 23·4		49 27·4 S 22 59·9		127 05·1 N 2 32·7		276 39·9 N 9 15·7		Rasalhague	96 37·1	N 12 34·6
07	320 05·4	311 41·6	22·8	64 29·9 23 00·0		142 07·7	32·8	291 42·1	15·8	Regulus	208 18·7	N 12 07·1
08	335 07·9	326 44·1	22·2	79 32·4	00·1	157 10·3	32·8	306 44·2	15·9	Rigel	281 44·3	S 8 14·2
S 09	350 10·4	341 46·6 ··	21·5	94 34·8 ··	00·2	172 13·0 ··	32·9	321 46·4 ··	16·0	Rigil Kent.	140 36·9	S 60 42·6
U 10	5 12·8	356 49·0	20·9	109 37·3	00·3	187 15·6	33·0	336 48·6	16·1	Sabik	102 50·5	S 15 41·5
N 11	20 15·3	11 51·5	20·3	124 39·8	00·4	202 18·3	33·0	351 50·7	16·2			
D 12	35 17·8	26 53·9 N 7 19·7		139 42·3 S 23 00·5		217 20·9 N 2 33·1		6 52·9 N 9 16·3		Schedar	350 19·4	N 56 22·0
A 13	50 20·2	41 56·4	19·0	154 44·7	00·6	232 23·5	33·2	21 55·1	16·5	Shaula	97 06·9	S 37 05·1
Y 14	65 22·7	56 58·8	18·4	169 47·2	00·8	247 26·2	33·3	36 57·2	16·6	Sirius	259 03·3	S 16 40·4
15	80 25·1	72 01·2 ··	17·8	184 49·7 ··	00·9	262 28·8 ··	33·3	51 59·4 ··	16·7	Spica	159 06·1	S 11 00·3
16	95 27·6	87 03·7	17·2	199 52·2	01·0	277 31·5	33·4	67 01·6	16·8	Suhail	223 17·1	S 43 18·7
17	110 30·1	102 06·1	16·6	214 54·7	01·1	292 34·1	33·5	82 03·7	16·9			
18	125 32·5	117 08·5 N 7 15·9		229 57·1 S 23 01·2		307 36·7 N 2 33·5		97 05·9 N 9 17·0		Vega	81 01·4	N 38 44·8
19	140 35·0	132 10·9	15·3	244 59·6	01·3	322 39·4	33·6	112 08·0	17·1	Zuben'ubi	137 42·1	S 15 55·1
20	155 37·5	147 13·4	14·7	260 02·1	01·4	337 42·0	33·7	127 10·2	17·2		S.H.A.	Mer. Pass.
21	170 39·9	162 15·8 ··	14·1	275 04·6 ··	01·5	352 44·6 ··	33·7	142 12·4 ··	17·3		° ′	h m
22	185 42·4	177 18·2	13·5	290 07·1	01·6	7 47·3	33·8	157 14·5	17·4	Venus	351 34·3	10 17
23	200 44·9	192 20·6	12·9	305 09·6	01·7	22 49·9	33·9	172 16·7	17·6	Mars	104 24·9	2 47
Mer. Pass.	h m 9 43·1	v 2·5	d 0·7	v 2·4	d 0·1	v 2·6	d 0·1	v 2·2	d 0·1	Jupiter	181 56·6	21 33
										Saturn	331 45·9	11 36

Figure 2403b: Sample left hand page of Nautical Almanac.

1969 APRIL 25, 26, 27 (FRI., SAT., SUN.)

G.M.T.	SUN G.H.A.	SUN Dec.	MOON G.H.A.	MOON v	MOON Dec.	MOON d	MOON H.P.
d h	° ′	° ′	° ′	′	° ′	′	′
25 00	180 29·4	N13 03·7	82 44·6	12·5	N22 39·6	9·3	54·7
01	195 29·5	04·5	97 16·1	12·6	22 30·3	9·5	54·7
02	210 29·7	05·4	111 47·7	12·6	22 20·8	9·5	54·7
03	225 29·8 ··	06·2	126 19·3	12·7	22 11·3	9·6	54·7
04	240 29·9	07·0	140 51·0	12·7	22 01·7	9·6	54·7
05	255 30·0	07·8	155 22·7	12·8	21 51·9	9·9	54·8
06	270 30·1	N13 08·6	169 54·5	12·8	N21 42·0	9·9	54·8
07	285 30·2	09·4	184 26·3	12·9	21 32·1	10·1	54·8
08	300 30·3	10·3	198 58·2	12·9	21 22·0	10·1	54·8
F 09	315 30·4 ··	11·1	213 30·1	12·9	21 11·9	10·3	54·8
R 10	330 30·5	11·9	228 02·0	13·0	21 01·6	10·3	54·8
I 11	345 30·6	12·7	242 34·0	13·1	20 51·3	10·5	54·9
D 12	0 30·7	N13 13·5	257 06·1	13·1	N20 40·8	10·5	54·9
A 13	15 30·9	14·3	271 38·2	13·2	20 30·3	10·7	54·9
Y 14	30 31·0	15·1	286 10·4	13·2	20 19·6	10·7	54·9
15	45 31·1 ··	16·0	300 42·6	13·2	20 08·9	10·8	55·0
16	60 31·2	16·8	315 14·8	13·3	19 58·1	11·0	55·0
17	75 31·3	17·6	329 47·1	13·3	19 47·1	11·0	55·0
18	90 31·4	N13 18·4	344 19·4	13·4	N19 36·1	11·1	55·0
19	105 31·5	19·2	358 51·8	13·4	19 25·0	11·2	55·0
20	120 31·6	20·0	13 24·2	13·5	19 13·8	11·3	55·1
21	135 31·7 ··	20·8	27 56·7	13·5	19 02·5	11·4	55·1
22	150 31·8	21·6	42 29·2	13·5	18 51·1	11·4	55·1
23	165 31·9	22·5	57 01·7	13·6	18 39·7	11·6	55·1
26 00	180 32·0	N13 23·3	71 34·3	13·6	N18 28·1	11·7	55·2
01	195 32·1	24·1	86 06·9	13·7	18 16·4	11·7	55·2
02	210 32·2	24·9	100 39·6	13·7	18 04·7	11·8	55·2
03	225 32·3 ··	25·7	115 12·3	13·8	17 52·9	11·9	55·2
04	240 32·5	26·5	129 45·1	13·7	17 41·0	12·0	55·3
05	255 32·6	27·3	144 17·8	13·9	17 29·0	12·1	55·3
06	270 32·7	N13 28·1	158 50·7	13·8	N17 16·9	12·2	55·3
07	285 32·8	28·9	173 23·5	13·9	17 04·7	12·2	55·3
S 08	300 32·9	29·7	187 56·4	13·9	16 52·5	12·4	55·4
A 09	315 33·0 ··	30·5	202 29·3	14·0	16 40·1	12·4	55·4
T 10	330 33·1	31·3	217 02·3	14·0	16 27·7	12·5	55·4
U 11	345 33·2	32·1	231 35·3	14·0	16 15·2	12·6	55·4
R 12	0 33·3	N13 32·9	246 08·3	14·1	N16 02·6	12·6	55·5
D 13	15 33·4	33·7	260 41·4	14·1	15 50·0	12·7	55·5
A 14	30 33·5	34·5	275 14·5	14·1	15 37·3	12·9	55·5
Y 15	45 33·6 ··	35·4	289 47·6	14·1	15 24·4	12·9	55·5
16	60 33·7	36·2	304 20·7	14·2	15 11·5	12·9	55·6
17	75 33·8	37·0	318 53·9	14·2	14 58·6	13·1	55·6
18	90 33·9	N13 37·8	333 27·1	14·3	N14 45·5	13·1	55·6
19	105 34·0	38·6	348 00·4	14·2	14 32·4	13·2	55·7
20	120 34·1	39·4	2 33·6	14·3	14 19·2	13·2	55·7
21	135 34·2 ··	40·2	17 06·9	14·3	14 06·0	13·4	55·7
22	150 34·3	41·0	31 40·2	14·4	13 52·6	13·4	55·7
23	165 34·4	41·8	46 13·6	14·3	13 39·2	13·5	55·8
27 00	180 34·5	N13 42·6	60 46·9	14·4	N13 25·7	13·5	55·8
01	195 34·6	43·4	75 20·3	14·4	13 12·2	13·7	55·8
02	210 34·7	44·2	89 53·7	14·4	12 58·5	13·6	55·9
03	225 34·8 ··	45·0	104 27·1	14·4	12 44·9	13·8	55·9
04	240 34·9	45·8	119 00·5	14·5	12 31·1	13·8	55·9
05	255 35·0	46·6	133 34·0	14·5	12 17·3	13·9	55·9
06	270 35·1	N13 47·4	148 07·5	14·5	N12 03·4	14·0	56·0
07	285 35·2	48·2	162 41·0	14·5	11 49·4	14·0	56·0
08	300 35·3	49·0	177 14·5	14·5	11 35·4	14·1	56·0
S 09	315 35·4 ··	49·7	191 48·0	14·5	11 21·3	14·2	56·0
U 10	330 35·5	50·5	206 21·5	14·6	11 07·1	14·2	56·1
N 11	345 35·6	51·3	220 55·1	14·5	10 52·9	14·3	56·1
D 12	0 35·7	N13 52·1	235 28·6	14·6	N10 38·6	14·3	56·2
A 13	15 35·8	52·9	250 02·2	14·6	10 24·3	14·4	56·2
Y 14	30 35·9	53·7	264 35·8	14·6	10 09·9	14·5	56·2
15	45 36·0 ··	54·5	279 09·4	14·6	9 55·4	14·5	56·3
16	60 36·1	55·3	293 43·0	14·6	9 40·9	14·6	56·3
17	75 36·2	56·1	308 16·6	14·6	9 26·3	14·6	56·3
18	90 36·3	N13 56·9	322 50·2	14·6	N 9 11·7	14·7	56·4
19	105 36·4	57·7	337 23·8	14·6	8 57·0	14·8	56·4
20	120 36·5	58·5	351 57·4	14·6	8 42·2	14·8	56·4
21	135 36·6	59·3	6 31·0	14·6	8 27·4	14·8	56·5
22	150 36·7	14 00·1	21 04·6	14·6	8 12·6	14·9	56·5
23	165 36·8	00·9	35 38·2	14·6	7 57·7	15·0	56·5
	S.D. 15·9	d 0·8	S.D. 15·0		15·1		15·3

Lat.	Twilight Naut.	Twilight Civil	Sun-rise	Moonrise 25	Moonrise 26	Moonrise 27	Moonrise 28
°	h m	h m	h m	h m	h m	h m	h m
N 72	////	////	02 32	□	09 06	11 58	14 15
N 70	////	00 56	03 00	□	09 57	12 17	14 21
68	////	01 53	03 22	07 44	10 28	12 31	14 26
66	////	02 26	03 38	08 44	10 51	12 42	14 30
64	00 48	02 49	03 51	09 18	11 09	12 52	14 33
62	01 39	03 07	04 03	09 43	11 23	13 00	14 36
60	02 09	03 22	04 12	10 02	11 35	13 07	14 38
N 58	02 31	03 35	04 21	10 18	11 46	13 13	14 41
56	02 48	03 45	04 28	10 32	11 55	13 19	14 43
54	03 03	03 55	04 35	10 43	12 03	13 23	14 44
52	03 15	04 03	04 41	10 53	12 10	13 28	14 46
50	03 25	04 10	04 46	11 03	12 17	13 32	14 47
45	03 47	04 26	04 57	11 22	12 31	13 40	14 50
N 40	04 03	04 38	05 07	11 37	12 42	13 47	14 53
35	04 16	04 48	05 15	11 50	12 52	13 53	14 55
30	04 27	04 57	05 22	12 02	13 00	13 58	14 57
20	04 45	05 11	05 34	12 21	13 15	14 07	15 01
N 10	04 58	05 23	05 45	12 38	13 27	14 15	15 04
0	05 08	05 33	05 54	12 54	13 39	14 23	15 06
S 10	05 18	05 42	06 04	13 09	13 51	14 30	15 09
20	05 26	05 52	06 14	13 26	14 03	14 38	15 12
30	05 33	06 01	06 26	13 45	14 17	14 47	15 16
35	05 36	06 06	06 32	13 56	14 25	14 52	15 17
40	05 40	06 12	06 40	14 08	14 34	14 58	15 20
45	05 43	06 18	06 48	14 23	14 45	15 04	15 22
S 50	05 47	06 25	06 59	14 41	14 58	15 12	15 25
52	05 48	06 28	07 03	14 50	15 04	15 16	15 27
54	05 50	06 32	07 09	14 59	15 11	15 20	15 28
56	05 52	06 35	07 15	15 10	15 18	15 24	15 30
58	05 53	06 39	07 21	15 22	15 26	15 29	15 32
S 60	05 55	06 44	07 28	15 36	15 36	15 35	15 34

Lat.	Sun-set	Twilight Civil	Twilight Naut.	Moonset 25	Moonset 26	Moonset 27	Moonset 28
°	h m	h m	h m	h m	h m	h m	h m
N 72	21 29	////	////	□	06 12	04 52	04 09
N 70	20 59	23 16	////	□	05 19	04 32	04 00
68	20 37	22 09	////	05 55	04 46	04 16	03 53
66	20 20	21 34	////	04 54	04 22	04 02	03 46
64	20 06	21 10	23 21	04 19	04 03	03 51	03 41
62	19 55	20 51	22 22	03 53	03 47	03 42	03 36
60	19 45	20 36	21 50	03 33	03 34	03 33	03 32
N 58	19 36	20 23	21 28	03 17	03 23	03 26	03 29
56	19 29	20 12	21 10	03 03	03 13	03 20	03 25
54	19 22	20 02	20 55	02 50	03 04	03 14	03 22
52	19 16	19 54	20 43	02 40	02 56	03 09	03 20
50	19 11	19 46	20 32	02 30	02 49	03 04	03 17
45	18 59	19 31	20 10	02 09	02 33	02 54	03 12
N 40	18 49	19 18	19 53	01 53	02 21	02 45	03 07
35	18 41	19 08	19 40	01 39	02 10	02 38	03 04
30	18 34	18 59	19 29	01 26	02 00	02 31	03 00
20	18 22	18 45	19 11	01 05	01 44	02 20	02 54
N 10	18 11	18 33	18 58	00 47	01 29	02 10	02 49
0	18 01	18 23	18 49	00 30	01 16	02 00	02 44
S 10	17 52	18 13	18 38	00 12	01 02	01 50	02 38
20	17 41	18 04	18 30	24 47	00 47	01 40	02 33
30	17 30	17 54	18 22	24 30	00 30	01 28	02 26
35	17 23	17 49	18 19	24 20	00 20	01 21	02 23
40	17 15	17 43	18 15	24 08	00 08	01 13	02 19
45	17 07	17 37	18 12	23 55	25 04	01 04	02 14
S 50	16 56	17 30	18 08	23 38	24 53	00 53	02 08
52	16 51	17 27	18 06	23 30	24 47	00 47	02 05
54	16 46	17 23	18 05	23 21	24 42	00 42	02 02
56	16 40	17 19	18 03	23 11	24 35	00 35	01 59
58	16 34	17 15	18 01	23 00	24 28	00 28	01 55
S 60	16 26	17 11	18 00	22 47	24 19	00 19	01 51

Day	SUN Eqn. of Time 00h	SUN Eqn. of Time 12h	SUN Mer. Pass.	MOON Mer. Pass. Upper	MOON Mer. Pass. Lower	MOON Age	MOON Phase
	m s	m s	h m	h m	h m	d	
25	01 58	02 03	11 58	19 05	06 42	09	
26	02 08	02 13	11 58	19 49	07 27	10	
27	02 18	02 23	11 58	20 33	08 11	11	

Figure 2403c: Sample right hand page of Nautical Almanac.

Nautical Almanac,
left page.

Specifically, the left page gives the GHA of Aries (♈), and the magnitude, GHA, Dec., and time of meridian passage of the navigational planets, Venus, Mars, Jupiter, and Saturn, for each hour of GMT. All tabulations are in degrees, minutes, and tenths of a minute of arc. A list of 57 selected stars, arranged in alphabetical order together with SHA and declination to the nearest one-tenth minute, is also given. These are the prime navigational stars selected for their magnitude and distribution in the heavens, and are the ones most frequently observed by the navigator.

Nautical Almanac,
right page.

"v" and "d."

Data for the sun and moon are presented on the right hand page with GHA and Dec., tabulated to one-tenth minute of arc for each hour. For the moon, additional values for the horizontal parallax (H.P.) and of "v" and "d" are tabulated for each hour. The moon's rate of change of GHA and Dec. varies considerably. The "d" values are the amount in arc by which Dec. changes during each hour; "v" values are the amount in arc by which GHA departs from the basic rate used in the almanac interpolation tables. The "v" and "d" values are for use with the interpolation tables, which are based on a constant rate of change. These latter tables, explained in the following paragraph, are included to facilitate the interpolation of GHA and Dec., respectively for intermediate times. For the sun "v" is omitted entirely and "d" is given only once at the bottom of the page for every three days. For the planets "v" and "d" are given for every three days, as they change very slowly.

To establish GHA and declination of the body for a time of observation other than the exact hour of GMT it is necessary to interpolate, i.e., calculate intermediate values between those which appear in the hourly tabulation. For the intermediate time, stated in minutes and seconds past the whole hour printed in the tables, the change in GHA and Dec. are assumed to be at a uniform rate. This is not strictly true; however, the error involved is negligible when using the stars. The "v" and "d" corrections listed in the previous paragraph are applied for greater accuracy when using bodies within the solar system.

These increments and corrections are printed on tinted pages to facilitate locating them. A partial sample page is shown in Figure 2403d. The computations are based on standard apparent motions of the heavenly bodies around the earth, at the rate of 15° per hour for the sun and planets, 15°02'.46 for Aries and 14°19'.0 for the moon. The values of the correction for "v" and "d" are then the excesses of the actual hourly motions over the above adopted values. They are generally positive, and therefore additive, except for the "v" factor for Venus, which is sometimes negative. Entry is made at the top of the page for minutes of GMT, and in the left hand column for seconds. This correction for time is taken from the appropriate column for the body observed, and combined with the "v" or "d" correction where appropriate.

Star positions.

The SHA and declination of 173 selected stars, including 57 navigational stars listed on the daily pages, are tabulated for each month near the end of the white section of the *Almanac.* No interpolation is needed and the data can be used in precisely the same way as those selected stars on the daily pages. The stars are arranged in ascending order of SHA.

Accuracy.

2404. The tabulated values are in most cases correct to the nearest one-tenth minute, the exception being the sun's GHA, which is deliberately adjusted by up to 0'.15 to reduce the error caused by omitting the "v" correction. The largest

INCREMENTS AND CORRECTIONS

56ᵐ s	SUN PLANETS	ARIES	MOON	v or Corrⁿ d	v or Corrⁿ d	v or Corrⁿ d
00	14 00·0	14 02·3	13 21·7	0·0 0·0	6·0 5·7	12·0 11·3
01	14 00·3	14 02·6	13 22·0	0·1 0·1	6·1 5·7	12·1 11·4
02	14 00·5	14 02·8	13 22·2	0·2 0·2	6·2 5·8	12·2 11·5
03	14 00·8	14 03·1	13 22·4	0·3 0·3	6·3 5·9	12·3 11·6
04	14 01·0	14 03·3	13 22·7	0·4 0·4	6·4 6·0	12·4 11·7
05	14 01·3	14 03·8	13 22·9	0·5 0·5	6·5 6·1	12·5 11·8
06	14 01·5	14 03·8	13 23·2	0·6 0·6	6·6 6·2	12·6 11·9
07	14 01·8	14 04·1	13 23·4	0·7 0·7	6·7 6·3	12·7 12·0
08	14 02·0	14 04·3	13 23·6	0·8 0·8	6·8 6·4	12·8 12·1
09	14 02·3	14 04·6	13 23·9	0·9 0·8	6·9 6·5	12·9 12·1
10	14 02·5	14 04·8	13 24·1	1·0 0·9	7·0 6·6	13·0 12·2
11	14 02·8	14 05·1	13 24·4	1·1 1·0	7·1 6·7	13·1 12·3
12	14 03·0	14 05·3	13 24·6	1·2 1·1	7·2 6·8	13·2 12·4
13	14 03·3	14 05·6	13 24·8	1·3 1·2	7·3 6·9	13·3 12·5
14	14 03·5	14 05·8	13 25·1	1·4 1·3	7·4 7·0	13·4 12·6
15	14 03·8	14 06·1	13 25·3	1·5 1·4	7·5 7·1	13·5 12·7
16	14 04·0	14 06·3	13 25·6	1·6 1·5	7·6 7·2	13·6 12·8
17	14 04·3	14 06·6	13 25·8	1·7 1·6	7·7 7·3	13·7 12·9
18	14 04·5	14 06·8	13 26·0	1·8 1·7	7·8 7·3	13·8 13·0
19	14 04·8	14 07·1	13 26·3	1·9 1·8	7·9 7·4	13·9 13·1
20	14 05·0	14 07·3	13 26·5	2·0 1·9	8·0 7·5	14·0 13·2
21	14 05·3	14 07·6	13 26·7	2·1 2·0	8·1 7·6	14·1 13·3
22	14 05·5	14 07·8	13 27·0	2·2 2·1	8·2 7·7	14·2 13·4
23	14 05·8	14 08·1	13 27·2	2·3 2·2	8·3 7·8	14·3 13·5
24	14 06·0	14 08·3	13 27·5	2·4 2·3	8·4 7·9	14·4 13·6
25	14 06·3	14 08·6	13 27·7	2·5 2·4	8·5 8·0	14·5 13·7
26	14 06·5	14 08·8	13 27·9	2·6 2·4	8·6 8·1	14·6 13·7
27	14 06·8	14 09·1	13 28·2	2·7 2·5	8·7 8·2	14·7 13·8
28	14 07·0	14 09·3	13 28·4	2·8 2·6	8·8 8·3	14·8 13·9
29	14 07·3	14 09·6	13 28·7	2·9 2·7	8·9 8·4	14·9 14·0
30	14 07·5	14 09·8	13 28·9	3·0 2·8	9·0 8·5	15·0 14·1
31	14 07·8	14 10·1	13 29·1	3·1 2·9	9·1 8·6	15·1 14·2
32	14 08·0	14 10·3	13 29·4	3·2 3·0	9·2 8·7	15·2 14·3
33	14 08·3	14 10·6	13 29·6	3·3 3·1	9·3 8·8	15·3 14·4
34	14 08·5	14 10·8	13 29·8	3·4 3·2	9·4 8·9	15·4 14·5
35	14 08·8	14 11·1	13 30·1	3·5 3·3	9·5 8·9	15·5 14·6
36	14 09·0	14 11·3	13 30·3	3·6 3·4	9·6 9·0	15·6 14·7
37	14 09·3	14 11·6	13 30·6	3·7 3·5	9·7 9·1	15·7 14·8
38	14 09·5	14 11·8	13 30·8	3·8 3·6	9·8 9·2	15·8 14·9
39	14 09·8	14 12·1	13 31·0	3·9 3·7	9·9 9·3	15·9 15·0
40	14 10·0	14 12·3	13 31·3	4·0 3·8	10·0 9·4	16·0 15·1
41	14 10·3	14 12·6	13 31·5	4·1 3·9	10·1 9·5	16·1 15·2
42	14 10·5	14 12·8	13 31·8	4·2 4·0	10·2 9·6	16·2 15·3
43	14 10·8	14 13·1	13 32·0	4·3 4·0	10·3 9·7	16·3 15·3
44	14 11·0	14 13·3	13 32·2	4·4 4·1	10·4 9·8	16·4 15·4
45	14 11·3	14 13·6	13 32·5	4·5 4·2	10·5 9·9	16·5 15·5
46	14 11·5	14 13·8	13 32·7	4·6 4·3	10·6 10·0	16·6 15·6
47	14 11·8	14 14·1	13 32·9	4·7 4·4	10·7 10·1	16·7 16·0
48	14 12·0	14 14·3	13 33·2	4·8 4·5	10·8 10·2	16·8 15·8
49	14 12·3	14 14·6	13 33·4	4·9 4·6	10·9 10·3	16·9 15·9
50	14 12·5	14 14·8	13 33·7	5·0 4·7	11·0 10·4	17·0 16·0
51	14 12·8	14 15·1	13 33·9	5·1 4·8	11·1 10·5	17·1 16·1
52	14 13·0	14 15·3	13 34·1	5·2 4·9	11·2 10·5	17·2 16·2
53	14 13·3	14 15·6	13 34·4	5·3 5·0	11·3 10·6	17·3 16·3
54	14 13·5	14 15·8	13 34·6	5·4 5·1	11·4 10·7	17·4 16·4
55	14 13·8	14 16·1	13 34·9	5·5 5·2	11·5 10·8	17·5 16·5
56	14 14·0	14 16·3	13 35·1	5·6 5·3	11·6 10·9	17·6 16·6
57	14 14·3	14 16·6	13 35·3	5·7 5·4	11·7 11·0	17·7 16·7
58	14 14·5	14 16·8	13 35·6	5·8 5·5	11·8 11·1	17·8 16·8
59	14 14·8	14 17·1	13 35·8	5·9 5·6	11·9 11·2	17·9 16·9
60	14 15·0	14 17·3	13 36·1	6·0 5·7	12·0 11·3	18·0 17·0

57ᵐ s	SUN PLANETS	ARIES	MOON	v or Corrⁿ d	v or Corrⁿ d	v or Corrⁿ d
00	14 15·0	14 17·3	13 36·1	0·0 0·0	6·0 5·8	12·0 11·5
01	14 15·3	14 17·6	13 36·3	0·1 0·1	6·1 5·8	12·1 11·6
02	14 15·5	14 17·8	13 36·5	0·2 0·2	6·2 5·9	12·2 11·7
03	14 15·8	14 18·1	13 36·8	0·3 0·3	6·3 6·0	12·3 11·8
04	14 16·0	14 18·3	13 37·0	0·4 0·4	6·4 6·1	12·4 11·9
05	14 16·3	14 18·6	13 37·2	0·5 0·5	6·5 6·2	12·5 12·0
06	14 16·5	14 18·8	13 37·5	0·6 0·6	6·6 6·3	12·6 12·1
07	14 16·8	14 19·1	13 37·7	0·7 0·7	6·7 6·4	12·7 12·2
08	14 17·0	14 19·3	13 38·0	0·8 0·8	6·8 6·5	12·8 12·3
09	14 17·3	14 19·6	13 38·2	0·9 0·9	6·9 6·6	12·9 12·4
10	14 17·5	14 19·8	13 38·4	1·0 1·0	7·0 6·7	13·0 12·5
11	14 17·8	14 20·1	13 38·7	1·1 1·1	7·1 6·8	13·1 12·6
12	14 18·0	14 20·3	13 38·9	1·2 1·2	7·2 6·9	13·2 12·7
13	14 18·3	14 20·6	13 39·2	1·3 1·2	7·3 7·0	13·3 12·7
14	14 18·5	14 20·9	13 39·4	1·4 1·3	7·4 7·1	13·4 12·8
15	14 18·8	14 21·1	13 39·6	1·5 1·4	7·5 7·2	13·5 12·9
16	14 19·0	14 21·4	13 39·9	1·6 1·5	7·6 7·3	13·6 13·0
17	14 19·3	14 21·6	13 40·1	1·7 1·6	7·7 7·4	13·7 13·1
18	14 19·5	14 21·9	13 40·3	1·8 1·7	7·8 7·5	13·8 13·2
19	14 19·8	14 22·1	13 40·6	1·9 1·8	7·9 7·6	13·9 13·3
20	14 20·0	14 22·4	13 40·8	2·0 1·9	8·0 7·7	14·0 13·4
21	14 20·3	14 22·6	13 41·1	2·1 2·0	8·1 7·8	14·1 13·5
22	14 20·5	14 22·9	13 41·3	2·2 2·1	8·2 7·9	14·2 13·6
23	14 20·8	14 23·1	13 41·5	2·3 2·2	8·3 8·0	14·3 13·7
24	14 21·0	14 23·4	13 41·8	2·4 2·3	8·4 8·1	14·4 13·8
25	14 21·3	14 23·6	13 42·0	2·5 2·4	8·5 8·1	14·5 13·9
26	14 21·5	14 23·9	13 42·3	2·6 2·5	8·6 8·2	14·6 14·0
27	14 21·8	14 24·1	13 42·5	2·7 2·6	8·7 8·3	14·7 14·1
28	14 22·0	14 24·4	13 42·7	2·8 2·7	8·8 8·4	14·8 14·2
29	14 22·3	14 24·6	13 43·0	2·9 2·8	8·9 8·5	14·9 14·3
30	14 22·5	14 24·9	13 43·2	3·0 2·9	9·0 8·6	15·0 14·4
31	14 22·8	14 25·1	13 43·4	3·1 3·0	9·1 8·7	15·1 14·5
32	14 23·0	14 25·4	13 43·7	3·2 3·1	9·2 8·8	15·2 14·6
33	14 23·3	14 25·6	13 43·9	3·3 3·2	9·3 8·9	15·3 14·7
34	14 23·5	14 25·9	13 44·2	3·4 3·3	9·4 9·0	15·4 14·8
35	14 23·8	14 26·1	13 44·4	3·5 3·4	9·5 9·1	15·5 14·9
36	14 24·0	14 26·4	13 44·6	3·6 3·5	9·6 9·2	15·6 15·0
37	14 24·3	14 26·6	13 44·9	3·7 3·5	9·7 9·3	15·7 15·0
38	14 24·5	14 26·9	13 45·1	3·8 3·6	9·8 9·4	15·8 15·1
39	14 24·8	14 27·1	13 45·4	3·9 3·7	9·9 9·5	15·9 15·2
40	14 25·0	14 27·4	13 45·6	4·0 3·8	10·0 9·6	16·0 15·3
41	14 25·3	14 27·6	13 45·8	4·1 3·9	10·1 9·7	16·1 15·4
42	14 25·5	14 27·9	13 46·1	4·2 4·0	10·2 9·8	16·2 15·5
43	14 25·8	14 28·1	13 46·3	4·3 4·1	10·3 9·9	16·3 15·6
44	14 26·0	14 28·4	13 46·5	4·4 4·2	10·4 10·0	16·4 15·7
45	14 26·3	14 28·6	13 46·8	4·5 4·3	10·5 10·1	16·5 15·8
46	14 26·5	14 28·9	13 47·0	4·6 4·4	10·6 10·2	16·6 15·9
47	14 26·8	14 29·1	13 47·3	4·7 4·5	10·7 10·3	16·7 16·0
48	14 27·0	14 29·4	13 47·5	4·8 4·6	10·8 10·4	16·8 16·1
49	14 27·3	14 29·6	13 47·7	4·9 4·7	10·9 10·4	16·9 16·2
50	14 27·5	14 29·9	13 48·0	5·0 4·8	11·0 10·5	17·0 16·3
51	14 27·8	14 30·1	13 48·2	5·1 4·9	11·1 10·6	17·1 16·4
52	14 28·0	14 30·4	13 48·5	5·2 5·0	11·2 10·7	17·2 16·5
53	14 28·3	14 30·6	13 48·7	5·3 5·1	11·3 10·8	17·3 16·6
54	14 28·5	14 30·9	13 48·9	5·4 5·2	11·4 10·9	17·4 16·7
55	14 28·8	14 31·1	13 49·2	5·5 5·3	11·5 11·0	17·5 16·8
56	14 29·0	14 31·4	13 49·4	5·6 5·4	11·6 11·1	17·6 16·9
57	14 29·3	14 31·6	13 49·7	5·7 5·5	11·7 11·2	17·7 17·0
58	14 29·5	14 31·9	13 49·9	5·8 5·6	11·8 11·3	17·8 17·1
59	14 29·8	14 32·1	13 50·1	5·9 5·7	11·9 11·4	17·9 17·2
60	14 30·0	14 32·4	13 50·4	6·0 5·8	12·0 11·5	18·0 17·3

*Figure 2403d:
Correction tables.*

error that can occur in GHA or Dec. of any body other than the sun or moon is less than two-tenths minutes; it may reach 0'.25 for the GHA of the sun, and 0'.3 for the moon. Additional data on errors, and explanations are given within the *Almanac*.

2405. A table is included within the *Almanac* for correcting sextant observations for atmospheric refraction. This table is based on standard conditions of barometric pressure and temperature; a second table gives additional corrections for non-standard conditions. Tables for correcting for the dip of the horizon under standard conditions and a special table for moon correction are also included. These tables for correcting the sextant altitude are discussed in more detail in

*Additional tables in
the* Almanac.

Chapter 22. These values do not change as a function of time as do the ephemeristic data in the *Almanac*.

The tables for determining the times of twilight and of the rising and setting phenomena of the sun and moon will be discussed in Chapter 28.

Use of the tables.

2406. Figure 2406 illustrates the method of extracting and recording the data for the sun, moon, the planet Mars and the star Denebola. The data are extracted from the daily pages illustrated in Figures 2403b and 2403c and from the increments and corrections section from Figure 2403d. Step by step solution is as follows to determine the values shown in Figure 2406:

Figure 2406:
Tabular solutions.

Body	SUN	MOON	DENEBOLA	MARS
GMT	13-56-35	20-57-04	22-56-08	08-57-05
Date (G)	26 APRIL	26 APRIL	26 APRIL	26 APRIL
"v" factor	—	14.3	—	2.4
Tab GHA	15° 33'.4	2° 33'.6	184° 43'.3	78° 33'.5
Corr. m s +	14° 08'.8	13° 37'.0	14° 04'.3	14° 16'.3
"v" corr. +	—	13'.7	—	2'.3
SHA +	—	—	183° 07'.3	—
			381° 54'.9	
GHA	29° 42'.2	16° 24'.3	21° 54'.9	92° 52'.1
"d" factor	+ 0.8	− 13.2	—	+ 0.1
Tab Dec.	13° 33'.7 N	14° 19'.2 N	14° 44'.6 N	22° 57'.6 S
"d" corr.	+ 0.8	− 12.7	—	+ 0.1
Dec.	13° 34'.5 N	14° 06'.5 N	14° 44'.6 N	22° 57'.7 S

Example: (Figure 2406, sun column)

A navigator located at approximately 30° North latitude and 60° W longitude on 26 April ZT 09 56 35 (+4) having observed the sun, needs to determine the GHA and Dec. from the *Nautical Almanac*.

Solution: (1) Enter column headed GMT, of the right hand daily page for correct date (26 April) and whole hour (13) of GMT. (2) Reading across from GMT, in column headed SUN, pick out and record GHA (15°33'.4) and Dec. (N13°33'.7) for whole hour and note whether Dec. is increasing or decreasing at the next later hour (+). (3) At the bottom of the column pick out and record the "d" factor (0.8). (4) Turn to yellow pages (Figure 2403d) for increments and corrections, and find correct page for 56 minutes of GMT listed at top of the page. Pick out incremental correction to GHA, (14°08'.8) under column headed SUN and PLANETS, opposite seconds of GMT (35) in left column. If timing was to greater accuracy than whole seconds, interpolate between lines by eye. (5) In the adjacent column, under the columns headed "v" or "d" corrections, enter with a "d" factor (0.8) from (3) above and pick out correction (0.8) to apply to declination. If Dec. on the daily pages was decreasing with time the correction is subtractive, if increasing it is additive. (6) Add GHA values from (2) and (4) above to obtain GHA sun (29°42'.2) for 13-56-35 GMT. (7) Add Dec. from step (2) and correction from step (5) to obtain declination of sun (N13°34'.5) for 13-56-35 GMT.

Referring to Figure 2406 and the above procedure for extracting data for the sun, a similar procedure is followed for the other bodies. Following through the problem it will be noted that there is both a "v" and "d" correction for the moon in addition to the correction for minutes and seconds of time after the whole hour of GMT. The north declination of the moon was decreasing with time resulting in the "d" correction being minus. In the Denebola problem the GHA ♈ plus SHA star produced a GHA Denebola of 381°54'.9 with the result that 360° is subtracted to produce GHA 21°54'.9. For the Mars observation, the south Dec. was increasing with time and the "d" correction was therefore (+). In both the moon and Mars observations the Dec. was changing toward the south. In the first case there is a decrease of N Dec., and in the latter an increase in S Dec.

Comments on solutions.

2407. The coordinates of celestial bodies are tabulated in the *Nautical Almanac* with respect to Greenwich mean time. Using the GMT of an observation, the navigator extracts the GHA and Dec. of the body observed. The position of the body establishes one vertex of the navigational triangle: the navigator solves this triangle to obtain a line of position.

Nautical Almanac. Summary.

The GHA of the sun, moon, planets and Aries are tabulated in the *Nautical Almanac* for each hour of GMT, and tables of increments permit interpolation for the minutes and seconds of an observation. A small "v" correction factor applying to the GHA is also shown on the daily pages. The sum of the tabulated GHA, together with the increment for excess minutes and seconds, and the value of the "v" correction for these minutes and seconds, is the GHA of the body at the time of observation. The SHA of a star is added to the GHA of Aries to obtain the star's GHA. The SHA of the star is taken from the almanac without interpolation.

The declinations of the sun, moon, and planets are also tabulated in the daily pages of the *Nautical Almanac* for GMT, as is a "d" factor. The correction to the declination for "d" is obtained from the table of increments for the excess minutes and seconds over the tabulated value. The declination of a star is taken from the *Almanac* without any correction.

In practice, the navigator always obtains *all* values of GHA and Dec., plus associated data, from the daily pages during one book opening. He then turns to the increments and corrections tables for the remaining data. This procedure materially shortens the time required to reduce observations.

2408. The *Air Almanac* contains basically the same data as that of the *Nautical Almanac*. The arrangement is designed primarily for the use of aviators, giving a more convenient arrangement for a fast solution; however, inaccuracies result for some bodies. It is becoming increasingly popular with surface navigators, but its use is not recommended for this purpose when maximum accuracy is required in all observations. In the past the *Air Almanac* rounded off listings for GHA and Dec., together with the correcting factors, to the nearest minute of arc. In recent editions the sun's GHA and declination, and the GHA of Aries are tabulated to a tenth of a minute. With this arrangement it should be mentioned that the sun's GHA can now be determined more accurately by means of the *Air*

Air Almanac. Contents.

GHA and Dec.

GREENWICH A. M. 1969 APRIL 26 (SATURDAY)

GMT	SUN GHA	SUN Dec.	ARIES GHA ♈	VENUS −4.0 GHA	VENUS Dec.	MARS −1.0 GHA	MARS Dec.	JUPITER −1.9 GHA	JUPITER Dec.	MOON GHA	MOON Dec.
00 00	180 32.0	N13 23.3	213 49.0	205 23	N 7 43	318 14	S22 57	35 46	N 2 31	71 35	N18 27
10	183 02.0	23.4	216 19.5	207 54		320 44		38 16		74 00	25
20	185 32.0	23.5	218 49.9	210 24		323 15		40 47		76 25	23
30	188 02.0 ·	23.7	221 20.3	212 55 ·		325 45 · ·		43 17 ·		78 51 ·	21
40	190 32.1	23.8	223 50.7	215 25		328 16		45 47		81 16	19
50	193 02.1	23.9	226 21.1	217 56		330 46		48 18		83 42	17
01 00	195 32.1	N13 24.1	228 51.5	220 26	N 7 42	333 16	S22 57	50 48	N 2 31	86 07	N18 15
10	198 02.1	24.2	231 21.9	222 56		335 47		53 19		88 33	13
20	200 32.1	24.3	233 52.3	225 27		338 17		55 49		90 58	12
30	203 02.1 ·	24.5	236 22.7	227 57 ·		340 48 · ·		58 20 ·		93 24 ·	10
40	205 32.2	24.6	238 53.2	230 28		343 18		60 50		95 49	08
50	208 02.2	24.7	241 23.6	232 58		345 48		63 21		98 14	06
02 00	210 32.2	N13 24.9	243 54.0	235 29	N 7 42	348 19	S22 57	65 51	N 2 31	100 40	N18 04
10	213 02.2	25.0	246 24.4	237 59		350 49		68 21		103 05	02
20	215 32.2	25.1	248 54.8	240 29		353 20		70 52		105 31	18 00
30	218 02.2 ·	25.3	251 25.2	243 00 ·		355 50 · ·		73 22 ·		107 56	17 58
40	220 32.3	25.4	253 55.6	245 30		358 21		75 53		110 22	56
50	223 02.3	25.6	256 26.0	248 01		0 51		78 23		112 47	54
03 00	225 32.3	N13 25.7	258 56.4	250 31	N 7 41	3 21	S22 57	80 54	N 2 31	115 13	N17 52
10	228 02.3	25.8	261 26.9	253 02		5 52		83 24		117 38	50
20	230 32.3	26.0	263 57.3	255 32		8 22		85 55		120 04	48
30	233 02.4 ·	26.1	266 27.7	258 02 ·		10 53 · ·		88 25 ·		122 29 ·	46
40	235 32.4	26.2	268 58.1	260 33		13 23		90 55		124 55	44
50	238 02.4	26.4	271 28.5	263 03		15 53		93 26		127 20	42
04 00	240 32.4	N13 26.5	273 58.9	265 34	N 7 40	18 24	S22 57	95 56	N 2 31	129 45	N17 40
10	243 02.4	26.6	276 29.3	268 04		20 54		98 27		132 11	38
20	245 32.4	26.8	278 59.7	270 35		23 25		100 57		134 36	36
30	248 02.5 ·	26.9	281 30.1	273 05 ·		25 55 · ·		103 28 ·		137 02 ·	34
40	250 32.5	27.0	284 00.5	275 35		28 25		105 58		139 27	32
50	253 02.5	27.2	286 31.0	278 06		30 56		108 28		141 53	30
05 00	255 32.5	N13 27.3	289 01.4	280 36	N 7 40	33 26	S22 57	110 59	N 2 31	144 18	N17 28
10	258 02.5	27.4	291 31.8	283 07		35 57		113 29		146 44	26
20	260 32.5	27.6	294 02.2	285 37		38 27		116 00		149 09	24
30	263 02.6 ·	27.7	296 32.6	288 08 ·		40 57 · ·		118 30 ·		151 35 ·	22
40	265 32.6	27.8	299 03.0	290 38		43 28		121 01		154 00	20
50	268 02.6	28.0	301 33.4	293 08		45 58		123 31		156 26	18
06 00	270 32.6	N13 28.1	304 03.8	295 39	N 7 39	48 29	S22 57	126 02	N 2 31	158 51	N17 16
10	273 02.6	28.2	306 34.2	298 09		50 59		128 32		161 17	14
20	275 32.7	28.4	309 04.7	300 40		53 29		131 02		163 42	12
30	278 02.7 ·	28.5	311 35.1	303 10 ·		56 00 · ·		133 33 ·		166 07 ·	10
40	280 32.7	28.6	314 05.5	305 41		58 30		136 03		168 33	08
50	283 02.7	28.8	316 35.9	308 11		61 01		138 34		170 58	06
07 00	285 32.7	N13 28.9	319 06.3	310 41	N 7 38	63 31	S22 58	141 04	N 2 31	173 24	N17 04
10	288 02.7	29.0	321 36.7	313 12		66 01		143 35		175 49	02
20	290 32.8	29.2	324 07.1	315 42		68 32		146 05		178 15	17 00
30	293 02.8 ·	29.3	326 37.5	318 13 ·		71 02 · ·		148 36 ·		180 40	16 58
40	295 32.8	29.5	329 07.9	320 43		73 33		151 06		183 06	56
50	298 02.8	29.6	331 38.3	323 13		76 03		153 36		185 31	54
08 00	300 32.8	N13 29.7	334 08.8	325 44	N 7 38	78 34	S22 58	156 07	N 2 31	187 57	N16 51
10	303 02.8	29.9	336 39.2	328 14		81 04		158 37		190 22	49
20	305 32.9	30.0	339 09.6	330 45		83 34		161 08		192 48	47
30	308 02.9 ·	30.1	341 40.0	333 15 ·		86 05 · ·		163 38 ·		195 13 ·	45
40	310 32.9	30.3	344 10.4	335 46		88 35		166 09		197 39	43
50	313 02.9	30.4	346 40.8	338 16		91 06		168 39		200 04	41
09 00	315 32.9	N13 30.5	349 11.2	340 47	N 7 37	93 36	S22 58	171 10	N 2 31	202 30	N16 39
10	318 02.9	30.7	351 41.6	343 17		96 06		173 40		204 55	37
20	320 33.0	30.8	354 12.0	345 47		98 37		176 10		207 21	35
30	323 03.0 ·	30.9	356 42.5	348 18 ·		101 07 · ·		178 41 ·		209 46 ·	33
40	325 33.0	31.1	359 12.9	350 48		103 38		181 11		212 12	31
50	328 03.0	31.2	1 43.3	353 19		106 08		183 42		214 37	29
10 00	330 33.0	N13 31.3	4 13.7	355 49	N 7 36	108 38	S22 58	186 12	N 2 31	217 03	N16 27
10	333 03.1	31.5	6 44.1	358 19		111 09		188 43		219 28	25
20	335 33.1	31.6	9 14.5	0 50		113 39		191 13		221 54	23
30	338 03.1 ·	31.7	11 44.9	3 20 ·		116 10 · ·		193 44 ·		224 19 ·	20
40	340 33.1	31.9	14 15.3	5 51		118 40		196 14		226 45	18
50	343 03.1	32.0	16 45.7	8 21		121 10		198 44		229 10	16
11 00	345 33.1	N13 32.1	19 16.2	10 52	N 7 36	123 41	S22 58	201 15	N 2 31	231 36	N16 14
10	348 03.2	32.3	21 46.6	13 22		126 11		203 45		234 01	12
20	350 33.2	32.4	24 17.0	15 52		128 42		206 16		236 27	10
30	353 03.2 ·	32.5	26 47.4	18 23 ·		131 12 · ·		208 46 ·		238 52 ·	08
40	355 33.2	32.7	29 17.8	20 53		133 42		211 17		241 18	06
50	358 03.2	32.8	31 48.2	23 24		136 13		213 47		243 43	04

Moonrise

Lat.	Moon-rise	Diff.
N	h m	m
72	09 06	*
70	09 57	*
68	10 28	72
66	10 51	60
64	11 09	54
62	11 23	49
60	11 35	46
58	11 46	44
56	11 55	42
54	12 03	40
52	12 10	39
50	12 17	37
45	12 31	35
40	12 42	33
35	12 52	31
30	13 00	29
20	13 15	27
10	13 27	24
0	13 39	22
10	13 51	20
20	14 03	18
30	14 17	16
35	14 25	14
40	14 34	13
45	14 45	10
50	14 58	08
52	15 04	07
54	15 11	05
56	15 18	04
58	15 26	02
60	15 36	00
S		

Moon's P. in A.

Alt °	Corr +	Alt °	Corr +
0	55	56	30
9	54	57	29
14	53	58	28
18	52	60	27
21	51	61	26
24	50	62	25
26	49	63	24
28	48	64	23
30	47	65	22
32	46	67	21
34	45	68	20
36	44	69	19
38	43	70	18
39	42	71	17
41	41	72	16
42	40	73	15
44	39	75	14
45	38	76	13
47	37	77	12
48	36	79	11
50	35	80	10
51	34		
52	33		
54	32		
55	31		
56	30		
57			

Sun SD 15.9
Moon SD 15'
Age 9d

Figure 2408a: Sample left hand page of Air Almanac.

GREENWICH P. M. 1969 APRIL 26 (SATURDAY)

GMT	☉ SUN GHA	Dec.	ARIES GHA ♈	VENUS −4.0 GHA	Dec.	MARS −1.0 GHA	Dec.	JUPITER −1.9 GHA	Dec.	◑ MOON GHA	Dec.
h m											
12 00	0 33.2	N13 32.9	34 18.6	25 54	N 7 35	138 43	S22 58	216 18	N 2 32	246 09	N16 02
10	3 03.3	33.1	36 49.0	28 25		141 14		218 48		248 34	15 59
20	5 33.3	33.2	39 19.4	30 55		143 44		221 18		251 00	57
30	8 03.3 ·	33.3	41 49.8	33 25 ·		146 14 ·		223 49 ·		253 25 ·	55
40	10 33.3	33.5	44 20.3	35 56		148 45		226 19		255 51	53
50	13 03.3	33.6	46 50.7	38 26		151 15		228 50		258 16	51
13 00	15 33.3	N13 33.7	49 21.1	40 57	N 7 34	153 46	S22 58	231 20	N 2 32	260 42	N15 49
10	18 03.4	33.9	51 51.5	43 27		156 16		233 51		263 07	47
20	20 33.4	34.0	54 21.9	45 57		158 47		236 21		265 33	45
30	23 03.4 ·	34.1	56 52.3	48 28 ·		161 17 ·		238 51 ·		267 58 ·	43
40	25 33.4	34.3	59 22.7	50 58		163 47		241 22		270 24	40
50	28 03.4	34.4	61 53.1	53 29		166 18		243 52		272 49	38
14 00	30 33.4	N13 34.5	64 23.5	55 59	N 7 34	168 48	S22 58	246 23	N 2 32	275 15	N15 36
10	33 03.5	34.7	66 54.0	58 30		171 19		248 53		277 40	34
20	35 33.5	34.8	69 24.4	61 00		173 49		251 24		280 06	32
30	38 03.5 ·	34.9	71 54.8	63 30 ·		176 19 ·		253 54 ·		282 31 ·	30
40	40 33.5	35.1	74 25.2	66 01		178 50		256 25		284 57	28
50	43 03.5	35.2	76 55.6	68 31		181 20		258 55		287 22	25
15 00	45 33.6	N13 35.4	79 26.0	71 02	N 7 33	183 51	S22 58	261 25	N 2 32	289 48	N15 23
10	48 03.6	35.5	81 56.4	73 32		186 21		263 56		292 13	21
20	50 33.6	35.6	84 26.8	76 03		188 51		266 26		294 39	19
30	53 03.6 ·	35.8	86 57.2	78 33 ·		191 22 ·		268 57 ·		297 05 ·	17
40	55 33.6	35.9	89 27.7	81 03		193 52		271 27		299 30	15
50	58 03.6	36.0	91 58.1	83 34		196 23		273 58		301 56	13
16 00	60 33.7	N13 36.2	94 28.5	86 04	N 7 32	198 53	S22 58	276 28	N 2 32	304 21	N15 10
10	63 03.7	36.3	96 58.9	88 35		201 23		278 58		306 47	08
20	65 33.7	36.4	99 29.3	91 05		203 54		281 29		309 12	06
30	68 03.7 ·	36.6	101 59.7	93 35 ·		206 24 ·		283 59 ·		311 38 ·	04
40	70 33.7	36.7	104 30.1	96 06		208 55		286 30		314 03	02
50	73 03.7	36.8	107 00.5	98 36		211 25		289 00		316 29	15 00
17 00	75 33.8	N13 37.0	109 30.9	101 07	N 7 32	213 56	S22 59	291 31	N 2 32	318 54	N14 58
10	78 03.8	37.1	112 01.3	103 37		216 26		294 01		321 20	55
20	80 33.8	37.2	114 31.8	106 08		218 56		296 32		323 45	53
30	83 03.8 ·	37.4	117 02.2	108 38 ·		221 27 ·		299 02 ·		326 11 ·	51
40	85 33.8	37.5	119 32.6	111 08		223 57		301 32		328 36	49
50	88 03.8	37.6	122 03.0	113 39		226 28		304 03		331 02	47
18 00	90 33.9	N13 37.8	124 33.4	116 09	N 7 31	228 58	S22 59	306 33	N 2 32	333 27	N14 44
10	93 03.9	37.9	127 03.8	118 40		231 28		309 04		335 53	42
20	95 33.9	38.0	129 34.2	121 10		233 59		311 34		338 19	40
30	98 03.9 ·	38.2	132 04.6	123 41 ·		236 29 ··		314 05 ·		340 44 ·	38
40	100 33.9	38.3	134 35.0	126 11		239 00		316 35		343 10	36
50	103 03.9	38.4	137 05.5	128 41		241 30		319 06		345 35	34
19 00	105 34.0	N13 38.6	139 35.9	131 12	N 7 30	244 00	S22 59	321 36	N 2 32	348 01	N14 31
10	108 04.0	38.7	142 06.3	133 42		246 31		324 06		350 26	29
20	110 34.0	38.8	144 36.7	136 13		249 01		326 37		352 52	27
30	113 04.0 ·	39.0	147 07.1	138 43 ·		251 32 ·		329 07 ·		355 17 ·	25
40	115 34.0	39.1	149 37.5	141 13		254 02		331 38		357 43	23
50	118 04.0	39.2	152 07.9	143 44		256 32		334 08		0 08	20
20 00	120 34.1	N13 39.4	154 38.3	146 14	N 7 30	259 03	S22 59	336 39	N 2 32	2 34	N14 18
10	123 04.1	39.5	157 08.7	148 45		261 33		339 09		5 00	16
20	125 34.1	39.6	159 39.2	151 15		264 04		341 40		7 25	14
30	128 04.1 ·	39.8	162 09.6	153 46 ·		266 34 ·		344 10 ·		9 51 ·	12
40	130 34.1	39.9	164 40.0	156 16		269 04		346 40		12 16	09
50	133 04.1	40.0	167 10.4	158 46		271 35		349 11		14 42	07
21 00	135 34.2	N13 40.2	169 40.8	161 17	N 7 29	274 05	S22 59	351 41	N 2 32	17 07	N14 05
10	138 04.2	40.3	172 11.2	163 47		276 36		354 12		19 33	03
20	140 34.2	40.4	174 41.6	166 18		279 06		356 42		21 58	14 00
30	143 04.2 ·	40.6	177 12.0	168 48 ·		281 37 ·		359 13 ·		24 24	13 58
40	145 34.2	40.7	179 42.4	171 18		284 07		1 43		26 49	56
50	148 04.2	40.8	182 12.8	173 49		286 37		4 13		29 15	54
22 00	150 34.3	N13 41.0	184 43.3	176 19	N 7 28	289 08	S22 59	6 44	N 2 32	31 41	N13 51
10	153 04.3	41.1	187 13.7	178 50		291 38		9 14		34 06	49
20	155 04.3	41.2	189 44.1	181 20		294 09		11 45		36 32	47
30	158 04.3 ·	41.4	192 14.5	183 51 ·		296 39 ·		14 15 ·		38 57 ·	45
40	160 34.3	41.5	194 44.9	186 21		299 09		16 46		41 23	43
50	163 04.3	41.6	197 15.3	188 51		301 40		19 16		43 48	40
23 00	165 34.4	N13 41.8	199 45.7	191 22	N 7 28	304 10	S22 59	21 47	N 2 32	46 14	N13 38
10	168 04.4	41.9	202 16.1	193 52		306 41		24 17		48 40	36
20	170 34.4	42.0	204 46.5	196 23		309 11		26 47		51 05	34
30	173 04.4 ·	42.2	207 17.0	198 53 ·		311 41 ·		29 18 ·		53 31 ·	31
40	175 34.4	42.3	209 47.4	201 23		314 12		31 48		55 56	29
50	178 04.5	42.4	212 17.8	203 54		316 42		34 19		58 22	27

Moonset

Lat. N	Moon-set h m	Diff. m
72	06 12	*
70	05 19	*
68	04 46	−25
66	04 22	−13
64	04 03	−07
62	03 47	−03
60	03 34	00
58	03 23	+02
56	03 13	04
54	03 04	06
52	02 56	07
50	02 49	09
45	02 33	11
40	02 21	13
35	02 10	15
30	02 00	16
20	01 44	19
10	01 29	21
0	01 16	23
10	01 02	25
20	00 47	27
30	00 30	29
35	00 20	31
40	00 08	32
45	25 04	35
50	24 53	38
52	24 47	39
54	24 42	40
56	24 35	42
58	24 28	44
60	24 19	46
S		

Moon's P. in A.

Alt °	Corr +	Alt °	Corr +
0	56	55	31
3	55	56	30
11	54	57	29
15	53	59	28
19	52	60	27
22	51	61	26
24	50	62	25
27	49	63	24
29	48	65	23
31	47	66	22
33	46	67	21
35	45	68	20
36	44	69	19
38	43	70	18
40	42	71	17
41	41	72	16
43	40	73	15
44	39	74	14
46	38	75	13
47	37	77	12
48	36	78	11
50	35	79	10
51	34	80	
52	33		
54	32		
55	31		
56			

Sun SD 15.9
Moon SD 15′
Age 10d

Figure 2408b: Sample right hand page of Air Almanac.

Almanac than with the *Nautical Almanac*. The reason for this is that the latter publication, which tabulates data for every whole hour, lists GHA adjusted by up to 0'.15 to minimize the error caused by ignoring the "v" correction, as stated in article 2404.

The *Air Almanac* gives ephemeristic data for each ten minutes of GMT on the daily pages; and due to the great number of tabulations, it cannot conveniently appear as a single volume covering an entire year. It is issued three times a year, each volume covering a four-month period of time. Two pages, the front and back of a single sheet, cover one calendar day (Figures 2408a and 2408b). Thus, at any one opening, the left hand page contains the tabulation of data for every ten minutes of time from 12 hours 0 minutes GMT to 23 hours 50 minutes of one day. Data from 0 hours 0 minutes to 11 hours 50 minutes of the following day are presented on the right hand page. The daily data include GHA and Dec. of the sun, each to 0'.1, the GHA of Aries to 0'.1, and the GHA and Dec. of the navigational planets and of the moon to the nearest 1'.0. The volumes are bound with plastic rings to enable the aviator to tear out the daily pages for more convenient use. In addition, these daily pages give the time of moonrise and moonset, the moon's parallax in altitude, the semidiameters of the sun and moon, and the latter's age.

On the inside of the front cover is given a table to permit ready interpolation of GHA of the sun, Aries and planets on the one hand, and of the moon on the other, for time increments between the 10-minute tabulated values of GHA. This table is repeated on a flap which can be folded out from the book. Both of these tables state arc to the nearest whole minute. For greater precision there is also included in the white section in the back of the *Almanac* a separate page for the interpolation of GHA sun and one for interpolation GHA Aries, each giving values of 0'.1 of arc. A star index of the 57 navigational stars in alphabetical order with their magnitudes, SHA and Dec. to 1'.0 is given covering their average position for the 4-month period of the *Almanac*. For those desiring greater precision, or for stars other than the 57 principal ones, separate tables are included in the white section giving SHA and Dec. of 173 stars to 0'.1 of arc for each month of the period covered by the *Almanac*. They are listed in ascending order of SHA and are intended for use with the astro-tracker. The value of SHA is combined with GHA♈ from the daily pages, to obtain GHA of the star.

Miscellaneous Tables in Air Almanac.

2409. Various other tables, sky diagrams and other data are included in the back of the book. As far as possible they are arranged in inverse order of use, that is, the most commonly used data is directly inside the back cover, therefore most easily located. A table is included in the back of the volume to assist in interpolating the time of moonrise and moonset for longitude.

Additional data.

2410. Sample daily pages from the *Air Almanac* are shown in Figures 2408a and 2408b, and a partial interpolation table in Figure 2410a. For comparison purposes these are given for the same date as the sample pages of the *Nautical Almanac*.

Figure 2410b illustrates the extraction of data for the various bodies as taken from the *Air Almanac*. For comparison purposes the same times and celestial bodies are used that were illustrated in Figure 2406 for the *Nautical Almanac*.

444

Example: Obtain GHA and Dec. of the sun on 26 April ZT 09-56-35 (+4).

INTERPOLATION OF G.H.A.

Increment to be added for intervals of G.M.T. to G.H.A. of:
Sun, Aries (♈) and planets; Moon

SUN, etc.	° ′	MOON	SUN, etc.	° ′	MOON	SUN, etc.	° ′	MOON
m s		m s	m s		m s	m s		m s
00 00	0 00	00 00	03 17	0 50	03 25	06 37	1 40	06 52
01	0 01	00 02	21	0 51	03 29	41	1 41	06 56
05	0 02	00 06	25	0 52	03 33	45	1 42	07 00
09	0 03	00 10	29	0 53	03 37	49	1 43	07 04
13	0 04	00 14	33	0 54	03 41	53	1 44	07 08
17	0 05	00 18	37	0 55	03 45	06 57	1 45	07 13
21	0 06	00 22	41	0 56	03 49	07 01	1 46	07 17
25	0 07	00 26	45	0 57	03 54	05	1 47	07 21
29	0 08	00 31	49	0 58	03 58	09	1 48	07 25
33	0 09	00 35	53	0 59	04 02	13	1 49	07 29
37	0 10	00 39	03 57	1 00	04 06	17	1 50	07 33
41	0 11	00 43	04 01	1 01	04 10	21	1 51	07 37
45		00 47	05		04 14	25		07 42
33			53					
37	0 24	01 41	04 57	1 14	05 08	17	2 04	08 35
41	0 25	01 45	05 01	1 15	05 12	21	2 05	08 40
45	0 26	01 49	05	1 16	05 17	25	2 06	08 44
49	0 27	01 53	09	1 17	05 21	29	2 07	08 48
53	0 28	01 58	13	1 18	05 25	33	2 08	08 52
01 57	0 29	02 02	17	1 19	05 29	37	2 09	08 56
02 01	0 30	02 06	21	1 20	05 33	41	2 10	09 00
05	0 31	02 10	25	1 21	05 37	45	2 11	09 04
09	0 32	02 14	29	1 22	05 41	49	2 12	09 09
13	0 33	02 18	33	1 23	05 46	53	2 13	09 13
17	0 34	02 22	37	1 24	05 50	08 57	2 14	09 17
21	0 35	02 27	41	1 25	05 54	09 01	2 15	09 21
25	0 36	02 31	45	1 26	05 58	05	2 16	09 25
29	0 37	02 35	49	1 27	06 02	09	2 17	09 29
33	0 38	02 39	53	1 28	06 06	13	2 18	09 33
37	0 39	02 43	05 57	1 29	06 10	17	2 19	09 38
41	0 40	02 47	06 01	1 30	06 15	21	2 20	09 42
45	0 41	02 51	05	1 31	06 19	25	2 21	09 46
49	0 42	02 56	09	1 32	06 23	29	2 22	09 50
53	0 43	03 00	13	1 33	06 27	33	2 23	09 54
02 57	0 44	03 04	17	1 34	06 31	37	2 24	09 58
03 01	0 45	03 08	21	1 35	06 35	41	2 25	10 00
05	0 46	03 12	25	1 36	06 39	45	2 26	
09	0 47	03 16	29	1 37	06 44	49	2 27	
13	0 48	03 20	33	1 38	06 48	53	2 28	
17	0 49	03 25	37	1 39	06 52	09 57	2 29	
03 21	0 50	03 29	06 41	1 40	06 56	10 00	2 30	

*Figure 2410a:
Incremental corrections* Air Almanac.

Solution: (1) Enter column headed GMT, for the correct date (26 April) listed at the top of the page, and locate the hour and even 10 minutes (1350) of GMT. (2) Reading across from GMT, in column headed SUN, pick out and record GHA (28°03'.4) and Dec. (N13°34'.4). (3) Turn to the table for "Interpolation of GHA" on the inside front cover of the almanac and pick out incremental correction under SUN column for 6 minutes 35 seconds (1°39'). (4) Add the GHA values in (2) and (3) above to obtain GHA Sun (29°42'.4) for 13-56-35 GMT.

Figure 2410b:
Sample problems,
Air Almanac.

Body	SUN	MOON	DENEBOLA	MARS
GMT	13-56-35	20-57-04	22-56-08	08-57-05
Date (G)	26 APRIL	26 APRIL	26 APRIL	26 APRIL
Tab GHA	28° 03'.4	14° 42'	197° 15'.3	91° 06'
Corr.	1° 39'	1° 42'	1° 32'	1° 46'
SHA	—	—	183° 07'	—
			381° 54'.3	
GHA	29° 42'.4	16° 24'	21° 54'.3	92° 52'
Dec	N13° 34'.4	N14° 07'	N 14° 45'	S 22° 58'

In the *Air Almanac* tabulated declination is always used without interpolation, always using the tabular value for the GMT immediately *before* the time of observation.

To obtain GHA of a star the tabulated value of GHA♈ is taken from the daily pages for hours and tens of minutes. To this the correction for extra minutes and seconds of GMT, and the SHA of the star as listed on the inside front cover or fold out section are added. If the total value exceeds 360°, subtract 360° from the answer.

Other ephemeristic tabulations.

2411. In addition to the *Nautical Almanac* and the *Air Almanac* many special tabulations of ephemeristic data have been made for specific purposes. A number of attempts have also been made to produce a long term or perpetual almanac. Appendix X of Bowditch, H. O. 9, contains one version of a long-term almanac. In the explanation section of the *Nautical Almanac* a brief description is given of corrections which can be applied to use portions of the almanac in the succeeding year. These are generally considered to be emergency methods for use when a current edition of the almanac is not available to the navigator.

An excellent perpetual almanac is the one prepared in England by Her Majesty's Nautical Almanac Office. It is printed in the sight reduction tables, AP 3270, the British equivalent of H. O. 249. It is restricted to the sun and the entire ephemeris is presented in two pages. The presentation of data is both interesting and original.

CHAPTER 25

Sight Reduction

2501. Preceding chapters of this text have dealt individually with the aspects   *Introduction.*
of determining a line of position from an observation of a celestial body.

The purpose of this chapter is to explain how complete solutions for lines of
position may be obtained by means of the methods currently in widest use.
These are H. O. 214, with which the "$\triangle$d only" method will be used, H. O. 249,
H. O. 211 (Ageton), and the new tables, H. O. 229. Of these, H. O. 211 is
unique in that it is designed primarily for use with a dead reckoning, or estimated
position, rather than with an assumed position.

2502. The most widely used sight reduction method in the last century was   *Previous method.*
the time sight. A latitude line was obtained by means of an observation of
Polaris, or the transit of the sun or of some other body. This latitude line was advanced to the time of an observation of a body located well to the east or west
of the observer; the body most frequently used was the sun. With this assumed
latitude, a longitude was calculated, originally in time, which gave the time
sight its name. The accuracy of the time sight obviously depended on the
accuracy of the assumed latitude.

This method remained popular with the merchant service up to World War II.
The U. S. Navy was quick to see the advantages of the altitude intercept method
of solution conceived by Marcq St. Hilaire in 1875. For sight reduction by this
method, the "Cosine-Haversine" formulae were used for computed altitude
and azimuth.

These were derived from the classic formulae: *Sine-Cosine*
formula.

$$\sin H = \sin L \sin d \overset{+}{\underset{\sim}{}} \cos L \cos d \cos t \qquad \text{and} \qquad \sin Z = \frac{\cos d \sin t}{\cos H}$$

Note. In the first formula, the rules for naming the sign may be stated as:

1. If t is less than 90°:
    a. and L and Dec. have the same name, the sign is positive.
    b. and L and Dec. have opposite names, the lesser quantity is sub-
       tracted from the greater.

2. If t is greater than 90°:
    a. and L and Dec. have the same name, the lesser quantity is sub-
       tracted from the greater.
    b. and L and Dec. have opposite names, the sign is positive.   **447**

These formulae are used today, when accuracy in reduction is paramount, and many of the "short methods" currently in use are based on them. It may be noted that some Navy patrol plane navigators used them for slide rule navigation during World War II. When using bodies at low altitudes, the Hc's thus obtained were sufficiently accurate for air navigation.

Short methods.

The cosine-haversine method remained in general use in the Navy until about forty years ago, when Ogura, in Japan, developed a more convenient solution. This led to the production of other simplified methods, both in this country and abroad. These became known as the "short methods," and included among the American volumes, in the order of their development, the Weems "Line of Position Book," H. O. 208, by Dreisenstok, and H. O. 211, by Ageton. These volumes are still in wide use. The only mathematical skill they demand of the user is the ability to add, subtract, and to interpolate between numbers in a column. They are convenient, in that in each case one small volume permits solution for any latitude, any declination, and any altitude. However, they have now been largely superseded by the "inspection tables," described hereafter.

Inspection tables.

2503. Modern sight reduction tables are of the inspection type. They are so called because altitude and azimuth are extracted for a given latitude, meridian angle, and declination by inspection, and no calculation is required. Non-tabular inspection methods have also been developed. The Weems "Star Altitude Curves" were first published in 1928, and were widely used during World War II, chiefly by air navigators. These curves are a graphic method of obtaining a fix by inspection.

Of the inspection tables now in general use, H. O. 214 has found general acceptance for marine navigation, both in the Navy and the merchant service, while H. O. 249 has become the standard method for air navigation; it is also used at times by surface navigators. The latest inspection tables to be developed are H. O. 229. These various tables are produced by the U. S. Naval Oceanographic Office and are discussed below.

H. O. 214.

2504. These tables, titled "Tables of Computed Altitude and Azimuth," are generally referred to simply as "H. O. 214." They are designed primarily for efficiency when working from an assumed position, and this is the method of use discussed below. They can, however, be used from a DR or estimated position; instructions for such use are given in each volume. Currently they provide the most widely used method of sight reduction in marine navigation.

H. O. 214 Entering Arguments.

The tables consist of nine volumes, each covering a 10° band of latitude in increments of 1°. Page entry is by latitude, the other entering arguments being declination and meridian angle (t); however, the latter is named "H.A.," for hour angle, in these tables. Declination values are tabulated horizontally across the top of each page as column headings; the values are stated in half-degree increments from 0° to 29°. Above 29°, selected declinations are tabulated to provide solutions for the 57 selected stars in the *Nautical Almanac*, as well as the great majority of the other navigational stars. Separate declination tables are given, generally on facing pages, for declinations having the same name as the latitude, and those of opposite name, as south latitude and south declination, and south latitude and north declination. Meridian angle is tabulated vertically in whole degrees, from 0° at the top of the page to the maximum value at which the altitude is approximately 5°.

The student should note that the entering arguments (L, Dec., and t) in H. O. 214 are not designated as north, south, east, or west. The reason for this is illustrated in Figure 2504a, where four navigational triangles are shown on the surface of the earth. In each of the four triangles, the AP is at the same latitude north or south of the equator. If the numerical value of the latitude of the AP is assumed to be 33°, then the side between the AP and the pole in *each* triangle, the colatitude, is equal to 57°. Similarly, the GP in each triangle is at the same latitude, 14° (on the same side of the equator as the AP), making the polar distance in each triangle equal to 76°. Further, the four triangles illustrated are constructed so that the angular distance from the meridian of the AP to the meridian of the GP is equal in each case, making the numerical value of meridian angle, t, the same in all triangles. With the two sides and the included angle of all triangles being numerically equal, the values of computed altitude and azimuth angle obtained by solving each triangle will be numerically equal. Using $L = 33°$, Dec. $= 14°$, and assuming that $t = 34°$, the numerical value of "Alt." (53°44'.7) and Az (113°.4) can be obtained from the tabular extract of Figure 2504b.

Similar triangles.

In those cases where the entering arguments in H. O. 214 are exact *tabulated* values, as in the preceding example, the numerical values of "Alt." (ht) and Hc are identical, and ht becomes Hc for purposes of solution.

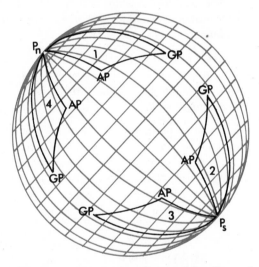

Figure 2504a: Four numerically equal celestial triangles.

To determine the intercept, a, for plotting the resulting lines of position, Hc is used in each case as obtained from the tables, but Az is usually converted to Zn, which differs for each triangle, since the true direction of the GP from the AP is different in each case. Referring to Figure 2504a, the Az in the first triangle is N and E, Zn therefore equals Az. In the second, the Az is S and E; Zn therefore equals 180° − Az. In the third, Az is S and W and Zn equals 180° + Az. In the fourth triangle Az is N and W; Zn therefore equals 360° − Az. When Zn and a are determined, the lines of position can be plotted using the methods described in Chapter 26.

The fact that four triangles can be solved by using one set of entering arguments makes it possible to save considerable space in an inspection table. Figure 2504a illustrates four such triangles, in each of which the AP and GP are on the same side of the equator; both north or both south. In these cases, the latitude and declination are said to have the *same name*. A *second set* of four triangles might be drawn such that in each triangle the AP is on one side of the equator, and the GP is on the other side. If the values of L, Dec., and t are numerically equal for each triangle, the resulting values of Hc and Az will also be numerically the same for all four triangles, and the solution of all four triangles can be achieved using one set of entering arguments, as before. For this second set of triangles, the latitude and declination are said to have *contrary names*, since they lie on opposite sides of the equator. The organization and format of H. O. 214 are based on the principles outlined above. Since each of the solutions obtained from the tables can apply to any of four triangles, the names north and south (for latitude and declination) or east and west (for meridian angle) are omitted in the tabulation, and must be applied by the navigator as appropriate for the particular triangle being solved. Solution is provided for both sets of triangles by means of the two sets of declination tables *"Dec., Same Name as L,"* and *"Dec., Contrary Name to L"* mentioned above.

The entering arguments in these tables are a whole degree of latitude, a whole or half degree of declination, and a whole degree of meridian angle. For the assumed latitude (aL), the user selects the whole degree nearest his DR or estimated position. The declination entry will be the tabulated declination *closest in value* to the actual declination, *and on the page appropriate for the name of the declination* ("same" or "opposite").

To obtain the meridian angle, the user assumes a longitude which, when applied to the GHA of the body, will yield a whole degree of meridian angle; *this assumed longitude (aλ) must lie within 30 minutes of arc of the best estimate of the ship's actual longitude at the time of the observation.*

Assumed longitude. It is obvious that when a number of celestial bodies are observed at about the same time, as in a round of star sights, a different longitude will have to be assumed to obtain a meridian angle for each body. In most cases, all the assumed positions will lie along the same assumed parallel of latitude. (The exception occurs when a ship approaches nearer to an adjoining whole degree while

Figure 2504b: Extract from "same name" page of H. O. 214.

DECLINATION SAME NAME AS LATITUDE

Lat. 33° H.A.	12° 00' Alt.	12° 00' Az.	12° 30' Alt.	12° 30' Az.	13° 00' Alt.	13° 00' Az.	13° 30' Alt.	13° 30' Az.	14° 00' Alt.	14° 00' Az.
	° ′ Ad Δt	°	° ′ Ad Δt	°	° ′ Ad Δt	°	° ′ Ad Δt	°	° ′ Ad Δt	°
00	69 00.0 1.0 02	180.0	69 30.0 1.0 02	180.0	70 00.0 1.0 02	180.0	70 30.0 1.0 02	180.0	71 00.0 1.0 02	180.0
1	68 58.8 1.0 06	177.3	69 28.8 1.0 06	177.2	69 58.8 1.0 06	177.2	70 28.7 1.0 06	177.1	70 58.7 1.0 06	177.0
2	68 55.2 1.0 10	174.6	69 25.1 1.0 10	174.4	69 55.0 1.0 10	174.3	70 24.9 1.0 11	174.2	70 54.8 1.0 11	174.1
3	68 49.3 99 14	171.9	69 19.0 99 14	171.7	69 48.8 99 14	171.5	70 18.5 99 15	171.3	70 48.3 99 15	171.1
4	68 41.0 99 18	169.2	69 10.6 99 18	169.0	69 40.2 99 18	168.7	70 09.7 99 19	168.5	70 39.2 98 19	168.2
05	68 30.4 98 21	166.5	68 59.8 98 22	166.3	69 29.1 98 22	166.0	69 58.4 98 23	165.7	70 27.7 98 23	165.4
6	68 17.6 97 25	164.0	68 46.7 97 25	163.6	69 15.8 97 26	163.3	69 44.8 97 26	162.9	70 13.8 97 27	162.6
7	68 02.6 96 28	161.4	68 31.4 96 29	161.0	69 00.2 96 30	160.6	69 28.9 96 30	160.2	69 57.6 95 31	159.8
8	67 45.5 95 32	158.9	68 14.0 95 32	158.5	68 42.5 95 33	158.1	69 10.8 94 34	157.6	69 39.1 94 34	157.1
9	67 26.4 94 35	156.5	67 54.6 94 36	156.0	68 22.6 93 36	155.6	68 50.6 93 37	155.1	69 18.5 93 38	154.6
10	67 05.4 93 38	154.1	67 33.2 92 39	153.6	68 00.9 92 39	153.1	68 28.4 92 40	152.6	68 55.9 91 41	152.0
1	66 42.5 91 41	151.8	67 09.9 91 42	151.3	67 37.2 91 42	150.8	68 04.4 90 43	150.2	68 31.4 90 44	149.6
2	66 17.9 90 44	149.6	66 44.9 90 44	149.1	67 11.8 89 45	148.5	67 38.5 89 46	147.9	68 05.1 88 47	147.3
3	65 51.7 89 46	147.4	66 18.2 88 47	146.9	66 44.6 88 48	146.3	67 10.9 87 49	145.7	67 37.0 87 49	145.0
4	65 23.8 87 49	145.4	65 49.9 87 50	144.8	66 15.9 86 50	144.2	66 41.8 86 51	143.5	67 07.4 85 52	142.9
30	55 27.3 67 73	120.4	55 47.4 67 73	119.7	56 07.2 66 74	119.1	56 26.9 65 74	118.4	56 46.3 64 75	117.7
1	54 43.6 66 74	119.3	55 03.4 66 74	118.6	55 23.0 65 74	117.9	55 42.4 64 75	117.3	56 01.5 63 75	116.6
2	53 59.5 65 74	118.2	54 19.0 65 75	117.5	54 38.3 64 75	116.8	54 57.4 63 76	116.2	55 16.3 63 76	115.5
3	53 14.9 65 75	117.1	53 34.2 64 75	116.4	53 53.2 63 76	115.8	54 12.1 62 76	115.1	54 30.7 62 77	114.5
4	52 29.9 64 76	116.0	52 48.9 63 76	115.4	53 07.7 62 76	114.8	53 26.3 62 77	114.1	53 44.7 61 77	113.4

observations are being made.) The longitudes assumed should all fall within about 60 minutes of one another, except when the vessel's course and speed result in a rapid change of longitude, and the period required to obtain the observations is rather protracted.

To illustrate the use of the tables, assume that in DR latitude 33°15'.0 N, the navigator observes a body towards the west, with a declination of 12°41'.4 N, and a GHA that yields a meridian angle of 32° W. He enters volume IV of H. O. 214, which covers the latitude band 30°–39° in the section indexed for latitude 33°, and finds the page tabulating Dec. 12°30', and for declination same name as latitude. The appropriate portion of this page is reproduced in Figure 2504b. He then finds the meridian angle column, under the heading "H.A.," along the left hand edge of the page, and moves down this to 32°, the body's meridian angle. Then he moves horizontally to the right, into the vertical column headed "12°30'."

Four groups of figures appear in this column. The first, which is printed in bold type under the heading "Alt." is the tabulated altitude (ht) stated to the nearest 0'.1 ; it is 54°19'.0. The second set of figures, under the heading "Δd," is *65*; this is a correction factor to adjust the altitude for a difference of 1'.0 between the true declination, and the tabulated declination. The third group of figures, under the heading "Δt" may be ignored when working from an assumed position; it is a correction factor for 1'.0 change of meridian angle used when working from a DR position. The values tabulated in the Δd column are expressed as hundredths of a minute, without the decimal point being shown, except where the altitude changes a full minute for a change in one minute of Dec.; in this case the Δd value is stated as 1.0. *Always* insert the decimal point when recording the value of Δd. The group of figures, under the heading "Az." is azimuth angle, stated to the nearest 0°.1 ; it is 117°.5.

H. O. 214 Tabulated values.

The next step is to correct the altitude obtained from the table for the difference between the tabulated and the actual declination. This is done by means of the correction factor (Δd) and a multiplication table given on the inside back cover of each volume of H. O. 214. A portion of this table is reproduced in Figure 2504c. The table is entered in the vertical column under the heading of

MULTIPLICATION TABLE

Δ	1'	2'	3'	4'	5'	6'	7'	8'	9'	10'	11'	12'	13'	14'	15'	Δ	0.1'	0.2'	0.3'	0.4'	0.5'	0.6'	0.7'	0.8'	0.9'	Δ
	DEC. DIFF. OR H. A. DIFF. (minutes of arc)																DEC. DIFF. OR H. A. DIFF. (tenths of minutes)									

Figure 2504c: Correction table for Δd.

451

Corrections for
minutes of Dec.

the appropriate whole minute of arc, in this instance it is 11' (12°41'.4–12°30'.0 = 11'.4). He moves down this column to the △d factor .65, which was found in the main table, and finds the value 7'.2. However, the declination difference was in fact 11'.4, so he moves further horizontally to the vertical column headed 0'.4, where he finds 0'.3. The total correction to the tabulated altitude will therefore be 7'.2 plus 0'.3, or 7'.5. The sign for this correction is determined by comparing the altitude extracted from the table with the adjoining *left* hand column if the actual declination is *less* than the tabulated, and the next *right* hand column, if it is *greater*. In this instance, the sign is plus, as the altitude in the 13° declination column is greater. The Hc is therefore 54°19'.0 + 7'.5, or 54°26'.5.

This Hc may now be compared with the Ho to obtain an altitude intercept (a). However, before this could be plotted, it would be necessary to determine the

Azimuth angle (Az).

true azimuth from the azimuth angle, Az. The prefix for the azimuth angle has the same name as the observer's latitude, which in this case is north; the suffix is determined by its direction from his meridian, which is west. The azimuth angle will therefore be written N117°.5 W, which would be stated as Zn 242°.5, (360° – 117°.5 = 242°.5). For greater accuracy, Az may be interpolated by inspection between adjoining Declination columns.

As a further illustration, assume that the same body, with a declination of 12°41'.4 N was observed from a ship in latitude 33° S. The meridian angle in this instance is 32° E. Enter the same volume (Figure 2504d) with the same latitude, 33°, but in this instance the *declination* is of *contrary name* to the latitude. In the declination column headed 12°30 against an H. A. of 32°, the navigator finds a tabulated altitude of 35°12'.3, a △d of .84, and an azimuth angle of 140°.7, which will be termed S 140°.7 E. Note that the altitude in the adjoining 13° declination column is less than 35°12'.3; the △d correction will therefore be subtractive.

The data obtained from H. O. 214 would then be corrected as follows:

Alt	35°12'.3	Az	S140°.7E
△d .84 × 11'.4 – 9'.5			
Hc	35°02'.8	Zn	039°.3 (180°–140°.7)

H. O. 214 is a convenient and highly satisfactory reduction table for the navigator. However, when the utmost accuracy is desired, there are three possible sources of small error, which he should bear in mind.

First, he should correct the azimuth angle by interpolation for the actual value of the declination. The other two sources of possible minor error, each of which may amount to 0'.1, affect the value of Hc. The first of these may arise because the value of △d is tabulated to permit correction of the tabulated altitude for an actual declination *less* than the value used in entering the table, while the altitude may not change equally with an increase in declination. For example, in the first illustration used, the tabulated value of △d is .65, but for an increase in declination it should be .64, as shown in the Dec. 13° column. The declination difference in the illustration is (+)11'.4, and correcting for this, using the factor of .65 and the multiplication table, 7'.5 is obtained, whereas 11'.4 × .64 is 7'.3 by the table.

DECLINATION **CONTRARY** NAME TO LATITUDE

H.A.	12° 00' Alt.	Δd Δt	Az.	12° 30' Alt.	Δd Δt	Az.	13° 00' Alt.	Δd Δt	Az.	13° 30' Alt.	Δd Δt	Az.	14° 00' Alt.	Δd Δt	Az.
00	45 00.0	1.0 01	180.0	44 30.0	1.0 01	180.0	44 00.0	1.0 01	180.0	43 30.0	1.0 01	180.0	43 00.0	1.0 01	180.0
1	44 59.4	1.0 03	178.6	44 29.4	1.0 03	178.6	43 59.4	1.0 03	178.6	43 29.4	1.0 03	178.7	42 59.4	1.0 03	178.7
2	44 57.6	1.0 05	177.2	44 27.6	1.0 05	177.3	43 57.6	1.0 05	177.3	43 27.6	1.0 05	177.3	42 57.7	1.0 05	177.3
3	44 54.5	1.0 07	175.9	44 24.6	1.0 07	175.9	43 54.7	1.0 07	175.9	43 24.7	1.0 07	176.0	42 54.8	1.0 07	176.0
4	44 50.3	1.0 09	174.5	44 20.4	1.0 09	174.5	43 50.5	1.0 09	174.6	43 20.6	1.0 09	174.6	42 50.7	1.0 09	174.7
05	44 44.9	99 11	173.1	44 15.0	99 11	173.2	43 45.2	99 11	173.2	43 15.3	99 11	173.3	42 45.5	1.0 11	173.4
6	44 38.2	99 13	171.7	44 08.4	99 13	171.8	43 38.7	99 13	171.9	43 08.9	99 13	172.0	42 39.1	99 12	172.1
7	44 30.4	99 15	170.4	44 00.7	99 15	170.5	43 31.0	99 15	170.6	43 01.3	99 15	170.7	42 31.6	99 14	170.8
8	44 21.4	99 17	169.0	43 51.8	99 17	169.1	43 22.2	99 17	169.2	42 52.6	99 16	169.4	42 23.0	99 16	169.5
9	44 11.2	98 19	167.7	43 41.7	98 19	167.8	43 12.2	98 18	167.9	42 42.7	98 18	168.1	42 13.2	98 18	168.2
10	43 59.9	98 21	166.3	43 30.5	98 21	166.5	43 01.2	98 20	166.6	42 31.7	98 20	166.8	42 02.3	98 20	166.9
1	43 47.5	98 23	165.0	43 18.2	98 22	165.2	42 49.0	98 22	165.3	42 19.7	98 22	165.5	41 50.4	98 22	165.6
2	43 33.9	97 24	163.7	43 04.8	97 24	163.9	42 35.7	97 24	164.0	42 06.5	97 24	164.2	41 37.3	97 24	164.3
3	43 19.2	97 26	162.4	42 50.3	97 26	162.6	42 21.3	97 26	162.7	41 52.2	97 26	162.9	41 23.2	97 25	163.1
4	43 03.5	96 28	161.1	42 34.7	96 28	161.3	42 05.8	96 28	161.5	41 36.9	96 27	161.7	41 08.1	96 27	161.8
30	36 40.2	85 52	142.4	36 14.6	85 51	142.8	35 48.9	86 51	143.1	35 23.2	86 51	143.4	34 57.5	86 50	143.7
1	36 09.1	84 53	141.4	35 43.8	85 53	141.7	35 18.3	85 52	142.1	34 52.9	85 52	142.4	34 27.3	85 51	142.7
2	35 37.4	84 54	140.4	35 12.3	84 54	140.7	34 47.1	84 53	141.0	34 21.8	84 53	141.4	33 56.5	84 53	141.7
3	35 05.0	83 55	139.4	34 40.1	83 55	139.7	34 15.1	83 54	140.1	33 50.0	84 54	140.4	33 25.0	84 54	140.7
4	34 31.9	82 56	138.4	34 07.2	82 56	138.7	33 42.4	83 55	139.1	33 17.6	83 55	139.4	32 52.8	83 55	139.8

Lat. 33°

Figure 2504d: Extract from "contrary name" page of H.O. 214.

The other source of possible error arises from the navigator's use of the multiplication table, by which he first multiplies whole minutes of arc, and then tenths, rather than by making a single multiplication. To illustrate, 15'.6 × .75, using the table, is 11'.8 (11'.3 + 0'.5), whereas the correct answer is 11'.70. These errors are too small to be of consequence in the practice of general navigation; they merit consideration when accuracy is of prime importance.

2505. H. O. Pub. No. 229 is entitled "*Sight Reduction Tables for Marine Navigation*"; it is usually referred to simply as "H. O. 229." It is an inspection table, and was prepared as an international cooperative effort of the U. S. Naval Oceanographic Office, the U. S. Naval Observatory, and H. M. Nautical Almanac Office. It is published in six volumes, arranged by latitude. Each volume contains data for a 15° band of latitude north or south, and there is an overlap of 1° between volumes; in each volume, the latitude is separated into two zones, as in the following:

H.O. 229.

The complete celestial solution using H. O. 229 is given in the appendix.

Vol. No.	First zone of latitude	Second zone of latitude
1	0°–7°	8°–15°
2	15°–22°	23°–30°
3	30°–37°	38°–45°
4	45°–52°	53°–60°
5	60°–67°	68°–75°
6	75°–82°	83°–90°

It is designed to provide calculated altitudes correct to the nearest 0'.1, when all corrections are employed, and azimuth angle to 0°.1, for all combinations of latitude, local hour angle (measured westward through 360°), and declination at a uniform interval of 1° in each of these arguments. It may be used for reduction from a DR position to the same degree of precision, and directions for such reduction are given in each volume. However, it is primarily intended to be used with an assumed position. The latitude of the latter is the integral degree nearest the vessel's DR or EP; its longitude is selected to give a whole degree of *local hour angle* (not meridian angle). Among today's tables it is unique, in that it offers both the maximum degree of precision required by the navigator and also

Purpose of H.O. 229 tables.

permits the reduction of an observation of *any* navigational body, at *any* altitude, including those of negative value.

Entering arguments. The primary entering argument (page entry) within each zone of latitude is the local hour angle; it is prominently displayed at the top and bottom of each page. The horizontal argument heading each column is latitude, and the vertical argument is declination. For each value of the local hour angle, LHA, in the range 0° to 90° or 270° to 360° there is an opening of two facing pages, which contain the tabulations for Dec. of 0° to 90° and for 8° of latitude.

For each opening, the left hand page is always limited to the tabulations for declination and latitude of the same name. On the upper portion of the right hand page are stated the tabulations for declination and latitude of contrary name; in the lower portions of these right hand pages are stated tabulations

29°, 331° L.H.A. — LATITUDE SAME NAME AS DECLINATION

N. Lat. $\begin{cases} \text{LHA greater than } 180°...Zn = Z \\ \text{LHA less than } 180°........Zn = 360° - Z \end{cases}$

Dec.	75° Hc	d	Z	76° Hc	d	Z	77° Hc	d	Z	78° Hc	d	Z	79° Hc	d	Z	80° Hc	d	Z	81° Hc	d	Z	82° Hc	d	Z	Dec.
0	13 05.0	+59.5	150.2	12 12.9	+59.6	150.3	11 20.8	+59.6	150.4	10 28.6	+59.7	150.5	9 36.4	+59.7	150.5	8 44.1	+59.8	150.6	7 51.8	+59.9	150.7	6 59.5	+59.9	150.8	0
1	14 04.5	59.5	150.0	13 12.5	59.6	150.1	12 20.4	59.7	150.3	11 28.3	59.7	150.4	10 36.1	59.8	150.5	9 43.9	59.8	150.5	8 51.7	59.8	150.6	7 59.4	59.8	150.7	1
65	76 11.4	+50.4	120.9	75 39.1	+52.4	124.2	75 04.0	+54.0	127.3	74 26.4	+55.4	130.2	73 46.7	+56.4	132.8	73 04.9	+57.3	135.2	72 21.5	+58.0	137.5	71 36.6	+58.5	139.5	65
66	77 01.8	49.0	118.5	76 31.5	51.2	122.2	75 58.0	53.1	125.6	75 21.8	54.6	128.7	74 43.1	55.9	131.6	74 02.2	57.0	134.2	73 19.5	57.7	136.6	72 35.1	58.4	138.8	66
67	77 50.8	47.3	115.9	77 22.7	49.9	119.9	76 51.1	52.1	123.6	76 16.4	53.9	127.0	75 39.0	55.4	130.2	74 59.2	56.5	133.0	74 17.2	57.5	135.6	73 33.5	58.2	138.0	67
68	78 38.1	45.1	112.8	78 12.6	48.3	117.3	77 43.2	50.9	121.4	77 10.3	53.0	125.1	76 34.4	54.6	128.5	75 55.7	56.0	131.7	75 14.7	57.1	134.5	74 31.7	57.9	137.1	68
69	79 23.2	42.5	109.4	79 00.9	46.2	114.3	78 34.1	49.2	118.8	78 03.3	51.8	122.9	77 29.0	53.8	126.7	76 51.7	55.4	130.1	76 11.8	56.6	133.3	75 29.6	57.6	136.1	69
70	80 05.7	+39.4	105.4	79 47.1	+43.6	110.8	79 23.3	+47.3	115.8	78 55.1	+50.3	120.4	78 22.8	+52.7	124.6	77 47.1	+54.6	128.4	77 08.4	+56.2	131.8	76 27.2	+57.3	134.9	70
71	80 45.1	35.4	100.9	80 30.7	40.5	106.8	80 10.6	44.8	112.3	79 45.4	48.4	117.4	79 15.5	51.4	122.1	78 41.7	53.7	126.4	78 04.6	55.4	130.2	77 24.5	56.8	133.6	71
72	81 20.5	30.6	95.7	81 11.2	36.4	102.1	80 55.4	41.7	108.3	80 33.8	46.0	114.0	80 06.9	49.6	119.2	79 35.4	52.4	124.0	79 00.0	54.6	128.3	78 21.3	56.2	132.1	72
73	81 51.1	24.8	89.8	81 47.6	31.6	96.7	81 37.1	37.6	103.5	81 19.8	42.9	109.9	80 56.5	47.3	115.8	80 27.8	50.8	121.2	79 54.6	53.5	126.0	79 17.5	55.5	130.3	73
74	82 15.9	18.2	83.2	82 19.2	25.6	90.6	82 14.7	32.6	98.0	82 02.7	39.0	105.1	81 43.8	44.3	111.7	81 18.6	48.7	117.8	80 48.1	52.0	123.3	80 13.0	54.6	128.1	74
89	75 52.0	52.0	2.0	76 52.0	52.0	2.1	77 51.9	51.9	2.3	78 51.9	51.9	2.5	79 51.8	51.8	2.8	80 51.7	51.7	3.1	81 51.6	51.6	3.4	82 51.5	51.5	3.9	89
90	75 00.0	-52.9	0.0	76 00.0	-52.9	0.0	77 00.0	-53.0	0.0	78 00.0	-53.0	0.0	79 00.0	-53.1	0.0	80 00.0	-53.1	0.0	81 00.0	-53.2	0.0	82 00.0	-53.3	0.0	90

75° — 76° — 77° — 78° — 79° — 80° — 81° — 82°

29°, 331° L.H.A. — LATITUDE SAME NAME AS DECLINATION

Figure 2505a: Portion of a "same name" page H.O. 229.

for the supplementary values of LHA (those larger than 90° but less than 270°), for declinations of the same name as latitude. The upper and lower sections of the page are clearly marked with a line where the altitude reaches zero. Portions of a left and right hand page are shown in Figures 2505a and 2505b, respectively.

To use the tables, the volume which includes the assumed latitude is selected, and the two pages listing the required LHA are found within the appropriate latitude zone of this volume. The appropriate page is then selected for a declination having the same or the contrary name as the latitude. On this page, the vertical column headed by the integral degree of assumed latitude is next found. Declination is listed in vertical columns at the outer edges of each page; the integral whole degree of declination numerically *less* in value to the actual declination is located in this column. Horizontally across from this, in the latitude column, three sets of numerical values are tabulated. The first, under the sub-heading "Hc," is the calculated altitude stated to the nearest 0'.1; in the next column sub-headed "d," in smaller type, is the actual difference, with sign, to the tabulated altitude for the next higher degree of declination. The third column, subheaded "Z", tabulates the azimuth angle to the nearest 0°.1.

Column arrangement H.O. 229.

Rules are given on each page for converting Z to Zn. Interpolation tables, given on four pages, are provided to permit correcting the tabulated altitude for the first difference "d" between the actual declination, and the integral degree of declination, used as an entering argument. The interpolation tables are also designed to permit, where required, correction for the effect of a second difference; this allows full precision to be obtained in the calculated altitude. In those cases in which second differences are significant, that is, where failing to correct for the second difference may cause an error in excess of 0'.25 in the calculated altitude, the value of "d" is printed in italics, and is followed by a dot.

Portions of these interpolation tables are shown in Figure 2505c. The main argument in entering these tables is the excess of the actual declination over the integral degree of declination used to enter the main body of the tables. This difference is tabulated in the vertical column at the left hand edge of each table, under the heading "Dec. Inc." The other argument is the tabulated altitude difference "d," which for convenience is divided into two parts, the first being a multiple of 10'(10', 20', 30', 40', or 50'), and the second the remainder in the range 0'.0 to 9'.9 by tenths of minutes. This interpolation table is a great convenience to the navigator. Its use may occasionally lead to a small error in the

LATITUDE CONTRARY NAME TO DECLINATION — L.H.A. 29°, 331°

Dec.	75° Hc d Z	76° Hc d Z	77° Hc d Z	78° Hc d Z	79° Hc d Z	80° Hc d Z	81° Hc d Z	82° Hc d Z	Dec.
0	13 05.0 −59.5 150.2	12 12.9 −59.5 150.3	11 20.8 −59.6 150.4	10 28.6 −59.7 150.5	9 36.4 −59.7 150.5	8 44.1 −59.7 150.6	7 51.8 −59.8 150.7	6 59.5 −59.9 150.8	0
1	12 05.5 59.5 150.3	11 13.4 59.6 150.4	10 21.2 59.7 150.5	9 28.9 59.6 150.6	8 36.7 59.8 150.6	7 44.4 59.8 150.7	6 52.0 59.8 150.8	5 59.6 59.8 150.8	1
2	11 06.0 59.5 150.4	10 13.8 59.6 150.5	9 21.5 59.6 150.6	8 29.3 59.7 150.7	7 36.9 59.7 150.7	6 44.6 59.8 150.8	5 52.2 59.8 150.9	4 59.8 59.9 150.9	2
3	10 06.5 59.5 150.5	9 14.2 59.6 150.6	8 21.9 59.6 150.7	7 29.6 59.7 150.8	6 37.2 59.7 150.8	5 44.8 59.8 150.9	4 52.4 59.9 150.9	3 59.9 59.9 151.0	3
4	9 07.0 59.5 150.7	8 14.6 59.5 150.7	7 22.3 59.7 150.8	6 29.9 59.7 150.9	5 37.5 59.8 150.9	4 45.0 59.8 151.0	3 52.5 59.8 151.0	3 00.0 59.8 151.0	4
5	8 07.5 −59.6 150.8	7 15.1 −59.6 150.9	6 22.6 −59.6 150.9	5 30.2 −59.7 151.0	4 37.7 −59.7 151.0	3 45.2 −59.8 151.1	2 52.7 −59.8 151.1	2 00.2 −59.9 151.1	5
6	7 07.9 59.5 150.9	6 15.5 59.6 151.0	5 23.0 59.6 151.0	4 30.5 59.7 151.1	3 38.0 59.8 151.1	2 45.4 59.8 151.1	1 52.9 59.8 151.2	1 00.3 59.8 151.2	6
7	6 08.4 59.5 151.1	5 15.9 59.6 151.1	4 23.4 59.7 151.1	3 30.8 59.7 151.2	2 38.2 59.7 151.2	1 45.6 59.7 151.2	0 53.1 −59.9 151.2	0 00.5 −59.9 151.2	7
8	5 08.9 59.5 151.2	4 16.3 59.6 151.2	3 23.7 59.6 151.3	2 31.1 59.7 151.3	1 38.5 59.8 151.3	0 45.9 −59.8 151.3	0 06.8 +59.8 28.7	0 59.4 +59.9 28.7	8
9	4 09.4 59.5 151.3	3 16.7 59.5 151.3	2 24.1 59.7 151.4	1 31.4 59.7 151.4	0 38.7 −59.7 151.4	0 13.9 +59.8 28.6	1 06.6 59.8 28.6	1 59.3 59.8 28.6	9
10	3 09.9 −59.6 151.4	2 17.2 −59.6 151.5	1 24.4 −59.6 151.5	0 31.7 −59.7 151.5	0 21.0 +59.7 28.5	1 13.7 +59.8 28.5	2 06.4 +59.9 28.5	2 59.1 +59.9 28.6	10
11	2 10.3 59.5 151.6	1 17.6 59.6 151.6	0 24.8 −59.6 151.6	0 28.0 +59.7 28.4	1 20.7 59.8 28.4	2 13.5 59.8 28.4	3 06.3 59.8 28.5	3 59.0 59.9 28.5	11
12	1 10.8 59.5 151.7	0 18.0 −59.6 151.7	0 34.8 +59.7 28.3	1 27.7 59.7 28.3	2 20.5 59.7 28.3	3 13.3 59.8 28.4	4 06.1 59.8 28.4	4 58.9 59.8 28.4	12
13	0 11.3 −59.5 151.8	0 41.6 +59.6 28.2	1 34.5 59.7 28.2	2 27.4 59.7 28.2	3 20.2 59.8 28.2	4 13.1 59.8 28.3	5 05.9 59.8 28.3	5 58.7 59.9 28.4	13
14	0 48.2 +59.6 28.1	1 41.2 59.6 28.1	2 34.1 59.7 28.1	3 27.1 59.6 28.1	4 20.0 59.7 28.1	5 12.9 59.7 28.2	6 05.7 59.9 28.2	6 58.6 59.8 28.3	14
90	75 00.0+52.0 0.0	76 00.0+52.0 0.0	77 00.0+51.9 0.0	78 00.0+51.9 0.0	79 00.0+51.8 0.0	80 00.0+51.7 0.0	81 00.0+51.6 0.0	82 00.0+51.5 0.0	90

| | 75° | 76° | 77° | 78° | 79° | 80° | 81° | 82° |

S. Lat. { L.H.A. greater than 180°...Zn = 180° − Z ; L.H.A. less than 180°.........Zn = 180° + Z } **LATITUDE SAME NAME AS DECLINATION** — L.H.A. 151°, 209°

Figure 2505b: Portion of a contrary name page H. O. 229.

First difference correction.

Hc not exceeding 0'.1; such error is acceptable in the course of ordinary navigation.

The major portion of the correction to convert the tabulated altitude to the calculated altitude is called the first difference correction. It is obtained as the sum of two quantities:

> The tabulated value corresponding to the "Dec. Inc.," and the tens of minutes of the altitude difference "d," and

> The tabulated value corresponding to the "Dec. Inc.," and the remainder of "d" in units and tenths. The units are to the right of the tens; note that the decimals here are a vertical argument.

The sum of these two quantities is applied to the tabulated altitude with the sign as shown in the "d" column of the main tables.

Double-second difference.

The minor portion of the correction is for the double-second difference. This is the difference between the tabulated altitude differences ("d") on the line directly above and the one directly below the value of "d" extracted from the table for the first difference. To illustrate: enter the main tables with L 76° N, LHA 29°, and Dec. 69° N. Note that the value of d is 46'.2, and that it is printed in italics, and followed by a dot; the double-second difference correction is therefore important. The value of d, for Dec. 68° (one line above the selected

455

INTERPOLATION TABLE

Left half

Dec. Inc.	10'	20'	30'	40'	50'	Dec.	0'	1'	2'	3'	4'	5'	6'	7'	8'	9'
28.0	4.6	9.3	14.0	18.6	23.3	.0	0.0	0.5	0.9	1.4	1.9	2.4	2.8	3.3	3.8	4.3
28.1	4.7	9.3	14.0	18.7	23.4	.1	0.0	0.5	1.0	1.5	1.9	2.4	2.9	3.4	3.8	4.3
28.2	4.7	9.4	14.1	18.8	23.5	.2	0.1	0.6	1.0	1.5	2.0	2.5	2.9	3.4	3.9	4.4
28.3	4.7	9.4	14.1	18.9	23.6	.3	0.1	0.6	1.1	1.6	2.0	2.5	3.0	3.5	3.9	4.4
28.4	4.7	9.5	14.2	18.9	23.7	.4	0.2	0.7	1.1	1.6	2.1	2.6	3.0	3.5	4.0	4.5
28.5	4.8	9.5	14.3	19.0	23.8	.5	0.2	0.7	1.2	1.7	2.1	2.6	3.1	3.6	4.0	4.5
28.6	4.8	9.5	14.3	19.1	23.8	.6	0.3	0.8	1.2	1.7	2.2	2.7	3.1	3.6	4.1	4.6
28.7	4.8	9.6	14.4	19.2	23.9	.7	0.3	0.8	1.3	1.8	2.2	2.7	3.2	3.7	4.1	4.6
28.8	4.8	9.6	14.4	19.2	24.0	.8	0.4	0.9	1.3	1.8	2.3	2.8	3.2	3.7	4.2	4.7
28.9	4.9	9.7	14.5	19.3	24.1	.9	0.4	0.9	1.4	1.9	2.3	2.8	3.3	3.8	4.2	4.7

Double Second Diff. and Corr.: 0.8 / 2.4 0.1 / 4.0 0.2 / 5.6 0.3 / 7.2 0.4 / 8.8 0.5 / 10.4 0.6 / 12.0 0.7 / 13.6 0.8 / 15.2 0.9 / 16.8 1.0

Dec. Inc.	10'	20'	30'	40'	50'	Dec.	0'	1'	2'	3'	4'	5'	6'	7'	8'	9'
34.0	5.6	11.3	17.0	22.6	28.3	.0	0.0	0.6	1.1	1.7	2.3	2.9	3.4	4.0	4.6	5.2
34.1	5.7	11.3	17.0	22.7	28.4	.1	0.1	0.6	1.2	1.8	2.4	2.9	3.5	4.1	4.7	5.2
34.2	5.7	11.4	17.1	22.8	28.5	.2	0.1	0.7	1.3	1.8	2.4	3.0	3.6	4.1	4.7	5.3
34.3	5.7	11.4	17.1	22.9	28.6	.3	0.2	0.7	1.3	1.9	2.5	3.0	3.6	4.2	4.8	5.3
34.4	5.7	11.5	17.2	22.9	28.7	.4	0.2	0.8	1.4	2.0	2.5	3.1	3.7	4.3	4.8	5.4
34.5	5.8	11.5	17.3	23.0	28.8	.5	0.3	0.9	1.4	2.0	2.6	3.2	3.7	4.3	4.9	5.5
34.6	5.8	11.5	17.3	23.1	28.8	.6	0.3	0.9	1.5	2.1	2.6	3.2	3.8	4.4	4.9	5.5
34.7	5.8	11.6	17.4	23.2	28.9	.7	0.4	1.0	1.6	2.1	2.7	3.3	3.9	4.4	5.0	5.6
34.8	5.8	11.6	17.4	23.2	29.0	.8	0.5	1.0	1.6	2.2	2.8	3.3	3.9	4.5	5.1	5.6
34.9	5.9	11.7	17.5	23.3	29.1	.9	0.5	1.1	1.7	2.2	2.8	3.4	4.0	4.5	5.1	5.7
35.0	5.8	11.6	17.5	23.3	29.1	.0	0.0	0.6	1.2	1.8	2.4	3.0	3.5	4.1	4.7	5.3
35.1	5.8	11.7	17.5	23.4	29.2	.1	0.1	0.7	1.2	1.8	2.4	3.0	3.6	4.2	4.8	5.4
35.2	5.8	11.7	17.6	23.4	29.3	.2	0.1	0.7	1.3	1.9	2.5	3.1	3.7	4.3	4.9	5.5
35.3	5.9	11.8	17.6	23.5	29.4	.3	0.2	0.8	1.4	2.0	2.5	3.1	3.7	4.3	4.9	5.5
35.4	5.9	11.8	17.7	23.6	29.5	.4	0.2	0.8	1.4	2.0	2.6	3.2	3.8	4.4	5.0	5.6
35.5	5.9	11.8	17.8	23.7	29.6	.5	0.3	0.9	1.5	2.1	2.7	3.3	3.8	4.4	5.0	5.6
35.6	5.9	11.9	17.8	23.7	29.7	.6	0.4	0.9	1.5	2.1	2.7	3.3	3.9	4.5	5.1	5.7
35.7	6.0	11.9	17.9	23.8	29.8	.7	0.4	1.0	1.6	2.2	2.8	3.4	4.0	4.6	5.1	5.7
35.8	6.0	12.0	17.9	23.9	29.9	.8	0.5	1.1	1.7	2.2	2.8	3.4	4.0	4.6	5.2	5.8
35.9	6.0	12.0	18.0	24.0	30.0	.9	0.5	1.1	1.7	2.3	2.9	3.5	4.1	4.7	5.3	5.9

Double Second Diff. and Corr.: 0.8 / 2.5 0.1 / 4.1 0.2 / 5.8 0.3 / 7.4 0.4 / 9.1 0.5 / 10.7 0.6 / 12.3 0.7 / 14.0 0.8 / 15.6 0.9 / 17.3 1.0 / 18.9 1.1 / 20.6 1.2 / 22.2 1.3 / 23.9 1.4 / 25.5 1.5 / 27.2 1.6 / 28.8 1.7 / 30.4 1.8 / 32.1 1.9 / 33.7 2.0 / 35.4 2.1

Right half

Dec. Inc.	10'	20'	30'	40'	50'	Dec.	0'	1'	2'	3'	4'	5'	6'	7'	8'	9'
36.0	6.0	12.0	18.0	24.0·	30.0	.0	0.0	0.6	1.2	1.8	2.4	3.0	3.6	4.3	4.9	5.5
36.1	6.0	12.0	18.0	24.0	30.1	.1	0.1	0.7	1.3	1.9	2.5	3.1	3.7	4.3	4.9	5.5
36.2	6.0	12.0	18.1	24.1	30.1	.2	0.1	0.7	1.3	1.9	2.6	3.2	3.8	4.4	5.0	5.6
36.3	6.0	12.1	18.1	24.2	30.2	.3	0.2	0.8	1.4	2.0	2.6	3.2	3.8	4.4	5.0	5.7
36.4	6.1	12.1	18.2	24.3	30.3	.4	0.2	0.9	1.5	2.1	2.7	3.3	3.9	4.5	5.1	5.7
36.5	6.1	12.2	18.3	24.3	30.4	.5	0.3	0.9	1.5	2.1	2.7	3.3	4.0	4.6	5.2	5.8
36.6	6.1	12.2	18.3	24.4	30.5	.6	0.4	1.0	1.6	2.2	2.8	3.4	4.0	4.6	5.2	5.8
36.7	6.1	12.3	18.4	24.5	30.6	.7	0.4	1.0	1.6	2.3	2.9	3.5	4.1	4.7	5.3	5.9
36.8	6.2	12.3	18.4	24.6	30.7	.8	0.5	1.1	1.7	2.3	2.9	3.5	4.1	4.7	5.4	6.0
36.9	6.2	12.3	18.5	24.6	30.8	.9	0.5	1.2	1.8	2.4	3.0	3.6	4.2	4.8	5.4	6.0

Double Second Diff. and Corr.: 0.8 / 2.5 0.1 / 4.2 0.2 / 5.9 0.3 / 7.6 0.4 / 9.3 0.5 / 11.0 0.6 / 12.7 0.7 / 14.4 0.8 / 16.1 0.9 / 17.8 1.0

Dec. Inc.	10'	20'	30'	40'	50'	Dec.	0'	1'	2'	3'	4'	5'	6'	7'	8'	9'
42.0	7.0	14.0	21.0	28.0	35.0	.0	0.0	0.7	1.4	2.1	2.8	3.5	4.2	5.0	5.7	6.4
42.1	7.0	14.0	21.0	28.0	35.1	.1	0.1	0.8	1.5	2.2	2.9	3.6	4.3	5.0	5.7	6.4
42.2	7.0	14.0	21.1	28.1	35.1	.2	0.1	0.8	1.6	2.3	3.0	3.7	4.4	5.1	5.8	6.5
42.3	7.0	14.1	21.1	28.2	35.2	.3	0.2	0.9	1.6	2.3	3.0	3.8	4.5	5.2	5.9	6.6
42.4	7.1	14.1	21.2	28.3	35.3	.4	0.3	1.0	1.7	2.4	3.1	3.8	4.5	5.2	5.9	6.7
42.5	7.1	14.2	21.3	28.3	35.4	.5	0.4	1.1	1.8	2.5	3.2	3.9	4.6	5.3	6.0	6.7
42.6	7.1	14.2	21.3	28.4	35.5	.6	0.4	1.1	1.8	2.5	3.3	4.0	4.7	5.4	6.1	6.8
42.7	7.1	14.3	21.4	28.5	35.6	.7	0.5	1.2	1.9	2.6	3.3	4.0	4.7	5.5	6.2	6.9
42.8	7.2	14.3	21.4	28.6	35.7	.8	0.6	1.3	2.0	2.7	3.4	4.1	4.8	5.5	6.2	6.9
42.9	7.2	14.3	21.5	28.6	35.8	.9	0.6	1.3	2.1	2.8	3.5	4.2	4.9	5.6	6.3	7.0
43.0	7.1	14.3	21.5	28.6	35.8	.0	0.0	0.7	1.4	2.2	2.9	3.6	4.3	5.1	5.8	6.5
43.1	7.2	14.3	21.5	28.7	35.9	.1	0.1	0.8	1.5	2.2	3.0	3.7	4.4	5.1	5.9	6.6
43.2	7.2	14.4	21.6	28.8	36.0	.2	0.1	0.9	1.6	2.3	3.0	3.8	4.5	5.2	5.9	6.7
43.3	7.2	14.4	21.6	28.9	36.1	.3	0.2	0.9	1.7	2.4	3.1	3.8	4.6	5.3	6.0	6.7
43.4	7.2	14.5	21.7	28.9	36.2	.4	0.3	1.0	1.7	2.5	3.2	3.9	4.6	5.4	6.1	6.8
43.5	7.3	14.5	21.8	29.0	36.3	.5	0.4	1.1	1.8	2.5	3.3	4.0	4.7	5.4	6.2	6.9
43.6	7.3	14.5	21.8	29.1	36.3	.6	0.4	1.2	1.9	2.6	3.3	4.1	4.8	5.5	6.2	7.0
43.7	7.3	14.6	21.9	29.2	36.4	.7	0.5	1.2	2.0	2.7	3.4	4.1	4.9	5.6	6.3	7.0
43.8	7.3	14.6	21.9	29.2	36.5	.8	0.6	1.3	2.0	2.8	3.5	4.2	4.9	5.7	6.4	7.1
43.9	7.4	14.7	22.0	29.3	36.6	.9	0.7	1.4	2.1	2.8	3.6	4.3	5.0	5.7	6.5	7.2

Double Second Diff. and Corr.: 1.0 / 3.0 0.1 / 4.9 0.2 / 6.9 0.3 / 8.9 0.4 / 10.8 0.5 / 12.8 0.6 / 14.8 0.7 / 16.7 0.8 / 18.7 0.9 / 20.7 1.0 / 22.7 1.1 / 24.6 1.2 / 26.6 1.3 / 28.6 1.4 / 30.5 1.5 / 32.5 1.6 / 34.5 1.7 / 36.4 1.8

The Double-Second-Difference correction (Corr.) is always to be added to the tabulated altitude.

Figure 2505c: H.O. 229 Interpolation Tables.

entry) is 48'.3, and for Dec. 70° (one line below) it is 43'.6; the difference of these values is 4'.7.

The interpolation tables also provide for obtaining the actual value of the double-second difference correction; it is obtained from the vertical column to the extreme right, headed "Double Second Diff. and Corr." This is a critical-type table. Enter it with the 4'.7 difference, found above, and obtain the actual value of the correction, 0'.3. *This correction is always additive.*

The value of the azimuth angle at times changes very materially with each degree of declination. It must, therefore, be corrected by interpolation for the actual value of the declination.

The following example illustrates the use of H. O. 229; it is based on those portions of the tables shown in Figures 2505a and 2505c.

The calculated altitude and azimuth are required for an observation of a body having a declination of 69°34'.8 north, and a local hour angle of 29°; the assumed latitude is 76° north.

Solution by H.O. 229.

LHA	29°	
aL	76°N	
aDec.	69°N	
Dec.	69°34'.8N	
Hc	79°00'.9	
First Diff Corr 1	+ 23'.2	$(34'.8 \times \frac{40'}{60})$
First Diff Corr 2	+ 3'.6	$(34'.8 \times \frac{6'.2}{60})$
Second Diff Corr	+ 0'.3	
Hc	79°28'.0	

Tabulated Z   N114°.3W

Z   N112°.3W $(34'.8 \times \frac{3°.5}{60}) = 2°$

Zn   247°.7

H. O. 229 also permits a reduction from a DR position. Entry in the tables is made as in the above example with the integral degree of latitude, LHA, and declination, and the tabulated Hc, *d*, and Z are extracted. In these tables the tabulated altitude is called Hc.

DR solution by H. O. 229.

In this instance, Hc must be corrected for increments of minutes of latitude and LHA, in addition to those of the declination. Hc is first corrected for the minutes of declination, as described above, using the Interpolation Tables. Correction to Hc for the increments of latitude and LHA are made by means of diagrams, which are included in each volume. Instructions for their use are included.

The azimuth angle, Z, may in most instances be corrected by mental interpolation for increments of latitude, LHA, and declination.

2506. H. O. 229 and H. O. 214, when used with an assumed position, offer sight reductions which are mathematically accurate. However, as with any sight reduction methods designed for use with an assumed position, and which tabulate latitude and meridian or hour angle by integral degrees, resulting lines of position may be somewhat in error under certain conditions. These errors tend to arise when the intercepts are long; they are caused by plotting the intercept and the line of position as rhumb lines on the chart, rather than as arcs of a great and small circle, respectively. These errors are not sufficiently large to require consideration in the ordinary practice of navigation at sea.

Possible errors arising from plotting from an assumed position.

It has been found that for any given distance between the true and assumed position, the maximum perpendicular distance from the true position to the plotted line of position is roughly proportional to the tangent of the altitude. The error tends to increase with the altitude of the body, and it is roughly proportional to the square of the difference between the true and assumed positions. Other factors being equal, the error decreases as the latitude increases. In the vicinity of the equator, for an altitude of 75°, and a true position differing in both latitude and longitude by 30′ from the assumed position, the error will not exceed 1.0 miles; at latitude 60°, it will not exceed 0.7 miles, and the probable error would not exceed 0.3 miles. For an altitude of 60°, near the equator, the error will not exceed 0.5 miles. If the difference in both latitude and longitude between the true and assumed positions is reduced to 20′, the errors quoted above would be reduced by more than half.

2507. These tables are entitled *"Sight Reduction Tables for Air Navigation,"* however, they are generally referred to simply as H. O. 249. As their name implies, they are designed for the use of air navigators. They have found some favor with surface navigators in cases where their convenience offsets the less precise data they supply.

H. O. 249.

These tables are published in three volumes. Like H. O. 214, they are inspection tables designed for use with an assumed position, but they differ from the latter publication in that altitude is stated only to the nearest whole minute of arc, and azimuth values are stated to the nearest whole degree. The first volume is designed for use with certain selected stars on a world wide basis; all integral

H. O. 249, Volume I using selected stars.

degrees of latitude, from 89° north to 89° south are included. The arguments for entering the tables in Volume I are the nearest whole degree of latitude with name, the LHA Aries (Υ) (*not* meridian angle) and the name of the star observed; with this entry, a calculated altitude, named Hc, and a true azimuth (Zn) rather than azimuth angle, are obtained. The LHAΥ is obtained by applying to the GHAΥ such an assumed longitude as will give a whole degree of LHAΥ.

For each degree of latitude and of LHAΥ, seven stars are tabulated. These stars are selected chiefly for good distribution in azimuth, for their magnitude and altitude, and for continuity both in latitude and hour angle. An extract from Volume I is reproduced in Figure 2507a.

H. O. 249, Volume II and III entering arguments.

Volumes II and III are generally similar to H. O. 214, but differ in format in that LHA, rather than meridian angle is tabulated. Both volumes list declination by integral degrees from 0° to 29° thereby covering all bodies of the solar system. It is assumed Vol. I will usually be used for star sights, although stars with Dec. of 29° or less can be used with Vol. II and Vol. III; 29 of the 57 selected stars fall into this category. Volume II covers latitudes 0° to 39°, and Volume III covers latitude 40° to 89°. A portion of a page from Volume II is reproduced in Figure 2507b. The entering arguments are a whole degree of latitude, without name in these volumes, a whole degree of declination of same or contrary name to the latitude, and a whole degree of LHA. In the design of the tables it is intended that the *next smaller value* of declination be used. The tabulated values of LHA provide for negative altitudes, because of the large value of the dip at the high operating altitudes of modern planes, which permit the observation of bodies below the celestial horizon.

For each single set of entering arguments, the tables state an altitude expressed to the nearest whole minute of arc, under the heading "Hc." Adjoining this, under the heading "d," is a value with sign, which is the difference in minutes between the tabulated altitude, and the altitude for a declination one degree higher, but at the same latitude, and for the same LHA. The third item, under the heading "Z", is the azimuth angle (not Zn as in Vol. I). The rule for converting Z to Zn is given on each page.

To correct the tabulated altitude for the difference between the true declination and that used as an entering argument, a multiplication table is included at the back of the book; a sample section is shown in Figure 2507c. By means of this table, the "d" value is multiplied by the difference between the true and tabulated declinations, and applied to the tabulated altitude according to the sign shown in the main table.

H. O. 249 is an excellent reduction method for the air navigator. At present long distance flight altitudes, cloud cover rarely presents a problem, and the seven stars selected for any given time are usually all visible during the hours of darkness. It furnishes an accuracy in keeping with that obtained by means of a sextant using a pendulous mirror, or some other artificial horizon, such as the bubble.

It is also a satisfactory method for small vessels making long ocean voyages. Stowage space in such ships is limited, and the three volumes give world wide coverage. Of the 173 navigational stars tabulated in the Nautical Almanac, 75 are suitable for use with Volumes II and III; 29 of these 75 are among the

LAT 42°N

LHA ♈	Hc Zn *Alpheratz	Hc Zn ALTAIR	Hc Zn Nunki	Hc Zn *ANTARES	Hc Zn ARCTURUS	Hc Zn *Alkaid	Hc Zn Kochab
270	17 43 067	49 00 136	20 34 167	18 23 202	37 33 263	46 27 302	51 19 341
271	18 24 067	49 30 138	20 43 168	18 06 203	36 48 263	45 49 303	51 05 341
272	19 05 068	50 00 139	20 52 169	17 48 204	36 04 264	45 12 303	50 50 341
273	19 46 068	50 29 140	21 00 170	17 30 204	35 20 265	44 34 303	50 36 341
274	20 28 069	50 57 142	21 07 171	17 11 205	34 35 265	43 57 304	50 21 341
275	21 10 070	51 24 143	21 14 172	16 52 206	33 51 266	43 20 304	50 06 340
276	21 51 070	51 51 145	21 20 173	16 32 207	33 06 267	42 43 304	49 51 340
277	22 34 071	52 16 146	21 25 174	16 11 208	32 22 268	42 06 304	49 36 340
278	23 16 071	52 41 147	21 29 175	15 50 209	31 37 268	41 29 305	49 21 340
279	23 58 072	53 04 149	21 33 176	15 28 210	30 53 269	40 53 305	49 06 340
280	24 40 072	53 27 150	21 36 177	15 06 210	30 08 270	40 16 305	48 50 340
281	25 23 073	53 48 152	21 38 178	14 43 211	29 23 270	39 40 306	48 35 340
282	26 06 074	54 09 154	21 39 179	14 20 212	28 39 271	39 04 306	48 19 339
283	26 48 074	54 28 155	21 40 180	13 56 213	27 54 272	38 28 306	48 04 339
284	27 31 075	54 46 157	21 40 181	13 31 214	27 10 272	37 52 307	47 48 339

LHA ♈	Hc Zn *Mirfak	Hc Zn Alpheratz	Hc Zn *ALTAIR	Hc Zn Rasalhague	Hc Zn *ARCTURUS	Hc Zn Alkaid	Hc Zn Kochab
285	13 24 033	28 14 075	55 03 158	55 05 219	26 25 273	37 16 307	47 32 339
286	13 48 033	28 58 076	55 19 160	54 37 220	25 41 274	36 41 307	47 16 339
287	14 13 034	29 41 076	55 34 162	54 08 222	24 56 274	36 05 308	47 00 339
288	14 37 034	30 24 077	55 47 163	53 37 223	24 12 275	35 30 308	46 44 339
289	15 03 035	31 08 077	55 59 165	53 06 225	23 27 275	34 55 308	46 28 339
290	15 28 035	31 51 078	56 10 167	52 35 226	22 43 276	34 20 309	46 12 339
291	15 54 036	32 35 079	56 19 169	52 02 227	21 59 277	33 45 309	45 56 339
292	16 20 036	33 19 079	56 27 170	51 29 229	21 14 277	33 10 309	45 40 339

Figure 2507a: Extract from H. O. 249, Volume I.

Figure 2507b: Extract from H. O. 249, Volume II.

DECLINATION (19°-29°) CONTRARY NAME TO LATITUDE

LHA	19° (Hc d Z)	20° (Hc d Z)	21° (Hc d Z)	22° (Hc d Z)	23° (Hc d Z)	24° (Hc d Z)	25° (Hc d Z)	26° (Hc d Z)	27° (Hc d Z)	28° (Hc d Z)	29° (Hc d Z)	LHA
14	3618 58 164	3520 58 164	3422 58 164	3324 58 164	3226 58 165	3128 59 165	3029 58 165	2931 58 166	2833 59 166	2734 58 166	2636 59 166	346
13	3632 58 165	3534 58 165	3436 59 165	3337 58 166	3239 59 166	3140 58 166	3042 59 166	2943 59 167	2844 58 167	2746 59 167	2647 58 167	347
12	3645 58 166	3547 59 166	3448 59 166	3349 58 167	3251 59 167	3152 59 167	3053 59 167	2954 59 168	2856 59 168	2757 59 168	2658 59 168	348
11	3657 59 167	3558 59 167	3459 59 167	3400 58 168	3302 59 168	3203 59 168	3104 59 168	3005 59 169	2906 59 169	2807 59 169	2708 59 169	349
10	3708 −59 168	3609 −59 168	3510 −59 169	3411 −59 169	3312 −59 169	3213 −60 169	3113 −59 169	3014 −59 170	2915 −59 170	2816 −59 170	2717 −59 170	350
9	3718 60 169	3618 59 170	3519 59 170	3420 59 170	3321 59 170	3222 60 170	3122 59 170	3023 59 171	2924 60 171	2824 59 171	2725 59 171	351
8	3727 60 171	3627 59 171	3528 60 171	3428 59 171	3329 59 171	3230 60 171	3130 59 172	3031 60 172	2931 59 172	2832 60 172	2732 59 172	352
7	3734 59 172	3635 60 172	3535 59 172	3436 60 172	3336 59 172	3237 60 172	3137 59 173	3038 60 173	2938 60 173	2838 59 173	2739 60 173	353
6	3741 59 173	3642 60 173	3542 60 173	3442 59 173	3343 60 174	3243 60 174	3143 59 174	3044 60 174	2944 60 174	2844 60 174	2744 59 174	354
5	3747 −60 174	3647 −60 174	3547 −59 174	3448 −60 174	3348 −60 175	3248 −60 175	3148 −59 175	3049 −60 175	2949 −60 175	2849 −60 175	2749 −60 175	355
4	3752 60 175	3652 60 175	3552 60 175	3452 60 176	3352 60 176	3252 59 176	3153 60 176	3053 60 176	2953 60 176	2853 60 176	2753 60 176	356
3	3755 60 176	3655 60 177	3555 59 177	3456 60 177	3356 60 177	3256 60 177	3156 60 177	3056 60 177	2956 60 177	2856 60 177	2756 60 177	357
2	3758 60 178	3658 60 178	3558 60 178	3458 60 178	3358 60 178	3258 60 178	3158 60 178	3058 60 178	2958 60 178	2858 60 178	2758 60 178	358
1	3800 60 179	3700 60 179	3600 60 179	3500 60 179	3400 60 179	3300 60 179	3200 60 179	3100 60 179	3000 60 179	2900 60 179	2800 60 179	359
0	3800 −60 180	3700 −60 180	3600 −60 180	3500 −60 180	3400 −60 180	3300 −60 180	3200 −60 180	3100 −60 180	3000 −60 180	2900 −60 180	2800 −60 180	360

DECLINATION (19°-29°) CONTRARY NAME TO LATITUDE — LAT 33°

LAT 33°

TABLE III.—Correction to Tabulated Altitude for Minutes of Declination

d / '	1 2 3	4 5 6	7 8 9	10 11 12	13 14 15	16 17 18	19 20 21	37 38 39	40 41 42	43 44 45	46 47 48	49 50 51	52 53 54	55 56 57	58 59 60	d / '
0	0 0 0	0 0 0	0 0 0	0 0 0	0 0 0	0 0 0	0 0 0	0 0 0	0 0 0	0 0 0	0 0 0	0 0 0	0 0 0	0 0 0	0 0 0	0
1	0 0 0	0 0 0	0 0 0	0 0 0	0 0 0	0 0 0	1 1 1	1 1 1	1 1 1	1 1 1	1 1 1	1 1 1	1 1 1	1 1 1	1 1 1	1
2	0 0 0	0 0 0	0 0 0	0 0 0	1 1 1	1 1 1	1 1 1	1 1 1	1 1 1	1 1 2	2 2 2	2 2 2	2 2 2	2 2 2	2 2 2	2
3	0 0 0	0 0 0	0 0 0	1 1 1	1 1 1	1 1 1	1 1 1	2 2 2	2 2 2	2 2 2	2 2 3	3 3 3	3 3 3	3 3 3	3 3 3	3
4	0 0 0	0 0 0	0 1 1	1 1 1	1 1 1	1 1 1	1 1 1	2 3 3	3 3 3	3 3 3	3 3 3	4 4 4	4 4 4	4 4 4	4 4 4	4
35	1 1 2	2 3 4	4 5 5	6 6 7	8 8 9	9 10 10	11 12 12	22 23 23	23 24 24	25 26 26	27 27 28	29 29 30	30 31 32	32 33 33	34 34 35	35
36	1 1 2	2 3 4	4 5 5	6 6 7	8 8 9	10 10 11	11 12 13	22 23 23	24 25 25	26 26 27	28 28 29	29 30 31	31 32 32	33 33 34	35 35 36	36
37	1 1 2	2 3 4	4 5 6	6 7 7	8 9 9	10 10 11	12 12 13	23 23 24	25 25 26	27 27 28	28 29 30	30 31 31	32 33 33	34 34 35	36 36 37	37
38	1 1 2	3 3 4	4 5 6	6 7 8	8 9 10	10 11 11	12 13 13	23 24 25	25 26 27	27 28 28	29 30 30	31 32 32	33 34 34	35 35 36	37 37 38	38
39	1 1 2	3 3 4	5 5 6	6 7 8	8 9 10	10 11 12	12 13 14	24 25 25	26 27 27	28 29 29	30 31 31	32 32 33	34 34 35	36 36 37	38 38 39	39

Figure 2507c: Extract from H. O. 249 correction table.

"selected stars." In accuracy, H. O. 249 is compatible with the accuracy of the sextant observations that can be obtained aboard a small craft in rough water. The Navy navigator, however, can and should obtain a higher order of accuracy in his celestial navigation than is possible by the use of H. O. 249. H. O. 214 or H. O. 229 should be the reduction methods of his choice.

′	30° 00′ A	30° 00′ B	30° 30′ A	30° 30′ B	31° 00′ A	31° 00′ B	31° 30′ A	31° 30′ B	32° 00′ A	32° 00′ B	′
0	30103	6247	29453	6468	28816	6693	28191	6923	27579	7158	30
	30092	6251	29442	6472	28806	6697	28181	6927	27569	7162	
1	30081	6254	29432	6475	28795	6701	28171	6931	27559	7166	29
	30070	6258	29421	6479	28785	6705	28161	6935	27549	7170	
22	29625	6409	28985	6633	28357	6862	27741	7095	27137	7333	8
	29614	6412	28974	6637	28346	6865	27731	7099	27127	7337	
23	29604	6416	28964	6640	28336	6869	27721	7103	27117	7341	7
	29593	6420	28953	6644	28326	6873	27711	7107	27107	7345	
24	29582	6423	28942	6648	28315	6877	27701	7111	27098	7349	6
	29571	6427	28932	6652	28305	6881	27690	7115	27088	7353	
25	29560	6431	28921	6655	28295	6885	27680	7118	27078	7357	5
	29550	6435	28911	6659	28284	6889	27670	7122	27068	7361	
26	29539	6438	28900	6663	28274	6893	27660	7126	27058	7365	4
	29528	6442	28890	6667	28264	6896	27650	7130	27048	7369	
27	29517	6446	28879	6671	28253	6900	27640	7134	27038	7373	3
	29507	6449	28869	6674	28243	6904	27630	7138	27028	7377	
28	29496	6453	28858	6678	28233	6908	27619	7142	27018	7381	2
	29485	6457	28848	6682	28222	6912	27609	7146	27008	7385	
29	29475	6461	28837	6686	28212	6916	27599	7150	26998	7389	1
	29464	6464	28827	6690	28202	6920	27589	7154	26988	7393	
30	29453	6468	28816	6693	28191	6923	27579	7158	26978	7397	0
′	A	B	A	B	A	B	A	B	A	B	′
′	149° 30′		149° 00′		148° 30′		148° 00′		147° 30′		′

Figure 2508a: Extract from page of H.O. 211.

Figure 2508b: The triangle as solved in H.O. 211.

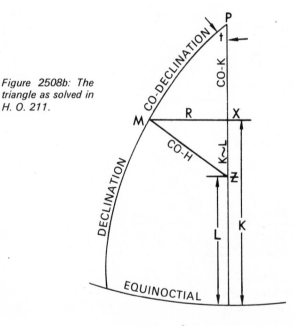

P. Pole.

Z. Zenith of observer. The azimuth (angle (PZM) is also called Ƶ.

M. Heavenly body observed.

L. Latitude of observer.

d. Declination of body M.

t. (or LHA). Local hour angle of body M.

H. Altitude of body M.

R. Perpendicular let fall from M on PZ. This is an auxiliary part.

X. Intersection of R with PZ.

K. Arc from X to the equinoctial. This is an auxiliary part introduced to facilitate solution.

The following formulae have been derived:

From triangle PMX—

1. csc R = csc t sec d.

2. $\csc K = \dfrac{\csc d}{\sec R}$

From triangle ZMX—

3. csc Hc = sec R sec (K ~ L).

4. $\csc Ƶ = \dfrac{\csc R}{\sec Hc}$

H.O. 211.

2508. This publication is entitled *"Dead Reckoning Altitude and Azimuth Table."* It is popularly referred to as "H. O. 211," or "Ageton" after its designer. It is a small volume of only 49 pages, containing a single table of log secants and log cosecants (×100,000), stated for each 0′.5 of arc. It is suitable for worldwide use with any declination, and any altitude. As its name implies, it is intended for use from a DR position. A partial page is shown in Figure 2508a.

In this method, two right triangles are formed by dropping a perpendicular from the celestial body to the celestial meridian of the observer. The right angle falls on the celestial meridian at a point which may lie either inside or outside of the navigational triangle. The right triangles are then solved for altitude and azimuth angle from formulae derived from Napier's rules.

In Figure 2508b the navigational triangle is shown with the parts of the triangle lettered.

In right triangle *PMX*, *t* and *d* are known. *R* may be found from formula (1). Knowing *R* and *d*, *K* may be found by formula (2). *K* is then combined algebraically with *L* to obtain $(K \sim L)$.

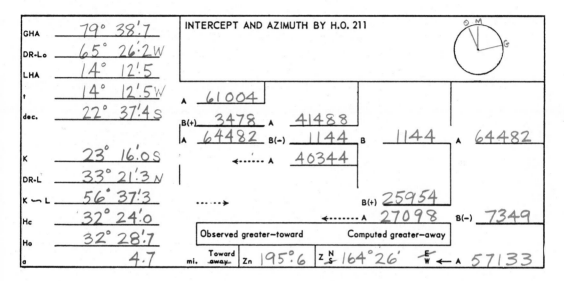

		INTERCEPT AND AZIMUTH BY H.O. 211	
GHA	79° 38′.7		
DR-Lo	65° 26′.2 W		
LHA	14° 12′.5		
t	14° 12′.5 W	A 61004	
dec.	22° 37′.4 S	B(+) 3478 A 41488	
		A 64482 B(−) 1144 B 1144 A 64482	
		⟵····· A 40344	
K	23° 16′.0 S		
DR-L	33° 21′.3 N		
K ⌣ L	56° 37′.3	·····⟶ B(+) 25954	
Hc	32° 24′.0	⟵······· A 27098 B(−) 7349	
Ho	32° 28′.7	Observed greater—toward Computed greater—away	
a	4.7	Toward away Zn 195°.6 Z N S 164° 26′ E W ⟵ A 57133	

Figure 2508c: Form with sample H.O. 211 solution.

In triangle *ZMX*, sides *R* and $(K \sim L)$ are now known. Hc may be found by formula (3). The azimuth, Z, is computed by formula (4).

All formulae are in terms of secants and cosecants. The table is arranged in parallel "A" and "B" columns, the "A" columns containing log cosecants multiplied by 100,000 and the "B" columns log secants multiplied by 100,000. This device has greatly simplified the arithmetic of solution.

The A and B columns.

The tabulation of functions for every half minute of arc throughout the table is employed so that, in ordinary use, interpolation will not be necessary.

The procedure necessary to obtain the calculated altitude and azimuth by the use of H. O. 211 is outlined in the volume itself with 14 steps involved. The example shown in Figure 2508c illustrates the reduction of an observation by this method; the work form used will be found convenient, as it indicates where the A or B values taken from the tables are entered and how they are combined.

Example: A navigator whose DR position is L 33°21′.3 N, λ 65°26′.2 W observes the sun at a time when its *t* is 14°12′.5 W, and its Dec., is 22°37′.4 S. After appropriate corrections are applied to the hs, the Ho is 32°28′.7. In obtaining Hc and Z, he elects not to interpolate.

Celestial Lines of Position

Introduction.

2601. A prior chapter has shown how the navigator, having obtained an altitude of a celestial body, can determine the circle of equal altitude passing through his position. Only seldom is he able to plot this circular line of position directly on his chart; he must, therefore, be able to construct a portion of the circle on his chart in the vicinity of the ship's DR position. The purpose of this chapter is to explain the techniques whereby celestial altitudes are converted into celestial lines of position, and how fixes and running fixes are obtained from such lines. Celestial lines of position are usually plotted on special charts

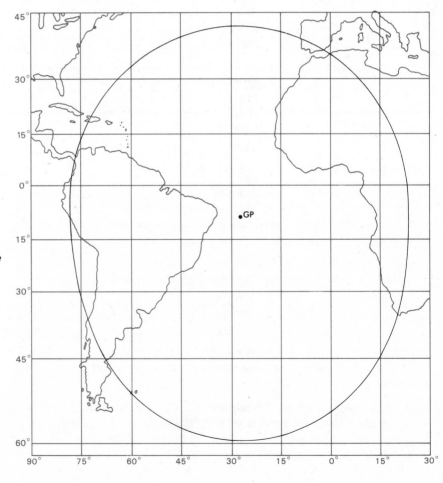

Figure 2603a: Circle of equal altitude plotted on a Mercator chart.

called *plotting sheets*. In the interest of simplification, the term "chart" will be used throughout this chapter.

2602. In piloting, the navigator may obtain a line of position in any of several ways; usually such lines represent bearings of a land- or sea-mark. In celestial navigation a line of position is a small segment of a circle, which represents distance in nautical miles from the GP of the observed body; it is somewhat similar to the circular line of position obtained from a radar range in piloting. This distance is obtained by converting the altitude of the observed body into miles on the surface of the earth; this distance must then be transformed into a line of position which can be plotted on the appropriate chart. Both celestial and terrestrial lines of position are used in essentially the same manner, and may be advanced or retired as required.

Terrestrial and celestial lines of position compared.

2603. As shown in Chapter 20, the radius of a circle of equal altitude is equal to the coaltitude, or 90° minus the altitude. If a body is observed at a very high altitude, the radius will be small, and the resulting circle of equal altitude can be plotted directly on a chart. The center of this circle will be the GP of the body, and the radius will equal the coaltitude. In practice, only that portion of the circle which lies in the vicinity of the ship's DR position is drawn.

Lines of position from high altitude observations.

There are two reasons why this direct method of plotting celestial lines of position is not suitable for most celestial observations. The first is that the radii of most circles of equal altitude are very long. For example, for an altitude of 50°, the coaltitude, and therefore the radius, is 40°, which equals 2,400 nautical miles, and for an altitude of 20°, the radius is 4,200 miles. A chart which would permit plotting radii of such magnitudes would be of such small scale that it would not yield the accuracy in position required in practical navigation.

Secondly, distortion is apparent on the commonly used Mercator projection, and increases with the latitude of the GP. The distortion of such a circle is illustrated in Figure 2603a.

However, if the body is very high in altitude, the coaltitude will be small enough to plot on a navigational chart, and the distortion will be negligible. There is no precise answer as to how great the altitude should be to permit direct plotting as a "high altitude" observation. At the U. S. Naval Academy, all sights with an observed altitude of 87° or more are treated as high altitude observations, and the resulting LOP is plotted directly.

Example: The 1137 DR position of an observer is L 5°30'.5 N, λ 139°57'.7 E, at which time he determines the Ho of the sun to be 88°14'.5. The GP of the sun for this time is determined from the Almanac to be L 7°14'.9 N, λ 140°26'.2 E.

Required: The plot of the 1137 LOP.

Solution: (Figure 2603b) Plot and label the 1137 DR position and the GP, using the latitudes and longitudes given. Since the radius of the circle of equal altitude equals the coaltitude, subtract the observed altitude from 90°, and convert the difference into minutes of arc, which equal nautical miles.

	90°00'.0
Ho	88°14'.5
Radius	1°45'.5 = 105 .5 nautical miles

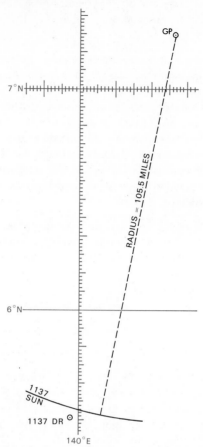

Figure 2603b: Plot of the LOP from a high altitude observation.

Using a radius of 105.5 miles (shown by the broken line), construct an arc with the GP as the center, drawing only that segment which lies in the vicinity of the DR position. Label the resulting line of position as shown. The radius shown in this figure is normally not drawn.

In actual practice, it is difficult to obtain accurate observations at very high altitudes, as when the sextant is rocked, the observed body travels almost horizontally along the horizon, making it difficult to establish the vertical. However, at midday in the tropics, the navigator must make his LAN observation of the sun, regardless of its altitude, in order to obtain a latitude line of position.

Lines of position from other than high altitude observations.

2604. The great majority of celestial observations are made at altitudes which do not permit direct plotting, as described above; for these a different method must be employed. This method is usually based on the use of an assumed position (AP), and the solution of the navigational triangle associated with it.

It has been stated that the navigational triangle may be defined by the AP, the elevated pole, and the GP of the body. By solving the triangle, the altitude and azimuth of the body at the AP at the time of observation may be computed. In Figure 2604a the circle represents the circle of equal altitude for an observer at M and the point AP is the assumed position selected for the particular observation. By solving the triangle containing AP, the navigator determines the length of the side AP-GP, or coaltitude, which is the radius of the circle of equal altitude through the AP (not shown in Figure 2604a).

464

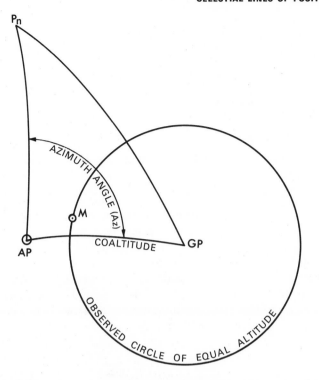

Figure 2604a: A circle of equal altitude and the navigational triangle associated with one AP.

If the altitude (Ho) obtained by the observer at M is greater than the altitude computed (Hc) by solving the triangle, the observer must be closer to the GP than is the AP; if it is less, he must be farther away. Also, the difference in the radii of the two circles of equal altitude, as illustrated in Figure 2604b, is equal to the difference between the coaltitudes obtained from Ho and Hc, respectively. *This difference is the intercept (a), and is expressed* in nautical miles, which equals the difference expressed in minutes of arc.

In solving the triangle, the value of the *azimuth angle* (Az) is also obtained; this is used to determine the true direction or *azimuth* (Zn) of the body from the AP. If the Ho is greater than the Hc, a line representing Zn is plotted from the AP toward the GP; if Hc is the greater, the line will be plotted as the reciprocal of Zn, or away from the GP. This line is a part of the radius of a circle of equal altitude; by laying off a distance equal to (a) along this line, a point on the observed circle of equal altitude is determined. If Ho is greater than Hc, (a) is always labeled T (toward); if it is less, the label is A (away). A useful memory aid in labeling (a) is *Coast Guard Academy* for *Computed Greater Away.*

Azimuth for the LOP.

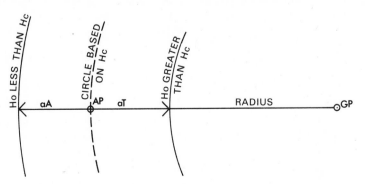

Figure 2604b: The relationship of the altitude difference, (a), to the AP, and the observed circle of equal altitude.

465

To sum up, to plot a celestial LOP the following must be known:

The position of the AP;

Azimuth of the body, Zn;

The intercept, a.

The intercept, (a), lies along a partial radius of a circle of equal altitude; it is plotted from the AP in the direction Zn, or towards the body, if labeled T (Ho greater than Hc). If labeled A (Hc greater than Ho), it is plotted in the direction of the reciprocal of Zn. The length of (a) in miles is equal to the difference between Ho and Hc in minutes of arc.

The line of position on which the observer is located is perpendicular to the intercept and passes through its terminus. Actually, this LOP is an arc of a circle of equal altitude; however, for most observations, the radius of the circle is so large that the curvature of the LOP is not significant. The LOP resulting from all but very high altitude observations may, therefore, be drawn as a straight line; the resulting error is insignificant in the ordinary practice of navigation. Figure 2604c illustrates the approximation made by using a straight line rather than an arc for plotting a celestial LOP.

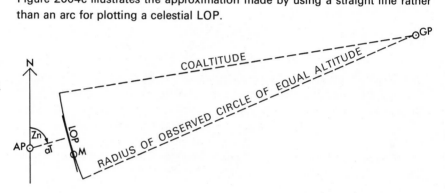

Figure 2604c: Plot of the same LOP from the AP and GP.

The following example will illustrate that portion of the navigator's work which has just been discussed. The actual plot, as laid down on the chart, is shown in Figure 2604d. Note that only two lines are drawn; the dashed line, from the AP, which is the intercept, and the heavy line, which is the LOP. The latter is labeled in accordance with standard practice, the ship's time of the observation being shown above, and the name of the body observed below.

Example: At 0623 a navigator determines the Ho of the star Procyon to be 12°37'.4. Selecting a point at L 35°00'.0 S and λ 76°27'.1 W as his assumed position, he computes Hc to be 12°17'.4 and Zn to be 329°.2.

Required: The plot of the 0623 celestial LOP.

Solution: (Figure 2604d).

First, determine (a) by comparison of Hc and Ho, and label it T or A as Ho or Hc, respectively, is the greater. Plot the AP, using the aL and aλ given. From the AP draw a broken line either toward or away from the direction of the GP, as indicated by Zn and the label of (a). Measure the distance (a) along this line, and at the point so determined, construct a perpendicular. This perpendicular is the 0623 LOP, and should be labeled as shown.

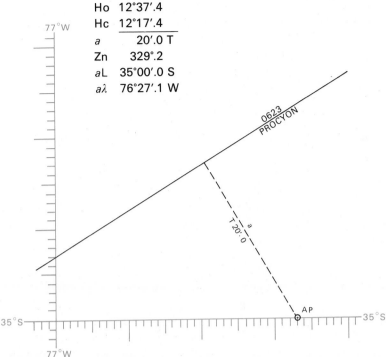

Ho 12°37'.4
Hc 12°17'.4
a   20'.0 T
Zn   329°.2
aL 35°00'.0 S
aλ 76°27'.1 W

77°W

0623
PROCYON

T 20'.0
a

AP

35°S

35°S

77°W

Figure 2604d: Plot of a celestial LOP.

2605. In piloting, a navigator can fix his position by taking bearings of two or more landmarks or other aids to navigation in rapid succession. For practical purposes, it is assumed that these bearings are taken simultaneously, and no adjustment of the lines of position is required. In celestial navigation, observations cannot be taken as rapidly as in piloting, with the result that the lines of position obtained must usually be adjusted for the travel of the ship between sights. This means that what is termed a "fix" in celestial navigation is actually constructed using the principles of the running fix used in piloting, since lines of position are advanced or retired to a common time. It is customary to consider the position resulting from observations obtained during a single round of sights as a fix, with the term "running fix" being reserved for a position obtained from observations separated by a considerable interval of time.

The celestial fix.

Each celestial line of position requires an AP, a segment of the radius (determined by Zn) equal to (a) in length, and the actual LOP constructed perpendicular to the Zn line through the point found using (a) (unless the high altitude technique is used). If three successive celestial observations were taken with small time intervals between them, the resulting APs with their associated lines of position could readily be plotted. To obtain a celestial fix, however, each would have to be advanced or retired to the time desired for the fix, making proper allowance for the travel of the ship during the intervening time. This could be done, as in piloting, by moving each LOP for the correct distance and direction. Because of the large number of lines required to plot a celestial fix in this manner in a comparatively small area of the chart or plotting sheet, many navigators prefer to *advance the AP rather than the line of position,* thereby plotting the LOP only once. This is the method prescribed for use at the United States Naval Academy, and will be used in examples throughout this text. It is illustrated in the following examples.

467

Example 1: The 0515 DR position of a ship on course 176°, speed 14.5 knots, is L 35°09'.2 S, λ 119°13'.7 E. About this time the navigator observes the stars Antares, Acrux, and Regulus, with the following results:

Body	ANTARES	ACRUX	REGULUS
Time	0515	0519	0525
a	20.3 T	18.1 T	7.0 A
Zn	093°.6	189°.5	311°.0
aL	35°00'.0 S	35°00'.0 S	35°00'.0 S
aλ	118°56'.0 E	119°17'.9 E	119°27'.9 E

Required: The plot of the 0525 celestial fix.

Solution: (Figure 2605a) Plot the 0515 DR position, and the DR track from 0515 to 0525. Plot the DR position for the time of each observation. Plot the AP of the earlier sight (Antares) and advance it in the direction and for the distance corresponding to the travel of the ship between the 0515 DR position and the 0525 DR position (2.4 miles in direction 176°). From the advanced AP so obtained, plot the 0515–0525 LOP, labeling it as shown. Note that the line joining the original AP and the advanced AP is plotted as a solid line, and that the advanced AP is *not* labeled. Next, plot the AP of Acrux and advance it for the direction and distance the ship has traveled between 0519 and 0525 (1.4 miles in direction 176°). Plot and label the 0519–0525 Acrux LOP from the advanced AP. Finally, plot the AP for the Regulus sight, and from it plot the 0525 Regulus LOP. The intersection of the three lines of position (or the center of the small triangle so formed) is the 0525 fix.

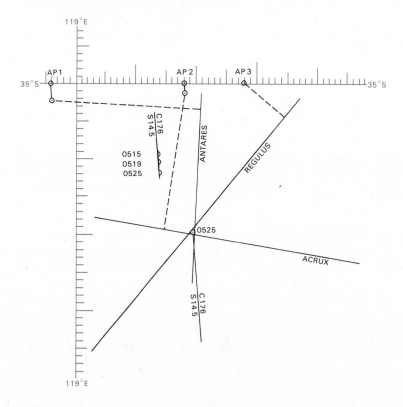

Figure 2605a: A three star celestial fix.

Example 2: The 0500 DR position of a ship on course 250°, speed 20 knots, is L 35°11'.0 N, λ 78°17'.0 W. At 0535 course is changed to 190°. During morning twilight the navigator observes two bodies with results as follows:

Body	DENEB	VENUS
Time	0525	0550
a	8.1 A	5.3 T
Zn	058°.5	123°.9
aL	35°00'.0 N	35°00'.0 N
aλ	78°09'.0 W	78°27'.5 W

Required: The plot of the 0550 celestial fix.

Solution: (Figure 2605b) Plot the 0500 DR position and the DR track until 0550, indicating the DR position for the time of each observation. Plot the AP of the earlier sight (Deneb) and advance it in the direction and for the distance corresponding to the travel of the ship between the 0525 DR position and the 0550 DR position (7.3 miles in direction 212°.5, as shown by the broken line marked "track").

From the advanced AP so obtained, plot the 0525–0550 LOP, labeling it as shown. Plot the AP of the Venus sight, and from it plot the 0550 LOP. The intersection of the two lines of position is the 0550 fix.

When a change of course or speed occurs between the times of the observations used in plotting a celestial fix, the procedure used for advancing or retiring a line of position is the same as that used in piloting (article 1112).

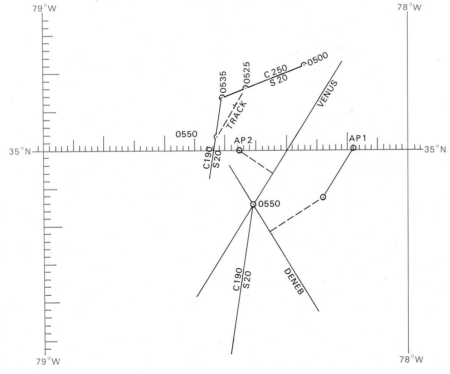

Figure 2605b: A celestial fix with a change of course between observations.

A fix obtained using the results of high altitude observations is plotted in a manner similar to that described above, except that the GP of the body is adjusted if necessary. The method of advancing a high altitude celestial line of position by advancing its GP is explained in the following example.

Example 3: The 1200 DR position of a ship on course 270°, speed 20.0 knots, is L 23°20'.0 N λ 75°08'.4 W. About this time, the navigator observes the sun twice, with the following results:

Body	SUN	SUN
Time	1154	1206
Ho	88°33'.6	88°00'.8
L GP	22°07'.7 N	22°07'.7 N
λ GP	74°04'.2 W	77°04'.2 W

Required: The plot of the 1206 fix.

Solution: (Figure 2605c) Plot the DR track from 1154 to 1206, indicating the 1154 and 1206 DR positions. Plot the 1154 position of the sun's GP, and advance it for the direction and distance from the 1154 DR position to the 1206 DR position (4.0 miles in direction 270°). Determine the radius of the observed circle of equal altitude about the GP by subtracting the Ho from 90°00'.0. The radius is 86.4 miles (since 90°00'.0 – 88°33'.6 = 1°26'.4 = 86.4 mi.). With this radius, and using the advanced GP as the center, swing an arc through the area containing the DR position. This is the 1154–1206 line of position, and is labeled as shown. Plot the 1206 GP of the sun, and determine the radius of the circle of equal altitude about it by subtracting the Ho from 90°00'.0. The radius is 119.2 miles (since 90°00'.0–88°00'.8 = 1°59'.2 = 119.2 mi.). With

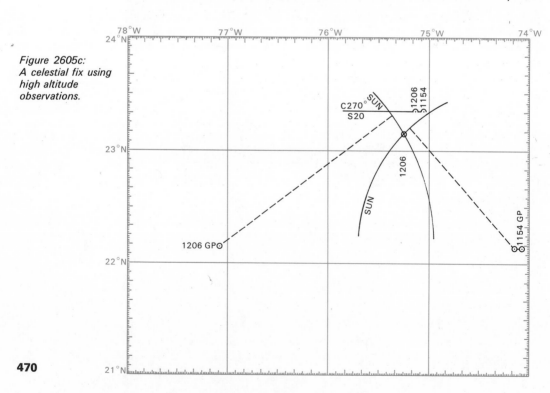

Figure 2605c: A celestial fix using high altitude observations.

this radius, and using the 1206 GP as a center, swing an arc through the area containing the DR position. The intersection of the two lines of position is the 1206 fix.

Note that there are two possible intersections of two circles of equal altitude, only one of which is shown. In ordinary circumstances, that intersection nearer the DR position is the fix. In the case shown in Figure 2605c there is no doubt as to the correct intersection, as the body passed to the south of the observer, and the intersection to the north of the GP used must be the fix. Where doubt exists and the navigator is unable to determine which intersection to use, commence a DR track from both positions, assuming the ship to be on the DR track which is more dangerous, until confirmation is obtained.

2606. When the times of the observations used are separated by a considerable interval, the result is a running celestial fix. The observations may be of different bodies, or successive sights of the same body. Since the time elapsed between observations used to obtain a running fix is usually at least an hour, and frequently considerably longer, the LOP obtained from the earlier observation is plotted for the information it provides. This LOP is then advanced (rather than the AP) to the time of the later observation to establish the R fix, using the same methods employed in establishing a R fix in piloting. *Running celestial fix.*

There is no arbitrary limit on the time interval between observations used for a running fix. This must be left to the discretion of the navigator; however, three hours might be considered the upper limit in most cases.

It should be noted that in summer, when the sun transits at high altitudes, it changes azimuth very rapidly before and after transit; excellent running fixes may thus be obtained within reasonable periods of time.

Example 1: The 0930 DR position of a ship on course 064°, speed 18.0 knots, is L 33°06'.4 N, λ 146°24'.5 W. The navigator observes the sun twice during the morning, with results as follows:

Body	SUN	SUN
Time	0942	1200
a	6.2 A	27.9 A
Zn	134°.2	182°.5
aL	33°00'.0 N	33°00'.0 N
aλ	146°24'.9 W	145°38'.0 W

Required: The plot of the 1200 running fix.

Solution: (Figure 2606a) Plot the 0930 DR position, and the DR track to 1200, indicating the 0942 and the 1200 DR positions. Plot the AP with its associated LOP for 0942. Advance the LOP for the distance and direction from the 0942 DR position to the 1200 DR position (41.4 miles in direction 064°), and label it as shown. Plot the AP and from it the LOP for the 1200 sun observation, labeling it as shown. The intersection of the 0942–1200 LOP and the 1200 LOP is the 1200 running fix.

When a change of course or speed occurs between the times of the observations used for obtaining a running celestial fix, the procedures used are the same as those employed in advancing the first LOP to obtain a running fix in piloting.

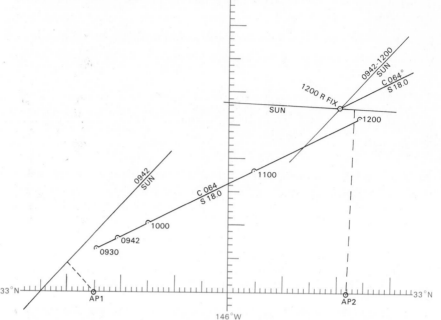

Figure 2606a: A running celestial fix.

Using the same observations as in example 1, the following example illustrates how a running fix is obtained when both course and speed are changed between observations.

Example 2: The 0930 DR position of a ship on course 064°, speed 18.0 knots, is L 33°06'.4 N, λ 146°24'.5 W. At 1100 course is changed to 030°, and speed is reduced to 13.5 knots. During the morning, the navigator observes the sun twice, with results as follows:

Body	SUN	SUN
Time	0942	1200
a	6.2 A	27.9 A
Zn	134°.2	182°.5
aL	33°00'.0 N	33°00'.0 N
aλ	146°24'.9 W	145°38'.0 W

Required: The plot of the 1200 running fix.

Solution: (Figure 2606b) Plot the 0930 DR position and the DR track to 1200, indicating the 0942 and the 1200 DR positions. Plot the 0942 LOP, and advance it for the distance and direction from the 0942 DR position to the 1200 DR position (35.8 miles in the direction 051°). Label it as shown. Plot and label the 1200 LOP. The intersection of the 0942–1200 LOP and the 1200 LOP is the 1200 running fix.

Where a current of known set and drift exists, the position of the running fix may be adjusted to allow for the effect of the current during the time elapsed between the first and second observation.

The errors inherent in the running celestial fix are the same as those for the terrestrial running fix. However, the magnitude of the errors tends to be greater.

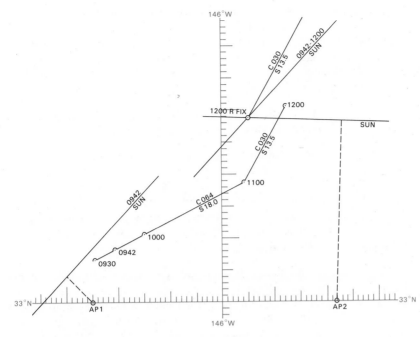

Figure 2606b: A running celestial fix with change of course and speed between observations.

in the celestial fix. There are three reasons for this:

The celestial LOP is rarely as accurate as the terrestrial LOP;

Information on set and drift is not available at sea to the same degree of accuracy as is usual along a coast or in pilot waters; and

In celestial navigation, the time required to obtain the running fix is usually longer than that required in piloting, thus errors in courses and distances made good affect the accuracy to a greater extent. However, a running celestial fix is frequently the best obtainable indication of position at sea, and can be most helpful to the navigator.

2607. A neat, carefully labeled plot of navigational information is character-istic of a good navigator. All lines of position and fixes should be drawn and labeled in such a way that no doubt ever exists as to their meaning. The illustra-tions of this chapter are all drawn and labeled in conformance with the standards used for purposes of instruction at the U. S. Naval Academy. These are as follows:

Labeling celestial lines of position and fixes.

Assumed position or geographical position. The AP or GP used with an LOP is always marked by an encircled dot and labeled "AP" or "GP," as appropriate.

Advanced AP or GP. The direction and distance an AP or GP is advanced is always shown by a solid line or lines, the end point of which is en-circled but not labeled. This is the advanced AP or GP from which an advanced LOP is plotted.

Azimuth line. The direction of the LOP from the AP used to plot the line is always shown by a broken line extending from the AP to the LOP, as indicated by the value and direction of (*a*).

473

Line of position. A line of position, whether a straight line or an arc, is always shown by a solid line and labeled with the ship's time of the observation "above" the line and the name of the body observed "below" the line. If the LOP has been advanced or retired, the time of the observation and the time to which it is adjusted are both shown, as "1927–1934" for a 1927 line of position advanced to 1934.

Running fix. The position found by a running fix is encircled and labeled with the time and the kind of position, as "1628 R FIX."

Fix. The position found by a fix is encircled and labeled with the time as "0724."

Fixes involving celestial and other lines of position.

2608. A line of position, however obtained, is merely an indication of the position of a ship, and must be crossed with one or more other lines to fix the position. The principal objective of all navigation is the determination of position; the navigator, therefore, should utilize any lines of position he can obtain.

Thus, the navigator might cross a Loran or Omega LOP with an LOP obtained from a celestial body. The LOP resulting from Consol or Consolan bearings may be similarly employed. Similarly, a navigator making a landfall might cross a celestial or some other LOP with a depth curve shown on his chart, determining by echo sounder the time when the curve is crossed. When only one LOP is obtainable at sea, a sounding or series of soundings may be helpful in determining the general area of the ship's position. Article 1118 describes how soundings may be used in this connection.

All LOPs will not be of the same order of accuracy, but with experience the navigator learns to evaluate the resulting fix. *It is vital that no opportunity be lost to acquire information which may be helpful in determining the ship's position.*

Summary.

2609. The first step in obtaining a celestial LOP is to measure the altitude of the body above the horizon. Ordinarily, the navigator then solves the navigational triangle containing his AP. The difference between the altitude thus computed and the observed altitude is the intercept, (*a*).

The intercept is then measured from the AP in the direction determined by Zn; Zn is the direction of the body's GP from the AP. The intercept will be measured toward (T) the body's GP from the AP if Ho is greater than Hc; it will be measured along the reciprocal (A) if Hc is the greater. A line drawn perpendicular to (*a*) at its terminus is the LOP.

A fix is obtained when two or more lines of position are crossed, and adjusted to a common time. If the observations are obtained in less than an hour, this is usually done by advancing the APs of the earlier observations for the ship's run to the time of the final observation; the LOPs are then plotted from the advanced APs. The resulting position is termed a *fix.* If the observations are obtained over a longer period of time, the first LOP is plotted when it is obtained, and is then advanced to the time of the later observation, as in piloting. The intersection of the first with the second LOP yields a *running fix.*

The careful navigator will seize every opportunity to acquire information which will be of help in fixing the ship's position. In addition to celestial lines of position, he may use lines obtained by electronics, and from soundings. At twilight, in clear weather, he will observe a minimum of five stars, well distributed in azimuth. He will make three observations of each body; normally, only one will be reduced to obtain a line of position. Should the resulting LOP seem to be in error, he may then reduce one of the other observations as a check. The rate of change of altitude in a series of observations of the same body should be directly proportional to the period of time between them. This gives a good check on the consistency of observations and, therefore, of their probable reliability.

CHAPTER 27

The Complete Celestial Solution

Introduction.

The complete celestial solution using H. O. 229 and the Nautical Almanac *is given in the Appendix.*

2701. Preceding chapters have dealt individually with all aspects of determining a line of position from an observation of a celestial body. The purpose of this chapter is to present the complete solution for a line of position, using the *Nautical Almanac*, and the H. O. 214 " $\triangle d$ only" method. The steps involved will be reviewed briefly in the order in which they are usually taken. The examples will include solutions for the sun, moon, a planet and a star, as well as an observation of Polaris for a latitude LOP.

It should be noted that these observations are reduced in a columnar format.

This format is highly recommended, as it permits a logically progressive reduction. In addition, it permits multiple reductions on a single page. The forms illustrated are those in use at the U. S. Naval Academy.

The combined coordinate systems.

2702. In Chapter 20 the theory of the navigational triangle was explained with reference to positions on the earth's surface; in this case, the vertices of the triangle were the elevated pole, the position of the observer, and the GP of the body. However, in some respects, it is more convenient to consider the triangle with reference to positions on the celestial sphere. In this sense, it is formed by a combination of the celestial equator system of coordinates, and the horizon system of coordinates. The vertices of the triangle are now the celestial pole, the observer's zenith, and the body itself, which is located by its coordinates. Note that the navigational triangle as envisioned on the celestial sphere is simply a projection of the navigational triangle as envisioned on the earth. Angles and angular distances are identical in each case.

On the celestial sphere shown in Figure 2702 the blue lines and labels refer to the triangle portrayed on the sphere, and the black lines and labels refer to the triangle depicted on the earth. In solving the navigational triangle, the navigator first obtains the position of the celestial body at a given time with reference to the celestial equator system of coordinates, by obtaining GHA and Dec. from the *Nautical Almanac*. This establishes the position of the body (and the GP), and defines the relationship of that position to both of the celestial poles. The navigator then selects the proper AP, which is in the near vicinity of his DR position. This selection establishes two points on the celestial sphere, both of which may be located in either the celestial equator or the horizon system of coordinates. One point is that occupied by the AP (and its zenith), and the other is the celestial pole nearer the AP. The celestial pole selected is identical with one of the poles used in conjunction with declination in the celestial equator system, and is used in determining both the colatitude and

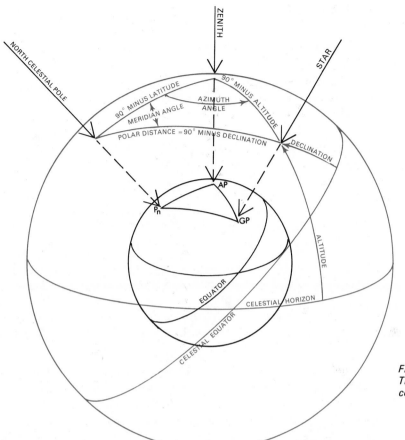

Figure 2702:
The combined
coordinate systems.

the polar distance sides of the navigational triangle. The pole used is usually called the *elevated pole*, as it is the one elevated above the horizon of the observer. The meridian angle, defined when the AP is selected, determines the angle at the pole between the great circle joining the pole and the zenith, and the great circle joining the pole and the celestial body. Knowing the colatitude, the polar distance, and the meridian angle, the triangle can be solved in terms of the horizon system of coordinates to determine the angle at the zenith, which is azimuth angle, and the arc from the zenith to the body, which is the computed coaltitude. By converting the computed coaltitude to computed altitude (Hc) and comparing it with the observed altitude (Ho) to obtain the altitude difference (*a*), and by converting the azimuth angle (Az) to true azimuth (Zn), the navigator is able to plot the resulting line of position.

2703. The student will save time if he extracts the pertinent data for all bodies from the daily pages of the *Nautical Almanac* at one page opening, when working multiple sights for a fix. Similarly, the *v* and *d* corrections as well as the increments of GHA for minutes and seconds for each body should be obtained at a single opening of the increments and corrections table.

Complete solutions for celestial observations.

While no additional corrections for non-standard atmospheric conditions are used in the following examples, the student must bear in mind that these should be used when weather conditions warrant.

Complete solution
for a sun
observation.

2704. When observing the sun, the navigator measures the sextant altitude of either the upper or lower limb of the body, and records the time and date of the observation. He also records the index error of the sextant.

He then converts the time to GMT and Greenwich date, and enters the appropriate daily pages of the *Nautical Almanac* to obtain the GHA and declination at the whole hours of GMT, and the *d* value for the period (noting the sign of the *d* value by inspection). If maximum accuracy were desired, he would also note the SD of the sun from the daily pages. The values of I and IC, with their appropriate signs, would be entered in the form, as would the correction for D, obtained from the *Nautical Almanac*. These would be combined with hs to obtain ha. The R correction, taken from Stars and Planets Table, and if required, a further correction from the Altitude Correction Tables—Additional Corrections, would be combined with ha to obtain Ho; see articles 2228 and 2231. However, in the following example the use of the critical Sun Table, which combines average value of SD with corrections for R and P, will be illustrated.

Having entered the GHA and declination for the whole hours of GMT, the navigator now turns to the appropriate page of the Increments of Corrections table, and obtains the increments of GHA for minutes and seconds, and the correction to the declination for the *d* value. Applying these values to those obtained from the daily pages, he obtains the GHA and Dec of the sun at the time of the observation.

With the *Nautical Almanac* still open, the navigator notes the value of IC (as determined from the sextant) and extracts the appropriate value of D. These are combined with hs to obtain ha. The appropriate correction for ☉ , or ☉ , taken from the Sun Table, is then applied to ha to obtain Ho.

The navigator then selects the AP, based on the best estimate of his position, and uses the *a*λ to determine LHA in whole degrees, which he converts to *t*.

Entering H. O. 214 with aL, Dec., and *t*, he obtains the tabulated altitude for the nearest value of the entering arguments, Δd and its sign, and Az. The correction to tabulated altitude for Δd and *d* diff. is then taken from the multiplication table at the back of H. O. 214, and applied to ht to obtain Hc.

Hc is then compared with Ho to determine (*a*). By converting Az to Zn, the navigator can then use Zn and (*a*) to plot the LOP from the AP.

Example: On 25 April, 1969, the 1300 DR position of a ship is Lat. 33°02'.8 N. Long. 34°05'.0 E. At 13-01-26 ZT an observation of the sun's lower limb is obtained from a height of eye of 38 feet, with a sextant having no IC. The sextant altitude is 62°53'.1.

Required: The (*a*), Zn, and AP, using H. O. 214 and the *Nautical Almanac.*

Answer: (Solution shown in column 1, page 479.)

a   Away 2'.9
Zn 227°.1
aL 33°00'.0 N
aλ 34°07'.9 E

Complete solution
for a moon
observation.

2705. When observing the moon, the navigator measures the sextant altitude of either the upper or lower limb of the body, and records the time and date of

Cus. _____

Spd. _____

BODY	☉	☾
DR L	33° 02'·8 N	33° 02'·8 N
DR λ	34° 05'·0 E	34° 05'·0 E
DATE (L)	25 APR. 69	25 APR. 69
W		
WE		
ZT	13-01-26	12-55-43
ZD (+ or −)	(−) 2	(−) 2
GMT	11-01-26	10-55-43
DATE (G)	25 APR. 69	25 APR. 69
v		13'·0
Tab. GHA	345° 30'·6	228° 02'·0
GHA incr'm't	21'·5	13° 14'·7
v corr./SHA		12'·0
GHA	345° 52'·1	241° 31'·7
aλ	34° 07.9 E	34° 28'·3 E
LHA	20° 00'·0	276° 00'·0
t (H.A.)	20° W	84° E
d (+ or −)	(+) 0'·8	(−) 10'·3
Tab. Dec.	13° 12'·7 N	21° 01'·6 N
d corr.	0'·0	(−) 9'·5
Dec.	13° 12'·7 N	20° 52'·1 N
H.P. ☾	+ −	+ 54'·9 −
IC	O	O
Dip (Ht 38 ')	(−) 6'·0	(−) 6'·0
Sum	(−) 6'·0	(−) 6'·0
hs	62° 53'·1	15° 19'·7
ha	62° 47'·1	15° 13'·7
Refr. Corr.	(−) 0'·5	(+) 62'·8
L/U ☾☉/♀♂	(+) 15'·9	(+) 1'·7 (−) 30'·0
TB (ha < 10°)		
Sum	+ 15'·9 (−) 0'·5	+ 64'·5 (−) 30'·0
Corr.	(+) 15'·4	(+) 34'·5
ha	62° 47'·1	15 13'·7
Ho	63° 02'·5	15 48'·2
Dec. Diff.	12'·7	7'·9
Δd (+ or −)	(+) ·78	(−) ·5
ht (Alt.)	62° 55'·5	16° 05'·0
corr.	(+) 9'·9	(−) 4'·0
Hc	63° 05'·4	16° 01'·0
Ho	63° 02'·5	15° 48'·2
a	A 2.9	A 12'·8
Az (see L & t)	N 132°·9 W	N 075°·1 E
Zn	227°·1	075°·1
aL	33° 00'·0 N	33° 50'·0 N
aλ	34° 07'·9 E	34 28'·3 E

Celestial Navigation Sight Worksheet.

479

the observation. He also checks the index error of the instrument.

He then converts the time to GMT and Greenwich date, and enters the appropriate daily pages of the *Nautical Almanac* to obtain the GHA, *v* value and its sign, declination, *d* value (noting the sign of the *d* value by inspection), and HP at the whole hours of GMT. HP is selected from the nearest whole hour of GMT. Turning to the appropriate Increments and Corrections table, he obtains the increments of GHA for minutes and seconds, and the corrections to GHA and declination for the *v* and *d* values, respectively. Applying these values to those obtained from the daily pages, he obtains the GHA and Dec. of the moon at the time of the observation.

With the *Nautical Almanac* still open, the navigator notes the value of IC (as determined from the sextant), extracts the D, R, and L (or U and (−)30′) corrections from the appropriate sections of the almanac and combines them with hs to obtain ha and Ho.

The navigator then selects the AP, based on the best estimate of his position, and uses the *a*λ to determine LHA in whole degrees, which he converts to *t*.

Entering H. O. 214 with *a*L, Dec., and *t*, he obtains the tabulated altitude for the nearest value of the entering argument, Δ*d* and its sign, and Az. The correction to tabulated altitude for Δ*d* and *d* diff. is then taken from the multiplication table at the back of H. O. 214, and applied to ht to obtain Hc.

Hc is then compared with Ho to determine (*a*). By converting Az to Zn, the navigator can then use Zn and (*a*) to plot the LOP from the AP.

Example: On 25 April 1969 the 1300 DR position of a ship is Lat. 33°02′.8 N, Long. 34°05′.0 E. At 12-55-43 ZT an observation of the moon's upper limb is obtained from a height of eye of 38 feet, with a sextant having no IC. The sextant altitude is 15°19′.7.

Required: The (*a*) Zn, and AP using H. O. 214 and the *Nautical Almanac*.

Answer: (Solution shown in column 2, page 479.)

a	Away 12′.8
Zn	075°.1
aL	33°00′.0 N
aλ	34°28′.3 E

Complete solution for a planet observation.

2706. When observing a planet, the navigator measures the sextant altitude of the center of the body and records the time and date of the observation. He also checks the index error of the instrument.

He then converts the time to GMT and Greenwich date, and enters the appropriate daily pages of the *Nautical Almanac* to obtain the GHA and declination at the whole hours of GMT, and the *v* and *d* values for the period (noting the sign of the *d* value by inspection). Turning to the appropriate Increments and Corrections table, he obtains the increments of GHA for minutes and seconds, and the corrections to GHA and declination for the *v* and *d* values, respectively. Applying these values to those obtained from the daily pages, he obtains the GHA and Dec. of the planet at the time of observation.

With the *Nautical Almanac* still open, the navigator notes the value of IC (as determined from the sextant), extracts the D and R (plus the "add'l" for Venus and Mars) corrections from the appropriate sections of the almanac, and combines them with hs to obtain ha and Ho.

The navigator then selects the AP, based on the best estimate of his position, and uses the aλ to determine LHA in whole degrees, which he converts to t.

Entering H. O. 214 with aL, Dec., and t, he obtains the tabulated altitude for the nearest value of the entering argument, Δd and its sign, and Az. The correction to tabulated altitude for Δd and d diff. is then taken from the multiplication table at the back of H. O. 214, and applied to ht to obtain Hc.

Hc is then compared with Ho to determine (a). By converting Az to Zn, the navigator can then use Zn and (a) to plot the LOP from the AP.

Example: On 26 April 1969, the 0600 position of a ship is Lat. 32°56'.3 S, Long. 60°07'.8 W. At 06-19-24 ZT, shortly before sunrise, an observation of Venus is obtained from a height of eye of 47 feet, with a sextant having an IC of (+) 0'.7. The sextant altitude is 20°40'.3.

Required: The (a), Zn, and AP, using H. O. 214 and the *Nautical Almanac.*

Answer: (Solution shown in column 1, page 482.)

a	Away 19'.1
Zn	065°.5
aL	33°00'.0 S
aλ	59°40'.8 W

2707. When observing a star, the navigator measures the sextant altitude of the body and records the time and date of the observation. He also checks the index error of the instrument.

Complete solution for a star observation.

He then converts the time to GMT and Greenwich date, and enters the appropriate daily pages of the *Nautical Almanac* to obtain the GHA of Aries at the whole hours of GMT, and the SHA and declination of the star for that period. Turning to the appropriate Increments and Corrections table, he obtains the increments of GHA of Aries for minutes and seconds. Adding this value to the GHA of Aries and SHA of the star obtained from the daily pages, he obtains the GHA at the time of the observation. The Dec. is the value tabulated on the daily page.

With the *Nautical Almanac* still open, the navigator notes the value of IC (as determined from the sextant), extracts the D and R corrections from the appropriate sections of the almanac, and applies them to hs to obtain ha and Ho.

The navigator then selects the AP, based on the best estimate of his position, and uses the aλ to determine LHA in whole degrees, which he converts to t.

Entering H. O. 214 with aL, Dec., and t, he obtains the tabulated altitude for the nearest value of the entering argument, Δd and its sign, and Az. The correction to tabulated altitude for Δd and d diff. is then taken from the multiplication table at the back of H. O. 214, and applied to ht to obtain Hc.

Hc is then compared with Ho to determine (a). By converting Az to Zn, the navigator can then use Zn and (a) to plot the LOP from the AP.

Example: On 26 April 1969, the 1915 DR position of a ship is Lat. 32°56'.4 N, Long. 29°49'.6 W. At 19-19-51 ZT the star Arcturus is observed from a height

Cus. _____		
Spd. _____		
BODY	VENUS ♀	ARCTURUS
DR L	32° 56'.3 S	32° 56'.4 N
DR λ	60° 07'.8 W	29° 49'.6 W
DATE (L)	26 APR 69	26 APR 69
W		
WE		
ZT	06-19-24	19-19-51
ZD (+ or −)	(+) 4	(+) 2
GMT	10-19-24	21-19-51
DATE (G)	26 APR 69	26 APR 69
v	2.5	
Tab. GHA	355° 49'.0	169° 40'.8
GHA incr'm't	4° 51'.0	4° 58'.6
v corr./SHA	0'.8	146° 25'.7
GHA	000° 40'.8	321° 05'.1
aλ	59° 40'.8 W	30° 05'.1
LHA	301° 00'.0	291° 00'.0
t (H.A.)	59° E	69° E
d (+ or −)	(−) 0.7	
Tab. Dec.	7° 36'.5 N	19° 20'.3 N
d corr.	(−) 0'.2	
Dec.	7° 36'.3 N	19° 20'.3 N
H.P. ☾	+ −	+ −
IC	(+) 0'.7	(+) 0'.5
Dip (Ht 47 ')	(−) 6'.6	(63') (−) 7.7'
Sum	(−) 5'.9	(−) 7'.2
hs	20° 40'.3	27° 47'.0
ha	20° 34'.4	27° 39'.8
Refr. Corr.	(−) 2'.6	− 1'.8
L/U ☾ ⊙/♀ ♂	(+) 0'.7	
TB (ha < 10°)		
Sum	+ 0'.7 2'.6 −	+ −
Corr.	(−) 1'.9	(−) 1'.8
ha	20° 34'.4	27° 39'.8
Ho	20° 32'.5	27° 38'.0
Dec. Diff.	6'.3	9'.7
△ (+ or −)	(−).64	(−).47
ht (Alt.)	20° 55'.6	27° 43'.1
corr.	(−) 4'.0	(−) 4'.5
Hc	20° 51'.6	27° 38'.6
Ho	20° 32'.5	27° 38'.0
a	A 19'.1	A 0'.6
Az (see L & t)	S 114°.5 E	N 083°.8 E
Zn	065°.5	083°.8
aL	33° 00'.0 S	33° 00'.0 N
aλ	59° 40'.8 W	30° 05'.1 W

Celestial Navigation Sight Worksheet.

of eye of 63 feet with a sextant having an IC of (+) 0'.5. The sextant altitude is 27°47'.0.

Required: The (*a*), Zn, and AP, using H. O. 214, and the *Nautical Almanac.*

Answer: (Solution shown in column 2, page 482.)

    a   Away 0.6
    Zn   083°.8
    aL   33°00'.0 N
    aλ   30°05'.1 W

2708. A latitude line of position is obtained from an observation of Polaris, and only the *Nautical Almanac* is required to reduce the observation (see article 2806). An azimuth may also be obtained.

Complete solution for a Polaris observation.

As with any body, the sextant altitude is obtained, and the time and date are recorded. The index error is checked.

Using the GMT and Greenwich date, the appropriate daily pages of the almanac are entered, and the GHA of Aries for the minutes and seconds are obtained. These are added to the tabulated value to obtain the GHA of Aries at the time of the observation.

The DR longitude at the time of the observation is applied to the GHA of Aries, to obtain LHA Aries. The Polaris Tables at the back of the almanac are entered at the top with LHA Aries in the appropriate vertical column, and the value a_0 is obtained, interpolating when necessary. Next a_1 is taken from the same vertical column, latitude being the other argument. Finally, a_2 is found in the same column in the lower part of the table, using the current month as the second argument. No interpolation is required to obtain a_1 and a_2.

These three corrections, a_0, a_1, and a_2, are all *additive* and are applied to the sextant altitude together with the IC and the D and R correctons; a final constant correction of *1°* *is subtractive.* The resultant sum will be the latitude.

To obtain the azimuth, the navigator follows down the same column of LHA Aries he used to obtain a_0, a_1, and a_2 to the section at the bottom of the page headed Azimuth. Entering this column with his DR latitude, and interpolating if necessary, he extracts the azimuth of Polaris. When the azimuth of Polaris is to the east of true north, the first two zeros are omitted, and it is stated simply as "0°.8," or "1°.9."

DR L	32° 56'.4 N
DR λ	29° 49'.6 W
DATE (L)	26 APR 69
ZT	19-21-02
ZD (+ or −)	(+) 2
GMT	21-21-02
DATE (G)	26 APR 69
Tab. GHA ♈	169° 40'.8
Incr'm't	5° 16'.4
GHA ♈	174° 57'.2
DR λ	29° 49'.6 W
LHA ♈	145° 07'.6
IC	+ 0'.5 −
Dip (Ht 63')	(−) 7.7
Sum	(−) 7'.2
hs	32° 46'.7
ha	32° 39'.5
TB (ha<10°)	
Refr. Corr.	(−) 1'.5
Ao	(+) 1° 21'.0
A1	0'.4
A2	0'.9
Add'l.	− 60.0
Sum	+ 82.3 61.5
Corr.	(+) 20'.8
ha	32° 39'.5
Lat.	33° 00'.3
Azimuth	359°.1 °T
Gyro. Brg.	358°.6 °pgc
Gyro. Error	0°.5 E

Latitude by Polaris.

Note that an assumed position is not used in obtaining a latitude line or an azimuth Polaris.

Example: On the evening of 26 April 1969, the 1915 DR position of a ship is Lat. 32°56'.4 N, Long. 29°49'6 W. Shortly after observing Arcturus, at 19-21-02 ZT Polaris is observed from a height of eye of 63 feet, with a sextant having an IC of (+) 0'.5. The sextant altitude is 32°46'.7. At the same time, the bearing of Polaris is 358°.6 by gyro.

Required: The latitude, and the gyro error, *using the Nautical Almanac.*

Answer: Lat. 33°00'.3 N
Gyro error 0°.5 E

Summary.

2709. In this chapter some of the routine celestial navigation work at sea has been reviewed. While typical, it is far from all inclusive, and only a few examples of all the work done by the navigator and his assistants have been given.

The technique of advancing celestial lines of position to allow for the ship's run to the time the final LOP is obtained is described in article 2605. The subject is mentioned here as a reminder that multiple LOPs must be advanced in order to obtain a valid fix; this is particularly important if the ship is steaming at high speed, or if considerable time elapsed between sights.

CHAPTER 28

Celestial Navigation: Special Cases and Phenomena

SPECIAL CASES

2801. A latitude observation is obtained when the celestial body is either due north or south of the observer. When reduced, such an observation yields a LOP extending in an east-west direction; this is termed a *latitude line*. A longitude observation is obtained when the observed body is either east or west of the observer. The resulting LOP is termed a *longitude line*, as it extends in a north-south direction. The former will be discussed first in this section; it has much to recommend it, as a celestial body changes altitude very slowly at transit, except at very high altitudes. Ordinarily, a skilled observer can obtain a considerable number of observations of a transiting body which will be almost identical in altitude. When one of these observations is reduced, great reliance can be placed in its accuracy.

Introduction.

Any celestial body will yield a latitude line when observed at transit. However, the two bodies most commonly used are the sun and Polaris. The sun transits the observer's meridian at *local apparent noon* (LAN); the *LAN observation is extremely important* in navigation, chiefly *because it can usually be relied on to yield the most dependable LOP of the day*. The sun should be observed at LAN as a matter of routine aboard every vessel.

Should it be deemed desirable, a latitude may be obtained from any observation made within 28 minutes of the time of either upper or lower transit, provided the altitude is between 6° and 86°, the latitude is not more than 60°, and the declination is not greater than 63°. This is termed a *reduction to the meridian;* the reduction is made by means of tables 29 and 30 in Bowditch. Instructions for their use are included with the tables.

2802. To determine the time of LAN accurately, the navigator, while the sun is still well to his east, enters the *Nautical Almanac* for the appropriate day, and finds the tabulated GHA which is nearest to, but east of his DR longitude, and the GMT of this entry. He then turns to his chart, and for this GMT determines his best estimate of the ship's longitude. Following this, he determines the difference of longitude in minutes between the sun's GHA and the ship's longitude at the hour of GMT found in the *Nautical Almanac*. This difference is meridian angle east (tE). The next step is to determine the instant when the sun's hour circle will coincide with the ship's longitude; this establishes

Determining the time of LAN.

the time of LAN, and is accomplished by combining the rate of the sun's change of longitude with that of the ship. The sun changes longitude at an almost uniform rate of 15°, or 900′ per hour. The rate of the ship's change of longitude per hour is usually determined by measurement on the chart.

If the ship is steaming towards the east, its hourly rate of change of longitude is added to that of the sun; if it is steaming west, the rate of change is subtracted from that of the sun.

All that remains is to divide the meridian angle east expressed in minutes, found above, by the combined rate of change of longitude. The answer, which will be in decimals of an hour, should be determined to three significant places. Multiplied by 60, minutes and decimals of minutes are obtained; the latter may be converted to seconds by again multiplying by 60. The answer will be mathematically correct to about four seconds; when added to the hour of GMT obtained from the *Nautical Almanac,* it will give the GMT of the sun's transit (LAN) at the ship. Any error in DRλ will, of course, affect the accuracy. The zone description may be employed to convert the GMT of LAN to ship's time. The above procedure can conveniently be written as a formula:

$$\text{Interval to LAN} = \frac{tE \text{ in minutes of arc}}{900' \text{arc} \pm \text{ship's movement in longitude per hour}}$$

This procedure is illustrated in the following example.

Example: On 25 April the navigator of a ship steaming on course 287°, speed 21.0 knots, plans to observe the sun at LAN. At 1145 (−6), he notes that the 1200 DR position will be Lat. 31°34′.6 S, Long. 82°44′.9 E.

Required: the ZT of transit.

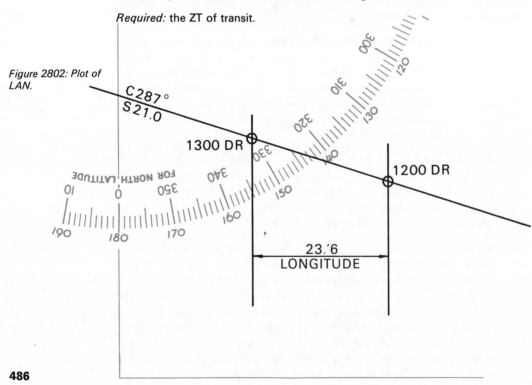

Figure 2802: Plot of LAN.

Solution: (Figure 2802) The ship's 1200 DR longitude will be 82°44'.9 E. This, converted to angular distance west of Greenwich, is 360° − 82°44'.9, or 277°15'.1. Entering the *Nautical Almanac* for the date, by inspection he finds the next tabulated GHA ☉ less than (east of) this to be 270°30'.1; it is for GMT 0600, which will be 1200 ship's time.

The difference in longitude between the ship and the sun, at 1200 (−6) equals 277°15'.1 − 270°30'.1, or 6°45'.0, or 405'.0. This latter figure is tE.

By inspection of the ship's predicted DR longitudes for 1200 and 1300, as plotted on the chart, the ship's hourly rate of change of longitude in minutes of arc is found to be 23'.6. This change is in a *westerly* direction; it will therefore be *subtracted* from the sun's change, which equals 900' per hour. The combined hourly rate of change then is 900' − 23'.6, or 876'.4. The value of tE is next divided by the combined rate 405'/876'.4 to find the time, in decimals of an hour, after 1200 ship's time, at which transit will occur. The answer, rounded off, is 0.462 hours, which, multiplied by 60 will give the time in minutes—0.462 × 60 equals 27.72 minutes, or 27 minutes 43 seconds. This added to 1200 (−6) gives the ship's time of transit, or LAN.

Answer: LAN will occur at 12-27-43 ZT.

Precision in determining the time of LAN is especially necessary when a ship is steaming on a generally northerly or southerly course at speed. For a ship proceeding towards the south, the sun will continue to increase its altitude for a considerable period *after* it actually has crossed the ship's meridian, and an observation made at the moment when it reaches its maximum altitude will yield a latitude which may be considerably in error.

Under most conditions, however, the sun will appear to "hang" for an appreciable period of time at LAN; that is, it will not change perceptibly in altitude. To obtain a latitude line at LAN, the navigator usually starts observing about two minutes before the time of transit, and continues to obtain sights until the altitude begins to decrease. The average of the three or four highest altitudes will be used for reduction. On a northerly or southerly course, several altitudes may be taken before and after transit, to insure that an unacceptable random error did not occur in the sight taken at the instant of transit.

2803. While meridian altitudes may be routinely solved by means of the inspection tables, such as H. O. 214 or H. O. 229, using an assumed latitude, LHA 0°, and a tabulated declination as entering arguments, such tables are not necessary to obtain a solution.

Solution for meridian altitudes.

In this article solution of upper branch meridian altitudes are discussed; lower branch meridian altitudes are covered in article 2804.

The method of solution is the same for all celestial bodies observed on the upper branch of the meridian; at this instant each azimuth is precisely 000°.0, or 180°.0. In terms of the navigational triangle, it is a special case, in that the elevated pole, the observer's zenith, and the celestial body are all on the same great circle. The LOP obtained from a meridian observation is an exact latitude line.

The semi-circle in Figure 2803a represents that half of the observer's meridian extending from the north point to the south point of his celestial horizon; it is also occupied by a celestial body (in this case the sun) at the instant of transit. This article will discuss the transit of the sun, as it is most frequently observed. However, any celestial body observed when precisely on the navigator's meridian may be used, and the method of reduction would be the same as that outlined here for the sun.

In this diagram, Z represents the observer's zenith, Q is the equator, P_n is the north pole, here the elevated pole, N and S represents the north and south points of the observer's horizon, respectively, and ☉ the sun on the meridian. The angle z is the zenith distance of the sun, that is, 90° minus the observed altitude; L, Dec., and Ho are the observer's latitude, the declination, and the observed altitude, respectively. This same labeling is used in all diagrams on the plane of the observer's meridian.

Zenith distance (z). In reductions to the meridian, *z is named for the direction of the observer from the body*, that is, if the observer is south of the body, the z is named south. The latitude may then be obtained by applying the angular value of the z to the declination, *adding if they are of the same name, and subtracting the smaller from the larger if the names are contrary*. The latitude will have the same name as the remainder; for example, if the z is 40° N and the declination is 20° S, the latitude equals 40° N − 20° S, or 20° N.

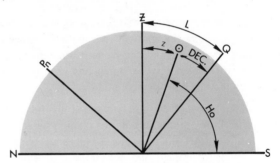

Figure 2803a:
Lat. = z + Dec.

Figure 2803a is drawn for an observer in north latitude, who is north of the sun; the observed altitude of the sun at transit is 70°. The z, therefore, is 90° −70°, or 20° N. The sun's declination at the time of transit is 20° N; as the declination is north, and as the observer is north of the sun, z and Dec. are added (20° N + 20° N) to give the observer's latitude, 40° N.

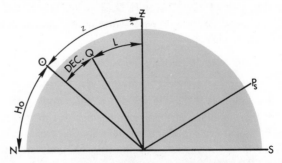

Figure 2803b:
Lat. = z − Dec.

Figure 2803b illustrates a case where the observer's latitude and the declination are of opposite name. The Ho is 40°, and the sun is north of the observer, giving a z of 50° S, and the declination is 20° N. In this case Dec. is subtracted from the z (50° S − 20° N) to yield a latitude of 30° S.

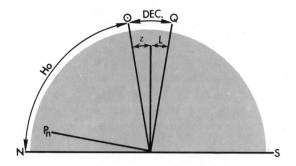

Figure 2803c: Lat. = Dec − z.

Figure 2803c shows an L and Dec. of the same name, but Dec. greater than L. The Dec. is 20° N; Ho is 80°, giving a z of 10° S. Therefore z is subtracted from Dec. (20° N − 10° S) to yield a latitude of 10° N.

2804. When a body is observed at *lower transit*, or on the lower branch of the meridian, the solution differs from that for the upper branch, in that polar distance (p) is used, rather than z; p is the angular distance of the body from the pole or 90° − Dec. At lower transit, the observer's latitude is equal to the observed altitude plus the polar distance, or L = Ho + p. In Figure 2804 a star with a declination of 50° N is observed at lower transit at an Ho of 20°. L therefore equals 20° + 40°, or 60° N.

Solution for lower branch meridian altitudes.

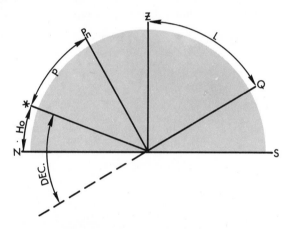

Figure 2804: Lat. = Ho + p.

2805. The latitude of a place is equal to the altitude of the elevated pole, as is illustrated in Figure 2805. Both the latitude of the observer, *QOZ* and the altitude of the pole *NOPn* equal 90° − *PnOZ*. Thus if a star were located exactly at each celestial pole, the corrected altitude of the star would equal the observer's latitude.

Latitude by Polaris.

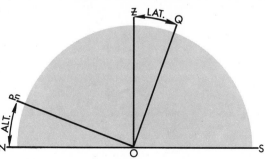

Figure 2805: Latitude equals altitude of elevated pole.

No star is located exactly at either pole, but Polaris is less than a degree from the north celestial pole. Like all stars, it alternately transits the upper and lower branches of each celestial meridian in completing its diurnal circle. Twice during every 24 hours, as it moves in its diurnal circle, Polaris is at the same altitude as the pole, and at that moment no correction would be required to its observed altitude to obtain latitude. At all other times a correction, constantly changing in value, must be applied. The value for any instant may be obtained from the Polaris tables in the *Nautical Almanac*, the entering argument being LHA♈. The correction is tabulated in three parts; the first is the basic correction applicable under all conditions. The second correction is for the DR latitude of the observer, and corrects for the angle at which he views the star's diurnal circle. The third is for the date, and corrects for the small variations in the position of the star in its diurnal circle in the course of the year.

Solution of a Polaris observation.

2806. The three Polaris correction tables comprise the last three white pages at the back of the *Nautical Almanac*. A portion of these tables, showing the arrangement of the three corrections a_0, a_1, and a_2, is reproduced in Figure 2806. It must be borne in mind that *these three corrections are in addition to the usual corrections applied to all sextant observations to obtain Ho.*

To solve a Polaris observation for latitude find the value of LHA♈ in the top horizontal column of the tables; these are divided into groups of 10°. Then follow down this column until opposite the single degree value of LHA♈, tabulated in the left hand column. The exact value of a_0 is then found for the

POLARIS (POLE STAR) TABLES, 1969
FOR DETERMINING LATITUDE FROM SEXTANT ALTITUDE AND FOR AZIMUTH

Figure 2806: Extract from Nautical Almanac— Polaris tables.

L.H.A. ARIES	240°– 249°	250°– 259°	260°– 269°	270°– 279°	280°– 289°	290°– 299°	300°– 309°	310°– 319°	320°– 329°	330°– 339°	340°– 349°	350°– 359°
	a_0	a_0	a_0	a_0	a_0	a_0	a_0	a_0	a_0	a_0	a_0	a_0
0	1 44·5	1 39·5	1 33·1	1 25·8	1 17·6	1 08·9	0 59·8	0 50·7	0 41·8	0 33·4	0 25·8	0 19·2
1	44·1	38·9	32·4	25·0	16·7	08·0	58·9	49·8	40·9	32·6	25·1	18·6
2	43·6	38·3	31·7	24·2	15·9	07·1	58·0	48·9	40·1	31·8	24·4	18·0
9	40·0	33·8	26·6	18·4	09·8	1 00·7	51·6	42·6	34·2	26·5	19·8	14·3
10	1 39·5	1 33·1	1 25·8	1 17·6	1 08·9	0 59·8	0 50·7	0 41·8	0 33·4	0 25·8	0 19·2	0 13·8
Lat.	a_1	a_1	a_1	a_1	a_1	a_1	a_1	a_1	a_1	a_1	a_1	a_1
0	0·5	0·4	0·3	0·2	0·2	0·1	0·1	0·2	0·2	0·3	0·4	0·4
10	·5	·4	·3	·3	·2	·2	·2	·2	·3	·3	·4	·5
20	·5	·4	·4	·3	·3	·3	·3	·3	·3	·4	·4	·5
30	·5	·5	·4	·4	·4	·4	·4	·4	·4	·4	·5	·5
66	·7	·8	·9	0·9	1·0	1·0	1·0	1·0	0·9	·9	·8	·7
68	0·8	0·8	0·9	1·0	1·1	1·1	1·1	1·1	1·0	0·9	0·9	0·8
Month	a_2	a_2	a_2	a_2	a_2	a_2	a_2	a_2	a_2	a_2	a_2	a_2
Jan.	0·5	0·5	0·5	0·6	0·6	0·6	0·6	0·6	0·6	0·6	0·6	0·7
Feb.	·4	·4	·4	·4	·4	·4	·5	·5	·5	·5	·6	·6
Mar.	·4	·4	·4	·4	·3	·3	·3	·3	·4	·4	·4	·4
Apr.	0·5	0·5	0·4	0·4	0·3	0·3	0·3	0·3	0·3	0·3	0·3	0·3
May	·7	·6	·6	·5	·4	·4	·3	·3	·2	·2	·2	·2
June	·8	·8	·7	·6	·6	·5	·4	·4	·3	·3	·2	·2
Oct.	0·8	0·9	0·9	1·0	1·0	1·0	1·0	1·0	0·9	0·9	0·9	0·8
Nov.	·7	·8	·8	0·9	0·9	1·0	1·0	1·0	1·0	1·0	1·0	1·0
Dec.	0·5	0·6	0·7	0·8	0·8	0·9	1·0	1·0	1·0	1·0	1·1	1·0

Latitude = corrected sextant altitude $-1° + a_0 + a_1 + a_2$

The table is entered with L.H.A. Aries to determine the column to be used; each column refers to a range of 10°. a_0 is taken, with mental interpolation, from the upper table with the units of L.H.A. Aries in degrees as argument; a_1, a_2 are taken, without interpolation, from the second and third tables with arguments latitude and month respectively. a_0, a_1, a_2 are always positive. The final table gives the azimuth of *Polaris*.

DR L	26° 37'.0 N	
DR λ	133° 28'.1 W	
Date (L)	27 APRIL 1969	
ZT	04 - 56	
ZD	+ 9	
GMT	13 - 56 - 19	
Date (G)	27 APRIL 1969	
tab GHA ♈	50° 20'.2	
Incrm't	14° 07'.1	
GHA ♈	64° 27'.3	
DR λ	133° 28'.1 W	
LHA ♈	290° 59'.2	
IC	+ —	—
Dip (Ht 39')		6'.1
Sum	(-) 6'.1	
hs	26° 40'.1	
ha	26° 34'.0	
TB (ha < 10°)	—	
Refr. Corr.		1'.9
Ao	68'.0	
A1	0'.4	
A2	0'.3	
Add'l	+ — 60'.0 —	
Sum	68'.7	61'.9
Corr.	(+) 6'.8	
ha	26° 34'.0	
Lat.	26° 40'.8	

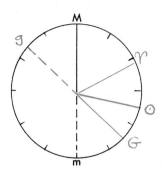

Latitude by Polaris.

minutes of LHA by interpolation. The value of a_1 is then found for the nearest tabulated latitude, without interpolation; next the a_2 correction for the current month is found, again with no interpolation. The arrangement of the tables is such that these three corrections are always *positive, but an additional constant negative of 1° is finally applied* to determine the total correction at the time and latitude of the observation. The total correction is negative at times.

Customarily, the navigator uses the latitude thus obtained to draw a latitude LOP. If his DR longitude is reasonably accurate, this latitude line will yield acceptable accuracy. If there is considerable uncertainty as to the ship's longitude, the azimuth of Polaris should be determined. This will be found at the bottom of the Polaris tables, the entering arguments being the nearest 10° of LHA ♈, and the nearest tabulated latitude; no interpolation is required. The LOP is then drawn through the computed latitude and the DR longitude, perpendicular to this azimuth.

Example: During morning twilight on 27 April 1969, at approximately 0456 (+9) time, a navigator observes Polaris. The ship's DR position is Lat. 26°37'.0 N, Long. 133°28'.1 W. His sextant had no I.C., the height of eye was 39 feet. The GMT of the observation was 13-56-19; the sextant altitude was 26°40'.1. The latitude at the time of the observation is required.

Solution: (Figure 2806). Knowing the GMT of the observation, by constructing a time diagram the navigator determines that the Greenwich date is also 27 April. He next obtains the LHA ♈ from the almanac for the GMT of the ob-

491

servation, which in this case was 13-56-19 on 27 April. He next corrects the hs for IC and D to obtain ha to which he applies refraction and the corrections from the Polaris Tables in the almanac to determine the latitude. In this case, there is no IC, and from the Dip Table, the D correction is $(-)6'.1$. The Refraction table gives the value of the R correction as $(-)1'.9$. The latitude corrections from the LHA ♈ 290°–299° column of the Polaris Tables are $(+)1°08'.0$, or $68'.0$ for a_0 (LHA ♈ 290°59.2), $(+)\ 0'.4$ for a_1 (Lat 30°), $(+)\ 0'.3$ for a_2 (Apr.), and the constant $(-)\ 60'.0$ additional correction. Finally, he determines the algebraic sum of these corrections $(+6.8)$ and applies it to ha to determine the latitude.

Observations for longitude.

2807. Longitude observations were in general use until the altitude difference or intercept method, devised in 1875 by Marcq de Saint-Hilaire, was accepted. The longitude obtained was predicated on a latitude; the latter was usually obtained from a LAN sun observation, and carried forward or back by DR to obtain the longitude. The calculated longitude was therefore accurate only if the DR latitude was accurate. Subsequently, as the accuracy of chronometers was improved, celestial bodies were observed on the *prime vertical*, that is, when their azimuth was exactly 090°.0 or 270°.0; this method yielded considerably increased accuracy.

Presently, observations intended solely to yield longitude are seldom required or made. If one is to be made, the most convenient method involves the use of an inspection table, such as H. O. 214, to determine the time at which the observation should be obtained. In the case of H. O. 214, it is entered with latitude and declination, and the meridian angle of the body is determined at the time the azimuth angle equals 90°.0. The GMT at which this meridian angle, converted to GHA by applying DR longitude, occurs can then be obtained from the *Nautical Almanac*. For the best results, interpolation should be made for t, Dec. and L.

Observations on the beam, bow, and stern.

2808. Observations made directly on the beam are helpful in determining whether the ship is on the desired track line, while observations obtained dead ahead or astern show how far she has advanced. The sun is the body most commonly used in making such observations. Here, again, H. O. 214 may be used to advantage. It is entered with the appropriate latitude and declination, as outlined in article 2807, and the desired azimuth angle, relative to the ship's head, stern, or beam is found. The time for the observation is then determined as for a longitude observation.

Summary, latitude, longitude, and special case observations.

2809. Observations yielding latitude lines are conventional aids used to assist in determining position at sea. The bodies most frequently observed for this purpose are the sun and Polaris. The sun, observed at transit, yields a latitude line, which ordinarily can be relied on as the most accurate LOP of the day, as the horizon at noon is usually very well defined, and the sun's rate of change of altitude is then usually very slow. Any celestial body may be observed on the meridian, and a latitude line obtained, as with the sun.

Polaris observations, when fully corrected, yield a LOP which ordinarily may be plotted as a latitude line.

Observations, usually of the sun, when made dead ahead or astern, or on the beam, yield information which can be very helpful to the navigator.

PHENOMENA

2810. Sunrise is the first appearance of the sun's *upper* limb above the visible horizon; similarly, sunset is the disappearance of the upper limb below the horizon. Due chiefly to the effect of refraction, as the upper limb appears to touch the horizon, it is actually more than 30'.0 below the celestial horizon. The times of moonrise and moonset are similarly determined, by the contact of the upper limb with the horizon.

Introduction.

Sunrise and sunset.

Moonrise and moonset.

Twilight is the period before sunrise when darkness is giving way to daylight, and after sunset, when the opposite is true. Three kinds of twilight are defined below, although the navigator is ordinarily concerned only with the first two. The darker limit of twilight occurs when the center of the sun is the stated number of degrees below the celestial horizon.

Twilight.

Twilight	Lighter Limit	Darker Limit	At Darker Limit
Civil	⊙ 0°	−6°	Horizon clear and bright stars visible
Nautical	⊙ 0°	−12°	Horizon vague
Astronomical	⊙ 0°	−18°	Full night

Twilight designations.
Duration of twilight.

The conditions at the darker limits are relative and vary considerably under different atmospheric conditions. The duration of twilight is chiefly a function of the observer's latitude; it increases with an increase in latitude.

In the *Nautical Almanac*, the GMT of sunrise and sunset, and the beginnings of morning and endings of evening civil and nautical twilight are tabulated for every three day period, at various latitudes along the meridian of Greenwich (0° λ), the mid day of the three being the reference day. The GMT of moonrise and moonset for 0° λ are similarly tabulated in a separate column for each day.

The Local Mean Time (LMT) of sunrise, sunset, and twilight for a given date and latitude are essentially the same in any longitude. This is due to the fact that for a period of one day the change in declination, and more important, the rate of change in hour angle, of the sun is comparatively small. For moonrise and moonset an additional interpolation for longitude is needed. In the back of the *Air Almanac*, tables containing the times of sunrise and sunset, and the beginning and end of civil twilight are given. Times of moonrise and moonset are given on the daily pages. As in the *Nautical Almanac*, all tabulated times are GMT of the phenomenon for the Greenwich meridian. In addition, the *Tide Tables* (published by the U. S. Coast and Geodetic Survey), include tables for the LMT of sunrise and sunset, with a convenient table for the reduction of LMT to ZT. Moonrise and moonset are tabulated daily for specific cities rather than by latitude.

2811. The GMT of sunrise and sunset for the middle day of the three on each page opening in the *Nautical Almanac*, is tabulated to the nearest minute for selected intervals of latitude from 72° N to 60° S. An extract from this table is shown in Figure 2811a. The tabulated times are generally used to obtain the ZT of the phenomena by one of two possible methods. The GMT of sunrise or sunset may be considered to be its LMT, and therefore its ZT on the standard meridian of any zone. To obtain the ZT of the phenomena at the ship, it is only necessary to convert the difference of longitude between the standard meridian

Sunrise and sunset.

Lat.	Sun-set	Twilight		Moonset			
		Civil	Naut.	25	26	27	28
°	h m	h m	h m	h m	h m	h m	h m
N 72	21 29	////	////	▢	06 12	04 52	04 09
N 70	20 59	23 16	////	▢	05 19	04 32	04 00
68	20 37	22 09	////	05 55	04 46	04 16	03 53
66	20 20	21 34	////	04 54	04 22	04 02	03 46
64	20 06	21 10	23 21	04 19	04 03	03 51	03 41
62	19 55	20 51	22 22	03 53	03 47	03 42	03 36
60	19 45	20 36	21 50	03 33	03 34	03 33	03 32
N 58	19 36	20 23	21 28	03 17	03 23	03 26	03 29
56	19 29	20 12	21 10	03 03	03 13	03 20	03 25
54	19 22	20 02	20 55	02 50	03 04	03 14	03 22
52	19 16	19 54	20 43	02 40	02 56	03 09	03 20
50	19 11	19 46	20 32	02 30	02 49	03 04	03 17
45	18 59	19 31	20 10	02 09	02 33	02 54	03 12
N 40	18 49	19 18	19 53	01 53	02 21	02 45	03 07
35	18 41	19 08	19 40	01 39	02 10	02 38	03 04
30	18 34	18 59	19 29	01 26	02 00	02 31	03 00
20	18 22	18 45	19 11	01 05	01 44	02 20	02 54
N 10	18 11	18 33	18 58	00 47	01 29	02 10	02 49
0	18 01	18 23	18 47	00 30	01 16	02 00	02 44
S 10	17 52	18 13	18 38	00 12	01 02	01 50	02 38
20	17 41	18 04	18 30	24 47	00 47	01 40	02 33
30	17 30	17 54	18 22	24 30	00 30	01 28	02 26
35	17 23	17 49	18 19	24 20	00 20	01 21	02 23
40	17 15	17 43	18 15	24 08	00 08	01 13	02 19
45	17 07	17 37	18 12	23 55	25 04	01 04	02 14
S 50	16 56	17 30	18 08	23 38	24 53	00 53	02 08
52	16 51	17 27	18 06	23 30	24 47	00 47	02 05
54	16 46	17 23	18 05	23 21	24 42	00 42	02 02
56	16 40	17 19	18 03	23 11	24 35	00 35	01 59
58	16 34	17 15	18 01	23 00	24 28	00 28	01 55
S 60	16 26	17 11	18 00	22 47	24 19	00 19	01 51

Day	SUN			MOON			
	Eqn. of Time		Mer. Pass.	Mer. Pass.		Age	Phase
	00ʰ	12ʰ		Upper	Lower		
	m s	m s	h m	h m	h m	d	
25	01 58	02 03	11 58	19 05	06 42	09	◖
26	02 08	02 13	11 58	19 49	07 27	10	
27	02 18	02 23	11 58	20 33	08 11	11	

*Figure 2811a:
Extract from daily
page of* Nautical
Almanac.

and the ship into time, adding this difference if the ship is west of the standard meridian and subtracting if it is east. Each degree of longitude will be 4 minutes of time, and each 15' of longitude 1 minute of time. The same result can be obtained by taking from the table the GMT at the required latitude, and applying to this the longitude converted to time, to give GMT of the phenomena at the local meridian, and finally applying the zone description with the sign reversed. Interpolation for latitude is made by means of a table near the back of the *Nautical Almanac;* a portion of this is reproduced in Figure 2811b. When more precise times of sunrise and sunset are desired, they may be obtained by interpolating for the correct day, in addition to the regular interpolation for latitude.

At times, in high latitudes, the sun remains continuously either below, or above the horizon. In the former case, the symbol ■ appears in place of a time; in the latter the symbol ▢ is substituted for the time.

To determine the time at a latitude which is not tabulated, Table 1 is entered, following the instructions listed below the table. It should be pointed out that the correction table is not linear and that information from the daily pages is always taken for the tabulated latitude smaller than the actual latitude. The entering arguments are:

TABLES FOR INTERPOLATING SUNRISE, MOONRISE, ETC.

TABLE I—FOR LATITUDE

Tabular Interval			Difference between the times for consecutive latitudes															
10°	5°	2°	5m	10m	15m	20m	25m	30m	35m	40m	45m	50m	55m	60m	1h 05m	1h 10m	1h 15m	1h 20m
° ′	° ′	° ′	m	m	m	m	m	m	m	m	m	m	m	m	h m	h m	h m	h m
0 30	0 15	0 06	0	0	1	1	1	1	1	2	2	2	2	2	0 02	0 02	0 02	0 02
1 00	0 30	0 12	0	1	1	2	2	3	3	3	4	4	4	5	05	05	05	05
1 30	0 45	0 18	1	1	2	3	3	4	4	5	5	6	7	7	07	07	07	07
2 00	1 00	0 24	1	2	3	4	5	5	6	7	7	8	9	10	10	10	10	10
2 30	1 15	0 30	1	2	4	5	6	7	8	9	9	10	11	12	12	13	13	13
5 30	2 45	1 06	3	5	8	11	13	16	18	20	22	24	26	28	0 29	0 30	0 31	0 32
6 00	3 00	1 12	3	6	9	12	14	17	20	22	24	26	29	31	32	33	34	36
6 30	3 15	1 18	3	6	10	13	16	19	22	24	26	29	31	34	36	37	38	40
7 00	3 30	1 24	3	7	10	14	17	20	23	26	29	31	34	37	39	41	42	44
7 30	3 45	1 30	4	7	11	15	18	22	25	28	31	34	37	40	43	44	46	48
10 00	5 00	2 00	5	10	15	20	25	30	35	40	45	50	55	60	1 05	1 10	1 15	1 20

Table I is for interpolating the L.M.T. of sunrise, twilight, moonrise, etc., for latitude. It is to be entered, in the appropriate column on the left, with the difference between true latitude and the nearest tabular latitude which is *less* than the true latitude; and with the argument at the top which is the nearest value of the difference between the times for the tabular latitude and the next higher one; the correction so obtained is applied to the time for the tabular latitude; the sign of the correction can be seen by inspection. It is to be noted that the interpolation is not linear, so that when using this table it is essential to take out the tabular phenomenon for the latitude *less* than the true latitude.

TABLE II—FOR LONGITUDE

Long. East or West	Difference between the times for given date and preceding date (for east longitude) or for given date and following date (for west longitude)																	
	10m	20m	30m	40m	50m	60m	1h + 10m	20m	30m	1h + 40m	50m	60m	2h 10m	2h 20m	2h 30m	2h 40m	2h 50m	3h 00m
°	m	m	m	m	m	m	m	m	m	m	m	m	h m	h m	h m	h m	h m	h m
0	0	0	0	0	0	0	0	0	0	0	0	0	0 00	0 00	0 00	0 00	0 00	0 00
10	0	1	1	1	1	2	2	2	2	3	3	3	04	04	04	04	05	05
20	1	1	2	2	3	3	4	4	5	6	6	7	07	08	08	09	09	10
30	1	2	2	3	4	5	6	7	7	8	9	10	11	12	12	13	14	15
40	1	2	3	4	6	7	8	9	10	11	12	13	14	16	17	18	19	20
50	1	3	4	6	7	8	10	11	12	14	15	17	0 18	0 19	0 21	0 22	0 24	0 25
130	4	7	11	14	18	22	25	29	32	36	40	43	47	51	54	0 58	1 01	1 05
140	4	8	12	16	19	23	27	31	35	39	43	47	51	54	0 58	1 02	1 06	1 10
150	4	8	13	17	21	25	29	33	38	42	46	50	0 54	0 58	1 03	1 07	1 11	1 15
160	4	9	13	18	22	27	31	36	40	44	49	53	0 58	1 02	1 07	1 11	1 16	1 20
170	5	9	14	19	24	28	33	38	42	47	52	57	1 01	1 06	1 11	1 16	1 20	1 25
180	5	10	15	20	25	30	35	40	45	50	55	60	1 05	1 10	1 15	1 20	1 25	1 30

Figure 2811b: Interpolation tables for rising and setting of the sun and moon.

Table II is for interpolating the L.M.T. of moonrise, moonset and the Moon's meridian passage for longitude. It is entered with longitude and with the difference between the times for the given date and for the preceding date (in east longitudes) or following date (in west longitudes). The correction is normally *added* for west longitudes and *subtracted* for east longitudes, but if, as occasionally happens, the times become earlier each day instead of later, the signs of the corrections must be reversed.

Time difference between the times of the occurrence at the tabulated latitudes on either side of the one for which the information is desired, and

Latitude difference between the tabulated latitude and the actual one.

Latitude correction.

This difference is then found in one of the three vertical columns headed "Tabular Interval"; the columns are subheaded 10°, 5°, and 2°, and the latitude difference is located in the appropriate one. That is, if the interval between tabulated latitudes is 2°, and the latitude for which the information is desired is 0°24′ greater than the smaller tabulated latitude, the "Tabular Interval" column headed 2° is entered, 0°24′ is found on the fourth line down. If the tabular interval were 5°, a latitude difference of 0°24′ would be located approximately on the second line down; if it were 10°, this same latitude difference would be located approximately on the first line. Having located the appropriate horizontal line of the table, the desired correction is then found under the appropriate number of minutes for the difference between the times for consecutive latitudes. Interpolation may be made in the table as necessary to obtain the time of the phenomenon to the nearest minute. The correction thus obtained is applied to the GMT of the phenomenon for the smaller tabulated latitude, originally extracted from the daily pages; the sign of the correction is determined by inspection.

To this sum, the longitude converted from arc to time is applied as described, to obtain the ZT of the phenomena for the latitude and longitude.

Sample problem, sunset.

Example: Find the ZT of sunset on 26 April 1969 at Lat. 17°15'.5 S, Long. 150°54'.6 E, using the *Nautical Almanac.*

Solution: Enter the appropriate daily page of the *Nautical Almanac* (Figure 2811a) and extract and record the LMT of sunset for the next smaller tabulated latitude. In this case, the next smaller tabulated latitude is 10° S, and the LMT of sunset at that latitude is 1752. Then note the difference of latitude between the tabulated values on either side of the latitude for which the information is desired, and the difference in the time of the phenomenon between the smaller and the larger tabulated latitudes, with its sign. In this case the tabular intervals is 10°, and the difference in time is (−)11ᵐ (1752 at Lat. 10° S and 1741 at Lat. 20° S). Next enter Table I and obtain the correction to the tabulated LMT. In this case the correction is (−)8ᵐ. Finally, apply the correction to the LMT of the smaller tabulated latitude to obtain the LMT of sunset at the given latitude, and convert this time to ZT. In this case, the LMT at Lat. 17°15'.5 S is 1744, and the ZT is 1740.

Answer: ZT 1740.

Figure 2811c: The Sunrise-Sunset Computer.

Sunset	
S 10°	1752
S 20°	1741
Diff. for 10°	− 11 min.
Table 1 Lat. Corr.	− 8 min.
1752−8 min.	=1744
Long. Corr.	− 4 min.
	1740

The procedure for obtaining the time of sunrise from the *Nautical Almanac* is the same as that explained above for sunset.

Sunrise-Sunset Computer.

In addition to the tabular methods discussed here the data can be determined to an accuracy better than 2 minutes by the use of a special Sunrise-Sunset Computer (Figure 2811c). Ephemeristic data for the sun are printed on the back of the computer and for purposes of this problem can be considered to be repetitive each year. Declination and *G* are tabulated, *G* being the GHA of the sun for 1200 GMT with the first two figures omitted for brevity. For example GHA of 359°.1 would be 9°.1 and 001°.7 would be 1°.7. With this ephemeristic data and the DR latitude and longitude, the four entering arguments are set on the face of the computer in accordance with the printed instructions. The time of meridian passage of the sun is also indicated on the computer.

2812. In celestial navigation, morning and evening twilight are the most im- *Twilight.*
portant times of the day, as ordinarily these are the only periods during which a
fix may be obtained by nearly simultaneous lines of position from observations
of a number of celestial bodies. At the darker limit of nautical twilight, when the
sun's center is 12° below the celestial horizon, the horizon is usually dimly
visible, except to an observer with dark-adapted vision, or using a telescope of
superior light gathering power. At the darker limit of civil twilight, when the
sun's center is 6° below the celestial horizon, during good weather the bright
stars are readily discernible to the practiced eye, and the horizon is clearly defined. This is approximately the mid-time of the period during which star observations should ordinarily be made.

The time of the darker limit of civil or nautical twilight is obtained from the
Nautical Almanac in the same manner that sunrise and sunset data are obtained.
The GMT of the phenomenon at the closest tabulated latitude is taken from
the daily pages, interpolation for latitude is made in Table 1, and the ZT of the
phenomenon at the desired latitude is then obtained by applying the longitude
in time, as discussed in article 2811.

When twilight lasts all night, as happens at times in high latitudes, the symbol
//// is shown in place of a time.

Example: Find the ZT of the ending of civil twilight from the *Nautical Almanac*
tables, in Figures 2811a and b, at Lat. 52°27'.4 N, Long. 38°07'.0 W.

Solution: Enter the appropriate daily page of the *Nautical Almanac* (Figure
2811a), and extract and record the LMT of civil twilight for the next smaller
tabulated latitude.

In this case the next smaller tabulated latitude is 52° N, and the LMT at that
latitude is 1954. Then note the difference between the tabulated values of
latitude on either side of the latitude for which the information is desired, and
the difference in the time of the phenomenon between the smaller and larger
tabulated latitudes, with its sign. In this case the tabular interval is 2°, and the
difference in time is (+)8^m (1954 at Lat. 52° N and 2002 at Lat. 54° N). Next
enter Table I (Figure 2811b), and obtain the correction to the tabulated LMT,
(+)2^m. Finally, apply the correction to the LMT of the smaller latitude to obtain
the LMT at the desired latitude, and convert this time to ZT. In this case, the
LMT of civil twilight at Lat. 52°27'.4 N is 1956 and the ZT is 1928.

Civil Twilight

52° N	1954
Tab. I	(+) 2
LMT	1956
dλ	(−) 28
ZT	1928

Answer: ZT of the ending of civil twilight is 1928.

2813. The time of moonrise and moonset is found by first interpolating for the *Moonrise and*
latitude at which it is required, as with the sun phenomena. However, there *moonset.*
must be a second interpolation for longitude, as the time of moonrise and
moonset differs considerably from day to day, and at any longitude other than

0° these phenomena will fall somewhere between the times tabulated for consecutive days on the 0° meridian. This is due to the fact that the change in hourly rate of increase of GHA for the moon is not precisely 15° per hour which would be assumed if longitude were merely converted to time as in the case of the sun.

It must be borne in mind that the tabulated time of moonrise and moonset is the GMT of these phenomena at the longitude of Greenwich; an observer in east longitude will experience each phenomenon before it occurs at 0° longitude. The GMT of moonrise and moonset in *east* longitude is found by interpolating between the tabulated time for the given day, and the tabulated time for the *preceding* day. For *west* longitude the reverse holds true, and the GMT at a given meridian in west longitude is found by interpolating between the tabulated time for the given day, and the tabulated time for the *following* day.

However, before interpolating for longitude; the times of the required phenomenon on the two days involved must first be interpolated for the required latitude using Table 1, Figure 2811b. The interpolating for longitude is then made using Table II of the "Tables for Interpolating Sunrise, Moonrise, Etc." An extract from this table is shown in the lower part of Figure 2811b. GMT is converted to ZT in the usual manner.

Sample problem, moonset.

Example: Find the ZT of moonset on 27 April 1969 at Lat. 63°09'.2 N, Long. 126°44'.4 W, using the *Nautical Almanac* extracts in Figures 2811a and b.

Solution: Enter the appropriate daily page of the *Nautical Almanac* and extract and record, for the next smaller tabulated latitude, the LMT of the phenomenon at the Greenwich meridian on the given date. In this case the LMT at Greenwich, tabulated for Lat. 62° N, is 0342 on 27 April. Then extract the equivalent time on the *preceding day if in east longitude,* or on the *following day if in west longitude.* In this case the LMT at Greenwich, again tabulated for Lat. 62° N, is 0336 on 28 April, the later day being taken because the position for which information is desired is in west longitude. Then determine the interval between tabulated values of latitude on either side of the one for which information is desired, and the time difference and its sign between the tabulated LMT at each of these latitudes for each of the two days involved. In this case the tabular interval for both days is 2°, and the difference in time is (+)9ᵐ on 27 April and (+)5ᵐ on 28 April. Next enter Table I and obtain the correction for latitude to the tabulated LMT at the longitude of Greenwich. The correction is (+)5ᵐ on 27 April, and (+)3ᵐ on 28 April. Then apply these corrections to the LMT at the smaller tabulated latitude, thus completing the interpolation to the nearest minute for latitude on each day. In this case, the LMT at the longitude of Greenwich at Lat. 63°09'.2 N is 0347 on 27 April, and 0339 on 28 April.

To interpolate for longitude, enter Table II with the longitude (east or west) in the left-hand column, and the difference between the LMT at each date in the line at the top of the table. In this case the longitude is approximately 127°, and the time difference is 8ᵐ (since 0347 − 0339 = 8ᵐ). Then obtain the correction from the table, using eye interpolation as necessary. In this case the correction to the nearest minute is 3ᵐ. Apply the correction to the LMT of the phenomenon on the date for which the information is desired, in such a way that the time arrived at falls between the LMT at Greenwich on the two dates in question. In most cases this will mean that the correction is added if the longitude is west, and subtracted if it is east. In this case the correction is sub-tracted, making the LMT of moonset at the observer's meridian 0344 (since 0347 − 3 = 0344) on 27 April. Finally, convert this LMT to ZT.

Moonset

62° N	0342	27 April
Tab. I	(+) 5	
LMT (G)	0347	27 April
62° N	0336	28 April
Tab. I	(+) 3	
LMT (G)	0339	28 April
LMT (G)	0347	27 April
diff.	(−) 8	
Tab. II	(−) 3	
LMT (G)	0347	27 April
LMT (L)	0344	27 April
dλ	(+)27	
ZT	0411	27 April

Answer: Moonset at Lat. 63°09'.2 N, Long. 126°44'.4 W, is at ZT 0411 on 27 April.

The procedure for obtaining the time of moonrise from the *Nautical Almanac* is the same as that explained above for moonset.

The moon appears to make a revolution about the earth in a period averaging 24h 50m; that is to say that moonrise and moonset occur, *on the average*, about fifty minutes later on successive days. However, any given period may vary considerably from the average, and under certain conditions moonrise may occur twice during one day or not at all. In the former case, both times are tabulated in the almanac, as (0002/2355), and in the latter case, the time of the next occurrence is tabulated relative to the given day, as 2415. This means that moonrise at the tabulated latitude will not occur at all on the stated day, but at 0015 on the next day. As discussed in article 1914, the phenomena can occur earlier on successive days. Considerable care must be exercised in interpolation.

2814. In the preceding articles, the methods of obtaining the times of these phenomena at a fixed position have been discussed. Usually, the navigator must determine these times aboard a moving ship.

Determining the time of phenomena aboard a moving ship.

To obtain the required time, he first examines his DR track in conjunction with the latitudes and GMT tabulated for the desired phenomenon in the *Nautical Almanac*. He selects the tabulated latitude nearest his DR position for the approximate time of the phenomenon and notes the tabulated GMT. This GMT he treats as his ZT (i.e. GMT 1144 he writes as ZT 1144), and determines the DR position for this ZT. Since LMT and ZT seldom differ by more than 30 minutes this method is sufficiently accurate for the initial DR. Using the latitude and longitude thus found, he determines the ZT of the phenomenon for this position, as described in the preceding articles. This is his first estimate.

The navigator next determines a new DR position for the ZT of the first estimate, and calculates the time of the phenomenon for this new position, interpolating for date, latitude, and longitude as may be necessary; this is the second estimate.

499

Ordinarily, this second estimate will give an acceptable accurate time for the phenomenon. However, if the two DR positions should prove to differ considerably in longitude, a new determination of the first estimate should be made.

Usually at sea, the maximum obtainable precision is required only for the time of sunrise and sunset; ordinarily, 2 or 3 minutes leeway are permissible in predicting the times of the other phenomena. The "Tables for Interpolating Sunrise, Moonrise, Etc." in the back of the *Nautical Almanac* are used, and longitude to the nearest 15' may be used in converting to time, i.e. to the nearest minute.

Example: The 1500 DR position of a ship is Lat. 33°23'.3 N, Long. 65°19'.4 W 26 April 1969. The ship is on course 255°, speed 20 knots. Find the ZT of sunset, to the nearest whole minute, using the *Nautical Almanac* excerpts in Figures 2811a and b.

	1841	L33°04'.2 N
	DR	λ66°46'.2 W

	Sunset	
LMT	1834	
Tab. I	(+) 4	
LMT	1838	
dλ	(+)27	
ZT	1905	1st est.
LMT	1838	
dλ	(+)28	
ZT	1906	2nd est.

Solution: (Figure 2814) By examination of the DR plot and the almanac, the navigator notes that in the band of latitude between 30° and 35°, sunset will occur at some time after 1830. At that time, the tabulated latitude closest to his DR is 35° N. He notes that for this latitude sunset occurs at 1841; he also notes that for L 30° N, it occurs at 1834, or seven minutes earlier.

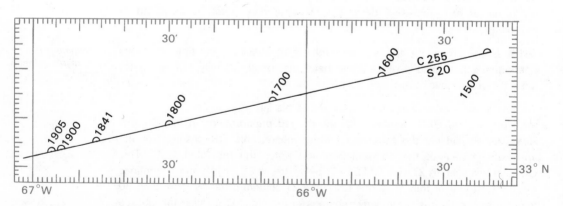

Figure 2814: Finding the time of sunset in a moving ship

He next plots his expected DR position for 1841; it proves to be L 33°04'.2 N, λ 66°46'.2 W.

Using this DR position he computes the time of sunset by entering the table on the daily page and extracts the time of 1834 for latitude 30° N. The latitude correction from Table 1 is (+)4 and the correction for difference in longitude between the DR and the standard meridian is (+)27 minutes (dλ 6°46'.2). This results in a ZT of 1905 as the first estimate.

By plotting the 1905 DR position, the navigator finds that the difference of longitude from the central meridian of the zone for the new position (computed to the nearest 15' of arc) is 7°00', resulting in a recomputed value of dλ of (+) 28 minutes.

Answer: ZT of sunset 1906.

Problems involving the time of sunrise, moonrise, moonset, and twilight for a moving ship are solved in a similar manner.

2815. Moonrise or moonset would be determined aboard ship by combining the method set forth in article 2813 with the above. The following example illustrates the solution.

Finding the time of moonset on a moving ship.

Example: (Figure 2815) On the evening of 26 April 1969, a ship's 2200 DR position is Lat. 16°52'.6 N, Long. 62°19'.4 W. The course is 063°, speed 20 knots. Find the ZT of moonset for the night of the 26th using data from the *Nautical Almanac* as reproduced in Figure 2811a.

Solution: An inspection of the moonset tables for 26 April shows that moonset in Lat. 10° N and on the Greenwich meridian occurred at 0129. For the night of 26 April the following moonset (tabulated for 27 April) will therefore have to be used; in Lat. 10° N and 0° Long. this occurs at 0210. Plot the DR position for 0210 on the chart; it will be Lat. 17°30'.5 N, Long. 61°02'.0 W. Next compute the time of moonset for this position, to obtain the first estimate of moonset as 0227 ZT.

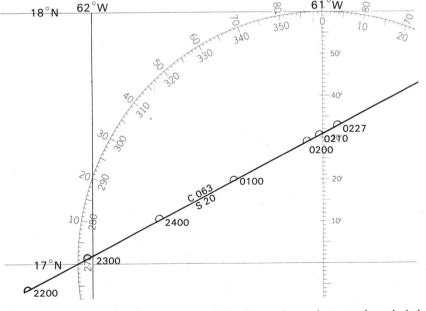

Figure 2815: Plot of moonset solution on moving vessel.

The ship's DR position for the time of the first estimate is next plotted; it is Lat. 17°33'.2 N, Long. 60°56'.8 W. Recompute the time of moonset for this new position, using the same procedures employed in obtaining the first estimate; this gives the second estimate of moonset, which proves to be 0227.

501

		Moonset	
L 10° N		0210	(27)
Lat. corr 7°.5		7	
LMT 0° λ		0217	(27)
L 10° N		0249	(28)
Lat. corr 7°.5 (Table 1)		4	
LMT 0° λ		0253	(28)
" " "		0217	(27)
diff	(+)	36	
Corr for λ (Table 2)	(+)	6.0 min	
LMT 0° λ		0217	(27)
	(+)	6	
LMT at ship		0223	(27)
dλ 1°02' W of meridian	(+)	4	
1st Est. ZT Moonset		0227	(27)
L 10° N		0210	(27)
Lat corr 7°5	(+)	7	
LMT 0° λ		0217	(27)
L 10° N		0249	(28)
Lat corr 7°.5	(+)	4	
LMT 0° λ		0253	(28)
LMT 0° λ		0217	(27)
diff	(+)	36	
Corr for λ	(+)	6 min	
LMT 0° λ		0217	(27)
	(+)	6	
LMT at ship		0223	(27)
dλ 0°56'.8 W of meridian	(+)	4	
2nd Est. ZT Moonset		0227	(27)

Summary.

2816. The GMT of the phenomena at various latitudes along the Greenwich meridian are tabulated on the daily pages of the almanac. For the sun phenomena, these values of GMT are almost exactly equal to the ZT along the standard meridian of each time zone, as the rotation of the earth causes the sun to appear to move westward at the rate of 15° per hour and the standard meridians of the time zones are established at 15° intervals. The navigator first determines the GMT of the desired phenomenon for the required latitude along the meridian of Greenwich and applies the difference in longitude—converted to time—between his position and the standard meridian to obtain the Zone Time.

For moonrise and moonset, the tabulated LMT must be interpolated for both latitude and longitude to obtain the LMT at the required position; it is then converted to ZT.

To find the time of these phenomena for a moving ship, the DR latitude is first determined for the approximate expected time of the required phenomenon. The tabulated latitude nearest to the DR latitude is located in the *Nautical Almanac* and the tabulated time is used to establish a DR position for that time. A *first estimate* of the time of the phenomena is then computed from the tables. Using the ZT thus obtained, a new DR position is plotted, and the time is corrected for the difference between the first and second DR positions.

CHAPTER 29

Compass Error at Sea

2901. Navy Regulations require that when a ship is under way and weather permits, the error of the compasses must be obtained once each day. However, good practice calls for a compass check twice a day, whenever possible; a check should be made immediately if there is reason to suppose a compass has sustained any damage, or is malfunctioning. Thus far the celestial navigation part of this text has been concerned with the solution of the navigational triangle to obtain an LOP. It is frequently necessary for the navigator to solve the navigational triangle for other purposes. The purpose of this chapter is to explain the solution to determine true azimuth, for use in determining compass error at sea.

Introduction.

Compass error at sea is determined by azimuth observations of celestial bodies; the sun is the body observed most frequently. Such observations should be made when the sun is low in altitude, preferably under 20°. All quartermasters should be trained to obtain accurate azimuth observations, and such observations should be made at least twice a day, when possible.

2902. Azimuth observations of celestial bodies are made using an *azimuth circle*, bearing circle, or similar device. An azimuth circle (Figure 1004) is an instrument whose principal components are a small, hinged, concave mirror and a shielded prism which is located on the ring opposite the mirror. When the instrument is used to observe the sun's azimuth, the azimuth circle is fitted over a gyrocompass repeater, or the bowl of a magnetic compass, and aligned so that the prism is directly between the mirror and the sun. When the hinged mirror is properly adjusted in the plane of the vertical circle of the sun, a thin, vertical beam of sunlight is cast upon a slit in the prism shield and refracted downward into the compass card. The line of sunlight on the card indicates the compass azimuth of the sun at that time. Two leveling bubbles are provided with the azimuth circle, as the instrument must be horizontal to indicate an accurate compass azimuth.

Azimuth observations.

An azimuth observation of a star or planet is made using the sight vanes of an azimuth circle or bearing circle, in a manner similar to that used for observing terrestrial bearings (article 1004). The moon may be observed for azimuth using either the mirror-prism method or the sight vane method. Because of the difficulty in seeing the leveling bubbles during darkness, azimuth observations are usually restricted to the sun. A pelorus can also be used to determine the azimuth measurements.

In practice, the navigator observes the azimuth of a celestial body and notes the time of the observation. He then solves the navigational triangle for his position, and determines the true azimuth of the body at the time of the observation. The difference between the true and observed azimuths, properly labeled E or W, is the compass error.

In general, the lower the celestial body, the more accurate the azimuth observation. For most practical purposes an accuracy to the nearest one-half degree is normally sufficient.

Exact azimuth by inspection tables.

2903. The inspection tables, such as H. O. 214, and H. O. 229, make excellent azimuth tables. As the solution for azimuth is generally similar for both these

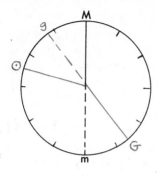

EXACT AZIMUTH
USING H. O. 214

Figure 2903: Extracts from H.O 214.

Body	SUN	Closest Tab		Exact	Next Tab
DR L	33° 25'.2 S	t	63°	62° 44'.7	62°
DR λ	139° 22'.8 W	Dec	13° N	13° 04'.9	13° 30' N
Date (L)	24 APRIL	L	33° S	33° 25'.2	34° S
ZT	16-26-32		Interpolation For Azimuth Angle (Az)		
ZD (-) +9					
GMT	01-26-32			CORR:	
Date (G)	25 APRIL				
Tab GHA	195° 29'.5	$\text{t diff} (0'.7) \times \left(\frac{15.3}{60}\right)$			+ 0°.2
Incm't	6° 38'.0				
SHA/v corr.		$\text{Dec diff} (0°.4) \times \left(\frac{04.9}{36}\right)$			+ 0°.1
GHA	202° 07'.5				
DR λ	139° 22'.8	$\text{L diff} (0°.3) \times \left(\frac{25.2}{60}\right)$			+ 0°.1
LHA	62° 44'.7				
t	62° 44'.7 W			Sum/Corr	0°.4
d (-)	+ 0'.8			Tab Az	116°.3
Tab Dec	13° 04'.5 N			Exact Az S	116°.7 W
d corr.	+ 0'.4			Exact Zn	296°.7
Dec	13° 04'.9 N			Gyro/Compass Brg	297°.5
				Gyro/Compass Error	0°.8 W

methods, only the use of the former will be discussed in this chapter. Sample problems using H. O. 229 will be found in the Appendix on page 687.

When H. O. 214 is used to determine true azimuth for the purpose of checking the compass, triple linear interpolation usually must be made in order to obtain the required accuracy. The $\triangle$ values in H. O. 214 apply only to *altitude*, and should not be used when interpolating for azimuth.

Example: The navigator of a ship observes the azimuth of the sun at 16-26-32 ZT on 24 April 1969. The 1627 DR position of the ship is Lat. 33°25'.2 S, Long. 139°22'.8 W. The azimuth obtained using the gyro repeater (GB) is 297°.5.

Required: Gyro error, using H. O. 214 to obtain true azimuth.

Solution: It is first necessary to determine the exact values of *t*, Dec., and L for the instant of observation of the azimuth. These values are determined as for working a sight, except that the *actual* position of the ship is used rather than an assumed position. Thus the DR longitude is used to determine the exact value of *t* at the time of observation, which is found to be 62°44'.7 W. The exact value of Dec. is found to be 13°04'.9 N by consulting the *Nautical Almanac* (Figure 2403c) in the usual manner. The DR latitude is taken as the exact value of L at the time of observation.

With the exact values of *t*, Dec., and L determined, enter the appropriate section of H. O. 214, and record as the "tab." values those tabulated entering arguments nearest to the exact values. In this case they are *t* 63° W, Dec. 13° N, and L 33° S. With these "tab." values as entering arguments, enter the proper section (the "contrary name" section in this case), and extract and record the tabulated azimuth angle, Az 116°.3 (Figure 2903). This value of Az is the *tabulated* ("tab.") value, to which the corrections resulting from the necessary inter-polation are applied to obtain the azimuth angle for the exact values of *t*, Dec., and L at the moment of observation. Interpolation is made separately for the difference between each of the exact values and the corresponding "tab." values of *t*, Dec., and L; and the algebraic sum of the resulting corrections is applied to the value of tab. Az to obtain the exact azimuth angle at the moment of observation. It is normally considered sufficiently accurate to reduce these corrections to the nearest tenth of a degree.

The *t* is interpolated from 63° (Az 116°.3) to 62° (Az 117°.0), indicating a change of (+)0°.7 for a change of 1° (60') in the entering value of *t*. This is known as the "*t* diff." Since the exact value of *t* is 62°44'.7, which is 15'.3 less than the "tab." value of *t*, the difference in the value of Az corresponding to this variation in *t* is only 15'.3/60' of the change for a 1° change in *t*. Thus, "*t* corr.," which is the correction to apply to the value of tab. Az for the variation of the exact value of *t* from the value of tab. *t* is equal to (+)0°.7 × 15'.3/60', which equals (+)0°.2.

The Dec. is interpolated from 13° (Az 116°.3) to 13°30' (Az 116°.7), indicating a change of (+)0°.4 for a change of 30' in the entering value of Dec. This is known as the "Dec. diff." Since the exact value of Dec. is 13°04'.9 and is 4'.9 more than the "tab." value of Dec., the difference in the value of Az corresponding to this variation in Dec. is only 4'.9/30' of the change for a 30' change in Dec. Thus the "Dec. corr.," which is the correction to apply to the value of tab. Az for the variation of the exact value of Dec. from the value of tab. Dec., is equal to (+)0°.4 × 4'.9/30', which, to the nearest tenth of a degree, equals 0°.1.

The L is interpolated from 33° (Az 116°.3) to 34° (Az 116°.6), indicating a change of (+)0°.3 in Az for a change of 1° (60') in the entering value of L. This is known as the "L diff." Since the exact value of L (33°25'.2) is 25'.2 greater than the "tab." value of L (33°), the difference in the value of Az corresponding to this change in L is only 25'.2/60' of the difference for a 1° change in L. Thus, "L corr.," which is the correction to apply to the value of Tab. Az for the variation of the exact value of L from the value of Tab. L, is equal to (+)0°.3 × 25'.2/60', which equals (+)0°.1.

By applying the algebraic sum of the t, Dec., and L corrections, as determined above, to the tab. Az, the value of the exact azimuth angle at the moment of observation is found to be S 116°.7 W, which converts to a Zn of 296°.7. The gyro error is determined by comparing this exact azimuth with that obtained by observation.

Answer: Gyro error 0°.8 W.

In solving problems for exact azimuth using H. O. 214, the multiplication of the fractional amount by the amount of the "diff." to obtain the appropriate correction can be accomplished most readily by establishing a proportion with dividers on a log scale of speed or distance, such as is found on some charts and on Maneuvering Board paper, and is discussed briefly in article 1304. In establishing the fractions involved, it is well to remember that the denominator of the fractional part for t and L is always 60', since the tabulated entering arguments of t and L are always 1° apart. The denominator of the fractional part for Dec., must always be established by inspection, since the interval between tabulated entering arguments varies from 30' at lower declinations up to several degrees at some higher declinations.

Azimuth by other tabular methods.

2904. Exact azimuths may also be obtained by using H. O. 211, H. O. 208, or by the use of various other tables, such as the Weems *Line of Position Book.* As with the inspection tables, these methods permit simultaneous solution for both azimuth and altitude.

Other tables which may be used to obtain azimuth are H. O. 260, *Azimuth Tables of the Sun,* and H. O. 261, *Azimuths of Celestial Bodies.* H. O. 260, known generally as the "Red Azimuth Tables" because of the color of the binding used for most printings, and H. O. 261, usually called the "Blue Azimuth Tables" for a similar reason, contain tabulations of azimuth to the nearest minute of arc, for every ten minutes of time. Unfortunately, with present equipment azimuth cannot be observed to anything approaching this standard of accuracy. Instructions for their use are given in H. O. 260.

H. O. 249 is of no value for obtaining exact azimuths, as tabulations are only to the nearest whole degree.

Azimuth by amplitude.

2905. When using an azimuth to check a compass, a low altitude is most desirable, as it is both easy to observe and gives the most accurate results. An *amplitude* observation is one made when the center of the observed body is either on the *celestial* or *visible horizon,* i.e., it is in the act of rising or setting. In the latter case a correction is applied to the observation in order to obtain the corresponding amplitude when the center of the body is on the celestial horizon. The sun is the body most frequently observed in obtaining an amplitude. However, the moon, a planet or a bright star having a declination not exceeding

24° may also be used. Amplitudes should be avoided in high latitudes.

Amplitude may be defined as angular distance measured N or S from the prime vertical to the body on the celestial horizon. It is given the prefix E (east) if the body is rising, and W (west) if it is setting; the suffix is N if the body rises or sets north of the prime vertical, as it does with a northerly declination, and S if it rises or sets south of the prime vertical, having a southerly declination.

If a body is observed when its center is on the celestial horizon, the amplitude may be taken directly from table 27 in Bowditch (Figure 2905a).

When observing amplitudes at normal bridge heights, two assumptions may be made which yield sufficiently accurate results for practical purposes. The first is that when the *sun's* center is on the celestial horizon, its *lower limb* is about two-thirds of a diameter above the visible horizon. The second is that when the center of the *moon* is on the celestial horizon, its *upper limb* is on the visible horizon. This apparent anomaly is due to the sun's parallax being very small (0'.1) as compared to the refraction, which at this altitude amounts to about 34'.5, whereas the moon parallax is large (between 54'.0 and 61'.5, depending on the date), while the refraction is about 34'.5.

When planets or stars are on the celestial horizon, they are about one *sun* diameter, or some 32'.0 above the visible horizon.

Latitude	Declination													Latitude
	18°.0	18°.5	19°.0	19°.5	20°.0	20°.5	21°.0	21°.5	22°.0	22°.5	23°.0	23°.5	24°.0	
0	18.0	18.5	19.0	19.5	20.0	20.5	21.0	21.5	22.0	22.5	23.0	23.5	24.0	0
10	18.3	18.8	19.3	19.8	20.3	20.8	21.3	21.8	22.4	22.9	23.4	23.9	24.4	10
15	18.7	19.2	19.7	20.2	20.7	21.3	21.8	22.4	22.8	23.3	23.9	24.4	24.9	15
20	19.2	19.7	20.3	20.8	21.3	21.9	22.4	23.0	23.5	24.0	24.6	25.1	25.6	20
25	19.9	20.5	21.1	21.6	22.2	22.7	23.3	23.9	24.4	25.0	25.5	26.1	26.7	25
45	25.9	26.7	27.4	28.2	28.9	29.7	30.5	31.2	32.0	32.8	33.5	34.3	35.1	45
46	26.4	27.2	27.9	28.7	29.5	30.3	31.1	31.8	32.6	33.4	34.2	35.0	35.8	46
47	26.9	27.7	28.5	29.3	30.1	30.9	31.7	32.5	33.3	34.1	35.0	35.8	36.6	47
48	27.5	28.3	29.1	29.9	30.7	31.6	32.4	33.2	34.0	34.9	35.7	36.6	37.4	48
49	28.1	28.9	29.8	30.6	31.4	32.3	33.1	34.0	34.8	35.7	36.6	37.4	38.3	49
50	28.7	29.6	30.4	31.3	32.1	33.0	33.9	34.8	35.6	36.5	37.4	38.3	39.3	50
51	29.4	30.3	31.2	32.0	32.9	33.8	34.7	35.6	36.5	37.5	38.4	39.3	40.3	51
52	30.1	31.0	31.9	32.8	33.7	34.7	35.6	36.5	37.5	38.4	39.4	40.4	41.3	52
53	30.9	31.8	32.8	33.7	34.6	35.6	36.5	37.5	38.5	39.5	40.5	41.5	42.5	53
54	31.7	32.7	33.6	34.6	35.6	36.6	37.6	38.6	39.6	40.6	41.7	42.7	43.8	54

Figure 2905a: Excerpt from Amplitude Table, 27, Bowditch.

Latitude	Declination													Latitude
	0°	2°	4°	6°	8°	10°	12°	14°	16°	18°	20°	22°	24°	
0	0.0	0.0	0.0	0.0	0.0	0.0	0.0	0.0	0.0	0.0	0.0	0.0	0.0	0
10	0.1	0.1	0.1	0.1	0.1	0.1	0.1	0.1	0.1	0.1	0.1	0.1	0.1	10
15	0.2	0.2	0.2	0.2	0.2	0.2	0.2	0.2	0.2	0.2	0.2	0.2	0.2	15
20	0.3	0.3	0.3	0.3	0.3	0.3	0.3	0.3	0.3	0.3	0.3	0.3	0.3	20
25	0.3	0.3	0.3	0.3	0.3	0.4	0.3	0.3	0.3	0.3	0.3	0.3	0.3	25
40	0.6	0.6	0.6	0.6	0.6	0.6	0.6	0.6	0.6	0.6	0.7	0.7	0.7	40
42	0.6	0.6	0.6	0.6	0.7	0.7	0.7	0.7	0.7	0.7	0.7	0.7	0.7	42
44	0.7	0.7	0.7	0.6	0.6	0.7	0.7	0.7	0.8	0.8	0.8	0.8	0.9	44
46	0.7	0.7	0.7	0.7	0.7	0.8	0.8	0.8	0.8	0.8	0.8	0.9	0.9	46
48	0.8	0.8	0.8	0.8	0.8	0.8	0.8	0.8	0.9	0.9	1.0	1.0	1.0	48
50	0.8	0.8	0.8	0.8	0.9	0.9	0.9	0.9	0.9	1.0	1.0	1.1	1.0	50
51	0.8	0.8	0.8	0.8	0.9	0.9	0.9	0.9	0.9	1.0	1.1	1.1	1.1	51
52	0.9	0.9	0.9	0.9	0.9	0.9	1.0	1.0	1.0	1.1	1.1	1.1	1.3	52
53	0.9	0.9	0.9	0.9	0.9	0.9	1.0	1.0	1.0	1.1	1.2	1.2	1.3	53
54	1.0	1.0	1.0	1.0	1.0	1.0	1.1	1.1	1.1	1.2	1.2	1.3	1.3	54

Figure 2905b: Excerpt from Correction Table. 28, Bowditch.

If a body is observed on the *visible horizon*, the *observed* value is corrected by the value taken from Table 28, according to the rule: For the *sun*, a *planet*, or a *star* apply the correction to the observed amplitude in the direction away from the elevated pole thus increasing the azimuth angle; for the *moon*, apply *half* the correction *toward* the elevated pole. The entering arguments for both tables are latitude and declination (Figure 2905b).

If desired, the correction can be applied with reversed sign to the value taken from Table 27, for comparison with the uncorrected observed value. This is the procedure used if amplitude or azimuth is desired when the celestial body is on the visible horizon.

Example: The DR latitude of a ship is 16°03'.6 S at a time when the sun's declination is 20°09'.1 N. The sun, when centered on the visible horizon, bears 069°.5 by gyro, giving a compass amplitude of E 20°.5 N.

Required: (1) The gyro error.

Solution: (Interpolating in tables)

Amplitude by compass E 20°.5 N
Correction   0°.3 N (away from elevated pole) (Table 28)
Observed amplitude   E 20°.8 N (=Zn 069°.2)
True Amplitude   E 21°.0 N (=Zn 069°.0)   (Table 27)
(1) Gyro error   0°.2 W (Zn 069°.2 – 069°.0)

Azimuth by Polaris. **2906.** The true azimuth of Polaris is tabulated in the *Nautical Almanac* for northern latitudes up to 65°. Polaris, the "north star," is always within about 2° of true north in these latitudes, and observations of it provide a convenient means of checking the compass, with little interpolation needed. An extract from the *Nautical Almanac* Polaris azimuth table, which appears in the almanac at the foot of the Polaris latitude tables, is shown in Fig. 2906.

The entering arguments in the *Nautical Almanac* azimuth table for Polaris are: (1) LHA of Aries and (2) latitude (at intervals of 5°, 10°, or 20°). Eye interpolation is made if necessary.

Example: The navigator of a ship at Lat. 62°24'.5 N, Long. 62°07'.8 W observes Polaris when the GHA Aries is 333°09'.5. The observed azimuth by gyro repeater (GB) is 359°.5.

Required: Gyro error by Polaris, using the *Nautical Almanac* Polaris Table.

Polaris

DR L   62°24'.5 N
DR λ   62°07'.8 W

GHA ♈   333°09'.5
DR λ   62°07'.8 W
LHA ♈   271°01'.7

Zn   001°.7
GB   359°.5
GE   2°.2 E (rounded off : 2°.0 E)

POLARIS (POLE STAR) TABLES, 1969

FOR DETERMINING LATITUDE FROM SEXTANT ALTITUDE AND FOR AZIMUTH

L.H.A. ARIES	240°– 249°	250°– 259°	260°– 269°	270°– 279°	280°– 289°	290°– 299°	300°– 309°	310°– 319°	320°– 329°	330°– 339°	340°– 349°	350°– 359°
Lat.						AZIMUTH						
°	°	°	°	°	°	°	°	°	°	°	°	°
0	0·5	0·6	0·7	0·8	0·8	0·9	0·9	0·8	0·8	0·7	0·6	0·5
20	0·5	0·7	0·8	0·8	0·9	0·9	0·9	0·9	0·8	0·8	0·7	0·5
40	0·6	0·8	0·9	1·0	1·1	1·1	1·1	1·1	1·0	0·9	0·8	0·7
50	0·8	0·9	1·1	1·2	1·3	1·4	1·4	1·3	1·2	1·1	1·0	0·8
55	0·9	1·0	1·2	1·4	1·5	1·5	1·5	1·5	1·4	1·3	1·1	0·9
60	1·0	1·2	1·4	1·6	1·7	1·7	1·7	1·7	1·6	1·5	1·3	1·0
65	1·1	1·4	1·6	1·8	2·0	2·0	2·1	2·0	1·9	1·7	1·5	1·2

Figure 2906: Extract from the Nautical Almanac Polaris azimuth table.

Solution: Using the exact DR longitude (note that an assumed position is *not* used), determine the LHA ♈ for the time of observation. Turn to the three pages of Polaris Tables located just forward of the yellow pages, toward the back of the *Nautical Almanac,* and locate the column heading encompassing the computed value of LHA♈. In this case it occurs on the third page of Polaris tables, an extract of which is given in Figure 2906. (In this figure the azimuth tables appear directly below the columnar headings, whereas the azimuth portion of the tables is actually at the extreme bottom of the table.) Using the column with a heading of LHA ♈ 270°–279°, follow down the column to the appropriate latitude. Using eye interpolation for latitude, the value of 1°.7, or 001°.7, is extracted as the true azimuth. The gyro error is determined by comparing this with the azimuth observed using the gyro repeater.

Answer: Gyro error 2°.2 E. Due to the limitations in the accuracy with which the compass, or a repeater can be read, this would be rounded off to the nearest half-degree, or 2°.0 E.

In practice, it is difficult to observe Polaris accurately for azimuth unless the ship is in a lower latitude, due to the difficulty of observing accurate azimuths at higher altitudes; this difficulty is increased if the ship is rolling. However, Polaris serves as a useful check on the compass at any time it can be observed, as an azimuth observation of approximately 000° indicates that the compass is reasonably free of error.

2907. The deviation of a magnetic compass on various headings is determined by *swinging ship.* During the process of swinging ship at sea, it is desirable to be able to obtain the magnetic azimuth of the sun at any moment, without the delay that would result if it were necessary to select each azimuth by triple interpolation from the tables. For this reason, it is common practice to determine in advance the magnetic azimuth at intervals during the period of swing, and to plot these against time on cross section paper, fairing a curve through the points. The curve may be constructed by means of azimuths from H. O. 214 or from other appropriate tables.

Curve of magnetic azimuths.

To construct the curve, the navigator first determines the true azimuth for the approximate mid-time of the period during which the ship is to be swung, using the method of article 2903. During the time devoted to swinging the ship, the latitude and declination remain essentially constant, and the only one of the three entering arguments to change appreciably is meridian angle. Since meridian angle changes at the nearly constant rate of 1° for each four minutes of time, the

509

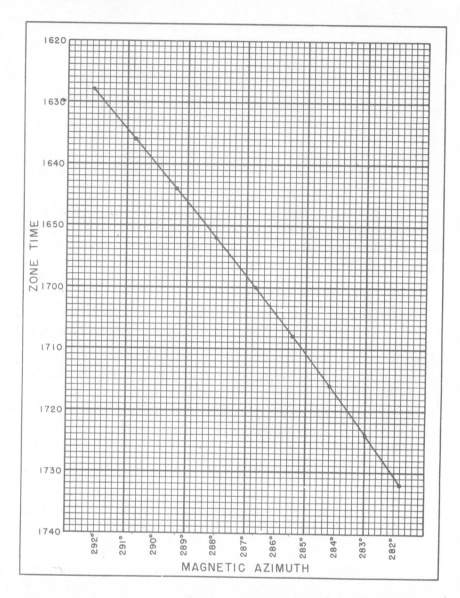

Figure 2907: A curve of magnetic azimuths.

azimuth at a time four minutes before or after the mid-time of the swing can be obtained by entering H. O. 214 with the same values of Dec. and L used previously, but with a *t* 1° greater or less, and applying the same correction to the tabulated value as that used for the mid-time. In practice, the change in azimuth in four minutes (1° of *t*) is usually quite small, and sufficient accuracy is obtained by determining the azimuth at intervals of eight minutes (2° of *t*). Thus, having determined the correction to the tabulated azimuth for the mid-time of the swing, the navigator has only to enter H. O. 214 with the same values of declination and latitude, and a meridian angle two degrees greater or less, and apply the previously-found correction to the tabulated Az to determine the true Az eight minutes earlier or later. A series of such computations provides values of true azimuth at intervals throughout the swing. By converting these values to magnetic azimuth, the navigator can plot this information on cross-section paper and fair a curve through the points, from which the magnetic azimuth can be taken at any time during the period. The above method will provide acceptable accuracy if the total time period is not overly long, or close to the time of LAN. For more accurate results, the determination of a separate correction for each solution is recommended.

Example: A ship is to be swung between 1630 and 1730 ZT to determine compass error. The 1700 DR latitude is 33°25'.2 S. At that time the declination of the sun will be 12°55'.8 N and its meridian angle will be 62°43'.8 W. The variation in the area is 9°45' E.

Required: A curve of magnetic azimuth for use during the swing.

ZT	t	Tab.	Tab. Az.	Corr.	Az	Zn	Var.	Magn. Zn
	°	°	°		°	°		°
1628	54.7	55°	121.7	↑	S 121.9 W	301.9	↑	292.1
1636	56.7	57°	120.3		120.5	300.5		290.7
1644	58.7	59°	118.9		119.1	299.1		289.3
1652	60.7	61°	117.6		117.8	297.8		288.0
1700	62.7	63°	116.3	(+)0°.2	116.5	296.5	9°.8 E	286.7
1708	64.7	65°	115.1		115.3	295.3		285.5
1716	66.7	67°	113.8		114.0	294.0		284.2
1724	68.7	69°	112.6		112.8	292.8		283.0
1732	70.7	71°	111.4	↓	111.6	291.6	↓	281.8

Solution: Determine the correction to tabulated azimuth angle and the true azimuth for the mid time of the swing. The correction to tabulated azimuth angle is (+)0°.2 and the true azimuth is 296°.5. Record this information on the middle line of a form such as that shown above, and then record ZT at eight-minute intervals before and after the mid-time to provide for the full period of the swing. In this case the time range is from 1628 to 1732. Next to each ZT, record *t* at that time. Since the sun is setting during the period of swing, *t* increases with time in this case, from 54°.7 to 70°.7. Take the nearest whole degree value, which is the tab. *t* value in each case. Then obtain the tabulated Az from H. O. 214 for each tab. *t* and the constant values of Dec. and L (which are 13° N and 33° S, respectively, in this case), and apply the correction for the mid-time, ((+)0°.2 in this case) to each tabulated Az to obtain the exact Az for each ZT. Next, convert each Az to Zn and apply the variation for the locality to determine the magnetic azimuth of the sun at each ZT. Finally, plot the magnetic azimuths against zone time on cross-section paper, as shown in Figure 2907.

Answer: See Figure 2907.

For an explanation of the use of magnetic azimuths in obtaining deviations of the magnetic compasses aboard ship, see article 917.

2908. Various azimuth diagrams have been produced over the years, to permit a graphic determination of azimuth; the Weir diagram was long used by the Navy.

Azimuths by diagram.

Currently the most commonly used azimuth diagram is that designed by Armistead Rust, a portion of which is reproduced in Figure 2908. This diagram

511

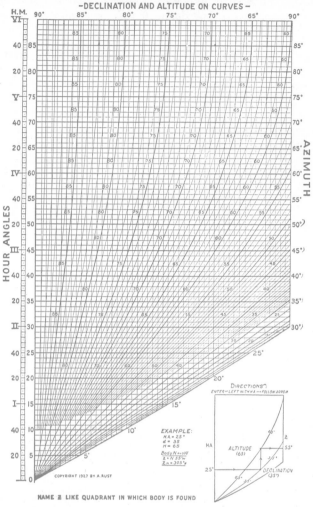

Figure 2908: Armistead Rust azimuth diagram—Left half. Declination and altitude on curves.

is included in the Weems *Line of Position Book*, as an alternate to computation for determining azimuth.

Summary.

2909. Compass error is determined at sea by observing the azimuth of a celestial body and comparing the observed value with the exact value, as obtained by computation. The azimuth as obtained for plotting an LOP is not sufficiently accurate for this purpose, and interpolation must be made for *t*, Dec., and L to obtain the exact azimuth from tables such as H. O. 214. This is done by triple linear interpolation, with entering arguments to the nearest 0°.1. The exact azimuth of Polaris, which is always close to 000° (for latitudes up to 65° N) can be obtained from tables in the *Nautical Almanac*. In solutions for exact azimuth by H. O. 214 or by Polaris, the best estimate of the ship's position is always used rather than an assumed position. A reasonably accurate curve of magnetic azimuths, for use in swinging ship, is conveniently obtained by determining the exact azimuth for the mid-time of the period, and applying a constant correction to the tabulated values for the Dec. and L of the mid-time, and for *t* values which differ from that of the mid-time by whole numbers of degrees.

CHAPTER 30

The Practice of
Navigation at Sea

3001. Chapter 15, "The Practice of Piloting," explained the navigation of a ship from its berth or anchorage to the point where it took its departure, and from its landfall off the next port to its berth or anchorage there. This chapter is concerned with the practice of navigation on the high seas, when out of sight of land and seamarks. At sea, the proper practice of celestial navigation is of the utmost importance. Even in areas of good electronic navigational coverage, celestial navigation must not be neglected; electronic aids may suddenly become unavailable. The good navigator uses every available means of determining his position.

Introduction.

3002. At sea, it is usually impossible to fix position with the same accuracy as can be obtained in piloting; however, the navigator must make every effort to obtain the most accurate fixes possible, and to maintain an accurate DR and EP between fixes. Every opportunity to obtain celestial observations should be seized.

Navigation at sea.

Every available means of obtaining positioning data must be employed; the echo sounder, Consol and Consolan, the radio direction finder, Omega, Loran, radar and other electronic aids are utilized whenever conditions permit.

3003. In the following article, a typical minimum day's work is outlined. Aboard many naval vessels, a considerable share of this work will be performed by the quartermasters. For example, the senior quartermaster usually winds and compares the chronometers, and azimuth observations are usually made and reduced by quartermasters, who usually also prepare the lists of stars to be observed. The organization of the navigation team, and the duties of the individual quartermasters who comprise it, will depend on their training and natural abilities.

The navigation team.

The senior quartermasters are frequently good sextant observers, and their sights can be most helpful in augmenting those of the navigator. The navigator should encourage and train his quartermasters to become proficient in all aspects of navigation, and particularly so as celestial observers. The greatest limiting factor on the accuracy of celestial navigation is the quality of the sextant observation, and consistently reliable observations can only be obtained after much practice. A quartermaster who can obtain good celestial observations is of the utmost value to his ship, and to the Navy.

Training in this field should start with LAN sights when the sun is moving slowly in altitude. Next, observations should be made when its altitude is chang-

Practice sights.

ing more rapidly; with practice, sights should be obtained every 10 to 15 seconds. These may be plotted on graph paper, using $\frac{1}{2}$ inch or 1 inch to a minute of arc, and to 10 seconds of time; a "line of best fit" is then drawn in, which serves to indicate the random errors of the individual observations. Such graphing will soon enable the navigator to identify his best qualified observers.

The navigator should also see to it that the quartermasters are trained as recorders. An observation is worthless if the altitude or time is misrecorded.

The training of quartermasters may be considered to be one of the highly important duties of the navigator.

The day's work.

3004. Details of the navigating team's work during a day at sea vary with the navigator and the ship, as well as other factors, but a typical *minimum* day's work during good weather might include the following:

> Plot of dead reckoning throughout the day.
>
> Computation of the time of the beginning of morning civil twilight, and preparation of a list of stars and planets in favorable positions for observation at that time, with the approximate altitude and azimuth of each body.
>
> Observation of selected celestial bodies and solution of the observations for a fix during morning twilight.
>
> Preparation of a position report based upon the morning twilight fix.
>
> Winding of chronometers, and determination of chronometer error, by radio time ticks.
>
> Azimuth of the sun to determine compass error.
>
> Observation of the sun for a morning sun line (and of Venus and the moon, if available).
>
> Observation of the sun at LAN (and of the moon if it is available) to obtain a ZT 1200 position (running fix or fix), or as near LAN as possible in the event of overcast.
>
> Computation of the day's run, from the preceding noon to the present noon.
>
> Preparation of a position report based upon the ZT 1200 position.
>
> Observation of the sun for an afternoon sun line (and of Venus and the moon, if available).
>
> Azimuth of the sun to determine compass error.
>
> Computation of the time of ending of evening civil twilight, and preparation of a list of stars and planets in favorable positions for observation at that time, with the approximate altitude and azimuth of each body.
>
> Observations of the celestial bodies selected and solution of the observations for a fix during evening twilight. If only one or two bodies can be obtained, the afternoon sun line can be advanced and combined with the evening stars for a running fix.
>
> Preparation of a 2000 position report based upon the evening twilight fix and any other positioning data.
>
> Preparation of the check-off list for the Captain's Night Order Book.

Notes on the day's work.

Venus may frequently be observed in the morning, when it is well west and higher than the sun. Similarly, it may be observed in the afternoon, if it is well east, and therefore considerably higher than the sun.

When the sun is high at transit, it is changing rapidly in azimuth. This permits excellent running fixes to be obtained by combining late morning and early afternoon sun lines with LAN.

During prolonged periods of overcast, the sun often does break through for a short time. Under such conditions, an observer and a sextant should both be available to obtain an observation without delay. Under such conditions, the sun should be observed even if it is veiled by thin cirrus; rarely does such blurring of the sun's limb cause an error of one minute of arc.

3005. The LMT of the beginning of morning nautical and civil twilights, and of sunrise, are tabulated in the *Nautical Almanac*, and they are used by the navigator principally to assist him in planning for morning twilight observations. He does this by determining the time at which civil twilight begins (article 2812), and obtaining LHA ♈ for that time. By setting his star finder for that LHA♈, he can determine the approximate altitudes and azimuths of celestial bodies which will be visible at that time.

Morning twilight observations.

A table such as is shown in Figure 3005a is useful in preparing to observe celestial bodies during twilight, as it is of great assistance in locating them in both azimuth and altitude. In addition, it permits the selection of bodies with azimuths which will be particularly helpful. A body ahead or astern will yield an LOP which makes a *speed line*, thus giving a check on the ship's advance. Similarly, a body observed on the beam will produce an approximate *course line*.

In general, the bodies selected should be well distributed in azimuth. Good practice calls for observing a minimum of five bodies; six or seven are more desirable. Of these, four should be reduced, and the resulting LOPs should be advanced for the run between observations. If the resulting quadrangle is of reasonable size, its center is taken as the position of the fix; if not, the other observations are reduced to obtain data for a better position. However, when all the bodies observed lie within 180° of azimuth, the *bisector method*, described in article 3009, should be used in establishing the fix, which may be *external* rather than *internal*.

The table should include many more bodies than the navigator expects to observe, as some may be obscured by cloud cover. Bodies in the altitude range between 15° and 65° are in general the most satisfactory to observe. Azimuth should also be taken into consideration, so that the bodies observed differ by roughly equal amounts in azimuth. The most desirable bodies for observation may be marked by asterisks on the star table, to signify that they are the first choice for observation, as is shown in Figure 3005a. The marked stars were selected to get good distribution in azimuth, and as being at good altitudes for observation. Polaris, which should be observed, both for a line of position and for a check on the compass, is not on the list, as its azimuth will be within about a degree of north, and its altitude will be about the same as the DR latitude.

When there is broken cloud cover, considerable time is often consumed in obtaining observations of a round of stars. As daylight increases, the stars become increasingly difficult to locate, particularly with the naked eye, and allowance must be made for the change in their altitudes. Bodies to the east or west will change altitude much more rapidly than those to the north or

Rate of change of altitude.

Figure 3005a:
Morning stars—
26 April 1969.
Civil twilight 0448.
DR Lat. 35°N.

Star	Magnitude	H.	Zn.
* Schedar	2.5	32°	041°
Deneb	1.3	69°	054°
Alpheratz	2.2	27°	073°
* Markab	2.6	33°	095°
Enif	2.5	46°	115°
* Altair	0.9	61°	156°
Nunki	2.1	28°	183°
Kaus Australis	2.0	20°	189°
Shaula	1.7	15°	199°
Sabik	2.6	33°	209°
Antares	1.2	19°	217°
* Rasalhague	2.1	60°	228°
Zuben'ubi	2.9	11°	242°
Alphecca	2.3	45°	275°
* Arcturus	0.2	25°	277°
Alkaid	1.9	32°	311°
Alioth	1.7	27°	322°
Dubhe	2.0	18°	336°
* Kochab	2.2	41°	342°

Figure 3005a:
Morning stars—
26 April 1969.
Civil twilight 0448.
DR Lat. 35°N.

south; for example, in the list, Arcturus with an azimuth of 277° at twilight will be decreasing in altitude at a rate of about 12'.2 per minute of time, while Kochab's rate is only about 3'.8. Arcturus therefore could well have moved out of the field of view of the sextant telescope, if no allowance is made for its motion. The rate of change of altitude in a minute of time may be obtained by the formula:

$$\triangle H \text{ per minute} = 15 \times \cos \text{Lat} \times \sin Z, \text{ where } Z$$
is the angle between the meridian and the body.

This formula was used in preparing the nomogram shown in Figure 3005b, which has been found to be helpful.

During morning twilight, the eastern horizon is the first to become sharply defined, and as a general rule, bodies in that direction are observed first. This procedure may be modified by the brightness of a particular body, which may make it visible in the east for some time after all other bodies are hidden from view by the approaching daylight. Conversely, it may be desirable to observe a relatively dim star to the westward as soon as the horizon is clear under it, as it may otherwise be lost to view. In general, the later a star or planet is observed during morning twilight, the more accurate will be its LOP, as the observation will then be made with the most sharply defined horizon. The inexperienced navigator must, however, guard against waiting too long, as the body may then be too faint to observe. For this reason, it is often desirable to make an observation when the limiting condition has nearly been reached, and the second one as late as possible.

No difficulty should be experienced in identifying the bodies observed during morning twilight, as the navigator usually has ample opportunity to study them before taking his sights. If any doubt does exist, its azimuth should be noted and recorded for possible use in identifying the body later.

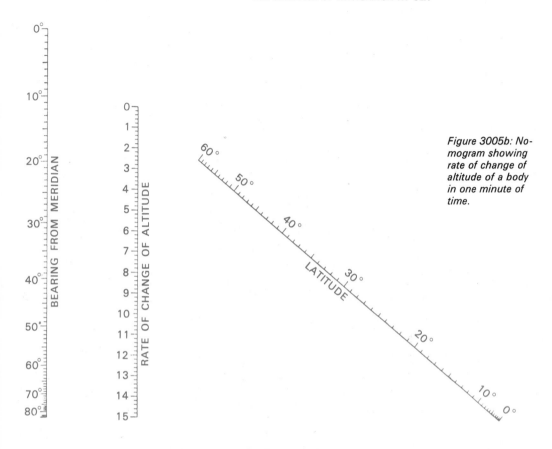

Figure 3005b: Nomogram showing rate of change of altitude of a body in one minute of time.

In checking the index error of the sextant, one should use a moderately bright star before making the observations, or the clearest part of the horizon after making the observations.

3006. The usual observations made at sea include two azimuths made for compass checks.

Daylight observations.

The sun is the body most frequently used for this purpose; the most accurate observations may be made when it is rising or setting as it is then moving comparatively slowly in azimuth, and minimal error is introduced by any tilt in the azimuth circle. Under conditions where it is very difficult to obtain accurate azimuths with an azimuth circle, it is wise to make an amplitude observation.

Azimuth observations.

If H. O. 229 is available, azimuths may be obtained down to 0° in altitude; if H. O. 214 is used, the altitude must be in excess of 5°.

When quartermasters who are capable observers are available, it is good practice to observe the sun at frequent and regular intervals; some ships make hourly observations. Even if all these sights are not reduced immediately, it does make valuable data available in the event of sudden overcast.

Altitude sights.

As stated in article 3004, Venus and the moon should be observed whenever possible in conjunction with the sun to obtain a forenoon fix.

If only one morning sun sight is to be observed it should be taken with two thoughts in mind. One is that the resulting LOP is to be advanced to noon to

Noon fix.

obtain a running fix, and the other is that the LAN observation will yield a latitude line, or an approximate latitude line in the event that the sun cannot be observed exactly at LAN. It is desirable that the two LOPs intersect at an angle of 45° or more; on the other hand, the morning sun observation should not be obtained so early that there can be. much error due to uncertainty as to the ship's speed in advancing it to noon. The two factors depend on the latitude of the observer and the sun's declination. H. O. 214 or H. O. 229 may be used to determine the rate of change of the sun's azimuth, and therefore how long before noon the observation should be made.

LAN should be observed as a matter of routine aboard all ships. It offers the most accurate celestial line of position, as the sun is not changing altitude perceptibly at LAN, and the horizon is usually sharply defined. In addition to the LAN sight, it may be desirable to obtain a sun line exactly at ZT 1200, so that it will not have to be adjusted to determine the ZT 1200 position, or it may be obtained at another convenient time. Many navigators prefer to make an observation at about ZT 1145, so that it and the morning sun line can be advanced to 1200 and the running fix at that time determined and submitted by 1200. A meridian altitude observation must, of course, be obtained at the time of transit.

The conditions governing the afternoon sun line observations are similar to those which apply to the morning sun line. A longitude line in the afternoon is useful for determining the time to be used in making evening twilight observations, and, since in mid-latitudes it generally will be taken rather late in the afternoon, it affords a good speed check for a vessel on an easterly or westerly course.

The above discussion is based upon the assumption that good weather prevails, and that the navigator can observe the sun at any time. If the sky is overcast, he does not ignore the possibility of obtaining an LOP at any time when the sun might be visible. With skillful use of the sextant shade glasses, the sun often can be observed when behind thin clouds.

If the moon can be observed during daylight, its LOP should be crossed with a sun line obtained at the same time, unless the two bodies are at nearly the same or reciprocal azimuths. Care must sometimes be taken in observing the moon that the correct limb is observed. Venus can often be seen during daylight, when it is higher in altitude than the sun, if the navigator knows its approximate altitude and azimuth, and less frequently Mars and Jupiter can be seen.

A small error, due to phase and parallax, will occur in daytime observations of Venus if the formula given in the "Explanation" section of the *Nautical Almanac* is not employed. For observations of Venus and Mars obtained between sunset and sunrise, the "additional correction," found inside the front cover of the almanac, should be used to compensate for phase and parallax.

Sun correction tables.

The *Sun Correction Tables*, on the inside front cover of the *Nautical Almanac* should be used for correcting sextant altitudes except when maximum accuracy is desired. The semi-diameter of the sun is averaged in the tables for two six month periods. Greater accuracy can be obtained by using the refraction correction, listed under "Stars and Planets," and the sun's semidiameter obtained from the bottom of the appropriate page in the almanac. To these, a parallax correction (+) 0'.1 should be added for altitudes up to 65°.

Low altitude sun sights, that is, observations of the sun in the altitude range of from 0° to 5°, have acquired a reputation for unreliability that they do not deserve. Refraction is somewhat uncertain at low altitudes; however, except under very unusual atmospheric conditions, such sights usually yield acceptable results. To illustrate: 266 observations of the sun were made at altitudes between 0° and 5°; 183 of these yielded LOPs that there within 0.5 miles of the true position, 53 lay between 0.5 and 1.0 miles, 30 were in error by more than 1.0 miles, and only two were in error by more than 2.0 miles, the greatest error being 2.2 miles. These observations were, of course, fully and carefully corrected.

Low altitude sights.

Low altitude sun sights must be corrected carefully. The fixed sextant error, the IC and the dip are applied to the sextant altitude (hs) before the refraction correction is taken from the Star and Planet tables (A_3), the semi-diameter is taken from the daily pages of the almanac, and (+) 0'.1 is used as the parallax correction. The "Additional Corrections" to the Altitude Correction Tables in the *Nautical Almanac* should also be used for all low altitude observations.

It should be noted here for some observers that the upper limb of the sun is both easier to observe and yields somewhat more accurate results at low altitudes than does the lower limb.

High altitude sun observations, at altitudes greater than 80° are generally hard to obtain accurately, due to the difficulty of establishing the vertical. However, a high altitude LAN observation may frequently be obtained with considerable accuracy.

When the sun's declination is near the ship's latitude, morning sun observations make it possible to determine longitude with precision. This, in turn, makes it possible to predict the time of LAN with accuracy.

High altitude sights.

An azimuth circle is placed on a gyro repeater on the side of the bridge on which the sun will transit, and is aligned with the north-south points of the gyro repeater card. The sextant index arm is set to the expected altitude at LAN, and the observer then steps back from the pelorus, and places himself so that the azimuth circle vanes are in line, when seen through the horizon glass of the sextant. The sun's altitude is obtained for LAN when its image is in contact with the horizon at a point directly above the vanes.

Such a high altitude LAN observation can be of considerable value, as under such conditions, all other sun lines obtained during the day will lie generally in a north-south direction.

Sea-air temperature difference correction. (article 2227). A difference between the sea surface temperature and that of the air in contact with it tends to affect the value of the dip correction. The latter is calculated for "standard conditions," and these are distorted when the air in contact with the sea is warmed or cooled by the water. The result is not serious when a number of bodies, well distributed in azimuth are observed, as it may generally be assumed that the anomaly is constant, and will apply equally to each of the bodies observed.

Sea-air temperature.

However, when only the sun is available for observation, as is usually the case in the daytime, this anomaly can affect the accuracy of the LOP. This is equally true for several bodies located in a limited sector of azimuth; however, in such a case, the use of bisectors (article 3009) will be helpful.

519

For best results sea water should be picked up in a canvas dip bucket at some point well forward in the ship; in actual practice, the intake water temperature, as obtained from the engine room, is used. This is compared with the dry bulb temperature measured at the level where the observations are made. The correction is subtractive when the air is colder than the water (i.e. the sextant altitude will be too great), and additive when the water is colder than the air (article 2227). This correction should be used only when experienced judgment indicates that it will result in improved observations.

Evening twilight observations.

3007. Evening twilight observations are similar to morning twilight observations, with the important difference to the inexperienced navigator that there is little opportunity to identify the bodies in advance of observation. Under these conditions, the approximate altitude and azimuth are particularly helpful in locating the bodies, and the azimuth of a body which has been observed for altitude, but not positively identified, should always be noted.

In the evening the stars and planets in the east are usually observed first, subject to their brightness, as that area of the sky darkens first.

Dark adapted vision.

Night observations. Star observations can be made successfully on clear nights, provided the observer's vision is *dark adapted* and if the sextant telescope and mirrors have reasonably good optical qualities. During World War II it was found that if the human eye was exposed to no light other than dull red for a considerable period of time, its night perception was considerably increased. This proved to be of great value to many navigators in the fleet submarines, which, when in enemy waters, could surface only during the hours of complete darkness. With dark adapted vision, and using a sextant fitted with a prismatic telescope having a 30 mm objective lens, and a magnification of 6×, they obtained satisfactory star fixes. The 6 × 30 telescope is acceptable for night use, but the 7 × 50 is superior, as it has about twice the light gathering power of the 6 × 30.

In making night observations, it is vital that the readout light on the sextant and the recorder's flashlight be fitted with red bulbs. Red lamp dye is available commercially, and flashlight bulbs dipped in it have proven satisfactory for night use.

Light amplification telescopes.

Light amplification or night vision telescopes developed as sniper-scopes for the Army will, when mounted on a sextant, provide a view of the horizon on a dark night.

Astigmatizing shade.

When observing bright stars or planets with a dim horizon, it is often desirable to use a pale sun shade to reduce the body's brilliance. An *astigmatizing shade* is also frequently helpful under such conditions. This is a prism which elongates the image of a star into a thin horizontal line. Astigmatizers are fitted on many sextants.

There is considerable risk of obtaining a false altitude when observing a brilliant moon, or a star or planet near the moon in azimuth, as the moonlight may give a false horizon. This risk is reduced if such observations are made from a point as low as possible in the ship, and it is also wise to have the recorder check the horizon under the moon through 7 × 50 binoculars to see if the illuminated water is actually at the horizon.

3008. The accuracy of an LOP obtained by celestial navigation is only rarely equal to that of the average LOP obtained in piloting. The reasons for this are numerous, and the major ones have been commented upon at appropriate places in this text. Ordinarily, therefore, a navigator should consider a single celestial LOP to be accurate only within about two miles in either direction. This is considering error in altitude measurement only, and might be increased by a mistake in timing, computation, or plotting. With experience and the cultivation of sound judgment in such matters, the navigator will be able to evaluate some sights as being more accurate than this, and some as probably being less accurate. Also, the accuracy of celestial observations increases with practice; a research program disclosed some years ago that the accuracy of observers in making celestial observations continued to improve after more than 2,000 observations had been made. Expert observers, such as those in the Coast and Geodetic Survey, under good conditions expect a multiple star fix to yield an accuracy within a quarter of a mile.

Accuracy of celestial lines of position and fixes.

The following discussion of the theory of error may be helpful in evaluating positioning data.

A fix or running fix in celestial navigation is determined by two or more lines of position, each of which may be in error. If two lines are crossed at an angle of 90° and each has a possible error of two miles, the situation illustrated in Figure 3008a results.

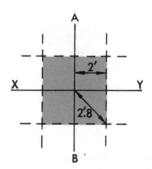

Figure 3008a: Possible error in a fix from two lines of position differing in azimuth by 90°, if each LOP has a possible error of two miles.

The navigator selects the point where LOP *A-B* intersects LOP *X-Y* as his fix, but if each line is in error by two miles, he will be at one of the corners of the square shown by the broken lines, 2.8 miles from his fix. If one of the lines is in error by two miles and the other is without error, his actual position will be at the intersection of one of the solid lines and one of the broken lines, 2.0 miles from his fix.

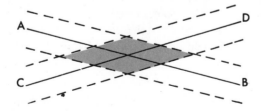

Figure 3008b: Possible error in a fix from two lines of position differing in azimuth by 30°, if each LOP has a possible error of two miles.

If two lines are crossed at an angle of 30° and each has a possible error of two miles, the situation illustrated in Figure 3008b results. The navigator selects the point where LOP *A-B* intersects LOP *C-D* as his fix, but if each line is in error by two miles, he will be at one of the corners of the parallelogram shown by the broken lines, either 2.1 or 7.7 miles from his fix. If one of the lines is in error by two miles and the other is without error, his actual position will be at the intersection of one of the solid lines and one of the broken lines, or 4.0 miles from his fix.

From the above discussion it can be seen that, when two lines of position are obtained, the navigator may place most confidence in the resulting fix when the lines intersect at angles of 90°, or nearly 90°, all other factors being equal. A 90° intersection in a *running fix* however, may not give as reliable a position as can be obtained from two lines of a *fix* which cut at a smaller angle, because of the possible error in advancing the earlier LOP for a running fix.

Whenever possible, the navigator uses at least three lines of position to obtain a fix. If these lines intersect at angles of 60° and each has a possible error of two miles, the situation illustrated in Figure 3008c results. The navigator selects the point where the three lines intersect as his fix, but if each line is subject to error of up to two miles, his actual position may be anywhere within the shaded hexagon of the figure, at a maximum distance of 2.3 miles from the plotted fix.

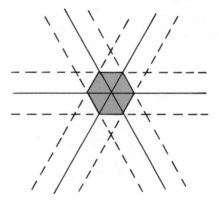

Figure 3008c: Possible error in a fix from three lines of position differing in azimuth by 120°, if each has a possible error of two miles.

The accuracy of a fix is not materially increased by plotting more than four lines of position, if the lines can be relied on to be equally accurate, and are approximately evenly distributed in azimuth. In practice, the usable stars are never perfectly located in azimuth, and five or more lines will usually yield a better idea of the most probable position, than will three. When the bodies observed all lie within 180° of azimuth of one another, *bisectors*, which are discussed below, should be employed.

In Figure 3008c the three solid lines are shown intersecting at a point. In practice, this rarely happens, and the navigator takes the center of the small figure usually formed as being his fix. The point selected is equidistant from all sides of the figure. It can be determined geometrically or by computation, but in practice the navigator estimates it by eye. The size of the figure obtained is not necessarily an indication of the accuracy of the fix.

When the navigator can select three or more bodies to be observed for a fix (as when observing stars), he can guard against a *constant* error in altitude by observing bodies at equal intervals of *azimuth*. A constant error in altitude causes all lines of position to be in error by the same amount and in the same direction, relative to the bodies being observed. When bodies are observed at equal intervals of azimuth, a constant error will either increase or decrease the size of the figure formed when the lines are plotted, but will have no effect on the center of the figure. Thus, four stars differing in azimuth by 90° should be observed, or five stars differing by 72°, etc. Theoretically, a four-star fix from bodies differing in azimuth by 90° (as N, S, E, and W) should produce only two lines of position, but in all probability a small rectangle will be the result.

The factor that has the greatest effect on a single observation is usually *random error*. The reliability of an individual line of position can be considerably improved by making several observations of the same body, and averaging the times and altitudes before solving for an LOP; this tends to average out the random errors. Alternately, if five or more observations of the same body are taken in quick succession, and its azimuth is noted by gyro, the accuracy of the individual observations may be determined by comparing the change of altitude between observation; the rate of change in altitude per second of time being equal to 0.25 × cos Latitude × sine of the angle between the body and the meridian. If the rate of change is steady for several sights one of these should be selected for reduction. This formula may be solved extremely rapidly with a slide rule.

An alternate method is to make three observations in quick succession and to solve and plot each one. If two LOPs are then in close agreement and a third differs considerably, it is usually safe to assume that the correct LOP lies midway between the two lines which are in agreement. The method is not as tedious as it may at first seem, particularly if solutions are made in parallel columns, as usually the only difference in the solutions are in minutes and seconds of time, and the resulting differences in GHA and $a\lambda$. Ordinarily, multiple observations are limited to sun lines, as the several bodies observed for a twilight fix serve as a check on each other.

In fixing or estimating the position of a ship, the navigator should not ignore the DR or EP, as these positions are based on other navigational information which may be more or less accurate than a given LOP. A DR or EP should be considered a *circle* with radius equal to the navigator's estimate of its accuracy, if knowledge of course and speed are considered to be equally good. If the navigator believes that one of these is known more accurately than the other, the DR or EP should be considered a small *ellipse*, with minor axis extending in the direction indicated by the more accurately known quantity and major axis extending in the direction indicated by the less accurately known quantity.

From the above, it can be seen that the interpretation of celestial lines of position can be a complex subject—one which calls for sound judgment on the part of an experienced navigator.

3009. When a number of bodies, with azimuths all lying within a 180° sector of arc, are observed, a constant error may yield misleading results, if the fix is assumed to lie within the polygon formed by the LOPs. Such constant errors are frequently caused by unusual terrestrial refraction, which causes the value of the dip, as obtained from the *Nautical Almanac,* to be considerably in error. This may lead to the fix lying outside the polygon, resulting in an *exterior fix,* rather than the usual interior one. Where multiple LOPs well distributed in azimuth are obtained, this problem does not arise, as in this case the error may

LOP bisectors.

523

be assumed to affect all LOPs about equally.

Where three or more observations are made of bodies with azimuths within 180° of each other, it is wise to use *LOP bisectors* to determine the fix. Each angle formed by a pair of position lines is bisected, the bisector being drawn in the direction of *the mean of the azimuths* of the two bodies.

For example, assume that due to cloud cover, it was possible to observe only three stars, the respective azimuths being as follows: star No. 1. 224°, No. 2. 000°, and No. 3. 256°. The resulting LOPs are plotted in Figure 3009.

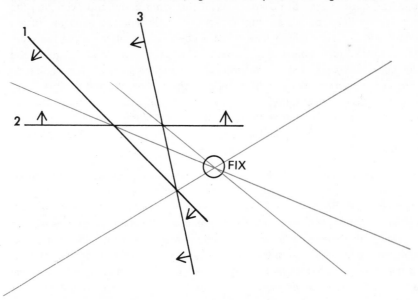

Figure 3009: The use of bisectors, showing the exterior fix (LOPs in black, bisectors in blue).

LOPs 1 and 2 will be bisected in the direction 292°—112°:

$$\frac{(224° + 000°)}{2} = 112°$$

LOPs 1 and 3 will be bisected in the direction 240°—060°:

$$\frac{(224° + 256°)}{2} = 240°$$

and LOPs 2 and 3 will be bisected in the direction 308°—128°. In Figure 3009 these bisectors are drawn in as light lines.

The most probable position for the fix lies at the center of the small triangle formed by the three bisectors, rather than in the triangle formed by the three LOPs.

Errors introduced in plotting by long intercepts.

3010. A small error in positioning may arise when working from an assumed position and the intercepts are long. This is caused by plotting the intercept and the LOP on the chart as rhumb lines, rather than as arcs of great and small circles, respectively. The errors tend to increase with altitude, being roughly proportional to the tangent of the altitude, and with the distance of the AP from the true position, being approximately proportional to the square of the difference between the two positions. The resulting error is greatest at the equator, and decreases with an increase in latitude.

A careful investigation made some years ago in Great Britain showed that for an observer located at the equator when the difference between the true and assumed positions is 30' in both latitude and longitude, and the altitude of the body observed was 75°, the maximum error will not exceed 1.0 mile; this maximum error will not exceed 0.7 miles at latitude 60°, and the probable error would be about half this amount. For an altitude of 60° at the equator the error will not exceed 0.5 miles. Being roughly proportional to the square of the difference between the true and assumed positions, if the true position is within 20' of latitude and longitude of the AP, the errors would be less than half those cited.

It is obvious that these errors are of no concern in the ordinary course of navigation. They are cited only to show that under special conditions, when the utmost accuracy is required, a reduction from the EP should be employed. Five place log tables, interpolated, will, under most conditions, yield an accuracy to 0'.1.

3011. The navigator customarily submits position reports to the commanding officer at least three times daily. In the U. S. Navy this is done at ZT 0800, *Position reports.*

```
SHIP'S POSITION
NAVSHIPS-1111 (REV. 5-62)

TO:
COMMANDING OFFICER, USS  GLENNON (DD 840)

AT (Time of day)                    DATE
   ZT 1200                             26 April 1969
LATITUDE              LONGITUDE              DETERMINED AT
34° 12'. 0 N         60° 07'. 3W           1200
BY (Indicate by check in box)
[X] CELESTIAL   [ ] D. R.   [ ] LORAN   [ ] RADAR   [ ] VISUAL
SET          DRIFT         DISTANCE MADE GOOD SINCE (time) (mi.)
130°         1.2 k.         70.6 mi. since 0800
DISTANCE TO                    MILES        ETA
Ambrose Channel L.T.          732.5       280600
TRUE HDG.   ERROR                                  VARIATION
303°              GYRO 0.°5     GYRO °           20.°6W
MAGNETIC COMPASS HEADING (Check one)
[ ] STD   [X] STEER-   [ ] REMOTE              320 °
              ING           IND     [ ] OTHER
DEVIATION    1104 TABLE DEVIATION    DG: (Indicate by check in box)
3.6E         3.8E                    [ ] ON   [X] OFF
REMARKS


RESPECTFULLY SUBMITTED (navigator)

CC:
```

Figure 3011:
A position report.

ZT 1200, and ZT 2000, using the form shown in Figure 3011. The information required is the name of the ship; the zone time and date of the report; the latitude and longitude, and the time the position was last determined; the method used (where a combination of methods are used it is customary to indicate the method having the predominant effect upon the accuracy of the position); the set and drift since the last well-determined position; distance made good since the last report (indicate time of last report, and distance in miles); the destination, its distance in miles, and the ETA (use date/time as explained in article 2311); the true heading; the error of the master gyro (of both master gyros if two are installed); the variation; the magnetic compass heading, with an indication of which compass is in use; the deviation as most recently determined; the deviation according to the current NavShips 1104; whether or not degaussing is energized; and any appropriate remarks, such as the clocks having been advanced or retarded since the last report.

The use of this form is generally self-explanatory. The latitude and longitude given are always for the time of the report, while the time at which the last well-determined position was obtained is given in the "determined at" block. Some commanding officers prefer that the time given in connection with the distance made good be the preceding 1200 rather than the time of the last report, since this gives a ready indication of the miles steamed during the elapsed portion of the "navigational day."

The distance made good and distance to go are ordinarily obtained by measurement on the chart, with dividers, if the distance is not too great, or they can be computed, as explained in Chapter 5.

Gyro and magnetic compass errors are based upon the most recent accurate azimuth observation. Variation is obtained from the pilot chart or sailing chart.

Summary.   **3012.** In this chapter the routine celestial navigation work of the navigator at sea has been listed. While typical, it is not all inclusive, and all of the work done by the navigator and his assistants has not been described.

Only the mechanics of the practice of navigation can be given in a book, and the student who has mastered this book has mastered *only* the mechanics. The efficiency, accuracy, and judgment of a good professional navigator come only with experience.

CHAPTER 31

Omega Navigation System

3101. The Omega navigation system, when fully implemented, will provide a world-wide, all-weather positioning system for ships, aircraft, and submarines, both surfaced and submerged, with a nominal accuracy of one mile in day time, and two miles at night. It has been developed by the U. S. Navy to meet the general navigational requirements of all branches of the service. The system will also have extensive application in civilian craft, both commercial and private.

Introduction.

Omega is a very low frequency (VLF) hyperbolic system, using phase difference measurements of continuous wave (CW) radio signals. These VLF signals can be transmitted over great distances; only six transmitting stations will make the system available in all parts of the globe, with two additional stations for redundancy and coverage during repair of an inoperative station.

3102. Omega differs from most other hyperbolic systems, such as Loran A, in that it uses a phase-difference technique, rather than a time-difference principle. The basic Omega measurement is the phase-difference of a 10.2 kHz signal transmitted from two stations. This phase-difference measurement yields a hyperbolic line of position (article 1710). A fix may be determined by using additional LOPs obtained from additional phase-difference measurements.

The Omega system.

The wavelength of the 10.2 kHz signal is approximately 16 miles; phase readings repeat twice with the wavelength, or every eight miles (Figure 3102a).

These eight-mile intervals between zero phase readings are called *lanes*. The phase-difference establishes a line of position within one of these lanes; the lanes are numbered on the Oceanographic Office Omega charts. Counters, on the phase indicators on the ship's receiver, are set at the beginning of a voyage, and subsequently count the numbers of lanes traversed. In the more sophisticated receivers provisions are made for resolving lane ambiguities and deriving a fix without prior knowledge of position (article 3103).

As the hyperbolic lines represent the locus of points at which the difference in the distances from the transmitting stations are equal, and as these distances are measured in units of time, representing distances traveled by the radio waves, the relative times of the transmission of signals from all Omega stations is determined with the utmost precision. Each station transmits, in turn, a signal for approximately one second every ten seconds; all transmissions, continuous wave at 10.2 kHz, are phase-locked to a common time standard.

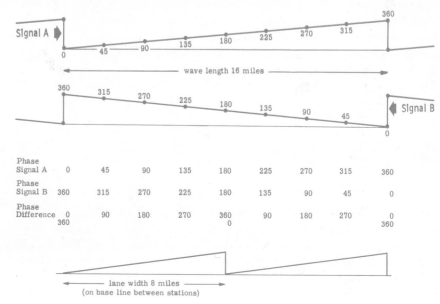

Phase Signal A	0	45	90	135	180	225	270	315	360
Phase Signal B	360	315	270	225	180	135	90	45	0
Phase Difference	0 360	90	180	270	360 0	90	180	270	0 360

Figure 3102a: 10.2 kHz phase difference measurement.

The older navigation systems use pulses emitted in the required time relationship, as in Loran, or continuous harmonically related carrier frequencies, in which the phase relationship conveys the time information, as in Decca. With a pulse system, all stations in a network can transmit on the same radio frequency at different times. However, when continuous carriers are employed, the frequencies used by the various stations must differ, so that they can be identified, while retaining a common basis in time. This leads to the requirement for the harmonic relationship.

Omega to some extent combines both methods. The measurements are made of relative phase of bursts of a steady carrier transmitted at the same radio frequency at different times. The use of a single frequency is advantageous, since phase shifts within the receiver are of no concern, as they remain the same for all signals. Aside from the very low frequency employed, the chief

Figure 3102b: Omega signal format.

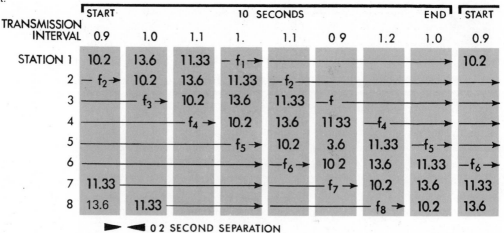

TRANSMISSION INTERVAL	START 0.9	1.0	1.1	1.	1.1	0 9	1.2	END 1.0	START 0.9
STATION 1	10.2	13.6	11.33	— f_1 →				→	10.2
2	— f_2 →	10.2	13.6	11.33	— f_2 —			→	→
3		— f_3 →	10.2	13.6	11.33	—f		→	→
4			— f_4 →	10.2	13.6	11 33	—f_4 —	→	→
5				— f_5 →	10.2	3.6	11.33	—f_5 →	→
6					—f_6 →	10 2	13.6	11.33	—f_6 →
7	11.33			→		— f_7 →	10.2	13.6	11.33
8	13.6	11.33		→			f_8 →	10.2	13.6

10 SECONDS

► ◄ 0 2 SECOND SEPARATION

distinction between Omega and the older systems is the time-sharing of con-tinuous carrier bursts of relative phase. Each Omega station transmits in a fixed sequence pattern, so only one signal is transmitted at a time. Eight stations can share a ten-second period, and the receiver can identify each station by its place in the sequence as well as by the exact time duration of its signal (Figure 3102b).

In addition, Omega differs from other hyperbolic navigation systems in that any two stations from which signals can be received may be paired to furnish a line of position. The navigator may therefore select stations whose signals will yield lines of position crossing nearly at right angles. This geometrical excellence, coupled with the range of choices available to the navigator, results in an accuracy in positioning that varies little with geographical location.

In the Omega system, the transmitting stations are located approximately 6,000 miles from one another. With a network of eight stations, at least four stations would be available to the navigator at any point on earth, thus yielding a mini-mum of six possible LOPs.

3103. As discussed above, the measurement of the difference in phase of two received signals, which were synchronized in time at the transmitting station, can produce a line of position which can be positively identified within a band or lane one-half the wavelength in width (Figure 3103a). It is therefore man-datory to know in which lane the vessel is located. The Omega receiver provides a counter, or printout on a graph, to furnish the navigator with data on the number of lanes which have been crossed since the start of the counter. Lane identification for surface ships therefore presents no serious problem.

Lane identification.

Any ambiguity in lane identification can be resolved by repeating the trans-mission from two stations on a second Omega frequency, 13.6 kHz. This fre-quency has a wavelength which is exactly one-third shorter than that of the basic frequency, 10.2 kHz. The phase synchronization is adjusted so that one contour of the higher frequency coincides with one contour of the lower fre-

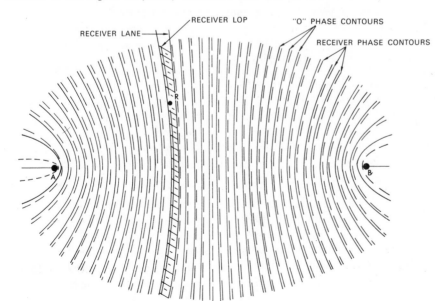

RECEIVER LOP
RECEIVER LANE
"O" PHASE CONTOURS
RECEIVER PHASE CONTOURS

Figure 3103a: Omega lane pattern.

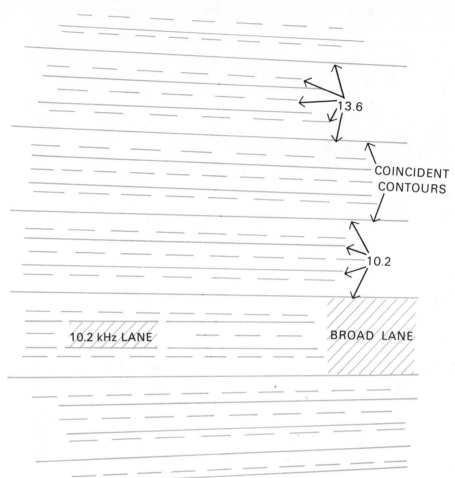

13.6

COINCIDENT
CONTOURS

10.2

10.2 kHz LANE

BROAD LANE

Figure 3103b:
Principles of lane
resolution.

quency. Every *fourth* 13.6 kHz contour will now coincide with every *third* 10.2 kHz contour, thus establishing a pattern of broad lanes, each extending over three lanes of the basic 10.2 kHz pattern, or over a width of twenty-four miles. This is illustrated in Figure 3103b.

It can thus be determined from the difference of the two phase indications in which of the three 10.2 kHz lanes forming the broad lane the observer is located. If the difference is less than one-third hertz, he is in the first lane; if between one and two-thirds, he is in the middle lane; and if between two-thirds and one hertz, he is in the third lane. A third set of transmissions at 11.33 kHz would similarly establish a lane seventy-two miles in width, within which the observer could locate himself.

Station choice.

3104. As in any navigation system in which lines of position are used to determine position, it is desirable to obtain a distribution in azimuth of these lines so that they cross each other at as nearly 90° as possible. If three lines of position are employed, the angle formed by the intersection of each pair should ideally be 60°, etc. Figure 3104a shows the distances and bearings of eight possible Omega stations from a location near Hawaii; each station is numbered. Figure 3104b shows the distribution of fifteen possible lines of position ob-

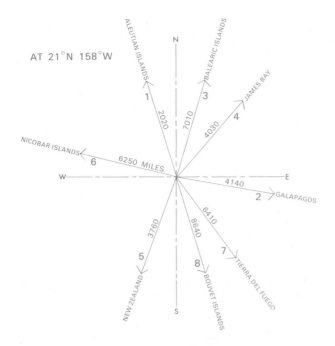

AT 21°N 158°W

Figure 3104a:
Directions and
distances of eight
stations from a
point near Hawaii.

tained at this location, using six of these stations. Stations numbers 3 and 8
are excluded, as probably too distant to provide satisfactory signal strength.
Each line of position is labeled with the numbers of the two stations from
which it is derived; for the sake of clarity, the lines of position are shown
radiating from the fix, rather than drawn through it, in the conventional manner.

It is obvious that a sufficient choice of lines of position to yield a good fix will
be available anywhere on the surface of the globe, as a line of position can be
obtained from *any* two stations located within about 6,500 miles of the observer. The transmission of signals from all stations is synchronized; and is
therefore not limited to the use of coupled pairs, as in Loran.

AT 21°N 158°W

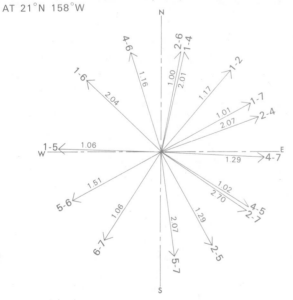

Figure 3104b: Di-
rections and relative
separation of posi-
tion lines from six
stations at a point
near Hawaii.

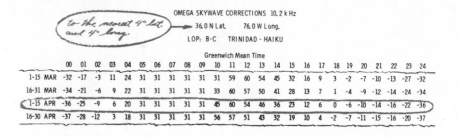

to the nearest 4° lat. and 4° long.

OMEGA SKYWAVE CORRECTIONS 10.2 k Hz

36.0 N Lat.   76.0 W Long.

LOP: B-C   TRINIDAD - HAIKU

	00	01	02	03	04	05	06	07	08	09	10	11	12	13	14	15	16	17	18	19	20	21	22	23	24
1-15 MAR	-32	-17	-3	11	24	31	31	31	31	31	31	59	60	54	45	32	16	9	3	-2	-7	-10	-13	-27	-32
16-31 MAR	-34	-21	-6	9	22	31	31	31	31	31	33	60	57	50	41	28	13	7	1	-4	-9	-12	-14	-24	-34
1-15 APR	-36	-25	-9	6	20	31	31	31	31	31	45	60	54	46	36	23	12	6	0	-6	-10	-14	-16	-22	-36
16-30 APR	-37	-28	-12	3	18	31	31	31	31	31	56	57	51	43	32	19	10	4	-2	-7	-11	-15	-16	-20	-37

Greenwich Mean Time

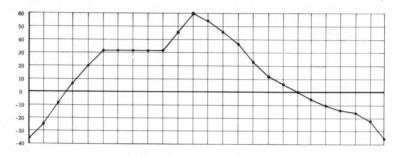

Figure 3105: Omega skywave corrections 10.2 kHz.

Correction of Omega signals.

3105. The very low frequency Omega signals radiate from the transmitting stations to the receiver along the normal channel between the earth's surface and the ionosphere. As the ionosphere changes its height from day to night, the path of wave travel varies, and the apparent signal speed also varies from day to night. The Omega charts are constructed using standard daytime phase velocity of propagation. Correction must be made for variations from this standard velocity. Computations for these diurnal corrections are published as Omega propagation correction tables by the Oceanographic Office. A sample extract is shown in Figure 3105; a graph constructed from this table is shown drawn in. Such graphing is of convenience to the navigator when remaining in the same general vicinity for some time.

This is the only correction which needs to be applied to the receiver display in order to obtain valid readings.

Receivers.

3106. In using Omega, a receiver on board the vessel must be capable of determining the phase of the Omega signals in the presence of the usual ambient noise and interference. The format of the signal permits many different modes of receiver operation ranging from an oscilloscope display of the signal timing, with manual alignment of the multiplexing function, to computer-type receivers capable of performing all functions, and presenting position in the form of geographical coordinates without external aid.

To determine position the operator and receiver must be able to:

Recognize the total transmitted pattern to identify the transmission of a given set of stations,

Isolate the signal components,

Determine the relative phases of the isolated signal components with accuracy,

Use the phase reading to determine a line of position or a fix.

Figure 3106a: AN/ SRN-12 Omega shipboard naviga- tion receiver.

To obtain a line of position when the approximate DR position is known. it is only necessary to read the receiver display, note the Greenwich Mean Time, and note these data on the work sheet. The appropriate correction table for the general area is then entered, and the diurnal correction for the GMT and date are extracted, and noted on the work sheet. This correction is added to the reading taken from the receiver display; the sum provides the required datum for plotting the line of position on the Omega chart. A fix can be ob- tained in two or three minutes, and it is a simple matter for the quartermaster of the watch to obtain an Omega position every hour.

Figure 3106a shows a typical Omega receiver. In this particular unit the AN/SRN-12, the receiver, controls and displays are contained in the bottom drawer which slides out to permit access for maintenance. Built-in test cir-

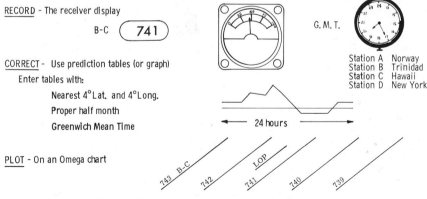

RECORD - The receiver display

       B-C (741)

G. M. T.

Station A Norway
Station B Trinidad
Station C Hawaii
Station D New York

CORRECT - Use prediction tables (or graph)
  Enter tables with:
      Nearest 4° Lat. and 4° Long.
      Proper half month
      Greenwich Mean Time

◀——— 24 hours ———▶

PLOT - On an Omega chart

Figure 3106b: Omega operation.

743 B-C   742   LOP 741   740   739

REPEAT - Obtain second line of position and plot for "fix".

OMEGA WORK SHEET				
Greenwich Mean Time			Date: 12 Apr	Time: 1925
Receiver	B-D	A-D	A-C	B-C 741.49
Correction				− .08
Line of Position				741.41

cuitry is included. Graphic recorders that provide a visual historical record of the lines of position, and an oscilloscope to aid in synchronization and trouble shooting are contained in the upper drawer. Should the recorders and oscilloscope not be desired, the receiver only (the lower drawer) is a complete operating unit. Figure 3106b is a schematic illustrating the simplicity of operation. The lane count of a pair of stations, B and C, is read from the counter, the phase-difference within the lane is read from the dial, and the Greenwich time is noted. The appropriate correction is then taken from the tables or the graph that has been prepared, and finally the line of position is plotted on the Omega chart. This process would be repeated on other pairings of stations to obtain a fix.

Differential Omega.   **3107.** For a given area, accuracy can be improved by using differential Omega, a technique in which two or more receivers are compared and the separation distance of the receivers is determined by the difference in their reading. If one is located at a known position ashore and its readout is broadcast or telemetered to vehicles operating in the vicinity, and compared to the receiver on the vessel, the long distance propagation error can be eliminated.

Advantages and disadvantages.   **3108.** The advantages and disadvantages of Omega are in general very similar to those listed for Loran in Chapter 18. However, when completely implemented, Omega will be a world wide system, and accuracy is not closely related to the distance from the transmitting system.

The navigator must always bear in mind that any electronic navigational method or system is subject to sudden failure due to any of a number of possible causes and he should not depend entirely on one system as a sole method of navigation. However, the Omega System provides considerable redundancy in that, in an eight station system, one has available at least four stations, and only three are required to produce a fix.

Summary.   **3109.** Omega, when the system is fully established, promises to yield a positioning accuracy of acceptable quality for ships, aircraft, and submarines on a world-wide basis.

From the user's point of view, its simplicity of operation, its accuracy, and its global coverage make it a most desirable adjunct to the navigator's tools.

CHAPTER 32

Loran-C and D

3201. Loran-C is a pulsed, hyperbolic long-range navigational aid system (Chapter 17), similar in operational concepts to Loran-A (Chapter 18). It operates in the internationally allocated frequency spectrum of 90 to 110 kHz, the long range navigation frequency spectrum as set up by International Radio Regulatory Considerations of the Geneva (1959) Radio Regulations, and is centered on a carrier frequency of 100 kHz. *Loran-C.*

The need for an accurate long-range navigation system was recognized during World War II, after the development of Loran-A. Between 1952 and 1956 extensive tests were conducted on this system, and the first operational chain was established along the East Coast of the United States in 1957. Since then Loran-C coverage has been greatly expanded, with the area of coverage in mid-1967 shown in Figure 3201. *Figure 3201: Loran-C coverage.*

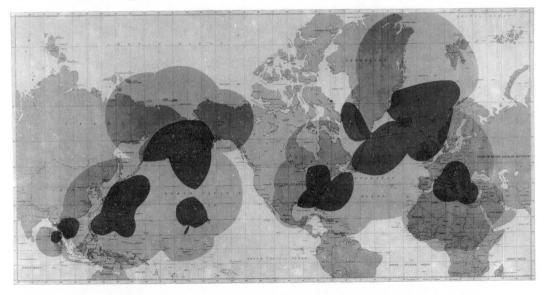

3202. Loran-C is similar to Loran-A, in that it is a pulsed, hyperbolic system of radio navigation available to ships and aircraft by day or night, in all weather conditions, over land and sea. In Loran-A a single RF pulse is transmitted in each repetition interval. In Loran-C a multipulse transmission is used. Each station radiates eight pulses spaced 1,000 microseconds apart. Additionally the master station transmits a ninth pulse principally for identification. Loran-C can *Characteristics.*

supply position information to a higher degree of accuracy and at greater distances than can be obtained with Loran-A.

In both Loran-A and Loran-C the time-difference reading is accomplished by comparing the arrival time of signals from two stations. In addition, Loran-C employs a phase comparison technique.

An approximate position is obtained by the difference in arrival time of the pulsed signals and this is refined by a comparison of the phase of the signal within the pulse. The phase comparison is accomplished automatically within the receiver and does not involve a separate operation by the navigator.

Due to its lower frequency, 100 kHz versus 2 MHz, as compared to Loran-A and its greater base line distance—500 to 700 miles, as compared to 100 to 200 miles—Loran-C is able to provide reasonably accurate information up to 1,200 miles by means of ground waves and over 3,000 miles with sky waves.

Basic principles. **3203.** In a Loran-C network there are three or more stations transmitting pulses which are radiated in all directions. One of these stations is designated as the "master" station, which sends out the master signal, and the remainder are "slave" stations. In the present Loran systems the signals are not sent simultaneously and the slave station signal is delayed by a controlled amount. Therefore the master station pulse is always received first and the time-differences increase from a minimum at the slave station to a maximum at the master station. When the master pulse is received by the "slave" stations the transmitters at these stations are actuated and, after the appropriate delay, they in turn transmit similar groups of pulses, accurately synchronized with the received signals. The constant time-difference between the reception aboard ship of the master and slave pulses establishes the Loran LOP.

The time-difference remains constant along a hyperbolic line and a series of lines of constant time-difference are computed for each pair of stations and the data made available in the form of charts and tables. When the navigational position of a vessel is desired the time-difference of a pair of stations is determined from the Loran receiver, and, by consulting the charts and/or tables, interpolating where necessary, the LOPS can be plotted corresponding to the measured values.

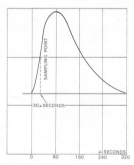

Figure 3203a:
Loran-C
pulse shape.

When a pulse is transmitted the amplitude starts at zero, rises to a maximum and recedes back to zero. This pulse shape can be varied. In Loran-C there is a fast build-up of amplitude to the peak, and the leading edge of the pulse is used for timing signals. Figure 3203a illustrates a theoretical pulse shape and the sampling point which can be determined by the electronics of the receiver.

The purpose of this sampling point being on the leading edge of the pulse is to differentiate between sky and ground waves. The ground wave path is always shorter than the reflected path from the ionosphere, and will be received first. The sky wave delay is so short, between 25 and 55 microseconds, that it is necessary to use the leading edge of the pulse to assure that the ground wave is received before being contaminated by the effects of the sky wave. The ability to use ground waves without contamination from the sky wave permits use of visual techniques in time-difference measurements, and permits the use of long base lines with high accuracy synchronization between master and slave stations.

Within each of the multipulse groups from the master and slave stations, the phase of the RF carrier is changed with respect to the pulse envelope in a systematic manner from pulse-to-pulse. The phase of each pulse in an eight or nine-pulse group is changed in accordance with a prescribed code so that it is either in phase (+) or 180° out of phase (−) with a stable 100 kHz reference signal. The phase code used at a master station is different from the phase code used at a slave, but all slave stations use the same code.

The use of phase-coded pulses by the system provides a measure of protection against interference from outside sources, and also reduces contamination of the ground wave of pulses transmitted subsequent to sky waves from preceding pulses; i.e., the sky wave of the first pulse arriving at the same time as the ground wave of the second pulse. Contamination by preceding sky waves without phase coding would nullify the effect of sampling only the ground wave, thereby degrading the inherent accuracy of the system. The use of phase coding also provides the receiver with necessary logical information for automatic search for the master and slave signals. Automatic search can be utilized for convenience or when the signal-to-noise ratio of the received signals precludes visual identification.

A large percentage of the Loran-C rates are compatible with the Loran-A system rates and, with proper modification of the Loran-A receiver to permit reception of the 100 kHz signal, envelope matching of these signals is possible. Since RF cycle matching is not incorporated in Loran-A receivers, a "fine" time-difference measurement is not possible with the Loran-A receiver and, consequently, the accuracy is less than when the 100 kHz signal is received on a standard Loran-C receiver.

Use of multipulses for Loran-C makes possible the sharing of the same RF channel by all stations in the system. Identification of particular groups of stations must be provided by some means other than channel selection. Accordingly, provision has been made in Loran-C equipment for 48 different pulse recurrence intervals or rates. The 48 rates are divided into six basic rates, each subdivided into eight specific rates. The *Basic Pulse Recurrence Rates* are shown in Figure 3203b, while the specific pulse recurrence rates are shown in Figure 3203c.

Basic pulse recurrence rates.

The combination of numbers and letters in the designation of a Loran-C line indicates the basic pulse recurrence rate, the specific pulse recurrence rate, station type designator of a particular station pair, and the time-difference in microseconds found on charts, tables, and indicators.

537

Figure 3203b:
Basic pulse
recurrence rates
(Loran-C frequency
100 kHz).

H	————————————————————	$33\frac{1}{3}$ pulses per second
L	————————————————————	25 pulses per second
S	————————————————————	20 pulses per second
SH	————————————————————	$16\frac{2}{3}$ pulses per second
SL	————————————————————	$12\frac{1}{2}$ pulses per second
SS	————————————————————	10 pulses per second

Figure 3203c:
Specific pulse
recurrence rates.

SPECIFIC PRR	BASIC PRR					
	SS	SL	SH	S	L	H
0	100,000	80,000	60,000	50,000	40,000	30,000
1	99,900*	79,900*	59,900*	49,900	39,900	29,900
2	99,800	79,800	59,800	49,800	39,800	29,800
3	99,700*	79,700*	59,700*	49,700	39,700	29,700
4	99,600	79,600	59,600	49,600	39,600	29,600
5	99,500*	79,500*	59,500*	49,500	39,500	29,500
6	99,400	79,400	59,400	49,400	39,400	29,400
7	99,300*	79,300*	59,300*	49,300	39,300	29,300

* Not compatible for reception on Loran-A receivers converted for radio frequency only.

Specific Pulse Recurrence Rates assigned for identification (following H, L, S, SH, SL, or SS) : 0, 1, 2, 3, 4, 5, 6, 7.

Station Type Designators (not station letter designators) and Transmission Sequence : M—Master, X—Slave, Y—Slave.

For example, the complete legend SO-X-13300 denotes the following : basic pulse recurrence rate, 20 pulses per second; specific pulse recurrence rate, 0; station type designator, slave X; and time-difference reading, 13,300 ms.

Station location.

3204. A Loran-C network is composed of one master station and two or more slave stations. The transmitting stations may be arranged in triads (Figure 3204a) stars, (Figure 3204b) or squares to provide optimum geometric ac-

Figure 3204a:
Loran-C triad
configuration.

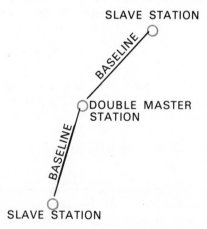

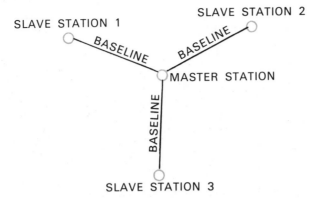

SLAVE STATION 2

SLAVE STATION 1

BASELINE   BASELINE

MASTER STATION

BASELINE

SLAVE STATION 3

Figure 3204b:
Loran-C star chain.

curacy for position fixing in the desired coverage area. Stations are so located that signals from two or more pairs of stations may be received in the coverage area.

The accuracy of this system depends upon the transmitting stations keeping their signals properly timed or synchronized. Since each slave station transmits a series of eight pulses and the master station nine pulses, a built-in master station identification and warning system exists. In case of loss of synchronization the ninth pulse from the master station blinks back and forth thus warning the operator of a receiver that the signal is not valid.

The inherent accuracy capability of this system makes it extremely useful for additional purposes, besides precise electronic navigation. Some of these uses are:

It can serve as a long-range time distribution system with an accuracy in the order of one microsecond.

It permits microsecond-order relative time standardization between widely separated receiving locations.

It is useful for electromagnetic wave propagation studies.

Since these services can be performed in conjunction with, and without affecting, navigational accuracy, the precise locations of the transmitting stations are classified, and normally are only available to military units and defense contractors, having a requirement for this information. Utilization of this time standard, with knowledge of the exact location of the transmitting stations, allows up-dating of SINS (Chapter 36).

3205. Ground wave coverage may be considered to be a function of propagation strength, and the strength of signal to noise ratio. During periods of favorable atmospheric conditions ground wave range approximates 2,000 miles. However, during periods of high noise and interference, this range may decrease to less than 1,000 miles. As a general rule, at peak pulse powers of 300 KW, the ground wave range for reliable signals may be taken as 1,200 miles. It is this favorable power output plus the low frequency of the system that allows reception by submerged vessels.

Loran-C ground and sky wave ranges.

First-hop sky waves (article 1703) extend out to about 2,300 miles, and second-hop sky wave signals have been picked up and used at a range of 3,400 miles from the transmitting stations.

539

Accuracy.

3206. The accuracy of Loran-C is dependent upon atmospheric conditions, noise and interference. Consequently ground wave accuracy is on the order of 0.1 per cent of the distance traveled, and sky wave accuracy is between 3 and 5 nautical miles.

It is the phase comparison and the longer baseline between stations which give Loran-C its greatly increased coverage and accuracy compared with the earlier hyperbolic navigational systems.

Receivers.

3207. Loran-C receivers are specifically designed for this particular system, and must be capable of accepting a carrier frequency of 100 kHz, with a band width of approximately 25 kHz. They are fitted with manual controls for selecting the proper recurrence rate; the remainder of the operations, including synchronization, may be accomplished manually or by automatic means. Phase measurement is automatically performed and once the receiver has been synchronized on a master and slave signal, the arrival time-difference is directly and continuously displayed as the receiver moves in the service area of the stations. The time-difference is then translated into geographic coordinates by plotting on charts, by the use of tables (H. O. Pub. No. 221 series), or by a computer.

Figure 3208: Section of Loran-C chart VLC30-22 showing sky wave corrections.

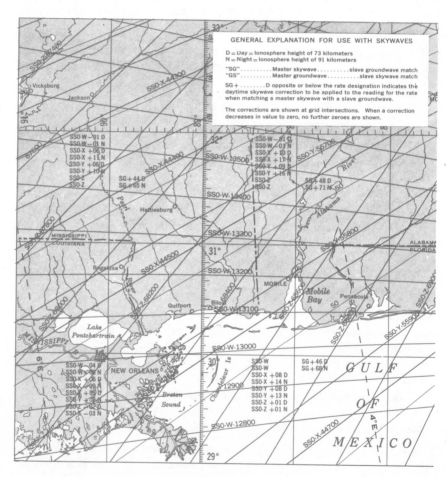

3208. When using a receiver specifically designed for Loran-C, it is not neces- *Charting Loran-C.*
sary to advance or retard Loran-C lines of position because all readings are
taken simultaneously. A single observation provides readings which establish
lines of position for all of the pairs within the particular network being used.
Normally these lines will not coincide with the lines printed on the charts and
interpolation, similar to that used with Loran-A, will be required. Loran-C
readings obtained by a modified Loran-A receiver will need to be advanced or
retarded.

When maximum accuracy is required, the appropriate Loran-C tables should
be used. From these tables the latitude and longitude of two points are obtained. These points are computed close enough so that a straight line drawn
between them gives an acceptable line of position. Sky wave corrections are
printed at numerous grid intersections on the chart (Figure 3208). Corrections
are given for both daytime and night time operations and also for matching
ground waves with sky waves during both of these periods. The corrections
are applied directly to the reading of the Loran-C receiver after necessary
interpolation.

3209. The extremely high order of stability in the Loran-C system has gener- *Timing.*
ated considerable interest in its use for time-measurement. The National Bureau
of Standards and the U. S. Naval Observatory have indicated that emissions
from the Loran-system provide the capability for synchronizing and setting
clocks to an accuracy of better than one microsecond in the areas covered by
ground waves. Such timing information is approximately 1,000 times better
than service available by most other means.

3210. To obtain high position accuracy over long transmission paths, receivers *Operation of*
must be designed specifically for Loran-C system use. With the proper equip- *Loran-C receivers.*
ment, the user is capable of obtaining the maximum amount of information
available from the transmitted Loran-C signals. The procedure for obtaining
this information follows:

> The receiver is designed to accept a carrier frequency of 100 kHz with a
> band width commensurate with requirements for pulse type reception
> (approximately 25 kHz).
>
> The receiver operator selects the pulse recurrence rate of the Loran-C
> chain to be observed. This selection aligns timing within the receiver to
> the timing of the signals to be observed. When the received signals are
> of sufficient amplitude to be observed on an oscilloscope swept at the
> rate of transmission, the received signals appear stationary. Signals on
> rates other than that selected at the receiver drift through the stationary
> signals.
>
> After selecting the proper recurrence rate, the operator then syn-
> chronizes the receiver with the master signals. Synchronization can be
> accomplished in either of two ways on most Loran-C receivers. In the
> first method, the operator utilizes the ninth pulse of the master station
> for visual identification of the time sequence of transmission. In the
> second method, the automatic search feature of the receiver is used.
> Automatic search is made possible through the use of the phase-coded
> pulses and logic circuits in the receiver. In either of the two methods, the

sampling gates are aligned in time with the receiver master pulses allowing the receiver to commence automatic tracking of these signals.

Synchronization of the receiver on slave signals is then accomplished by visual or automatic means.

When the receiver has synchronized on a master and a slave signal, the arrival time-difference is directly and continuously displayed as the receiver moves in the service area. These time-difference readings are then translated into geographic coordinates by the use of computers, charts, or tables.

Automatic alarms have been incorporated in most receivers to inform the operator when the receiver is tracking on a combined ground wave-sky wave signal. Alarms also inform the operator when the receiver has lost a particular signal either through improper sampling or when a transmitting station is off-air.

Loran-C charts are prepared and sold by the U. S. Naval Oceanographic Office, Washington, D. C. The charts are standard projections and show the chain rate identification, isogonic lines, and the first-hop sky wave corrections for day and night. The ionosphere heights for day and night corrections are assumed to be 73 and 91 kilometers, respectively. The hyperbolic lines of position, the main feature of the charts, are spaced approximately 10 to 50 microseconds apart depending on the local geometric accuracy potential of the area. Scale of the VLC-30 series is 1 : 2,188,800.

Loran-C was selected, in 1974, as the government-provided radio navigation system for the coastal/confluence zone of the U.S. This zone is defined as extending from the harbor entrances to an outer boundary of 50 nautical miles offshore, or to the edge of the continental shelf, whichever is greater. Loran-A chains will be phased out on a scheduled basis.

Loran-D.

3211. Some years ago, the need developed for a low frequency hyperbolic navigation system which would be semi-mobile. Loran-D, a pulsed-type system, was developed to fill this need. It is designed to be readily transportable, so that new lines of position can be furnished in a new area as the need develops, and to minimize down time to correct equipment failures.

Like Loran-C, Loran-D operates in the low-frequency band, in the range 90–110 kHz, and its signal characteristics are very similar to those of Loran-C. Three or four transmitting stations operate together on a time-shared basis to provide ground wave signals of high accuracy over a range of about 500 miles. Under good conditions it will establish position to one-tenth of a mile at a range of 250 miles from the transmitters. Its signals are equally dependable, whether over land or water.

Primarily, Loran-D differs from Loran-C in its signal, which uses repeated groups of 16 pulses, spaced 500 microseconds apart.

The system is highly resistant to electronic jamming. This characteristic, and its extreme mobility—stations can be set up anywhere within 24 hours—make it extremely useful when areas of operation are changing rapidly. The system is equally satisfactory for use aboard naval vessels and high speed aircraft.

CHAPTER 33

Electronic Systems for Hydrographic Surveying

3301. *Hydrography* may be defined as that science which deals with the measurement of the physical features of waters and their marginal land areas, with special reference to the elements that affect safe navigation, and the publication of such information in a form suitable for the use of navigators. *Hydrographic surveying* in the strict sense is defined merely as the surveying of a water area; in common practice, however, it has come to include such matters as the study and measurement, in a given survey area, of the magnetic variation and dip, the tides, currents, and meteorological characteristics.

Introduction.

Probably the most important requirement in any survey is to establish the position of each feature measured. To do this, the location of a reference point must first be very precisely determined, for all other positions are located relative to this reference point, which is called the *origin.*

3302. The navigator often places almost unquestioning reliance on his nautical chart. Consequently the hydrographer needs to use the utmost accuracy when conducting surveys. In hydrographic surveying it is extremely important to be able to comb an area, following lines with a fixed spacing in order to insure that no possible underwater obstacle has been missed, and that the area has been systematically covered. An error or inaccuracy in charted information may result in a marine disaster and possible loss of life and property.

Accuracy for surveying.

The accuracy of a given survey depends on the purpose for which it is intended. Accuracy ranges from one part in 5,000 to one in 100,000; the latter extremely high standard being necessary for missile and space craft control. The principal function of a hydrographic survey is to determine depths of water; the positions at which soundings are obtained can best be determined by accurate reference to known points on shore. This locates the points at their correct geographic positions, and also results in the land and marine features being placed in correct relationship to each other. This is an important consideration as the mariner, when near the coast, also uses reference positions on land to locate himself.

3303. In hydrographic surveying, the term *control*, when referred to a survey vessel, is used to mean the accurate location of the vessel within the survey area. *Visual control* is the determination of position by visual reference to conspicuous landmarks whose positions are established relative to the *origin*. The method most commonly used is to obtain horizontal sextant angles between landmarks or accurately located beacons on the shore. Position is then plotted by means of a three-arm protractor, described in article 1110.

Control for survey vessels.

543

Electronic control.

At present, visual control is supplemented by *electronic control*, which permits operation in periods of low visibility, as well as beyond visual range. To be acceptable for this use, the electronic equipment must have great inherent accuracy; it must be operated within the closest practicable tolerances.

Any electronic system meeting the requirements of accuracy might be used for control. Radio acoustic ranging, radar in conjunction with transponder beacons, and the electronic position indicator have been employed for control.

Hyperbolic systems.

Some of the electronic systems which are currently widely used in the United States are *Raydist, Decca, Shoran* and *Hiran.* Numerous other systems, operating with similar techniques, are also available. Various modes of operation are therefore possible for surveying. These consist of *hyperbolic* systems, *elliptical* systems, *circular* or *range* systems, named from the curves of equal value generated on the chart when the signals received from the transmitting stations in the system are charted, and, in some cases, a combination of these. The range or distance measuring systems offer the advantage that they require no special charts.

Lanes.

A hyperbolic curve represents a locus of points where the *difference* of times required for the signals from two transmitting stations to be received is equal. The chief limitation on the accuracy of these systems is caused by the geometry of the hyperbolae. The *lane* is the unit of measurement in these systems; its width is equal to half a wave length. When using a phase comparison system the lane is further subdivided. The best resolution that can be expected along the base line is about one one-hundredth of a lane; at 2 MHz, this is about three feet, and at 10 kHz it is about 450 feet. As the vessel departs from the base line, the lanes expand and are successively wider.

Circular systems.

In a *circular* system, the vessel uses the signal from only one station at a time; the range to the station is based on the length of time of signal travel. There is no deterioration in signal accuracy due to position relative to the transmitter, as the signals spread outward over the earth's surface as a series of equispaced concentric rings.

Elliptical systems.

In an *elliptical* system, the *sum* of the times of transmission of signals from two stations would be used. A line representing a locus of points where these sums are equal would take the form of an ellipse.

The elliptical system is seldom used. In one of the Raydist configurations described hereafter a combination of the circular and elliptical system is employed but the ellipses are transformed electronically into a range.

These systems are discussed in the following articles. The navigator's responsibilities are not limited to the aforementioned equipment, but are increased to include using any publication or instrument, electronic or manual, that will allow him to navigate the vessel safely. Operation of this special instrumentation is also a responsibility of the navigator and his assistants.

Raydist.

3304. Raydist is the name given to a series of transportable and highly accurate positioning systems in which the phases of two continuous-wave (CW) radio signals are used to determine the position of a mobile station. Various modes of operation are available differing according to the system. Raydist operates in the 1.6 to 5.0 MHz frequency range, which permits the use of small efficient

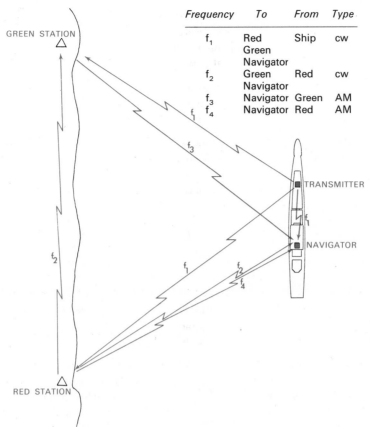

Frequency	To	From	Type
f_1	Red Green Navigator	Ship	cw
f_2	Green Navigator	Red	cw
f_3	Navigator	Green	AM
f_4	Navigator	Red	AM

Figure 3304a: Raydist DM system.

portable transmitters and antennae. The systems are not limited to line-of-sight operations, and may be used at distances in excess of 150 nautical miles with a sensitivity of approximately 1 meter when sufficient power is available. The design of the Raydist systems permits presentation of positioning data in various forms: range, elliptical, and hyperbolic or in a combination of any two of these. The DM Raydist using the range-elliptical combination has been widely employed by the Coast and Geodetic Survey.

Distance measuring systems using circular coordinates have a greater potential for accurate positioning than do the hyperbolic systems. This is because of the geometry involved; lane widths remain constant with increased range in a circular system, while they increase very rapidly with range in a hyperbolic system.

This is a system requiring four radio frequencies for use by three stations as indicated in Figure 3304a. Two of these frequencies are distance-measuring CW frequencies, and the two others are amplitude modulated (AM) to transmit information back to the ship concerning the phase relationship of the CW transmissions received at each station. The AM frequencies do not enter into the determination of distance; however, interference on any of the four frequencies will adversely affect operation of the lane counters in the phase meter.

DM Raydist.

A CW transmitter located at the Red station operates at a frequency 200 Hz higher or lower than half the frequency used by the ship. A special purpose,

545

dual-frequency receiver is also used at both the Red and Green shore stations. The receiver at each shore station accepts the transmission from both the vessel and from the Red shore station, doubles the lower frequency and heterodynes it with the higher frequency to generate the 400 Hz audio beat note. Separate audio notes are then returned to the mobile station by the Red and Green stations as a modulation of two additional and completely independent frequencies (the AM frequencies). These signals are phase-compared with an internally generated beat note, by an instrument called the *"Navigator"* aboard the survey vessel. A comparison of the Red signal with the local mobile frequency yields a reading on the phase meter of the range (distance) to the Red station. The Green station compares the phase relationship of the signals from the mobile and Red stations yielding a measurement in elliptical coordinates which the phase meter then converts into distance of the Green station from the mobile station. The *"Navigator"* receives the data from all stations and converts them to a usable output of position coordinates.

Since the system is completely automatic, the distance from the shore station can be read directly off the dials. By heterodyning the transmitted frequencies the equipment has computed the distance traveled by both transmitted frequencies, and properly located the position of the vessel.

DR Raydist.

Since, with the DM Raydist, land or other obstacles between the two shore stations can cause sufficient interference to limit the accuracy of the system, a DR Raydist system is often employed. With this system the Red and Green stations are identically equipped, each having its own CW transmitter operating so closely in frequency as to be considered a single frequency. In this range-range system the distance between the shore stations, plus the features of the terrain, are no longer a hindrance, since there is no transmission of signals between the shore stations. This allows the user to have available all-weather, around-the-clock information for positional data. The latest DR system is the DR-S with single sideband transmitters requiring only two frequencies.

Figure 3304b: Raydist DR base station being positioned on shore.

The most widely used Raydist systems—the DM, DR, and DR-S—are capable of providing position information simultaneously to a number of users. They are high-accuracy ranging systems which operate over the horizon with multi-user capability.

The heterodyne tone, as it is received at the two shore stations, is returned to the *"Navigator"* and compared phase-wise with the same tone as it is detected directly in the *"Navigator."* The tone being relayed back from the Red station is compared with the tone detected locally in the *"Navigator"* to determine the range to the Red station; this process is concurrently repeated to determine the range of the Green station. Since the heterodyned frequency is derived from a fixed transmitter and the mobile transmitter, its phase, as it is detected at the shore stations, will be dependent upon the location of the mobile transmitter. Therefore as the mobile station moves, the relative phase of the heterodyne tone changes, causing the phasemeter, or *Position Indicator* dials to rotate.

Any phase-comparison system produces position within a lane; as in most surveying systems, Raydist does not identify the lane. A starting position must therefore be known. A lane counter, an integral part of the equipment, then counts the lanes crossed from the starting position.

A typical Raydist DR system base station is shown in Figure 3304b; and a Raydist *"Navigator"* and the *Automatic Position Plotter* as installed in the cabin of a small survey launch are shown in Figure 3304c.

The base stations for the new DR-S Raydist system, as well as some of the older Raydist systems, are designed to operate from conventional automobile-type storage batteries; the high-powered systems are generally operated from 110 volt, 60 cycle sources. The conventional batteries can operate up to 24 hours without recharging and provide a reliable power source. For longer operations, larger capacity batteries are used.

Figure 3304c: Raydist Navigator and automatic plotter installed in cabin of small vessel.

Shoran and Hiran.

3305. *Shoran* (for SHort RAnge Navigation) is a secondary radar system using two transponder beacons, located ashore, and a single indicator aboard the vessel to measure the distance from each beacon. This system is a pulse-modulated, ultra-high frequency (230 to 310 MHz) distance measuring system used primarily in survey work. Its operation is based on the assumption that the velocity of electromagnetic waves is known to within a few miles per second.

In operation the two transponder beacons are positioned and the distance between them established. Then the vessel transmits pulse type signals alternately on frequencies of 230 and 250 MHz. These signals actuate the transmitters at the transponder beacons and, after a pre-set time delay, the stations transmit the signal back to the vessel, pulse for pulse, on a frequency of 310 MHz. The returning pulses are matched with a fixed index, thus automatically converting the elapsed time for the round trip to distances in statute miles. The distance readout is calibrated in hundredths of a mile; distance can be read with an accuracy of from 30 to 60 feet, except at extreme ranges.

After reception of the distances from both shore stations the navigator plots distance circles and the intersection of these circles marks his location. Due to the high frequency used the distances at which the system can be utilized is limited by the curvature of the earth.

A higher precision version of Shoran, called *Hiran* (from HIgh precision RAnge Navigation) was developed to meet the most exacting survey requirements. Hiran is similar to Shoran but signals are kept at a constant amplitude to prevent an error in the time of triggering the signal from the transponder. Hiran also has a greater accuracy, the smallest division of the counter being one five-hundredths of a mile, rather than one one-hundredth as in Shoran.

Decca.

3306. Decca HI-FIX, as used in survey work, uses essentially the same principle as Decca (article 1814). It is light weight and compact, thus providing high mobility for erecting stations for survey work. HI-FIX has a maximum range of about 100 miles, the range depending upon the radiating power of the station, and provides lane identification, in addition to the phase comparison, in one of the configurations available. It can be used either in a two-range version or in a hyperbolic system. A master and two slave stations share a common carrier frequency on a time-multiplex basis in the 2 MHz frequency region.

CHAPTER 34

Radio Astronomy for Navigation

3401. The brief introduction to nautical astronomy in Chapter 19 described how light rays from the sun, moon and planets of the solar system as well as major stars in this galaxy are used in the practice of celestial navigation. It was also pointed out that as yet uncounted millions of other galaxies composed of stars and other matter exist in the universe although most of these are too distant to be seen by the naked eye or with the low powered telescopes used on navigational sextants.

Introduction.

It is now a well established fact that many celestial bodies and groups of bodies in the form of galaxies emit radio waves as well as light waves. Some of the presently located sources of radio energy are at such vast distances that they are beyond the reach of the largest optical telescopes, and cannot be determined to originate in any visible source. This is true even though the radio emission from a galaxy is weaker than the optical emission by a very large factor; it illustrates the increased distances which can now be probed by the astronomer with the *radio telescope*, as compared to even the largest optical telescope. The radio telescope is designed to pick up even the most faint radio wave emissions from outer space, and to determine as closely as possible the declination and sidereal hour angle describing the location of the emitting source.

With the discovery that many celestial bodies emitted radio waves, a new science was born. How this science can serve the navigator is described in this chapter.

3402. The existence of extra-terrestrial radio emissions or "noise" was first discovered in 1932 by Karl G. Jansky, while studying atmospheric static at a wavelength of 14.6 meters. Detection of radio waves from the sun was first announced in 1944. Since then the science of radio astronomy has progressed rapidly. Celestial X-ray energy sources were discovered in 1962. Although energy at many wavelengths is being continually emitted from the sun, moon, and stars, the earth's atmosphere is opaque to these radiations except for two "windows." One of these permits the visible range of the spectrum—those wavelengths to which the eye is sensitive—to pass through. The other is transparent to the short wavelengths in the microwave radio band; that is the band from a few millimeters to approximately thirty meters, corresponding to radio frequencies between about 50 GHz (gigahertz) to 10 MHz.

Background.

3403. In radio astronomy, any source emitting radio waves, whether it be a single body or an entire galaxy of stars, usually is termed a *radio star;* some such stars are too distant to be seen optically; other sources transmit no visible light but emit radiation of far greater wavelengths, which falls within the radio wave

Sources of radio energy.

portion of the frequency spectrum. The first radio star to be identified with an optically known object was the Crab nebula in the constellation Taurus; it is the gaseous remains of the super-Nova of 1054 A.D. observed by the Chinese. The size and shape of the associated radio source at meter wavelengths coincides with the nebula as photographed through a telescope. As pointed out above, there are many discrete radio sources known as radio stars, although they generally are not stars by strict astronomical definition. To date, the sun is the only radio star which can also be defined astronomically as a star; in other words, it is the only body meeting the astronomer's definition of a star, from which radio emissions have been detected.

The only radio emissions presently available to the navigator are those generated by the sun and moon; the *radio sextant*, described in article 3406, has been developed to permit using the radio emissions from these two bodies in navigation. Radio waves in the meter wavelength are emitted from many other discrete sources, and measurements have been made at several wavelengths on the same source. These show a steady decrease in emission with decreasing wavelength, and they can be identified only by a large and complex antenna system, which is not suitable for shipboard use. Fortunately, the radiation from the sun and moon becomes stronger at the shorter wavelengths.

Emission processes. **3404.** The processes of radio emission are not completely understood. Bright hydrogen regions in which the radio emission is generated thermally by the collision of free electrons with positive ions have been investigated by observations in the centimeter band with some success. Any hot object radiates electromagnetic energy in accordance with Planck's law, which summarizes the wavelengths of the radiated power; this law is described in detail in most physics tests.

The source of radio waves lies in the hot gases of the sun's atmosphere, the microwave spectrum coming primarily from the region 30,000 to 50,000 miles from the photosphere, while the longer wavelength radiation originates farther out in the sun's atmosphere. Apparently there are two basically different causes for these radio radiations. In the first place, any hot object radiates electromagnetic energy in accordance with Planck's law. The hot gas near the photosphere emits a spectrum characteristic of an object with temperature between 6,000° and 10,000° Kelvin, depending on the exact region under consideration. The radiations from this region having wavelengths greater than approximately one half-meter do not escape from the sun because the ionized gas farther out in the sun's atmosphere refracts them so much that they are, in effect, trapped. However, radiations in the millimeter and centimeter region can propagate through the sun's atmosphere and can be observed on earth. The second general type of mechanism is that of coherent ion motion in the sun's atmosphere. Large scale circulation of ionized solar gases actually constitutes an electrical current similar to that in an antenna, which radiates a radio spectrum varying in characteristics according to the nature of the current. Such radiations are observed over a wide range of wavelengths, but are most pronounced in the meter wavelength range.

Any body which is hotter than its surroundings will radiate energy in the form of heat. The higher the temperature, the more heat is radiated, and at sufficiently high temperatures visible light, at shorter wavelengths than heat or infrared, will also be radiated. This can be seen in heated iron, which first glows red and eventually white as the temperature increases. A body heated to extremely high temperatures—the sun, for example—will produce a complete spectrum of progressively longer wavelengths from light to heat to radio and will produce detectable radio waves. Radio emissions from the moon, which has a much lower temperature, are also detectable and are usable with sensitive receivers now being produced, even though the radiation is about fifty times weaker than that of the sun.

3405. With the detection of radio waves emanating from discrete sources outside our solar system, the interest of astronomers throughout the world was aroused. Much effort has been devoted to the design of radio telescopes for the exploration of outer space, as well as for study of emissions from the sun and moon.

Radio telescopes.

Except in frequency, radio waves are identical to light waves, and many radio telescope antennae are quite similar in form to modern optical reflecting telescopes. The optics of a typical reflecting telescope are shown in Figure 3405a.

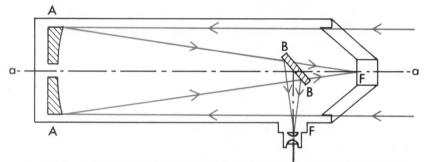

Figure 3405a: Optics of a typical reflecting telescope.

Figure 3405b: NRL's 50 ft. parabolic reflector radio telescope.

Figure 3405b shows the 50-foot precision parabolic reflector of the Naval Research Laboratory's radio telescope, which focuses the incoming radio waves on the central sensor, or pickup. This radio telescope was designed primarily for study of emissions from the sun and moon, and operates with a 9.4 centimeter microwave radio receiver. This instrument, which can be exactly trained in azimuth and altitude, went into operation late in 1953. Since radio wavelengths are longer than those of visible light, the radio telescope must be larger. Optical telescopes must be ground and polished to very exacting tolerances; for radio telescopes the required tolerances are considerably reduced. It is doubtful if an optical reflector much bigger than the 200-inch diameter Hale instrument at Mount Palomar can be built. However, there is no such limit on the size of radio telescopes; the Jodrell Bank telescope in England, which is designed to permit exploration of the universe, has a reflecting surface 250 feet in diameter. For practical shipboard installation an antenna cannot exceed a few feet in diameter, thus limiting the wavelength of the signals which can be received. The radio sextant antenna is in the form of a concave reflecting surface which focuses the incoming signals on a small sensing antenna mounted above the reflecting surface.

Navigation by radio astronomy.

3406. The classic method of optical celestial navigation still offers many advantages despite the development of more sophisticated systems. It is a completely self-contained method, requiring no external inputs, it is passive, and for an experienced navigator, it often permits extreme accuracy. However, its use is frequently limited by clouds or fog which make it impossible to obtain observations.

The discovery that the sun and moon emitted radio waves of lengths that could be received by antenna arrays of acceptable size for shipboard use suggested that these emissions might be used to augment conventional celestial navigation. Research was begun with a view to developing satisfactory receivers, as well as miniature radio telescopes capable of defining precisely the circumference of the disc of the sun or moon, from which the signals emanate. Instrumentation capable of sensing the vertical accurately was also required, as the primary purpose was to develop a celestial system which could be used when poor visibility made it impossible to obtain optical observations.

The radio sextant.

The Collins Radio Company was a leader in working towards developing such instrumentation. It was found that both the sun and the moon emitted radiation in the area of 9 cm and 2 cm wavelengths, and that these were suitable for marine navigation, the latter yielding stronger signals during periods of rain. Work began on producing a *radio sextant* or radiometric sextant as it is sometimes called, which would be satisfactory for marine use. As radio waves entering the earth's atmosphere are refracted in a manner similar to light waves, refraction under various conditions of atmospheric conditions was studied, and radio refraction correction tables were prepared.

Various models were tested, and an experimental model suitable for service testing aboard ship was installed aboard the USS *Arneb*. Extensive tests were conducted in 1957–58 during a cruise which included 1,400 miles of steaming in Antarctic ice. This radio sextant was limited to tracking solar signals. For this installation, a Mark IV Mod O deck-mounted stabilization system was employed to supply the vertical reference. This system was not designed for this specific purpose, and it required considerable modification; its performance left a good deal to be desired. Despite the errors introduced by the vertical system, and sometimes unsatisfactory performance of the time pieces employed, the results achieved by the radio sextant in tracking the sun permitted navigation of acceptable accuracy. These results were particularly impressive, as much of the time in the Antarctic no other method of positioning was available, and it was considered that further work in this area was well warranted. The experience gained during these trials led to the development of the modern equipment described in the following article.

Figure 3407a:
Radiometric
acquisition unit.

3407. The latest radio sextant produced by the Collins Radio Co. operates in the area of the 2.2 cm wavelength. It forms part of the *Ship's Self-Contained Navigation System* (SSCNS), developed for the Navy by the A.C. Electronics Division of the General Motors Corporation. As the radio sextant is integrated into the SSCNS, the latter will be described briefly.

Ship's Self-Contained Navigation System (SSCNS).

The SSCNS includes many features which make it highly acceptable for installation aboard naval vessels. It provides almost global navigational coverage both by day and night, regardless of weather conditions, and it is *self-contained*, passive and highly immune to countermeasures. In addition to the radio sextant, it includes an inertial system and computer, and makes precise all-weather solar and lunar altitude and bearing data available to the navigator. The system operates satisfactorily when celestial radio inputs are interrupted; during such periods other navigational data may be inserted for updating the inertial system.

The new radio sextant is the first designed as a production model, rather than for experimental use. Weight and volume have been greatly decreased compared to previous models, and it is far more convenient to operate. The sextant consists of three units, which can be installed in three different locations. The deck-mounted radiometric acquisition unit consists of a roll, pitch, bearing, and altitude gimbal structure, a microwave radiometer, and an antenna covered by a rigid spherical radome. This unit, without the radome, is shown in Figure 3407a.

The new radio sextant.

An air conditioning unit is mounted below decks and furnishes heating or cooling as required. The third unit, the control console, can be installed at a remote location. The radio sextant operates in close relationship to the Inertial Measurement Unit (IMU) which can be mounted on the under side of the sextant bedplate. The vertical, as well as pitch, roll, heading and computed solar-lunar altitude and azimuth data are furnished to the sextant by the IMU and its associated computer. This mounting arrangement minimized structural deflection and alignment errors, which degrade total system operation.

A new gimbal design was developed for this sextant. All four axes intersect at a point which coincides with the center of the 54-inch diameter radome, which is made of fiberglass in honeycomb construction (Figure 3407b). This arrangement minimized dome refraction for a radome of given size, as the symmetry axis of the antenna is always perpendicular to the radome surface.

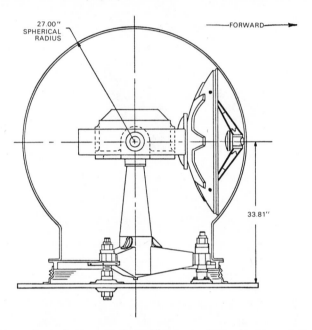

Figure 3407b: Acquisition unit within the radome.

The sextant is designed for ease of maintenance and reliability. Three levels of maintenance and operational monitoring are provided. Built-in test equipment continuously monitors operation and automatically detects any system performance fault. In addition, many test points are available for detailed observation. In most instances, the fault may be speedily identified as occurring in a certain circuit card, and a new card can be inserted immediately.

A simplified block diagram showing the principal features of this radio sextant is shown in Figure 3407c. The sextant employs a solid state superheterodyne radio receiver, or radiometer, operating in the 15.350–15.400 GHz radio astronomy band.

SSCNS radio sextant operation.

3408. When the sun or moon is to be tracked, the computer uses the ship's DR position, as supplied by the inertial system, and for the current time obtains ephemeristic data for the selected body from the memory or storage section of the computer. With these data, it computes both altitude and azimuth, and then automatically trains the antenna on the computed position of the body. The

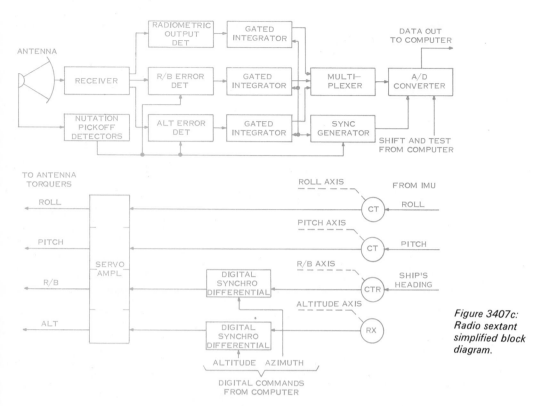

Figure 3407c:
Radio sextant
simplified block
diagram.

instrument next originates a search pattern, and locks on to the body as soon as it is acquired. The difference between the observed and computed altitudes and azimuths are used to update the inertial system. Once the body is acquired, the sextant continues to track the body, and the computer then furnishes azimuth and refraction-corrected altitude of the sun or moon at two minute intervals. Tracking is continued until the body sets below the horizon.

As in optical celestial navigation with the marine sextant, the sun and moon, unlike the stars, are not point sources of energy emission when observed with the radio sextant. However, in reducing the observation the position of the center of the body must be used. When using the marine sextant, a limb of the body is made tangent to the horizon, and the semi-diameter of the body for the time of the observation is applied to the sextant altitude to obtain the altitude of the body's center, thus in effect converting the sight to a point source observation. Similarly, in radio sextant navigation, the center of the body must be determined, as though it were a point source of emission of microwave radio energy, rather than emitting energy from its entire surface. This is achieved automatically with the radio sextant, in part by the frequency employed by the receiver, and also by the electronics of the system in the scan operation of tracking, and the averaging technique employed. The radio emissive centers of both the sun and moon coincide with the geometrical centers to the precision required for navigation.

Refraction occurs as the radio waves enter the atmosphere; correction data for this effect is stored in the computer's memory section. The altitude is corrected automatically and continuously, when atmospheric pressure and the dry and wet bulb temperatures are entered in the computer. The repeatability of the

Refraction.

555

refraction effect, that is, the consistency of its value under similar conditions, is acceptable for navigational purposes. Short-lived abberations in refraction are minimized as the radio sextant observation is an average of angular measurement over a period of about a minute. This averaging process is necessary as the source of the radiation subtends an angle of about 30' as measured from the earth.

Another effect for which the instrumentation provides correction is *atmospheric pulling,* which may be described as pseudo-refraction. The natural radio emission (noise) from the atmosphere depends on atmospheric temperature and attenuation, and therefore varies with direction. More radiation is received from areas near the horizon than is received from the vicinity of the zenith; the scanning system therefore encounters an extraneous, additive modulation from this variable atmospheric emission. The effect is usually negligible when the sun is observed; however it is an important factor for lunar observations. For the latter, the actual atmosphere modulation is measured by observing the atmosphere on each side of the source. Variations which are linear over a four minute time period and a 7° pointing interval are automatically corrected by introducing a bias or offset equivalent to the variation.

Position fixing by radio sextant.

3409. In the SSCNS, the radio sextant serves to update the position recorded by the inertial component of the system. This is achieved by feeding in continuous altitude and azimuth data. Essentially, it may be considered as determining position by providing a series of accurate *running fixes* (articles 1111 and 2606) obtained from observations of a single body, and integrated over a considerable period of time. This single-body method of operation is necessitated by the fact that only for very limited periods of the month are the sun and moon both above the horizon, and satisfactorily situated in azimuth to supply a conventional two-body fix. In essence, when observing a body, the SSCNS may be likened to a navigator obtaining observations of a single body and reducing them almost instantaneously, averaging the results, plotting the resulting lines of position, and advancing these for the run with the utmost precision. The SSCNS, however, does not require plotting to determine position; the observed data from the radio sextant are automatically applied as a reset torque for updating the position indicated by the inertial portion of the system.

Summary.

3410. The modern radio sextant, as used in the SSCNS, is provided with highly sensitive and accurate stabilization to establish the vertical reference necessary for all celestial altitude observations. It is able to track the sun or moon automatically under almost any weather conditions, when either body is above the horizon. Continuing altitude and azimuth data of a high quality are thus available for updating the inertial portion of the system.

The use of discrete celestial sources of microwave radiation other than the sun and moon for marine navigation does not at present appear feasible, chiefly because of the extremely large antenna system which is required.

The obvious advantage offered by the radio sextant is that it provides a passive, continuous all-weather system of acceptably accurate navigation whenever the sun or moon is above the horizon. The principal limitation is that it is limited in use to only two celestial bodies, and that neither of these bodies may be above the horizon for considerable periods of time.

CHAPTER 35

Doppler Navigation

3501. If the direction and distance traveled by a ship relative to the earth could be continuously and accurately determined, position would be known at all times. Several methods of making such measurements are now being developed for marine navigation. Among them are *Doppler* and *Inertial Navigation;* the latter is discussed in Chapter 36. Doppler navigation using electromagnetic wave transmission has proven highly satisfactory in aircraft; inertial navigation is used with success in aircraft, submarines, and surface ships.

Introduction.

The Doppler method, based on a change of frequency caused by motion, is named for Christian Doppler, who described the frequency change, or shift, in 1842. The classic example used to illustrate the Doppler shift is the sound of a fast moving locomotive's whistle. As the locomotive approaches the pitch of the sound seems to rise; as the locomotive moves away, the pitch seems to sink. For a long time the Doppler shift was of real interest only to astronomers. However, when technology had progressed to the point where acoustic and electromagnetic radiation could be produced and controlled, it was realized that the Doppler effect could be used to measure velocity.

Doppler navigational systems are capable of giving a constant readout of latitude and longitude to a very high degree of accuracy. The limiting factor on the use of such equipment is the depth of water under the ship; it cannot be used in depths much greater than 100 fathoms when using the ocean floor as the reflector for the signals. Nevertheless, it can be used to great advantage on certain missions.

3502. In order to comprehend the principles of Doppler navigation, the mechanics of the Doppler shift must be understood. The same principles hold good regarding the Doppler shift for all waves of the frequency spectrum, whether they be the waves of visible light, with which the astronomer is concerned, the electromagnetic waves used by the jet aircraft navigator, or the acoustic or sound waves used in marine navigation.

Mechanics of the Doppler shift.

For purposes of illustration, this article will first consider the sound energy as being transmitted horizontally through the water, rather than diagonally downwards, as is the case in marine Doppler navigation. If the sonic projector shown in Figure 3502a is considered as being stationary in the water while transmitting sound on a frequency f, the transmitted radiation in the form of sound waves moves away from the transmitter at the speed of sound, C. This speed is affected primarily by the temperature, salinity and density of the sea water. The transmitted radiation travels outward in the form of waves, alternating between pressure crests and troughs. The distance between consecutive crests or troughs is

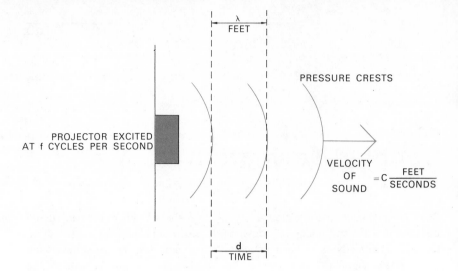

*Figure 3502a:
Pattern of
acoustic wave
transmitted from
stationary under-
water projector.*

the *wavelength, λ,* of the acoustic wave.

The wavelength is equal to the speed of sound divided by the frequency or $\lambda = C/f$. Therefore, in a period of time *t* each pressure crest travels a distance *d* equal to *C* multiplied by *t*. In the illustration it can be seen that the wavelength in feet (λ) and the distance (*d*) that a given pressure crest has traveled are one and the same.

Figure 3502b depicts a ship carrying the projector moving through the water at a velocity *V*, and the resulting wave being monitored at a fixed point some distance away from the projector. When transmitted at a fixed frequency the waves, with their pressure crests, are still generated at the same time intervals or frequency. The pressure crests are closer together in the medium due to the velocity of the vessel. The new compressed wavelengths λ' are equal to the undisturbed wavelengths minus the distance traveled at velocity *V* between pressure crests. Since frequency and wavelength vary inversely, in a direct proportion, in a medium having a given speed of sound, the change in wavelength caused by ship's velocity results in a change in frequency as received at the monitoring point. This change in frequency is known as the Doppler shift.

*Figure 3502b:
Pattern of
acoustic wave
transmitted from
a moving under-
water projector.*

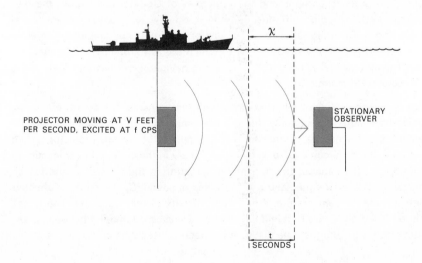

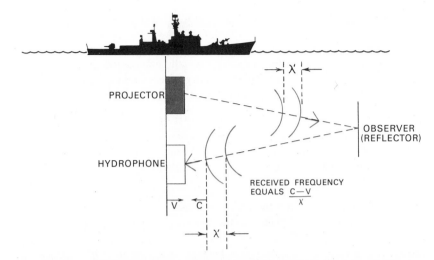

RECEIVED FREQUENCY
EQUALS $\frac{C-V}{\lambda}$

Figure 3502c: Pattern of acoustic wave reflected back to moving transmitter/receiver.

If the stationary observer in Figure 3502b is replaced by a reflector, as shown in Figure 3502c, the transmitted energy will be reflected back to the ship. By adding a hydrophone, or receiver, the distance to the object can be determined by measuring the elapsed time between transmission of an outgoing signal and the return of the echo, a sonar distance. In addition, by measuring the Doppler shift of the echo, the ship's speed relative to the reflector can be determined.

In Doppler navigation the ocean floor is normally used as a reflector, as no reflective surfaces are available in the horizontal plane. The sound projector and hydrophone are therefore depressed to a predetermined angle below the horizontal. If a second projector and hydrophone, facing in the opposite direction to the first pair and depressed to the same angle, are added, the Doppler shift, as received by the two hydrophones can be compared. If the Doppler shift, as obtained from the after hydrophone is subtracted from the shift as obtained from the forward hydrophone, the value of the shift, due to horizontal motion will be doubled ; in addition, any shift due to vertical motion will be cancelled. It follows that if four projectors and hydrophones, equally distributed in bearing are employed, relative direction and distance measurements can be very precisely determined.

3503. So far, only the Doppler shift has been considered, with no thought to the medium—sea water—through which it is transmitted. The existing characteristics of the water can have a significant effect on Doppler navigation, the major considerations being their effect on the *speed of sound*, on *signal attenuation*, and on *volume reverberation*.

Sonic signals transmitted through sea water.

As was stated in article 3502, the wavelength, λ, of a transmitted sound wave is equal to the speed of sound, C, divided by the frequency, f, or $\lambda = C/f$. The *speed of sound* in water is affected by such factors as salinity, temperature, and pressure, which increases with depth. It can vary by approximately 3 per cent on either side of the standard value, which is generally taken as 4,935 feet per second in sea water near the surface with a temperature of 60° F and salinity of 34 parts per thousand.

Speed of sound.

A discrepancy of this magnitude could cause an intolerable error in a Doppler navigational system. Errors due to this cause can be largely eliminated by transmitting a signal on a constant wavelength rather than on a constant frequency, or by constantly adjusting the depression angle of the transmitter and hydrophone array to compensate for a change in the velocity of sound. Both methods offer certain advantages, and neither is generally considered to be the ultimate answer to the problem. The two methods have been combined with considerable success in some Doppler instrumentation.

Signal attenuation.

The acoustic energy of the sonic signal is dissipated as it passes through the water; this phenomenon is called *signal attenuation.* As path losses increase with increased frequency, due to signal attenuation, tradeoffs between power and frequency must always be taken into consideration in the design of Doppler navigational equipment.

Volume reverberation.

Volume reverberation is the term used to describe the acoustic energy that is returned from debris, bubbles, minute marine life or thermal gradients in the water, rather than from the bottom. The noise caused by volume reverberation can at times drown out the echo reflected from the bottom. This effect is used to advantage with some types of Doppler equipment, as discussed in article 3505.

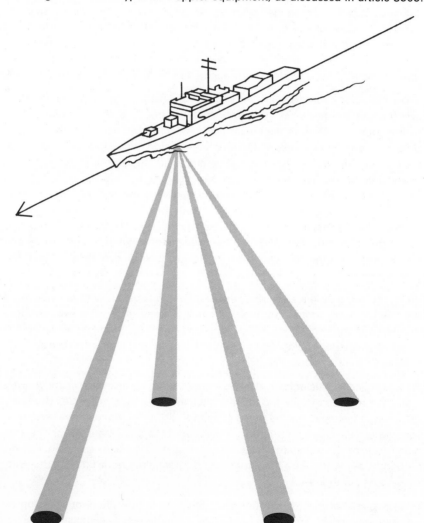

Figure 3504a: Doppler navigation principle.

Figure 3504b:
Distance indicator.

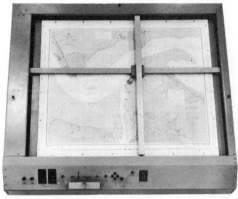

Figure 3504c:
Automatic plotter.

3504. The Doppler navigational system as originally developed by the Raytheon Company (Figure 3504a) employs four beams of sonic energy, spaced 90° apart. These beams are directed outward and downward at equal angles of inclination from the horizontal. The sonic energy is transmitted from *transducers,* which are activated by an electrical signal from the transmitter. In addition to radiating the outgoing sonic signal, the transducers serve as hydrophones, in that they also pick up the echo of the signal, reflected from the ocean floor, and convert the acoustic echo into electrical energy. This energy passes into the receiver, where it is amplified, and the input from the four transducers are compared to produce the Doppler frequency. It also determines the relative height of the frequencies, thus providing a sense of motion and its direction.

The Doppler navigator.

If the transducer array remained fixed in bearing relative to the ship's center line, motion would be stated relative to the ship's coordinate system; that is, the readout would show motion relative to the vessel's heading and would indicate speed over the bottom and cross track errors (lateral displacement relative to the track). To make it a true navigational system, the transducer array is constantly oriented to true north by the ship's gyrocompass, which also serves to stabilize the array, and maintain it in a horizontal plane, regardless of any roll or pitch. Motion is now indicated in the north-south and east-west directions, and readout is both the true direction and distance traveled from a point of departure expressed as distance north or south and east or west as shown in Figure 3504b. Therefore the system can present a constant indication of position, expressed as latitude and longitude, and can also continuously plot position on a chart, using an X-Y coordinate plotter, as shown in Figure 3504c.

Accuracy.

Geometric arrangement and sonic factors, both of which affect the performance of the system, have been discussed briefly. Another limitation on the accuracy of the system is the heading accuracy supplied by the gyrocompass employed. A high quality gyrocompass under good operational conditions will have a bearing uncertainty of 0°.1, or about six minutes of arc. The Doppler navigational system using a heading reference in which this error remained constant would indicate a position to about 0.17 per cent of the distance traveled from the departure, and the ship might be to the right or left of the intended track by this amount. As the errors introduced by the gyro usually tend to be random, rather than constant, they average out to a considerable extent. Many runs have been made with this equipment to a considerably higher degree of accuracy than the 0.17 per cent error would seem to indicate.

The chief limitation in Doppler navigation using the ocean floor as a reflector is not system accuracy, but rather that it is effective only in depths not exceeding approximately 100 fathoms due to signal attenuation.

Doppler naviga-tional system for maintaining an accurate DR plot at sea.

3505. Volume reverberation was mentioned in article 3503 as sometimes having an adverse effect on the Doppler navigational system, as the echo returning from the ocean floor was masked by an echo from thermal gradients, stratified layers of minute marine life, etc. Because of this volume reverberation in sonar transmissions, with a CW transmitter, part of the acoustic energy is reflected back and produces a signal level, at the receiver, that is higher than the noise level. Consequently Doppler navigation is possible relative to the water mass, regardless of water depth.

Volume reverberation is not an unmixed liability, as it makes possible use of the Doppler navigational system as a highly accurate DR system at any sea depths. Motion is sensed relative to the water mass, and is accurately read out as a change in position. This equipment can be extremely helpful at sea in indicating aberrations from the intended heading, due to steering errors, wind drift, etc.

Second generation Doppler naviga-tional equipment.

3506. A new generation of Doppler navigational instrumentation has been developed with two very different types of vessels primarily in mind; these are the "super-jumbo" tankers, displacing 200,000 tons or more, and research submarines, often termed deep-submergence vehicles.

These two highly diverse types have one characteristic in common—they are little affected by wave action. At its operating depths, the deep submergence vehicle will be quite unaffected by surface conditions, while the giant tanker, due to its enormous size, is much less affected than are most other surface ships.

Due to this greatly improved stability, the Doppler system developed for these ships does not employ the gyro-stabilized pendulous array of transducers de-scribed in the preceding articles. Instead, the four transducers are rigidly affixed to the ship's bottom plating, in such a position that under normal conditions of loading, their axes are directed downwards at a specific angle; usually they are located well forward of the midships point. Stabilization is achieved internally by electronic means.

This system of mechanically fixed transducers will perform the same functions and permit the same degree of accuracy as discussed above, and the system should greatly benefit both types of vessels. The deep submergence vehicle, operating in a medium which cuts off almost all conventional types of navigation, is no longer at the mercy of bottom currents of unknown set and drift. It can complete an accurate and detailed survey of the ocean floor, and return to the point from which the survey was started.

For the giant tanker, this equipment furnishes a continuous and accurate DR plot at sea; it is of even greater benefit when entering or operating in port. Due to the great draft of these ships, often well in excess of 50 feet, they cannot rely on the usual channel markers to keep in safe waters. Instead, they must often restrict their movements to a limited portion of the normally used channel. The Doppler system will be of the greatest assistance in such operations, and can often warn of potential trouble before it can be detected by plotting visual bearings.

3507. Pilots and conning officers have frequently experienced difficulty in sensing slight lateral motion in these big ships during the final stages of coming alongside a fueling berth. Due to the tremendous inertia involved, serious damage can result from even a comparatively slight contact with a pier or camel.

Doppler in docking tankers.

To detect such motion, a pair of transducers may be installed well aft. These are placed on the athwartships axis, and are intended solely to detect lateral or turning motion when coming alongside a pier, and when the engines are stopped. Propeller noise would seriously affect their efficiency when underway.

3508. Marine Doppler navigation systems are still in the early stages of development. It seems highly probable that their performance and efficiency will be further improved. Doppler navigation will probably be limited in use to specialized ships, but for them it should prove to be a most useful adjunct to their overall navigational equipment.

Conclusion.

CHAPTER 36

Inertial Navigation

3601. *Inertial navigation* as defined by J. M. Slater in *Newtonian Navigation,* is the process of directing the movements of a rocket, ship, aircraft, or other vehicle from one point to another, based on sensing acceleration of the vehicle in a known spatial direction with the aid of instruments that mechanize the Newtonian Laws of Motion, and integrating acceleration to determine velocity and position.

3602. The *Ship's Inertial Navigation System* (SINS) has been developed as an accurate all-weather dead reckoning system. It employs gyroscopes, accelerometers, and associated electronics to sense turning rates and accelerations associated with the rotation of the earth, and with ship's movement relative to the surface of the earth.

Since Newton's Laws of Motion remain valid throughout the entire range of speeds of any naval vessel, inertial navigation, which is based on these laws, can be of tremendous assistance to the navigator. The inertial systems can furnish a wide range of information in addition to position coordinates. They provide a continuous readout of latitude, longitude, and ship's heading, as well as information on roll, pitch, and velocity, which is useful for the stabilization of other instruments. They are capable of extreme accuracy; their accuracy depends directly on how faithfully the component gyroscopes and accelerometers mechanize the laws of motion. Constant advances are being made both in the design and manufacturing processes of this precision instrumentation. In addition, every effort is made to locate and eliminate every possible source of error, no matter how minute. The SINS system is of necessity extremely complex compared to other navigational methods—consequently, it has a high initial cost and requires the use of expert maintenance and operating personnel.

3603. Inertial navigation systems were originally developed for aircraft; subsequently they came into use in spacecraft. The Ship's Inertial Navigation System was developed for the Polaris submarines; its use has now been extended to include surface ships and attack class submarines.

This text is intended to introduce the student to the basic principles of SINS, so that he may better understand its advantages and disadvantages, and its relationship to modern surface navigation. No mechanical or electronic system should ever be relied upon to give absolute continuous solution of the navigational problem, but rather to present intelligent information to assist the navigator in the performance of his duties.

Among the earliest applications of inertial navigation was the installation by Sperry Gyroscope Division of Sperry Rand Corporation of an MIT designed Ships Inertial Navigation System aboard the USS *Compass Island* in the fall of 1956. This was part of an evaluation program which led to the design and fabrication of SINS systems for submarines. Practical inertial navigation for shipboard use was inaugurated with the installation of the N6A Inertial Navigators, built by Autonetics, a Division of North American Aviation, Inc., in the submarines *Nautilus* and *Skate,* for their transpolar voyages in 1958. These units had originally been designed for missile use but were found acceptable for use in submarines.

3604. Inertial systems derive their basic name from the fact that gyroscopes   *Concept.*
and accelerometers (described in article 3605) have a sense of inertia in that they have a tendency to maintain their orientation in accordance with Newton's Laws. Any deviation from their original orientation can be sensed and measured with proper instrumentation. Accelerometers measure the individual components of horizontal and vertical accelerations, while the gyroscopes stabilize the accelerometers in a desired orientation. A computer, which is also included in the system, determines position and velocity by integrating the acceleration components sensed in the vehicle and also calculates orientation corrections caused by motion over the earth, rotation of the earth, and other factors.

Chapter 9 discussed the basic concept of the gyroscope, in introducing the principles of the north-seeking gyrocompass. In inertial systems three gyro axes (article 3606) are used to establish a stable platform for the accelerometers. The platform must remain horizontal with reference to the surface of the earth, while the gyroscopes, in their gimbaled mounts, are generally torqued so as to have two horizontal axes and one vertical axis. They are generally not fixed in space, although they could be in certain configurations. Certain errors in SINS increase with time, so that after an extended period the readout data become unacceptable; the system must then be corrected or updated. This is achieved by the *systems approach*, in which the inertial system with its own internal monitoring is supplemented by external sources of data on position, attitude, and velocity. These data sources have limited errors which are not a function of elapsed time; they include celestial trackers, radiometric sextants, Loran and other electronic navigation systems, navigation satellites, speed logs, etc.

3605. Inertial navigation is based on the sensing of movement of the vehicle   *Accelerometers.*
and integrating this movement or acceleration with respect to time to determine velocity and position. The stable platform established by means of gyroscopes is used to establish the horizontal for the accelerometers. In actual practice the accelerometers need not be physically mounted on the gyro platform; they can be installed on an accelerometer platform controlled by the gyros.

Acceleration sensing instruments may be of three basic types:

An *accelerometer* in which the output is a measure of acceleration,

A *velocity meter*—a single integrating device with an output signal proportional to velocity, and

A *distance meter*—a double integrating device with an output signal proportional to distance traveled.

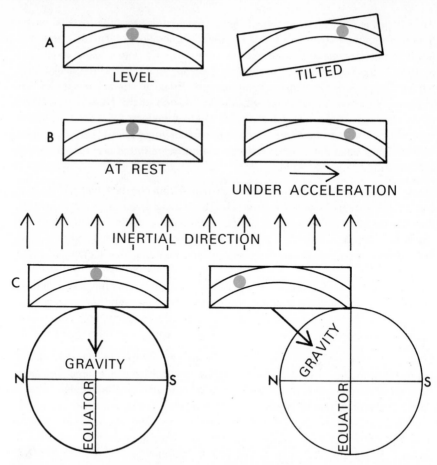

Figure 3605a: Gravity and acceleration effects on a bubble.

The term *accelerometer* is often used to denote any one of these instruments. The principle of the accelerometer may be illustrated by the use of a pendulum or a leveling bubble. Although a simple bubble would not measure acceleration to an accuracy needed in an inertial navigation system, it can be used to illustrate the basic concept of the effects of acceleration. For this illustration consider the bubble in an ordinary carpenter's level. Like the accelerometer, it cannot distinguish between the force of gravity and that of acceleration caused by movement. In Figure 3605a at A, the level is shown both at rest and with one end raised. In the latter case the bubble moves to a new position due to the force of gravity. At B, the same unit is shown both at rest and in motion in the direction of the arrow. The bubble moves off-center only during a change in velocity, that is during a period of acceleration or deceleration; at a constant velocity it remains centered.

The gyro-stabilized platform, or the gimbaled gyros, with no torque applied, will remain fixed relative to space rather than relative to the surface of the earth. If this were the case, then in Figure 3605a at C, the arrows would indicate the direction in space to which a platform is aligned. The accelerometer, represented by the level, is shown level with the earth at the equator. The direction of the gravity vector is 90° from the plane of the gyro platform, and points to the center of the earth. As the vehicle changes latitude the direction of the gravity vector will still be toward the center of the earth, but it will no longer be 90° from a

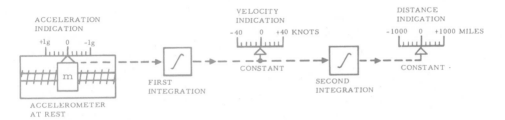

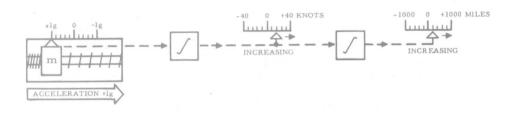

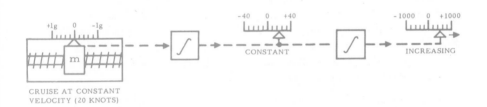

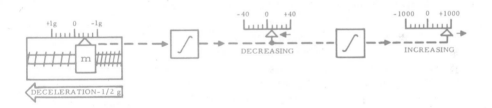

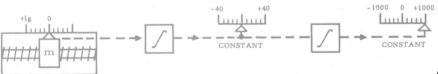

Figure 3605b: Illustrations of accelerometer action and integration for velocity and distance.

space oriented platform, thus creating a movement of the bubble by the force of gravity in a similar manner as shown at A. To avoid sensing this gravity component, the platform is generally maintained level as it is moved over the surface of the earth. This is accomplished by appropriate torquing of the gyroscopes. An actual accelerometer is much more complex than the carpenter's level, but it is similar in that it usually has only one sensitive axis, like the bubble which can only move along the glass tube.

Figure 3605b illustrates the principle of the accelerometer integrated for velocity and distance. Velocity in the technical sense is a measure both of speed and direction. Acceleration similarly is a measure both of magnitude and direction. In this case the mass (*m*) in the accelerometer is illustrated as free to move along a rod which determines the sensitive axis, but with the mass operating against a spring restraint. Such an instrument could be calibrated in terms of gravity by orienting the rod vertically with respect to the earth's surface, rather than horizontally. If the accelerometer is neither vertical nor horizontal with respect to the earth, the mass will be deflected to indicate a component of acceleration proportional to the sine of the tilt angle.

In the horizontal position, and while undergoing acceleration, the mass moves against the spring restraint until a point of equilibrium is reached whereby force (*f*) is equal to mass (*m*) multiplied by acceleration (*a*), or $f = ma$. This formula is universally valid in inertial space, except where velocity approaches the speed of light, when mass no longer remains constant. In Figure 3605b the accelerometer indication will be zero when the vehicle is stationary, or when it moves at a constant velocity. An accelerometer with double integration will give a readout for distance as well as for velocity. By following through the illustrations in Figure 3605b, the sequence of events is listed in five steps, as the accelerometer senses acceleration of 1*g* from rest, through a velocity of 20 knots, and deceleration at $\frac{1}{2}g$ to a stop, after traveling a distance of 1,000 miles. Velocity and distance readouts are illustrated as the results of the first and second integration of the accelerometer with respect to time.

In an inertial system the accelerometer will normally contain at least the first stage of integration to produce a signal indicating velocity. The instrument can then be referred to as a velocity meter. The second integration is readily performed in the computer of the SINS system to give distance. The sensing element in the accelerometer is subject to various vibrations and accelerations, so that if an elementary accelerometer were used, the signal strength would change rapidly and would indicate frequent shifts from acceleration to deceleration. This can be seen if a bubble level is moved across a table by hand; the bubble will fluctuate rapidly back and forth. The integrating accelerometer smooths out these rapid changes, and produces a steady velocity signal which is more readily accommodated by the system's digital computer.

An ideal accelerometer is unaffected by rotation around its sensitive axis. It measures the force, or a vector of the forces, along the direction of the sensitive axis.

The method of centering the floating element is generally accomplished by torque feedback.

Gyroscopes.   **3606.** A gyroscope is, in effect, a miniaturized version of the earth, used to hold the inertial platform in alignment. When affected by disturbing torques it cannot maintain direction in space as well as the earth does, due to its much smaller mass, which is only partially offset by its much higher speed of rotation. For this reason it is necessary to use several motors and gear drives or direct drive torquers to drive the gimbals in response to the gyroscopes signals to maintain platform stabilization. A "package" consisting of three gyroscopes, two for the horizontal axes, and one for azimuth can control the alignment of a platform from which accelerometer measurements are made. The velocity meters (ac-

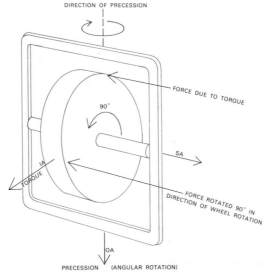

DIRECTION OF PRECESSION

FORCE DUE TO TORQUE

90°

SA

IA

TORQUE

FORCE ROTATED 90° IN DIRECTION OF WHEEL ROTATION

OA

PRECESSION   (ANGULAR ROTATION)

Figure 3606a: The rule for precession.

celerometers) can be mounted on the gyro stabilized platform. Velocity signals from these accelerometers are used to precess or torque the gyroscopes in their respective axes. This feedback from one instrument to the other produces an oscillation, which can best be visualized by considering a simple pendulum which has motion across the vertical when any force is applied to it, rather than simply moving to a new position and stopping. The inertial system is so designed that the oscillatory period T equals $2\pi(R/g)^{\frac{1}{2}}$, where R is earth's radius and g is the surface acceleration of gravity; this is the so-called *Schuler period,* or *84-minute pendulum.* With the system tuned to this 84-minute period, as the platform is moved at any angular velocity in any direction about the earth, the leveling gyroscopes are torqued to cause precesssion at exactly the same velocity, and thereby maintain the accelerometer platform in a level plane.

Schuler period.

Three rate gyros are normally used on the platform, the z axis of the platform being vertical. Axes x and y may be aligned north and east or in other azimuthal directions, depending upon the coordinates used in designing the system.

The basic sensing element of a modern SINS system, such as the Mark III Mod 5, is the *rate integrating gyroscope* (Figure 3606b). The accuracy of the SINS data output depends largely upon the ability of the gyro to maintain its orientation; this ability, while based to a great extent on the internal construction of the gyro, also depends upon the accuracy of calibration and alignment of the system, which are the responsibility of the shipboard operator. Basic information on gyroscopic precession was given in Chapter 9. It is summarized here, and is illustrated in Figure 3606a when applied to a gyroscope having a single degree of freedom. For a given torque around the input axis (IA), a given angular rate of precession about the output axis (OA) is generated, assuming the angular momentum of the wheel stays constant. The rule for precession is: a spin axis (SA) precesses about the output axis (OA) towards the input axis (IA) about which the torque is applied. In other words, with the force exerted by a torque acting directly on the wheel, the precession of the wheel is in the direction of the force rotated around 90° in the direction of wheel rotation, as shown in Figure 3606a.

Rate integrating gyroscope.

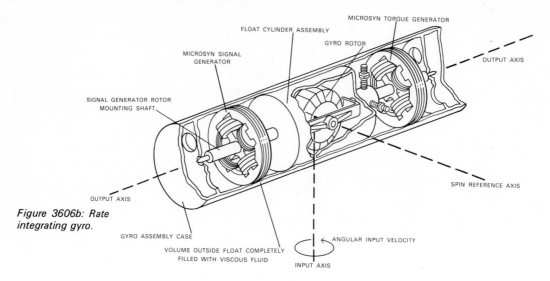

MICROSYN TORQUE GENERATOR

FLOAT CYLINDER ASSEMBLY

GYRO ROTOR

MICROSYN SIGNAL
GENERATOR

OUTPUT AXIS

SIGNAL GENERATOR ROTOR
MOUNTING SHAFT

SPIN REFERENCE AXIS

OUTPUT AXIS

*Figure 3606b: Rate
integrating gyro.*

GYRO ASSEMBLY CASE

ANGULAR INPUT VELOCITY

VOLUME OUTSIDE FLOAT COMPLETELY
FILLED WITH VISCOUS FLUID

INPUT AXIS

The gyroscope is damped to cause the rate of precession to match linearly the rate of input axis rotation. For example, for a *10 arc minute per hour* input rate the gyro precesses at 10 arc minutes every hour. The high precision gyroscopes used in SINS are capable of precessing linearly in response to input torques covering a range of seconds of arc per hour to several degrees of arc per second of time. The first value defines the minimum sensitivity of the unit, and the latter the maximum rate of roll, pitch, or azimuthal rate change, to which the gyro is designed to respond. The total displacement about the output axis is the same as the total angle through which the input axis is rotated. The rate integrating gyroscope (Figure 3606b) derives its name from the fact that the output of the pickoff signal is the summation, or integration, of all the rates causing precession ; the output angle is the integral of the input rate integral. The gyro pickoff output signal represents the total displacement of the *float* element, containing the spinning wheel and its supporting gimbal, with respect to its case. This displacement is caused by applied control precessional torques, gyro drift, and external angular rates acting on the case about the input axis.

*Figure 3606c:
Schematic of rate
gyroscope.*

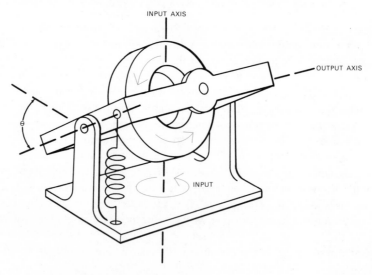

INPUT AXIS

OUTPUT AXIS

θ

INPUT

The gyro output drives a gimbal which applies a rotation about the input axis, always restoring the gyro output to a null. Thus the sum of the rates applied to and acting on the gyro must be zero.

A simplified schematic of a *rate gyroscope,* having a single degree of freedom, is shown in Figure 3606c. The precessional rotation about the output axis is restrained by a spring. The amount of precession around the output axis is in this case a function of the *rate* of rotational motion around the input axis rather than the *amount* of rotation, as in the integrating rate gyroscope. The rate of rotation around the input axis results in an output torque which is opposed by a restraining force illustrated by the spring device. The gyro will precess through angle θ until the precessional torque is balanced by the force exerted by the spring. It follows, then, that as long as the *rate* of input remains constant the gyro will maintain its position. When the rate of input decreases the gyro will feel the force of the spring applied as an input torque, and this torque will cause the rotor to return to its normal position. The angle θ is always proportional to the angular input rate.

Rate gyroscope.

3607. Two basic principles can be stated which summarize the use of gyroscopes and accelerometers in an inertial system.

The assembled system.

> *Linear momentum* of a mass remains constant unless an external force is applied.

> *Angular momentum* of a rotating mass remains constant unless an external torque is applied.

By practical application of the first principle, if acceleration is precisely measured, by integrating time, the distance traveled can be determined. Applying the second principle a gyroscope can be used to determine the direction of travel. Having determined both distance and direction, a dead reckoning navigation system is created.

Figure 3607a shows the schematic of a gimbaled inertial design using separate gyroscopes and accelerometers for the three axes *x, y,* and *z.*

Figure 3607b shows a complete inertial navigation system, the Autonetics N7A *Inertial Autonavigator.* The arrangement of the internal component parts is

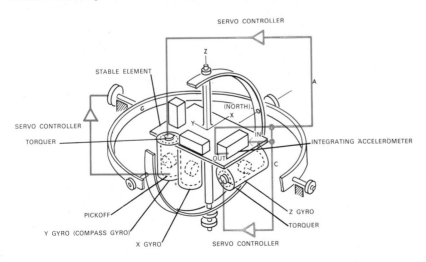

Figure 3607a: Components of an inertial guidance platform.

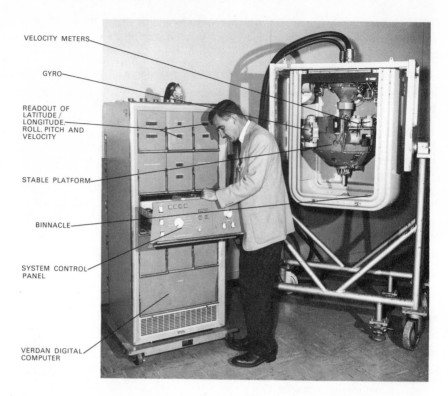

VELOCITY METERS

GYRO

READOUT OF
LATITUDE /
LONGITUDE,
ROLL, PITCH AND
VELOCITY

STABLE PLATFORM

BINNACLE

SYSTEM CONTROL
PANEL

VERDAN DIGITAL
COMPUTER

Figure 3607b:
N7A Inertial
Autonavigator.

visible, with the cover removed from the binnacle. In the cabinet at the left of the photograph the top section contains windows for the readout of latitude, longitude, roll, pitch, and velocity. The central section contains the system control panel, and the lower section holds a digital computer designated VERDAN (Versatile Digital Differential Analyzer).

Figure 3607c shows the Sperry Mark III Mod 4 SINS installed aboard ship. The binnacle is shown at the left, the various consoles, with their functions marked, are shown at the right.

Errors in inertial
navigation.

3608. Inertial systems are not subject to the various errors of dead reckoning navigation outlined in article 712, grouped together under the heading "current." In theory the inertial system is limited in ultimate accuracy only by the degree of perfection of the instrumentation used. Imperfections can, of course, arise in many of the various parts of the assembled system.

When the inertial system is used aboard ship over a considerable period of time, the dominant error sources are the gyro loop uncompensated drift rates. These drift rates are composed of many variables, depending on the mechanization and configuration of the system. They may be due to imperfections in manufacturing, to instabilities arising subsequent to the installation of the system, or they can be caused by vehicle movement or position. The ultimate result, however, is that they appear as gyro platform drift, causing erroneous presentation of the output data. The principal known causes of this apparent gyro drift are outlined below.

Article 3605 stated that an accelerometer is sensitive only to acceleration along one axis. If two accelerometers are mounted with their sensitive axes at right

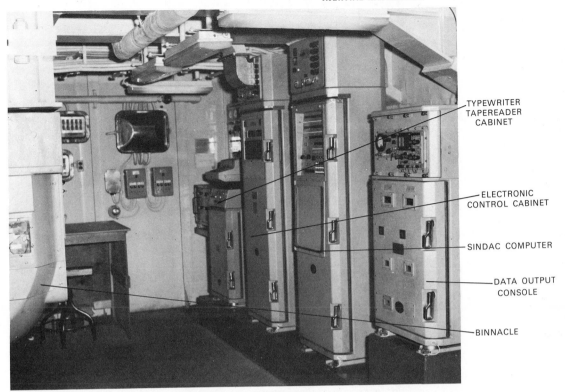

TYPEWRITER
TAPEREADER
CABINET

ELECTRONIC
CONTROL CABINET

SINDAC COMPUTER

DATA OUTPUT
CONSOLE

BINNACLE

angles to one another, they can be used to measure any arbitrary acceleration in the plane in which they are mounted. Assuming for the sake of simplicity that the system is so designed that one accelerometer is mounted with a north-south axis while the other is in the east-west axis, then in measuring accelerations along any course each will measure one component of the acceleration. These components can be integrated separately and interpreted as distances traveled north-south or east-west from the assumed starting point. Obviously, an exact initial alignment of the platform is necessary. If there is a misalignment in azimuth of the system, and the ship is steaming on a precise course of 000°, the east-west accelerometer will detect a very slight signal which will produce an erroneous indication that the ship has moved slightly either to the east or west, and the north distance readout will be slightly too low.

Figure 3607c: Mark III Mod 4 SINS.

Errors in alignment.

As the earth completes one rotation about its axis in 24 hours, the accelerometer platform must be continuously adjusted to remain level with respect to the earth during this entire period. If the platform is permitted to tilt, the accelerometer will sense a component of gravity. This adjustment for the computed earth rate is automatically applied to the platform by the computer system. While the computed earth rate may equal in *magnitude* the true earth rate, if its *direction* is incorrect due to a misalignment of the platform in heading, there will be an error in the rate supplied to the platform. The resultant error in the accelerometer platform position is generally known as the 24-hour error since it is based upon erroneous sensing of the daily rotation of the earth.

Earth rate.

The fact that the computed earth rate must match the true is used in aligning the inertial platform. With the system at rest the platform is leveled and aligned as closely as possible in azimuth. The accelerometer outputs are then monitored,

Aligning the platform using earth rate.

573

and any indicated acceleration is considered to be due to platform tilt caused by residual error in the azimuth alignment. Azimuth alignment is then corrected until no measurable platform tilt occurs. When this procedure is followed, the platform has been aligned by using the earth's rate of rotation as a reference.

The inertial package when carried over the surface of the earth is affected by both the curvature of the earth and by gravity. When the computer arrives at an incorrect value of the angular distance traveled by the vehicle, due to incorrect alignment or because of other errors in the system, it will supply an incorrect signal to the drive motor used for leveling the accelerometer platform. This causes the accelerometer, which cannot distinguish between gravity and vehicle acceleration, to sense a gravity component, and an erroneous acceleration signal is fed back through the closed loop. This attempt of the system to correct itself produces an undamped oscillation which, in a properly designed system, would have a period approaching 24 hours (Figure 3608).

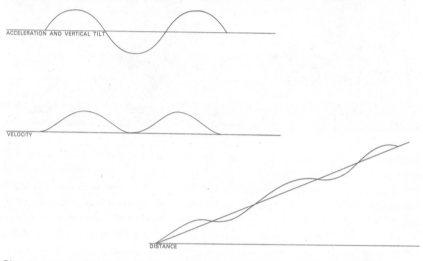

Figure 3608:
System errors.

Gyro drift.

Since a gyroscope cannot be constructed to be mechanically perfect, some drift rate will always be present. This drift of the platform tends to produce an acceleration error which increases linearly with time. Due to the closed feedback loop the earth curvature is actually an asset rather than a liability. The accelerometer platform oscillates about a zero mean error as described in the preceding paragraph rather than building up a linear error. Nevertheless, as indicated in Figure 3608, there will be a consistent and often random build-up of error with respect to time, due to gyro drift, producing a position error.

Miscellaneous errors.

The precise requirements of an inertial system make it necessary to take secondary effects into account; these are caused by Coriolis effect, and the earth's shape, which is not perfectly spherical. These error sources are automatically compensated for by the computer. For long periods of inertial navigation, dynamic coupling between various parts of the system produces a small rate error which must also be considered.

It must be realized that error sources can better be described statistically than as constants. Using this concept, the long-term build-up of errors can be determined and reduced more readily than by attempting to evaluate and use only constant error sources.

3609. The early methods of resetting the system were based on the assumption that the drift rate remained constant during the sampling period. This did not prove entirely satisfactory because accurate drift rate calculations can be made only periodically, and the rate must remain nearly constant or the random drift must be reasonably well known. External position information is needed from outside sources, such as a Loran or celestial fix, to recalibrate or reset the SINS, regardless of the reset technique. These data are fed through the computer which computes and applies proper torquing to the stabilized platforms. All of the data fed to the computers needs to be smoothed out, as frequent resetting, or the use of data which may itself be inaccurate can create errors in determining and correcting the drift rate of the system. A theory developed by R. E. Kalman and generally referred to as the "Kalman filter" makes it feasible to include the randomness of the system as well as of the reference source in the reset formula. A detailed explanation of the theory is beyond the scope of this text. It involves complex differential equations; in practice these are solved by the computer.

Reset procedure.

Kalman filter theory.

3610. New methods of monitoring the SINS gyros are constantly being developed. One method of determining the drift rate is by employing a *monitoring gyro.*

Monitoring gyro.

Including a monitor (a rate gyro) in the system improves performance because it senses and supplies data to the computer on any uncompensated fixed or slowly varying components of drift in the *x* and *y* gyros; a significant reduction in the random error component is also obtained. The monitoring technique utilizes a redundant gyro mounted on a rotating platform. An integrating rate gyro, with high gain feedback from pickoff to torquer, is used to effectively yield an accurate rate gyro. This platform, an integral part of the *heading* gimbal, rotates about an axis parallel to the heading gimbal axis, and does not compensate the *z* axis, or *heading* gyro. Reversal of the direction of the input axis of the monitor inertial component, with respect to the navigational component, represents the basic technique used. Case reversal is instrumented by successively positioning the monitor table to each of the four quadrant positions, under control of the computer program. The monitoring gyro provides an output at each quadrant which is equal to the difference between the gyro-applied torque and the sensed torque. The torque applied from the computer to the monitor gyro is the same as the torque computed for the gyro being monitored. Since the SINS system computes the ship's position from accelerations resulting from the ship's movement it is important that gyro drift be known as accurately as possible. The monitoring gyro improves overall performance of the system by detecting gyro drift that has not been compensated.

3611. Due to the errors just discussed, inertial navigation systems must have the capability of being updated or reset through the computer. Continuous compensation can be made for a known gyro drift. Discrete position information, obtained, for example, from a Loran, celestial, NAVSAT, or bathymetric fix, can also be used to damp the system by manual or automatic insertion of the position into the computer.

Stellar inertial navigation.

The study of navigation involves various coordinate systems. Regardless of the system of coordinates chosen for the internal operation of the system, the computer must deal with three reference systems, as well as with the vector angles defining the angular relationship of the reference systems. These vector angles can be described in an overly simplified manner as follows:

1. The vector angle relating the platform coordinate system, defined by the sensitive axes of the inertial instruments on the platform, to a true coordinate system such as latitude and longitude.

2. The vector angle relating the computer coordinate system, defined by information available to the computer, to a true coordinate system.

3. The vector angle relating the platform coordinate system to the computer coordinate system.

This latter vector angle can in part be attributed to the mis-alignment of the platform, resulting in a slightly different set of coordinates than those programmed in the computer. The interrelationship of vector angles in the coordinate systems outlined above can always be stated as:

$$\text{vector no. 1} = \text{no. 2} + \text{no. 3}$$

It is often assumed that a star tracker mounted on an inertial system is intended primarily for determining a celestial fix. It can also be used to determine the platform drift rate representing a major portion of the vector angle described in no. 3. The star tracker could be physically mounted on the stable element of the inertial system; in actual use it is often remotely located. A computer in the system can automatically compute elevation angle or altitude, and azimuth angle, from the ephemeristic data stored in its memory section, and from its knowledge of ship's position. Disregarding errors in driving the telescope, it would be possible to point the telescope directly at the star, provided the coordinate system stored in the computer and the platform coordinates were coincident. The platform-mounted telescope will, however, have a pointing error equivalent to vector angle no. 3.

The telescope on the star tracker generally scans around or across the line of sight to the star. In this process it does have the ability to track the star, thereby permitting a determination of the deviation in altitude and azimuth angles from those computed. These error data, extrapolated over a period of time, can be used in determining drift rate of the gyro platform. In this monitoring system it is necessary to use either two trackers tracking different stars, or one tracker alternately tracking two stars. This is because the star tracker, when used as a monitor, must be capable of measuring the angular deviation between the actual line of sight to the star and the computed line. The tracker can measure only components normal to the line of sight; it cannot detect angular errors about the line of sight. However, the error components obtained from two stars can be resolved in the computer to determine the total error.

Since the stellar-monitored system has the capability of determining a gyro drift rate, it can be used for *alignment* of the platform attitude, as well as to correct the *computed* azimuth orientation without physically rotating the platform. It must be remembered that the stellar monitor system will introduce its own slight error caused by refraction compensation errors, ephemeristic errors, timing errors and mechanical pointing errors. They may be considered as essentially constant, while tracking a star for a short period of time. While alternately tracking two stars, the stellar monitoring error will generally be random in nature. The *radio sextant* (Chapter 34) is also used with an inertial system in a manner similar to the star trackers to provide a celestial updating system under adverse weather conditions.

3612. Previous articles have mentioned various coordinate systems relating to inertial navigation. The gyros in the inertial system are the inertial instruments which define the frame of reference in which acceleration is measured. This frame of reference is mathematically described by the particular coordinate system chosen, and mechanically defined by causing the gyro to precess at angular rates as dictated by the coordinate system. The design and arrangement of components and the coordinate system employed within the instrumentation is not strictly a navigational function and will not be discussed in detail. The readout on a SINS system is normally given in the familiar terms of latitude and longitude even though the computer may go through various conversions and computations to arrive at this readout. The operating manual for the SINS Mark III Mod 5 explains the operation of that particular instrumentation on the basis of the following three coordinate systems, which are familiar to the navigator, and will be reviewed only briefly.

Coordinate systems.

The *ship's coordinate system* which is defined by the longitudinal axis, the athwartship axis, and the vertical or deck-to-keel axis, which, in the case of the submarine, can be defined as the optical axis of the main periscope. The angular quantities measured in the ship coordinate system are relative bearing or relative azimuth, and elevation—the angle measured in a vertical plane from the deck plane to the line of sight. The ship's coordinate system is related to the horizontal plane in the local geographic coordinate system by the angles of roll, pitch, and heading.

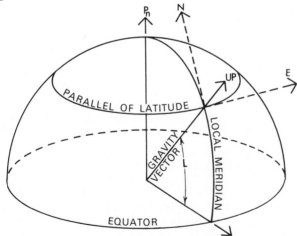

Figure 3612a: Geographical coordinate system.

The *local geographic coordinate system* is located at the ship's position and is based on the direction of the vertical and the direction of north (Figure 3612A). The quantities measured in the local geographic system are velocity north, velocity east, and *depth* when used in a submarine. Heading is measured about the vertical from north clockwise to the projection in the horizontal plane of the ship's fore and aft axis. It can be considered as a local coordinate system, and the angle relating this system to the equatorial coordinate system is latitude.

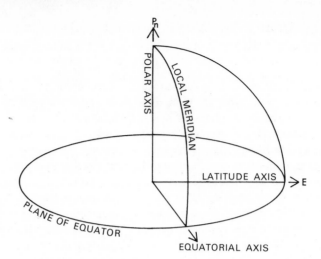

The *equatorial coordinate system* consists of the earth's polar axis, the intersection of the plane of the ship's local meridian with the plane of the equator, and an axis directed east perpendicular to both these axes (Figure 3612B). The intersection of the equatorial coordinate system axes is therefore at the center of the earth. The latitude axis and the east axis of the local geographic system are parallel. Ship's motion in longitude is measured about the polar axis of this system, while motion in latitude is measured about the latitude axis.

Computers.

3613. Due to the technical and mathematical complexity of inertial navigation systems, a computer must be included as an integral part of the overall system. Within this chapter various references have been made to the functions of the computer. The computers used in modern SINS systems are usually general purpose digital computers, but they are used in a very special purpose application. The words "general purpose" merely imply that the computer could be programmed without a hardware change to solve any general problem instead of the specific computations related to inertial navigation.

The computer for a SINS system could be analog rather than digital although the digital type is at present the more widely used, and its functions will vary somewhat depending upon the acceleration instruments employed, the system accuracy required, and the choice of coordinate system. In general, the computer will send torquing signals to the gyros and accelerometers, in addition to computing present position and velocity.

Navigational computers are further discussed in Chapter 39. For use with SINS they must have at least five major functional components. These consist of a storage or memory unit, control unit, arithmetical unit, input unit, and output unit. The navigator is directly concerned only with the latter two functions. Input to the memory is generally in the form of perforated typed tape. Control inputs are electronic signals generated automatically. The output unit is designed on demand to furnish *readout* on a tape, and to *indicate* a numerical display on the control panel.

Conclusion.

3614. Inertial navigation is a field in which technology advances rapidly. A great variety of systems are already in existence ranging from those designed for ballistic missiles, in which guidance is necessary only for a very short period of time which can be measured in seconds, to those designed for nuclear submarines, which may cruise for many weeks. It is difficult to predict the optimum configurations which will be used in any future system.

In addition to providing a self-contained navigation system, data from SINS can be used for other navigational applications. The Navy Navigation Satellite System requires an input of ship's motion into the solution, and this can be obtained accurately from the SINS. On aircraft carriers, SINS is used to transfer precise ship's velocity and position to the inertially-equipped aircraft before launching. This transfer of information is required for gyrocompass alignment of the aircraft inertial systems.

Gyroscopes are normally thought of as physically spinning masses in the form of a wheel. New instrumentation now under development indicates the ultimate feasibility of using other principles, such as laser gyros. On gyros currently in production, improvements such as gas bearings are used to reduce bearing friction. R&D units using electrostatic support for a gyro sphere have also been developed.

Instrumentation in this field has caused many formidable technological problems, and formulation and analysis of the systems has involved very complicated mathematical calculations which would be almost impossible to complete without the present advanced computer technology.

It must be remembered that for all the accuracy of inertial systems, the output is merely an accurate DR and not a fix. Only external means (bearings, NAVSAT, celestial, etc.) will provide the exact location of the ship at a given time. The best inertial equipment must be updated at regular intervals. The navigator who puts blind faith in the output of his inertial systems invites disaster.

CHAPTER 37

Satellite Navigation

Introduction.

3701. The *Navy Navigation Satellite System* developed for the U. S. Navy is generally referred to as NAVSAT. It originated within the Navy as Project Transit and was developed to fulfill a requirement established by the Chief of Naval Operations with an objective stated as follows: "Develop a satellite system to provide accurate all weather, world-wide navigation for naval surface ships, aircraft, and submarines." The system was then developed by the Applied Physics Laboratory of the Johns Hopkins University under a Navy contract. It is a highly accurate, passive, all-weather, world-wide navigational system, suitable for subsurface and surface navigation, as well as for use in aircraft. It is coming into increasingly wide use in the fleet, and is also available to commercial interests.

Doppler shift.

3702. The measurement of radio signals transmitted by NAVSAT is based on the *Doppler shift* phenomenon—the apparent change in frequency of the radio waves received when the distance between the source of radiation (in this case the satellite) and the receiving station, is increasing or decreasing because of the motion of either or both. The amount of shift in either case is proportional to the velocity of approach or recession. The frequency is shifted upward as the satellite approaches the receiving station and shifted downward as the satellite passes and recedes. The amount of this shift depends on the exact location of the receiving station with respect to the path of the satellite. Accordingly, if the satellite positions (orbits) are known, it is possible by a very exact measure of the Doppler shift in frequency to calculate the location of the receiver on earth. The Doppler shift is also affected by the earth's rotation, but this effect is allowed for and corrected by the computer in providing the fix.

The accuracy obtained by using this Doppler shift technique is possible because the quantities measured, frequency and time, can readily be determined to an accuracy of one part in a billion.

Components of the system.

3703. The NAVSAT system (Figure 3703a) consists of one or more satellites, ground tracking stations, a computing center, an injection station, Naval Observatory time signals, and the shipboard receiver and computer.

Satellite data.

Each satellite is placed in a nominally circular polar orbit at an altitude of about 600 nautical miles, orbiting the earth in approximately 105 minutes. Only one satellite is used at any given time to determine position. The satellite stores data which is updated from a ground station approximately every twelve hours and it broadcasts the following data every two minutes:

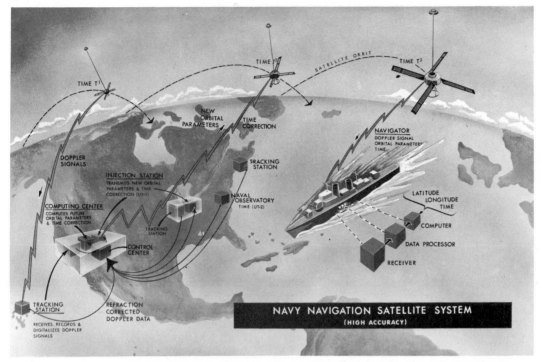

Figure 3703a:
Components of
NAVSAT system.

Fixed and variable parameters describing its own orbit.

A time reference.

Two frequencies, 150 and 400 MHz, are employed because the ionosphere which is a dispersion medium bends and also stretches radio waves, causing the satellite to seem closer than it actually is. Each frequency is somewhat differently affected, and by comparing the Doppler signals received on the two frequencies, precise allowance can be made for the ionosphere's effect on the waves.

The parameters describe the satellite orbit as a function of time and are correct only for the 2-minute time interval for which they are transmitted by the satellite, and for those intervals immediately preceding and following that period. In each 2-minute transmitting period, data on eight periods is given, four before and four after the time of the message. The time reference is synchronized with corrected GMT (UT_2) from the Naval Observatory. A block diagram of the satellite function is shown in Figure 3703b.

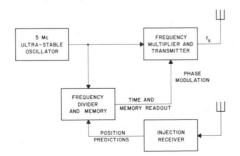

Figure 3703b:
Block diagram
transit satellite.

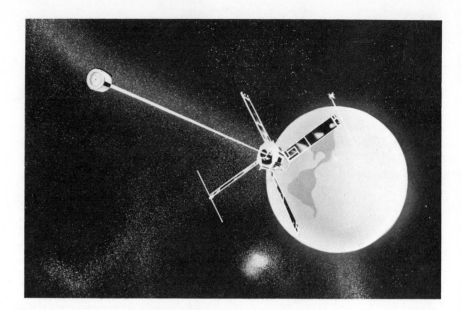

Figure 3703c:
Transit satellite.

The satellites (Figure 3703c) sometimes referred to as "birds," are completely transistorized; they are octagonal in shape, and have four windmill-like vanes, which carry solar cells. They are gravity-gradient stabilized, so that the directional antennae are always pointed downwards, towards the earth.

Position fixing.

A satellite fix may be obtained when the satellite's maximum altitude, relative to the observer, is above 15°, and less than 75°. As a general rule, each satellite will yield four fixes a day—two on successive orbits, and two more on successive orbits some twelve hours later. However, this sequence may be disturbed, as the satellite, while above the horizon, may pass at too great or too small an altitude relative to the observer to permit obtaining a position. Figure 3703d shows four satellites in orbit around the earth; it is obvious that an increase in the number of satellites will increase the frequency with which fixes may be obtained.

Figure 3703d:
Coverage with
four satellites.

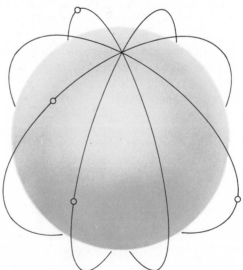

NAVSAT users are kept informed as to the operational status of the satellites, of the insertion of new satellites into service, and the withdrawal of satellites by SPATRAK messages originated by the U. S. Naval Astronautics Group, Pt. Mugu, California.

3704. A planet in deep space follows a fixed path around its parent body in accordance with Newton's Laws of Motion. Its orbit is Keplerian, or perfectly elliptical, and its position can be predicted exactly for any given future instant of time. A NAVSAT satellite moves under the earth's gravitational attraction in accordance with the same laws, but as it operates at an altitude of about 600 miles, it is subjected to external forces which produce orbital irregularities, or *perturbations*. To make the system acceptable, these perturbations must be accurately predicted, so that the satellite's position can be determined for any instant of time.

The need for daily satellite updating.

The most important of these forces is caused by the earth's shape; the earth is not a sphere, but an oblate spheroid, and, in addition, its gravitational field is irregular. Figure 3704 shows the earth's gravity model, as sensed by a NAVSAT satellite. The satellite is also subject to slight atmospheric drag, as it is not operating in a complete vacuum. Other external forces which affect it are the gravitational attraction of the sun and the moon, solar photon pressure and solar wind, electrostatic and electromagnetic forces caused by the satellite's interaction with charged particles in space, and in the earth's magnetic field.

Figure 3704: Contour plot of mean sea level deviations.

Fortunately, all the forces causing perturbations are either sufficiently constant or so localized that they can be reduced to formulae which can be programmed into orbital computations.

Satellite tracking stations.

To determine the precise orbit of each satellite in the system, ground tracking stations are established at exactly determined positions in Hawaii, California, Minnesota, and Maine. These stations regularly monitor the Doppler signal as a function of time. Concurrently, the U. S. Naval Observatory monitors the satellite's time signal for comparison with corrected universal time (UT_2). The resulting information is transmitted to the computing center for processing.

As the satellite is essentially moving as a planet, and as the perturbations in its orbit are determined by the computer, of all the possible paths permitted by Newton's Laws, only one can result in a particular curve of Doppler shift. Thus, at any instant of time, the position of the satellite relative to the known location of the tracking station can be determined very precisely.

The computing center, having received these data, computes an orbit for the satellite that best fits the Doppler curve obtained from the tracking stations. This orbital information is extrapolated to give satellite positions for each two minutes of UT_2 for the following sixteen hours, and these data are supplied to the injection station, for transmission to the satellite about every twelve hours, for storage and retransmission on schedule. The satellite is in effect a relay station which stores and transmits the data computed at ground stations and which are inserted in its memory system.

Shipboard NAVSAT equipment.

3705. Typical NAVSAT shipboard equipment used by the navigator consists of a receiver, a computer, and a tape readout unit. Complete operator instructions are supplied in the operator's manual. A prototype system, the AN/SRN-9 (XN-5) built by APL, Johns Hopkins University, is shown in Figure 3705a. The BRN-3 equipment (Figure 3705b) used in fleet ballistic missile submarines is larger and somewhat more complex, as both the operation and self-test capability are more fully automated. The BRN-3 is not an integrating Doppler system, as it obtains approximately 1 second samples of the signal rather than integrating over a longer period. However, from the navigator's viewpoint they perform similar functions, as do other commercially produced receivers.

Figure 3705a: AN/ SRN-9 shipboard equipment.

NAVIGATION SET, RADIO
AN/BRN-3

*Figure 3705b:
BRN-3 shipboard
equipment.*

3706. To obtain a fix, the ship's *estimated position* and *velocity* or movement must be entered in the computer. The accuracy of the estimated position is not of great importance; however, the accuracy with which the velocity can be established is important, as will be seen in the following discussion.

Ship motion computer inputs.

On ships equipped with the Ships Inertial Navigation System (SINS) described in Chapter 36, the two minute synchronization signal received from the satellite can be transmitted to SINS. In some installations this signal causes the SINS to print out ship's position data coinciding with the two-minute Doppler count. In other installations the SINS general purpose computer is used to solve the NAVSAT problem rather than employing a separate computer.

If inertial equipment is not available to supply automatic information on the ship's movement to the computer, the course and speed from the gyrocompass and EM log are inserted in the computer. This, of course, is a potential source of error, as the system, for high accuracy, requires an input of the ship's true velocity; that is, her speed and direction of travel relative to the surface of the earth. Unfortunately, accurate information on the existence of a current and its set and drift are rarely available to the navigator. In round numbers, the error in a NAVSAT fix will be about 0.25 miles for every knot of unknown velocity. A velocity north (or south) error causes a considerably larger error in the fix than a velocity east error.

3707. The computer insertions can be made in various forms. They may be in the form of an estimated position at a given time plus course and speed, estimated positions at two minute intervals, distance moved in X-Y coordinates, etc. The geographic accuracy of an estimated position is not of vital importance, but accurate velocity *is* required. Thus, when two estimated positions are used, the location of the second position must be accurately described relative to the first.

Required shipboard computer input.

+ 0	3	9	0	0	0	0		Estimated Latitude (39°00.00' North)
						5		Accepted
− 0	7	6	0	0	0	0		Estimated Longitude (76°00.00 West)
						5		Accepted
+ 0	0	0	8	2	0	0		Antenna Height (82 Meters)
						5		Accepted
+ 2	0	2	0	0	7	5		Time (20 Hours and 20 Minutes GMT—Day 75)
						5		Accepted
+ 1	5	6	2	2	7	5		Ship's Motion (15.6 Knots at 227.5° Azimuth)
						5		Accepted

Figure 3707: Typical ship's data entered in the SRN-9 computer.

Figure 3707 shows typical taped data as it might appear for insertion on the SRN-9, together with an explanation of the coding. The antenna height entry states its height above the *geoid*, which is the assumed shape of the earth, as used by the computer. It combines the antenna height above the water with a correction for the shape of the earth in the immediate area. This correction is obtained from a chart supplied with the operating instructions.

How a fix is obtained

3708. The fix determined by the ship's computing system is based on the Doppler frequency shift which occurs whenever the relative distance between a transmitter and a receiver is changing. Such a change occurs whenever a transmitting satellite passes within range of a radio receiver on earth, and consists of a combination of the motion of the satellite in its orbit, the motion of the vessel over the surface of the earth, and the rotation of the earth about its axis. Each of these motions contributes to the overall Doppler frequency shift in a characteristic way. An increase in frequency occurs as the satellite approaches the ship, in effect compressing the waves en route. The received frequency exactly equals the transmitted frequency at the point of closest satellite approach, where for an instant of time there is no relative motion directly along the vector from the satellite to the receiver. The received frequency then decreases as the satellite recedes from the ship's position thereby expanding the radio waves between them. The shape of the curve of frequency differences and its time of reception depend both on the receiver's position on earth and the satellite's location in space. The reception of these Doppler signals and the resulting computer computations form the basis of the satellite navigation system.

Figure 3708a: Integrated Doppler measurement.

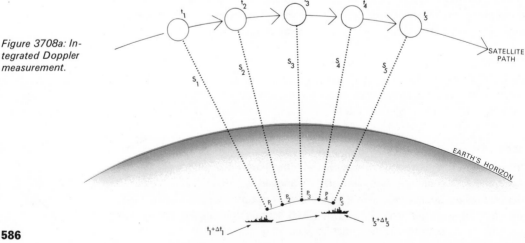

Figure 3708a shows in a simplified form the relationship of time, range, and position. In the diagram, t_1 through t_5 represent the position of the satellite in orbit at the successive transmissions which occur at two minute intervals. S_1 through S_5 represent the slant range between the satellite and the ship. p_1 through p_5 represent the position of the ship referenced to the time at which the receiver recognizes the satellite synchronization signal $t_1 + \triangle t_1$ through $t_5 + \triangle t_5$, where $\triangle t$ represents the time interval for the signal to travel from the satellite to the receiver aboard ship.

The integral Doppler measurements (Figure 3708b) are simply the count N 1–2 of the number of cycles received between $t_1 + \triangle t_1$, and $t_2 + \triangle t_2$, the count N 2–3 of the number of Doppler cycles between $t_2 + \triangle t_2$ and $t_3 + \triangle t_3$, and so on for all two-minute intervals during the satellite pass.

Frequency

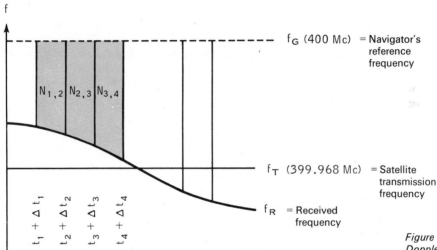

Figure 3708b: Doppler frequency variation with time producing slant range change.

Four or five two-minute Doppler counts are obtained during a typical satellite pass. Each Doppler count consists of a constant plus a measured slant range difference between the receiver and the satellite at positions defined by the navigation message. The measured range differences are truly known only if the constant but unknown frequency difference, $\triangle F$, between the satellite's oscillator and the receiver's reference oscillator can be determined.

To calculate a position fix, the Doppler counts and the satellite message are fed to a digital computer. The computer is also provided with an initial estimate of the ship's latitude and longitude and an estimate of the frequency difference $\triangle F$. The computer then compares calculated range differences from the known satellite positions to the estimated ship's position with those measured by the Doppler counts, and the navigation fix is obtained by searching for and finding those values of latitude, longitude, and $\triangle F$ which make the calculated range differences agree best with the measured range differences. Because the geometry is complicated, only simple, linearized equations are used, and the computations are performed repeatedly until the solution converges. Many repetitions are normally required, and a fix is obtained within a few minutes on typical small digital computers.

587

The SRN-9
receiver.

3709. The SRN-9 receiver uses a tape printout of all information received; a portion of this tape printout is shown in Figure 3709a with an explanation of the data; other receivers use different formats for the data. However, the tape printout shown is typical of the presentation of information. The navigation computer uses these data to compute a fix automatically, which is also presented as a tape readout. An example of the printed fix is shown in Figure 3709b.

	Units	Title and Symbol
++ 1 2 8 1.0 8 1 5	Minutes	Time of Perigee (t_p)
+ .4 2 7 5 8 1 7	Deg/Min	Mean Satellite Motion − 3 $(\dot{M} - 3)$
+ 3 2 0.2 0 3 4	Degrees	Argument of Perigee (ϕ_p)
+ .0 0 2 1 4 3 1	Deg/Min	Argument of Perigee Change Rate $(1\dot{\phi}1)$
+ 0.0 1 1 1 1 5	None	Eccentricity
+ 0 7 3 7 4.0 1	Kilom.	Orbit Semi Major Axis (A_0)
+ 2 1 1.8 4 8 2	Degrees	Right Ascension of the Ascending Node (ω_N)
− .0 0 0 0 6 3 6	Deg/Min	Right Ascension Change Rate $(\dot{\omega}_N)$
+ 0.0 1 5 7 0 7	None	Cosine of the Inclination Angle
+ 1 3 4.2 8 0 2	Degrees	Right Ascension of Greenwich at Time of Perigee (ω_G)
+ 0.9 9 9 8 7 7	None	Sine of the Inclination Angle
3 9 7 7 4 9 2.	Cycles	(Doppler Count)

Figure 3709a: Tape printout of receiver showing satellite orbit.

Figure 3709b: Tape printout of ship's position.

+ 0 3 9 0 9 7 7		Latitude: 39°09.7782' North
8 2		
− 0 7 6 5 3 8 3	Fix Result	Longitude: 76°53.8350' West
5 0		
+ 3 1 9 6 2 1 9		Offset Frequency: 31,962.19 Cycles

Time signals.

3710. The time signal transmitted by the satellite, which occurs at the two-minute mark, is accurate to better than 0.02 seconds. It may be used conveniently as an accurate chronometer check. With the NAVSAT receiver locked to the satellite signal, the two minute signal will be heard as a "beep."

Conclusion.

3711. Since it became operational in January 1964, the Navy Navigation Satellite System has fulfilled the requirements originally established by CNO. It has proven itself to be both extremely accurate and reliable as a navigational system, and has contributed greatly to our knowledge of the earth's shape, and its gravitational field.

As with any highly sophisticated equipment, it requires expert maintenance, and all operating personnel must be thoroughly trained in its use.

CHAPTER 38

Advanced Celestial Observing Instruments

3801. The hand-held sextant is the principal observing instrument used for celestial navigation afloat. More highly sophisticated optical instruments have recently been developed for use aboard special purpose vessels and for submerged navigation at periscope depth. These instruments will be described briefly; for the theory of celestial navigation the student is referred to the appropriate preceding chapters.

Introduction.

3802. The introduction of high speed jet aircraft equipped with gyroscopic heading references led to the development of the astro tracker; automatic star tracking systems were soon extended to marine and space use. The astro tracker is capable of acquiring and tracking the image of a star; it contains a gyroscopic unit for establishing a horizontal reference plane from which altitude and azimuth measurements can be made. In small self-contained units the greatest single error generally is caused by faulty establishment of the horizontal plane. Nevertheless, acceptable results are achieved in obtaining star azimuths for correcting the heading reference, and in obtaining altitudes for lines of position.

Astro trackers.

Performance levels of automatic star tracking systems are specified in terms of tracking capability and accuracy of star measurements from which track and present position are obtained. In present state-of-the-art systems star catalogs of 100 stars can be acquired and tracked in the daytime or nighttime sky. Position accuracies within one nautical mile are obtainable. Like all celestial techniques, star tracking systems are error bounded; i.e. position and track accuracies do not degrade with time or distance traveled.

A typical daylight Star Tracker Assembly is shown in Figure 3802a. The central element, the photoelectric telescope, contains the optics, scanner and photosensitive solid state sensor. The telescope is servo articulated in bearing and altitude. This assembly is installed upon pitch and roll gimbals which provide base motion isolation for the photoelectric tracking process.

Solid state photoelectric telescope.

A typical photoelectric telescope is gimbaled to provide freedom of movement in bearing and elevation. Telescope gimbal freedom is unlimited in bearing and restricted in the unit illustrated to elevations of from 30 to 80 degrees. Synchro resolvers or digital angle transducers on each gimbal provide an electrical readout of gimbal position. Incident starlight is received through the telescope aperture. The light is focused by a combination of lenses and mirrors onto the photodetector plane. A modulator located in the light path imparts intelligence to the star acquisition and tracking process by determining star image position

589

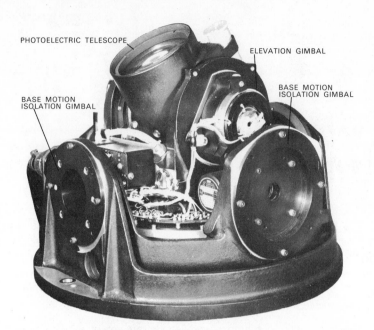

PHOTOELECTRIC TELESCOPE

ELEVATION GIMBAL

BASE MOTION
ISOLATION GIMBAL

BASE MOTION
ISOLATION GIMBAL

Figure 3802a: Star tracker assembly.

with respect to the center of the field of view. Modulation in the solid state telescope shown in Figure 3802b is accomplished by using a nutating fiber optics ''wand'' which articulates the focused star image over the solid state photosensor. This sensor, mounted in the focal plane, is designed to convert the light energy into electrical signals and to yield high signal sensitivity and daylight background gradient cancellation. This is accomplished by specially designed patterned sensor geometry. The electrical outputs of the sensor are processed to provide for star recognition, acquisition and tracking.

Figure 3802b: Optics of solid state telescope.

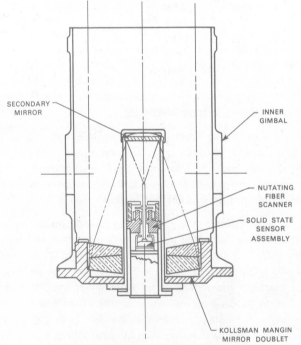

SECONDARY
MIRROR

INNER
GIMBAL

NUTATING
FIBER
SCANNER

SOLID STATE
SENSOR
ASSEMBLY

KOLLSMAN MANGIN
MIRROR DOUBLET

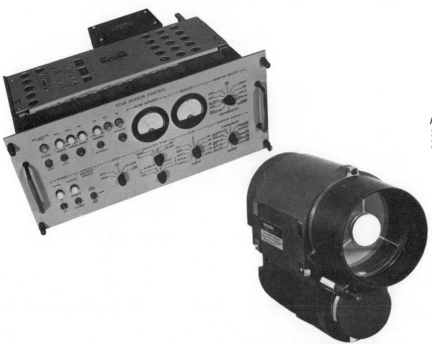

Figure 3803a: NCN 121 Daylight Star Tracker.

3803. Another type of daytime star tracker for shipboard use has been developed which employs a TV-type Vidicon tube as the sensitive element. The National Aeronautics and Space Administration (NASA) currently uses the tracker aboard Range Instrumentation Ships (RIS) employed in the Apollo program, as a component of the Integrated Navigation System (INS) installed in these vessels. It is capable of detecting the light from stars having a magnitude of (+) 2.5 or better against a daytime sky having a brilliance of 1,000 foot-Lamberts. At night, stars with a magnitude as low as (+) 3.5 may be tracked.

Shipboard star tracker.

The Vidicon Tracker is a multiple element sensor, having great inherent ability to overcome noise signals caused by a bright and non-uniform sky background. Each small element of area of the sensor is capable of storing the energy it receives from one electron beam sweep to the next, in effect making it the equivalent of a large number of sensors. The advantage of the vidicon tube is lost if there is excessive star image motion; the tracker must be kept pointed directly at the star, and this requires the use of a three-axis gyro-stabilized platform.

Vidicon Tracker.

Since the unit is extremely sensitive to light, damage would result if it were accidentally pointed toward the sun. An automatic light-activated sun filter is included which moves over the vidicon tube when excessive light enters the system, in order to prevent such damage.

The Nortronics NCN 121 daylight star tracker is shown in Figure 3803a together with the star sensor control panel. This unit is a precision vidicon fast-acquisition system for providing azimuth and elevation (star altitude) tracking data in daytime or at night. The use of two-star mode tracking permits the inertial system to be updated (article 3611). The vidicon daylight star tracker's relatively small field of view of approximately 10 arc minutes, which is necessary for sensitivity in daylight star acquisition, necessitates the use of a computer system to precompute star positions, and to align the tracker in the proper direction to detect the star. When aligned to the approximate position of the star, search and acquisition

591

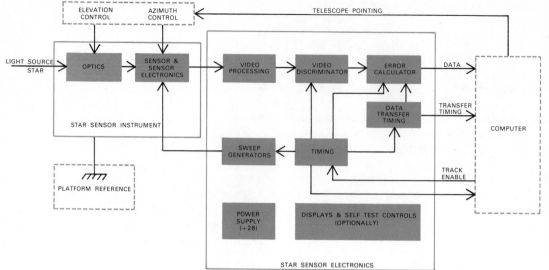

Figure 3803b: Block diagram.

are completed within a few seconds of time. Instrumental accuracy of the star tracker is within a few arc-seconds. A block diagram of the functions of the system is shown in Figure 3803b.

Star Tracker and Inertial System.

3804. Aboard ship, the magnitude and frequency of motion in roll, pitch, and yaw greatly exceed those in jet aircraft at operational altitudes. A greatly improved stable platform to provide the vertical was therefore required. In the range instrumentation ships designed for NASA, vertical reference and stability about three axes have been obtained by combining the star tracker with a deck-mounted Ship's Inertial Navigation System (SINS), an integral part of the INS. Experience has shown that the cooperative action of different types of navigation systems permits attaining an overall performance considerably better than the sum of the outputs of the individual systems. This synergistic advantage is particularly appropriate when a star tracking system is combined with an inertial system. A combination of this type permits bounding of inertial system errors, which accumulate as a function of time, and complete realignment of the inertial system when required.

The combining of the two units therefore produces improved overall results. A typical placement of the stellar-inertial system is shown in Figure 3804, in which the electronic instrumentation of a range tracking ship is illustrated. The

Figure 3804: Shipboard stellar inertial system.

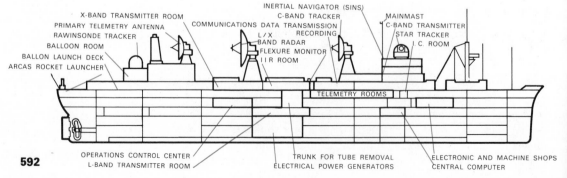

star tracker is mounted on top of a bedplate which is fixed to the ship with the SINS mounted on the bottom of the bedplate. This arrangement eliminates errors caused by flexure of the ship which would occur if the two units were separately installed at different locations.

The vertical established by SINS is a precision reference essentially free of bias errors; it is achieved by accelerometer monitoring.

A microelectronic general purpose digital computer, called the *Miniature Inertial Navigation Digital Automatic Computer* (MINDAC) is incorporated in the INS complex. It performs all necessary computations both for star tracking and for SINS. Star altitude data obtained from the star tracker is reduced to positioning information in MINDAC, which can store ephemeristic data for 80 of the brightest stars in both the northern and southern hemispheres in its memory section. Memory capacity for storing a Loran-C program or other data can also be added.

Orientation data from SINS processed through the computer and combined with star position data is used to initially align the star tracker telescope to the star position. After the star has been detected by the tracker, tracker error signals, measured by the star sensor, are used to torque the tracker's traverse and elevation gyros to center the star on the tracker line of sight. After being aligned by signals from SINS the star tracker remains space oriented to the line of sight to the star by the use of gyros mounted on each gimbaled axis. This orientation is maintained even though the ship's motion is constantly moving the bedplate. MINDAC then takes a series of star shots by freezing (simultaneously sampling) tracker train and elevation readouts and reduces these data from several stars to reset SINS.

3805. A periscope (from the Greek *peri*—all around and *skopos*—watcher) is an optical instrument which permits viewing along a displaced or deflected axis, providing an observer with a view he could not otherwise obtain. *Periscopes.*

Many such instruments designed for use in submarines during the last century could be described in the literal sense as periscopes, as they presented the observer with an annular image of 360° showing the entire horizon to a limited height, projected on a white background. Subsequently, an instrument was developed which substantially constituted the submarine periscope as now in use, in that it showed the observer a magnified view of a limited sector of the horizon, but could be rotated to permit scanning the entire horizon. *All-purpose periscope.*

The Kollmorgen Corporation—originally the Kollmorgen Optical Co.—pioneered the production of periscopes in the U. S. prior to World War I. Subsequently the need was felt for an attack periscope as an adjunct to the general purpose instrument, and the installation of two periscopes became standard practice. The neck of the Type-2 attack periscope, used during the second World War, was less than $1\frac{1}{2}$ inches in diameter, to minimize its wake when above the surface, and a split-objective stadimeter was included to obtain improved ranging and target course-angle determination. Because of the advent of aircraft in anti-submarine warfare, the general-purpose periscope had to be capable of scanning from the zenith to about 10° below the horizon. With the increase in size of submarines and greater operating depths, periscopes increased both in length and diameter, and were encased in full-length stainless steel forgings. The rigidity of this generation of periscopes is attested by the fact *Attack periscope.*

that they have been used as towing bits for rubber life rafts, to tow downed aviators out of range of shore fire, before the submarine surfaced to take them aboard. To prevent internal fogging, they were filled with dry nitrogen. The Type-4 periscope, which had excellent night vision capability, was next introduced; it was unique in that, in addition to its excellent optical qualities, it also served as an antenna for an ST radar set. The Type-2 and Type-4 periscopes are shown in Figure 3805.

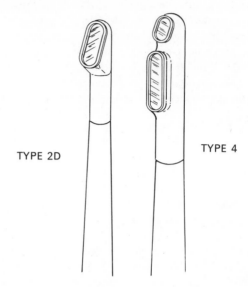

TYPE 2D

TYPE 4

Figure 3805:
Type 2-D attack
periscope.

Type-4 attack
periscope.

Submarine Celestial
Altitude Recorder
(SCAR).

3806. During World War II, in enemy patrolled waters, U. S. submarines were forced to rely heavily on DR navigation. At times, on clear nights, the navigator could obtain a round of star sights using a marine sextant; with dark-adapted vision and a high quality sextant, good star fixes could often be obtained. However, the submarine was subject to visual and radar detection, and considerable risk was involved. A definite need was established for instrumentation that would permit obtaining celestial observations by means of a periscope while submerged. This argument led to the development of a periscope suitable for celestial navigation and the Submarine Celestial Altitude Recorder (SCAR). This equipment was intended to demonstrate the feasibility of obtaining celestial observations from below the surface.

In conventional celestial navigation, the altitude of the body is referred to the horizontal for measurement. This may be the visible horizon, as when the marine sextant is used, or a bubble or pendulous mirror in air navigation. SCAR employed a new intermediate reference, the *deck plane.* The deck plane is an imaginary longitudinal plane drawn through the submarine. It is horizontal when roll and pitch angles are zero. At sea, with the submarine exposed to wave motion, it is seldom parallel to the true horizontal plane due to pitch and roll; in making observations, allowance must therefore be made for *deck plane tilt.* The angular inclination of the tilt is established by gyroscopic reference, such as that furnished by the Mark XIX gyro compass. A correction must be made for yaw, the changing error in the submarine's heading, as it affects the relative magnitude of the pitch and roll components of deck plane tilt, relative to the line of sight to the star.

It is obvious from the geometry of two intersecting planes, one of which is constantly in motion, that the most simplified solution of deck plane tilt occurs when the submarine is heading directly toward or away from the celestial body being observed, or has it on either beam. When a celestial body having a relative bearing of 0°, 90°, 180°, or 270° is observed the roll or pitch angle output of the Mark XIX, or of a similar gyro-established vertical, gimbaled in roll or pitch, can be directly applied to the elevation to obtain the sextant altitude.

With SCAR it was necessary to pre-compute the altitude and azimuth of the star and to change the heading of the submarine to produce a periscopic train angle of 0°, 90°, 180°, or 270° in order to use available data without performing a coordinate transformation. With the proper elevation set in, the star would appear in the field of view of the periscope, but the image would seem to move constantly with respect to the index line or reticle in the optics. Tracking the image to keep it continuously centered was not considered practical, and a *mark switch* was used which was closed by the navigator when the star image crossed the index mark. The altitude of the star was printed out together with GMT by a celestial altitude recorder. The appropriate value of either roll or pitch, as obtained from the gyrocompass, was applied to the elevation of the periscopic line of sight from the deck plane. This value was then combined with a computed cross-level correction from the remaining component of deck plane tilt, to relate elevation to the horizontal plane. The sextant altitude, hs, was thereby obtained.

SCAR had only limited use in the Navy, however, it demonstrated the feasibility of submerged celestial navigation, and led to the vastly improved systems described in the succeeding articles.

TYPE 8B

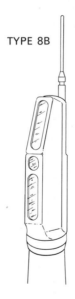

Figure 3807: All-purpose Type-8B periscope.

3807. Nuclear submarines established need for a new all-purpose periscope, which in addition to having excellent optics for ordinary viewing, would also have improved capability for celestial observation. The Type-8B periscope, shown in Figure 3807, was developed to meet these requirements. A cylinder,

Type-8B all-purpose periscope.

14 inches in diameter, called the *Electric and Electronic Adapter* is attached to its base, and contains the Type-3 sextant, developed by Sperry, as well as electronic gear, and an electric torque motor, which assists in driving the periscope in train for viewing at any desired angle relative to the fore and aft axis.

As a navigational instrument, the Type-8B periscope system is similar to the Type-8 periscope with SCAR in that it is a general purpose instrument, which can be used for measuring celestial altitudes, and as it is limited to making single observations of a body, rather than to tracking it. It differs in that the Type-3 sextant contains its own gyroscopic horizontal reference which trains with the periscope thus permitting celestial observations to be made on any relative bearing without the need for coordinate transformation. As with the Type-8 periscope and SCAR, a mark switch is closed when the image of the body is brought to the reticle, and the sextant altitude and its GMT are printed out numerically.

The type-8B periscope and its direct descendants remain in wide use in U. S. submarine forces.

Type-11 star tracker periscope.

3808. The concept of the Fleet Ballistic Missile nuclear submarines indicated the requirement for a celestial position fixing capability to a very high order of accuracy, obtained while the submarine remained submerged, and on any heading relative to the desired star's azimuth. The order of the required accuracy approached that obtainable by a fine theodolite, erected on shore.

This requirement led to the Kollmorgen Corporation's design of the Type-11 star tracker periscope which is integrated into a complete celestial navigational complex consisting of a *Stabilization Data Computer* (SDC), a *Navigation Data Assimilation Computer* (NAVDAC), which has its own Greenwich mean time source and which stores ephemeristic data on a great number of stars in its memory section, and a *Ship's Inertial Navigation System* (SINS). The SDC serves as the connecting link between the periscope and NAVDAC and SINS. The latter is the basic instrument of the complex; it can function for limited periods without reference to external data. The input of celestial data, obtained by means of periscopic observations, serves to correct accumulated error periodically.

The instrumentation employed for celestial navigation in the FBM submarines is shown in simplified schematic form in Figure 3808.

When star observations are to be obtained, SINS supplies the submarine's DR position to NAVDAC. Using these data, as well as the current instant of GMT and the stored ephemeristic data on the selected star, NAVDAC supplies the star's computed altitude and azimuth and their rate of change to the SDC. Concurrently, SINS establishes the vertical by feeding continuous information on yaw, roll and pitch angle to SDC, which combines this information with the star data to keep the periscope's line of sight continuously pointed in the star's direction. Star acquisition is obtained immediately, due to the accuracy inherent in the system. As the field of view is small, ordinarily the desired star will be the only one to appear.

The observer overrides or coerces the system by manipulating a *joystick,* and brings the star image to the center of the reticle. The system then is allowed to track the star for about 30 seconds. Continuous data on observed altitude and

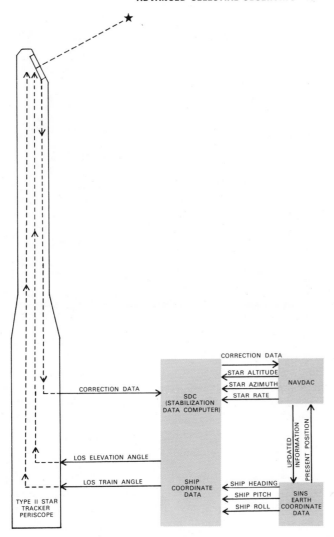

Figure 3808:
Schematic of FBM
submarine naviga-
tion system.

azimuth are obtained and fed back through the system for comparison with the calculated data. The difference between the observed altitude and azimuth and those calculated by NAVDAC is used to realign SINS.

Periscopes of the Type-11 family bear only superficial resemblance to conventional periscopes. They were designed for the sole purpose of providing coordinate data of celestial bodies to the FBM submarine celestial navigation system; the operation of this system is almost entirely automatic. The observer serves to "close the loop" by eyeball and actuating a correction control to permit the system to compare predicted celestial coordinates with those observed. The system permits an extremely high order of navigational accuracy.

3809. *Gyro Erected Optical Navigation* (GEON) is a passive celestial navigation system, capable of operating on a world-wide basis, and requires no computer. Observations are by eye; they can be made both by day and by night, subject to the availability of suitable stars.

GEON.

The prototype instrument consisted of a MK XIX, Mod 3 gyro compass, which was especially adapted and refined for this use. A Kern model DKM-2 theodolite

597

Figure 3809: GEON.

is equatorially mounted on this compass. All the essential movements of the theodolite are retained, but a third degree of movement was added to permit varying the tilt of the polar axis for latitude. All angular readouts are by microscope. The telescope has a magnification of 30 power and a 45 mm objective lens; this telescope permits the observation of daylight stars, suitably situated in azimuth relative to the sun, and having a magnitude of better than (+) 1.0. By night, stars with a magnitude of (+) 4.0 may be observed. Figure 3809 shows the telescope mounted on the compass.

Having set the declination of the star to be observed on the vertical circle, the star image is centered on the telescope's cross hairs, and the time is noted. Latitude is then read directly off the latitude scale, local hour angle is read from the horizontal scale, and azimuth is read from the compass. All that then remains to obtain a position is to compare the LHA with the corrected GHA of the body, as taken from the *Nautical Almanac*. Using this single-star method, fixes may be obtained at intervals of about two minutes.

The gyro's error in establishing the vertical is considerably less than its small error in azimuth. To minimize the effect of the error in azimuth, the instrument was originally used to observe bodies situated within 15° of the zenith. These observations yielded underway fixes with a radial mean square root (RMS) error of between 0.6 and 1.8 miles. Subsequently, the gyro performance was much refined and currently fixes are reported with a radial RMS error of the nature of 0.3 mile; these fixes in many instances were obtained from non-circumzenith stars.

It seems most probable that GEON may also be used for obtaining a conventional fix derived from observations of several stars well distributed in azimuth Such a mode of operation should yield excellent results; the primary source of error being a possible slight constant bias error in determination of the vertical. However, the multi-star method of obtaining a fix would be rather more time consuming than the one-star mode.

CHAPTER 39

Navigational Computers

3901. The basic art and science of obtaining navigational positioning information have not changed appreciably over the years, although some of the tools or instruments have. Acronyms and terms such as NAVDAC, MINDAC, VERDAN, MARDAN, SINS, INS, ANALOG, and DIGITAL, are necessary to the navigator's vocabulary. These terms relate to computers; how computers affect the navigator, and some of the computers used in navigation, are described in this chapter.

Introduction.

3902. A computer is an electronic calculator especially designed for the solution of complex mathematical problems. When separate subsystems are combined to make a single complex navigational system, such as SINS (Chapter 36), the solution becomes much too involved and lengthy for the navigator to undertake using the old conventional methods. Therefore computers, with their essential mathematical programming and information storage capability, are employed to do the navigator's work. Computers are now installed in aircraft, submarines, and, in limited numbers, in surface vessels. They may be programmed for one specific task, as for Loran-C supplying a continuous latitude-longitude readout on an *x-y* plotter or on dials, or for a series of tasks, as when used in the *Integrated Navigation System* or INS (article 3907). In order to provide answers to the various navigational problems either an *analog* or a *digital* computer, or a combination of both, may be required.

Computers in navigation.

3903. The *analog computer* solves a particular physical problem instantaneously through the use of an equivalent electrical circuit which is mathematically identical to the physical problem; that is, the electrical circuit selected is *analogous* to the problem.

Analog computers.

It should be noted that the solution of the physical problem by the analog computer is instantaneous; in other words, the electrical analog produces a continuous solution at every instant of time. Generalizing, analog computers may be said to yield instantaneous solutions to time-varying physical problems. The analog computer is not versatile; if the physical problem itself, rather than merely its parameters, is changed, a new analog must be designed. Analog computers are therefore usually designed to furnish repeated solutions for a very specific type of problem. It is obvious that the accuracy of the solution of a physical problem by an electrical analog is limited by the circuit component tolerances. The limited versatility and accuracy of analog computers has led to the recent rapid development of digital computers.

Digital computers. **3904.** The *digital computer* may be defined as a machine which calculates the solution of a mathematical problem to any desired degree of numerical accuracy through a prearranged sequence of simple arithmetic operations such as addition, subtraction, multiplication, and division. Most digital computers employ the *binary* (two variables) code which uses only two digits, 0 and 1.

Several important advantages and disadvantages inherent in digital computers should be noted. The digital computer forms the solution through a sequence of arithmetic operations known as *instructions.* A *program* is defined as an ordered sequence of instructions. The digital computer performs only one of these operations or instructions at a time.

Clearly, the digital computer solution is *not* instantaneous, as it obviously requires a finite time to form and sum the first terms of the series expansion. However, it is important to note that the solution can be made more accurate by merely summing more terms. Finally the input variable need not be continuous; that is, the independent variable is treated as a discrete value, and the solution is the numerical result of the summation for that value.

The finite time required for the digital computer solution must be less than the time between significant changes of the input variable; otherwise, the solution will be seriously in error. Fortunately, the computation frequency of a digital computer can be made much greater than the frequency of changes for most variables in the real world. The functions are accomplished at the rate of 1,000,000 or more operations per second.

An unseen advantage of the digital computer over the analog computer is its versatility. Analog computers usually require a hardware change to solve a new problem of a different form, but the digital computer, may be reprogrammed to solve a new problem merely by rearranging the existing instructions already fed into the computer. In other words, a new problem of a different form merely requires a "soft-ware" change to the program of a digital computer. A comparison of the characteristics of the analog and digital computers is given in Figure 3904.

Figure 3904: General computer characteristics.

Computer Type		Characteristic			
	Input Output Data Type	Accuracy	Solution Time	Solution Form	Versatility
DIGITAL	Discrete numeric	Unlimited	Limited variable access time	Arithmetic (Add, Subtract, Multiply, Divide, etc.)	New program requires software program change
ANALOG	Continuous signal	Restricted by circuit components	Instantaneous	Electrical circuit analogous to physical problem	New problem requires hardware computer change

3905. The *NAV*igation *D*ata *A*ssimilation *C*omputer (NAVDAC) is a real-time (precise time or clock time), general purpose digital computer originally designed for the Polaris submarine program. This computer has four primary functions:

NAVDAC.

> *Coordination*—the control of all equipment in the entire system.

Functions.

> *Data gathering* for fixes from external fix sources.

> *Processing* of fix data for reduction to SINS reset parameters.

> *Resetting* SINS and *monitoring* results.

From these four functions it can be seen that NAVDAC is an integrator for the various navigational instruments, including the inertial system, velocity measuring devices, gyrocompass, radio aids such as Loran and celestial altitude measuring instruments, etc. It is, in fact, the central system for combining the individual components into a single operating system. Data from the individual input sources are processed by NAVDAC, drawing, when necessary, on its data storage or "memory" component, and the resultant information is used to determine the corrections to be applied to SINS, to indicate ship's position, etc. The data storage component has a tremendous capacity; for example, it stores the sidereal hour angle and declination for each of about 200 stars. All data are regularly updated, as required.

Since NAVDAC uses more than one fix-determining input, it is able to filter the data received, correlate and weight it, make logical and statistical decisions, perform coordinate conversions, and generate control functions. Consequently, a standard of accuracy and reliability previously unattainable is possible by means of the redundancy from multiple data sources. In addition to all this, the computer is able to carry out self-checking procedures for verifying the large number of computations that it has undertaken. NAVDAC has provided the accuracies commensurate with the requirements of marine navigation.

Figure 3905a shows the role of NAVDAC in the operational system, together with its inputs and outputs, as well as its employment of both analog and

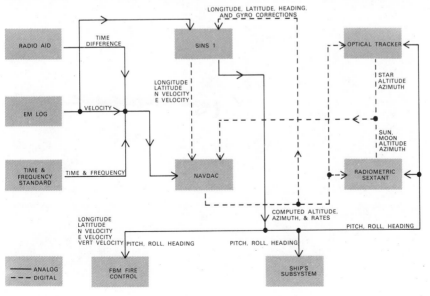

Figure 3905a:
Block diagram of navigation system with NAVDAC.

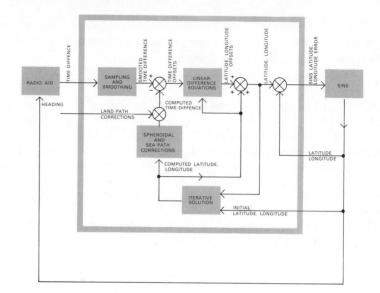

Figure 3905b:
NAVDAC operation
with radio aid.

digital computer information. Figure 3905b shows the NAVDAC organized for use with a radio aid. Operation with any other input would differ only in the source and type of input. The function of the NAVDAC computer has been described as it is representative of the computer solution required for navigation of modern nuclear submarines. Other computers provide similar solutions. The VERDAN computer used with the Autonetics N7A Inertial Navigation System is shown in Figure 3905c as installed aboard ship. A later version, the MARDAN computer, used with the Autonetics N7F SINS, has a self-contained buffer

Figure 3905c:
Verdan computer.

READOUT
DISPLAY

COMPUTER
KEYBOARD

allowing intercommunication with the other computers. It has a capacity of 4,096 words and a speed of up to 400 iterations per second. The Sperry SINDAC computer was shown in Figure 3607c, in a shipboard installation.

3906. The *M*iniature *I*nertial *N*avigation *D*igital *A*utomatic *C*omputer (MINDAC) is a general-purpose digital computer in a SINS system designed primarily to calculate present ship's position from heading and velocity input data, and to provide appropriate bias and torquing signals to the gyros in order to maintain the SINS inertial platform aligned to the vertical. In addition, it provides periodic readout of the ship's velocity and position to the central data processor, and resets the platforms to the correct position when necessary at the operator's command.

MINDAC.

While there are other computers that perform these same functions, MINDAC is the primary inertial platform alignment computer designed for use in the Integrated Navigation System described hereafter. It is also used aboard submarines and aircraft carriers with the Sperry Mk III Mod 6 SINS.

3907. The *I*ntegrated *N*avigation *S*ystem (INS) consists of a Ship's Inertial Navigation System (SINS), to which are added an automatic star tracker, a multi-speed repeater, and instrumentation to provide accurate data on attitude (roll, pitch, and heading) for radar stabilization. The system also supplies velocity (north, east, or vertical), and latitude and longitude coordinates for ship control and navigation. The system is used aboard the NASA range instrumentation ships, which supplement the range tracking stations established ashore in various parts of the world. For effective space vehicle tracking and control, the positions of the tracking stations must be established to the closest possible tolerance; the navigational accuracy requirements for the range instrumentation ships are therefore unusually stringent.

INS-Integrated Navigation System.

As may be seen in Figure 3907, the INS receives inputs from a number of sources, processes the data, positions the star tracker (for day and night observations) and gives an output of navigation data and heading. This enables the proper positioning of the tracking equipment (radar) for immediate acquisition of the spacecraft. INS is a subsystem of the complete *S*hip's *P*osition and *A*ttitude *M*easurement System, the components of which are also shown in Figure 3907.

3908. Other navigational computers are being developed; many of these are of a less sophisticated type than those described. Such computers fall under two headings—those designed solely for navigation and those intended for general shipboard use on a shared time basis. The latter type appears to be of very considerable interest to operators of large commercial vessels, as it fits in well with the present trend towards automation in such ships.

Future computer use.

It seems probable that all naval vessels of the destroyer type as well as many of the larger military planes, will, within the next decade, be equipped with digital computers designed for navigation. Such a computer might give a continuous DR readout in latitude and longitude, based on inputs from the gyrocompass and ship's log, as does the *D*ead *R*eckoning *A*nalyzer *I*ndicator (DRAI) currently in use. However, with the computer, the DR position should be updated on command from the navigator, based on any navigational data obtained, even a

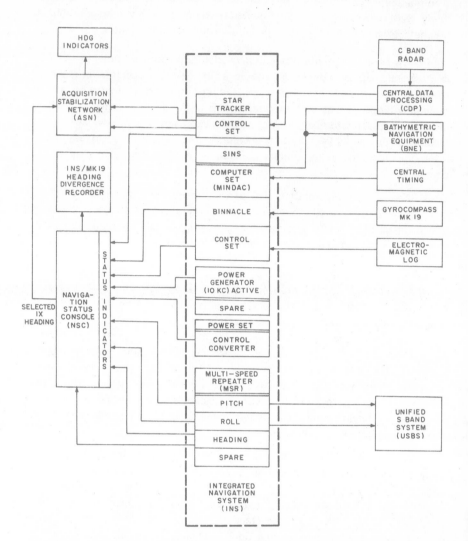

Figure 3907: INS data and signals inputs/outputs to external equipments.

single line of position; in such a case, the computer would select the most probable position, and give, in effect, an EP. The computer would have its own time source, probably in the form of a quartz crystal clock, and a memory section capable of storing the SHA and Declination of a limited number of stars—those currently in use for morning and evening observations. GHA and Dec of the sun, moon, and planets would be entered in the computer by means of a typewriter keyboard as required.

The computer would have a remote electronic readout of the altitude shown on the sextant; the latter would be fitted with a button to signal when the body was on the horizon, and the computer would note both time and altitude, and almost instantaneously reduce the sight for computed altitude and azimuth, and determine the intercept. Several observations would yield a satisfactory fix automatically, the computer being able to differentiate between an internal and external fix (article 3009).

The navigator could thus take a considerable number of observations of each body, without ever losing it from view, and these observations would be averaged by the computer in order to determine an excellent fix.

When used with an electronic navigational system, such as Omega or Loran-C it is possible for the computer to update position automatically and continuously, based on signals received from two or more stations. Such computers, programmed for use with Loran-C, are currently in use in aircraft.

Such a computer would have the capability of solving both plane and spherical triangles. Given ranges and bearings, obtained by radar, of a moving ship, it could determine the range, bearing and time of the closest point of approach, and enable the conning officer to determine any required change in course or speed well before any danger of collision arose. Maneuvering board problems could be solved with equal speed. Great circle distance and the initial heading for any destination from the ship's present position could be determined almost instantaneously.

3909. *Data loggers* have been used with success to monitor the performance of both the main and auxiliary power plants aboard merchant ships for many years. Their function is to scan perhaps 300 or more test points at a rate of between 2 to 25 or so points per second, depending on the required control. The scanning sensors are transducers which have high speed response, and which convert measurements into electrical signals. These signals are converted by the data logger for display, and an alarm may be actuated if any signal exceeds a safe value.

Computers in the merchant service.

Data loggers.

The data logger has greatly increased power plant efficiency; however, unlike the computer, it cannot exert any control function. The growing trend towards automation in the merchant service, and the decreasing cost of computers, combined with increased reliability, versatility and flexibility all lead towards increased use of computers in merchantmen. These computers are generally of the multi-purpose type, and are programmed to serve several or all the ship's departments. In the engine room, such a computer can carry out all the functions of a data logger, and, in addition, it can be programmed to take immediate corrective action when required. The fresh water supply can be monitored, and the evaporators started as needed. All in all, it can replace many men in the engine room.

The computer can also be extremely valuable for navigation. In merchantmen, the mate on watch traditionally has performed all the navigator's duties during his tour on the bridge. Sight reduction and plotting can be time consuming, and sometimes had to be slighted when other immediate problems demanded attention. The computer can be programmed to do all this; in fact, if desired, it could be designed to perform all the navigational functions described in article 3908.

Of particular interest to commercial operators is the use of the computer for optimum track ship routing (Chapter 43). The computer's memory section can store data on the ship's resistance moment, performance under various conditions of load, draft, sea state and the resulting motion. Based on these data, and an input of weather and sea state reports, the computer can supply an immediate recommendation on the optimum course and speed to be employed.

605

It is expected that this ability of the computer to recommend optimum course and speed under conditions of adverse weather, as well as the improved accuracy in navigation it permits, will lead to greatly increased economy in operation.

*Trend to
automation.*

The trend towards automation in the merchant marine is world-wide, and is resulting in increasing economy of operation. A new Japanese super-tanker of 205,000 deadweight tons operates with a crew of only 32 men, as compared to the 42-man crew required for a slightly older 130,000-ton tanker. The SS *Mormacargo* in 1964 was the first U. S. flag merchant ship to have engine controls operated directly from the bridge, thus permitting complete ship control by one man. It seems probable that in the future merchantmen will have all monitoring and computer readouts presented in consoles in the wheelhouse.

Summary.

3910. The computers discussed in this chapter have yielded standards of accuracy and speed of solution which would have seemed incredible to the navigator only a few years ago; they are representative of the finest navigational computers presently available. However, the state of the art in the field of computers is advancing extremely rapidly, particularly in microminiaturization, and new computers, combining greater accuracy, versatility, reliability, and speed with smaller space and lower power requirements are becoming available. The navigator can expect greatly improved instrumentation in this field in the comparatively near future.

CHAPTER 40

Lifeboat Navigation

4001. The preceding chapters have dealt with navigation as practiced aboard a *Introduction.* well-equipped vessel. Lifeboat navigation is very different; only minimal facilities are available for the navigator, and even the basic instruments, such as a sextant, may be lacking. In addition, lifeboat navigation differs in that it is impossible to travel any considerable distance to windward even in a powered lifeboat, and that the destination must be carefully selected; it is also impossible to bring a life-boat in to a beach through heavy surf, without risking the loss of all hands.

As long as ships ply the seas, ships will be lost, and the prudent navigator must plan ahead to the possibility that his ship may be one of them. He cannot expect that there will be sufficient time to organize his equipment after the word is passed to abandon ship. In addition to being thoroughly familiar with the use of available equipment he must be able to improvise, and must know what is possible if either sextant, watch, reduction tables, or almanac is lost.

The first consideration after abandoning ship is to determine whether to remain as close as possible to the scene, or try to reach land or a heavily traveled steamer lane. This decision will generally depend on whether or not a distress signal was sent, and receipted for, before the ship was abandoned, and when help might be expected.

If no assistance can be expected, the navigator must always bear in mind that long voyages in poorly equipped lifeboats have and can be made, as proved by Captain Bligh, of HMS *Bounty*, who sailed 3,000 miles when cast adrift in an open boat. He must also remember that morale is a factor of the highest importance, if a long journey is to be completed successfully.

4002. The best way to lessen the degree of an emergency is to always be pre- *Preparation for an* pared for it. When the emergency occurs, it may be too late to plan. There are *emergency.* several ways to prepare for the emergency of abandoning ship. The surest way is to make up an emergency navigational kit for each lifeboat and life raft, place it in a waterproof container, and lash it securely in place. The following items are desirable even if they cannot all be included in a kit for each lifeboat.

Charts. The best charts for lifeboat use are pilot charts for the area to be traveled. Both winter and summer charts should be included. The aircraft position charts, published by the U. S. Coast and Geodetic Survey, are also excellent. They are prepared on the Lambert conformal conic projection; in addition to variation, they give data permitting the plotting of lines of position from Consol stations, if within an area of coverage, and if a radio receiver is available.

Sextant. In addition to conventional marine sextants, inexpensive plastic ones are available, which are capable of acceptable accuracy for lifeboat use.

Almanac and star chart. If at all possible a *Nautical Almanac* and a *Star Finder* should be available. Failing the latter, charts in the *Nautical Almanac* may be used, although many navigators prefer the star chart included in the *Air Almanac;* the star chart from an old almanac may be saved for emergency use. A *Long-Term Almanac* is included as *Appendix X* of *Bowditch.* With the necessary instructions and auxiliary tables, it comprises five pages, and supplies ephemeristic data on the sun and forty-five of the selected stars. It is valid over a period of many years, and surprisingly accurate; the maximum error in altitude computed by it should not exceed 2'.0 for the sun, and 1'.3 for the stars. It is wise to have these five pages photostated, and to include them in each set of sight reduction tables to be used in boats. Include with them copies of the refraction and dip tables from the *Nautical Almanac,* as these tables are not found in the *Long Term Almanac.*

Tables. Although *Bowditch* is a large volume, a copy should be taken in the boat if possible. In addition to the *Long Term Almanac* mentioned above, it contains all tables necessary for sight reduction, and a wealth of material concerning all facets of navigation, as well as Appendix V, the list of maritime positions.

H. O. Pub. 211 is ideal for emergency use, as it is a very small volume which provides a computed altitude and azimuth angle for any celestial observation, including those having a negative altitude (article 4012). In addition, it permits reduction from the DR position, which sometimes is an asset in small craft navigation.

A 10-inch slide rule with sine scale permits a rapid reduction of observations for altitude and azimuth. Altitudes to 30° may be solved to an accuracy of about 2'.0 if care is used; an accuracy of about 5'.0 may be obtained to 50°. Such a rule was used aboard some Navy patrol bombers during World War II for sight reduction. The formulae for obtaining altitude and azimuth by slide rule are given in article 4012.

Transistorized battery radio. Such a radio can be invaluable in obtaining time signals, particularly if it has a short-wave band.

Radar reflector. Folding radar reflectors are available, made of metal mesh or aluminum sheets. Such a reflector returns a strong echo, and will make it much easier for search craft to locate a lifeboat by radar, particularly if the reflector is elevated. Aluminum kitchen foil may serve as a substitute.

Plastic bags. Fairly heavy plastic bags, such as are used for packaging ice cubes, are invaluable for storing books, instruments, radio, etc., and keeping them dry in a lifeboat.

Notebook. Various items of general information from this chapter and any other desired information should be copied. *Do not depend on the memory.* Enough blank pages should be left to permit computations and a log to be kept.

Plotting equipment. Be sure to include pencils, erasers, a protractor (very important), and some kind of straightedge, preferably one graduated in inches. Dividers and compasses may prove useful, but are not essential. Several small area plotting sheets, or paper for making them, such as cross section paper, preferably graduated in 10 squares per inch, may be useful.

Miscellaneous. Sun glasses are useful to protect the eyes. A small bottle of medicine to combat seasickness may prove invaluable. It has been found that the entire crew of a lifeboat is usually seasick during the first few days and sometimes no one is well enough to perform any navigational duties or to give a signal if help should be within sight. A pad of maneuvering board forms may be useful. A Bible is excellent for morale purposes. This list assumes that a compass and flashlight will be included as part of the regular boat equipment.

If it proves impractical to keep such a kit in each lifeboat, it may be possible to have one available for taking along. However, this is less satisfactory, for in the confusion of the last few minutes aboard it might be overlooked; it could be misplaced and there may be no time for a search. The least that can be done is to provide a check-off list of equipment to assemble at the last minute if time permits.

Various items of knowledge are useful and may prove invaluable under some conditions. Among these are the following:

Positions. The approximate latitude and longitude of several ports, islands, etc., in the area in which the ship or plane operates. This will prove useful if no chart is available. In addition, the approximate position of the ship or aircraft should be known at all times. A general knowledge of the charts of the region in which the ship or plane operates is often useful.

Currents. A general knowledge of the principal ocean currents in the operating area is valuable if no current chart is available.

Weather. A general knowledge of weather is useful. The particular information of value in emergencies is a knowledge of prevailing winds at different seasons in the operating area, and the ability to detect early signs of approaching storms and predict their paths relative to the course of the lifeboat.

Stars. The ability to identify stars may prove valuable, particularly if no star chart is available.

Whatever plan is adopted for preparation in case of an emergency, be sure there is a definite plan. Do not wait until the order to "abandon ship" to decide what to do. It may be too late.

American flag merchant ships are required by law to keep much equipment in their lifeboats; however, this is all survival gear, and includes no navigational equipment. In addition to water, rations, and equipment such as boathooks, buckets, etc., the required equipment includes a first aid kit, two signaling mirrors, storm oil, a sea anchor or drogue, a fishing kit, lifesaving signals or flares, and a desalting kit.

4003. When the abandon ship order is given, the amount of preparation that can be made for navigation will depend on the time available. There is usually some warning. There are some things that must of necessity be left to the last moment, but it is not wise to add unnecessarily to the list. *Abandoning ship.*

A check-off list should be available without a search. The number of items on it will depend on the degree of preparation that has been made. The following minimum list assumes that a full navigational kit is available in the lifeboat. Anything short of this should be taken into consideration in making the check-off list. Before leaving the ship, check the following :

Watch error. Determine the error and write it down. Be sure you know what kind of time your watch is keeping. Do not attempt to set it, but see that it is wound. It may be possible to take along a chronometer.

Date. Check the date and write it down.

Position. Write down the position of the ship. If possible, record also the set and drift of the current and the latitude and longitude of the nearest land in several directions. It may be easier to take along the chart or plotting sheet giving this information.

Navigational equipment. Check the navigational equipment in the boat. Look particularly to see that there is a compass, chart, and watch. If anything is missing, is it possible to get it from the ship? Do not abandon the ship's sextant. If a portable radio is available, take it along.

See that all equipment is properly secured before lowering the boat.

Do not abandon any clothing, regardless of the temperature. It is important that the body be protected from exposure.

Getting organized. **4004.** The first few hours in a lifeboat may prove the most important. If medicine for seasickness is available, take it at once, even before leaving the ship, if possible.

There must be a definite understanding of who is to be in charge, not to exercise autocratic rule, but to regulate the cramped life in the lifeboat and avoid confusion. Extreme fairness and equality are important if good teamwork and high morale are to be maintained.

If there are several boats in the water, considerable advantage is to be gained by their staying close together, if possible.

Before setting out on any course, it is important to make an *estimate of the situation.* Do not start out until you know where you are going, and determine this carefully and deliberately. This may be the most important decision of the entire journey. Make it carefully.

First, determine the number of watches available and determine as accurately as possible the error of each watch. Learn from each owner all that is available regarding the rate and reliability of his timepiece. Record this information and establish a regular routine for winding the watches and checking them.

Record the best known latitude and longitude of the point of departure and the time of day. Let this be the beginning of a carefully kept log.

In choosing the first course, carefully study all factors. *Do not set the course until you are sure the best possible one has been determined.*

A number of factors will influence the decision. If a pilot chart is available, study it minutely and be sure you are thoroughly familiar with the average current to be expected and prevailing winds. Consider the motive power available and the probable speed. It may be better to head for land some distance away, if wind and current will help, than for nearby land which will be difficult to reach.

Note the location of the usually traveled shipping routes. These are shown on the pilot chart. If more than one suitable course is available, choose the one that will take you nearest to well traveled shipping routes. Remember, in selecting a course, that the upwind range of even a powered lifeboat is very limited. Captain Bligh knew that there were islands within about 200 miles upwind, but he knew he could not reach them; his decision to take the long 3000-mile downwind journey made survival possible.

Consider the size and height of the nearby land, and the navigation equipment available. Remember that the horizon is quite close when the observer is standing in a lifeboat: the distance to the horizon in miles is about 1.15 times the square root of the height of eye in feet. Determine the probable accuracy with which positions can be determined. A small low island some distance away may be extremely hard to find with crude navigational methods.

Will accurate time be available? Remember that the latitude can be determined accurately without time, but the longitude will be no more accurate than the time. If there is any question of the ability to maintain reasonably accurate time (each four seconds error in time results in 1' error in the longitude), do not head straight for the destination, but for a point that is certain to take the boat to the east or west of the destination, and when the latitude of the destination has been reached, head due east or west and maintain the latitude. This method was successfully used for centuries before the invention of the chronometer.

If adequate distress signals were sent before abandoning ship, and it is to be expected that rescue ships or planes will conduct a search, it is best to remain near to the last reported position of the ship.

Having decided upon the course to follow and the probable average speed, including help from current and wind, estimate the time of reaching the destination and set the ration accordingly.

Determine the knowledge, ability, and aptitude of all aboard and assign each definite responsibilities. *Establish a definite routine.*

4005. An important part of the trip back to safety is the maintaining of a high morale. With a great determination and cool judgment almost any difficulty can be overcome. This is proved by many great tales of the sea. The story of Captain Bligh, previously mentioned, is perhaps one of the greatest illustrations of the value of patience and determination. *Morale.*

A regular routine and a definite assignment of duties is valuable from the standpoint of morale. Include in the routine regular periods for reading aloud from the Bible. This will not only provide a means of occupying time, but will constitute a source of encouragement and add to the faith and determination of the crew. Remember, also, the high value placed on prayer by those who have been through the experience of abandoning a ship or aircraft at sea.

4006. *Dead reckoning* is always important, but never more so than when in a lifeboat. Determine as accurately as possible the point of departure and keep a record of courses, speeds, estimated currents and leeway. Do not be too quick *Dead reckoning.*

to abandon a carefully determined EP for an uncertain fix by crude methods. Unless really accurate methods of navigation are available, consider all positions as EP's and carefully evaluate all information available. The real test of a navigator is how accurately he can evaluate the information at hand and from it determine the true position of his vessel. Upon this ability may depend the question of whether the lifeboat arrives at its destination.

Take full advantage of all conditions. When the wind is favorable, make all the distance possible in the desired direction. It may sometimes be advantageous to change course slightly to make greater speed in a direction differing somewhat from the desired course. If the wind is definitely unfavorable, put out a sea anchor and reduce the leeway.

Attempt to keep a plot of the track of the boat. Plotting in an open boat may be difficult; it may be easier to keep account of movements mathematically by means of the simplified traverse table in article 4009.

Direction. **4007.** At the very start of the voyage it is well to check the accuracy of the compass on the course to be steered. The variation can be determined from the pilot chart, but to find the deviation, if this is not accurately known, locate a bit of wreckage in the water or throw overboard a life preserver or other object that will not drift too much with the wind and head on the reciprocal magnetic course to that desired. After this has been followed for some distance (a half mile to a mile), turn and steer for the object. If there is no deviation, the compass course will be the reciprocal of that first steered. If it is not, the desired compass course is half way between the reciprocal of the first course and the compass course back to the object.

Underway the compass error should be checked at regular intervals. In the northern hemisphere Polaris can be considered to be due north except in very high latitudes (above L 60° N the maximum error is greater than 2°). When Polaris is directly above or below the pole the azimuth is 000° in any latitude. When the sun, or any body, reaches its highest altitude, it can be considered to be on the celestial meridian, bearing 180° or 000°. These are true directions, and yield compass error directly, not deviation.

If an almanac and method of computation is available, the true direction of any body can be determined at any time, by the usual methods of computing azimuth.

If a compass is not available, an approximation of a straight course can be steered by towing a line secured at the gunwhale amidships. If the boat deviates from a straight track, the line will move away from its neutral position approximately parallel to the side of the boat. With a cross sea this method is least accurate but may be better than nothing at all.

At night the boat can be kept on a reasonably straight course north or east or west by steering for Polaris or a body near the prime vertical.

Speed. **4008.** Throughout the trip, speed should be determined as accurately as possible. Ability to estimate speed will be developed by practice. One crude method of measuring the speed is to throw a floating object overboard at the bow and note the time required for the boat to pass it. For this purpose a definite distance should be marked off along the gunwale. Make this as long as convenient, but an easily used length—25 feet, 16.7 feet, 20 feet, 10 feet, etc.—some length divisible into 100 feet a whole number of times is preferable.

If a boat travels 100 feet per minute, it is moving at the rate of 1 knot. If the length marked off is 25 feet and an object is thrown over at the forward mark, it should be opposite the second mark in 15 seconds if the boat is making 1 knot, 7.5 seconds if 2 knots, 5 seconds if 3 knots, etc. If the distance is 16.7 feet, the time should be 10 seconds for 1 knot, 5 seconds for 2 knots, etc. A table or curve of speed vs. time can easily be made. Speed determined in this way is relative to the *water* and not speed over the ground.

Since the objects available for throwing overboard may be scarce, attach a light line to the object and secure the other end to the boat, so that it can be recovered and used again. A small drogue can be improvised from light cloth and light cord, such as a fishing line, which makes a good log line. Knot the line at intervals similar to those listed above or multiples of these. As the drogue is streamed aft, with the line permitted to run out freely, the time between the passage of two knots through the hand is noted. The drogue should be some distance astern before starting to take time; the knot at which time is started should therefore be 25 feet or so forward of the drogue. *Be sure the line can run out freely.*

Even without a watch, the method can still be used. A member of the crew who has practiced with a chronometer, such as a quartermaster who has been responsible for checking a comparing watch with a chronometer, may have become quite proficient at counting seconds and half seconds. A half second counter can be improvised by making a simple pendulum. Attach any small heavy weight to a light line. If the pendulum is 9.8 inches long (to the center of the weight, the period (over and back) is 1 second. If the length is 39.1 inches long, the period is 2 seconds.

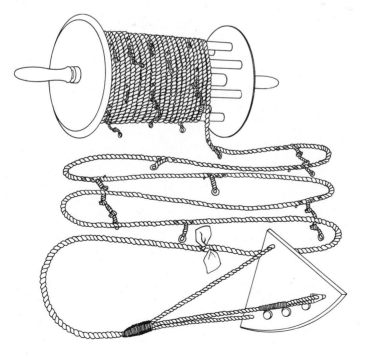

Figure 4008:
Chip log.

Traverse table.

4009. A simple traverse table may have many uses. In the table below the course is given in the first four columns, the difference of latitude in minutes per mile distance along the course in the fifth, and the departure or miles east or west per mile distance in the sixth. To find *l* and *p* multiply the tabulated value by the distance.

Course				*l*	*p*
°	°	°	°		
000	180	180	360	1.00	0.00
005	175	185	355	1.00	0.09
010	170	190	350	0.98	0.17
015	165	195	345	0.97	0.26
020	160	200	340	0.94	0.34
025	155	205	335	0.91	0.42
030	150	210	330	0.87	0.50
035	145	215	325	0.82	0.57
040	140	220	320	0.77	0.64
045	135	225	315	0.71	0.71
050	130	230	310	0.64	0.77
055	125	235	305	0.57	0.82
060	120	240	300	0.50	0.87
065	115	245	295	0.42	0.91
070	110	250	290	0.34	0.94
075	105	255	285	0.26	0.97
080	100	260	280	0.17	0.98
085	095	265	275	0.09	1.00
090	090	270	270	0.00	1.00

This table can be used for the solution of any right triangle. For the distance covered by a lifeboat during one day, the earth can be considered a plane without appreciable error. Apply the difference in latitude to the latitude at the beginning of the run. To convert *p* to DLo, multiply the *p* by the factor taken from the table below. The mid latitude is the entering argument. Both difference of latitude and difference of longitude are in minutes. The course indicates the direction in which to apply them.

Lm	p to DLo	Lm	p to DLo	Lm	p to DLo
°		°		°	
0	1.00	30	1.15	60	2.00
5	1.00	35	1.22	65	2.37
10	1.02	40	1.30	70	2.92
15	1.04	45	1.41	75	3.86
20	1.06	50	1.56	80	5.76
25	1.10	55	1.74	85	11.47

Example: A lifeboat leaves L 28°37'.4 S, λ 160°12'.6 E and follows course 240° for 80 miles.

Required: The latitude and longitude at the end of the run.

Solution: Enter the first table with C 240° and find *l* 0.50, and *p* 0.87. Since the distance is 80 miles, the difference of latitude is 80 × 0.50 = 40'.0. Since the course is 240°, this is a component to the southward. Hence, the latitude after the run is 28°37'.4 S + 40'.0 S = 29°17'.4 S. Enter the second table with the mid latitude, 29°.0 S, and take out "*p* to DLo," 1.14. The DLo is then 80 × 0.87 × 1.14 = 79'.3. Hence the longitude after the run is 160°12'.6 E − 79'.3 W = 158°53'.3 E, since the course has a component to westward.

Answer: L 29°17'.4 S, λ 158°53'.3 E.

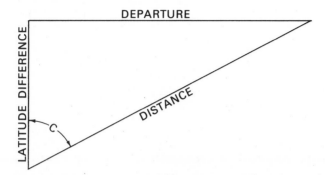

DEPARTURE

LATITUDE DIFFERENCE

DISTANCE

C

Figure 4009a: Traverse sailing.

If desired, the values of *l* and *p* can be found graphically by constructing the triangle of Figure 4009a. A maneuvering board (Chapter XIII) is useful for this purpose, but not essential. The conversion from *p* to DLo can also be made graphically, as shown in Figure 4009b. However, it is usually as easy to plot directly on a chart or plotting sheet as to make graphical solutions in the way just described.

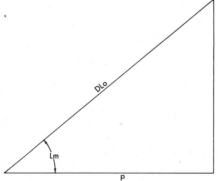

DLo

Lm

P

Figure 4009b: Converting p to DLo graphically.

4010. If a sextant is available, altitudes of celestial bodies are measured as described in Chapter 22. Be sure to determine the index correction. To assure optimum observations, when using a sextant in a lifeboat, or in any other small craft, the observer should obtain his altitude at the instant the crest of a wave is directly under his position in the boat. If no sextant is available altitudes can be measured in several ways, including the following:

Measuring altitudes.

Protractor. A protractor, a maneuvering board fastened securely to a board, or any graduated circle or semicircle can be used in any of several ways. The astrolabe used before the sextant was invented employed the same principle as the methods described hereafter.

In Figure 4010a a weight is attached to the center of curvature by a string that crosses the outer scale. If an AN plotter (article 312) is used, a hole for attaching

615

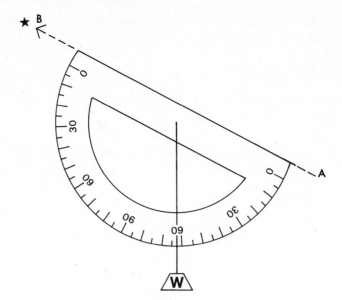

Figure 4010a: Measuring zenith distance with a protractor.

the string is already provided. The observer sights along the straightedge of the protractor, *AB*, at the body. An assistant reads the scale at the point where it is crossed by the string. This is the zenith distance if the protractor is graduated as shown in Figure 4010a. The altitude is 90° minus this reading. The altitude shown in Fig. 4010a is 28°. Several readings should be made, the protractor reversed and several more taken and all readings averaged. This method should not be used for the sun unless the eyes are adequately protected.

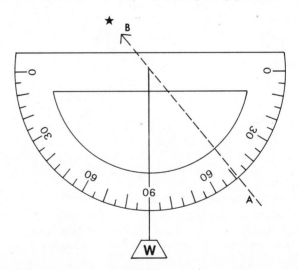

Figure 4010b: Measuring altitude with a protractor.

In Figure 4010b the weight is attached to a pin at the center of curvature and the protractor held horizontally, as indicated by the string crossing at 90°. The assistant holds the protractor and keeps the string on 90°. The observer moves a pin, pencil point, or other thin object along the scale until this pin and the center one are in line with the body. The body is then in direction AB. When the protractor is used in this way, the altitude is indicated directly. In Figure 4010b an altitude of about 48° is being measured. This method should not be used for the sun unless the eyes are protected.

For the sun either of the above methods can be used if a pin is mounted at the plane of the protractor. In the first method the reading is made when the shadow of the pin falls on 0°. In the second method the reading is made at the shadow.

There are several other variations of the use of the protractor. In the second method the weight can be omitted and the assistant can sight along the straight-edge at the horizon. An observation can be made without the assistant if the weight is attached at the scale at 90° and a loop of string placed over the pin at the center of curvature for holding the device. If preferred, the handle can be attached at 90° on the scale and the weight at the center of curvature, the pro-tractor being inverted. The first method can be used without an assistant if the string is secured in place by the thumb and forefinger when the observation is made.

If no scale graduated in degrees is available, place two pins or nails in a board and attach a weight to B by means of a string (Figure 4010c). Sight along AB and line up the two pins with the body. If the sun is being observed, hold the board so that the shadow of B falls on A. When A and B are lined up with the body, secure the string in place with the thumb and forefinger. From A draw AC perpendicular to the string. The traverse table can then be used to find the angle, entering the difference of latitude column with length BC or the de-parture column with AC. In either case the length is given in units of AB. That is, if AB is 10 inches, the length BC or AC in inches is divided by 10 before entering the table. A simpler way is to divide AC by BC and use the table below, entering the L/H column with AC/BC.

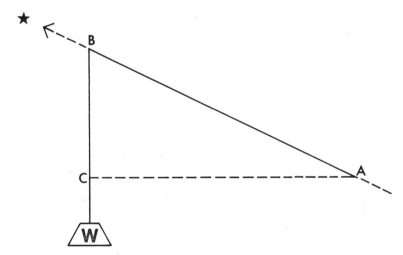

Figure 4010c:
Measuring altitude
without a protractor.

Length of shadow. If a bucket or other container is available, altitudes of the sun can be determined by measuring the length of a shadow. Drive a nail or other pointer in a board and float the board on water. The top of the pointer should be pointed for accurate results. If a nail is used, drive it through the board and turn the board over. Measure carefully the length of the shadow. Turn the board approximately 180° in azimuth and measure again. Divide the average of the two readings by the height of the pin and enter the following table (or any table of natural cotangents) to find the altitude.

Alt.	L/H	Alt.	L/H	Alt.	L/H
°		°		°	
5	11.430	35	1.428	65	0.466
10	5.671	40	1.192	70	0.364
15	3.732	45	1.000	75	0.268
20	2.747	50	0.839	80	0.176
25	2.145	55	0.700	85	0.087
30	1.732	60	0.577	90	0.000

In this table L is the length of the shadow and H is the height of the pin.

Example: The length of the shadow of a pin 4 inches long is 6.3 inches.

Required: The altitude of the sun.

Solution: L/H = 6.3/4 = 1.575. Interpolating in the table, the altitude is found to be 32°.6.

Answer: h 32°.6.

When using any of the methods described, several observations should be made and the average used, with the average time. If possible, reverse the device for half the readings.

Whatever method is used, *measure* the altitude, however crude the method. Do not attempt to estimate it, for estimates are seldom as accurate as the crudest measurement. If a damaged sextant is available, try to repair it. If the mirrors are broken, plain glass held in place by chewing gum or anything else available will usually be satisfactory.

Before leaving the measurement of altitudes, it might be well to point out that at sunrise or sunset the observed altitude (Ho) is (−) 50'. To this must be added (numerically) the dip correction.

Correction of measured altitudes. **4011.** If altitudes are measured from the visible horizon, they are corrected in the usual way, as explained in Chapter 22. Altitudes of the sun should be corrected for refraction, mean semidiameter, and dip. Altitudes of stars should be corrected for refraction and dip. If a weight is used to establish the vertical, or if the length of a shadow is measured, there is no correction for dip. If the sun's altitude is measured by means of a shadow, whether the length of the shadow is measured or the shadow falls across a scale or another pin, the center of the sun is measured, and hence no correction for semidiameter is needed. Approximate altitude corrections can be found as follows:

Alt. °	5	6	7	8	10	12	15	21	33	63	90
Corr. '	10	9	8	7	6	5	4	3	2	1	0

Refraction. The accompanying critical type table provides refraction corrections from 5° to 90°. If crude methods of observing the altitudes are employed, it may be sufficiently accurate to apply the correction only to the nearest 0°.1. For this purpose, altitudes above 20° can be considered to have no correction and those between 5° and 20° to have a correction of 0°.1. Observations below 5° should not be made if they can be avoided. The correction for refraction is

618

always subtractive, and must be applied to observations of all bodies, regardless of the method used.

If a slide rule is available, the refraction correction for altitudes above 10° may be found accurately by multiplying the cotangent of the altitude by 0.96.

Mean semidiameter. The mean semidiameter of the sun is 16' and the actual value does not differ from this by more than 0'.3. If the lower limb is observed, the correction is (+) and if the upper limb is observed, the correction is (−).

Dip. The correction for dip, in minutes of arc, is equal to the square root of the height of eye in feet, to sufficient accuracy for lifeboat use. This correction is used for all bodies whenever the visible horizon is used as a reference and is always (−). Dip may be determined exactly with a slide rule, by multiplying the square root of the height of eye in feet by 0.97.

Parallax. No correction is made for parallax, unless the moon is used, for it is too small to be a consideration for lifeboat navigation when other bodies are observed.

4012. A line of position may be obtained without a sextant or other altitude measuring instrument by noting the time a celestial body makes a contact with the visible horizon. The body most suitable for such observations is the Sun, and either the upper or lower limb may be used; the best practice would be to time both when they contact the horizon, and use the mean of the two resulting intercepts. A pair of binoculars, if available, will assist in determining the instant of contact. *Horizon sights.*

Such observations will usually yield surprisingly accurate results; they will certainly be more satisfactory than lines of position obtained from measurements made by improvised altitude measuring devices.

The uncorrected altitude is noted as 0°0', and carefully corrected for dip, refraction, and semidiameter. The correction for dip is made by adding its value numerically to the value of the refraction correction. Thus if the semidiameter is 16'.0, and the height of eye is 6 feet 6 inches, the corrections to an upper limb sun horizon sight would be as follows:

Height of eye 6'6"	Dip	− 2.5
0° H, Refraction		−34.5
☉ ,	S.D.	−16.0
		———
Correction		53'.0

The corrected altitude would be 0° − 53'.0, or −0°53'.0. Under nonstandard atmospheric conditions, the additional corrections for temperature and barometric pressure should be applied, if a thermometer and barometer are available.

The sight may be reduced in the ordinary manner by H. O. 211, or H. O. 229. H. O. 214 cannot be used, as no altitudes below about 5° are tabulated. It must be borne in mind that when both Ho and Hc are negative, the intercept will be named *towards if Ho is numerically less than Hc*, and vice versa.

Very low altitude sights may also be reduced very rapidly by means of a slide rule having a sine scale, and using the formula:

$$\sin Hc = \sin L \sin d \underset{\scriptscriptstyle\mp}{\pm} \cos L \cos d \cos t.$$

Hc is negative, if its sine is negative. Accurate solutions may be obtained at very low latitudes; as at altitudes below 2°, a sine may be read to about 0'.2 on a 10-inch slide rule. Azimuth angle may be obtained by means of the formula:

$$\sin Z = \frac{\cos d \sin t}{\cos Hc}$$

At very low altitudes, the division by cosine Hc may be ignored, as in such cases the cosine approaches unity. (See page 447 for naming the sign.)

Any low altitude observations may yield results that are in error by a few miles under conditions of abnormal terrestrial refraction. However, Captain P. V. H. Weems, USN (Ret.) made 10 horizon sights at sea on six different occasions, which gave an average error of 1.95 miles, and a maximum error of 4.0 miles.

An azimuth of the sun should be obtained at the same time the horizon sight is made, as a check on the accuracy of the compass.

The green flash. The *green flash* is a common phenomenon in the tropics, and occurs at the moment the sun's upper limb touches the horizon. It is caused by refraction of the light waves from the sun, as they pass through the earth's atmosphere. These light waves are not refracted, or bent, equally, the longer waves of red light being least refracted, the shorter blue and violet waves being more refracted. The red, orange and yellow light is cut off by the horizon when the blue and violet light is still momentarily visible. These blue and violet rays cause the green flash.

It is estimated that at sea in the tropics, the green flash may be seen as often as 50 percent of the time; it is, of course, easier to observe at sunset. The green flash usually lasts for a period of between one-half and one second.

Using the time of the green flash to obtain a line of position is merely a variation of the horizon sight described in the previous article. It is somewhat easier to determine the time of the flash than to determine the instant the sun's upper limb disappears below the horizon, when there is no green flash.

The green flash sight is corrected and reduced similarly to the horizon sight, described above.

Lines of position. **4013.** If tables are available for computation of Hc, lines of position are used in the usual way, as explained in Chapter 26. However, if no such tables are available, latitude and longitude should be determined separately, as was done before the discovery of the line of position by Captain Sumner in 1837.

If accurate time is not available, it will not be possible to determine the longitude. In this case no attempt should be made to steer directly for the destination, unless a whole continent is involved. Instead, the course should be set for a point well to the eastward or westward of the destination and when the latitude has been reached, a course of 090° or 270°, as appropriate, should be followed, as mentioned earlier in the chapter. If a single wrist watch is used for time and the journey is likely to be a long one, the time may be of questionable accuracy before the end of the voyage. If the watch is in error by 1 minute, the longitude will be inaccurate by 15'. If the destination is a small island, the course should be set for a point 50 to 100 miles or more, according to the maximum reasonable error in time, to the eastward or westward. In making this estimate allow for large watch rates, since the rate in a lifeboat will probably not be the same as aboard ship.

4014. The latitude can be determined in the northern hemisphere by means of an altitude of Polaris and in any latitude by means of meridian altitudes, as explained in Chapter 27.

Finding the latitude.

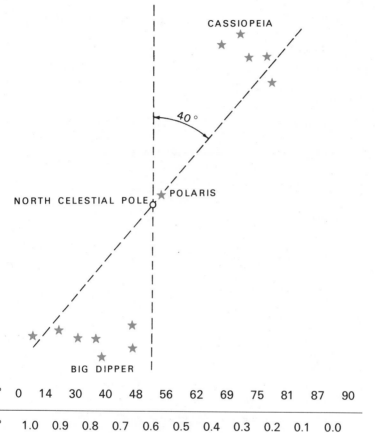

*Figure 4014a:
Estimating the
Polaris correction.*

Angle °	0	14	30	40	48	56	62	69	75	81	87	90
Corr. °	1.0	0.9	0.8	0.7	0.6	0.5	0.4	0.3	0.2	0.1	0.0	

Latitude by Polaris. If no Polaris correction table is available, the correction can be estimated in the following way: A line through Polaris and the north celestial pole, if extended, passes between ε *Cassiopeiae* and Ruchbah (the two left-hand stars of *Cassiopeia* when it appears as a W) on one side and Alkaid and Mizar (the last two stars in the handle of the big dipper) on the other. In both constellations these are the trailing stars in the counterclockwise motion about the pole. Polaris is on the side of the pole toward *Cassiopeia.* The correction depends only on the angle this line makes with the vertical. The accompanying critical type table gives the correction. If *Cassiopeia* is above Polaris, the correction is (−); if the big dipper is above, the correction is (+). If no correction table is available, it may be possible to estimate the correction from the relative positions of the two constellations. In Figure 4014a the angle is 40° and from the table the correction is found to be 0°.8. Since *Cassiopeia* is above the pole, the correction is (−) 0°.8.

Meridian altitude. At lifeboat speed most accurate results by the meridian altitude method are usually obtained by observing the highest altitude. For this purpose a number of observations should be made before and after meridian transit. If cross section paper is available, plot the altitude vs. time and fair a curve through the points. A typical curve is shown in Figure 4014b. Although the highest altitude measured is 40°.0, the meridian altitude is found to be 39°58′. For this plot altitudes were observed to the nearest 0°.1 at 5 minute intervals. If preferred, altitudes can be observed at less frequent intervals, perhaps each half hour, during the entire day. At a stationary point the curve should be symmetrical before and after meridian transit. At lifeboat speeds it should approach symmetry. The highest altitude is independent of time, which is used only to space the observations. If time is not available, make the observations at any desired interval. Approximately equal intervals can be estimated by using a pendulum, as explained in article 4008, or by counting at an even speed to any desired amount.

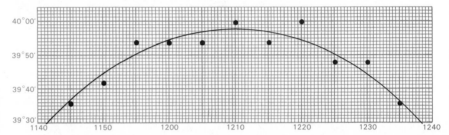

Figure 4014b: Typical curve of altitudes near meridian transit.

When the meridian altitude has been determined, combine it with the body's declination to find the latitude, as explained in Chapter 28.

The latitude can also be found by the duration of daylight, as described in article 4015.

Obtaining the longitude.

4015. In Figure 4014b the highest point on the curve represents meridian transit, or LAN; it can be seen that the time of transit is 1210. At this moment, the sun is the same distance west of Greenwich as the observer, and if a table of GHA of the sun is available, or if the equation of time is known, the approximate longitude can be determined. Without a fairly accurate timepiece there is of course no method for determining longitude.

The time of meridian transit can be found by picking off two points on this curve at which the altitude is the same, and noting the respective times; meridian transit occurs midway between them.

Greater accuracy may be obtained if the observations for equal altitude are made when the sun's rate of change of altitude is greater than that shown in Figure 4014b; say an hour before and after transition in this case. The curve as illustrated is not necessary. The best practice would be to obtain a series of altitudes before transit, plotting them against time then drawing in a line of best fit, which, over a period of a few minutes would be represented by a straight line. Then, after transit, the sextant would be reset to the last and highest altitude obtained before LAN, and when the sun reached this altitude, a new series of sights would be begun. These also should be plotted. Note that actual observations do not have to be used; equal altitudes, with their times, may be taken from the lines of best fit.

This method can be used with any body. If no means of measuring an altitude is available, the instant at which the body bears 180° or 000° true should be noted.

If a star is used, it is necessary to have its GHA. If its SHA is known, its GHA can be found approximately, by knowing that GHA ♈ in time units equals GMT on 23 September. GHA ♈ in time units is 90° more than GMT on 22 December, 180° more on 21 March, and 270° more on 22 June. GHA ♈ in time units gains approximately 4 minutes per day on GMT. The GHA of a star is equal to GHA ♈ + SHA.

The equation of time can be found approximately from the following table:

Date	Eq. T	Date	Eq. T	Date	Eq. T.
	m s		m s		m s
Jan. 10	−7 29	May 10	+3 41	Sept. 10	+2 53
20	11 02	20	3 39	20	6 25
30	13 21	30	2 42	30	9 51
Feb. 10	14 21	June 10	0 50	Oct. 10	12 51
20	13 53	20	−1 16	20	15 05
28	12 43	30	3 23	30	16 15
Mar. 10	10 30	July 10	5 08	Nov. 10	16 04
20	7 41	20	6 10	20	14 25
30	4 39	30	6 19	30	11 25
Apr. 10	1 27	Aug. 10	5 19	Dec. 10	7 20
20	+1 01	20	3 24	20	2 33
30	2 47	30	0 43	30	−2 25

Linear interpolation in this table does not produce very accurate results because of the uneven variation of the equation of time. The value varies from year to year, also, as does declination, but almost repeats every four years. If an almanac is available, it should be used.

Example: The altitude of the sun is 30° at $11^h21^m14^s$ and again at $12^h06^m32^s$ on 15 July. The watch is keeping (+) 9 ZT.

Required: Find the longitude, using the equation of time table above.

Solution: The time of transit is midway between the two times given, or at $11^h43^m53^s$. The GMT is 9 hours later, or $20^h43^m53^s$. The equation of time on 15 July is (−) 5^m39^s. Hence, the Greenwich apparent time (GAT) is $20^h43^m53^s$ − $5^m39^s = 20^h38^m14^s$. The GHA is equal to GAT ± 12^h, or $8^h38^m14^s = 129°33'.5$. This is the longitude.

Answer: λ 129°33'.5 W.

The longitude found in this way is the value at the time of meridian transit.

If the only watch should run down, it can be started again approximately by working this problem in reverse. That is, start with the best estimated longitude and find the GAT, then the GMT, and finally the ZT. Set the watch according to this time. Do this at the first opportunity after the watch runs down, while the EP is still reasonably good.

Longitude can also be determined by the time of sunrise or sunset, if a sunrise-sunset table is available. The process is somewhat similar to that just described for meridian transit. Find the LMT of sunrise or sunset from the table. Note the exact watch time of the phenomenon and from this find the GMT. The difference between GMT and LMT is the longitude. This depends on a knowledge of the latitude. It has the advantage that no equipment but a watch and sunrise-sunset table is needed. However, it is not very accurate, and the longitude obtained will not be as reliable as that taken from a horizon sight line of position, using the same latitude.

The latitude can be determined in this way, too, but even less accurately. Near the equinox, it is practically worthless and of little value at any time near the equator. To use the method the time of sunrise *and* sunset are noted and the total period of daylight determined. This is a function of the latitude on any given date. The latitude having this length of daylight is determined from the almanac. This is perhaps the least accurate way of finding the latitude and should be used only when there is no means of measuring the altitude. The time need not be accurate, for only the *duration* of daylight is needed.

Estimating distance. **4016.** If land or a ship is seen, it may be of value to know its approximate distance. To determine this, it is necessary to know approximately its height or some other dimension. If an object of known height (such as a mountain peak) appears over the horizon, the distance in nautical miles from the top of the object to the horizon is equal to $1.15\sqrt{H}$, where H is the height of the object above sea level. This is approximately equal to $\frac{8}{7}$ of the square root of the height of the object. To this must be added the distance from the observer to his horizon, found in the same way.

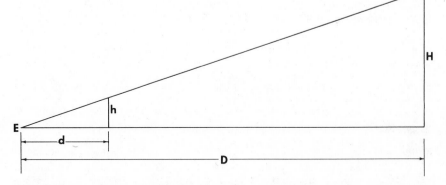

Figure 4016: Finding distance by simple proportion.

Example: A mountain peak 2000 feet high appears over the horizon of an observer whose eye is 8 feet above sea level.

Required: The distance of the mountain peak from the observer.

Solution: The distance from the top of the mountain to the horizon is $1.15\sqrt{2000}$ = 51.4 miles. The distance from the observer to the horizon is $1.15\sqrt{8} = 3.3$ miles. Hence, the distance of the mountain is 51.4 + 3.3 = 54.7 miles.

Answer: d 54.7 mi.

If an object is fully visible and its height is known, or if the length between two visible points is known, the distance can be found by simple proportion. Hold a scale at arm's length and measure the length subtended by the known height or length. Distance is then found by the proportion

$$\frac{D}{d} = \frac{H}{h} \qquad \text{or} \qquad D = \frac{dH}{h}$$

where D is the distance in feet, d is the distance in inches of the rule from the eye, H is the height (or length) of the object in feet and h is the length of the rule subtended by the object in inches. See Figure 4016. If H is in miles, the distance D is also in miles. If H is in feet and D is desired in nautical miles, the formula becomes

$$D = \frac{dH}{6000h}.$$

Example: An island 1.2 miles long subtends a length of 3.5 inches for an observer holding a rule 21 inches from his eye.

Required: The distance of the island from the observer.

Solution: Solving the formula,

$$D = \frac{dH}{h} = \frac{21 \times 1.2}{3.5} = 7.2 \text{ miles.}$$

Answer: D = 7.2 mi.

In using this method with a length, be careful to use the length *at the visible height* (the shore line and a low beach may be below the horizon) and be sure that the length is perpendicular to the line of sight (which may not be the same as the greatest length). If a height is employed, be sure the *visible* height is used.

A variation is to measure the angle subtended and determine the length graphically. That is, in Figure 4016, if the angle at E is known, the distance D at height H can be determined by drawing a figure to scale.

4017. The position of the celestial equator is indicated in the sky by any *Miscellaneous.* body of 0° declination. The sun's declination is 0° about 21 March and 23 September. The star δ *Orionis* (the northernmost star of *Orion's* belt) is nearly on the celestial equator. Such a body indicates the approximate east point of the horizon at rising and the west point at setting, at any latitude.

A great circle through Polaris, Caph (the leading star in *Cassiopeia*), and the eastern side of the square of *Pegasus* (Alpheratz and Algenib) represents approximately the hour circle of the vernal equinox. The local hour angle of this circle is the LHA ♈. The LHA ♈ in time units can also be determined approximately by knowing that at the autumnal equinox (about 23 September) LHA ♈ and LMT are identical. Every half a month thereafter the LHA ♈ in time units *gains* one hour on LMT. Hence, on 15 January it is approximately 7^h30^m fast on LMT.

Protect the watch and wind it regularly. If a water tight container is available, that is a good place for keeping the watch, especially while launching the lifeboat.

In the interest of being picked up at the earliest possible time, remember that metal is a better radar reflector than wood, and the higher the reflector the greater the range at which it might be picked up. If there is a possibility that radar equipped planes or ships are searching for your lifeboat, try to rig up some kind of metal corner reflector that will produce a stronger pip on the rescuer's radar screen. Also, do not forget to weigh the possibility of rescue in determining to leave the vicinity of the stricken ship and in setting the course.

Keep out of the direct rays of the sun as much as possible, to avoid sunburn, dehydration of the body, eye infection, and eye strain.

Rig a sail, even if one must be improvised.

Before going to sea consult a good seamanship book on the handling of a small boat, particularly in a surf. Landing in a surf is treacherous and should be thoroughly understood. There is no *need* to negotiate safely a thousand miles of unfriendly ocean in an open boat, only to be killed or seriously injured through lack of knowledge of the principles of making a landing on an open beach from seaward.

Keep a sharp lookout at all times and do not pass up any chance of rescue.

Work as a team and make the wisest use of all information and aids available.

Navigation without instruments.
4018. The ancient Polynesians were able to navigate successfully, without mechanical instruments or time pieces, by using their knowledge of the heavens and the lore of the sea. Few persons today have acquired this knowledge, hence this chapter has been principally devoted to using, or improvising, instruments and methods familiar to most naval and merchant marine officers, and quartermasters.

The declination of any star is equal to the latitude of the point on earth directly beneath the star, the GP, and for lifeboat accuracy the declination of the stars can be assumed to remain fixed. This is the key to no-instrument celestial navigation. In the South Atlantic, for example, Alphard will pass overhead at Ascension Island. Farther north Alkaid passes over Land's End, England; Newfoundland; Vancouver Island; south of the Aleutians and over the Kuril Islands, north of Japan.

A rough determination of latitude can therefore be made by observing the passing of a star of known declination directly overhead. By comparing the star's Dec., with the known latitude of land areas a position east or west of the land areas can be determined. Ancient navigators were able to sail to the proper latitude then east or west to a known island by this process.

Directions to land can be determined by observing the flight of birds or by typical cloud formations over islands. A steady course can be steered by maintaining a constant angle with the direction of swells or wave motion. Nearby land can sometimes be detected by sounds or even by a particular smell. A complete dissertation on using the lore of the sea and sky for navigation is beyond the space limitation of this text but is mentioned to illustrate the necessity of using any available data or knowledge when routine navigation methods are not available.

4019. Anyone spending a part of his life at sea or over the water should con- *Summary.* sider it good insurance to be adequately prepared for an emergency. A man does not refuse to buy fire insurance for his house just because he hopes it will never burn down, or even because relatively few houses do burn. The cost of insurance is too inexpensive and the consequences of a fire too great to ignore this important item. As long as there is a possibility, however remote, of having to abandon ship, a suitable preparation for this emergency is good insurance. His very life and those of others may depend on his preparation. It may be too late when the order to abandon ship is given.

One of the essential items of preparation is a thorough knowledge of *fundamentals*. Practically all of the information given in this chapter consists of applications of fundamentals.

Once you have boarded a lifeboat or life raft, make a careful estimate of the situation. The methods to be used and the procedure to be followed depend on the particular situation. Use the most accurate methods available. Use imagination and ingenuity in making use of the materials at hand. If more than one method of doing anything is available, check one method against another.

Establish a regular routine and keep busy. *Navigate* with whatever means are available; do not guess if there is any way of making a measurement or estimate.

Maintain good morale at all cost. Be *determined* to get back and do not permit conversation to become pessimistic. Good leadership qualities are never more important than at such a time.

CHAPTER 41

Bathymetric Navigation

Introduction.

4101. *Bathymetric Navigation* may be defined as the branch of navigation that utilizes the topography of the ocean floor to obtain positioning data by sonic or ultrasonic echoes returned from the ocean floor at even the greatest depths. Since time immemorial, the mariner's major concern has been grounding; the hand lead is probably the oldest navigational instrument. From this developed the deep-sea lead, often called the "blue pigeon," which could be used at greater depths. The base of this lead was concave, so that the hollow could be "armed" with tallow, thus yielding both a sounding and a sample of the bottom sediment to assist in determining position. Such soundings could be obtained in the vicinity of the continental shelf but only at comparatively long intervals, due to the time consumed in recovering a fifty or seventy pound lead and a hundred or more fathoms of line by hand. Today, the navigator can obtain a continuous flow of soundings; these may even be presented graphically, as a profile of the sea bed over which the ship has passed.

Principles of echo sounding.

4102. The *depth finder*, also called Fathometer and echo sounder, generates an underwater sound wave signal, and measures the duration of the time elapsing between the generation of the signal and the reception of the echo returned from the bottom; this time lapse is converted to a readout of units of depth, usually stated in fathoms, although feet are used in many echo sounders designed for small craft. The U. S. Naval Oceanographic Office is using the metric system to indicate depths on all new charts and a readout in meters is desirable when using these new charts. Most echo sounders operate in the audible range of about 20 to 20,000 cycles per second; these are termed *sonic* depth finders. However, the trend is towards using higher frequencies, in order to reduce interference from ship noise, and such instruments are termed *ultrasonic*.

The speed of sound through sea water varies with the salinity of the water, its temperature, and the pressure (depth). This variation is not very great, and most echo sounding equipment of American manufacture is calibrated for a speed of sound of 4,800 feet per second. At sea, the actual speed of travel of sound is nearly always greater than this calibrated speed, and the error introduced lies on the side of safety, except where the water is fresh, or extremely cold.

Transducer.

The *transducer*, located on a horizontal portion of a ship's bottom plating, near the keel, transmits the acoustic signal when activated electrically. The sound energy used to determine depth is projected in the shape of a cone. Aboard most U. S. naval vessels the echo sounding equipment generates a cone of about 60°; the area of the bottom covered by the cone of sound is a function of the depth, and in deep water it can be quite large. The returning echo is picked up by the transducer, converted into electrical energy, amplified and presented visually. Elapsed time between the outgoing and the returning signal is read directly as depth. The depth finder usually gives depth under the keel, so that the actual depth of the water is equal to the depth under the keel plus the draft of the ship. Alternately, it may be calibrated to indicate the depth of water as measured from the surface.

The readout of depth is presented in somewhat different form by the various manufacturers. In a typical instrument, a circular electric light tube is mounted vertically; this tube flashes briefly at the instant the sonic signal is transmitted, and again when the echo is received. In front of the light tube, and mounted concentrically with it, is an opaque shield, which rotates at a predetermined speed. This shield has a narrow radial slot, which allows the light to be seen at only one point each time it flashes. Adjacent to the shield is a circular scale calibrated in units of depth. The depth finder shows the first flash of light at the zero point on the scale, and the second flash indicates the depth of water. Different scales may be available for use at various depths; the speed of rotation of the opaque shield is adjusted to match the scale being used. The U. S. Navy's AN/UQN-1 depth finder is shown in Figure 1015a. The new, redesigned and improved AN/UQN-4 is shown in Figure 4102a, and is described in article 4103.

Readout.

Some echo sounders are also equipped with a *recorder* which produces a graphic trace of the depths encountered; this trace is called a *bottom profile*. The recorder consists of a wide paper tape, graduated in depth and time units, and a moving arm equipped with a stylus, which makes one sweep over the

Figure 4102a: AN/UQN-4 Depth finder.

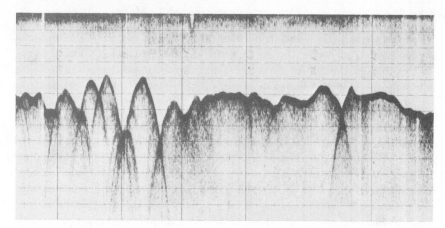

Figure 4102b:
A typical bottom
profile.

tape for each sounding. When the echo is received, the stylus marks a short line on the tape. A typical bottom profile is shown in Figure 4102b.

In theory, echos are returned from the bottom from all points within the sound cone; in actual use, the first echoes tend to mask the later ones, and there may be an appreciable delay between the return of the first and the later echoes. It must be borne in mind that the first return will come from that portion of the bottom which is nearest the ship, and that *this portion is not necessarily directly below the ship*. This phenomenon is known as a *side echo*. Subsequent returns will be from other portions of the bottom. In comparatively shallow water, *multiple returns* may occur when the bottom is a good sound reflector. The echo returns from the bottom and is recorded as the depth, but it is also reflected downwards from the water surface to the bottom, and then back up. Two or more returns can occur. Figure 4102c shows an example of multiple returns; the upper trace represents the actual bottom, while the lower trace, showing twice the depth, is caused by multiple return. Reducing the echo sounder gain will usually remove indications of multiple return.

Side echo.

Multiple returns.

Another phenomenon which may be puzzling is the appearance at times of a false bottom, suspended in the water. This is caused by echoes returned from the *deep scattering layer*, also called the *phantom bottom*. In daytime it is encountered at depths of about 200 fathoms; it usually moves nearer the surface at night. It is believed to be caused by echoes reflected from light-shunning plankton and other minute marine life. At times, this layer is sufficiently dense to mask echoes from the actual bottom.

Figure 4102c:
Multiple bottom
returns as seen on
the recorder.

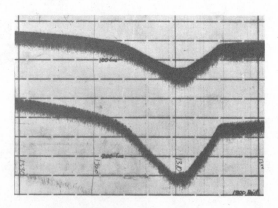

Schools of fish also return an echo, making the echo sounder particularly useful to fishermen. Any sharp discontinuity within the water causes sound to be reflected, and an echo sounder often can detect the boundary of a layer of fresh water overlaying the heavier salt water.

A rocky bottom reflects almost all the sound striking its surface, while soft mud tends to absorb it, thus returning a weaker signal. A layer of mud or silt overlaying rock frequently yields two echoes.

The navigator must always bear in mind that depths shown on charts may be inaccurate due to changing bottom conditions, such as silting or the formation of sand bars, since the survey was made. It is also possible that protruding underwater obstacles may have been missed during the survey. It is important to use the depth sounder continuously in a deep draft vessel approaching shallow water or operating on soundings. Modern surveys are, however, much more accurate and reliable than those conducted before the introduction of the electronic positioning systems discussed in Chapter 33. Electronic systems permit not only an accurate establishment of the survey vessel's position but extend the range of operations further from shore. Most important, they are able to maintain an automatic plot of positions related to time. By use of a depth sounder in place of the old hand lead a continuous recording of depths is made and is correlated with the position of the survey vessel.

4103. The AN/UQN-4 precision echo sounder shown in Figure 4102a is the successor to the UQN-1 series; instruments of this latter series are installed in many vessels, and have proved very satisfactory.

The AN/UQN-4 echo sounder.

The UQN-4 is essentially an improved version of the basic UQN-1, described in article 1015. Like the latter instruments, it transmits on a frequency of 12 kHz; it differs from them primarily in that both the transmitting and receiving circuitry are entirely solid state, and in that the cathode ray tube readout has been replaced by a numerical readout, which shows the depth stated either in feet or fathoms.

The transducer beam width is 30°. The signal frequency is crystal controlled; emission consists of a pulsed CW signal, with a maximum peak output of 1,000 watts. The pulse duration and repetition rate are given in the following table. Two pulse lengths are available for each of the deeper range settings.

Range	Short Pulse	Long Pulse	Pulse Repetition Rate
600 feet	0.33 ms		120 per minute
600 fathoms	2.46 ms	26.67 ms	20 per minute
6,000 fathoms	20.00 ms	160.00 ms	2 per minute

In lieu of automatic transmission (auto pinging), the operator can key a single signal manually. In addition to the numerical depth readout, the UQN-4 has a strip chart recorder, which is greatly improved over previous models.

The UQN-4 has two additional features which are not available on its predecessors. It is fitted with a draft adjustment, which permits the depth readout to be adjusted so that it states depth below the lowest portion of the ship, such as a sonar dome, and provision is made for automatic tracking. A selected depth is set manually into the numerical depth readout circuit. A *Lost Tracking Indicator* is illuminated whenever a depth 200 feet greater or less than the preset depth is encountered.

The echo sounder as a navigational aid.

4104. Soundings shown on the U. S. Naval Oceanographic Office charts are obtained by echo sounder, and are uncorrected for any variation in salinity, density, or temperature. Since conditions in any given area remain reasonably constant, echo sounder readings may therefore be compared directly with the charted values.

Article 4102 stated that the sound energy was projected from the transducer in the shape of a cone; the base of this cone covers a considerable area of the bottom, but it is represented by the echo sounder as a single value of depth. This is advantageous, as a minimum depth is recorded even if the ship is not directly above the point from which the echo is received. As stated above, in theory, echoes are returned from the bottom at all points within the cone; in practice the first echo received masks the subsequent ones.

Line of soundings.

In ordinary navigation when using the echo sounder, the *line of soundings* method may be used to advantage as an aid in determining position. The manner of employing this method depends largely on the chart covering the area.

Either of the two methods requires a piece of transparent paper or plastic, on which is drawn a straight line representing the ship's course. If bottom contour lines are printed on the chart, the depth values of the contour lines should be noted; assume that these are given for every 20 fathoms. The echo sounder is now turned on, and when a sounding of a multiple of 20 fathoms true depth is obtained, a mark is made at one end of the heading line on the tracing paper, the depth is noted opposite the mark at one side of the line, and the time at the other. When the depth changes by 20 fathoms, the time is again noted, and using the latitude scale of the chart, the ship's run for the time interval is calculated, and another mark is made at the appropriate distance from the first, and depth and time are again noted. After this process has been repeated several times, the paper is placed on the chart in the vicinity of the ship's DR position, with the ship's heading line oriented in the proper direction. It is now moved across the chart, with the heading line always oriented in the proper direction, until the depth marks on the paper agree with the contour lines on the chart. The ship's position may now usually be determined with considerable accuracy.

Note that if the echo sounder reads depth under the keel, the soundings must be adjusted to represent depth below the surface. In this case, if the vessel draws 24 feet (4 fathoms), use echo sounder readings of 16 fathoms, 36 fathoms, 56 fathoms, etc.

When contour lines are not shown on the chart, it is best to mark off the line on the paper in equal distances, each distance representing the ship's advance for a convenient period of time. On small scale charts these distances should be greater than when a large scale chart is used. When a number of soundings have been recorded, the paper is oriented and moved across the chart in the same manner as described above, to determine the most probable position.

The Coast and Geodetic Survey is producing bathymetric maps of the waters adjacent to the coast line of the United States. These maps extend seaward

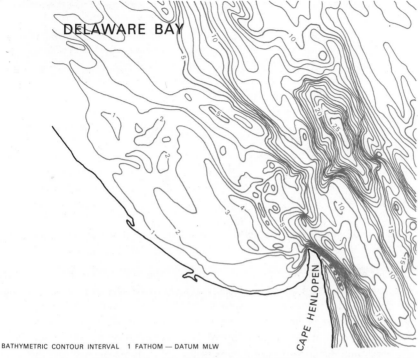

DELAWARE BAY

CAPE HENLOPEN

BATHYMETRIC CONTOUR INTERVAL   1 FATHOM — DATUM MLW

*Figure 4104:
Section of
bathymetric map.*

somewhat beyond the one hundred fathom curve, and show the contour of the
bottom in considerable detail. A portion of such a map is reproduced in Figure
4014. These maps can be of great assistance in fixing position by means of the
depth finder.

4105. Charted "landmarks" on the ocean floor can often assist the navigator
in determining position. Such marks include *submarine canyons, trenches,
troughs, escarpments, ridges, seamounts,* and *guyots.* These terms in general
describe submarine topographical features which are similar to their counterparts found on dry land. An escarpment is a long steep face of rock, or long submarine cliff. A seamount is an elevation of relatively small horizontal extent
rising steeply towards, but not reaching, the surface. A guyot is a flat-topped
seamount, rather similar to the mesas found in the southwestern United States.
Canyons are found off most continental slopes; they are relatively steepsided,
and their axes descend steadily. A canyon, when crossed approximately at right
angles, is easily recognized on the recorder. It will serve to establish a line of
position, and the maximum depth recorded, when crossing the axis, may further
aid in determining position. Trenches, troughs, ridges and escarpments are often
found on the ocean bottom, which may be otherwise featureless; they can also
be useful in yielding a line of position. Many guyots occur in the Pacific, and are
useful in positioning. A line of position may also be obtained when crossing the
line of demarcation between an ocean basin, which is usually very flat, and the
surrounding bottom mass.

*Use of bottom
"land marks" in
navigation.*

4106. If the apex of an isolated seamount is located by means of the echo
sounder, a precise position can be determined. If several seamounts are located
in the same area, identification must be made by individual shape as well as
minimum depth.

*Precise positioning
by means of
seamounts.*

633

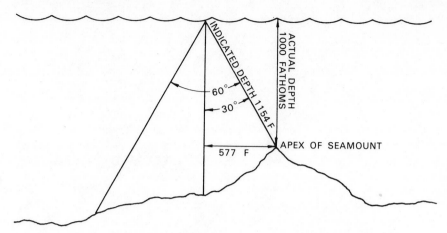

60°

30°

INDICATED DEPTH 1154 F

ACTUAL DEPTH 1000 FATHOMS

APEX OF SEAMOUNT

577 F

Figure 4106a: The geometry of a 60° sound cone.

Article 4102 stated that the echo sounders on most naval vessels generated a 60° cone of sound. The geometry of such a cone should now be considered.

The first echo return comes from the portion of the sea bed which is nearest the ship, and this portion is not necessarily directly below the ship; in such a case, the depth finder is indicating a side echo. This can be very helpful because, if the seamount apex lies within the sound cone the depth recorded by the depth finder cannot exceed the depth of the apex multiplied by 1.154. In addition, the horizontal distance from the apex to the ship cannot exceed half the depth indicated by the depth finder (Figure 4106a).

The 60° sound cone.

Ordinarily, to obtain a fix by means of locating the summit of a seamount, a position some distance away is determined as accurately as possible, and then a course is set for the apex. The distance of the departure position from the apex will depend in part on the existing current, sea and wind conditions.

Figure 4106b shows the contour lines surrounding the apex of a seamount. Assume that a ship obtained a good running fix due south of the apex, and is approaching on a course of 000°. It is possible that this course will take the ship directly over the summit, in which case the depth finder will give a minimum reading of 1126 fathoms (the depth at the summit), and provide a fix. Unfortunately, this occurs but seldom.

Figure 4106c shows the DR plot, as the ship approaches the location of the summit. Soundings are recorded every minute on the plot as is also the minimum sounding obtained; times are omitted in this figure for clarity. The shallowest sounding obtained is 1169 fathoms, and a line is drawn at right angles to the heading line for this sounding. As the soundings begin to increase it is obvious the ship has passed the area of the summit, a right turn is made to come to a course of 270°, crossing the original track at an angle of 90°. The turn to starboard is adjusted so that the new course that will pass as close as possible to the summit's assumed position. Soundings are again noted every minute, as is the minimum sounding, which is 1149 fathoms. A perpendicular to the ship's course line is again drawn for this minimum sounding.

The intersection of the two perpendicular lines passing through the minimum recorded depths locates the summit of the seamount relative to the ship; the direction and distance separating the intersection of these two lines from the

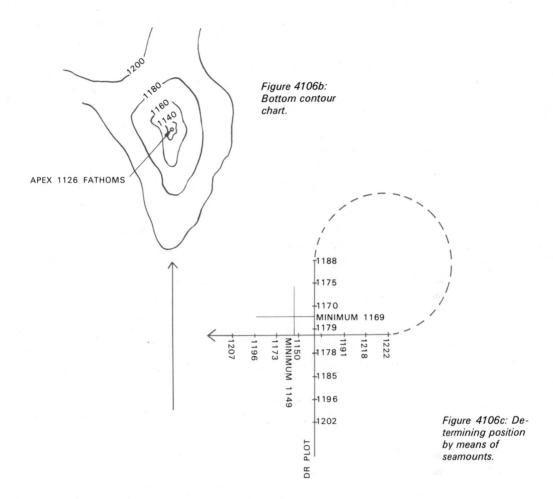

Figure 4106b:
Bottom contour
chart.

APEX 1126 FATHOMS

Figure 4106c: De-
termining position
by means of
seamounts.

charted position of the seamount is the offset of the ship's track from the seamount. Adjustment of the track may be accomplished by shifting all recorded
times and soundings by the direction and distance of the offset.

If there is any doubt in placing the ship's position relative to the summit, or when
extreme accuracy is desired, a third transit is made. This is usually made on a
heading 45° from the first two transits. If the ship does not pass over the summit,
a perpendicular is again drawn through the point where the minimum sounding
was obtained, and an analysis of the three perpendiculars will usually clarify the
ship's location relative to the apex. This method of locating the apex of a seamount may be adapted for use with a sound cone of any given width.

4107. A highly refined system of bathymetric navigation has been developed *Refined bathymet-*
for use aboard the National Aeronautics and Space Administration's range in- *ric navigation.*
strumentation ships (RIS).

Essentially, this system requires that a very precise topographic bottom survey
first be made of the area in which these ships are to operate, and that this survey
be referred to precisely determined position coordinates.

635

This system is based on accurately located surveys in areas with a depth of between 200 and 4000 fathoms and a topographical variation of at least 12 fathoms. The sites selected are square areas 4 miles on each side. Positional information, while surveying the area, is determined by means of transponder beacons of a sonar reference system, positioned specifically for this purpose. The transponders are placed on the ocean floor and are located precisely in latitude and longitude by means of SINS, Loran C and NAVSAT fixes. When the survey is completed, the beacons are recovered, utilizing an acoustic release mechanism.

With the transponder beacons in place the actual survey is conducted by the survey ship steaming down one side of the area, taking soundings commencing before entry into the area, and continuing across the square on reciprocally alternating tracks 500 yards apart. The depth data are accumulated at an interval spacing ranging from 1 to 5 seconds per sounding, depending on the actual depth of the water. As the depth data are acquired from the depth finder they are converted to digital form and transferred to a central computer where they are "time-tagged" and stored on magnetic tape. At the same time the positional data are recorded and also stored on time-tagged magnetic tape.

The central computer accepts the depth data recorded during the survey operation and converts them into punched tape for use later when required for positioning information. In order to produce this matrix the computer must interpolate between data points on adjacent tracks to predict the most probable depths at locations in the matrix where depth data are lacking, as shown in Figure 4107. The result is a grid representing a continuous, three-dimensional profile of the ocean floor in the surveyed area, stored in the computer.

To utilize the system, the ship must first identify the four mile square area in which it is located. Incoming echoes from the ship's echo sounder, as she moves on a given heading, are then compared by the computer with the stored sounding data for the area, until a match is obtained.

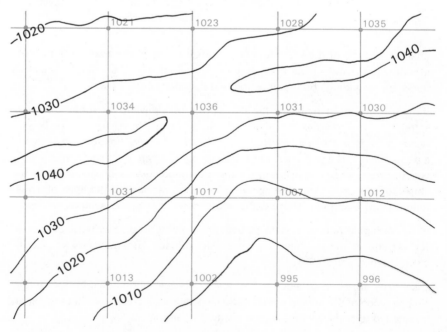

Figure 4107: Probable depth matrix superimposed on contour map (fathoms).

The specifications call for the ship to locate herself with a 50 per cent probability of accuracy within a circle 100 yards in diameter. In addition to its navigational accuracy, the system offers the advantage of requiring no external inputs.

4108. *Sonar* (SOund NAvigation Ranging) operates in the same manner as the echo sounder, except that it radiates its signal in a generally horizontal, rather than a vertical direction. Excellent ranges on underwater objects may be obtained with sonar, and as the sonar transducer can be rotated horizontally, accurate bearings may also be obtained. *Sonar in piloting.*

Sonar can be of great assistance in piloting in thick weather, particularly in rocky areas.

For example, when the harbor of Newport, Rhode Island, is closed due to very heavy fog, a ship returning to port can come to anchor out of the channel south of Brenton Reef and west of Seal Ledge, in a very precisely determined position. Subsequent changes in sonar ranges and bearings would give immediate notice, should she drag her anchor (Figure 4108).

Figure 4108: Sonar in piloting.

In arctic regions, sonar is sometimes helpful in locating ice when steaming at slow speed, as approximately nine-tenths of the ice mass is located below the water surface. Large bergs may sometimes be detected at a range of 6,000 yards or more, but the service range is usually less. Growlers may be picked up at ranges of between 1,000 and 2,000 yards; even smaller pieces may be detected in time to avoid them.

During the latter part of World War II sonar made it possible for U. S. submarines to penetrate defensive mine fields laid by the Japanese. Moving submerged at slow speeds, the submarines were able to detect the anchored mines, and thus thread their way through the fields.

4109. Bathymetric navigation is still in its infancy as a method of ship positioning. The instrumentation developed for the National Aeronautics and Space Administration's RIS is only a first step in the use of modern technology in this field. An interesting device developed by the Navy for its Deep Submersible Rescue Vehicle program is the altitude/depth (A/D) sonar, which shows the vehicle's altitude above the ocean bottom, and the depth below the surface for cruising and search purposes. *Summary.*

Further improvements and refinements in this field may be expected.

CHAPTER 42

Polar Navigation

The polar regions. **4201.** No single definition is completely satisfactory in defining the limits of the *polar regions*. Astronomically, the parallels of latitude at which the sun becomes circumpolar, at about latitudes 67°.5 north and south, are considered the lower limits. Meteorologically, the limits are irregular lines which, in the Arctic, coincide approximately with the tree line. For purposes of this text, the polar regions will be considered to extend from the geographical poles to latitude 70°. The *subpolar regions* are a transitional area extending for an additional 10° to latitude 60°.

Arctic geography. **4202.** The *Arctic Ocean* is a body of water, a little smaller in area than the

Figure 4202: The north polar region, or Arctic.

United States, which is almost completely surrounded by land, as shown in Figure 4202. Some of this land is high and rugged, and covered with permanent ice caps; part of it is low and marshy when thawed. Underlying permanently frozen ground, called *permafrost*, prevents adequate drainage, resulting in large numbers of lakes and ponds, and extensive areas of *muskeg*, soft spongy ground with characteristic growths of certain mosses, and tufts of grass or sedge. There are also large areas of *tundra*, low treeless plains with vegetation consisting of mosses, lichens, shrubs, willows, etc., and usually having an underlying layer of permafrost.

Greenland is mountainous, and notable for its many *fjords*, long narrow and often deep arms of the sea lying between mountains. Its northern portion is covered with a heavy ice cap. The northernmost point of land is Kap Morris Jesup, which is about 380 miles from the geographic pole.

Greenland.

The central part of the Arctic Ocean is a basin with an average depth of about 12,000 feet; the bottom is not level, and there are a number of seamounts and deeps. The greatest depth is probably something over 16,000 feet; at the pole, the depth is 14,150 feet. Surrounding the polar basin is an extensive continental shelf, broken only in the area between Greenland and Spitsbergen. The many islands of the Canadian archipelago lie on this shelf. The Greenland Sea, east of Greenland, Baffin Bay, west of Greenland, and the Bering Sea, north of the

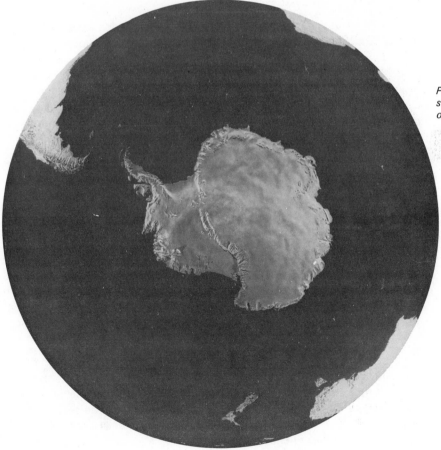

Figure 4203: The south polar region, or Antarctic.

639

Aleutians, each has its independent basin. Due to ice conditions surface ships cannot penetrate to the pole but have successfully reached quite high latitudes.

Antarctic geography.

4203. The *Antarctic*, or south polar region, is in marked contrast to the Arctic in physiographical features. It is a high mountainous land mass, about twice the area of the United States, surrounded by the Atlantic, Pacific, and Indian Oceans, as shown in Figure 4203. An extensive polar plateau, covered with snow and ice, is about 10,000 feet high. The average height of Antarctica is about 6,000 feet, which is higher than any other continent, and there are several mountain ranges with peaks rising to more than 13,000 feet. The height at the south pole is about 9,500 feet.

The barrier presented by land and tremendous *ice shelves* in the Ross Sea prevents ships from reaching very high latitudes. Much of the coast of Antarctica is high and rugged, with few good harbors or anchorages.

Polar coordinates.

4204. Many of the concepts of measurement which are used in normal navigation take on new meanings, or lose their meaning entirely, in the polar regions. In temperate latitudes man speaks of north, south, east, and west when he refers to direction; of latitude and longitude; of time; of sunrise and sunset; and of day and night. Each of these terms is normally associated with specific concepts and relationships. In the polar regions, however, each of these terms has a somewhat different significance, requiring a reappraisal of the concepts and relationships involved.

In temperate latitudes, the lengths of a degree of latitude and a degree of longitude are roughly comparable, and meridians are thought of as parallel lines, as they appear on a Mercator chart, or as nearly parallel lines. Not so in polar regions, where meridians radiate outward from the pole like great spokes of a gigantic wheel, and longitude becomes a coordinate of direction. A plane circling the pole might cover 360° of longitude in a couple of minutes. Each of two observers might be north (or south) of the other if the north (or south) pole were between them. At the north pole all directions are south, and at the south pole all directions are north. A visual bearing of a mountain peak can no longer be considered a rhumb line. It is a great circle, and because of the rapid convergence of meridians, must be plotted as such.

Time as used in temperate zones has little meaning in polar regions. As the meridians converge, so do the time zones. A mile from the pole the time zones are but a quarter of a mile apart. At the pole the sun rises and sets once each year, the moon once a month. Stars never set, but circle the sky always at essentially the same altitude. A day of 24 hours at the pole is not marked by the usual periods of daylight and darkness, and "morning" and "afternoon" have no significance. In fact, the day is not marked by any observable phenomenon except that the sun makes one complete circle around the sky, maintaining essentially the same altitude and always bearing south (or north).

Our system of coordinates, direction, and many of the concepts so common to our daily lives are man-made. They have been used because they have proved useful. If they are discarded near the poles, it is because their usefulness does not extend to these regions. A new concept must be devised for use in the polar regions. It should differ as little as possible from familiar methods, while taking full cognizance of changed conditions.

4205. Probably the only real trick to navigating in higher latitudes is to use every known method, and evaluate the results by weighing the value of each shred of positional evidence gathered. No method used is really new or unique, rather the application of method to unique problems.

Navigational problems in polar and subpolar regions are most easily considered in these categories: chart projections, environmental factors, determining direction, determining distance, and fixing position.

4206. The familiar Mercator chart projection will normally not be used in higher latitudes since distortion becomes so great as the poles are approached. Variations of the Mercator projection can be used, thus retaining some advantages without the unacceptable distortion imposed by having tangency of the cylinder occur at the Equator. This is done *by rotating the tangent cylinder through 90°*. If this is done, the cylinder is tangent to a meridian, which becomes the "fictitious equator." Parallels of latitude become oval curves, with the sinusoidal meridians extending outward from the pole. The meridians change their direction of curvature at the pole. Within the polar regions the parallels are very nearly circles and the meridians diverge but slightly from straight lines. The distortion at L 70° is comparable to that at L 20° on an ordinary Mercator chart. Within this region a straight line can be considered a great circle with but small error. If the cylinder is tangent to a meridian, the projection is called *transverse Mercator*. If it is placed tangent to an oblique great circle, the projection is termed *oblique Mercator*.

Other projections used in polar regions are the stereographic, gnomonic or great circle, azimuthal equidistant (Figure 4206) and the modified Lambert conformal. Near the pole, all of these and the transverse Mercator projection are so nearly alike as to be difficult to distinguish by eye. All are suitable, and all can be used with a grid. On the gnomonic chart a great circle is a straight line, and on the others it is very nearly so. Distance and grid direction are measured in the accustomed manner.

In practical usage these polar charts are used in a manner similar to the Lambert for measuring course and distance and plotting position (Chapter 3).

The real problem of polar charts does not involve the projection to be used. The latitude and longitude lines can be drawn to the same accuracy as on any other chart, but the other information shown on polar charts is sometimes far from accurate. These regions are being traveled more and more, and pilots and charts are improving, but many areas have not been accurately surveyed. The result is that in less-traveled areas coast lines are inaccurate or missing, topography is unreliable, and soundings are sparse. Lines of magnetic variation are located principally by extrapolation. Even the positions of the magnetic poles are not accurately known. One of the major problems of navigation is the production of accurate charts for polar regions. The navigator must, therefore, be acutely aware of the accuracy (or lack of accuracy) of his charts, and take greater than usual precautions to ensure that a safe course is steered. Any advance warning device is most useful, and should be fully used. Coastal topography or irregular soundings may presage pinnacles some distance offshore, and if ice conditions permit sonar or a forward-looking echo sounder, these should be employed.

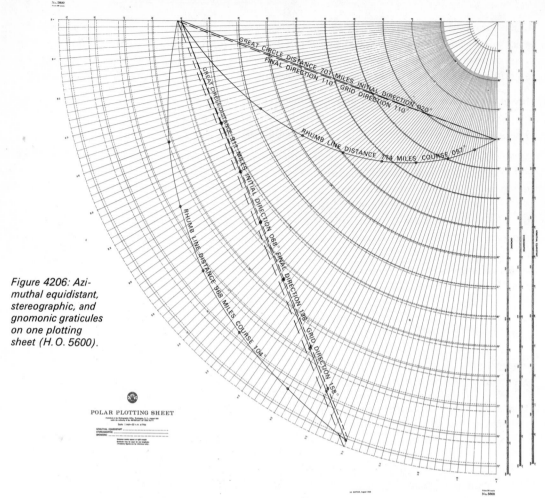

Figure 4206: Azimuthal equidistant, stereographic, and gnomonic graticules on one plotting sheet (H.O. 5600).

A straight line across a polar chart can be considered a great circle within the limits of practical navigation. On the transverse Mercator chart this is a fictitious rhumb line making the same angle with fictitious meridians.

The most easily used projection for polar ship operations is usually considered to be the Lambert *conformal.* Plotting is a bit of a problem, but land masses are most accurately portrayed, and courses steamed in ice being somewhat tortuous, the advantages of a rhumb line course being a straight line are not missed. For this or any other of the usual high-latitude chart projections, an aircraft or AN plotter is most convenient (article 1020).

Grid direction.   **4207.** Some navigators consider that in polar regions it is convenient to discard the conventional directions of true north, east, etc., except for celestial navigation, and substitute grid north, grid east, etc. That is, directions can be given in relation to the common direction of all fictitious grid meridians across the chart. The relationship between grid direction and true direction depends on the orientation of the grid. The system generally accepted places grid north in the direction of the north pole from Greenwich, or 000° on the Greenwich meridian is 000° grid (at both poles). With this orientation the interconversion of true and grid directions is very simple. If G is grid direction and T is true direction, in the northern hemisphere,

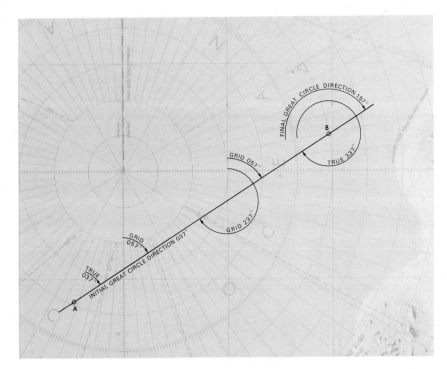

$$G = T + \lambda\, W$$

$$G = T - \lambda\, E$$

$$T = G - \lambda\, W$$

$$T = G + \lambda\, E.$$

In the southern hemisphere the signs are reversed. It is not necessary to remember all of these formulae, for the last three follow naturally from the first. Grid direction of a straight line remains constant for its entire length, while true direction changes continually.

In Figure 4207a the grid direction from A to B is 057° and from B to A is 237°, the reciprocal. However, the true direction from A to B is 037°, but from B to A is 337°.

It is most convenient to give all directions in relation to grid north. Even azimuths of celestial bodies can be converted to grid directions, if desired, both for plotting lines of position and for checking the directional gyro. If wind directions are given in terms of the grid, confusion is minimized, for a wind blowing in a constant grid direction is following widely different true directions over a relatively short distance near the pole. Since drift correction angle relative to a grid course is desired, wind direction should be given on the same basis. A grid direction is indicated by the letter G following the direction, as Zn 068° G, or by placing the letter G before the nature of the direction, as GH 144°, for grid heading 144°.

The lines of equal magnetic variation all pass through the magnetic pole and the geographic pole, the former because it is the origin of such lines, and the latter because of the convergence of the meridians at that point. However, con-

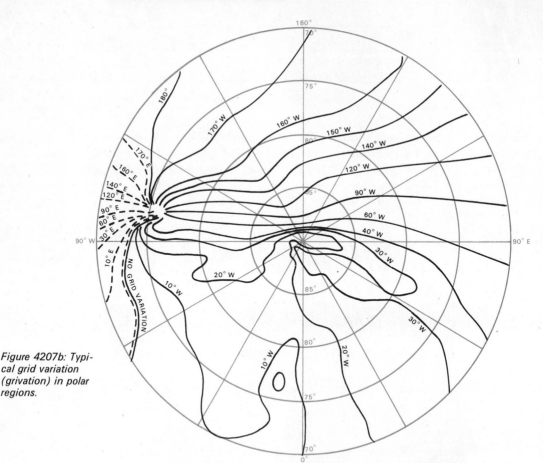

Figure 4207b: Typical grid variation (grivation) in polar regions.

vergency can be combined with variation to obtain the difference between grid direction and magnetic direction at any point. This difference is called *grid variation* or *grivation*. Lines of equal grid variation can be shown on a polar chart instead of lines of ordinary variation. These lines pass through the magnetic pole but disregard the geographic pole. See Figure 4207b and 4207c. Hence, even when a magnetic compass is used, grid navigation is easier than attempting to maintain true directions.

Grid sailing as described may be useful for air navigation but is not likely to be needed for surface ship operations, because 82° N is the probable limit of navigation and speeds are usually so low that other more normal plotting methods can be effectively used.

Environmental factors.

4208. *Environmental factors.* The effects of polar operations in navigation are many and varied. A thorough study of *Sailing Directions* or *Coast Pilots* is necessary, including those available from other countries. For example, the Danish Pilot for Greenland contains some excellent land profiles, *Aircraft charts* can also be very useful, since the topography shown is an essential factor in marine navigation. The *Ice Atlas* gives good average seasonal data although current information from satellite, long range aircraft, or helicopter ice reconnaissance is more useful. In some areas, it may be necessary to work from aerial photographs or preliminary charts, and soundings will be lacking. Whatever the circumstance, the navigator must plan ahead and obtain all information from whatever source.

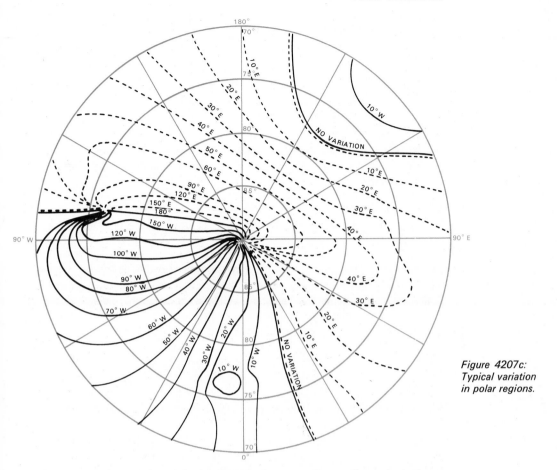

Figure 4207c:
*Typical variation
in polar regions.*

Occasionally, a review of old *Cruise Reports*, or even accounts by early explorers will yield useful data. A volume of *Sailing Directions* (*Coast Pilot*), H. O. 27 has been published for Antarctica. It contains a surprising amount of information which recent expeditions into the area have proved to be quite accurate, if incomplete.

Rather than paraphrase the many authoritative references available on the higher latitudes a brief summary of the more prevalent features is presented as a reminder of the general environment in which navigation will be accomplished.

Seasonal conditions. Normally cruises will be scheduled during the daylight periods, that is, during the summer months for the area involved. During these periods the sun may not set at all, and consequently there may be no navigational twilight. Ice conditions will be more favorable, as will the weather generally except at the turn of the seasons. Fog at the ice edge is frequently encountered, and good radar navigation is imperative. Warm water currents also cause fog, not just at the ice edge but near cooler land masses as well. There may be days with below freezing temperatures, or raw and damp days, but for the most part the weather will be cool and pleasant. Gales are few. Cold weather precautions should be taken, but mosquitos may be encountered in Northern Ellesmere Island in August. Aside from the *Sailing Directions* and other sources already suggested, there are several Army Engineer manuals on cold weather operations, the *Naval Arctic Operations Handbook* (in two parts),

645

and H. O. 551 (*Manual of Ice Seamanship*). There is additional help in the ATP, NWP and NWIP series for those to whom these publications are available.

Cruising in the off season, though unlikely, is possible and is apt to increase as ship capabilities and the needs of commerce expand. Severe low temperatures, ice conditions and gales may be expected, especially at the turn of the season. During the dark period, there may be enough light to take good celestial sights although there may be no actual navigational twilight. The mid-winter period will probably be clear and very cold. Bare flesh will stick to metal instruments. Elaborate cold weather precautions are essential for engineering equipment as well as personnel.

Magnetic anomalies and *storms* are prevalent, the *Aurora* (Borealis and Australis) will be visually attractive but troublesome to communications and magnetic compasses.

Mirage effect. This phenomena, due to abnormal refractions, occur whenever there is a severe discontinuity between surface and air temperatures. In summer in the north, for example, when the water and ice is much colder than the air above, multiple images may be seen, each inverted to the other. Landfalls may be made many miles before they are expected.

Piloting and DR. Unknown tides and currents, or ice conditions, will make a good DR very hard to keep. Close observations for any clues of set and drift are most useful; for example, grounded icebergs may show tidal erosion as well as a wake. If observed for long periods, they serve as a rough tide gauge. Depth can also be estimated from grounded bergs, using 1 foot above the waterline as equal to 6 feet below. Pit logs may not be practical, but timing objects passing alongside can give a rough indication of speed through the water or ice.

In entering a harbor or unfamiliar waters it is good practice to send a small boat ahead with a portable fathometer and radio telephone for communication.

One of the principal hazards to marine navigation in polar regions is ice. In some regions icebergs are very numerous. In the upper part of Baffin Bay, for instance, south of Cape York, literally hundreds of icebergs may be visible at one time. During periods of darkness or low visibility radar is essential in avoiding collision. This method is usually quite adequate, icebergs often being picked up before they are visible on a clear day. *Growlers* are the chief hazard to marine navigation. These are small icebergs, about the size of a small house, usually broken from larger ones. When the sea is smooth, it is usually possible to detect growlers in time to avoid them without difficulty, but if the sea is rough, they may not be picked up because of excessive sea return near the ship. It must be remembered that about 90 percent of an iceberg is *below* the surface of the water, so that in a rough sea, a growler is practically awash. Sonar has proved useful in detecting the presence of such ice. Broken ice presents no particular difficulty, but when heavy pack ice is encountered, further progress is usually impossible. Sometimes a *lead* or strip of open water where the ice has cracked and drifted apart permits a ship to continue for some distance into pack ice.

Fog is somewhat frequent in some polar regions during the summer, but is seldom of long duration. Most of the precipitation in the summer is in the form of rain, which is quite plentiful in some areas and is usually light but steady. Overcast conditions can persist for days.

To summarize, piloting in polar regions is fraught with difficulties and at best yields only a general indication of position. However, it is a most important method of marine navigation.

4209. *Determining direction* is perhaps the single most difficult problem. Magnetic compasses become largely useless due to the large and somewhat unpredictable variations and magnetic storms encountered. Gyrocompasses with proper speed and latitude corrections entered are reasonably accurate, but directive force weakens as the poles are approached. Flux-gate gyros have been recommended, but are usually available only in aircraft. *Direction.*

Any gyroscopic device will degrade in accuracy in higher latitudes. It is therefore necessary to take almost continuous error observations on a celestial body, normally the sun. One practical method is to mount an *astro compass* on and oriented along the ship's centerline (if offset, mount lubbers line parallel to the center line). An astro compass is illustrated in Figure 4209. A sun compass can be useful, but needs a shadow from the sun to give useful data. The astro compass can be used with the sun or *any other body*.

Figure 4209: Astro compass.

The *sky compass,* operating on polarized sunlight, has been successfully used. It is useful in that the sun need not be seen, therefore an overcast does not mean a loss of direction. The usual azimuths can also be used, of course, and precomputed tables or curves make the process practical and timely. Since acceleration errors in gyrocompasses (turns or rapid speed changes) are greater in higher latitudes, timely error determination is essential.

Bearing.

Bearings may be difficult to plot over long distances, due to the problems encountered with chart projections, but considering the bearings as great circles and plotting them as such according to the chart projection employed will solve the problem (use radio bearing correction procedure). Bearings generally may be a problem due to poor charting. In this case, redundancy of observations is important, and an attempt to fix the position of objects with the ship stopped, to give good visual or radar navigational references for a stretch of steaming, is recommended. Piloting practices should be thoroughly reviewed.

Distance.

4210. Determining distance may also require some ingenuity. *Distance off* may be measured by radar, or by stadimeter or sextant if heights are known. *Distance to go* will depend on good fixes and good charts. *Distance run* will require the use of some of the older piloting techniques (such as doubling the angle on the bow if running on a steady course and speed), or a chip log, or timing the passage of objects alongside the ship for a known distance. Fixed, or almost stationary objects such as bergs, can also be used, and plotted on a maneuvering board as known fixed targets to solve for own course and speed; radar can be useful for this purpose. Recall, however, that drifting bergs are offset by Coriolis force, the rule of thumb being that the offset is 30° to 40° to the right of the wind in the northern hemisphere. In open water, pit logs or engine turns can be used as usual, with only normal problems as to accuracy. Don't forget to retract pit logs or retractable sonar gear when entering ice.

Dead Reckoning.

4211. A DR plot must be carefully and attentively kept, particularly in ice. Every movement of the vessel must be recorded with the best possible accuracy. Some ships operating in ice detail one or two men full time to this task alone. At times the ship's movements may be too erratic to permit plotting, and the average course and speed must be carefully estimated. An *automatic course recorder* is very useful if the gyro corrections are known. Speed must be estimated or obtained as described above. With practice, a useful estimate of speed can be made by an experienced man. Since many polar cruises require close navigation, it is better to keep up all plots rather than to prepare historical records after the fact. These records are also desirable, but timely fixes and good DR projections are operationally necessary for safe navigation at the present moment. It is frequently good practice to proceed very deliberately, or even stop, in order not to lose track. If a DRT has a dummy log input, speed estimates can be entered and a track without set can be developed easily.

Fixing position.

4212. *Fixing position* can be quite an adventure, and occasionally there will be considerable doubt. Skillful piloting is essential, in addition to a good DR plot. The navigator must never miss an opportunity for an LOP; he can not know when there will be another available. An alert conning officer may notice uncharted dangers or those on track if the ship is off course. Occasionally land, water or ice reflections can be useful in navigating as well as conning, and the OOD may be the one to observe them first.

Visual methods of position fixing are always good, particularly as charts improve. Radar can serve as a warning device as well as for navigation. A good rule is to use only radar ranges. One helpful technique, particularly in first establishing a position in an unfamiliar area, is to prepare a tracing of the PPI picture, which can then be matched with the chart. Many targets should be plotted on the tracing; target separation should, when possible, be about 5°. This will simplify matching the tracing to the chart, as any error in bearings will not affect the accuracy of determining the ship's position; position is determined by matching the contours on the tracing to those on the chart, rather than by the use of bearings.

One useful wrinkle when using radar in ice is to reduce radiated power. This reduces range but increases ice definition (resolution), so that leads are more easily perceived. Some radars have an automatic setting for this, others would require reducing magnetron current. Short wavelength radars now available also give better resolution, and vessels may have sets of this type available.

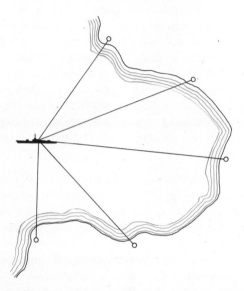

Figure 4212: Use of radar ranges.

4213. Celestial navigation is of prime importance in polar regions, although its practice may be very different from that to which the navigator is accustomed. He must acquire new techniques, familiarize himself with new tools, accustom himself to functioning in a very different environment, and never miss the opportunity to obtain a line of position.

Celestial navigation.

Tools and techniques which have been found useful will be discussed in the following paragraphs. But first consider *time*, on which all celestial navigation is based, as the importance of time itself is somewhat affected in the polar regions.

In previous chapters the importance of time was stressed, since each four seconds of error of the navigational watch may introduce an error of as much as one minute of longitude. At the equator this is a mile; at latitude 60°, it is 0.5 mile; at latitude 88°, it is only 0.035 miles. Thus, at this latitude, a watch error of 2 minutes would introduce a maximum error of about one mile. That is, the maximum change of altitude of a body, at a fixed point of observation, is one minute of arc in two minutes of time, and the average error is not more than half this amount. Thus, for celestial navigational purposes precise time is of little consequence in polar regions. At the pole all bodies circle the sky at a constant altitude, except for the slow change due to a change in declination. Since time zones lose their significance near the poles, it is customary to keep all timepieces set to GMT in polar regions.

Time.

Navigators in temperate climates usually avoid observations of bodies below 15° and most of them never observe bodies lower than 10°. In polar regions the only available body may not exceed an altitude of 10° for several weeks. At the pole the maximum altitude of the sun is 23°27' and the moon and planets may exceed this value by a few degrees. Hence, in polar regions there is no lower limit to observations.

The reason for avoiding low altitudes in temperate latitudes is the variable amount of refraction to be expected. In polar regions refraction varies over much wider limits than in lower latitudes. Because of the low temperatures in polar regions, the refraction correction for sextant altitudes should be adjusted for temperature, or a special refraction table for this area should be used. Refraction is known to vary with temperature and barometric pressure, but there are other factors which are imperfectly known. Refractions of several *degrees* have occasionally been observed, resulting in the sun appearing several days before it was expected in the spring, or continuing to appear for days after it should have disappeared below the horizon. Since abnormal refraction affects both the refraction and dip corrections, bubble sextant altitudes, if the average of a number of observations is used, are sometimes more reliable in polar regions than marine sextant observations.

Tools and techniques.

The marine sextant is the basic tool for polar navigation, although it is difficult at times to obtain a good horizon. Sun and moon observations will usually be made at lower altitudes than the navigator is accustomed to using; they must be carefully corrected for refraction. As for all observations made in the polar regions, the "Additional Corrections" for non-standard temperature and barometric pressure, contained in the *Nautical Almanac*, should be applied. When the horizon is poorly defined and a star at high altitude is visible, it may be desirable to make both direct and over-the-shoulder observations; however, practice is required to obtain good sights by the latter method. An artificial horizon can be improvised when required. The conventional mercury horizon can rarely be used even aboard a stationary ship; it can, however, be used to advantage on the ice. For ship use, a pan of lubricating oil makes an acceptable horizon. It may be placed on a leveled gyro repeater, and should be shielded from the wind, if necessary.

Bubble sextant.

An aircraft bubble sextant, or a marine sextant with bubble attachment (article 2206) can be used advantageously in the polar regions. It takes some practice to become accustomed to its use, and a considerable number of sights of each body should always be taken and averaged. Results obtained with the bubble sextant will be improved if there is no ship's motion; it may be desirable to take all way off the ship while sights are being made. Some navigators find it helpful to suspend the bubble sextant from a spring, to help damp out undesired motion.

The best celestial fixes are obtained by erecting a theodolite on shore, or on firm ice. If it is equipped with a 30-power telescope, high magnitude fixed stars, situated at reasonably high altitudes, should be visible on clear days, even with the sun above the horizon. This is particularly true if they lie approximately 90° from the sun in azimuth. For nighttime star observations, the theodolite serves best if it is fitted with a prismatic astrolabe.

During the long polar day, which at Thule, Greenland, in latitude 76°32' N, lasts for four months, the only body regularly available is the sun, which circles the sky, changing azimuth about 15° each hour. The moon will at times give a second line of position; when it is near the new or full phase, such a line will be nearly parallel to the sun line. An average of several observations of the sun, obtained every two hours, provides a series of running fixes. Even better practice is to make observations every hour, and establish the most probable position for each hour.

The best celestial fixes are usually obtained from star observations made during twilight. With increased latitude, the period of twilight lengthens, permitting additional time for observation. With this increase the period when the sun is just below the horizon also lengthens, and it may be difficult to pick up stars or planets unless a sextant fitted with a high-magnification telescope and large mirrors is available.

In the Arctic, with such an instrument, Capella, Deneb, and Vega should be among the first stars visible, particularly when situated approximately at right angles in azimuth to the position of the sun below the horizon. In the Antarctic, the first stars to look for are Rigel Kentaurus, Acrux, Canopus, Hadar, and Achernar. The brighter planets will be the next bodies to become visible, if they are high in declination. A bright aurora may delay the observation of stars and planets after sunset; at times, however, it may assist in defining the horizon. With dark-adapted vision, and good sextants, navigators can frequently obtain excellent observations throughout the polar night. The moon should, of course, be observed whenever it is available.

Other conditions, beside long periods of darkness, complicate the problem of locating the horizon in high latitude. Low fog, frost smoke, or blowing snow may veil the horizon when the sun is clearly visible. Nearby land, hummocked sea ice, or an extensive ice foot may be troublesome, particularly at low heights of eye. As previously stated an artificial horizon sextant can be most helpful under such conditions, and can supply good lines of position, if the observer is practiced in its use, and averages a number of observations.

When using the marine sextant aboard ship, the value of the dip correction should be determined by the height of eye above the ice at the horizon. This can usually be established with reasonable accuracy by observing nearby ice. Due to the frequently considerable anomalies in refraction, the tabulated refraction should always be corrected for temperature and barometric pressure. When stars are available, several, well distributed in azimuth, should be observed to minimize errors due to abnormal refraction. Other difficulties experienced aboard ship are the fact that false horizons sometimes appear, and during summer, when ships are most likely to be in polar regions, the sky in some areas is usually overcast. Also, a geographical position is not as important to a ship as a position relative to adjacent land, which may not be accurately charted. When stars are available, it is good practice to observe those of relatively high altitudes, since they are least affected by abnormal refraction.

The plotting of lines of position in polar regions is no more difficult than elsewhere. However, it must be remembered that an azimuth line is in reality a great circle. In moderate latitudes it is approximated on a Mercator chart by a rhumb line. Over the short distance involved no appreciable error is introduced by this

651

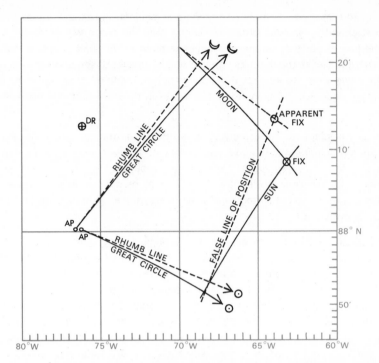

Figure 4213a:
A high-latitude
celestial fix plotted
on a Mercator
plotting sheet.

practice. Similarly, the line of position, actually part of a small circle on the earth, is also drawn as a straight line without loss of accuracy unless the altitude is very high, when it is actually drawn as a circle. These are discussed in more detail in Chapter 26.

In polar regions rhumb lines are not suitable because they no longer approximate great circles. This is shown in Figure 4213a in which a fix is plotted on a Mercator plotting sheet in the usual way. The solid lines show the actual lines that should be used. In Figure 4213b this same fix is shown plotted on a transverse Mercator chart. Note that both the azimuth line and the line of position are plotted as straight lines, as on a Mercator chart near the equator. The AP is selected as in any latitude and located by means of the graticule of actual latitude and longitude. The fix is also given in terms of geographical coordinates. In

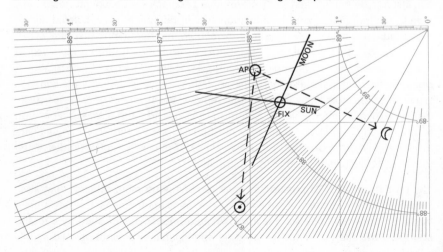

Figure 4213b: The
celestial fix of Fig-
ure 4213a plotted
on a transverse
Mercator chart.

plotting the azimuth line, the direction can be converted to grid azimuth, or plotted directly by means of true azimuth. If the latter method is used, be careful to measure the direction from the meridian of the AP. An aircraft plotter or protractor is usually used for this purpose.

Sextant altitudes are corrected the same in polar regions as elsewhere, except that refraction should be corrected for temperature, or a special refraction table used, as indicated above. Coriolis corrections, needed for bubble sextant observations made from a moving craft, reach extreme values near the poles and should not be neglected.

Computed altitude can be calculated in polar regions by any of several methods, including H.O. 211. It can be determined more easily by means of H.O. 229, Vol. 6, H.O. 214, Vols. VIII and IX may be used; although the tables do not extend below 5°, they may be used for altitudes less than this value as explained in Bowditch. H.O. 249 offers a rapid reduction, if its standard of accuracy is acceptable; however, Volume I is restricted to a limited number of stars. The Weems *Star Altitude Curves* are available for the north polar regions. These are printed on the Mercator projection from latitude 50° S to latitude 80° N, and on the stereographic projection between latitude 80° N and the north pole. These, also, are restricted to certain stars.

If a body near the zenith is observed, the line of position is plotted as a circle, with the GP as the center, as in any latitude.

One special method of plotting lines of position is available only in polar regions. By this method the pole is used as the AP. The Hc can then be determined by means of the almanac. The altitude of a body is its angular distance from the horizon; the declination is its angular distance from the celestial equator. At the pole the horizon and celestial equator coincide, making the altitude equal to the declination. This is why a body with fixed declination circles the sky without change in altitude. At the pole all directions are south (or north) and hence azimuth has no significance. The lines radiating outward from the pole, similar to azimuth lines in moderate latitudes, are meridians. Hence, in place of azimuth, GHA is used, for it indicates which "direction" the body is from the pole.

Pole as assumed position.

To plot a sight by this method, enter the almanac with GMT and determine the body's declination and GHA. Using the declination as Hc, compare it with Ho. If Ho is greater, it is a "Toward" case, as usual. Measure the altitude difference, *a*, from the pole along the meridian indicated by the GHA, and at the point so found erect a perpendicular to the meridian. If Hc is greater, an "Away" case, measure *a* along the meridian 180° from that indicated by the GHA, or *away* from the body (Figure 4213c).

This method was first suggested at least as early as 1892, but there is no evidence of its having been used until some 30 years later. In the early days of air exploration in polar regions the method was quite popular, but with the development of modern tabular methods, it has fallen into disuse, except within 2° of the pole, or above latitude 88°, where it is sometimes used. This, of course, is a very small area. If a ship is near the meridian of the GP of the body (or its reciprocal), the method is entirely accurate at any latitude, even though the altitude difference might be quite large, for this is simply a different way to plot meridian altitudes. However, the straight line used as the line of position is actually the arc of a

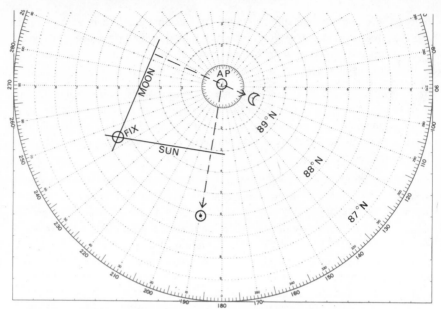

Figure 4213c: The celestial fix of Figure 4213a plotted on a maneuvering board used as an azimuthal equidistant chart. The pole is used as the assumed position.

small circle on the earth. The radius of the circle depends on the altitude of the body. For bodies near the horizon, the straight line of position, a close approximation of a great circle, can be used for some distance from the meridian of the GP without appreciable error. However, as the altitude increases, the discrepancy becomes larger. Tables have been prepared to show the distance from the straight line to the circle of equal altitude at different altitudes and for several hundred miles from the meridian of the GP, on a polar stereographic projection. With modern methods available, the pole is not generally used as the AP in an area where such a correction is needed.

Lines of position are advanced in the same manner as in lower latitudes. If a grid course is being followed, the AP or line of position is advanced along the grid course. The use of the pole as the AP does not complicate this practice.

Various other methods of using celestial navigation in polar regions have been suggested. Among these is the use of sets of altitude curves for different bodies printed on transparent paper or plastic, to be used as a template over the chart; and various types of computers.

Generally speaking, tables such as H. O. 214, H. O. 229, or H. O. 249 are best for celestial navigation in polar regions.

Electronic navigation.

4214. Other means of fixing position are electronic systems, radiating from sources external to the ship:

Radiobeacons, when available, can be used. Watch for plotting errors due to chart projection, and for attenuation over ice or snow.

Consol or *Consolan,* available in a small portion of the polar regions, is useful but not precise, as is true of any bearing device at extreme range.

Loran-A (1750–2000 kHz) is usable in the Arctic, but the coverage is greatly restricted. Ground-wave coverage extends into the edge of the sub-Arctic in several places, but into the Arctic in the Baffin Bay, Denmark Straits and Norwegian Sea only, as shown on H. O. 15308. The sky-wave coverage extends for some distance beyond that of the ground-wave.

Loran-C (90–110 kHz) is available in portions of the polar regions, and is quite precise when properly used. See H. O. 15308-1 for coverage.

Omega (10–14 kHz) is a VLF hyperbolic system, somewhat similar to Loran. When fully deployed it should give an accuracy similar to that of Loran-A over most of the earth, including the polar regions.

Navigational satellites give excellent fixes, but not continuously, with good precision and reliability. They are essential for polar vessels, and receiver-computers are now available to civilian navigators.

One other *self-contained* system not previously discussed is an inertial navigator. Ships so equipped will find this a very useful device, although updating by external means is periodically required. It is the primary system used aboard submarines transiting the pole under ice (Chapter 36).

4215. Sunrise, sunset, moonrise, and moonset, as stated in article 4204, do not have the same significance in polar regions as in lower latitudes. At the pole the change in altitude of a body is occasioned only by a change in declination. Since the maximum rate of change of declination of the sun is about 1' per hour, and the sun is about 32' in diameter, the entire sun would not be visible for about 32 hours after "sunrise," or the moment of first appearance of the upper limb, if refraction remained constant. In a plane high above the pole the sun might be visible more than a week before it appears on the ground. Because of large variations in refraction, even the *day* of sunrise is difficult to predict in polar regions.

Sunrise, sunset, moonrise, moonset.

Ordinary sunrise, sunset, moonrise and moonset tables are not available for polar regions, nor would they be of real value there. The method usually used is that provided by the graphs of the *Air Almanac*, shown in Figures 4215a, 4215b, and 4215c.

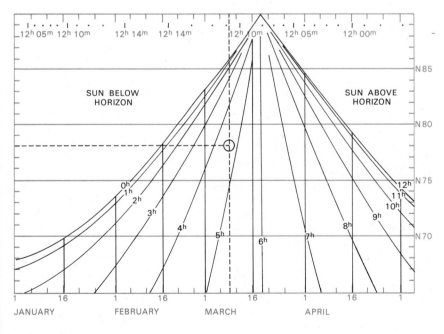

Figure 4215a: Semi-duration of sunlight graph from the Air Almanac.

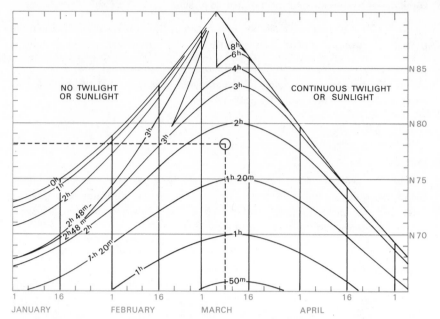

Figure 4215b: Duration of twilight graph from the Air Almanac.

The semiduration of sunlight is found by means of the graph of Figure 4215a. The manner of its use is illustrated by the dashed lines.

Example: Find the LMT of sunrise and sunset at L 78° on March 8. Find the GMT if the observer is in λ 93° W.

Solution: From 8 March on the scale at the bottom of the graph draw a line vertically upward to the top of the diagram. To the nearest minute the time indicated by the dots is 1211. This is the LMT of meridian transit, or the center of the period of sunlight. Next, draw a horizontal line from L 78° N at the left (or right) margin to intersect the vertical line. At the point of intersection interpolate by eye between the curves. The semiduration of sunlight so found is 4h40m. Hence, the sun will rise 4h40m before meridian transit, or at 0731, and set 4h40m after meridian transit, or at 1651. The GMT is 6h12m *later*, so that sunrise occurs at 1343 and sunset 2303. These values, of course, are approximations.

Answers: Sunrise, LMT 0731, GMT 1343; sunset, LMT 1651, GMT 2303.

The duration of civil twilight is found in a similar manner by the use of Figure 4215b.

Example: Find the LMT and GMT of beginning of morning twilight and ending of evening twilight for the example above.

Solution: Draw a vertical line through 8 March and a horizontal line through L 78° N. at the intersection interpolate between the two curves. The value found is about 1h45m. Hence, morning twilight begins 1h45m before sunrise and evening twilight ends 1h45m after sunset.

Answers: Morning twilight, LMT 0546, GMT 1158; evening twilight, LMT 1836, GMT 2448 or 0048 the following day.

The time of moonrise and moonset is found from Figure 4215c in a manner similar to finding sunrise and sunset. The time of transit of the moon, of course,

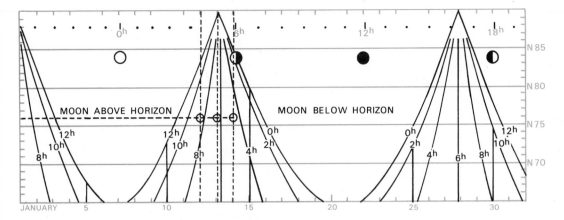

Figure 4215c: Semi-duration of moon-light graph from the Air Almanac.

is not always near 1200 but may be any time during the day. The phase of the moon is shown by its symbol, the open symbol being full moon and the black symbol new moon.

Example: Find the LMT, ZT, and GMT of both moonrise and moonset at L 76° N, λ 70° W on 12 January, and the phase this day.

Solution: The vertical line through 12 January indicates that the moon will be on the celestial meridian at LMT 0425. The semiduration of moonlight is 8ʰ00ᵐ. Hence, moonrise occurs 8 hours before the LMT of 0425 or at 2025 the day before and moonset at 1225. Similarly, for the following day moonrise occurs at 2230 the day before and moonset occurs at 1130. The next moonrise will occur at 0100 on 14 January.

	Moonrise			Moonset	
Tab.	2230	12 Jan.	Tab.	1225	12 Jan.
Tab.	0100	14 Jan.	Tab.	1130	13 Jan.
Diff.	150		Diff.	55	
150 × 70.0/360	(+) 29		55 × 70.0/360	(−) 11	
LMT	2259		LMT	1214	
dλ	(−) 20		dλ	(−) 20	
ZT	2239	12 Jan.	ZT	1154	12 Jan.
ZD	(+) 5		ZD	(+) 5	
GMT	0339	13 Jan.	GMT	1654	12 Jan.

The phase is gibbous, about two days before last quarter.

Answers: Moonrise, LMT 2259, ZT 2239, GMT 0339 (13 Jan.); moonset, LMT 1214, ZT 1154, GMT 1645; phase, gibbous, about two days before last quarter.

There are comparable graphs for sunlight, twilight, and moonlight for the south polar region. These are not printed in the almanacs but are available free from the U. S. Naval Observatory in Washington, D. C., in U. S. Naval Observatory Circular No. 120.

4216. Land navigation of vehicles which cross the surface of the ice is not essentially different from that of aircraft or marine vessels, with one important exception. The navigator of the ice vehicle can stop and obtain a stable platform for

Land navigation.

measuring altitudes, directions, etc., without being bothered by bubble acceleration or vibration.

Navigation of such vehicles usually consists of proceeding by dead reckoning for a convenient period (often several days) and checking the position by accurate celestial observation at favorable times. At such times the accuracy of the compass is also checked. An aircraft type flux gate compass is generally most suitable for maintaining direction, except in the immediate vicinity of the magnetic poles, where it is usually necessary to steer for prominent landmarks and check the direction at frequent intervals, Dead reckoning in land vehicles is complicated by the necessity of frequently changing course to avoid obstructions.

Summary. **4217.** Throughout this chapter emphasis has been placed on the problems and difficulties to be encountered in polar regions, not to frighten people away, but to emphasize the need for an understanding of the conditions to be met and for adequate planning and preparation before entering the regions. This having been done the polar regions can be navigated with confidence.

Planning is important in any operation; it is vital to the success of polar navigation. The first step to adequate planning is the acquisition of maximum data on the operational area. Sailing directions should be procured. The U. S. Naval Oceanographic Office and the Arctic and Cold Weather Coordinating Office of the Chief of Naval Operations should be consulted with a view to obtaining pertinent data. Planning should not be confined solely to navigational matters; the navigator should seek information on ice, climate, and weather, as well as information gathered from previous operations in the area. A bubble sextant should be obtained, and the navigator should familiarize himself with its operation. Forecasts on anticipated ice and weather conditions should be obtained before departure, and updated by radio whenever possible. The entire cruise may well be unusual and interesting, as well as professionally challenging. The navigator's role is vital to the safety of the vessel, and his skillful and ingenious use of a variety of navigation methods will contribute significantly to the success of the operation.

CHAPTER 43

Optimum Track Ship Routing

4301. *Optimum track routing* has been defined as the selection of the optimum track for a trans-oceanic crossing by the application of long range predictions of wind, waves and currents to the routed vessel's performance characteristics. It has been defined more generally as the art of taking advantage of all available meteorological and hydrographic information in order to obtain the safest and most economical passage for a ship. The idea of navigating by taking advantage of weather conditions is not new. In 1847, Matthew Fontaine Maury began to compile data on winds, currents, and weather conditions obtained from ships' logs, and inaugurated a program calling for the reporting of these data by ship-masters. Maury's published studies provided a sound basis for the selection of the probable best track, based on average wind and current conditions, for a given voyage; his recommendations were almost universally adopted by ocean-going sailing vessels.

The introduction of steam made it possible for ships to become independent of fair winds, and to proceed more directly towards their destinations, and the art of "playing the weather" fell largely into disuse. However, the Pilot Charts still show recommended tracks for both full and low powered steamers, based on the average wind and current conditions expected during the period for which the chart is prepared. *Routing*, based on existing conditions, and those expected to develop in the near future, came into use for airplanes after World War II. *Pressure pattern flying* and *single heading flight* were widely adopted for long air passages, particularly those across the Atlantic. Such routings were based on the current weather conditions, as well as on forecasts as to how they would develop during the period of each flight. In long flights, determination of the "least time" track is generally of prime importance, and this depends almost entirely on taking advantage of favorable winds.

4302. As previously stated, the shortest distance between two points on the surface of the earth is the arc of the great circle connecting them. Although this represents the shortest linear distance, it may not represent the most desirable track for the vessel; another route may produce a least time track. In the case of passenger vessels, the optimum route is quite often one which will maintain the maximum conditions of passenger safety and comfort. In other operations minimum fuel consumption may be the determining factor, or in the case of some cargo vessels, particularly those carrying deck loads, the optimum track may be one which will present the least hazard to the cargo. In general, routes are prepared which combine these advantages as far as possible. It has always been recognized by seamen that waves, whether seas or swells, are the one

Introduction.

Purpose of optimum track routing.

659

element having the greatest adverse effect on the movement of the ship through the water. Optimum track routing is therefore normally used to route ships along a track to avoid areas where the waves are the highest.

The desirability of optimum track routing cannot be overemphasized. During the month of February, 1965, a group of insurance underwriters reported that due to bad weather, 105 merchant ships sustained hull or cargo damage of sufficient seriousness to result in insurance claims. During the same month bad weather was a contributing factor in the total loss of 7 and partial loss of 253 ships due to abandonment, shipwreck, or stranding.

Predictions of sea conditions.

4303. The ship routing technique developed by the Navy at the U. S. Naval Oceanographic Office and employed by the Naval Weather Service, uses a five-day forecast of surface weather conditions issued by the U. S. Weather Bureau. Standard wave forecasting techniques are used to derive predictions of wave height from the isobaric pattern of winds on the weather chart. Empirical tests have been made to determine ship speed versus wave conditions for various types of vessels and this information is further divided into the effect of head seas, following seas, and beam seas. Figure 4303a shows a typical graph presenting this information.

Figure 4303a: Relationship between ship's speed and wave heights.

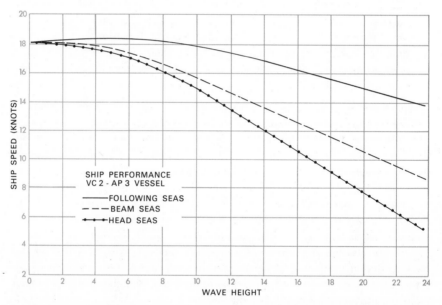

Synoptic wave charts are prepared showing the size and type of waves over large areas of the ocean. Data for the preparation of these charts is gathered from reporting commercial and military vessels, and from the meteorological services of various governments. *Prognostic* wave charts are more widely used than the synoptic charts for route selection, as wind and wave conditions often change rapidly at a given point, as in the vicinity of a rapidly moving cold front. They are prepared from sea level atmosphere charts, as well as from data in the synoptic charts. Figure 4303b is a section of a typical prognostic wave chart of the North Atlantic.

Figure 4303c shows a surface pressure system lying along a ship's proposed track A-B, and the distribution and direction of waves connected with this

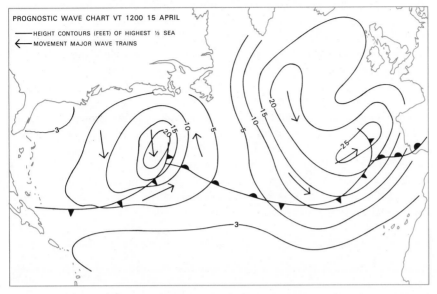

Figure 4303b: Prognostic wave chart.

pressure system. The wave heights are in feet. The *isopleth* lines give the mean wave heights for waves within each area. The pressure system and wave pattern is assumed to remain static for each 24-hour period.

In addition to the routing service provided by the Navy for its vessels, several commercial organizations provide a similar service to the shipping industry, and techniques of forecasting sea conditions are constantly being improved. The use of upper air charts and jet stream analysis has proven valuable for longer term predictions covering the duration of a voyage. Significant upper air meteorological features often appear on the upper level charts before they are reflected in surface conditions, thus permitting analysis of and the forecasting of marine weather. Ocean areas that will become hazardous may thus be determined before the condition actually develops.

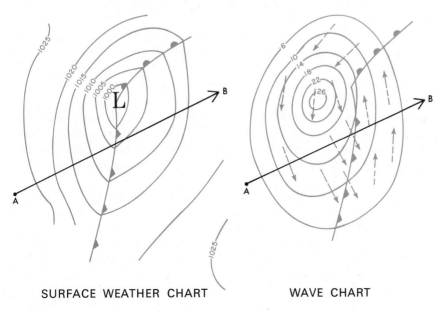

Figure 4303c: Surface pressure system and associated wave heights.

SURFACE WEATHER CHART   WAVE CHART   **661**

Currents, wind
and waves.

4304. The effects of ocean currents on the movement of a ship in relation to the earth would be easy to determine if the exact current set and drift were known; as the ship moves through the water the entire water mass is also being moved by the current effect. By adding the vectors representing the ship's course and speed and the set and drift of the current, the ship's movement relative to the earth could be precisely determined. This is quite similar to the wind drift problem of an aircraft in which the track of the aircraft over the earth is the result of the two vectors representing heading and air speed, and wind direction and velocity.

Current.

However, there is one important difference affecting a ship in the ocean current problem. The ship is not completely immersed in the moving medium; approximately one-third of the hull is immersed and affected by the current, while the remainder of the hull is being affected by air resistance. This latter effect is negligible at low speeds and in no-wind conditions, but it becomes more serious as the relative wind speed increases. Ship movement can be aided by a favorable current, but the prediction of the location and velocity of such a current at a given time is not in most cases accurate enough to be the determining factor in optimum track ship routing. Currents are of assistance in the final determination of a route where wind and wave conditions otherwise provide an almost equal choice.

Wind effect.

Wind effect on the movement of a vessel is difficult to compute. It varies with ship type and loading, and on the direction and strength of the wind relative to the exposed hull and superstructure. It is known that for a given wind velocity, a head wind will slow the movement of a vessel more than a following wind will increase her speed. In addition to these factors, wave action has a considerable effect on a ship's speed.

Wave effect.

The wave effect on a vessel is also difficult to determine and the computations of mathematical models seldom agree with empirically derived values. This is due in part to the fact that uniform wave heights are used in computation while a great range of heights are actually present in a given storm situation, and also because a commanding officer often decreases ship's speed to avoid the adverse effects of violent motion. Prediction of wave effects on different types of vessels represents the result of large numbers of empirical tests analyzed to produce average values. A combination of reported wave heights and wind values from prognostic charts are used to draw isopleths, or lines of equal wave heights, on the chart. Details of theory and the construction of wave charts to apply these values to actual operations is beyond the scope of this text.

Construction of a
least time track.

4305. With the advent of facsimile equipment to reproduce chart information by radio the navigator can construct "least-time" tracks at sea in the same manner as those produced ashore prior to the voyage, by the routing service. The basic concept involves the determination of a day's run that would be obtained on various courses. A great circle is normally drawn on the chart between point of departure or present position if at sea, and the destination. Diverging lines radiating from the point of origin represent the possible tracks, as shown in Figure 4305a. Using a chart of average wave height and the ship's performance curve to determine speed on the various tracks, a 24-hour travel can be computed for each possible track. The points on each line representing a 24-hour travel are then connected with a smooth curve which represents the loci of possible positions of the vessel after one day's travel. Additional diverging

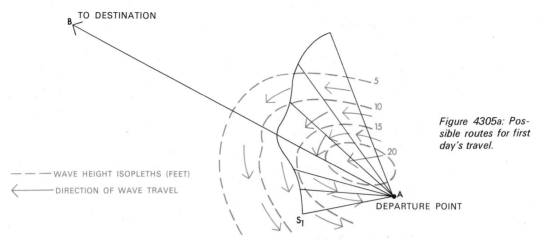

TO DESTINATION

WAVE HEIGHT ISOPLETHS (FEET)

DIRECTION OF WAVE TRAVEL

DEPARTURE POINT

Figure 4305a: Possible routes for first day's travel.

tracks are then drawn, the origin of each being perpendicular to curve S_1 at its starting point. Using the wave chart for the second day, the second day's run is constructed and a curve S_2 is drawn through these points. A point of tangency of an arc, centered at the destination B, to curve S_2 would indicate the point nearest the destination which can be reached after two days steaming.

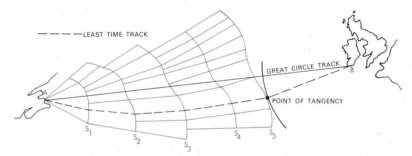

LEAST TIME TRACK

GREAT CIRCLE TRACK

POINT OF TANGENCY

Figure 4305b: Least-time track computed for five days travel.

When good meteorological forecasts are available, least time tracks can be prepared for several days in advance. Figure 4305b shows a plot carried forward for five successive days. The least time track is plotted in reverse to the point of origin from the farthest point of advance for the number of days involved. Each section of the intended track will be perpendicular to the respective curves.

Computers now being introduced aboard merchant vessels will digest weather and sea data inputs, and present an almost instantaneous accommodation as to the optimum course and speed to permit maximum safety and economy. The use of computers aboard ship is further discussed in Chapter 39.

4306. For an extended trip it may be impossible to avoid all storms; sometimes the vessel will be able to avoid the actual storm center, but not all the storm seas and swell associated with the system. The use of long range forecasts and all available weather data for storm avoidance is an art which is mastered by a thorough understanding of navigation and meteorology. The following examples illustrate the use of weather routing on a long voyage using the forecasts of the movements of storm centers expected to be encountered.

Routing for storm avoidance.

Figure 4306a shows a developed semistationary storm and a series of deepening lows in the northern hemisphere. A ship is bound to the westward from A to B.

663

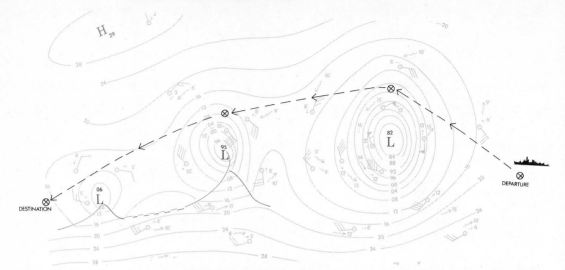

Figure 4306a:
Storm avoidance.

Prolonged heavy head seas are to be expected to the south and southwest of the storm center, and moderate head seas to the south and southwest of the center of the second low pressure area.

To avoid these head seas, a marked diversion to the north of the storm center is indicated; this new path, shown as a dotted line, should also take the ship to the north of the second low.

Figure 4306b: Divergence from track to avoid heavy seas.

Figure 4306b shows the track of a rapidly deepening storm in the northern hemisphere. In this case, it is not possible to pass safely to the north of the storm. The ship therefore should divert well to the south. This will cause continuous head winds, and increase the distance steamed, but will avoid possible damage due to heavy seas.

Transmission of weather data.

4307. Navy radio station NSS transmits facsimile weather charts and other

Figure 4307:
Marine radio
facsimile recording
system.

data on a regular schedule. Figure 4307 shows a facsimile receiver suitable for shipboard use. Regular weather broadcasts by radio are made from various locations. H. O. Pub. 118, *Radio Weather Aids*, furnishes a complete listing of all official broadcasts.

4308. Experience indicates a considerable saving in time and fuel may usually be obtained by optimum track ship routing, and that damage can frequently be avoided. The many variables involved, and the uncertainty of the time which would have been used in following a great circle make exact comparisons impossible. From the experience gained in thousands of crossings, it is apparent that the saving in time, fuel, and passenger and cargo safety, as well as reduced cargo and ship damage, have made this system very much worthwhile, and the navigator should familiarize himself with the techniques required for optimum ship routing. In order to gain this familiarization the U. S. Naval Oceanographic Office Special Publication, SP-1, *Application of Wave Forecasts to Marine Navigation,* should be consulted.

Effects of optimum ship routing.

665

CHAPTER 44

Air Navigation

Introduction.

4401. In the early days of aviation, navigation was principally based on marine navigation equipment and methods which were adopted for the new vehicle. The expanding range of operations and greatly increased speeds soon forced the development of specialized instruments and techniques. Both government and industry-financed development programs have been carried on at great expense. As a result, the science of air navigation has outstripped surface navigation and now generally employs a higher degree of automation, as well as a wider use of systems concepts. Marine navigators have benefited from these programs, in that many of the electronic systems as well as other concepts, such as inertial and the Doppler effect, have been adapted to marine use.

The subject of air navigation cannot be covered fully in this text. This chapter is intended only to illustrate the principal differences in requirements between air and marine navigation, and to describe briefly, for the surface navigator, some of the techniques and equipment employed by his counterpart in the air.

Requirements: comparisons between marine and air navigation.

4402. The most obvious difference in navigational requirements between the marine and air environments is the addition of the third dimension—height above the earth—which must be taken into consideration in air navigation. Altitude measurements must be added to the traditional direction and distance measurements used on board ship. The introduction of the altitude factor not only adds the requirement for new sensing devices but also modifies the other navigational problems. The range of line-of-sight measurements, whether visual or electronic, is greatly increased with an increase in altitude. Speed measuring devices are in most cases affected by the density of the medium in which used and must be adjusted to allow for great variations in density. Distance measurements, when made by electronic signals, become slant range measurements, rather than horizontal distances, as the signals travel along the hypotenuse of a triangle defined by horizontal distance, altitude, and slant range. Direction sensing instruments are affected by the forces created by increased aircraft velocity, and to some extent by the position in which it is necessary to mount them in the aircraft. The visible horizon, which defines the vertical for celestial observations in marine navigation, must be replaced by an artificial horizon. Wind velocities affecting the drift and speed of an aircraft are of far greater magnitude than the current which effects a ship. They vary both in direction and velocity with change in altitude but are to some extent more easily predicted and measured. Time available for computing and plotting fixes, whether visual, electronic or celestial, is limited, necessitating a greater amount of precomputation, or of automation in the sensing and measuring devices. Charts must cover larger areas and therefore must be smaller in scale, thus limiting the data which can be depicted while still maintaining readability.

Perhaps the greatest difference between the demands made on the air navigator and the marine navigator is that the air environment is less forgiving of errors. Even if the navigator is uncertain of his position in the large ocean areas, a ship can usually continue underway for a considerable period of time without endangering crew or vessel. The air navigator *must* be certain of his position at all times if he is to arrive safely at his destination, or return to a base or carrier.

4403. Aeronautical charts produced by the U. S. Coast & Geodetic Survey, the U. S. Air Force, and by commercial organizations are, with a few exceptions for specialized use, based on the Lambert projection. The U. S. Naval Oceanographic Office produces several series on the Mercator projection; they are mainly small scale long range charts. A description of the features of various chart projections and the method of use is given in Chapter 3. Direction and distance in the air are almost universally measured with an aircraft plotter, consisting of a protractor and fixed distance scales to match the chart scales.   *Charts.*

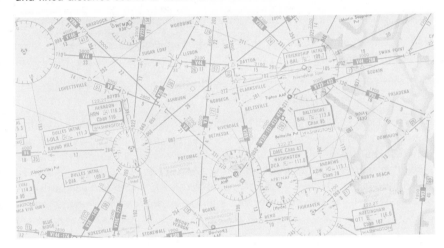

Figure 4403: IFR chart.

In light aircraft and those operating under Visual Flight Rules (VFR), three principal chart series are used. These consist of local charts using a scale of 1 : 250,000, and covering areas around principal airports in the U. S., sectional charts at 1 : 500,000 which give complete U. S. coverage, and World Aeronautical Charts (WAC) or Operational Navigational Charts (ONC), which give complete world coverage at a scale of 1 : 1,000,000. Long range charts designed for jet aircraft use varying scales from 1 : 2,000,000 to 1 : 6,250,000. These give terrain information, including ground elevation and principal ground features, both natural and man-made, which are recognizable from the air. The amount of detail depends upon the scale of the chart, but radio navigational data are always included. Elevation was traditionally shown by contour lines, but illustrated relief, giving a more realistic presentation of mountains and valleys, is now widely used. Charts for use under Instrument Flight rules (IFR) are published by the government as well as by commercial organizations; they employ various scales for use at different altitudes. Such en-route charts and approach charts omit practically all terrain information, but give complete radio data outlining the airways, approach procedures, etc. (Figure 4403).

667

Dead reckoning.

4404. In air navigation dead reckoning has a slightly different connotation than in marine navigation, where course and speed alone are used to define the parameters. In air navigation the wind vector is almost invariably included in the dead reckoning problem. Once the wheels of an aircraft are off the runway, wind drift affects a powered aircraft exactly as it would a free balloon. If the wind is from the north (000°) at 20 knots any aircraft, regardless of its speed, will drift precisely 20 nautical miles south in a period of one hour. Wind direction is given as the true direction *from* which the wind is blowing. Definitions of terms involving direction and speed in the air differ slightly in meaning from the same terms when used in surface navigation; their meanings, incidentally, are also much more standardized. These terms, briefly defined below, include:

DR definitions.

Heading—the horizontal direction in which an aircraft is pointed.

Course—the intended horizontal direction of travel.

Track—The rhumb line direction of an actual flight path over the ground.

Air speed—speed of an aircraft with respect to the air.

Ground speed—speed of an aircraft with respect to the surface of the earth.

Drift angle—the angle between the heading of an aircraft and its track or flight path over the ground.

Drift correction angle—the angle between the heading line and the course line, or the anticipated drift angle.

Over the continental U. S. and in many other areas of the world, weather stations are constantly taking meteorological measurements on which predictions can be based. Although wind direction and velocity vary with altitude, predictions are usually quite accurate, and the wind vector is therefore allowed for in-flight planning. If wind data are not available a *no-wind* plot can be carried on the chart, similar to the DR plot for surface vessels. Where the wind is known, the vector diagram takes the form shown in Figure 4404a. On some aircraft

Figure 4404a: Wind vector diagram, wind is known.

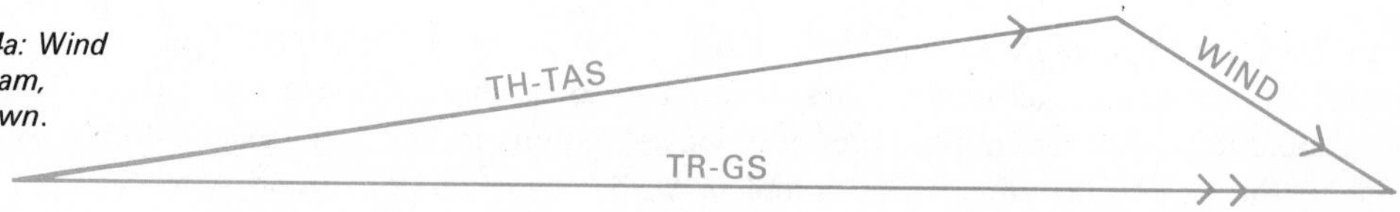

Figure 4404b: Wind vector diagram, true heading and wind direction is plotted from center of board.

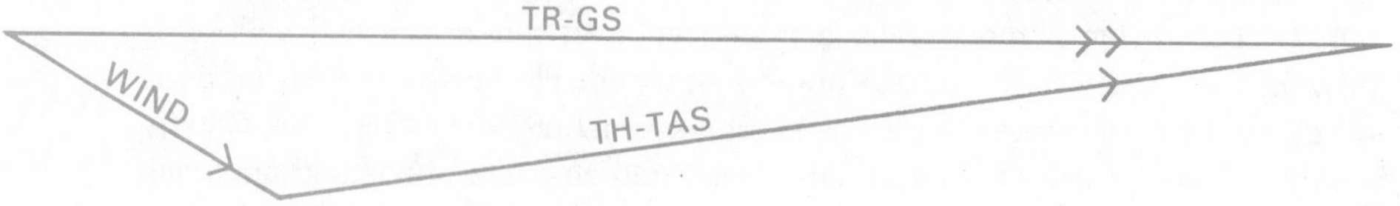

plotting boards, where true heading and wind direction are plotted from the center of the board, the vector diagram would appear as in Figure 4404b. In either case the track, or course, and ground speed vector represent the resultant of vector addition of the TH-TAS and wind vectors. In air navigation the problem is almost invariably solved on a computer similar in design to that shown in

Figure 4404c. In this figure the vectors are shown as an overprint for purposes of illustration; in practice the only mark on the computer face would be a dot representing the end of the wind vector. For the carrier-based pilot an additional vector representing the carrier's motion must be added; if he is to fly a search pattern involving several legs, a vector must also be drawn for each leg. However, once the principle of the vector diagram is mastered, additional vectors present no real problem, as all vectors are employed in the same manner. In problems where several vectors are required, a plastic aircraft plotting board is generally used in preference to the computer shown in Figure 4404c. These plotting boards are similar to the plastic maneuvering boards used aboard naval vessels as described in article 1304.

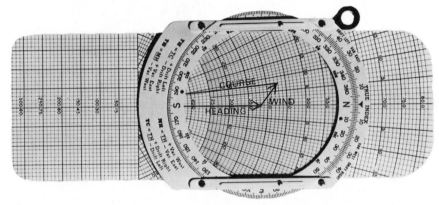

Figure 4404c: Typical aircraft computer.

4405. *Speed-time-distance* computations are made on the circular slide rule side of the computer. A slide rule uses proportions; as a result, it is equally satisfactory for use with statute miles which are still the standard for most private pilots, or with nautical miles which are used by the military and the airlines. On the computer, miles per hour or knots are thought of as "miles per sixty minutes," and the speed is read at the sixty minute index, with the distance on the outer scale set opposite minutes on the inner scale (Figure 4405a).

Speed, time, distance.

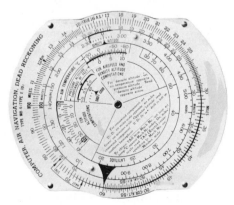

Figure 4405a: Computer slide rule.

The pilot is interested in converting all measurements into units of time. When distance can be measured from the chart in time units rather than in miles the computational step is eliminated. The USAF has for many years used *navigational proportional dividers* for this purpose; they can be used at any speed, on any chart, regardless of the chart scale. With speed set on the sliding pivot the instrument is opened out, similar to a pair of dividers and the long points are set on the two requisite positions on the chart. The short points are then set on the distance scale of the chart, and by calling the units minutes instead of miles, time in minutes is read directly (Figure 4405b). By setting elapsed time on the sliding pivot, ground speed can be read from the chart distance scales for any portion of the flight.

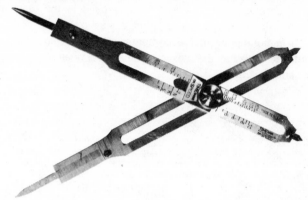

Figure 4405b: Navigational proportional dividers.

Piloting.

4406. Piloting in marine navigation, which is based on bearings and distances from objects of known location, does not have an exact counterpart in air navigation. No visual or optical observing instruments comparable to the pelorus, azimuth circle, range finder or stadimeter, are used in the air; electronic or radio navigation instruments are used instead. However, when flying VFR, a form of pilotage is employed, based on constant reference to identifiable objects on the ground, but the reference is by eye rather than by precise measurements of angles as aboard ship. The time of crossing over any road, river, railroad, or other identifiable line on the earth establishes a line of position. Time over a recognizable point on the ground such as a small town, the intersection of a river and road, etc., establishes a fix. It is common practice to draw a course line on the chart before takeoff, noting the estimated times of passing identifiable objects. These estimated times are used to determine where to look for appropriate landmarks. Actual times are then used to determine ground speed and drift. Air pilotage is based on accurate chart reading and ability to relate the physical appearance of the ground and of landmarks to the pictorial symbols appearing on the charts.

Altitude.

4407. A *sensitive altimeter* is normally used to determine altitude. It operates from a pitot tube measuring air pressure; essentially, it is similar to an aneroid barometer, except that the dial is calibrated to read altitude rather than inches of mercury. The altimeter therefore measures altitude above a given plane of reference, which is normally sea level. If the instrument were to read altitude above the ground (an absolute altimeter) it would vary constantly while flying level over land areas, due to the hills and valleys below. When flying over land the sensitive altimeter is universally used. It is calibrated to read zero, at sea level, under standard conditions of air pressure of 29.92 inches of mercury and a temperature of 15° Centigrade. Because standard conditions rarely exist, the altimeter has a provision for setting it to a pressure other than 29.92 inches.

Pressure altimeter.

For takeoff and landing operations from a given airport it is desirable to know the altitude of the aircraft above the airport. The altimeter can be used for this purpose by setting in the known barometric pressure at the airport; the instrument then reads altitude above this artificially established plane.

Correct altitude above sea level will be indicated only when temperature is decreasing with altitude at a standard rate. This condition will seldom exist, so that indicated altitude is seldom the true altitude; however, if all aircraft in the same area are using the same altimeter setting, vertical separation between aircraft can be maintained.

Indicated altitude, when corrected for any instrumental error, is known as *calibrated altitude. Pressure altitude* is, in effect, the calibrated altitude with the barometric scale set to the standard sea level pressure of 29.92 inches. Aircraft navigational computers use this pressure altitude together with the outside air temperature at flight level as the parameters for determining true altitude. The scales on the computer are so arranged that when temperature and pressure altitude are used as the entering arguments, true altitude is read on the outer scale opposite the calibrated altitude (Figure 4405a).

For operations over water, an *absolute* or *radar altimeter* is often used. A radar signal is transmitted vertically downwards from the instrument, and altitude is indicated by the length of time it takes the signal to reach the surface and return to the receiver. This instrument produces true altitude above sea level. When used in conjunction with a sensitive altimeter the horizontal variation in pressure, or the slope of a plane passing through points of equal pressure, can be determined (Figure 4407). From these data the wind components can be determined which are required for *pressure pattern flight,* a method of navigation on over-water flights to take advantage of existing wind conditions.

Absolute altitude.

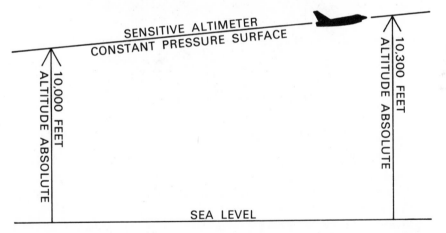

Figure 4407:
Absolute altitude measurement.

4408. *Air speed* is measured by an air speed indicator using a pitot-static tube opening forward. It compares the static pressure with total or *ram pressure*, which is the sum of the static pressure of the atmosphere plus the dynamic atmospheric pressure caused by the aircraft movement. The instrument dial is calibrated in either miles per hour or knots. Air speed indicators are calibrated for standard atmospheric conditions at sea level. The atmosphere becomes less dense with an increase in altitude, and also varies at any altitude with changes in temperature. This change in density of the air produces an erroneous air speed indicator reading which is corrected by use of the aircraft computer (Figure

Air speed.

4405a). Pressure altitude is set in the window opposite air temperature to obtain a reading of true air speed opposite calibrated air speed on the slide rule scales. The calibrated air speed is the reading of the air speed indicator corrected for any instrumental errors. At high speed, *compressibility* causes an error in reading, as the air in front of the pitot tube is literally compressed by the motion of the aircraft. The compressibility correction can also be determined by means of an aircraft computer designed for high speed use, or it can be read from a table.

Some aircraft are equipped with a *true air speed indicator* in which additional diaphragms and mechanisms compensate for these errors. This device has "true air speed" marked on the face of the dial.

Jet aircraft carry an additional instrument called a *mach meter.* The *mach number* is the relationship of the aircraft speed to the speed of sound; the latter varies with air density, so that the measurement is actually a function of altitude. Mach 1 being the speed of sound, subsonic jets will have a reading on the mach meter which is a percentage of the speed of sound; for example, mach .82 indicates the aircraft has a speed which is 82 percent of the speed of sound under the atmospheric conditions existing at the flight level of the aircraft. In determining distance traveled, the mach number must be converted to true air speed which, multiplied by time, gives distance. The mach to air speed conversion, or vice versa, is made on the aircraft computer, as a direct relationship of calibrated air speed, pressure altitude, and mach number.

Figure 4409: Aircraft magnetic compass.

Direction instruments.

4409. As in marine navigation, the magnetic compass is the airplane's basic directional or heading instrument. In aircraft only limited space is available on the instrument panel, and small front reading compasses, having a compass card with a vertical graduated dial are used (Figure 4409). The lubber line is at the after rather than the forward edge of the card, thus reversing the *apparent* motion of the card as the craft turns. The numerals become numerically greater from right to left on the visible portion of the card.

Fluxgate compass.

As the instrument panel is a poor location for a magnetic compass, because of the proximity of many instruments which adversely affect compass performance, remote indicating compasses are used almost entirely in larger aircraft. These instruments, referred to as *fluxgate compasses,* produce an induced current varying with the aircraft heading, which is transmitted to a dial indicator on the instrument panel. The compass proper can be located in the tail, a wing tip, or in some other area relatively free from deviation.

The *gyrosyn compass* uses the *fluxgate magnetic compass* as the direction sensing instrument and complements this with a directional gyro. This arrangement produces a steady and accurate compass as it eliminates the oscillations and turning errors present in a simple aircraft magnetic compass. As the small gyroscope has no north directional properties, it is automatically and continuously reset by the fluxgate compass; the gyro, which will for short periods maintain a heading, serves to steady the compass.

Gyrosyn compass.

Directional gyros can be used in aircraft compass systems without being slaved to the magnetic compass. A directional gyro is not a north-pointing gyro, it merely tends to hold its position horizontally in space; it has a movable ring around the indicator, which can be set to any desired heading. Precision gyros with low *drift rates* (precession) are available for this purpose, and corrections for *wander*, which is proportional to latitude, can be applied. Drift is determined by frequent observations of the azimuths of celestial bodies. Such directional gyros can operate in the free gyro mode; alternately, they can be slaved to some directional force, such as the magnetic compass. The procedures for determining and correcting drift rate is given in instrument manuals and air navigation texts.

Directional gyros.

In high latitudes, where the magnetic compass is unreliable and where geographic meridians converge rapidly, the directional gyro using *grid headings* is often used. The grid heading refers to an artificial grid on the chart rather than to true north. This mode of operation has been found to be the most practical for long flights at high latitudes. The drift is monitored by azimuths of celestial bodies.

The true north gyrocompass used on all major surface ships is not adaptable for aircraft use.

4410. U. S. aircraft making long range over-water flights are almost invariably equipped either with Loran-A (Chapter 18), with the newer long range Loran-C (Chapter 32) or with Omega (Chapter 31). As the range of these systems is not limited by line-of-sight distance, the areas of signal reception are approximately the same as for surface use. The instrumentation is similar to marine models except that an electronic computer is often used with Loran-C or Omega, to give automatic readout of latitude and longitude. The high speed of jet aircraft makes it highly desirable that there be a continuous readout of position, rather than that a fix be obtained from lines of position plotted on a chart. At 600 knots, if ten minutes were required to process data and plot a fix the aircraft would be 100 miles beyond the fix. Projecting this to even higher supersonic speeds makes the requirement for automation even more stringent.

Electronic aids to navigation.

Loran-C and Omega.

For domestic operation, and in some other areas of the world, Omnirange (VOR) is the standard system for air navigation. The VOR stations operate in the VHF frequency band of 108 to 118 mHz. At these frequencies, VOR is a line of sight system and the distances at which the signals can be received is a function of altitude as well as of transmitter power. Two signals are transmitted, one fixed and one rotating. The aircraft receiver compares the phase of the signals and produces a readout indicating the magnetic bearing of the station. Whether the bearing is *to* or *from* the station is also indicated on the receiver. This permits the navigator to know whether he is approaching or leaving the station; ambiguity in this respect was a weakness in older types of radio navigation aids. Several

Omni (VOR).

673

hundred Omni stations are located along the airways of the U. S., and give almost blanket coverage. A bearing from one station gives a line of position, bearings from two stations produce a fix. Each transmitting station identifies itself by transmitting a three-letter code; this code is shown on the chart at the station location. VOR bearings are magnetic bearings, as the north reference of the station transmitter is offset from true north by the amount of the local variation. This is a convenience for the navigator as most aircraft use a magnetic heading reference.

DME.

Most VOR stations are equipped for *distance measuring equipment* (DME). Using DME, the aircraft interrogates the station by transmitting a group of paired pulses which the transponder at the ground station receives and retransmits. As in radar type equipment, the time between signal transmission and its return is measured and converted into units of distance by the electronics within the receiver. When using VOR-DME, bearing and distance provide a continuous indication of position and constitutes a *rho-theta system* (see article 1711).

TACAN.

The military version of this equipment is called *TACAN*, which operates in the UHF frequencies; it is employed by the pilot or navigator in the same manner as VOR. Many VOR transmitting stations are equipped to respond on TACAN distance measuring frequencies; they are called *VORTAC* stations. TACAN is also installed aboard some aircraft carriers as a homing device for returning planes. A TACAN antenna is shown in Figure 4410.

Figure 4410: TACAN antenna atop mast of aircraft carrier.

The Omni receiver can be considered as a special type of direction finder. As in marine navigation, the simple *radio direction finder* (RDF) is also used in aviation to obtain bearings on L/MF transmitting stations. The aircraft installation is usually in the form of an automatic direction finder (ADF) in which the loop antenna is rotated automatically. With the frequency of the transmitting station set in the receiver, the indicator, generally in the form of a pointer rotating through 360°, automatically and continuously indicates the direction of the radio station *from* the aircraft.

4411. All celestial observations, whether made afloat or in the air, depend on establishment of the vertical.

Celestial navigation.

In marine navigation this is accomplished by viewing the sea horizon to establish a horizontal plane perpendicular to the vertical. A different technique is required in air navigation, as the horizon is often invisible and almost never readily observable. Over a land mass, no useful horizon is available. In addition, the dip angle would be excessive, and depend upon a knowledge of absolute altitude. The aircraft sextant therefore uses an artificial horizon. Many such horizon systems have been proposed, but the bubble and the pendulous mirror are the only two in general use. Hand-held bubble sextants of many designs have been produced but with the introduction of pressurized aircraft and with jet propulsion greatly increasing both altitude and speed, the periscopic sextant has come into wide use. Only the small observing head of the instrument protrudes through the aircraft fuselage. A schematic plan of the optical system of the periscopic sextant is shown in Figure 4411. Various other optical arrangements are possible, provided the image of the bubble is in the field of view, and properly collimated to the optical system.

Artificial horizon.

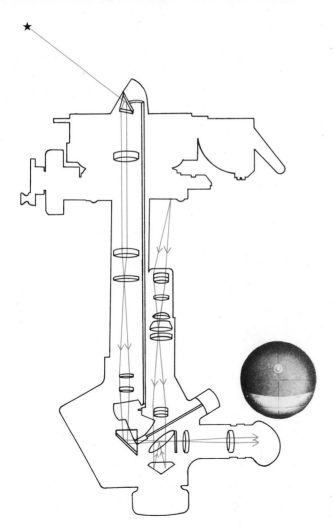

*Figure 4411:
Periscopic sextant
optical schematic.*

Averaging device.

As acceleration can cause a large random error in a single celestial observation made with an artificial horizon, an averaging device is fitted to the sextant. Such devices generally average the altitude over a period of two minutes while the navigator keeps the image of the observed body centered in the bubble. Other time periods can be used on some sextants, but the two-minute period is generally accepted as satisfactory, as it exceeds the natural oscillation period of most aircraft.

Sights must be reduced more rapidly than aboard ship, and a lesser degree of accuracy is acceptable as a trade-off against solution time. For sight reduction, H. O. 249 (see article 2507) is generally used, together with the *Air Almanac* (article 2408). Precomputation is often employed with the reduction made ahead of time; the observations are then obtained at predetermined times.

Automatic star trackers are also employed on some aircraft, primarily in military types. The star tracker can continuously measure altitude and azimuth of a celestial body, but it is used principally as an automatic astro compass to provide a continuous check on the heading reference. At operational altitudes of jet aircraft stars are generally visible during the hours of darkness. Daylight star trackers have also been developed which can track the brighter stars against a daylight sky background.

Doppler.

4412. The determination of wind drift, which affects both track and ground speed, proved difficult on long over-water flights, as coverage by electronic navigational aids is limited in many areas. *Doppler* navigational equipment has proven to be an excellent solution for this problem.

Figure 4412:
Three beam
Antenna
Configuration.

GROUND PATH

Doppler navigation is based on the shift between a transmitted and received frequency due to the relative motion of either the transmitter or receiver. A more detailed explanation of the phenomenon is given in Chapter 37 on satellite navigation. In the aircraft application, there is no relative motion between the units, as both are mounted in the aircraft. To use the Doppler effect the transmitted signals are directed in a narrow beam at a known angle down to the earth's surface whence they are reflected back to the receiver. The motion of the aircraft during the time of signal travel causes a Doppler shift. Through the use of multiple beams of microwave energy, directed towards the earth at several angles from the aircraft, combined with a heading reference, a self-contained and highly accurate navigational system has been developed. The Doppler shift is proportional to the velocity of the aircraft.

At least three beams of energy (Figure 4412) are required to create a Doppler navigational system. These three or more velocity signals are combined as a computer function within the receiver to produce a readout of ground speed and drift angle. These two values, added to the heading obtained from the compass yield a solution of the navigational problem. Continuous plotting of this DR information on a chart is laborious and time consuming; a Doppler navigator computer is therefore generally employed. This is a complex unit which, given the starting position, presents output in the form of latitude and longitude on a continuing basis. Other versions present data relative to an assumed track, in terms of distance to go, and cross-track difference perpendicular to the prescribed track. These data can, in turn, be fed into an automatic pilot to provide automated flight along a selected track.

4413. Air navigation, due to the ever increasing speeds involved, is becoming highly automated. The B-58 supersonic bomber, for example, contains a computer to integrate and solve all navigational problems, but carries a fulltime navigator to operate it. For the great majority of aircraft operations the navigator or pilot-navigator performs the principal computer functions. Although he may have available a considerable number of sensing instruments to produce useful data, for safe navigation he must exercise his own good judgment. Inertial navigational systems, since they are similar in concept to their marine counterparts, have not been described here. Other systems under development will undoubtedly increase both the accuracy and efficiency of future air navigation. The concepts outlined in this chapter are those which are basic to air navigation, and are presented to give the marine navigator some understanding of the differences involved in navigation in the two media.

Conclusion.

CHAPTER 45

Space Navigation

4501. The exploration of space is probably the most ambitious project ever undertaken by man. The manning of space vehicles for this exploration has required completely new concepts as well as unique equipment to support the various missions. Manned space flight demands support in a completely new medium involving a new dimension, where man is free of gravity, wind, atmosphere and other familiar terrestrial phenomena. The vast distances in space also raise problems. Whereas we think of light and radio waves as traveling from point to point almost instantaneously, it takes 8.3 minutes for light from the sun to reach the surface of the earth; it takes 6 minutes for radar beams bounced off Mars to return to earth.

A multitude of problems have to be met and solved by new thinking and new concepts. One of these new concepts lies in the field of space navigation and guidance, where position cannot be described by the familiar coordinates of latitude and longitude. As previously mentioned, a new dimension must be allowed for, and new developments in the field of navigation must compensate for it. Space navigation is best performed using a combination of on-board, and of earth-based navigation instrumentation. This chapter cannot give the

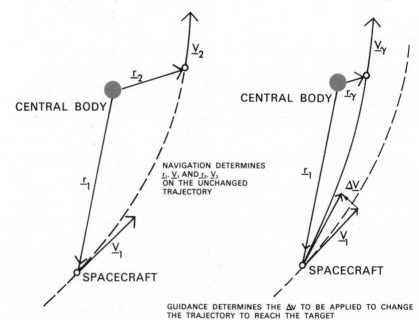

Figure 4502: Navigation and guidance concepts.

NAVIGATION DETERMINES r_1, V_1 AND r_2, V_2 ON THE UNCHANGED TRAJECTORY

GUIDANCE DETERMINES THE ΔV TO BE APPLIED TO CHANGE THE TRAJECTORY TO REACH THE TARGET

student complete coverage on space navigation; it is intended to relate basic space navigation to its counterpart on the surface of the earth.

4502. Although the terms "navigation" and "guidance" are often used synonymously, they are in fact only related. The function of *space navigation* is twofold; it must determine the *state* of the spacecraft; the state of the spacecraft at any given instant of time may be defined as describing completely the motion of the spacecraft in a free-fall trajectory.

Navigation and guidance.

In addition, space navigation involves determination and indication of the position and velocity of the craft relative to reference coordinates at a given moment. The guidance problem is to determine what trajectory changes to make to control the position and velocity in order to reach some terminal point; it arises when the navigation problem has been solved. Guidance is the process of moving the center of mass of the vehicle along some desired path; stability and control are associated with motions about the center of mass. The relationships between navigation and guidance are illustrated in Figure 4502.

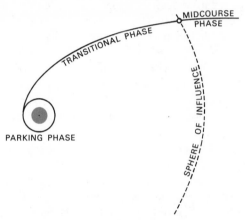

Figure 4503: Orbital phases.

4503. Navigation in space cannot be as clearly defined as in marine or aircraft practice. An orbital flight is ordinarily divided into three phases and navigation must be adapted to each of these phases with their differing parameters. The orbital phases are the *parking phase,* the *transitional phase,* and the *midcourse phase.* Figure 4503 shows the three orbital phases of a spaceflight. In all phases of vehicular flight one of the most important requirements is that the navigator maintain a good DR plot. As will be seen in article 4504, this is particularly important during the parking phase.

Orbital phases.

The complex mathematics of orbital flight, involving space mechanics, and the high velocities involved in space travel, necessitate the use of a computer for on-board navigation. The navigator is an important link in the system, to make observations, enter data in the computer, to exercise judgment and initiate guidance action. Complex computations involving velocity and position are best solved by the computer.

The trend in space navigation system development has been toward the use of redundant instrumentation for measurements and relatively sophisticated computers for statistical estimation techniques to resolve sensor data to navigational information. Current navigational accuracy limits are set by the computational complexity rather than by the tracking accuracy.

679

Parking phase.

4504. In the parking phase the spacecraft is in a captured orbit about a celestial body with the gravitational attraction of that body having the primary attraction on the orbit. In this phase the on-board navigation is probably the most complicated, since it depends on a planet-fixed reference system for either surveillance or for landing. Normally, little or no guidance is required while in a parking orbit.

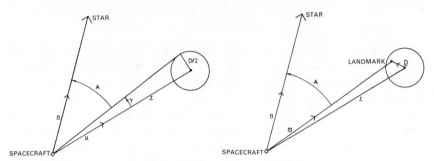

Figure 4504a: Star elevation angle measurement (measuring angle A).

Figure 4504b: Star landmark angle measurement (measure angle A).

On-board navigation can be accomplished by any one of several methods while in the parking phase of the flight. One method is to measure the angle included between the line-of-sight to a star and the limb of a planet disc. Thus far practical tests have of course been limited to the planet earth. Figure 4504a shows the geometry of this measurement. Another method is to determine the angular measurement between the line-of-sight to a star and a discernible landmark on a near planet, as illustrated in Figure 4504b. A third method consists of determining the time at which a star is occluded by a nearby planet (Figure 4504c). A fourth method is by measurement of the angle subtended by the diameter of the visible disc of a nearby planet when the planet radius is known, similar in principle to obtaining a stadiametric distance in marine navigation. With this information the distance of the spacecraft from the planet center can be computed. Figure 4504d shows the geometry of this measurement. Uncertainty in planet diameters can cause errors of sizeable proportions in this method.

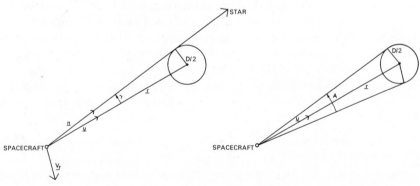

Figure 4504c: Star occultation time measurement.

Figure 4504d: Body subtended angle measurement.

Still another method of navigation in the near vicinity of a planet, when in the parking phase, is to track discernible landmarks on the planet's surface. The actual procedures to be followed in this latter method depend upon whether the location of the landmarks on the planet are known. One or more landmarks may be used to give orbital parameters after successive observations are taken during a series of orbits of the planet. The primary advantage of this method lies in its presentation of the spacecraft's position relative to a coordinate system referenced to the planet, and following the planet's motion; its major disadvantage is that landmarks may not always be clearly discernible when the planet has an atmosphere. Data obtained from the Gemini flights show that earth landmarks are not always visible even in a low altitude orbit. With each method cited, and particularly with the last, it is of extreme importance to keep a good DR plot in order to determine what guidance action may be required.

4505. The space craft is in the transitional phase of spaceflight when it is escaping or approaching a celestial body. In this phase, its orbit is primarily affected by the gravitational field of the body, but it has sufficient energy to override the influence of the body. On-board navigation while in the transitional phase has as its reference the center of the celestial body. The methods employed are similar to marine celestial position fixing, using an instrument basically similar to the marine sextant. A space sextant is illustrated in Figure 4505.

Transitional phase.

For navigation in the vicinity of a planet or during the transitional phase, on-board techniques have many distinct advantages over earth-based navigation. The primary advantage lies in the previously mentioned communication delay caused by the extreme distances involved. Another advantage is that the space-craft is positioned relative to the body concerned, rather than relative to earth.

Figure 4505: Apollo Optical Unit or space sextant.

4506. Once the spacecraft has escaped from the gravitational influence of a celestial body, the orbital parameters are primarily affected by the gravitational pull of the sun. In this phase the vehicle is in an orbit around the sun, and on-board navigation coordinates are generally chosen to be sun-centered, using the same instruments as in the transitional phase.

Midcourse phase.

4507. Navigation methods discussed so far have been based upon accomplishment aboard the spacecraft. But while these on-board techniques are being employed earth-based facilities also check on the position of the spacecraft. Techniques for this earth-based navigation are based on radar tracking of the vehicle. Command guidance is supplied by radio. While this method has proved to be extremely reliable in the past, and it is included in the plans for all future manned and unmanned missions, it does have some definite disadvantages. The primary disadvantage lies in the time delay between receipt, processing and relaying of information for other than near-earth orbits.

Earth-based navigation.

Another disadvantage is that earth-based tracking radars indicate spacecraft distances and speeds relative to a point on the earth's surface, even though the spacecraft might, for example, be approaching, or be in orbit around the moon. Small uncertainties or errors in the measurement made at the earth-based location can yield large uncertainties in the precise navigation required at the position of the spacecraft. On-board navigation is therefore a definite requirement for manned missions; earth-based navigation, the primary system for earth orbiting flights, will perhaps serve more as a back up system on long future missions. On-board equipment provides accurate angle data while ground radars provide more precise ranging information.

Dead reckoning.

4508: As mentioned previously, DR plays an extremely important role in keeping abreast of the guidance commands required during various phases of spacecraft orbit. Space DR differs from shipboard DR chiefly in the terminology used, and because of the additional dimension in which the craft travels. While the surface navigator is chiefly concerned with the time versus speed ratio, the astronaut must in addition apply orbital parameters of gravitational attraction and centrifugal force. By proper application of these parameters, which vary with the orbital phase of the flight, the orbit DR track can be accurately computed and compared to the prescribed orbit, in order to determine any guidance procedures which may be required.

Inertial navigation.

4509. Precision inertial navigation is applicable to space flight primarily during times when a major power application is taking place, such as launch, landing, and during any major orbit change maneuver. An inertial navigator provides the primary reference during launch to inject the vehicle properly into orbit. Inertial navigation is not practical for long term, deep space navigation; primarily because inertial accelerometers indicate only non-gravitational acceleration. They cannot measure the primary acceleration, gravity, applied to a vehicle traveling in space. No suitable gravity model of the solar system has been computed, as the exact distribution of mass in the solar system is unknown.

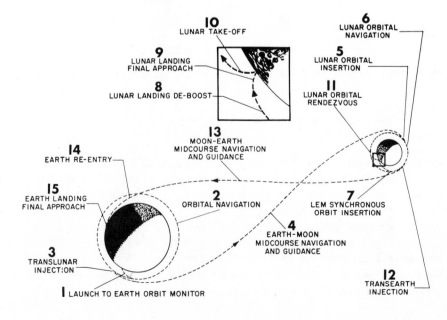

Figure 4510a:
Apollo navigation
and guidance
phase summary.

10 LUNAR TAKE-OFF

9 LUNAR LANDING FINAL APPROACH

8 LUNAR LANDING DE-BOOST

6 LUNAR ORBITAL NAVIGATION

5 LUNAR ORBITAL INSERTION

11 LUNAR ORBITAL RENDEZVOUS

13 MOON-EARTH MIDCOURSE NAVIGATION AND GUIDANCE

14 EARTH RE-ENTRY

15 EARTH LANDING FINAL APPROACH

2 ORBITAL NAVIGATION

7 LEM SYNCHRONOUS ORBIT INSERTION

4 EARTH-MOON MIDCOURSE NAVIGATION AND GUIDANCE

3 TRANSLUNAR INJECTION

1 LAUNCH TO EARTH ORBIT MONITOR

12 TRANSEARTH INJECTION

4510. The previous articles have described the three major phases of spacecraft navigation. Since the manned spacecraft program has so far been principally involved in flights under positive ground control, it is impossible to ascertain with certainty what methods of navigation will prove most satisfactory. Consequently, the concepts and techniques designed for the Apollo flights, and which are expected to meet all requirements, will be covered briefly.

Apollo Program manned spacecraft navigation.

Since this program covers a moon exploration project, guidance and navigation are quite closely related. In carrying out the primary mission the vehicle passes through fifteen distinct guidance and navigation phases. Of these fifteen, only eleven are directly concerned with the Apollo vehicle itself; the others are for navigation and guidance of the Lunar Excursion Module (LEM), which lands on the moon (Figure 4510a).

Since these flights are taking place relatively near the earth, as compared to planned future exploration of the solar system and deep space, primary navigation, including the prediction of future orbital information, is by means of the earth-based tracking system. This system, using radar and visual tracking information, and both radio and voice for relaying information and guidance commands, is a proved system, as was shown in the Mercury, Mariner, Surveyor and

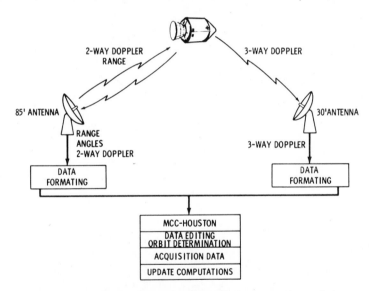

Figure 4510b: Radar tracking system.

Gemini flights. A schematic representation of the operation of the manned space flight network tracking system (MSFN) is shown in Figure 4510b. The vehicle is tracked by an 85-foot antenna which provides range, angles, and velocity. This information is transmitted to the Mission Control Center in Houston from which navigation information is determined. The vehicle can also be tracked by a 30-foot antenna which uses three-way Doppler information to provide position and velocity data.

Distance is determined by modulating the carrier with random digits (0 and 1). The signal is received by transponders in the spacecraft or the LEM and retransmitted. The measurement of transit time of the signal is a measure of the distance of the spacecraft. Velocity is determined by measuring the Doppler shift in the signal returned by the spacecraft.

An on-board system is also essential on the Apollo flights. This is not meant to be a back-up system, but rather an independent system with the same capabilities as the earth-based system. It is not subject to possible jamming, and can take over when the vehicle is inaccessible to earth control, as when on the far side of the moon. The space sextant shown in Figure 4505 is used in this mode of navigation. The optical system is used to align the inertial system, and for navigation in earth orbit, lunar orbit, and cislunar space. The inertial measurement unit is used as a primary attitude reference and is used for guidance purposes during all maneuvers and during re-entry. Data are obtained by simultaneous lines-of-sight observations on two celestial bodies or by superimposing a star image on a landmark. Time and angular measurement are read out electronically, and are fed into the computer. The optical system of the space sextant is shown in Figure 4510c.

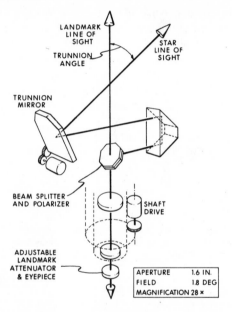

Figure 4510c: Space sextant optical system schematic.

The astronaut uses a sextant to position the star accurately over the landmark or horizon. When the star and landmark are superimposed, the astronaut presses a button and the angles between the two, and the time, are entered into the computer automatically. The geometry of measuring a navigational fix in cislunar space differs from that of traditional marine or air navigation. The angles measured using three stars and their angles from a landmark or horizon form three cones in space. These may be thought of as cones of position rather than as traditional lines of position. The intersection of two of these cones forms a line and the intersection with the third cone forms a point.

Computation is performed automatically in the computer. Apollo does not use the conventional method of computation performed by mariners for many centuries, i.e., computation based upon two or more star sightings and running the earlier sightings forward to the last sighting and computing a fix. This could be defined as a "deterministic" technique. In Apollo, recursive navigation techniques are used (involving Kalman filter theory). Under this concept the accuracy of position and velocity determination is improved as more and more sightings are taken and the uncertainties are reduced with each sighting. This method involves statistical mathematics techniques. Fixes as they are known in maritime navigation are not obtained in Apollo.

Two major advantages are offered by optical navigation, as compared to other possible methods such as radar and inertial, in that it does not impose a heavy electrical power demand, and it is not subject to cumulative errors which might be excessive in long duration non-accelerating flights as in the coasting period during the mid-course phase of the orbit. Additionally photometric sensors are incorporated within the sextant to allow for automatic star tracking and detection of light in the visual wave length which is radiated from the atmosphere at the earth's bright horizon. The computer that is used for solving sights needs minimum programming and can be used simultaneously for other jobs such as reducing data received from earth.

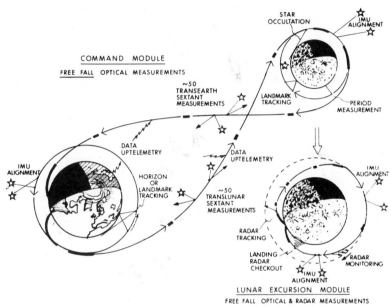

Figure 4510d: Navigation mission phases for Apollo.

Problems have been posed by the need for on-board navigation and guidance for spacecraft which are without precedent in the field of navigation. The astronaut must have full independent capability for positioning his vehicle without help from or without reference to the earth. There will always be a need for a simple manual method by which an astronaut can return to earth in the event of an emergency situation. Figure 4510d shows the navigation mission phases for the Apollo spacecraft and its capabilities; also shown are the navigation phases for the Lunar Excursion Module (not covered in this chapter), which include the use of radar to accomplish its mission. The drawing illustrates the use of optical measurements for navigation and for alignment of the inertial measurement unit (IMU).

4511. All manned space flights prior to the Apollo project involved earth orbits which are equivalent to the parking phase of lunar space flights. On these flights, navigation was at a minimum, as the spacecraft was operating under the inflexible natural laws governing orbiting bodies. A review of the elementary concepts of space mechanics illustrates the basic laws governing orbital space flight.

Basic orbit parameters.

685

A spacecraft will remain in the same plane in which it was injected at launch if no force is applied. At any instant of time, this plane would trace a great circle on the surface of the earth, at a fixed angle of inclination to the earth's equatorial plane. However, the rotation of the earth within the plane of the orbit causes an apparent westward movement of the orbit plane around the earth at the rate of approximately 15° per hour.

In free fall centrifugal force is exactly offset by gravity. The spacecraft can neither return to earth nor escape from its gravitational field; there can, therefore, be only one velocity for a given orbit height. The shape of the orbit is either circular or elliptical. The radial distance of the spacecraft from the center of the earth at *perigee,* its point of nearest approach, together with the orbital eccentricity, defines the size of the orbit.

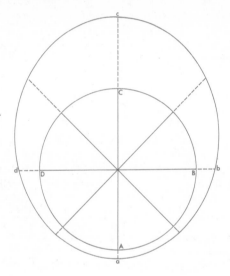

*Figure 4511:
Relationship of
circles and ellipses.*

A spacecraft in orbit will sweep equal areas of the orbital plane in equal times. In an elliptical orbit this results in a varying velocity at different points in the orbit, the change being greater as the ellipse is elongated, and least when it approaches a circle. Figure 4511 illustrates the relationship of a circle and an ellipse. An object traveling at constant velocity around the circle would sweep an even number of degrees and an equal area in equal minutes, A to B, B to C, etc. Arcs a to b, and b to c on the ellipse obviously do not represent equal areas; the spacecraft therefore cannot consume the same length of time for sweeping the two sections.

A spacecraft traveling in an elliptical orbit is therefore constantly changing its velocity. If the velocity at any given instant is changed by the pilot, the height and/or shape of the orbit is changed.

Considering these facts, the orbit of a satellite about an isolated, spherical body having no atmosphere would be an ellipse lying in a plane whose direction was fixed relative to the stars. The ellipse would remain fixed in size, shape and orientation. The orbit of a satellite around the real earth departs from this ideal concept as the result of four main perturbations, caused by the departures of the earth's gravitational field from spherical symmetry, the influence of atmospheric drag, lunar and solar gravitational attractions, and solar radiation pressure.

The Complete Celestial Solution Using H.O. 229

Chapter 27 dealt at length with sight reduction, using H.O. 214 and the *Nautical Almanac*. This appendix covers sight reduction using H.O. 229, *Sight Reduction Tables for Marine Navigation*, again with the *Nautical Almanac*. The H.O. 229 was described in article 2505.

Introduction.

Before proceeding, the student may find it desirable to review articles 2702 and 2703, which discuss the combined coordinate systems and the efficient use of the *Nautical Almanac*.

The arrangement of this appendix differs slightly from that of Chapter 27 in that the reduced celestial observations represent a single day's work for a navigator, and the resulting lines of position are plotted (see page 693). The hypothetical ship is a fleet tug, accompanying a damaged freighter; she is on C 288°.5, S 6.75 K. At 0400 (+1), on 1 August 1972, the tug's DR position is Lat. 41°02'.8 N, Long. 14°38'.0 W.

When observing a planet, the navigator measures the sextant altitude of the center of the body and records the time and date of the observation. He also checks the index error of the instrument.

Complete solution for a planet observation.

He then converts the time to GMT and Greenwich date, and enters the appropriate daily pages of the *Nautical Almanac* to obtain the GHA and declination at the whole hours of GMT, and the *v* and *d* values for the period, noting the sign of the *d* value by inspection. The *v* is always plus except for Venus when it can be either plus or minus. Turning to the appropriate "Increments and Corrections Table," he obtains the increments of GHA for minutes and seconds, and the corrections to GHA and declination for the *v* and *d* values, respectively. Applying these values to those obtained from the daily pages, he obtains the GHA and Dec. of the planet at the time of observation.

The extract from the Nautical Almanac *used in this Appendix starts on page 696.*

With the *Nautical Almanac* still open, the navigator notes the value of IC (as determined from the sextant), extracts the D and R (plus the "add'l" for Venus and Mars) corrections from the appropriate sections of the almanac, and combines them with hs to obtain ha and Ho.

The navigator then selects the AP, based on the best estimate of his position, and uses the *a*λ to determine LHA in whole degrees.

Entering H.O. 229 with integral degrees of LHA, *a*L, and Dec., he obtains the tabulated altitude for the value of the entering arguments, *d*, and its sign, and Z. Z is corrected by visual interpolation for the actual value of the declination.

The extract from H.O. 229 begins on page 703.

The correction to the tabulated altitude for Dec. Inc. and *d* is then taken from a multiplication table inside the cover of H.O. 229 and is applied to ht, as is the double second difference correction if *d* is printed in italic type, to obtain Hc.

Hc is then compared with Ho to determine (*a*). By converting Z to Zn, the navigator can use Zn and (*a*) to plot the LOP from the AP.

Example: On 1 August 1972 the 0447 DR position of the ship is Lat. 41°04'.5 N, Long. 14°44'.6 W. At 04-47-13 ZT the planet Venus is observed from a height of eye of 21 feet, with a sextant having an IC of (+) 0'.2. The sextant altitude is 31°13'.2.

Required: The (*a*), Zn, and AP, using H.O. 229 and the *Nautical Almanac*.

Answer: (Solution shown in column 1, page 689.)

a	Away 23'.6
Zn	092°.2
aL	41°00'.0 N
aλ	14°15'.7 W

Complete solution for a moon observation.

When observing the moon, the navigator measures the sextant altitude of either the upper or lower limb of the body, and records the time and date of the observation. He also checks the index error of the instrument.

He then converts the time to GMT and Greenwich date, and enters the appropriate daily pages of the *Nautical Almanac* to obtain the GHA, *v* value, which for the moon is always (+), declination, *d* value (noting the sign of the *d* value by inspection), and HP for the nearest whole hour of GMT. Turning to the appropriate "Increments and Corrections Table," he obtains the increments of GHA for minutes and seconds, and the corrections to GHA and declination for the *v* and *d* values, respectively. Applying these values to those obtained from the daily pages, he obtains the GHA and Dec. of the moon at the time of the observation.

With the *Nautical Almanac* still open, the navigator notes the value of IC (as determined from the sextant), and extracts the D correction and the corrections for altitude and HP from the "Altitude Correction Tables—Moon." The latter two corrections are always additive, but if the upper limb is observed, an additional correction of (−) 30' is made. These corrections are combined with hs to obtain ha and Ho.

The navigator then selects the AP, based on the best estimate of his position, and uses the aλ to determine LHA in whole degrees.

Entering H.O. 229 with integral degrees of LHA, aL and Dec., he obtains the tabulated altitude for the value of the entering arguments, *d* and its sign, and Z. Z is corrected by visual interpolation for the actual value of the declination. The correction to the tabulated altitude for Dec. Inc. and *d* is then taken from a multiplication table inside the cover of H.O. 229 and applied to ht, as is the double second difference correction if *d* is printed in *italic* type, to obtain Hc.

Hc is then compared with Ho to determine (*a*). By converting Z to Zn, the navigator can then use Zn and (*a*) to plot the LOP from the AP.

Example: On 1 August 1972, the 0611 DR position of the ship is Lat. 41°07'.5 N, Long. 14°56'.3 W. At 06-11-03 ZT the lower limb of the moon is observed from

Sight Reduction using H.O. 229

Cus:

Spd:

Body	VENUS	☾	☉
IC	+ 0·2 −	+ 0·2 −	+ 0·2 −
Dip (Ht 21 ')	4·4	4·4	4·4
Sum	− 4·2	− 4·2	− 4·2
hs	31° 13·2	57° 06·5	12° 38·2
ha	31° 09·1	57° 02·3	12° 34·0
Alt. Corr	1·6	41·4	0·1 4·3
Add'l.	0·3		15·8 ∞
H. P. (59·1)		6·1	0·5 ᴛʙ
Corr. to ha	− 1·3	+47·5	+12·1
Ho (Obs Alt)	31° 07·7	57° 49·8	12° 46·1
Date	1 AUG 72	1 AUG 72	1 AUG 72
DR Lat	41° 04·5 N	41° 07·5 N	41° 07·5 N
DR Long	14° 44·6 W	14° 56·3 W	14° 56·3 W
Obs. Time			
WE (S+, F−)			
ZT	04 47 13	06 11 03	06 11 56
ZD (W+, E−)	+ 1	+ 1	+ 1
GMT	05 47 13	07 11 03	07 11 56
Date (GMT)	1 AUG 72	1 AUG 72	1 AUG 72
Tab GHA V	298 26·8 0·7	33 31·5 9·6	283 26·2
GHA incr'mt.	11 48·3	2 38·2	2 59·0
SHA or V Corr.	0·6	1·8	
GHA	310° 15·7	36° 11·5	286 25·2
± 360 if needed			
aλ (−W, +E)	14° 15·7 W	15° 11·5 W	15° 25·2 W
LHA	296°	21°	271°
Tab Dec d	N 18° 35·9 +0·2	N 14° 41·4 +13·1	N 17° 58·8 −0·6
d Corr (+ or −)	+ 0·2	+ 2·5	− 0·1
True Dec	N 18° 36·1	N 14° 43·6	N 17° 58·7
a Lat (N or S)	N 41 (Same) Cont.	N 41 (Same) Cont.	N 41 (Same) Cont.
Dec Inc (±)d	36·1 +36·4	43·6 +51·6	58·7 +38·1
Hc (Tab. Alt.)	31° 09·4	57° 23·5	11° 47·7
tens DS Diff.	18·0	36·3	29·4
units DS Corr.	3·9 +	1·2 +	7·9 +
Tot. Corr. (+ or −)	+ 21·9	+ 37·5	37·3
Hc (Comp. Alt.)	31° 31·3	58° 01·0	12° 25·0
Ho (Obs. Alt.)	31° 07·7	57° 49·8	12° 46·1
a (Intercept)	23·6 A	11·2 A	21·1 T
Z	92·2	139·1	76·8
Zn (°T)	092°·2	220°·9	076°·8

H.O. 229 worksheet.

a height of eye of 21 feet with a sextant having an IC of (+) 0'.2. The sextant altitude is 57°06'.5.

Required: The (*a*), Zn, and AP, using H.O. 229 and the *Nautical Almanac.*

Answer: (Solution shown in column 2, page 689.)

> *a* Away 11'.2
> Zn   220°.9
> *a*L   41°00'.0 N
> *a*λ   15°11'.5 W.

Complete solution for a sun observation.

When observing the sun, the navigator measures the sextant altitude of either the upper or lower limb of the body, and records the time and date of the observation. He also records the index error of the sextant.

He then converts the time to GMT and Greenwich date, and enters the appropriate daily pages of the *Nautical Almanac* to obtain the GHA and declination at the whole hours of GMT, and the *d* value for the period (noting the sign of the *d* value by inspection). If maximum accuracy were desired, he would also note the SD of the sun from the daily pages. The values of I and IC, with their appropriate signs, would be entered in the form, as would the correction for D, obtained from the *Nautical Almanac.* These would be combined with hs to obtain ha.

Ordinarily, the ha is corrected by means of the sun altitude correction tables inside the front cover of the *Nautical Almanac,* which include corrections for an average value of semi-diameter, refraction, and parallax. Alternatively, the value of the semi-diameter found at the bottom of the sun column in the daily pages of the *Nautical Almanac* may be used together with the value of the refraction correction found under the heading "Stars and Planets," and an additional correction of (+)0'.1 for parallax to be used for altitudes of 65° and less.

Having entered the GHA and declination for the whole hours of GMT, the navigator now turns to the appropriate page of the "Increments and Corrections table," and obtains the increments of GHA for minutes and seconds and the correction to the declination for the *d* value. Applying these values to those obtained from the daily pages, he obtains the GHA and Dec. of the sun at the time of the observation.

With the *Nautical Almanac* still open, the navigator notes the value of IC (as determined from the sextant) and extracts the appropriate value of D. These are combined with hs to obtain ha. The appropriate correction for ☉, or ☉, taken from the Sun Table, is then applied to ha to obtain Ho.

The navigator then selects the AP, based on the best estimate of his position, and uses the *a*λ to determine LHA in whole degrees.

Entering H.O. 229 with integral degrees of LHA, *a*L, and Dec., he obtains the tabulated altitude for the value of the entering arguments, *d* and its sign, and Z. Z is corrected by visual interpolation for the actual value of the declination. The correction to the tabulated altitude for Dec. Inc. and *d* is then taken from a multiplication table inside the cover of H.O. 229 and is applied to ht, as is the double second difference correction if *d* is printed in *italic* type, to obtain Hc.

Hc is then compared with Ho to determine (*a*). By converting Z to Zn, the navigator can use Zn and (*a*) to plot the LOP from the AP.

Example: On 1 August 1972, the 0611 DR position of the ship is Lat. 41°07'.5 N, Long. 14°56'.3 W. At 06-11-56 ZT the lower limb of the sun is observed from a height of eye of 21 feet with a sextant having an IC of (+) 0'.2. The sextant altitude is 12°38'.2. The dry bulb temperature is 88° F, and the barometer reads 29.76 inches.

Because of the sun's comparatively low altitude, the individual corrections for refraction, semi-diameter and parallax, as well as the additional correction for nonstandard temperature and barometric pressure are to be applied to ha in this instance.

Required: The (*a*), Zn, and AP, using H.O. 229 and the *Nautical Almanac.*

Answer: (Solution shown in column 3, page 689.)

a	T 21'.1
Zn	076°.8
*a*L	41°00'.0 N
*a*λ	15°25'.2 W

When observing a star, the navigator measures the sextant altitude of the body and records the time and date of the observation. He also checks the index error of the instrument.

Complete solution for a star observation.

He then converts the time to GMT and Greenwich date, and enters the appropriate daily pages of the Nautical Almanac to obtain the GHA of Aries at the whole hours of GMT, and the SHA and declination of the star for that period. Turning to the appropriate "Increments and Corrections" table, he obtains the increments of GHA of Aries for minutes and seconds. Adding this value to the GHA of Aries and SHA of the star obtained from the daily pages, he obtains the star's GHA at the time of the observation. The Dec. is the value tabulated on the daily page.

With the *Nautical Almanac* still open, the navigator notes the value of IC (as determined from the sextant), extracts the D and R corrections from the appropriate sections of the almanac, and applies them to hs to obtain ha and Ho.

The navigator then selects the AP, based on the best estimate of his position, and uses the *a*λ to determine LHA in whole degrees.

Entering H.O. 229 with integral degrees of LHA, *a*L, and Dec., he obtains the tabulated altitude for the value of the entering argument, *d* and its sign, and Z. The correction to tabulated altitude for *d* and Dec. Inc. is then taken from the multiplication table in H.O. 229, and applied to ht, as is the double second difference correction if *d* is printed in *italic* type, to obtain Hc. He corrects Z by visual interpolation for the actual value of the declination.

Hc is then compared with Ho to determine (*a*). By converting Z to Zn, the navigator can then use Zn and (*a*) to plot the LOP from the AP.

Two star observations are included in the following examples. The Vega reduction (Example 2) requires a double second difference correction, while Antares' declination is of contrary name to the observer's latitude.

In the Antares reduction (Example 1), note that the value of *d* as found in the tables is (−) 60'.0; this being the case, the full value of Dec. Diff. is applied to ht to obtain Hc.

Sight Reduction using H.O. 229

Cus:

Spd:

		ANTARES	VEGA	
Body		ANTARES	VEGA	
IC		+ 0·2 −	+ 0·2 −	+ −
Dip (Ht 21 ')		4·4	4·4	
Sum		− 4·2	− 4·2	
hs		22° 06'·5	64° 44'·5	
ha		22° 02'·3	64° 40·3	
Alt. Corr		2·4	0·5	
Add'l.				
H. P. ( )				
Corr. to ha		−2·4	−0·5	
Ho (Obs Alt)		21° 59'·9	64 39'·8	
Date		1 AUG 72	1 AUG 72	
DR Lat		41° 36'·7 N	41° 36'·7 N	
DR Long		16° 52'·8 W	16° 52'·8 W	
Obs. Time				
WE (S+, F−)				
ZT		19 47 56	19 48 50	
ZD (W+, E−)		+ 1	+ 1	
GMT		20 47 56	20 48 50	
Date (GMT)		1 AUG 72	1 AUG 72	
Tab GHA	V	250° 31'·2	250° 31'·2	
GHA incr'mt.		12 01·0	12 14·5	
SHA or V Corr.		113 03·7	80 59·3	
GHA		375° 35'·9	343° 45'·0	
±360 if needed		15° 35'·9		
aλ (−W, +E)		W 16° 35'·9	W 16° 45'·0	
LHA		359	327	
Tab Dec	d			
d Corr (+ or −)				
True Dec		S 26° 22'·5	N 38 45'·6	
a Lat (N or S)		N 42° Same Cont.	N 42° Same Cont.	Same Cont.
Dec Inc (±)d		22·5 −60	45·6 +19·1	
Hc (Tab. Alt.)		21° 59'·6	64° 34'·0	
tens	DS Diff.		7·6 4	
units	DS Corr.	+	6·9 +0·2	+
Tot. Corr. (+ or −)		−22·5	+ 14·7	
Hc (Comp. Alt.)		21° 37'·1	64° 48'·7	
Ho (Obs. Alt.)		21 59·9	64 39.8	
a (Intercept)		22·8 T	8·9 A	A T
Z		N 179 E	N 86·3 E	
Zn (°T)		179°	086°·3	

H.O. 229 worksheet.

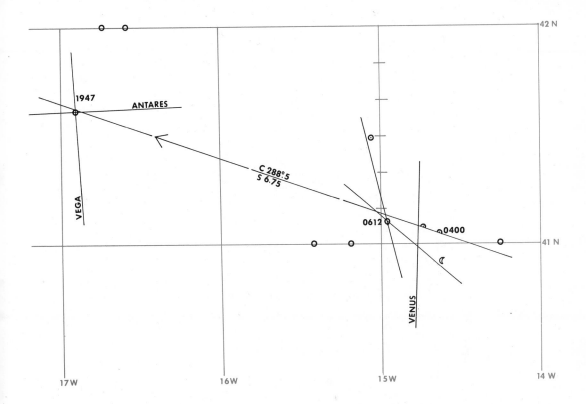

Example 1: On 1 August 1972, the 1947 DR position of the ship is Lat. 41°36'.7   *LOP plotting sheet.*
N, Long. 16°52'.8 W. At 19-47-56 the star Antares is observed from a height of
eye of 21 feet with a sextant having an IC of (+) 0'.2. The sextant altitude is
22°06'.5.

Required: The (*a*), Zn, and AP, using H. O. 229, and the *Nautical Almanac*.

Answer: (Solution shown in column 1, page 692.)

> *a*   Towards 22'.8
> Zn   179°.0
> *a*L   42°00'.0 N
> *a*λ   16°35'.9 W

Example 2: On 1 August 1972 the 1948 DR position of the ship is Lat. 41°36'.7
N, Long. 16°52'.8 W. At 19-48-50 ZT the star Vega is observed from a height of
eye of 21 feet with a sextant having an IC of (+) 0'.2. The sextant altitude is
64°44'.5.

Required: The (*a*), Zn, and AP, using H. O. 229, and the *Nautical Almanac*.

Answer: (Solution shown in column 2, page 692.)

> *a*   Away 8'.9
> Zn   086°.3
> *a*L   42°00'.0 N
> *a*λ   16°45'.0 W

The need for regular determination of compass error, and methods of making   *Exact azimuth*
azimuth observations at sea are described in detail in articles 2901 and 2902.   *H. O. 229.*
The method of calculating the azimuth by means of H. O. 229 is discussed next.   **693**

H.O. 229 makes an excellent azimuth table. When H.O. 229 is used to determine true azimuth for the purpose of checking the compass, triple linear interpolation usually must be made in order to obtain the required accuracy. The "d" values in H.O. 229 apply only to *altitude*, and should not be used when interpolating for azimuth.

Example: The azimuth of the sun is observed at 06-11-56 ZT on 1 August 1972. The 0612 DR position is Lat. 41°07'.5 N, Long. 14°56'.3 W. The azimuth obtained using a gyro repeater is 077°.5.

Required: Gyro error, using H.O. 229 to obtain true azimuth.

Solution: It is first necessary to determine the exact values of LHA, Dec., and L for the instant of observation of the azimuth. These values are determined as for working a sight, except that the *actual* position of the ship is used rather than an assumed position. Thus the DR longitude, 14°56'.3 W, is used to determine the exact value of LHA at the time of observation. The exact value of Dec. is found to be N 17°58'.7 by consulting the *Nautical Almanac* in the usual manner. The DR latitude is taken as the exact value of L at the time of observation.

With the exact values of LHA, Dec., and L determined, enter the appropriate section of H.O. 229, with the "tab." values, those tabulated entering arguments *nearest* to the exact values. In this case they are LHA 271°, Dec. N 18°, and L 41° N. With these "tab." values as entering arguments, enter the proper section (the "same name" section in this case), and extract and record the tabulated

EXACT AZIMUTH USING H.O. 229

H.O. 229 Azimuth worksheet.

Body	☉
DR L	41° 07'.5 N
DR λ	14° 56'.3 W
Date (L)	1 AUG. 72
ZT	06 11 56
ZD (+ or −)	+ 1
GMT	07 11 56
Date (G)	1 AUG 72
Tab GHA	283° 26'.2
Inc'mt	2° 59'.0
GHA	286° 25'.2
DR λ	14° 56'.3
LHA	271° 28'.9
Tab Dec	N 17 58'.8 d 0'.6
d corr	− 0'.1
Dec	N 17° 58'.7

	EXACT Deg	EXACT Min	Z DIFF (+ or −)	CORR (+ or −)
LAT	41	07.5	+0.3	0
LHA	271	28.9	+0.7	+0.3
DEC	17	58.7	+0.8	0

Total (+)	+0.3
Tab Z	76.8
Exact Z	N 77°.1 E
Exact Zn	077°.1
Gyro/Compass Brg	077°.5
Gyro/Compass Error	W 0°.4

NORTH LAT

LHA greater than 180° .... Zn = Z
LHA less than 180° .... Zn = 360° − Z

SOUTH LAT

LHA greater than 180° .... Zn = 180° − Z
LHA less than 180° .... Zn = 180° + Z

694

azimuth angle, Z 76°.8. This value of Z is the *tabulated* ("tab.") value, to which the corrections resulting from the necessary interpolation are applied to obtain the azimuth angle for the exact values of LHA, Dec., and L at the moment of observation. Interpolation is made separately for the difference between each of the exact values and the corresponding "tab." values of LHA, Dec., and L; and the algebraic sum of the resulting corrections is applied to the value of tab. Z to obtain the exact azimuth angle at the moment of observation. It is normally considered sufficiently accurate to reduce these corrections to the nearest tenth of a degree.

The LHA is interpolated from 271° (Z 76°.8) to 272° (Z 77°.5), indicating a change of (+) 0°.7 for a change of 1° (60') in the entering value of LHA known as the "LHA diff." Since the exact value of LHA is 271°28'.9, which is 28'.9 more than the "tab." value of LHA, the difference in the value of Z corresponding to this variation in LHA is 28'.9/60' of the change for a 1° change in LHA. Thus, "LHA corr.", which is the correction to apply to the value of tab. Z for the variation of the exact value of LHA from the value of tab. LHA is equal to (+) 0°.7 × 28'.9/60' which equals (+) 0°.3.

The Dec. is interpolated from 18° (Z 76°.8) to 17° (Z 77°.6), indicating a change of (+) 0°.8 for a change of 60' in the entering value of Dec. This is known as the "Dec. diff." Since the exact value of Dec. is 17°58'.7 and is 1'.3 less than the "tab." value of Dec., the difference in the value of Z corresponding to this variation in Dec. is only 1'.3/60' of the change for 60' change in Dec. Thus the "Dec. corr.," which is the correction to apply to the value of tab. Z for the variation of the exact value of Dec. from the value of tab. Dec., is equal to (+) 0°.8 × 1'.3/60', which, to the nearest tenth of a degree, equals 0°.0.

The L is interpolated from 41° (Z 76°.8) to 42° (Z 77°.1), indicating change of (+) 0°.3 in Z for a change of 1° (60') in the entering value of L. This is known as the "L diff." Since the exact value of L (41°07'.5) is 7'.5 greater than the "tab." value of L (41°), the difference in the value of Z corresponding to this change in L is only 7'.5/60 of the difference for a 1° change in L. Thus, "L corr.," which is the correction to apply to the value of Tab. Z for the variation of the exact value of L from the value of Tab. L, is equal to (+) 0°.3 × 7'.5/60', which equals (+) 0°.0.

By applying the algebraic sum of the LHA, Dec., and L corrections, as determined above, to the tab. Z, the value of the exact azimuth angle at the moment of observation is found to be N 77°.1 E, which converts to a Zn of 077°.1. The gyro error is determined by comparing this exact azimuth with that obtained by observation, 077°.5.

Answer: Gyro error 0°.4 W

In solving problems for exact azimuth using H. O. 229, the multiplication of the fractional amount by the amount of the "diff." to obtain the appropriate correction can be accomplished most readily by establishing a proportion with dividers on a log scale of speed or distance, such as is found on some charts and on Maneuvering Board paper, and is discussed briefly in article 1304. In establishing the fractions involved, it is well to remember that the denominator of the fractional part of LHA, Dec., and L is always 60', since the tabulated entering arguments of LHA, Dec., and L are always 1° apart.

1972 AUGUST 1, 2, 3 (TUES., WED., THURS.)

G.M.T.	ARIES G.H.A.	VENUS −4.2 G.H.A.	Dec.	MARS +2.0 G.H.A.	Dec.	JUPITER −2.1 G.H.A.	Dec.	SATURN +0.4 G.H.A.	Dec.	STARS Name	S.H.A.	Dec.
1 00	309 41.9	223 23.0	N18 35.1	165 50.0	N15 33.5	40 21.2	S23 20.6	233 21.0	N21 18.3	Acamar	315 41.5	S 40 24.4
01	324 44.4	238 23.7	35.2	180 50.9	33.0	55 23.9	20.6	248 23.3	18.3	Achernar	335 49.1	S 57 22.1
02	339 46.9	253 24.5	35.4	195 51.8	32.5	70 26.6	20.6	263 25.5	18.4	Acrux	173 44.3	S 62 57.2
03	354 49.3	268 25.3 ..	35.5	210 52.7 ..	32.0	85 29.2 ..	20.6	278 27.7 ..	18.4	Adhara	255 36.9	S 28 55.9
04	9 51.8	283 26.0	35.7	225 53.6	31.5	100 31.9	20.6	293 29.9	18.4	Aldebaran	291 24.7	N 16 27.4
05	24 54.3	298 26.8	35.9	240 54.5	30.9	115 34.6	20.6	308 32.1	18.4			
T 06	39 56.7	313 27.5	N18 36.0	255 55.4	N15 30.4	130 37.2	S23 20.6	323 34.3	N21 18.4	Alioth	166 47.5	N 56 06.7
U 07	54 59.2	328 28.3	36.2	270 56.3	29.9	145 39.9	20.6	338 36.5	18.5	Alkaid	153 22.9	N 49 27.2
E 08	70 01.7	343 29.0	36.4	285 57.2	29.4	160 42.5	20.6	353 38.7	18.5	Al Na'ir	28 21.5	S 47 05.4
S 09	85 04.1	358 29.8 ..	36.5	300 58.1 ..	28.9	175 45.2 ..	20.6	8 40.9 ..	18.5	Alnilam	276 17.7	S 1 12.9
D 10	100 06.6	13 30.5	36.7	315 59.1	28.4	190 47.9	20.6	23 43.1	18.5	Alphard	218 26.5	S 8 32.3
A 11	115 09.0	28 31.3	36.8	331 00.0	27.9	205 50.5	20.6	38 45.3	18.5			
Y 12	130 11.5	43 32.0	N18 37.0	346 00.9	N15 27.3	220 53.2	S23 20.6	53 47.5	N21 18.6	Alphecca	126 36.8	N 26 48.5
13	145 14.0	58 32.7	37.2	1 01.8	26.8	235 55.8	20.6	68 49.7	18.6	Alpheratz	358 15.1	N 28 56.4
14	160 16.4	73 33.5	37.3	16 02.7	26.3	250 58.5	20.6	83 51.9	18.6	Altair	62 37.8	N 8 47.8
15	175 18.9	88 34.2 ..	37.5	31 03.6 ..	25.8	266 01.2 ..	20.7	98 54.1 ..	18.6	Ankaa	353 45.5	S 42 26.9
16	190 21.4	103 35.0	37.7	46 04.5	25.3	281 03.8	20.7	113 56.3	18.6	Antares	113 03.7	S 26 22.5
17	205 23.8	118 35.7	37.8	61 05.4	24.8	296 06.5	20.7	128 58.6	18.7			
18	220 26.3	133 36.4	N18 38.0	76 06.3	N15 24.2	311 09.1	S23 20.7	144 00.8	N21 18.7	Arcturus	146 23.6	N 19 19.5
19	235 28.8	148 37.1	38.1	91 07.3	23.7	326 11.8	20.7	159 03.0	18.7	Atria	108 32.8	S 68 59.1
20	250 31.2	163 37.9	38.3	106 08.2	23.2	341 14.4	20.7	174 05.2	18.7	Avior	234 31.3	S 59 25.2
21	265 33.7	178 38.6 ..	38.5	121 09.1 ..	22.7	356 17.1 ..	20.7	189 07.4 ..	18.7	Bellatrix	279 05.1	N 6 19.7
22	280 36.2	193 39.3	38.6	136 10.0	22.2	11 19.8	20.7	204 09.6	18.8	Betelgeuse	271 34.7	N 7 24.3
23	295 38.6	208 40.0	38.8	151 10.9	21.6	26 22.4	20.7	219 11.8	18.8			
2 00	310 41.1	223 40.7	N18 39.0	166 11.8	N15 21.1	41 25.1	S23 20.7	234 14.0	N21 18.8	Canopus	264 10.2	S 52 40.6
01	325 43.5	238 41.4	39.1	181 12.7	20.6	56 27.7	20.7	249 16.2	18.8	Capella	281 20.1	N 45 58.3
02	340 46.0	253 42.2	39.3	196 13.6	20.1	71 30.4	20.7	264 18.4	18.8	Deneb	49 52.0	N 45 11.0
03	355 48.5	268 42.9 ..	39.4	211 14.6 ..	19.6	86 33.0 ..	20.7	279 20.6 ..	18.9	Denebola	183 05.0	N 14 43.6
04	10 50.9	283 43.6	39.6	226 15.5	19.1	101 35.7	20.7	294 22.8	18.9	Diphda	349 26.4	S 18 07.9
05	25 53.4	298 44.3	39.8	241 16.4	18.5	116 38.3	20.7	309 25.0	18.9			
W 06	40 55.9	313 45.0	N18 39.9	256 17.3	N15 18.0	131 41.0	S23 20.8	324 27.3	N21 18.9	Dubhe	194 29.4	N 61 54.1
E 07	55 58.3	328 45.7	40.1	271 18.2	17.5	146 43.7	20.8	339 29.5	18.9	Elnath	278 51.6	N 28 35.2
D 08	71 00.8	343 46.4	40.2	286 19.1	17.0	161 46.3	20.8	354 31.7	19.0	Eltanin	91 00.0	N 51 29.6
N 09	86 03.3	358 47.1 ..	40.4	301 20.0 ..	16.5	176 49.0 ..	20.7	9 33.9 ..	19.0	Enif	34 16.9	N 9 45.0
E 10	101 05.7	13 47.8	40.6	316 21.0	15.9	191 51.6	20.7	24 36.1	19.0	Fomalhaut	15 57.3	S 29 45.8
S 11	116 08.2	28 48.5	40.7	331 21.9	15.4	206 54.3	20.8	39 38.3	19.0			
D 12	131 10.7	43 49.2	N18 40.9	346 22.8	N15 14.9	221 56.9	S23 20.8	54 40.5	N21 19.0	Gacrux	172 35.6	S 56 57.9
A 13	146 13.1	58 49.9	41.1	1 23.7	14.4	236 59.6	20.8	69 42.7	19.1	Gienah	176 24.1	S 17 23.5
Y 14	161 15.6	73 50.5	41.2	16 24.6	13.9	252 02.2	20.8	84 44.9	19.1	Hadar	149 31.7	S 60 14.9
15	176 18.0	88 51.2 ..	41.4	31 25.5 ..	13.3	267 04.9 ..	20.8	99 47.1 ..	19.1	Hamal	328 35.4	N 23 20.1
16	191 20.5	103 51.9	41.5	46 26.4	12.8	282 07.5	20.8	114 49.3	19.1	Kaus Aust.	84 24.1	S 34 24.0
17	206 23.0	118 52.6	41.7	61 27.4	12.3	297 10.2	20.8	129 51.6	19.1			
18	221 25.4	133 53.3	N18 41.9	76 28.3	N15 11.8	312 12.8	S23 20.8	144 53.8	N21 19.2	Kochab	137 18.2	N 74 16.3
19	236 27.9	148 54.0	42.0	91 29.2	11.3	327 15.5	20.8	159 56.0	19.2	Markab	14 08.6	N 15 03.6
20	251 30.4	163 54.6	42.2	106 30.1	10.7	342 18.1	20.8	174 58.2	19.2	Menkar	314 47.1	N 3 59.2
21	266 32.8	178 55.3 ..	42.3	121 31.0 ..	10.2	357 20.8 ..	20.8	190 00.4 ..	19.2	Menkent	148 43.9	S 36 14.4
22	281 35.3	193 56.0	42.5	136 31.9	09.7	12 23.4	20.8	205 02.6	19.2	Miaplacidus	221 47.4	S 69 36.3
23	296 37.8	208 56.6	42.7	151 32.8	09.2	27 26.1	20.8	220 04.8	19.3			
3 00	311 40.2	223 57.3	N18 42.8	166 33.8	N15 08.6	42 28.7	S23 20.8	235 07.0	N21 19.3	Mirfak	309 24.5	N 49 45.8
01	326 42.7	238 58.0	43.0	181 34.7	08.1	57 31.4	20.8	250 09.2	19.3	Nunki	76 35.9	S 26 20.0
02	341 45.1	253 58.6	43.1	196 35.6	07.6	72 34.0	20.8	265 11.4	19.3	Peacock	54 06.6	S 56 49.4
03	356 47.6	268 59.3 ..	43.3	211 36.5 ..	07.1	87 36.7 ..	20.8	280 13.7 ..	19.3	Pollux	244 05.4	N 28 05.7
04	11 50.1	284 00.0	43.5	226 37.4	06.6	102 39.3	20.8	295 15.9	19.4	Procyon	245 32.1	N 5 17.9
05	26 52.5	299 00.6	43.6	241 38.3	06.0	117 42.0	20.8	310 18.1	19.4			
T 06	41 55.0	314 01.3	N18 43.8	256 39.3	N15 05.5	132 44.6	S23 20.8	325 20.3	N21 19.4	Rasalhague	96 34.6	N 12 34.8
H 07	56 57.5	329 01.9	43.9	271 40.2	05.0	147 47.2	20.9	340 22.5	19.4	Regulus	208 16.3	N 12 06.2
U 08	71 59.9	344 02.6	44.1	286 41.1	04.5	162 49.9	20.9	355 24.7	19.4	Rigel	281 41.7	S 8 13.7
R 09	87 02.4	359 03.2 ..	44.3	301 42.0 ..	03.9	177 52.5 ..	20.9	10 26.9 ..	19.5	Rigil Kent.	140 33.7	S 60 43.7
S 10	102 04.9	14 03.9	44.4	316 42.9	03.4	192 55.2	20.9	25 29.1	19.5	Sabik	102 47.5	S 15 41.6
D 11	117 07.3	29 04.5	44.6	331 43.8	02.9	207 57.8	20.9	40 31.3	19.5			
A 12	132 09.8	44 05.2	N18 44.7	346 44.8	N15 02.4	223 00.5	S23 20.9	55 33.6	N21 19.5	Schedar	350 15.4	N 56 23.2
Y 13	147 12.3	59 05.8	44.9	1 45.7	01.8	238 03.1	20.9	70 35.8	19.5	Shaula	97 03.2	S 37 05.3
14	162 14.7	74 06.5	45.1	16 46.6	01.3	253 05.8	20.9	85 38.0	19.5	Sirius	259 01.0	S 16 40.5
15	177 17.2	89 07.1 ..	45.2	31 47.5 ..	00.8	268 08.4 ..	20.9	100 40.2 ..	19.6	Spica	159 03.7	S 11 01.2
16	192 19.6	104 07.7	45.4	46 48.4	15 00.3	283 11.0	20.9	115 42.4	19.6	Suhail	223 15.5	S 43 19.3
17	207 22.1	119 08.4	45.5	61 49.3	14 59.7	298 13.7	20.9	130 44.6	19.6			
18	222 24.6	134 09.0	N18 45.7	76 50.3	N14 59.2	313 16.3	S23 20.9	145 46.8	N21 19.6	Vega	80 59.3	N 38 45.6
19	237 27.0	149 09.6	45.9	91 51.2	58.7	328 19.0	20.9	160 49.0	19.6	Zuben'ubi	137 39.4	S 15 55.9
20	252 29.5	164 10.3	46.0	106 52.1	58.2	343 21.6	20.9	175 51.3	19.7		S.H.A.	Mer. Pass.
21	267 32.0	179 10.9 ..	46.2	121 53.0 ..	57.6	358 24.3 ..	20.9	190 53.5 ..	19.7	Venus	272 59.7	9 05
22	282 34.4	194 11.5	46.3	136 53.9	57.1	13 26.9	20.9	205 55.7	19.7	Mars	215 30.7	12 54
23	297 36.9	209 12.1	46.5	151 54.8	56.6	28 29.5	20.9	220 57.9	19.7	Jupiter	90 44.0	21 11
Mer. Pass.	3 16.7	v 0.7	d 0.2	v 0.9	d 0.5	v 2.7	d 0.0	v 2.2	d 0.0	Saturn	283 32.9	8 22

Extract from the Nautical Almanac.

1972 AUGUST 1, 2, 3 (TUES., WED., THURS.)

G.M.T.	SUN G.H.A.	Dec.	MOON G.H.A.	v	Dec.	d	H.P.
d h	° ′	° ′	° ′	′	° ′	′	′
1 00	178 26.0	N18 03.2	292 09.2	10.1	N13 07.2	13.7	59.1
01	193 26.0	02.6	306 38.3	10.1	13 20.9	13.5	59.1
02	208 26.0	02.0	321 07.4	9.9	13 34.4	13.5	59.1
03	223 26.1	·· 01.3	335 36.3	9.9	13 47.9	13.4	59.1
04	238 26.1	00.7	350 05.2	9.9	14 01.3	13.3	59.1
05	253 26.2	18 00.1	4 34.1	9.7	14 14.6	13.3	59.1
06	268 26.2	N17 59.4	19 02.8	9.7	N14 27.9	13.2	59.1
T 07	283 26.2	58.8	33 31.5	9.6	14 41.1	13.1	59.1
U 08	298 26.3	58.2	48 00.1	9.5	14 54.2	13.0	59.1
E 09	313 26.3	·· 57.5	62 28.6	9.5	15 07.2	13.0	59.1
S 10	328 26.4	56.9	76 57.1	9.4	15 20.2	12.8	59.2
D 11	343 26.4	56.3	91 25.5	9.3	15 33.0	12.8	59.2
A 12	358 26.4	N17 55.7	105 53.8	9.2	N15 45.8	12.7	59.2
Y 13	13 26.5	55.0	120 22.0	9.1	15 58.5	12.6	59.2
14	28 26.5	54.4	134 50.1	9.1	16 11.1	12.5	59.2
15	43 26.6	·· 53.7	149 18.2	8.9	16 23.6	12.4	59.2
16	58 26.6	53.1	163 46.1	8.9	16 36.0	12.3	59.2
17	73 26.6	52.5	178 14.0	8.9	16 48.3	12.3	59.2
18	88 26.7	N17 51.8	192 41.9	8.7	N17 00.6	12.1	59.2
19	103 26.7	51.2	207 09.6	8.6	17 12.7	12.1	59.2
20	118 26.8	50.6	221 37.2	8.6	17 24.8	11.9	59.2
21	133 26.8	·· 49.9	236 04.8	8.5	17 36.7	11.8	59.2
22	148 26.9	49.3	250 32.3	8.4	17 48.5	11.8	59.2
23	163 26.9	48.6	264 59.7	8.3	18 00.3	11.6	59.2
2 00	178 26.9	N17 48.0	279 27.0	8.2	N18 11.9	11.6	59.2
01	193 27.0	47.4	293 54.2	8.2	18 23.5	11.4	59.3
02	208 27.0	46.7	308 21.4	8.0	18 34.9	11.3	59.3
03	223 27.1	·· 46.1	322 48.4	8.0	18 46.2	11.2	59.3
04	238 27.1	45.4	337 15.4	7.9	18 57.4	11.1	59.3
05	253 27.2	44.8	351 42.3	7.8	19 08.5	11.0	59.3
06	268 27.2	N17 44.2	6 09.1	7.7	N19 19.5	10.9	59.3
W 07	283 27.2	43.5	20 35.8	7.6	19 30.4	10.7	59.3
E 08	298 27.3	42.9	35 02.4	7.6	19 41.1	10.7	59.3
D 09	313 27.3	·· 42.2	49 29.0	7.4	19 51.8	10.5	59.3
N 10	328 27.4	41.6	63 55.4	7.4	20 02.3	10.4	59.3
E 11	343 27.4	40.9	78 21.8	7.3	20 12.7	10.3	59.3
S 12	358 27.5	N17 40.3	92 48.1	7.2	N20 23.0	10.1	59.3
D 13	13 27.5	39.6	107 14.3	7.1	20 33.1	10.1	59.3
A 14	28 27.6	39.0	121 40.4	7.0	20 43.2	9.9	59.3
Y 15	43 27.6	·· 38.4	136 06.4	7.0	20 53.1	9.8	59.3
16	58 27.7	37.7	150 32.4	6.9	21 02.9	9.6	59.3
17	73 27.7	37.1	164 58.3	6.7	21 12.5	9.5	59.3
18	88 27.8	N17 36.4	179 24.0	6.7	N21 22.0	9.4	59.3
19	103 27.8	35.8	193 49.7	6.7	21 31.4	9.3	59.3
20	118 27.9	35.1	208 15.4	6.5	21 40.7	9.1	59.3
21	133 27.9	·· 34.5	222 40.9	6.4	21 49.8	9.0	59.3
22	148 27.9	33.8	237 06.3	6.4	21 58.8	8.8	59.3
23	163 28.0	33.2	251 31.7	6.3	22 07.6	8.7	59.3
3 00	178 28.0	N17 32.5	265 57.0	6.2	N22 16.3	8.6	59.3
01	193 28.1	31.9	280 22.2	6.1	22 24.9	8.4	59.4
02	208 28.1	31.2	294 47.3	6.1	22 33.3	8.3	59.4
03	223 28.2	·· 30.6	309 12.4	5.9	22 41.6	8.1	59.4
04	238 28.2	29.9	323 37.3	5.9	22 49.7	8.0	59.4
05	253 28.3	29.2	338 02.2	5.8	22 57.7	7.9	59.4
06	268 28.3	N17 28.6	352 27.0	5.8	N23 05.6	7.7	59.4
T 07	283 28.4	27.9	6 51.8	5.7	23 13.3	7.5	59.4
H 08	298 28.4	27.3	21 16.5	5.5	23 20.8	7.4	59.4
U 09	313 28.5	·· 26.6	35 41.0	5.6	23 28.2	7.3	59.4
R 10	328 28.6	26.0	50 05.6	5.4	23 35.5	7.0	59.4
S 11	343 28.6	25.3	64 30.0	5.4	23 42.5	7.0	59.4
D 12	358 28.7	N17 24.7	78 54.4	5.3	N23 49.5	6.8	59.4
A 13	13 28.7	24.0	93 18.7	5.2	23 56.3	6.6	59.4
Y 14	28 28.8	23.3	107 42.9	5.2	24 02.9	6.4	59.4
15	43 28.8	·· 22.7	122 07.1	5.1	24 09.3	6.3	59.4
16	58 28.9	22.0	136 31.2	5.1	24 15.6	6.2	59.4
17	73 28.9	21.4	150 55.3	5.0	24 21.8	6.0	59.4
18	88 29.0	N17 20.7	165 19.3	4.9	N24 27.8	5.8	59.4
19	103 29.0	20.0	179 43.2	4.8	24 33.6	5.7	59.4
20	118 29.1	19.4	194 07.0	4.8	24 39.3	5.4	59.4
21	133 29.1	·· 18.7	208 30.8	4.8	24 44.7	5.4	59.4
22	148 29.2	18.0	222 54.6	4.7	24 50.1	5.1	59.4
23	163 29.2	17.4	237 18.3	4.6	24 55.2	5.0	59.4
S.D.	15.8	d 0.6	S.D. 16.1		16.2		16.2

Moonrise

Lat.	Twilight Naut.	Civil	Sunrise	Moonrise 1	2	3	4
°	h m	h m	h m	h m	h m	h m	h m
N 72	□	□	□	18 31	□	□	□
N 70	////	////	01 35	19 21	□	□	□
68	////	////	02 20	19 53	19 02	□	□
66	////	00 37	02 49	20 16	19 58	□	□
64	////	01 45	03 11	20 35	20 31	20 27	20 23
62	////	02 19	03 28	20 51	20 56	21 09	21 42
60	00 33	02 43	03 43	21 04	21 16	21 37	22 18
N 58	01 35	03 02	03 55	21 15	21 32	21 59	22 44
56	02 06	03 17	04 05	21 25	21 46	22 17	23 05
54	02 29	03 31	04 15	21 34	21 58	22 32	23 22
52	02 47	03 42	04 23	21 42	22 09	22 46	23 37
50	03 01	03 52	04 30	21 49	22 18	22 57	23 50
45	03 30	04 13	04 46	22 04	22 38	23 22	24 16
N 40	03 52	04 29	04 59	22 17	22 55	23 41	24 37
35	04 09	04 42	05 10	22 27	23 09	23 58	24 55
30	04 23	04 54	05 19	22 37	23 21	24 12	00 12
20	04 45	05 12	05 36	22 53	23 42	24 36	00 36
N 10	05 02	05 28	05 52	23 08	24 00	00 00	00 57
0	05 16	05 41	06 03	23 21	24 18	00 18	01 17
S 10	05 28	05 54	06 16	23 35	24 35	00 35	01 37
20	05 40	06 06	06 29	23 50	24 50	00 50	01 58
30	05 51	06 19	06 45	24 07	00 07	01 15	02 23
35	05 56	06 27	06 54	24 17	00 17	01 28	02 37
40	06 02	06 35	07 04	24 29	00 29	01 43	02 54
45	06 09	06 44	07 16	24 42	00 42	02 00	03 15
S 50	06 16	06 55	07 30	24 59	00 59	02 22	03 40
52	06 19	07 00	07 37	25 07	01 07	02 32	03 53
54	06 22	07 05	07 44	25 15	01 15	02 44	04 07
56	06 26	07 11	07 52	25 25	01 25	02 58	04 24
58	06 29	07 17	08 02	00 00	01 37	03 14	04 44
S 60	06 33	07 24	08 12	00 09	01 50	03 33	05 09

Moonset

Lat.	Sunset	Twilight Civil	Naut.	Moonset 1	2	3	4
°	h m	h m	h m	h m	h m	h m	h m
N 72	□	□	□	15 20	□	□	□
N 70	22 31	////	////	14 33	□	□	□
68	21 48	////	////	14 02	16 48	□	□
66	21 20	23 21	////	13 40	15 53	□	□
64	20 59	22 23	////	13 22	15 21	17 27	19 40
62	20 42	21 50	////	13 08	14 57	16 46	18 21
60	20 28	21 27	23 26	12 56	14 38	16 18	17 45
N 58	20 16	21 09	22 33	12 45	14 22	15 57	17 19
56	20 05	20 53	22 03	12 36	14 09	15 39	16 58
54	19 56	20 40	21 41	12 28	13 57	15 24	16 41
52	19 48	20 29	21 24	12 21	13 47	15 11	16 26
50	19 41	20 21	21 09	12 15	13 38	14 59	16 13
45	19 25	19 59	20 41	12 01	13 19	14 36	15 47
N 40	19 13	19 43	20 20	11 50	13 04	14 17	15 26
35	19 02	19 30	20 03	11 40	12 51	14 01	15 09
30	18 53	19 18	19 49	11 32	12 39	13 47	14 54
20	18 37	19 00	19 28	11 18	12 20	13 24	14 29
N 10	18 23	18 45	19 11	11 05	12 03	13 04	14 07
0	18 10	18 31	18 57	10 53	11 48	12 46	13 46
S 10	17 57	18 19	18 44	10 42	11 32	12 27	13 26
20	17 43	18 06	18 33	10 29	11 16	12 07	13 04
30	17 28	17 53	18 22	10 15	10 57	11 44	12 38
35	17 19	17 46	18 16	10 07	10 46	11 31	12 23
40	17 09	17 38	18 10	09 58	10 33	11 15	12 06
45	16 57	17 29	18 04	09 47	10 18	10 57	11 45
S 50	16 43	17 18	17 57	09 34	10 00	10 34	11 19
52	16 36	17 13	17 54	09 28	09 52	10 23	11 07
54	16 29	17 08	17 51	09 22	09 42	10 11	10 52
56	16 21	17 02	17 48	09 15	09 32	09 57	10 35
58	16 11	16 56	17 44	09 06	09 19	09 40	10 15
S 60	16 01	16 49	17 40	08 57	09 05	09 20	09 49

Day	SUN Eqn. of Time 00h	12h	Mer. Pass.	MOON Mer. Pass. Upper	Lower	Age	Phase
	m s	m s	h m	h m	h m	d	
1	06 16	06 14	12 06	04 41	17 07	22	
2	06 12	06 10	12 06	05 34	18 02	23	
3	06 08	06 05	12 06	06 31	19 01	24	◗

Extract from the Nautical Almanac.

ALTITUDE CORRECTION TABLES 10°–90°—SUN, STARS, PLANETS

OCT.—MAR. SUN APR.—SEPT.

App. Alt.	Lower Limb / Upper Limb (Oct.–Mar.)	App. Alt.	Lower Limb / Upper Limb (Apr.–Sept.)
9 34	+10.8 −21.5	9 39	+10.6 −21.2
9 45	+10.9 −21.4	9 51	+10.7 −21.1
9 56	+11.0 −21.3	10 03	+10.8 −21.0
10 08	+11.1 −21.2	10 15	+10.9 −20.9
10 21	+11.2 −21.1	10 27	+11.0 −20.8
10 34	+11.3 −21.0	10 40	+11.1 −20.7
10 47	+11.4 −20.9	10 54	+11.2 −20.6
11 01	+11.5 −20.8	11 08	+11.3 −20.5
11 15	+11.6 −20.7	11 23	+11.4 −20.4
11 30	+11.7 −20.6	11 38	+11.5 −20.3
11 46	+11.8 −20.5	11 54	+11.6 −20.2
12 02	+11.9 −20.4	12 10	+11.7 −20.1
12 19	+12.0 −20.3	12 28	+11.8 −20.0
12 37	+12.1 −20.2	12 46	+11.9 −19.9
12 55	+12.2 −20.1	13 05	+12.0 −19.8
13 14	+12.3 −20.0	13 24	+12.1 −19.7
13 35	+12.4 −19.9	13 45	+12.2 −19.6
13 56	+12.5 −19.8	14 07	+12.3 −19.5
14 18	+12.6 −19.7	14 30	+12.4 −19.4
14 42	+12.7 −19.6	14 54	+12.5 −19.3
15 06	+12.8 −19.5	15 19	+12.6 −19.2
15 32	+12.9 −19.4	15 46	+12.7 −19.1
15 59	+13.0 −19.3	16 14	+12.8 −19.0
16 28	+13.1 −19.2	16 44	+12.9 −18.9
16 59	+13.2 −19.1	17 15	+13.0 −18.8
17 32	+13.3 −19.0	17 48	+13.1 −18.7
18 06	+13.4 −18.9	18 24	+13.2 −18.6
18 42	+13.5 −18.8	19 01	+13.3 −18.5
19 21	+13.6 −18.7	19 42	+13.4 −18.4
20 03	+13.7 −18.6	20 25	+13.5 −18.3
20 48	+13.8 −18.5	21 11	+13.6 −18.2
21 35	+13.9 −18.4	22 00	+13.7 −18.1
22 26	+14.0 −18.3	22 54	+13.8 −18.0
23 22	+14.1 −18.2	23 51	+13.9 −17.9
24 21	+14.2 −18.1	24 53	+14.0 −17.8
25 26	+14.3 −18.0	26 00	+14.1 −17.7
26 36	+14.4 −17.9	27 13	+14.2 −17.6
27 52	+14.5 −17.8	28 33	+14.3 −17.5
29 15	+14.6 −17.7	30 00	+14.4 −17.4
30 46	+14.7 −17.6	31 35	+14.5 −17.3
32 26	+14.8 −17.5	33 20	+14.6 −17.2
34 17	+14.9 −17.4	35 17	+14.7 −17.1
36 20	+15.0 −17.3	37 26	+14.8 −17.0
38 36	+15.1 −17.2	39 50	+14.9 −16.9
41 08	+15.2 −17.1	42 31	+15.0 −16.8
43 59	+15.3 −17.0	45 31	+15.1 −16.7
47 10	+15.4 −16.9	48 55	+15.2 −16.6
50 46	+15.5 −16.8	52 44	+15.3 −16.5
54 49	+15.6 −16.7	57 02	+15.4 −16.4
59 23	+15.7 −16.6	61 51	+15.5 −16.3
64 30	+15.8 −16.5	67 17	+15.6 −16.2
70 12	+15.9 −16.4	73 16	+15.7 −16.1
76 26	+16.0 −16.3	79 43	+15.8 −16.0
83 05	+16.1 −16.2	86 32	+15.9 −15.9
90 00		90 00	

STARS AND PLANETS

App. Alt.	Corrn
9 56	−5.3
10 08	−5.2
10 20	−5.1
10 33	−5.0
10 46	−4.9
11 00	−4.8
11 14	−4.7
11 29	−4.6
11 45	−4.5
12 01	−4.4
12 18	−4.3
12 35	−4.2
12 54	−4.1
13 13	−4.0
13 33	−3.9
13 54	−3.8
14 16	−3.7
14 40	−3.6
15 04	−3.5
15 30	−3.4
15 57	−3.3
16 26	−3.2
16 56	−3.1
17 28	−3.0
18 02	−2.9
18 38	−2.8
19 17	−2.7
19 58	−2.6
20 42	−2.5
21 28	−2.4
22 19	−2.3
23 13	−2.2
24 11	−2.1
25 14	−2.0
26 22	−1.9
27 36	−1.8
28 56	−1.7
30 24	−1.6
32 00	−1.5
33 45	−1.4
35 40	−1.3
37 48	−1.2
40 08	−1.1
42 44	−1.0
45 36	−0.9
48 47	−0.8
52 18	−0.7
56 11	−0.6
60 28	−0.5
65 08	−0.4
70 11	−0.3
75 34	−0.2
81 13	−0.1
87 03	0.0
90 00	

App. Alt. / Additional Corrn

1972

VENUS

App. Alt.	Additional Corrn
Jan. 1–Feb. 29	
0°	
42	+0.1
Mar. 1–Apr. 15	
0°	
47	+0.2
Apr. 16–May 12	
0°	
46	+0.3
May 13–May 27	
0°	
11	+0.4
41	+0.5
May 28–June 5	
0°	
6	+0.5
20	+0.6
31	+0.7
June 6–June 29	
0°	
4	+0.6
12	+0.7
22	+0.8
June 30–July 8	
0°	
6	+0.5
20	+0.6
31	+0.7
July 9–July 24	
0°	
11	+0.4
41	+0.5
July 25–Aug. 19	
0°	
46	+0.3
Aug. 20–Oct. 5	
0°	
47	+0.2
Oct. 6–Dec. 31	
0°	
42	+0.1

MARS

App. Alt.	Additional Corrn
Jan. 1–Dec. 31	
0°	
60	+0.1

DIP

Ht. of Eye (m)	Corrn	Ht. of Eye (ft)	Ht. of Eye (m)	Corrn
2.4	−2.8	8.0	1.0	− 1.8
2.6	−2.8	8.6	1.5	− 2.2
2.8	−2.9	9.2	2.0	− 2.5
3.0	−3.0	9.8	2.5	− 2.8
3.2	−3.1	10.5	3.0	− 3.0
3.4	−3.2	11.2	See table	
3.6	−3.3	11.9		
3.8	−3.4	12.6	m	
4.0	−3.5	13.3	20	− 7.9
4.3	−3.6	14.1	22	− 8.3
4.5	−3.7	14.9	24	− 8.6
4.7	−3.8	15.7	26	− 9.0
5.0	−3.9	16.5	28	− 9.3
5.2	−4.0	17.4		
5.5	−4.1	18.3	30	− 9.6
5.8	−4.2	19.1	32	−10.0
6.1	−4.3	20.1	34	−10.3
6.3	−4.4	21.0	36	−10.6
6.6	−4.5	22.0	38	−10.8
6.9	−4.6	22.9		
7.2	−4.7	23.9	40	−11.1
7.5	−4.8	24.9	42	−11.4
7.9	−4.9	26.0	44	−11.7
8.2	−5.0	27.1	46	−11.9
8.5	−5.1	28.1	48	−12.2
8.8	−5.2	29.2		
9.2	−5.3	30.4	ft.	
9.5	−5.4	31.5	2	− 1.4
9.9	−5.5	32.7	4	− 1.9
10.3	−5.6	33.9	6	− 2.4
10.6	−5.7	35.1	8	− 2.7
11.0	−5.8	36.3	10	− 3.1
11.4	−5.9	37.6	See table	
11.8	−6.0	38.9		
12.2	−6.1	40.1	ft.	
12.6	−6.2	41.5	70	− 8.1
13.0	−6.3	42.8	75	− 8.4
13.4	−6.4	44.2	80	− 8.7
13.8	−6.5	45.5	85	− 8.9
14.2	−6.6	46.9	90	− 9.2
14.7	−6.7	48.4	95	− 9.5
15.1	−6.8	49.8		
15.5	−6.9	51.3	100	− 9.7
16.0	−7.0	52.8	105	− 9.9
16.5	−7.1	54.3	110	−10.2
16.9	−7.2	55.8	115	−10.4
17.4	−7.3	57.4	120	−10.6
17.9	−7.4	58.9	125	−10.8
18.4	−7.5	60.5		
18.8	−7.6	62.1	130	−11.1
19.3	−7.7	63.8	135	−11.3
19.8	−7.8	65.4	140	−11.5
20.4	−7.9	67.1	145	−11.7
20.9	−8.0	68.8	150	−11.9
21.4	−8.1	70.5	155	−12.1

App. Alt. = Apparent altitude = Sextant altitude corrected for index error and dip.

For daylight observations of Venus, see page 260.

ADDITIONAL REFRACTION CORRECTIONS FOR NON-STANDARD CONDITIONS

Temperature

| −20°F. | −10° | 0° | +10° | 20° | 30° | 40° | 50° | 60° | 70° | 80° | 90° | 100°F. |

| −30°C. | | −20° | | −10° | | 0° | | +10° | | 20° | | 30° | | 40°C. |

Pressure in millibars: 1050, 1030, 1010, 990, 970

Pressure in inches: 31·0, 30·5, 30·0, 29·5, 29·0

Zone letters (left to right): A B C D E F G H J K L M N

App. Alt.	A	B	C	D	E	F	G	H	J	K	L	M	N	App. Alt.
0 00	−6·9	−5·7	−4·6	−3·4	−2·3	−1·1	0·0	+1·1	+2·3	+3·4	+4·6	+5·7	+6·9	0 00
0 30	5·2	4·4	3·5	2·6	1·7	0·9	0·0	0·9	1·7	2·6	3·5	4·4	5·2	0 30
1 00	4·3	3·5	2·8	2·1	1·4	0·7	0·0	0·7	1·4	2·1	2·8	3·5	4·3	1 00
1 30	3·5	2·9	2·4	1·8	1·2	0·6	0·0	0·6	1·2	1·8	2·4	2·9	3·5	1 30
2 00	3·0	2·5	2·0	1·5	1·0	0·5	0·0	0·5	1·0	1·5	2·0	2·5	3·0	2 00
2 30	−2·5	−2·1	−1·6	−1·2	−0·8	−0·4	0·0	+0·4	+0·8	+1·2	+1·6	+2·1	+2·5	2 30
3 00	2·2	1·8	1·5	1·1	0·7	0·4	0·0	0·4	0·7	1·1	1·5	1·8	2·2	3 00
3 30	2·0	1·6	1·3	1·0	0·7	0·3	0·0	0·3	0·7	1·0	1·3	1·6	2·0	3 30
4 00	1·8	1·5	1·2	0·9	0·6	0·3	0·0	0·3	0·6	0·9	1·2	1·5	1·8	4 00
4 30	1·6	1·4	1·1	0·8	0·5	0·3	0·0	0·3	0·5	0·8	1·1	1·4	1·6	4 30
5 00	−1·5	−1·3	−1·0	−0·8	−0·5	−0·2	0·0	+0·2	+0·5	+0·8	+1·0	+1·3	+1·5	5 00
6	1·3	1·1	0·9	0·6	0·4	0·2	0·0	0·2	0·4	0·6	0·9	1·1	1·3	6
7	1·1	0·9	0·7	0·6	0·4	0·2	0·0	0·2	0·4	0·6	0·7	0·9	1·1	7
8	1·0	0·8	0·7	0·5	0·3	0·2	0·0	0·2	0·3	0·5	0·7	0·8	1·0	8
9	0·9	0·7	0·6	0·4	0·3	0·1	0·0	0·1	0·3	0·4	0·6	0·7	0·9	9
10 00	−0·8	−0·7	−0·5	−0·4	−0·3	−0·1	0·0	+0·1	+0·3	+0·4	+0·5	+0·7	+0·8	10 00
12	0·7	0·6	0·5	0·3	0·2	0·1	0·0	0·1	0·2	0·3	0·5	0·6	0·7	12
14	0·6	0·5	0·4	0·3	0·2	0·1	0·0	0·1	0·2	0·3	0·4	0·5	0·6	14
16	0·5	0·4	0·3	0·3	0·2	0·1	0·0	0·1	0·2	0·3	0·3	0·4	0·5	16
18	0·4	0·4	0·3	0·2	0·2	0·1	0·0	0·1	0·2	0·2	0·3	0·4	0·4	18
20 00	−0·4	−0·3	−0·3	−0·2	−0·1	−0·1	0·0	+0·1	+0·1	+0·2	+0·3	+0·3	+0·4	20 00
25	0·3	0·3	0·2	0·2	0·1	−0·1	0·0	+0·1	0·1	0·2	0·2	0·3	0·3	25
30	0·3	0·2	0·2	0·1	0·1	0·0	0·0	0·0	0·1	0·1	0·2	0·2	0·3	30
35	0·2	0·2	0·1	0·1	0·1	0·0	0·0	0·0	0·1	0·1	0·1	0·2	0·2	35
40	0·2	0·1	0·1	0·1	−0·1	0·0	0·0	0·0	+0·1	0·1	0·1	0·1	0·2	40
50 00	−0·1	−0·1	−0·1	−0·1	0·0	0·0	0·0	0·0	0·0	+0·1	+0·1	+0·1	+0·1	50 00

The graph is entered with arguments temperature and pressure to find a zone letter; using as arguments this zone letter and apparent altitude (sextant altitude corrected for dip), a correction is taken from the table. This correction is to be applied to the sextant altitude in addition to the corrections for standard conditions (for the Sun, stars and planets from page A2 and for the Moon from pages xxxiv and xxxv).

ALTITUDE CORRECTION TABLES 35°-90°—MOON

App. Alt.	35°–39° Corrⁿ	40°–44° Corrⁿ	45°–49° Corrⁿ	50°–54° Corrⁿ	55°–59° Corrⁿ	60°–64° Corrⁿ	65°–69° Corrⁿ	70°–74° Corrⁿ	75°–79° Corrⁿ	80°–84° Corrⁿ	85°–89° Corrⁿ	App. Alt.
00	35 56·5	40 53·7	45 50·5	50 46·9	55 43·1	60 38·9	65 34·6	70 30·1	75 25·3	80 20·5	85 15·6	00
10	56·4	53·6	50·4	46·8	42·9	38·8	34·4	29·9	25·2	20·4	15·5	10
20	56·3	53·5	50·2	46·7	42·8	38·7	34·3	29·7	25·0	20·2	15·3	20
30	56·2	53·4	50·1	46·5	42·7	38·5	34·1	29·6	24·9	20·0	15·1	30
40	56·2	53·3	50·0	46·4	42·5	38·4	34·0	29·4	24·7	19·9	15·0	40
50	56·1	53·2	49·9	46·3	42·4	38·2	33·8	29·3	24·5	19·7	14·8	50
00	36 56·0	41 53·1	46 49·8	51 46·2	56 42·3	61 38·1	66 33·7	71 29·1	76 24·4	81 19·6	86 14·6	00
10	55·9	53·0	49·7	46·0	42·1	37·9	33·5	29·0	24·2	19·4	14·5	10
20	55·8	52·8	49·5	45·9	42·0	37·8	33·4	28·8	24·1	19·2	14·3	20
30	55·7	52·7	49·4	45·8	41·8	37·7	33·2	28·7	23·9	19·1	14·1	30
40	55·6	52·6	49·3	45·7	41·7	37·5	33·1	28·5	23·8	18·9	14·0	40
50	55·5	52·5	49·2	45·5	41·6	37·4	32·9	28·3	23·6	18·7	13·8	50
00	37 55·4	42 52·4	47 49·1	52 45·4	57 41·4	62 37·2	67 32·8	72 28·2	77 23·4	82 18·6	87 13·7	00
10	55·3	52·3	49·0	45·3	41·3	37·1	32·6	28·0	23·3	18·4	13·5	10
20	55·2	52·2	48·8	45·2	41·2	36·9	32·5	27·9	23·1	18·2	13·3	20
30	55·1	52·1	48·7	45·0	41·0	36·8	32·3	27·7	22·9	18·1	13·2	30
40	55·0	52·0	48·6	44·9	40·9	36·6	32·2	27·6	22·8	17·9	13·0	40
50	55·0	51·9	48·5	44·8	40·8	36·5	32·0	27·4	22·6	17·8	12·8	50
00	38 54·9	43 51·8	48 48·4	53 44·6	58 40·6	63 36·4	68 31·9	73 27·2	78 22·5	83 17·6	88 12·7	00
10	54·8	51·7	48·2	44·5	40·5	36·2	31·7	27·1	22·3	17·4	12·5	10
20	54·7	51·6	48·1	44·4	40·3	36·1	31·6	26·9	22·1	17·3	12·3	20
30	54·6	51·5	48·0	44·2	40·2	35·9	31·4	26·8	22·0	17·1	12·2	30
40	54·5	51·4	47·9	44·1	40·1	35·8	31·3	26·6	21·8	16·9	12·0	40
50	54·4	51·2	47·8	44·0	39·9	35·6	31·1	26·5	21·7	16·8	11·8	50
00	39 54·3	44 51·1	49 47·6	54 43·9	59 39·8	64 35·5	69 31·0	74 26·3	79 21·5	84 16·6	89 11·7	00
10	54·2	51·0	47·5	43·7	39·6	35·3	30·8	26·1	21·3	16·5	11·5	10
20	54·1	50·9	47·4	43·6	39·5	35·2	30·7	26·0	21·2	16·3	11·4	20
30	54·0	50·8	47·3	43·5	39·4	35·0	30·5	25·8	21·0	16·1	11·2	30
40	53·9	50·7	47·2	43·3	39·2	34·9	30·4	25·7	20·9	16·0	11·0	40
50	53·8	50·6	47·0	43·2	39·1	34·7	30·2	25·5	20·7	15·8	10·9	50

H.P.	L	U	L	U	L	U	L	U	L	U	L	U	L	U	L	U	L	U	L	U	L	U	H.P.
54·0	1·1	1·7	1·3	1·9	1·5	2·1	1·7	2·4	2·0	2·6	2·3	2·9	2·6	3·2	2·9	3·5	3·2	3·8	3·5	4·1	3·8	4·5	54·0
54·3	1·4	1·8	1·6	2·0	1·8	2·2	2·0	2·5	2·3	2·7	2·5	3·0	2·8	3·2	3·0	3·5	3·3	3·8	3·6	4·1	3·9	4·4	54·3
54·6	1·7	2·0	1·9	2·2	2·1	2·4	2·3	2·6	2·5	2·8	2·7	3·0	3·0	3·3	3·2	3·5	3·5	3·8	3·7	4·1	4·0	4·3	54·6
54·9	2·0	2·2	2·2	2·3	2·3	2·5	2·5	2·7	2·7	2·9	2·9	3·1	3·2	3·3	3·4	3·5	3·6	3·8	3·9	4·0	4·1	4·3	54·9
55·2	2·3	2·3	2·5	2·4	2·6	2·6	2·8	2·8	3·0	2·9	3·2	3·1	3·4	3·3	3·6	3·5	3·8	3·7	4·0	4·0	4·2	4·2	55·2
55·5	2·7	2·5	2·8	2·6	2·9	2·7	3·1	2·9	3·2	3·0	3·4	3·2	3·6	3·4	3·7	3·5	3·9	3·7	4·1	3·9	4·3	4·1	55·5
55·8	3·0	2·6	3·1	2·7	3·2	2·8	3·3	3·0	3·5	3·1	3·6	3·3	3·8	3·4	3·9	3·6	4·1	3·7	4·2	3·9	4·4	4·0	55·8
56·1	3·3	2·8	3·4	2·9	3·5	3·0	3·6	3·1	3·7	3·2	3·8	3·3	4·0	3·4	4·1	3·6	4·2	3·7	4·4	3·8	4·5	4·0	56·1
56·4	3·6	2·9	3·7	3·0	3·8	3·1	3·9	3·2	3·9	3·3	4·0	3·4	4·1	3·5	4·3	3·6	4·4	3·7	4·5	3·8	4·6	3·9	56·4
56·7	3·9	3·1	4·0	3·1	4·1	3·2	4·1	3·3	4·2	3·3	4·3	3·4	4·3	3·5	4·4	3·6	4·5	3·7	4·6	3·8	4·7	3·8	56·7
57·0	4·3	3·2	4·3	3·3	4·3	3·3	4·4	3·4	4·4	3·4	4·5	3·5	4·5	3·5	4·6	3·6	4·7	3·6	4·7	3·7	4·8	3·8	57·0
57·3	4·6	3·4	4·6	3·4	4·6	3·4	4·6	3·5	4·7	3·5	4·7	3·5	4·7	3·6	4·8	3·6	4·8	3·6	4·8	3·7	4·9	3·7	57·3
57·6	4·9	3·6	4·9	3·6	4·9	3·6	4·9	3·6	4·9	3·6	4·9	3·6	4·9	3·6	4·9	3·6	5·0	3·6	5·0	3·6	5·0	3·6	57·6
57·9	5·2	3·7	5·2	3·7	5·2	3·7	5·2	3·7	5·2	3·7	5·1	3·6	5·1	3·6	5·1	3·6	5·1	3·6	5·1	3·6	5·1	3·6	57·9
58·2	5·5	3·9	5·5	3·8	5·5	3·8	5·4	3·8	5·4	3·7	5·4	3·7	5·3	3·7	5·3	3·6	5·2	3·6	5·2	3·5	5·2	3·5	58·2
58·5	5·9	4·0	5·8	4·0	5·8	3·9	5·7	3·9	5·6	3·8	5·6	3·8	5·5	3·7	5·5	3·6	5·4	3·6	5·3	3·5	5·3	3·4	58·5
58·8	6·2	4·2	6·1	4·1	6·0	4·1	6·0	4·0	5·9	3·9	5·8	3·8	5·7	3·7	5·6	3·6	5·5	3·5	5·4	3·5	5·3	3·4	58·8
59·1	6·5	4·3	6·4	4·3	6·3	4·2	6·2	4·1	6·1	4·0	6·0	3·9	5·9	3·8	5·8	3·6	5·7	3·5	5·6	3·4	5·4	3·3	59·1
59·4	6·8	4·5	6·7	4·4	6·6	4·3	6·5	4·2	6·4	4·1	6·2	3·9	6·1	3·8	6·0	3·7	5·8	3·5	5·7	3·4	5·5	3·2	59·4
59·7	7·1	4·6	7·0	4·5	6·9	4·4	6·8	4·3	6·6	4·1	6·5	4·0	6·3	3·8	6·2	3·7	6·0	3·5	5·8	3·3	5·6	3·2	59·7
60·0	7·5	4·8	7·3	4·7	7·2	4·5	7·0	4·4	6·9	4·2	6·7	4·0	6·5	3·9	6·3	3·7	6·1	3·5	5·9	3·3	5·7	3·1	60·0
60·3	7·8	5·0	7·6	4·8	7·5	4·7	7·3	4·5	7·1	4·3	6·9	4·1	6·7	3·9	6·5	3·7	6·3	3·5	6·0	3·2	5·8	3·0	60·3
60·6	8·1	5·1	7·9	5·0	7·7	4·8	7·6	4·6	7·3	4·4	7·1	4·2	6·9	3·9	6·7	3·7	6·4	3·4	6·2	3·2	5·9	2·9	60·6
60·9	8·4	5·3	8·2	5·1	8·0	4·9	7·8	4·7	7·6	4·5	7·3	4·2	7·1	4·0	6·8	3·7	6·6	3·4	6·3	3·2	6·0	2·9	60·9
61·2	8·7	5·4	8·5	5·2	8·3	5·0	8·1	4·8	7·8	4·5	7·6	4·3	7·3	4·0	7·0	3·7	6·7	3·4	6·4	3·1	6·1	2·8	61·2
61·5	9·1	5·6	8·8	5·4	8·6	5·1	8·3	4·9	8·1	4·6	7·8	4·3	7·5	4·0	7·2	3·7	6·9	3·4	6·5	3·1	6·2	2·7	61·5

10ᵐ

10 ᵐ (s)	SUN PLANETS	ARIES	MOON	v or Corrⁿ d		v or Corrⁿ d		v or Corrⁿ d	
00	2 30·0	2 30·4	2 23·2	0·0	0·0	6·0	1·1	12·0	2·1
01	2 30·3	2 30·7	2 23·4	0·1	0·0	6·1	1·1	12·1	2·1
02	2 30·5	2 30·9	2 23·6	0·2	0·0	6·2	1·1	12·2	2·1
03	2 30·8	2 31·2	2 23·9	0·3	0·1	6·3	1·1	12·3	2·2
04	2 31·0	2 31·4	2 24·1	0·4	0·1	6·4	1·1	12·4	2·2
05	2 31·3	2 31·7	2 24·4	0·5	0·1	6·5	1·1	12·5	2·2
06	2 31·5	2 31·9	2 24·6	0·6	0·1	6·6	1·2	12·6	2·2
07	2 31·8	2 32·2	2 24·8	0·7	0·1	6·7	1·2	12·7	2·2
08	2 32·0	2 32·4	2 25·1	0·8	0·1	6·8	1·2	12·8	2·2
09	2 32·3	2 32·7	2 25·3	0·9	0·2	6·9	1·2	12·9	2·3
10	2 32·5	2 32·9	2 25·6	1·0	0·2	7·0	1·2	13·0	2·3
11	2 32·8	2 33·2	2 25·8	1·1	0·2	7·1	1·2	13·1	2·3
12	2 33·0	2 33·4	2 26·0	1·2	0·2	7·2	1·3	13·2	2·3
13	2 33·3	2 33·7	2 26·3	1·3	0·2	7·3	1·3	13·3	2·3
14	2 33·5	2 33·9	2 26·5	1·4	0·2	7·4	1·3	13·4	2·3
15	2 33·8	2 34·2	2 26·7	1·5	0·3	7·5	1·3	13·5	2·4
16	2 34·0	2 34·4	2 27·0	1·6	0·3	7·6	1·3	13·6	2·4
17	2 34·3	2 34·7	2 27·2	1·7	0·3	7·7	1·3	13·7	2·4
18	2 34·5	2 34·9	2 27·5	1·8	0·3	7·8	1·4	13·8	2·4
19	2 34·8	2 35·2	2 27·7	1·9	0·3	7·9	1·4	13·9	2·4
20	2 35·0	2 35·4	2 27·9	2·0	0·4	8·0	1·4	14·0	2·5
21	2 35·3	2 35·7	2 28·2	2·1	0·4	8·1	1·4	14·1	2·5
22	2 35·5	2 35·9	2 28·4	2·2	0·4	8·2	1·4	14·2	2·5
23	2 35·8	2 36·2	2 28·7	2·3	0·4	8·3	1·5	14·3	2·5
24	2 36·0	2 36·4	2 28·9	2·4	0·4	8·4	1·5	14·4	2·5
25	2 36·3	2 36·7	2 29·1	2·5	0·4	8·5	1·5	14·5	2·5
26	2 36·5	2 36·9	2 29·4	2·6	0·5	8·6	1·5	14·6	2·6
27	2 36·8	2 37·2	2 29·6	2·7	0·5	8·7	1·5	14·7	2·6
28	2 37·0	2 37·4	2 29·8	2·8	0·5	8·8	1·5	14·8	2·6
29	2 37·3	2 37·7	2 30·1	2·9	0·5	8·9	1·6	14·9	2·6
30	2 37·5	2 37·9	2 30·3	3·0	0·5	9·0	1·6	15·0	2·6
31	2 37·8	2 38·2	2 30·6	3·1	0·5	9·1	1·6	15·1	2·6
32	2 38·0	2 38·4	2 30·8	3·2	0·6	9·2	1·6	15·2	2·7
33	2 38·3	2 38·7	2 31·0	3·3	0·6	9·3	1·6	15·3	2·7
34	2 38·5	2 38·9	2 31·3	3·4	0·6	9·4	1·6	15·4	2·7
35	2 38·8	2 39·2	2 31·5	3·5	0·6	9·5	1·7	15·5	2·7
36	2 39·0	2 39·4	2 31·8	3·6	0·6	9·6	1·7	15·6	2·7
37	2 39·3	2 39·7	2 32·0	3·7	0·6	9·7	1·7	15·7	2·7
38	2 39·5	2 39·9	2 32·2	3·8	0·7	9·8	1·7	15·8	2·8
39	2 39·8	2 40·2	2 32·5	3·9	0·7	9·9	1·7	15·9	2·8
40	2 40·0	2 40·4	2 32·7	4·0	0·7	10·0	1·8	16·0	2·8
41	2 40·3	2 40·7	2 32·9	4·1	0·7	10·1	1·8	16·1	2·8
42	2 40·5	2 40·9	2 33·2	4·2	0·7	10·2	1·8	16·2	2·8
43	2 40·8	2 41·2	2 33·4	4·3	0·8	10·3	1·8	16·3	2·9
44	2 41·0	2 41·4	2 33·7	4·4	0·8	10·4	1·8	16·4	2·9
45	2 41·3	2 41·7	2 33·9	4·5	0·8	10·5	1·8	16·5	2·9
46	2 41·5	2 41·9	2 34·1	4·6	0·8	10·6	1·9	16·6	2·9
47	2 41·8	2 42·2	2 34·4	4·7	0·8	10·7	1·9	16·7	2·9
48	2 42·0	2 42·4	2 34·6	4·8	0·8	10·8	1·9	16·8	2·9
49	2 42·3	2 42·7	2 34·9	4·9	0·9	10·9	1·9	16·9	3·0
50	2 42·5	2 42·9	2 35·1	5·0	0·9	11·0	1·9	17·0	3·0
51	2 42·8	2 43·2	2 35·3	5·1	0·9	11·1	1·9	17·1	3·0
52	2 43·0	2 43·4	2 35·6	5·2	0·9	11·2	2·0	17·2	3·0
53	2 43·3	2 43·7	2 35·8	5·3	0·9	11·3	2·0	17·3	3·0
54	2 43·5	2 43·9	2 36·1	5·4	0·9	11·4	2·0	17·4	3·0
55	2 43·8	2 44·2	2 36·3	5·5	1·0	11·5	2·0	17·5	3·1
56	2 44·0	2 44·4	2 36·5	5·6	1·0	11·6	2·0	17·6	3·1
57	2 44·3	2 44·7	2 36·8	5·7	1·0	11·7	2·0	17·7	3·1
58	2 44·5	2 45·0	2 37·0	5·8	1·0	11·8	2·1	17·8	3·1
59	2 44·8	2 45·2	2 37·2	5·9	1·0	11·9	2·1	17·9	3·1
60	2 45·0	2 45·5	2 37·5	6·0	1·1	12·0	2·1	18·0	3·2

11ᵐ

11 ᵐ (s)	SUN PLANETS	ARIES	MOON	v or Corrⁿ d		v or Corrⁿ d		v or Corrⁿ d	
00	2 45·0	2 45·5	2 37·5	0·0	0·0	6·0	1·2	12·0	2·3
01	2 45·3	2 45·7	2 37·7	0·1	0·0	6·1	1·2	12·1	2·3
02	2 45·5	2 46·0	2 38·0	0·2	0·0	6·2	1·2	12·2	2·3
03	2 45·8	2 46·2	2 38·2	0·3	0·1	6·3	1·2	12·3	2·4
04	2 46·0	2 46·5	2 38·4	0·4	0·1	6·4	1·2	12·4	2·4
05	2 46·3	2 46·7	2 38·7	0·5	0·1	6·5	1·2	12·5	2·4
06	2 46·5	2 47·0	2 38·9	0·6	0·1	6·6	1·3	12·6	2·4
07	2 46·8	2 47·2	2 39·2	0·7	0·1	6·7	1·3	12·7	2·4
08	2 47·0	2 47·5	2 39·4	0·8	0·2	6·8	1·3	12·8	2·5
09	2 47·3	2 47·7	2 39·6	0·9	0·2	6·9	1·3	12·9	2·5
10	2 47·5	2 48·0	2 39·9	1·0	0·2	7·0	1·3	13·0	2·5
11	2 47·8	2 48·2	2 40·1	1·1	0·2	7·1	1·4	13·1	2·5
12	2 48·0	2 48·5	2 40·3	1·2	0·2	7·2	1·4	13·2	2·5
13	2 48·3	2 48·7	2 40·6	1·3	0·2	7·3	1·4	13·3	2·5
14	2 48·5	2 49·0	2 40·8	1·4	0·3	7·4	1·4	13·4	2·6
15	2 48·8	2 49·2	2 41·1	1·5	0·3	7·5	1·4	13·5	2·6
16	2 49·0	2 49·5	2 41·3	1·6	0·3	7·6	1·5	13·6	2·6
17	2 49·3	2 49·7	2 41·5	1·7	0·3	7·7	1·5	13·7	2·6
18	2 49·5	2 50·0	2 41·8	1·8	0·3	7·8	1·5	13·8	2·6
19	2 49·8	2 50·2	2 42·0	1·9	0·4	7·9	1·5	13·9	2·7
20	2 50·0	2 50·5	2 42·3	2·0	0·4	8·0	1·5	14·0	2·7
21	2 50·3	2 50·7	2 42·5	2·1	0·4	8·1	1·6	14·1	2·7
22	2 50·5	2 51·0	2 42·7	2·2	0·4	8·2	1·6	14·2	2·7
23	2 50·8	2 51·2	2 43·0	2·3	0·4	8·3	1·6	14·3	2·7
24	2 51·0	2 51·5	2 43·2	2·4	0·5	8·4	1·6	14·4	2·8
25	2 51·3	2 51·7	2 43·4	2·5	0·5	8·5	1·6	14·5	2·8
26	2 51·5	2 52·0	2 43·7	2·6	0·5	8·6	1·6	14·6	2·8
27	2 51·8	2 52·2	2 43·9	2·7	0·5	8·7	1·7	14·7	2·8
28	2 52·0	2 52·5	2 44·2	2·8	0·5	8·8	1·7	14·8	2·8
29	2 52·3	2 52·7	2 44·4	2·9	0·6	8·9	1·7	14·9	2·9
30	2 52·5	2 53·0	2 44·6	3·0	0·6	9·0	1·7	15·0	2·9
31	2 52·8	2 53·2	2 44·9	3·1	0·6	9·1	1·7	15·1	2·9
32	2 53·0	2 53·5	2 45·1	3·2	0·6	9·2	1·8	15·2	2·9
33	2 53·3	2 53·7	2 45·4	3·3	0·6	9·3	1·8	15·3	2·9
34	2 53·5	2 54·0	2 45·6	3·4	0·7	9·4	1·8	15·4	3·0
35	2 53·8	2 54·2	2 45·8	3·5	0·7	9·5	1·8	15·5	3·0
36	2 54·0	2 54·5	2 46·1	3·6	0·7	9·6	1·8	15·6	3·0
37	2 54·3	2 54·7	2 46·3	3·7	0·7	9·7	1·9	15·7	3·0
38	2 54·5	2 55·0	2 46·6	3·8	0·7	9·8	1·9	15·8	3·0
39	2 54·8	2 55·2	2 46·8	3·9	0·7	9·9	1·9	15·9	3·0
40	2 55·0	2 55·5	2 47·0	4·0	0·8	10·0	1·9	16·0	3·1
41	2 55·3	2 55·7	2 47·3	4·1	0·8	10·1	1·9	16·1	3·1
42	2 55·5	2 56·0	2 47·5	4·2	0·8	10·2	2·0	16·2	3·1
43	2 55·8	2 56·2	2 47·7	4·3	0·8	10·3	2·0	16·3	3·1
44	2 56·0	2 56·5	2 48·0	4·4	0·8	10·4	2·0	16·4	3·1
45	2 56·3	2 56·7	2 48·2	4·5	0·9	10·5	2·0	16·5	3·2
46	2 56·5	2 57·0	2 48·5	4·6	0·9	10·6	2·0	16·6	3·2
47	2 56·8	2 57·2	2 48·7	4·7	0·9	10·7	2·1	16·7	3·2
48	2 57·0	2 57·5	2 48·9	4·8	0·9	10·8	2·1	16·8	3·2
49	2 57·3	2 57·7	2 49·2	4·9	0·9	10·9	2·1	16·9	3·2
50	2 57·5	2 58·0	2 49·4	5·0	1·0	11·0	2·1	17·0	3·3
51	2 57·8	2 58·2	2 49·7	5·1	1·0	11·1	2·1	17·1	3·3
52	2 58·0	2 58·5	2 49·9	5·2	1·0	11·2	2·2	17·2	3·3
53	2 58·3	2 58·7	2 50·1	5·3	1·0	11·3	2·2	17·3	3·3
54	2 58·5	2 59·0	2 50·4	5·4	1·0	11·4	2·2	17·4	3·3
55	2 58·8	2 59·2	2 50·6	5·5	1·1	11·5	2·2	17·5	3·4
56	2 59·0	2 59·5	2 50·8	5·6	1·1	11·6	2·2	17·6	3·4
57	2 59·3	2 59·7	2 51·1	5·7	1·1	11·7	2·2	17·7	3·4
58	2 59·5	3 00·0	2 51·3	5·8	1·1	11·8	2·3	17·8	3·4
59	2 59·8	3 00·2	2 51·6	5·9	1·1	11·9	2·3	17·9	3·4
60	3 00·0	3 00·5	2 51·8	6·0	1·2	12·0	2·3	18·0	3·5

47ᵐ	SUN PLANETS	ARIES	MOON	v or Corrⁿ d	v or Corrⁿ d	v or Corrⁿ d
s	° ′	° ′	° ′	′ ′	′ ′	′ ′
00	11 45·0	11 46·9	11 12·9	0·0 0·0	6·0 4·8	12·0 9·5
01	11 45·3	11 47·2	11 13·1	0·1 0·1	6·1 4·8	12·1 9·6
02	11 45·5	11 47·4	11 13·4	0·2 0·2	6·2 4·9	12·2 9·7
03	11 45·8	11 47·7	11 13·6	0·3 0·2	6·3 5·0	12·3 9·7
04	11 46·0	11 47·9	11 13·8	0·4 0·3	6·4 5·1	12·4 9·8
05	11 46·3	11 48·2	11 14·1	0·5 0·4	6·5 5·1	12·5 9·9
06	11 46·5	11 48·4	11 14·3	0·6 0·5	6·6 5·2	12·6 10·0
07	11 46·8	11 48·7	11 14·6	0·7 0·6	6·7 5·3	12·7 10·1
08	11 47·0	11 48·9	11 14·8	0·8 0·6	6·8 5·4	12·8 10·1
09	11 47·3	11 49·2	11 15·0	0·9 0·7	6·9 5·5	12·9 10·2
10	11 47·5	11 49·4	11 15·3	1·0 0·8	7·0 5·5	13·0 10·3
11	11 47·8	11 49·7	11 15·5	1·1 0·9	7·1 5·6	13·1 10·4
12	11 48·0	11 49·9	11 15·7	1·2 1·0	7·2 5·7	13·2 10·5
13	11 48·3	11 50·2	11 16·0	1·3 1·0	7·3 5·8	13·3 10·5
14	11 48·5	11 50·4	11 16·2	1·4 1·1	7·4 5·9	13·4 10·8
15	11 48·8	11 50·7	11 16·5	1·5 1·2	7·5 5·9	13·5 10·7
16	11 49·0	11 50·9	11 16·7	1·6 1·3	7·6 6·0	13·6 10·8
17	11 49·3	11 51·2	11 16·9	1·7 1·3	7·7 6·1	13·7 10·8
18	11 49·5	11 51·4	11 17·2	1·8 1·4	7·8 6·2	13·8 10·9
19	11 49·8	11 51·7	11 17·4	1·9 1·5	7·9 6·3	13·9 11·0
20	11 50·0	11 51·9	11 17·7	2·0 1·6	8·0 6·3	14·0 11·1
21	11 50·3	11 52·2	11 17·9	2·1 1·7	8·1 6·4	14·1 11·2
22	11 50·5	11 52·4	11 18·1	2·2 1·7	8·2 6·5	14·2 11·2
23	11 50·8	11 52·7	11 18·4	2·3 1·8	8·3 6·6	14·3 11·3
24	11 51·0	11 52·9	11 18·6	2·4 1·9	8·4 6·7	14·4 11·4
25	11 51·3	11 53·2	11 18·8	2·5 2·0	8·5 6·7	14·5 11·5
26	11 51·5	11 53·4	11 19·1	2·6 2·1	8·6 6·8	14·6 11·6
27	11 51·8	11 53·7	11 19·3	2·7 2·1	8·7 6·9	14·7 11·6
28	11 52·0	11 53·9	11 19·6	2·8 2·2	8·8 7·0	14·8 11·7
29	11 52·3	11 54·2	11 19·8	2·9 2·3	8·9 7·0	14·9 11·8
30	11 52·5	11 54·5	11 20·0	3·0 2·4	9·0 7·1	15·0 11·9
31	11 52·8	11 54·7	11 20·3	3·1 2·5	9·1 7·2	15·1 12·0
32	11 53·0	11 55·0	11 20·5	3·2 2·5	9·2 7·3	15·2 12·0
33	11 53·3	11 55·2	11 20·8	3·3 2·6	9·3 7·4	15·3 12·1
34	11 53·5	11 55·5	11 21·0	3·4 2·7	9·4 7·4	15·4 12·2
35	11 53·8	11 55·7	11 21·2	3·5 2·8	9·5 7·5	15·5 12·3
36	11 54·0	11 56·0	11 21·5	3·6 2·9	9·6 7·6	15·6 12·4
37	11 54·3	11 56·2	11 21·7	3·7 2·9	9·7 7·7	15·7 12·4
38	11 54·5	11 56·5	11 22·0	3·8 3·0	9·8 7·8	15·8 12·5
39	11 54·8	11 56·7	11 22·2	3·9 3·1	9·9 7·8	15·9 12·6
40	11 55·0	11 57·0	11 22·4	4·0 3·2	10·0 7·9	16·0 12·7
41	11 55·3	11 57·2	11 22·7	4·1 3·2	10·1 8·0	16·1 12·7
42	11 55·5	11 57·5	11 22·9	4·2 3·3	10·2 8·1	16·2 12·8
43	11 55·8	11 57·7	11 23·1	4·3 3·4	10·3 8·2	16·3 12·9
44	11 56·0	11 58·0	11 23·4	4·4 3·5	10·4 8·2	16·4 13·0
45	11 56·3	11 58·2	11 23·6	4·5 3·6	10·5 8·3	16·5 13·1
46	11 56·5	11 58·5	11 23·9	4·6 3·6	10·6 8·4	16·6 13·1
47	11 56·8	11 58·7	11 24·1	4·7 3·7	10·7 8·5	16·7 13·2
48	11 57·0	11 59·0	11 24·3	4·8 3·8	10·8 8·6	16·8 13·3
49	11 57·3	11 59·2	11 24·6	4·9 3·9	10·9 8·6	16·9 13·4
50	11 57·5	11 59·5	11 24·8	5·0 4·0	11·0 8·7	17·0 13·5
51	11 57·8	11 59·7	11 25·1	5·1 4·0	11·1 8·8	17·1 13·5
52	11 58·0	12 00·0	11 25·3	5·2 4·1	11·2 8·9	17·2 13·6
53	11 58·3	12 00·2	11 25·5	5·3 4·2	11·3 8·9	17·3 13·7
54	11 58·5	12 00·5	11 25·8	5·4 4·3	11·4 9·0	17·4 13·8
55	11 58·8	12 00·7	11 26·0	5·5 4·4	11·5 9·1	17·5 13·9
56	11 59·0	12 01·0	11 26·2	5·6 4·4	11·6 9·2	17·6 13·9
57	11 59·3	12 01·2	11 26·5	5·7 4·5	11·7 9·3	17·7 14·0
58	11 59·5	12 01·5	11 26·7	5·8 4·6	11·8 9·3	17·8 14·1
59	11 59·8	12 01·7	11 27·0	5·9 4·7	11·9 9·4	17·9 14·2
60	12 00·0	12 02·0	11 27·2	6·0 4·8	12·0 9·5	18·0 14·3

48ᵐ	SUN PLANETS	ARIES	MOON	v or Corrⁿ d	v or Corrⁿ d	v or Corrⁿ d
s	° ′	° ′	° ′	′ ′	′ ′	′ ′
00	12 00·0	12 02·0	11 27·2	0·0 0·0	6·0 4·9	12·0 9·7
01	12 00·3	12 02·2	11 27·4	0·1 0·1	6·1 4·9	12·1 9·8
02	12 00·5	12 02·5	11 27·7	0·2 0·2	6·2 5·0	12·2 9·9
03	12 00·8	12 02·7	11 27·9	0·3 0·2	6·3 5·1	12·3 9·9
04	12 01·0	12 03·0	11 28·2	0·4 0·3	6·4 5·2	12·4 10·0
05	12 01·3	12 03·2	11 28·4	0·5 0·4	6·5 5·3	12·5 10·1
06	12 01·5	12 03·5	11 28·6	0·6 0·5	6·6 5·3	12·6 10·2
07	12 01·8	12 03·7	11 28·9	0·7 0·6	6·7 5·4	12·7 10·3
08	12 02·0	12 04·0	11 29·1	0·8 0·6	6·8 5·5	12·8 10·3
09	12 02·3	12 04·2	11 29·3	0·9 0·7	6·9 5·6	12·9 10·4
10	12 02·5	12 04·5	11 29·6	1·0 0·8	7·0 5·7	13·0 10·5
11	12 02·8	12 04·7	11 29·8	1·1 0·9	7·1 5·7	13·1 10·6
12	12 03·0	12 05·0	11 30·1	1·2 1·0	7·2 5·8	13·2 10·7
13	12 03·3	12 05·2	11 30·3	1·3 1·1	7·3 5·9	13·3 10·8
14	12 03·5	12 05·5	11 30·5	1·4 1·1	7·4 6·0	13·4 10·8
15	12 03·8	12 05·7	11 30·8	1·5 1·2	7·5 6·1	13·5 10·9
16	12 04·0	12 06·0	11 31·0	1·6 1·3	7·6 6·1	13·6 11·0
17	12 04·3	12 06·2	11 31·3	1·7 1·4	7·7 6·2	13·7 11·1
18	12 04·5	12 06·5	11 31·5	1·8 1·5	7·8 6·3	13·8 11·2
19	12 04·8	12 06·7	11 31·7	1·9 1·5	7·9 6·4	13·9 11·2
20	12 05·0	12 07·0	11 32·0	2·0 1·6	8·0 6·5	14·0 11·3
21	12 05·3	12 07·2	11 32·2	2·1 1·7	8·1 6·5	14·1 11·4
22	12 05·5	12 07·5	11 32·4	2·2 1·8	8·2 6·6	14·2 11·5
23	12 05·8	12 07·7	11 32·7	2·3 1·9	8·3 6·7	14·3 11·6
24	12 06·0	12 08·0	11 32·9	2·4 1·9	8·4 6·8	14·4 11·6
25	12 06·3	12 08·2	11 33·2	2·5 2·0	8·5 6·9	14·5 11·7
26	12 06·5	12 08·5	11 33·4	2·6 2·1	8·6 7·0	14·6 11·8
27	12 06·8	12 08·7	11 33·6	2·7 2·2	8·7 7·0	14·7 11·9
28	12 07·0	12 09·0	11 33·9	2·8 2·3	8·8 7·1	14·8 12·0
29	12 07·3	12 09·2	11 34·1	2·9 2·3	8·9 7·2	14·9 12·0
30	12 07·5	12 09·5	11 34·4	3·0 2·4	9·0 7·3	15·0 12·1
31	12 07·8	12 09·7	11 34·6	3·1 2·5	9·1 7·4	15·1 12·2
32	12 08·0	12 10·0	11 34·8	3·2 2·6	9·2 7·4	15·2 12·3
33	12 08·3	12 10·2	11 35·1	3·3 2·7	9·3 7·5	15·3 12·4
34	12 08·5	12 10·5	11 35·3	3·4 2·7	9·4 7·6	15·4 12·4
35	12 08·8	12 10·7	11 35·6	3·5 2·8	9·5 7·7	15·5 12·5
36	12 09·0	12 11·0	11 35·8	3·6 2·9	9·6 7·8	15·6 12·6
37	12 09·3	12 11·2	11 36·0	3·7 3·0	9·7 7·8	15·7 12·7
38	12 09·5	12 11·5	11 36·3	3·8 3·1	9·8 7·9	15·8 12·8
39	12 09·8	12 11·7	11 36·5	3·9 3·2	9·9 8·0	15·9 12·9
40	12 10·0	12 12·0	11 36·7	4·0 3·2	10·0 8·1	16·0 12·9
41	12 10·3	12 12·2	11 37·0	4·1 3·3	10·1 8·2	16·1 13·0
42	12 10·5	12 12·5	11 37·2	4·2 3·4	10·2 8·2	16·2 13·1
43	12 10·8	12 12·8	11 37·5	4·3 3·5	10·3 8·3	16·3 13·2
44	12 11·0	12 13·0	11 37·7	4·4 3·6	10·4 8·4	16·4 13·3
45	12 11·3	12 13·3	11 37·9	4·5 3·6	10·5 8·5	16·5 13·3
46	12 11·5	12 13·5	11 38·2	4·6 3·7	10·6 8·6	16·6 13·4
47	12 11·8	12 13·8	11 38·4	4·7 3·8	10·7 8·6	16·7 13·5
48	12 12·0	12 14·0	11 38·7	4·8 3·9	10·8 8·7	16·8 13·6
49	12 12·3	12 14·3	11 38·9	4·9 4·0	10·9 8·8	16·9 13·7
50	12 12·5	12 14·5	11 39·1	5·0 4·0	11·0 8·9	17·0 13·7
51	12 12·8	12 14·8	11 39·4	5·1 4·1	11·1 9·0	17·1 13·8
52	12 13·0	12 15·0	11 39·6	5·2 4·2	11·2 9·1	17·2 13·9
53	12 13·3	12 15·3	11 39·8	5·3 4·3	11·3 9·1	17·3 14·0
54	12 13·5	12 15·5	11 40·1	5·4 4·4	11·4 9·2	17·4 14·1
55	12 13·8	12 15·8	11 40·3	5·5 4·4	11·5 9·3	17·5 14·1
56	12 14·0	12 16·0	11 40·6	5·6 4·5	11·6 9·4	17·6 14·2
57	12 14·3	12 16·3	11 40·8	5·7 4·6	11·7 9·5	17·7 14·3
58	12 14·5	12 16·5	11 41·0	5·8 4·7	11·8 9·5	17·8 14·4
59	12 14·8	12 16·8	11 41·3	5·9 4·8	11·9 9·6	17·9 14·5
60	12 15·0	12 17·0	11 41·5	6·0 4·9	12·0 9·7	18·0 14·6

	38°			39°			40°			41°			42°			43°			44°			
Dec.	Hc	d	Z	Hc	d	Z	Hc	d	Z	Hc	d	Z	Hc	d	Z	Hc	d	Z	Hc	d	Z	Dec.
°	° '	'	°	° '	'	°	° '	'	°	° '	'	°	° '	'	°	° '	'	°	° '	'	°	°
0	20 12.5	+39.3	106.7	19 55.1	+40.0	107.1	19 37.3	+40.9	107.4	19 19.2	+41.6	107.7	19 00.7	+42.4	108.1	18 42.0	+43.1	108.4	18 22.9	+43.8	108.7	0
1	20 51.8	39.0	105.9	20 35.1	39.9	106.3	20 18.2	40.6	106.6	20 00.8	41.4	107.0	19 43.1	42.2	107.3	19 25.1	42.9	107.7	19 06.7	43.7	108.0	1
2	21 30.8	38.8	105.1	21 15.0	39.6	105.5	20 58.8	40.4	105.8	20 42.2	41.2	106.2	20 25.3	42.0	106.6	20 08.0	42.8	106.9	19 50.4	43.5	107.3	2
3	22 09.6	38.5	104.3	21 54.6	39.4	104.7	21 39.2	40.2	105.0	21 23.4	41.0	105.4	21 07.3	41.8	105.8	20 50.8	42.5	106.2	20 33.9	43.3	106.5	3
4	22 48.1	38.3	103.4	22 34.0	39.1	103.8	22 19.4	39.9	104.2	22 04.4	40.8	104.6	21 49.1	41.5	105.0	21 33.3	42.4	105.4	21 17.2	43.1	105.8	4
5	23 26.4	+38.0	102.6	23 13.1	+38.8	103.0	22 59.3	+39.7	103.4	22 45.2	+40.5	103.8	22 30.6	+41.4	104.3	22 15.7	+42.1	104.7	22 00.3	+42.9	105.0	5
6	24 04.4	37.7	101.8	23 51.9	38.6	102.2	23 39.0	39.5	102.6	23 25.7	40.3	103.0	23 12.0	41.1	103.5	22 57.8	41.9	103.9	22 43.2	42.7	104.3	6
7	24 42.1	37.4	100.9	24 30.5	38.3	101.4	24 18.5	39.2	101.8	24 06.0	40.0	102.2	23 53.1	40.8	102.7	23 39.7	41.6	103.1	23 25.9	42.4	103.5	7
8	25 19.5	37.2	100.0	25 08.8	38.1	100.5	24 57.7	38.9	101.0	24 46.0	39.8	101.4	24 33.9	40.6	101.9	24 21.3	41.5	102.3	24 08.3	42.2	102.8	8
9	25 56.7	36.8	99.2	25 46.9	37.7	99.6	25 36.6	38.6	100.1	25 25.8	39.4	100.6	25 14.5	40.3	101.1	25 02.8	41.1	101.5	24 50.5	42.0	102.0	9
10	26 33.5	+36.5	98.3	26 24.6	+37.4	98.8	26 15.2	+38.2	99.3	26 05.2	+39.2	99.8	25 54.8	+40.1	100.2	25 43.9	+40.9	100.7	25 32.5	+41.7	101.2	10
11	27 10.0	36.1	97.4	27 02.0	37.0	97.9	26 53.4	38.0	98.4	26 44.4	38.9	98.9	26 34.9	39.7	99.4	26 24.8	40.6	99.9	26 14.2	41.5	100.4	11
12	27 46.1	35.8	96.5	27 39.0	36.8	97.0	27 31.4	37.7	97.5	27 23.3	38.5	98.1	27 14.6	39.5	98.6	27 05.4	40.3	99.1	26 55.7	41.2	99.6	12
13	28 21.9	35.4	95.6	28 15.8	36.3	96.1	28 09.1	37.3	96.7	28 01.8	38.3	97.2	27 54.1	39.1	97.7	27 45.7	40.0	98.2	27 36.9	40.8	98.8	13
14	28 57.3	35.0	94.7	28 52.1	36.0	95.2	28 46.4	36.9	95.8	28 40.1	37.9	96.3	28 33.2	38.8	96.9	28 25.7	39.7	97.4	28 17.7	40.6	97.9	14
15	29 32.3	+34.7	93.7	29 28.1	+35.7	94.3	29 23.3	+36.6	94.9	29 18.0	+37.5	95.4	29 12.0	+38.4	96.0	29 05.4	+39.4	96.5	28 58.3	+40.3	97.1	15
16	30 07.0	34.2	92.8	30 03.8	35.2	93.4	29 59.9	36.2	94.0	29 55.5	37.1	94.5	29 50.4	38.1	95.1	29 44.8	39.0	95.7	29 38.6	39.9	96.2	16
17	30 41.2	33.8	91.8	30 39.0	34.8	92.4	30 36.1	35.8	93.0	30 32.6	36.8	93.6	30 28.5	37.8	94.2	30 23.8	38.7	94.8	30 18.5	39.6	95.4	17
18	31 15.0	33.4	90.9	31 13.8	34.4	91.5	31 11.9	35.4	92.1	31 09.4	36.4	92.7	31 06.3	37.3	93.3	31 02.5	38.3	93.9	30 58.1	39.2	94.5	18
19	31 48.4	33.0	89.9	31 48.2	34.0	90.5	31 47.3	35.0	91.1	31 45.8	36.0	91.8	31 43.6	37.0	92.4	31 40.8	37.9	93.0	31 37.3	38.9	93.6	19
20	32 21.4	+32.4	88.9	32 22.2	+33.5	89.6	32 22.3	+34.5	90.2	32 21.8	+35.5	90.8	32 20.6	+36.5	91.5	32 18.7	+37.5	92.1	32 16.2	+38.5	92.7	20
21	32 53.8	32.0	87.9	32 55.7	33.0	88.6	32 56.8	34.1	89.2	32 57.3	35.1	89.9	32 57.1	36.1	90.5	32 56.2	37.1	91.2	32 54.7	38.0	91.8	21
22	33 25.8	31.5	86.9	33 28.7	32.5	87.6	33 30.9	33.6	88.2	33 32.4	34.6	88.9	33 33.2	35.7	89.6	33 33.3	36.7	90.2	33 32.7	37.7	90.9	22
23	33 57.3	31.0	85.9	34 01.2	32.1	86.6	34 04.5	33.1	87.2	34 07.0	34.2	87.9	34 08.9	35.1	88.6	34 10.0	36.2	89.3	34 10.4	37.2	89.9	23
24	34 28.3	30.4	84.9	34 33.3	31.5	85.5	34 37.6	32.6	86.2	34 41.2	33.6	86.9	34 44.0	34.8	87.6	34 46.2	35.7	88.3	34 47.6	36.8	89.0	24
25	34 58.7	+29.9	83.8	35 04.8	+31.0	84.5	35 10.2	+32.1	85.2	35 14.8	+33.2	85.9	35 18.8	+34.2	86.6	35 21.9	+35.3	87.3	35 24.4	+36.3	88.0	25
26	35 28.6	29.3	82.7	35 35.8	30.4	83.5	35 42.3	31.5	84.2	35 48.0	32.6	84.9	35 53.0	33.7	85.6	35 57.2	34.8	86.3	36 00.7	35.8	87.0	26
27	35 57.9	28.8	81.7	36 06.2	29.9	82.4	36 13.8	31.0	83.1	36 20.6	32.1	83.8	36 26.7	33.1	84.6	36 32.0	34.2	85.3	36 36.5	35.3	86.1	27
28	36 26.7	28.1	80.6	36 36.1	29.3	81.3	36 44.8	30.4	82.0	36 52.7	31.5	82.8	36 59.8	32.7	83.5	37 06.2	33.7	84.3	37 11.8	34.8	85.0	28
29	36 54.8	27.5	79.5	37 05.4	28.7	80.2	37 15.2	29.8	81.0	37 24.2	30.9	81.7	37 32.5	32.0	82.5	37 39.9	33.2	83.2	37 46.6	34.2	84.0	29
30	37 22.3	+26.9	78.4	37 34.1	+28.0	79.1	37 45.0	+29.2	79.9	37 55.1	+30.4	80.6	38 04.5	+31.5	81.4	38 13.1	+32.5	82.2	38 20.8	+33.7	83.0	30
31	37 49.2	26.3	77.2	38 02.1	27.4	78.0	38 14.2	28.5	78.8	38 25.5	29.7	79.5	38 36.0	30.8	80.3	38 45.6	32.0	81.1	38 54.5	33.1	81.9	31
32	38 15.5	25.5	76.1	38 29.5	26.7	76.9	38 42.7	27.9	77.6	38 55.2	29.0	78.4	39 06.8	30.2	79.2	39 17.6	31.4	80.0	39 27.6	32.5	80.8	32
33	38 41.0	24.9	74.9	38 56.2	26.1	75.7	39 10.6	27.3	76.5	39 24.2	28.4	77.3	39 37.0	29.6	78.1	39 49.0	30.7	78.9	40 00.1	31.8	79.7	33
34	39 05.9	24.2	73.8	39 22.3	25.3	74.6	39 37.9	26.5	75.4	39 52.6	27.7	76.2	40 06.6	28.9	77.0	40 19.7	30.0	77.8	40 31.9	31.2	78.6	34
35	39 30.1	+23.4	72.6	39 47.6	+24.7	73.4	40 04.4	+25.8	74.2	40 20.3	+27.1	75.0	40 35.5	+28.2	75.8	40 49.7	+29.4	76.7	41 03.1	+30.6	77.5	35
36	39 53.5	22.7	71.4	40 12.3	23.9	72.2	40 30.2	25.1	73.0	40 47.4	26.2	73.8	41 03.7	27.4	74.7	41 19.1	28.7	75.5	41 33.7	29.8	76.4	36
37	40 16.2	22.0	70.2	40 36.2	23.1	71.0	40 55.3	24.4	71.8	41 13.6	25.6	72.6	41 31.1	26.8	73.5	41 47.8	27.9	74.3	42 03.5	29.2	75.2	37
38	40 38.2	21.1	69.0	40 59.3	22.4	69.8	41 19.7	23.5	70.6	41 39.2	24.8	71.4	41 57.9	26.0	72.3	42 15.7	27.2	73.1	42 32.7	28.4	74.0	38
39	40 59.3	20.4	67.7	41 21.7	21.5	68.5	41 43.2	22.8	69.4	42 04.0	23.9	70.2	42 23.9	25.2	71.1	42 42.9	26.4	71.9	43 01.1	27.6	72.8	39
40	41 19.7	+19.5	66.5	41 43.2	+20.8	67.3	42 06.0	+21.9	68.1	42 27.9	+23.2	69.0	42 49.1	+24.3	69.8	43 09.3	+25.6	70.7	43 28.7	+26.8	71.6	40
41	41 39.2	18.7	65.2	42 04.0	19.9	66.0	42 27.9	21.2	66.9	42 51.1	22.3	67.7	43 13.4	23.6	68.6	43 34.9	24.8	69.5	43 55.5	26.1	70.4	41
42	41 57.9	17.8	63.9	42 23.9	19.0	64.8	42 49.1	20.2	65.6	43 13.4	21.5	66.4	43 37.0	22.7	67.3	43 59.7	24.0	68.2	44 21.6	25.2	69.1	42
43	42 15.7	17.0	62.6	42 42.9	18.2	63.5	43 09.3	19.4	64.3	43 34.9	20.6	65.2	43 59.7	21.9	66.0	44 23.7	23.1	66.9	44 46.8	24.3	67.8	43
44	42 32.7	16.1	61.3	43 01.1	17.3	62.2	43 28.7	18.5	63.0	43 55.5	19.8	63.9	44 21.6	20.9	64.7	44 46.8	22.2	65.6	45 11.1	23.4	66.5	44
45	42 48.8	+15.1	60.0	43 18.4	+16.3	60.9	43 47.2	+17.6	61.7	44 15.3	+18.8	62.5	44 42.5	+20.1	63.4	45 09.0	+21.2	64.3	45 34.5	+22.6	65.2	45
46	43 03.9	14.3	58.7	43 34.7	15.5	59.5	44 04.8	16.6	60.4	44 34.1	17.8	61.2	45 02.6	19.1	62.1	45 30.2	20.4	63.0	45 57.1	21.6	63.9	46
47	43 18.2	13.3	57.4	43 50.2	14.5	58.2	44 21.4	15.7	59.0	44 51.9	16.9	59.9	45 21.7	18.1	60.7	45 50.6	19.4	61.6	46 18.7	20.6	62.6	47
48	43 31.5	12.4	56.0	44 04.7	13.5	56.8	44 37.1	14.8	57.7	45 08.8	16.0	58.5	45 39.8	17.2	59.4	46 10.0	18.4	60.3	46 39.3	19.7	61.2	48
49	43 43.9	11.4	54.7	44 18.2	12.6	55.5	44 51.9	13.7	56.3	45 24.8	14.9	57.1	45 57.0	16.1	58.0	46 28.4	17.4	58.9	46 59.0	18.6	59.8	49
50	43 55.3	+10.4	53.3	44 30.8	+11.6	54.1	45 05.6	+12.8	54.9	45 39.7	+14.0	55.8	46 13.1	+15.2	56.6	46 45.8	+16.3	57.5	47 17.6	+17.6	58.4	50
51	44 05.7	9.5	52.0	44 42.4	10.5	52.7	45 18.4	11.7	53.5	45 53.7	12.9	54.4	46 28.3	14.1	55.2	47 02.1	15.3	56.1	47 35.2	16.6	57.0	51
52	44 15.2	8.4	50.6	44 52.9	9.6	51.3	45 30.1	10.7	52.1	46 06.6	11.9	53.0	46 42.4	13.0	53.8	47 17.4	14.3	54.7	47 51.8	15.4	55.6	52
53	44 23.6	7.4	49.2	45 02.5	8.6	50.0	45 40.8	9.7	50.7	46 18.5	10.8	51.5	46 55.4	12.0	52.4	47 31.7	13.2	53.2	48 07.2	14.4	54.1	53
54	44 31.0	6.5	47.8	45 11.1	7.5	48.6	45 50.5	8.6	49.3	46 29.3	9.7	50.1	47 07.4	10.9	50.9	47 44.9	12.1	51.8	48 21.6	13.3	52.7	54
55	44 37.5	+5.4	46.4	45 18.6	+6.4	47.1	45 59.1	+7.5	47.9	46 39.0	+8.7	48.7	47 18.3	+9.8	49.5	47 57.0	+10.9	50.3	48 34.9	+12.1	51.2	55
56	44 42.9	4.3	45.0	45 25.0	5.4	45.7	46 06.6	6.5	46.5	46 47.7	7.5	47.2	47 28.1	8.7	48.0	48 07.9	9.8	48.9	48 47.0	11.0	49.7	56
57	44 47.2	3.4	43.6	45 30.4	4.4	44.3	46 13.1	5.4	45.0	46 55.2	6.5	45.8	47 36.8	7.5	46.6	48 17.7	8.7	47.4	48 58.0	9.9	48.2	57
58	44 50.6	2.3	42.2	45 34.8	3.3	42.9	46 18.5	4.3	43.6	47 01.7	5.3	44.3	47 44.3	6.5	45.1	48 26.4	7.5	45.9	49 07.9	8.6	46.7	58
59	44 52.9	1.2	40.8	45 38.1	2.2	41.5	46 22.8	3.2	42.1	47 07.0	4.3	42.9	47 50.8	5.2	43.6	48 33.9	6.4	44.4	49 16.5	7.4	45.2	59
60	44 54.1	+0.2	39.4	45 40.3	+1.1	40.0	46 26.0	+2.1	40.7	47 11.3	+3.1	41.4	47 56.0	+4.1	42.1	48 40.3	+5.1	42.9	49 23.9	+6.3	43.7	60
61	44 54.3	−0.8	38.0	45 41.4	+0.1	38.6	46 28.1	+1.0	39.2	47 14.4	1.9	39.9	48 00.1	3.0	40.6	48 45.4	4.0	41.4	49 30.2	5.0	42.1	61
62	44 53.5	1.9	36.6	45 41.5	−1.0	37.2	46 29.1	−0.1	37.8	47 16.3	+0.9	38.5	48 03.1	1.8	39.1	48 49.4	2.8	39.9	49 35.2	3.8	40.6	62
63	44 51.6	2.9	35.1	45 40.5	2.0	35.7	46 29.0	1.1	36.3	47 17.2	−0.3	37.0	48 04.9	+0.6	37.6	48 52.2	1.6	38.3	49 39.0	2.6	39.1	63
64	44 48.7	3.9	33.7	45 38.5	3.2	34.3	46 27.9	2.3	34.9	47 16.9	1.4	35.5	48 05.5	−0.5	36.1	48 53.8	+0.4	36.8	49 41.6	1.3	37.5	64
65	44 44.8	−5.0	32.3	45 35.3	−4.2	32.9	46 25.6	−3.4	33.4	47 15.5	−2.6	34.0	48 05.0	−1.7	34.7	48 54.2	−0.9	35.3	49 42.9	+0.1	36.0	65
66	44 39.8	6.0	30.9	45 31.1	5.2	31.4	46 22.2	4.5	32.0	47 12.9	3.7	32.6	48 03.3	2.9	33.2	48 53.3	2.0	33.8	49 43.0	−1.1	34.4	66
67	44 33.8	7.0	29.5	45 25.9	6.4	30.0	46 17.7	5.6	30.5	47 09.2	4.8	31.1	48 00.4	4.0	31.7	48 51.3	3.2	32.3	49 41.9	2.4	32.9	67
68	44 26.8	8.1	28.1	45 19.5	7.3	28.6	46 12.1	6.7	29.1	47 04.4	5.9	29.6	47 56.4	5.2	30.2	48 48.1	4.4	30.7	49 39.5	3.6	31.3	68
69	44 18.7	9.0	26.8	45 12.2	8.4	27.2	46 05.4	7.7	27.7	46 58.5	7.1	28.2	47 51.2	6.3	28.7	48 43.7	5.6	29.2	49 35.9	4.8	29.8	69
70	44 09.7	−10.1	25.4	45 03.8	−9.4	25.8	45 57.7	−8.8	26.2	46 51.4	−8.1	26.7	47 44.9	−7.5	27.2	48 38.1	−6.7	27.7	49 31.1	−6.0	28.3	70
71	43 59.6	11.0	24.0	44 54.4	10.5	24.4	45 48.9	9.8	24.8	46 43.3	9.2	25.3	47 37.4	8.6	25.7	48 31.4	8.0	26.2	49 25.1	7.3	26.7	71
72	43 48.6	11.9	22.6	44 43.9	11.4	23.0	45 39.1	10.9	23.4	46 34.1	10.4	23.8	47 28.8	9.7	24.3	48 23.4	9.0	24.7	49 17.8	8.4	25.2	72
73	43 36.7	13.0	21.3	44 32.5	12.4	21.6	45 28.2	11.9	22.0	46 23.7	11.3	22.4	47 19.1	10.8	22.8	48 14.4	10.3	23.2	49 09.4	9.6	23.7	73
74	43 23.7	13.9	19.9	44 20.1	13.4	20.3	45 16.3	12.9	20.6	46 12.4	12.4	21.0	47 08.3	11.9	21.4	48 04.1	11.3	21.8	48 59.8	10.8	22.2	74
75	43 09.8	−14.8	18.6	44 06.7	−14.4	18.9	45 03.4	−13.9	19.2	46 00.0	−13.5	19.6	46 56.4	−12.9	19.9	47 52.8	−12.5	20.3	48 49.0	−12.0	20.7	75
76	42 55.0	15.7	17.3	43 52.3	15.3	17.6	44 49.5	14.9	17.9	45 46.5	14.5	18.2	46 43.5	14.1	18.5	47 40.3	13.5	18.8	48 37.0	13.0	19.2	76
77	42 39.3	16.6	16.0	43 37.0	16.3	16.2	44 34.6	15.9	16.5	45 32.0	15.4	16.8	46 29.4	15.0	17.1	47 26.8	14.7	17.4	48 24.0	14.2	17.7	77
78	42 22.7	17.5	14.7	43 20.7	17.1	14.9	44 18.7	16.8	15.1	45 16.6	16.5	15.4	46 14.4	16.1	15.7	47 12.1	15.7	16.0	48 09.8	15.3	16.3	78
79	42 05.2	18.3	13.4	43 03.6	18.1	13.6	44 01.9	17.7	13.8	45 00.1	17.4	14.0	45 58.3	17.1	14.3	46 56.4	16.7	14.5	47 54.5	16.4	14.8	79
80	41 46.9	−19.2	12.1	42 45.5	−18.9	12.3	43 44.2	−18.7	12.5	44 42.7	−18.3	12.7	45 41.2	−18.0	12.9	46 39.7	−17.8	13.1	47 38.1	−17.5	13.4	80
81	41 27.7	20.0	10.8	42 26.6	19.8	11.0	43 25.5	19.5	11.2	44 24.4	19.3	11.4	45 23.2	19.1	11.5	46 21.9	18.7	11.8	47 20.6	18.4	12.0	81
82	41 07.7	20.8	9.6	42 06.8	20.6	9.7	43 06.0	20.4	9.9	44 05.1	20.2	10.0	45 04.1	19.9	10.2	46 03.2	19.8	10.4	47 02.2	19.5	10.6	82
83	40 46.9	21.6	8.3	41 46.2	21.4	8.4	42 45.6	21.3	8.6	43 44.9	21.1	8.7	44 44.2	20.9	8.9	45 43.4	20.6	9.0	46 42.7	20.5	9.2	83
84	40 25.3	22.4	7.1	41 24.8	22.3	7.2	42 24.3	22.1	7.3	43 23.8	21.9	7.4	44 23.3	21.8	7.6	45 22.8	21.6	7.7	46 22.2	21.4	7.8	84
85	40 02.9	−23.2	5.9	41 02.5	−23.0	6.0	42 02.2	−22.9	6.1	43 01.9	−22.8	6.2	44 01.5	−22.6	6.3	45 01.2	−22.6	6.4	46 00.8	−22.4	6.5	85
86	39 39.7	23.9	4.7	40 39.5	23.8	4.7	41 39.3	23.7	4.8	42 39.1	23.6	4.9	43 38.9	23.5	5.0	44 38.6	23.3	5.1	45 38.4	23.3	5.1	86
87	39 15.8	24.5	3.5	40 15.7	24.5	3.5	41 15.6	24.4	3.6	42 15.5	24.4	3.6	43 15.4	24.3	3.7	44 15.3	24.3	3.8	45 15.1	24.2	3.8	87
88	38 51.3	25.3	2.3	39 51.2	25.2	2.3	40 51.2	25.3	2.4	41 51.1	25.2	2.4	42 51.1	25.2	2.5	43 51.0	25.1	2.5	44 50.9	25.0	2.5	88
89	38 26.0	26.0	1.1	39 26.0	26.0	1.2	40 25.9	25.9	1.2	41 25.9	25.9	1.2	42 25.9	25.9	1.2	43 25.9	25.9	1.2	44 25.9	25.9	1.3	89
90	38 00.0	−26.6	0.0	39 00.0	−26.6	0.0	40 00.0	−26.7	0.0	41 00.0	−26.7	0.0	42 00.0	−26.7	0.0	43 00.0	−26.7	0.0	44 00.0	−26.7	0.0	90
	38°			39°			40°			41°			42°			43°			44°			

64°, 296° L.H.A. LATITUDE SAME NAME AS DECLINATION

Extract from H.O. 229.

Dec.	38° Hc	d	Z	39° Hc	d	Z	40° Hc	d	Z	41° Hc	d	Z	42° Hc	d	Z	43° Hc	d	Z	44° Hc	d	Z	Dec.
°	° ′	′	°	° ′	′	°	° ′	′	°	° ′	′	°	° ′	′	°	° ′	′	°	° ′	′	°	°
0	47 21.8	+54.5	148.1	46 30.8	+54.7	148.6	45 39.4	+55.1	149.2	44 47.7	+55.4	149.7	43 55.8	+55.7	150.2	43 03.7	+55.9	150.6	42 11.3	+56.2	151.1	0
1	48 16.3	54.2	147.4	47 25.5	54.6	148.0	46 34.5	54.9	148.6	45 43.1	55.3	149.1	44 51.5	55.5	149.6	43 59.6	55.8	150.1	43 07.5	56.0	150.6	1
2	49 10.5	54.0	146.8	48 20.1	54.4	147.4	47 29.4	54.7	148.0	46 38.4	55.0	148.6	45 47.0	55.4	149.1	44 55.4	55.7	149.6	44 03.5	56.0	150.1	2
3	50 04.5	53.8	146.1	49 14.5	54.2	146.8	48 24.1	54.6	147.4	47 33.4	54.9	148.0	46 42.4	55.2	148.5	45 51.1	55.5	149.1	44 59.5	55.8	149.6	3
4	50 58.3	53.4	145.4	50 08.7	53.9	146.1	49 18.7	54.3	146.7	48 28.3	54.7	147.4	47 37.6	55.0	148.0	46 46.6	55.3	148.5	45 55.3	55.6	149.1	4
5	51 51.7	+53.3	144.7	51 02.6	+53.6	145.4	50 13.0	+54.1	146.1	49 23.0	+54.5	146.7	48 32.6	+54.9	147.4	47 41.9	+55.2	148.0	46 50.9	+55.5	148.5	5
6	52 45.0	52.9	143.9	51 56.2	53.4	144.7	51 07.1	53.8	145.4	50 17.5	54.2	146.1	49 27.5	54.6	146.7	48 37.1	55.0	147.4	47 46.4	55.3	148.0	6
7	53 37.9	52.6	143.1	52 49.6	53.1	143.9	52 00.9	53.6	144.7	51 11.7	54.0	145.4	50 22.1	54.4	146.1	49 32.1	54.8	146.8	48 41.7	55.2	147.4	7
8	54 30.5	52.2	142.3	53 42.7	52.8	143.2	52 54.5	53.2	144.0	52 05.7	53.7	144.7	51 16.5	54.2	145.4	50 26.9	54.6	146.1	49 36.9	54.9	146.8	8
9	55 22.7	51.9	141.5	54 35.5	52.4	142.3	53 47.7	53.0	143.2	52 59.4	53.5	144.0	52 10.7	53.9	144.7	51 21.5	54.3	145.5	50 31.8	54.8	146.2	9
10	56 14.6	+51.5	140.6	55 27.9	+52.1	141.5	54 40.7	+52.6	142.4	53 52.9	+53.2	143.2	53 04.6	+53.6	144.0	52 15.8	+54.1	144.8	51 26.6	+54.5	145.5	10
11	57 06.1	51.0	139.6	56 20.0	51.7	140.6	55 33.3	52.3	141.5	54 46.1	52.8	142.4	53 58.2	53.4	143.3	53 09.9	53.8	144.1	52 21.1	54.2	144.8	11
12	57 57.1	50.5	138.7	57 11.7	51.2	139.7	56 25.6	51.9	140.7	55 38.9	52.5	141.6	54 51.6	53.0	142.5	54 03.7	53.6	143.3	53 15.3	54.1	144.1	12
13	58 47.6	50.1	137.6	58 02.9	50.8	138.7	57 17.5	51.5	139.7	56 31.4	52.1	140.7	55 44.6	52.7	141.7	54 57.3	53.2	142.5	54 09.4	53.7	143.4	13
14	59 37.7	49.5	136.5	58 53.7	50.3	137.7	58 09.0	51.0	138.8	57 23.5	51.6	139.8	56 37.3	52.3	140.8	55 50.5	52.9	141.7	55 03.1	53.4	142.6	14
15	60 27.2	+48.8	135.4	59 44.0	+49.7	136.6	59 00.0	+50.5	137.8	58 15.1	+51.3	138.9	57 29.6	+51.9	139.9	56 43.4	+52.5	140.9	55 56.5	+53.1	141.8	15
16	61 16.0	48.3	134.2	60 33.7	49.1	135.5	59 50.5	49.9	136.7	59 06.4	50.7	137.9	58 21.5	51.5	139.0	57 35.9	52.1	140.0	56 49.6	52.7	141.0	16
17	62 04.3	47.5	133.0	61 22.8	48.5	134.3	60 40.4	49.4	135.6	59 57.1	50.3	136.8	59 13.0	51.0	138.0	58 28.0	51.7	139.1	57 42.3	52.4	140.1	17
18	62 51.8	46.7	131.6	62 11.3	47.8	133.1	61 29.8	48.8	134.4	60 47.4	49.6	135.7	60 04.0	50.4	136.9	59 19.7	51.3	138.1	58 34.7	51.9	139.2	18
19	63 38.5	45.8	130.3	62 59.1	47.0	131.8	62 18.6	48.0	133.2	61 37.0	49.0	134.5	60 54.4	49.9	135.8	60 11.0	50.7	137.0	59 26.6	51.5	138.2	19
20	64 24.3	+45.0	128.8	63 46.1	+46.2	130.4	63 06.6	+47.3	131.9	62 26.0	+48.4	133.3	61 44.3	+49.3	134.7	61 01.7	+50.2	136.0	60 18.1	+51.0	137.2	20
21	65 09.3	43.9	127.2	64 32.3	45.2	128.9	63 53.9	46.5	130.5	63 14.4	47.5	132.0	62 33.6	48.7	133.4	61 51.9	49.5	134.8	61 09.1	50.4	136.1	21
22	65 53.2	42.7	125.6	65 17.5	44.2	127.4	64 40.4	45.5	129.0	64 01.9	46.8	130.6	63 22.3	47.8	132.2	62 41.4	48.9	133.6	61 59.5	49.9	135.0	22
23	66 35.9	41.6	123.8	66 01.7	43.1	125.7	65 25.9	44.6	127.5	64 48.7	45.9	129.2	64 10.1	47.1	130.8	63 30.3	48.2	132.3	62 49.4	49.2	133.8	23
24	67 17.5	40.2	122.0	66 44.8	41.9	124.0	66 10.5	43.4	125.9	65 34.6	44.8	127.6	64 57.2	46.2	129.3	64 18.5	47.4	131.0	63 38.6	48.5	132.5	24
25	67 57.7	+38.8	120.0	67 26.7	+40.6	122.1	66 53.9	+42.3	124.1	66 19.4	+43.8	126.0	65 43.4	+45.2	127.8	65 05.9	+46.5	129.5	64 27.1	+47.7	131.1	25
26	68 36.5	37.1	118.0	68 07.3	39.1	120.2	67 36.2	40.9	122.3	67 03.2	42.6	124.3	66 28.6	44.1	126.2	65 52.4	45.6	128.0	65 14.8	46.8	129.7	26
27	69 13.6	35.4	115.8	68 46.4	37.5	118.1	68 17.1	39.5	120.3	67 45.8	41.3	122.5	67 12.7	43.0	124.5	66 38.0	44.4	126.4	66 01.6	45.9	128.2	27
28	69 49.0	33.5•	113.5	69 23.9	35.8	115.9	68 56.6	37.9	118.3	68 27.1	39.9	120.5	67 55.7	41.7	122.6	67 22.4	43.4	124.7	66 47.5	44.8	126.6	28
29	70 22.5	31.4•	111.1	69 59.7	33.9•	113.6	69 34.5	36.1	116.1	69 07.0	38.2	118.4	68 37.4	40.2	120.7	68 05.8	42.0	122.8	67 32.3	43.7	124.9	29
30	70 53.9	+29.2•	108.5	70 33.6	+31.7•	111.2	70 10.6	+34.3•	113.8	69 45.2	+36.6	116.3	69 17.6	+38.6	118.6	68 47.8	+40.6	120.9	68 16.0	+42.4	123.1	30
31	71 23.1	26.7•	105.8	71 05.3	29.6•	108.6	70 44.9	32.1•	111.3	70 21.8	34.6•	113.9	69 56.2	37.0	116.4	69 28.4	39.1	118.8	68 58.4	41.0	121.1	31
32	71 49.8	24.1•	102.9	71 34.9	27.0•	105.9	71 17.0	29.9•	108.7	70 56.4	32.6•	111.5	70 33.2	35.0•	114.1	70 07.5	37.3	116.6	69 39.4	39.5	119.0	32
33	72 13.9	21.3•	100.0	72 01.9	24.5•	103.0	71 46.9	27.5•	106.0	71 29.0	30.2•	108.9	71 08.2	32.9•	111.6	70 44.8	35.4	114.3	70 18.9	37.7	116.8	33
34	72 35.2	18.4•	96.9	72 26.4	21.6•	100.0	72 14.4	24.8•	103.1	71 59.2	27.9•	106.1	71 41.1	30.7•	109.0	71 20.2	33.4•	111.8	70 56.6	35.9•	114.5	34
35	72 53.6	+15.2•	93.7	72 48.0	+18.7•	96.9	72 39.2	+21.9•	100.1	72 27.1	+25.1•	103.2	72 11.8	+28.2•	106.2	71 53.6	+31.0•	109.2	71 32.5	+33.7•	112.0	35
36	73 08.8	11.9•	90.4	73 06.7	15.4•	93.7	73 01.1	19.0•	96.9	72 52.2	22.3•	100.1	72 40.0	25.5•	103.3	72 24.6	28.6•	106.4	72 06.2	31.5•	109.4	36
37	73 20.7	8.5•	87.0	73 22.1	12.2•	90.3	73 20.1	15.7•	93.6	73 14.5	19.2•	97.0	73 05.5	22.7•	100.2	72 53.2	25.9•	103.4	72 37.7	29.0•	106.5	37
38	73 29.2	5.1•	83.5	73 34.3	8.7•	86.9	73 35.8	12.4•	90.3	73 33.7	16.0•	93.6	73 28.2	19.5•	97.0	73 19.1	23.0•	100.3	73 06.7	26.3•	103.6	38
39	73 34.3	+ 1.5•	80.0	73 43.0	5.2•	83.3	73 48.2	8.8•	86.8	73 49.7	12.6•	90.2	73 47.7	16.3•	93.7	73 42.1	19.9•	97.1	73 33.0	23.3•	100.4	39
40	73 35.8	− 2.1•	76.4	73 48.2	+ 1.5•	79.8	73 57.0	+ 5.3•	83.2	74 02.3	+ 9.1•	86.7	74 04.0	+12.8•	90.2	74 02.0	+16.5•	93.7	73 56.3	+20.2•	97.1	40
41	73 33.7	5.5•	72.9	73 49.7	− 2.0•	76.2	74 02.3	+ 1.7•	79.6	74 11.4	5.4•	83.1	74 16.8	9.2•	86.6	74 18.5	13.0•	90.2	74 16.5	16.8•	93.7	41
42	73 28.2	9.1•	69.4	73 47.7	5.6•	72.6	74 04.0	− 2.0•	76.0	74 16.8	+ 1.7•	79.4	74 26.0	5.5•	82.9	74 31.5	9.4•	86.5	74 33.3	13.2•	90.1	42
43	73 19.1	12.4•	65.9	73 42.1	9.1•	69.1	74 02.0	5.7•	72.3	74 18.5	− 2.0•	75.7	74 31.5	+ 1.8•	79.2	74 40.9	5.6•	82.8	74 46.5	9.6•	86.4	43
44	73 06.7	15.7•	62.5	73 33.0	12.6•	65.5	73 56.3	9.2•	68.7	74 16.5	5.8•	72.0	74 33.3	− 2.1•	75.5	74 46.5	+ 1.8•	79.0	74 56.1	5.7•	82.7	44
45	72 51.0	−18.8•	59.2	73 20.4	−15.9•	62.1	73 47.1	−12.8•	65.2	74 10.7	− 9.3•	68.4	74 31.2	− 5.7•	71.7	74 48.3	− 2.0•	75.2	75 01.8	+ 1.9•	78.8	45
46	72 32.2	21.7•	56.1	73 04.5	19.0•	58.8	73 34.3	16.0•	61.7	74 01.4	12.9•	64.7	74 25.5	9.5•	68.0	74 46.3	5.9•	71.4	75 03.7	− 2.1•	74.9	46
47	72 10.5	24.5•	53.0	72 45.5	22.0•	55.5	73 18.3	19.3•	58.3	73 48.5	16.3•	61.2	74 16.0	13.1•	64.3	74 40.4	9.6•	67.6	75 01.6	6.0•	71.1	47
48	71 46.0	27.2•	50.0	72 23.5	24.8•	52.4	72 59.0	22.2•	55.0	73 32.2	19.5•	57.8	74 02.9	16.5•	60.8	74 30.8	13.3•	63.9	74 55.6	9.8•	67.2	48
49	71 18.8	29.5•	47.2	71 58.7	27.4•	49.5	72 36.8	25.1•	51.9	73 12.7	22.5•	54.5	73 46.4	19.8•	57.3	74 17.5	16.7•	60.3	74 45.8	13.5•	63.5	49
50	70 49.3	−31.7•	44.5	71 31.3	−29.8•	46.6	72 11.7	−27.7•	48.9	72 50.2	−25.4•	51.3	73 26.6	−22.8•	53.9	74 00.8	−20.1•	56.8	74 32.3	−17.0•	59.8	50
51	70 17.6	33.8•	42.0	71 01.5	32.0•	43.9	71 44.0	30.2•	46.0	72 24.8	28.0•	48.3	73 03.8	25.7•	50.7	73 40.7	23.2•	53.4	74 15.3	20.4•	56.2	51
52	69 43.8	35.7	39.6	70 29.5	34.1•	41.4	71 13.8	32.3•	43.3	71 56.8	30.5•	45.4	72 38.1	28.4•	47.7	73 17.5	26.1•	50.1	73 54.9	23.5•	52.8	52
53	69 08.1	37.4	37.3	69 55.4	36.0	38.9	70 41.5	34.5•	40.7	71 26.3	32.8•	42.6	72 09.7	30.9•	44.8	72 51.4	28.7•	47.0	73 31.4	26.5•	49.5	53
54	68 30.7	38.9	35.1	69 19.4	37.7	36.6	70 07.0	36.3	38.3	70 53.5	34.8	40.1	71 38.8	33.1•	42.0	72 22.7	31.2•	44.1	73 04.9	29.1•	46.4	54
55	67 51.8	−40.5	33.1	68 41.7	−39.3	34.5	69 30.7	−38.1	36.0	70 18.7	−36.6	37.6	71 05.7	−35.2	39.4	71 51.5	−33.5•	41.3	72 35.8	−31.6•	43.4	55
56	67 11.3	41.7	31.1	68 02.4	40.8	32.4	68 52.6	39.6	33.8	69 42.1	38.5	35.3	70 30.5	37.0	36.9	71 18.0	35.6	38.7	72 04.2	33.9•	40.6	56
57	66 29.6	43.0	29.3	67 21.6	42.0	30.5	68 13.0	41.1	31.7	69 03.6	39.9	33.1	69 53.5	38.8	34.6	70 42.4	37.4	36.2	71 30.3	36.0•	38.0	57
58	65 46.6	44.0	27.6	66 39.6	43.3	28.6	67 31.9	42.3	29.8	68 23.7	41.4	31.0	69 14.7	40.3	32.4	70 05.0	39.2	33.9	70 54.3	37.9	35.5	58
59	65 02.6	45.1	25.9	65 56.3	44.3	26.9	66 49.6	43.6	28.0	67 42.3	42.7	29.1	68 34.4	41.8	30.3	69 25.8	40.7	31.7	70 16.4	39.5	33.2	59
60	64 17.5	−46.0	24.4	65 12.0	−45.4	25.3	66 06.0	−44.7	26.2	66 59.6	−43.9	27.3	67 52.6	−43.0	28.4	68 45.1	−42.1	29.6	69 36.9	−41.1	31.0	60
61	63 31.5	46.8	22.9	64 26.6	46.3	23.7	65 21.3	45.6	24.6	66 15.7	45.0	25.6	67 09.6	44.3	26.6	68 03.0	43.4	27.7	68 55.8	42.5	28.9	61
62	62 44.7	47.6	21.6	63 40.3	47.1	22.3	64 35.7	46.6	23.1	65 30.7	45.9	23.9	66 25.3	45.2	24.9	67 19.6	44.6	25.9	68 13.3	43.8	27.0	62
63	61 57.1	48.4	20.2	62 53.2	47.8	20.9	63 49.1	47.3	21.6	64 44.8	46.9	22.4	65 40.1	46.3	23.3	66 35.0	45.6	24.2	67 29.5	44.9	25.2	63
64	61 08.7	48.9	19.0	62 05.4	48.6	19.6	63 01.8	48.1	20.3	63 57.9	47.6	21.0	64 53.8	47.1	21.7	65 49.4	46.6	22.6	66 44.6	45.9	23.4	64
65	60 19.8	−49.6	17.8	61 16.8	−49.2	18.4	62 13.7	−48.9	19.0	63 10.3	−48.4	19.6	64 06.7	−48.0	20.3	65 02.8	−47.4	21.0	65 58.7	−46.9	21.8	65
66	59 30.2	50.1	16.7	60 27.6	49.8	17.2	61 24.8	49.4	17.7	62 21.9	49.1	18.3	63 18.7	48.6	18.9	64 15.4	48.2	19.6	65 11.8	47.8	20.3	66
67	58 40.1	50.6	15.6	59 37.8	50.3	16.1	60 35.4	50.0	16.6	61 32.8	49.7	17.1	62 30.1	49.4	17.7	63 27.2	49.0	18.3	64 24.0	48.5	18.9	67
68	57 49.5	51.1	14.6	58 47.5	50.9	15.0	59 45.4	50.6	15.5	60 43.1	50.3	15.9	61 40.7	49.9	16.4	62 38.2	49.6	17.0	63 35.5	49.2	17.6	68
69	56 58.4	51.6	13.6	57 56.6	51.3	14.0	58 54.8	51.1	14.4	59 52.8	50.7	14.8	60 50.8	50.5	15.3	61 48.6	50.2	15.8	62 46.3	49.9	16.3	69
70	56 06.8	−51.9	12.7	57 05.3	−51.7	13.0	58 03.7	−51.5	13.4	59 02.1	−51.3	13.8	60 00.3	−51.1	14.2	60 58.4	−50.8	14.6	61 56.4	−50.5	15.1	70
71	55 14.9	52.3	11.8	56 13.6	52.1	12.1	57 12.2	51.9	12.4	58 10.8	51.7	12.8	59 09.2	51.5	13.2	60 07.6	51.2	13.5	61 05.9	51.0	14.0	71
72	54 22.6	52.6	11.0	55 21.5	52.5	11.2	56 20.3	52.3	11.5	57 19.1	52.2	11.8	58 17.7	51.9	12.2	59 16.4	51.8	12.5	60 14.9	51.5	12.9	72
73	53 30.0	53.0	10.1	54 29.0	52.8	10.4	55 28.0	52.7	10.7	56 26.9	52.5	10.9	57 25.8	52.3	11.2	58 24.6	52.1	11.5	59 23.4	52.0	11.9	73
74	52 37.0	53.3	9.4	53 36.2	53.2	9.6	54 35.3	53.0	9.8	55 34.4	52.8	10.1	56 33.5	52.7	10.3	57 32.5	52.6	10.6	58 31.4	52.4	10.9	74
75	51 43.7	−53.5	8.6	52 43.0	−53.4	8.8	53 42.3	−53.3	9.0	54 41.6	−53.2	9.2	55 40.8	−53.1	9.5	56 39.9	−52.9	9.7	57 39.0	−52.7	10.0	75
76	50 50.2	53.8	7.9	51 49.6	53.7	8.1	52 49.0	53.6	8.2	53 48.4	53.5	8.4	54 47.7	53.4	8.6	55 47.0	53.2	8.9	56 46.3	53.1	9.1	76
77	49 56.4	54.0	7.2	50 55.9	53.9	7.3	51 55.4	53.8	7.5	52 54.9	53.8	7.7	53 54.3	53.6	7.9	54 53.8	53.6	8.1	55 53.2	53.5	8.3	77
78	49 02.4	54.3	6.5	50 02.0	54.2	6.7	51 01.6	54.1	6.8	52 01.1	54.0	7.0	53 00.7	54.0	7.1	54 00.2	53.8	7.3	54 59.7	53.7	7.5	78
79	48 08.1	54.4	5.9	49 07.8	54.4	6.0	50 07.5	54.4	6.1	51 07.1	54.3	6.3	52 06.7	54.1	6.4	53 06.4	54.1	6.5	54 06.0	54.1	6.7	79
80	47 13.7	−54.7	5.3	48 13.4	−54.6	5.4	49 13.1	−54.5	5.5	50 12.8	−54.4	5.6	51 12.6	−54.5	5.7	52 12.3	−54.4	5.8	53 11.9	−54.2	6.0	80
81	46 19.0	54.9	4.7	47 18.8	54.8	4.7	48 18.6	54.8	4.8	49 18.4	54.7	4.9	50 18.1	54.6	5.0	51 17.9	54.6	5.1	52 17.7	54.6	5.3	81
82	45 24.1	55.0	4.1	46 24.0	55.0	4.1	47 23.8	54.9	4.2	48 23.7	54.9	4.3	49 23.5	54.9	4.4	50 23.3	54.8	4.5	51 23.1	54.7	4.6	82
83	44 29.1	55.2	3.5	45 29.0	55.1	3.6	46 28.9	55.1	3.6	47 28.8	55.1	3.7	48 28.6	55.0	3.8	49 28.5	55.0	3.9	50 28.4	55.0	3.9	83
84	43 33.9	55.3	3.0	44 33.9	55.3	3.0	45 33.8	55.3	3.1	46 33.7	55.3	3.1	47 33.6	55.2	3.2	48 33.5	55.2	3.2	49 33.4	55.1	3.3	84
85	42 38.6	−55.5	2.4	43 38.6	−55.5	2.5	44 38.5	−55.4	2.5	45 38.4	−55.4	2.6	46 38.4	−55.4	2.6	47 38.3	−55.3	2.7	48 38.3	−55.4	2.7	85
86	41 43.1	55.6	1.9	42 43.1	55.6	1.9	43 43.1	55.6	2.0	44 43.0	55.5	2.0	45 43.0	55.5	2.1	46 43.0	55.6	2.1	47 42.9	55.5	2.1	86
87	40 47.5	55.7	1.4	41 47.5	55.7	1.4	42 47.5	55.7	1.5	43 47.5	55.7	1.5	44 47.5	55.7	1.5	45 47.4	55.6	1.5	46 47.4	55.6	1.6	87
88	39 51.8	55.8	0.9	40 51.8	55.8	0.9	41 51.8	55.8	1.0	42 51.8	55.8	1.0	43 51.8	55.8	1.0	44 51.8	55.8	1.0	45 51.8	55.9	1.0	88
89	38 56.0	56.0	0.5	39 56.0	56.0	0.5	40 56.0	56.0	0.5	41 56.0	56.0	0.5	42 56.0	56.0	0.5	43 56.0	56.0	0.5	44 55.9	55.9	0.5	89
90	38 00.0	−56.1	0.0	39 00.0	−56.1	0.0	40 00.0	−56.1	0.0	41 00.0	−56.1	0.0	42 00.0	−56.1	0.0	43 00.0	−56.1	0.0	44 00.0	−56.1	0.0	90
	38°			39°			40°			41°			42°			43°			44°			

Dec.	38°			39°			40°			41°			42°			43°			44°			Dec.
	Hc	d	Z	Hc	d	Z	Hc	d	Z	Hc	d	Z	Hc	d	Z	Hc	d	Z	Hc	d	Z	
°	° ′	′	°	° ′	′	°	° ′	′	°	° ′	′	°	° ′	′	°	° ′	′	°	° ′	′	°	°
0	0 47.3	+36.9	90.6	0 46.6	+37.8	90.6	0 46.0	+38.5	90.6	0 45.3	+39.3	90.7	0 44.6	+40.1	90.7	0 43.9	+40.9	90.7	0 43.2	+41.6	90.7	0
1	1 24.2	36.9	89.8	1 24.4	37.7	89.9	1 24.5	38.6	89.9	1 24.6	39.4	89.9	1 24.7	40.2	89.9	1 24.8	40.9	90.0	1 24.8	41.7	90.0	1
2	2 01.1	36.9	89.0	2 02.1	37.7	89.1	2 03.1	38.5	89.1	2 04.0	39.3	89.1	2 04.9	40.1	89.2	2 05.7	40.9	89.2	2 06.5	41.6	89.3	2
3	2 38.0	36.9	88.2	2 39.8	37.7	88.3	2 41.6	38.5	88.3	2 43.3	39.3	88.4	2 45.0	40.1	88.4	2 46.6	40.8	88.5	2 48.1	41.7	88.5	3
4	3 14.9	36.8	87.5	3 17.5	37.7	87.5	3 20.1	38.5	87.6	3 22.6	39.3	87.6	3 25.1	40.0	87.7	3 27.4	40.9	87.8	3 29.8	41.6	87.8	4
5	3 51.7	+36.8	86.7	3 55.2	+37.6	86.7	3 58.6	+38.4	86.8	4 01.9	+39.2	86.9	4 05.1	+40.0	86.9	4 08.3	+40.8	87.0	4 11.4	+41.5	87.1	5
6	4 28.5	36.8	85.9	4 32.8	37.6	86.0	4 37.0	38.4	86.0	4 41.1	39.2	86.1	4 45.1	40.0	86.2	4 49.1	40.7	86.3	4 52.9	41.5	86.4	6
7	5 05.3	36.6	85.1	5 10.4	37.5	85.2	5 15.4	38.3	85.3	5 20.3	39.1	85.4	5 25.1	39.9	85.4	5 29.8	40.7	85.5	5 34.4	41.4	85.6	7
8	5 41.9	36.7	84.3	5 47.9	37.4	84.4	5 53.7	38.2	84.5	5 59.4	39.0	84.6	6 05.0	39.8	84.7	6 10.5	40.6	84.8	6 15.8	41.4	84.9	8
9	6 18.6	36.5	83.5	6 25.3	37.4	83.6	6 31.9	38.2	83.7	6 38.4	39.0	83.8	6 44.8	39.8	83.9	6 51.1	40.5	84.1	6 57.2	41.3	84.2	9
10	6 55.1	+36.5	82.7	7 02.7	+37.2	82.8	7 10.1	+38.1	82.9	7 17.4	+38.9	83.1	7 24.6	+39.7	83.2	7 31.6	+40.5	83.3	7 38.5	+41.3	83.5	10
11	7 31.6	36.3	81.9	7 39.9	37.2	82.0	7 48.2	38.0	82.2	7 56.3	38.8	82.3	8 04.3	39.6	82.4	8 12.1	40.4	82.6	8 19.8	41.2	82.7	11
12	8 07.9	36.3	81.1	8 17.1	37.1	81.2	8 26.2	37.9	81.4	8 35.1	38.8	81.5	8 43.9	39.5	81.7	8 52.5	40.3	81.8	9 01.0	41.0	82.0	12
13	8 44.2	36.2	80.3	8 54.2	37.1	80.4	9 04.1	37.9	80.6	9 13.9	38.6	80.8	9 23.4	39.4	80.9	9 32.8	40.2	81.1	9 42.0	41.0	81.2	13
14	9 20.4	36.0	79.5	9 31.3	36.8	79.6	9 42.0	37.7	79.8	9 52.5	38.5	80.0	10 02.8	39.4	80.1	10 13.0	40.1	80.3	10 23.0	40.9	80.5	14
15	9 56.4	+36.0	78.7	10 08.1	+36.8	78.8	10 19.7	+37.6	79.0	10 31.0	+38.4	79.2	10 42.2	+39.2	79.4	10 53.1	+40.0	79.6	11 03.9	+40.7	79.8	15
16	10 32.4	35.8	77.9	10 44.9	36.7	78.0	10 57.3	37.4	78.2	11 09.4	38.3	78.4	11 21.4	39.0	78.6	11 33.1	39.9	78.8	11 44.6	40.7	79.0	16
17	11 08.2	35.7	77.0	11 21.6	36.5	77.2	11 34.7	37.4	77.4	11 47.7	38.1	77.6	12 00.4	39.0	77.8	12 13.0	39.7	78.0	12 25.3	40.5	78.3	17
18	11 43.9	35.6	76.2	11 58.1	36.4	76.4	12 12.1	37.2	76.6	12 25.8	38.1	76.8	12 39.4	38.8	77.1	12 52.7	39.6	77.3	13 05.8	40.4	77.5	18
19	12 19.5	35.4	75.4	12 34.5	36.2	75.6	12 49.3	37.0	75.8	13 03.9	37.8	76.0	13 18.2	38.7	76.3	13 32.3	39.5	76.5	13 46.2	40.3	76.7	19
20	12 54.9	+35.2	74.6	13 10.7	+36.1	74.8	13 26.3	+36.9	75.0	13 41.7	+37.7	75.2	13 56.9	+38.5	75.5	14 11.8	+39.3	75.7	14 26.5	+40.1	76.0	20
21	13 30.1	35.1	73.7	13 46.8	35.9	74.0	14 03.2	36.8	74.2	14 19.4	37.6	74.4	14 35.4	38.4	74.7	14 51.1	39.2	75.0	15 06.6	39.9	75.2	21
22	14 05.2	34.9	72.9	14 22.7	35.7	73.1	14 40.0	36.5	73.4	14 57.0	37.4	73.6	15 13.8	38.2	73.9	15 30.3	39.0	74.2	15 46.5	39.8	74.4	22
23	14 40.1	34.7	72.1	14 58.4	35.6	72.3	15 16.5	36.4	72.6	15 34.4	37.2	72.8	15 52.0	38.0	73.1	16 09.3	38.8	73.4	16 26.3	39.6	73.7	23
24	15 14.8	34.5	71.2	15 34.0	35.4	71.5	15 52.9	36.2	71.7	16 11.6	37.0	72.0	16 30.0	37.8	72.3	16 48.1	38.6	72.6	17 05.9	39.4	72.9	24
25	15 49.3	+34.4	70.4	16 09.4	+35.1	70.6	16 29.1	+36.0	70.9	16 48.6	+36.8	71.2	17 07.8	+37.6	71.5	17 26.7	+38.4	71.8	17 45.3	+39.3	72.1	25
26	16 23.7	34.1	69.5	16 44.5	35.0	69.8	17 05.1	35.8	70.1	17 25.4	36.6	70.4	17 45.4	37.5	70.7	18 05.1	38.3	71.0	18 24.6	39.0	71.3	26
27	16 57.8	33.9	68.7	17 19.5	34.7	68.9	17 40.9	35.6	69.2	18 02.0	36.4	69.5	18 22.9	37.2	69.8	18 43.4	38.0	70.2	19 03.6	38.8	70.5	27
28	17 31.7	33.7	67.8	17 54.2	34.6	68.1	18 16.5	35.3	68.4	18 38.4	36.2	68.7	19 00.1	37.0	69.0	19 21.4	37.8	69.3	19 42.4	38.6	69.7	28
29	18 05.4	33.4	66.9	18 28.8	34.2	67.2	18 51.8	35.2	67.5	19 14.6	36.0	67.9	19 37.1	36.7	68.2	19 59.2	37.6	68.5	20 21.0	38.4	68.9	29
30	18 38.8	+33.2	66.0	19 03.0	+34.1	66.4	19 27.0	+34.8	66.7	19 50.6	+35.7	67.0	20 13.8	+36.5	67.3	20 36.8	+37.3	67.7	20 59.4	+38.1	68.0	30
31	19 12.0	33.0	65.2	19 37.1	33.8	65.5	20 01.8	34.6	65.8	20 26.3	35.4	66.2	20 50.3	36.3	66.5	21 14.1	37.1	66.8	21 37.5	37.9	67.2	31
32	19 45.0	32.7	64.3	20 10.9	33.5	64.6	20 36.4	34.4	64.9	21 01.7	35.2	65.3	21 26.6	36.0	65.6	21 51.2	36.8	66.0	22 15.4	37.6	66.4	32
33	20 17.7	32.4	63.4	20 44.4	33.2	63.7	21 10.8	34.1	64.1	21 36.9	34.9	64.4	22 02.6	35.7	64.8	22 28.0	36.6	65.2	22 53.0	37.4	65.5	33
34	20 50.1	32.1	62.5	21 17.6	33.0	62.8	21 44.9	33.8	63.2	22 11.8	34.6	63.5	22 38.3	35.5	63.9	23 04.6	36.2	64.3	23 30.4	37.1	64.7	34
35	21 22.2	+31.9	61.6	21 50.6	+32.7	61.9	22 18.7	+33.5	62.3	22 46.4	+34.3	62.7	23 13.8	+35.1	63.0	23 40.8	+36.0	63.4	24 07.5	+36.8	63.8	35
36	21 54.1	31.5	60.7	22 23.3	32.4	61.0	22 52.2	33.2	61.4	23 20.7	34.1	61.8	23 48.9	34.9	62.2	24 16.8	35.7	62.5	24 44.3	36.5	63.0	36
37	22 25.6	31.2	59.8	22 55.7	32.0	60.1	23 25.4	32.9	60.5	23 54.8	33.7	60.9	24 23.8	34.5	61.3	24 52.5	35.3	61.7	25 20.8	36.1	62.1	37
38	22 56.8	30.9	58.8	23 27.7	31.7	59.2	23 58.3	32.5	59.6	24 28.5	33.4	60.0	24 58.3	34.2	60.4	25 27.8	35.0	60.8	25 56.9	35.9	61.2	38
39	23 27.7	30.6	57.9	23 59.4	31.4	58.3	24 30.8	32.2	58.7	25 01.9	33.0	59.0	25 32.5	33.9	59.5	26 02.8	34.7	59.9	26 32.8	35.5	60.3	39
40	23 58.3	+30.2	57.0	24 30.8	+31.1	57.3	25 03.0	+31.9	57.7	25 34.9	+32.7	58.1	26 06.4	+33.5	58.5	26 37.5	+34.4	59.0	27 08.3	+35.1	59.4	40
41	24 28.5	29.8	56.0	25 01.9	30.6	56.4	25 34.9	31.5	56.8	26 07.6	32.3	57.2	26 39.9	33.2	57.6	27 11.9	33.9	58.0	27 43.4	34.8	58.5	41
42	24 58.3	29.5	55.1	25 32.5	30.3	55.4	26 06.4	31.1	55.8	26 39.9	32.0	56.2	27 13.1	32.7	56.7	27 45.8	33.6	57.1	28 18.2	34.4	57.6	42
43	25 27.8	29.1	54.1	26 02.8	30.0	54.5	26 37.5	30.8	54.9	27 11.9	31.5	55.3	27 45.8	32.4	55.7	28 19.4	33.2	56.2	28 52.6	34.1	56.6	43
44	25 56.9	28.7	53.1	26 32.8	29.5	53.5	27 08.3	30.3	53.9	27 43.4	31.2	54.3	28 18.2	32.0	54.8	28 52.6	32.8	55.2	29 26.7	33.6	55.7	44
45	26 25.6	+28.4	52.1	27 02.3	+29.1	52.5	27 38.6	+30.0	52.9	28 14.6	+30.8	53.4	28 50.2	+31.6	53.8	29 25.4	+32.4	54.3	30 00.3	+33.2	54.7	45
46	26 54.0	27.9	51.2	27 31.4	28.7	51.6	28 08.6	29.5	52.0	28 45.4	30.3	52.4	29 21.8	31.1	52.8	29 57.8	32.0	53.3	30 33.5	32.8	53.8	46
47	27 21.9	27.4	50.2	28 00.1	28.3	50.6	28 38.1	29.1	51.0	29 15.7	29.9	51.4	29 52.9	30.7	51.9	30 29.8	31.5	52.3	31 06.3	32.3	52.8	47
48	27 49.3	27.1	49.2	28 28.4	27.8	49.6	29 07.2	28.6	50.0	29 45.6	29.4	50.4	30 23.6	30.3	50.9	31 01.3	31.1	51.3	31 38.6	31.9	51.8	48
49	28 16.4	26.5	48.1	28 56.2	27.4	48.6	29 35.8	28.2	49.0	30 15.0	29.0	49.4	30 53.9	29.7	49.9	31 32.4	30.5	50.3	32 10.5	31.4	50.8	49
50	28 42.9	+26.2	47.1	29 23.6	+26.9	47.5	30 04.0	+27.7	48.0	30 44.0	+28.5	48.4	31 23.6	+29.3	48.8	32 02.9	+30.1	49.3	32 41.9	+30.9	49.8	50
51	29 09.1	25.6	46.1	29 50.5	26.4	46.5	30 31.7	27.2	46.9	31 12.5	28.0	47.4	31 52.9	28.8	47.8	32 33.0	29.6	48.3	33 12.8	30.4	48.8	51
52	29 34.7	25.2	45.1	30 16.9	26.0	45.5	30 58.9	26.7	45.9	31 40.5	27.4	46.3	32 21.7	28.3	46.8	33 02.6	29.1	47.3	33 43.2	29.8	47.7	52
53	29 59.9	24.6	44.0	30 42.9	25.4	44.4	31 25.6	26.2	44.8	32 07.9	27.0	45.3	32 50.0	27.7	45.7	33 31.7	28.5	46.2	34 13.0	29.4	46.7	53
54	30 24.5	24.2	43.0	31 08.3	24.9	43.4	31 51.8	25.6	43.8	32 34.9	26.4	44.2	33 17.7	27.3	44.7	34 00.2	28.0	45.1	34 42.4	28.8	45.6	54
55	30 48.7	+23.6	41.9	31 33.2	+24.3	42.3	32 17.4	+25.1	42.7	33 01.3	+25.9	43.2	33 45.0	+26.6	43.6	34 28.2	+27.5	44.1	35 11.2	+28.2	44.6	55
56	31 12.3	23.1	40.8	31 57.5	23.9	41.2	32 42.5	24.6	41.6	33 27.2	25.3	42.1	34 11.6	26.1	42.5	34 55.7	26.8	43.0	35 39.4	27.6	43.5	56
57	31 35.4	22.5	39.7	32 21.4	23.2	40.1	33 07.1	24.0	40.6	33 52.5	24.8	41.0	34 37.7	25.5	41.4	35 22.5	26.2	41.9	36 07.0	27.0	42.4	57
58	31 57.9	22.0	38.6	32 44.6	22.7	39.0	33 31.1	23.4	39.5	34 17.3	24.1	39.9	35 03.2	24.8	40.3	35 48.7	25.7	40.8	36 34.0	26.4	41.3	58
59	32 19.9	21.3	37.5	33 07.3	22.1	37.9	33 54.5	22.8	38.4	34 41.4	23.5	38.8	35 28.0	24.3	39.2	36 14.4	25.0	39.7	37 00.4	25.7	40.2	59
60	32 41.2	+20.8	36.4	33 29.4	+21.5	36.8	34 17.3	+22.2	37.2	35 04.9	+22.9	37.7	35 52.3	+23.6	38.1	36 39.4	+24.3	38.5	37 26.1	+25.1	39.0	60
61	33 02.0	20.2	35.3	33 50.9	20.9	35.7	34 39.5	21.5	36.1	35 27.8	22.3	36.5	36 15.9	23.0	37.0	37 03.7	23.7	37.4	37 51.2	24.4	37.9	61
62	33 22.2	19.6	34.2	34 11.8	20.2	34.6	35 01.0	21.0	35.0	35 50.1	21.6	35.4	36 38.9	22.3	35.8	37 27.4	23.0	36.3	38 15.6	23.8	36.7	62
63	33 41.8	19.0	33.1	34 32.0	19.6	33.4	35 22.0	20.2	33.8	36 11.7	20.9	34.2	37 01.2	21.6	34.6	37 50.4	22.3	35.1	38 39.4	23.0	35.5	63
64	34 00.8	18.3	31.9	34 51.6	19.0	32.3	35 42.2	19.6	32.7	36 32.6	20.3	33.1	37 22.8	20.9	33.5	38 12.7	21.6	33.9	39 02.4	22.3	34.4	64
65	34 19.1	+17.7	30.8	35 10.6	+18.2	31.1	36 01.8	+18.9	31.5	36 52.9	+19.5	31.9	37 43.7	+20.2	32.3	38 34.3	+20.9	32.7	39 24.7	+21.5	33.2	65
66	34 36.8	17.0	29.6	35 28.8	17.7	30.0	36 20.7	18.2	30.3	37 12.4	18.9	30.7	38 03.9	19.5	31.1	38 55.2	20.1	31.5	39 46.2	20.8	31.9	66
67	34 53.8	16.3	28.4	35 46.5	16.9	28.8	36 38.9	17.6	29.1	37 31.3	18.1	29.5	38 23.4	18.7	29.9	39 15.3	19.3	30.3	40 07.0	20.0	30.7	67
68	35 10.1	15.7	27.3	36 03.4	16.2	27.6	36 56.5	16.7	27.9	37 49.4	17.3	28.3	38 42.1	18.0	28.7	39 34.6	18.6	29.1	40 27.0	19.2	29.5	68
69	35 25.8	14.9	26.1	36 19.6	15.5	26.4	37 13.2	16.1	26.7	38 06.7	16.6	27.1	39 00.1	17.2	27.5	39 53.2	17.8	27.8	40 46.2	18.4	28.2	69
70	35 40.7	+14.3	24.9	36 35.1	+14.7	25.2	37 29.3	+15.3	25.5	38 23.3	+15.9	25.9	39 17.3	+16.4	26.2	40 11.0	+17.0	26.6	41 04.6	+17.5	27.0	70
71	35 55.0	13.5	23.7	36 49.8	14.1	24.0	37 44.6	14.5	24.3	38 39.2	15.0	24.6	39 33.7	15.5	25.0	40 28.0	16.1	25.3	41 22.1	16.7	25.7	71
72	36 08.5	12.8	22.5	37 03.9	13.2	22.8	37 59.1	13.8	23.1	38 54.2	14.3	23.4	39 49.2	14.8	23.7	40 44.1	15.3	24.1	41 38.8	15.9	24.4	72
73	36 21.3	12.0	21.3	37 17.1	12.5	21.6	38 12.9	13.0	21.8	39 08.5	13.5	22.1	40 04.0	14.0	22.5	40 59.4	14.5	22.8	41 54.7	14.9	23.1	73
74	36 33.3	11.3	20.1	37 29.6	11.8	20.3	38 25.9	12.1	20.6	39 22.0	12.6	20.9	40 18.0	13.1	21.2	41 13.9	13.5	21.5	42 09.6	14.1	21.8	74
75	36 44.6	+10.6	18.8	37 41.4	+11.0	19.1	38 38.0	+11.4	19.3	39 34.6	+11.8	19.6	40 31.1	+12.2	19.9	41 27.4	+12.7	20.2	42 23.7	+13.2	20.5	75
76	36 55.2	9.8	17.6	37 52.4	10.1	17.8	38 49.4	10.6	18.1	39 46.4	11.0	18.3	40 43.3	11.4	18.6	41 40.1	11.9	18.9	42 36.9	12.2	19.2	76
77	37 05.0	9.0	16.4	38 02.5	9.4	16.6	39 00.0	9.7	16.8	39 57.4	10.1	17.1	40 54.7	10.5	17.3	41 52.0	10.9	17.6	42 49.1	11.3	17.9	77
78	37 14.0	8.3	15.1	38 11.9	8.6	15.3	39 09.7	9.0	15.6	40 07.5	9.3	15.8	41 05.2	9.6	16.0	42 02.9	9.9	16.3	43 00.4	10.4	16.5	78
79	37 22.3	7.4	13.9	38 20.5	7.7	14.1	39 18.7	8.0	14.3	40 16.8	8.4	14.5	41 14.8	8.8	14.7	42 12.8	9.1	14.9	43 10.8	9.4	15.2	79
80	37 29.7	+6.7	12.6	38 28.2	+7.0	12.8	39 26.7	+7.3	13.0	40 25.2	+7.5	13.2	41 23.6	+7.8	13.4	42 21.9	+8.1	13.6	43 20.2	+8.5	13.8	80
81	37 36.4	5.8	11.4	38 35.2	6.1	11.5	39 34.0	6.3	11.7	40 32.7	6.6	11.9	41 31.4	6.9	12.1	42 30.0	7.2	12.2	43 28.7	7.4	12.4	81
82	37 42.2	5.1	10.1	38 41.3	5.3	10.3	39 40.3	5.5	10.4	40 39.3	5.8	10.6	41 38.3	6.0	10.7	42 37.2	6.3	10.9	43 36.1	6.5	11.1	82
83	37 47.3	4.3	8.9	38 46.6	4.4	9.0	39 45.8	4.7	9.1	40 45.1	4.8	9.3	41 44.3	5.0	9.4	42 43.5	5.2	9.5	43 42.6	5.5	9.7	83
84	37 51.6	3.4	7.6	38 51.0	3.6	7.7	39 50.5	3.8	7.8	40 49.9	4.0	7.9	41 49.3	4.2	8.1	42 48.7	4.3	8.2	43 48.1	4.5	8.3	84
85	37 55.0	+2.6	6.3	38 54.6	+2.8	6.4	39 54.3	+2.9	6.5	40 53.9	+3.0	6.6	41 53.5	+3.1	6.7	42 53.0	+3.4	6.8	43 52.6	+3.5	6.9	85
86	37 57.6	1.9	5.1	38 57.4	1.9	5.1	39 57.2	2.0	5.2	40 56.9	2.1	5.3	41 56.6	2.3	5.4	42 56.4	2.3	5.5	43 56.1	2.5	5.6	86
87	37 59.5	1.0	3.8	38 59.3	1.1	3.9	39 59.2	1.1	3.9	40 59.0	1.3	4.0	41 58.9	1.3	4.0	42 58.7	1.4	4.1	43 58.6	1.5	4.2	87
88	38 00.5	+0.1	2.5	39 00.4	+0.2	2.6	40 00.3	+0.3	2.6	41 00.3	+0.3	2.7	42 00.2	+0.4	2.7	43 00.1	+0.5	2.7	44 00.1	+0.4	2.8	88
89	38 00.6	−0.6	1.3	39 00.6	−0.6	1.3	40 00.6	−0.6	1.3	41 00.6	−0.6	1.3	42 00.6	−0.6	1.3	43 00.6	−0.6	1.4	44 00.5	−0.5	1.4	89
90	38 00.0	−1.5	0.0	39 00.0	−1.5	0.0	40 00.0	−1.5	0.0	41 00.0	−1.5	0.0	42 00.0	−1.5	0.0	43 00.0	−1.5	0.0	44 00.0	−1.6	0.0	90
	38°			39°			40°			41°			42°			43°			44°			

LATITUDE **CONTRARY** NAME TO DECLINATION L.H.A. 1°, 359°

	39°			40°			41°			42°			43°			44°			45°			
Dec.	Hc	d	Z	Hc	d	Z	Hc	d	Z	Hc	d	Z	Hc	d	Z	Hc	d	Z	Hc	d	Z	Dec.
°	° ′	′	°	° ′	′	°	° ′	′	°	° ′	′	°	° ′	′	°	° ′	′	°	° ′	′	°	°
0	50 59.4	-60.0	178.4	49 59.4	-60.0	178.4	48 59.4	-60.0	178.5	47 59.4	-60.0	178.5	46 59.4	-60.0	178.5	45 59.5	-60.0	178.6	44 59.5	-60.0	178.6	0
1	49 59.4	60.0	178.4	48 59.4	60.0	178.5	47 59.4	60.0	178.5	46 59.4	60.0	178.5	45 59.4	59.9	178.6	44 59.5	60.0	178.6	43 59.5	60.0	178.6	1
2	48 59.4	60.0	178.5	47 59.4	60.0	178.5	46 59.4	60.0	178.5	45 59.4	59.9	178.6	44 59.5	60.0	178.6	43 59.5	60.0	178.6	42 59.5	60.0	178.6	2
3	47 59.4	60.0	178.5	46 59.4	60.0	178.5	45 59.4	60.0	178.6	44 59.5	60.0	178.6	43 59.5	60.0	178.6	42 59.5	60.0	178.6	41 59.5	60.0	178.7	3
4	46 59.4	60.0	178.5	45 59.4	60.0	178.6	44 59.4	59.9	178.6	43 59.5	60.0	178.6	42 59.5	60.0	178.6	41 59.5	60.0	178.7	40 59.5	60.0	178.7	4
5	45 59.4	-60.0	178.6	44 59.4	-60.0	178.6	43 59.5	-60.0	178.6	42 59.5	-60.0	178.6	41 59.5	-60.0	178.7	40 59.5	-60.0	178.7	39 59.5	-60.0	178.7	5
6	44 59.4	60.0	178.6	43 59.4	59.9	178.6	42 59.5	60.0	178.6	41 59.5	60.0	178.7	40 59.5	60.0	178.7	39 59.5	60.0	178.7	38 59.5	60.0	178.7	6
7	43 59.4	60.0	178.6	42 59.5	60.0	178.6	41 59.5	60.0	178.7	40 59.5	60.0	178.7	39 59.5	60.0	178.7	38 59.5	60.0	178.7	37 59.5	60.0	178.7	7
8	42 59.4	59.9	178.6	41 59.5	60.0	178.7	40 59.5	60.0	178.7	39 59.5	60.0	178.7	38 59.5	60.0	178.7	37 59.5	60.0	178.7	36 59.5	60.0	178.8	8
9	41 59.5	60.0	178.7	40 59.5	60.0	178.7	39 59.5	60.0	178.7	38 59.5	60.0	178.7	37 59.5	60.0	178.7	36 59.5	60.0	178.8	35 59.5	59.9	178.8	9
10	40 59.5	-60.0	178.7	39 59.5	-60.0	178.7	38 59.5	-60.0	178.7	37 59.5	-60.0	178.8	36 59.5	-60.0	178.8	35 59.5	-60.0	178.8	34 59.6	-60.0	178.8	10
11	39 59.5	60.0	178.7	38 59.5	60.0	178.7	37 59.5	60.0	178.8	36 59.5	60.0	178.8	35 59.5	60.0	178.8	34 59.5	59.9	178.8	33 59.6	60.0	178.8	11
12	38 59.5	60.0	178.7	37 59.5	60.0	178.8	36 59.5	60.0	178.8	35 59.5	60.0	178.8	34 59.5	60.0	178.8	33 59.6	60.0	178.8	32 59.6	60.0	178.8	12
13	37 59.5	60.0	178.8	36 59.5	60.0	178.8	35 59.5	60.0	178.8	34 59.5	60.0	178.8	33 59.5	59.9	178.8	32 59.6	60.0	178.8	31 59.6	60.0	178.9	13
14	36 59.5	60.0	178.8	35 59.5	60.0	178.8	34 59.5	60.0	178.8	33 59.5	59.9	178.8	32 59.6	60.0	178.8	31 59.6	60.0	178.9	30 59.6	60.0	178.9	14
15	35 59.5	-60.0	178.8	34 59.5	-60.0	178.8	33 59.5	-60.0	178.8	32 59.6	-60.0	178.8	31 59.6	-60.0	178.9	30 59.6	-60.0	178.9	29 59.6	-60.0	178.9	15
16	34 59.5	60.0	178.8	33 59.5	60.0	178.8	32 59.5	59.9	178.9	31 59.6	60.0	178.9	30 59.6	60.0	178.9	29 59.6	60.0	178.9	28 59.6	60.0	178.9	16
17	33 59.5	60.0	178.8	32 59.5	59.9	178.9	31 59.6	60.0	178.9	30 59.6	60.0	178.9	29 59.6	60.0	178.9	28 59.6	60.0	178.9	27 59.6	60.0	178.9	17
18	32 59.5	60.0	178.9	31 59.6	60.0	178.9	30 59.6	60.0	178.9	29 59.6	60.0	178.9	28 59.6	60.0	178.9	27 59.6	60.0	178.9	26 59.6	60.0	178.9	18
19	31 59.5	59.9	178.9	30 59.6	60.0	178.9	29 59.6	60.0	178.9	28 59.6	60.0	178.9	27 59.6	60.0	178.9	26 59.6	60.0	178.9	25 59.6	60.0	178.9	19
20	30 59.6	-60.0	178.9	29 59.6	-60.0	178.9	28 59.6	-60.0	178.9	27 59.6	-60.0	178.9	26 59.6	-60.0	178.9	25 59.6	-60.0	179.0	24 59.6	-60.0	179.0	20
21	29 59.6	60.0	178.9	28 59.6	60.0	178.9	27 59.6	60.0	178.9	26 59.6	60.0	179.0	25 59.6	60.0	179.0	24 59.6	60.0	179.0	23 59.6	60.0	179.0	21
22	28 59.6	60.0	178.9	27 59.6	60.0	178.9	26 59.6	60.0	179.0	25 59.6	60.0	179.0	24 59.6	60.0	179.0	23 59.6	60.0	179.0	22 59.6	60.0	179.0	22
23	27 59.6	60.0	179.0	26 59.6	60.0	179.0	25 59.6	60.0	179.0	24 59.6	60.0	179.0	23 59.6	60.0	179.0	22 59.6	60.0	179.0	21 59.6	60.0	179.0	23
24	26 59.6	60.0	179.0	25 59.6	60.0	179.0	24 59.6	60.0	179.0	23 59.6	60.0	179.0	22 59.6	60.0	179.0	21 59.6	60.0	179.0	20 59.6	60.0	179.0	24
25	25 59.6	-60.0	179.0	24 59.6	-60.0	179.0	23 59.6	-60.0	179.0	22 59.6	-60.0	179.0	21 59.6	-60.0	179.0	20 59.6	-60.0	179.0	19 59.6	-60.0	179.0	25
26	24 59.6	60.0	179.0	23 59.6	60.0	179.0	22 59.6	60.0	179.0	21 59.6	60.0	179.0	20 59.6	60.0	179.0	19 59.6	60.0	179.0	18 59.6	59.9	179.0	26
27	23 59.6	60.0	179.0	22 59.6	60.0	179.0	21 59.6	60.0	179.0	20 59.6	60.0	179.0	19 59.6	60.0	179.1	18 59.6	59.9	179.1	17 59.7	60.0	179.1	27
28	22 59.6	60.0	179.0	21 59.6	60.0	179.0	20 59.6	60.0	179.1	19 59.6	60.0	179.1	18 59.6	60.0	179.1	17 59.7	60.0	179.1	16 59.7	60.0	179.1	28
29	21 59.6	60.0	179.1	20 59.6	60.0	179.1	19 59.6	60.0	179.1	18 59.6	60.0	179.1	17 59.6	59.9	179.1	16 59.7	60.0	179.1	15 59.7	60.0	179.1	29
30	20 59.6	-60.0	179.1	19 59.6	-60.0	179.1	18 59.6	-60.0	179.1	17 59.6	-59.9	179.1	16 59.7	-60.0	179.1	15 59.7	-60.0	179.1	14 59.7	-60.0	179.1	30
31	19 59.6	60.0	179.1	18 59.6	60.0	179.1	17 59.6	60.0	179.1	16 59.7	60.0	179.1	15 59.7	60.0	179.1	14 59.7	60.0	179.1	13 59.7	60.0	179.1	31
32	18 59.6	60.0	179.1	17 59.6	60.0	179.1	16 59.6	59.9	179.1	15 59.7	60.0	179.1	14 59.7	60.0	179.1	13 59.7	60.0	179.1	12 59.7	60.0	179.1	32
33	17 59.6	60.0	179.1	16 59.6	59.9	179.1	15 59.7	60.0	179.1	14 59.7	60.0	179.1	13 59.7	60.0	179.1	12 59.7	60.0	179.1	11 59.7	60.0	179.1	33
34	16 59.6	59.9	179.1	15 59.7	60.0	179.1	14 59.7	60.0	179.1	13 59.7	60.0	179.1	12 59.7	60.0	179.1	11 59.7	60.0	179.2	10 59.7	60.0	179.2	34
35	15 59.7	-60.0	179.1	14 59.7	-60.0	179.2	13 59.7	-60.0	179.2	12 59.7	-60.0	179.2	11 59.7	-60.0	179.2	10 59.7	-60.0	179.2	9 59.7	-60.0	179.2	35
36	14 59.7	60.0	179.2	13 59.7	60.0	179.2	12 59.7	60.0	179.2	11 59.7	60.0	179.2	10 59.7	60.0	179.2	9 59.7	60.0	179.2	8 59.7	60.0	179.2	36
37	13 59.7	60.0	179.2	12 59.7	60.0	179.2	11 59.7	60.0	179.2	10 59.7	60.0	179.2	9 59.7	60.0	179.2	8 59.7	60.0	179.2	7 59.7	60.0	179.2	37
38	12 59.7	60.0	179.2	11 59.7	60.0	179.2	10 59.7	60.0	179.2	9 59.7	60.0	179.2	8 59.7	60.0	179.2	7 59.7	60.0	179.2	6 59.7	60.0	179.2	38
39	11 59.7	60.0	179.2	10 59.7	60.0	179.2	9 59.7	60.0	179.2	8 59.7	60.0	179.2	7 59.7	60.0	179.2	6 59.7	60.0	179.2	5 59.7	60.0	179.2	39
40	10 59.7	-60.0	179.2	9 59.7	-60.0	179.2	8 59.7	-60.0	179.2	7 59.7	-60.0	179.2	6 59.7	-60.0	179.2	5 59.7	-60.0	179.2	4 59.7	-60.0	179.2	40
41	9 59.7	60.0	179.2	8 59.7	60.0	179.2	7 59.7	60.0	179.2	6 59.7	60.0	179.2	5 59.7	60.0	179.2	4 59.7	60.0	179.2	3 59.7	60.0	179.2	41
42	8 59.7	60.0	179.2	7 59.7	60.0	179.2	6 59.7	60.0	179.3	5 59.7	60.0	179.3	4 59.7	60.0	179.3	3 59.7	60.0	179.3	2 59.7	60.0	179.3	42
43	7 59.7	60.0	179.3	6 59.7	60.0	179.3	5 59.7	60.0	179.3	4 59.7	60.0	179.3	3 59.7	60.0	179.3	2 59.7	60.0	179.3	1 59.7	60.0	179.3	43
44	6 59.7	60.0	179.3	5 59.7	60.0	179.3	4 59.7	60.0	179.3	3 59.7	60.0	179.3	2 59.7	60.0	179.3	1 59.7	60.0	179.3	0 59.7	-60.0	179.3	44
45	5 59.7	-60.0	179.3	4 59.7	-60.0	179.3	3 59.7	-60.0	179.3	2 59.7	-60.0	179.3	1 59.7	-60.0	179.3	0 59.7	-60.0	179.3	0 00.3	+60.0	0.7	45
46	4 59.7	60.0	179.3	3 59.7	60.0	179.3	2 59.7	60.0	179.3	1 59.7	60.0	179.3	0 59.7	-60.0	179.3	0 00.3	+60.0	0.7	1 00.3	60.0	0.7	46
47	3 59.7	60.0	179.3	2 59.7	60.0	179.3	1 59.7	60.0	179.3	0 59.7	-60.0	179.3	0 00.3	+60.0	0.7	1 00.3	60.0	0.7	2 00.3	59.9	0.7	47
48	2 59.7	60.0	179.3	1 59.7	60.0	179.3	0 59.7	-60.0	179.3	0 00.3	+60.0	0.7	1 00.3	60.0	0.7	2 00.3	59.9	0.7	3 00.2	60.0	0.7	48
49	1 59.7	60.0	179.3	0 59.7	-60.0	179.3	0 00.3	+60.0	0.7	1 00.3	60.0	0.7	2 00.3	59.9	0.7	3 00.2	60.0	0.7	4 00.2	60.0	0.7	49
50	0 59.7	-60.0	179.4	0 00.3	+60.0	0.6	1 00.3	+59.9	0.6	2 00.3	+59.9	0.6	3 00.2	+60.0	0.6	4 00.2	+60.0	0.6	5 00.2	+60.0	0.6	50
51	0 00.3	+60.0	0.6	1 00.3	59.9	0.6	2 00.2	60.0	0.6	3 00.2	60.0	0.6	4 00.2	60.0	0.6	5 00.2	60.0	0.6	6 00.2	60.0	0.6	51
52	1 00.3	59.9	0.6	2 00.2	60.0	0.6	3 00.2	60.0	0.6	4 00.2	60.0	0.6	5 00.2	60.0	0.6	6 00.2	60.0	0.6	7 00.2	60.0	0.6	52
53	2 00.2	60.0	0.6	3 00.2	60.0	0.6	4 00.2	60.0	0.6	5 00.2	60.0	0.6	6 00.2	60.0	0.6	7 00.2	60.0	0.6	8 00.2	60.0	0.6	53
54	3 00.2	60.0	0.6	4 00.2	60.0	0.6	5 00.2	60.0	0.6	6 00.2	60.0	0.6	7 00.2	60.0	0.6	8 00.2	60.0	0.6	9 00.2	60.0	0.6	54
55	4 00.2	+60.0	0.6	5 00.2	+60.0	0.6	6 00.2	+60.0	0.6	7 00.2	+60.0	0.6	8 00.2	+60.0	0.6	9 00.2	+60.0	0.6	10 00.2	+60.0	0.6	55
56	5 00.2	60.0	0.6	6 00.2	60.0	0.6	7 00.2	60.0	0.6	8 00.2	60.0	0.6	9 00.2	60.0	0.6	10 00.2	60.0	0.6	11 00.2	60.0	0.6	56
57	6 00.2	60.0	0.5	7 00.2	60.0	0.5	8 00.2	60.0	0.5	9 00.2	60.0	0.6	10 00.2	60.0	0.6	11 00.2	60.0	0.6	12 00.2	60.0	0.6	57
58	7 00.2	60.0	0.5	8 00.2	60.0	0.5	9 00.2	60.0	0.5	10 00.2	60.0	0.5	11 00.2	60.0	0.5	12 00.2	60.0	0.5	13 00.2	60.0	0.5	58
59	8 00.2	60.0	0.5	9 00.2	60.0	0.5	10 00.2	60.0	0.5	11 00.2	60.0	0.5	12 00.2	60.0	0.5	13 00.2	60.0	0.5	14 00.2	60.0	0.5	59
60	9 00.2	+60.0	0.5	10 00.2	+60.0	0.5	11 00.2	+60.0	0.5	12 00.2	+60.0	0.5	13 00.2	+60.0	0.5	14 00.2	+60.0	0.5	15 00.2	+60.0	0.5	60
61	10 00.2	60.0	0.5	11 00.2	60.0	0.5	12 00.2	60.0	0.5	13 00.2	60.0	0.5	14 00.2	60.0	0.5	15 00.2	60.0	0.5	16 00.2	60.0	0.5	61
62	11 00.2	60.0	0.5	12 00.2	60.0	0.5	13 00.2	60.0	0.5	14 00.2	60.0	0.5	15 00.2	60.0	0.5	16 00.2	60.0	0.5	17 00.2	60.0	0.5	62
63	12 00.2	60.0	0.5	13 00.2	60.0	0.5	14 00.2	60.0	0.5	15 00.2	60.0	0.5	16 00.2	60.0	0.5	17 00.2	60.0	0.5	18 00.2	60.0	0.5	63
64	13 00.2	60.0	0.4	14 00.2	60.0	0.5	15 00.2	60.0	0.5	16 00.2	60.0	0.5	17 00.2	60.0	0.5	18 00.2	60.0	0.5	19 00.2	60.0	0.5	64
65	14 00.2	+60.0	0.4	15 00.2	+60.0	0.4	16 00.2	+60.0	0.4	17 00.2	+60.0	0.4	18 00.2	+60.0	0.4	19 00.2	+60.0	0.4	20 00.2	+60.0	0.4	65
66	15 00.2	60.0	0.4	16 00.2	60.0	0.4	17 00.2	60.0	0.4	18 00.2	60.0	0.4	19 00.2	60.0	0.4	20 00.2	60.0	0.4	21 00.2	60.0	0.4	66
67	16 00.2	60.0	0.4	17 00.2	60.0	0.4	18 00.2	60.0	0.4	19 00.2	60.0	0.4	20 00.2	60.0	0.4	21 00.2	60.0	0.4	22 00.2	60.0	0.4	67
68	17 00.2	60.0	0.4	18 00.2	60.0	0.4	19 00.2	60.0	0.4	20 00.2	59.9	0.4	21 00.2	59.9	0.4	22 00.2	59.9	0.4	23 00.2	59.9	0.4	68
69	18 00.2	59.9	0.4	19 00.2	59.9	0.4	20 00.2	59.9	0.4	21 00.1	60.0	0.4	22 00.1	60.0	0.4	23 00.1	60.0	0.4	24 00.1	60.0	0.4	69
70	19 00.1	+60.0	0.4	20 00.1	+60.0	0.4	21 00.1	+60.0	0.4	22 00.1	+60.0	0.4	23 00.1	+60.0	0.4	24 00.1	+60.0	0.4	25 00.1	+60.0	0.4	70
71	20 00.1	60.0	0.3	21 00.1	60.0	0.3	22 00.1	60.0	0.4	23 00.1	60.0	0.4	24 00.1	60.0	0.4	25 00.1	60.0	0.4	26 00.1	60.0	0.4	71
72	21 00.1	60.0	0.3	22 00.1	60.0	0.3	23 00.1	60.0	0.3	24 00.1	60.0	0.3	25 00.1	60.0	0.3	26 00.1	60.0	0.3	27 00.1	60.0	0.3	72
73	22 00.1	60.0	0.3	23 00.1	60.0	0.3	24 00.1	60.0	0.3	25 00.1	60.0	0.3	26 00.1	60.0	0.3	27 00.1	60.0	0.3	28 00.1	60.0	0.3	73
74	23 00.1	60.0	0.3	24 00.1	60.0	0.3	25 00.1	60.0	0.3	26 00.1	60.0	0.3	27 00.1	60.0	0.3	28 00.1	60.0	0.3	29 00.1	60.0	0.3	74
75	24 00.1	+60.0	0.3	25 00.1	+60.0	0.3	26 00.1	+60.0	0.3	27 00.1	+60.0	0.3	28 00.1	+60.0	0.3	29 00.1	+60.0	0.3	30 00.1	+60.0	0.3	75
76	25 00.1	60.0	0.3	26 00.1	60.0	0.3	27 00.1	60.0	0.3	28 00.1	60.0	0.3	29 00.1	60.0	0.3	30 00.1	60.0	0.3	31 00.1	60.0	0.3	76
77	26 00.1	60.0	0.3	27 00.1	60.0	0.3	28 00.1	60.0	0.3	29 00.1	60.0	0.3	30 00.1	60.0	0.3	31 00.1	60.0	0.3	32 00.1	60.0	0.3	77
78	27 00.1	60.0	0.2	28 00.1	60.0	0.2	29 00.1	60.0	0.2	30 00.1	60.0	0.2	31 00.1	60.0	0.2	32 00.1	60.0	0.2	33 00.1	60.0	0.2	78
79	28 00.1	60.0	0.2	29 00.1	60.0	0.2	30 00.1	60.0	0.2	31 00.1	60.0	0.2	32 00.1	60.0	0.2	33 00.1	60.0	0.2	34 00.1	60.0	0.2	79
80	29 00.1	+60.0	0.2	30 00.1	+60.0	0.2	31 00.1	+60.0	0.2	32 00.1	+60.0	0.2	33 00.1	+60.0	0.2	34 00.1	+60.0	0.2	35 00.1	+60.0	0.2	80
81	30 00.1	60.0	0.2	31 00.1	60.0	0.2	32 00.1	60.0	0.2	33 00.1	60.0	0.2	34 00.1	60.0	0.2	35 00.1	60.0	0.2	36 00.1	60.0	0.2	81
82	31 00.1	60.0	0.2	32 00.1	60.0	0.2	33 00.1	60.0	0.2	34 00.1	60.0	0.2	35 00.1	60.0	0.2	36 00.1	60.0	0.2	37 00.1	60.0	0.2	82
83	32 00.1	60.0	0.1	33 00.1	60.0	0.1	34 00.1	60.0	0.1	35 00.1	60.0	0.1	36 00.1	60.0	0.2	37 00.1	59.9	0.2	38 00.1	59.9	0.2	83
84	33 00.1	59.9	0.1	34 00.1	59.9	0.1	35 00.1	59.9	0.1	36 00.1	59.9	0.1	37 00.1	59.9	0.1	38 00.0	60.0	0.1	39 00.0	60.0	0.1	84
85	34 00.0	+60.0	0.1	35 00.0	+60.0	0.1	36 00.0	+60.0	0.1	37 00.0	+60.0	0.1	38 00.0	+60.0	0.1	39 00.0	+60.0	0.1	40 00.0	+60.0	0.1	85
86	35 00.0	60.0	0.1	36 00.0	60.0	0.1	37 00.0	60.0	0.1	38 00.0	60.0	0.1	39 00.0	60.0	0.1	40 00.0	60.0	0.1	41 00.0	60.0	0.1	86
87	36 00.0	60.0	0.1	37 00.0	60.0	0.1	38 00.0	60.0	0.1	39 00.0	60.0	0.1	40 00.0	60.0	0.1	41 00.0	60.0	0.1	42 00.0	60.0	0.1	87
88	37 00.0	60.0	0.0	38 00.0	60.0	0.0	39 00.0	60.0	0.0	40 00.0	60.0	0.0	41 00.0	60.0	0.0	42 00.0	60.0	0.0	43 00.0	60.0	0.0	88
89	38 00.0	60.0	0.0	39 00.0	60.0	0.0	40 00.0	60.0	0.0	41 00.0	60.0	0.0	42 00.0	60.0	0.0	43 00.0	60.0	0.0	44 00.0	60.0	0.0	89
90	39 00.0	+60.0	0.0	40 00.0	+60.0	0.0	41 00.0	+60.0	0.0	42 00.0	+60.0	0.0	43 00.0	+60.0	0.0	44 00.0	+60.0	0.0	45 00.0	+60.0	0.0	90
	39°			40°			41°			42°			43°			44°			45°			

706 LATITUDE **SAME** NAME AS DECLINATION L.H.A. 179°, 181°

Dec.	38°			39°			40°			41°			42°			43°			44°			Dec.
	Hc	d	Z	Hc	d	Z	Hc	d	Z	Hc	d	Z	Hc	d	Z	Hc	d	Z	Hc	d	Z	
°	° ′	′	°	° ′	′	°	° ′	′	°	° ′	′	°	° ′	′	°	° ′	′	°	° ′	′	°	°
0	41 22.0	+49.1	133.5	40 40.5	+49.7	134.1	39 58.5	+50.2	134.7	39 16.1	+50.7	135.3	38 33.2	+51.3	135.9	37 50.0	+51.7	136.4	37 06.3	+52.2	136.9	0
1	42 11.1	48.7	132.7	41 30.2	49.3	133.4	40 48.7	49.9	134.0	40 06.8	50.5	134.6	39 24.5	51.0	135.2	38 41.7	51.5	135.8	37 58.5	52.0	136.3	1
2	42 59.8	48.5	131.9	42 19.5	49.0	132.6	41 38.6	49.7	133.2	40 57.3	50.2	133.9	40 15.5	50.7	134.5	39 33.2	51.2	135.1	38 50.5	51.7	135.7	2
3	43 48.3	48.0	131.1	43 08.5	48.7	131.8	42 28.3	49.3	132.5	41 47.5	49.9	133.2	41 06.2	50.5	133.8	40 24.4	51.1	134.4	39 42.2	51.5	135.0	3
4	44 36.3	47.7	130.3	43 57.2	48.4	131.0	43 17.6	49.0	131.7	42 37.4	49.6	132.4	41 56.7	50.2	133.1	41 15.5	50.7	133.7	40 33.7	51.3	134.3	4
5	45 24.0	+47.3	129.4	44 45.6	+48.0	130.2	44 06.6	+48.6	130.9	43 27.0	+49.3	131.6	42 46.9	+49.9	132.3	42 06.2	+50.5	133.0	41 25.0	+51.1	133.7	5
6	46 11.3	46.8	128.5	45 33.6	47.6	129.3	44 55.2	48.3	130.1	44 16.3	49.0	130.8	43 36.8	49.6	131.6	42 56.7	50.2	132.3	42 16.1	50.7	132.9	6
7	46 58.1	46.5	127.6	46 21.2	47.2	128.4	45 43.5	48.0	129.3	45 05.3	48.6	130.0	44 26.4	49.2	130.8	43 46.9	49.9	131.5	43 06.8	50.5	132.2	7
8	47 44.6	45.9	126.7	47 08.4	46.7	127.5	46 31.5	47.5	128.4	45 53.9	48.2	129.2	45 15.6	48.9	130.0	44 36.8	49.5	130.7	43 57.3	50.2	131.5	8
9	48 30.5	45.5	125.7	47 55.1	46.3	126.6	47 19.0	47.0	127.5	46 42.1	47.8	128.3	46 04.5	48.6	129.2	45 26.3	49.2	129.9	44 47.5	49.9	130.7	9
10	49 16.0	+44.9	124.7	48 41.4	+45.8	125.7	48 06.0	+46.6	126.6	47 29.9	+47.4	127.4	46 53.1	+48.1	128.3	46 15.5	+48.9	129.1	45 37.4	+49.5	129.9	10
11	50 00.9	44.4	123.7	49 27.2	45.3	124.7	48 52.6	46.2	125.6	48 17.3	47.0	126.5	47 41.2	47.8	127.4	47 04.4	48.5	128.3	46 26.9	49.2	129.1	11
12	50 45.3	43.8	122.6	50 12.5	44.7	123.7	49 38.8	45.6	124.6	49 04.3	46.4	125.6	48 29.0	47.2	126.5	47 52.9	48.0	127.4	47 16.1	48.8	128.3	12
13	51 29.1	43.1	121.6	50 57.2	44.1	122.6	50 24.4	45.1	123.6	49 50.7	46.0	124.6	49 16.2	46.9	125.6	48 40.9	47.7	126.5	48 04.9	48.4	127.4	13
14	52 12.2	42.5	120.4	51 41.3	43.6	121.5	51 09.5	44.5	122.6	50 36.7	45.5	123.6	50 03.1	46.3	124.6	49 28.6	47.1	125.6	48 53.3	47.9	126.5	14
15	52 54.7	+41.8	119.3	52 24.9	+42.8	120.4	51 54.0	+43.9	121.5	51 22.2	+44.8	122.6	50 49.4	+45.8	123.6	50 15.7	+46.7	124.6	49 41.2	+47.5	125.6	15
16	53 36.5	41.0	118.1	53 07.7	42.2	119.2	52 37.9	43.2	120.4	52 07.0	44.3	121.5	51 35.2	45.2	122.6	51 02.4	46.2	123.6	50 28.7	47.1	124.6	16
17	54 17.5	40.3	116.8	53 49.9	41.4	118.0	53 21.1	42.6	119.2	52 51.3	43.6	120.4	52 20.4	44.7	121.5	51 48.6	45.6	122.6	51 15.8	46.5	123.7	17
18	54 57.8	39.4	115.5	54 31.3	40.7	116.8	54 03.7	41.8	118.0	53 34.9	43.0	119.2	53 05.1	44.0	120.4	52 34.2	45.0	121.5	52 02.3	46.0	122.6	18
19	55 37.2	38.6	114.2	55 12.0	39.8	115.5	54 45.5	41.1	116.8	54 17.9	42.2	118.1	53 49.1	43.3	119.3	53 19.2	44.4	120.4	52 48.3	45.4	121.6	19
20	56 15.8	+37.6	112.9	55 51.8	+39.0	114.2	55 26.6	+40.2	115.5	55 00.1	+41.4	116.8	54 32.4	+42.6	118.1	54 03.6	+43.7	119.3	53 33.7	+44.8	120.5	20
21	56 53.4	36.6	111.4	56 30.8	38.0	112.8	56 06.8	39.4	114.2	55 41.5	40.7	115.6	55 15.0	41.9	116.9	54 47.3	43.0	118.1	54 18.5	44.1	119.4	21
22	57 30.0	35.6	110.0	57 08.8	37.0	111.4	56 46.2	38.4	112.9	56 22.2	39.7	114.2	55 56.9	41.0	115.6	55 30.3	42.3	116.9	55 02.6	43.4	118.2	22
23	58 05.6	34.4	108.5	57 45.8	36.0	110.0	57 24.6	37.4	111.4	57 01.9	38.9	112.9	56 37.9	40.2	114.3	56 12.6	41.5	115.6	55 46.0	42.7	117.0	23
24	58 40.0	33.3	106.9	58 21.8	34.9	108.5	58 02.0	36.4	110.0	57 40.8	37.9	111.5	57 18.1	39.3	112.9	56 54.1	40.6	114.3	56 28.7	41.9	115.7	24
25	59 13.3	+32.0	105.3	58 56.7	+33.7	106.9	58 38.4	+35.3	108.5	58 18.7	+36.8	110.0	57 57.4	+38.3	111.5	57 34.7	+39.7	113.0	57 10.6	+41.0	114.4	25
26	59 45.3	30.8	103.6	59 30.4	32.4	105.3	59 13.7	34.2	106.9	58 55.5	35.7	108.5	58 35.7	37.3	110.0	58 14.4	38.7	111.6	57 51.6	40.1	113.0	26
27	60 16.1	29.3	101.9	60 02.8	31.2	103.6	59 47.9	32.9	105.3	59 31.2	34.6	106.9	59 13.0	36.1	108.5	58 53.1	37.7	110.1	58 31.7	39.2	111.6	27
28	60 45.4	28.0	100.1	60 34.0	29.8	101.9	60 20.8	31.5	103.6	60 05.8	33.3	105.3	59 49.1	35.0	107.0	59 30.8	36.6	108.6	59 10.9	38.1	110.2	28
29	61 13.4	26.4	98.3	61 03.8	28.3	100.1	60 52.3	30.2	101.9	60 39.1	32.0	103.6	60 24.1	33.8	105.3	60 07.4	35.4	107.0	59 49.0	37.1	108.7	29
30	61 39.8	+24.8	96.4	61 32.1	+26.8	98.3	61 22.5	+28.8	100.1	61 11.1	+30.6	101.9	60 57.9	+32.4	103.6	60 42.8	+34.2	105.4	60 26.1	+35.9	107.1	30
31	62 04.6	23.2	94.5	61 58.9	25.2	96.4	61 51.3	27.2	98.2	61 41.7	29.2	100.1	61 30.3	31.1	101.9	61 17.0	32.9	103.7	61 02.0	34.6	105.4	31
32	62 27.8	21.4	92.5	62 24.1	23.6	94.4	62 18.5	25.6	96.3	62 10.9	27.6	98.2	62 01.4	29.6	100.1	61 49.9	31.5	101.9	61 36.6	33.3	103.7	32
33	62 49.2	19.6	90.5	62 47.7	21.8	92.4	62 44.1	23.9	94.4	62 38.5	26.0	96.3	62 31.0	28.0	98.2	62 21.4	30.0	100.1	62 09.9	32.0	102.0	33
34	63 08.8	17.8	88.4	63 09.5	19.9	90.4	63 08.0	22.2	92.4	63 04.5	24.3	94.3	62 59.0	26.4	96.3	62 51.4	28.5	98.2	62 41.9	30.4	100.1	34
35	63 26.6	+15.8	86.3	63 29.4	+18.1	88.3	63 30.2	+20.3	90.3	63 28.8	+22.6	92.3	63 25.4	+24.7	94.3	63 19.9	+26.8	96.3	63 12.3	+28.9	98.2	35
36	63 42.4	13.9•	84.1	63 47.5	16.2•	86.1	63 50.5	18.4	88.2	63 51.4	20.6	90.2	63 50.1	22.9	92.2	63 46.7	25.1	94.3	63 41.2	27.2	96.3	36
37	63 56.3	11.8•	81.9	64 03.7	14.1•	83.9	64 08.9	16.5•	86.0	64 12.0	18.8	88.1	64 13.0	21.0	90.1	64 11.8	23.3	92.2	64 08.4	25.5	94.3	37
38	64 08.1	9.7•	79.7	64 17.8	12.0•	81.7	64 25.4	14.4•	83.8	64 30.8	16.7•	85.9	64 34.0	19.1•	88.0	64 35.1	21.3	90.1	64 33.9	23.7	92.2	38
39	64 17.8	7.6•	77.4	64 29.8	10.0•	79.4	64 39.8	12.2•	81.5	64 47.5	14.7•	83.6	64 53.1	17.0•	85.7	64 56.4	19.4	87.9	64 57.6	21.7•	90.0	39
40	64 25.4	+5.4•	75.1	64 39.8	+7.7•	77.1	64 52.0	+10.2•	79.2	65 02.2	+12.5•	81.3	65 10.1	+15.0•	83.5	65 15.8	+17.4•	85.6	65 19.3	+19.7•	87.8	40
41	64 30.8	3.2•	72.8	64 47.5	5.6•	74.8	65 02.2	7.9•	76.9	65 14.7	10.4•	79.0	65 25.1	12.7•	81.1	65 33.2	15.2•	83.3	65 39.0	17.6•	85.5	41
42	64 34.0	+1.1•	70.5	64 53.1	3.3•	72.5	65 10.1	5.7•	74.5	65 25.1	8.1•	76.6	65 37.8	10.6•	78.8	65 48.4	13.0•	81.0	65 56.6	15.5•	83.2	42
43	64 35.1	-1.2•	68.1	64 56.4	+1.2•	70.1	65 15.8	3.5•	72.2	65 33.2	5.8•	74.3	65 48.4	8.2•	76.4	66 01.4	10.7•	78.6	66 12.1	13.3•	80.8	43
44	64 33.9	3.4•	65.8	64 57.6	-1.2•	67.8	65 19.3	+1.2•	69.8	65 39.0	3.5•	71.8	65 56.6	6.0•	74.0	66 12.1	8.4•	76.1	66 25.4	10.9•	78.4	44
45	64 30.5	-5.5•	63.5	64 56.4	-3.3•	65.4	65 20.5	-1.2•	67.4	65 42.5	+1.3•	69.4	66 02.6	+3.6•	71.5	66 20.5	+6.1•	73.7	66 36.3	+8.6•	75.9	45
46	64 25.0	7.7•	61.2	64 53.1	5.6•	63.0	65 19.3	3.3•	65.0	65 43.8	-1.1•	67.0	66 06.2	+1.3•	69.1	66 26.6	3.7•	71.2	66 44.9	6.1•	73.4	46
47	64 17.3	9.9•	58.9	64 47.5	7.8•	60.7	65 16.0	5.7•	62.6	65 42.7	3.4•	64.6	66 07.5	-1.1•	66.6	66 30.3	+1.3•	68.7	66 51.0	3.8•	70.9	47
48	64 07.4	11.9•	56.6	64 39.7	10.0•	58.4	65 10.3	7.8•	60.2	65 39.3	5.8•	62.1	66 06.4	3.5•	64.1	66 31.6	-1.1•	66.2	66 54.8	+1.3•	68.3	48
49	63 55.5	13.9•	54.4	64 29.7	12.0•	56.1	65 02.5	10.1•	57.9	65 33.5	7.9•	59.7	66 02.9	5.8•	61.7	66 30.5	3.6•	63.7	66 56.1	-1.2•	65.8	49
50	63 41.6	-16.0•	52.2	64 17.7	-14.2•	53.8	64 52.4	-12.3•	55.5	65 25.6	-10.3•	57.3	65 57.1	-8.1•	59.2	66 26.9	-5.9•	61.2	66 54.9	-3.6•	63.2	50
51	63 25.6	17.9	50.0	64 03.5	16.1	51.6	64 40.1	14.3•	53.2	65 15.3	12.4•	55.0	65 49.0	10.4•	56.8	66 21.0	8.3•	58.7	66 51.3	6.0•	60.7	51
52	63 07.7	19.7	47.9	63 47.4	18.1	49.4	64 25.8	16.4•	51.0	65 02.9	14.5•	52.6	65 38.6	12.6•	54.4	66 12.7	10.5•	56.2	66 45.3	8.5•	58.2	52
53	62 48.0	21.5	45.8	63 29.3	20.0	47.2	64 09.4	18.3	48.8	64 48.4	16.7•	50.4	65 26.0	14.8•	52.0	66 02.2	12.9•	53.8	66 36.8	10.8•	55.7	53
54	62 26.5	23.3	43.8	63 09.3	21.8	45.1	63 51.1	20.3	46.6	64 31.7	18.6	48.1	65 11.2	16.9•	49.7	65 49.3	15.1•	51.4	66 26.0	13.1•	53.2	54
55	62 03.2	-24.9	41.8	62 47.5	-23.6	43.1	63 30.8	-22.1	44.5	64 13.1	-20.6	45.9	64 54.3	-19.0•	47.4	65 34.2	-17.2•	49.1	66 12.9	-15.4•	50.8	55
56	61 38.3	26.5	39.9	62 23.9	25.2	41.1	63 08.7	23.9	42.4	63 52.5	22.4	43.8	64 35.3	20.9	45.2	65 17.0	19.2•	46.8	65 57.5	17.5•	48.4	56
57	61 11.8	28.0	38.0	61 58.7	26.8	39.2	62 44.8	25.5	40.4	63 30.1	24.2	41.7	64 14.4	22.7	43.0	64 57.8	21.3	44.5	65 40.0	19.6•	46.0	57
58	60 43.8	29.5	36.2	61 31.9	28.4	37.3	62 19.3	27.2	38.4	63 05.9	25.9	39.6	63 51.7	24.6	40.9	64 36.5	23.1	42.3	65 20.4	21.6•	43.8	58
59	60 14.3	30.8	34.4	61 03.5	29.8	35.4	61 52.1	28.7	36.5	62 40.0	27.6	37.7	63 27.1	26.3	38.9	64 13.4	25.0	40.2	64 58.8	23.6	41.5	59
60	59 43.5	-32.1	32.7	60 33.7	-31.1	33.6	61 23.4	-30.2	34.7	62 12.4	-29.0	35.7	63 00.8	-27.9	36.9	63 48.4	-26.7	38.1	64 35.2	-25.4	39.4	60
61	59 11.4	33.3	31.0	60 02.6	32.5	31.9	60 53.2	31.5	32.9	61 43.4	30.6	33.9	62 32.9	29.5	34.9	63 21.7	28.4	36.1	64 09.8	27.1	37.3	61
62	58 38.1	34.6	29.4	59 30.1	33.7	30.3	60 21.7	32.9	31.1	61 12.8	31.9	32.1	62 03.4	31.0	33.1	62 53.3	29.9	34.1	63 42.7	28.8	35.3	62
63	58 03.5	35.6	27.9	58 56.4	34.9	28.6	59 48.8	34.1	29.5	60 40.9	33.3	30.3	61 32.4	32.3	31.3	62 23.4	31.4	32.2	63 13.9	30.4	33.3	63
64	57 27.9	36.7	26.4	58 21.5	36.0	27.1	59 14.7	35.2	27.8	60 07.6	34.5	28.6	61 00.1	33.7	29.5	61 52.0	32.8	30.4	62 43.5	31.8	31.4	64
65	56 51.2	-37.6	24.9	57 45.5	-37.0	25.6	58 39.5	-36.4	26.3	59 33.1	-35.7	27.0	60 26.4	-34.9	27.8	61 19.2	-34.1	28.7	62 11.7	-33.3	29.6	65
66	56 13.6	38.6	23.5	57 08.5	38.0	24.1	58 03.1	37.4	24.7	58 57.4	36.7	25.4	59 51.5	36.1	26.2	60 45.1	35.3	27.0	61 38.4	34.6	27.8	66
67	55 35.0	39.5	22.1	56 30.5	39.0	22.7	57 25.7	38.4	23.3	58 20.7	37.8	23.9	59 15.4	37.2	24.6	60 09.8	36.6	25.3	61 03.8	35.8	26.1	67
68	54 55.5	40.3	20.8	55 51.5	39.8	21.3	56 47.3	39.3	21.9	57 42.9	38.8	22.5	58 38.2	38.2	23.1	59 33.2	37.6	23.7	60 28.0	37.0	24.5	68
69	54 15.2	41.1	19.5	55 11.7	40.7	20.0	56 08.0	40.2	20.5	57 04.1	39.8	21.0	58 00.0	39.3	21.6	58 55.6	38.6	22.2	59 51.0	38.0	22.9	69
70	53 34.1	-41.8	18.3	54 31.0	-41.4	18.7	55 27.8	-41.1	19.2	56 24.3	-40.5	19.7	57 20.7	-40.1	20.2	58 17.0	-39.7	20.8	59 13.0	-39.2	21.3	70
71	52 52.3	42.6	17.1	53 49.6	42.2	17.5	54 46.7	41.8	17.9	55 43.8	41.5	18.4	56 40.6	41.0	18.8	57 37.3	40.5	19.3	58 33.8	40.0	19.9	71
72	52 09.7	43.2	15.9	53 07.4	42.9	16.3	54 04.9	42.5	16.7	55 02.3	42.1	17.1	55 59.6	41.8	17.5	56 56.8	41.4	18.0	57 53.8	41.0	18.5	72
73	51 26.5	43.8	14.8	52 24.5	43.5	15.1	53 22.4	43.2	15.5	54 20.2	42.9	15.8	55 17.8	42.5	16.2	56 15.4	42.2	16.7	57 12.8	41.9	17.1	73
74	50 42.7	44.4	13.7	51 41.0	44.2	14.0	52 39.2	43.9	14.3	53 37.3	43.6	14.7	54 35.3	43.3	15.0	55 33.2	43.0	15.4	56 30.9	42.6	15.8	74
75	49 58.3	-44.9	12.7	50 56.8	-44.7	12.9	51 55.3	-44.5	13.2	52 53.7	-44.3	13.5	53 52.0	-44.0	13.8	54 50.2	-43.7	14.2	55 48.3	-43.4	14.5	75
76	49 13.4	45.5	11.6	50 12.1	45.3	11.9	51 10.8	45.1	12.1	52 09.4	44.8	12.4	53 08.0	44.6	12.7	54 06.5	44.4	13.0	55 04.9	44.1	13.3	76
77	48 27.9	46.0	10.6	49 26.8	45.8	10.9	50 25.7	45.6	11.1	51 24.6	45.4	11.3	52 23.4	45.2	11.6	53 22.1	44.9	11.8	54 20.8	44.7	12.1	77
78	47 41.9	46.4	9.7	48 41.0	46.3	9.9	49 40.1	46.1	10.1	50 39.2	46.0	10.3	51 38.2	45.8	10.5	52 37.2	45.6	10.7	53 36.1	45.4	11.0	78
79	46 55.5	46.9	8.8	47 54.7	46.7	8.9	48 54.0	46.6	9.1	49 53.2	46.4	9.3	50 52.4	46.3	9.5	51 51.6	46.1	9.7	52 50.7	45.9	9.9	79
80	46 08.6	-47.3	7.8	47 08.0	-47.2	8.0	48 07.4	-47.1	8.1	49 06.8	-46.9	8.3	50 06.1	-46.7	8.5	51 05.5	-46.7	8.7	52 04.8	-46.5	8.9	80
81	45 21.3	47.7	7.0	46 20.8	47.6	7.1	47 20.3	47.4	7.2	48 19.9	47.4	7.4	49 19.4	47.3	7.5	50 18.8	47.1	7.7	51 18.3	47.0	7.8	81
82	44 33.6	48.1	6.1	45 33.2	48.0	6.2	46 32.9	47.9	6.3	47 32.5	47.8	6.4	48 32.1	47.7	6.6	49 31.7	47.6	6.7	50 31.3	47.5	6.8	82
83	43 45.5	48.5	5.3	44 45.2	48.3	5.4	45 45.0	48.3	5.5	46 44.7	48.2	5.6	47 44.4	48.1	5.7	48 44.1	48.0	5.8	49 43.8	48.0	5.9	83
84	42 57.0	48.7	4.5	43 56.9	48.7	4.5	44 56.7	48.7	4.6	45 56.5	48.6	4.7	46 56.3	48.5	4.8	47 56.1	48.5	4.9	48 55.8	48.3	5.0	84
85	42 08.3	-49.1	3.7	43 08.2	-49.1	3.7	44 08.0	-49.0	3.8	45 07.9	-48.9	3.9	46 07.8	-48.9	3.9	47 07.6	-48.8	4.0	48 07.5	-48.8	4.1	85
86	41 19.2	49.4	2.9	42 19.1	49.3	2.9	43 19.0	49.3	3.0	44 19.0	49.3	3.0	45 18.9	49.3	3.1	46 18.8	49.2	3.2	47 18.7	49.2	3.2	86
87	40 29.8	49.7	2.1	41 29.8	49.7	2.2	42 29.7	49.6	2.2	43 29.7	49.6	2.3	44 29.6	49.5	2.3	45 29.6	49.6	2.3	46 29.5	49.5	2.4	87
88	39 40.1	49.9	1.4	40 40.1	49.9	1.4	41 40.1	49.9	1.5	42 40.1	49.9	1.5	43 40.1	49.9	1.5	44 40.0	49.8	1.5	45 40.0	49.8	1.6	88
89	38 50.2	50.2	0.7	39 50.2	50.2	0.7	40 50.2	50.2	0.7	41 50.2	50.2	0.7	42 50.2	50.2	0.7	43 50.2	50.2	0.8	44 50.2	50.2	0.8	89
90	38 00.0	-50.4	0.0	39 00.0	-50.4	0.0	40 00.0	-50.4	0.0	41 00.0	-50.5	0.0	42 00.0	-50.5	0.0	43 00.0	-50.5	0.0	44 00.0	-50.5	0.0	90
	38°			39°			40°			41°			42°			43°			44°			

INTERPOLATION TABLE

Dec. Inc.	10'	20'	30'	40'	50'	Dec.	0'	1'	2'	3'	4'	5'	6'	7'	8'	9'
	Tens					Decimals →	Units									
36.0	6.0	12.0	18.0	24.0	30.0	.0	0.0	0.6	1.2	1.8	2.4	3.0	3.6	4.3	4.9	5.5
36.1	6.0	12.0	18.0	24.0	30.1	.1	0.1	0.7	1.3	1.9	2.5	3.1	3.7	4.3	4.9	5.5
36.2	6.0	12.0	18.1	24.1	30.1	.2	0.1	0.7	1.3	1.9	2.6	3.2	3.8	4.4	5.0	5.6
36.3	6.0	12.1	18.1	24.2	30.2	.3	0.2	0.8	1.4	2.0	2.6	3.2	3.8	4.4	5.0	5.7
36.4	6.1	12.1	18.2	24.3	30.3	.4	0.2	0.9	1.5	2.1	2.7	3.3	3.9	4.5	5.1	5.7
36.5	6.1	12.2	18.3	24.3	30.4	.5	0.3	0.9	1.5	2.1	2.7	3.3	4.0	4.6	5.2	5.8
36.6	6.1	12.2	18.3	24.4	30.5	.6	0.4	1.0	1.6	2.2	2.8	3.4	4.0	4.6	5.2	5.8
36.7	6.1	12.3	18.4	24.5	30.6	.7	0.4	1.0	1.6	2.3	2.9	3.5	4.1	4.7	5.3	5.9
36.8	6.2	12.3	18.4	24.6	30.7	.8	0.5	1.1	1.7	2.3	2.9	3.5	4.1	4.7	5.4	6.0
36.9	6.2	12.3	18.5	24.6	30.8	.9	0.5	1.2	1.8	2.4	3.0	3.6	4.2	4.8	5.4	6.0
43.0	7.1	14.3	21.5	28.6	35.8	.0	0.0	0.7	1.4	2.2	2.9	3.6	4.3	5.1	5.8	6.5
43.1	7.2	14.3	21.5	28.7	35.9	.1	0.1	0.8	1.5	2.2	3.0	3.7	4.4	5.1	5.9	6.6
43.2	7.2	14.4	21.6	28.8	36.0	.2	0.1	0.9	1.6	2.3	3.0	3.8	4.5	5.2	5.9	6.7
43.3	7.2	14.4	21.6	28.9	36.1	.3	0.2	0.9	1.7	2.4	3.1	3.8	4.6	5.3	6.0	6.7
43.4	7.2	14.5	21.7	28.9	36.2	.4	0.3	1.0	1.7	2.5	3.2	3.9	4.6	5.4	6.1	6.8
43.5	7.3	14.5	21.8	29.0	36.3	.5	0.4	1.1	1.8	2.5	3.3	4.0	4.7	5.4	6.2	6.9
43.6	7.3	14.5	21.8	29.1	36.3	.6	0.4	1.2	1.9	2.6	3.3	4.1	4.8	5.5	6.2	7.0
43.7	7.3	14.6	21.9	29.2	36.4	.7	0.5	1.2	2.0	2.7	3.4	4.1	4.9	5.6	6.3	7.0
43.8	7.3	14.6	21.9	29.2	36.5	.8	0.6	1.3	2.0	2.8	3.5	4.2	4.9	5.7	6.4	7.1
43.9	7.4	14.7	22.0	29.3	36.6	.9	0.7	1.4	2.1	2.8	3.6	4.3	5.0	5.7	6.5	7.2
44.0	7.3	14.6	22.0	29.3	36.6	.0	0.0	0.7	1.5	2.2	3.0	3.7	4.4	5.2	5.9	6.7
44.1	7.3	14.7	22.0	29.4	36.7	.1	0.1	0.8	1.6	2.3	3.0	3.8	4.5	5.3	6.0	6.7
44.2	7.3	14.7	22.1	29.4	36.8	.2	0.1	0.9	1.6	2.4	3.1	3.9	4.6	5.3	6.1	6.8
44.3	7.4	14.8	22.1	29.5	36.9	.3	0.2	1.0	1.7	2.4	3.2	3.9	4.7	5.4	6.2	6.9
44.4	7.4	14.8	22.2	29.6	37.0	.4	0.3	1.0	1.8	2.5	3.3	4.0	4.7	5.5	6.2	7.0
44.5	7.4	14.8	22.3	29.7	37.1	.5	0.4	1.1	1.9	2.6	3.3	4.1	4.8	5.6	6.3	7.0
44.6	7.4	14.9	22.3	29.7	37.2	.6	0.4	1.2	1.9	2.7	3.4	4.2	4.9	5.6	6.4	7.1
44.7	7.5	14.9	22.4	29.8	37.3	.7	0.5	1.3	2.0	2.7	3.5	4.2	5.0	5.7	6.5	7.2
44.8	7.5	15.0	22.4	29.9	37.4	.8	0.6	1.3	2.1	2.8	3.6	4.3	5.0	5.8	6.5	7.3
44.9	7.5	15.0	22.5	30.0	37.5	.9	0.7	1.4	2.2	2.9	3.6	4.4	5.1	5.9	6.6	7.3
45.0	7.5	15.0	22.5	30.0	37.5	.0	0.0	0.8	1.5	2.3	3.0	3.8	4.5	5.3	6.1	6.8
45.1	7.5	15.0	22.5	30.0	37.6	.1	0.1	0.8	1.6	2.4	3.1	3.9	4.6	5.4	6.1	6.9
45.2	7.5	15.0	22.6	30.1	37.6	.2	0.2	0.9	1.7	2.4	3.2	3.9	4.7	5.5	6.2	7.0
45.3	7.5	15.1	22.6	30.2	37.7	.3	0.2	1.0	1.7	2.5	3.3	4.0	4.8	5.5	6.3	7.1
45.4	7.6	15.1	22.7	30.3	37.8	.4	0.3	1.1	1.8	2.6	3.3	4.1	4.9	5.6	6.4	7.1
45.5	7.6	15.2	22.8	30.3	37.9	.5	0.4	1.1	1.9	2.7	3.4	4.2	4.9	5.7	6.4	7.2
45.6	7.6	15.2	22.8	30.4	38.0	.6	0.5	1.2	2.0	2.7	3.5	4.2	5.0	5.8	6.5	7.3
45.7	7.6	15.3	22.9	30.5	38.1	.7	0.5	1.3	2.0	2.8	3.6	4.3	5.1	5.8	6.6	7.4
45.8	7.7	15.3	22.9	30.6	38.2	.8	0.6	1.4	2.1	2.9	3.6	4.4	5.2	5.9	6.7	7.4
45.9	7.7	15.3	23.0	30.6	38.3	.9	0.7	1.4	2.2	3.0	3.7	4.5	5.2	6.0	6.7	7.5
58.0	9.6	19.3	29.0	38.6	48.3	.0	0.0	1.0	1.9	2.9	3.9	4.9	5.8	6.8	7.8	8.8
58.1	9.7	19.3	29.0	38.7	48.4	.1	0.1	1.1	2.0	3.0	4.0	5.0	5.9	6.9	7.9	8.9
58.2	9.7	19.4	29.1	38.8	48.5	.2	0.2	1.2	2.1	3.1	4.1	5.1	6.0	7.0	8.0	9.0
58.3	9.7	19.4	29.1	38.9	48.6	.3	0.3	1.3	2.2	3.2	4.2	5.2	6.1	7.1	8.1	9.1
58.4	9.7	19.5	29.2	38.9	48.7	.4	0.4	1.4	2.3	3.3	4.3	5.3	6.2	7.2	8.2	9.2
58.5	9.8	19.5	29.3	39.0	48.8	.5	0.5	1.5	2.4	3.4	4.4	5.4	6.3	7.3	8.3	9.3
58.6	9.8	19.5	29.3	39.1	48.8	.6	0.6	1.6	2.5	3.5	4.5	5.5	6.4	7.4	8.4	9.4
58.7	9.8	19.6	29.4	39.2	48.9	.7	0.7	1.7	2.6	3.6	4.6	5.6	6.5	7.5	8.5	9.5
58.8	9.8	19.6	29.4	39.2	49.0	.8	0.8	1.8	2.7	3.7	4.7	5.7	6.6	7.6	8.6	9.6
58.9	9.9	19.7	29.5	39.3	49.1	.9	0.9	1.9	2.8	3.8	4.8	5.8	6.7	7.7	8.7	9.7
59.0	9.8	19.6	29.5	39.3	49.1	.0	0.0	1.0	2.0	3.0	4.0	5.0	5.9	6.9	7.9	8.9
59.1	9.8	19.7	29.5	39.4	49.2	.1	0.1	1.1	2.1	3.1	4.1	5.1	6.0	7.0	8.0	9.0
59.2	9.8	19.7	29.6	39.4	49.3	.2	0.2	1.2	2.2	3.2	4.2	5.2	6.1	7.1	8.1	9.1
59.3	9.9	19.8	29.6	39.5	49.4	.3	0.3	1.3	2.3	3.3	4.3	5.3	6.2	7.2	8.2	9.2
59.4	9.9	19.8	29.7	39.6	49.5	.4	0.4	1.4	2.4	3.4	4.4	5.4	6.3	7.3	8.3	9.3
59.5	9.9	19.8	29.8	39.7	49.6	.5	0.5	1.5	2.5	3.5	4.5	5.5	6.4	7.4	8.4	9.4
59.6	9.9	19.9	29.8	39.7	49.7	.6	0.6	1.6	2.6	3.6	4.6	5.6	6.5	7.5	8.5	9.5
59.7	10.0	19.9	29.9	39.8	49.8	.7	0.7	1.7	2.7	3.7	4.7	5.7	6.6	7.6	8.6	9.6
59.8	10.0	20.0	29.9	39.9	49.9	.8	0.8	1.8	2.8	3.8	4.8	5.8	6.7	7.7	8.7	9.7
59.9	10.0	20.0	30.0	40.0	50.0	.9	0.9	1.9	2.9	3.9	4.9	5.9	6.8	7.8	8.8	9.8
	10'	20'	30'	40'	50'		0'	1'	2'	3'	4'	5'	6'	7'	8'	9'

Double Second Diff. and Corr.

Block 36 / 43:

Diff	Corr.
0.8	0.1
2.5	0.2
4.2	0.3
5.9	0.4
7.6	
9.3	0.5
11.0	0.6
12.7	0.7
14.4	0.8
16.1	0.9
	1.0
18.7	0.9
20.7	1.0
22.7	1.1
24.6	1.2
26.6	1.3
28.6	1.4
30.5	1.5
32.5	1.6
34.5	1.7

Block 44 / 45:

Diff	Corr.
1.1	
3.2	0.1
5.3	0.2
7.5	0.3
9.6	0.4
11.7	0.5
13.9	0.6
16.0	0.7
18.1	0.8
20.3	0.9
22.4	1.0
24.5	1.1
26.7	1.2
28.8	1.3
30.9	1.4
33.1	1.5
35.2	1.6

Block 58:

Diff	Corr.
8.2	0.1
24.6	
41.0	0.2

Block 59:

Diff	Corr.
16.2	0.1
48.6	
0.0	0.0
48.2	

The Double-Second-Difference correction (Corr.) is always to be added to the tabulated altitude.

Abbreviations and Symbols

Included in this appendix are the abbreviations and symbols that are commonly used in the practice of navigation. The abbreviations and symbols used on charts are described in H. O. Chart No. 1, which is included at the end of this book.

ABBREVIATIONS

A   amplitude; augmentation; away (altitude difference).

a   altitude difference (Ho~Hc); assumed.

a₀, a₁, a₂ First, second and third Polaris sight reduction correction (from Nautical Almanac).

AA Air Almanac.

AC alternating current.

ADF automatic direction finder.

AF audio frequency.

aL assumed latitude.

AM amplitude modulation; ante meridian (before noon).

Amp amplitude.

Amps amperes.

AP assumed position.

App apparent.

approx approximate.

atm atmosphere.

AU astronomical unit.

Aug augmentation.

Az azimuth angle. (Z also used.)

aλ assumed longitude.

B   barometric pressure correction; bearing.

BFO beat frequency oscillator.

Bn beacon.

C   Centigrade (celsius); chronometer time; compass; correction; course (vessel), course angle.

C & GS Coast and Geodetic Survey.

CC chronometer correction; compass course.

CE chronometer error; compass error.

CH compass heading.

CIC Combat Information Center.

cm centimeter.

Cn course (as distinguished from course angle).

CNO Chief of Naval Operations.

co- the complement of.

co-L colatitude.

COG Course Over Ground.

comp compass.

corr correction.

cos cosine.

cot cotangent.

cm centimeter.

CPA closest point of approach.

Cpgc course per gyro compass.

cps cycles per second.

Cpsc course per standard compass.

CP stg c course per steering compass.

CRT cathode ray tube.

csc   cosecant.

Cus   course (aircraft). (The following are preferable: CC, GC, MC, TC).

CW   continuous wave.

C-W   chronometer time minus watch time.

D   deviation; dip (of horizon); distance; drift (current).

d   declination; difference; distance.

DB   danger bearing.

DC   direct current.

dec   declination.

deg   degree.

Dep   departure.

Dest   destination

Dev   deviation.

DG   degaussing.

diff   difference.

dist   distance.

DLo   difference of longitude.

DMA   Defense Mapping Agency

DME   distance measuring equipment.

DR   dead reckoning, dead reckoning position.

Dr   drift.

DRA   dead reckoning analyzer.

DRAI   dead reckoning analyzer indicator.

DRM   direction of relative movement.

DRT   dead reckoning tracer.

DST   daylight saving time.

dur   duration.

dλ difference of longitude.

E   East; error.

e   Earth (wind triangle and relative movement problems).

EHF   extremely high frequency.

EM log   electro-magnetic log.

EP   estimated position.

EPI   electronic position indicator.

ESSA   Environmental Science Services Administration.

Eq. T   equation of time.

est   estimated.

ETA   estimated time of arrival.

ETD   estimated time of departure.

F   Fahrenheit; fast; phase correction (altitude).

f   frequency; latitude factor.

fath   fathom, fathoms.

FBM   Fleet Ballistic Missile (submarine).

FM   frequency modulation.

fm   fathom, fathoms.

ft   foot, feet.

FTC   fast time constant (radar).

G   Greenwich, Greenwich meridian (upper branch); grid.

g   Greenwich meridian (lower branch).

GAT   Greenwich apparent time.

GB   grid bearing.

GC   grid course.

GE   gyro error.

GH   grid heading.

GHA   Greenwich hour angle.

GHz   gigahertz.

GMT   Greenwich mean time.

Govt   government.

GP   geographical position.

Gr   Greenwich.

GST   Greenwich sidereal time.

GV   grid variation.

GZn   grid azimuth.

H   height.

HA   hour angle.

ha   apparent altitude.

Hc   computed altitude.

Hd   head.

Hdg   heading.

HE   height of eye.

HF   high frequency.

HHW   higher high water.

HLW   higher low water.

H.O.   Hydrographic Office (now called Oceanographic Office).

Ho   observed altitude.

Hor   horizontal.

HP   horizontal parallax.

hr   hour.

hrs   hours.

hs   sextant altitude.

Ht   height.

ht   tabulated altitude.

Ht. eye   height of eye.

HW   high water.

Hz   Hertz (cycle per second).

I   instrument correction.

IC	index correction.	**mag**	magnetic; magnitude.
IFF	identification friend or foe.	**max**	maximum.
IFR	instrument flight rules.	**MB**	magnetic bearing.
IMU	inertial measurement unit.	**mb**	millibars.
in	inch, inches.	**MC**	magnetic course.
INS	integrated navigation system.	**mc**	megacycles.
ITR	intended track.	**MF**	medium frequency.
J	irradiation correction.	**MH**	magnetic heading.
K	knot, knots.	**MHHW**	mean higher high water.
kc	kilocycles.	**MHW**	mean high water.
kHz	kilohertz.	**MHWN**	mean high water neaps.
km	kilometer, kilometers.	**MHWS**	mean high water springs.
kn	knot, knots.	**MHz**	megahertz.
kt	knot.	**mi**	mile, miles.
kts	knots.	**mid**	middle.
kw	kilowatt.	**min**	minute, minutes.

L latitude; lower limb correction for Moon (from *Nautical Almanac*).

MINDAC Miniature Inertial Navigation Digital Automatic Computer.

L_1	latitude of departure.	**MLLW**	mean lower low water.
L_2	latitude of destination.	**MLW**	mean low water.
l	difference of latitude.	**MLWN**	mean low water neaps.
LAN	local apparent noon.	**MLWS**	mean low water springs.
LAT	local apparent time.	**mm**	millimeter.
lat	latitude.	**mph**	miles (statute) per hour.
LEM	lunar excursion module.	**MPP**	most probable position.
LF	low frequency.		

LHA local hour angle.

MSFN manned space flight network.

LHW	lower high water.	**ms**	millisecond.
LL	lower limb.	**MZn**	magnetic azimuth.
LLW	lower low water.	**N**	North.
Lm	mid-latitude.	**NA**	Nautical Almanac.
LMT	local mean time.	**Na**	nadir.
Lo(λ)	longitude.		

NASA National Aeronautics and Space Administration.

long	longitude.	**naut**	nautical.
LOP	line of position.		

NAVDAC Navigation Data Assimilation Computer.

LST	local sidereal time.
Lv	latitude of vertex.

NAVSAT Navy navigation satellite system.

LW	low water.	**nm**	nautical mile, nautical miles.
λ_1	longitude of departure.	**n mi**	nautical mile, nautical miles.
λ_2	longitude of destination.	**Nt M**	nautical mile.
λv	longitude of vertex.		

M magnetic; maneuvering ship (in relative plot of relative movement problems; meridian (upper branch); meridional parts.

ONC Operational Navigational Charts.

P atmospheric pressure; parallax; planet; pole.

m maneuvering ship (in speed triangle of relative movement problems); meridian (lower branch); meridional difference; meters.

p	departure; polar distance.
PC	personal correction.
PD	polar distance; position doubtful.
pgc	per gyro compass.

P in A parallax in altitude.

Pit log Pitot-static log.

PM post meridian (after noon); pulse modulation.

Pn North pole; North celestial pole.

Pos position.

posit position.

PPI plan position indicator.

PRR pulse repetition rate.

Ps South pole; South celestial pole.

psc per standard compass.

p stg c per steering compass.

Pt point.

pub publication.

PV prime vertical.

Q Polaris correction.

QQ' celestial equator; equator.

R reference craft (relative movement problems); refraction.

r reference ship (in speed triangle of relative movement problems).

RA right ascension.

RB relative bearing.

RDF radio direction finder.

rel relative.

rev reversed.

RF radio frequency.

R Fix running fix.

RIS range instrumentation ship.

RMS root mean square.

RPM revolution per minute.

S sea-air temperature difference correction; slow; South; speed.

SCAR submarine celestial altitude recorder.

SD semidiameter.

sec secant; second, seconds.

SH ship's head (heading).

SHA sidereal hour angle.

SHF super high frequency.

sin sine.

SINS ship's inertial navigation system.

SMG speed made good.

SOA speed of advance.

SOG speed over the ground.

SRM speed of relative movement.

SSCNS Ship's Self-Contained Navigation System.

STC sensitivity time control.

St.M statute mile.

T air temperature correction; temperature; time; toward (altitude difference); true (direction).

t meridian angle; elapsed time.

Tab tabulated value.

TACAN tactical air navigation.

tan tangent.

TB true bearing; combined temperature-barometric correction.

TC true course.

T_G ground-wave reading (Loran).

T_{GS} ground-wave-sky-wave reading (Loran).

TH true heading.

TR track.

Tr transit.

T_S sky-wave reading (Loran).

T_{SG} sky-wave-ground-wave reading (Loran).

TZn true azimuth.

U upper limb correction for Moon (from *Nautical Almanac*).

UHF ultra high frequency.

UL upper limb.

UPS universal plotting sheet.

USC&GS United States Coast and Geodetic Survey.

UT universal time, (UT_0, UT_1, UT_2, etc.).

V variation, volts.

Var variation.

vel velocity.

VFR visual flight rules.

VHF very high frequency.

vis visibility.

VLF very low frequency.

VOR very high frequency omnirange.

VORTAC very high frequency omnirange—TACAN (combined system).

W watch time; West.

w wind (wind triangle problems).

WAC	World Aeronautical Chart.	z	zenith distance; zone meridian (lower branch).
WE	watch error.		
X	parallactic angle.	ZD	zone description.
yd	yard.	Zn	azimuth (as distinguished from azimuth angle).
yds	yards.		
Z	azimuth angle; zenith; zone meridian (upper branch).	ZT	zone time.

CELESTIAL BODIES

⊙	Sun	☆	Star	◑	First quarter
☾	Moon	♈	Aries	◐	Gibbous moon
♀	Venus	⊖☾	Center	○	Full moon
⊕	Earth	☱ ☾	Lower limb	◓	Gibbous moon
♂	Mars	☵ ☾	Upper limb	◑	Last quarter
♃	Jupiter	●	New moon	◕	Crescent moon
♄	Saturn	◑	Crescent moon		

MISCELLANEOUS SYMBOLS

d	Days; example: 4^d	∞	Infinity
h	Hours; example: 20^h	°	Degrees
m	Minutes of time; example: 15^m	′	Minutes of arc
s	Seconds of time; example: 24^s	″	Seconds of arc
■	Remains below horizon	□	Remains above horizon
±	Plus or minus according to appropriate rule	////	Twilight all night
		*	Interpolation impractical
~	Absolute difference, i.e., smaller subtracted from larger	>	is greater than
		<	is less than
		Δ	Delta (unit change)
		μs	microseconds

Conversion Table For Meters, Feet, and Fathoms

Extract from H.O. 9 Bowditch.

Meters	Feet	Fathoms	Meters	Feet	Fathoms	Feet	Meters	Feet	Meters	Fathoms	Meters	Fathoms	Meters
1	3.28	0.55	61	200.13	33.36	1	0.30	61	18.59	1	1.83	61	111.56
2	6.56	1.09	62	203.41	33.90	2	0.61	62	18.90	2	3.66	62	113.39
3	9.84	1.64	63	206.69	34.45	3	0.91	63	19.20	3	5.49	63	115.21
4	13.12	2.19	64	209.97	35.00	4	1.22	64	19.51	4	7.32	64	117.04
5	16.40	2.73	65	213.25	35.54	5	1.52	65	19.81	5	9.14	65	118.87
6	19.69	3.28	66	216.54	36.09	6	1.83	66	20.12	6	10.97	66	120.70
7	22.97	3.83	67	219.82	36.64	7	2.13	67	20.42	7	12.80	67	122.53
8	26.25	4.37	68	223.10	37.18	8	2.44	68	20.73	8	14.63	68	124.36
9	29.53	4.92	69	226.38	37.73	9	2.74	69	21.03	9	16.46	69	126.19
10	32.81	5.47	70	229.66	38.28	10	3.05	70	21.34	10	18.29	70	128.02
11	36.09	6.01	71	232.94	38.82	11	3.35	71	21.64	11	20.12	71	129.84
12	39.37	6.56	72	236.22	39.37	12	3.66	72	21.95	12	21.95	72	131.67
13	42.65	7.11	73	239.50	39.92	13	3.96	73	22.25	13	23.77	73	133.50
14	45.93	7.66	74	242.78	40.46	14	4.27	74	22.56	14	25.60	74	135.33
15	49.21	8.20	75	246.06	41.01	15	4.57	75	22.86	15	27.43	75	137.16
16	52.49	8.75	76	249.34	41.56	16	4.88	76	23.16	16	29.26	76	138.99
17	55.77	9.30	77	252.62	42.10	17	5.18	77	23.47	17	31.09	77	140.82
18	59.06	9.84	78	255.91	42.65	18	5.49	78	23.77	18	32.92	78	142.65
19	62.34	10.39	79	259.19	43.20	19	5.79	79	24.08	19	34.75	79	144.48
20	65.62	10.94	80	262.47	43.74	20	6.10	80	24.38	20	36.58	80	146.30
21	68.90	11.48	81	265.75	44.29	21	6.40	81	24.69	21	38.40	81	148.13
22	72.18	12.03	82	269.03	44.84	22	6.71	82	24.99	22	40.23	82	149.96
23	75.46	12.58	83	272.31	45.38	23	7.01	83	25.30	23	42.06	83	151.79
24	78.74	13.12	84	275.59	45.93	24	7.32	84	25.60	24	43.89	84	153.62
25	82.02	13.67	85	278.87	46.48	25	7.62	85	25.91	25	45.72	85	155.45
26	85.30	14.22	86	282.15	47.03	26	7.92	86	26.21	26	47.55	86	157.28
27	88.58	14.76	87	285.43	47.57	27	8.23	87	26.52	27	49.38	87	159.11
28	91.86	15.31	88	288.71	48.12	28	8.53	88	26.82	28	51.21	88	160.93
29	95.14	15.86	89	291.99	48.67	29	8.84	89	27.13	29	53.04	89	162.76
30	98.43	16.40	90	295.28	49.21	30	9.14	90	27.43	30	54.86	90	164.59
31	101.71	16.95	91	298.56	49.76	31	9.45	91	27.74	31	56.69	91	166.42
32	104.99	17.50	92	301.84	50.31	32	9.75	92	28.04	32	58.52	92	168.25
33	108.27	18.04	93	305.12	50.85	33	10.06	93	28.35	33	60.35	93	170.08
34	111.55	18.59	94	308.40	51.40	34	10.36	94	28.65	34	62.18	94	171.91
35	114.83	19.14	95	311.68	51.95	35	10.67	95	28.96	35	64.01	95	173.74
36	118.11	19.69	96	314.96	52.49	36	10.97	96	29.26	36	65.84	96	175.56
37	121.39	20.23	97	318.24	53.04	37	11.28	97	29.57	37	67.67	97	177.39
38	124.67	20.78	98	321.52	53.59	38	11.58	98	29.87	38	69.49	98	179.22
39	127.95	21.33	99	324.80	54.13	39	11.89	99	30.18	39	71.32	99	181.05
40	131.23	21.87	100	328.08	54.68	40	12.19	100	30.48	40	73.15	100	182.88
41	134.51	22.42	101	331.36	55.23	41	12.50	101	30.78	41	74.98	101	184.71
42	137.80	22.97	102	334.65	55.77	42	12.80	102	31.09	42	76.81	102	186.54
43	141.08	23.51	103	337.93	56.32	43	13.11	103	31.39	43	78.64	103	188.37
44	144.36	24.06	104	341.21	56.87	44	13.41	104	31.70	44	80.47	104	190.20
45	147.64	24.61	105	344.49	57.41	45	13.72	105	32.00	45	82.30	105	192.02
46	150.92	25.15	106	347.77	57.96	46	14.02	106	32.31	46	84.12	106	193.85
47	154.20	25.70	107	351.05	58.51	47	14.33	107	32.61	47	85.95	107	195.68
48	157.48	26.25	108	354.33	59.06	48	14.63	108	32.92	48	87.78	108	197.51
49	160.76	26.79	109	357.61	59.60	49	14.94	109	33.22	49	89.61	109	199.34
50	164.04	27.34	110	360.89	60.15	50	15.24	110	33.53	50	91.44	110	201.17
51	167.32	27.89	111	364.17	60.70	51	15.54	111	33.83	51	93.27	111	203.00
52	170.60	28.43	112	367.45	61.24	52	15.85	112	34.14	52	95.10	112	204.83
53	173.88	28.98	113	370.73	61.79	53	16.15	113	34.44	53	96.93	113	206.65
54	177.17	29.53	114	374.02	62.34	54	16.46	114	34.75	54	98.76	114	208.48
55	180.45	30.07	115	377.30	62.88	55	16.76	115	35.05	55	100.58	115	210.31
56	183.73	30.62	116	380.58	63.43	56	17.07	116	35.36	56	102.41	116	212.14
57	187.01	31.17	117	383.86	63.98	57	17.37	117	35.66	57	104.24	117	213.97
58	190.29	31.71	118	387.14	64.52	58	17.68	118	35.97	58	106.07	118	215.80
59	193.57	32.26	119	390.42	65.07	59	17.98	119	36.27	59	107.90	119	217.63
60	196.85	32.81	120	393.70	65.62	60	18.29	120	36.58	60	109.73	120	219.46

Index

This edition of **Dutton's** is indexed by **article** number instead
of page number. It is felt that this
will make the book more convenient for both the student and
the practicing navigator.

Credit by figure number is acknowledged to the following individuals and organizations:
WEEMS & PLATH, INC.: 103a, 710a, 902b, 1020a, 1020b, 1110c, 2202, 2203, 2206, 2214c, 2214d, 2303, 2304, 2312b, 2811c, 2815, 1805, 4405b. **C. PLATH**: 908c, 2214d. **PEABODY MUSEUM**: 103b. **THE INSTITUTE OF NAVIGATION, LONDON**: 4303a, 4303b, 4305a, 4305b. **CONVAIR DIVISION, GENERAL DYNAMICS**: 202a, 202b, 202c, 204a, 204b, 205a, 205b, 302, 310, 312a, 502, 2003a, 2003b, 2003c, 2004a, 2004b, 2004c, 2005, 2221, 2303, 2304, 2403a. **NATIONAL OCEAN SURVEY**: 304b, 314a, 315, 316, 4403. **U.S. COAST GUARD**: 607, 609. **U.S. NAVY**: 944, 1013, 1015b, 1912c, 3011, 3405b, 4102b, 4102c, 4410. **DANFORTH/WHITE**: 908d. **SPERRY RAND CORPORATION**: 926a, 926b, 934, 936a, 936b, 937, 3606a, 3606b, 3606c, 3607c, 3612, 3905a, 3905b, 3907. **CHESAPEAKE INSTRUMENT CORPORATION**: 1010a, 1010b, 1615a, 1615b. **ALDEN ELECTRONIC & IMPULSE RECORDING EQUIPMENT CO., INC.**: 4307. **ROBERT A. RAGUSO**: 4306a, 4306b. **MASSACHUSETTS INSTITUTE OF TECHNOLOGY, EXPERIMENTAL ASTRONOMY LABORATORY**: 4502, 4503, 4504a, 4504b, 4504c, 4504d. **MASSACHUSETTS INSTITUTE OF TECHNOLOGY, INSTRUMENTATION LABORATORY**: 4510a, 4510c, 4510d. **NATIONAL AERONAUTICS AND SPACE ADMINISTRATION**: 4510b. **RAND McNALLY & COMPANY**: 4202, 4203, (©R.L. No. 69 GP 27). **KENYON MARINE**: 1012. **EDO CANADA, LTD.**: 1015a, 4102a. **HARTMAN-HUYCK SYSTEMS COMPANY, INC.**: 1023a, 1023b. **INTERNATIONAL TELEPHONE AND TELEGRAPH CORPORATION, FEDERAL TELECOMMUNICATIONS LABORATORIES**: 4410 **DECCA SYSTEMS, INC.**: 1814a, 1814b, 1814c. **KELVIN HUGHES AMERICA CORPORATION**: 1616. **HAMILTON WATCH COMPANY**: 2320. **F. W. KEATOR**: 3005b. **NORTHROP NORTRONICS**: 3102a, 3105, 3106a, 3106b, 3803a, 3803b, 3804. **HASTINGS-RAYDIST, INC.**: 3304a, 3304b, 3304c. **COLLINS RADIO COMPANY**: 3407a, 3407b, 4412. **RAYTHEON**: 1614a, 1614b, 1614c, 1614d, 3504b, 3504c. **AUTONETICS DIVISION OF NORTH AMERICAN AVIATION**: 3605b, 3607a, 3607b, 3905c. **APPLIED PHYSICS LABORATORY, THE JOHNS HOPKINS UNIVERSITY**: 3703a, 3703c, 3704, 3705. **KOLLSMAN INSTRUMENT CORPORATION**: 3802a, 3802b, 4409, 4411, 4505. **KOLLMORGAN CORPORATION**: 3805, 3807, 3808. **WOODS HOLE OCEANOGRAPHIC INSTITUTION**: 3809. **U.S. NAVAL OCEANOGRAPHIC OFFICE**: 312b, 811a, 811b, 811c, 815a, 815b, 1705, 1708b, 1710, 1905a, 4202, 4203, 4209.

MR. G. D. DUNLAP is president of Weems & Plath, Inc., a company engaged in the design, development, and sale of navigation instruments, charts, and publications. Mr. Dunlap has designed over twenty navigation instruments and is the author of numerous articles in technical journals and magazines. In recent years he has conducted navigational studies for the U.S. Navy and Coast Guard and he has been a member of the Institute of Navigation since 1946. He has written the following books: *America's Cup Defenders* and *Navigating and Finding Fish with Electronics*.

CAPTAIN HENRY H. SHUFELDT, USNR (Retired) is consultant to Weems & Plath, Inc. His years of study and experience as navigator and commanding officer aboard various ships qualify him to write authoritatively about navigation. He has written articles, primarily on celestial navigation, for the *Journal of the U.S. Institute of Navigation, The Journal of the British Institute of Navigation, U.S. Naval Institute Proceedings, The Skipper, Yachting,* and *Rudder*. He is the author of *Slide Rule for the Mariner*.

Mr. Dunlap and Captain Shufeldt are co-authors of *Piloting and Dead Reckoning*.

THE TYPE USED THROUGHOUT THIS BOOK IS MONOPHOTO UNIVERS. THE BOOK IS PRINTED OFFSET ON FIFTY-POUND BANTA PIGMENTED PAPER AND WAS COMPOSED, PRINTED, AND BOUND BY THE GEORGE BANTA COMPANY, INC., MENASHA, WISCONSIN, USA. DESIGNED BY MELBOURNE SMITH.

THE ENDSHEETS FOR THIS BOOK WERE TAKEN FROM A FACSIMILE OF THE *ATLAS DE FERNÃO VAZ DOURADO*, ORIGINALLY PUBLISHED IN 1571 AND REPRODUCED IN 1948 BY THE INSTITUTO PARA A ALTA CULTURO, PORTUGAL.

Nautical Chart Symbols and Abbreviations

United States of America

Prepared jointly by

DEFENSE MAPPING AGENCY
Hydrographic Center

and

DEPARTMENT OF COMMERCE,
National Oceanic and
Atmospheric Administration,
National Ocean Survey

GENERAL REMARKS

This publication (CHART No. 1) contains symbols and abbreviations which have been approved for use on nautical charts published by the United States of America (USA). Terms, symbols, and abbreviations are numbered in accordance with a standard form approved by a 1952 resolution of the International Hydrographic Organization (IHO). Although the use of IHO approved symbols and abbreviations is not mandatory, the USA has cooperated to adopt many IHO approved symbols for standard use on USA nautical charts. Alphanumeric style differences in the first column of the following pages indicate symbol and abbreviation status as follows:

VERTICAL FIGURES indicate those items for which the symbol and abbreviation are in accordance with resolutions of the IHO.

SLANTING FIGURES indicate those symbols for which no IHO resolution has been adopted.

SLANTING FIGURES UNDERSCORED indicate IHO and USA symbols do not agree.

SLANTING FIGURES ASTERISKED indicate that no symbol has been adopted by the USA.

SLANTING FIGURES IN PARENTHESIS indicate that the items are in addition to those appearing in the 1952 IHO approved standard form.

† All changes since the June 1968 edition of this publication are indicated by the dagger symbol in the margin immediately adjacent to the item identification of the symbol or abbreviation affected.

BUILDINGS. A conspicuous feature on a building may be shown by a landmark symbol with a descriptive label (See I 8b, 36, 44, 72). Prominent buildings that are of assistance to the mariner may be shown by actual shape as viewed from above (See I 3a, 5, 47, 66).

BUOYS and BEACONS. On entering a channel from seaward, buoys on starboard side are red with even numbers, on port side black with odd numbers. Lights on buoys on starboard side of channel are red or white, on port side white or green. Mid-channel buoys have black-and-white vertical stripes. Junction or obstruction buoys, which may be passed on either side, have red-and-black horizontal bands. This system does not always apply to foreign waters. The dot of the buoy symbol, the small circle of the light vessel and mooring buoy symbols, and the center of the beacon symbol indicate their positions.

COLORS are optional for characterizing various features and areas in the charts.

DEPTH contours and soundings are shown in meters on an increasing number of new charts and new editions.

HEIGHTS of land and conspicuous objects are given in feet above Mean High Water, unless otherwise stated in the title of the chart.

IMPROVED CHANNELS are shown by limiting dashed lines with the depth and date of the latest examination placed adjacent to the channel except when the channel data is tabulated.

LETTERING styles and capitalization as indicated in Chart No. 1 are not always rigidly adhered to on the charts.

LONGITUDES are referred to the Meridian of Greenwich.

METRIC CHARTS show land tint in green.

OBSOLESCENT SYMBOLIZATION on charts will be revised to agree with the current preferred usage as soon as opportunity affords.

SCALES are computed on the middle latitude of each chart, or on the middle latitude of a series of charts.

SHORELINE is the line of Mean High Water, except in marsh and mangrove areas, where the apparent shoreline (outer edge of vegetation) is used. A heavy line (A-9) is used to represent a firm shoreline. A light line (A-7) represents an apparent shoreline.

U. S. COAST PILOTS, SAILING DIRECTIONS, LIGHT LISTS, RADIO AIDS, and related publications furnish information required by the navigator that cannot be shown conveniently on the nautical chart.

U. S. NAUTICAL CHART CATALOGS and INDEXES list nautical charts, auxiliary maps, and related publications, and include general information relative to the charts.

Some differences may be observed between Chart No. 1 and symbols shown on certain reproductions of foreign charts and special charts. Foreign symbols may be interpreted by reference to the Symbol Sheet or Chart No. 1 of the originating country. A glossary of foreign terms and abbreviations is generally given on charts on which they are used, as well as in the Sailing Directions.

TABLE OF CONTENTS

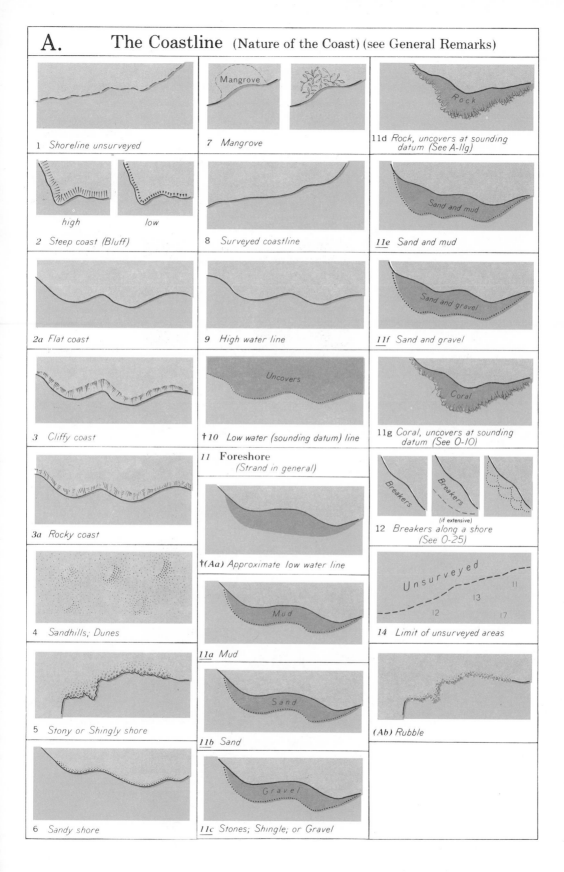

A. The Coastline (Nature of the Coast) (see General Remarks)

1   *Shoreline unsurveyed*

2   *Steep coast (Bluff)*
high   low

2a *Flat coast*

3   *Cliffy coast*

3a *Rocky coast*

4   *Sandhills; Dunes*

5   *Stony or Shingly shore*

6   *Sandy shore*

7   *Mangrove*

8   *Surveyed coastline*

9   *High water line*

†10 *Low water (sounding datum) line*

11 **Foreshore**
    (Strand in general)

†(Aa) *Approximate low water line*

11a *Mud*

11b *Sand*

11c *Stones; Shingle; or Gravel*

11d *Rock, uncovers at sounding datum (See A-11g)*

11e *Sand and mud*

11f *Sand and gravel*

11g *Coral, uncovers at sounding datum (See O-10)*

12 *Breakers along a shore (See O-25)*
Breakers   Breakers   (if extensive)

14 *Limit of unsurveyed areas*
Unsurveyed
11 13 17 12

(Ab) *Rubble*

1

B.	**Coast Features**		

1	*G*	Gulf
2	*B*	Bay
(Ba)	*B*	Bayou
3	*Fd*	Fjord
4	*•L*	Loch; Lough; Lake
5	*Cr*	Creek
5a	*C*	Cove
6	*In*	Inlet
7	*Str*	Strait
8	*Sd*	Sound
9	*Pass*	Passage; Pass
	Thoro	Thorofare
10	*Chan*	Channel
10a		Narrows
11	*Entr*	Entrance
12	*Est*	Estuary
12a		Delta
13	*Mth*	Mouth
14	*Rd*	Road; Roadstead
15	*Anch*	Anchorage
16	*Hbr*	Harbor
16a	*Hn*	Haven
17	*P*	Port
(Bb)	*P*	Pond
18	*I*	Island
19	*It*	Islet
20	*Arch*	Archipelago
21	*Pen*	Peninsula
22	*C*	Cape
23	*Prom*	Promontory
24	*Hd*	Head; Headland
25	*Pt*	Point
26	*Mt*	Mountain; Mount
27	*Rge*	Range
27a		Valley
28		Summit
29	*Pk*	Peak
30	*Vol*	Volcano
31		Hill
32	*Bld*	Boulder
33	*Ldg*	Landing
34		Table-land (Plateau)
35	*Rk*	Rock
36		Isolated rock
(Bc)	*Str*	Stream
(Bd)	*R*	River
(Be)	*Slu*	Slough
(Bf)	*Lag*	Lagoon
(Bg)	*Apprs*	Approaches
(Bh)	*Rky*	Rocky

C.	**The Land** (Natural Features)

1 Contour lines (Contours)

1a Contour lines, approximate (Contours)

2 Hachures

2a Form lines, no definite interval

2b Shading

†3 Glacier

4 Saltpans

5 Isolated trees

5a Deciduous or of unknown or unspecified type

5b Coniferous

5c Palm tree

5d Nipa palm

5e Filao

5f Casuarina

5g Evergreen tree (other than coniferous)

6 Cultivated fields

6a Grass fields

7 Paddy (rice) fields

7a Park; Garden

8 Bushes

8a Tree plantation in general

9 Deciduous woodland

10 Coniferous woodland

10a Woods in general

†11 Tree top height (above shoreline datum)

12 Lava flow

13 River; Stream

14 Intermittent stream

15 Lake; Pond

16 Lagoon (Lag)

Marsh Symbol used in small areas

17 Marsh; Swamp

18 Slough (Slu.)

19 Rapids

20 Waterfalls

21 Spring

2

D. Control Points

No.	Symbol		Description
1	△		Triangulation point (station)
1a			Astronomic Station
†2	⊙		Fixed point (landmark, position accurate)
(Da)	∘		Fixed point (landmark, position approx.)
3	· 256		Summit of height (Peak) (when not a landmark)
(Db)	◎ 256		Peak, accentuated by contours
(Dc)	☀ 256		Peak, accentuated by hachures
(Dd)	☀		Peak, elevation not determined
(De)	⊙ 256		Peak, when a landmark
4	⊕	Obs Spot	Observation spot
*5		BM	Bench mark
6	View X		View point
7			Datum point for grid of a plan
8			Graphical triangulation point
9		Astro	Astronomical
10		Tri	Triangulation
(Df)		C of E	Corps of Engineers
12			Great trigonometrical survey station
13			Traverse station
14		Bdy Mon	Boundary monument
(Dg)	◇		International boundary monument

E. Units

No.	Abbr.	Term	No.	Abbr.	Term
1	hr	Hour	14a		Greenwich
2	m; min	Minute (of time)	15	pub	Publication
3	sec	Second (of time)	16	Ed	Edition
4	m	Meter	17	corr	Correction
4a	dm	Decimeter	18	alt	Altitude
4b	cm	Centimeter	19	ht; elev	Height; Elevation
4c	mm	Millimeter	20	°	Degree
4d	m²	Square meter	21	′	Minute (of arc)
4e	m³	Cubic meter	22	″	Second (of arc)
5	km	Kilometer	23	No	Number
6	in	Inch	(Ea)	St M	Statute mile
7	ft	Foot	(Eb)	msec	Microsecond
8	yd	Yard	(Ec)	Hz	Hertz (cps)
9	fm	Fathom	(Ed)	kHz	Kilohertz (kc)
10	cbl	Cable length	(Ee)	MHz	Megahertz (Mc)
11	M	Nautical mile	(Ef)	cps	Cycles/second (Hz)
12	kn	Knot	(Eg)	kc	Kilocycle (kHz)
12a	t	Ton	(Eh)	Mc	Megacycle (MHz)
12b	cd	Candela (new candle)			
13	lat	Latitude			
14	long	Longitude			

F. Adjectives, Adverbs and other abbreviations

No.	Abbr.	Term
1	gt	Great
2	lit	Little
3	lrg	Large
4	sml	Small
5		Outer
6		Inner
7	mid	Middle
8		Old
9	anc	Ancient
10		New
11	St	Saint
12	conspic	Conspicuous
13		Remarkable
14	D . Destr	Destroyed
15		Projected
16	dist	Distant
17	abt	About
18		See chart
18a		See plan
19		Lighted; Luminous
20	sub	Submarine
21		Eventual
22	AERO	Aeronautical
23		Higher
23a		Lower
24	exper	Experimental
25	discontd	Discontinued
26	prohib	Prohibited
27	explos	Explosive
28	estab	Established
29	elec	Electric
30	priv	Private, Privately
31	prom	Prominent
32	std	Standard
33	subm	Submerged
34	approx	Approximate
35		Maritime
36	maintd	Maintained
37	aband	Abandoned
38	temp	Temporary
39	occas	Occasional
40	extr	Extreme
41		Navigable
42	N M	Notice to Mariners
(Fa)	L N M	Local Notice to Mariners
43		Sailing Directions
44		List of Lights
(Fb)	unverd	Unverified
(Fc)	AUTH	Authorized
(Fd)	CL	Clearance
(Fe)	cor	Corner
(Ff)	concr	Concrete
(Fg)	fl	Flood
(Fh)	mod	Moderate
(Fi)	bet	Between
(Fj)	1st	Fir
(Fk)	2nd	Second
(Fl)	3rd	Third
(Fm)	4th	Fourth
†(Fn)	DD	Deep Draft
†(Fo)	min	Minimum
†(Fp)	max	Maximum

1	⚓	*Anch*	*Anchorage (large vessels)*
2	⚓ ⚓	*Anch*	*Anchorage (small vessels)*
3		*Hbr*	*Harbor*
4		*Hn*	*Haven*
5		*P*	*Port*
6		*Bkw*	*Breakwater*
6a			*Dike*
7			*Mole*
8			*Jetty (partly below MHW)*
8a			*Submerged jetty*
(Ga)			*Jetty (small scale)*
9		*Pier*	*Pier*
10			*Spit*
11			*Groin (partly below MHW)*
12	ANCH PROHIBITED	*ANCH PROHIB*	*Anchorage prohibited (See P-25) (Screen Opt)*
12a			*Anchorage reserved*
12b	QUARANTINE ANCHORAGE	*QUAR ANCH*	*Quarantine anchorage*
13	Spoil Area		*Spoil ground*
(Gb)	Dumping Ground		*Dumping ground*
(Gc)	80 83 Disposal Area 85 Depths from survey of JUNE 1972 90 98		*Disposal area*
† (Gd)	Ⓟ		*Pump-out facilities*
14		*Fsh stks*	*Fisheries; Fishing stakes*
14a			*Fish trap; Fish weirs (actual shape charted)*
14b			*Duck blind*
15			*Tunny nets (See G-14a)*
15a	Oys	*Oys*	*Oyster bed*
16		*Ldg*	*Landing place*
17			*Watering place*
18		*Whf*	*Wharf*
19			*Quay*

20			*Berth*
20a	(14)		*Anchoring berth*
20b	3		*Berth number*
21	°	*Dol*	*Dolphin*
22			*Bollard*
23			*Mooring ring*
24			*Crane*
25			*Landing stage*
25a			*Landing stairs*
26		*Quar*	*Quarantine*
27			*Lazaret*
*28		Harbor Master	*Harbor master's office*
29		Cus Ho	*Customhouse*
30			*Fishing harbor*
31			*Winter harbor*
32			*Refuge harbor*
33		*B Hbr*	*Boat harbor*
34			*Stranding harbor (uncovers at LW)*
35			*Dock*
36			*Dry dock (actual shape on large-scale charts)*
37			*Floating dock (actual shape on large-scale charts)*
38			*Gridiron; Careening grid*
39			*Patent slip; Slipway; Marine railway*
39a		*Ramp*	*Ramp*
40	Lock		*Lock (point upstream) (See H-13)*
41			*Wet dock*
42			*Shipyard*
43			*Lumber yard*
44		Health Office	*Health officer's office*
45		*Hk*	*Hulk (actual shape on lrg scale charts) (See O-11)*
46	PROHIBITED AREA	*PROHIB AREA*	*Prohibited area (Screen Optional)*
46a	(10)		*Calling-in point for vessel traffic control*
47			*Anchorage for seaplanes*
48			*Seaplane landing area*
49	Under construction		*Work in progress*
50			*Under construction*
51			*Work projected*
(Ge)	Subm ruins		*Submerged ruins*

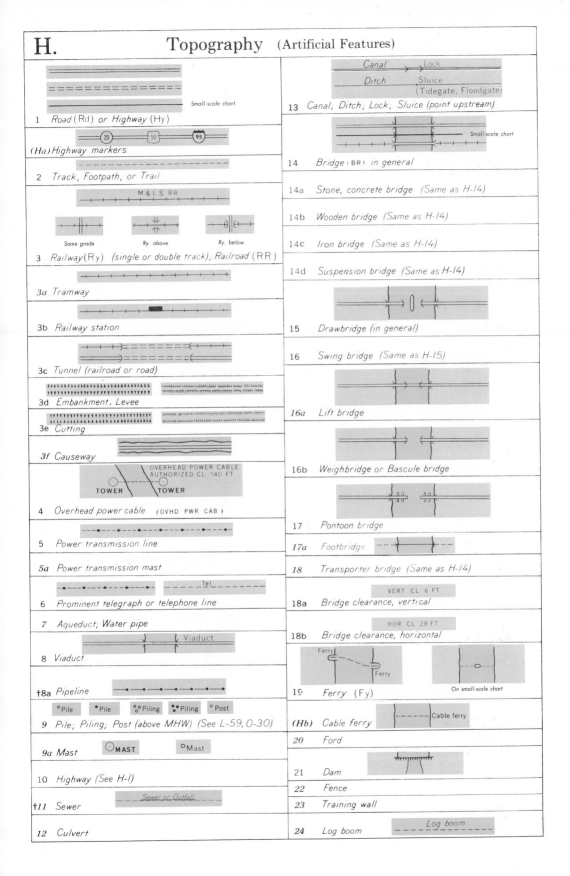

H. Topography (Artificial Features)

1 Road (Rd) or Highway (Hy) — *Small-scale chart*	13 Canal; Ditch; Lock; Sluice (point upstream) — *Canal, Lock, Ditch, Sluice (Tidegate, Floodgate)*
(Ha) Highway markers	14 Bridge (BR) in general — *Small-scale chart*
2 Track, Footpath, or Trail	14a Stone, concrete bridge (Same as H-14)
3 Railway (Ry) (single or double track); Railroad (RR) — M & L S RR; Same grade, Ry. above, Ry. below	14b Wooden bridge (Same as H-14)
3a Tramway	14c Iron bridge (Same as H-14)
3b Railway station	14d Suspension bridge (Same as H-14)
3c Tunnel (railroad or road)	15 Drawbridge (in general)
3d Embankment, Levee	16 Swing bridge (Same as H-15)
3e Cutting	16a Lift bridge
3f Causeway	16b Weighbridge or Bascule bridge
4 Overhead power cable (OVHD PWR CAB) — OVERHEAD POWER CABLE AUTHORIZED CL. 140 FT; TOWER, TOWER	17 Pontoon bridge
5 Power transmission line	17a Footbridge
5a Power transmission mast	18 Transporter bridge (Same as H-14)
6 Prominent telegraph or telephone line — Tel	18a Bridge clearance, vertical — VERT CL 6 FT
7 Aqueduct; Water pipe	18b Bridge clearance, horizontal — HOR CL 28 FT
8 Viaduct — Viaduct	19 Ferry (Fy) — Ferry, Ferry; On small-scale chart
†8a Pipeline	(Hb) Cable ferry — Cable ferry
9 Pile; Piling; Post (above MHW) (See L-59, 0-30) — °Pile, •Pile, °°Piling, •°Piling, °Post	20 Ford
9a Mast — ⊙MAST, °Mast	21 Dam
10 Highway (See H-1)	22 Fence
†11 Sewer — Sewer or Outfall	23 Training wall
12 Culvert	24 Log boom — Log boom

I. Buildings and Structures (see General Remarks)

1			City or Town (large scale)
(Ia)			City or Town (small scale)
2			Suburb
3		Vil	Village
3a			Buildings in general
4		Cas	Castle
5			House
6			Villa
7			Farm
8		Ch	Church
8a		Cath	Cathedral
8b	SPIRE	Spire	Spire; Steeple
9			Roman Catholic Church
10			Temple
11			Chapel
12			Mosque
12a			Minaret
(Ib)			Moslem Shrine
13			Marabout
14		Pag	Pagoda
15			Buddhist Temple; Joss-House
15a			Shinto Shrine
16			Monastery; Convent
17			Calvary; Cross
17a			Cemetery, Non-Christian
18	Cem		Cemetery, Christian
18a			Tomb
19			Fort (actual shape charted)
20			Battery
21			Barracks
22			Powder magazine
23	Airport		Airplane landing field
24			Airport, large scale (See P-13)
(Ic)			Airport, military (small scale)
(Id)			Airport, civil (small scale)
25			Mooring mast
26	King St	St	Street
26a	Locust Ave	Ave	Avenue
26b	Grand Blvd	Blvd	Boulevard
27		Tel	Telegraph
28		Tel Off	Telegraph office
29		P O	Post office
30		Govt Ho	Government house
31			Town hall
32		Hosp	Hospital
33			Slaughterhouse
34		Magz	Magazine
34a			Warehouse; Storehouse
35	MON	Mon	Monument
36	CUP	Cup	Cupola
37	ELEV	Elev	Elevator; Lift
(Ie)		Elev	Elevation; Elevated
38			Shed
39			Zinc roof
40	Ruins	Ru	Ruins
41	TR	Tr	Tower
(If)	ABAND LT HO		Abandoned lighthouse
42	WINDMILL		Windmill
43			Watermill
43a	WINDMOTOR		Windmotor
44	CHY	Chy	Chimney; Stack
45	S'PIPE	S'pipe	Water tower; Standpipe
†46			Oil tank
47		Facty	Factory
48			Saw mill
49			Brick kiln
50			Mine; Quarry
51	Well		Well
52			Cistern
†53	TANK	Tk	Tank
54			Noria
55			Fountain

I. Buildings and Structures (continued)

61		Inst	Institute	72	⊙GAB °Gab		Gable
62			Establishment	73			Wall
63			Bathing establishment	74			Pyramid
64		Ct Ho	Courthouse	75			Pillar
65	▮	Sch	School	76			Oil derrick
(Ig)	▮	H S	High school	(Ii)		Ltd	Limited
(Ih)	▮	Univ	University	(Ij)		Apt	Apartment
66	■ ▨ ▢	Bldg	Building	(Ik)		Cap	Capitol
67		Pav	Pavilion	(Il)		Co	Company
68			Hut	(Im)		Corp	Corporation
69			Stadium	†(In)	⊙TR		Landmark (position accurate)
70		T	Telephone	†(Io)	o Tr		Landmark (position approximate)
†71	⊕ ● ⊘		Gas tank; Gasometer	†(Ip)	⊙RA DOME o Ra dome		Radar Dome

J. Miscellaneous Stations

1	Sta	Any kind of station	13			Tide signal station
2	Sta	Station	14			Stream signal station
3	✖ C G	Coast Guard station (Similar to Lifesaving Sta.)	15			Ice signal station
			16			Time signal station
(Ja)	⊙C G WALLIS SANDS	Coast Guard station (when landmark)	16a			Manned oceanographic station
			16b			Unmanned oceanographic station
4	⊙LOOK TR	Lookout station; Watch tower	17			Time ball
5		Lifeboat station	18			Signal mast
6	✖LS S	Lifesaving station (See J-3)	19	⊙FS ⊙FP °FS °FP		Flagstaff; Flagpole
7	Rkt Sta	Rocket station	19a	⊙F TR °F Tr		Flag tower
8	◑ ⊙PIL STA	Pilot station	20			Signal
9	Sig Sta	Signal station	21		Obsy	Observatory
10	Sem	Semaphore	22		Off	Office
11	S Sig Sta	Storm signal station	(Jc)	°BELL		Bell (on land)
12		Weather signal station	(Jd)	°HECP		Harbor entrance control post
†(Jb)	⊙NWS SIG STA	Nat. Weather Service signal sta.				

†1		☆	Position of light	29	F Fl	Fixed and flashing light
2	Lt		Light	30	F Gp Fl	Fixed and group flashing light
†(Ka)			Riprap surrounding light	30a	Mo	Morse code light
3	Lt Ho		Lighthouse	31	Rot	Revolving or Rotating light
†4	AERO	AERO	Aeronautical light (See F-22)	41		Period
4a			Marine and air navigation light	42		Every
†5	Bn	Bn	Light beacon	43		With
†6			Light vessel; Lightship	44		Visible (range)
8			Lantern	(Kb)	M	Nautical mile (See E-11)
9			Street lamp	(Kc)	m; min	Minutes (See E-2)
10	REF		Reflector	(Kd)	sec	Seconds (See E-3)
†11	Ldg Lt	Ldg Lt	Leading light	45	Fl	Flash
†12	RED	RED	Sector light	46	Occ	Occultation
†13	GREEN RED	GREEN RED	Directional light	46a		Eclipse
14			Harbor light	47	Gp	Group
15			Fishing light	48	Occ	Intermittent light
16			Tidal light	49	SEC	Sector
†17	Priv maintd		Private light (maintained by private interests; to be used with caution)	50		Color of sector
21	F		Fixed light	51	Aux	Auxiliary light
22	Occ		Occulting light	52		Varied
23	Fl		Flashing light	61	Vi	Violet
23a	E Int		Isophase light (equal interval)	62		Purple
24	Qk Fl		Quick flashing (scintillating) light	63	Bu	Blue
25	Int Qk Fl I Qk Fl		Interrupted quick flashing light	64	G	Green
				65	Or	Orange
25a	S Fl		Short flashing light	66	R	Red
26	Alt		Alternating light	67	W	White
27	Gp Occ		Group occulting light	67a	Am	Amber
28	Gp Fl		Group flashing light	67b	Y	Yellow
28a	S-L Fl		Short-long flashing light	68	OBSC	Obscured light
28b			Group short flashing light	68a	Fog Det Lt	Fog detector light (See N-Nb)

K.   Lights   (continued)

69		Unwatched light	79		Front light
70	Occas	Occasional light	80	Vert	Vertical lights
71	Irreg	Irregular light	81	Hor	Horizontal lights
72	Prov	Provisional light	(Kf)	VB	Vertical beam
73	Temp	Temporary light	(Kg)	RGE	Range
(Ke)	D: Destr	Destroyed	(Kh)	Exper	Experimental light
74	Exting	Extinguished light	(Ki)	TRLB	Temporarily replaced by lighted buoy showing the same characteristics
75		Faint light	(Kj)	TRUB	Temporarily replaced by unlighted buoy
76		Upper light	(Kk)	TLB	Temporary lighted buoy
77		Lower light	(Kl)	TUB	Temporary unlighted buoy
78		Rear light			

L.   new optional symbols)   Buoys and Beacons
(see General Remarks)

†1		Position of buoy	17	RB / RB	Bifurcation buoy (RBHB)
†2		Light buoy	18	RB / RB	Junction buoy (RBHB)
†3	BELL / BELL	Bell buoy	19	RB / RB	Isolated danger buoy (RBHB)
†3a	GONG / GONG	Gong buoy	†20	RB / G / G / G / G	Wreck buoy (RBHB or G)
†4	WHIS	Whistle buoy	20a	RB / G	Obstruction buoy (RBHB or G)
†5	C	Can or Cylindrical buoy	21	Tel	Telegraph-cable buoy
†6	N	Nun or Conical buoy	†22		Mooring buoy (colors of mooring buoys never carried)
†7	SP	Spherical buoy	22a		Mooring
†8	S	Spar buoy	†22b	Tel / Tel	Mooring buoy with telegraphic communications
†8a	P	Pillar or Spindle buoy	†22c	T / T	Mooring buoy with telephonic communications
†9		Buoy with topmark (ball) (see L-70)	23		Warping buoy
†10		Barrel or Ton buoy	24	Y	Quarantine buoy
(La)		Color unknown	24a		Practice area buoy
(Lb)	FLOAT	Float	25	Explos Anch	Explosive anchorage buoy
†12	FLOAT / FLOAT	Lightfloat	25a	AERO	Aeronautical anchorage buoy
13		Outer or Landfall buoy	26	Deviation	Compass adjustment buoy
14	BW	Fairway buoy (BWVS)	27	BW	Fish trap (area) buoy (BWHB)
14a	BW	Mid-channel buoy (BWVS)	27a		Spoil ground buoy
15	R "2" / R "2"	Starboard-hand buoy (entering from seaward)	28	W	Anchorage buoy (marks limits)
16	"1"	Port-hand buoy (entering from seaward)	29	Priv maintd	Private aid to navigation (buoy) (maintained by private interests, use with caution)

†*29* (cont.)	!	R	Starboard-hand buoy (entering from seaward)
	!	B	Port-hand buoy
30			Temporary buoy (See Ki,j,k,l)
30a			Winter buoy
†*31*			Horizontal stripes or bands HB
†*32*			Vertical stripes VS
†*33*			Checkered Chec
33a		Diag	Diagonal bands
41		W	White
42		B	Black
43		R	Red
44		Y	Yellow
45		G	Green
46		Br	Brown
47		Gy	Gray
48		Bu	Blue
48a		Am	Amber
48b		Or	Orange
†*51*			Floating beacon
†*52*			Fixed beacon (unlighted or daybeacon)
	▲ Bn		Black beacon
	△ Bn		Color unknown
(Lc)			Private aid to navigation
53		Bn	Beacon, in general (See L-52)
54			Tower beacon

55			Cardinal marking system
56	△ Deviation Bn		Compass adjustment beacon
57			Topmarks (See L-9, 70)
58			Telegraph-cable (landing) beacon
59	Piles Piles		Piles (See O-30, H-9)
	⊥ ⊥		Stakes
	Stumps		Stumps (See O-30)
	⊥ ⊥		Perches
61	⊙CAIRN ○Cairn		Cairn
62			Painted patches
†63	⊙ TR		Landmark (position accurate) (See D-2)
†(Ld)	○ Tr		Landmark (position approximate)
64		REF	Reflector
65	⊙MARKER		Range targets, markers
(Le)	W Or W Or		Special-purpose buoys
†66			Oil installation buoy
†67			Drilling platform (See O-Ob, O-Oc)
70	Note:		TOPMARKS on buoys and beacons may be shown on charts of foreign waters. The abbreviation for black is not shown adjacent to buoys or beacons.
(Lf)	Ra Ref		Radar reflector (See M-13)

M. Radio and Radar Stations

1	°R Sta	Radio telegraph station	12	Racon	Radar responder beacon
2	°R T	Radio telephone station	13	Ra Ref	Radar reflector (See L-Lf)
3	R Bn	Radiobeacon	14	Ra (conspic)	Radar conspicuous object
4	R Bn	Circular radiobeacon	14a		Ramark
5	R D	Directional radiobeacon; Radio range	15	D F S	Distance finding station (synchronized signals)
6		Rotating loop radiobeacon	16	AERO R Bn 302 ▪·▪·▪	Aeronautical radiobeacon
7	R D F	Radio direction finding station	17	° Decca Sta	Decca station
(Ma)	TELEM ANT	Telemetry antenna	18	° Loran Sta Venice	Loran station (name)
(Mb)	R RELAY MAST	Radio relay mast	†19	CONSOL Bn 190 kHz MMF ▪▪▪	Consol (Consolan) station
(Mc)	MICRO TR	Microwave tower	(Md)	AERO R Rge 342 ▪·▪·▪	Aeronautical radio range
9	R MAST / R TR	Radio mast / Radio tower	(Me)	Ra Ref Calibration Bn	Radar calibration beacon
9a	TV TR	Television mast; Television tower	(Mf)	LORAN TR SPRING ISLAND	Loran tower (name)
†10	R TR (WBAL) 1090 kHz	Radio broadcasting station (commercial)	(Mg)	R TR F R Lt	Obstruction light
10a	°R Sta	Q.T.G. Radio station			
11	Ra	Radar station			

N. Fog Signals

1	Fog Sig	Fog-signal station	13	HORN	Fog horn
2		Radio fog-signal station	†13a	HORN	Electric fog horn
3	GUN	Explosive fog signal	14	BELL	Fog bell
4		Submarine fog signal	15	WHIS	Fog whistle
5	SUB-BELL	Submarine fog bell (action of waves)	16	HORN	Reed horn
6	SUB-BELL	Submarine fog bell (mechanical)	17	GONG	Fog gong
7	SUB-OSC	Submarine oscillator	18		Submarine sound signal not connected to the shore (See N-5,6,7)
8	NAUTO	Nautophone	18a		Submarine sound signal connected to the shore (See N-5,6,7)
9	DIA	Diaphone	(Na)	HORN	Typhon
10	GUN	Fog gun	(Nb)	Fog Det Lt	Fog detector light (See K 68a)
11	SIREN	Fog siren			
12	HORN	Fog trumpet			

Dangers

♂ (25)	**11** ⚓ *Wreck showing any portion of hull or superstructure (above sounding datum)*	**Obstruction (Fish haven)**
1 *Rock which does not cover (height above MHW) (See General Remarks)*		† *(Oc)* Fish haven (fishing reef)
		28 Wreck (See O-11 to 16)
✳ Uncov 2 ft **❀ Uncov 2 ft**	**Masts**	**Wreckage** **Wks**
✳ (2) **❀ (2)**	**12** *Wreck with only masts visible (above sounding datum)*	**29** Wreckage
2 *Rock which covers and uncovers, with height in feet above chart (sounding) datum*	**13** Old symbols for wrecks	**29a** Wreck remains (dangerous only for anchoring)
+	**13a** Wreck always partially submerged ⚓	**Subm piles**
†3 *Rock awash at (near) level of chart (sounding) datum*		**30** Submerged piling (See H-9, L-59)
Dotted line emphasizes danger to navigation	**†14** *Sunken wreck dangerous to surface navigation (less than 11 fathoms over wreck) (See O-6a)*	**Snags** **Stumps**
†(Oa) Rock awash (height unknown)		**30a** Snags; Submerged stumps (See L-59)
Dotted line emphasizes danger to navigation	**5½ Wk**	**31** Lesser depth possible
	15 *Wreck over which depth is known*	**32** Uncov Dries (See A-10; O-2, 10)
+	**2½ Wk**	**33** Cov Covers (See O-2, 10)
4 *Sunken rock (depth unknown)*	**15a** *Wreck with depth cleared by wire drag*	**34** Uncov Uncovers (See A-10; O-2, 10)
Dotted line emphasizes danger to navigation	**16** *Sunken wreck, not dangerous to surface navigation*	**3 Rep (1958)**
5 Rk	**Foul**	Reported (with date)
5 Shoal sounding on isolated rock	**17** Foul ground	**Eagle Rk (rep 1958)**
†6 *Sunken rock not dangerous to surface navigation (See O-4)*	**Tide Rips**	**35** Reported (with name and date)
	18 Overfalls or Tide rips *Symbol used only in small areas*	**36** Discol Discolored (See O-9)
2½ Rk **2½ Wk** **2½ Obstr**		**37** Isolated danger
6a *Sunken danger with depth cleared by wire drag (in feet or fathoms)*	**Eddies**	
	19 Eddies *Symbol used only in small areas*	**38** Limiting danger line
Reef	**Kelp**	**+ rky +**
7 Reef of unknown extent	**20** Kelp, Seaweed *Symbol used only in small areas*	**39** Limit of rocky area
	21 Bk Bank	**41** P A Position approximate
Sub Vol	**22** Shl Shoal	**42** P D Position doubtful
8 Submarine volcano	**23** Rf Reef (See A-11d,11g;O-10)	**43** E D Existence doubtful
	23a Ridge	**44** P Pos Position
Discol Water	**24** Le Ledge	**45** D Doubtful
9 Discolored water		**46** Unexamined
		†(Od) L D Least Depth
Coral **Co** **Co** **Co**	**25** Breakers (See A-12)	**Subm Crib** **Crib (above water)**
10 *Coral reef, detached (uncovers at sounding datum)*	**†26** Sunken rock (See O-4)	**(Oe)** Crib
+ Co 3½ Reef Line +	**5½ Obstr**	**Platform (lighted) HORN**
	27 Obstruction	**†(Of)** Offshore platform (unnamed)
Coral or Rocky reef, covered at sounding datum (See A-11d, 11g)	**+ Submerged Well**	**Hazel (lighted) HORN**
	†(Ob) Submerged Well (buoyed)	**†(Og)** Offshore platform (named)

P. Various Limits, etc.

#		Description
1		Leading line, Range line
2		Transit
3		In line with
4		Limit of sector
5		Channel, Course, Track recommended (marked by buoys or beacons) (See P-21)
(Pa)		Alternate course
6	—Ra——Ra—	Radar guided track
7		Submarine cable (power, telegraph, telephone, etc.)
†7a	Cable Area	Submarine cable area
7b		Abandoned submarine cable (includes disused cable)
†8		Submarine pipeline
8a	Pipeline Area	Submarine pipeline area
9		Maritime limit in general
(Pb)	RESTRICTED AREA	Limit of restricted area
10		Limit of fishing zone (fish trap areas)
(Pc)		U. S. Harbor Line
11		Limit of dumping ground, spoil ground (See P-9; G-13)
12		Anchorage limit
13		Limit of airport (See I-23, 24)
13a		Limit of military practice areas
14		Limit of sovereignty (Territorial waters)
15		Customs boundary
16		International boundary (also State boundary)
17		Stream limit
18		Ice limit
19		Limit of tide
20		Limit of navigation
21	> – – – –> / – <– – >–	Course recommended (not marked by buoys or beacons) (See P-5)
22		District or province limit
23		Reservation line
		(Options)
24	COURSE 053°00' TRUE / MARKERS MARKERS	Measured distance
25	PROHIBITED AREA	Prohibited area (See G-12,46) (Screen Optional)
(Pd)	SAFETY FAIRWAY	Shipping safety fairway
(Pe)		Directed traffic lanes

Q. Soundings

#		Description
1	SD	Doubtful sounding
2	65	No bottom found
3		Out of position
4		Least depth in narrow channels
5	30 FEET APR 1972	Dredged channel (with controlling depth indicated)
6	24 FEET MAY 1972	Dredged area
7		Swept channel (See Q-9)
8	6	Drying (or uncovering) heights; in feet above chart (sounding) datum
†9	17 / 119	Swept area, not adequately sounded (shown by green tint)
†9a	29 23 3 / 22 / 30 18 8 / 21 7	Swept area adequately sounded (swept by wire drag to depth indicated)
10		Hair-line depth figures
10a	8₂ 19	Figures for ordinary soundings
11	8₂ 19	Soundings taken from foreign charts
12	8₂ 19	Soundings taken from older surveys (or smaller scale chts)
13	8₂ 19	Echo soundings
14	8₂ 19	Sloping figures (See Q-12)
15	8₂ 19	Upright figures (See Q-10a)
16	(25) (2)	Bracketed figures (See O-1, 2)
17	6	Underlined sounding figures (See Q-8)
18	3₂ 6₁	Soundings expressed in fathoms and feet
22		Unsounded area
(Qa)	6 5 2ft	Stream

R. †Depth Contours and Tints (see General Remarks)

Feet	Fms/Meters				Feet	Fms/Meters			
0	0				300	50			
6	1				600	100			
12	2				1,200	200			
18	3				1,800	300			
24	4				2,400	400			
30	5				3,000	500			
36	6				6,000	1,000			
60	10				12,000	2,000			
120	20				18,000	3,000			
180	30				Or continuous lines, with values			5 — (blue or	
240	40						black) — 100		

S. Quality of the Bottom

No.	Abbr.	Term	No.	Abbr.	Term	No.	Abbr.	Term
1	Grd	Ground	24	Oys	Oysters	50	spk	Speckled
2	S	Sand	25	Ms	Mussels	51	gty	Gritty
3	M	Mud; Muddy	26	Spg	Sponge	52	dec	Decayed
4	Oz	Ooze	27	K	Kelp	53	fly	Flinty
5	Ml	Marl	28 {	Wd	Sea-weed	54	glac	Glacial
6	Cl	Clay	28 {	Grs	Grass	55	ten	Tenacious
7	G	Gravel	29	Stg	Sea-tangle	56	wh	White
8	Sn	Shingle	31	Spi	Spicules	57	bk	Black
9	P	Pebbles	32	Fr	Foraminifera	58	vi	Violet
10	St	Stones	33	Gl	Globigerina	59	bu	Blue
11	Rk; rky	Rock; Rocky	34	Di	Diatoms	60	gn	Green
11a	Blds	Boulders	35	Rd	Radiolaria	61	yl	Yellow
12	Ck	Chalk	36	Pt	Pteropods	62	or	Orange
12a	Ca	Calcareous	37	Po	Polyzoa	63	rd	Red
13	Qz	Quartz	38	Cir	Cirripeda	64	br	Brown
13a	Sch	Schist	38a	Fu	Fucus	65	ch	Chocolate
14	Co	Coral	38b	Ma	Mattes	66	gy	Gray
(Sa)	Co Hd	Coral head	39	fne	Fine	67	lt	Light
15	Mds	Madrepores	40	crs	Coarse	68	dk	Dark
16	Vol	Volcanic	41	sft	Soft			
(Sb)	Vol Ash	Volcanic ash	42	hrd	Hard	70	vard	Varied
17	La	Lava	43	stf	Stiff	71	unev	Uneven
18	Pm	Pumice	44	sml	Small	(Sc)	S/M	Surface layer and Under layer
19	T	Tufa	45	lrg	Large			
20	Sc	Scoriae	46	stk	Sticky			
21	Cn	Cinders	47	brk	Broken			
21a		Ash	47a	grd	Ground (Shells)	76		Fresh water springs in sea-bed
22	Mn	Manganese	48	rt	Rotten			
23	Sh	Shells	49	str	Streaky			

T.		**Tides and Currents**

1	HW	High water
1a	HHW	Higher high water
2	LW	Low water
(Ta)	LWD	Low water datum
2a	LLW	Lower low water
3	MTL	Mean tide level
4	MSL	Mean sea level
4a		Elevation of mean sea level above chart (sounding) datum
5		Chart datum (datum for sounding reduction)
6	Sp	Spring tide
7	Np	Neap tide
7a	MHW	Mean high water
8	MHWS	Mean high water springs
8a	MHWN	Mean high water neaps
8b	MHHW	Mean higher high water
8c	MLW	Mean low water
9	MLWS	Mean low water springs
9a	MLWN	Mean low water neaps
9b	MLLW	Mean lower low water
10	ISLW	Indian spring low water
11		High water full and change (vulgar establishment of the port)
12		Low water full and change
13		Mean establishment of the port
13a		Establishment of the port
14		Unit of height
15		Equinoctial
16		Quarter; Quadrature
17	Str	Stream
18	⟫⟫⟫ 2 kn →	Current, general, with rate
19	2 kn →	Flood stream (current) with rate
20	2 kn →	Ebb stream (current) with rate
21	○Tide gauge	Tide gauge; Tidepole; Automatic tide gauge
23	vel	Velocity; Rate
24	kn	Knots
25	ht	Height
26		Tide
27		New moon
28		Full moon
29		Ordinary
30		Syzygy
31	fl	Flood
32		Ebb
33		Tidal stream diagram
34	Ⓐ Ⓑ	Place for which tabulated tidal stream data are given
35		Range (of tide)
36		Phase lag
(Tb)		Current diagram, with explanatory note

U.		**Compass**

Compass Rose

The outer circle is in degrees with zero at true north. The inner circles are in points and degrees with the arrow indicating magnetic north.

1	N	North
2	E	East
3	S	South
4	W	West
5	NE	Northeast
6	SE	Southeast
7	SW	Southwest
8	NW	Northwest
9	N	Northern
10	E	Eastern
11	S	Southern
12	W	Western
21	brg	Bearing
22	T	True
23	mag	Magnetic
24	var	Variation
25		Annual change
25a		Annual change nil
26		Abnormal variation; Magnetic attraction
27	deg	Degrees (See E-20)
28	dev	Deviation

Index of Abbreviations

A

aband.	Abandoned	F 37
ABAND LT HO	Abandoned lighthouse	If
abt.	About	F 17
AERO	Aeronautical	F 22; K 4
AERO R. Bn.	Aeronautical radiobeacon	M 16
AERO R. Rge.	Aeronautical radio range	Md
alt.	Altitude	E 18
Alt	Alternating (light)	K 26
Am	Amber	K 67a; L 48a
anc.	Ancient	F 9
Anch	Anchorage	B 15; G 1,2
Anch prohib	Anchorage prohibited	G 12
approx.	Approximate	F 34
Apprs.	Approaches	Bg
Apt.	Apartment	Ij
Arch.	Archipelago	B 20
Astro.	Astronomical	D 9
AUTH.	Authorized	Fc
Aux	Auxiliary (light)	K 51
Ave.	Avenue	I 26a

B

B	Bay	B 2
B	Bayou	Ba
B	Black	L 42
Bdy. Mon.	Boundary monument	D 14
BELL	Fog Bell	N 14
bet.	Between	Fi
B Hbr	Boat harbor	G 33
Bk	Bank	O 21
bk	Black	S 57
Bkw.	Breakwater	G 6
Bld	Boulder	B 32
Bldg.	Building	I 66
Blds	Boulders	S 11a
Blvd.	Boulevard	I 26b
B.M.	Bench mark	D 5
Bn	Beacon (in general)	L 52,53
BR.	Bridge	H 14
Br	Brown	L 46
br	Brown	S 64
brg.	Bearing	U 21
brk	Broken	S 47
Bu	Blue	K 63; L 48
bu	Blue	S 59
BWHB	Black and white horizontal bands	L 27
BWVS	Black and white vertical stripes	L 14,14a

C

C	Can; Cylindrical (buoy)	L 5
C	Cape	B 22
C	Cove	B 5a
Ca	Calcareous	S 12a
Cap.	Capitol	Ik
Cas.	Castle	I 4
Cath.	Cathedral	I 8a
cbl.	Cable length	E 10
Cd	Candela	E12b
C. G.	Coast Guard	J 3, Ja

ch	Chocolate	S 65
Ch.	Church	I 8
Chan	Channel	B 10
Chec	Checkered (buoy)	L 33
CHY.	Chimney	I 44
Cir	Cirripeda	S 38
Ck	Chalk	S 12
Cl	Clay	S 6
CL.	Clearance	Fd
cm.	Centimeter	E 4b
Cn	Cinders	S 21
Co.	Company	Il
Co	Coral	S 14
Co Hd	Coral head	Sa
concr.	Concrete	Ff
conspic.	Conspicuous	F 12
C. of E.	Corps of Engineers	Df
cor.	Corner	Fe
Corp.	Corporation	Im
Cov	Covers	0 33
corr.	Correction	E 17
cps	Cycles/second	Ef
Cr.	Creek	B 5
crs	Coarse	S 40
Cswy.	Causeway	H 3f
Ct. Ho.	Courthouse	I 64
CUP.	Cupola	I 36
Cus. Ho.	Customhouse	G 29

D

D	Doubtful	O 45
DD	Deep Draft	Fm
D.; Destr.	Destroyed	F 14; Ke
dec.	Decayed	S 52
deg.	Degrees	U 27
dev.	Deviation	U 28
Diag	Diagonal bands	L 33a
D. F. S.	Distance finding station	M 15
Di	Diatoms	S 34
DIA	Diaphone	N 9
Discol	Discolored	O 36
discontd.	Discontinued	F 25
dist.	Distant	F 16
dk	Dark	S 68
dm.	Decimeter	E 4a
Dol	Dolphin	G 21

E

E.	East, Eastern	U 2,10
Ed.	Edition	E 16
E.D.	Existence doubtful	O 43
elec.	Electric	F 29
elev.	Elevation	E 19
ELEV.	Elevator, Lift	I 37
Elev.	Elevation, Elevated	Ie
Entr	Entrance	B 11
E Int	Isophase lt.(equal interval)	K 23a
Est	Estuary	B 12
estab.	Established	F 28
Exper	Experimental (light)	Kh
exper.	Experimental	F 24
explos.	Explosive	F 27

17

Explos Anch	Explosive Anchorage (buoy)	L 25
Exting	Extinguished (light)	K 74
extr.	Extreme	F 40

F

F	Fixed (light)	K 21
Facty.	Factory	I 47
Fd	Fjord	B 3
F Fl	Fixed and flashing (light)	K 29
F Gp Fl	Fixed and group flashing (light)	K 30
Fl	Flash, Flashing (light)	K 23, 45
fl.	Flood	Fg; T 31
fly	Flinty	S 53
fm	Fathom	E 9
fne	Fine	S 39
Fog Det Lt	Fog detector light	K 68a; Nb
Fog Sig.	Fog signal station	N 1
FP	Flagpole	J 19
Fr	Foraminifera	S 32
FS.	Flagstaff	J 19
Fsh stks	Fishing stakes	G 14
ft.	Foot	E 7
Ft.	Fort	I 19
F. TR.	Flag tower	J 19a
Fu	Fucus	S 38a
Fy.	Ferry	H 19

G

G	Gulf	B 1
G	Gravel	S 7
G	Green	K 64
G	Green	L 20, 20a, 45
GAB.	Gable	I 72
Gl	Globigerina	S 33
glac	Glacial	S 54
gn	Green	S 60
GONG	Fog gong	N 17
Govt. Ho.	Government House	I 30
Gp	Group	K 47
Gp Fl	Group flashing	K 28
Gp Occ	Group occulting	K 27
Grd, grd	Ground	S 1, 47a
Grs	Grass	S 28
gt.	Great	F 1
gty	Gritty	S 51
GUN	Explosive fog signal	N 3
GUN	Fog gun	N 10
Gy	Gray	L 47
gy	Gray	S 66

H

HB	Horizontal bands or stripes	L 31
Hbr	Harbor	B 16; G 3
Hd.	Head, Headland	B 24
HECP	Harbor entrance control post	Jd
Hk	Hulk	G 45
HHW	Higher high water	T 1a
Hn	Haven	B 16a; G 4
Hor	Horizontal lights	K 81

HOR. CL.	Horizontal clearance	H 18b
HORN	Fog trumpet; Fog horn; Reed horn; Typhon	N 12, 13, 13a, 16, Na
Hosp.	Hospital	I 32
hr.	Hour	E 1
hrd	Hard	S 42
H. S.	High School	Ig
ht.	Height	E 19; T 25
HW	High water	T 1
Hy.	Highway	H 1
Hz	Hertz	Ec

I

l.	Island	B 18
I Qk; Int Qk	Interrupted quick	K 25
in.	Inch	E 6
In	Inlet	B 6
Inst.	Institute	I 61
Irreg	Irregular	K 71
ISLW	Indian spring low water	T 10
Iso	Isophase	K23a
It.	Islet	B 19

K

K	Kelp	S 27
kc	Kilocycle	Eg
kHz	Kilohertz	Ed
km.	Kilometer	E 5
kn	Knots	E 12; T 24

L

L	Loch, Lough, Lake	B 4
La	Lava	S 17
Lag	Lagoon	Bf; C 16
lat.	Latitude	E 13
LD	Least Depth	Od
Ldg.	Landing; Landing place	B 33; G 16
Ldg. Lt.	Leading light	K 11
Le	Ledge	O 24
Lit	Little	F2
LLW	Lower low water	T 2a
L.N.M.	Local Notice to Mariners	Fa
long.	Longitude	E 14
LOOK. TR.	Lookout station; Watch tower	J 4
lrg	Large	F 3; S 45
LS. S.	Lifesaving station	J 6
Lt.	Light	K 2
lt	Light	S 67
Ltd.	Limited	Ii
Lt. Ho.	Lighthouse	K 3
LW	Low water	T 2
LWD	Low water datum	Ta

M

M	Nautical mile	E11; Kb
M	Mud, Muddy	S 3
m.	Meter	E 4, d, e
m²	Square meter	E4d
m³	Cubic meter	E4c
m. ; min.	Minute (of time)	E2; Kc
Ma	Mattes	S 38b
mag.	Magnetic	U 23
Magz.	Magazine	I 34
maintd.	Maintained	F 36
max	Maximum	Fp

Abbreviations

Mc	Megacycle	Eh	Pag.	Pagoda	I 14	
Mds	Madrepores	S 15	Pass	Passage, Pass	B 9	
MHHW	Mean higher high water	T 8b	Pav.	Pavilion	I 67	
MHW	Mean high water	T 7a	P. D.	Position doubtful	O 42	
MHWN	Mean high water neaps	T 8a	Pen.	Peninsula	B 21	
MHWS	Mean high water springs	T 8	PIL. STA.	Pilot station	J 8	
MHz	Megahertz	Ee	Pk.	Peak	B 29	
MICRO. TR.	Microwave tower	Mc	Pm	Pumice	S 18	
mid.	Middle	F 7	Po	Polyzoa	S 37	
min	Minimum	Fo	P. O.	Post Office	I 29	
Mkr	Marker	Lc	P.; Pos.	Position	O 44	
Ml	Marl	S 5	priv.	Private, Privately	F 30	
MLLW	Mean lower low water	T 9b	Priv. maintd.	Privately maintained K 17; L 29		
MLW	Mean low water	T 8c	Prohib.	Prohibited	F 26	
MLWN	Mean low water neaps	T 9a	prom.	Prominent	F 31	
MLWS	Mean low water springs	T 9	Prom.	Promontory	B 23	
mm.	Millimeter	E 4c	Prov	Provisional (light)	K 72	
Mn	Manganese	S 22	Pt.	Point	B 25	
Mo.	Morse code light	K 30a	Pt	Pteropods	S 36	
mod.	Moderate	Fh	pub.	Publication	E 15	
MON.	Monument	I 35	P. F.	Pump-out facitilies	G d	
Ms	Mussels	S 25	PWI	Potable water intake		
M. Sec.	Microsecond	Eb				
MSL	Mean sea level	T 4	**Q**			
Mt.	Mountain, Mount	B 26	Quar.	Quarantine	G 26	
Mth	Mouth	B 13	Qk Fl	Quick flashing (light)	K 24	
MTL	Mean tide level	T 3	Qz	Quartz	S 13	

N

N.	North; Northern	U 1, 9
N	Nun; Conical (buoy)	L 6
NAUTO	Nautophone	N 8
NE.	Northeast	U 5
N.M.	Notice to Mariners	F 42
No.	Number	E 23
Np	Neap tide	T 7
NW.	Northwest	U 8
NWS	National Weather Service Signal Station	Jb

R

R.	Red	K 66; L 15,43
R.	River	Bd
Ra	Radar station	M 11
Racon	Radar responder beacon	M 12
Ra (conspic)	Radar conspicuous object	M 14
Ra Ref	Radar reflector	Lf; M 13
RBHB	Red and black horizontal bands	L 17,18, 19, 20,20a
R Bn	Red beacon	L 52
R. Bn.	Radiobeacon	M 3,4,6
Rd	Radiolaria	S 35
rd	Red	S 63
Rd.	Road	H 1
Rd.	Road, Roadstead	B 14
R.D.	Directional Radiobeacon; Radio range	M 5
R. D. F.	Radio direction finding station	M 7
REF	Reflector	K 10; L 64
Rep.	Reported	O 35
Rf	Reef	O 23
Rge.	Range	B 27
RGE	Range	Kg
Rk.	Rock	B 35
Rk,rky	Rock, Rocky	S 11
Rky.	Rocky	Bh
R. MAST	Radio mast	M 9
Rot	Revolving; Rotating (light)	K 31
RR.	Railroad	H 3
R.RELAY MAST	**Radio relay mast**	M b
R. Sta.	Radio telegraph station; Q.T.G. Radio station	M1,10a
R. T.	Radio telephone station	M 2
rt	Rotten	S 48

O

OBSC	Obscured (light)	K 68
Obs. Spot	Observation spot	D 4
Obstr.	Obstruction	O 27
Obsy.	Observatory	J 21
Occ	Occulting (light); Occultation	K 22,46
Occ	Intermittent (light)	K 48
Occas	Occasional (light)	F 39; K 70
Off.	Office	J 22
or	Orange	S 62
Or	Orange	K 65; L48b
OVHD. PWR. CAB.	Overhead power cable	H 4
Oys	Oysters; Oyster bed	S 24; G 15a
Oz	Ooze	S 4

P

P.	Pebbles	S 9
P	Pillar (buoy)	L8a
P	Pond	Bb
P.	Port	B 17; G 5
P. A.	Position approximate	O 41

R. TR.	Radio tower	M 9	TB	Temporary buoy	L 30
Ru.	Ruins	I 40	Tel.	**Telegraph**	I 27; L 22b
RW Bn	Red and white beacon	L 52	**Telem Ant**	Telemetry antenna	Ma
Ry.	Railway	H 3	Tel. Off.	**Telegraph office**	I 28
			Temp	Temporary (light)	F 38; K 73
S			ten	Tenacious	S 55
S	Sand	S 2	Thoro	Thorofare	B 9
S	South; Southern	U 3, 11	Tk.	Tank	I 53
S	Spar (buoy)	L 8	TR.	Tower	I 41
Sc	Scoriae	S 20	**TRLB, TRUB, TLB, TUB**		Ki, j, k, l
Sch.	Schist	S 13a	Tri.	**Triangulation**	D 10
Sch.	School	I 65	TV TR.	Television tower (mast)	M 9a
Sd.	Sound	B 8			
SD	Sounding doubtful	Q 1	**U**		
SE.	Southeast	U 6	Uncov	Uncovers	O 2
sec.	Second (of time)	E 3	Uncov.	Uncovers; Dries	O 32, 34
sec	Seconds	Kd	Univ.	University	Ih
SEC	Sector	K 49	unverd.	Unverified	Fb
Sem.	Semaphore	J 10	**unev**	Uneven	S 71
S Fl	Short flashing (light)	K 25a			
sft	Soft	S 41	**V**		
Sh	Shells	S 23	var.	Variation	U 24
Shl	Shoal	O 22	**vard**	**Varied**	S 70
Sig. Sta.	Signal station	J 9	VB	Vertical beam	Kf
SIREN	Fog siren	N 11	vel.	Velocity	T 23
Sk	**Stroke**		Vert	Vertical (lights)	K 80
S-L Fl	Short-long flashing (light)	K 28a	VERT. CL.	Vertical clearance	H 18a
Slu	Slough	Be; C 18	Vi	Violet	K 61
sml	Small	F 4 : S 44	vi	Violet	S 58
Sn	Shingle	S 8	**View X**	**View point**	D 6
Sp	Spring tide	T 6	Vil.	Village	I 3
SP	Spherical (buoy)	L 7	Vol.	Volcano	B 30
Spg	Sponge	S 26	Vol	Volcanic	S 16
Spi	**Spicules**	S 31	Vol Ash	Volcanic ash	Sb
S'PIPE	Standpipe	I 45	VS	Vertical stripes	L 32
spk	Speckled	S 50			
S. Sig. Sta.	Storm signal station	J 11	**W**		
St.	Saint	F 11	W.	West; Western	U 4, 12
St.	Street	I 26	W	White	K 67; L 41
St	Stones	S 10	wh	White	S 56
Sta.	Station	J 1, 2	W Bn	White beacon	L 52
std.	Standard	F 32	Wd	Sea-weed	S 28
stf	Stiff	S 43	Whf.	Wharf	G 18
Stg	**Sea-tangle**	S 29	WHIS	Fog whistle	N 15
stk	Sticky	S 46	Wk	Wreck	O 15, 28
St. M.	Statute mile	Ea	Wks	Wreckage	O 29
Str	Strait	B 7	W Or	White and orange	Le
Str	Stream	Bc; T 17			
str	**Streaky**	S 49	**Y**		
sub	Submarine	F 20	Y	Yellow	L 24, 44
SUB-BELL	Submarine fog bell	N 5,6	yl	Yellow	S 61
subm	Submerged	F 33	yd.	Yard	E 8
Subm	Submerged	Oa,30			
Subm Ruins	Submerged ruins	Gd	1st	First	Fj
SUB-OSC	Submarine oscillator	N 7	2nd	Second	Fk
Sub Vol	Submarine volcano	O 8	3rd	Third	Fl
Subm.W.	Submerged Well	Ob	4th	Fourth	Fm
SW.					
T					
t	**Ton**	E12a	°	Degree	E 20
T.	Telephone	I 70; L 22c	′	Minute (of arc)	E 21
T	True	U 22	″	Second (of arc)	E 22
T	Tufa	S 19			

NAVIGATIONAL AIDS

IN

UNITED STATES WATERS

AIDS TO NAVIGATION ON NAVIGABLE WATERS
except Western Rivers and Intracoastal Waterway

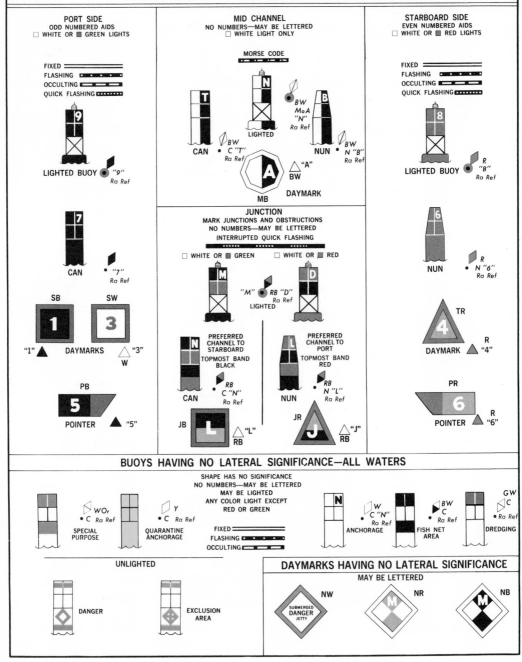

AIDS TO NAVIGATION ON THE INTRACOASTAL WATERWAY

AS SEEN ENTERING FROM NORTH AND EAST—PROCEEDING TO SOUTH AND WEST

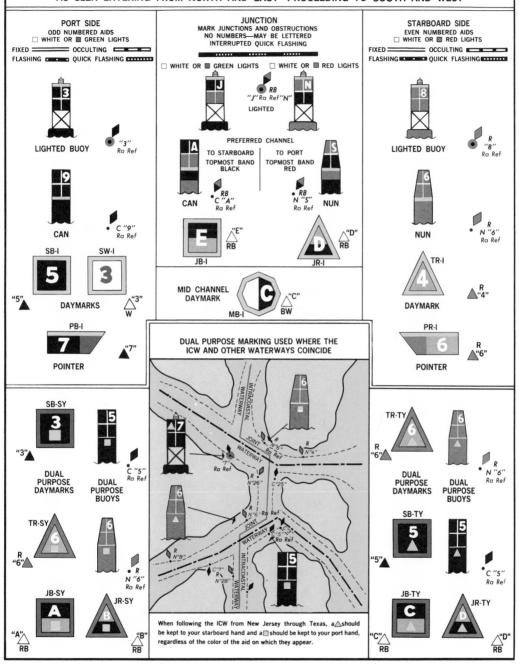

AIDS TO NAVIGATION ON WESTERN RIVERS

AS SEEN ENTERING FROM SEAWARD

PORT SIDE
☐ WHITE OR ■ GREEN LIGHTS
FLASHING

LIGHTED BUOY

CAN

SW

PASSING DAYMARK

CW

CROSSING DAYMARK

176.9

MILE BOARD

JUNCTION
MARK JUNCTIONS AND OBSTRUCTIONS
INTERRUPTED QUICK FLASHING

PREFERRED CHANNEL TO STARBOARD — TOPMOST BAND BLACK

PREFERRED CHANNEL TO PORT — TOPMOST BAND RED

☐ WHITE OR ■ GREEN LIGHTS

☐ WHITE OR ■ RED LIGHTS

LIGHTED

CAN

NUN

JB

JR

STARBOARD SIDE
☐ WHITE OR ■ RED LIGHTS
GROUP FLASHING (2)

LIGHTED BUOY

NUN

TR

PASSING DAYMARK

CR

CROSSING DAYMARK

123.5

MILE BOARD

RANGE DAYMARKS

| | KWB | KWR | KRW | KRB | KBW | KBR |

NAVIGABLE WATERS EXCEPT ICW

| | KWB-I | KWR-I | KRW-I | KRB-I | KBW-I | KBR-I |

INTRACOASTAL WATERWAY

MAY BE LETTERED

UNIFORM STATE WATERWAY MARKING SYSTEM

REGULATORY MARKERS

BOAT EXCLUSION AREA

EXPLANATION MAY BE PLACED OUTSIDE THE CROSSED DIAMOND SHAPE, SUCH AS DAM, RAPIDS, SWIM AREA, ETC.

DANGER

THE NATURE OF DANGER MAY BE INDICATED INSIDE THE DIAMOND SHAPE, SUCH AS ROCK, WRECK, SHOAL, DAM, ETC.

CONTROLLED AREA

TYPE OF CONTROL IS INDICATED IN THE CIRCLE, SUCH AS 5 MPH, NO ANCHORING, ETC.

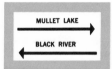

INFORMATION

FOR DISPLAYING INFORMATION SUCH AS DIRECTIONS, DISTANCES, LOCATIONS, ETC.

BUOY USED TO DISPLAY REGULATORY MARKERS

MAY SHOW WHITE LIGHT
MAY BE LETTERED

AIDS TO NAVIGATION

MAY SHOW WHITE REFLECTOR OR LIGHT

MOORING BUOY

WHITE WITH BLUE BAND

MAY SHOW WHITE REFLECTOR OR LIGHT

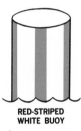

RED-STRIPED WHITE BUOY

MAY BE LETTERED
DO NOT PASS BETWEEN BUOY AND NEAREST SHORE

BLACK-TOPPED WHITE BUOY

MAY BE NUMBERED

PASS TO NORTH OR EAST OF BUOY

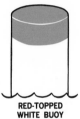

RED-TOPPED WHITE BUOY

PASS TO SOUTH OR WEST OF BUOY

CARDINAL SYSTEM

MAY SHOW GREEN REFLECTOR OR LIGHT

MAY SHOW RED REFLECTOR OR LIGHT

SOLID RED AND SOLID BLACK BUOYS

USUALLY FOUND IN PAIRS
PASS BETWEEN THESE BUOYS

PORT SIDE ———— LOOKING UPSTREAM ———— STARBOARD SIDE

LATERAL SYSTEM

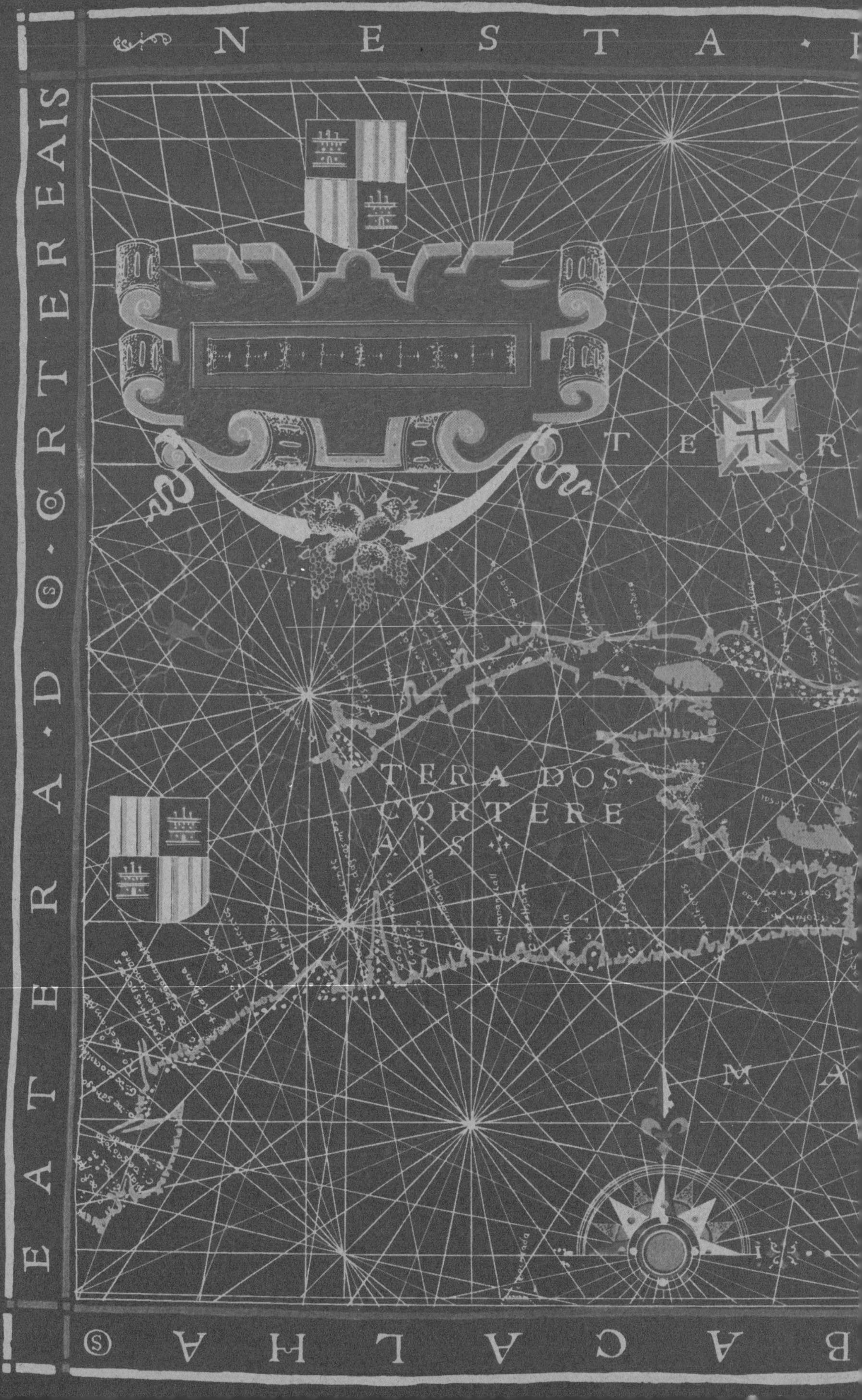
NESTA ·
EA TERA · DO · CORTEREAIS
BACALHAS
TER
TERA DOS CORTERE AIS
MA